Douglas Cobb's 1-2-3 Handbook, Release 2.2 Edition

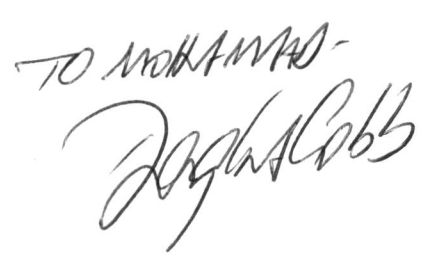

Douglas Cobb's 1-2-3 Handbook, Release 2.2 Edition

Douglas Cobb
with Steven S. Cobb and Gena Berg Cobb

BANTAM BOOKS
NEW YORK · TORONTO · LONDON · SYDNEY · AUCKLAND

DOUGLAS COBB'S 1-2-3 HANDBOOK, RELEASE 2.2 EDITION

A Bantam Book / November 1989

Paradox is a registered trademark of Borland International. Apple is a registered trademark of and Macintosh is a trademark licensed to Apple Computer, Inc. Ashton-Tate, dBASE II, dBASE III, dBase III Plus, and dBASE IV are registered trademarks of Ashton-Tate. Compaq is a registered trademark of and Compaq Plus, Compaq Deskpro, and Compaq Deskpro 286 are trademarks of Compaq Computer Corporation. SuperCalc is a registered trademark of Computer Associates, International. Dow Jones News/Retrieval is a registered service mark of Dow Jones & Company, Inc. Epson is a registered trademark of and Epson MX-80, Epson FX-80, Epson FX-100, and Epson LQ-1500 are trademarks of Epson America, Inc. 3-2-1 GOSUB is a trademark of Frontline Systems. Sideways is a registered trademark of and Allways, InWord, Noteworthy, and The Worksheet Utilities are trademarks of Funk Software, Inc. What's Best! is a trademark of General Optimization Inc. SOS is a trademark of Goldata Inc. Hayes is a registered trademark of and Smartmodem is a trademark of Hayes Microcomputer Products, Inc. Hercules is a registered trademark of and Hercules Graphics Card is a trademark of Hercules Computer Technology. HP LaserJet is a trademark of Hewlett Packard Company. Intel is a registered trademark of and Above is a trademark of Intel Corporation. IBM, IBM Personal Computer AT, Personal System/2, PS/2, and IBM Quietwriter are registered trademarks of and IBM PC, IBM PC XT, IBM Portable, IBM PC XT 286, and IBM Proprinter are trademarks of International Business Machines, Inc. 3D Graphics is a trademark of Intex Solutions. Lotus, 1-2-3, Freelance, Graphwriter, Symphony, and VisiCalc are registered trademarks of and SpeedUp, Learn, Spotlight, Lotus HAL, 1-2-3 Report Writer, and The Application Connection are trademarks of Lotus Development Corporation. Microsoft and Multiplan are registered trademarks of and MS-DOS and Microsoft Word are trademarks of Microsoft Corporation. WordStar is a trademark of MicroPro, Inc. Crosstalk is a trademark of Microstuff, Incorporated. Norton Utilities and UnErase are trademarks of Peter Norton Computing, Inc. Okidata is a registered trademark of Oki America, Inc. SeeMore and @BASE are trademarks of Personics. Note-It is a registered trademark of and 4VIEWS, 4Word The Add-In Word Processor, Cambridge Spreadsheet Analyst, Note-It Plus, Spellin', SQZ!, and The Budget Express are trademarks of Symantec. WordPerfect is a trademark of Wordperfect Corporation.

Production by Microtext Productions, Inc.

Throughout this book, the trade names and trademarks of many companies and products have been used, and no such uses are intended to convey endorsement of or other affiliations with the book.

All rights reserved.
Copyright © 1989 by Douglas Cobb.
Book Design by The Cobb Group, Inc.
Composed by Christopher Chabris and Sania Hamilton, Castle Productions Limited.

No part of this book may be reproduced or transmitted in any form or by any means, electronic or mechanical, including photocopying, recording, or by any information storage and retrieval system, without permission in writing from the publisher. For information address: Bantam Books.

ISBN 0-553-34867-1

Published simultaneously in the United States and Canada

Bantam Books are published by Bantam Books, a division of Bantam Doubleday Dell Publishing Group, Inc. Its trademark, consisting of the words "Bantam Books" and the portrayal of a rooster, is Registered in U.S. Patent and Trademark Office and in other countries. Marca Registrada, Bantam Books, 666 Fifth Avenue, New York, New York 10103

PRINTED IN THE UNITED STATES OF AMERICA

0 9 8 7 6 5 4 3 2 1

To Tom—DFC

To my son, Timothy Ford Cobb—SSC

To my mother, Ernestine Hilliard Berg—GBC

Acknowledgments

The authors wish to thank the following people, without whom this book would not have been possible: Marjorie Phifer, Linda Baughman, Maureen Pawley, Julie Tirpak, and Elayne Noltemeyer, for making it happen; Tom Cottingham, Lou Armstrong, Tracy Milliner, Mark Crane, Joe Pierce, Jeff Yocom, Peggy Zeillmann, David Schmitt, Jim Wooldridge, Linda Watkins, Jody Gilbert, Toni Bowers, Clyde Zellers, Duane Spurlock, Rose Fairfax, Beth Riggle, Tara Billinger, Ann Rockers, Tim Landgrave, Jon Pyles, Patty Flynn, Raven Sexton, Julia Bennett, Karen Pierce, Kathlene Lane, Lori Junkins, Becky Ledford, Trisha Shields, Doug Been, Beth Ording, Jeff Warner, Margaret Walz, Teresa Codey, Lori Houston, Luanne Flynn, Laura Heuser, Kellie Woods, Jenny Camacho, Pat Parr, Gordon Colby, Donald Fields, and Ginger Kepple, for keeping the ship afloat; Kenzi Sugihara, Stephen Guty, Terry Nasta, John Kilcullen, Debra Miller, and Jim Plumeri of Bantam Books; Michelle Cobb, for her understanding and encouragement; Tim Cobb, Wes Cobb, and David Cobb, for doing without their dads; Sharon Spickard and the staff at The Computer Shoppe of Louisville; CBM Computer Centers of Louisville; Dan McMillan, Julie Bingham, Ezra Gotthiel, Lex Crossett, and Alan Schlingenbaum of Lotus for their help and answers; and Mitch Kapor and Jonathan Sachs, for creating 1-2-3.

The LORD'S lovingkindnesses indeed never cease, for his compassions never fail. They are new every morning; Great is Thy faithfulness.
                                                            Lamentations 3:22-23

Table of Contents

Table of Tips xxiii

1 Introduction 1
   1-2-3 RELEASE 2.2 1
   ABOUT THIS BOOK 2
      A Note About Versions 2
      Organization 3
      Examples 4
      Tips 4
   CONVENTIONS 4
   CONCLUSION 5

2 1-2-3 Basics 7
   HARDWARE REQUIREMENTS 7
      Hardware Options 8
      Installing 1-2-3 8
   LOADING 1-2-3 9
   A TOUR OF THE SCREEN 10
      The Worksheet 11
      The Control Panel 12
      The Clock 13
      The Error Messages Area 13
      Status Indicators 13
   FUNCTION KEYS 14
   MOVING THE CELL POINTER 14
      The Arrow Keys 15
      Moving by Windows 19
      The [Home] Key 19
      The [End][Home] Combination 20
      The [Goto] Key 20
   MAKING CELL ENTRIES 21
      Entering Labels and Numbers 21
      Numbers 23
      Labels 25
      Formulas 28

EDITING ENTRIES 36
  Correcting Errors Before Your Lock in the Entry 36
  Correcting Errors After You Lock in the Entry 36
  Editing Formulas 39
COMMANDS 40
  Issuing Commands 40
  Cancelling Commands 44
THE [UNDO] KEY 44
MEMORY MANAGEMENT 45
  How Much Memory Remains? 46
  Memory-full Errors 47
  Recovering Memory 48
  Expanded Memory 49
RECALCULATION 50
  Minimal Recalculation 50
  The Method of Recalculation 50
  The Order of Recalculation 51
  Circular References 53
NAMING CELLS AND RANGES 57
  Creating Names 58
  Using Range Names 59
  The [Name] Key 59
  The / Range Name Table Command 60
  Deleting Names 62
  Changing Names 63
  The / Range Name Labels Command 63
ERASING THE WORKSHEET 65
GETTING HELP 65
EXITING FROM 1-2-3 66
CONCLUSION 67

3 Formatting the Worksheet 69
FORMATS 69
  The Global Format 69
  Formatting Cells and Ranges 71
  1-2-3's Format Options 77
  Changing the Default Format 88
ZERO SUPPRESSION 91
  The Label Option 93
  Restoring the Display of Zeros 93
  Notes 94
LABEL PREFIXES 94
  The Default Label Prefix 94
  Overriding the Default 95

　　　　The / Range Label Command 96
　　　　Changing the Default 98
　　CONCLUSION 99

4 Cut-and-Paste Commands 101
　　ADJUSTING COLUMN WIDTHS 101
　　　　Why Change Column Widths? 101
　　　　The / Worksheet Column Set-Width Command 102
　　　　Resetting the Width of a Column 105
　　　　Changing the Width of Multiple Columns 105
　　　　Changing the Global Column Width 106
　　　　Notes 109
　　　　Hiding Columns 109
　　　　Revealing Hidden Columns 111
　　ERASING ENTRIES 112
　　　　Erasing a Single Cell 112
　　　　Notes 112
　　　　Erasing a Range 114
　　　　Rejecting the Guess 115
　　INSERTING ROWS AND COLUMNS 116
　　　　Inserting Rows 116
　　　　Inserting Columns 119
　　　　Reference Effects 120
　　DELETING ROWS AND COLUMNS 121
　　　　Deleting Rows 121
　　　　Deleting Columns 122
　　　　Reference Effects 123
　　　　MOVING ENTRIES 124
　　　　Moving Single Entries 124
　　　　Moving More Than One Cell at a Time 126
　　　　Notes 127
　　　　Reference Considerations 127
　　COPYING ENTRIES 130
　　　　Copy Basics 130
　　　　A Simple Copy 130
　　　　Other FROM/TO Combinations 131
　　COPYING FORMULAS AND FUNCTIONS 135
　　　　Relative References 135
　　　　Absolute and Mixed References 138
　　　　Which to Use? 144
　　SPECIAL KINDS OF COPIES 145
　　　　The / Range Value Command 145
　　　　The / Range Trans Command 148
　　CONCLUSION 153

5 Functions 155
THE FORM OF FUNCTIONS 155
Function Names 155
Arguments 156
MATHEMATICAL FUNCTIONS 157
The @ABS Function 157
The @MOD Function 157
The @RAND Function 158
The @SQRT Function 158
The @ROUND Function 159
The @INT Function 160
Logarithmic Functions 162
Trigonometric Functions 164
STATISTICAL FUNCTIONS 166
The Form of Statistical Functions 166
The @SUM Function 167
The @COUNT Function 170
The @AVG Function 170
The @MAX and @MIN Functions 171
The @STD and @VAR Functions 171
FINANCIAL FUNCTIONS 172
Multiple Cash Flow Financial Functions 172
Single Cash Flow Financial Functions 182
Depreciation Functions 184
LOOKUP FUNCTIONS 186
The @CHOOSE Function 186
The @INDEX Function 188
The @VLOOKUP and @HLOOKUP Functions 189
LOGICAL FUNCTIONS 196
The @IF Function 196
Other Logical Functions 201
STRING FUNCTIONS 202
The @CHAR and @CODE Functions 203
The @FIND, @EXACT, and @REPLACE Functions 205
The @LEFT, @RIGHT, and @MID Functions 207
The @LENGTH Function 209
The @LOWER, @UPPER, and @PROPER Functions 210
The @STRING and @VALUE Functions 211
The @REPEAT Function 214
The @TRIM and @CLEAN Functions 215
OTHER FUNCTIONS 215
The @CELL and @CELLPOINTER Functions 216
The @COLS and @ROWS Functions 218
The @ERR Function 218

The @NA Function 219
The @N and @S Functions 219
The @@ Function 219
CONCLUSION 220

6 Worksheet Commands 221
CREATING TITLES 221
   An Example 223
   Notes 224
SPLITTING THE SCREEN 224
   An Example 225
   The [Window] Key 225
   Moving the Cell Pointer 226
   Synchronizing Windows 227
   The [Window] Key Revisited 230
   The Clear Option 230
   Notes 230
FILLING RANGES 232
   An Example 232
   Notes 232
   Filling a Rectangular Range 233
COMPUTING FREQUENCY DISTRIBUTIONS 235
   An Example 236
   Notes 237
DATA TABLES 237
   Basics 238
   A One-Variable Table 238
   The [Table] Key 240
   A Table with Two Equations 240
   A Two-Variable Table 241
   Notes 243
COMPUTING LINEAR REGRESSION 244
   An Example 245
   Using the Results 245
   Interpreting the Results 247
   Multiple Regression 248
   The Intercept Option 249
MATRIX MATHEMATICS 250
   The Multiply Option 250
   The Invert Option 252
THE / SYSTEM COMMAND 255
PROTECTION 256
   An Analogy 257
   Protecting the Worksheet 257

Reprotecting Cells 259
Unprotecting the Worksheet 259
CREATING INPUT FORMS 259
An Example 260
Notes 262
THE / RANGE JUSTIFY COMMAND 262
An Example 262
Notes 264
SEARCHING AND REPLACING 265
The Find Option 265
The Replace Option 269
Notes 269
CONCLUSION 271

7 Dates and Times 273

DATES 273
Entering Dates: The @DATE Function 274
Formatting Dates 275
Working with Date Values 279
Special Date Functions 280
Creating Date Series 282
TIMES 285
Entering Times: The @TIME Function 286
Formatting Times 287
Working with Time Values 290
Special Time Functions 291
COMBINED DATE/TIME ENTRIES 292
The @NOW Function 292
Formatting Combined Date/Time Entries 293
Creating Your Own Date/Time Entries 294
Working with Combined Date/Time Entries 295
CONVERTING LABELS INTO DATES AND TIMES 295
The @DATEVALUE Function 296
The @TIMEVALUE Function 297
CONCLUSION 298

8 Printing 299

HARDWARE SETUP 299
Choosing a Printer 300
Choosing an Interface 301
Changing the Auto-Linefeed Setting 302
PRINTING BASICS 302
An Example 303
Default Print Settings 304

The @NA Function	219
The @N and @S Functions	219
The @@ Function	219
CONCLUSION	220

6 Worksheet Commands 221

CREATING TITLES	221
An Example	223
Notes	224
SPLITTING THE SCREEN	224
An Example	225
The [Window] Key	225
Moving the Cell Pointer	226
Synchronizing Windows	227
The [Window] Key Revisited	230
The Clear Option	230
Notes	230
FILLING RANGES	232
An Example	232
Notes	232
Filling a Rectangular Range	233
COMPUTING FREQUENCY DISTRIBUTIONS	235
An Example	236
Notes	237
DATA TABLES	237
Basics	238
A One-Variable Table	238
The [Table] Key	240
A Table with Two Equations	240
A Two-Variable Table	241
Notes	243
COMPUTING LINEAR REGRESSION	244
An Example	245
Using the Results	245
Interpreting the Results	247
Multiple Regression	248
The Intercept Option	249
MATRIX MATHEMATICS	250
The Multiply Option	250
The Invert Option	252
THE / SYSTEM COMMAND	255
PROTECTION	256
An Analogy	257
Protecting the Worksheet	257

  Reprotecting Cells 259
  Unprotecting the Worksheet 259
 CREATING INPUT FORMS 259
  An Example 260
  Notes 262
 THE / RANGE JUSTIFY COMMAND 262
  An Example 262
  Notes 264
 SEARCHING AND REPLACING 265
  The Find Option 265
  The Replace Option 269
  Notes 269
 CONCLUSION 271

7 Dates and Times 273

 DATES 273
  Entering Dates: The @DATE Function 274
  Formatting Dates 275
  Working with Date Values 279
  Special Date Functions 280
  Creating Date Series 282
 TIMES 285
  Entering Times: The @TIME Function 286
  Formatting Times 287
  Working with Time Values 290
  Special Time Functions 291
 COMBINED DATE/TIME ENTRIES 292
  The @NOW Function 292
  Formatting Combined Date/Time Entries 293
  Creating Your Own Date/Time Entries 294
  Working with Combined Date/Time Entries 295
 CONVERTING LABELS INTO DATES AND TIMES 295
  The @DATEVALUE Function 296
  The @TIMEVALUE Function 297
 CONCLUSION 298

8 Printing 299

 HARDWARE SETUP 299
  Choosing a Printer 300
  Choosing an Interface 301
  Changing the Auto-Linefeed Setting 302
 PRINTING BASICS 302
  An Example 303
  Default Print Settings 304

How 1-2-3 Divides a Report into Pages 307
Aligning the Paper in the Printer 308
Printing Part of a Worksheet 309
Aborting a Print 310
FORMATTING PRINTED REPORTS 310
Margins 310
Changing the Page Length 313
Setup Strings 314
Headers and Footers 320
Borders 325
Saving Print Settings 330
Returning Print Settings to Their Defaults 330
Formatting—Final Comments 331
CHANGING THE DEFAULT PRINT SETTINGS 331
An Example 331
The Update Option 332
The Status Option 332
Forcing the Printer to Pause between Pages 332
INSERTING MANUAL PAGE BREAKS 333
An Example 333
Notes 334
UNFORMATTED REPORTS 335
LISTING THE WORKSHEET 335
CONCLUSION 338

9 File Management 339
SAVING WORKSHEETS 339
Saving a Worksheet for the First Time 339
File Names 341
Saving a Worksheet That Already Has Been Saved 342
Disk-Full Errors 344
RETRIEVING WORKSHEETS 345
A Caution 346
Retrieving a File with a Nonstandard Extension 346
Loading a Worksheet from the DOS Prompt 346
Automatic-Load Worksheets 347
ERASING A FILE 348
CHANGING THE DIRECTORY 351
Changing the Directory During Command Execution 351
Changing the Default Directory Temporarily 354
Changing the Default Directory Permanently 355
PASSWORD PROTECTING A WORKSHEET 356
An Example 356
Notes 356

THE / FILE XTRACT COMMAND 358
   Extract Basics 358
   The Formulas Option 359
   The Values Options 361
COMBINING WORKSHEETS 362
   Basics 362
   The Copy Option 363
   The Add and Subtract Options 366
   Combining a Range 371
   File Combine—Final Notes 374
LISTING FILES 374
THE / FILE ADMIN TABLE COMMAND 375
CONCLUSION 376

10 Creating Graphs 377

GRAPH BASICS 377
   The / Graph Command 377
   Data Ranges 378
   Creating a Graph 379
   Viewing Graphs 381
   Multiple-Range Graphs 382
   Graph Enhancements 384
   Naming Graphs 386
   Starting a New Graph 388
GRAPH TYPES 390
   Line Graphs 390
   Multiple-Range Line Graphs 391
   Bar Graphs 393
   Multiple-Range Bar Graphs 394
   Stacked-Bar Graphs 395
   Pie Graphs 397
   XY Graphs 400
ENHANCING GRAPHS 407
   Adding Titles 407
   Labeling the X-Axis 409
   The / Graph Options Scale Command 416
   Adding Data Labels 423
   The / Graph Options Format Command 427
   Using Color and Shading 430
   Adding Legends 432
   Removing a Legend 435
   Adding a Grid 435
SAVING A GRAPH FOR PRINTING 436
CONCLUSION 437

11 Printing Graphs 439
- PREPARING TO PRINT GRAPHS 439
- LOADING PRINTGRAPH 440
- CONFIGURING PRINTGRAPH 441
  - Choosing a Graphs Directory and a Fonts Directory 441
  - Choosing a Printer or Plotter 443
  - Choosing the Interface 444
  - Specifying Paper Size 445
  - The Pause and Eject Settings 446
- CHOOSING GRAPHS TO PRINT 447
- FORMATTING YOUR GRAPHS 448
  - Choosing a Text Font 448
  - Specifying the Size and Rotation of a Printed Graph 450
  - Choosing Colors in a Graph 456
  - Printing More Than One Graph 457
- PRINTING 459
  - An Example 460
  - Saving PrintGraph Settings 461
  - Leaving PrintGraph 463
- PRINTING GRAPHS IN 1-2-3 RELEASE 1A 463
- CONCLUSION 464

12 Data Base Management 465
- BASICS 465
  - The Structure of 1-2-3 Data Bases 466
  - The Size of 1-2-3 Data Bases 467
  - Data Base Entries 467
  - Cleaning Up a Data Base 468
  - Editing a Data Base 468
  - Saving and Printing a Data Base 469
  - Creating a 1-2-3 Data Base: An Example 469
- SORTING 471
  - Sort Basics 471
  - Sorting on a Single Field: An Example 473
  - Sorting on a Text Field 474
  - Sorting on Two Fields 476
- CRITERIA 478
  - The Criteria Range 478
  - Defining Criteria 479
  - Defining the Criteria Range 492
- QUERYING 492
  - Defining the Ranges 493
  - The / Data Query Find Command 496

Extracting Records 498
The / Data Query Delete Command 504
DATA BASE STATISTICAL FUNCTIONS 506
The Form of @D Functions 507
The @DSUM Function 508
The @DCOUNT Function 509
The @DAVG Function 510
The @DMAX and @DMIN Functions 510
The @DSTD and @VAR Functions 510
CONCLUSION 513

13 Macros 515
A SIMPLE EXAMPLE 516
Creating the Macro 516
Naming the Macro 517
Running the Macro 517
How It Works 518
MACRO BASICS 519
Macro Syntax 519
Naming Macros 523
Running Macros 525
Stopping Macros 525
Macros Are Worksheet Specific 527
Documenting Macros 529
Where to Place Macros 530
RECORDING MACROS 530
USING MENU COMMANDS IN MACROS 532
An Example 533
Another Example 534
Yet Another Example 536
Notes 539
DEBUGGING MACROS 542
Types of Errors 542
The STEP Mode 545
Editing Macros 546
AUTO-EXECUTING MACROS 547
An Example 547
Notes 548
CONCLUSION 549

14 Lotus Command Language Basics 551
COMMAND LANGUAGE BASICS 551
The Form of LCL Commands 555
Argument Types 556

  Using LCL Commands 557
  Conventions 558
 FUNDAMENTAL LCL TECHNIQUES 558
  Stopping Macros: The {Quit} Command 558
  Soliciting User Input 559
  Making Entries in Cells: The {Let} Command 564
  Conditional Testing 566
  Looping: The {For} Command 568
  Branching 573
  Subroutine Calls 576
  Creating Custom Menus: The {MenuBranch} and
   {MenuCall} Commands 584
 CONCLUSION 594

15 More LCL Techniques 595
 OTHER LCL COMMANDS 595
  Controlling the Interface 595
  Interacting with the User 602
  Controlling Program Flow 606
  Manipulating Information 612
  Working with Files 617
 ADVANCED TECHNIQUES 627
  Self-Modifying Macros 627
  Computed Macro Statements 628
 CONCLUSION 630

16 Add-in Applications 631
 USING ADD-IN APPLICATIONS 631
  Attaching Add-in Applications 632
  Invoking Add-in Applications 634
  Detaching Add-in Applications 634
  Auto-attaching and Auto-invoking Add-ins 635
  Using Add-in Applications in Releases 2 and 2.01 636
 ALLWAYS 636
  Installing Allways 637
  Attaching and Invoking Allways 638
  Formatting the Worksheet 641
  Altering the Column Widths and Row Heights 642
  Embedding a Graph Within a Worksheet 642
  Controlling the Layout of a Printed Worksheet 643
  Printing a Worksheet 643
  Controlling the Display 643
  Other Commands 644

Returning to 1-2-3	644
Saving Enhancements	644
THE MACRO LIBRARY MANAGER	645
Using the Macro Library Manager	645
Creating a Macro Library	646
Executing a Macro from a Library	648
Loading and Removing Macro Libraries	648
Editing Macro Libraries	649
Creating a Second Macro Library	653
Limitations	654
A Macro That Can Be Executed Only from a Library	654
Range Name Confusion	656
Macros That Use Other Libraries and the Worksheet	657
OTHER ADD-IN APPLICATIONS	661
CONCLUSION	662

Appendix 1: Exchanging Data with Other Programs 663

THE TRANSLATE UTILITY	663
Loading the Translate Program	664
Specifying the Translation	664
Built-in Help	665
Choosing the File to Translate	665
Changing the Directory	666
Specifying the Name for the Target File	667
Performing the Translation	668
Final Comments	669
EXCHANGING DATA BETWEEN DIFFERENT RELEASES OF 1-2-3	670
Translating 1-2-3 Release 1A Files into Releases 2, 2.01, and 2.2	670
Translating 1-2-3 Release 2, 2.01, and 2.2 Files into Release 1A	671
Exchanging Information with 1-2-3 Release 3	674
EXCHANGING DATA BETWEEN 1-2-3 AND SYMPHONY	675
Using Symphony Worksheets in 1-2-3	675
Using 1-2-3 Worksheets in Symphony	676
EXCHANGING DATA BETWEEN 1-2-3 AND dBASE	678
Translating a dBASE File into a 1-2-3 Worksheet	678
Translating from 1-2-3 into dBASE	682
WORKING WITH ASCII TEXT FILES	687
Creating ASCII Files in 1-2-3	687
Importing ASCII Text Files into 1-2-3	692
An Example	696
Parse Problems	702
OTHER KINDS OF DATA EXCHANGE	702
CONCLUSION	702

Appendix 2: The [Compose] Key 703
HOW COMPUTERS REPRESENT CHARACTERS 703
THE [COMPOSE] KEY 704
USING UPPER-LEVEL ASCII CHARACTERS 705

Appendix 3: Changing 1-2-3's Global and Default Settings 707
GLOBAL SETTINGS 707
DEFAULT SETTINGS 708
    Settings We've Explored Previously 709
    The Punctuation Setting 709
    The Currency Setting 711
    The Negative Setting 713
    The Help Setting 713
    The Clock Setting 715
    The Beep Setting 716
    Saving the Default Settings 716

Appendix 4: Using 1-2-3 on a Network 719
FILE RESERVATIONS 719
UPDATING LINKING FORMULAS 720

Appendix 5: Printing with an HP LaserJet 721
HARDWARE SETUP 721
    Running the Install Program 721
    Configuring the Printer 723
PRINTING WORKSHEETS 725
    Printing Basics 726
    Formatting Reports 729
PRINTING GRAPHS 745
    Configuring PrintGraph 745
    Graph Printing Basics 749
    Formatting the Graph 751
CONCLUSION 756

Index 757

Table of Tips

2 1-2-3 Basics
Special Number Characters 23
Blank Cells are Values 34
Pointing and Editing 39
Recalculate Before You Print 51
Recalculating Cells and Ranges 52

3 Formatting the Worksheet
Use Text Format to Create an Audit Copy of Your Worksheet 91
Use Spaces to Align Labels 98
Right-Alignment Quirk 98
Don't Type Label Prefixes 99

4 Cut-and-Paste Commands
Erasing a Cell that is Referred to by a String Formula 114
Erasing a Remote Cell or Range 116
A Potential Problem 119
Remote Moves and Copies 129
Including the From Range in the To Range 142
/ Range Value and Recalculation 147
Overlapping From and To Ranges 149

5 Functions
Computing Roots with the ^ Operator 159
Using @ROUND to Overcome Addition Errors 161
Include Extra Cells in @SUM Ranges 169
Don't Include Extra Cells in an @AVG Range 170
Use Zeros, not Blanks 171
What is Present Value Analysis? 174
What is the Period? 175
Using @NPV to Compute Present Value 177
Nesting @IF Functions 201
Using @FIND with @LEFT 208
Using @UPPER, @LOWER, and @PROPER 211
Using @STRING 213

7 Dates and Times
- Computing the Day of the Week 281
- Returning the Name of a Month 282
- Getting the Full Year 283
- Getting the Hour in 12-Hour Form 292
- Locking in the Current Date and Time 293

8 Printing
- Using [End] [Home] 307
- Left Margins and Indented Entries 311
- Hiding Rows and Columns 320
- Changing the Anchored Corner of a Range 328
- Printing Report Drafts 336

9 File Management
- Editing a File Name 343
- Using Wildcards 347
- Viewing File Names 350

10 Creating Graphs
- Graphing Discontinuous Data 379
- Setting the Lower Limit in XY Graphs 406
- Using Cell Entries as Titles 410
- Labelling Pie Segments 417
- Adding Information Labels to a Graph 428

11 Printing Graphs
- Print Density 444
- Previewing Graphs 448
- Assigning Colors to Pie Graphs 458
- Leave Your Printer Alone! 459
- Printing Graphs with Legends 462

12 Data Base Management
- Undoing a Sort 474
- Sorting Other Worksheet Entries 476
- Exact-Match Text Criteria 486
- Name the Cells of the First Record 487
- Blank Rows in a Criteria Range 495
- One-Row Output Ranges 500
- Extracting Formulas and Functions 502
- Using the [Query] Key 506
- Reusing Data Base Statistical Functions 509

Locating the Max and Min Values 511
Using a Data Table 512
Name the Ranges 513

13 Macros
Pausing Macros 526
Where is the Cell Pointer? 529
Use Range Names, not Cell References 540
Don't Forget the Label Prefix 541
Save the Worksheet Before Running a Macro for the First Time 544

14 Lotus Command Language Basics
Use Range Names as Location Arguments 557
Where is the Cell Pointer? 577
Automatic Recalculation with the /p Command 579
Don't Use Key Words as Subroutine Names 582
Use Single Word Names for Your Subroutines 584
Begin Each Option with a Different Letter 589
Place the Default Option First 589

15 More LCL Techniques
Pausing for a Specified Interval 608
Range Names with {Write} and {WriteLn} 626

Appendix 1: Exchanging Data with Other Programs
Spurious Error Messages 673
Marking the Print Range 689
Printing More than One Copy 691

1

Introduction

I first saw 1-2-3 in October of 1982. I had an office at 55 Wheeler Street in Cambridge, Massachusetts—the same building where a small startup software publisher called Lotus Development Corporation was quietly creating what would become Lotus 1-2-3. Marv Goldschmidt, a friend from my days at The Computer Store, was the VP of Marketing for Lotus. One day he invited me up to see 1-2-3.

I was blown away by what I saw. This new program had all of the capabilities of VisiCalc—then the dominant spreadsheet program—plus plenty of new commands and functions, a built-in data base, business graphics, and something called macros. It was powerful. It was fast. It was visual. It was easy to use. I didn't need a crystal ball to see that this program was going to be a big hit.

What's happened since then is now part of the lore of the PC industry: 1-2-3 was officially announced at Comdex in the fall of 1982, where it became the hit of the show. The program shipped in the last few days of January 1983. By February 1, Lotus Development had achieved break even. Within weeks, 1-2-3 had knocked VisiCalc from the top spot on the bestseller lists—a position VisiCalc had held for a couple of years. Within months, Lotus went public. Lotus 1-2-3 has since become the most popular business software ever sold, with millions of copies in use. Today 1-2-3 remains the top-selling business software in the world.

1-2-3 RELEASE 2.2

In July of 1989, Lotus introduced the latest version of 1-2-3: Release 2.2. This new release is a vast improvement over earlier releases. It includes new user-friendliness features, such as settings sheets, that make the new version a pleasure to work with. It offers a couple of new safety features, undo and automatic file backup, that help to protect your data. It integrates into 1-2-3 several capabilities, such as the ability to record macros and the minimal recalculation scheme, that were add-ins in prior versions. And it adds new features, such as the macro library manager and the /Range Search command, that were not available at all in earlier releases.

Interestingly, 1-2-3 2.2 was not the only version of 1-2-3 to debut in 1989. In the summer of 1989, Lotus announced and shipped 1-2-3 Release 3.0. This major new release offers capabilities far beyond the powers of earlier versions (including Release 2.2). The price of these new features, however, is that Release 3.0 demands more memory and more computing power than many 1-2-3 users have available to them. 1-2-3 2.2 is for those users who need a more modest upgrade that doesn't reguire them to purchase more memory or faster computers. We think Release 2.2 will be the upgrade of choice for most 1-2-3 users.

ABOUT THIS BOOK

Douglas Cobb's 1-2-3 Handbook is a reference guide and tutorial for Lotus 1-2-3. We wrote the first edition of the book in the summer of 1987. This new edition covers 1-2-3 Release 2.2.

How you use this book depends on how much experience you have with 1-2-3. If you are just starting out, you should begin with Chapter 2 and read straight through. The book presents 1-2-3 concepts in order of increasing complexity, beginning with the basics—such as making entries in cells and naming ranges—and building up to complex topics—such as macros and the Lotus Command Language.

If you are an advanced user, you probably won't need to read the book from cover to cover. Instead, you'll want to keep the book right beside your computer and use it as a reference guide. When you have a question, encounter a problem, or need to jog your memory, you can use the table of contents and the index to find the right answer. You can also read the Tips that you'll find throughout the book to pick up hints for using 1-2-3 more effectively.

I had two co-authors on this book: my brother Steve and my wife Gena. Both Steve and Gena are experienced 1-2-3 users. They are talented and experienced writers and have co-authored many other books with me, including *Mastering Symphony* and *Excel in Business*. Steve is the editor of the *1-2-3 User's Journal* and the *Symphony User's Journal*. Gena has been writing about spreadsheets for as long as I have—she was the co-author of my first book, *VisiCalc Models for Business*. Both co-authors have MBAs—Steve from the University of Chicago and Gena from Harvard.

To put it mildly, this book is much better with their contributions than it would have been without them.

A Note About Versions

This book is about 1-2-3 Release 2.2. Since Release 1A, Release 2, Release 2.01, and Release 2.2 are more similar than they are different, however, most of the book applies to all of those releases. Nearly all of the differences between Release 2.2 and earlier releases involve new features that are available only in Release 2.2. In those cases where the two releases do the same thing in different ways, we've concentrated on Release 2.2.

Throughout the book, we've used the marginal symbol that appears next to this paragraph to point out explanations of the differences between Release 2.2 and earlier releases. We also use the symbol ▶ to mark the beginning and the symbol ◀ to mark the end of these explanations. If you are upgrading from an earlier release to Release 2.2, you can scan through the book for these marginal notes. In addition, you can use the index to look up topics of interest.

RELEASE ▶ 2.2 ◀

Organization

This book is organized into 16 chapters and four appendices. Chapters 2 through 7 cover the 1-2-3 worksheet. Chapter 2, "1-2-3 Basics," explains the fundamentals: moving the cell pointer, making entries, naming ranges, and so on. This chapter also covers the concept of recalculation and tells you how 1-2-3 manages memory. In Chapter 3, "Formatting the Worksheet," we show you how to format and align the entries in your worksheets. In Chapter 4, "Cut-and-Paste Commands," you'll learn how to copy, move, and erase entries, how to insert and delete rows and columns, and how to change the widths of columns. Chapter 5, "Functions," explains 1-2-3's functions: @SUM, @NPV, and so on. Chapter 6, "Worksheet Commands," covers 1-2-3's worksheet commands, including /Data Table, /Data Regression, /Worksheet Titles, and /Range Protect. Chapter 7, "Dates and Times," explains how you can use dates and times in 1-2-3.

In Chapter 8, "Printing," we discuss the /Print command, which allows you to print worksheets. Chapter 9, "File Management," covers 1-2-3's File commands. In this chapter, we explain how to save and retrieve worksheets, erase files, extract a portion of a worksheet into a separate file, and combine all or part of one worksheet into another.

Chapters 10 and 11 cover 1-2-3 graphics. In Chapter 10, "Creating Graphs," we show you how to create each of 1-2-3's graph types, and how to add titles, legends, and other enhancements to a basic 1-2-3 graph. Chapter 11, "Printing Graphs," covers 1-2-3's PrintGraph utility, which allows you to print graphs.

Chapter 12, "Data Base Management," explains the 1-2-3 data base manager. In this chapter, we show you how to create a data base in 1-2-3, how to sort a data base, how to create and define criteria, how to query a data base, and how to use data base statistical functions.

Chapters 13, 14, and 15 explain macros and the Lotus Command Language. Chapter 13, "Macros," covers simple macros. Chapter 14, "Lotus Command Language Basics," explains the 15 most important Lotus Command Language commands. Chapter 15, "Other LCL Techniques," covers the remaining LCL commands. These three chapters include dozens of example macros.

Chapter 16, "Enhancing 1-2-3," covers the add-in manager, which allows you use to add-in programs with 1-2-3. In this chapter, we show you how to use the Add-in Manager. We also explain the add-ins that come with 1-2-3, the Macro Library Manager and Allways, in this chapter. Finally, we take a brief look at several third-party add-ins for 1-2-3.

Finally, our book includes five appendices. Appendix 1, "Exchanging Data with Other Programs," covers 1-2-3's Translate utility. In this appendix, we will show you how to import data from Symphony, dBASE II and III, and ASCII text files into

1-2-3, and also how to export data from 1-2-3 into other programs. Appendix 2, "The [Compose] Key," explains the use of the special function key [Compose]. Appendix 3, "Changing 1-2-3's Global and Default Settings," covers the / Worksheet Global Default command. Appendix 4, "Using 1-2-3 on a Network," explains a few issues that will come up when you use 1-2-3 on a network. Appendix 5, "Printing on an HP LaserJet," shows you how to print your 1-2-3 worksheets on Hewlett-Packard LaserJet printers.

Examples

The book includes examples of each of 1-2-3's commands and functions. We've tried our best to come up with realistic examples that show how you might actually use a particular command or function. For example, the discussion of the / Data Matrix command includes an example of how you would use this command to perform linear programming in 1-2-3. The discussion of the Lotus Command Language's file i/o commands includes an example that uses these commands to operate on a simple data base.

Tips

We've included over 100 tips for using 1-2-3 in this book. These tips, which are found throughout the book, are the result of our many years of work with 1-2-3. Some tips offer simple reminders, such as "Recalculate Before You Print." Others present sophisticated techniques, such as "Using @NPV to Compute Simple Present Value," and "Using Data Tables to Compute Data Base Statistical Functions." We expect that even the most experienced 1-2-3 user will find these tips valuable.

CONVENTIONS

Throughout this book, we use certain conventions to make the text easier to read and understand. To avoid confusion, we'd like to explain these conventions to you.

The contents of cells are displayed in one of two forms. If the entry appears on a separate line, it is presented in the same form 1-2-3 uses to display the contents of cells in the control panel:

A5: +A1/100

In this example, *A5* is the address of the cell that contains the entry and *+A1/100* is the entry. In general, we do not include formatting symbols, protection indicators, and column width indicators when we present the contents of cells in this way. If the reference to the entry is embedded in the text, we typically present it in italics, as in "cell A5 contains the formula *+A1/100*." When we refer to a label entry, we'll include its label prefix, and we'll usually present the label itself in italics, as in "the label *'Sales*."

The names of standard keys like [Enter], [Esc], [Ctrl], [Pg Up], and [Home] are enclosed in square brackets. So are the names of the "nameless" keys on the IBM PC keyboard: [Spacebar], [Backspace], [Tab], and [Shift]. The four arrow keys are represented by the symbols →, ←, ↓, and ↑.

When referring to function keys, we use the 1-2-3 names for those keys and enclose the names in brackets, like this: [Help], [Goto], and [Calc]. In addition, when we first refer to a key, we include a parenthetical reminder of the key location, as in "the [Calc] key ([F9])." When two or more keys must be pressed simultaneously, those key names are presented side-by-side, as in "press [Ctrl]→" or "press [Alt][F1]."

Command names are usually presented in full form, as in "the /Print Printer Range command." The name of the individual options in the command name are always capitalized. (Keep in mind that you can issue a command by simply typing the first letter of each word in the command.)

File names, range names, and function names always appear in capital letters, as in "the CUSTOMER file," "the range name PROFIT," and "the @MAX function." Unless we instruct you to do so, you do not need to use capital letters.

CONCLUSION

In this book, we've done our best to explain every facet of 1-2-3 in clear, understandable language. We hope you enjoy reading our book and that it helps you become a better 1-2-3 user. We do not think you can buy a better book about 1-2-3—we hope you agree.

2

1-2-3 Basics

In this chapter, we will cover the basics of using 1-2-3. We'll begin by telling you about the computer hardware you'll need to use 1-2-3. Next, we'll load 1-2-3 and take you on a brief tour of the screen. Then we'll explain how to move around in the worksheet and how to make and edit entries. We'll also show you how to create and use range names, and we'll discuss the concepts of memory management and recalculation. Finally, we'll show you how to quit from 1-2-3.

HARDWARE REQUIREMENTS

1-2-3 is designed to run on IBM, COMPAQ, Toshiba, and most other IBM-compatible personal computers. To use 1-2-3, you'll need to have DOS version 2.0 or later.

▶1-2-3 Release 2.2 requires that your computer have two floppy disk drives or one floppy drive and a hard disk.◀ (1-2-3 Releases 2 and 2.01 require at least one floppy disk drive. 1-2-3 Release 1A requires two floppy disk drives or one floppy drive and a hard disk.)

▶1-2-3 Release 2.2 requires at least 320K of memory.◀ (Earlier releases of 1-2-3 required only 256K of memory.) If your computer has only the minimum amount of memory, however, you probably won't be able to take full advantage of 1-2-3's capabilities. We recommend that you equip your computer with at least a full 640K to get the most from 1-2-3. (If you want to use Allways with 1-2-3, you'll need a minimum of 512K of memory.)

Of course, you must have a monitor and a display adaptor to use 1-2-3. If you plan to take advantage of 1-2-3's graphics capabilities, you'll need a graphics monitor and a graphics display adaptor. 1-2-3 supports all of the important display adapters: Monochrome, CGA, EGA, VGA, Hercules, and others. We'll talk about graphics display adaptors again when we cover graphs in Chapter 10.

If you want to print your 1-2-3 worksheets, you will also need a printer. If you want to print the graphs that you create, you will need a graphics printer or a plotter. 1-2-3 supports a wide range of printers, so the chances are good your printer is supported by 1-2-3.

RELEASE
▶ 2.2 ◀

RELEASE
▶ 2.2 ◀

Hardware Options

1-2-3 also supports several optional hardware devices. These options let you increase the speed and memory capacity of your computer.

First, 1-2-3 supports the Intel 8087, 80287, and 80387 math coprocessors. These chips are special microprocessors that perform arithmetic quickly and efficiently. When you install one of these chips in your computer, the main processor hands over all arithmetic to the coprocessor. Depending on the type of calculation being performed, a math coprocessor can increase the speed of calculation by two to 300 times. If you build large worksheets, or perform lots of complex financial computations (like present value calculations), you might want to consider a math coprocessor for your computer.

1-2-3 Releases 2, 2.01, and 2.2 also support the Lotus/Intel/Microsoft Expanded Memory Specification. The Lotus/Intel/Microsoft memory spec makes it possible to install up to 8 megabytes of expanded memory in your computer. We'll talk about the expanded memory spec later in this chapter when we talk about memory management.

Installing 1-2-3

Before you can run 1-2-3 Release 2.01 or 2.2 for the first time, you need to run a program called INIT that is delivered on your 1-2-3 System disk. This program initializes 1-2-3, recording your name and your company's name on the System disk. For more on INIT, see the booklet "Setting Up 1-2-3," which came with your copy of 1-2-3. (Earlier releases of 1-2-3 did not require you to run INIT.)

If your computer has a hard disk, you will probably want to copy the 1-2-3 program files onto that disk. Copying the program files to a hard disk lets you load 1-2-3 more quickly and allows you to avoid swapping disks when you go from 1-2-3 to the PrintGraph or Translate utility.

After you have copied 1-2-3 to your hard drive, you should install it for your computer hardware. Installing 1-2-3 tells the program about the hardware devices—the monitor, printer, and so on—it will be using. Although you can run 1-2-3 before you have installed the program, you will not be able to view graphs or print anything.

To install 1-2-3, you must run the Install program. The exact procedure you follow to install 1-2-3 depends on many factors, including the configuration of your hardware and whether or not you have copied 1-2-3 onto a hard disk. The booklet "Setting Up 1-2-3," which came with your copy of 1-2-3, does a thorough job of explaining the installation procedure.

The result of the installation procedure is a file called 123.SET, which contains the programs, called drivers, that allow 1-2-3 to work with your hardware. A copy of this file must reside on all of your 1-2-3 disks, or, if you use a hard disk, on the directory that contains your 1-2-3 program files.

If you want to, you can create more than one driver set for 1-2-3. For example, you could have a set named 123.SET and another called LASER.SET. To create the second and subsequent sets, you simply run the Install program and specify the name of the driver set in which you want 1-2-3 to save the driver programs. When 1-2-3 is loaded, it automatically looks for and reads the driver set 123.SET. If you want 1-2-3 to use a different driver set, you must type the name of that set next to the name 123 when you load the program. For example, to use the set LASER.SET, you'd type 123 LASER and press [Enter].

You can also use the Install program to modify an existing driver set. All you have to do is load the Install program and select the *Change Selected Equipment* option from the main Install menu.

LOADING 1-2-3

Once you have installed 1-2-3, you're ready to load the program. There are two basic approaches to loading 1-2-3. First, you can load 1-2-3 through the Lotus Access System. The Access System is simply a menu that links 1-2-3 with the two utility programs PrintGraph and Translate. To load 1-2-3 in this way, first change the current directory to the directory that contains the 1-2-3 program files, then type lotus and press [Enter]. After a moment, you'll see the screen shown in Figure 2-1. To load 1-2-3, just press [Enter].

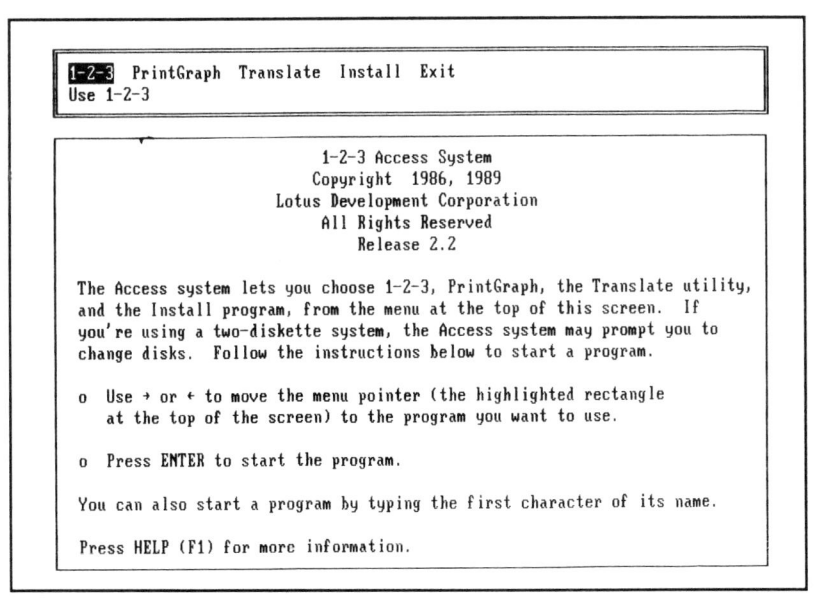

```
1-2-3  PrintGraph   Translate   Install   Exit
Use 1-2-3

                    1-2-3 Access System
                    Copyright 1986, 1989
                  Lotus Development Corporation
                     All Rights Reserved
                        Release 2.2

The Access system lets you choose 1-2-3, PrintGraph, the Translate utility,
and the Install program, from the menu at the top of this screen.  If
you're using a two-diskette system, the Access system may prompt you to
change disks.  Follow the instructions below to start a program.

o  Use → or ← to move the menu pointer (the highlighted rectangle
   at the top of the screen) to the program you want to use.

o  Press ENTER to start the program.

You can also start a program by typing the first character of its name.

Press HELP (F1) for more information.
```

FIGURE 2-1: The Lotus Access System

Instead of loading 1-2-3 through the Access System, you can load it directly. We prefer to load 1-2-3 directly since this method is a bit more efficient than using the Access System. To load 1-2-3 in this way, change the current directory to the directory that contains the 1-2-3 program files, type 123, and press [Enter]. For example, suppose that your 1-2-3 program files are on the directory C:\123. To load 1-2-3, type C: and press [Enter] to change the active disk to C, then type cd 123 and press [Enter] to make C:\123 the active directory. Next, type 123 and press [Enter].

Just how long it takes 1-2-3 to load depends on what type of computer you are using and whether or not you have a hard disk. Computers with hard disks can load 1-2-3 faster than those that use only floppy disks.

A TOUR OF THE SCREEN

After 1-2-3 is loaded, the screen of your computer will look like Figure 2-2. This main 1-2-3 screen has three distinct areas. The first three lines of this screen are called the control panel. The largest part of the screen—the part below and to the right of the inverse video bars—is called the worksheet. The last line includes the 1-2-3 clock, the error messages area, and the status indicator area. Before we go any further, let's take a brief tour of the screen.

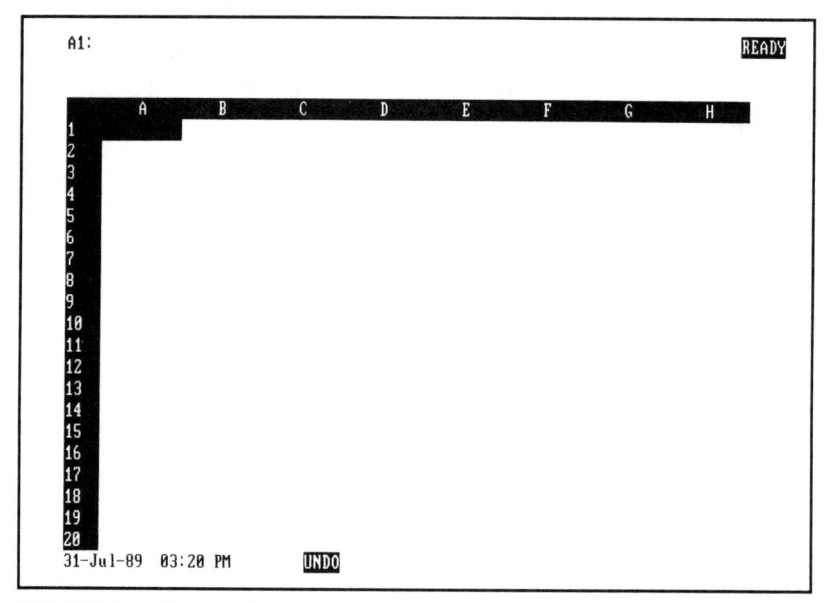

FIGURE 2-2: The 1-2-3 screen

The Worksheet

When you are using 1-2-3, a part of your computer's memory is configured as a huge grid. A 1-2-3 worksheet is 256 columns wide and 8192 rows deep. Each of the rows in the worksheet is identified by a number from 1 to 8192, and each of the columns is identified by a letter or letters from A to IV. These column letters and row numbers appear in the inverse video areas above and to the left of the worksheet area. For example, in Figure 2-2, columns A through H and rows 1 through 20 are visible on the screen.

Cells

The intersection of each row and column in the worksheet is called a cell. Each cell in the worksheet is identified by its row and column coordinates. For example, the cell at the intersection of column A and row 1 is called cell A1. Similarly, the cell at the intersection of column Z and row 100 is called cell Z100.

Cells are the basic building blocks of the 1-2-3 worksheet. Every entry you make into the worksheet is made into a cell (we'll show you how to make entries in a few pages). In addition, most commands operate on the contents of cells.

Since the 1-2-3 worksheet has 256 columns and 8192 rows, it is made up of more than two million individual cells! Keep in mind, however, that the number of cells you can use in 1-2-3 is limited by the memory capacity of the computer. We'll cover the concept of memory management later in this chapter.

The Cell Pointer

Notice that cell A1 in Figure 2-2 is highlighted (displayed in inverse video). This highlight is called the cell pointer. The cell pointer is like the point of your pencil—you use it to write information into the cells of the worksheet. Whenever you load 1-2-3, it will place the cell pointer in cell A1. Of course, you can easily move the cell pointer to any cell in the worksheet. We'll show you how to do that in a few pages.

Windows

Although the 1-2-3 worksheet is 256 columns wide and 8192 rows deep, only about 160 cells are visible in Figure 2-2. The rest of the cells are out of view to the right of and below the visible portion of the worksheet.

If you could view the entire 1-2-3 worksheet at once, like a paper worksheet, it would be more than 21 feet wide and 171 feet long! Because the screen of your PC is only nine or 12 inches wide (measured diagonally), it is impossible for you to see the entire worksheet at once on the screen. Instead, at any given time, you can see only about eight columns and 20 rows.

You can think about the screen of your computer as a window onto the 1-2-3 worksheet. Because the size of your computer's screen is limited, you can see only a small portion of the worksheet at any time through the window. If you want to see other parts of the worksheet, you must move the window. We'll show you how to do this in a few pages.

To understand this concept better, imagine cutting a one-inch square hole in a piece of cardboard and then placing that piece over this page. When the cardboard is on the page, you will be able to see only a one-inch square area at any time. By moving the cardboard around on the page, however, you could eventually view the entire page through the window in the cardboard.

Although you'll usually look at the worksheet through a single window, 1-2-3 allows you to divide the screen into two windows. Creating a second window makes it possible to view two separate parts of the worksheet at once on the screen. We'll show you how to create a second window in Chapter 6.

The Control Panel

The three lines of the screen above the column letters make up the control panel. The control panel performs many important roles in 1-2-3. For one thing, when you issue commands, 1-2-3 displays menus in the control panel. Similarly, when you make or edit cell entries, those entries appear in the control panel.

1-2-3 always displays the address of the cell pointer in the upper-left corner of the control panel. For example, the address *A1:* in the upper-left corner of the control panel in Figure 2-2 tells you that the cell pointer is located in cell A1. If the cell on which the cell pointer is positioned contains an entry, that entry will appear in the control panel next to the address indicator. If the cell has been assigned a format, or if the column that contains the cell has been assigned a special width, 1-2-3 will also display the width and the format in the control panel.

Notice the message READY in the upper-right corner of the control panel. This message, which indicates that 1-2-3 is ready for you to do something, appears in the Mode indicator. 1-2-3 uses the Mode indicator to let you know what it is up to. As you work with 1-2-3, the program will display various messages, such as VALUE, LABEL, WAIT, EDIT, and POINT, in the Mode indicator. Table 2-1 shows the meaning of each of 1-2-3's status indicators. We'll mention these messages at the appropriate spots throughout the book.

Indicator	Meaning
EDIT	You are editing a cell
ERROR	An error has occurred
FILES	1-2-3 is displaying a list of file names
FIND	You issued the / Data Query Find command
FRMT	You issued the / Data Parse Format-Line Edit command
HELP	You pressed [Help]
LABEL	You are entering a label
MENU	You have pressed / to active the menu
NAMES	1-2-3 is displaying a list of range names
POINT	You are pointing to define a cell reference
READY	1-2-3 is ready for you to take an action
STAT	You issued the / Worksheet Status command
VALUE	You are entering a value
WAIT	1-2-3 is completing a command or process

TABLE 2-1: Mode indicators

The Clock

1-2-3 displays the current date and time in the lower-left corner of the screen. For example, in Figure 2-2 the date/time *31-Jul-89 03:20 PM* appears in the clock display. 1-2-3 draws the date and time from your computer's clock, so if the system clock is incorrect, 1-2-3's clock will also be incorrect.

▶If you want to, you can tell 1-2-3 Release 2.2 not to display the clock at all, to display it in a different format, or to display the current filename instead of the clock. (In earlier releases, you cannot display the filename.) To do this, you issue the / Worksheet Global Default Other Clock command. We'll cover this command in detail in Appendix 3.◀

RELEASE
▶ 2.2 ◀

The Error Messages Area

If an error occurs while you are using 1-2-3, the program will replace the clock display with an error message. At the same time, the Mode indicator will display the message ERROR. For example, if you make too many entries in a worksheet, you might see the error message *Memory full*. If you see an error message like this one, you must press [Esc] to acknowledge the message, and then try to figure out what you did wrong. We'll cover 1-2-3's various error messages in the appropriate sections of this book.

Status Indicators

In addition, 1-2-3 uses the last line of the screen to display messages, called status indicators, that let you know the status of the keyboard or of the worksheet. Table 2-2 shows the meaning of each of 1-2-3's status indicators. We'll explain each of these indicators in detail in the appropriate parts of the book.

Indicator	Meaning
CALC	Worksheet needs to be recalculated
CAPS	[Caps Lock] key has been pressed
CMD	1-2-3 is pausing during a macro
CIRC	Circular reference exists
END	[End] key has been pressed, will affect next arrow key
LEARN	1-2-3 is in the LEARN mode
MEM	Available memory has fallen below 4096 bytes
NUM	[Num Lock] key has been pressed
OVR	1-2-3 is in Overwrite mode
RO	Worksheet is a read-only worksheet
SCROLL	[Scroll] key has been pressed
SST	A macro being executed in single-step mode is paused
STEP	1-2-3 is in STEP mode
UNDO	Undo is active and you can undo your last action

TABLE 2-2: Status indicators

FUNCTION KEYS

1-2-3 takes full advantage of the ten special function keys at the left edge of the IBM PC keyboard. 1-2-3 uses these keys to do such things as edit a cell, recalculate the worksheet, display a graph, or move the cell pointer to a selected cell. Table 2-3 lists each of these keys and briefly explains its purpose. We'll explain each of these keys fully in the appropriate chapters of this book.

We will use 1-2-3's names for these keys when we refer to them throughout the book. In addition, we will always enclose the names of function keys in brackets. For example, when we refer to the [F9] key, we'll call it [Calc].

Key	1-2-3 Name	Used to...
[F1]	[Help]	Access Help
[Alt][F1]	[Compose]	Enter special LICS characters in the worksheet
[F2]	[Edit]	Edit contents of current cell
[Alt][F2]	[Step]	Debug macros (places 1-2-3 in STEP mode)
[F3]	[Name]	Display list of range names
[Alt][F3]	[Run]	Runs a macro
[F4]	[Abs]	Create absolute and mixed references
[Alt][F4]	[Undo]	Reverses last action
[F5]	[Goto]	Jump the cell pointer to a cell
[Alt][F5]	[Learn]	[Activate] the LEARN mode
[F6]	[Window]	Move cell pointer from window to window
[F7]	[Query]	Process a query
[Alt][F7]	[App1]	Runs add-in application 1
[F8]	[Table]	Process a data table
[Alt][F8]	[App2]	Runs add-in application 2
[F9]	[Calc]	Recalculate the worksheet
[Alt][F9]	[App3]	Runs add-in application 3
[F10]	[Graph]	Display a graph
[Alt][F10]	[App4]	Runs add-in application 4

TABLE 2-3: Function keys

MOVING THE CELL POINTER

As we have explained, the cell pointer is like the point of your pencil—you use it to write information into the cells that make up the worksheet. When you first load 1-2-3, the cell pointer will always be in cell A1. In order to make an entry in another cell, you must first move the cell pointer to that cell. As you might expect, 1-2-3 offers a variety of tools that you can use to move the cell pointer.

The Arrow Keys

You can use the four arrow keys—→, ←, ↓, and ↑—to move the cell pointer one cell in any direction. For example, if you press → while the cell pointer is in cell A1, it will move to cell B1. If you press ↓ while the cell pointer is in cell B1, it will move to cell B2. Pressing ← with the cell pointer in cell B2 will move it to cell A2. Likewise, pressing ↑ with the cell pointer in cell A2 will return it to cell A1. As the cell pointer moves, the address indicator in the upper-left corner of the control panel will change to reflect the cell pointer's new position.

Of course, you can use the arrow keys to move the cell pointer many cells in any direction. For example, to move the cell pointer from cell A1 to cell C10, you would press → twice and ↓ nine times. To move it from cell C10 to cell H20, you would press → five times and ↓ ten times. (By the way, you don't have to press these keys in any particular order.)

Holding down an arrow key is the same as pressing it repeatedly. As long as you hold an arrow key, 1-2-3 will move the cell pointer from cell to cell in the indicated direction. In fact, 1-2-3 may continue to move the cell pointer for a moment or two after you release the key. This characteristic can cause you to overshoot your target cell when you are moving the cell pointer.

Moving Beyond the Edge of the Window

As we have explained, you'll never be able to see the entire worksheet on the screen at once. However, this limitation does not prevent you from moving the cell pointer to any cell in the worksheet. When you move the cell pointer to a cell that is beyond the edge of the window, 1-2-3 will shift the window to keep the cell pointer in view. In other words, no matter where the cell pointer is located on the worksheet, it will always be in view.

For example, suppose that the cell pointer is currently in cell H20. If you press →, 1-2-3 will move the cell pointer to cell I20. At the same time, the window will shift one column to the right so that column I is visible. As a result, column A will slide out of view off the left edge of the screen. If you press ↓ with the cell pointer in cell I20, 1-2-3 will move the cell pointer to cell I21. So that the cell pointer stays in view, 1-2-3 will shift the window down one row. This shift will bring row 21 into view but will move row 1 off the screen, as shown in Figure 2-3.

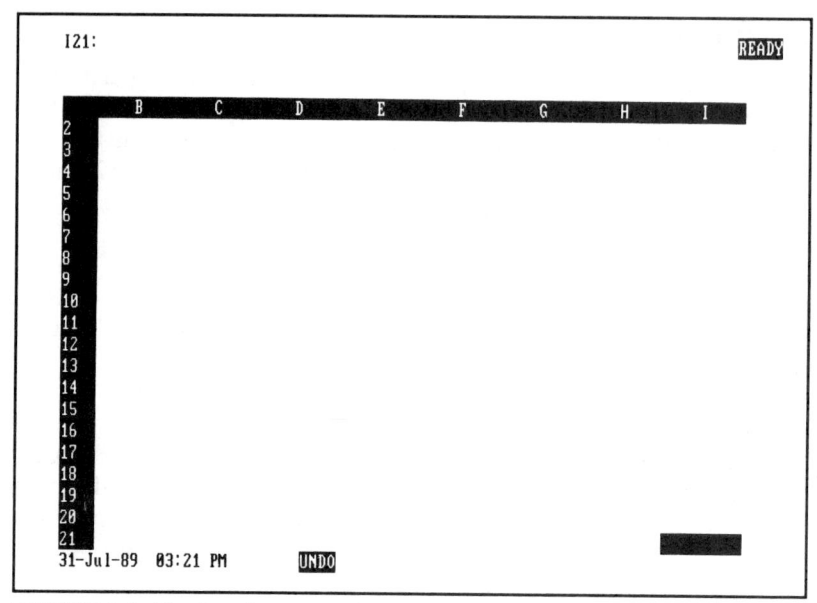

FIGURE 2-3: Moving the cell pointer

Although you can move the cell pointer past the edge of the window, you cannot move it beyond the borders of the worksheet. In other words, you cannot move the cell pointer up from row 1, down from row 8192, to the left from column A, or to the right from column IV. If you try to move the cell pointer past the edge of the worksheet, 1-2-3 will beep and the cell pointer will not move.

The [Num Lock] Key

As you probably know, the keys in the numeric keypad of the IBM PC and most compatible computers serve double duty. You can use these keys to move the cell pointer, or you can use them as a numeric keypad to type numbers.

When you first load 1-2-3, the keypad will be in the keypad mode. In this mode, you can use the keypad to enter numbers, and the arrow keys (as well as the [Home], [End], [Pg Up], and [Pg Dn] keys) are inactive. When 1-2-3 is in this mode, the status indicator NUM will appear at the bottom of the screen. If you want to use the keypad to move the cell pointer, you must press the [Num Lock] key. When you press this key, the status indicator NUM will disappear, and you'll be able to use the keypad to move the cell pointer. Since most computers these days have both a numeric keypad and a separate 4-key pad for moving the cell pointer, you may want to leave the keypad in the keypad mode all the time. On the other hand, if you like using the keypad to move the cell pointer, then you'll want to use the [Num Lock] key to change the keypad mode.

Once you have pressed the [Num Lock] key, it stays active until you press it again. If you use this key, remember to press it again to return the arrow keys to normal operation.

The [Scroll Lock] Key

Normally, when you press an arrow key, 1-2-3 will move the cell pointer. The [Scroll Lock] key changes this rule. If you press an arrow key after you press [Scroll Lock], 1-2-3 will not move the cell pointer. Instead, it will move the window one column or row in the indicated direction.

Let's consider an example. Suppose the cell pointer is in cell C2. If you press →, the cell pointer will move to cell D2. If you then press ↓, it will move to cell D3. Now let's look at the effect of [Scroll Lock]. First, move the cell pointer back to cell C2 and press [Scroll Lock]. When you press this key, 1-2-3 will display the status indicator SCROLL at the bottom of the screen. Now press →. Instead of moving the cell pointer to cell D2, 1-2-3 will leave the cell pointer in cell C2 but will shift the window one column to the right so that columns B through I are in view. Now press ↓. Again, the cell pointer will remain in cell C2, but the window will shift down one row so that rows 2 through 21 are now in view. Figure 2-4 shows the screen at this point.

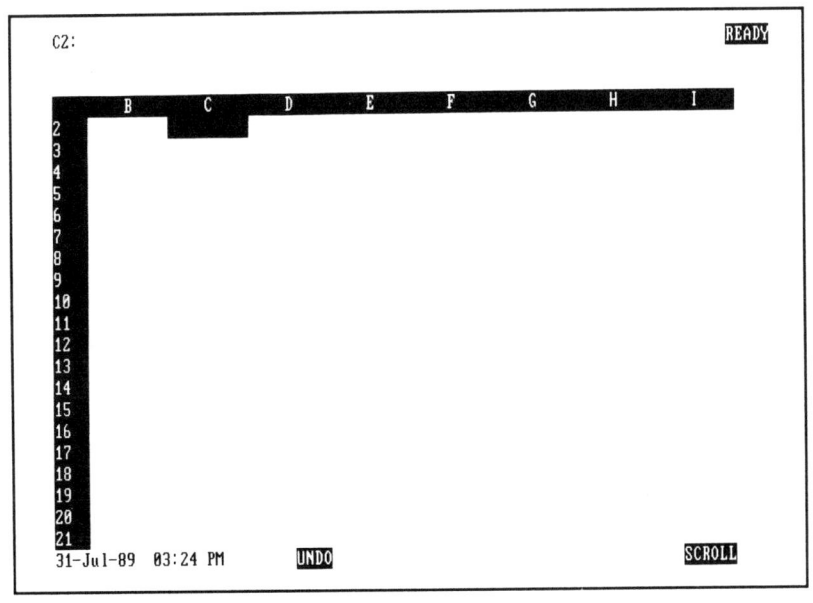

FIGURE 2-4: The [Scroll Lock] key

When the cell pointer reaches the edge of the window in the SCROLL mode, it will begin to move from cell to cell. For example, if you press ↓ one more time when the screen looks like Figure 2-4, the window will shift down one row so that rows 3 through 22 are in view. At the same time, the cell pointer will move from cell C2 to cell C3. If you then press ↑, the cell pointer will remain in cell C3, but the window will shift up one row, bringing row 1 back into view.

Like [Caps Lock] and [Num Lock], [Scroll Lock] stays active until you press it again. After you have used [Scroll Lock] to shift the screen, be sure to press it again to return the arrow keys to normal operation.

The [End] Key

The [End] key allows you to move the cell pointer to the end of a range of cells. Although the rule that describes how the [End] key works sounds complicated, the [End] key is really one of 1-2-3's most useful tools.

Here's the rule: Pressing [End] and an arrow key will move the cell pointer in the indicated direction to the cell at the next boundary between a cell that contains an entry and a blank cell. The cell pointer will always end up in a cell that contains an entry (if there is such a cell in the indicated direction). If there are no entries in the cells in the indicated direction, the cell pointer will move to the end of the worksheet.

Now that you've read the rule, let's use a few examples to make the effect of [End] more clear. First, suppose that the cell pointer is in cell A1 and that the worksheet is completely blank. If you press [End] ↓, the cell pointer will move to cell A8192—the last cell in column A. If you press [End] → with the cell pointer in cell A8192, it will move to cell IV8192. Pressing [End] ↑ at this point will move the cell pointer to cell IV1. Pressing [End] ← with the cell pointer in cell IV1 will return it to cell A1.

Now suppose that the worksheet contains a few entries, as shown in Figure 2-5 (we'll show you how to make entries in a few pages). Notice that cell A3, the current cell, contains an entry. If you press [End] →, the cell pointer will jump to cell D3—the cell at the next boundary between a cell that contains an entry (D3) and a blank cell (E3). Pressing [End] → again will move the cell pointer to cell F3—the cell at the next boundary between a cell that contains an entry (F3) and a blank cell (E3). Pressing [End] → again will move the cell pointer to cell G3.

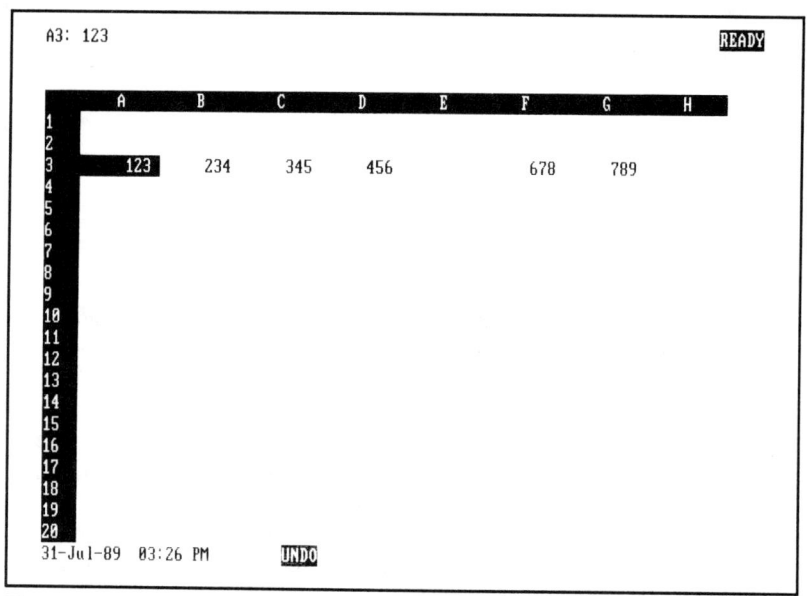

FIGURE 2-5: The [End] key

You will find that [End] comes in handy when you need to select ranges of cells—for example, when you define the FROM or TO ranges for the /Copy command. If you are like most 1-2-3 users, [End] will become one of your favorite 1-2-3 tools.

Moving by Windows

In addition to the arrow keys and the [End] key, 1-2-3 offers four tools that you can use to move through the worksheet a window at a time in any direction. These keys—[Pg Up], [Pg Dn], [Ctrl] → (or [Tab]), and [Ctrl] ← (or [Shift][Tab])—come in handy when you need to move large distances through the worksheet.

The [Pg Up] and [Pg Dn] keys move the cell pointer up or down through the worksheet one windowful at a time. For example, suppose the cell pointer is in cell A1 and that you can see rows 1 through 20 on the screen. Pressing [Pg Dn] will move the cell pointer to cell A21 and will bring rows 21 through 40 into view. Pressing [Pg Up] with the cell pointer in cell A21 will return it to cell A1 and will bring rows 1 through 20 back into view.

Since the one window you see when you first load 1-2-3 is 20 rows deep, pressing these keys will usually move the cell pointer 20 rows up or down. If you have used the /Worksheet Window Horizontal command to split the window horizontally, pressing [Pg Up] or [Pg Dn] will move the cell pointer up or down only by the height of the current window. (We'll show you how to divide the window in Chapter 6.)

The [Ctrl] → and [Ctrl] ← combination keys move the cell pointer left or right through the worksheet one windowful at a time. (Pressing [Tab] has the same effect as pressing [Ctrl] →; pressing [Shift][Tab] has the same effect as pressing [Ctrl] ←.) For example, suppose the cell pointer is in cell A1 and that you can see columns A through H on the screen. Pressing [Ctrl] → at this point will move the cell pointer to cell I1 and will bring columns I through P into view. Pressing [Ctrl] ← with the cell pointer in cell I1 will return it to cell A1 and will bring columns A through H back into view.

The [Ctrl] → and [Ctrl] ← combinations always move the cell pointer one full window. Exactly how far the cell pointer moves depends on two factors: the widths of the columns in the worksheet and the number of columns in the current window. Since the one window you see when you first load 1-2-3 is eight columns wide, pressing these keys will usually move the cell pointer eight columns to the left or right. If you have used the /Worksheet Window Vertical command to split the window vertically, pressing [Ctrl] → or [Ctrl] ← will move the cell pointer left or right only by the width of the current window. If you have changed the widths of the columns in the worksheet, pressing [Ctrl] → or [Ctrl] ← may move the cell pointer more or less than eight columns. (We'll show you how to change the widths of columns in Chapter 4.)

The [Home] Key

Pressing the [Home] key moves the cell pointer directly to cell A1. The [Home] key comes in handy when you want to return the cell pointer to the "home" position quickly.

The [End][Home] Combination

Pressing [End] and [Home] in sequence moves the cell pointer to the lower-right cell in the worksheet's active rectangle. You can use this technique to your advantage when you are defining Print ranges and other full-worksheet ranges.

The active rectangle is a range that includes every entry, formatted cell, and unprotected cell in the worksheet. The active rectangle always begins at cell A1 and includes every cell into which you have made an entry, assigned a format, or unprotected. For example, suppose you enter the number 100 in cell C12 of an otherwise empty, unformatted worksheet. The active rectangle in this worksheet is now A1..C12. If you press [End][Home] in this worksheet, 1-2-3 will move the cell pointer to cell C12. If you then enter the number 100 in cell Z100 or format that cell, the active area will become A1..Z100. If you press [End][Home] in this worksheet, 1-2-3 will move the cell pointer to cell Z100.

The [Goto] Key

The [Goto] key ([F5] on the IBM PC and most compatibles) allows you to move the cell pointer directly to any cell in the worksheet. When you press the [Goto] key, 1-2-3 will display the prompt *Enter address to go to:*, followed by the address of the current cell. When you see this prompt, you should type the address of the cell you want to move the cell pointer to, then press [Enter]. Immediately, 1-2-3 will move the cell pointer to the specified cell.

For example, suppose the cell pointer is in cell A1 and you want to move it to cell Z100. To do this, press [Goto], type Z100, and press [Enter]. Figure 2-6 shows the result. As you can see, the cell pointer is now in cell Z100.

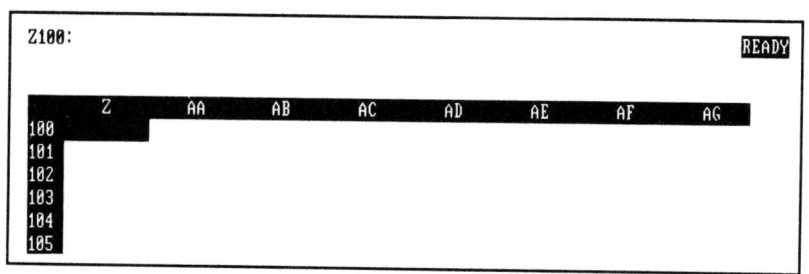

FIGURE 2-6: The [Goto] key

Notice that cell Z100 is in the upper-left corner of the screen in Figure 2-6. Whenever you use [Goto] to jump to a cell that isn't currently in view, 1-2-3 will place that cell in the upper-left corner of the screen. If the cell to which you want to move the cell pointer is in view when you press [Goto], however, 1-2-3 will simply move the cell pointer to that cell—it will not shift the screen.

Instead of using a cell address to define the cell you want to jump to, you can use a range name to define that cell. We'll cover range names later in this chapter.

MAKING CELL ENTRIES

To create your budgets, analyses, and so on in 1-2-3, you make entries into the cells of the 1-2-3 worksheet. 1-2-3 allows you to make three basic types of entries: labels, numbers, and formulas. Labels are simply text entries. Number entries are simply numbers. Formulas allow you to make computations and concatenations based on the entries in your worksheet. (Formulas and numbers are collectively referred to as values. We'll use the term *value* to describe number entries and formulas in this book.)

Entering Labels and Numbers

To enter a label or number into a cell, just move the cell pointer to that cell, type the label or number, and press [Enter]. For example, suppose you want to enter the value 123 in cell B2 in your worksheet. To begin, move the cell pointer to cell B2. Then type 123 and press [Enter]. Figure 2-7 shows this entry in place.

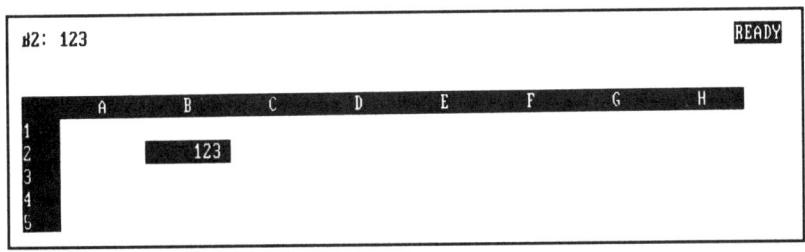

FIGURE 2-7: A number entry

1-2-3 uses the first character you type when you are making an entry to determine the type of the entry. If the first character is a numeral (0 to 9) or one of the symbols +, -, (, $, #, ., or @, 1-2-3 assumes that the entry is a value (a number or a formula). If the first character is anything other than a value character, 1-2-3 assumes that the entry is a label. In that case, the Mode indicator will change to LABEL.

▶The difference between values and labels is important. As you will see, 1-2-3 allows you to create formulas that link values and labels to labels. However, 1-2-3 Release 2 will not allow you to create a formula that links a value to a label. (1-2-3 Releases 2.01 and 2.2 will.) Any formula that attempts to do so will return an error result.◀

RELEASE
▶ 2.2 ◀

The flashing underline that appears in the control panel when you begin typing an entry is called the cursor. Later in this chapter, you'll see how to use this cursor to edit cell entries.

Locking in the Entry

As you are typing an entry, that entry will appear in the second line of the control panel (sometimes called the edit line). When you are finished typing an entry, you must lock in the entry. Locking in the entry transfers it from the control panel to the current cell.

There are several different ways to lock in an entry. The simplest is just to press the [Enter] key. When you press [Enter], the characters you have typed will disappear from the third line of the control panel. At the same time, the entry will appear in the current cell and in the first line of the control panel, next to the cell address.

For example, suppose you want to enter the value 234 into cell B3. To begin, move the cell pointer to cell B3, then type 234. As you type, the number 234 will appear on the second line of the control panel. Figure 2-8 shows the screen at this point. Now, press [Enter] to lock in the entry. Figure 2-9 shows the result. As you can see, the entry no longer appears on the second line of the control panel. However, it now appears in cell B3, and in the first line of the control panel next to the current cell indicator. As in this case, when you point to a cell, the contents of that cell will always appear in the control panel next to the address of that cell.

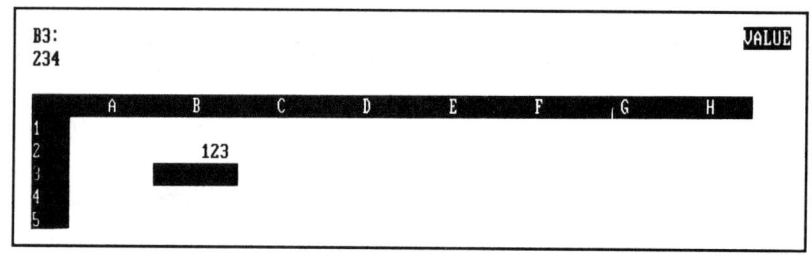

FIGURE 2-8: Making an entry

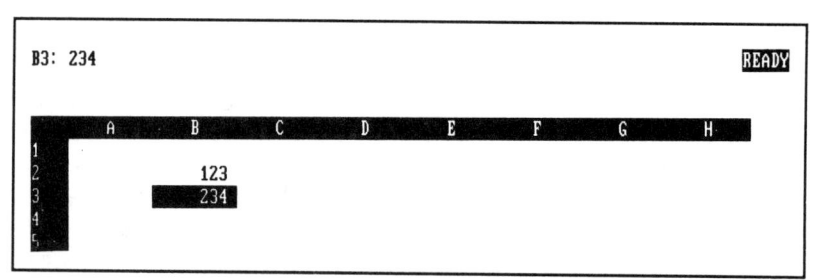

FIGURE 2-9: Locking in the entry

In addition, you can lock in an entry by pressing any of the cursor-movement keys, including →, ←, ↑, ↓, [Home], [End], [Tab], [Shift][Tab], [Ctrl]→, [Ctrl]←, [Pg Up] or [Pg Dn]. Pressing one of these keys will lock in the entry and move the cell pointer at the same time. For example, pressing → to lock in entry will an entry will lock in the entry and move the cell pointer one cell to the right. Pressing [Pg Dn] to lock in an entry will lock in the entry and move the cell pointer down twenty cells. If you are making a series of entries—for example, a series of labels across a row or a group of numbers down a column—you can save lots of keystrokes by using the cursor-movement keys to lock in the entries.

Cancelling an Entry

If you begin typing an entry, and then realize that you don't want to make an entry after all, just press [Esc]. Pressing [Esc] while you are making an entry cancels all of the keystrokes you have pressed and returns 1-2-3 to the READY mode.

Numbers

Number entries are nothing more than numbers in the cells of a worksheet. Number entries have several important properties. First, you can create formulas that use mathematical operators (+, -, *, /, and ^) to add, subtract, multiply, divide, and "exponentialize" numbers. (We'll show you how to create formulas in a few pages.) In addition, number entries can be formatted. When you format a number, it will be displayed in a special way. For example, you could format the number 1234.56 to display as $1,234.56, 1,234.56, or 1.23E3.

Value Characters

As we have said, 1-2-3 uses the first character in an entry to determine the type of the entry. If the first character is a numeral (0 to 9) or one of the symbols +, -, (, $, #, ., or @, 1-2-3 assumes that the entry is a value (a number or a formula). Normally, numbers begin with a numeral, a minus sign, an open parenthesis, or a decimal point. The other characters are used in formulas and functions.

If you begin a number entry with a plus sign, 1-2-3 will simply drop the plus sign. If you begin a number entry with a minus sign, 1-2-3 will interpret that entry as a negative number and will retain the minus sign. Similarly, if you begin and end a number entry with a parenthesis, 1-2-3 will interpret that entry as a negative number. For example, the entry *(123)* is equivalent to the entry *-123*. You'll begin decimal numbers by typing a decimal point. For example, to enter the value .33, you would type .33.

Number entries cannot contain spaces, commas, or any alphabetic characters. If you try to include one of these characters in an entry that begins with a value character, 1-2-3 won't accept the entry. Instead, when you press [Enter] to lock in the entry, 1-2-3 will beep and will display the message ERROR in the Mode indicator.

TIP: SPECIAL NUMBER CHARACTERS

In addition to the value characters +, -, (,), the numerals 0 to 9, and the characters $, #, ., and @, values can also include the characters *E* (or *e*) and %. The characters *E* and *e* can be used to enter a number in scientific notation. For example, if you make the entry 1E5 in a cell, 1-2-3 will interpret that entry as the number 100000 (or 10 to the 5th power). If you end a value entry with a percent sign (%), 1-2-3 will interpret that entry as a percentage and will divide the number you type by 100 before it stores it in the worksheet. For instance, if you type the entry 45%, 1-2-3 will interpret that number as .45.

Long Numbers

A number entry can be up to 240 characters long. Since the standard column width in 1-2-3 is just nine characters, however, it should be clear that 1-2-3 needs some rules for displaying long entries. If you enter a value into a cell that is too narrow to display the value in full, 1-2-3 will display the value in scientific notation. For example, if you enter the value 12345678901234 into cell B4, which is nine characters wide, 1-2-3 will display the value in scientific notation, as shown in Figure 2-10. (The number of digits that 1-2-3 will display in this sort of situation depends on the width of the column that contains the long number. If you change the width of the column that contains the long entries, 1-2-3 will change the displayed value according to the width of the cell. However, changing the column width affects only the displayed value of numbers on your worksheet. Column width has no effect on the actual number stored in the cell.)

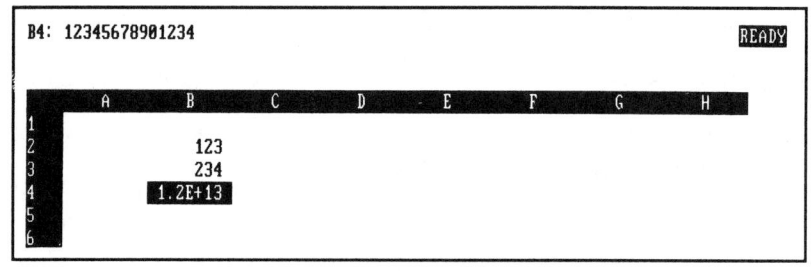

FIGURE 2-10: A long value entry

Display and Contents

If you look at the control panel in Figure 2-10, you'll see that cell B4 actually contains the number you entered, 12345678901234, even though the cell displays the value *1.2E+13*. Although 1-2-3 has changed the appearance of the entry in cell B4, the actual contents of cell B4 are still the same.

This is a very important concept. What is displayed in a cell and what is actually stored in the cell may be two entirely different things. We'll come back to this concept later in this chapter and again in Chapter 3, where you'll learn to control the way entries are displayed by assigning formats to cells.

Precision of Numeric Values

If you enter a very large or very small number into the worksheet, 1-2-3 may store that number in scientific notation. For example, if you enter a number like 123456789012345678 into a cell, 1-2-3 will display that number as 1.2E+17. In addition, 1-2-3 will store the number in scientific notation: 1.2345679E+17.

Similarly, if you enter a value smaller than .0000000001 into a cell, 1-2-3 will store that value in scientific notation. For instance, if you enter the value .0000000001 into a cell, 1-2-3 will display the value as 1.0E-10 and will store the value as 1.0000000E-10.

This is the one exception to the rule we stated in the previous section. Normally, when you enter a number in a cell, 1-2-3 will remember the actual number you enter, even if it changes the number for display purposes. If the number is very large, however, or very small, 1-2-3 will store an abbreviated version of the number.

You can enter values as large as 10^{99} or as small as 10^{-99} into a cell. 1-2-3 can calculate values as large as 10^{308} or as small as 10^{-308}, but will store any value greater than 999999999999999 or smaller than .0000000001 in scientific notation.

Labels

Labels are simple text entries. You'll use labels in your worksheets as column headers and row labels, as worksheet titles, and as notes and messages.

1-2-3 considers any entry that begins with a character other than one of the value characters to be a label. (Labels typically begin with a letter, a space, or a punctuation mark.) To enter a label into a cell, just move the cell pointer to that cell and type. When you are finished typing the entry, you can use any of the techniques discussed above to lock the entry.

For example, suppose you want to enter the label *Sales* in cell A2 of the worksheet in Figure 2-10. To do this, move the cell pointer to cell A2, type Sales, and press [Enter]. Figure 2-11 shows the result.

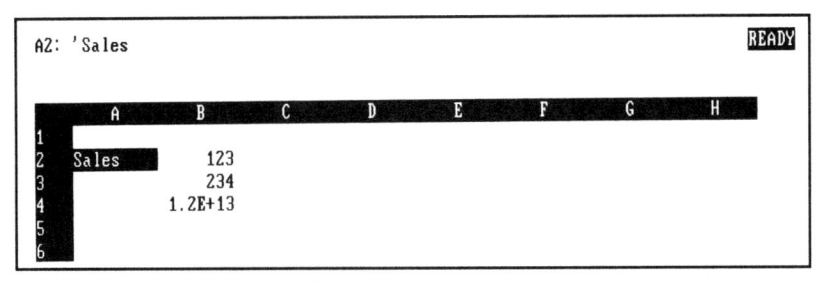

FIGURE 2-11: Entering a label

Label Prefixes

If you look at the control panel in Figure 2-11, you'll see an apostrophe (') in front of the entry in cell A2. This character is called a label prefix. Although you usually don't have to type a label prefix when you enter a label, every label must have a label prefix. Label prefixes control the alignment of labels in the cells of the worksheet.

1-2-3 offers four label prefixes: ' (left-aligned), " (right-aligned), ^ (centered), and \ (repeating). (There is a fifth prefix, |, which is used only in special circumstances; we'll cover it in Chapter 8, "Printing.") The left-aligned prefix, ', is the default label prefix.

If you enter a label without first typing a prefix, 1-2-3 automatically will give that label the default prefix. Provided that you have not changed the default prefix, the default prefix will be ', and the label will be left-aligned in the cell. For example, the label in cell A2, *'Sales*, which has the prefix ', is left-aligned. Even though we did not

type a label prefix when we entered this label, 1-2-3 supplied the default prefix '
automatically. (We'll show you how to change the default label prefix in Chapter 3.)

Changing Alignment

By using different label prefixes, you can align a label with the right edge of a cell or center it in a cell, or repeat a label so that it fills a cell. Figure 2-12 shows examples of left-aligned, right-aligned, centered, and repeating labels. For example, cell B1 contains the label *^Qtr 1*. Notice that this entry is centered in cell B1. To enter this label, we moved the cell pointer to cell B1, typed ^Qtr 1, and pressed [Enter]. Cell A6 contains the label *"Net*. To enter this label, we moved the cell pointer to cell A6, typed "Net, and pressed [Enter]. As you can see, this entry is aligned with the right edge of cell A6.

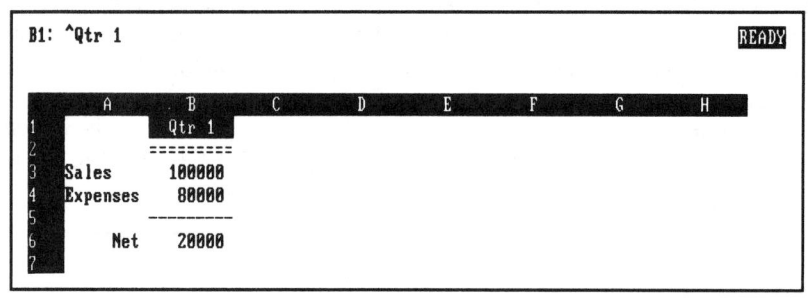

```
B1: ^Qtr 1                                                      READY

              A       B        C        D        E        F        G        H
                     Qtr 1
    1
    2              =========
    3      Sales    100000
    4      Expenses  80000
    5              ---------
    6          Net   20000
    7
```

FIGURE 2-12: Label alignment

Although we said that the label in cell A6 is right-aligned, it is actually offset one character from the right edge of the cell. 1-2-3 always offsets right-aligned labels one character from the right edge of cells.

Repeating Labels

The \ prefix causes 1-2-3 to repeat the label you specify enough times to fill the cell. This prefix is most often used to create underlines and dividers in the worksheet. For example, cells B2 and B5 in Figure 2-12 contain repeating labels. Cell B2 contains the label \=. To enter this label, we moved the cell pointer to cell B2, typed \=, and pressed [Enter]. Cell B5 contains the repeating label \-, which we entered by moving the cell pointer to cell B5, typing \-, and pressing [Enter]. In both cases, 1-2-3 has repeated the character that follows the backslash to fill the cell.

You can use the backslash prefix to repeat any character or combination of characters. For example, the label \=* would cause 1-2-3 to repeat the characters = and *. In addition, once you have used the backslash prefix to create a repeating label, you can use the / Copy command to copy that label into adjacent cells. The result is a divider that spans the worksheet. If you widen a cell that contains a repeating label, 1-2-3 will widen the label to account for the new column width. (We'll cover the / Copy command and the / Worksheet Column Set-Width command in Chapter 4.)

Long Labels

A label entry can be up to 240 characters long. If you create a label that is too long to be displayed in a single cell, 1-2-3 will allow that label to overlap into adjacent cells. For example, suppose you enter the label *This is a long label* into cell B2 in a blank worksheet, as shown in Figure 2-13.

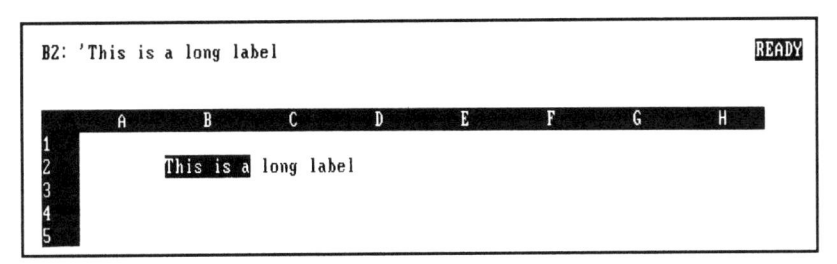

FIGURE 2-13: A long label

Notice that this label overlaps the right border of cell B2 and spills into cell C2. Although it looks like the label is now in two cells, the entire label is still stored in cell B2. If you move the cell pointer to cell C2 and look at the control panel, you'll see that this cell is still empty. The characters that seem to be contained in cell C2 are really stored in cell B2 and only seem to overlap into C2.

1-2-3 allows long labels to overlap into adjacent cells only if those cells are blank. If the adjacent cells contain entries, 1-2-3 will truncate the display of the long label. To see how this works, enter the label *'Another label* in cell C2. As you can see in Figure 2-14, this new entry prevents 1-2-3 from displaying the entire long label that is stored in cell B2.

FIGURE 2-14: Another label

It is important that you understand that entering the label in cell C2 did not affect the label in cell B2. If you were to move the cell pointer back to cell B2, you'd see the entire label *This is a long label* in the control panel. Entering the label in cell C2 simply prevents 1-2-3 from displaying the label in cell B2 in full.

Numeric Labels

As we have said, 1-2-3 uses the first character in an entry to determine the type of the entry. If the first character is a value character, 1-2-3 will assume that the entry is a value. But what if you want to enter a label that begins with a value character, such as the label *9999 Elm Street*? In that case, you must begin the entry by typing a label prefix.

For example, to enter this label into cell B4 in Figure 2-14, you would move the cell pointer to cell B4, type '9999 Elm Street, and press [Enter]. Because you begin this entry with a label prefix, 1-2-3 will consider it to be a label. (Of course, you could just as easily use the label prefix "or ^ to begin the entry.)

There are some text entries, like telephone numbers and zip codes, that are made up entirely of numbers. You must precede these types of entries with a label prefix when you enter them into the worksheet. For example, to enter the phone number 502-425-7756 into a cell, you would type '502-425-7756. If you forget the label prefix, 1-2-3 will assume that the entry is a formula: 502 minus 425 minus 7756—not at all what you had in mind.

Formulas

If you could enter only simple numbers and labels into the worksheet, 1-2-3 would be nothing more than an expensive notepad. The power of the 1-2-3 worksheet is its ability to use formulas to make calculations based on the numbers and labels in the worksheet.

Let's walk through a series of simple formulas to see how they work. To begin, move the cell pointer to cell B2 in a blank worksheet, type 7+4, and press [Enter]. As soon as you press [Enter], 1-2-3 will display the value 11 in cell B2. If you look at the control panel, however, you'll see that cell B2 actually contains the formula you typed: 7+4.

Now move the cell pointer to cell B3 and type 7-4. When you lock in this entry, 1-2-3 will display the value 3 in cell B3. Now enter the formula 7*4 in cell B4, the formula 7/4 in cell B5, and the formula 7^4 in cell B6. When you lock in these formulas, 1-2-3 will display the value 28 in cell B4, the value 1.75 in cell B5, and the value 2401 in cell B6. Figure 2-15 shows the worksheet with these formulas in place.

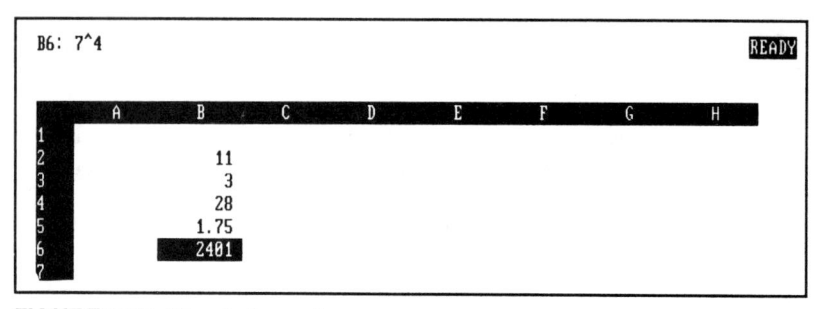

FIGURE 2-15: Simple formulas

Each of the formulas in Figure 2-15 uses one of 1-2-3's five mathematical operators. As you've probably already guessed, the plus sign (+) tells 1-2-3 to add, the minus sign (-) tells 1-2-3 to subtract, the asterisk (*) tells 1-2-3 to multiply, the slash (/) tells 1-2-3 to divide, and the carat (^) tells 1-2-3 to raise a number to a specified power.

Precedence of Operators

As you begin building complex formulas, you'll need to think about the precedence that 1-2-3 assigns to each operator. The term *precedence* simply refers to the order in which 1-2-3 performs calculations in complex formulas. As a general rule, 1-2-3 multiplies and divides before it adds and subtracts. For example, the formula *6+18/3* returns the value 12. When 1-2-3 computes this result, it calculates the value of *18/3* first, then adds 6 to that value.

When you are building long, complex formulas, it can often be difficult to predict exactly how 1-2-3 will calculate your formula. To get around this problem, you can use parentheses to override 1-2-3's built-in operator precedence and specify the order in which you want the elements of your formula to be evaluated. For example, each of the formulas in Table 2-4 uses the same values and operators. Only the parentheses are different. As you can see, however, the results are completely different.

Formula	Value
2*5+10/8-3	8.25
(2*5)+10/(8-3)	12
2*(5+10)/8-3	0.75
(2*5+10)/8-3	-0.5
2*(5+(10/(8-3)))	14

TABLE 2-4: Precedence of operators

Whenever you use parentheses in your formulas, make sure you include a closing parenthesis for each opening parenthesis. Otherwise, 1-2-3 will beep when you try to lock in the entry and will not accept it.

Using Cell References in Formulas

The simple example formulas we've considered so far have operated on literal numbers only. In most cases, however, the formulas you create will refer to the numbers in other cells of the worksheet. When you create a formula that contains cell references, you link that formula to other cells in the worksheet. As a result, the value of the formula always depends on the current values of the source cells. If you make a change to any of the source cells, the value of the formula will also change. You'll find this capability to be extremely valuable.

To enter a formula that begins with a cell reference, you must first type a value character—usually +, -, or (. If you forget to type the value character, 1-2-3 will assume that the formula is a label. Why? Because the first character in a cell reference is a letter.

For example, consider the worksheet in Figure 2-16. Cells B2, B3, and B4 in this worksheet contain the values 100, 50, and 25 respectively. Let's enter a few formulas into this worksheet. First, move the cell pointer to cell B6 and enter the formula +B2 (don't forget to type the plus sign). Notice in Figure 2-17 that this formula returns the value 100, which is the value of cell B2. The formula in cell B6 links cell B6 to cell B2 so that the value of cell B6 will always be equal to the value in cell B2.

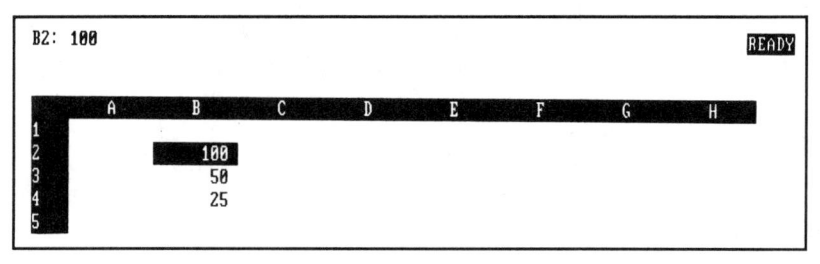

FIGURE 2-16: A simple worksheet

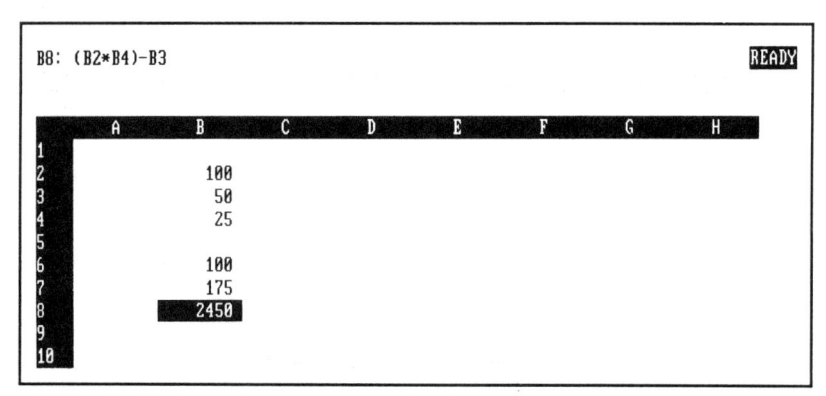

FIGURE 2-17: Formulas that use cell references

Now move the cell pointer to cell B7 and enter the formula +B2+B3+B4. In Figure 2-16, this formula returns the value 175, the sum of the values in cells B2, B3, and B4. This formula links cell B7 to cells B2, B3, and B4.

Finally, enter the formula (B2*B4)-B3 in cell B8. This formula tells 1-2-3 to multiply the value in cell B2 by the value in cell B4, and then to subtract the value in cell B3 from that result. In Figure 2-17, this formula returns the value 2450.

As we have said, if you make a change to one of the values on which a formula depends, the value of the formula will also change. If you make a change to B2, the value of the formulas in cells B6, B7, and B8 will also change. For example, suppose you move the cell pointer to cell B2 and change the entry there to 200. As you can see in Figure 2-18, when you change the value of cell B2, 1-2-3 automatically updates the values of cells B6, B7, and B8.

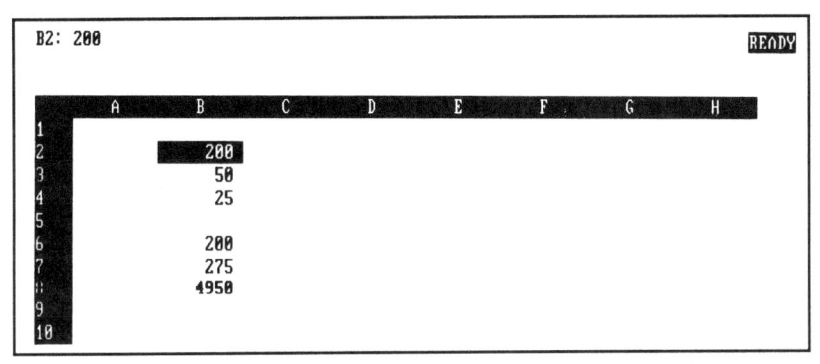

```
B2: 200                                                    READY

         A       B       C       D       E       F       G       H
    1
    2           200
    3            50
    4            25
    5
    6           200
    7           275
    8          4950
    9
   10
```

FIGURE 2-18: Changing the value on which a formula depends

For purposes of formulas, 1-2-3 assigns the value 0 to blank cells and cells that contain labels. If you create a formula that refers to a blank cell, or to a cell that contains a label, then the reference to that cell will have the value 0 in your formula. For example, if cell A1 contains the value 1000 and cell A2 contains the label *'test* (or if cell A2 is blank), then the formula +A1+A2 will return 1000. (In 1-2-3 Release 2, a formula that refers to a cell that contains a label will return the value ERR.)

Of course, you can create formulas in 1-2-3 that are much more complex than the simple examples we've given here. Your formulas can be up to 240 characters long and may contain dozens of operators, cell references, and parentheses. You'll see examples of formulas—both simple and complex—throughout the book.

Pointing

Instead of typing the cell references in your formulas, you can define the formulas by pointing to those cells. Pointing can save time and can help avoid typing errors. For example, suppose you want to create a formula in cell B9 that totals the values you entered in cells B2, B3, and B4. To do this, move the cell pointer to cell B9 and type a plus sign (+). Next, press ↑ to move the cell pointer to cell B2. As you press ↑, notice that the formula in the second line of the control panel changes from +B8 to +B7 to +B6, and so on. Also, notice that the Mode indicator reads POINT as you are pointing.

When the cell pointer is on cell B2, type another plus sign. At this point, the cell pointer will move back to cell B9 and the second line of the control panel will contain the partial formula *+B2+*. Now, press ↑ again to move the cell pointer to cell B3. When the cell pointer is in place, type another plus sign. Finally, press ↑ again to move the cell pointer to cell B4 and press [Enter]. As you can see in Figure 2-19, the finished formula is *+B2+B3+B4*. The result of the formula is 275.

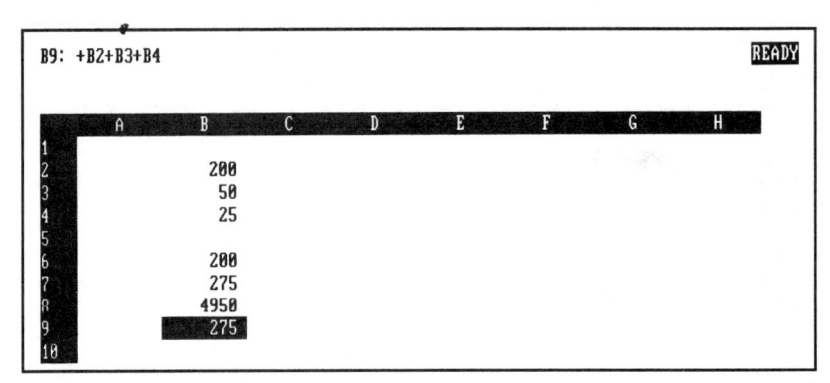

```
B9: +B2+B3+B4                                            READY

      A      B      C      D      E      F      G      H
 1
 2          200
 3           50
 4           25
 5
 6          200
 7          275
 8         4950
 9          275
10
```

FIGURE 2-19: Pointing to define a formula

You can use any of 1-2-3's cursor-movement keys—including →, ←, ↑, ↓, [Home], [End], [Pg Up], [Pg Dn], [Ctrl]→ and [Ctrl]←—while you are pointing to define a formula. Each of these keys has the same effect when you are pointing that it has when you are simply moving the cell pointer. As you might have noticed, when you point to cells, 1-2-3 doesn't place a cell reference in the formula you're building until you type a mathematical operator or press [Enter].

You can use this technique to create any formula. In fact, we greatly prefer pointing to typing for defining formulas. When you point, you don't have to remember the precise address of a cell, but only its relative location in the worksheet. This means that you can devote your attention to building your worksheet instead of to remembering the addresses of a bunch of cells.

Absolute and Relative References

In 1-2-3, there are three kinds of cell references: relative references, absolute references, and mixed references. The cell references in the sample formulas you have seen so far are relative references. When you use the / Copy command to copy a formula that contains a relative reference, the reference will change to reflect the location of the copy. 1-2-3 also allows you to create absolute references to other cells in your worksheet. Absolute references refer to other cells by their absolute position in the worksheet. When you copy a formula that contains an absolute reference, that reference will not change. Mixed references are half relative and half absolute.

The difference between absolute and relative references doesn't become very important until you begin using the / Copy command. For now, we'll just introduce the concept; we'll cover it again in Chapter 4.

You can specify absolute and mixed references in your formulas by typing a dollar sign ($) before the column and/or row coordinates of the cell address. For example, to enter an absolute reference to cell A1, you would type +$A$1. To enter a mixed reference to cell A1, you would type either +$A1 or +A$1.

You can also use the [Abs] key ([F4] on the IBM PC) to define absolute and mixed references. We'll show you how to use this key in Chapter 4.

String Formulas

1-2-3 also lets you create formulas that refer to cells containing labels. These formulas are called string formulas. 1-2-3 even offers a special operator, &, which allows you to concatenate labels and strings together. (1-2-3 Release 1A does not have the ability to create string formulas.)

An Example

Let's look at an example of a string formula. Cell B2 in Figure 2-20 contains the label *'Louisville* and cell B3 contains the label *'KY*. Cell B5 in this worksheet contains the formula +B2. This formula returns the string *Louisville*.

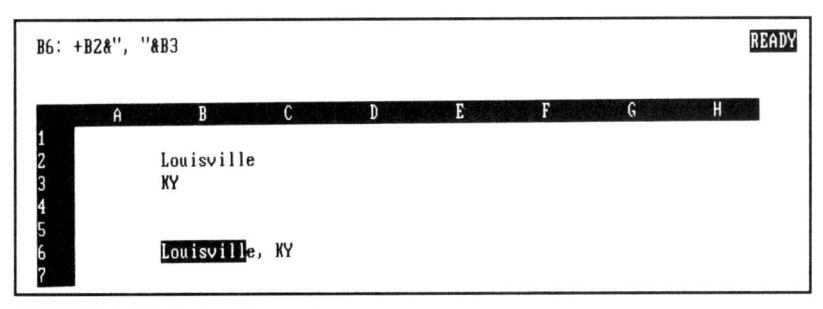

```
B6: +B2&", "&B3                                              READY

       A      B         C        D       E        F       G       H
   1
   2         Louisville
   3         KY
   4
   5
   6         Louisville, KY
   7
```

FIGURE 2-20: String formulas

Concatenation

You can use the concatenation operator, &, to concatenate, or string together, several labels or strings. For example, cell B6 in Figure 2-20 contains the formula *+B2&", "&B3*. As you can see, this formula returns the string *Louisville, KY*. In other words, this formula "strings together" the labels in cells B2 and B3.

The formula also includes a literal string—a comma and a space enclosed in quotation marks—to separate the two cell references. 1-2-3 allows you to use any literal string you want in a string formula. When you use a literal string in a string formula, you must enclose it in quotation marks.

You cannot use the concatenation operator to concatenate numeric values to labels or to concatenate values to other values. Nor can you use 1-2-3's mathematical operators (+, -, /, *, and ^) to link one label to another label.

> **TIP: BLANK CELLS ARE VALUES**
>
> For purposes of formulas, 1-2-3 assigns the value 0 to blank cells in the worksheet. This means that a string formula which tries to concatenate a string or label to a blank cell will always return the value ERR. This occurs because 1-2-3 will never allow you to create a formula that links a label or string to a value. For example, if cell B2 contains the label *'Expenses*, and cell B3 is blank, the formula *+B2&B3* will return the value ERR.

Error Values

Sometimes you will create formulas that will return error messages instead of values. Among the most common causes of errors are formulas that use a blank cell as the divisor in a division calculation. For example, suppose cell B2 contains the formula *+100/A2*. If cell A2 is blank, or if cell A2 contains the number 0, 1-2-3 will not be able to resolve the formula and will return the error value ERR.

You will also see an error if you use the / Worksheet Delete command to delete a row or column that contains cells that are referred to by a formula. For example, suppose you enter the formula *+A1+A2+A3* in cell A5. If you delete row 3 from the worksheet, the formula will change to *+A1+A2+ERR*, and the cell will display the error value *ERR*. (We'll cover the / Worksheet Delete command in Chapter 4.)

Linking Formulas

RELEASE ► 2.2 ◄

►1-2-3 Release 2.2 allows you to enter formulas that refer to cells in other worksheets. To create a formula that refers to a cell in another worksheet, simply enter a formula in the form

    +<<worksheet>>cell

into a cell, where *worksheet* is the name of the worksheet that contains the cell you want to refer to, and *cell* is the address (or name) of the cell. For example, you would use the reference

    +<<TEST1>>A1

to refer to cell A1 of the worksheet named TEST.WK1—as long as that worksheet is in the current directory. If the worksheet is not in the default directory, you must preface the name of the file with its path. For example, if TEST.WK1 is stored in the directory c:\12322\worksheets, and that directory is not the default directory, you would have to use the formula

    +<<C:\12322\WORKSHEETS\TEST1.WK1>>A1

to reference the entry in cell A1 of that worksheet.

As long as the worksheet you are referring to has the standard filename extension .WK1, you don't have to specify the filename extension when you are creating linking formulas. All you need to supply is the worksheet's filename. However, if the worksheet you want to refer to has a nonstandard extension (any extension other than .WK1 is nonstandard), then you'll have to provide the filename extension as well.

Limitations

There are several significant restrictions on the use of the linking references. First, linking references have to stand alone—they cannot be imbedded in formulas or functions. If you try to imbed a linking formula in a formula or function, 1-2-3 won't accept the formula or function. For example, 1-2-3 will balk if you try to enter the formula +<<TEST1>>A1+1 into your worksheet. To perform this calculation, you must enter the formula +<<TEST1>>A1 into one cell, then create a formula in another cell that refers to the cell that contains the linking formula.

Second, linking formulas can refer to only one cell in the remote worksheet. If you try to create a linking formula that references more than one cell, 1-2-3 will enter a reference to only a single cell. For example, if you type +<<TEST1.WK1>>A1..B5 and press [Enter], 1-2-3 will accept the formula +<<TEST1.WK1>>A1; if you type +<<TEST1.WK1>>B5..A1, 1-2-3 will accept the formula +<<TEST1.WK1>>B5.

Unfortunately, Release 2.2 doesn't adjust linking formulas when you delete or rename the worksheet that contains the referenced cell. For example, suppose that after entering the formula +<<TEST1.WK1>>A1 into a cell of a 1-2-3 Release 2.2 worksheet, you save the worksheet, retrieve TEST.WK1, resave it under the name FILE.WK1, and then erase the file named TEST.WK1. When you subsequently retrieve the original worksheet, you'll see that the linking formula is still +<<TEST1.WK1>>A1—not +<<FILE.WK1>>A1. Since TEST.WK1 no longer exists, this formula will return the value ERR. The same thing happens to linking formulas that do not specify a path when you change the default directory.

Release 2.2 also does not adjust linking formulas in the same way it does regular formulas when you move the referenced cell. For example, suppose that after entering the formula +<<TEST1.WK1>>A1 into cell A1 of a worksheet, you saved that worksheet, retrieved TEST1.WK1, used the / Move command to move the entry from cell A1 into cell B5, and resaved the file. When you subsequently retrieve the original worksheet, you'll see that the linking formula is still +<<TEST1.WK1>>A1—not +<<TEST1.WK1>>B5. Fortunately, this problem does not occur if you use range names instead of cell references in your linking formulas. (For more on the / Move command, see Chapter 4, "Cut and Paste Commands.")

The / File Admin Link-Refresh Command

1-2-3 recalculates the linking formulas in a worksheet when you retrieve that worksheet. However, it does not recalculate those formulas when it recalculates the worksheet. To recalculate linking formulas, you must use the / File Admin Link-Refresh command. When you issue this command, 1-2-3 Release 2.2 updates all the linking formulas in the current worksheet.

You'll probably only use the / File Admin Link-Refresh command if you use 1-2-3 on a network. Here's why: On single-user systems, only one worksheet can be open at a time. Consequently, there's no way to make changes to a worksheet that is referenced by a linking formula while the worksheet that contains the linking formula is open. This fact, combined with the fact that 1-2-3 recalculates the linking formulas in a worksheet whenever you retrieve a worksheet, means the result of a linking formula on a single-user system always will be up-to-date.

When 1-2-3 is used on a network, however, more than one person can work with the same worksheet at the same time. Consequently, another user can save changes to a file that is referenced by a linking formula in the worksheet you are using at the time. In situations of this sort, you may wish to update the linking formulas in your worksheet. Unless you issue the / File Admin Link-Refresh command, 1-2-3 won't recalculate the linking formulas until the next time you retrieve the worksheet. (For more about using 1-2-3 on a network, see Appendix 4.)◄

EDITING ENTRIES

No matter how good a typist you are, you'll occasionally make typos and other errors when you make cell entries. Fortunately, 1-2-3 makes it easy to edit entries.

Correcting Errors Before You Lock in the Entry

If you make typing errors as you are creating an entry, you can correct them in a couple of different ways. If your mistake is simple and you catch it quickly, you can use the [Backspace] key to erase it from the entry. For example, suppose that you are entering the label *1986 Sales Forecast* in cell A2 of a blank worksheet. To make this entry, you would move the cell pointer to cell A2 and begin typing. Suppose that as you type the entry, however, you type *1986 Sael*. To correct this error, you could press [Backspace] twice to erase the error, and then simply complete the entry. When you finished making the entry, you could press [Enter] to lock it in.

If the entry has several mistakes or if it is fairly short, you might be better off cancelling the entry and starting over rather than trying to edit out the mistakes. To cancel an entry, just press [Esc] before you lock in the entry. Once the entry has been cancelled, you can simply start over from scratch.

Correcting Errors After You Lock in the Entry

If you have already locked in the entry before you discover a mistake, you can take two different approaches to correcting the error. You can either replace the entry with a new entry or use the [Edit] key to enter the EDIT mode and edit the entry.

Replacing an Entry

If, like some labels and most numbers, the entry you want to change is fairly short, it is probably easier to replace the erroneous entry with a new entry. If you want to replace an entry in a cell with a new entry, just move the cell pointer to that cell, type the new entry, and press [Enter]. 1-2-3 will delete the old entry as soon as you press [Enter] to lock in the new entry. For example, suppose you wanted to enter the label *Sales* in cell A5, but instead you typed *Slaes*. To correct this error, just move the cell pointer to cell A5, type Sales, and press [Enter].

The [Edit] Key

If the entry you want to change is long or complex, you'll probably want to edit the entry instead of replacing it. To edit an entry, you must move the cell pointer to the cell that contains the entry and press the [Edit] key ([F2]). Pressing [Edit] puts 1-2-3 in the EDIT mode and brings the contents of the current cell into the second line of the control panel. Once you have pressed [Edit], you can edit the cell using the same techniques discussed in the previous section.

For example, suppose cell A2 contains the label *'1986 Sales Forecast*. To edit this label, move the cell pointer to cell A2 and press [Edit] ([F2]). Figure 2-21 shows the screen at this point. Notice that the label from cell A2 now appears in the control panel and the flashing cursor appears at the end of the entry.

```
A2: '1986 Sales Forecast                                          EDIT
'1986 Sales Forecast
         A         B         C         D         E         F         G         H
    1
    2  1986 Sales Forecast
    3
```

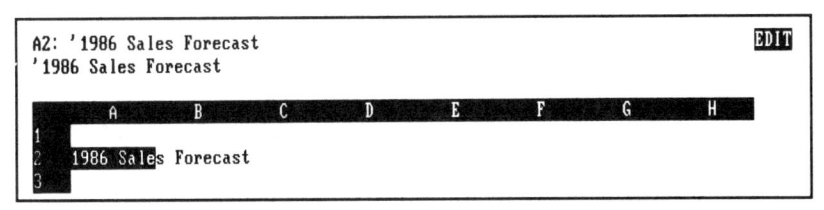

FIGURE 2-21: Editing an entry

Moving the Cursor

After you press [Edit], you can use the →, ←, [Home], [End], [Ctrl]→, and [Ctrl]← combinations to position the flashing cursor anywhere in the entry. As you might expect, pressing → will move the cursor one space to the right and pressing ← will move it one space to the left. You cannot move the cursor to the left beyond the first character in an entry or to the right beyond the space following the last entry. Pressing [Home] moves the cursor directly to the first character in the entry. Pressing [End] moves the cursor directly to the last character.

Pressing [Ctrl]→ moves the cursor five spaces to the right in the edit line, while pressing [Ctrl]← moves it five spaces to the left. These combinations, which very few people actually use, are great when you need to move large distances in a long entry quickly.

If you press the ↑ or ↓ keys (or [Pg Up] or [Pg Dn]) while you are editing an entry, 1-2-3 will lock in the entry and move the cell pointer the indicated distance in the indicated direction.

Inserting Characters

Once the cursor is in place, you can insert, delete, or replace characters. Often you'll want to add a few new characters to the label. For example, suppose you want to add the words *Unit and Dollar* to the label *1986 Sales Forecast* just before the word *Sales*. To add these characters to the entry, just press ← to move the cursor to the letter *S* in the word *Sales*, then type the words *Unit and Dollar*, followed by a single blank space. 1-2-3 will push the cursor—and any characters to its right—to the right as you type. Once you are done, you can press [Enter] to lock in the change.

Deleting Characters

You can also delete characters from the entry. For example, suppose that after you finish making this change, you decide that you want to remove the words *and Dollar* from the label *'1986 Unit and Dollar Sales Forecast*. To do this, you would move the cell pointer to cell A2 and press [Edit]. Next, press ← to move the cursor to the space just after the *r* in *Dollar* and press [Backspace] 11 times.

Instead of using [Backspace] to delete the unwanted characters, you could use the [Del] key. To do this, you would move the cursor to the first letter *a* in the phrase *and Dollar* and press [Del] 11 times.

Once you have made this change, you can press [Enter] to lock it in.

Replacing Characters

Now suppose that you want to change the date in the label *'1986 Unit Sales Forecast* from *1986* to *1987*. To begin, move the cell pointer to cell A2 and press [Edit]. Once you are in the EDIT mode, there are several ways to perform the replacement. First, you could move the cursor to the *6* in the date *1986*, press [Del] once, and type 7. Alternatively, you could move the cursor to the space after the date *1986*, press [Backspace] once, and type 7.

1-2-3 Release 2 offers yet another way to make this change. Instead of deleting and retyping the entry, you can press [Ins] to enter the Overwrite mode and simply "overtype" the character(s) you want to replace. Pressing the [Ins] key switches 1-2-3 out of the Insert mode and into the Overwrite mode. As a signal that it is now in the Overwrite mode, 1-2-3 will display the status indicator OVR at the bottom of the screen. To switch 1-2-3 back to the Insert mode, press [Ins] again.

When 1-2-3 is in the Insert mode, new characters you type when you are editing an entry will be inserted between the characters that make up the entry. On the other hand, when 1-2-3 is in the Overwrite mode, new characters you type will replace the existing characters in the entry. The Insert mode is the default, and you will probably find that it is best suited to your needs in most situations. However, there are times when the Overwrite mode can come in handy.

For example, you could use the Overwrite mode to change the date *1986* in the sample label *'1986 Unit Sales Estimate* to *1987*. To do this, first press [Ins] to enter the Overwrite mode. Then move the cursor to the *6* in the date *1986* and type 7. That's all there is to it. Once you have made the change, press [Enter] to lock it in.

Locking in the Change

Once you have made a change to an entry, you must lock in the change. As always, you can lock in the changes you have made to an entry just by pressing [Enter]. Alternatively, you can press ↑, ↓, [Pg Up], or [Pg Dn]. You cannot, however, press →, ←, [Ctrl]→, [Ctrl]←, [Home], or [End]. Pressing any of these keys will move the cursor within the entry in the control panel instead of locking in the entry and moving the cell pointer.

Editing Formulas

You can edit formulas just as you edit labels. If you have not yet locked in a formula, you can press [Backspace] to erase individual characters, or press [Esc] if you want to cancel the entire entry and start over. You can also change a formula once you have locked it in. If the formula is short or if it contains several errors, you might want to replace it with a new formula. To do this, just move the cell pointer to the cell that contains the formula and type a new formula.

If you want to edit the formula, move the cell pointer to the cell that contains the formula, then press [Edit] to enter the EDIT mode. Once you are in the EDIT mode, you can move the cursor to the character or characters you want to change, and insert, delete, or replace characters. For example, suppose cell C6 in your worksheet contains the formula +C2+C4. You decide that this formula should be +C3+C4. To correct the formula, first move the cell pointer to cell C6 and press [Edit]. Then simply move the cursor to the *2* in the reference *C2*, press [Backspace], type 3, and press [Enter].

You can also add cell references to formulas. All you have to do is edit the cell that contains the formula, move the cursor to the point in the formula where you want to add the reference, type an operator, and then type the cell reference you want to add to the formula. If you are adding a new reference in the middle of a formula, you must type the reference. If you want to add a cell reference to the end of a formula, however, you can define that reference by pointing. All you have to do is type an operator, press ↑, ↓, [Pg Up], or [Pg Dn] to enter the POINT mode, and point to the appropriate cell.

TIP: POINTING AND EDITING

There is one trick you will need to keep in mind if you want to point while you are editing a formula. Since →, ←, [Home], [End], [Ctrl]→, and [Ctrl]← are used to move the cursor around within the entry you are editing, you can't use these keys to point—unless you first press ↓, ↑, [Pg Up], or [Pg Dn] to enter the POINT mode. If you try to press →, ←, or one of the other keys to point while you are editing a formula, 1-2-3 will simply move the cursor within that formula. However, if you press ↓, ↑, [Pg Up], or [Pg Dn] first to enter the POINT mode, you can then use any of the other keys to point to another cell.

COMMANDS

Commands are the tools that you use to manipulate information in the worksheet. 1-2-3 offers commands that you can use to copy, move, and erase entries, to insert and delete rows and columns, to assign special formats to entries, to make calculations, and to perform other housekeeping and formatting chores. We'll cover these commands in the other chapters of this book. In this section, however, we'll show you how to issue and cancel commands.

Issuing Commands

To issue a command in 1-2-3, you must first press the slash key (/). When you press this key, 1-2-3's main menu will come into view in the control panel. Figure 2-22 shows this. Notice that the Mode indicator in Figure 2-22 now reads MENU.

```
A1:                                                              MENU
Worksheet Range Copy Move File Print Graph Data System Add-In Quit
Global   Insert Delete Column Erase Titles Window Status Page Learn
         A        B        C        D        E        F        G        H
1
2
3
4
5
6
7
8
9
10
11
12
13
14
15
16
17
18
19
20
```

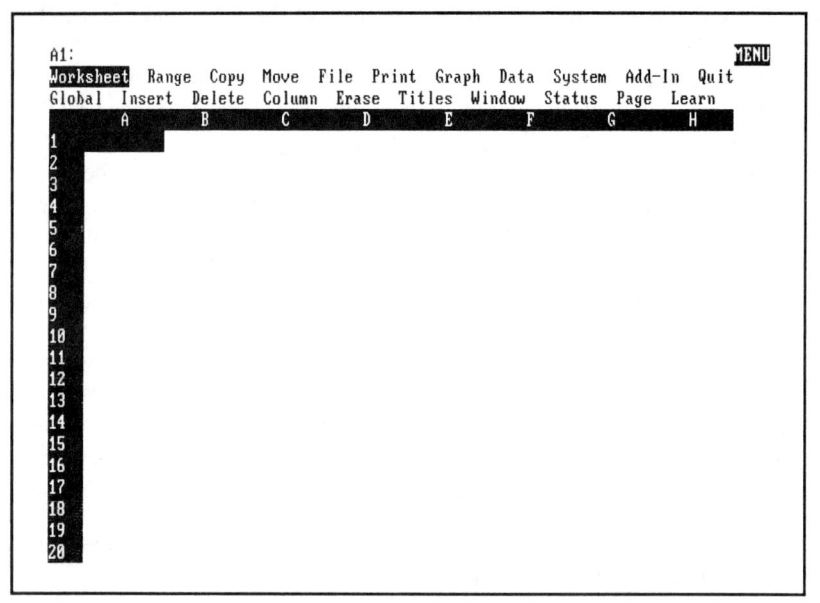

FIGURE 2-22: 1-2-3's main menu

The words in the second line of the control panel—Worksheet, Range, Copy, and so on—are the options you can choose from the main menu. Notice that the first option, Worksheet, is highlighted. The third line of the control panel displays a prompt that gives more information about the highlighted option. This prompt may show the next level of menu options, which you'll see if you select the highlighted command, or the prompt may contain an explanation of how the highlighted command works. For example, the prompt in the third line of the control panel in Figure 2-22

Global Insert Delete Column Erase Titles Window Status Page Learn

lists the options on the menu 1-2-3 will display if you choose Worksheet.

Choosing Commands

There are two different ways to issue commands in 1-2-3. First, you can point to the option you want to choose and press [Enter]. Alternatively, you can simply type the first letter in the name of the option you want to select.

When you first start out with 1-2-3, you'll probably find it easier to point to menu options. To choose an option in this way, just press the → and ← keys to move the highlight to the option you want to choose and press [Enter]. For example, to select the File command from the main menu, you could press → four times to move the cursor to the File option, then press [Enter].

If you press → when the highlight is on the last option in a menu, or if you press ← when the highlight is on the first option, the highlight will wrap around to the other end of the menu. For example, if you press ← when the cursor is on the Worksheet option in the main menu, it will wrap around to the Quit option at the end of the menu.

You can also use the [Home] and [End] keys to move the cursor in a menu. When you press [Home], the cursor will jump directly to the first option in the menu. When you press [End], it will move to the last option.

As you become more experienced with 1-2-3, you'll probably begin to issue commands by typing instead of by pointing. To issue a command in this way, you simply type the first letter in the name of the command you want to select. For example, to select the File option from the main menu, you would type either an *f* or an *F* (1-2-3 doesn't care about case when you are issuing commands).

Submenus

If you choose Worksheet, Range, File, Print, Graph, or Data from the main menu, 1-2-3 will display a submenu that offers more options. For example, if you choose File from the main menu, 1-2-3 will display the menu in Figure 2-23. As you can see, this menu has the same basic form as the main menu. The options you can choose appear in the second line of the control panel. The first option is highlighted. A prompt that explains the highlighted option appears in the third line of the control panel. All 1-2-3 menus have this same basic structure.

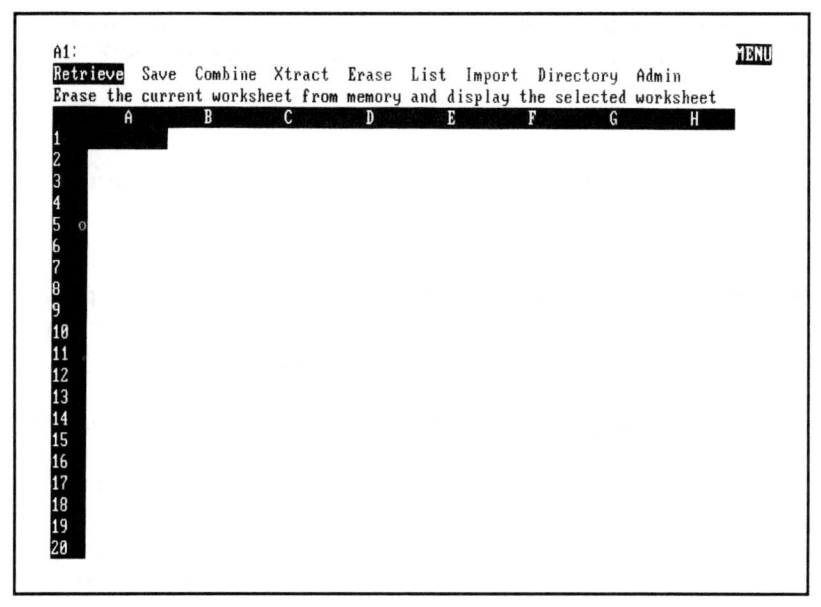

```
A1:                                                                    MENU
Retrieve Save Combine Xtract Erase List Import Directory Admin
Erase the current worksheet from memory and display the selected worksheet
         A        B        C        D        E        F        G        H
1
2
3
4
5   o
6
7
8
9
10
11
12
13
14
15
16
17
18
19
20
```

FIGURE 2-23: The File menu

You make selections from submenus in the same ways you make selections from the main menu. You can either point to the option you want to choose and press [Enter], or you can type the first letter in the option name.

Sometimes you will have to make selections from three or four menus before you get to the precise command you want to use. For example, to change the method of recalculation from automatic to manual, you press /, choose Worksheet from the main menu, Global from the Worksheet menu, Recalculation from the Global menu, and Manual from the Recalculation menu. In other words, you issue the / Worksheet Global Recalculation Manual command.

You can use the [Esc] key to back up from one submenu to the next highest menu. For example, suppose that you want to issue the / Range Format command, but that you instead issue the / File command. When you choose File, 1-2-3 will display the menu shown in Figure 2-23. To escape from this menu to the main menu, just press [Esc]. As soon as the main menu comes into view, you can choose Range and go ahead with the command.

Settings Sheets

RELEASE
▶ 2.2 ◀

▶1-2-3 Release 2.2 displays a settings sheet when you issue the following commands:

/ Worksheet Global
/ Worksheet Global Default
/ Graph
/ Print

/ Data Sort
/ Data Query
/ Data Regression
/ Data Parse

Setting sheets display all the settings controlled by a particular command on the screen at once. The changes you make to the settings controlled by that command are reflected in the setting sheet. This allows you to see at a glance just what the status of those settings is.

For example, Figure 2-24 shows the settings sheet 1-2-3 will display when you issue the / Worksheet Global Default command. Notice that this sheet lists every setting controlled by the options under the / Worksheet Global Default command: Printer settings, International settings, and so on.

```
A1:                                                                    MENU
Printer Directory Status Update Other Autoexec Quit
Specify printer interface and default settings
─────────────────────── Default Settings ───────────────────────
Printer:                              Directory: C:\12322
   Interface    Parallel 1
   Auto linefeed  No                  Autoexecute macros: Yes
   Margins
      Left 4  Right 76  Top 2  Bottom 2  International:
   Page length   60                      Punctuation    A
   Wait          No                      Decimal        Period
   Setup string                          Argument       Comma
   Name         HP 2686 LaserJet Se...   Thousands      Comma
                                         Currency       Prefix: $
Add-In:                                  Date format (D4)  A (MM/DD/YY)
   1                                     Time format (D8)  A (HH:MM:SS)
   2                                     Negative       Parentheses
   3
   4                                   Help access method: Removable
   5                                   Clock display:    None
   6                                   Undo:             Disabled
   7                                   Beep:             Yes
   8
```

FIGURE 2-24: The / Worksheet Global Default Settings Sheet

While you are viewing any settings sheet, you can toggle back to the worksheet simply by pressing the [Window] key ([F6]). Pressing the [Window] key a second time toggles the settings sheet back into view.◄

Defining Ranges

Some 1-2-3 commands ask you to define ranges. For example, when you choose Copy or Move from the main menu, 1-2-3 will prompt you to define a range to copy or move from, then a range to copy or move to.

A range in 1-2-3 is a rectangular group of adjacent cells. A range can be as small as a single cell, or as large as the entire worksheet. It can contain cells in only one row or column, or cells in several rows and columns. For example, cells A1, A2, B1, and B2 constitute a range, as do cells C10, C11, C12, and C13, and cells B5, B6, B7, and B8. However, cells A1, A2, and B1 do not constitute a range because this group of cells is not rectangular. Similarly, cells A1, A2, C1, and C2 do not constitute a range because they are not adjacent.

1-2-3 uses the addresses of the cells in the upper-left and lower-right corners of a range to designate the range. For example, 1-2-3 would use the notation A1..B2 to designate the range that contains the cells A1, A2, B1, and B2. Similarly, the range A1..Z100 contains all of the cells in the rectangular area that begins at cell A1 and ends at cell Z100, including cells Z1 and A100.

You can define a range in one of two ways: either by typing the addresses of the cells at its corners, separated by a period (.) and pressing [Enter], or by pointing to one of the corner cells, typing a period, pointing to the opposite corner, and pressing [Enter]. For example, to define the range A1..C10, you could type A1.C10 and press [Enter], or you could point to cell A1, type a period, point to cell C10, and press [Enter]. (Although you have to type only one period when you are defining a range, you can type two. If you choose to type just one period, 1-2-3 will add a second period for you.)

Cancelling Commands

You can cancel a command and return to the READY mode at any time by pressing [Ctrl][Break]. For example, suppose you have issued the / Worksheet Global Recalculation command, but you now realize you do not want to use this command at all. To cancel the command, press [Ctrl][Break]. Immediately, 1-2-3 will remove the Recalculation menu from the control panel and return to the READY mode.

THE [UNDO] KEY

RELEASE ► 2.2 ◄

►1-2-3 Release 2.2 offers a key, [Undo] ([Alt][F4]), that lets you "undo" certain actions you have performed in 1-2-3. This key makes it possible to undo many of your mistakes, returning your 1-2-3 worksheet to the state it was in before your error. For example, if you press [Undo] after erasing or overwriting a formula or function, 1-2-3 will restore the formula or function. Similarly, if you press [Undo] after issuing the / Worksheet Delete Row command, 1-2-3 will restore the deleted rows. You can even use the [Undo] key to restore a worksheet that you have erased accidentally using the / Worksheet Erase command.

Each time you issue a command (or perform an action) that may result in a change to the worksheet, 1-2-3 creates a temporary backup copy of the worksheet before it executes that command or takes that action. When you press the [Undo] key, 1-2-3 replaces the "current" worksheet with the backup—the version of the worksheet as it existed prior to the command or action.

Although you can use [Undo] to undo the effect of most commands and actions, some you cannot. 1-2-3 displays the indicator UNDO on the Status line when the [Undo] key can be used. (This indicator is visible in Figures 2-2 through 2-5.) When this indicator is visible, pressing the [Undo] key will reverse the previous action; if the indicator is not visible, pressing the [Undo] key will have no effect.

The [Undo] key returns the worksheet to the state it was in the last time 1-2-3 was in the READY mode. Consequently, a single press of the [Undo] key may undo multiple changes. For instance, if you issue the / Graph command, then make several changes to the graph settings prior to returning to the READY mode, 1-2-3 will undo all of those changes when you press [Undo]. Similarly, if you press [Undo] after running a macro, 1-2-3 will return the worksheet to its state prior to the execution of the macro.

As you can imagine, Release 2.2's Undo capability uses a lot of RAM. If you don't have expanded memory, 1-2-3 will reserve half of your computer's free conventional memory (the RAM not occupied by DOS, 1-2-3 program code, or add-in applications) as an Undo buffer. If you have expanded memory, 1-2-3 will use it instead of conventional memory for the Undo buffer; if there is not enough expanded memory for the entire Undo buffer, 1-2-3 will store as much of the buffer in expanded memory as it can, then store the remainder in conventional memory.

In some cases, the disadvantages of 1-2-3 Release 2.2's Undo capability (especially its appetite for RAM) outweigh its advantages. In those cases, you can use the / Worksheet Global Default Other Undo command to turn it off. When you issue this command, 1-2-3 offers two choices: Enable and Disable. Choosing Disable turns off the Undo capability (and doubles the amount of RAM available to your worksheets); choosing Enable turns it back on. The Undo status appears in the Default Settings settings sheet, which is visible on the screen when you issue any of the / Worksheet Global Default commands.

If you disable Undo, then retrieve a large worksheet, you may not be able to reenable Undo. If the worksheet uses any of the memory 1-2-3 needs to use for the Undo buffer, then 1-2-3 will not allow you to reenable Undo. ◄

MEMORY MANAGEMENT

►1-2-3 Release 2.2 and DOS consume about 270K of your computer's memory. By subtracting this number from the total memory capacity of your computer, you can determine how much memory is available to hold the values, labels, formulas, and functions you want to enter in the worksheet. If your computer has 640K of RAM, there will be about 370K of memory available for your worksheets. If you have only 512K, there will be about 140K of free memory. (You'll have even less memory if 1-2-3's Undo capability is active.)

1-2-3 Release 2.2 occupies approximately 33K more memory than 1-2-3 Release 2.01. Remember, though, that the add-in manager, optimal recalculation, and the ability to record macros are built into 1-2-3 Release 2.2. To get these features in 1-2-3 Release 2.01, you have to add the add-in manager to your driver set and attach two add-ins—LEARN.APP and SPEEDUP.APP—all of which requires 27K. In effect, then, the true difference in RAM usage between Release 2.01 and Release 2.2 is only about 6K. For this 6K, you get many features not available in previous releases

RELEASE
► 2.2 ◄

of 1-2-3, including file linking, a search and replace command, new macro commands and functionality, and improved graphics.)◄

As you might expect, every entry you make into the 1-2-3 worksheet uses memory. The amount of memory a given entry will consume depends on the type and length of the entry. Certain types of entries, such as formulas, consume more memory than other types, such as labels and integer values. In addition, long labels, formulas, and values use more memory than shorter entries, and decimal values consume more memory than integers.

1-2-3 Releases 2, 2.01, and 2.2 allocate memory in blocks of four vertical cells. For instance, cells A1, A2, A3, and A4 are a block, as are cells A5, A6, A7, and A8. If you make an entry into any cell in a block, or if you format any cell in the block (even if the cell is empty), 1-2-3 will reserve 4 bytes of memory for each of the four cells in the block, for a total of 16 bytes.

1-2-3 Releases 2.0, 2.01, and 2.2 do not allocate any memory to blank cells outside of active blocks. This means that the position of an entry in a Release 2, 2.01, or 2.2 worksheet has little to do with the amount of memory that entry consumes. You can make an entry anywhere you want—including cell IV8192—and that entry will consume no more memory than the same entry in cell B2. While it is still possible to use up all of the available memory, in general you don't have to keep track of blank cells. You should, however, try to limit the number of active blocks as much as possible, since 1-2-3 does allocate memory to each cell in an active block.

(In 1-2-3 Release 1A, every cell in the active rectangle of the worksheet—the smallest rectangle that includes every cell that contains an entry or has been assigned a format—consumes at least four bytes. This means that the amount of memory an entry consumes in Release 1A depends in part upon the location of that entry.)

Other things you do in the worksheet also consume memory. For example, every named graph you create consumes 464 bytes. Each range name you create consumes 34 bytes of memory. However, in most cases named graphs, range names, and the like do not consume enough memory to be a concern.

How Much Memory Remains?

RELEASE ► 2.2 ◄

►You can determine the amount of memory that is free at any time just by issuing the / Worksheet Status command or, in 1-2-3 Release 2.2 only, the / Worksheet Global command.◄ When you do so, 1-2-3 will display a screen, like the one in Figure 2-25, that reveals the current status of many of 1-2-3's default settings. The first two lines of this screen indicate the amount of memory that is currently free. After you have checked the amount of free memory, just press any key to return to the worksheet.

The first line shows the amount of conventional memory that is currently free, the total amount of conventional memory, and the percentage of the total that is currently free. (The second number indicates the amount of memory that is available after DOS, 1-2-3, and any RAM-resident programs have been loaded—not the total amount of memory installed in your computer.)

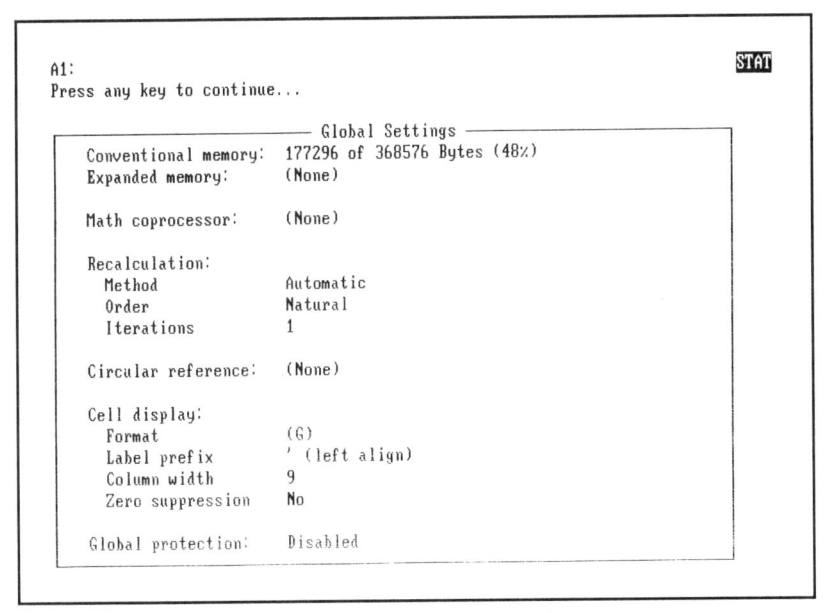

```
A1:                                                    STAT
Press any key to continue...
                        ── Global Settings ──
    Conventional memory:  177296 of 368576 Bytes (48%)
    Expanded memory:      (None)

    Math coprocessor:     (None)

    Recalculation:
      Method              Automatic
      Order               Natural
      Iterations          1

    Circular reference:   (None)

    Cell display:
      Format              (G)
      Label prefix        ' (left align)
      Column width        9
      Zero suppression    No

    Global protection:    Disabled
```

FIGURE 2-25: The / Worksheet Status command

The second line shows the amount of expanded memory that is available, if any. This statistic is important only if you have installed an expanded memory board in your computer. (Expanded memory takes advantage of the Lotus/Intel/Microsoft Extended Memory Specification, which allows certain programs, like 1-2-3, to access more than 640K of memory.) If your computer has expanded memory, this line will show the available expanded memory, the total expanded memory, and the percentage of the total that is available. If your computer does not have expanded memory, this line will read *(None)*.

Memory-full Errors

It is possible to make enough entries in a worksheet to consume all of the available memory. When the amount of available memory dips below 4096 bytes, the indicator *Mem* will appear at the bottom of the screen. When you see this indicator, you should begin to think about ways to free up some memory.

When the amount of available memory drops to 0, 1-2-3 will beep and display the error message *Memory full* at the bottom of the screen. When this happens, you're out of luck. First, you must press [Esc] to acknowledge the error. Then, before you do anything else, use the / File Save command to save the worksheet to disk. Once that is done, you need to try to free up some memory, or resume your work with a new worksheet.

In some circumstances, a *Memory full* message may occur when there is still a little bit of free memory. This happens when 1-2-3 finds that it does not have enough memory to complete the current operation—for instance, when you've asked 1-2-3 to copy a formula into several cells and there isn't enough free memory to hold all the copies. 1-2-3 may or may not partially complete the task before it stops and displays *Memory full*. If this occurs, you may still be able to make a few more entries in the worksheet before 1-2-3 absolutely runs out of memory.

Recovering Memory

RELEASE ► 2.2 ◄

If you begin to run short on memory, there are several things you can do to recover wasted memory. ►First, in 1-2-3 Release 2.2 you can use the / Worksheet Global Default Other Undo Disable command to turn off the Undo feature. Turning off Undo makes it impossible to undo your mistakes, but frees up lots of memory. For instance, the settings sheet in Figure 2-25 indicates that the Undo buffer for that worksheet is using about 190K of expanded memory. Turning off Undo in that worksheet would make that 190K available to the worksheet. If memory is more important to you than the safety offered by Undo, you'll want to turn off Undo to gain more free memory.◄

Second, you can use the / Range Erase command to erase unneeded entries (such as "null" labels—label prefixes without any text or label prefixes followed only by blank spaces) and the / Range Format Reset command to unformat formatted blank cells. The goal is to eliminate as many active blocks of four cells as possible. You'll recover 16 bytes for each active block you eliminate.

The biggest problem with both of these approaches is that null labels and formatted blank cells are hard to find. Unless you know where to look, you can spend a lot of time trying to find and eliminate these memory wasters. A better approach is to avoid making null label entries and formatting empty cells.

You may also be able to save some memory by tightening up your worksheet. Since 1-2-3 allocates memory by vertical blocks of four cells, empty rows that run across your worksheet may be wasting memory. Deleting these rows may allow you to recover a little memory.

If the worksheet contains lots of formulas, and some of those formulas have lived out their usefulness, you can save memory by converting the formulas to plain values. For example, suppose at the beginning of the current year you built a two-year budget worksheet for your company. It is now September, and you are beginning to run out of memory. Why not change the formulas for January, February, March, April, May, and June to values? You can use the / Range Values command to convert formulas to values. (We'll cover this command in Chapter 4.) You'll recover about 26 bytes for each formula you convert.

You can also get rid of any graph names and range names you no longer need. Each graph name you eliminate recovers 464 bytes and each range name you delete recovers 34 bytes.

If you are really desperate, you can remove any active memory-resident programs and detach any add-ins you are using. However, these steps will probably have a significant impact on your work—after all, if you are used to using an add-in, you won't feel too good about detaching it—so they should be saved until the bitter end.

Realizing the Savings

Sometimes, you will begin to realize memory savings as soon as you begin erasing entries, removing formats, and converting formulas to values. Usually, though, erasing an entry or removing a format will not have any impact on the amount of free memory. In any event, you won't fully recover the memory that has been allocated to those entries and formats until you save and retrieve the worksheet. As 1-2-3 saves the worksheet, it frees up the memory that had been allocated to the entries you changed. The next time you load the worksheet, that memory will be available for new entries. If you need to recover a lot of memory, you'll need to save and retrieve the worksheet after you erase, unformat, and convert but before you make any new entries in the worksheet.

Breaking up the Worksheet

If none of these techniques work, you can always use the / File Xtract command to break the large worksheet into several smaller, self-contained pieces. ►In 1-2-3 Release 2.2, you can then use linking formulas to build links between the individual pieces of the original worksheet. If you do this carefully, you'll be able to work with the cluster of worksheets almost as easily as you can the one large worksheet.◄ Earlier releases of 1-2-3 do not support linking formulas. In those releases, you can use the / File Combine command to combine and summarize the key data from the individual worksheets. We'll cover the / File Xtract and / File Combine commands in Chapter 9.

RELEASE
► 2.2 ◄

Expanded Memory

1-2-3 Releases 2, 2.01, and 2.2 support the Lotus/Intel/Microsoft Expanded Memory Specification—a bank-switching memory scheme that allows 1-2-3 to address up to 8 megabytes (that's 8 million bytes) of expanded memory. If you find that your worksheets are bumping up against the 640K limit, you'll want to consider using expanded memory. To use expanded memory, you'll need to install an expanded memory board in your computer. Expanded memory boards are available from a wide array of manufacturers.

The Lotus/Intel/Microsoft Expanded Memory Specification divides your computer's memory into two distinct parts: the lower 640K (called conventional memory) and all memory above 640K (called expanded memory). The 1-2-3 progam code, any memory-resident or add-in software, network software, and all integer entries, range names, and named graphs are stored in the lower 640K. Labels, floating point (noninteger) values, formulas, and functions are stored in the memory above 640K. ►In 1-2-3 Release 2.2, the Undo buffer is stored in expanded memory, if there is enough expanded memory to hold it, or in both expanded and conventional memory, if there is not. If your computer does not have expanded memory, then the Undo buffer is stored in conventional memory.◄

RELEASE
► 2.2 ◄

Because of the way the 1-2-3 divides the entries in a worksheet between lower and upper memory, it is possible to fill one segment of memory before the other is filled. For example, if you create a worksheet that contains a large number of integer values, you might fill the lower 640K of memory long before you fill the upper part of memory. Unfortunately, a memory-full error will occur whenever either part of memory becomes full. Once a memory-full error has occurred, you will not be able to make any new entries in the worksheet, even though there may be a great deal of available memory in the other part of memory.

RECALCULATION

As you know, you can enter formulas into your 1-2-3 worksheets that refer to the other cells in those worksheets. When you change the values in the cells that are referred to by a formula, 1-2-3 automatically updates the value of the formula as well. This process of updating the values of formulas is called recalculation.

Like most spreadsheets, 1-2-3 gives you control over several important aspects of recalculation. In 1-2-3, you can control the method of recalculation (Automatic or Manual) and the order of recalculation (Natural, Columnwise, or Rowwise). These settings are controlled by the / Worksheet Global Recalculation command. We'll explain these options in this section. In addition, we'll explain the concept of circular references in this section: what they are, how they affect your worksheet, and what you can do to solve them.

Minimal Recalculation

RELEASE 2.2 ▶Unlike previous releases of 1-2-3, Release 2.2 does not always recalculate every formula and function in a worksheet each time you press the [Calc] key (or when it recalculates the worksheet automatically). Instead, it recalculates only the formulas and functions that have been affected by changes you have made to the worksheet since it was last recalculated. As you can imagine, this saves a lot of time.

1-2-3 Release 2.2 uses this new system of recalculation (called minimal recalculation) whenever the Natural order of recalculation is specified. However, it still recalculates every formula and function in a worksheet when it is set for Columnwise or Rowwise recalculation. (We'll show you how to change the order of recalculation in a few pages.)◀

The Method of Recalculation

In 1-2-3, you can choose between two different methods of recalculation: Manual and Automatic. Automatic recalculation means that 1-2-3 will automatically recalculate the worksheet every time you make an entry in the worksheet. Automatic is the default method of recalculation.

RELEASE 2.2 Here's the problem with Automatic recalculation: When you are working with a large spreadsheet that contains many formulas, 1-2-3 may need several seconds (or even a couple of minutes) to recalculate the worksheet. ▶This is even true under 1-2-

3 Release 2.2's minimal recalculation scheme.◄ Since 1-2-3 will recalculate the worksheet every time you make an entry, you'll have to wait a couple of seconds every time you make an entry while 1-2-3 recalculates. Even in smaller worksheets, where the time required to recalculate is just a fraction of a second, the pauses will drive you crazy!

To save time, you may want to change the method of recalculation to Manual while you enter data. When recalculation is set to Manual, 1-2-3 does not recalculate the worksheet every time you make an entry. Instead, it will not recalculate until you tell it to do so. To set the method of recalculation to Manual, issue the / Worksheet Global Recalculation Manual command.

With the recalculation method set to Manual, you can enter and edit labels, numbers, and formulas without waiting for 1-2-3 to recalculate. When you are ready to recalculate the worksheet, all you have to do is press the [Calc] key ([F9]). When you press this key, 1-2-3 will update the formulas in the worksheet to reflect the changes you've made since you last recalculated.

Whenever the method of recalculation is Manual and you make or edit an entry in the worksheet, the message *CALC* will appear at the bottom of the screen. This message is 1-2-3's way of saying, "You've made an entry that may affect your formulas, but you haven't recalculated the worksheet yet." If you see this message, you know that the values in the worksheet may not be up-to-date.

Unfortunately, the CALC indicator is not very intelligent. If the method of recalculation is Manual, the indicator will appear whenever you make a change to the worksheet—even if the change you made had no effect on any formula.

As a general rule, we set the recalculation method to Manual as the very first step in building any new spreadsheet. We find that the Manual option saves time even in relatively small worksheets.

TIP: RECALCULATE BEFORE YOU PRINT

It may seem to be an obvious point, but lots of people have been burned by forgetting to recalculate a worksheet before they print it. Typically, the problem isn't discovered until the Departmental Manager (or the Chairman of the Board) is reviewing the printed worksheet and discovers that the numbers don't add up. Be careful! Remember to recalculate before you print.

The Order of Recalculation

1-2-3 offers three options for the order of recalculation: Natural, Columnwise, and Rowwise. The option you choose controls the order in which 1-2-3 recalculates the formulas in the worksheet.

> **TIP: RECALCULATING CELLS AND RANGES**
>
> There may be times in your work with 1-2-3 when you'll want to recalculate just a single cell or a range of cells without recalculating the entire worksheet. For example, suppose you are working in a large worksheet that takes several seconds to recalculate. You make a change to one assumption, and you want to see how that change affects three formulas. You don't want to have to wait several seconds to recalculate the entire worksheet.
>
> Fortunately, there are ways to recalculate just a single cell or a small range without recalculating the entire worksheet. All you have to do to recalculate a single cell is edit that cell—just move the cell pointer to that cell, press [Edit], and press [Enter]. To recalculate a range, just copy the range onto itself. For example, suppose you want to recalculate the range B100..F100 in a worksheet. To do this, move the cell pointer to cell B100, issue the /Copy command, select the range B100..F100 as the FROM range and cell B100 as the TO range, and press [Enter]. As 1-2-3 copies the entries on top of themselves, it will recalculate each of the entries as well. (For more on the /Copy command, see Chapter 4.)

RELEASE ► 2.2 ◄

The default order is Natural. When 1-2-3 recalculates a worksheet under Natural recalculation, it begins by calculating the cell that must be calculated first if the others are to be recalculated correctly. After that cell has been recalculated, 1-2-3 recalculates the next most fundamental cell, then the next most fundamental, and so on, until all of the cells in the worksheet have been recalculated. ►In 1-2-3 Release 2.2, only the cells that have been affected by the changes you have made since you last recalculated will be updated.◄

For example, suppose you have entered the following formulas into cells B2, B3, and B4 in a worksheet:

B2: +B3
B3: +B4+100
B4: +B1

Suppose further that cell B1 contains the number 100. When 1-2-3 recalculates this worksheet, it will recalculate cell B4 first. Why? Because cell B3 depends on cell B4, and cell B2 depends on cell B3. In other words, cell B4 is the most fundamental cell in the worksheet. After 1-2-3 recalculates cell B4, it will then recalculate B3 and then B2. Because cell B2 depends on cell B3, which depends on cell B4, it is recalculated last, even though cell B2 comes before the other cells in the worksheet.

The /Worksheet Global Recalculation command allows you to change the order of recalculation from Natural to Rowwise or Columnwise. When you choose one of these methods, 1-2-3 will recalculate the worksheet linearly, beginning with cell A1 and then proceeding row by row, or column by column, through the worksheet.

▶Choosing either of these recalculation orders in 1-2-3 Release 2.2 also turns off minimal recalculation.◀

RELEASE
▶ 2.2 ◀

In most circumstances, Rowwise and Columnwise will do as good a job of recalculating the worksheet as Natural. However, if your worksheet includes formulas that contain forward references, it won't recalculate correctly using the Rowwise and Columnwise orders. A forward reference is a reference to a cell that will be recalculated after the cell that contains the reference. For example, the reference to cell B4 in the formula in cell B3 above is a forward reference. Forward references cannot occur under Natural recalculation, where the relative positions of the cells make no difference. But they can and do occur frequently when you use Rowwise and Columnwise recalculation. For this reason, we recommend that you avoid these recalculation order options.

If you must use Rowwise and Columnwise recalculation, you can avoid problems with forward references by calculating the worksheet two or more times each time you recalculate. You can do this by pressing [Calc] two or three times, or you can use the / Worksheet Global Recalculation Iteration option to set an iteration count of 2 or 3. We'll cover this command in more detail in a few pages.

Circular References

Circular references occur when a cell contains a formula that refers to the cell itself. Circular references can create tremendous problems in your worksheets since they often make it impossible for 1-2-3 to recalculate a worksheet correctly.

Most circular references are the result of errors. Most references of this sort are unsolvable—no matter what you do, 1-2-3 will not be able to come up with the "right" answer for the formula that contains the circular reference. Other circular references are deliberate. Many of these references can be solved through the use of iterative recalculation.

Unsolvable Circular References

The most obvious type of circular reference occurs when you create a formula in a cell that contains a direct reference to that same cell. Usually this type of error is the result of a typographical error or a pointing error. Unfortunately, this type of circular reference is usually impossible to solve.

For example, if you enter the formula +B1-B2 in cell B2, you've created a circular reference. This formula contains a circular reference because it is in cell B2 and also refers to cell B2. When you enter this formula in the worksheet, 1-2-3 will display the CIRC status indicator at the bottom of the screen. Because cell B1 contains the number 100, the formula returns the value 100.

No matter how hard it tries, 1-2-3 can't solve this formula. Each time 1-2-3 arrives at a new value for the formula in cell B2, the value of cell B2 changes. When 1-2-3 evaluates the formula in cell B2 using this new value, the value in cell B2 changes again. Obviously, 1-2-3 could continue to go around this circle forever—like a cat chasing its tail—without ever really solving the formula.

The CIRC Indicator

When you enter a circular reference into the worksheet, 1-2-3 will display the indicator CIRC at the bottom of the screen. If the method of recalculation is Automatic, this indicator will come into view as soon as you make the entry. If recalculation is set to Manual, this indicator will not come into view until you press [Calc] to recalculate the worksheet.

Finding and Fixing Circular References

Because some circular references—like the one described here—are unsolvable, and because nearly all circular references are accidental, you should be very alert to the presence of the CIRC indicator. If you see this indicator, you should immediately try to locate the circular reference and correct it.

RELEASE ▶ 2.2 ◀ ▶1-2-3 Releases 2, 2.01, and 2.2 make it easy to find circular references. All you have to do is issue the / Worksheet Status command or, in 1-2-3 Release 2.2 only, the / Worksheet Global command.◀ The screen that appears when you issue this command includes a line, *Circular reference:*, which shows the location of the circular reference in the worksheet. (In 1-2-3 Release 1A, you are pretty much on your own when you are trying to locate circular references.)

For example, Figure 2-26 shows the screen that 1-2-3 will display if you issue / Worksheet Status command after entering the circular reference *+B1+B2* into cell B2. Notice the cell reference to B2 on the *Circular reference:* line of the status screen.

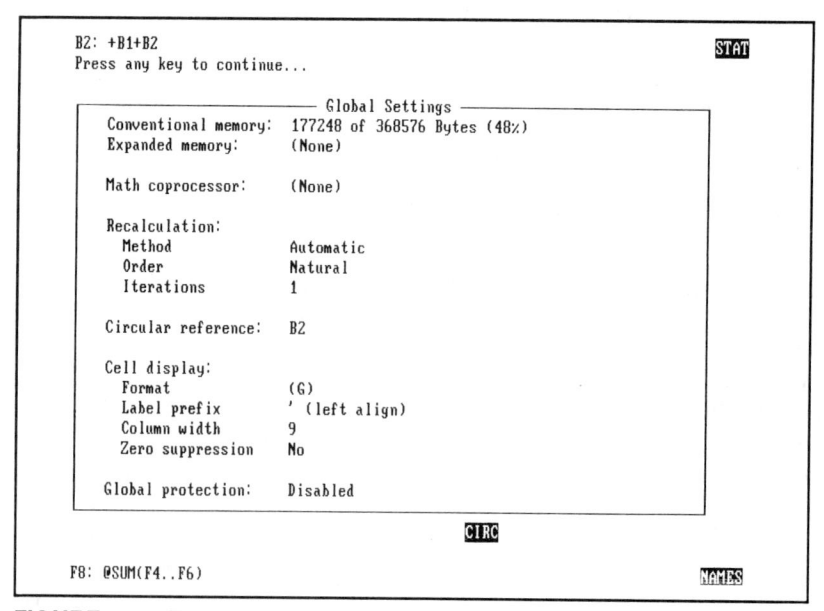

```
B2: +B1+B2                                                          STAT
Press any key to continue...
                        ─── Global Settings ───
      Conventional memory:  177248 of 368576 Bytes (48%)
      Expanded memory:      (None)

      Math coprocessor:     (None)

      Recalculation:
         Method             Automatic
         Order              Natural
         Iterations         1

      Circular reference:   B2

      Cell display:
         Format             (G)
         Label prefix       ' (left align)
         Column width       9
         Zero suppression   No

      Global protection:    Disabled
                                                   CIRC
   F8: @SUM(F4..F6)                                               NAMES
```

FIGURE 2-26: Finding circular references

Once you have used the / Worksheet Status command to locate a circular reference, you can correct it. In many cases, correcting circular references is easy. For instance, in this case you could correct the error just by editing cell B2 and removing the reference to cell B2 from the formula in that cell. Once you have made the correction, you can press [Enter] to lock in the change, then press [Calc] to recalculate the worksheet.

In other cases, however, circular references are not so easy to find and fix. Often, circular references are not as direct as the simple example we've considered so far. In some cases, circular references may involve many cells that are widely separated in the worksheet. For example, a circular reference would exist in a worksheet where cell C10 depends on cells C3 through C9, cells C3 through C9 depend on cells B3 through B9, cells B3 through B9 depend on cell A3, and cell A3 depends on cell C10. In cases like this, the cell that appears in the status screen may not contain a circular reference. Instead, it may just be one of the cells in the chain that creates the circle. For this reason, you may have a difficult time figuring out all of the relationships that lead to the circular reference.

Often a worksheet that contains one circular reference contains more than one. However, when you issue the / Worksheet Status command, 1-2-3 will display the address of only one of the cells that contain a circular reference. There are a couple of ways to deal with this limitation. First, after you correct the error in the cell referred to by the / Worksheet Status command, look in the cells around that cell for similar errors. Circular references are like wolves—they tend to travel in packs. If you find a circular reference in one cell, there are likely to be similar references in cells that contain similar formulas.

If the surrounding cells are clean, then you'll need to reissue the / Worksheet Status command. When you issue this command after correcting one circular reference, 1-2-3 will display the address of another cell that contains a circular reference (if another one exists). Once you have corrected that error, you can repeat the command again and continue this process until all the errors have been fixed.

Solvable Circular References

Unlike the previous example, many circular references can be resolved. In fact, from time to time you might deliberately create a circular reference. You can use the / Worksheet Global Recalculation Iteration command to overcome the problems created by this kind of circular reference.

For example, Figure 2-27 shows a worksheet that contains a solvable circular reference. Cell B1 in this worksheet contains the formula *+B2+B3*, cell B2 contains the value 100, and cell B3 contains the formula *.5*B1*. This set of formulas is circular because the formula in B1 depends on the value in B3, and the formula in B3 depends on the value in B1. Consequently, the CIRC indicator will appear as soon as you enter these formulas.

```
B3: 0.5*B1                                                    READY

        A       B       C       D       E       F       G       H
    1          100
    2          100
    3           50
    4
    5
```

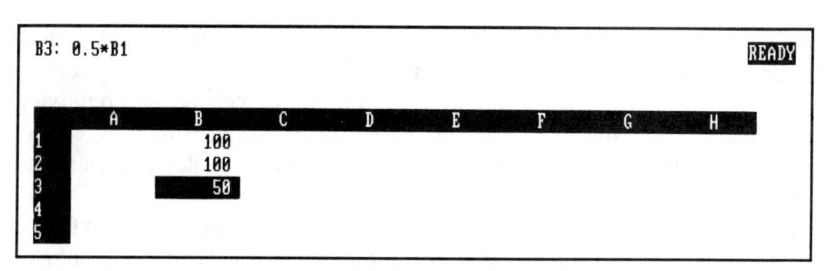

FIGURE 2-27: A circular reference

You can use the /Worksheet Global Recalculation Iteration command to solve this kind of circular reference. When this option is on, 1-2-3 will recalculate the worksheet a specified number of times each time you press [Calc]. To resolve the circular reference in the example, issue the / Worksheet Global Recalculation Iteration command. When you issue this command, 1-2-3 will display the prompt *Enter iteration count (1-50): 1*. Notice that the default iteration count is 1. This setting tells 1-2-3 to recalculate the worksheet once each time you press [Calc] or, if recalculation is set to Automatic, each time you make an entry.

You should type a number from 1 to 50 that represents the number of times you want the worksheet to be recalculated when you press [Calc]. In the example, you should type 10 and press [Enter], then press [Calc] to recalculate the worksheet.

Table 2-5 shows how the values in cells B1 and B3 will change as 1-2-3 recalculates the circular reference. Notice that the values in cells B1 and B3 change less with each iteration as 1-2-3 closes in on the correct answer. The final results in cells B1 and B3 are very close to correct since 99.95117 is almost exactly half of 199.9023.

| | B1 | B2 | B3 |
	(+B2+B3)	(100)	(+.5*B1)
literal value	100	100	50
iteration 1	150	100	75
iteration 2	175	100	87.5
iteration 3	187.5	100	93.75
iteration 4	193.75	100	96.875
iteration 5	196.875	100	98.4375
iteration 6	198.4375	100	99.21875
iteration 7	199.2187	100	99.60937
iteration 8	199.6093	100	99.80468
iteration 9	199.8046	100	99.90234
iteration 10	199.9023	100	99.95117

TABLE 2-5: Iterative recalculation

The recalculation stops after 10 iterations because you set the iteration number to 10. If you were to recalculate the worksheet again, 1-2-3 would recalculate the sheet 10 more times, and would further refine the values of B1 and B3.

As you might expect, iterative recalculation can be a very slow process. If your worksheet is of any size at all, and you set the number of iterations at 10 or higher, 1-2-3 might take several minutes to complete the entire recalculation process. Our suggestion is that you leave the iteration count setting at 1 except when you really need to solve circular references. For this same reason, we suggest that you make sure the recalculation method is set to Manual when you are using iterative calculation. We also suggest that you keep the iteration count as low as possible.

NAMING CELLS AND RANGES

In the previous examples, we have shown you how to create formulas that include references to cells in the worksheet. So far, these formulas have referred to the cells by their address: A1, D2, and so on. However, 1-2-3 also allows you to assign English-language names to the cells and ranges in your worksheet and to use those names in your formulas and commands.

Creating Names

To name a range, you issue the / Range Name Create command. When you issue this command, 1-2-3 will prompt you to supply the name you want to create. You should type the name and press [Enter]. The name you supply can be up to 15 characters long and can include any character, but it must begin with a letter.

Next, 1-2-3 will display the prompt *Enter range:*, followed by the address of the current cell as a range reference. For example, if the cell pointer is on cell A1 when you issue the / Range Name Create command, 1-2-3 will display the prompt *Enter Range: A1..A1*. The range reference is 1-2-3's guess at the range you want to name. You can either press [Enter] to accept this guess and assign the name to the current cell, use the cursor-movement keys to expand the guess range to include several cells, or press [Esc] to unanchor the range reference and point to a different range. Normally, you'll want to move the cell pointer to the cell you want to name (or, if you plan to name a range, to a cell at one of the corners of that range) before you issue the / Range Name Create command. That way, you can take advantage of 1-2-3's guess.

Examples

For example, suppose you want to assign the name *PROD1* to the range B4..E4 in Figure 2-28. To do this, move the cell pointer to cell B4 and issue the / Range Name Create command. When 1-2-3 prompts you to supply the name, type PROD1 and press [Enter]. Next, 1-2-3 will display the prompt *Enter range: B4..B4*. When you see this prompt, either press ➡ three times to select the range B4..E4 and press [Enter], or type B4..E4 and press [Enter].

```
A1: [W14]                                                           READY

            A          B         C         D         E         F          G
    1
    2                Qtr 1     Qtr 2     Qtr 3     Qtr 4     Total
    3                -------   -------   -------   -------   -------
    4   Product 1    1234      2345      3456      4567      11602
    5   Product 2    1111      2222      3333      4444      11110
    6   Product 3    1000      2000      3000      4000      10000
    7                -------   -------   -------   -------   -------
    8   Total        3345      6567      9789      13811     32712
    9                =======   =======   =======   =======   =======
    10
```

FIGURE 2-28: A sample worksheet

You can also assign names to single cells in your worksheet. For example, suppose you want to assign the name *GRAND TOTAL* to cell F8 in Figure 2-28. To do this, move the cell pointer to cell F8 and issue the / Range Name Create command, type GRAND TOTAL and press [Enter]. When you see the prompt *Enter range: F8..F8*, press [Enter] to assign the name to the current cell.

Range Name Rules

As we have said, range names may be up to 15 characters long and may include any character, including spaces, punctuation marks like colons, periods, commas, and special Lotus International Character Set (LICS) characters like £ and π. (For more on the LICS, see Appendix 1.) However, the name must begin with a letter. For example, the names TEST, HERE, MAY86, OP EXP and COBB,DOUG are all acceptable to 1-2-3. (Actually, 1-2-3 will allow you to create names that begin with characters other than letters. However, you won't be able to use these names in formulas or with commands.)

You also should never create a range name that looks like a cell address. For example, you would not want to create a range name like A1, PR12, or AA100. Again, although 1-2-3 will allow you to create a name that looks like a cell address, you won't be able to use that name in formulas or commands. When you try to use the name, 1-2-3 will assume that you are referring to a cell by its address instead of referring to a named range.

1-2-3 does not distinguish between upper- and lower-case letters in range names. To 1-2-3, the names *Actual*, *ACTUAL*, and *actual* are all identical. (For clarity, however, we'll present range names in all upper-case form.)

A given range name can exist only once in a worksheet. If you assign a range name that already exists to another cell or range in a worksheet, 1-2-3 will remove the name from the original cell or range when it assigns it to the new cell or range. (We'll show you how to change a range name in a few pages.)

You can give a single cell or range two or more names. For example, you could give the cell F8 in Figure 2-28 the name GRAND TOTAL and TOTAL. If a cell has two or more names, you can refer to that cell using any of its names.

Using Range Names

You can use range names just as you would use cell references in formulas, functions, and commands. For example, if the cell F8 has the name GRAND TOTAL, then the formula *+GRAND TOTAL* is identical to the formula *+F10*. Similarly, if the range B4..E4 is named PROD1, then the formula *@SUM(PROD1)* would be identical to *@SUM(B4..E4)*.

In fact, when you create range names, 1-2-3 will use those names instead of cell references in formulas whenever it can. For instance, suppose that, before you assigned any names to the worksheet in Figure 2-28, cell F4 contained the formula *@SUM(B4..E4)*. When you use the /Range Name Create command to assign the name PROD1 to the range B4..E4, this formula changes to *@SUM(PROD1)*.

You can also use range names to define ranges when you issue commands. For example, suppose you want to copy the contents of cell F8, which is named GRAND TOTAL, to cell G8. To do this, you would issue the / Copy command, then supply either the address F8 or the name GRAND TOTAL as the range to copy from.

You can also use range names with the [Goto] key to move the cell pointer. For instance, suppose that you have assigned the name GRAND TOTAL to cell F8, and you want to move the cell pointer to that cell. To do this, you could press [Goto] and type GRAND TOTAL. When you press [Enter], 1-2-3 will immediately move the cell pointer to cell F8. If you supply a name that applies to several cells when you use the [Goto] key, 1-2-3 will move the cell pointer to the upper-left corner of the named range.

Last but not least, range names can be used in several different ways in macros. We'll talk about using range names in macros in Chapter 13.

The [Name] Key

One of the problems with range names is that it is easy to forget exactly which names you have used in a worksheet. When you want to use a name—say, to define the destination for the [Goto] key or the range you want a command to operate on—you may not be able to remember its exact spelling. For this reason, 1-2-3 offers a special key, [Name] ([F3]), that you can use to bring a list of all the range names in a worksheet into view. You can use this key whenever 1-2-3 is prompting you for a range—for example, after you press the [Goto] key or after you issue commands like / Copy, / Range Erase, or / Print Printer Range. ►In 1-2-3 Release 2.2, you can also use this key when you are entering a formula.◄

RELEASE ► 2.2 ◄

For example, suppose you want to use the [Goto] key to move the cell pointer to the first cell in the range named PROD1. To begin, press [Goto] ([F5]). When you see the prompt *Enter address to go to:*, press [Name]. Figure 2-29 shows the screen at this point. As you can see, 1-2-3 is displaying a list of all the names in the worksheet (there are only three) on the third line of the control panel. At this point, you can use the ➡ key to point to the name PROD1 and press [Enter]. Immediately, 1-2-3 will move the cell pointer to the range named PROD1.

```
A1: [W14]                                                      NAMES
Enter address to go to:
GRAND TOTAL      PROD1          TOTAL
          A         B         C         D         E         F         G
 1
 2                          Qtr 1     Qtr 2     Qtr 3     Qtr 4     Total
 3                         -------   -------   -------   -------   -------
 4     Product 1            1234      2345      3456      4567      11602
 5     Product 2            1111      2222      3333      4444      11110
 6     Product 3            1000      2000      3000      4000      10000
 7                         -------   -------   -------   -------   -------
 8     Total                3345      6567      9789     13011      32712
 9                         =======   =======   =======   =======   =======
10
```

FIGURE 2-29: Pressing the [Name] key once

1-2-3 is able to display only five names at a time in the control panel. If there are more than five range names in the worksheet, you'll see the names of only the first five when you press [Name]. (The names will be displayed in alphabetical order.) You can use the cursor-movement keys →, ←, [Ctrl]→, [Ctrl]←, [Home], and [End] to move the cursor through the list and bring more names into view.

If you want to see the entire list of names on one screen, you need only press [Name] twice. For example, suppose you want to use / Copy to copy the contents of the cell named GRAND TOTAL. To begin, issue the / Copy command. When 1-2-3 prompts you to specify the FROM range, press [Name] twice. Figure 2-30 shows the resulting screen. As you can see, 1-2-3 is now displaying a "full-screen" list of range names. (Of course, there are only three range names in this worksheet. However, 1-2-3 can display as many as 105 names at a time in this screen.) Once this screen comes into view, you can use the cursor-movement keys →, ←, ↑, ↓, [Ctrl]→, [Ctrl]←, [Home], and [End] to point to the name you want to use, then press [Enter] to select that name.

The / Range Name Table Command

The / Range Name Table command allows you to create a list of range names in the worksheet. This command makes it easier to remember the name you have created in a worksheet and the ranges to which those names apply.

When you issue this command, 1-2-3 will display the prompt *Enter range for table:*, followed by the address of the current cell as a range reference. This prompt asks you where you want 1-2-3 to place the list, or table, of range names. The reference to the current cell is 1-2-3's guess at where you want to put the table. You can press [Enter] to accept the guess, or you can press [Esc], point to another cell, and press [Enter]. (You can also simply type the address of the cell where you want 1-2-3 to begin the table.) Normally, you'll move the cell pointer to the cell where you want the table to begin before you issue the / Range Name Table command. That way, you can take advantage of 1-2-3's guess.

You have to specify only one cell as the table range. 1-2-3 will create the range name table beginning at the selected cell.

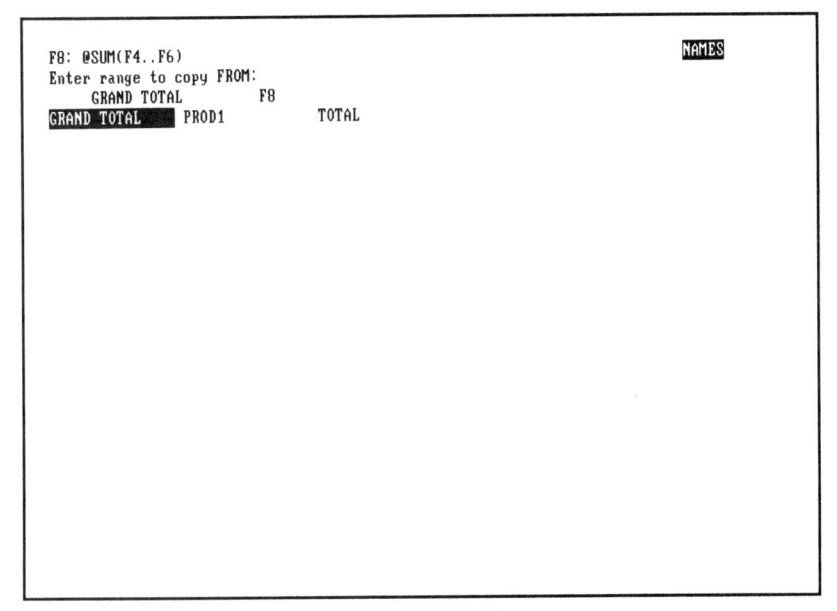

```
F8: @SUM(F4..F6)                                          NAMES
Enter range to copy FROM:
   GRAND TOTAL       F8
GRAND TOTAL    PROD1         TOTAL
```

FIGURE 2-30: Pressing the [Name] key again

An Example

For example, suppose you want to create a list of the range names in the example worksheet in Figure 2-28. You want the list to begin at cell A11. First, move the cell pointer to cell A11, then issue the /Range Name Table command. When 1-2-3 prompts you to specify the location of the table, press [Enter]. Figure 2-31 shows the result.

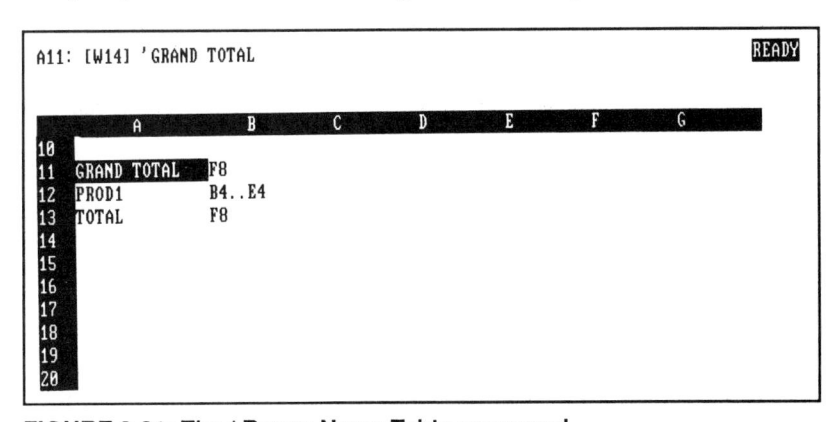

```
A11: [W14] 'GRAND TOTAL                                    READY

        A          B        C        D        E        F        G
10
11  GRAND TOTAL   F8
12  PROD1         B4..E4
13  TOTAL         F8
14
15
16
17
18
19
20
```

FIGURE 2-31: The / Range Name Table command

As you can see, 1-2-3 has created a list of the range names in the worksheet. The first column of the list (column A) contains each of the names. The second column

(column B) contains the addresses of the cells or ranges to which the names apply. The first name appears in cell A11, the cell you selected.

Notes

When 1-2-3 creates the range name list, it will overwrite any entries in the table range. You should be sure to select a range for the table that does not contain any important entries.

The table that 1-2-3 creates when you issue the /Range Name Table command is not dynamic—it will not change to reflect changes you make to the range names in the worksheet. In other words, if you add a new range name to the worksheet, that name will not be added to the table automatically. If you delete a name, that name will still appear in the table. To bring the list up-to-date, you'll need to reissue the /Range Name Table command.

Deleting Names

To delete a range name, just issue the /Range Name Delete command. When you issue this command, 1-2-3 will display the prompt *Enter name to delete:* and will display a list of all of the range names in the worksheet. To delete a name, you just point to the name in the list, or type the name, and press [Enter]. As soon as you press [Enter], 1-2-3 will delete the name. Be careful! 1-2-3 does not give you a chance to reconsider before it deletes the name. Once you have deleted a name, the only way to restore the name is to recreate it.

When you delete a range name, every formula in the worksheet that uses that name will be changed. Instead of referring to the range by name, the formulas will all refer to the range by its cell coordinates.

For example, suppose you want to delete the name PROD1 from the worksheet in Figure 2-29. To do this, you would issue the /Range Name Delete command and choose the name PROD1 from the list. When you press [Enter], 1-2-3 will delete this name from the worksheet. At the same time, the formula in cell F4 will change from *@SUM(PROD1)* to *@SUM(A4..E4)*.

The /Range Name Delete command allows you to delete only one name at a time. If you want to delete several names, you'll need to repeat the command once for every name. If you want to delete all of the names in a worksheet, you can issue the /Range Name Reset command. As soon as you choose the Reset command from the Range Name menu, 1-2-3 will delete every range name from the worksheet. As with the /Range Name Delete command, 1-2-3 does not offer any warning or ask for confirmation before it eliminates all of the range names. Also as with /Range Name Delete, when you use the /Range Name Reset command to delete every range name from a worksheet, every formula that referred to a range by name will change to refer to that range by address.

Changing Names

Once you have created a range name, you can change the range to which that name applies. To change a name's range, you issue the / Range Name Create command, choose that name from 1-2-3's list, and then specify a new range for the name.

For example, suppose you have assigned the name QTR1 to cell B2 in Figure 2-29. You want to change the range to which the name QTR1 applies from B2 to B4..B6. To do this, issue the / Range Name Create command and choose the name QTR1 from the list. When you choose this name, 1-2-3 will highlight the range to which the name currently applies—in this case, the range B2. To change the range, select the range B4..B6 and press [Enter].

Cautions

Although you can change the range to which a name applies, there are a couple of reasons why you might not want to do so. First, changing the range to which a name applies can mess up any formulas that refer to that name.

Second, if you have assigned two names to a range, and then you change the range to which one of the names applies, the range of the other name will change, too. For example, suppose cell F8 in Figure 2-29 has the names TOTAL and GRAND TOTAL. If you change the range of the name TOTAL to F11, the range described by the name GRAND TOTAL will also change to F11.

An Alternative Approach

Instead of changing the range to which a name applies with the / Range Name Create command, you're usually better off deleting the name you want to change and then redefining that name using the / Range Name Create command. Of course, deleting the name first adds an extra step to the process. By doing so, however, you avoid any possibility of damaging the formulas or the other range names in your worksheet.

The / Range Name Labels Command

The / Range Name Labels command uses the labels in a range of the worksheet to name the cells that are adjacent to that range. Before you can use this command, you must enter the labels you want to use as range names into the worksheet. (Often, the labels will be in place before you decide to use / Range Name Labels.) The labels should be arranged in the cells of one row or column.

Once the labels are in place, you issue the / Range Name Labels command. When you issue this command, 1-2-3 will present a menu with four options: Right, Down, Left, and Up. The option you choose from this menu determines which cells 1-2-3 will name. For example, if you choose Down, 1-2-3 will name the cells below the range of labels you select. If you choose Left, it will name the cells to the left of the range of labels you select.

Next, 1-2-3 will display the prompt *Enter label range:*, followed by the address of the current cell as a range reference. For example, if the cell pointer is on cell A1 when you issue the / Range Name Labels command, 1-2-3 will display the prompt *Enter label range: A1..A1*. The range reference is 1-2-3's guess at the range you want to name. You can either press [Enter] to accept this guess and use the label in the current cell to name an adjacent cell, use the cursor-movement keys to expand the guess range to include several cells, or press [Esc] to unanchor the range reference and point to a different range.

An Example

Suppose you want to use the labels in the range A3..A9 in Figure 2-32 to name the cells in the range B3..B9. To begin, move the cell pointer to cell A3 and issue the / Range Name Create command. Since you want to name the range B3..B9, when you see the Right/Down/Left/Up menu, you should then choose Right. When 1-2-3 prompts you to define the range of labels, press ↓ to point to cell A9 and press [Enter] to select the range A3..A9. (You could also type A3..A9 and press [Enter].) When you press [Enter], 1-2-3 will use the labels in the range A3..A9 to name each of the cells in the range B3..B9. For example, 1-2-3 will assign the name *John* to cell B3, the name *Mary* to cell B4, and so on.

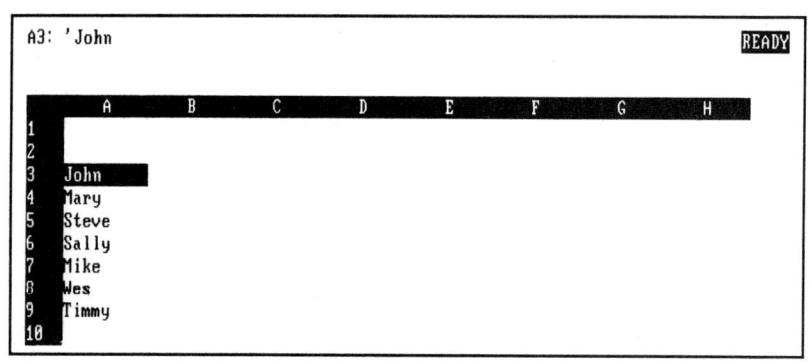

FIGURE 2-32: The / Range Name Labels command

Notes

The / Range Name Labels command names only one cell for each label in the label range. Similarly, this command always names the cells in the range immediately adjacent to the label range. There is no way to use this command to name several cells for each label in the label range, or to name a remote range. For example, you could not use the labels in the range A3..A9 in Figure 2-32 to name the range B3..E9 or to name the range E3..E9.

As we have explained, a given name can exist only once in a worksheet. If the label range contains duplicate labels—labels that are identical in every way—1-2-3 will not be able to use both of those labels to define range names. Instead, 1-2-3 will name the cell adjacent to the last (bottommost or rightmost) duplicate label. 1-2-3 will not name the cell adjacent to the other duplicate label. If one of the labels in the label range is identical to a range name that exists elsewhere in the worksheet, 1-2-3 will move the name to the cell next to the label.

If there are blank cells—or cells that contain values—in the label range, 1-2-3 will not name the cells adjacent to those cells. If there are no labels at all in the label range, the / Range Name Labels command will have no effect at all.

Remember that the maximum length of a range name in 1-2-3 is 15 characters. If any of the labels in the label range is more than 15 characters long, 1-2-3 will use the first 15 characters in that label to name the adjacent cell.

ERASING THE WORKSHEET

The / Worksheet Erase command allows you to erase the entire worksheet. This command erases all of the entries in the worksheet, any range names you have defined, any graphs you have created, any ranges you may have defined, and so on—in short, / Worksheet Erase erases everything in the worksheet.

When you issue this command, 1-2-3 will display the menu with two options: Yes and No. This menu gives you a chance to reconsider. If you choose No, then 1-2-3 will cancel the / Worksheet Erase command and return to the READY mode without erasing the worksheet. If you choose Yes, 1-2-3 will erase the entire worksheet instantly.

You should be very careful to save your work before you use the / Worksheet Erase command. If you do not save before you issue this command, all of your work will be lost. To save the worksheet, you just issue the / File Save command, supply a name for the file, and press [Enter]. We'll cover this command in detail in Chapter 9.

GETTING HELP

You can get help at any time when you are using 1-2-3 by pressing the [Help] key ([F1]). If you are in the middle of some operation —such as making an entry in a cell or issuing a command—when you press this key, 1-2-3 will display a help screen that offers assistance with the task you are performing. (The system isn't perfect— sometimes it will guess wrong about what it is you are actually doing.) For instance, you'll see the help screen shown in Figure 2-33 if you press [Help] in the middle of a / Copy command.

When you are finished reading the help screen 1-2-3 presents, you can press [Esc] to return to 1-2-3 and continue with your work exactly where you left off. If you need more help, you can select one of the index items in the help screen. You select an index item by moving the cursor to that item and pressing [Enter]. Choosing an index item brings up another help screen that offers more information about the selected topic. For instance, if you select the *cell or range references:* index item from the screen in Figure 2-33, 1-2-3 will present another screen that offers information about defining cell or range references.

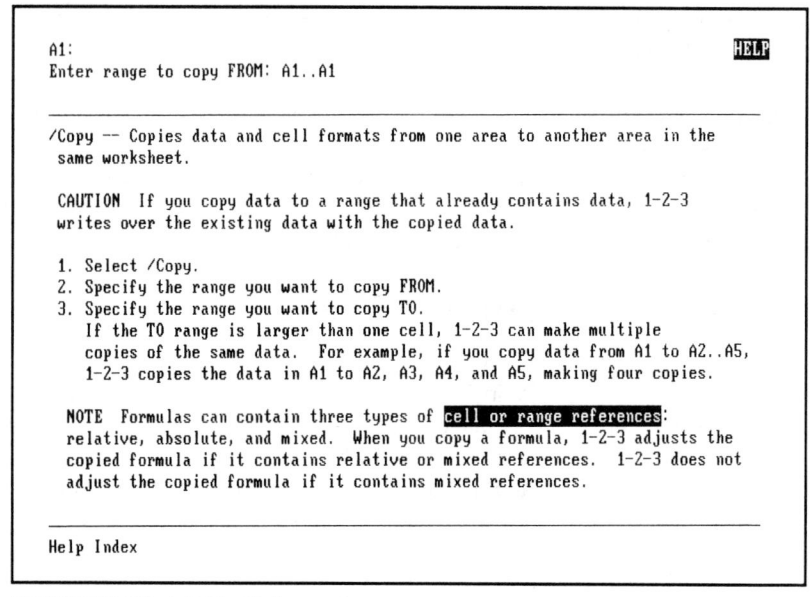

```
A1:                                                                    HELP
Enter range to copy FROM: A1..A1
─────────────────────────────────────────────────────────────────────────
/Copy -- Copies data and cell formats from one area to another area in the
same worksheet.

CAUTION  If you copy data to a range that already contains data, 1-2-3
writes over the existing data with the copied data.

1. Select /Copy.
2. Specify the range you want to copy FROM.
3. Specify the range you want to copy TO.
   If the TO range is larger than one cell, 1-2-3 can make multiple
   copies of the same data. For example, if you copy data from A1 to A2..A5,
   1-2-3 copies the data in A1 to A2, A3, A4, and A5, making four copies.

NOTE  Formulas can contain three types of cell or range references:
relative, absolute, and mixed. When you copy a formula, 1-2-3 adjusts the
copied formula if it contains relative or mixed references.  1-2-3 does not
adjust the copied formula if it contains mixed references.
─────────────────────────────────────────────────────────────────────────
Help Index
```

FIGURE 2-33: 1-2-3's Help system

One of the index items on every help screen is Help Index. Selecting this option will reveal the help index screen shown in Figure 2-34. (You'll also see this screen if you press [Help] when 1-2-3 is in the READY mode.) This screen lists all of the topics covered in 1-2-3's help system. You can get help about any of these topics by pointing to that topic and pressing [Enter].

EXITING FROM 1-2-3

When you have finished your work in 1-2-3, you'll usually want to save the work you have done into a worksheet file. To do this, you just issue the / File Save command, supply a name for the file, and press [Enter]. (For more on the / File Save command, see Chapter 9.) Once you've saved your work, you can exit from 1-2-3 and return to DOS. To exit 1-2-3, you issue the / Quit command. When you issue this command, 1-2-3 will display a simple Yes/No menu. This menu gives you one last chance to change your mind. If you wish to remain in 1-2-3, you should choose No. You might choose this option if you have forgotten to save your work. If you choose No, 1-2-3 will cancel the Quit command.

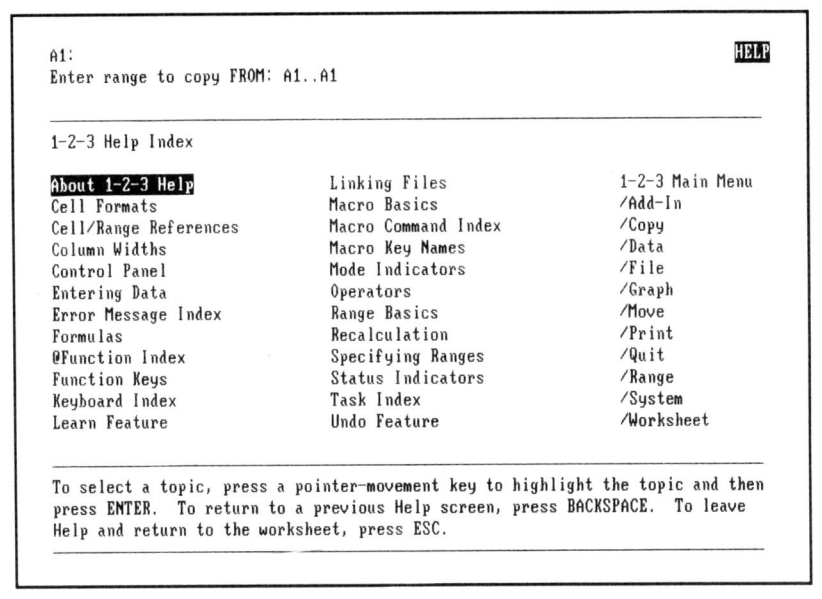

```
A1:                                                      HELP
Enter range to copy FROM: A1..A1


1-2-3 Help Index

About 1-2-3 Help        Linking Files           1-2-3 Main Menu
Cell Formats            Macro Basics            /Add-In
Cell/Range References   Macro Command Index     /Copy
Column Widths           Macro Key Names         /Data
Control Panel           Mode Indicators         /File
Entering Data           Operators               /Graph
Error Message Index     Range Basics            /Move
Formulas                Recalculation           /Print
@Function Index         Specifying Ranges       /Quit
Function Keys           Status Indicators       /Range
Keyboard Index          Task Index              /System
Learn Feature           Undo Feature            /Worksheet


To select a topic, press a pointer-movement key to highlight the topic and then
press ENTER. To return to a previous Help screen, press BACKSPACE. To leave
Help and return to the worksheet, press ESC.
```

FIGURE 2-34: 1-2-3's Help Index screen

If you want to leave 1-2-3, you should choose Yes. ►When you do this, 1-2-3 Release 2.2 will check to see if you have made changes to the worksheet since you last saved it. If you have not, 1-2-3 will return you to DOS. If the worksheet does contain unsaved changes, however, 1-2-3 Release 2.2 will beep, present the prompt *WORKSHEET CHANGES NOT SAVED! End 1-2-3 anyway?* and give you two choices: Yes and No. If you choose Yes, your screen will go blank, and and any changes that you made to the worksheet since you last saved it will be lost. If you entered 1-2-3 through the Lotus Access System, after a moment the Access System menu will appear on the screen. To return to DOS, choose the Exit option. If you entered 1-2-3 directly from DOS, after a moment the DOS prompt will appear on the screen. If you choose No, Release 2.2 will cancel the / Quit command and return you to the worksheet.◄ Earlier releases of 1-2-3 do not give you this last chance to save your work.

RELEASE ► 2.2 ◄

CONCLUSION

In this chapter, we have explained the basics of working with 1-2-3. We've demonstrated how to load 1-2-3, how to move the cell pointer, how to enter labels, numbers, and formulas into the worksheet, and how to create and use range names. We also explained how 1-2-3 allocates memory and how you can control recalculation. Finally, we explained how to exit from 1-2-3.

What you have learned so far, however, is just the beginning. In the next 14 chapters, you'll learn much more about using the 1-2-3 worksheet.

3

Formatting the Worksheet

In Chapter 2, we showed you how to enter values, labels, and formulas into a 1-2-3 worksheet. In this chapter, we'll show you how to format the values and how to align the labels in your worksheets. We'll also explain the / Worksheet Global Zero command, which allows you to hide all the zeros in your worksheets.

FORMATS

Formats allow you to change the way values are displayed. When you assign a format to a cell or range, 1-2-3 will display the values in that range in a different way. For example, if you assign the Currency format with two decimal places to a cell that contains the value 1234.56, that value will be displayed as $1,234.56. If you assign the Percent format with zero decimal places to a cell that contains the value .1234, that value will be displayed as 12%.

1-2-3 offers seven formats for values: Fixed, Sci, Currency, Comma (,), General, +/-, and Percent. Another format, Text, applies only to cells that contain formulas, and still another, Hidden, applies to both values and labels. We'll cover all of these formats in this chapter. In addition, 1-2-3 offers a group of formats that apply only to date and time entries. We'll cover Date and Time formats in Chapter 7.

The Global Format

Every 1-2-3 worksheet has a global format. Every value in a worksheet will be displayed in that worksheet's global format unless you assign the cell that contains that value a different format. (We'll show you how to assign a format to a cell or range later in this chapter.)

The Default Global Format: General

1-2-3's default global format is the General format. In the General format, values are displayed pretty much "as is." For example, Figure 3-1 shows a worksheet that contains several values, all of which are displayed in General format. Cell C4 in this worksheet contains the value 35000. As you can see, the value displayed in cell C4 is identical to the value contained in that cell. Similarly, cell C5 contains the value 9999.99, which is displayed as 9999.99. Cell C6 contains the value 4545.1, which is displayed as 4545.1 The results of formulas and functions are also displayed in General format. For example, cell C8 contains the formula

C8: +C4+C5+C6

The result of this function, 49545.09, is displayed in General format.

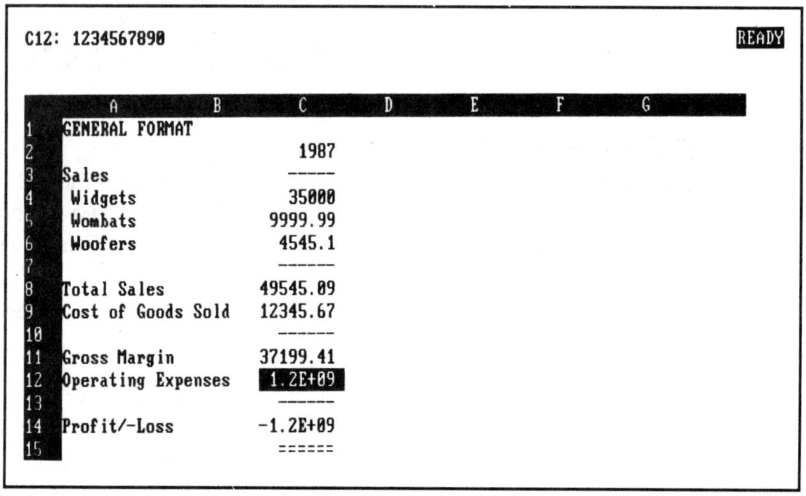

FIGURE 3-1: The General format

    As long as a value is short enough to be displayed in full, the General format will display that value "as is." If the value is too long, 1-2-3 will display as much of the value as it can. If the integer portion of the value (the portion to the left of the decimal place) is short enough to be displayed in full, 1-2-3 will display that part of the entry and will truncate the decimal portion of the entry. For example, cell C9 in Figure 3-1 contains the value 12345.6789, which is too long to be displayed in full. Since the integer portion of this value is short enough to be displayed in full, 1-2-3 displays this value as 12345.67.

    If 1-2-3 cannot display the integer portion of the entry in full, it will display the value in scientific, or exponential, notation. For example, cell C12 in Figure 3-1 contains the value 1234567890. Because column C is only nine characters wide, 1-2-3 cannot display this value in full. As a result, 1-2-3 displays this value in scientific form as 1.2E+09.

Changing Formats

1-2-3 gives you the option of changing the global format of any worksheet from General to one of 1-2-3's other formats. We'll show you how to do that later in this chapter. In addition, 1-2-3 allows you to assign formats to individual cells and ranges in your worksheets. We'll show you how to do that in the next section.

Formatting Cells and Ranges

As we have said, every 1-2-3 worksheet has a global format, which controls the display of every value in that worksheet. 1-2-3 also allows you to assign formats to individual cells and ranges in your worksheets. These formats override the global format, causing the values in the formatted cells to be displayed in a different way than the values in other cells. Unless you want every value in your worksheet to be displayed in the same way, you'll want to assign formats to ranges and cells in your worksheets.

The / Range Format Command

The / Range Format command allows you to assign a format to a cell or range. When you issue this command, 1-2-3 will display the menu shown in Figure 3-2, which lists 1-2-3's format options. You select the format you want to assign to the range from this menu.

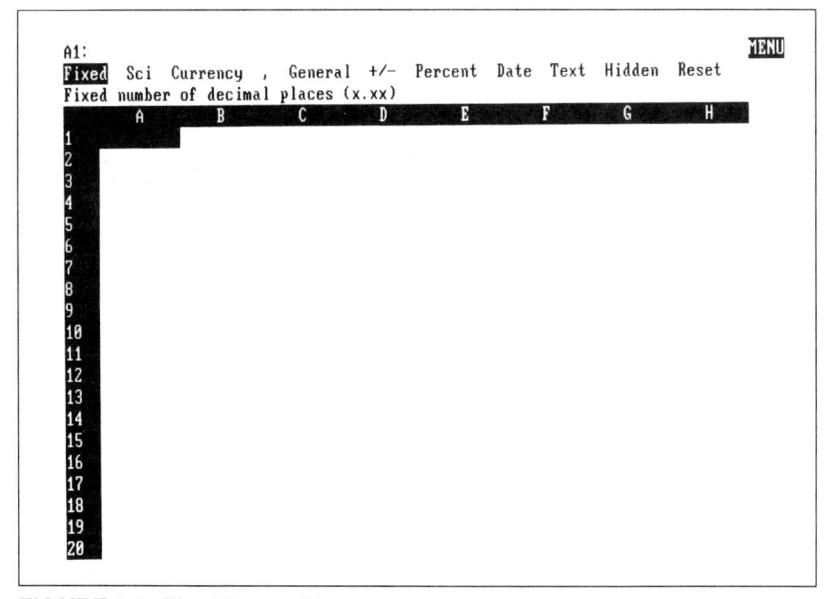

FIGURE 3-2: The / Range Format menu

If you select the Fixed, Sci, Currency, Comma (,), or Percent options, 1-2-3 will display the prompt *Enter number of decimal places (0..15):*, followed by the number

2. This prompt allows you to tell 1-2-3 how many decimal places it should display in the formatted values. The number 2 is simply 1-2-3's default. You can choose any number from 0 to 15. (If you choose any of the other options, 1-2-3 will not prompt you for the number of decimal places.)

After you select a format and specify the number of decimal places, 1-2-3 will display the prompt *Enter range to format:* in the control panel, followed by a range reference to the cell that contains the cell pointer. For instance, if the cell pointer is in cell A1 when you issue the /Range Format command, the reference *A1..A1* will appear next to the prompt. This range reference is 1-2-3's "guess" at the range you want to format. You can either press [Enter] to accept this guess and format the current cell, modify the guess to include several cells, or press [Esc] to reject the guess and specify a completely different cell or range.

Typically, you'll point to the cell you want to format (or, if you plan to format a range of cells, to a cell at one of the corners of the range) before you issue the /Range Format command. That way, you can take advantage of 1-2-3's guess.

An Example

For example, suppose you want to assign the Currency format with two decimal places to the range B7..B13 in the worksheet in Figure 3-3. To do this, move the cell pointer to cell B7 and issue the /Range Format command. When you see the Format menu, select the Currency option. When 1-2-3 prompts you to specify the number of decimal places, press [Enter] to accept the default option, 2. When 1-2-3 prompts you to define the range to be formatted, press ↓ six times to select the range B7..B13, and then press [Enter]. Figure 3-4 shows the result.

FIGURE 3-3: A sample worksheet

```
B7: (C2) 19.9                                                    READY


            A       B        C         D         E         F        G        H
     1  SALES FORECAST                                  Fiscal Year:      1989
     2
     3                      Qtr 1     Qtr 2     Qtr 3     Qtr 4    Total   Percent
     4                     -------   -------   -------   -------  -------  -------
     5  Widgets
     6   Units               400       452     510.76   577.1588 1939.918 0.234615
     7   Dollars   $19.90    7960     8994.8  10164.12  11485.46 38604.38 0.184328
     8  Wombats
     9   Units               555     582.75   611.8875  642.4818 2392.119 0.289305
    10   Dollars   $22.95 12737.25  13374.11  14042.81  14744.95 54899.13 0.262133
    11  Woofers
    12   Units               999     989.01   979.1199  969.3287 3936.458 0.476079
    13   Dollars   $29.45 29420.55  29126.34  28835.08  28546.73 115928.7 0.553538
    14                     -------   -------   -------   -------  -------
    15  Unit Sales          1954    2023.76   2101.767  2188.969 8268.496
    16  Dollar Sales      50117.8  51495.25   53042.02  54777.14 209432.2
    17                     =======   =======   =======   =======  =======
    18  Average Sale     25.64882
    19
    20
```

FIGURE 3-4: Formatting a range

Notes

Although we used the Currency format in this example, you use exactly the same technique to assign any format to any cell or range in any worksheet. All you have to do is issue the / Range Format command, choose the format you want to use, specify the desired number of decimal places (if necessary) and select the range you want to format.

Formats Affect Appearances Only

It is important that you understand that changing the format of a cell does not change the value that is actually contained in that cell. Even though the way that the value is displayed changes, the value itself stays the same. For example, when you assigned the Currency format with two decimal places to the range B7..B13, the appearance of the values in that range was changed. However, the values in cells B7, B10, and B13 did not change in any way. If you look at the control panel in Figure 3-4, you'll see that cell B7 still contains the value 19.9—even though the value displayed in cell B7 in the worksheet is $19.90. Remember, changing the format of a cell has no effect on the value in that cell.

Formats Apply to Cells, Not Values

When you assign a format to a cell, that format applies to the cell itself and not just to the value in that cell. If you replace that value in a formatted cell with another value, the new value will be displayed in the same format as the original value. For example, if you were to replace the entry in cell B7 in Figure 3-4, 19.9, with the entry 21.95, that new entry would be displayed as $21.95.

Similarly, you can assign formats to blank cells. If you format a blank cell and then enter a value in the cell, that value will be displayed in the format you have assigned to the cell. For example, remember that we included the blank cells B8, B9, B11, and B12 in the range we formatted in Figure 3-4. If you enter a value into any of these cells, it will be displayed in the Currency format with two decimal places.

Finally, using the / Range Erase command to erase the entry in a cell does not remove the format you have assigned to the cell. To unformat a cell or range, you must issue the / Range Format Reset command. We'll cover that command in a page or two.

Size of Format Range Unlimited

The size of the range you select after you issue the / Range Format command can be as small as a single cell or as large as the entire worksheet. Typically, the ranges you select to format will be just one cell or a small range of cells, but there may be times when you want to format a large range of cells.

You can use the / Range Format command to change the format of every cell in the worksheet, but there is a better way. Instead of issuing the / Range Format command, selecting a format, and selecting the entire worksheet as the range to be formatted, you can simply use the / Worksheet Global Format command to change the worksheet's global format. We'll cover this command in a few pages.

The Format Indicator

When the cell pointer is positioned on a formatted cell, 1-2-3 will display an indicator in the control panel that reveals the format you have assigned to the cell. For example, in Figure 3-4, the format indicator is (C2), indicating that cell B7 has been assigned the Currency format with two decimal places.

Copying Formatted Cells

When you use the / Copy command to make a copy of a formatted cell, that cell's format will be copied along with the contents of the cell. For example, cell C18 in Figure 3-4 contains the formula

+C16/C15

which computes the average sale amount for the first quarter. Suppose you want to assign the Currency format with two decimal places to this cell, and then copy the formula and format to the range D18..G18. To do this, move the cell pointer to cell C18, issue the / Range Format Currency command, press [Enter] to specify 2 decimal places, and press [Enter] again to assign the format to the current cell only. Figure 3-5 shows the worksheet at this point. Now, issue the / Copy command, press [Enter] to define the FROM range, select the range D18..G18 as the TO range, and press [Enter]. Figure 3-6 shows the result.

Chapter 3: Formatting the Worksheet

```
C18: (C2) +C16/C15                                                    READY

         A        B        C        D        E        F        G        H
1   SALES FORECAST                                  Fiscal Year:       1989
2
3                          Qtr 1    Qtr 2    Qtr 3    Qtr 4    Total   Percent
4                          -----    -----    -----    -----    -----   -------
5   Widgets
6     Units                  400      452   510.76 577.1588 1939.918 0.234615
7     Dollars   $19.90      7960   8994.8 10164.12 11485.46 38604.38 0.184328
8   Wombats
9     Units                  555   582.75 611.8875 642.4818 2392.119 0.289305
10    Dollars   $22.95  12737.25 13374.11 14042.81 14744.95 54899.13 0.262133
11  Woofers
12    Units                  999   989.01 979.1199 969.3287 3936.458 0.476079
13    Dollars   $29.45  29420.55 29126.34 28835.08 28546.73 115928.7 0.553538
14                         -----    -----    -----    -----    -----
15  Unit Sales              1954  2023.76 2101.767 2188.969 8268.496
16  Dollar Sales         50117.8 51495.25 53042.02 54777.14 209432.2
17                         =====    =====    =====    =====    =====
18  Average Sale    $25.65
19
20
```

FIGURE 3-5: The Currency format

```
C18: (C2) +C16/C15                                                    READY

         A        B        C        D        E        F        G        H
1   SALES FORECAST                                  Fiscal Year:       1989
2
3                          Qtr 1    Qtr 2    Qtr 3    Qtr 4    Total   Percent
4                          -----    -----    -----    -----    -----   -------
5   Widgets
6     Units                  400      452   510.76 577.1588 1939.918 0.234615
7     Dollars   $19.90      7960   8994.8 10164.12 11485.46 38604.38 0.184328
8   Wombats
9     Units                  555   582.75 611.8875 642.4818 2392.119 0.289305
10    Dollars   $22.95  12737.25 13374.11 14042.81 14744.95 54899.13 0.262133
11  Woofers
12    Units                  999   989.01 979.1199 969.3287 3936.458 0.476079
13    Dollars   $29.45  29420.55 29126.34 28835.08 28546.73 115928.7 0.553538
14                         -----    -----    -----    -----    -----
15  Unit Sales              1954  2023.76 2101.767 2188.969 8268.496
16  Dollar Sales         50117.8 51495.25 53042.02 54777.14 209432.2
17                         =====    =====    =====    =====    =====
18  Average Sale    $25.65   $25.45   $25.24   $25.02   $25.33
19
20
```

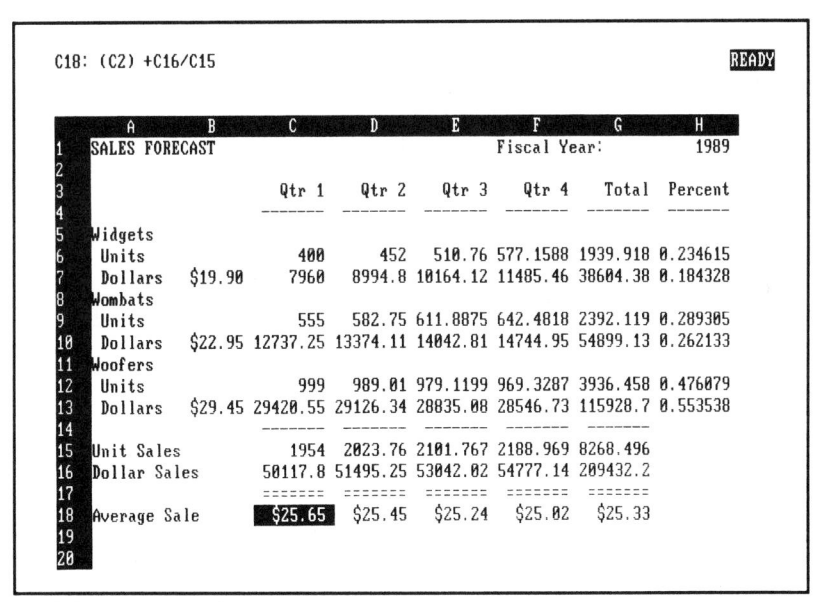

FIGURE 3-6: Copying formats

You can use this characteristic of 1-2-3 to your advantage. Whenever you need to format and copy, format first and then copy the formatted entry, instead of copying first and then formatting all of the copies. You'll save time by formatting first. We'll cover the / Copy command in detail in Chapter 4.

Column Widths and Formats

If the column that contains a formatted entry is so narrow that 1-2-3 can't display the formatted value in full, the value will be displayed as a series of asterisks. For example, suppose that you want to assign the Currency format with two decimal places to the range C16..G16. To do this, move the cell pointer to cell C16, issue the / Range Format Currency command, press [Enter] to accept the default number of decimal places, 2, select the range C16..G16, and press [Enter]. Figure 3-7 shows the result. As you can see, 1-2-3 now displays asterisks in cells C16 through G16, indicating that the formatted entries in these cells are too wide for it to display.

```
C16: (C2) +C13+C10+C7                                                    READY

        A         B        C         D        E         F        G        H
 1  SALES FORECAST                                Fiscal Year:          1989
 2
 3                               Qtr 1     Qtr 2    Qtr 3    Qtr 4    Total   Percent
 4                              -------   -------  -------  -------  -------  -------
 5  Widgets
 6     Units                      400       452   510.76  577.1588 1939.918 0.234615
 7     Dollars   $19.90          7960      8994.8 10164.12 11485.46 38604.38 0.184328
 8  Wombats
 9     Units                      555     582.75  611.8875 642.4818 2392.119 0.289305
10     Dollars   $22.95       12737.25   13374.11 14042.81 14744.95 54899.13 0.262133
11  Woofers
12     Units                      999     989.01  979.1199 969.3287 3936.458 0.476079
13     Dollars   $29.45       29420.55   29126.34 28835.08 28546.73 115928.7 0.553538
14                              -------   -------  -------  -------  -------
15  Unit Sales                   1954    2023.76  2101.767 2188.969 8268.496
16  Dollar Sales              **************************************
17                              -------   -------  -------  -------  -------
18  Average Sale               $25.65    $25.45   $25.24   $25.02   $25.33
19
20
```

FIGURE 3-7: Column widths and formats

In general, for 1-2-3 to display a formatted value, the column that contains the value must be one character wider than the formatted value. For example, 1-2-3 can display formatted values that are up to eight characters long (such as 1,234.56) in a standard nine-character-wide column. If the length of a formatted value exceeds the width of the column that contains the value, minus one, then 1-2-3 will display that value as a series of asterisks.

There are two ways to overcome this type of problem. First, you could use the / Worksheet Column Set-Width or / Worksheet Column Column-Group Set-Width commands to increase the width of the columns that contain the formatted entries. If you make the columns wide enough, 1-2-3 will be able to display the entries, no matter which format you have given them. We'll explain these commands in Chapter 4.

Alternatively, you could choose a narrower format for the cells that contain the offending entries. In the example, you could change the format of the range C16..G16 from Currency with two decimal places to Currency with zero decimal places. Figure 3-8 shows the result of making this change. Because the Currency format with zero decimal places requires three fewer characters than the same format with two decimal places, 1-2-3 is now able to display the values in these cells.

```
C16: (C0) +C13+C10+C7                                                    READY

          A         B          C         D         E         F         G        H
 1  SALES FORECAST                                              Fiscal Year:    1989
 2
 3                             Qtr 1     Qtr 2     Qtr 3     Qtr 4    Total   Percent
 4                             ------    ------    ------    ------   ------  ------
 5  Widgets
 6    Units                      400       452   510.76  577.1500  1939.918  0.234615
 7    Dollars     $19.90        7960    8994.8  10164.12  11405.46  38604.38  0.184328
 8  Wombats
 9    Units                      555    582.75  611.8875  642.4818  2392.119  0.289305
10    Dollars     $22.95     12737.25  13374.11  14042.81  14744.95  54899.13  0.262133
11  Woofers
12    Units                      999    989.01  979.1199  969.3287  3936.458  0.476079
13    Dollars     $29.45     29420.55  29126.34  28835.08  28546.73  115928.7  0.553538
14                             ------    ------    ------    ------   ------
15  Unit Sales                  1954   2023.76  2101.767  2188.969  8268.496
16  Dollar Sales             $50,118   $51,495   $53,042   $54,777  $209,432
17                            =======   =======   =======   =======  =======
18  Average Sale              $25.65    $25.45    $25.24    $25.02    $25.33
19
20
```

FIGURE 3-8: Changing formats to avoid width problems

Unformatting a Cell or Range

The / Range Format Reset command allows you to unformat a cell or range. When you issue this command, the cells in the affected range will revert to the global format.

For example, suppose you want to unformat the range C16..G16 in Figure 3-8. To do this, move the cell pointer to cell C16, issue the / Range Format Reset command, select the range C16..G16, and press [Enter]. The resulting worksheet will look just like Figure 3-6. The values in the range C16..G16 will once again be displayed in General format.

Of course, you can also change the format of a cell or range by issuing the / Range Format command and choosing a new format for the range.

1-2-3's Format Options

Now that you know how to format a cell or range, let's look at each of 1-2-3's formats in detail. In addition to the General format, 1-2-3 offers eight other formats: Fixed, Sci, Currency, Comma (,), +/-, Percent, Text, and Hidden.

Fixed

The Fixed format allows you to control the number of decimal places that 1-2-3 will display. Fixed is 1-2-3's simplest format—but also one of the most frequently used formats. Table 3-1 shows several examples of the Fixed format.

Value	Decimals	Display
123.456	4	123.4560
123.456	3	123.456
123.456	2	123.46
123.456	1	123.5
123.456	0	123
-123.456	2	-123.46

TABLE 3-1: The Fixed format

Suppose you want to assign the Fixed format with zero decimal places to the ranges C6..G6, C9..G9, and C12..G12 in Figure 3-6. To do this, move the cell pointer to cell C6, issue the / Range Format command, and choose the Fixed format option. When 1-2-3 prompts you to specify the number of decimal places it should display, type 0 and press [Enter]. Next, press → four times to select the range C6..G6 and press [Enter] to complete the command. Now, repeat this process for the ranges C9..G9 and C12..G12. Figure 3-9 shows the result.

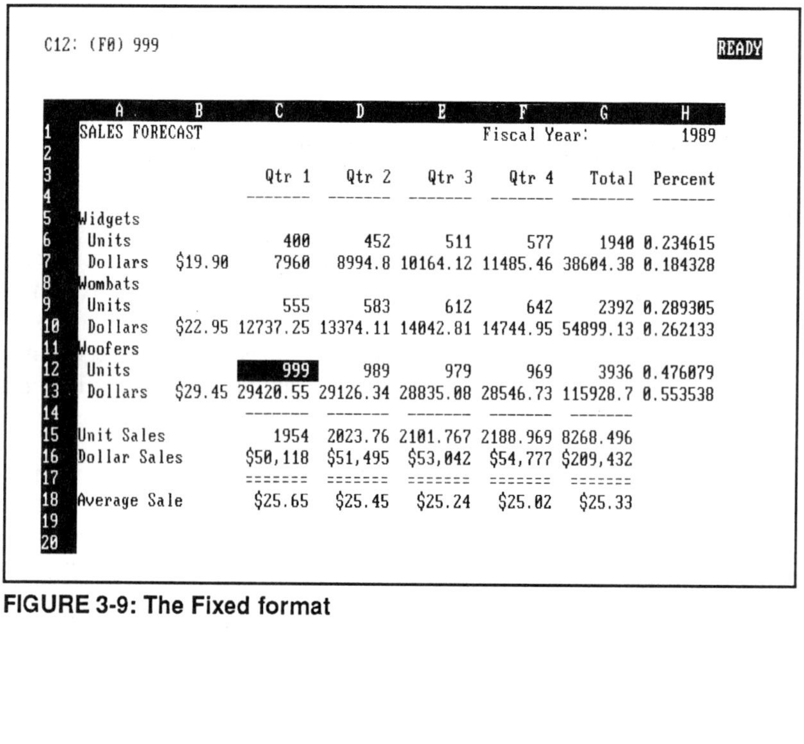

FIGURE 3-9: The Fixed format

Comma (,)

Like the Fixed format, the Comma (,) format allows you to control the number of decimal places that 1-2-3 will display. In addition, 1-2-3 inserts commas between the hundreds and thousands, thousands and millions, and so on, in values that are displayed in the Comma (,) format. (Actually, you can change the punctuation system. We'll show you how to do that in Appendix 3.) In addition, negative numbers are enclosed in parentheses. ▶(1-2-3 Release 2.2 can display negative values in the Comma (,) formatted with leading minus signs. We'll show you how to do that in Appendix 3 also.)◀ Table 3-2 shows several examples of this format.

RELEASE
▶ 2.2 ◀

Value	Decimals	Display
123456.789	4	123,456.7890
123456.789	3	123,456.789
123456.789	2	123,456.79
123456.789	1	123,456.8
123456.789	0	123,457
-123456.789	2	(123,456.79)
-123456.789	0	(123,457)

TABLE 3-2: The Comma (,) format

Suppose you want to assign the Comma (,) format with zero decimal places to the range C15..G15 in Figure 3-9. To do this, move the cell pointer to cell C15, issue the / Range Format command, and choose the , option. (You must either point to the comma (,) in the menu or type , to select this option.) When 1-2-3 prompts you to specify the number of decimal places, type 0 and press [Enter]. Next, select the range C15..G15 and press [Enter] to complete the command. Figure 3-10 shows the result.

Currency

As you have already seen, the Currency format allows you to display values as currency. 1-2-3 displays values in the Currency format with a dollar sign ($) and with commas between the hundreds and thousands, thousands and millions, and so on. (Actually, you can specify a different currency symbol and punctuation system if you wish. We'll show you how to do that in Appendix 3.) Negative numbers are enclosed in parentheses in Currency format. (▶1-2-3 Release 2.2 can display Currency-formatted negative values with leading minus signs. We'll show you how to do that in Appendix 3 also.)◀ Like the Fixed and Comma formats, the Currency format allows you to control the number of decimal places that 1-2-3 will display. Table 3-3 shows several examples of this format.

RELEASE
▶ 2.2 ◀

```
C15: (,0) +C12+C9+C6                                          READY

      A         B          C         D         E         F         G         H
 1  SALES FORECAST                                  Fiscal Year:        1989
 2
 3                         Qtr 1     Qtr 2     Qtr 3     Qtr 4    Total   Percent
 4                         -----     -----     -----     -----    -----   -------
 5  Widgets
 6    Units                  400       452       511       577     1940  0.234615
 7    Dollars   $19.90      7960    8994.8  10164.12  11485.46  38604.38 0.184328
 8  Wombats
 9    Units                  555       583       612       642     2392  0.289305
10    Dollars   $22.95  12737.25  13374.11  14042.81  14744.95  54899.13 0.262133
11  Woofers
12    Units                  999       989       979       969     3936  0.476079
13    Dollars   $29.45  29420.55  29126.34  28835.08  28546.73 115928.7  0.553538
14                         -----     -----     -----     -----    -----
15  Unit Sales            1,954     2,024     2,102     2,189     8,268
16  Dollar Sales         $50,118   $51,495   $53,042   $54,777  $209,432
17                       =======   =======   =======   =======   =======
18  Average Sale          $25.65    $25.45    $25.24    $25.02    $25.33
19
20
```

FIGURE 3-10: The Comma (,) format

Value	Decimals	Display
123456.789	4	$123,456.7890
123456.789	3	$123,456.789
123456.789	2	$123,456.79
123456.789	1	$123,456.8
123456.789	0	$123,457
-123456.789	2	($123,456.79)
-123456.789	0	($123,457)

TABLE 3-3: The Currency format

We've already assigned the Currency format with two decimal places to two ranges in Figure 3-10: B7..B13 and C18..G18. To assign these formats, we moved the cell pointer to cell B7, issued the / Range Format Currency command, typed 0 and pressed [Enter] to specify two decimal places, selected the range B7..B13 and pressed [Enter]. Then we moved the cell pointer to cell C18, repeated the / Range Format Currency command, specified two decimal places, selected the range C18..G18, and pressed [Enter].

As we pointed out previously, if 1-2-3 cannot display a formatted value in full in a cell, it will instead display a series of asterisks. This problem is particularly acute with the Currency format, because this format adds as many as seven characters to the width of an entry. For example, the value -12345 is only six characters long. But in the Currency format with two decimal places, this entry will be displayed as ($12,345.00), for a total length of 12 characters. Unless the column that contains the formatted entry is 13 or more characters wide, the entry will be displayed as a series of asterisks.

The best way to avoid this problem is to choose zero decimal places for the Currency format whenever you can. Getting rid of the decimal places decreases the width of the formatted value by three characters.

Percent

The Percent format causes 1-2-3 to display decimal values as percentages. 1-2-3 displays values in the Percent format with a percent sign (%). Like the Fixed, Comma (,) and Currency formats, the Percent format allows you to control the number of decimal places that 1-2-3 will display. Table 3-4 shows several examples of this format.

Value	Decimals	Display
.6789	3	67.890%
.6789	2	67.89%
.6789	1	67.9%
.6789	0	68%
1.6789	2	167.89%
-.6789	2	-67.89%
-.6789	0	-68%

TABLE 3-4: The Percent format

Suppose you want to assign the Percent format with one decimal place to the range H6..H13 in Figure 3-10. To do this, move the cell pointer to cell H6 and issue the /Range Format Percent command. When 1-2-3 prompts you to specify the number of decimal places it should display, you should type 1 and press [Enter]. Then select the range H6..H13 and press [Enter] to complete the command. The result is shown in Figure 3-11.

There is one trick to keep in mind when you are working with the Percent format. 1-2-3 expects the values to which you assign the Percent format to be decimal values like .125 and .5. When 1-2-3 displays a number in Percent format, it "shifts" the decimal point two places to the right. Thus the value .125 is displayed as 12.5% in Percent format with one decimal place and the value .5 as 50% in Percent format with zero decimal places. When you apply this format to a number that is greater than 1, you'll end up with a percentage over 100%. For example, the value 25 would be displayed as 2500% in the Percent format with zero decimal places.

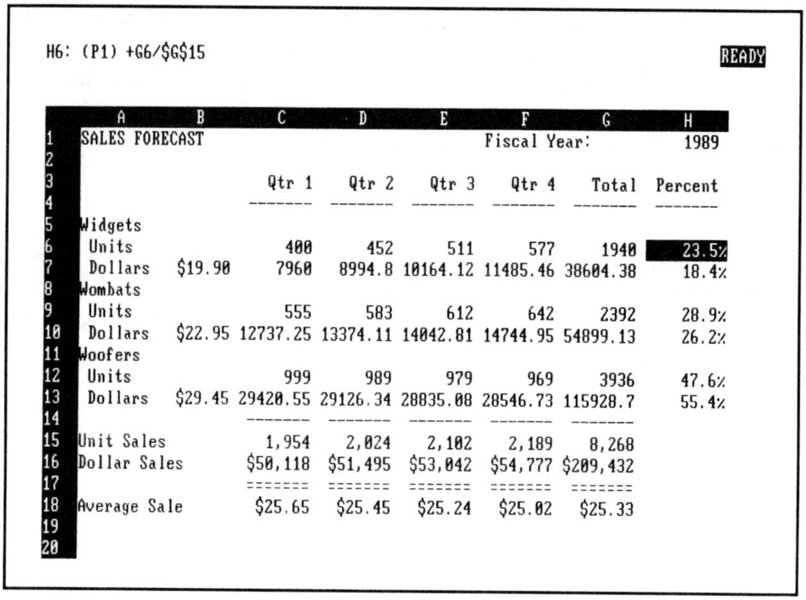

```
H6: (P1) +G6/$G$15                                          READY

        A        B        C        D        E        F        G        H
1  SALES FORECAST                                  Fiscal Year:      1989
2
3                         Qtr 1    Qtr 2    Qtr 3    Qtr 4    Total  Percent
4                         -------  -------  -------  -------  -------  -------
5  Widgets
6    Units                   400      452      511      577     1940    23.5%
7    Dollars   $19.90       7960    8994.8 10164.12 11485.46 38604.38   18.4%
8  Wombats
9    Units                   555      583      612      642     2392    28.9%
10   Dollars   $22.95   12737.25 13374.11 14042.81 14744.95 54899.13    26.2%
11 Woofers
12   Units                   999      989      979      969     3936    47.6%
13   Dollars   $29.45   29420.55 29126.34 28035.08 28546.73 115928.7    55.4%
14                      -------  -------  -------  -------  -------
15 Unit Sales            1,954    2,024    2,102    2,189    8,268
16 Dollar Sales        $50,118  $51,495  $53,042  $54,777  $209,432
17                      =======  =======  =======  =======  =======
18 Average Sale         $25.65   $25.45   $25.24   $25.02   $25.33
19
20
```

FIGURE 3-11: The Percent format

Sci (Scientific)

RELEASE ► 2.2 ◄

▶The Sci format causes 1-2-3 Release 2.2 to display values in scientific, or exponential, notation. (This format is called *Scientific* in earlier releases of 1-2-3).◀ This format also lets you to control the number of decimal places 1-2-3 will display. The Sci format comes in handy when you need to present very large or very small numbers in a compact and understandable form.

In the Sci format, values are represented as powers of 10. For example, the value 1230 would be represented as

1.23E+3

in the Sci format with two decimal places. The letter *E* in this display stands for the words *10 raised to the power of,* so this display can be read *1.23 times 10 raised to the power of 3*. Since 10 raised to the third power is 10 times 10 times 10, or 1000, and 1.23 times 1000 is 1230, you can see that this display is equivalent to the value 1230.

You can also represent very small numbers in the Sci format. For example, the value .00005 would be displayed as

5.00E-5

in Scientific format with two decimal places. The expression *E-5* in this display means *10 raised to the -5 power*. Since raising a number to a negative power is the same as dividing the number by itself, this expression is equivalent to the formula

10/10/10/10/10/10/10

or .00001. Five times .00001 equals .00005, our original value. Table 3-5 shows several other examples of Scientific format.

Value	Decimals	Display
10	0	1E+1
123	0	1E+2
123	2	1.23E+2
1234567	0	1E+6
1234567	2	1.23E+6
-1234567	2	-1.23E+6
.00000501	0	5E-6
.00000501	2	5.01E-6

TABLE 3-5: The Sci format

Figure 3-12 shows a worksheet that contains two very large numbers and one very small number. Suppose you want to assign the Sci format with three decimal places to these values. To do this, move the cell pointer to cell B3, issue the /Range Format command, choose Sci, enter 3 as the number of decimal places, and press [Enter]. Then select the range B3..B4 and press [Enter]. Figure 3-13 shows the result.

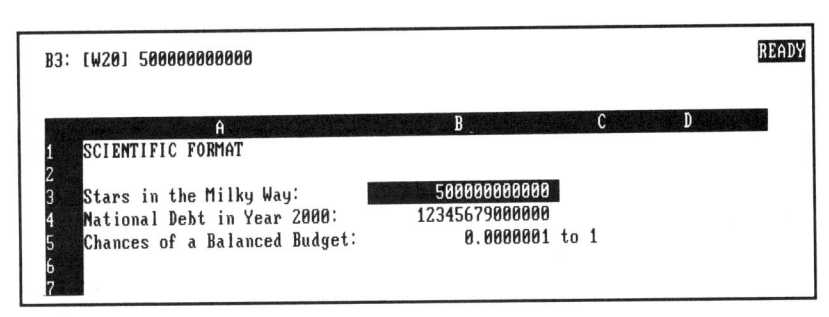

FIGURE 3-12: A sample worksheet

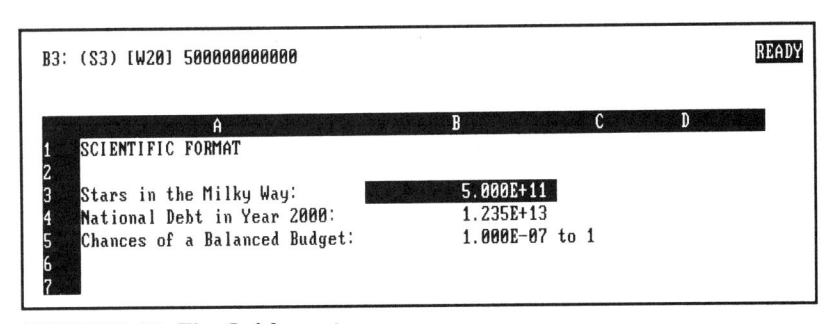

FIGURE 3-13: The Sci format

+/- (Bar Graph) Format

The +/- format (sometimes also called the Bar Graph format) causes 1-2-3 to display values as a series of plus signs (+) and minus signs (-). In effect, this format allows you to create simple bar graphs in the cells of your worksheets. Although the +/- format is the least used of 1-2-3's formats (you may never use it, in fact), it has some interesting applications.

Let's look at how the +/- format works. Figure 3-14 shows a worksheet that contains a six-year profit history for XYZ Corp. Cells B6 through B11 contain the company's net income figures for each of the last six years, in millions of dollars. These cells have been assigned the Currency format with one decimal place. Now suppose you want to view these values as a simple bar graph. One way to do this is to assign the +/- format to these cells. Move the cell pointer to cell B6, issue the /Range Format command, choose the +/- option, select the range B6..B11, and press [Enter]. Figure 3-15 shows the result.

FIGURE 3-14: A sample worksheet

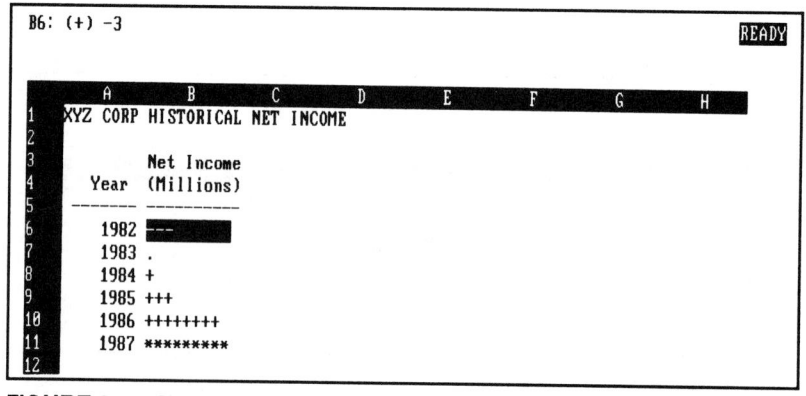

FIGURE 3-15: The +/- format

1-2-3 displays different numbers in different ways in the +/- format. Negative numbers are displayed as a series of minus signs. For example, the value -3 in cell B6 is displayed as a series of three minus signs in Figure 3-15. Similarly, positive numbers are displayed as a series of plus signs. For example, the value 1 in cell B8 is displayed as a single plus sign in Figure 3-15, and the value 8 in cell B10 is displayed as a series of eight plus signs. The value 0 is displayed as a single decimal point in +/- format, as you can see in cell B7 in Figure 3-15.

The +/- format always rounds a value down to the nearest integer for display purposes. For example, the value 3.7 in cell B9 is displayed as a series of only three plus signs in Figure 3-15.

As with 1-2-3's other numeric formats, in the +/- format, if the value in a cell is too wide to be fully displayed in that cell, 1-2-3 will display a series of asterisks instead. For example, because column B is only nine characters wide, the value 12 in cell B11 is displayed as a series of asterisks in Figure 3-15. This limitation is particularly troubling in the +/- format since the width of the column required to display an entry in +/- format increases by one character as the size of the value increases by 1. Of course, if you increased the width of column B to 12 or more characters, this value would be displayed as a series of 12 plus signs.

Because the 1-2-3 screen is only 72 characters wide, from a practical point of view the largest number that can be displayed in +/- format is 72. To display a number this large, of course, you would have to increase the width of the column that contains the value to 72 characters. Of course, you can display any value at all in the +/- format—you just won't be able to see the entire value at once.

If you want to display a number that is larger than 72 in the +/- format, you can factor that number down until it is small enough to be displayed effectively in the format. For example, notice that the numbers in column B in Figure 3-14 represent millions of dollars. Obviously, it is not practical to display a number like -3000000 in +/- format. To overcome that problem, we simply divided each net income number by 1000000 before we entered it into the worksheet.

Because the bar graphs that result from the +/- format are not nearly as attractive or useful as those you can create with the / Graph command, you probably won't use this format very often. Still, it does have some limited applications. For example, one clever application of this format makes it possible to create PERT charts in your worksheets.

The Hidden Format

The Hidden format hides the values and labels in selected cells. (This format is not available in 1-2-3 Release 1A.) When you assign the Hidden format to a cell or range, 1-2-3 will stop displaying the entries in that range. When you look at the worksheet, the cells to which you have assigned the Hidden format will appear to be blank. The cells are not blank, of course—their entries are simply hidden.

Let's consider an example of the Hidden format. Suppose you want to hide the contents of the range H3..H13 in Figure 3-11. To do this, move the cell pointer to cell H3, issue the / Range Format Hidden command, select the range H3..H13, and press

[Enter]. Figure 3-16 shows the result. As you can see, the entries in the range H3..H13 are now hidden from view.

```
H3: (H) "Percent                                                              READY

         A          B         C         D         E         F         G         H
 1  SALES FORECAST                                      Fiscal Year:         1989
 2
 3                            Qtr 1     Qtr 2     Qtr 3     Qtr 4     Total
 4                           -------   -------   -------   -------   -------
 5  Widgets
 6    Units                    400       452       511       577      1940
 7    Dollars     $19.90      7960    8994.8  10164.12  11485.46  38604.38
 8  Wombats
 9    Units                    555       583       612       642      2392
10    Dollars     $22.95  12737.25  13374.11  14042.81  14744.95  54899.13
11  Woofers
12    Units                    999       989       979       969      3936
13    Dollars     $29.45  29420.55  29126.34  28835.08  28546.73  115928.7
14                           -------   -------   -------   -------   -------
15  Unit Sales               1,954     2,024     2,102     2,189     8,268
16  Dollar Sales           $50,118   $51,495   $53,042   $54,777  $209,432
17                          =======   =======   =======   =======   =======
18  Average Sale            $25.65    $25.45    $25.24    $25.02    $25.33
19
20
```

FIGURE 3-16: The Hidden format

The Hidden format hides labels as well as values. For example, cell H3 in Figure 3-11 contains the label 'Percent. As you can see, this label is hidden in Figure 3-16. The Hidden format is the only one of 1-2-3's formats that has any effect on cells that contain labels.

Unfortunately, assigning the Hidden format to a cell does not completely hide the contents of that cell. When you point to a cell to which you have assigned the Hidden format, the contents of that cell will be visible on the first line of the control panel. For example, cell H3 in Figure 3-16 has been given the Hidden format. If you look at the control panel, you'll see that the contents of this cell are visible there. All releases of 1-2-3 display the contents of a hidden cell on the formula line when you move the cell pointer to that cell and press the [Edit] key—even if the cell is protected and global protection is enabled.

RELEASE ▶ 2.2 ◀
▶In 1-2-3 Release 2.2, the contents of protected cells that have been assigned the Hidden format will not appear in the Control Panel if global protection has been enabled. We'll talk about protection—and its effect on hidden cells—in Chapter 6.◀

To unhide a range of cells, just issue the /Range Format Reset command and select that range. For example, to unhide the entries in the range H3..H13 in Figure 3-16, you would move the cell pointer to cell H3, issue the / Range Format Reset command, select the range H3..H13, and press [Enter]. Immediately, 1-2-3 would bring the hidden cells back into view. Instead of being in the Percent format, however, these cells would once again be in the default format—General. If you want to restore the Percent format to these cells, you would have to reissue the /Range Format command.

As with all of 1-2-3's other formats, the Hidden format has absolutely no effect on the contents of cells; assigning the Hidden format to a cell does not alter the contents of that cell. Similarly, assigning the Hidden format to a cell does not affect any formulas that refer to the hidden cell.

There are several clever uses for the Hidden format. For one thing, you can use the Hidden format to hide comments or explanatory notes that you might include in your worksheets so that those comments don't clutter the worksheet. You can also use the Hidden format to hide proprietary or confidential data.

1-2-3 includes another command, / Worksheet Column Hide, that allows you to hide entire columns. For more on this command, see Chapter 4.

The Text Format

The Text format allows you to view the actual contents of cells. In Chapter 2, we explained that when you enter a formula or a function in a cell, 1-2-3 will display the result of the formula or function in that cell instead of the formula or function itself. When you assign the Text format to a cell that contains a formula or function, however, 1-2-3 will display the formula or function itself and not the results of that formula or function.

For example, suppose you want to view the contents of cells C16..G16 in Figure 3-16. To bring the contents of these cells into view, move the cell pointer to cell C16, issue the /Range Format command, choose the Text option, select the range C16..G16, and press [Enter]. Figure 3-17 shows the result.

```
C16: (T) +C13+C10+C7                                              READY

        A        B        C         D         E         F         G       H
1  SALES FORECAST                                   Fiscal Year:         1989
2
3                         Qtr 1     Qtr 2     Qtr 3     Qtr 4     Total
4                         ------    ------    ------    ------    ------
5  Widgets
6    Units                 400       452       511       577      1940
7    Dollars   $19.90     7960     8994.8  10164.12  11485.46  38604.38
8  Wombats
9    Units                 555       583       612       642      2392
10   Dollars   $22.95  12737.25  13374.11  14042.81  14744.95  54899.13
11 Woofers
12   Units                 999       989       979       969      3936
13   Dollars   $29.45  29420.55  29126.34  28835.08  28546.73  115928.7
14                        ------    ------    ------    ------    ------
15 Unit Sales             1,954    2,024     2,102     2,189     8,268
16 Dollar Sales         +C13+C10  +D13+D10  +E13+E10  +F13+F10  +G13+G10
17                        ======    ======    ======    ======    ======
18 Average Sale           $25.65   $25.45    $25.24    $25.02    $25.33
19
20
```

FIGURE 3-17: The Text format

There are a couple of limitations on the Text format that you should be aware of. For one thing, unless the formula or function in a cell is very short, or the column that contains the cell is very wide, you probably won't be able to see the entire contents of the cell. For example, the formula in cell C16 in Figure 3-17 is *+C13+C10+C7*. Because column C is only nine characters wide, however, you can see only the first part of this formula. The same is true for the formulas in cells D16 through G16. Of course, if you want to view these formulas in their entirety, you could use the /Worksheet Column Set-Width command to increase the width of columns C through G. (For more on this command, see Chapter 4.)

In addition, notice that the formula in cell G16 does not "spill over" into cell H16 as it would if it were a long label. In the Text format, 1-2-3 will display only as much of a formula as will fit in a single cell.

While you can assign the Text format to cells that contain labels or literal values, there is not much point in doing so. The Text format has absolutely no effect on the way labels and literal values are displayed.

Changing the Default Format

As we have said, 1-2-3's default global format is General. However, there may be times when you'll want to change the default format for a worksheet from General to one of 1-2-3's other formats so that the values in that worksheet will be displayed in a format other than General.

You can change the default format for a given worksheet from General to any of 1-2-3's other formats—Currency, Percent, and so on. The command that allows you to change the default format is the /Worksheet Global Format command. ►When you issue this command, 1-2-3 will display the menu and settings sheet shown in Figure 3-18. (1-2-3 Releases 1A, 2, and 2.01 display only the menu.)◄ As you can see, this menu is very similar to the one you see when you issue the /Range Format command. To change the default format for the worksheet, you just choose one of the options from this menu.

RELEASE
► 2.2 ◄

If you choose the Fixed, Sci, Currency, Comma (,) or Percent option, then 1-2-3 will display the prompt *Enter number of decimal places (0..15):*, followed by the default number of decimal places, 2. You should type the number of decimal places you want 1-2-3 to use in the default format and press [Enter].

An Example

For example, suppose you want to change the default format for the worksheet in Figure 3-17 to Currency with zero decimal places. To make this change, issue the /Worksheet Global Format command, choose the Currency option, type 0, and press [Enter]. Immediately, 1-2-3 will change the format of all values in cells that have not been assigned a specific format to Currency with zero decimal places. Figure 3-19 shows the result.

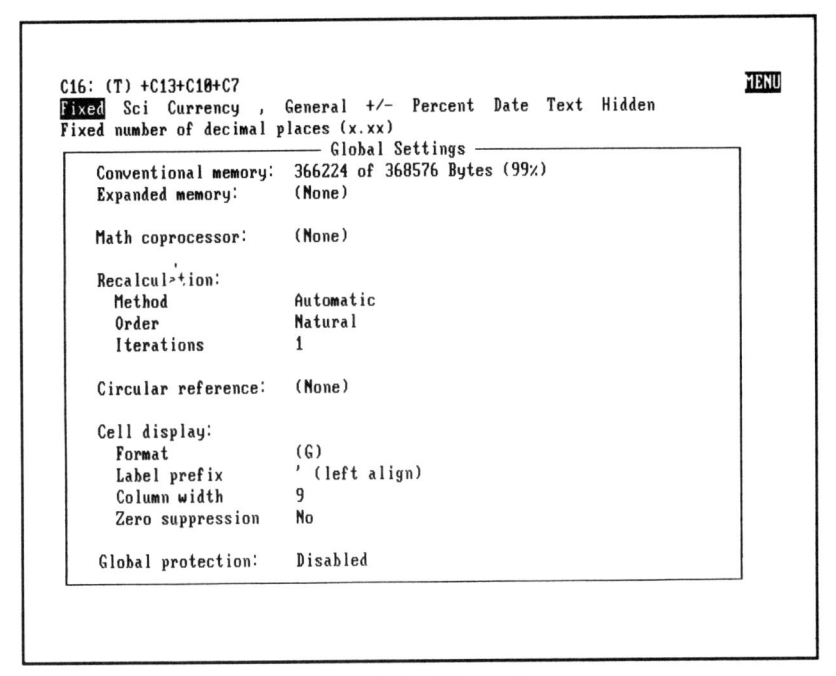

```
C16: (T) +C13+C10+C7                                          MENU
Fixed  Sci  Currency , General +/- Percent Date Text Hidden
Fixed number of decimal places (x.xx)
                    ─── Global Settings ───
    Conventional memory:  366224 of 368576 Bytes (99%)
    Expanded memory:      (None)

    Math coprocessor:     (None)

    Recalculation:
      Method              Automatic
      Order               Natural
      Iterations          1

    Circular reference:   (None)

    Cell display:
      Format              (G)
      Label prefix        ' (left align)
      Column width        9
      Zero suppression    No

    Global protection:    Disabled
```

FIGURE 3-18: The / Worksheet Global Format menu

```
C16: (T) +C13+C10+C7                                          READY

       A       B        C        D        E        F        G        H
 1  SALES FORECAST                              Fiscal Year:   $1,989
 2
 3                    Qtr 1    Qtr 2    Qtr 3    Qtr 4    Total
 4                   -------  -------  -------  -------  -------
 5  Widgets
 6    Units              400      452      511      577     1940
 7    Dollars  $19.90  $7,960   $8,995  $10,164  $11,485  $38,604
 8  Wombats
 9    Units              555      583      612      642     2392
10    Dollars  $22.95 $12,737  $13,374  $14,043  $14,745  $54,899
11  Woofers
12    Units              999      989      979      969     3936
13    Dollars  $29.45 $29,421  $29,126  $28,835  $28,547 $115,929
14                   -------  -------  -------  -------  -------
15  Unit Sales         1,954    2,024    2,102    2,189    8,268
16  Dollar Sales     +C13+C10 +D13+D10 +E13+E10 +F13+F10 +G13+G10
17                   =======  =======  =======  =======  =======
18  Average Sale      $25.65   $25.45   $25.24   $25.02   $25.33
19
20
```

FIGURE 3-19: Changing the Global Format

Notes

As we have said, the formats you assign to cells and ranges with the / Range Format command will override the worksheet's default format. For this reason, when you change a worksheet's default format, the format of values in cells that have been given specific formats will not change. For example, notice that all of the cells in Figure 3-19 to which we have assigned formats were not affected by the change in the default format.

On the other hand, changing the global format does change the way values in any cells that have not been given specific formats are displayed. This includes any cells that do not yet contain entries, and even any cells that you insert into the worksheet with the / Worksheet Insert Row or Column commands.

Sometimes changing the default format will affect the worksheet in ways you don't expect. For example, notice that the value 1989 in cell H1 in Figure 3-19 is displayed as $1,989—hardly the result you wanted. To overcome this problem, you'll have to assign a specific format (probably the Fixed format with zero decimal places) to cell H1.

If you change the default format and then issue the / Range Format Reset command to reset the format of a range, the cells in that range will be displayed in the new default format. For example, if you issue the / Range Format Reset command and select the range C16..G16, the entries in that range will appear in Currency format with zero decimal places, as shown in Figure 3-20.

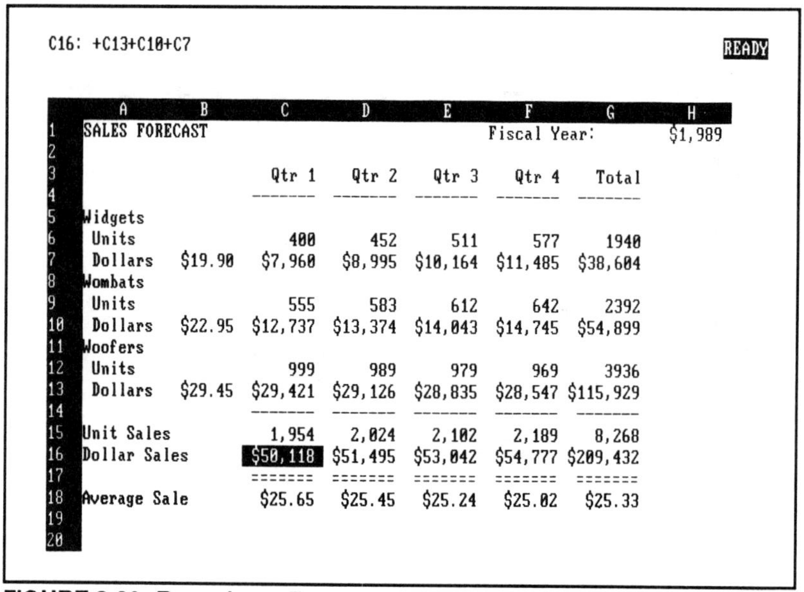

FIGURE 3-20: Resetting a Range Format

To change the global format back to General (or to any other format, for that matter), simply reissue the / Worksheet Global Format command and choose the General option (or the option you want to use as the global format).

> **TIP: USE TEXT FORMAT TO CREATE AN AUDIT COPY OF YOUR WORKSHEET**
>
> If you change the default format for a worksheet to Text, 1-2-3 will display the contents of every cell that contains a formula or function instead of the results of those formulas and functions (unless you've specifically formatted those cells). If you then use the /Worksheet Global Default Column-Width command to increase the default column width so that all of every formula is visible, and print the worksheet, you'll have an audit copy of the worksheet.

ZERO SUPPRESSION

The / Worksheet Global Zero command allows you to hide (suppress) all of the zeros in a worksheet. (This command is not available in 1-2-3 Release 1A.) ►When you issue this command, 1-2-3 Release 2.2 will present a menu with three options: No, Yes, and Label. (Earlier releases do not offer the Label option.).◄ The / Worksheet Global Zeros command affects cells that contain formulas and functions that return zeros, as well as cells that contain literal zeros.

RELEASE ► 2.2 ◄

If you choose Yes from the / Worksheet Global Zeros menu, 1-2-3 will immediately "hide" every zero in the worksheet. This improves the appearance (and understandability) of worksheets that contain large numbers of meaningless zeros. For example, consider the worksheet in Figure 3-21, which shows a simplified version of a 1-2-3 check register. The formulas in the range E6..H10 in this worksheet use the account codes in column D and row 4 to "post" each check to the proper account. (These formulas use 1-2-3's @IF function, which we'll cover in Chapter 5.)

Notice that each check in the worksheet is posted to only one account. 1-2-3 displays zeros in the other three columns of each row, making the worksheet unattractive and difficult to understand. To remove these zeros, we need only issue the / Worksheet Global Zero Yes command. Figure 3-22 shows the result.

As you can see, all the zeros visible in Figure 3-21 are hidden in Figure 3-22. This includes the zeros in the range E6..H11, which are the results of formulas, and the literal zero in cell C11. As a result, the worksheet in Figure 3-22 is far more attractive and far easier to understand than the one in Figure 3-21.

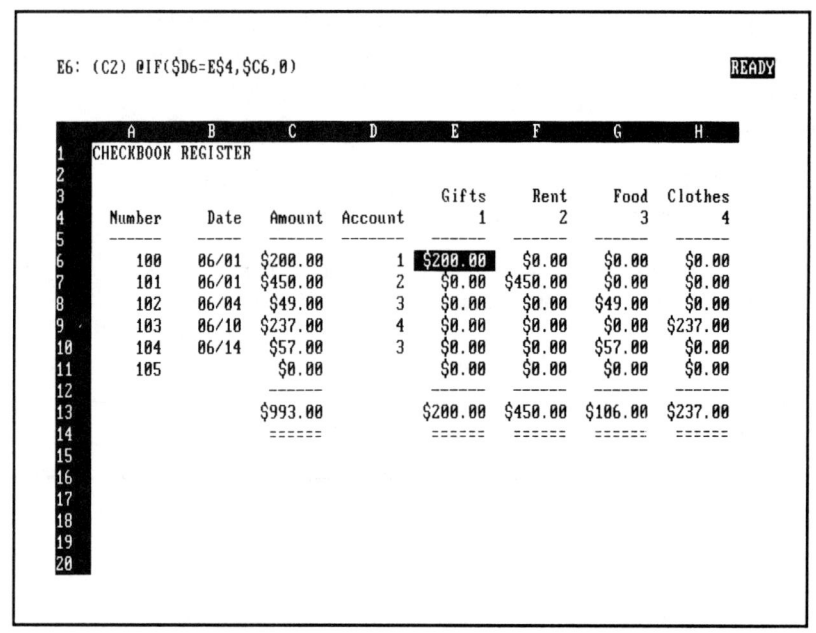

```
E6: (C2) @IF($D6=E$4,$C6,0)                                        READY

         A         B         C         D         E         F         G         H
 1  CHECKBOOK REGISTER
 2
 3                                             Gifts     Rent      Food    Clothes
 4    Number     Date     Amount   Account       1         2         3         4
 5    ------    -----    -------   -------    -------   -------   -------   -------
 6      100     06/01    $200.00      1       $200.00     $0.00     $0.00     $0.00
 7      101     06/01    $450.00      2         $0.00   $450.00     $0.00     $0.00
 8      102     06/04     $49.00      3         $0.00     $0.00    $49.00     $0.00
 9      103     06/10    $237.00      4         $0.00     $0.00     $0.00   $237.00
10      104     06/14     $57.00      3         $0.00     $0.00    $57.00     $0.00
11      105                $0.00                $0.00     $0.00     $0.00     $0.00
12                       -------                -------   -------   -------   -------
13                       $993.00               $200.00   $450.00   $106.00   $237.00
14                       =======                =======   =======   =======   =======
15
16
17
18
19
20
```

FIGURE 3-21: A worksheet with lots of zeros

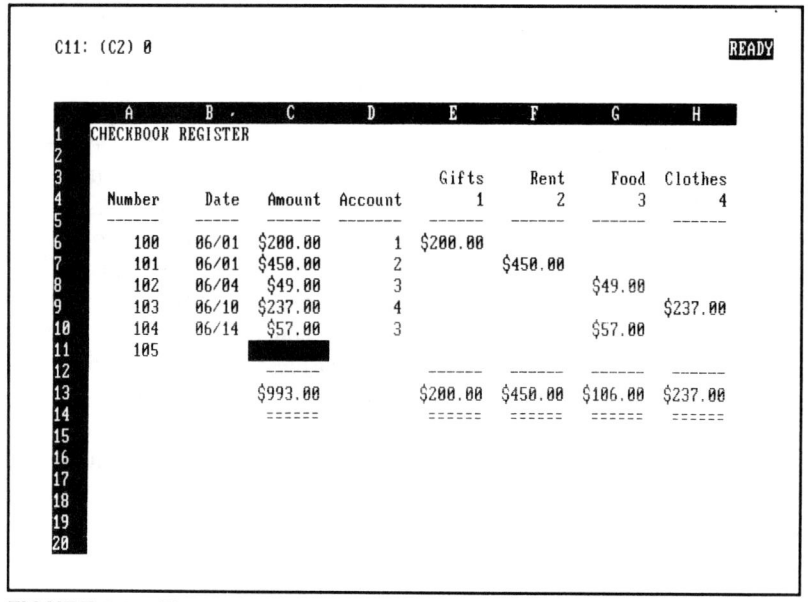

```
C11: (C2) 0                                                         READY

         A         B         C         D         E         F         G         H
 1  CHECKBOOK REGISTER
 2
 3                                             Gifts     Rent      Food    Clothes
 4    Number     Date     Amount   Account       1         2         3         4
 5    ------    -----    -------   -------    -------   -------   -------   -------
 6      100     06/01    $200.00      1       $200.00
 7      101     06/01    $450.00      2                 $450.00
 8      102     06/04     $49.00      3                            $49.00
 9      103     06/10    $237.00      4                                      $237.00
10      104     06/14     $57.00      3                            $57.00
11      105
12                       -------                -------   -------   -------   -------
13                       $993.00               $200.00   $450.00   $106.00   $237.00
14                       =======                =======   =======   =======   =======
15
16
17
18
19
20
```

FIGURE 3-22: Zero suppression

The Label Option

▶1-2-3 Release 2.2's / Worksheet Global Zero command offers an option—Label—that allows you to specify what 1-2-3 should display in place of zero values. (This option is not available in earlier releases.) When you issue the / Worksheet Global Zero Label command, 1-2-3 will display the prompt *Enter label (can include label prefix):* at the top of the screen, and wait for your reply. In response to this prompt, you can type any entry up to 239 characters in length. Unless you specify otherwise, the entry will be left-aligned. To right-align, center, or repeat the entry, you must preface it with the prefix ", ^, or \, respectively. As soon as you press [Enter], 1-2-3 will begin displaying the entry you specified in any cells that contain or return the value 0.

For example, Figure 3-23 shows the effect on the worksheet shown in Figure 3-21 of issuing the / Worksheet Global Zero Label command, typing "xxx, and pressing [Enter]. As you can see, 1-2-3 displays the right-aligned characters *xxx* in every cell that contains or returns the value 0.◄

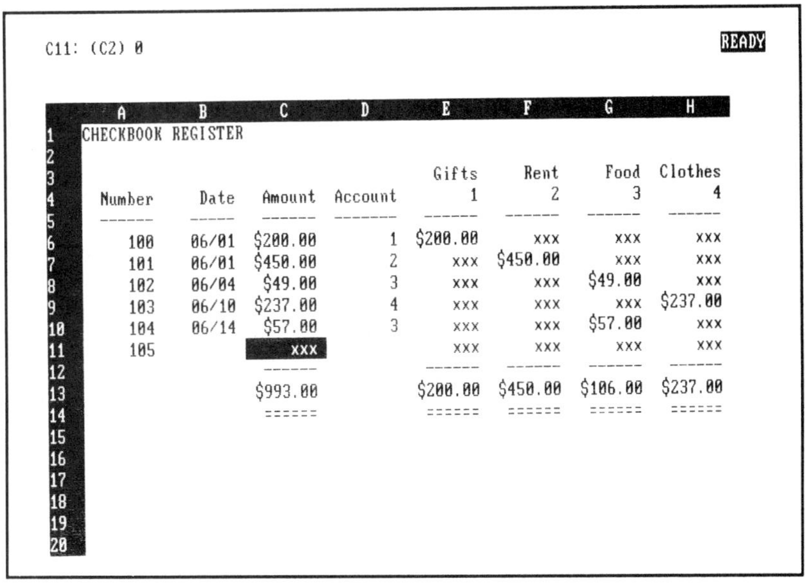

RELEASE
▶ 2.2 ◄

FIGURE 3-23: The / Worksheet Global Zero Label command

Restoring the Display of Zeros

To bring the zeros in a worksheet back into view, you need only issue the / Worksheet Global Zero command and choose the No option. Immediately, 1-2-3 will bring every zero in the worksheet back into view, whether the display of zeros was suppressed with the Yes option or altered with the Label option.

Notes

When you save a worksheet in which you have suppressed or altered the display of zeros, 1-2-3 does not save the Zero-Suppression setting with the worksheet. Consequently, all of the zeros in the worksheet will be visible the next time you retrieve it. To hide (or alter the display of) the zeros in the worksheet, you must reissue the / Worksheet Global Zero (or Label) command after you retrieve it. (If you want 1-2-3 to suppress the display zeros automatically when you retrieve a worksheet, you can create an auto-executing macro that issues the / Worksheet Global Zero Yes or Label command. We'll show you how in Chapter 13.)

Although the / Worksheet Global Zero command can radically alter the appearance of the worksheet, it has no effect on the substance of the worksheet. The / Worksheet Global Zero Yes command does not erase the cells that contain zeros; it merely hides those zeros from view. Similarly, turning on zero suppression does not change the format of any cell. Furthermore, references to cells that contain or return the value 0 will still return the value 0.

When you point to a cell that contains a "hidden" zero, the contents of that cell will be visible in the control panel. For example, in Figures 3-22 and 3-23, the cell pointer is on cell C11, which contains a suppressed zero. Notice that the contents of this cell is visible in the control panel.

We can think of two disadvantages to using zero suppression. First, hiding all of the zeros in a worksheet may make it hard for you to find your way around in that worksheet. Second, since you won't be able to spot the cells that contain zeros when zero suppression is on, if you aren't careful, you can easily erase ranges or delete rows or columns that contain zeros. Be careful.

LABEL PREFIXES

As we explained in Chapter 2, every label in 1-2-3 must begin with a label prefix. 1-2-3 offers four label prefixes: ' (left-aligned), " (right-aligned), ^ (centered), and \ (repeating). The label prefix you use to start a label determines the alignment of that label in the cell that contains the label. For example, if you begin a label with the prefix ", it will be aligned with the right edge of the cell. If you begin a label with the prefix ^, it will be centered in the cell.

The Default Label Prefix

Although every label must begin with a label prefix, you usually won't need to type a label prefix when you type a label. If the entry you are making begins with a letter, 1-2-3 will assume that the entry is a label and will automatically supply a prefix—the default prefix—for the label.

The original default label prefix is ' (left-aligned). Whenever you enter a label without a label prefix, 1-2-3 will supply the prefix ' for that label, and the label will be left-aligned. For example, suppose you want to enter the left-aligned label *Total* into cell A9 in Figure 3-24. To do this, just move the cell pointer to cell A9, type Total, and press [Enter]. Figure 3-25 shows the result.

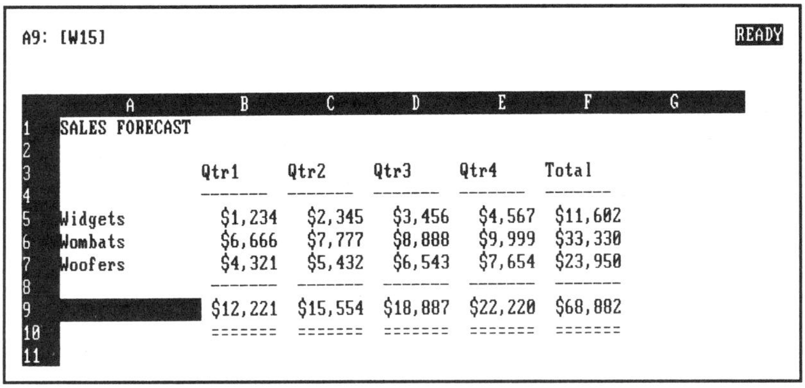

```
A9: [W15]                                                        READY

       A          B       C       D       E       F       G
 1  SALES FORECAST
 2
 3              Qtr1    Qtr2    Qtr3    Qtr4    Total
 4              ------- ------- ------- ------- -------
 5  Widgets     $1,234  $2,345  $3,456  $4,567  $11,602
 6  Wombats     $6,666  $7,777  $8,888  $9,999  $33,330
 7  Woofers     $4,321  $5,432  $6,543  $7,654  $23,950
 8              ------- ------- ------- ------- -------
 9              $12,221 $15,554 $18,887 $22,220 $68,882
10              ======= ======= ======= ======= =======
11
```

FIGURE 3-24: A sample worksheet

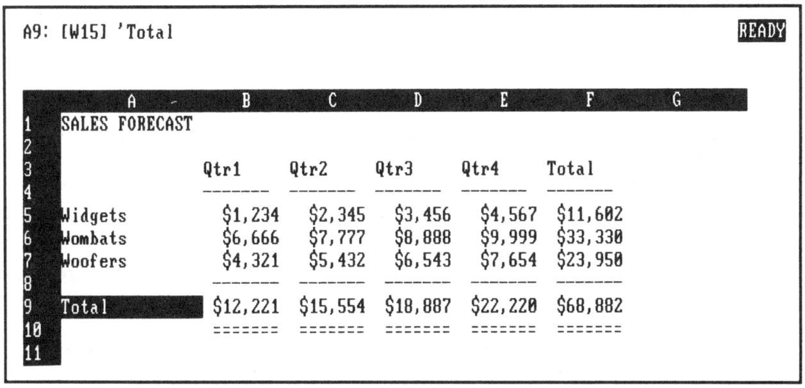

```
A9: [W15] 'Total                                                 READY

       A          B       C       D       E       F       G
 1  SALES FORECAST
 2
 3              Qtr1    Qtr2    Qtr3    Qtr4    Total
 4              ------- ------- ------- ------- -------
 5  Widgets     $1,234  $2,345  $3,456  $4,567  $11,602
 6  Wombats     $6,666  $7,777  $8,888  $9,999  $33,330
 7  Woofers     $4,321  $5,432  $6,543  $7,654  $23,950
 8              ------- ------- ------- ------- -------
 9  Total       $12,221 $15,554 $18,887 $22,220 $68,882
10              ======= ======= ======= ======= =======
11
```

FIGURE 3-25: The default label prefix

Overriding the Default

If you want to enter a label with a nondefault alignment, you just type the appropriate prefix at the beginning of the label. For example, suppose you want to enter the right-aligned label *Percent* into cell A11 in Figure 3-25. We'll assume that the default label prefix in this worksheet is ' (left-aligned). If you simply type the label *Percent* into cell A11, 1-2-3 will give that label the prefix ', and the label will be left-aligned. To right-align the label, you must type *"Percent*. By typing the label prefix " at the beginning of this label, you tell 1-2-3 you want the label to be right-aligned. Figure 3-26 shows the resulting worksheet.

```
A11: [W15] "Percent                                                          READY

        A           B         C         D         E         F         G
1   SALES FORECAST
2
3                  Qtr1      Qtr2      Qtr3      Qtr4      Total
4                  -------   -------   -------   -------   -------
5   Widgets        $1,234    $2,345    $3,456    $4,567    $11,602
6   Wombats        $6,666    $7,777    $8,888    $9,999    $33,330
7   Woofers        $4,321    $5,432    $6,543    $7,654    $23,950
8                  -------   -------   -------   -------   -------
9   Total          $12,221   $15,554   $18,887   $22,220   $68,882
10                 =======   =======   =======   =======   =======
11        Percent
12
```

FIGURE 3-26: Overriding the default label prefix

The / Range Label Command

What if you want to change the alignment of several labels that are already in place? In that case, you'll need to use the / Range Label command. This command changes the label prefixes of the labels in the range you specify.

When you issue this command, 1-2-3 will display the menu that is shown in Figure 3-27. The three options on this menu—Left, Right, and Center—allow you to specify the alignment of the labels in the range you will select. When you make a choice from this menu, 1-2-3 will display the prompt *Enter range of labels:* in the control panel, followed by a range reference to the cell that contains the cell pointer. This range reference is 1-2-3's guess at the range of labels you want to realign. You can either press [Enter] to accept this guess and assign a label alignment to the current cell, modify the guess to include several cells, or press [Esc] to reject the guess and specify a completely different cell or range to realign. Typically, you'll point to the first cell in the range of labels you want to realign before you issue / Range Label. That way, you can take advantage of 1-2-3's guess.

For example, notice that the labels in the range B3..F4 in the worksheet in Figure 3-26 are left-aligned. You want to center these labels. To do this, you should move the cell pointer to cell B3, issue the / Range Label command, choose Center from the Label menu, select the range B3..F4, and press [Enter]. Figure 3-28 shows the result.

Notice that the labels in the range B3..F4 in Figure 3-28 are now centered. In fact, 1-2-3 has actually changed the label prefix of each of these labels from ' to ^. For example, if you look at the control panel in Figure 3-28, you'll see that the label prefix for the label in cell B3 is now ^.

You cannot use the / Range Label command to "pre-set" the alignment of a range of cells. That is, you cannot use this command to assign an alignment to a range of cells before you enter labels in those cells. The / Range Label command can only be used to change the alignment of labels that are already in place.

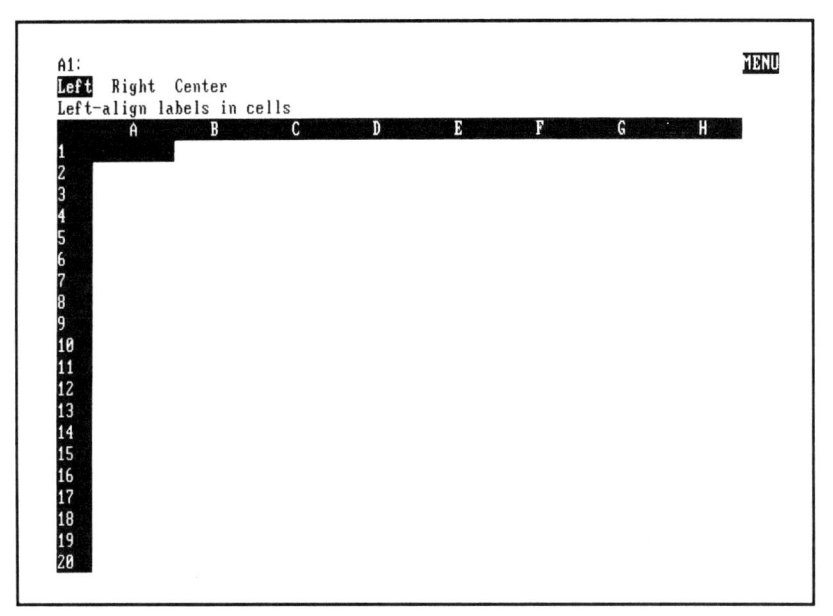

```
A1:                                                    MENU
Left  Right  Center
Left-align labels in cells
      A         B        C       D        E       F       G       H
 1
 2
 3
 4
 5
 6
 7
 8
 9
10
11
12
13
14
15
16
17
18
19
20
```

FIGURE 3-27: The / Range Label menu

```
B3: [W9] ^Qtr1                                              READY

        A         B        C        D        E        F       G
 1  SALES FORECAST
 2
 3            Qtr1     Qtr2     Qtr3     Qtr4    Total
 4            -------  -------  -------  -------  -------
 5  Widgets  $1,234   $2,345   $3,456   $4,567  $11,602
 6  Wombats  $6,666   $7,777   $8,888   $9,999  $33,330
 7  Woofers  $4,321   $5,432   $6,543   $7,654  $23,950
 8            -------  -------  -------  -------  -------
 9  Total    $12,221  $15,554  $18,887  $22,220 $60,882
10            =======  =======  =======  =======  =======
11      Percent
12
```

FIGURE 3-28: The / Range Label command

TIP: USE SPACES TO ALIGN LABELS

Instead of using the label prefixes " and ^ to change the alignment of labels, we often include preceding spaces in our labels that change their alignment. For example, the labels in rows 8 and 10 in Figure 3-24 are left-aligned, but we have included a single space before the first character in each label to shift the label one space to the right. For instance, the label in cell B8 is ' -------. We prefer this method to the use of label prefixes because it gives us more control over the alignment of labels and because it's a lot easier to type a space or two than it is to type ^ or ".

TIP: RIGHT-ALIGNMENT QUIRK

If you look carefully at Figure 3-26, you'll see that the label in cell A11, which is supposedly right-aligned, is actually offset one space from the right edge of the cell. In fact, right-aligned labels are always offset one space from the right edge of cells. This is done to match the display of values. The final digit in any value entry is one space to the left of the left edge of the cell that contains it; the final space is reserved for the closing parenthesis on values assigned the Currency or Comma (,) formats.

To force a label to be flush with the right edge of a cell, you must enter it as a left-aligned label with enough preceding spaces to shift it to the right the required number of spaces. For example, to force the label *Percent* in cell A11 to be flush with the right edge of the cell, you'd have to replace it with the label *'   Percent*. We left eight spaces in this label before the letter *P*. These spaces shift the label to the right far enough so that the letter *t* is flush with the right edge of the cell.

Changing the Default

As you might expect, you can change the default label prefix from ' to " (right-aligned) or ^ (centered). (1-2-3 does not allow you to use the \ (repeating) prefix as the default prefix.) To do this, you just issue the / Worksheet Global Label-Prefix command. When you issue this command, 1-2-3 will display the same menu shown in Figure 3-27. The three choices on this menu—Left, Right, and Center—are the three options for the default label prefix. To change the default prefix, you just choose one of these options.

Changing the default label prefix has no effect on any labels that are already in the worksheet. Those labels will retain the prefix they were given when you entered them into the worksheet. The new default label prefix you specify will only affect any labels you enter into the worksheet after changing the default.

For example, suppose you want to change the default label prefix for the worksheet in Figure 3-28 from ' (left-aligned) to " (right-aligned). To do this, issue the / Worksheet Global Label-Prefix command and choose the Right option. After you change the default prefix, the worksheet will still look just like Figure 3-28. Changing the default label prefix has not changed the alignment of any of the labels that were already in the worksheet.

However, any new labels you enter into the worksheet will have the new default prefix. For example, suppose you move the cell pointer to cell A12, type Increase, and press [Enter]. Figure 3-29 shows this label in the worksheet. As you can see, this new label is right-aligned.

```
A12: [W15] "Increase                                            READY

        A          B        C        D        E        F       G
1  SALES FORECAST
2
3              Qtr1    Qtr2    Qtr3    Qtr4    Total
4              ------- ------- ------- ------- -------
5  Widgets     $1,234  $2,345  $3,456  $4,567  $11,602
6  Wombats     $6,666  $7,777  $8,888  $9,999  $33,330
7  Woofers     $4,321  $5,432  $6,543  $7,654  $23,950
8              ------- ------- ------- ------- -------
9  Total       $12,221 $15,554 $18,887 $22,220 $68,882
10             ======= ======= ======= ======= =======
11         Percent
12         Increase
```

FIGURE 3-29: Changing the default label prefix

Once you have changed the default label prefix, you can restore the original default simply by repeating the / Worksheet Global Label-Prefix command and choosing the Left option.

TIP: DON'T TYPE LABEL PREFIXES

Typing endless label prefixes is laborious and time-consuming, so as a rule, we prefer not to type label prefixes. If we need to enter a series of labels with an alignment other than the default, we enter the labels with the default alignment (which means we don't have to type any prefix at all); then, after all the labels are in place, we use the / Range Label command to change their alignment. This approach saves keystrokes and cuts down on mistakes.

CONCLUSION

In this chapter, we've shown you how to format the entries in your worksheets. First, we showed you how to change the format of values using the / Range Format and / Worksheet Global Format commands. Then we showed you how to suppress the display of extraneous zeros in your worksheets with the / Worksheet Global Zero command. Finally, we showed you how to use label prefixes, the / Range Label command, and the / Worksheet Global Label-Prefix command to change the alignment of labels.

4

Cut-and-Paste Commands

Editing an old-fashioned paper spreadsheet is a tedious and time-consuming process. To edit a paper spreadsheet, you need four tools—a pair of scissors, a jar of glue, an eraser, and a pencil—as well as a lot of patience. You use the scissors and glue to remove entire rows and columns, insert entire rows and columns, move sections of the worksheet and adjust the width of columns. You use the pencil to make entries and to copy information, and the eraser to erase mistakes. You use the patience to maintain your sanity during the process.

1-2-3 has fourteen commands that can take the place of these four editing tools. These commands are: / Worksheet Column Set-Width, / Worksheet Column Reset-Width, / Worksheet Column Hide, / Worksheet Column Display, and ▶/ Worksheet Column Column-Range◀; / Worksheet Delete Column and / Worksheet Delete Row; / Worksheet Insert Column and / Worksheet Insert Row; / Move, / Copy, / Range Value, / Range Trans, and / Range Erase. These are the tools that you will use to edit 1-2-3's electronic worksheet.

RELEASE
▶ 2.2 ◀

ADJUSTING COLUMN WIDTHS

1-2-3's / Worksheet Column and / Worksheet Global Column-Width commands allow you to change the widths of the columns in your worksheets. As you'll see in this section, these commands allow you to narrow or widen one column or every column in the worksheet. ▶In 1-2-3 Release 2.2, you can change the width of a group of adjacent columns with a single command.◀ You can also use these commands to hide selected columns.

RELEASE
▶ 2.2 ◀

Why Change Column Widths?

There are several reasons why you might want to change the widths of the columns in a worksheet. As discussed in Chapters 2 and 3, the width of a column in a worksheet affects how 1-2-3 will display information in the cells of that column. To display a value entry correctly, the column that contains the entry must be one space wider than the number of characters in the formatted entry. Otherwise, 1-2-3 will display that value as a series of asterisks (*). In some cases, you'll need to widen a column to eliminate these asterisks.

In Chapter 2, we talked about long labels. As you probably recall, a long label from one cell will overlap the cells to its right, as long as those cells are empty. If the cells to the right are occupied, however, only a portion of the long label will be visible. To bring the entire label into view, you'll need to widen the column that contains the label.

Although you will often use 1-2-3's / Worksheet Column and / Worksheet Global Column-Width commands to solve display problems, you also will use them simply to improve the appearance of a worksheet. In some cases, for example, you'll want to widen a column to separate the information in that column from the information in an adjacent column. In other cases, you'll want to decrease the width of a column or two so that you can see more information on the screen at once.

The / Worksheet Column Set-Width Command

The / Worksheet Column Set-Width command lets you adjust the width of one column at a time. You can use this command to decrease the width of any column to as little as one character or to increase its width to as many as 240 characters. (In 1-2-3 Release 1A, the maximum column width is 72 characters.) Using the / Worksheet Column Set-Width command is a four-step process. First, you position the cell pointer in any cell of the column whose width you want to adjust. When the cell pointer is in place, you issue the / Worksheet Column Set-Width command. Then you must specify the new width of the column, either by pointing or by typing a number. Finally, you press [Enter] to lock in the new width.

Examples

For example, suppose that you want to increase the width of column A of the worksheet shown in Figure 4-1 so that the labels in cells A6, A7, and A8 are fully visible. Currently, 1-2-3 is displaying only the first nine characters of these labels because column A is nine spaces wide (1-2-3's default width), and cells B5, B6, B7, and B8 contain entries.

To increase the width of column A in this worksheet, first position the cell pointer anywhere in that column, then issue the / Worksheet Column Set-Width command. When you issue this command, you'll see the prompt *Enter column width (1..240): 9* on the second line of the control panel and the indicator [W9] on the first line. Both messages indicate the current width of the column. (This indicator does not appear in 1-2-3 Release 1A.)

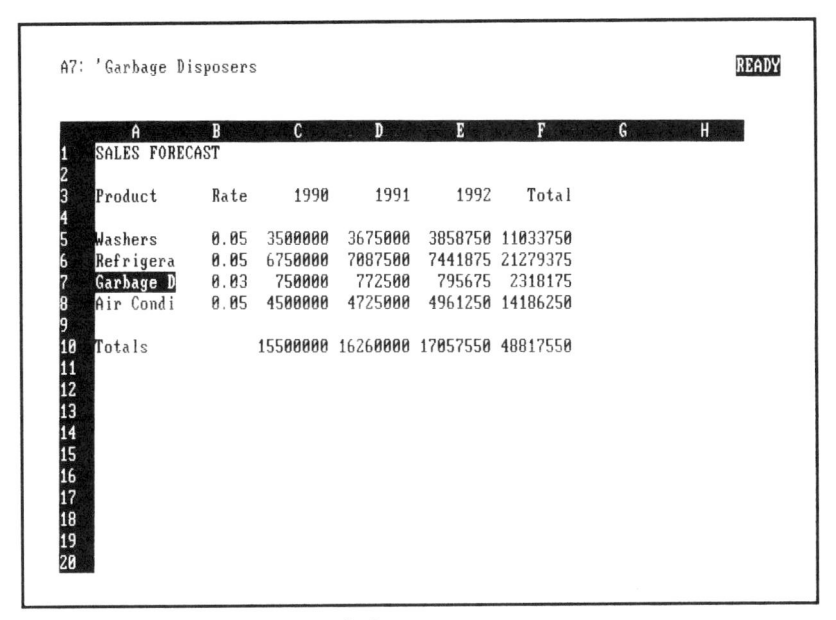

```
A7: 'Garbage Disposers                                          READY

       A         B       C        D        E        F       G     H
 1 SALES FORECAST
 2
 3 Product     Rate    1990     1991     1992    Total
 4
 5 Washers     0.05  3500000  3675000  3858750 11033750
 6 Refrigera   0.05  6750000  7087500  7441875 21279375
 7 Garbage D   0.03   750000   772500   795675  2318175
 8 Air Condi   0.05  4500000  4725000  4961250 14186250
 9
10 Totals           15500000 16260000 17057550 48817550
11
12
...
20
```

FIGURE 4-1: An example worksheet

Once you see this prompt, you can adjust the width of the column in one of two ways. First, you can type a new width and press [Enter]. This method is most useful when you know exactly how wide you want the column to be. Alternatively, you can press the → or ← keys to change the width of the column. Pressing → will increase the width of the column by one character, while pressing ← will decrease the column width by one character. This method is most useful when you don't know exactly how wide the column must be to display formatted values and long labels entirely.

Since in the example you aren't sure of exactly how wide the column should be (but only that it should be wide enough to display the labels in full), you probably will want to use the → key to expand the column. If you press → one time, 1-2-3 will increase the width of column A to ten characters. The change will be reflected by the indicator on the first line of the control panel, which will change to [W10] and by the prompt on the second line. In addition, 1-2-3 will display ten characters from each of the labels in the range A6..A8. As you continue to press →, more letters will appear in each of those cells. In order to see all of the labels in column A, you'll have to increase the width of column A to 17 characters. To do this, you'll have to press → eight times, then press [Enter] to lock in the new width. Figure 4-2 shows the worksheet after column A has been widened.

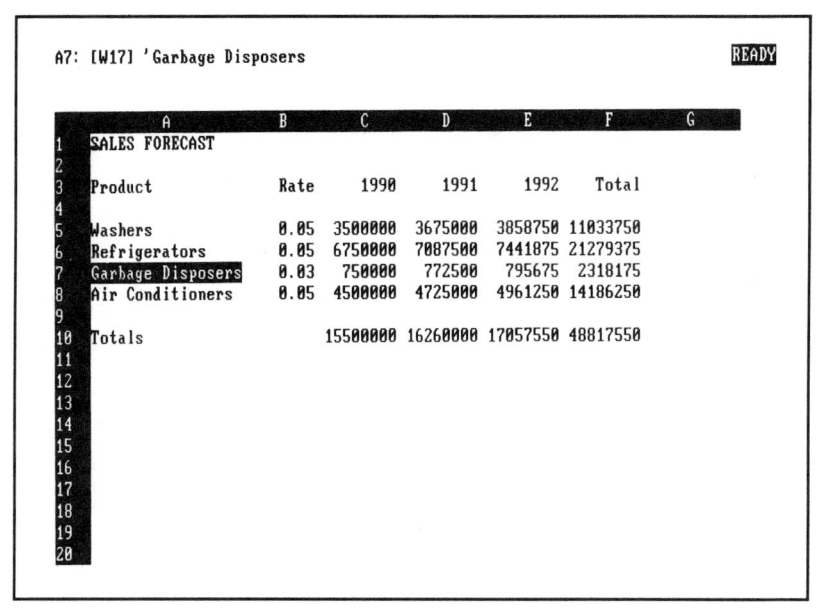

```
A7: [W17] 'Garbage Disposers                                              READY

                A           B        C        D        E         F        G
  1    SALES FORECAST
  2
  3    Product              Rate    1990     1991     1992     Total
  4
  5    Washers              0.05  3500000  3675000  3858750  11033750
  6    Refrigerators        0.05  6750000  7087500  7441875  21279375
  7    Garbage Disposers    0.03   750000   772500   795675   2318175
  8    Air Conditioners     0.05  4500000  4725000  4961250  14186250
  9
 10    Totals                    15500000 16260000 17057550  48817550
 11
 12
 13
 14
 15
 16
 17
 18
 19
 20
```

FIGURE 4-2: Widening a column

Notice the indicator [W17] in the first line of the control panel. This indicator specifies the new width of column A. You'll see this indicator only when the cell pointer is in a column to which you have assigned a custom width, or when you use the / Worksheet Column command to change the width of a column. (This indicator does not appear in 1-2-3 Releases 1A.)

Now suppose you want to reduce the width of column B in Figure 4-2 to six characters. To do this, move the cell pointer to any cell in column B and issue the / Worksheet Column Set-Width command. When 1-2-3 prompts you to enter the new column width, type 6 and press [Enter]. Figure 4-3 shows the resulting worksheet. Notice that column B is now just six characters wide, and that the prompt [W6] now appears in the control panel.

It's important to note that you must position the cell pointer in the column whose width you want to change before you issue the / Worksheet Column Set-Width command. Most of 1-2-3's cut-and-paste commands (including the / Column commands that allow you to hide columns and set the width of more than one column at a time) allow you to select the range you want to operate on after you issue the command. However, the / Worksheet Column Set-Width command (and, as we will explain next, the / Worksheet Column Reset-Width command) requires you to position the cell pointer before you issue them.

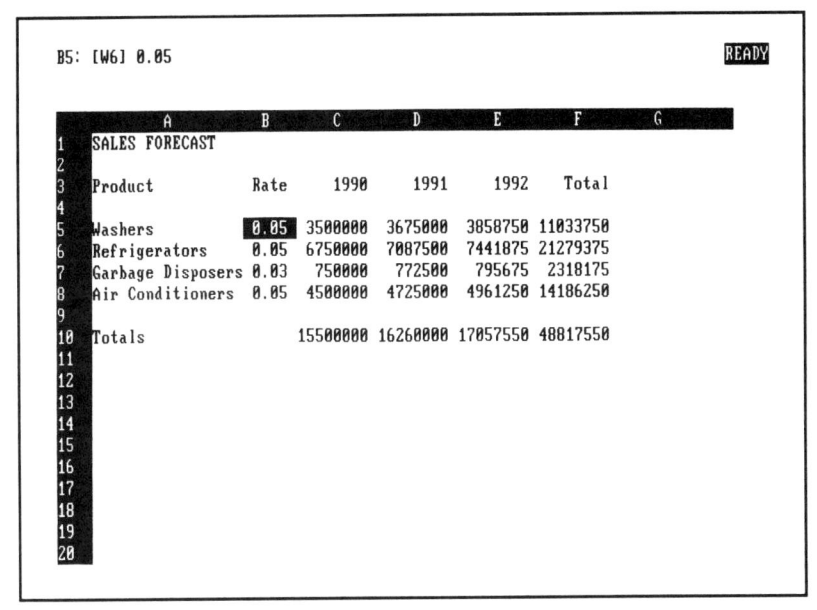

```
B5: [W6] 0.05                                              READY

         A            B       C        D        E        F        G
  1  SALES FORECAST
  2
  3  Product          Rate    1990     1991     1992     Total
  4
  5  Washers          0.05    3500000  3675000  3858750  11033750
  6  Refrigerators    0.05    6750000  7087500  7441875  21279375
  7  Garbage Disposers 0.03    750000   772500   795675   2318175
  8  Air Conditioners 0.05    4500000  4725000  4961250  14186250
  9
 10  Totals                  15500000 16260000 17057550  48817550
 11
 12
 ...
 20
```

FIGURE 4-3: Narrowing a column

Resetting the Width of a Column

After you use the / Worksheet Column Set-Width command to adjust the width of a column, you may wish to return it to its original width. To do this, you could reissue the / Worksheet Column Set-Width command, specify the original width (in our example, nine spaces), and press [Enter]. As an alternative, you can use 1-2-3's / Worksheet Column Reset-Width command. When you issue this command, 1-2-3 resets the width of the current column to the global column width (usually nine spaces). Just like the / Worksheet Column Set-Width command, this command requires you to select the column whose width you want to change ahead of time.

For example, if you were to position the cell pointer anywhere in column B of the worksheet in Figure 4-3, and then issue the / Worksheet Column Reset-Width command, 1-2-3 would reset the width of column B to nine characters. The resulting worksheet would look just like Figure 4-2.

Changing the Width of Multiple Columns

▶The / Worksheet Column Set-Width command allows you to change the width of only one column at a time. To change the width of more than a single column, you must repeat the / Worksheet Column Set-Width command for each column whose width you want to change—except in 1-2-3 Release 2.2. Unlike previous releases of 1-2-3, 1-2-3 Release 2.2 offers a command that allows you to set the width of any number of adjacent columns at the same time: / Worksheet Column Column-Range. To set the width of nonadjacent columns, you must issue the / Worksheet Column Set-Width or

RELEASE
▶ 2.2 ◀

/ Worksheet Column Column-Range commands multiple times—no matter which release of 1-2-3 you are using.

When you issue the / Worksheet Column Column-Range command, 1-2-3 Release 2.2 gives you two choices: Set-Width and Reset-Width. If you want to change the width of a group of columns to a width other than the default width for the worksheet, you should choose Set-Width; if you want to set the width of the columns to the default width, you should choose Reset-Width. In either case, 1-2-3 Release 2.2 will then ask you to select the columns whose width you want to alter. At that point, you should select a range that contains one (or, if you wish, more) cells in each column whose width you want to alter, either by pointing or typing.

What happens next depends on whether you selected Set-Width or Reset-Width from the / Worksheet Column Column-Range menu. If you selected Reset-Width, 1-2-3 will set the columns you selected to the worksheet's current default column width. If you selected the Set-Width, 1-2-3 Release 2.2 will ask you to specify the width for the selected columns. You can do this either by typing or pointing. (If you point, 1-2-3 will change the width of every column you specified each time you press the ← or →|keys.) Once you have specified the width, you should press [Enter]. When you do, 1-2-3 will set the width of the all the columns you selected to the width you specified.

For example, suppose you want to set the width of columns C, D, E, and F of the worksheet shown in Figure A to 10 spaces each. To do this, you would issue the / Worksheet Column Column-Range Set-Width command, highlight (or type the coordinates of) a range that includes at least on cell in each of columns C, D, E, and F (for example, C1..F1), and press [Enter], either type 10 or press the - key once, and then press [Enter]. To reset the width of those columns to the default width for the worksheet, you would issue the / Worksheet Column Column-Range Reset-Width command, point to a range that included cells in only columns A, B, and C, and press [Enter].◄

Changing the Global Column Width

RELEASE
► 2.2 ◄

In addition to changing the widths of individual columns in a worksheet one at a time ►(or, in 1-2-3 Release 2.2, as a group)◄, you can adjust the width of every column in the worksheet at once. To do this, you use 1-2-3's / Worksheet Global Column-Width command. When you issue this command, 1-2-3 will display the prompt *Enter global column width (1..240):* in the control panel, followed by the current global width. Unless you have changed it previously, this global width will be nine characters. You can specify a new global width either by typing the width or by pressing the → and ← keys.

An Example

For example, suppose you want to display the values in the range C5..F10 of the worksheet shown in Figure 4-3 in the Currency format with zero decimal places. To do this, you would issue the / Range Format Currency command, choose 0 decimal places, specify the range C5..F10, and press [Enter]. Figure 4-4 shows the result. As you can see, the formatted values in columns C, D, E, and F are too wide for 1-2-3 to display. Consequently, 1-2-3 displays a series of nine asterisks in each cell.

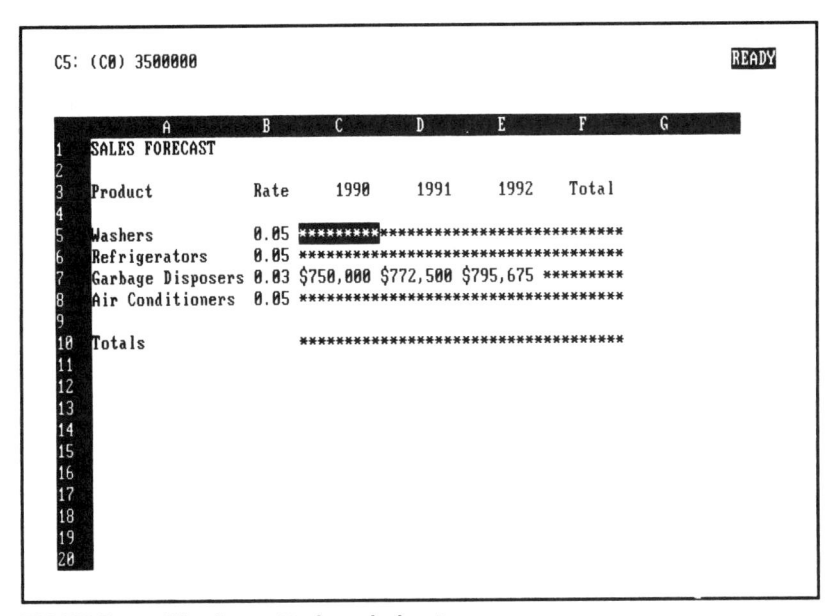

```
C5: (C0) 3500000                                               READY


           A          B       C         D        E        F       G
   1   SALES FORECAST
   2
   3   Product        Rate    1990      1991     1992     Total
   4
   5   Washers        0.05    *********************************
   6   Refrigerators  0.05    *********************************
   7   Garbage Disposers 0.03 $750,000 $772,500 $795,675 *********
   8   Air Conditioners 0.05  *********************************
   9
   10  Totals                 *********************************
   11
   12
   13
   14
   15
   16
   17
   18
   19
   20
```

FIGURE 4-4: The formatted worksheet

To display the formatted values instead of these asterisks, you must widen columns C, D, E, and F. To do this, you could use the / Worksheet Column Set-Width command four times—once for each of the four columns you want to widen, or the / Worksheet Column Column-Range Set-Width command once. Alternatively, you can use the / Worksheet Global Column-Width command to increase the width of every column in the worksheet. When you issue this command, 1-2-3 will display the prompt *Enter global column width (1..240): 9*. To adjust the widths of the columns in the worksheet, press the ➡ key until the columns are wide enough to display the formatted values. Each time you press ➡, 1-2-3 will increase the default column width by one character.

In this case, a column width of 12 is required to display all of these values with their assigned formats. Figure 4-5 shows the result of setting the global column width to 12. As you can see, 1-2-3 has set the width of every column except column A to the new global width. Why not column A? Because we previously used the / Worksheet Column Set-Width command to change the width of that column. The / Worksheet Global Column-Width command has no effect on columns that have previously been assigned a width with the / Worksheet Column Set-Width command—unless you subsequently reset the width of those columns. That's why the / Worksheet Column Set-Width command changed the width of column B. Remember—we reset the width of column B to the default prior to issuing the / Worksheet Global Column-Width command.

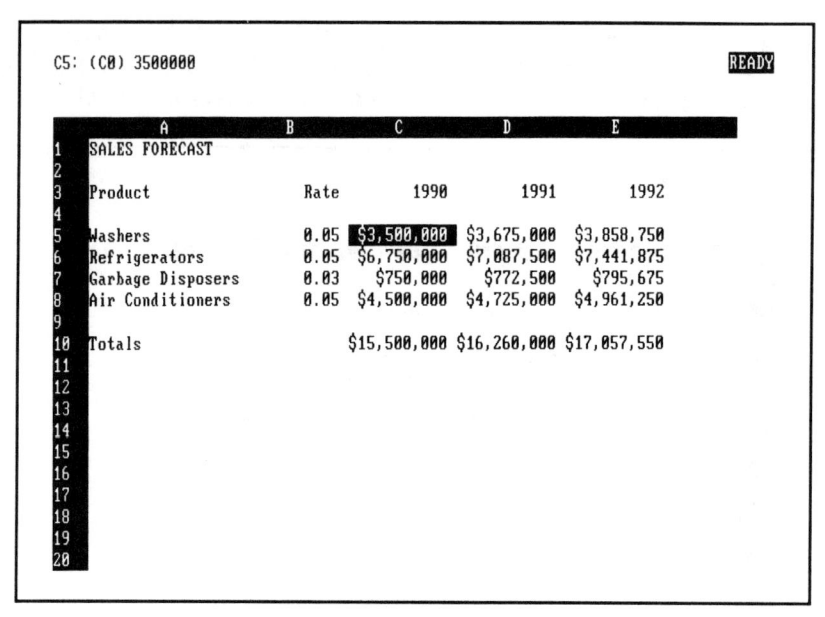

```
C5: (C0) 3500000                                                         READY

            A           B       C          D          E
    1  SALES FORECAST
    2
    3  Product          Rate    1990       1991       1992
    4
    5  Washers          0.05    $3,500,000 $3,675,000 $3,858,750
    6  Refrigerators    0.05    $6,750,000 $7,087,500 $7,441,875
    7  Garbage Disposers 0.03    $750,000   $772,500   $795,675
    8  Air Conditioners 0.05    $4,500,000 $4,725,000 $4,961,250
    9
   10  Totals                   $15,500,000 $16,260,000 $17,057,550
   11
   ...
   20
```

FIGURE 4-5: A global column width of 12

Also remember that when you use the / Worksheet Global Column-Width command, you change the width of every column in the worksheet (except for those that, like column A, have been assigned their own widths). As a result, when you issue this command, you may change the widths of columns that you would rather not change. If you encounter this problem, you can overcome it by using the / Worksheet Column Set-Width command to restore the widths of those columns individually. For example, in this case you might want to use this command to set the width of column B back to six characters.

The Reset-Width Command Revisited

As we stated previously, the / Worksheet Column Reset-Width command resets the width of a column to the current global width for the worksheet. If you adjust the width of a column individually, then alter the global column width, and then use the / Worksheet Column Reset-Width command to reset the width of that one column, 1-2-3 will set the width of that column to the new global width—not to the global width that was active when you originally adjusted the width of that column. For example, if you issue the / Worksheet Column Reset-Width command while the cell pointer is in column A of the worksheet shown in Figure 4-5, then 1-2-3 will set the width of that column to 12 spaces—not to its original width of nine spaces.

Notes

You can use the /Worksheet Column Set-Width, /Worksheet Column Column-Range Set-Width, and / Worksheet Global Column-Width commands to set a column width as narrow as one character or as wide as 240 characters. However, since 1-2-3 can't display numbers in a one-character-wide column (even one-digit numbers are displayed as asterisks in one-character-wide columns), you won't decrease the width of a column below two or three characters in most cases. Since the 1-2-3 screen can only display 72 characters of the worksheet at one time, you usually won't increase column widths to more than about 70 characters.

Hiding Columns

Although one character is the minimum width that you can specify when using the / Worksheet Column Set-Width command, it is possible to reduce the width of a column to 0 using the / Worksheet Column Hide command. (This command is not available in 1-2-3 Release 1A.) Hiding a column prevents it from being displayed on the screen. It also prevents 1-2-3 from printing the entries in that column—a topic we'll cover in Chapter 8.

Hiding a single column is easy. You just issue the / Worksheet Column Hide command, point to the column you want to hide, and press [Enter]. When you do this, 1-2-3 will remove the column from view so that the columns to the left and right of that column appear side-by-side. For example, suppose you want to hide column B of the worksheet in Figure 4-6. To do this, first issue the / Worksheet Column Hide command. When you issue this command, 1-2-3 will display the prompt *Specify column to hide:*, followed by the address of the current cell (the one on which the cell pointer was positioned when you issued the command). To hide column B, position the cell pointer anywhere in column B and press [Enter]. Figure 4-7 shows the result. As you can see, column B is no longer visible, and columns A and C appear side-by-side.

```
C5: (C2) +B5*1.5                                               READY

           A           B           C           D      E      F      G
 1  Price List
 2
 3                          Cost        Price
 4
 5  Product 1            $123.45     $185.18
 6  Product 2             $99.95     $149.93
 7  Product 3             $14.27      $21.41
 8  Product 4             $52.31      $78.47
 9  Product 5             $54.89      $82.34
10
11
12
```

FIGURE 4-6: A sample worksheet

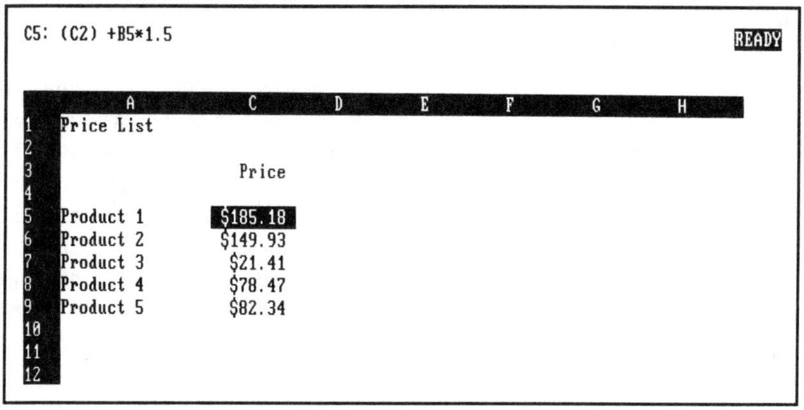

```
C5: (C2) +B5*1.5                                              READY

       A             C         D         E         F         G         H
  1  Price List
  2
  3                 Price
  4
  5  Product 1    $185.18
  6  Product 2    $149.93
  7  Product 3     $21.41
  8  Product 4     $78.47
  9  Product 5     $82.34
 10
 11
 12
```

FIGURE 4-7: Hiding a column

Unlike the / Worksheet Column Set-Width and / Column Reset-Width commands (but like the / Worksheet Column Column-Range commands), the / Worksheet Column Hide command allows you to act upon any number of adjacent columns—not just one column at a time. To do this, simply define a range that includes at least one cell in each column you want to hide. For example, to hide columns B and C in Figure 4-6, you would issue the / Worksheet Column Hide command, move the cell pointer to any cell in column B, press the [period] key (.), point to any cell in column C, and press [Enter].

Hiding a column does not remove it from the worksheet entirely; it just hides that column from view and prevents it from printing. Consequently, any references to the cells of the column are still valid. As you can see in Figure 4-7, for example, the formulas in column C, which refer to the cells of column B, still return the same values as they did in Figure 4-6.

As a general rule, you cannot move the cell pointer into a hidden column. However, 1-2-3 will reveal temporarily any and all hidden columns in the worksheet whenever it is in the POINT mode. You can enter the POINT mode by issuing any command that calls for you to define a range (such as / Copy or / Range Name Create) or by pressing one of the arrow keys while you are defining a formula or function. 1-2-3 places an asterisk to the right of the column letter of any hidden column to let you know which columns are hidden and which are not. As soon as you leave the POINT mode, the columns will disappear from view.

Because 1-2-3 reveals hidden columns while it is in the POINT mode, you can create formulas that refer to cells in hidden columns or issue commands that affect cells in these columns. For example, suppose you want to enter the formula +B5/C5 in cell D5 after you have hidden column B. To enter this formula, move to cell D5, type +, and press ← to begin pointing to column B. As soon as you do this, column B will come back into view, as shown in Figure 4-8. Now, you can point to cell B5 just as you normally would, type /, point to cell C5, and press [Enter] to complete the formula. As soon as you press [Enter], column B will disappear from view.

```
C5: (C2) +B5*1.5                                              POINT
+C5
```

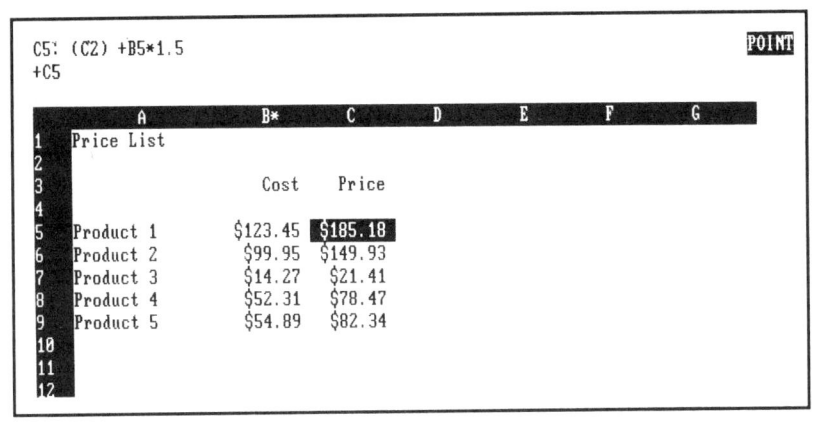

```
       A        B*      C        D        E        F       G
  1 Price List
  2
  3                   Cost    Price
  4
  5 Product 1       $123.45  $185.18
  6 Product 2        $99.95  $149.93
  7 Product 3        $14.27   $21.41
  8 Product 4        $52.31   $78.47
  9 Product 5        $54.89   $82.34
 10
 11
 12
```

FIGURE 4-8: Revealing a hidden column

Revealing Hidden Columns

Once you've hidden a column, you can reveal it by issuing the / Worksheet Column Display command. When you issue this command, 1-2-3 will enter the POINT mode and will bring all of the hidden columns in the worksheet into view. 1-2-3 will always place an asterisk to the right of the letter at the top of any hidden column. To "unhide" a column, just position the cell pointer in that column and press [Enter].

For example, suppose you want to unhide column B in Figure 4-7. To do this, first issue the / Worksheet Column Display command. Figure 4-9 shows the result of issuing this command. Notice that column B is in view and is marked with an asterisk. To unhide column B, position the cell pointer in any cell in the column and press [Enter]. When you press [Enter], 1-2-3 will reveal column B, and your worksheet will look like Figure 4-6.

```
C5: (C2) +B5*1.5                                              POINT
Specify column to unhide: C5
```

```
       A        B*      C        D        E        F       G
  1 Price List
  2
  3                   Cost    Price
  4
  5 Product 1       $123.45  $185.18
  6 Product 2        $99.95  $149.93
  7 Product 3        $14.27   $21.41
  8 Product 4        $52.31   $78.47
  9 Product 5        $54.89   $82.34
 10
 11
 12
```

FIGURE 4-9: Unhiding a column

To unhide two or more columns at once, just issue the / Worksheet Column Display command and define a range that includes all of the columns you want to unhide. Since the Display command has no effect on unhidden columns, it's all right to highlight cells in columns that are not hidden. When you press [Enter], 1-2-3 will reveal any hidden columns in the specified range.

ERASING ENTRIES

1-2-3's /Range Erase command allows you to erase entries from the cells of your worksheets in much the same way as you would use an eraser to remove information from a paper spreadsheet. If you are like most 1-2-3 users, you'll probably find /Range Erase to be one of your most frequently used commands.

When you issue the /Range Erase command, 1-2-3 will display the prompt *Enter range to erase:* in the control panel, followed by a range reference to the cell that contains the cell pointer. For instance, if the cell pointer is in cell A1 when you issue the /Range Erase command, the reference *A1..A1* will appear next to the prompt. This range reference is 1-2-3's "guess" at the range you want to erase. You can press [Enter] to accept this guess and erase the current cell, modify the guess to include several cells, or press [Esc] to reject the guess and specify a completely different cell or range to erase.

Typically, you'll point to the cell you want to erase (or, if you plan to erase a range, to one of the cells at the corners of that range) before you issue the /Range Erase command. That way, you can take advantage of 1-2-3's guess.

Erasing a Single Cell

You'll often use /Range Erase to erase a single cell. For example, suppose you want to erase the contents of cell C5 from the worksheet in Figure 4-10. To do this, move the cell pointer to cell C5—the cell you want to erase. Next, issue the /Range Erase command. As soon as you issue this command, 1-2-3 will display the prompt E*nter range to erase:* in the control panel, followed by the range reference *C5..C5*. To erase the contents of only this cell, just press [Enter]. In this case, 1-2-3 will remove the entry from cell C5. Figure 4-11 shows the worksheet after cell C5 has been erased.

Notes

The /Range Erase command does not remove any formats you have assigned to the cells in the Erase range. For example, notice the message *C5: (C0)* in the control panel in Figure 4-11. This message indicates that cell C5 is empty, but that it still retains its Currency format with zero decimal places. To remove the format from a range of cells, you must issue the /Range Format Reset command, select the cells you want to unformat, and press [Enter]. (For more on this command, refer back to Chapter 3.)

Chapter 4: Cut-and-Paste Commands

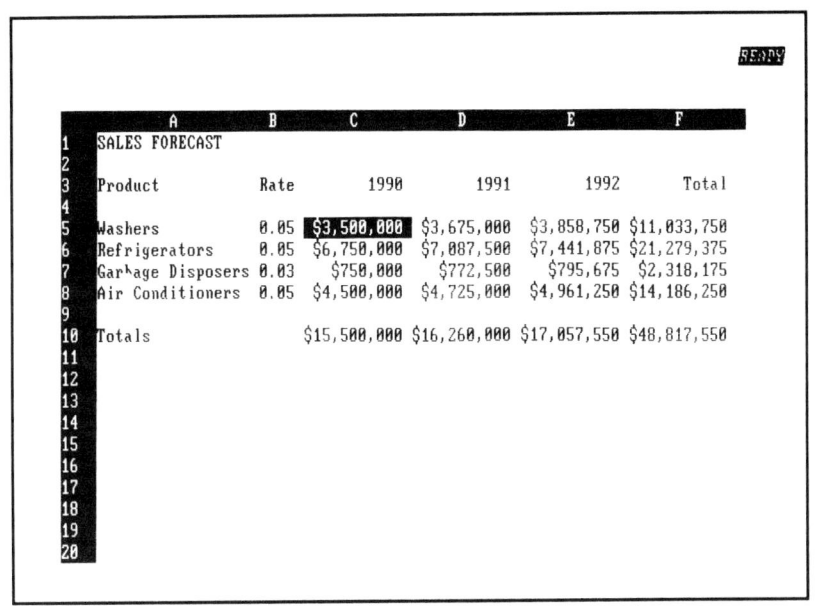

FIGURE 4-10: A sample worksheet

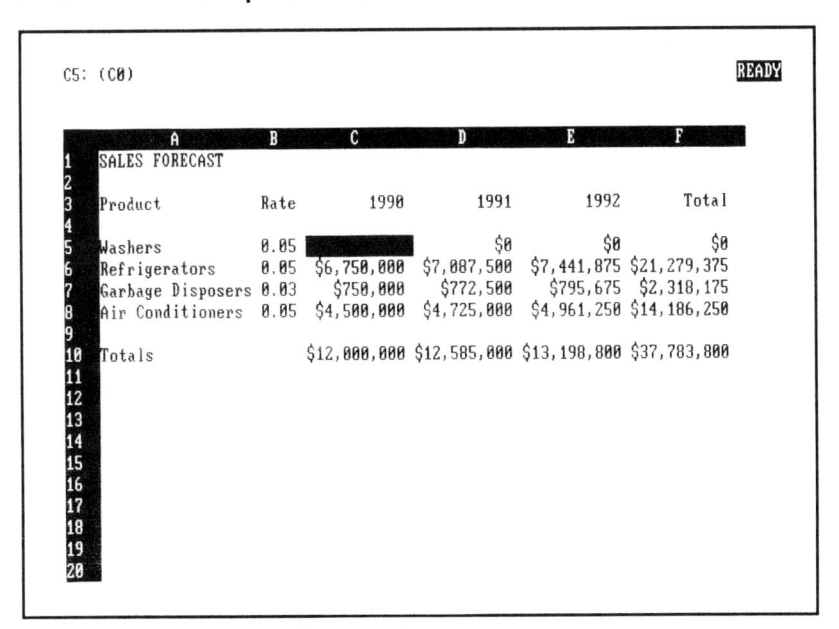

FIGURE 4-11: Erasing a single cell

When you erase a cell that is referred to by a formula or function, then the value of that cell in the formula or function will become 0. For example, in Figure 4-10 the result of the formula in cell C10 is 15500000. In Figure 4-11, however, the result of the formula is only 12000000. Similarly, the formulas in cells D5, E5, and F5, all of which depend on cell C5, now return the value 0. The difference? Cell C5, which contained the value 3500000 in Figure 4-10, is blank in Figure 4-11. As a result, the formulas in cells C10, D5, E5, and F5 assign this cell the value 0.

> **TIP: ERASING A CELL THAT IS REFERRED TO BY A STRING FORMULA**
>
> In most cases, erasing the contents of a cell will not cause any problems in your worksheet. However, erasing a label from a cell that is referred to by a string formula or string function is a notable exception to this rule. For example, suppose that cell A2 contains the label *'John* and cell B2 contains the label *'Jones*. If cell C2 contains the string formula +A2&" "&B2, it will return the string *John Jones*. If you erase the entry from cell A2, cell B2, or both, however, this formula will return the value ERR. Why? Because 1-2-3 assigns the value 0 to any blank cell, and it does not allow you to concatenate a value to a label. Beware of this potential problem when you erase entries from a worksheet that contains string formulas.

Erasing a Range

You can also use the /Range Erase command to erase a range of cells. Typically, you'll move the cell pointer to a cell at one of the corners of the range you want to erase before you issue the /Range Erase command. That way, you can use the arrow keys to point to the opposite corner of the range, then press [Enter] to erase the contents of the selected cells.

For example, suppose that you want to erase the contents of the range C5..E8 from the worksheet in Figure 4-11. Begin by positioning the cell pointer on cell C5 or any of the other three corners of the range (E5, E8, or C8). Next, issue the /Range Erase command. Assuming the cell pointer is in cell C5, when you issue this command 1-2-3 will display the prompt *Enter range to erase: C5..C5* in the control panel.

At this point, you can specify the Erase range in either of two ways. First, you can type the range reference C5..E8. Because the first character you type removes 1-2-3's suggested range from the prompt, the control panel now will display the message *Enter range to erase: C5..E8*. Alternatively, you can specify the range by pointing. Since the cursor is anchored on cell C5, you can select the range C5..E8 simply by pressing the → key two times and the ↓ key three times. When you do this, the range reference *C5..E8* will appear in the control panel.

After you have selected the range you want to erase, press [Enter]. 1-2-3 will immediately erase the contents of the selected cells, as shown in Figure 4-12.

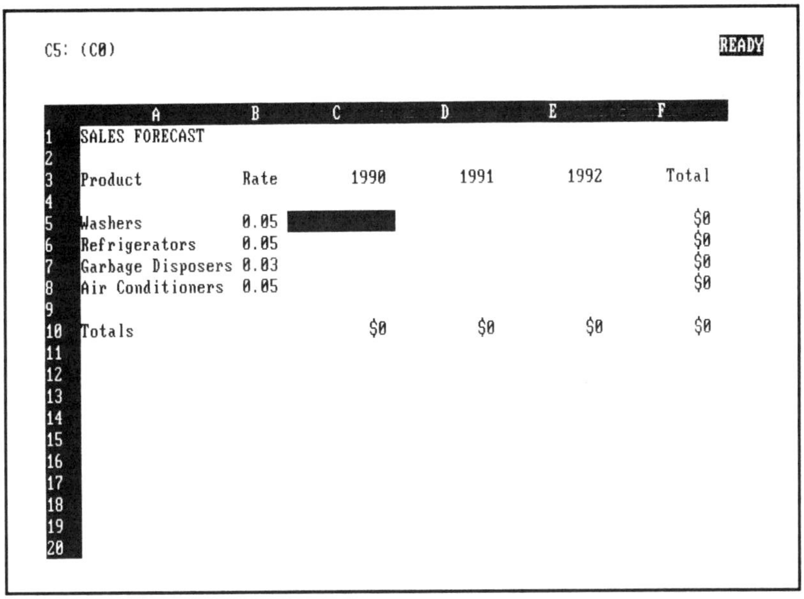

```
C5: (C0)                                                    READY

           A          B         C         D         E         F
    1  SALES FORECAST
    2
    3  Product       Rate      1990      1991      1992     Total
    4
    5  Washers       0.05                                     $0
    6  Refrigerators 0.05                                     $0
    7  Garbage Disposers 0.03                                 $0
    8  Air Conditioners  0.05                                 $0
    9
   10  Totals                   $0        $0        $0       $0
   11
   12
   ...
   20
```

FIGURE 4-12: Erasing a range

Rejecting the Guess

As you have seen, 1-2-3 automatically supplies the address of the cell in which the cell pointer is positioned as a part of the / Range Erase prompt. When you want to erase only a single cell, therefore, you'll usually find it convenient to position the cell pointer on that cell before you issue the / Range Erase command. Similarly, when you want to erase a range, you probably will want to position the cell pointer in one of the corners of that range. However, you don't have to accept 1-2-3's Erase range guess. If you want to, you can press [Esc] after you issue the / Range Erase command to reject the guess, then supply a different Erase range.

For example, suppose the cell pointer is in cell A1 and you want to erase cell F10. To do this, you could point to cell F10, issue the / Range Erase command, and then press [Enter] to accept 1-2-3's Guess range, F10..F10. Alternatively, you could issue the / Range Erase command while the cell pointer is still in cell A1. If you do this, 1-2-3 will display the prompt *Enter the range to erase: A1..A1*. At this point, you can specify the Erase range in one of two ways. First, you can just type F10 and press [Enter]. On the other hand, you can press [Esc] to unanchor the range A1..A1, point to cell F10, and press [Enter]. Either way, 1-2-3 will erase cell F10, then return the cell pointer to cell A1.

> ### TIP: ERASING A REMOTE CELL OR RANGE
>
> Normally, you will find it easier to point to the cell you want to erase, then issue the / Range Erase command. However, in some circumstances it is better to issue the / Range Erase command, then point to the cell you want to erase.
>
> For example, suppose that the cell pointer is in cell A123 and that you want to erase an entry that is somewhere in row 10 (you don't know its precise address). After this cell has been erased, you want to resume working in the vicinity of cell A123. To do this, you could move the cell pointer to the cell you want to erase, issue the / Range Erase command, and press [Enter]. Alternatively, you could issue the / Range Erase command while the cell pointer is still in cell A123. When you do this, 1-2-3 will display the prompt *Enter range to erase: A123..A123* at the top of the screen. At this point, you can press [Esc] to unanchor the cell pointer, use the cursor-movement keys to move the cell pointer to the cell you want to erase, and press [Enter]. It works either way.
>
> The key difference between these two methods is the position of the cell pointer after the / Range Erase command is completed. If you point to the cell you want to erase, then issue the / Range Erase command, the cell pointer will be in the cell you erase after the command is completed. To resume your work in row 123, you'll have to press [Pg Dn] and ↓ several times.
>
> However, if you issue the / Range Erase command, then press [Esc] and point to the cell you want to erase, after the command is completed the cell pointer will return to the cell it was in when you issued the / Range Erase command. In this case, the cell pointer will end up in cell A123 after the cell is erased. You can then start work without moving the cell pointer again.

INSERTING ROWS AND COLUMNS

1-2-3 offers two commands, / Worksheet Insert Row and / Worksheet Insert Column, that allow you to add new blank columns and rows anywhere within a worksheet. These commands allow you to add new information to a worksheet or remove information from a worksheet quickly and easily.

Inserting Rows

1-2-3's / Worksheet Insert Row command allows you to insert one or more blank rows into a worksheet. To insert one or more rows into a worksheet, you simply issue the / Worksheet Insert Row command, point to the range of rows you want to insert, and press [Enter]. When you choose / Worksheet Insert Row, 1-2-3 will display the prompt *Enter row insert range:* in the control panel, followed by a range reference to the cell that contains the cell pointer. For example, if the cell pointer is in cell A1 when you issue / Worksheet Insert Row, the cell reference *A1..A1* will appear next to the prompt. This range reference is 1-2-3's guess at the range you want to insert. You can either press [Enter] to accept this guess and insert a row above the current row, modify the guess to include several rows, or press [Esc] to reject the guess and specify a completely different Insert range.

Typically, you'll move the cell pointer to a cell in the row above which you want to insert a row before you issue the / Worksheet Insert Row command. That way, you can take advantage of 1-2-3's guess. However, you can reject 1-2-3's guess by pressing [Esc] and then inserting one or more rows in a remote location.

A Simple Example

For example, suppose you want to insert a single row between the current rows 5 and 6 in the worksheet shown in Figure 4-10 so that you can add a new product. To insert this row, just position the cell pointer anywhere in row 6 (the row above which you want to add the new row), issue the / Worksheet Insert Row command, and press [Enter]. Figure 4-13 shows the result. As you can see, 1-2-3 has inserted a blank row immediately above the row that contained the cell pointer (row 6). In the process, 1-2-3 has pushed the entries in row 6 and the rows that follow down one row.

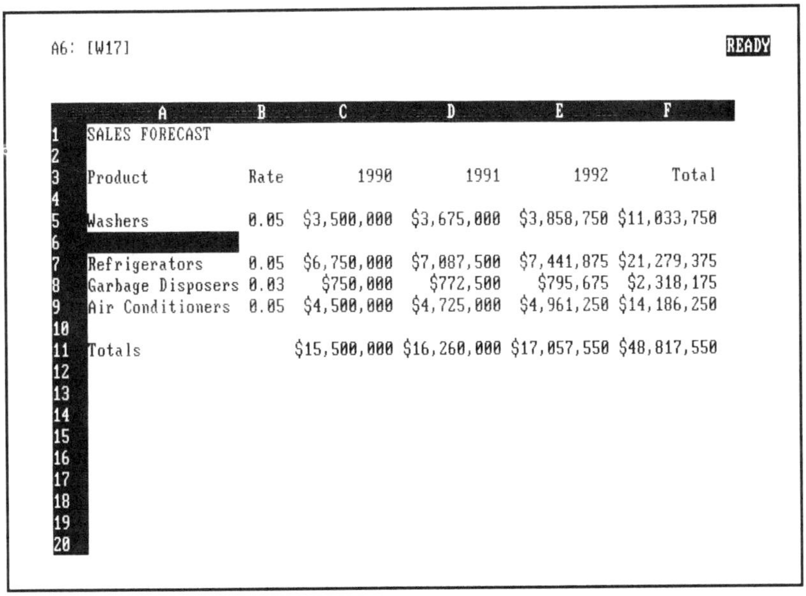

FIGURE 4-13: Inserting a row

Inserting More Than One Row

In the previous example, we inserted only a single row into a worksheet. You can insert more than one row at a time, however. To do this, its best to begin by moving the cell pointer to a cell in the row above which you want to insert the rows before you issue the / Worksheet Insert Row command. That way, when 1-2-3 prompts you to specify the rows you want to insert, you can simply expand the cell pointer to cover the number of rows that you want to add, then press [Enter].

For example, suppose that you want to insert three blank rows between rows 8 and 9 of the worksheet shown in Figure 4-13. To do this, position the cell pointer somewhere in row 9 (the row above which you want 1-2-3 to insert the new rows). When you issue the / Worksheet Insert Row command, 1-2-3 will display the prompt *Enter row insert range:*, followed by the coordinates of the current cell, stated as a range. If the cell pointer is on cell A9, for example, 1-2-3 will display the reference *A9..A9*.

In this case, you want to insert three rows. Therefore, you should press ↓ two times so that the cell pointer covers the range A9..A11. When you press [Enter], 1-2-3 will perform the insertion. Figure 4-14 shows the resulting worksheet. Since you highlighted three rows, 1-2-3 inserted three new rows into the worksheet.

```
A9: [W17]                                                              READY

         A              B         C         D         E         F
 1  SALES FORECAST
 2
 3  Product          Rate       1990      1991      1992      Total
 4
 5  Washers          0.05   $3,500,000 $3,675,000 $3,858,750 $11,033,750
 6
 7  Refrigerators   0.05   $6,750,000 $7,087,500 $7,441,875 $21,279,375
 8  Garbage Disposers 0.03  $750,000   $772,500   $795,675   $2,318,175
 9
10
11
12  Air Conditioners 0.05  $4,500,000 $4,725,000 $4,961,250 $14,186,250
13
14  Totals                $15,500,000 $16,260,000 $17,057,550 $48,817,550
15
16
17
18
19
20
```

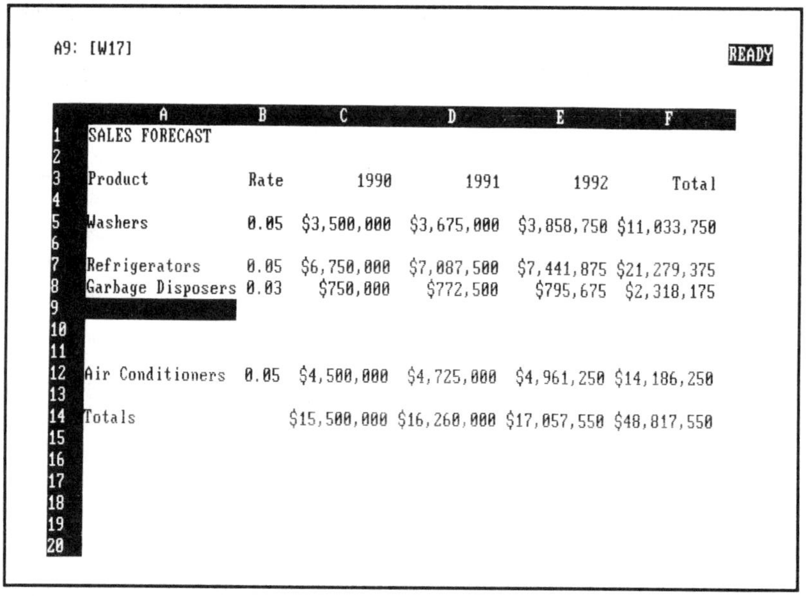

FIGURE 4-14: Inserting more than one row

Since row 9 was the top row that you highlighted, 1-2-3 inserted all of the rows between rows 8 and 9. However, if you had selected the range A9..A7 in response to 1-2-3's prompt, 1-2-3 would have inserted the three new rows above row 7. 1-2-3 will always insert the number of rows you specify *above the topmost row* of the range you specify.

To insert three new rows into the worksheet shown in Figure 4-13, we highlighted only one cell in each of three rows. Although you can highlight more than one cell in each row, these additional cells do not affect the insertion. For example, 1-2-3 would have produced the worksheet shown in Figure 4-14 if you had highlighted cells A9..A11, cells A9..Z11, cells D9..F11, or any other combination of cells in rows 9, 10, and 11.

TIP: A POTENTIAL PROBLEM

To insert a new row into a worksheet, 1-2-3 has to push a row off the bottom of that sheet. To insert a new column, 1-2-3 has to move one column off the right edge of the worksheet. When 1-2-3 inserted three rows into the worksheet shown in Figure 4-14, for example, it had to remove rows 8190, 8191, and 8192 from that worksheet.

1-2-3 will push only empty rows and columns off the worksheet, however. If the insertion of a row would require 1-2-3 to push a row that contains an entry off the bottom of the worksheet, or if the insertion of a column will cause 1-2-3 to push a column that contains entries off the right edge of the worksheet, 1-2-3 will beep, flash the word ERROR in the Mode indicator, display the message

Cannot Move or Copy data beyond worksheet boundaries

at the bottom of the screen, and refuse to perform the insertion. Pressing [Esc] when you see this message will return you to the READY mode. If you still want to make the insertion, you must move the contents of the cells in the bottom rows or rightmost columns of the worksheet away from the edges of the worksheet. We'll cover the / Move command later in this chapter.

Inserting Columns

Inserting new blank columns into a worksheet is not much different than inserting new blank rows. To insert one or more new columns, simply issue the / Worksheet Insert Column command, point to the range of columns you want to insert, and press [Enter].

When you issue the / Worksheet Insert Column command, 1-2-3 will display the prompt *Enter column insert range:*, followed by a range reference to the current cell. This range reference is 1-2-3's guess at the range of columns you want to insert. You can either press [Enter] to accept this guess, modify the guess to include several columns, or press [Esc] to reject the guess and specify a completely different Insert range.

1-2-3 always inserts new columns to the left of the leftmost column in the range you specify. For that reason, you will usually want to move the cell pointer to a cell in the column to the left of which you want to insert new columns before you issue the / Worksheet Column Insert command.

Let's look at how the / Worksheet Insert Column command works. Suppose you want to insert columns for the years 1993 and 1994 into the worksheet shown in Figure 4-14, between column E (which contains the data for FY 1992) and column F (which contains the totals for the worksheet). To do this, move the cell pointer to any cell in column F and issue the / Worksheet Insert Column command. When 1-2-3 prompts you to define the Insert range, press ➡ once, then press [Enter]. When you do this, 1-2-3 will insert two columns into the worksheet. Figure 4-15 shows the result.

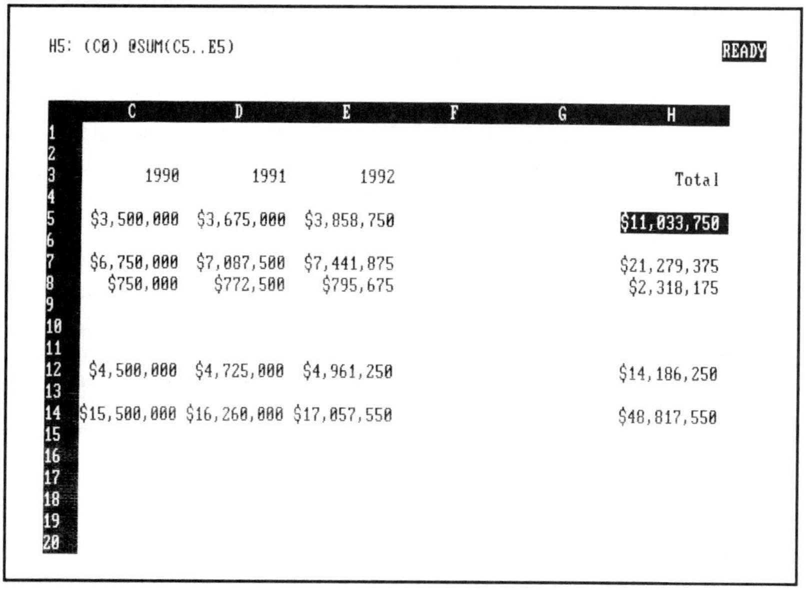

```
H5: (C0) @SUM(C5..E5)                                                    READY

        C           D           E           F           G           H
 1
 2
 3     1990        1991        1992                                Total
 4
 5   $3,500,000  $3,675,000  $3,858,750                          $11,033,750
 6
 7   $6,750,000  $7,087,500  $7,441,875                          $21,279,375
 8     $750,000    $772,500    $795,675                           $2,318,175
 9
10
11
12   $4,500,000  $4,725,000  $4,961,250                          $14,186,250
13
14  $15,500,000 $16,260,000 $17,057,550                          $48,817,550
15
16
17
18
19
20
```

FIGURE 4-15: Inserting two columns

There are several things to notice about Figure 4-15. First, because you high lighted two columns, 1-2-3 inserted two columns into the worksheet. 1-2-3 inserted these new columns to the left of column F—the leftmost column of the range you specified. As a result of inserting two new columns, 1-2-3 has pushed the contents of the cells in columns F through IV two columns to the right and has pushed columns IU and IV off the right edge of the worksheet.

Reference Effects

As you have seen, inserting a row into a worksheet pushes the remaining rows in that sheet down one row. For example, the entry in cell C7 in Figure 4-13 used to be in cell C6, the entry in cell D8 used to be in cell D7, and so forth. Similarly, inserting a new column pushes the remaining columns to the right one column.

Fortunately, if the worksheet contains formulas or functions that refer to cells that have been relocated by the insertion of a row or column, 1-2-3 will adjust those formulas or functions to reflect the new location of those cells. For example, suppose cell G5 of the worksheet in Figure 4-10 contains the formula +*F10/4*. After you insert a new row 6 in the worksheet, this formula would change to +*F11/4*. After you insert new rows 9, 10, and 11 into the worksheet, the formula will be +*F14/4*. After you insert columns F and G, the formula will change to +*H14/11*. In addition, because cell G5 is to the right of the inserted columns, the formula will be in cell I5 after you insert the new columns.

If you insert a new row within the boundaries of a range, 1-2-3 will expand that range to encompass the new row or column. For example, as you can see, cell C10 in Figure 4-10 contains the function *@SUM(C5..C8)*. After you insert a new row between rows 5 and 6, this formula will have moved to cell C11 and will have changed to *@SUM(C5..C9)*. After you insert rows 9, 10, and 11, this formula will be in cell C14 and will have changed to *@SUM(C5..C12)*. 1-2-3 expands the range to include the new row.

Similarly, if you had used the / Range Name Create command to assign the name TEST to the range C5..C8 prior to the insertion, the range would be changed to C5..C9 after the new row 6 was inserted. After you inserted the new rows 9, 10, and 11, this range would be C5..C12.

1-2-3 will not expand a range to include rows or columns that you add to the worksheet outside of the range's boundaries. For example, the @SUM functions in the range F5..F10 in Figure 4-10 sum the contents of the appropriate cells in columns C, D, and E. Cell F5 in Figure 4-10 contains the function *@SUM(C5..E5)*. Because the new columns F and G were inserted outside of the range referenced by these @SUM functions, 1-2-3 didn't adjust those functions to include the new columns. For example, the function in cell H5 in Figure 4-15, *@SUM(C5..E5)*, is identical to the function in cell F5 in Figure 4-10.

DELETING ROWS AND COLUMNS

It is as easy to delete rows and columns from a worksheet as it is to insert them into a worksheet. Two commands make it possible to delete rows and columns: / Worksheet Delete Row and / Worksheet Delete Column. These two commands instruct 1-2-3 to remove entire rows or columns from a worksheet. Unlike the / Range Erase command, which removes only the contents of the cells you select, the / Worksheet Delete commands actually remove the cells in the selected rows or columns from the worksheet. Using these commands on 1-2-3's electronic worksheet is like using scissors to cut rows and columns from a paper spreadsheet.

Deleting Rows

1-2-3's / Worksheet Delete Row command deletes one or more adjacent rows from a worksheet. When you issue this command, 1-2-3 will display the prompt *Enter range of rows to delete:* in the control panel, followed by the address of the current cell, stated as a range reference. If the cell pointer is on cell H9 when you issue this command, for example, 1-2-3 will display the range reference H9..H9. This range reference is 1-2-3's guess at the row you want to delete. When you see this reference, you can press [Enter] to delete the single row indicated, use the ↑ or ↓ arrow keys to mark more than one row, or press [Esc] and then select a remote row or group of rows. Typically, you'll move the cell pointer to one of the cells in the row or rows you want to delete before you issue the / Worksheet Delete Row command.

For example, suppose that you want to delete rows 9, 10, and 11 from the worksheet shown in Figure 4-15. To do this, you would first move the cell pointer to any cell in row 9 (we'll use H9), then issue the / Worksheet Delete Row command. When 1-2-3 prompts you to define the Delete range, you should press ↓ twice to highlight cells H9, H10, and H11, and then press [Enter].

Figure 4-16 shows the results of this deletion. As you can see, 1-2-3 has removed the old rows 9, 10, and 11 from the worksheet. To fill the space vacated by these rows, it has shifted the former rows 12 through 8192 up three rows and has added three new blank rows to the bottom of the worksheet so that the worksheet still contains 8192 rows. In addition, it has renumbered the rows of the worksheet so that the old row 12 is now row 9, the old row 13 is now row 10, the old row 14 is now row 11, and so forth.

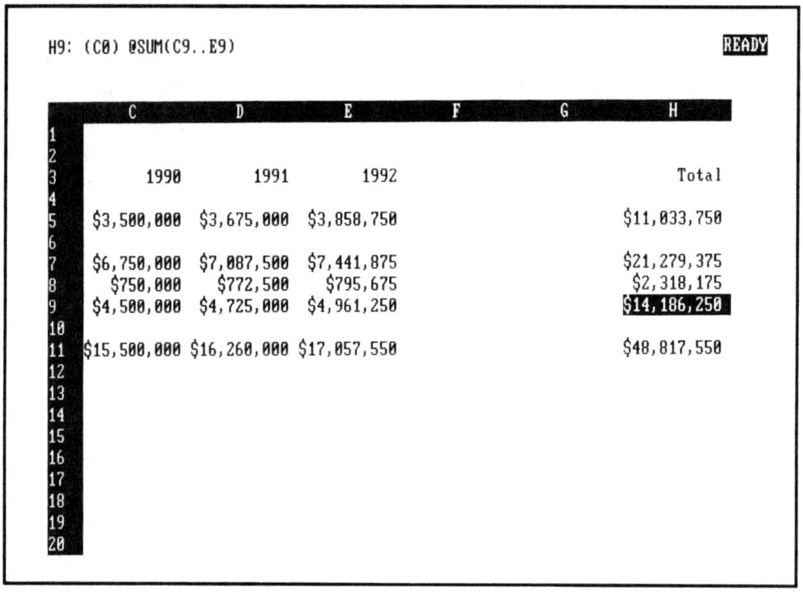

```
H9: (C0) @SUM(C9..E9)                                              READY

          C           D           E         F         G         H
 1
 2
 3        1990        1991        1992                          Total
 4
 5     $3,500,000  $3,675,000  $3,858,750                    $11,033,750
 6
 7     $6,750,000  $7,087,500  $7,441,875                    $21,279,375
 8       $750,000    $772,500    $795,675                     $2,318,175
 9     $4,500,000  $4,725,000  $4,961,250                    $14,186,250
10
11    $15,500,000 $16,260,000 $17,057,550                    $48,817,550
12
13
14
15
16
17
18
19
20
```

FIGURE 4-16: Deleting rows

In the example, we used the range H9..H11 to define the rows to be deleted. Actually, we could have used any range that included at least one cell in each of rows 9, 10, and 11, including A9..A11, A9..Z11, or H9..IV11. Although you can highlight more than one cell in each of the rows you want to delete, it is not necessary to do so.

Deleting Columns

Deleting columns from a worksheet is not much different than deleting rows. To delete one or more columns from a worksheet, simply issue the / Worksheet Delete Column command, point to the range of columns you want to delete, and press [Enter]. When you issue the / Worksheet Delete Column command, 1-2-3 will automatically offer a range reference to the current cell as the range to be deleted. Consequently, the easiest way to delete a column is to move the cell pointer to a cell in the column you want to delete before you issue the / Worksheet Delete Column command. You can delete one or more columns in a remote location, however, by using the [Esc] and [period] keys to unanchor and reanchor the cursor after you issue the / Worksheet Delete Column command.

To demonstrate this command, suppose that you want to delete columns F and G from the worksheet shown in Figure 4-16. To do this, just move the cell pointer to any cell in column F (we'll use F9) and issue the / Worksheet Delete Column command. Next, press ➡ to define the range F9..G9 as the Delete range and press [Enter] to delete columns F and G. Once these columns have been deleted, the worksheet will again look like Figure 4-13.

Reference Effects

When you delete a row or column from a worksheet, 1-2-3 revises all references to the cells in the rows and columns that were shifted as a result of the deletion. For example, suppose cell I5 in Figure 4-15 contains the reference *+H14/4*. After you delete rows 9, 10, and 11, this reference will change to *+H11/4*. After you delete columns E and F, the formula will be *+F11/4*. In addition, because the deletion causes 1-2-3 to shift the contents of columns H through IV two columns to the left, this formula will be in cell G5 after the deletion. As you can see, these are the same types of adjustments that 1-2-3 makes when you insert a row or column into a worksheet.

Deleting a Referenced Cell

Problems result when you delete a row or column that contains a referenced cell, however. For example, suppose that cell I5 in Figure 4-16 contains the formula *+H11/4*. If you use the / Worksheet Delete Row command to delete row 11, or the / Worksheet Delete Column command to delete column H, this formula will change to *+ERR/4* and will display the value ERR. Why does this happen? Because, by deleting row 11 or column H, you have eliminated the cell to which the formula refers. Whenever you delete a cell that is referred to by a formula or function, the reference to that cell will be replaced with the value ERR, and that formula or function will return the value ERR. To avoid this situation, be very careful not to delete rows and columns that are referred to by formulas or functions elsewhere in the worksheet. Instead of deleting a row or column that includes cells that are referred to by formulas, you might try simply erasing those cells with the / Range Erase command.

Deleting a Cell of a Range

In our discussion of the / Worksheet Insert command, we explained that 1-2-3 automatically expands ranges when you insert a row or column within the boundaries of that range. In a similar way, 1-2-3 will contract a range when you delete a row or column in the middle of a range. In Figure 4-15, cell C14 contains the function *@SUM(C5..C12)*. When you deleted rows 9, 10, and 11 to produce the worksheet shown in Figure 4-16, 1-2-3 changed this function to *@SUM(C5..C9)*. (Of course, this function now will appear in cell C11.) As you can see, 1-2-3 has adjusted this range to account for the removal of the old rows 9, 10, and 11 from the worksheet.

You'll run into problems if you delete a row or column that contains one of the endpoints ("anchor cells") of a range. Since 1-2-3 keeps track of a range by the addresses of its anchor cells, deleting the anchor cell of a range causes 1-2-3 to forget where that range is located. If we had deleted row 5 or row 12 from the worksheet shown in Figure 4-15, for example, 1-2-3 would have replaced the function *@SUM(C5..C12)* with the function *@SUM(ERR)*, which returns the value ERR. This occurs because we deleted the row that contained one of the endpoints of the range C5..C12.

MOVING ENTRIES

1-2-3's / Move command allows you to move the contents of a cell or range to another location in the worksheet. / Move is one of the most frequently used cut-and-paste commands.

To move the contents of a cell or range, you issue the / Move command, select the range you want to move from, press [Enter], then select the range you want to move to and press [Enter] again. When you issue the / Move command, 1-2-3 will display the prompt *Enter the range to move FROM:*, followed by the address of the current cell, stated as a range. For example, if the cell pointer is on cell A1 when you issue the / Move command, the range reference will be *A1..A1*. This range is 1-2-3's guess at the range you want to move from. You can press [Enter] to accept this guess and use the current cell as the FROM range or you can use the arrow keys to highlight additional cells and then press [Enter]. You can also press [Esc] to unanchor the cell pointer and define a completely different FROM range.

You'll usually want to position the cell pointer on the cell that you want to move (or, if you want to move a range, on one of the cells at the corners of that range) before you issue the / Move command. This allows you to take advantage of 1-2-3's guess.

After you define the FROM range, 1-2-3 will display the prompt *Enter range to move TO:*, followed by the address of the current cell. When you see this prompt, you can either type the address of the cell or range to which you wish to move, or point to define that range. Since the cell pointer is not anchored, you should not press [Esc] before you begin pointing. Once you define the TO range, press [Enter] to complete the move.

Moving Single Entries

Suppose that you have entered the function *@DATE(90,1,1)* into cell C1 of the worksheet in Figure 4-17 and have assigned that cell the Date 3 format. Now you want to move that entry to cell F1. To do this, first place the cell pointer on cell C1 and issue the / Move command. When 1-2-3 prompts you to supply the FROM range, just press [Enter] to accept the current cell as the FROM range. To define the TO range, point to cell F1 (or type the cell reference F1) and press [Enter]. As soon as you do this, 1-2-3 will move the function *@DATE(90,1,1)* to cell F1 and assign that cell the D3 format. After the move, cell C1 will be empty and will no longer be assigned a special format. As you can see, Figure 4-18 shows the worksheet after the move is completed.

FIGURE 4-17: A sample worksheet

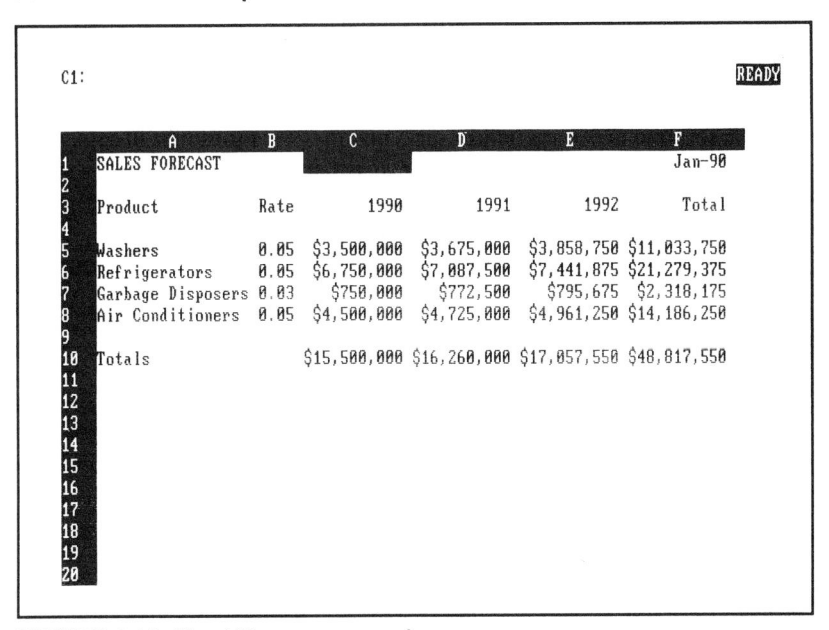

FIGURE 4-18: The / Move command

You can also use the /Move command to move labels from one cell to another. For example, suppose you want to move the label *'Product* from cell A3 in Figure 4-18 to cell A4. To move this label, place the cell pointer on cell A3, issue the /Move command, press [Enter] to specify cell A3 as the FROM range, press ↓ once to point to cell D4, and then press [Enter] to complete the move. After the move, cell A3 will be empty and cell A4 will contain the label *'Product*.

Moving More Than One Cell at a Time

You also can use the /Move command to move multiple-cell ranges. For example, suppose that you want to move the contents of the range A3..F3 in Figure 4-18 to the range A4..F4. To do this, place the cell pointer on cell B3 and issue the /Move command. When 1-2-3 prompts you for the FROM range, press → four times to select the range A3..F3, then press [Enter].

Once you have specified the FROM range, 1-2-3 will prompt you to specify the TO range. You could define the range by pointing to the range A4..A4 and pressing [Enter]. However, when you are moving a range of cells from one location to another, you do not have to specify the full dimensions of the TO range. Instead, you only need to select the upper-left cell of that range. In this case, then, you could define the TO range by pointing to cell A4 and pressing [Enter].

Figure 4-19 shows the worksheet after the move is completed. As you can see, 1-2-3 has moved the entries from the range A3..F3 to the range A4..F4. The cells of the FROM range are now empty.

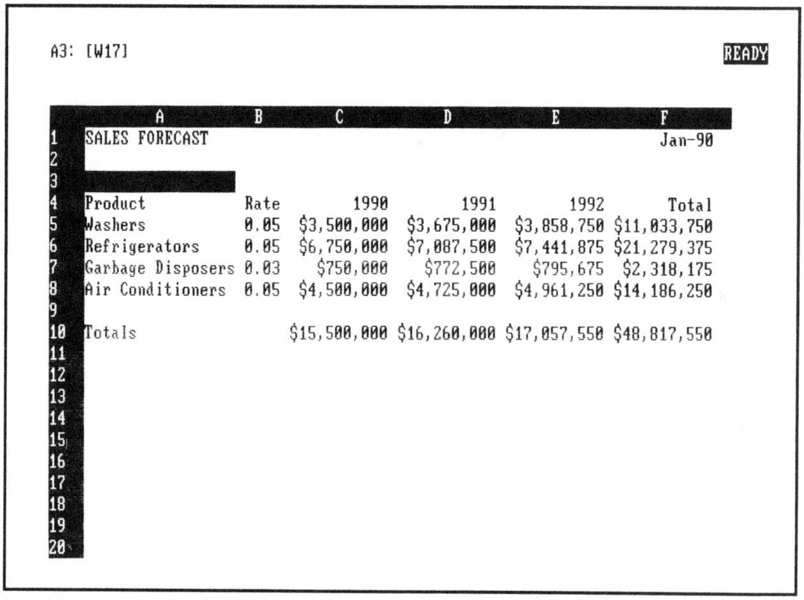

```
A3: [W17]                                                              READY

         A              B         C          D          E          F
 1  SALES FORECAST                                                 Jan-90
 2
 3
 4  Product           Rate       1990       1991       1992       Total
 5  Washers           0.05   $3,500,000  $3,675,000  $3,858,750 $11,033,750
 6  Refrigerators     0.05   $6,750,000  $7,087,500  $7,441,875 $21,279,375
 7  Garbage Disposers 0.03     $750,000    $772,500    $795,675  $2,318,175
 8  Air Conditioners  0.05   $4,500,000  $4,725,000  $4,961,250 $14,186,250
 9
10  Totals                  $15,500,000 $16,260,000 $17,057,550 $48,817,550
11
12
...
20
```

FIGURE 4-19: Moving more than one entry

You can use the / Move command to move a range of any size or shape. In the example, we used the / Move command to move a partial row into another partial row. You can also use / Move to move a partial column of entries into another partial column, or a rectangular range into another range. When you use / Move, the size and shape of the TO range will always be identical to the size and shape of the FROM range. Remember, though, that when you are defining the TO range, you need only point to the upper-left cell in that range.

Notes

Besides moving the contents of the FROM range to the TO range, the / Move command also moves any formats assigned to the cells in the FROM range to the TO range. After a move, therefore, the cells of the FROM range will be blank and unformatted. The cells of the TO range will include the contents of the cells in the FROM range and any formats that were assigned to those cells.

If the cells in the TO range of a move contain entries, have been assigned formats, or both, 1-2-3 will overwrite those entries and replace those formats when it performs the move. This can lead to some problems, as you'll see in a few pages. You may need to use the / Worksheet Insert command to insert a few rows or columns at the move destination to avoid overwriting information that is already in the worksheet.

Reference Considerations

What happens to the cell references in the formulas in your worksheet when you use the / Move command? There are two important rules to keep in mind. First, when you move a value or label that is referred to by formulas elsewhere in the worksheet, 1-2-3 will adjust those references to account for the new location of the entry you have moved. For example, cell C3 in Figure 4-17 contains the formula *1900+@YEAR(C1)*. After you move the @DATE function in cell C1 to cell F1, this formula will be *1900+@YEAR(F1)*.

When you use the / Move command to move a formula or function that contains cell references, that formula or function will not change in any way. For example, cell C3 in Figure 4-18 contains the formula *1900+@YEAR(F1)*. When you moved the range B3..F3 into the range B4..F4, this formula was moved to cell C4, as shown in Figure 4-19. However, the formula in cell C4 in Figure 4-19 is still *1900+@YEAR(F1)*.

▶Unfortunately, 1-2-3 does not adjust references to cells in other worksheets when you use the / Move command to move those cells. For example, suppose that after entering the formula *+<<TEST1.WK1>>A1* into cell A1 of a worksheet, you saved that worksheet, retrieved TEST.WK1, and used the / Move command to move the entry from cell A1 into cell B5. When you subsequently resave TEST1.WK1 and retrieve the original worksheet, you'll see that the linking formula is still *+<<TEST1.WK1>>A1*—not *+<<TEST1.WK1>>B5*. This problem does not occur if you use range names instead of cell references in your linking formulas.◄

RELEASE
▶ 2.2 ◀

A Potential Problem

1-2-3 has problems when you move an entry into a cell that is referred to by a formula or function. For example, cell D10 in Figure 4-19 contains the function *@SUM(D5..D8)*, and cell E5 contains the formula *+D5*B5*. Suppose you use the / Move command to move the contents of cell C5 (or any other cell, for that matter) to cell D5. Figure 4-20 shows the resulting worksheet. As you can see, the formula in cell D10 is now *@SUM(ERR)*. Similarly, the formula in cell E5 contains the formula *+ERR*B5*. Because the formula in cell E5 returns the value ERR, the formulas in cells F5, E10, and F10 also return that value.

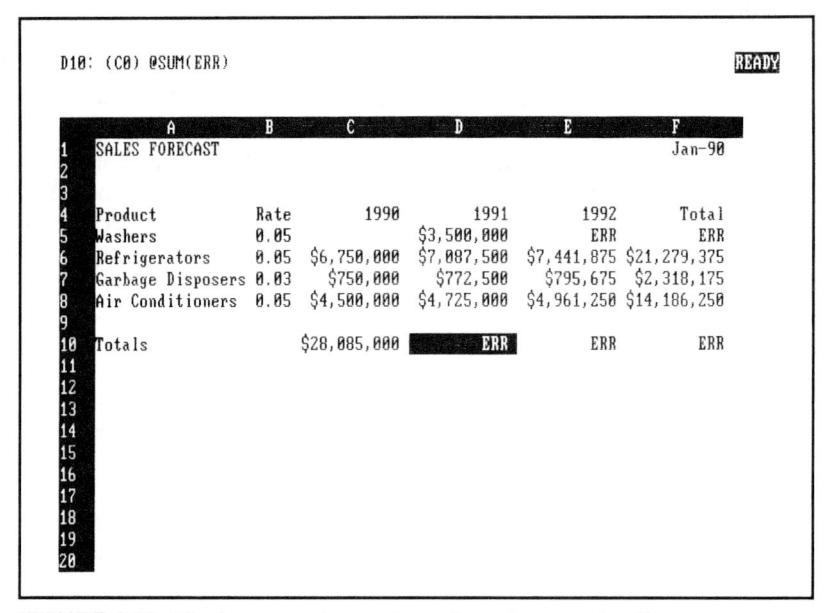

```
D10: (C0) @SUM(ERR)                                                   READY

              A          B         C          D          E          F
 1  SALES FORECAST                                               Jan-90
 2
 3
 4  Product           Rate       1990        1991       1992      Total
 5  Washers           0.05              $3,500,000        ERR        ERR
 6  Refrigerators     0.05  $6,750,000  $7,087,500 $7,441,875 $21,279,375
 7  Garbage Disposers 0.03    $750,000    $772,500   $795,675  $2,318,175
 8  Air Conditioners  0.05  $4,500,000  $4,725,000 $4,961,250 $14,186,250
 9
10  Totals                 $28,085,000        ERR        ERR        ERR
11
12
13
14
15
16
17
18
19
20
```

FIGURE 4-20: Moving an entry on top of a referenced cell

These problems occurred because the contents of cell C5 have replaced the contents of cell D5. Since the function in cell D10 and the formula in cell E5 cannot locate the original contents of cell D5, the references to cell D5 in that formula and function change to ERR. In general, whenever you move the contents of one cell into a cell that is referred to by a formula or function, the reference to that cell in the formula will change to ERR.

Of course, after you move the contents of cell C5 to cell D5, the function in cell C10 will change to *@SUM(D5..C8)*. Similarly, the function in cell F5, which is *@SUM(C5..E5)* in Figure 4-19, will become *@SUM(D5..E5)*. Both of these functions change to reflect the new position of the contents of cell C5.

Range Names

If the cell that contains the entry you move has been assigned a range name, that name will move with the contents of the cell. For instance, suppose cell C1 in Figure 4-17 had been assigned the name TEST. After you move the contents of cell C1 to cell F1, the name TEST will apply to cell F1.

If you move the contents of a cell that is at one of the corners of a named range, 1-2-3 will change the definition of the named range to reflect the move. For example, suppose you have assigned the name RANGE to the range C1..D2 in Figure 4-17. After you move the contents of cell C1 to cell F1, this name would apply to the range F1..D2. As this demonstrates, moving a cell that defines one corner of a named range usually will thoroughly goof up the range name.

If the TO range of a move is a cell that has been assigned a name, or is a cell at the upper-left or lower-right corner of a named range, then the move will destroy the range name. For example, suppose you had assigned the range name 1991 to the range D5..D8 in Figure 4-17. If you move the contents of cell C5 to cell D5, the range name 1991 will no longer apply to the range D5..D8. The name continues to exist; however, it just doesn't apply to any cells.

> ### TIP: REMOTE MOVES AND COPIES
>
> Most of the time, you'll move the cell pointer to the cell whose contents you want to move or copy before you issue the / Move or / Copy command. You don't have to do so, however. If you want to use a remote range as the FROM range, just press [Esc] when 1-2-3 prompts you to define the FROM range, then point to the cells you want to move or copy from.
>
> There is one situation in which using a remote FROM range makes sense. Suppose you are working in row 100 of a worksheet and want to move or copy the contents of a row in the upper part of the worksheet (you aren't sure if it is row 9 or 10) to row 100. You can move the cell pointer to row 9 or 10, then issue the / Move or / Copy command and use 1-2-3's guess as the basis for your FROM range. Then, to define your TO range, you would have to point to row 100—the row you had been working in. Moreover, after the move or copy is completed, the cell pointer will be in row 9 or 10. If you want to resume your work in row 100, you'll have to move the cell pointer back to that row manually.
>
> Suppose, on the other hand, that you issue the / Move or / Copy command while the cell pointer is still in row 100, then press [Esc] and move to row 9 or 10 to define the FROM range. When you press [Enter] to lock in that range, the cell pointer will return to row 100, so defining the TO range is a snap. In addition, once the move or copy is completed, the cell pointer will be in row 100, so you can resume your work without moving the cell pointer.

COPYING ENTRIES

1-2-3's /Copy command allows you to copy the contents of one or more cells to other cells in the same worksheet. Because copying can be a tricky process, we'll explore the different ways you can make copies one at a time. First, we'll work through the various combinations of sources and destinations as we copy simple values and labels. Then we'll show you how 1-2-3 copies formulas and functions.

Copy Basics

To copy the contents of a cell or range, you issue the /Copy command, select the range you want to copy from, press [Enter], then select the range you want to copy to and press [Enter] again. When you issue the / Copy command, 1-2-3 will display the prompt *Enter the range to copy FROM:*, followed by the address of the current cell stated as a range. For example, if the cell pointer is on cell A1 when you issue the /Copy command, the range reference will be *A1..A1*. This range is 1-2-3's guess at the range you want to copy from. You can press [Enter] to accept this range and use the current cell as the FROM range, or you can use the arrow keys to highlight additional cells and then press [Enter]. You can also press [Esc] to unanchor the cell pointer and define a completely different FROM range.

You will usually move the cell pointer to the cell you want to copy (or, if you want to copy a range instead, to one of the corners of that range) before you issue the /Copy command. That way, you can take advantage of 1-2-3's guess.

After you define the FROM range, 1-2-3 will display the prompt *Enter range to copy TO:*, followed by the address of the current cell. When you see this prompt, you can either type the address of the cell or range to which you wish to copy, or point to define that range. Since the cell pointer is not anchored, you should not press [Esc] before you begin pointing. Once you have defined the TO range, press [Enter] to complete the copy.

A Simple Copy

Suppose you want to copy the label *Total* from cell F5 in Figure 4-21 into cell A11. To do this, first move the cell pointer to cell F5 and issue the / Copy command. Then press [Enter] to accept the default FROM range. After you specify a FROM range, 1-2-3 will prompt you to define the TO range. To designate cell A11 as the TO range, you can either point to it and press [Enter] or type A11 and press [Enter]. Either way, 1-2-3 will copy the label *Total* from cell F5 into cell A11.

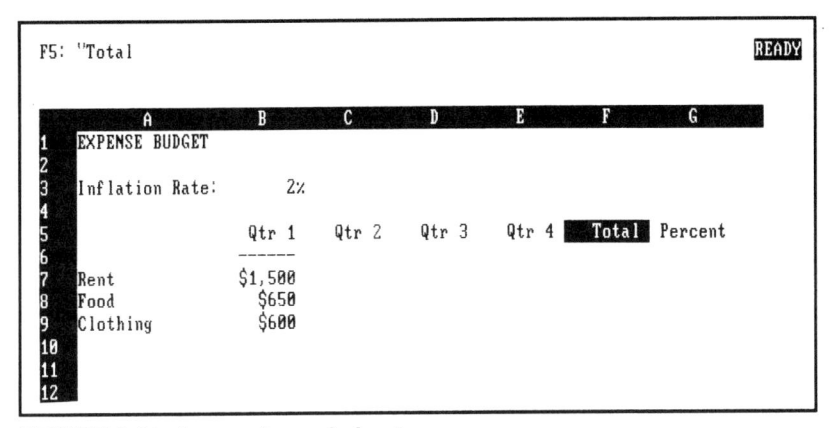

```
F5: "Total                                                    READY

        A           B        C        D        E        F        G
1  EXPENSE BUDGET
2
3  Inflation Rate:     2%
4
5                    Qtr 1    Qtr 2    Qtr 3    Qtr 4    Total   Percent
6                   ------
7  Rent             $1,500
8  Food               $650
9  Clothing           $600
10
11
12
```

FIGURE 4-21: A sample worksheet

Figure 4-22 shows the resulting worksheet. As you can see, the entry in cell A11 is an identical copy of the entry in cell F5—even the label prefix is the same, as you can tell from the alignment of the entry in A11. Also notice that, unlike the / Move command, the / Copy command does not erase the contents of the FROM range.

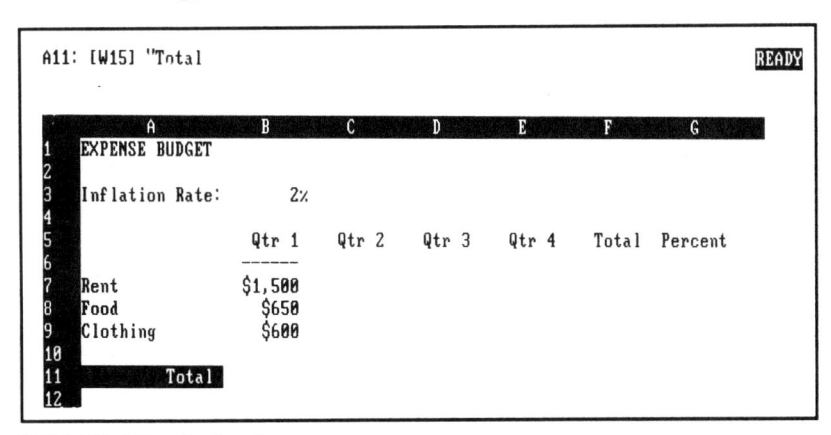

```
A11: [W15] "Total                                              READY

        A           B        C        D        E        F        G
1  EXPENSE BUDGET
2
3  Inflation Rate:     2%
4
5                    Qtr 1    Qtr 2    Qtr 3    Qtr 4    Total   Percent
6                   ------
7  Rent             $1,500
8  Food               $650
9  Clothing           $600
10
11        Total
12
```

FIGURE 4-22: A simple copy

Although in this example we used / Copy to copy a simple label, you can also use the command to copy a value. In fact, the process of copying a value from one cell to another is identical to the process of copying a label—you simply issue the / Copy command, specify the FROM range, press [Enter], specify the TO range, and press [Enter] again. When you copy a value from a cell that has been assigned a format, that format will be copied to the TO range as well.

Other FROM/TO Combinations

In the simple copy we just performed, both the FROM range and the TO range were single cells. There are six other possible combinations of FROM and TO ranges, however. These combinations are summarized in Table 4-1. Let's consider examples of some of these types of copies.

FROM Range	TO Range	Example
single cell	single cell	A1 to B1
single cell	multiple cells	A1 to B1..D1
		A1 to A2..A5
		A1 to B2..D5
single row	single row	A1..D1 to A2..D2
single column	single column	A1..A5 to B1..B5
single row	multiple rows	A1..D1 to A2..D5
single column	multiple columns	A1..A5 to B1..E5
rectangular range	rectangular range	A1..D5 to J1..M5

TABLE 4-1: FROM/TO copy combinations

Copying from One Cell to More Than One Cell

You can use the /Copy command to copy an entry from a single cell to more than one cell. For example, suppose that you want to copy the label '------ from cell B6 of the worksheet shown in Figure 4-22 into the range C6..G6 of the same worksheet. To do this, move the cell pointer to cell B6, issue the /Copy command, and press [Enter] to specify cell B6 as the FROM range. When 1-2-3 presents the *Enter range to copy TO:* prompt, use the arrow keys to move the cell pointer to cell C6, press the [period] key to anchor the cell pointer, and then press → four times to select the range C6..G6. When you press [Enter], 1-2-3 will place a copy of the label from cell B6 into the cells in the range C6..G6. Figure 4-23 shows the resulting worksheet.

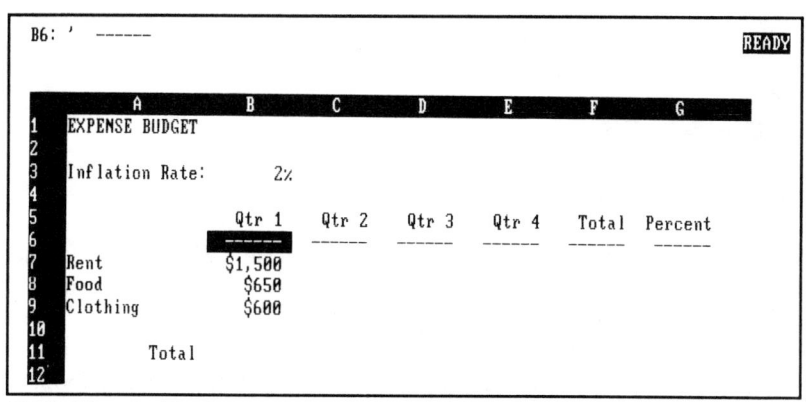

FIGURE 4-23: Multiple copies of a single entry

Copying from a Single Row to a Single Row

You also can use the /Copy command to copy information from a single row to another single row. For example, suppose you want to copy the entries from the range B6..F6 of the worksheet in Figure 4-23 into the range B10..F10. To do this, move the cell pointer to cell B6, issue the / Copy command, press → four times and press [Enter] to select the range B6..F6 as the FROM range.

To specify the TO range, point to cell B10 and press [Enter]. Figure 4-24 shows the resulting worksheet. Although you could point to the entire range B10..F10, you don't have to. When you are copying from a range to another range, it is only necessary to highlight the upper-left cell of the TO range—in this case, cell B10.

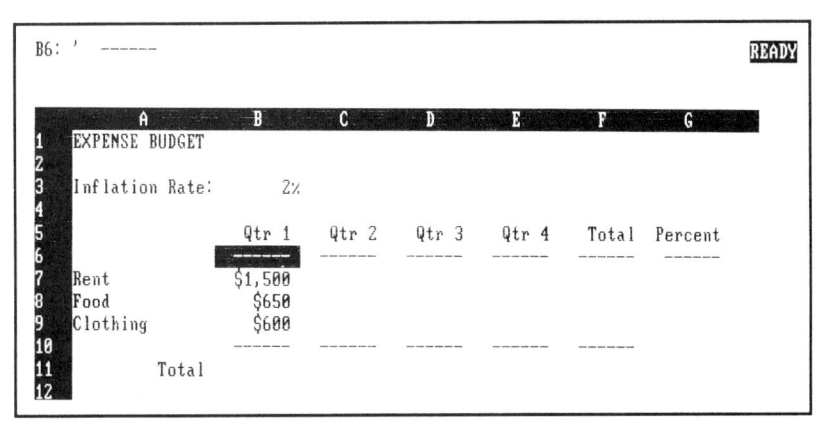

```
B6: '  ------                                              READY


        A           B       C       D       E       F       G
1  EXPENSE BUDGET
2
3  Inflation Rate:    2%
4
5                    Qtr 1   Qtr 2   Qtr 3   Qtr 4   Total   Percent
6                    ------  ------  ------  ------  ------  ------
7  Rent              $1,500
8  Food                $650
9  Clothing            $600
10                   ------  ------  ------  ------  ------
11         Total
12
```

FIGURE 4-24: Copying a single row into a single row

Copying from a Single Column to a Single Column

You can copy information from a single column into another single column in much the same way that you copy a row of information into another single row. For example, suppose that you want to copy the entries from the range A7..A9 in Figure 4-24 into the range A16..A18. To do this, move the cell pointer to cell A7, issue the / Copy command, and press ↓ twice to select cells A7..A9 as the FROM range. To select cells A16..A18 as the TO range, you should point to cell A16—the upper-left cell in the range—and press [Enter]. When you press [Enter], 1-2-3 will place a single copy of the entries from the range A7..A9 into the range A16..A18. Figure 4-25 shows the result.

Copying from a Single Row to Multiple Rows

1-2-3 also lets you copy entries from a single row into two or more rows. To make this kind of copy, you must select a row of entries as the FROM range and a range that spans two or more rows as the TO range. To define the TO range, you can select the entire range that will be filled by the copy; however, it is only necessary to highlight the leftmost cell in each row of the TO range.

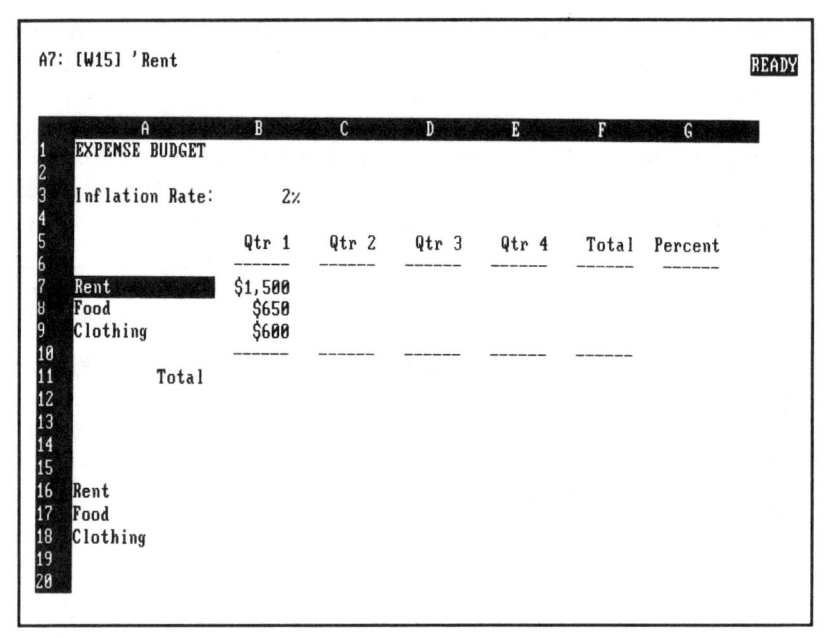

```
A7: [W15] 'Rent                                                                READY

     A              B         C         D         E         F         G
 1  EXPENSE BUDGET
 2
 3  Inflation Rate:    2%
 4
 5                   Qtr 1     Qtr 2     Qtr 3     Qtr 4     Total    Percent
 6                  ------    ------    ------    ------    ------   -------
 7  Rent           $1,500
 8  Food             $650
 9  Clothing         $600
10                  ------    ------    ------    ------    ------
11          Total
12
13
14
15
16  Rent
17  Food
18  Clothing
19
20
```

FIGURE 4-25: Copying a single column into a single column

Copying from a Single Column to Multiple Columns

Copying information from the cells of a single column into the cells of two or more adjacent columns is similar to copying the contents of the cells in a single row into more than one row. To make this kind of copy, you must select a column of entries as the FROM range and a range that spans two or more columns as the TO range. To define the TO range, you can select the entire range that will be filled by the copy; however, it is only necessary to highlight the topmost cell in each column of the TO range.

Copying a Range to a Range

You can also copy a multiple-column, multiple-row range into another range. For example, suppose you want to copy the entries in the range B5..E6 in Figure 4-25 into the range B14..E15. To do this, you would move the cell pointer to cell B5, issue the /Copy command, select the range B5..E6, and press [Enter] to define the FROM range.

Next, 1-2-3 will prompt you to define the TO range. As with most other types of copies, you only need to select the upper-left cell of the TO range (in this case, cell B14). However, you can select the entire range (in this case, the range B14..E15) if you wish. When you press [Enter], 1-2-3 will make a single copy of the FROM range, as shown in Figure 4-26.

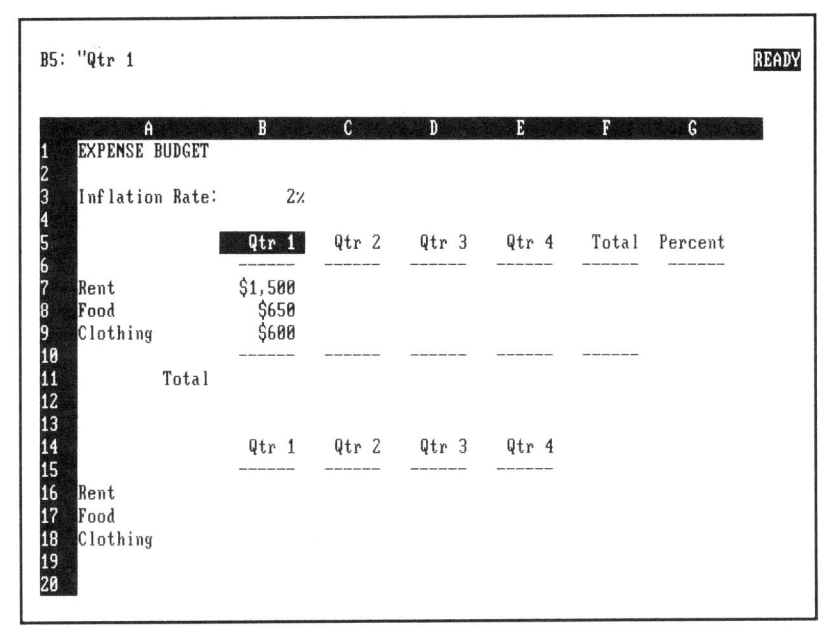

```
B5: "Qtr 1                                                    READY

         A            B         C        D        E        F        G
   1  EXPENSE BUDGET
   2
   3  Inflation Rate:      2%
   4
   5                     Qtr 1     Qtr 2    Qtr 3    Qtr 4   Total   Percent
   6                     ------    ------   ------   ------  ------  ------
   7  Rent             $1,500
   8  Food               $650
   9  Clothing           $600
  10                     ------    ------   ------   ------  ------
  11         Total
  12
  13
  14                     Qtr 1     Qtr 2    Qtr 3    Qtr 4
  15                     ------    ------   ------   ------
  16  Rent
  17  Food
  18  Clothing
  19
  20
```

FIGURE 4-26: Copying a multiple-cell range

COPYING FORMULAS AND FUNCTIONS

So far, we've copied labels and values as we have demonstrated the different source/destination combinations that you can use with the / Copy command. As you might expect, you can also use the / Copy command to copy formulas and functions. In fact, you will probably use / Copy to copy formulas and functions more often than you will use it to copy simple values and labels.

Because formulas and functions typically contain references to other cells, copying formulas and functions is trickier than copying simple labels and values. When you copy a formula, 1-2-3 must decide what to do with the cell references in that formula. Should the cell references in each copy be adjusted to reflect the location of that copy? Or should the references in each copy continue to refer to the same cells as the original formula?

The way 1-2-3 handles the cell references in the formulas you copy is determined by the type of those references. As we mentioned in Chapter 2, 1-2-3 offers three types of cell references: relative references, absolute references, and mixed references. It is important that you understand how each of these types of references works if you are to understand how 1-2-3 copies formulas.

Relative References

The default type of cell reference in 1-2-3 is a relative reference. Nearly all of the references you've seen so far in this book are relative references. For example, the formula *+F11/4* includes a relative reference to cell F11. The function *@SUM(B7..B9)* includes a relative reference to the range B7..B9.

When you copy a formula that includes a relative reference to another location, the copy of the formula will not refer to the same cell as the original formula. Instead, 1-2-3 will adjust the reference to reflect the location of the copy. For example, suppose that you enter the simple formula *+A1* in cell A2 of a blank worksheet (the reference to cell A1 in this formula is a relative reference). If you copy that formula from cell A2 to cell B2, cell B2 will contain the formula *+B1*. Just as cell A1 is the cell one row above cell A2, cell B1 is the cell one row above cell B2. Although these two references do not refer to the same cell, they refer to cells that are in the same location relative to the cells that contain the references.

Let's look at an example of copying relative references. Suppose that you want to enter these functions into the range B11..F11 of the worksheet in Figure 4-25:

B11: @SUM(B7..B9)   E11: @SUM(E7..E9)
C11: @SUM(C7..C9)   F11: @SUM(F7..F9)
D11: @SUM(D7..D9)

You also want to give these cells the Currency format with zero decimals.

To do this, you could move the cell pointer to each of these cells individually and type the appropriate function manually, then use the / Range Format command to format the range B11..F11. An easier way, however, would be to enter the function *@SUM(B7..B9)* into cell B11 and assign that cell the Currency format. Then you could use the / Copy command to copy the formula and format into cells C11 through F11. Figure 4-27 shows the results of this copy.

As you can see, the functions in cells C11 through F11 do not return the same result as the function in cell B11. Why not? Because the functions in these cells are not identical to the function in cell B11. Instead, cell C11 contains the function *@SUM(C7..C9)*, cell D11 contains the function *@SUM(D7..D9)*, and so on. Because the reference to the range B7..B9 in the formula in cell B11 is relative, 1-2-3 changed the reference in each copy. (Since the cells in the range C7..F9 are blank, these formulas return the value 0.)

Here's another way to think about it. 1-2-3 interprets the function *@SUM(B7..B9)* in cell B11 in this way: "Sum the values in the three-cell range that begins with the cell four rows above this cell and ends with the cell two rows above this cell." If you think about it for a moment, you'll see that each of the formulas in cells C11, D11, E11, and F11 gives 1-2-3 exactly the same instruction. For instance, the formula in cell D11, *@SUM(D7..D9)*, tells 1-2-3 to sum the values in the three-cell range that begins with the cell four rows above the cell that contains this function (cell D7) and ends with the cell two rows above the cell that contains this function (cell D9).

```
B11: (C0) @SUM(B7..B9)                                                    READY

           A          B        C        D        E        F        G
    1  EXPENSE BUDGET
    2
    3  Inflation Rate:      2%
    4
    5                     Qtr 1    Qtr 2    Qtr 3    Qtr 4    Total   Percent
    6                     ------   ------   ------   ------   ------  ------
    7  Rent              $1,500
    8  Food                $650
    9  Clothing            $600
   10                     ------   ------   ------   ------
   11          Total     $2,750      $0       $0       $0       $0
   12
   13
   14                     Qtr 1    Qtr 2    Qtr 3    Qtr 4
   15                     ------   ------   ------   ------
   16  Rent
   17  Food
   18  Clothing
   19
   20
```

FIGURE 4-27: An example worksheet

Also notice that 1-2-3 copied the format of cell B11 as it copied the formula. Whenever you copy a value or formula that has been assigned a format, that format will be copied as well.

Let's consider another example. Suppose you want to enter a series of formulas in cells F7, F8, and F9 that sum the cells in columns B, C, D, and E. First enter the formula +B7+C7+D7+E7 in cell F7 and give that cell the Currency format with zero decimal places. Then, with the cell pointer on cell F7, issue the /Copy command, press [Enter] and use the ↓ key to select F8..F9 as the TO range. When you press [Enter] to lock in the TO range, 1-2-3 will copy the formula in cell F7 into cells F8 and F9. Figure 4-28 shows the worksheet that will result.

Because the references to cells B7, C7, D7, and E7 in the formula in cell F7 are relative references, the references in the formulas in cells F8 and F9 will be different than those in the original formula. For example, the formula in cell F8 in Figure 4-28 is *+B8+C8+D8+E8*. The formula in cell F9 is *+B9+C9+D9+E9*.

```
F7: (C0) +B7+C7+D7+E7                                              READY

         A          B         C         D         E         F         G
 1 EXPENSE BUDGET
 2
 3 Inflation Rate:    2%
 4
 5                  Qtr 1     Qtr 2     Qtr 3     Qtr 4     Total   Percent
 6                  ------    ------    ------    ------    ------  ------
 7 Rent            $1,500                                  $1,500
 8 Food              $650                                    $650
 9 Clothing          $600                                    $600
10                  ------    ------    ------    ------    ------
11         Total   $2,750        $0        $0        $0   $2,750
12
13
14                  Qtr 1     Qtr 2     Qtr 3     Qtr 4
15                  ------    ------    ------    ------
16 Rent
17 Food
18 Clothing
19
20
```

FIGURE 4-28: Copying formulas

Absolute and Mixed References

In most cases, you'll want to use relative references in your formulas. In some situations, though, you won't want a reference to change when you copy it, as relative references do. In these cases, you'll need to use absolute or mixed references. Unlike relative references, absolute and mixed references "fix" a reference's column or row coordinate, or both, so that it does not change when the reference is copied.

Absolute References

Unlike relative references, which change as you copy them, absolute references do not change as they are copied. To define an absolute reference, you simply include dollar signs ($) before the column and row portions of the reference. For example, to enter an absolute reference to cell A1 in cell A2, you would move the cell pointer to cell A2 and type +$A$1. The dollar signs in this reference define this as an absolute reference.

Now suppose you use the /Copy command to copy this formula to cell B2. The result of the copy in cell B2 will be the formula *+$A$1*—exactly the same formula that is in cell A2. Because the reference to cell A1 is an absolute reference, it does not change when you copy it. No matter where you copy an absolute reference in a worksheet, the copy always will refer to the same cell as the original formula.

Defining Absolute References

As we have said, you define absolute references by including dollar signs ($) in front of the row and column portions of the reference. You can either type the dollar signs, or you can use the [Abs] key ([F4] on the IBM PC) to define them. You can use this key to change any reference to an absolute reference while you are typing a reference, pointing to define a reference, or editing a formula that contains a reference. (In 1-2-3 Release 1A, you can use the [Abs] key only while you are in the POINT mode.)

For example, suppose you want to enter an absolute reference to cell A1 in cell A2. To do this, move the cell pointer to cell A2, type +, and point to cell A1. When you do this, 1-2-3 will display the reference *+A1* on the edit line. To make this relative reference into an absolute reference, just press the [Abs] key. When you do this, 1-2-3 will insert dollar signs in the reference so that the edit line displays the reference as *+$A$1*. If you press [Enter] at this point, 1-2-3 will lock the absolute reference into cell A2.

If instead of pressing [Enter] you press [Abs] again, the reference in the edit line will change to *+A$1*. Pressing [Abs] again will change the reference to *+$A1*. Notice that in both of these references a dollar sign appears in front of only the column or the row portion of the reference—not both. These references are examples of mixed references. We'll cover mixed references in a few pages. If you press [Abs] a fourth time, 1-2-3 will make the reference relative again. If you continue to press [Abs], the cycle will repeat.

You can also use the [Abs] key in the VALUE mode. For example, suppose you want to enter an absolute reference to cell A1 in cell A2. To do this, move the cell pointer to cell A2 and type +A1 and press the [Abs] key. When you do this, 1-2-3 will insert dollar signs in front of the row and column portions of the reference so that the edit line displays the reference as *+$A$1*. If you press [Enter] at this point, 1-2-3 will lock the absolute reference into cell A2.

You can also use the [Abs] key in the EDIT mode. For example, suppose you have entered the formula *+A1+A2* into cell A3, and now you want to change the references in this formula to absolute references. To do this, move the cell pointer to cell A3 and press [Edit] to enter the EDIT mode. Now, press the [Abs] key. This will change the formula to *+A1+$A$2*. Notice that only the last reference in the formula has changed. Before you can use the [Abs] key in the EDIT mode, you must position the cursor under the reference you want to change or under the character following that reference. Since the cursor was under the character after the reference to cell A2, that reference was changed when you pressed [Abs]. To change the reference to cell A1 to an absolute reference, you should move the cursor so that it is under that reference and press [Abs] again. This will change the formula in cell A3 to *+$A$1+$A$2*. If you press [Enter] at this point, 1-2-3 will lock in the changed formula.

Range references can also be absolute. For example, the function *@SUM($A$1..$A$5)* contains an absolute reference to the range A1..A5. Suppose you want to enter this function into cell A6. To do this, you could move the cell pointer to cell A6 and type @SUM($A$1..$A$5). Alternatively, you could type @SUM(A1..A5), then press the [Abs] key. When you press this key, the function in cell A6 will change to @SUM($A$1..$A$5). Whenever you use the [Abs] key to define an absolute reference to a range, the references to both anchor cells will be absolute. If you want one end of the range to be absolute and the other to be relative, as in the function @SUM($A$1..A5), you'll have to type the range reference.

You can also define absolute references to named ranges. For example, suppose the range A1..A5 has been assigned the name TEST. To define an absolute reference to this range, you would type a dollar sign before the range name, as in the function @SUM($TEST).

An Example

Here's a situation in which you would want to use an absolute reference. Cells B7 through B9 in Figure 4-28 contain values that represent expense estimates for rent, food, and clothing, in the first quarter of the year. You expect that inflation will cause each expense to increase by 2% per quarter. You've entered this rate in cell B3. You now want to enter formulas in the range C7..E9 that compute estimates for these expense categories for second, third, and fourth quarters.

To perform these calculations, you could enter each of these formulas individually. For example, you could enter the formula +B7*(1+B3) into cell C7, enter the formula +C7*(1+B3) into cell D7, enter the formula +D8*(1+B3) into cell E8, and so forth. This process would be very tedious, however.

Instead of entering each of these formulas manually, you could enter the formula +B7*(1+B3) into cell C7 then copy it into the range C7..E9. Figure 4-29 shows the worksheet that would result from this copy.

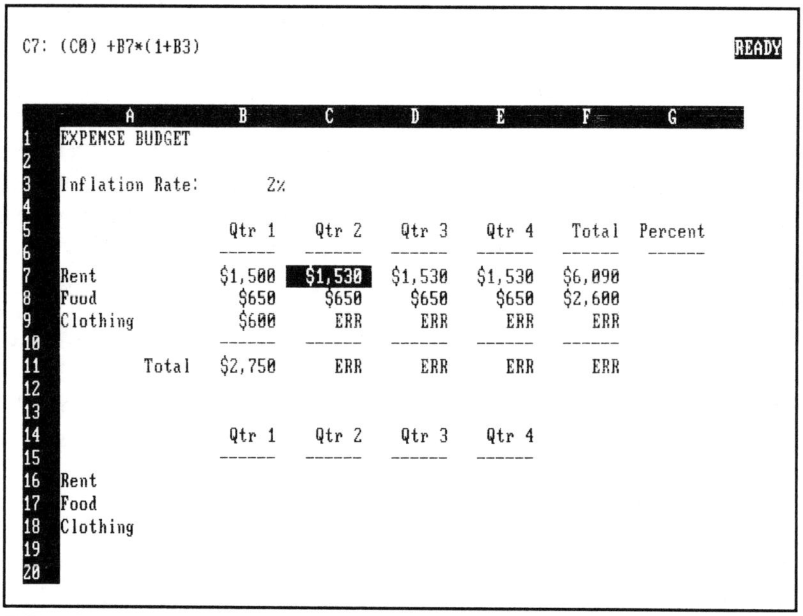

FIGURE 4-29: A worksheet with problems

Unfortunately, all is not well in the worksheet in Figure 4-29. Here's why: Because the reference to cell B3 in the formula in cell C7 is relative, 1-2-3 adjusted it as it was copied. For example, the formula in cell C8 is *+B8*(1+B4)*. The formula in cell D7 is *+C7*(1+C3)*. Notice that neither of these formulas refers to cell B3, the cell that contains the inflation rate. In fact, none of the cells in the range C7..E7 (except for the formula in cell C7 itself) refers to cell B3. As a result, none of the formulas returns the correct result, and a few return ERR.

Because you want all the copies of the formula to refer to cell B3, you should change the reference to cell B3 in cell C7 to an absolute reference. After you make this change, the formula would look like this: *+B7*(1+$B$3)*. The absolute reference $B$3 assures that 1-2-3 will not change the reference to cell B3 as it copies the formula into different rows and columns of the worksheet. Once you have changed the formula, you can issue the / Copy command, select cell C7 as the FROM range, select C7..E7 as the TO range, and press [Enter] to make the copies.

Figure 4-30 shows the corrected worksheet. All of the formulas in cells C7 through E9 now refer to cell B3. For example, the formula in cell C8 is *+B8*(1+$B$3)*. The formula in cell D7 is *+C7*(1+$B$3)*. Because the reference to cell B3 in the formula in cell C7 is absolute, that reference did not change when we copied the formula.

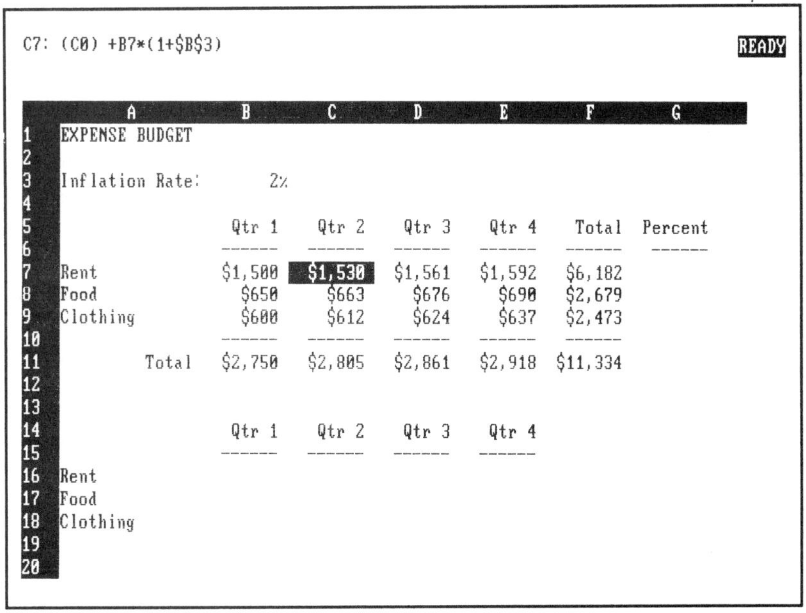

```
C7: (C0) +B7*(1+$B$3)                                              READY

              A           B         C         D         E         F         G
 1    EXPENSE BUDGET
 2
 3    Inflation Rate:     2%
 4
 5                        Qtr 1     Qtr 2     Qtr 3     Qtr 4     Total     Percent
 6                        ------    ------    ------    ------    ------    ------
 7    Rent                $1,500    $1,530    $1,561    $1,592    $6,182
 8    Food                  $650      $663      $676      $690    $2,679
 9    Clothing              $600      $612      $624      $637    $2,473
10                        ------    ------    ------    ------    ------
11            Total       $2,750    $2,805    $2,861    $2,918   $11,334
12
13
14                        Qtr 1     Qtr 2     Qtr 3     Qtr 4
15                        ------    ------    ------    ------
16    Rent
17    Food
18    Clothing
19
20
```

FIGURE 4-30: Copying absolute references

> **TIP: INCLUDING THE FROM RANGE IN THE TO RANGE**
>
> To create the formulas in the range C7..E9 in Figure 4-30, we entered a formula into cell C7, issued the / Copy command, selected cell C7 as the FROM range, and selected C7..E7 as the TO range. Notice that the FROM and TO ranges in this copy overlap. Although you usually will select separate FROM and TO ranges, these two ranges can overlap. Most commonly, you will include the entire FROM range within the TO range. This allows you to create a formula in the first cell of a range and then copy the formula into the other cells in that range.

Mixed References

In addition to relative and absolute references, 1-2-3 offers a third type of reference: mixed references. As the name implies, mixed references are hybrids. In a mixed reference, either the row portion or the column portion of the reference is absolute. The other portion of the reference is relative. When you copy a mixed reference, the absolute half of the reference remains constant, but the relative half changes.

Like absolute references, mixed references are marked by dollar signs ($). The position of the $ within a mixed reference determines which portion of that reference is fixed. A $ in front of the column letter portion of the reference means that the column portion of the reference is absolute. For example, the reference *+$A1* will always refer to a cell in column A, no matter where it is copied. Suppose you enter this formula in cell A2, then copy the formula to cell B3. After the copy, the formula in cell B3 will be *+$A2*. If you copy the formula in cell A2 to cell D5, the formula in D5 will be *+$A4*. Notice that, as you copy this formula, the column portion of the reference remains fixed, but the row portion is adjusted relative to the position of the copy.

A $ in front of the row number portion of a reference means that the row portion of the entry is fixed. For example, the reference *+A$1* will always refer to a cell in row 1, no matter where it is copied in the worksheet. Suppose you enter this formula in cell A2, then copy the formula to cell B3. After the copy, the formula in cell B3 will be *+B$1*. If you copy the formula in cell A2 to cell D5, the reference in D5 will be *+D$1*. Notice that, as you copy this formula, the row portion of the reference remains fixed, but the column portion changes.

Defining Mixed References

You can define mixed references in the same of the ways you define absolute references: You can either type the $ signs in the appropriate spots when you enter a reference, or you can use the [Abs] key. If you use the [Abs] key, keep in mind that pressing [Abs] twice fixes the row portion of the reference, while pressing [Abs] three times fixes the column portion of the reference. All of the same tricks and rules you learned for using [Abs] to define absolute references also apply to mixed references.

An Example

You'll want to use mixed references in situations where you want the row or column coordinate of a reference to remain fixed as you copy it. For example, cells F7 through F9 in Figure 4-30 contain functions that compute the total for each expense category for the year. Cell F11 contains the function *@SUM(F7..F9)*, which computes the total of all expenses for the year. Suppose that you want to enter formulas in the range G7..G9 that calculate the percentage of total expenses accounted for by each of the three expense categories. To do this, enter the formula *+F7/F$11* in cell G7. As you can see, the reference to cell F11 in this formula is a mixed reference. The reference to cell F7 is relative.

When you copy this formula into cells G8 and G9, 1-2-3 will not adjust the row portion of the reference to cell F11. Consequently, the formula in cell G8 will be *+F8/F$11*, as you can see in Figure 4-31, and the formula in cell G9 will be *+F9/F$11*. Because the reference to cell F11 is a mixed reference, the row portion of the reference remains constant when you copy the formula into cell G8 and cell G9.

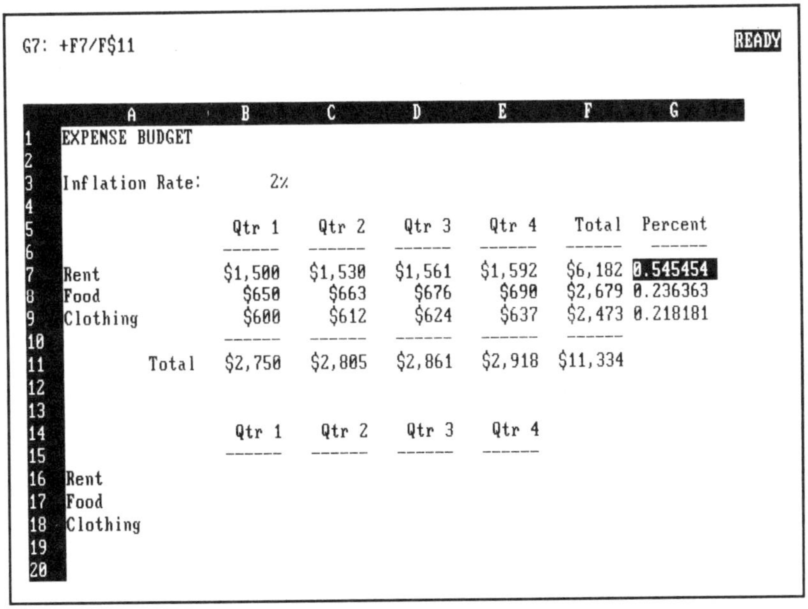

```
G7: +F7/F$11                                                            READY

           A          B         C         D         E         F         G
  1  EXPENSE BUDGET
  2
  3  Inflation Rate:        2%
  4
  5                       Qtr 1     Qtr 2     Qtr 3     Qtr 4    Total   Percent
  6                       -----     -----     -----     -----    -----   -------
  7  Rent                $1,500    $1,530    $1,561    $1,592   $6,182   0.545454
  8  Food                  $650      $663      $676      $690   $2,679   0.236363
  9  Clothing              $600      $612      $624      $637   $2,473   0.218181
 10                       -----     -----     -----     -----   ------
 11           Total       $2,750    $2,805    $2,861    $2,918  $11,334
 12
 13
 14                       Qtr 1     Qtr 2     Qtr 3     Qtr 4
 15                       -----     -----     -----     -----
 16  Rent
 17  Food
 18  Clothing
 19
 20
```

FIGURE 4-31: Copying mixed references

You may wonder why we didn't use the formula *+F7/$F$11* in cell G7. In fact, this formula, which includes an absolute reference to cell F11, would work just as well as the mixed reference. However, there are cases where you will not be able to use the mixed and absolute forms of a formula interchangeably, so it's a good idea to get in the habit of using the proper form.

Which to Use?

The hardest part of working with relative, absolute, and mixed references is determining exactly which type of reference you should use in a given situation. For example, suppose you want to enter a formula into cell B16 that computes the percentage of total expenses for the first quarter accounted for by Rent. This formula would include references to cells B7 and B11. After you enter this formula, you want to copy it into the range B16..E18 so that you can determine the percentages of total expenses represented by each type of expense in each quarter. How should you define the references in the formula in cell B15?

The correct form of this formula is *+B7/B$11*. When you copy this formula into the range B16..E18, every cell in that range will contain a formula that computes the percentage of total expenses represented by a particular type of expense in a particular quarter. Figure 4-32 shows the worksheet after the copy. Cell C16 in this worksheet contains the formula *+C7/C$11*. Cell D17 contains the formula *+D8/D$11*.

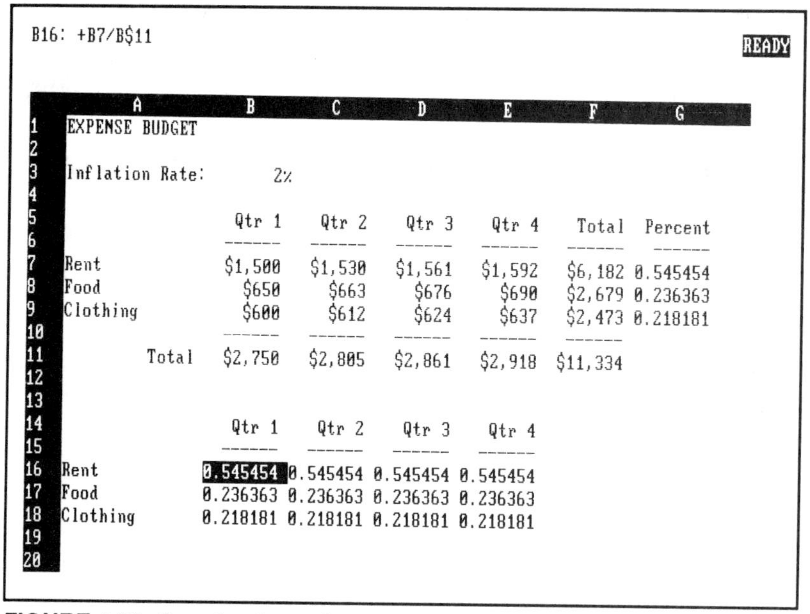

```
B16: +B7/B$11                                                    READY

         A            B         C         D         E        F         G
    1  EXPENSE BUDGET
    2
    3  Inflation Rate:     2%
    4
    5                     Qtr 1     Qtr 2     Qtr 3     Qtr 4   Total   Percent
    6                     ------    ------    ------    ------  ------
    7  Rent               $1,500    $1,530    $1,561    $1,592  $6,182  0.545454
    8  Food                 $650      $663      $676      $690  $2,679  0.236363
    9  Clothing             $600      $612      $624      $637  $2,473  0.218181
   10                     ------    ------    ------    ------  ------
   11        Total        $2,750    $2,805    $2,861    $2,918  $11,334
   12
   13
   14                     Qtr 1     Qtr 2     Qtr 3     Qtr 4
   15                     ------    ------    ------    ------
   16  Rent             0.545454  0.545454  0.545454  0.545454
   17  Food             0.236363  0.236363  0.236363  0.236363
   18  Clothing         0.218181  0.218181  0.218181  0.218181
   19
   20
```

FIGURE 4-32: Copying formulas

If you didn't get the formula for cell B16 right the first time, don't worry—we had to try twice to get it. In fact, you will often use a trial-and-error approach to figure out which type of reference to use in a particular situation. As you become more experienced with 1-2-3, however, your intuition in this area will improve. Keep practicing!

SPECIAL KINDS OF COPIES

So far, we have demonstrated how you can use the / Copy command to copy the contents of one cell or range to another cell or range. In addition to the / Copy command, 1-2-3 Releases 2, 2.01, and 2.2 also offer two commands that let you make special kinds of copies. The first command, / Range Value, allows you to convert formulas and functions to their current values as you copy them. ►The second command, / Range Trans, allows you to copy a column of entries into a row or a row of entries into a column. (The / Range Trans command has the name / Range Transpose in 1-2-3 Release 2 and 2.01. The / Range Value and / Range Trans commands are not available in 1-2-3 Release 1A.)◄

RELEASE
► 2.2 ◄

The / Range Value Command

1-2-3's / Range Value command copies the current values of formulas and functions into the range you define. Only the results—the current values—of the formulas and functions are copied—not the formulas and functions themselves. In every other way, the / Range Value command is identical to the / Copy command. To copy the current values of a range of formulas, you issue the / Range Value command, select the range to copy from, press [Enter], then select the range to copy to and press [Enter] again. The process is identical to copying or moving entries. Only the results are different.

An Example

For example, suppose that you want to copy the current values of the functions in the range B11..F11 of the worksheet in Figure 4-32 into the range B12..F12. Cell B11 contains the function *@SUM(B7..B9)*, which adds the values in cells B7..B9. Cells C11, D11, E11, and F11 contain similar functions.

To begin, move the cell pointer to cell B11 and issue the / Range Value command. When 1-2-3 prompts you to define the FROM range, press ➡ four times to select the range B11..F11 as the FROM range. As soon as you press [Enter], 1-2-3 will present the prompt *Enter range to copy TO:*, followed by the address of the current cell. To define the TO range, you could highlight the entire range B12..F12 or just cell B12 (the cell at the upper-left corner in the range). When you press [Enter], 1-2-3 will copy the values of the formulas in the range B11..F11 into the range B12..F12, as shown in Figure 4-33.

```
B11: (C0) @SUM(B7..B9)                                              READY

           A              B         C         D         E         F         G
    1  EXPENSE BUDGET
    2
    3  Inflation Rate:    2%
    4
    5                    Qtr 1     Qtr 2     Qtr 3     Qtr 4     Total    Percent
    6                    ------    ------    ------    ------    ------   -------
    7  Rent              $1,500    $1,530    $1,561    $1,592    $6,182   0.545454
    8  Food                $650      $663      $676      $690    $2,679   0.236363
    9  Clothing            $600      $612      $624      $637    $2,473   0.218181
   10                    ------    ------    ------    ------    ------
   11          Total     $2,750    $2,805    $2,861    $2,918   $11,334
   12                    $2,750    $2,805    $2,861    $2,918   $11,334
   13
   14                    Qtr 1     Qtr 2     Qtr 3     Qtr 4
   15                    ------    ------    ------    ------
   16  Rent             0.545454  0.545454  0.545454  0.545454
   17  Food             0.236363  0.236363  0.236363  0.236363
   18  Clothing         0.218181  0.218181  0.218181  0.218181
   19
   20
```

FIGURE 4-33: The / Range Value command

As you can see, the cells in the range B12..F12 in Figure 4-33 seem to contain the same entries as the cells in the range B11..F11. However, while the cells in the range B11..E11 contain functions that return values, the cells in the range B12..F12 contain pure values only. For example, cell B11 contains the function @SUM(B7..B9), but cell B12 contains the value 2750—the result of the function in cell B11 at the time you issued the / Range Value command.

Notes

The / Range Value command works just as the / Copy command would if you used it on cells that contain values or labels. If you include a cell that contains a simple value or a label in the FROM range of a / Range Value command, 1-2-3 will simply copy it to the appropriate cell of the TO range. If the TO range of a / Range Value command contains any entries, 1-2-3 will overwrite those entries.

Uses for the / Range Value Command

Why would you want to transform formulas and functions into values? First, you can use the / Range Value command to "freeze" the current results of a formula so you can compare those results to updated results of the same formulas. For example, Figure 4-34 shows the worksheet shown in Figure 4-33 after we have revised the inflation rate in cell B3 and then recalculated the worksheet. (As you recall, the formulas in the range B7..F9 depend on the value in cell B3.) Because the cells in the range B11..F11 contain

@SUM functions, 1-2-3 has changed their results to reflect the new rate. However, the values in the range B12..F12, which we created with the /Range Value command, are not affected by the changes. Consequently, this worksheet displays both the "before" and "after" totals.

```
B3: (P0) 0.01                                                        READY

              A         B         C         D         E         F         G
  1  EXPENSE BUDGET
  2
  3  Inflation Rate:      1%
  4
  5                    Qtr 1     Qtr 2     Qtr 3     Qtr 4     Total   Percent
  6                    -----     -----     -----     -----     -----   -------
  7  Rent             $1,500    $1,515    $1,530    $1,545    $6,091  0.545454
  8  Food               $650      $657      $663      $670    $2,639  0.236363
  9  Clothing           $600      $606      $612      $618    $2,436  0.218181
 10                    -----     -----     -----     -----     -----
 11         Total     $2,750    $2,778    $2,805    $2,833   $11,166
 12                   $2,750    $2,805    $2,861    $2,918   $11,334
 13
```

FIGURE 4-34: Before and after worksheets

As you learned in Chapter 2, values consume less memory than functions and formulas. Therefore, you can save memory by using the /Range Value command to convert formulas and functions to values. To do this, you'd issue the /Range Value command and specify the same cells as the FROM and TO ranges. When you press [Enter], 1-2-3 will copy the current values of the formulas in the FROM range into the TO range. In other words, 1-2-3 will replace the formulas in the FROM range with the current values of those formulas.

Of course, you would only want to use this technique to convert formulas that no longer need to be dynamic. When you use the /Range Value command to replace a formula with the current value of that formula, the formula will no longer be updated each time you recalculate. There is no way to restore the formula short of reentering it manually.

TIP: / RANGE VALUE AND RECALCULATION

When you use the / Range Value command to copy the current value of a formula or function, 1-2-3 copies the value that is currently displayed in the cell that contains that formula or function. 1-2-3 does not recalculate formulas or functions before it copies their values. If your worksheet is set for Manual recalculation, the results of some of the functions and formulas you are copying may not be up-to-date. Consequently, 1-2-3 may copy an incorrect value when you issue the /Range Value command. To avoid this problem, always press the [Calc] key prior to issuing the / Range Value command.

The / Range Trans Command

RELEASE
► 2.2 ◄

►1-2-3's / Range Trans command switches the orientation of a range by 90 degrees as it copies that range. (This command has the name / Range Transpose in Releases 2 and 2.01, and is not available in 1-2-3 Release 1A.)◄ In other words, / Range Trans allows you to copy the information from a row into a column or copy the information from a column into a row. To transpose a range, you issue the / Range Trans command, select the range to copy from, press [Enter], then select the range to copy to and press [Enter] again. The process is identical to that of copying entries.

An Example

For example, suppose you began creating a worksheet by entering the labels '*January*, '*February*, '*March*, and so forth, into cells A3 through A14, as shown in Figure 4-35. After doing this, you realize that you want these labels to appear across row 2 instead. To place these entries into the range B2..M2, you could reenter them, one by one, or use the / Copy command 12 times to copy each label individually. Alternatively, you can use 1-2-3's / Range Trans command.

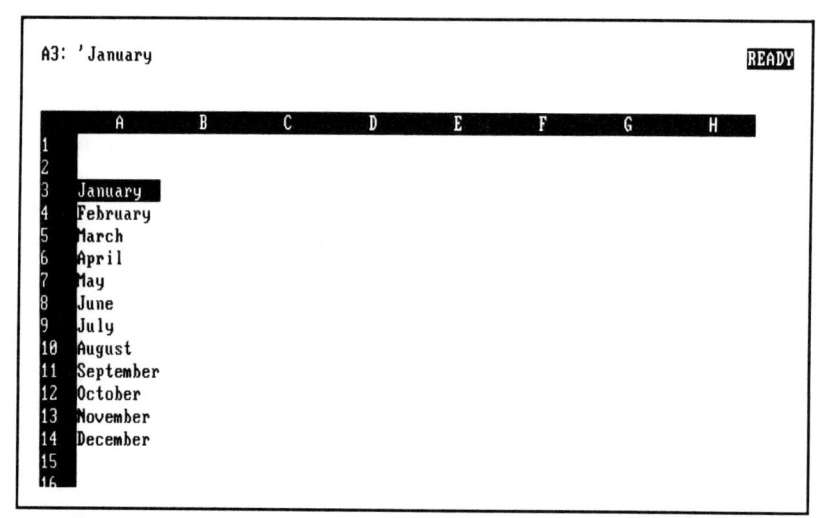

FIGURE 4-35: A sample worksheet

To transpose these twelve entries, first move the cell pointer to cell A3, then issue the / Range Trans command. When 1-2-3 prompts you to define the FROM range, select the range A3..A14. When you press [Enter] to lock in the FROM range, 1-2-3 will prompt you to define the TO range. As with the / Copy command and the / Range Value command, you only need to specify the upper-left corner of the range. In this case, you should choose B2.

When you press [Enter], 1-2-3 will copy the entries from the range A3..A14 into the range B2..M2, as shown in Figure 4-36. As you can see, 1-2-3 has copied the entries from the first cell of the FROM range (A3) into the first cell of the TO range (B2), the second cell of the FROM range (A4) into the second cell of the TO range (C2), and so forth. Since the information was copied from a single column, 1-2-3 copied it into a single row.

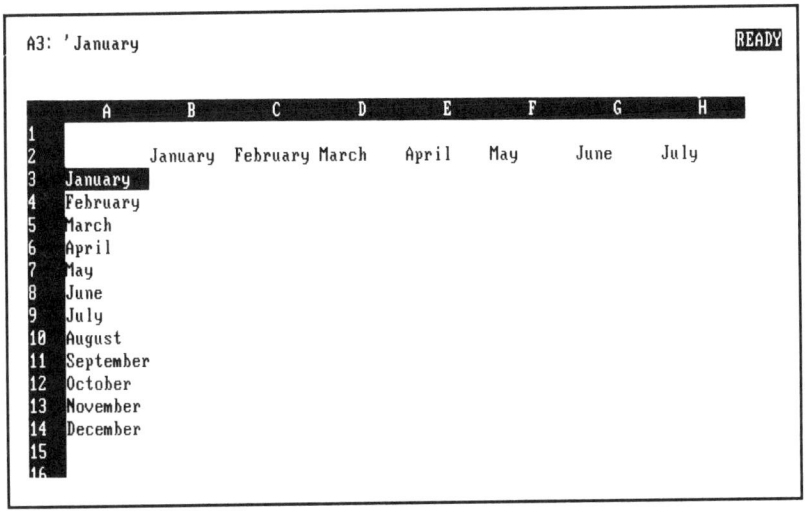

```
A3: 'January                                                    READY

      A       B        C        D      E      F      G      H
1
2             January February March  April  May   June   July
3    January
4    February
5    March
6    April
7    May
8    June
9    July
10   August
11   September
12   October
13   November
14   December
15
16
```

FIGURE 4-36: The / Range Trans command

Notes

Notice that the /Range Trans command did not erase the entries in the range A3..A14 as it copied those entries to the range B2..M2. This is as it should be; after all, /Range Trans is a special form of the /Copy command, and the /Copy command does not erase the contents of the FROM range. If you want to remove the entries in the FROM range after you've used the / Range Trans command, you must erase them.

You can also use the / Range Trans command to transpose a range of entries that are in a row into a column. In fact, if the FROM range consists of a single row of entries, the / Range Trans command will always copy those entries into a single column.

TIP: OVERLAPPING FROM AND TO RANGES

As a general rule, you should avoid overlapping the FROM and TO ranges in a /Range Trans command. There is one situation in which overlapping ranges are useful and work well, however—"pivoting" a single-column or single-row range at its upper-left cell. In that event, the first cell in the FROM range and the first cell in the TO range can overlap. In any other circumstances, overlapping the FROM and TO ranges will not produce the result you want.

Transposing Blocks of Entries

Although you commonly will use / Range Trans to transpose single columns and single rows, you also can transpose blocks of cells that contain several rows and several columns. For example, suppose you want to copy the values in the range A2..E6 of the worksheet shown in Figure 4-37 into the range A8..E12. To do this, issue the / Range Trans command, select cells A2 through E6 as the FROM range, and select cell A8 as the TO range (remember—you only need to specify the upper-left cell of the TO range in any copy process). Figure 4-38 shows the result of this transposition. As you can see, 1-2-3 has copied the entries from the first row of the FROM range (A2..E2) into the first column of the TO range (A8..A12), has copied the entries from the second row of the FROM range (A3..E3) into the second column of the TO range (B8..B12), and so forth.

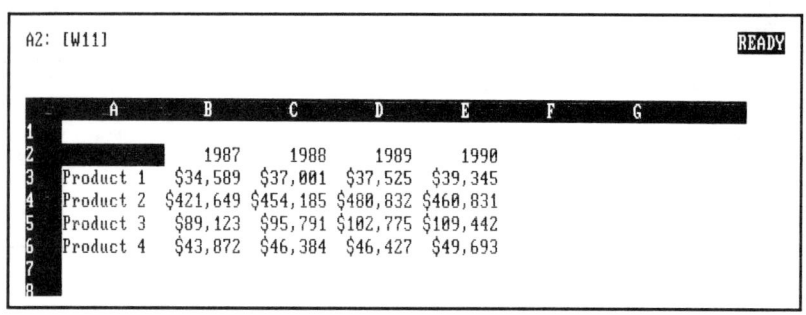

FIGURE 4-37: A sample worksheet

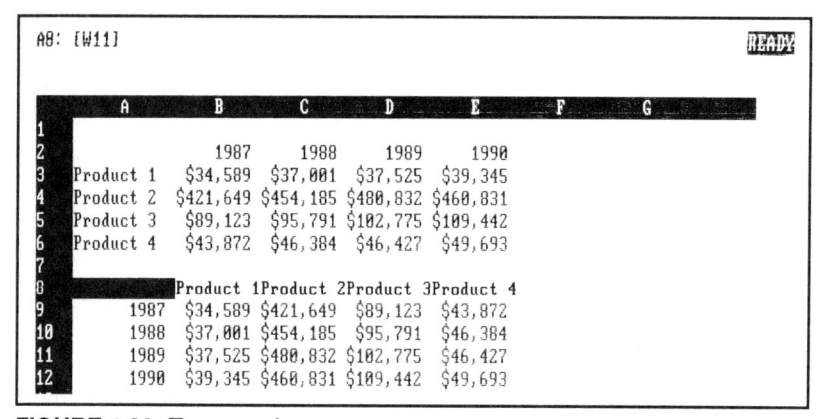

FIGURE 4-38: Transposing a range

Transposing Formulas and Functions

RELEASE ► 2.2 ◄ ▶So far, we have used / Range Trans to copy ranges that contain only values and labels. However, you also can use the / Range Trans command to copy formulas and functions. When you do, the result you'll get depends on which release of 1-2-3 you are using. 1-2-3 Releases 2 and 2.01 will copy the formulas and functions themselves, just like they do when you issue the / Copy command. 1-2-3 Release 2.2's / Range Trans command copies the results of the formulas and functions, rather than their results—just like the / Range Values command does.

To demonstrate the difference this makes, lets use the / Range Trans command to copy the formulas

　　B3: +A3+1
　　B4: +A4+1
　　B5: +A5+1
　　B6: +A6+1
　　B7: +A7+1

in cells B3..B7 of the worksheet shown in Figure 4-39 into cells C2..G2 of that worksheet. (Cells A3..A7 contain the values 1, 3, 5, 7, and 9, respectively.) To do this, you would issue the / Range Trans command, highlight cells B3..B7, press [Enter], highlight cell C2, and press [Enter] again.

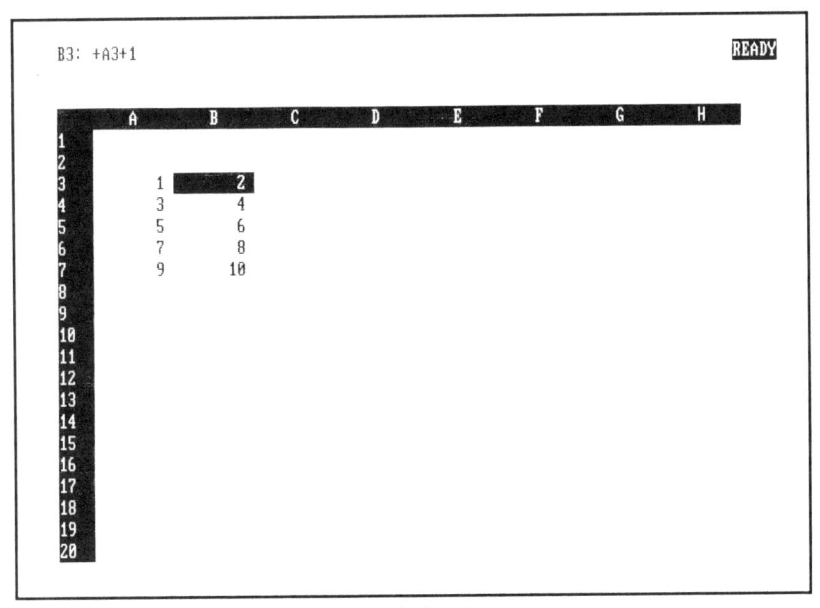

FIGURE 4-39: Another sample worksheet

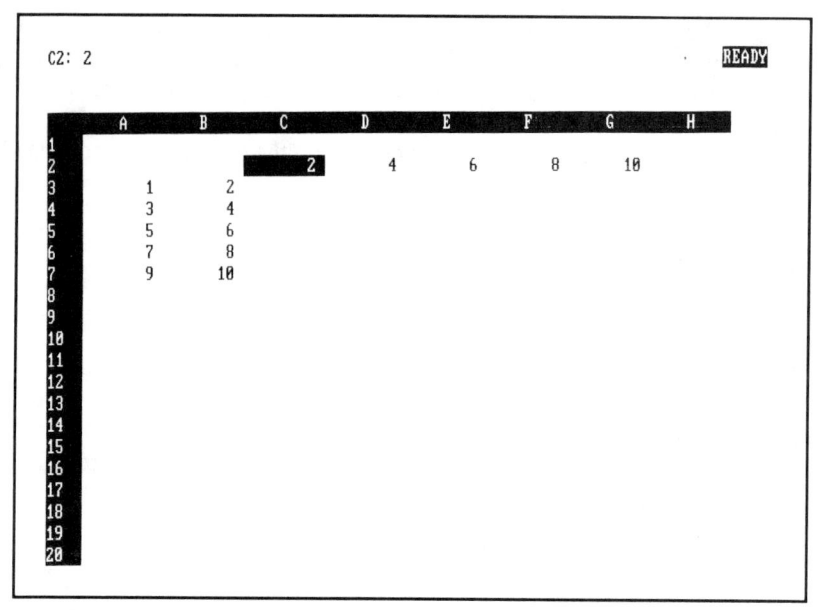

```
C2: 2                                                          READY

          A         B         C         D         E         F         G         H
    1
    2                         2         4         6         8         10
    3         1         2
    4         3         4
    5         5         6
    6         7         8
    7         9         10
    8
    9
   10
   11
   12
   13
   14
   15
   16
   17
   18
   19
   20
```

FIGURE 4-40: Transposing formulas in 1-2-3 2.2

Figure 4-40 shows the result of transposing these formulas in 1-2-3 Release 2.2. As you can see, cells C2..G2 contain the values 2, 4, 6, 8, and 10, respectively—the results of the formulas in cells B3..B7. Figure 4-41 shows the result of this operation in 1-2-3 Releases 2 and 2.01. Instead of containing values, cells C2..G2 contain the formulas

C2: +B2+1
D2: +C2+1
E2: +D2+1
F2: +E2+1
G2: +F2+1

Since the references in the formulas in cells B3..B7 are relative, the references in the copies of the formulas are different than the ones in the original formulas. However, instead of referring to the cells immediately above themselves, each of the copies refers to the cell immediately to its left—just like the formulas in cells B3..B7 do. Consequently, they return the values 1, 2, 3, 4, and 5.◄

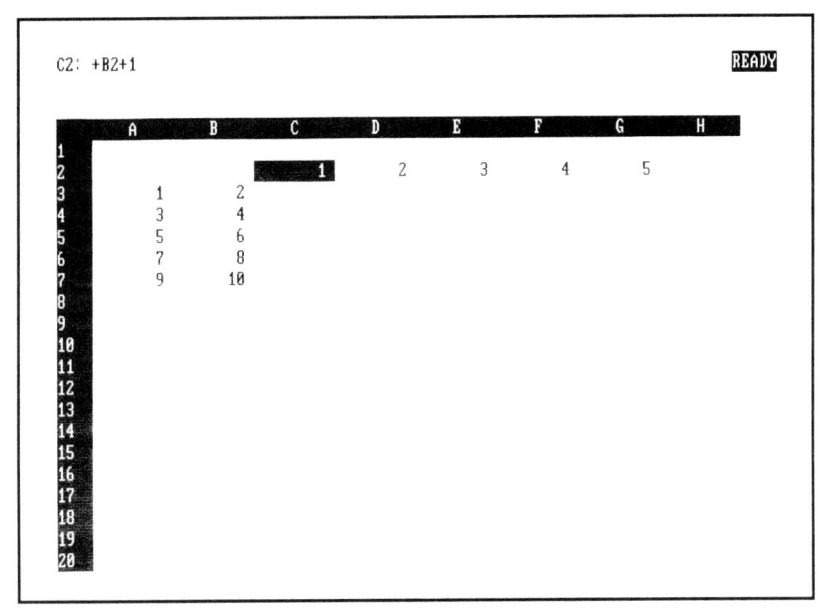

```
C2: +B2+1                                              READY

        A       B       C       D       E       F       G       H
    1
    2                           1       2       3       4       5
    3       1       2
    4       3       4
    5       5       6
    6       7       8
    7       9      10
    8
    ...
```

FIGURE 4-41: Transposing formulas in 1-2-3 Releases 2 and 2.01

CONCLUSION

1-2-3 offers a variety of commands that allow you to edit a worksheet. These commands are 1-2-3's equivalent of the scissors, glue, pencil, and eraser that you would use to edit a paper spreadsheet. Using these commands, you can erase entries, add rows and columns to a worksheet, delete rows and columns from a worksheet, move entries from one place to another, and make copies of entries. If you are like most 1-2-3 users, you will use these commands all the time.

5

Functions

Functions are built-in tools that allow you to perform complex calculations and manipulations quickly and efficiently. For example, you can use the @SQRT function to calculate the square root of a value, the @NPV function to compute the net present value of a series of cash flows, or the @LENGTH function to determine the length of a label. You can think of functions as shortcuts that simplify operations that would be difficult or impossible to do with conventional formulas—similar to the special function keys on business calculators.

In this chapter, we'll cover all of 1-2-3's functions except for date/time functions, which we'll cover in Chapter 7, and data base functions, which we'll cover in Chapter 12. Before we look at any functions, however, let's take a moment to examine a few fundamental concepts.

THE FORM OF FUNCTIONS

While functions can perform many different tasks, all functions have similar forms. For one thing, all 1-2-3 functions have *names*. A function's name is a short, descriptive word that identifies what the function does. In addition, most functions have one or more *arguments*. A function's arguments define what the function is to act upon. For example, in the function

@SUM(C4..C9)

the function name is @SUM and the argument is (C4..C9). This function instructs 1-2-3 to sum, or add, the values of the entries in the range C4 to C9.

Function Names

Most function names are an abbreviation of the purpose of the function. For example, the function @SUM computes the sum of several values. Similarly, the function @NPV computes the net present value of a series of values.

Function names always begin with the character @. This character tells 1-2-3 that the entry is a function and not a label. If you forget to type the @ symbol as you are entering a function, 1-2-3 will consider the entry to be a label. For instance, if you type *SUM(C4..C9)* instead of *@SUM(C4..C9)*, 1-2-3 will record your entry as the *label 'SUM(C4..C9)*. This happens because the first character in the entry *SUM(C4..C9)* is a letter.

Arguments

Most functions require one or more arguments. A function's argument tells 1-2-3 what you want the function to operate on. For example, the single argument of the function *@SUM(C4..C9)* is the range reference C4..C9. This function commands 1-2-3 to add the values contained in cells C4, C5, C6, C7, C8, and C9. As in this example, a function's arguments are always enclosed in parentheses.

Some functions require more than one argument. If a function requires more than one argument, those arguments must be separated from one another by commas. For example, the function *@MOD(A1,3)* has two arguments: the cell reference A1 and the value 3. This function computes the remainder of dividing the value in cell A1 by 3.

Notice that the two arguments of this function are enclosed in a single set of parentheses and are separated from one another by a single comma. By default, you can use a comma or a semicolon to separate the arguments of a multi-argument function. If you wish, you can use the / Worksheet Global Default Other International Punctuation command to change the default argument separator. We'll show you how in Appendix 3.

A few functions do not require arguments at all. For example, the function @PI, which returns the value of π, accepts no arguments, nor does the function @NA, which allows you to enter the value NA (Not Available) into a cell.

The arguments of functions can be literal values, references to cells or ranges, range names, formulas, or even other functions. For example, in the function *@MOD(A1,3)*, the first argument is a cell reference and the second argument is a literal value. Similarly, in the function *@ABS(-5)*, the single argument is the literal value -5. This function will return the absolute value of the number -5.

You can also use range names as the arguments of your functions. For example, if you assign the range name TEST to cells C4..C9, you could use the function *@SUM(TEST)* to add the values in those cells.

Although you will use literals and cell or range references as the arguments of most of your functions, you can use formulas and other functions as well. For example, the first argument of the @CHOOSE function

@CHOOSE(@MOD(DATECELL,7),"Saturday","Sunday","Monday", "Tuesday","Wednesday","Thursday","Friday")

is another function: @MOD. The technique of using one function as the argument of another function is called *nesting*. (By the way, this function returns the day of the week that corresponds to the date in the cell named DATECELL. We'll explain how this function works in Chapter 7.)

Although the arguments of most functions will be values (or references to cells that contain values), a few functions require strings as arguments. These functions are called *string functions*. For example, the single argument of the function @LENGTH must be a string, a reference to a cell that contains a string, or a formula or function that returns a string. The arguments of a few other functions (called logical functions) must be conditional tests. For example, the first argument of the function @IF must be a conditional test. We'll cover string functions and logical functions later in this chapter.

MATHEMATICAL FUNCTIONS

Mathematical functions are 1-2-3's simplest functions. There are seventeen functions in this group. They are: @ABS, @MOD, @RAND, @SQRT, @ROUND, @INT, @LOG, @LN, @EXP, @PI, @SIN, @COS, @TAN, @ASIN, @ACOS, @ATAN, and @ATAN2. These functions operate on values and return value results.

The @ABS Function

1-2-3's @ABS function returns the absolute value (the positive equivalent) of the value specified by its argument. The form of this function is

@ABS(*value*)

For example, as you can see, cell B3 in Figure 5-1 contains the value -123. The function in cell B5

B5: @ABS(B3)

returns the value 123. If cell B3 contained a positive value, such as 123, this function would have returned that value unaltered.

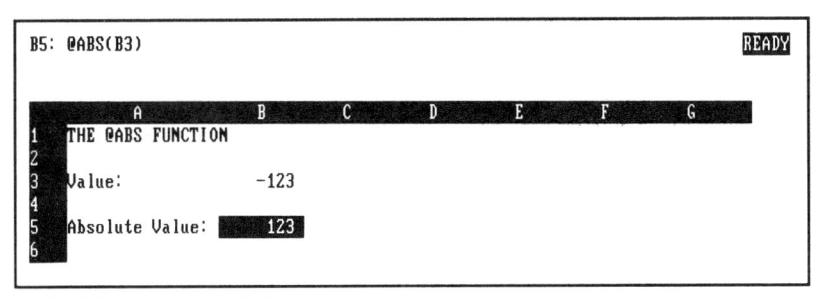

FIGURE 5-1: The @ABS function

The @MOD Function

1-2-3's @MOD function computes the modulus, or remainder, that results from dividing one value by another. The form of this function is

@MOD(*dividend,divisor*)

The result of the function is the remainder that results from dividing *dividend* by *divisor*. For example, cell B3 of the worksheet in Figure 5-2 contains the value 10 and cell B4 contains the value 3. Cell B6 contains the function

    B6: @MOD(B3,B4)

Since 10 divided by 3 equals 3 with a remainder of 1, this function returns 1. @MOD is frequently used in calculations that involve dates. We'll discuss this function further in Chapter 6.

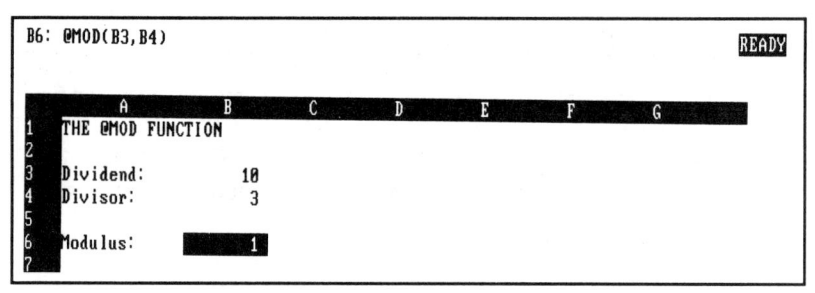

```
B6: @MOD(B3,B4)                                                    READY

         A          B          C        D        E        F        G
   1  THE @MOD FUNCTION
   2
   3  Dividend:       10
   4  Divisor:         3
   5
   6  Modulus:         1
   7
```

FIGURE 5-2: The @MOD function

The @RAND Function

1-2-3's @RAND function lets you generate random numbers in your worksheets. The form of the @RAND function is simply @RAND—it requires no arguments. The @RAND function always returns a random value between 0 and 1. In 1-2-3 Releases 2, 2.01, and 2.2, the @RAND function is truly random. (In 1-2-3 Release 1A, the @RAND function was not truly random. Instead, @RAND returned a predictable series of values, beginning with the same value—.147506—at the beginning of each 1-2-3 session.)

Each time you press the [Calc] key (or each time you make or edit an entry while 1-2-3 is set for Automatic recalculation), the value of any @RAND functions in the worksheet will change. In many cases, you will want to use 1-2-3's / Range Value command to "freeze" a random number once you have used an @RAND function to generate it.

The @SQRT Function

1-2-3's @SQRT function makes it easy to compute the square root of a value. The form of this function is

    @SQRT(*value*)

The result of the function is the square root of *value*. For example, the function in cell B5 in Figure 5-3

    B5: @SQRT(B3)

returns the value 5 since cell B3 contains the value 25.

```
B5: @SQRT(B3)                                              READY

            A           B        C        D        E        F        G
    1  THE @SQRT FUNCTION
    2
    3  Value:          25
    4
    5  Square Root:     5
    6
    7
```

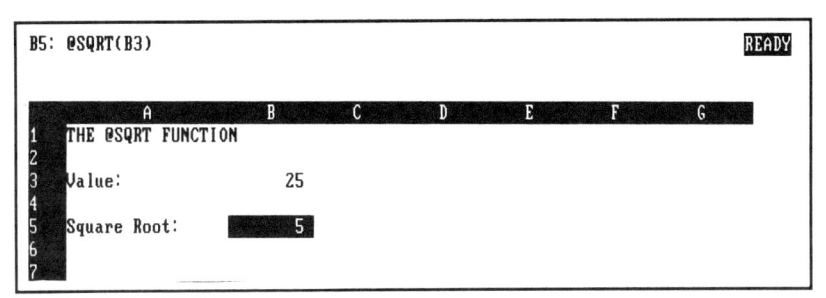

FIGURE 5-3: The @SQRT function

TIP: COMPUTING ROOTS WITH THE ^ OPERATOR

You also can use 1-2-3's ^ operator to calculate the square root of a number. To calculate a number's square root, just raise that number to the 1/2 power. For example, the formula *25^(1/2)* returns the value 5, the same result as the function *@SQRT(25)*. You can use this technique to calculate other roots of a number as well. For example, the formula *8^(1/3)* returns the value 2, the third root of the number 8. Similarly, the formula *81^(1/4)* returns the value 3, the fourth root of the value 81. (The parentheses are necessary to override the default order of precedence.)

The @ROUND Function

1-2-3's @ROUND function rounds a value to the number of decimal places you specify. The form of this function is

@ROUND(*value,# of decimal places*)

where *# of decimal places* is a number from 16 to -16 that specifies the number of decimal places to which you want to round the *value* argument. The @ROUND function follows the same rules for rounding that you learned in grade school. Digits less than 5 are rounded down (towards zero), while digits 5 or greater are rounded up (away from zero).

Cells C3 through C10 in Figure 5-4 contain basic examples of the @ROUND function. Because cell A3 contains the value 1234.567 and cell B3 contains the value 2, the function in cell C3

C3: @ROUND(A3,B3)

returns the value 1234.57. Since cell B4 contains the value 1, however, the function in cell C4, *@ROUND(A4,B4)*, returns the value 1234.6. Similarly, the function in cell C5, *@ROUND(A5,B5)*, returns the value 1235.

Although the *# of decimal places* argument of most @ROUND functions will be a positive number, it can be a negative number. A negative *# of decimal places* argument instructs 1-2-3 to "round" to the right of the decimal place. For instance, because cell B7 contains the value -2, the function *@ROUND(A7,B7)* in cell C7 returns the value 1200.

You can also use @ROUND to round negative numbers. For instance, cell A10 contains the value -1234.56. The function *@ROUND(A10,B10)* in cell C10 returns the value -1235. Remember, rounding a number up means rounding away from 0, no matter whether the number is positive or negative.

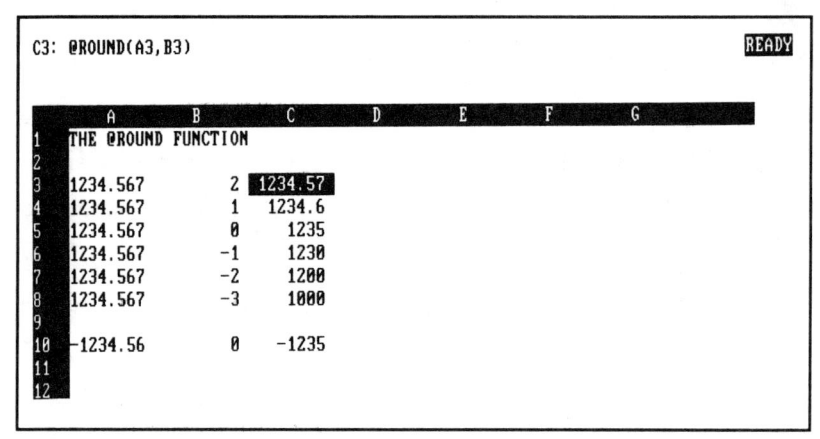

```
C3: @ROUND(A3,B3)                                          READY

         A           B          C         D        E        F        G
  1   THE @ROUND FUNCTION
  2
  3   1234.567        2      1234.57
  4   1234.567        1      1234.6
  5   1234.567        0      1235
  6   1234.567       -1      1230
  7   1234.567       -2      1200
  8   1234.567       -3      1000
  9
 10   -1234.56        0     -1235
 11
 12
```

FIGURE 5-4: The @ROUND function

The @INT Function

Like the @ROUND function, 1-2-3's @INT function can be used to adjust the number of decimal places in a value. Unlike @ROUND, however, which rounds values to a specified number of decimal places, @INT simply truncates a value to integer form. The form of this function is

@INT(*value*)

For example, cell B3 in Figure 5-5 contains the value 1234.567. The function in cell B5

B5: @INT(B3)

returns the integer value 1234.

TIP: USING @ROUND TO OVERCOME ADDITION ERRORS

In Chapter 4, you learned that assigning a format to a value changes the appearance of the value but not the value itself. For instance, if you assign the Fixed format with zero decimal places to a cell that contains the value 100.45, that value will be displayed as 100. The actual value in the cell will remain 100.45, however.

Figure A illustrates a problem that can arise from formatting values. Cells B3 and B4 in this worksheet both contain the value 100.45. Both cells have been assigned the Fixed format with two decimal places, so both cells display the value 100. Cell B6 in this worksheet contains the formula +B3+B4, which returns the value 200.90. Because this cell has also been given the Fixed format with two decimal places, this value is displayed as 201. The problem is that the formatted value in cell B6, 201, is not the sum of the formatted values in cells B3 and B4. Even though 1-2-3's math is correct, it appears to be wrong.

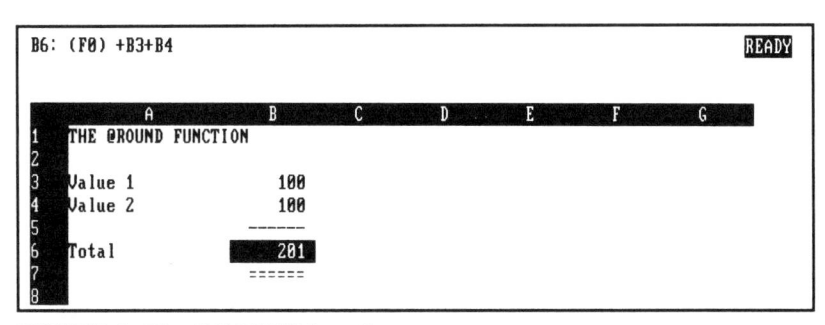

```
B6: (F0) +B3+B4                                                    READY

              A           B           C           D           E           F           G
 1    THE @ROUND FUNCTION
 2
 3    Value 1            100
 4    Value 2            100
 5                      ------
 6    Total              201
 7                      ======
 8
```

FIGURE A: The @ROUND function

If you use 1-2-3 very much, you've probably run across a similar problem. Fortunately, this problem is easy to solve. All you have to do is change the formula in cell B6 to

B6: @ROUND(B3,0)+@ROUND(B4,0)

The @ROUND functions in this formula round the values in B3 and B4 to zero decimal places. As a result, the values added by the formula agree with the values displayed in cells B3 and B4. This new formula will return the value 200, the "correct" sum for the values displayed in cells B3 and B4.

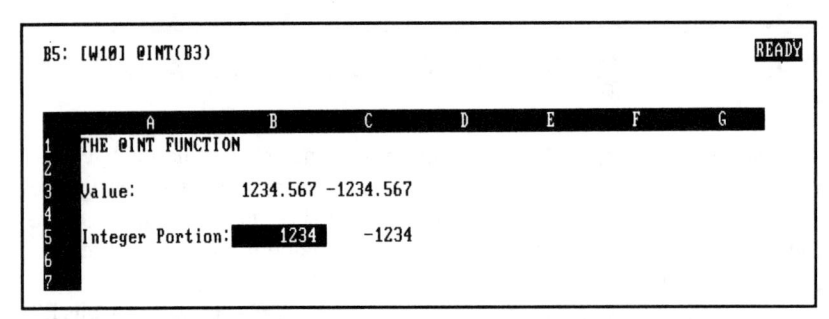

```
B5: [W10] @INT(B3)                                                    READY

         A          B          C          D          E          F          G
1  THE @INT FUNCTION
2
3  Value:        1234.567   -1234.567
4
5  Integer Portion:  1234       -1234
6
7
```

FIGURE 5-5: The @INT function

Notice the difference between this result and the result of the function @ROUND(A5,B5) in cell C5 in Figure 5-4. While the @ROUND function rounds the value to the nearest integer, the @INT function simply truncates the decimal portion of the number.

You can also use @INT to truncate negative numbers. For example, cell C3 in Figure 5-5 contains the value -1234.567. The function in cell C5, *@INT(B5)*, returns the value -1234.

Logarithmic Functions

1-2-3 features a group of three logarithmic functions that are of interest primarily to engineers and scientists. These functions—@LOG, @LN, and @EXP—allow you to work with base 10 and natural logarithms within a 1-2-3 worksheet.

The @LOG Function

1-2-3's @LOG function calculates the base 10 logarithm of a value. The base 10 log of a value is the power of 10 that equals that value. Since 10^2=100, for example, the base 10 log of 100 is 2. The form of the @LOG function is

@LOG(*value*)

The result of the function is the base 10 log of *value*.

Figure 5-6 shows an example of the @LOG function. Cell B3 in this worksheet contains the value 123. The function in cell B5

B5: @LOG(B3)

calculates the base 10 logarithm of the value in cell B3: 2.089905.

The @LN Function

In much the same way that the @LOG function calculates the base 10 logarithm of a value, 1-2-3's @LN function calculates the natural logarithm of a value. The natural, or base *e*, logarithm of a value is the power of the constant *e* (2.71828) that produces the original value. The form of this function is

@LN(*value*)

The result of the function is the natural log of *value*.

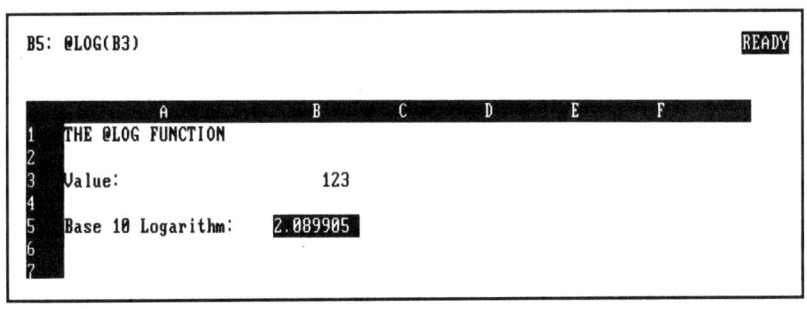

```
B5: @LOG(B3)                                              READY

              A           B         C         D         E         F
1    THE @LOG FUNCTION
2
3    Value:              123
4
5    Base 10 Logarithm:  2.089905
6
7
```

FIGURE 5-6: The @LOG function

Cell B5 in Figure 5-7 contains an example of the @LN function. This function

B5: @LN(B3)

computes the natural logarithm of the value 123: 4.812184.

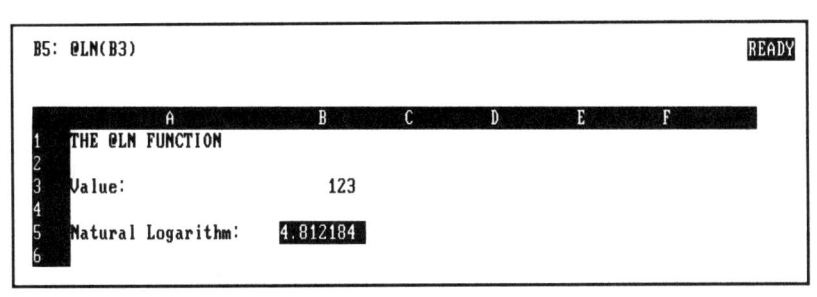

```
B5: @LN(B3)                                               READY

              A           B         C         D         E         F
1    THE @LN FUNCTION
2
3    Value:              123
4
5    Natural Logarithm:  4.812184
6
```

FIGURE 5-7: The @LN function

The @EXP Function

1-2-3's final geometric function, @EXP, is the inverse to the @LN function. The @EXP function has the form

@EXP(*value*)

The @EXP function raises the constant *e* to the power specified by *value*. For example, the function in cell B7 in Figure 5-8

B7: @EXP(B5)

returns the value 123, the value of *e* raised to the 4.812184 power.

```
B7: @EXP(B5)                                                    READY

          A              B         C         D         E       F
    1  THE @EXP FUNCTION
    2
    3  Value:           123
    4
    5  Natural Logarithm: 4.812184
    6
    7  Exponential       123
    8
    9
```

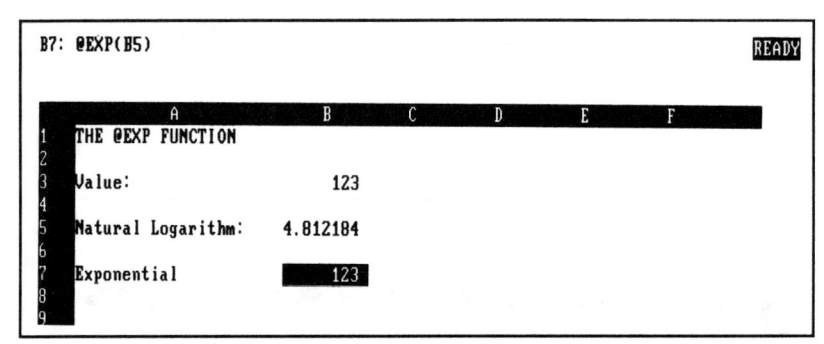

FIGURE 5-8: The @EXP function

Trigonometric Functions

Trigonometric functions compute common trigonometric values, such as the sine or cosine of an angle. This group contains eight functions: @PI, @SIN, @COS, @TAN, @ASIN, @ACOS, @ATAN, and @ATAN2.

The @PI Function

1-2-3's simplest trigonometric function, @PI, returns the value of the constant π, accurate to ten decimal places. The form of this function is simply @PI; it accepts no arguments. Whenever you enter this function into a cell, it will return the value 3.1415926536.

The @SIN, @COS, and @TAN Functions

1-2-3's @SIN, @COS, and @TAN functions return the sine, cosine, and tangent, respectively, of an angle. The forms of these functions are

@SIN(*angle*)
@COS(*angle*)
@TAN (*angle*)

where the single argument, *angle*, is the measure of an angle (in radians) whose sine, cosine, or tangent you want 1-2-3 to compute. This measure must be stated in radians, not in degrees. To convert an angle from degrees to radians, just multiply the number of degrees by .0175 (pi/180).

Cells B5 through B7 of the worksheet shown in Figure 5-9 contain examples of these functions. As you can see, cell B3 contains the value .523598—the radian measure of a 30-degree angle. Cell B5, which contains the function *@SIN(B3)*, returns the value .5—the sine of a 30-degree angle. Cell B6, which contains the function *@COS(B3)*, returns the value .866025—the cosine of a 30-degree angle. Cell B7, which contains the function *@TAN(B3)*, returns the value .577350—the tangent of that angle.

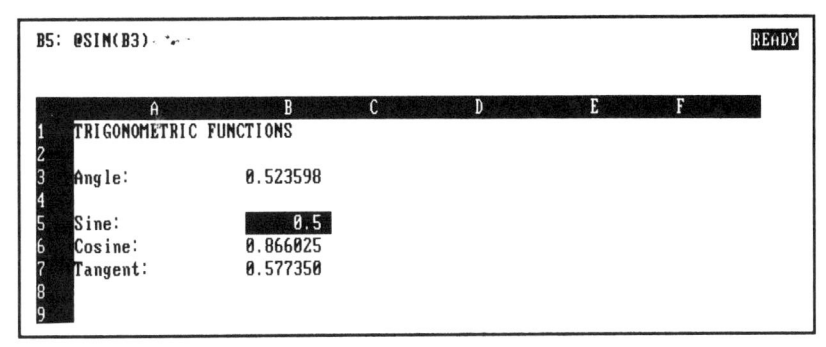

```
B5: @SIN(B3)                                                    READY

        A           B           C           D           E           F
1   TRIGONOMETRIC FUNCTIONS
2
3   Angle:      0.523598
4
5   Sine:          0.5
6   Cosine:     0.866025
7   Tangent:    0.577350
8
9
```

FIGURE 5-9: Trigonometric functions

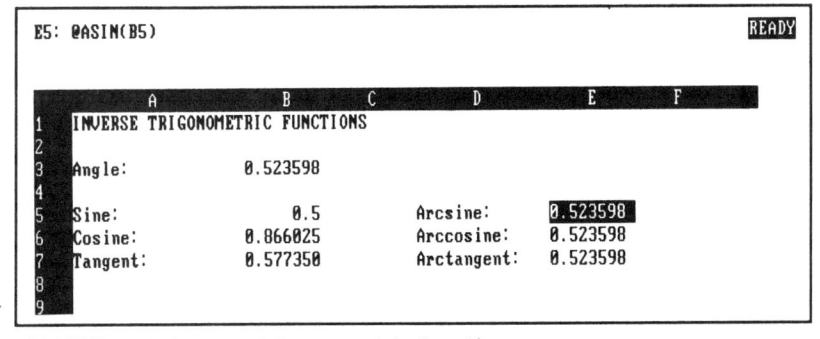

The Inverse Trigonometric Functions

As we just explained, 1-2-3's @SIN, @COS, and @TAN functions return the sine, cosine, and tangent, respectively, of the angle specified by their arguments. To complement these functions, 1-2-3 features four functions that perform the opposite task: they return an angle, given its sine, cosine, or tangent. These functions—@ASIN, @ACOS, @ATAN, and @ATAN2—are called arc functions.

The @ASIN, @ACOS, and @ATAN Functions

1-2-3's @ASIN, @ACOS, and @ATAN functions return the angle whose sine, cosine, or tangent, respectively, is specified by their argument. Cells E5 through E7 of the worksheet shown in Figure 5-10 contain examples of these functions. The function

E5: @ASIN(B5)

in cell E5 returns the angle (measured in radians) whose sine is returned by the @SIN function in cell B5. In a similar manner, the function *@ACOS(B6)* in cell E6 returns the angle whose cosine is returned by the @COS function in cell B6, and the function *@ATAN(B7)* in cell E7 returns the angle whose tangent is returned by the @TAN function in cell B7. Since the functions in the range B5..B7 act upon the value .523598 in cell B3, the functions in cells E5 through E7 return that same value.

```
E5: @ASIN(B5)                                                   READY

        A           B           C           D           E           F
1   INVERSE TRIGONOMETRIC FUNCTIONS
2
3   Angle:      0.523598
4
5   Sine:          0.5        Arcsine:       0.523598
6   Cosine:     0.866025      Arccosine:     0.523598
7   Tangent:    0.577350      Arctangent:    0.523598
8
9
```

FIGURE 5-10: Inverse trigonometric functions

The @ATAN2 Function

The @ATAN2 function computes a four-quadrant arctangent. Like 1-2-3's other three arc functions, this function returns the radian measure of an angle. Unlike the @ASIN, @ACOS, and @ATAN functions, however, the @ATAN2 function requires two arguments:

@ATAN2(*x-coordinate,y-coordinate*)

The function's arguments specify the absolute position of a point in terms of its relationship to the x- and y-axes, respectively. For example, suppose that you want to measure the four-quadrant arctangent defined by a point with an x-coordinate of 3 and a y-coordinate of -3. To do this, you would use the function

@ATAN2(3,-3)

which returns the value -.78539.

STATISTICAL FUNCTIONS

1-2-3's statistical functions give you an easy way to calculate statistics, such as the sum, average, and standard deviation, about the values in a worksheet. 1-2-3 offers seven statistical functions: @SUM, @COUNT, @AVG, @MIN, @MAX, @STD, and @VAR.

The Form of Statistical Functions

1-2-3's statistical functions all have similar forms. All of these functions can accept one or more arguments. If you want to calculate a statistic about a group of values that are adjacent to one another in a worksheet, you can use a single argument that specifies the dimensions of that range. To compute the sum of the values in cells A1, A2, and A3 of a worksheet, for example, you could use the function *@SUM(A1..A3)*. To compute the average of those same values, you could use the function *@AVG(A1..A3)*. You'll use this form of statistical functions most often.

You also can list each of the cells whose values you want to include in the statistic as separate arguments in the statistical function. For example, the function *@SUM(A1,A2,A3)* is equivalent to the function *@SUM(A1..A3)*. You can even use a mixture of range references and cell references as the arguments of a statistical function. For example, the functions *@SUM(A1..A2,A3)* and *@SUM(A1,A2..A3)* would return the same result as the function *@SUM(A1..A3)*. You usually will use multiple arguments only to compute statistics about the values in a discontinuous range, however. For example, you would use the function *@SUM(A1,B10,C20)* to add the values in cells A1, B10, and C20, or the function *@AVG(A1,B10,C20)* to compute the average of those values.

The @SUM Function

1-2-3's @SUM function allows you to sum values. This function provides an efficient alternative to the + operator for adding the values in a range. For example, suppose that you want to add the values in cells B4..B13 of the worksheet shown in Figure 5-11. To do this, you could enter the function

B15: @SUM(B4..B13)

in cell B15. As you can see, this function returns the value 866—the result of adding the values in this ten-cell range.

@SUM offers a more efficient way to add a group of values than does the + operator. For example, you could use the formula

+B4+B5+B6+B7+B8+B9+B10+B11+B12+B13

instead of an @SUM function to total the values in the range B4..B13. However, this formula is more cumbersome than the function and would take longer to enter.

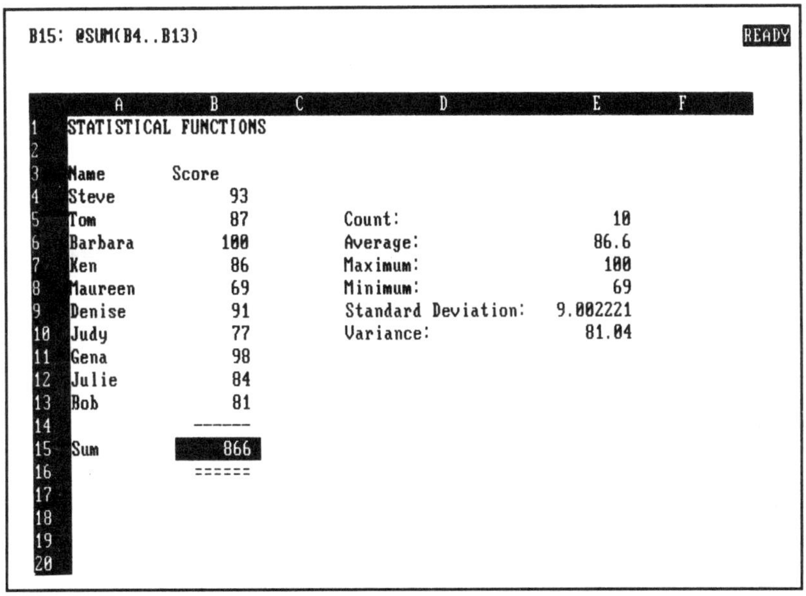

```
B15: @SUM(B4..B13)                                              READY

         A         B        C          D              E         F
  1  STATISTICAL FUNCTIONS
  2
  3  Name      Score
  4  Steve        93
  5  Tom          87      Count:                    10
  6  Barbara     100      Average:                86.6
  7  Ken          86      Maximum:                 100
  8  Maureen      69      Minimum:                  69
  9  Denise       91      Standard Deviation: 9.002221
 10  Judy         77      Variance:              81.04
 11  Gena         98
 12  Julie        84
 13  Bob          81
 14              ----
 15  Sum          866
 16              ====
 17
 18
 19
 20
```

FIGURE 5-11: Statistical functions

There are a couple of other advantages to using @SUM instead of the + operator. As you learned in Chapter 4, when you insert or delete rows or columns from within the range specified by the argument of an @SUM function, that range will shrink or grow to adjust for the insertion or deletion. For example, suppose you use the / Worksheet Insert Row command to insert a new row between rows 12 and 13 in the worksheet in Figure 5-11. The @SUM function in cell B16 (it was in B15 before the row was inserted) will change to *@SUM(B4..B14)*. If you instead used a formula to sum these values, it would be

+B4+B5+B6+B7+B8+B9+B10+B11+B12+B14

after the row is inserted. Although the formula has been adjusted to account for the new row (the reference to cell B13 has changed to B14), it does not automatically include the new cell B13. The flexibility of @SUM is a big plus.

Second, the argument of an @SUM function can refer to cells that contain labels and cells that contain values at the same time. For example, the function *@SUM(B3..B14)* in cell B15 in Figure 5-12, which refers to cells B3 through B14, returns the value 866. Because 1-2-3 assigns a value of 0 to cells that contain labels when they are referred to by an @SUM function, including them in the function's argument has no effect on the function's result.

RELEASE ► 2.2 ◄

►On the other hand, in 1-2-3 Release 2 the formula

+B3+B4+B5+B6+B7+B8+B9+B10+B11+B12+B13+B14

which seems to be identical to the function *@SUM(B3..B14)*, will return the value ERR in 1-2-3 Release 2. This occurs because the formula refers to cells that contain labels and to cells that contain values. (In 1-2-3 Release 1A, 2.01, and 2.2, this formula would return the value 866, just like the @SUM function.)◄

```
B15: @SUM(B3..B14)                                                    READY

         A          B          C              D              E         F
 1  STATISTICAL FUNCTIONS
 2
 3  Name       Score
 4  Steve         93
 5  Tom           87        Count:                          10
 6  Barbara      100        Average:                      86.6
 7  Ken           86        Maximum:                       100
 8  Maureen       69        Minimum:                        69
 9  Denise        91        Standard Deviation:       9.002221
10  Judy          77        Variance:                    81.04
11  Gena          98
12  Julie         84
13  Bob           81
14             ------
15  Sum           866
16             ======
17
18
19
20
```

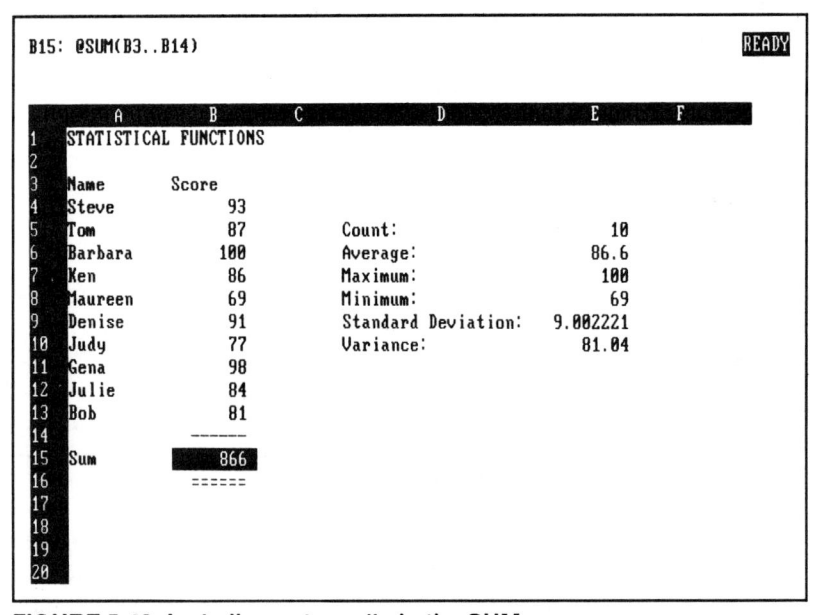

FIGURE 5-12: Including extra cells in the SUM range

TIP: INCLUDE EXTRA CELLS IN @SUM RANGES

We always make it a point to include an extra cell at the top and bottom of the argument range of our @SUM functions. This helps to make the functions more adaptable to insertions and deletions of rows.

For example, suppose you use the /Worksheet Insert Row command to add a new row to the worksheet between rows 3 and 4 in Figure 5-12. Figure A shows the resulting worksheet. The function in cell B16 is now *@SUM(B3..B15)*. If you entered a new value in cell B4, it would automatically be included in the total. By including cells B3 and B14 in the sum range, we allow the function to adjust for the insertion and deletion of rows before the first value or after the last value in the column.

```
B16: @SUM(B3..B15)                                              READY

         A          B        C              D              E         F
 1  STATISTICAL FUNCTIONS
 2
 3  Name        Score
 4
 5  Steve          93
 6  Tom            87        Count:                        10
 7  Barbara       100        Average:                      86.6
 8  Ken            86        Maximum:                     100
 9  Maureen        69        Minimum:                      69
10  Denise         91        Standard Deviation:    9.002221
11  Judy           77        Variance:                     81.04
12  Gena           98
13  Julie          84
14  Bob            81
15              -------
16  Sum            866
17              =======
18
19
20
```

FIGURE A: Inserting a row in the SUM range

Since @SUM assigns the value 0 to any labels in the range specified by its argument, including these cells in the sum range has no effect on the result of the function. By including them, however, you can make the @SUM function far more flexible.

The @COUNT Function

1-2-3's @COUNT function counts the number of nonblank cells in the range specified by its argument. For example, the function in cell E5 in Figure 5-11

    E5: @COUNT(B4..B13)

counts the number of entries in the range B4..B13 of the worksheet shown in Figure 5-11. Since all of the cells in this ten-cell range contain entries (in this case, values), this function returns the value 10.

Since @COUNT returns the number of nonblank cells in a range, for purposes of the @COUNT function, labels are the same as values. For example, the function *@COUNT(B4..B15)*, which includes the label-containing cell B14 and the @SUM function in cell B15, would return the value 12. The @COUNT function ignores blank cells, however. For example, the function *@COUNT(B4..B17)* returns the value 13 since there are only 13 nonblank cells in the range B4..B17.

There is one quirk of @COUNT that is worth pointing out. @COUNT will always return the result 1 if the range referred to by its argument is a single cell. For example, the function *@COUNT(A1)* will always return 1—even if cell A1 is blank. You'll want to keep this peculiarity in mind as you work with @COUNT.

The @AVG Function

1-2-3's @AVG function calculates the average (arithmetic mean) of a group of values. As you probably know, the mean of a group of values is simply the sum of those values divided by the number of values in the group. For example, the function in cell E6 in Figure 5-11

    E6: @AVG(B4..B13)

calculates the average of the values in the range B4..B13 and returns 86.6.

TIP: DON'T INCLUDE EXTRA CELLS IN AN @AVG RANGE

When you use @AVG to calculate the average of the values in a range, be sure not to include any cells that contain labels in that range. If you do, 1-2-3 will return an average that is erroneously low. As you recall, 1-2-3's @COUNT function counts cells that contain labels as well as cells that contain values, and the @SUM function assigns cells that contain labels a value of 0. @AVG works the same way. If you include a cell that contains a label in the range of an @AVG function, therefore, the average will be too low. For example, the function *@AVG(B3..B13)* would return the value 72.72, the result of dividing the sum of the entries in the range B3..B13, 866, by the number of entries in that range, 11. This result is wrong because the label in cell B3 increases the count of entries referred to by @AVG by 1, to 11, without increasing the sum.

TIP: USE ZEROS, NOT BLANKS

If you want to assign the value 0 to a cell in the range referred to by an @AVG function, put a zero in that cell. Just leaving the cell blank won't do the trick. If you leave the cell blank, it will not be counted by the @AVG function, and the resulting average will be too high. Just like @COUNT, the @AVG function does not count empty cells. When you include a blank cell in the range referred to by an @AVG function, that cell will be ignored. Entering a zero in the cell assures that it will be counted by @AVG and used to compute the average.

The @MAX and @MIN Functions

1-2-3's @MAX and @MIN functions return the highest and lowest values, respectively, from the range specified by their arguments. Cells E7 and E8 in the worksheet shown in Figure 5-11 contain examples of these functions. The function in cell E7

E7: @MAX(B4..B13)

returns the value 100—the highest value in this range. The function in cell E8

E8: @MIN(B4..B13)

returns the value 69—the lowest value in the range.

Unfortunately, 1-2-3 does not point out the location of the cell that contains the value returned by an @MAX or @MIN function. If you want to locate the source of the value, you must track it down yourself. In this case, the minimum value (69) comes from cell B8, and the maximum value (100) comes from cell B6.

When 1-2-3 evaluates an @MAX or @MIN function, it assigns the value 0 to any cell that contains a label or a string. Consequently, any @MIN function that acts upon a range that contains a label or string will return the value 0 (unless that range also contains a negative value). If you entered the function *@MIN(B3..B13)* in the worksheet in Figure 5-11, for example, it would return the value 0 because cell B3 contains a label. The @MAX and @MIN functions ignore blank cells.

The @STD and @VAR Functions

1-2-3's @STD and @VAR functions compute two important statistics: the standard deviation and the variance of the values in a range. Both the standard deviation and the variance measure the dispersion of the values in the specified range. (In fact, the two measures are very closely related since the standard deviation is simply the square root of the variance.)

The @STD Function

The @STD function computes the standard deviation of the values in the range you specify. The standard deviation of a group of values is a measure of the extent to which the values in that range are dispersed from the mean for that range. About 68% of the individuals in a normally distributed group will be within one standard deviation from the mean, and about 95% will be within two standard deviations from the mean. A low standard deviation indicates that values in the range are clustered closely around the mean. A high standard deviation means that the values are widely dispersed.

Cell E9 in Figure 5-11 contains an example of the @STD function. This function

E9: @STD(B4..B13)

returns the value 9.002221—the standard deviation of the values in the ten-cell range B4..B13.

The @VAR Function

1-2-3's @VAR function calculates the variance of a range of values. The statistical variance is simply the square of the standard deviation. To calculate the variance of the values in the range B4..B13, then, you could use the function in cell E10:

E10: @VAR(B4..B13)

Alternatively, you could use the formula *@STD(B4..B13)^2*. Both functions return the value 81.04.

FINANCIAL FUNCTIONS

Financial functions make it possible to perform sophisticated financial computations, such as calculating the monthly payment on a mortgage without developing long, complex formulas. 1-2-3 offers eleven financial functions: @PV, @NPV, @IRR, @PMT, @FV, @TERM, @CTERM, @RATE, @SLN, @DDB, and @SYD. For purposes of explanation, we will divide these functions into three groups: functions that analyze multiple cash flow investments, functions that analyze single cash flow investments, and functions that calculate depreciation.

Multiple Cash Flow Financial Functions

1-2-3's @PV, @NPV, @IRR, @PMT, @FV, and @TERM functions analyze investments that consist of a series of cash flows. These types of investments are called *annuities*. Although the cash flows in an annuity may be of the same or different amounts, they must occur at consistent increments of time. Examples of annuities include bonds, which produce periodic cash inflows in exchange for a single cash outflow (the amount required to purchase the bond) and most consumer loans, like auto loans and home mortgages, which involve periodic payments.

The @PV Function

@PV probably is 1-2-3's most-used financial function. This function calculates the present value of a stream of equally spaced constant cash flows. The form of this function is

@PV(*payments,rate,term*)

The first argument, *payments*, specifies the amount of equal payments generated by the annuity. The second argument, *rate*, specifies the discount rate. The third argument, *term*, specifies the number of cash flows that the annuity will pay.

An Example

Suppose you want to determine the present value of an investment that will pay you five equal yearly payments of $1000 beginning one year from today. Let's assume that 10% per year is the best rate you can earn elsewhere and thus is an appropriate discount rate. The worksheet shown in Figure 5-13 solves this problem. As you can see, cell B3 contains the value 1000 (the amount of each payment), cell B4 contains the value .10 (the discount rate), and cell B5 contains the value 5 (the number of periods). The function

B8: @PV(B3,B4,B5)

in cell B8 uses the values in these cells to calculate the present value of this investment: 3790.79. The result of this function indicates that you shouldn't pay more than $3790.79 for this investment opportunity.

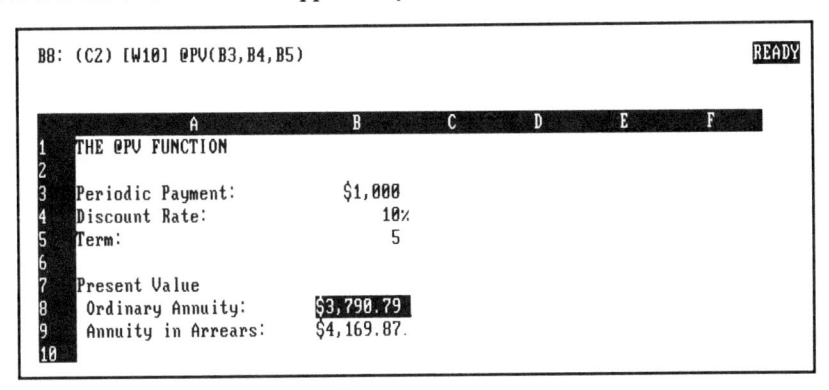

```
B8: (C2) [W10] @PV(B3,B4,B5)                                    READY

              A               B         C      D       E      F
1      THE @PV FUNCTION
2
3      Periodic Payment:     $1,000
4      Discount Rate:          10%
5      Term:                    5
6
7      Present Value
8         Ordinary Annuity:  $3,790.79
9         Annuity in Arrears: $4,169.87
10
```

FIGURE 5-13: The @PV function

Timing Assumptions

1-2-3's @PV function assumes that the first cash flow of the specified annuity occurs one period from the current date. This is the correct assumption for an ordinary annuity, like the one described above. In some situations, however, the first cash flow of an investment occurs on the date of the analysis, not one year from that date. This type of investment is called an *annuity due* or an *annuity in arrears*. The payments you make to a set-contribution savings plan (such as an IRA) are examples of this type of investment.

TIP: WHAT IS PRESENT VALUE ANALYSIS?

Present value analysis is a useful way of determining the attractiveness of an investment opportunity. The best way to understand present value is to consider a simple example. Suppose someone offers you an investment: He will pay you $1.03 in one year if you will give him $1.00 today. Is this an attractive investment? Probably not. Since you can invest your dollar at a rate of 5% per year at the local Savings and Loan, you can have about $1.05 in a year. All other things being equal, why would you invest your money at 3% when you can invest it at 5%?

Another way to look at this problem is to compute the present value of the $1.03 you have been promised. To compute the present value of an investment, you *discount* the cash inflows from that investment back to the present time. If the present value of the investment is greater than its price, it is an attractive investment.

The present value of an investment is based on three facts: the discount rate, the term of the investment, and the amounts of the payments. The discount rate is usually equal to the rate that the best alternative investment could earn. In this simple example, we have said that the best alternative investment can earn 5% per year, so the discount rate is 5%. To compute the present value of the $1.03 you've been promised, then, you'd use the formula

1.03/(1+.05)

This formula returns the value .98, which is the present value of $1.03 received one year from now, assuming a discount rate of 5%. Since the present value of the investment is less than its price—$1.00—this is not an attractive investment.

Another closely related tool for measuring the attractiveness of an investment is net present value analysis. The net present value of an investment is the present value of the cash inflows it will generate minus the present value of any cash outflows. Typically, there is only one cash outflow: the price you pay to buy the investment. If the net present value of an investment is greater than 0, it is an attractive investment. A net present value less than 0 indicates that you would be better off to place your money in an alternative investment.

To compute the net present value of our $1.03 investment, we would simply subtract the cost of the investment, $1.00, from the present value of the cash inflow, $.98. (Since the cost occurs today, it does not need to be discounted.) The result, -$.02, is the net present value of this investment. Since this number is less than 0, this is not an attractive investment.

Of course, these examples are trivial. Most investments are more complex and involve many cash flows. Thanks to 1-2-3's @PV and @NPV functions, however, computing the present value of even the most complex investments is simple.

Although the @PV function does not calculate the present value of an annuity due, you can modify this function to adjust for this alternative timing assumption. For example, suppose that the cash flow, rate, and term in cells B3, B4, and B5 of the worksheet shown in Figure 5-13 describe an investment that will generate five annual payments of $1000—one today, one a year from today, one two years from today, one three years from today, and one four years from today. To calculate the present value of this opportunity, you'd use the formula

B9: @PV(B3,B4,B5-1)+B3

in cell B9 in Figure 5-13. This formula calculates the present value over four years instead of five years, and then adds the first year's payment to the result. In other words, this adjusted PV formula does not discount the first year's payment of $1000 since that payment occurs today instead of one year in the future. As you can see, moving each cash flow ahead one period increases the present value of the investment by some $379.

TIP: WHAT IS THE PERIOD?

1-2-3 does not have any way to know whether the number you use as the rate argument in an @PV function is a monthly rate or an annual rate, or whether the number you use as the term argument is stated in weeks, months, or years. It simply uses the three arguments you supply to compute the present value of the *payments* at the periodic rate *rate* across *term* periods of time. This is also true for the @FV, @PMT, @NPV, and @TERM functions.

For this reason, it is important that the three arguments of the @PV function (and the @FV, @PMT, @NPV, and @TERM functions) are all based on the same period of time. If the cash flows occur monthly, for example, the *rate* argument should specify a monthly interest rate and the *term* argument should specify a number of months. If the arguments do not agree, then the function's result will be incorrect.

The @NPV Function

Like the @PV function, 1-2-3's @NPV function calculates the present value of a series of equally spaced cash flows. Unlike the @PV function, however, the @NPV function can compute the present value of a stream of unequal cash flows. The form of the @NPV function is

@NPV(*rate,range of cash flows*)

where *rate* is the periodic rate of interest and *range of cash flows* is a range that contains the cash flows that occur at each period during the term of the investment. The *range of cash flows* argument must be in the form of a range, such as B5..B8. Unlike 1-2-3's statistical functions, the @NPV function will not accept a series of cell references in place of this single range reference.

Because the @NPV function can analyze a stream of unequal cash flows, you can include negative flows in the range of the worksheet referred to by the *range of cash flows* argument. Typically, the first cash flow in a net present value analysis—the cash flow required to purchase the investment—will be negative. However, you also can use the @NPV function to calculate the simple present value of a stream of uneven positive cash flows.

An Example

As an example of this function, suppose that you want to calculate the net present value of the stream of cash flows contained in cells B5 through B8 of the worksheet in Figure 5-14 at a periodic rate of 12%. To do this, you would use the function in cell B11:

B11: @NPV(B3,B5..B8)

As you can see, this function returns the value 277.94. This positive net present value indicates that this investment is a better opportunity than the best available alternative.

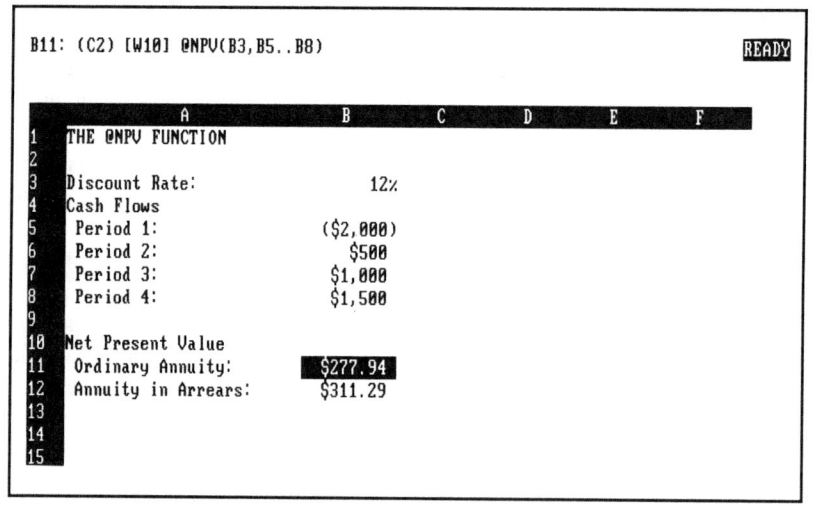

```
B11: (C2) [W10] @NPV(B3,B5..B8)                                    READY

            A                B          C        D        E        F
1    THE @NPV FUNCTION
2
3    Discount Rate:          12%
4    Cash Flows
5      Period 1:         ($2,000)
6      Period 2:            $500
7      Period 3:          $1,000
8      Period 4:          $1,500
9
10   Net Present Value
11     Ordinary Annuity:   $277.94
12     Annuity in Arrears: $311.29
13
14
15
```

FIGURE 5-14: The @NPV function

Timing Considerations

Like the @PV and @PMT functions, 1-2-3's @NPV assumes that the first cash flow occurs one period from the date of the analysis, the second cash flow occurs two periods from the date of the analysis, and so forth. When 1-2-3 evaluates the function in cell B11, then, it assumes that the $2000 outflow occurs not on the date of the analysis, but one year after the date of the analysis. Similarly, the first inflow ($500) occurs two years from the date of the analysis, the second inflow three years from the date of the analysis, and the third inflow four years from the date of the analysis.

To calculate a net present value that assumes that cash flows occur at the beginning of each period, you must adjust 1-2-3's basic @NPV formula. Specifically, you should use the @NPV function to calculate the present value of the second through last cash flows, then add the initial flow to the result. To calculate this correct net present value of the cash flows in cells B5 through B8 using the rate contained in B3, then, you would use the formula in cell B12:

B12: @NPV(B3,B6..B8)+B5

As you can see, this formula returns the value 311.29—approximately $33 more than the result of the original calculation. Both calculations return a value greater than 0, however, indicating that these are attractive investments.

TIP: USING @NPV TO COMPUTE PRESENT VALUE

You can also use the @NPV function to compute present value (as opposed to net present value). The advantage of @NPV over @PV is that @NPV can compute the present value of an unequal stream of cash flows.

For example, we've set up Figure A to analyze an investment that will pay $1000 at the end of the first year, $2000 at the end of the second year, and $3000 at the end of the third year. Cells B5 through B7 contain these values. The value in cell B3, .12, is the discount rate. Cell B10 contains the formula

B10: @NPV(B3,B5..B7)

The result of this function, 4622.59, is the present value of this stream of cash flows. Since @PV requires that all of the periodic cash flows be equal, you could not use that function to make this computation.

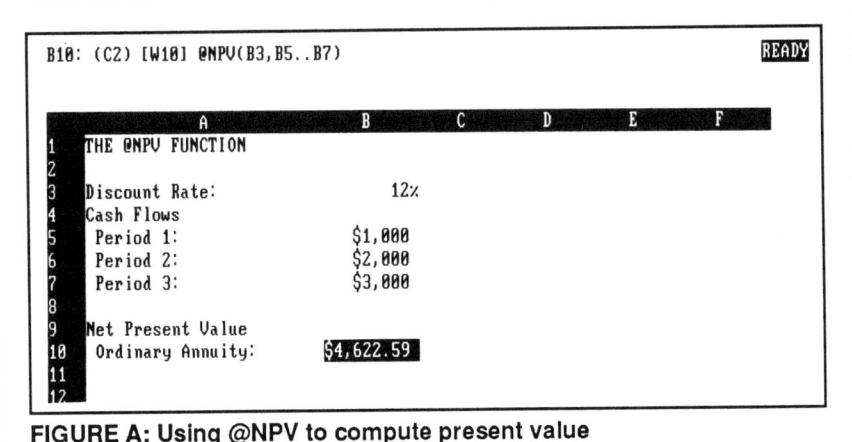

```
B10: (C2) [W10] @NPV(B3,B5..B7)                                    READY

            A              B         C         D         E         F
   1   THE @NPV FUNCTION
   2
   3   Discount Rate:        12%
   4   Cash Flows
   5     Period 1:        $1,000
   6     Period 2:        $2,000
   7     Period 3:        $3,000
   8
   9   Net Present Value
  10     Ordinary Annuity: $4,622.59
  11
  12
```

FIGURE A: Using @NPV to compute present value

The @IRR Function

1-2-3's @IRR function calculates the internal rate of return of an investment. The internal rate of return on an investment is the rate of return implied by its cost and stream of cash flows. The concepts of internal rate of return and net present value are closely related. Specifically, the internal rate of return is the rate of interest at which the net present value of an investment is zero. Another way to say this is that the IRR of an investment is that rate which makes the present value of the cash inflows from that investment exactly equal to the initial cash outflow.

To determine the attractiveness of an investment, you just compare the internal rate of return on that investment to the best alternative rate. Assuming equal risk, the alternative with the higher IRR is the better investment.

The form of the @IRR function is

@IRR(*rate guess,range of cash flows*)

The *rate guess* argument needs to be an approximation of the internal rate of return. 1-2-3 uses this guess as the starting point of its iterative process of calculating the IRR. The *range of cash flows* argument must be the range of the worksheet that contains the cash flows you want to analyze. The first value in this range must be negative, indicating a negative cash flow or investment.

Cell B10 of the worksheet in Figure 5-15 contains an example of this function. The function in this cell

B10: @IRR(B3,B5..B8)

returns the value .194377. This indicates that the implied rate of return for the stream of cash flows in the range B5..B8 is approximately 19%.

```
B10: (P4) [W10] @IRR(B3,B5..B8)                                    READY


           A                B         C         D         E         F
  1  THE @NPV FUNCTION
  2
  3  Guess Rate:           12%
  4  Cash Flows
  5    Period 1:       ($2,000)
  6    Period 2:          $500
  7    Period 3:        $1,000
  8    Period 4:        $1,500
  9
 10  Internal Rate of Return:  19.4377%
 11
 12
```

FIGURE 5-15: The @IRR function

When 1-2-3 calculates an @IRR function, it works in much the same way you would if you had to do the calculation by hand. It begins by calculating the net present value of the stream, using your guess as the discount rate. If the result is higher than 0, 1-2-3 chooses a higher rate and recalculates the NPV. If the result is lower than 0, then 1-2-3 chooses a lower rate and recalculates the NPV. 1-2-3 continues this iterative process until it pinpoints the rate that produces an NPV of 0. If 1-2-3 is able to find a rate that produces an NPV of less than .0000001 within 20 iterations, it returns that rate as the internal rate of return. If 1-2-3 is not able to achieve this result within 20 tries, it returns the value ERR. When this happens, you should specify a different guess and calculate the function again. (This problem arises very rarely.)

In this example, we used the discount rate from our previous net present value analysis (the value in cell B3) as the "guess" for the @IRR function. We could have used any value that is reasonably close to the final result, however.

The @IRR function uses the same timing assumption as the @NPV function. It calculates the internal rate of return as if the first cash flow occurred one year from the date of the analysis, and each subsequent cash flow occurred in one-year increments from that point. However, this assumption makes no difference in the outcome of the analysis. The result of an internal rate of return calculation would be the same no matter what timing assumption was used. Consequently, there is no need to adjust the @IRR function to account for different timing assumptions.

The @PMT Function

1-2-3's @PMT function calculates the periodic payment required to amortize (pay off) a loan. The form of this function is

@PMT(*amount borrowed,interest rate,term*)

where *amount borrowed* is the amount borrowed, *interest rate* is the periodic interest rate, and *term* is the number of periods over which you'll pay off the loan.

An Example

As an example of the use of the @PMT function, suppose you want to calculate the monthly payments on a 30-year, 10.5% APR, $100,000 mortgage. The worksheet shown in Figure 5-16 is set up for this calculation. Cell B3 contains the value 100000 (the amount borrowed), cell B4 contains the value .105 (the annual rate), and cell B5 contains the value 30 (the term of the loan, in years). The function

B8: @PMT(B3,B4/12,B5*12)

in cell B8 uses these values to calculate the monthly mortgage payments: $914.74. Because the payments occur on a monthly basis, we divided the annual rate by 12 to produce a monthly rate of interest. We multiplied the term of the loan in years by 12 for the same reason.

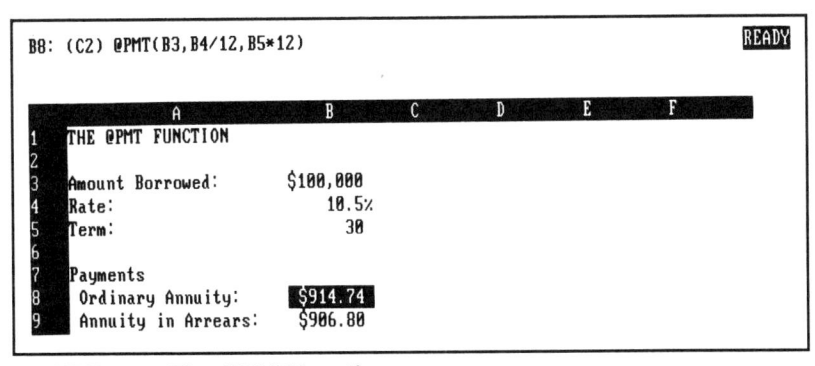

```
B8: (C2) @PMT(B3,B4/12,B5*12)                                    READY

         A                  B          C        D        E        F
1    THE @PMT FUNCTION
2
3    Amount Borrowed:    $100,000
4    Rate:                 10.5%
5    Term:                   30
6
7    Payments
8      Ordinary Annuity:   $914.74
9      Annuity in Arrears: $906.80
```

FIGURE 5-16: The @PMT function

Timing Assumptions

Like the @PV function, 1-2-3's @PMT function assumes that the payments required to amortize the principal amount start one period from the date of the analysis and occur at the end of each period thereafter. This assumption is correct for most installment loans, such as auto loans and home mortgages. In some cases, however, you may be required to make the first payment immediately. To correct for this alternative timing assumption, you must adjust the result of the @PMT function by dividing the @PMT function by the sum of 1 plus the periodic interest rate. In this case, then, you would use the formula in cell B9 of Figure 5-16:

B9: @PMT(B3,B4/12,B5*12)/(1+B4/12)

This formula returns the value 906.80—a difference of 7.94 per month.

The @FV Function

1-2-3's @FV function calculates the future value of an investment. The future value of an investment is its value at some specified future date, including all of the interest that it has earned up to that time. The form of the @FV function is

@FV(*payments,rate,term*)

where *payments* specifies the amount of the cash flows in the investment, *rate* specifies the rate of interest that you can earn on the investment, and *term* specifies the number of cash flows that will occur.

Suppose that you want to calculate the future value of contributing $2000 to an IRA each year for 30 years, given a 12% annual rate of interest. We have set up the worksheet shown in Figure 5-17 to perform this calculation. As you can see, cell B3 contains the value 2000—the amount of each contribution to the IRA. Cell B4 contains the value .12—the annual interest rate. Cell B5 contains the value 30—the term of the investment. The function in cell B8

B8: @FV(B3,B4,B5)

calculates the future value of the investment: 482655.

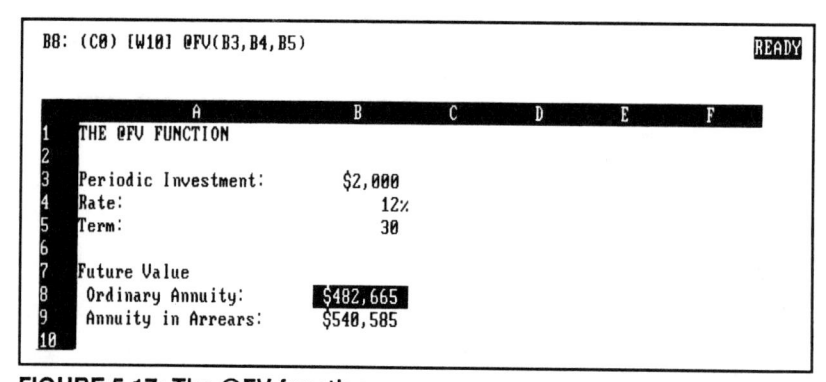

```
B8: (C0) [W10] @FV(B3,B4,B5)                                        READY

              A              B           C       D       E       F
 1     THE @FV FUNCTION
 2
 3     Periodic Investment:    $2,000
 4     Rate:                      12%
 5     Term:                       30
 6
 7     Future Value
 8       Ordinary Annuity:    $482,665
 9       Annuity in Arrears:  $540,585
10
```

FIGURE 5-17: The @FV function

Timing Assumptions

Like 1-2-3's other financial functions, the @FV function assumes that the first cash flow in the investment being analyzed occurs one period in the future—not on the date of the analysis. Unfortunately, this is not the assumption you are likely to want to use when performing this analysis. When 1-2-3 evaluates the function in cell B8, for example, it assumes that the first contribution of $2000 occurs not at the time of the analysis, but rather one year from that point. It is relatively easy to adjust this function to match the up-front timing assumption, however. To do this, just calculate the future value over one more period than you normally would, and then subtract an undiscounted payment from that result. In this case, you would use the formula in cell B9 in Figure 5-17

    B9: @FV(B3,B4,B5+1)-B3

As you can see, this formula returns the result 540585. Alternatively, you could use the formula *@FV(B3,B4,B5)*(1+B4)*, which returns the same result.

The @TERM Function

The @TERM function calculates the number of periods required for a stream of equal, evenly spaced investments to compound to a target amount, given a constant rate of interest. (This function is not available in Release 1A.) The form of this function is

    @TERM(*payment,rate,target value*)

where *payment* specifies the amount of each equal periodic investment, *rate* specifies the periodic rate of interest, and *target value* specifies the amount of money you want to have at some point in the future.

As you can see, the @TERM function is closely related to the @FV function. The @FV function computes a future value, given a rate of interest, a number of periods, and the amount of each payment. The @TERM function computes the number of periods, given a rate of interest, the amount of each payment, and a future value.

For example, suppose you want to determine how many years it would take for contributions of $2000 per year to an IRA to grow to $1,000,000, given a 12% rate of interest. We have set up the worksheet shown in Figure 5-18 to solve this problem. In cell B3, we have entered the amount to be invested each period: 2000. In cell B4, we have entered the annual rate: .12. Cell B5 contains the value 1000000—the target amount. In cell B8, we have entered the function

    B8: @TERM(B3,B4,B5)

which returns the value 36.27390411. This value indicates that it will take a little over 36 years for annual contributions of $2000 to compound to a value of $1,000,000.

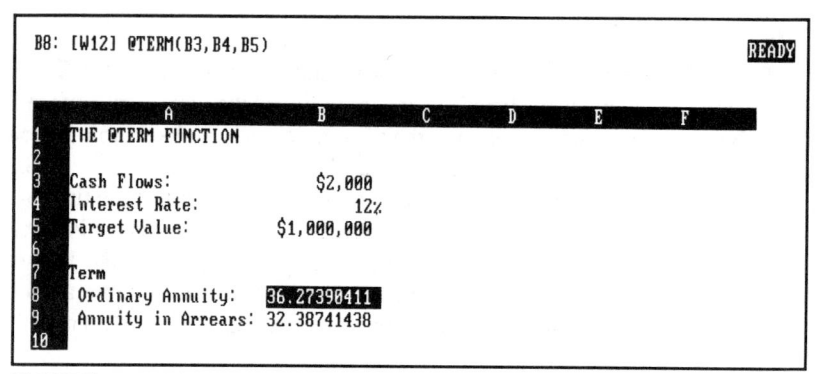

```
B8: [W12] @TERM(B3,B4,B5)                                          READY

              A              B           C         D         E        F
    1   THE @TERM FUNCTION
    2
    3   Cash Flows:          $2,000
    4   Interest Rate:          12%
    5   Target Value:    $1,000,000
    6
    7   Term
    8     Ordinary Annuity:  36.27390411
    9     Annuity in Arrears: 32.38741438
   10
```

FIGURE 5-18: The @TERM function

Timing Assumptions

Like 1-2-3's other financial functions, the @TERM function assumes that the cash flows being analyzed occur at the end of each period and that the first cash flow occurs at the end of the first period. Consequently, the @TERM function in cell B13 returns a value that is higher than it would be if it assumed that the first cash flow occurred on the date of the analysis. Fortunately, it is easy to modify the @TERM function to fit this assumption. To do this, just divide the result of the function by the sum of 1 plus the periodic rate. For example, the formula in B9

    B9: @TERM(B3,B4,B5)/(1+B4)

calculates the number of periods required for our example investment to grow to $1,000,000, assuming that the first contribution occurs on the day of the analysis. As you can see, this formula returns the value 32.38741438—about four years less than the result returned by the ordinary @TERM function.

Single Cash Flow Financial Functions

The six financial functions that we have discussed so far analyze annuities—investments that involve series of cash flows. Two other financial functions—@CTERM and @RATE—analyze investments that involve only a single cash flow. (These functions are not available in 1-2-3 Release 1A.) Investments of this type include a purchase of stock that is not expected to pay dividends, or the purchase of a work of art. In either of these cases, you would invest a lump sum of money at one time and withdraw it at another. Unlike most of 1-2-3's other financial functions, the @CTERM and @RATE functions are not affected by timing considerations.

The @CTERM Function

1-2-3's @CTERM function calculates the number of periods required for a single lump-sum investment to compound to a target value, given a fixed rate of interest. The form of this function is

@CTERM(*rate,target amount,starting amount*)

where *rate* specifies the fixed periodic rate of interest, *target amount* specifies the desired future value, and *starting amount* specifies the amount invested.

As an example of this function, suppose that you want to determine how many years it will take for $1000, invested at 12% per year, to grow to a value of $10,000. We have set up this problem in the worksheet shown in Figure 5-19. As you can see, cell B3 contains the value .12—the fixed rate of return. Cell B4 contains the value 10000—the target amount. Cell B5 contains the value 1000—the lump sum invested. The function

B7: @CTERM(B3,B4,B5)

in cell B7 uses the values in these cells to compute the result 20.31776—the number of years required for the initial amount to grow to the target.

```
B7: @CTERM(B3,B4,B5)                                        READY

           A            B         C        D        E        F
 1   THE @CTERM FUNCTION
 2
 3   Rate:               12%
 4   Target Amount:   $10,000
 5   Starting Amount:  $1,000
 6
 7   Periods Required: 20.31776
 8
 9
```

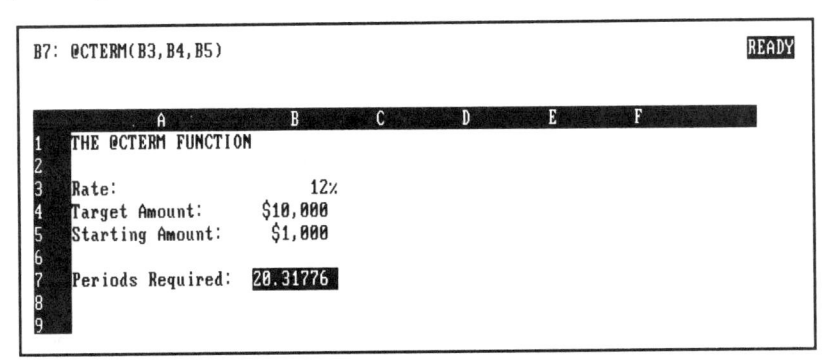

FIGURE 5-19: The @CTERM function

The @RATE Function

1-2-3's @RATE function calculates the periodic rate of interest required to compound a lump-sum investment to a target amount over a fixed number of periods. The form of this function is

@RATE(*target amount,initial amount,term*)

where *target amount* specifies the target amount (the desired future value of the investment), *initial amount* specifies the lump sum invested, and *term* specifies the number of periods over which the investment will compound.

For example, suppose you want to know the rate of return that would be required to increase an investment of $1000 to $10,000 in only ten years. We've set up Figure 5-20 to make this computation. Cell B3 contains the value 10000—the target amount. Cell B4 contains the value 1000—the amount of the initial investment. Cell B5 contains the value 10—the number of periods over which the investment will compound. Cell B7 contains the function

B7: @RATE(B3,B4,B5)

The result of this function—.258925—indicates that the investment will have to earn a return of nearly 26% to reach a total value of $10,000 in just ten years.

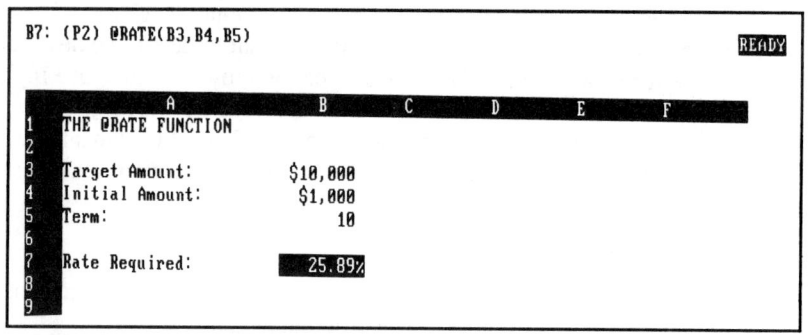

FIGURE 5-20: The @RATE function

Depreciation Functions

1-2-3 includes one more group of financial functions that provide convenient ways to calculate depreciation. The three functions in this group— @SLN, @DDB, and @SYD—each calculate depreciation according to a different method. The @SLN function calculates straight-line depreciation, the @DDB function calculates depreciation by the double-declining balance method, and the @SYD function calculates depreciation by the sum-of-the-years-digits method. (These functions are not available in 1-2-3 Release 1A.)

The worksheet that is shown in Figure 5-21 demonstrates these three functions. Cell B3 contains the value 1000, the depreciable value of an asset. Cell B4 contains the value 100, the salvage value of the asset. Cell B5 contains the value 5, the life of the asset.

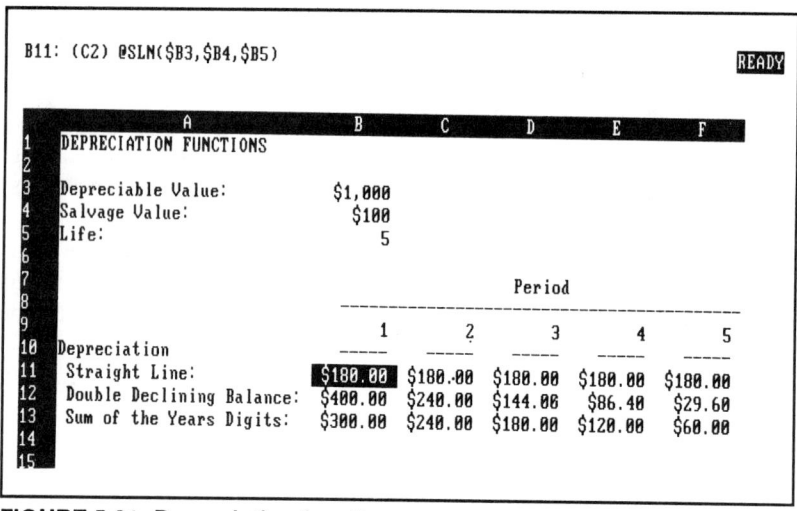

FIGURE 5-21: Depreciation function

Unfortunately, the methods of depreciation calculated by these functions have, for the most part, been replaced by the Accelerated Cost Recovery System of depreciation (ACRS). While you can create formulas that compute ACRS depreciation, 1-2-3 does not offer functions that will make the required computations automatically.

The @SLN Function

1-2-3's @SLN function calculates the straight-line depreciation for an asset. The form of this function is

@SLN(*cost of asset,salvage value,life of asset*)

The *cost of asset* argument specifies the depreciable value of the asset. The *salvage value* argument specifies the value of the asset at the end of its depreciable life. The *life of asset* argument specifies the life of the asset.

Cells B11 through F11 in Figure 5-21 contain examples of this function. The function in cell B11

B11: @SLN($B3,$B4,$B5)

computes the first-year straight-line depreciation for an asset with a $1000 depreciable value, a $100 salvage value, and a five-year life: $180.00. Since under the straight-line method, the depreciation expense is the same for all periods in the life of the asset, the functions in cells C11 through F11, which compute the depreciation for the second through fifth years in the asset's life, return the same result. (We used mixed references in the formula in cell B11 so that we could copy it into the range C11..F11.)

The @DDB Function

1-2-3's @DDB function calculates depreciation using the double-declining balance method. When you use the double-declining balance method, the depreciation expense for the first period will be higher than for the second period, the depreciation expense for the second period will be higher than for the third period, and so forth. Consequently, double-declining balance is called an *accelerated* depreciation method.

Because the double-declining depreciation method produces a different depreciation expense for each period during the life of an asset, 1-2-3's @DDB function requires an extra argument, as shown below:

@DDB(*cost of asset,salvage value,life of asset,current period*)

The first three arguments of this function are the same as the three arguments of the @SLN function. The fourth argument, *current period*, specifies the period for which you want to calculate the depreciation.

Cells B12 through F12 in Figure 5-21 contain examples of this function. The function in cell B12

B12: @DDB($B3,$B4,$B5,B9)

calculates the first-year double-declining balance depreciation for a $1000 asset with a $100.00 salvage value and a five-year life. As you can see, this function returns the value 400.00—significantly greater than the 180.00 returned by the @SLN function in cell B11. The function in cell C12, *@DDB($B3,$B4,$B5,C9)*, computes the second-year depreciation for this asset: $240.00.

The @SYD Function

1-2-3's third depreciation function, @SYD, calculates depreciation by the sum-of-the-years-digits method. Like the double-declining balance method, sum-of-the-years-digits is an accelerated method of depreciation. Consequently, the @SYD function requires four arguments, as shown below:

@SYD(*cost of asset,salvage value,life of asset,current period*)

The order and purpose of these four arguments is the same as for @DDB.

Cells B13 through F13 in Figure 5-21 contain examples of the use of the @SYD function. The function in cell B13

B13: @SYD($B3,$B4,$B5,B9)

computes the first-year depreciation for a $1000 asset with a salvage value of $100.00 and a life of five years. The result, 300.00, indicates that the sum-of-the-years-digits method does not accelerate depreciation quite as much as the double-declining balance method. The function in cell C13, *@SYD($B3,$B4,$B5,C9)*, computes the second-year depreciation for this asset: $240.00.

LOOKUP FUNCTIONS

1-2-3 features four functions that we call *lookup* functions: @CHOOSE, @INDEX, @VLOOKUP, and @HLOOKUP. These functions "look up" a value or string from a list or range. Unlike some other 1-2-3 functions, which make it easier to perform tasks that you could do with a complex formula, these functions let you do things within 1-2-3 that you simply could not do otherwise.

The @CHOOSE Function

The simplest lookup function, the @CHOOSE function, allows 1-2-3 to select a result from a list, based on the position of the result in that list. The form of this function is

@CHOOSE(*offset,item 1,item 2,item 3,...item n*)

where *item 1,item 2,item 3,...item n* is the list of results from which 1-2-3 will choose, and *offset* specifies the position within that list of the item you want to choose. The items in the list may be literal strings, literal values, cell references, other functions or formulas, or a mixture of these types of entries. The individual elements in the list must be separated from one another by commas.

The *offset* argument may be a literal value, a reference to a cell that contains or returns a value, or a formula or function that returns a value. This argument must specify a value between 0 and *n-1*, where *n* is the number of items in the list. The offset argument specifies the offset, or position relative to the first item, of the item in the list you want the function to return. The first item in the list has an offset of 0, the second item has an offset of 1, and so on. If you specify an offset of 0, 1-2-3 will choose the first item from the list, but if you specify an offset of 1, 1-2-3 will choose the second item from the list. If you specify an offset of $n-1$, 1-2-3 will choose the last item from the list. If you specify an offset value outside of the range from 0 to $n-1$, the function will return the result ERR.

Cell B5 of the worksheet shown in Figure 5-22 contains an example of the @CHOOSE function. This function

B5: @CHOOSE(B3,E1,E2,E3,E4,E5)

returns the value 12345 from cell E4. Since cell B3 (the offset argument) contains the value 3, 1-2-3 selects the item from the list with an offset of 3. In this case, the argument with an offset of 3 is the cell reference E4, so 1-2-3 returns the value from that cell: 12345.

```
B5: @CHOOSE(B3,E1,E2,E3,E4,E5)                                    READY

        A          B         C         D         E         F         G         H
1    THE @CHOOSE FUNCTION                                  2
2                                                         55
3    Offset:            3                                 35
4                                                      12345
5    Result:        12345                                100
6
7
```

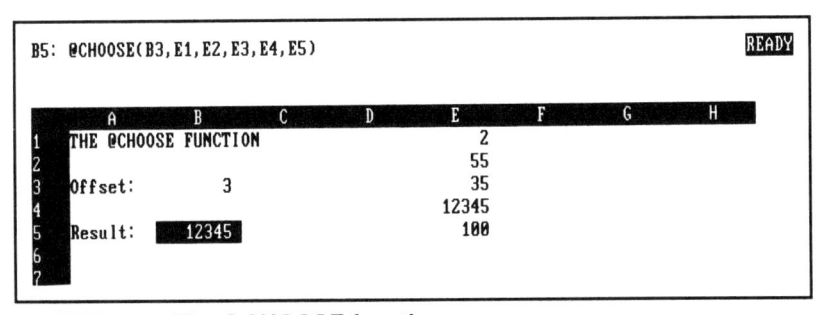

FIGURE 5-22: The @CHOOSE function

Although we used cell references as the arguments for the first @CHOOSE example, you are not required to do so. For example, the functions

@CHOOSE(3,E1,E2,E3,E4,E5)
@CHOOSE(3,2,55,35,12345,100)

return the same result as the function in cell B5 of Figure 5-22. You will often use literal values as the arguments of an @CHOOSE function.

In 1-2-3 Release 2, 2.01, and 2.2, you can also use @CHOOSE to look up strings or labels from a list. For example, cell B5 in Figure 5-23 contains the function

B5: @CHOOSE(B3,E1,E2,E3,E4,E5)

Notice that cells E1 through E5 in this figure contain the labels *John, Mary, Sally, Steve,* and *Mike*. Since the offset argument in cell B3, 2, tells the @CHOOSE function to return the entry from the cell in the list with an offset of 2, the function returns the string *Sally*.

```
B5: @CHOOSE(B3,E1,E2,E3,E4,E5)                                READY

        A         B         C         D         E         F         G         H
1    THE @CHOOSE FUNCTION                      John
2                                              Mary
3    Offset:       2                           Sally
4                                              Steve
5    Result:    Sally                          Mike
6
7
```

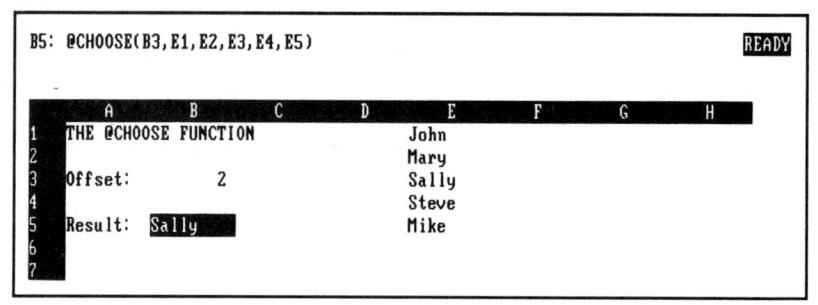

FIGURE 5-23: The @CHOOSE function

Just as you can use literal values as the arguments for numeric @CHOOSE functions, you can use literal strings as the arguments for your string @CHOOSE functions. If you do this, however, each of the strings must be enclosed in quotes, like this:

@CHOOSE(B3,"John","Mary","Sally","Steve","Mike")

Even though you can use strings as the item arguments in an @CHOOSE function, you must use a value or a reference to a cell that contains a value as the offset argument.

The @INDEX Function

@INDEX is another of 1-2-3's lookup functions. Unlike the @CHOOSE function, which locates a result from a one-dimensional list based on a single offset argument, the @INDEX function locates a result from a rectangular range of cells, based on both vertical and horizontal offset arguments. The form of this function is

@INDEX(*range,column offset,row offset*)

where *range* specifies the rectangular range of cells from which you want 1-2-3 to select a result, *column offset* specifies the column of the range that contains the result, and *row offset* specifies the row of the range that contains the result. The *range* argument may be either a range reference (like A1..B5) or a range name (like TABLE). The column and row offset arguments may be literal values, references to cells that contain or return values, or formulas or functions that return values. These arguments represent the offset, or position relative to the upper-left corner of the range, of the item you want to look up. 1-2-3 considers the first row and the first column in the range to have an offset of 0.

Cell B6 of the worksheet shown in Figure 5-24 contains an example of the @INDEX function. This function

B6: @INDEX(D2..G6,B3,B4)

returns the value 456 from cell E5. Since the column offset argument is a reference to cell B3, and B3 contains the value 1, 1-2-3 looks in column E—the column with an offset of 1 relative to the first column in the range. Since the row offset argument is a reference to cell B4, which contains the value 3, 1-2-3 looks in row 5—the row with an offset of 3 relative to the first row. Because cell E5 is at the intersection of the second column and fourth row of the index range, 1-2-3 returns the value 456 from that cell.

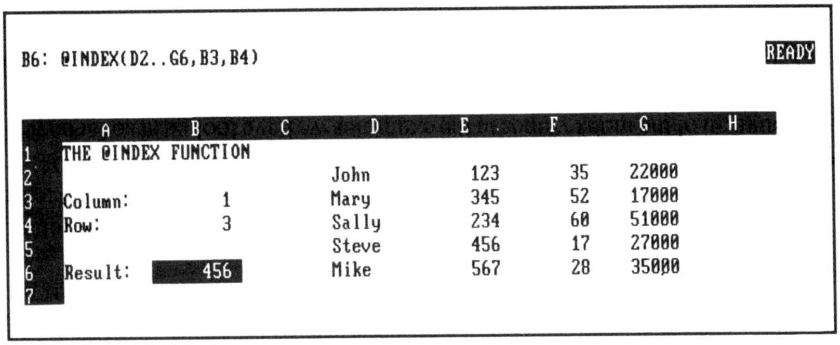

```
B6: @INDEX(D2..G6,B3,B4)                                          READY

        A          B       C       D       E       F       G       H
  1  THE @INDEX FUNCTION
  2                              John    123    35     22000
  3  Column:       1              Mary    345    52     17000
  4  Row:          3              Sally   234    60     51000
  5                              Steve   456    17     27000
  6  Result:      456             Mike    567    28     35000
  7
```

FIGURE 5-24: The @INDEX function

As with @CHOOSE, you can use @INDEX to look up strings and labels. For example, if you change the function in cell B6 to *@INDEX(D2..G6,0,3)*, then it will return the string *Steve*.

The @VLOOKUP and @HLOOKUP Functions

@VLOOKUP and @HLOOKUP are probably the most commonly used lookup functions. These two functions allow you to use a key value or string to look up an entry from a table that you have built in the worksheet. Although these functions are very similar, they are easier to understand if they are tackled one at a time. We'll begin with the @VLOOKUP function, which we'll use to explain the general principles of table lookups. After we've covered @VLOOKUP, we'll explain @HLOOKUP.

The @VLOOKUP Function

The form of 1-2-3's @VLOOKUP function is

@VLOOKUP(*key entry,table range,offset*)

The first argument, *key entry*, specifies the value 1-2-3 will look up in the table. The second argument, *table range*, must be the coordinates or name of the range that contains the entries you want to look up. The final argument, *offset*, specifies the column of the table that contains the function's result.

Lookup Tables

The @VLOOKUP function looks up values from a table you have built in the worksheet. The location of the table is defined by the function's *table range* argument. The lookup table referred to by the *table range* argument must include at least two partial columns. In 1-2-3 Releases 2, 2.01, and 2.2, the entries in the table range may be values or labels, or references, formulas, or functions that return values or labels. (In 1-2-3 Release 1A, the entries in the table range must be values or references, formulas, or functions that return values. If the table range includes labels, those labels will be assigned the value 0 by the @VLOOKUP function.)

@VLOOKUP works by comparing the key entry argument to the values in the leftmost column of the table range. The entries in this column are sometimes called the compare values or the index values, and this first column is sometimes called the index column. In 1-2-3 Releases 2, 2.01, and 2.2, the key entry and the index values may be labels or values. If the key entry is a value, all of the entries in the index column also should be values. If the key entry is a label, or a string, then all of the entries in the index column should be labels. Because the way that 1-2-3 evaluates an @VLOOKUP function depends on whether the key entry is a value or a label, we'll discuss those two cases separately. (In 1-2-3 Release 1A, the key entry and the index values must be values.)

Numeric Lookups

The worksheet shown in Figure 5-25 contains an example of an @VLOOKUP function that uses a value as its key entry. This function

B6: @VLOOKUP(B3,D3..F7,B4)

returns the value 31 from cell E4. Here's how it works: 1-2-3 uses the key entry to determine which row of the table contains the function's result. To determine this, 1-2-3 searches the index column for the first value that is greater than the key value. The result of the function will be in the row of the table immediately *above* the row that contains the first index value that is greater than the key value.

In this case, 1-2-3 begins evaluating the @VLOOKUP function by searching down the index column (cells D3 through D7 in this example) for the first value that exceeds the key entry value. The key entry in this example is a reference to cell B3, which contains the value 3. Cell D5 is the first cell in the index column of the lookup table that contains a value greater than 3. Therefore, 1-2-3 identifies the row above cell D5—row 4—as the row that contains the result of the function.

Once 1-2-3 has identified the row that contains the result, it uses the offset argument to determine which column contains the result. The first column of the table (the index column) has an offset of 0, the column immediately to the right of this column has an offset of 1, and so on. In this case, the offset of 1 tells 1-2-3 to look in the second column in the table range—column E—for the result. The result of the function is in cell E4. Because cell E4 contains the value 31, the function returns that value.

Another Example

It is important that you understand that 1-2-3 does not look for an exact match between the key value and one of the values in the index column. For example, if you replaced the value 3 in cell B3 of the worksheet shown in Figure 5-25 with the value 4, the function in cell B6 still would return the value 31 from cell E4. Once again, 1-2-3 begins evaluating this function by searching down the index column for the first value that exceeds the key value. Although the key value in cell B3 is now 4, the value in cell

D5, 5, is still the first index value that is greater than the key value. Since the result of the function is in the row above the the first row that contains an index value greater than the key value, once again 1-2-3 identifies row 4 as the row that contains the function's result. Since the offset argument in cell B4, 1, has not changed, the function still returns the entry from cell E4—the value 31.

```
B6: @VLOOKUP(B3,D3..F7,B4)                                    READY

         A            B         C        D        E        F        G
    THE @VLOOKUP FUNCTION
1
2
3   Key Value:         3                  1       32      35000
4   Offset:            1                  3       31      32000
5                                         5       28      17000
6   Result:           31                  7       54      65000
7                                         9       42      43000
8
```

FIGURE 5-25: The @VLOOKUP function

Rules

Since the result of a numeric @VLOOKUP function is determined by locating the first value in the index column that is greater than the key value, it is important that the values in the index column are in ascending numeric order. Even though 1-2-3 can evaluate an @VLOOKUP function even if the values in the index column of its table are not in ascending order, the results usually aren't very useful.

The worksheet shown in Figure 5-26 demonstrates such a situation. As you can see, this worksheet is set up in much the same way as the one shown in Figure 5-25. In fact, both worksheets have the same function in cell B6: *@VLOOKUP(B3,D3..F7,B4)*. Because the values in the key column of the table range are not arranged in ascending order, however, the results of these two functions are not the same.

```
B6: @VLOOKUP(B3,D3..F7,B4)                                    READY

         A            B         C        D        E        F        G
    THE @VLOOKUP FUNCTION
1
2
3   Key Value:         3                  1       32      35000
4   Offset:            1                  9       42      43000
5                                         7       54      65000
6   Result:           32                  5       28      17000
7                                         3       31      32000
8
9
```

FIGURE 5-26: The @VLOOKUP function

When 1-2-3 evaluates this function, it begins at the top of the index column (cell D3) and searches for the first value that is greater than the key, in this case, the value 9 in cell D4. Consequently, 1-2-3 determines that the result of the function is in row 3. Since the offset argument is 1, 1-2-3 returns the value 32 from cell E3. Because the values in the index column are not arranged in ascending order, 1-2-3 stops searching before it finds the correct index value, 3. Remember—when the key entry is a value, @VLOOKUP does not look for an exact match between the key value and an index value.

It is also important that no index value be repeated in a table. If two different rows in the same table have the same index value, then 1-2-3 will be unable to look up data from one or the other of those rows. Always be sure that there are no duplicate values in the index column of your lookup tables.

Other Things to Know

If the key value you specify is less than the first value in the index column, the @VLOOKUP function will return the value ERR. For example, the function in cell B6 in Figure 5-25, *@VLOOKUP(B3,D3..F7,B4)*, would return the value ERR if you entered a value less than 1 into cell B3.

If the key value you specify is greater than the largest value in the index column, @VLOOKUP will assume that the result of the function is in the last row of the table. For example, if you enter the value 10 (or any value greater than 9) in cell B3 in Figure 5-25, the function *@VLOOKUP(B3,D3..F7,B4)* will return the value 42 from cell E7.

The @VLOOKUP function will also return the value ERR if you specify an offset less than 0 or greater than the number of columns in the range, less one. For example, the function *@VLOOKUP(B3,D3..F7,B4)* would return the value ERR if you entered a value greater than 3 or less than 0 into cell B4.

If the offset argument in an @VLOOKUP function is 0, the function will return the appropriate value from the index column. If you changed the entry in cell B4 to 0, the function *@VLOOKUP(B3,D3..F7,B4)* would return the value 3 from cell D4.

Although all of the index values in the examples we have looked at so far have been positive, you can also use negative values in the index column. As always, the values in the index column should be arranged in ascending order: negative values first, followed by positive values.

Text Lookups

In 1-2-3 Releases 2, 2.01, and 2.2, the entries in the table range can be either values or labels, or a combination of values and labels. For example, Figure 5-27 displays a modified version of the lookup table from Figure 5-25. Notice that column E now contains the labels *'Doug*, *'Steve*, and so on. The function in cell B6

B6: @VLOOKUP(B3,D3..G7,B4)

returns the string *Steve*. Just as before, 1-2-3 uses the key value in cell B3 and the offset in cell B4 to determine that the result of the function is in row 4, the second row in the table range, and column E, the column with an offset of 1. Since cell E4 contains a label, the result of the function is a string—*Steve*. If you were to try to recreate this example in 1-2-3 Release 1A, the function would return the result ERR.

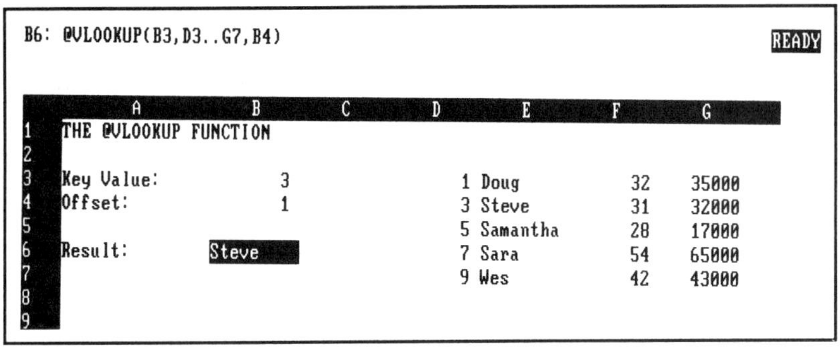

```
B6: @VLOOKUP(B3,D3..G7,B4)                                           READY

         A          B          C          D          E          F          G
   1  THE @VLOOKUP FUNCTION
   2
   3  Key Value:        3                     1 Doug         32      35000
   4  Offset:           1                     3 Steve        31      32000
   5                                          5 Samantha     28      17000
   6  Result:        Steve                    7 Sara         54      65000
   7                                          9 Wes          42      43000
   8
   9
```

FIGURE 5-27: Looking up a label

Using a String as the Key

In addition to looking up entries on the basis of a key value, 1-2-3 Releases 2, 2.01, and 2.2 can look up entries on the basis of a key label or string. Unlike numeric lookups, which locate a result by finding the first value in the index column that is greater than the key value, string lookups work on an exact-match basis.

Cell B6 in Figure 5-28 contains an example of a string lookup function. This function

B6: @VLOOKUP(B3,D3..G7,B4)

looks up an entry from the range D3..G7 based on the key entry 'Steve in cell B3 and the offset 1 in cell B4. As you can see, this function returns the value 3.

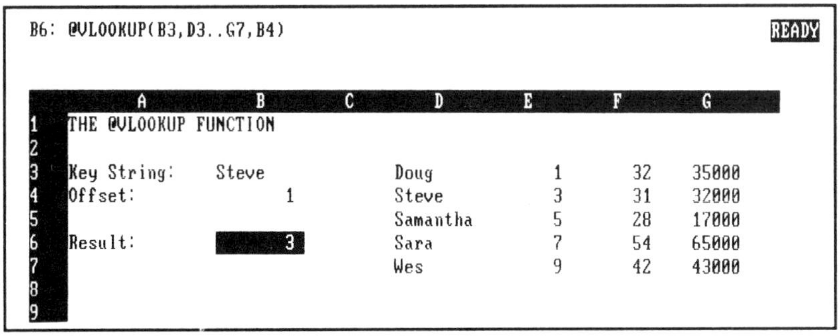

```
B6: @VLOOKUP(B3,D3..G7,B4)                                           READY

         A          B          C          D          E          F          G
   1  THE @VLOOKUP FUNCTION
   2
   3  Key String:   Steve                     Doug          1       32      35000
   4  Offset:           1                     Steve         3       31      32000
   5                                          Samantha      5       28      17000
   6  Result:           3                     Sara          7       54      65000
   7                                          Wes           9       42      43000
   8
   9
```

FIGURE 5-28: Using a label as the key of an @VLOOKUP function

When 1-2-3 evaluates a text @VLOOKUP function, it searches the index column for an entry that matches the key string exactly (capitalization *does not* count, however). In this case, 1-2-3 locates the label 'Steve in cell D4, establishing row 4 as the row that contains the result of the function. Once 1-2-3 locates the row, the offset argument tells it which column contains the result of the function. In this case, the offset value 1 in cell B4 instructs 1-2-3 to choose the entry from the second column of the table. Consequently, this function returns the value 3 from cell E4.

Notes

Like numeric lookup functions, string lookup functions return the value ERR when you specify an offset that is less than 0 or greater than the number of columns in the table range, minus one. In addition, string lookups return the value ERR if 1-2-3 can't find a match for the key entry in the index column.

If you specify an offset argument of 0 with a string key entry, the @VLOOKUP function will not, as you might expect, return a string. Instead, it will return a value that indicates the offset of the row that contains the index string that matches the key string. For example, if you changed the entry in cell B4 in Figure 5-28 to 0, the function in cell B6 would return the value 1. This value is the offset of the row in the table that both contains the index string, *Steve*, and matches the key string.

The @HLOOKUP Function

The @HLOOKUP function is identical to the @VLOOKUP function in every way save one: @HLOOKUP looks up entries from horizontal lookup tables. In a horizontal lookup table, the index values are in the top row of the table, and the data items being looked up are in the following rows.

The form of 1-2-3's @HLOOKUP function is

@HLOOKUP(*key entry,table range,offset*)

As with @VLOOKUP, the first argument, *key entry*, specifies the value 1-2-3 will look up in the table. The second argument, *table range*, must be the coordinates or name of the range that contains the entries you want to look up. The final argument, *offset*, specifies the column of the table that contains the function's result.

Cell B6 of the worksheet shown in Figure 5-29 contains an example of the @HLOOKUP function:

B6: @HLOOKUP(B3,C8..G10,B4)

This function uses the value from cell B3 as the key value and the value from cell B4 as the offset, just as the function in Figure 5-25 does. (In fact, this function is the horizontal equivalent of the vertical lookup function in cell B6 of Figure 5-25.)

As you can see, this function specifies the range C8..G10 as the table range. The lookup table referred to by the *table range* argument of @HLOOKUP must include at least two partial rows. In 1-2-3 Releases 2, 2.01, and 2.2, the entries in the table range may be values or labels—or references, formulas, or functions that return values or labels. (In 1-2-3 Release 1A, the entries in the table range must be values or references, formulas, or functions that return values.) If the table range includes labels, those labels will be assigned the value 0 by the @HLOOKUP function. Since this is a horizontal lookup table, the index values are in row 8. Rows 9 and 10 contain the entries to be looked up.

```
B6: @HLOOKUP(B3,C8..G10,B4)                                    READY

        A       B       C       D       E       F       G
   1  THE @HLOOKUP FUNCTION
   2
   3  Key Value:     3
   4  Offset:        1
   5
   6  Result:       31
   7
   8                         1       3       5       7       9
   9                        32      31      28      54      42
  10                     35000   32000   17000   65000   43000
  11
  12
```

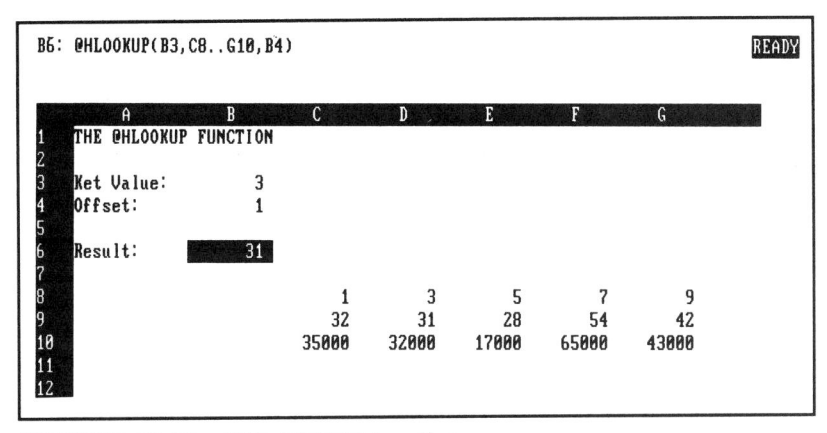

FIGURE 5-29: The @HLOOKUP function

When 1-2-3 evaluates an @HLOOKUP function, it uses the key value to determine which column of the table contains the function's result. The result will always be in the column to the left of the column that contains the first value that is greater than the key value. Once the column coordinate of the result is determined, 1-2-3 uses the offset argument to determine which row contains the result. The first row of the table (the index row) has an offset of 0, the next row an offset of 1, and so on.

To evaluate the function in cell B6, then, 1-2-3 searches the index row (C8..G8) for the first value that exceeds the key value. Since the value 5 in cell E8 is the first value that exceeds the key value 3 (the entry in cell B3), 1-2-3 determines that column D contains the result. The offset argument of 1 then pinpoints the second row of the table range (row 9). Consequently, the function returns the result 31.

In every other way, the @HLOOKUP function is identical to the @VLOOKUP function. In 1-2-3 Releases 2, 2.01, and 2.2, the key entry and the index values may be labels or values. (As with @VLOOKUP, in 1-2-3 Release 1A, the key entry and the index values must be values.) If the entries in the index row are values, they should be arranged in ascending order from left to right. As with @VLOOKUP, no index value should be repeated in a table.

If the key value you specify is less than the first value in the index row, or if you specify an offset less than 0 or greater than the number of rows in the range less one, the @HLOOKUP function will return the value ERR. If the key value you specify is greater than the largest value in the index row, @HLOOKUP will assume that the result of the function is in the last column of the table. If the offset argument in a numeric @HLOOKUP function is 0, the function will return a value from the index row.

In 1-2-3 Releases 2, 2.01, and 2.2, the entries in the table range can be either values or labels, or a combination of values and labels. In addition, these releases can look up entries on the basis of a key label. As with text @VLOOKUP functions, text @HLOOKUP functions work on an exact-match basis. Text lookups return the value ERR if 1-2-3 is unable to find a match for the key entry in the index row. If you specify an offset argument of 0 with a string key entry, the @HLOOKUP function will return a value that indicates the offset of the column in the table that contains the index string that matches the key.

LOGICAL FUNCTIONS

Logical functions allow you to build decision-making capabilities into your 1-2-3 worksheets. 1-2-3's logical functions include @IF, the conditional functions @ISERR, @ISNA, @ISSTRING, and @ISNUMBER, and the special functions @TRUE and @FALSE.

The @IF Function

1-2-3's principal logical function, @IF, allows 1-2-3 to use conditional tests to make decisions. The form of this function is

@IF(*conditional test,true result,false result*)

The first argument is a *conditional test*. If the conditional test is true, the function will return the *true result*. If the test is false, the function will return the *false result*.

Conditional Tests

A conditional test is an expression that makes a comparison between two values, labels, functions, or formulas, or that tests the contents of a particular cell or range for some characteristic (such as containing a string). The simplest conditional tests are expressions that make comparisons using one of 1-2-3's six conditional operators. Table 5-1 lists these conditional operators. For example, the expressions

    A1>5
    A1=A10
    ((A1+10)/A3)<=100
    @COUNT(TEST)>=A1
    A1="John Smith"

are all conditional tests.

Any expression that uses one of the conditional operators to make a comparison must be either true or false. For example, consider the conditional test *A1>5*. If A1 contains a value that is less than 5 (such as 3), this test will be false. If cell A1 contains the value 5, this test also will be false. If cell A1 contains a value greater than 5, however, this test will be true.

If you enter this test into a cell, you might be surprised at the result. If the conditional test is true, 1-2-3 will display the value 1 in the cell that contains the test. If the conditional test is false, 1-2-3 will display the value 0 in that cell. 1-2-3 always uses the value 1 to represent the result True and the value 0 to represent the result False.

Operator	Definition
>	Greater than
<	Less than
=	Equal to
<>	Not equal to
>=	Greater than or equal to
<=	Less than or equal to

TABLE 5-1: Conditional operators

An Example

Cells C4 through C6 of the worksheet shown in Figure 5-30 contain examples of the @IF function. The first function

C4: @IF(B4<30000,.03,.05)

compares the entry in cell B4 with the value 30000. This function says: If the value in B4 is less than 30000, then return .03; otherwise, return .05. Since cell B3 contains the value 45000, and since 45000 is not less than 30000, this function returns the value .05—the false result. The formula in cell D4, +B4*C4, uses this result to compute the total commission due to Steve.

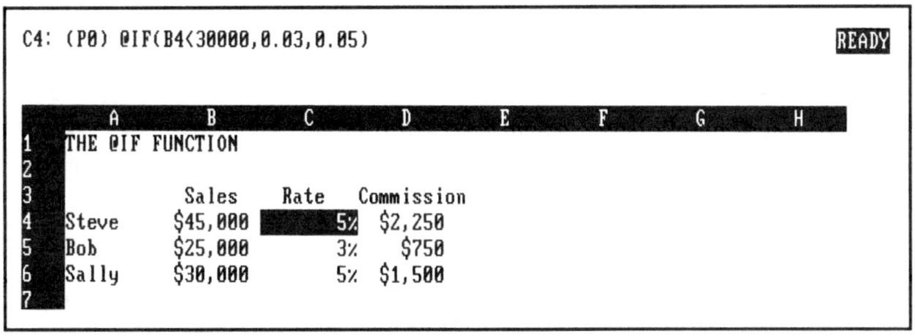

FIGURE 5-30: The @IF function

The function in cell C5, *@IF(B5<30000,.03,.05)*, compares the entry in cell B5, 25000, to the value 30000. Since 25000 is less than 30000, this function returns the value .03—the true value. Similarly, the function in cell C6, *@IF(B6<30000,.03,.05)*, tests to see if the entry in cell B6 is less than 30000. Since the entry in that cell, 30000, is not less than 30000 (they are equal), the function returns .05—the false value.

Another Example

Figure 5-31 shows another example of the @IF function. Cell E5 in this worksheet contains the @IF function

E5: @IF(D5=1,100,75)

which uses the Rate Code entry in cell D5 to compute the hourly rate for a given job. The function can be read in English like this: If the value in cell D5 equals 1, then return 100; otherwise, return 75. Since the value in cell D5 is 1, this function returns 100. The function in cell E6, *@IF(D6=1,100,75)*, computes the hourly rate for the second job in the table. Since cell D6 contains the value 2, this function returns the value 75.

```
E5: (C0) @IF(D5=1,100,75)                                        READY

         A         B         C         D         E         F         G         H
1    THE @IF FUNCTION
2
3                                       Rate
4    Client  Person   Hours    Code    Rate    Dollars
5       101  Doug        8        1    $100     $800
6       101  Steve      16        2    $75      $1,200
7       102  Karen       8        1    $100     $800
8
9
```

FIGURE 5-31: The @IF function

Using Text in an @IF Function

In the previous examples, the true and false arguments were values. In 1-2-3 Releases 2, 2.01, and 2.2, the arguments of an @IF function can also be strings or references to cells that contain labels. For example, the worksheet shown in Figure 5-32 contains several examples of @IF functions that return strings. As you can see, this simple worksheet lists three test scores and an attendance record for each of six students. The functions in the range F4..F9 determine whether each student passes or fails the course. The first function

F4: @IF(@AVG(B4..D4)>=75,"Pass","Fail")

determines whether Bill passed or failed the course. This function compares the average of Bill's three test scores (computed by the function *@AVG(B4..D4)*) to the value 75. Since Bill's average, 90.67, is greater than 75, the test is true, and the function returns the true result—the string *Pass*.

```
F4: @IF(@AVG(B4..D4))>=75,"Pass","Fail")                         READY

          A         B         C         D         E         F         G         H
1     THE @IF FUNCTION
2
3     Student  Test #1  Test #2  Test #3  Absences  Grade
4     Bill        93       84       95        3    Pass
5     Sue         84       63       77        2    Fail
6     John       100       66       84        0    Pass
7     Mary        88       95       73        1    Pass
8     Jim         73       69       92        2    Pass
9     Bob         92       93       81        5    Pass
10
```

FIGURE 5-32: The @IF function

Cells F5 through F9 contain similar formulas. For example, cell F5 contains the function @IF(@AVG(B5..D5)>=75,"Pass","Fail"). Because the result of the function @AVG(B5..D5) is only 74.6666, the conditional test is false, and 1-2-3 returns the false result—the string *Fail*.

You can also use strings or labels in the conditional test of an @IF function. For example, Figure 5-33 shows a simple worksheet that has been set up to manage a checkbook. Cell E5 contains the function

E5: (C0) @IF($D5=E$4,$C5,0)

This function says: If the entry in cell D5 matches the entry in cell E4, then return the value from C5; otherwise, return the value 0. Notice that both cell D5 and cell E4 contain the label *Rent*. Since these two entries match, the function returns the true value from cell C5: 450. The effect of the function is to "post" the entry from cell C5 into the appropriate column of the worksheet.

```
E5: (C0) @IF($D5=E$4,$C5,0)                                          READY

         A        B        C        D        E        F        G        H
  1  THE @IF FUNCTION
  2
  3  Check
  4  Number   Date     Amount   Account  Rent     Food     Clothing Car
  5     101   01-Jul   $450     Rent     $450     $0       $0       $0
  6     102   03-Jul   $25      Clothing $0       $0       $25      $0
  7     103   04-Jul   $60      Food     $0       $60      $0       $0
  8     104   07-Jul   $225     Car      $0       $0       $0       $225
  9     105   09-Jul   $10      Food     $0       $10      $0       $0
 10
```

FIGURE 5-33: The @IF function

Cells E5 through H9 all contain similar formulas that compare the code in column D to the account name in row 4. If the entry in column D does not match the entry in row 4, these functions return 0. For example, the function in cell E6, @IF($D6=E$4,$C6,0), returns the value 0 because the entries in cells D6 and E4 do not match.

Complex Conditional Operators

In addition to the six basic logical operators (=, >, <, >=, <=, and), 1-2-3 offers three "complex" logical operators: #AND#, #OR#, and #NOT#. These operators allow you to join simple conditional tests, like A1>5, into compound conditionals, like #NOT#(A1>5#AND#(B1<10#OR#C1=3)).

#AND#

1-2-3's #AND# operator allows you to join two conditional tests in a "logical AND" fashion. When you join two tests in this way, the combined test is true only when both of the component tests are true. If either or both of the component conditions are false, the combined test will be false.

For instance, suppose that in the example shown in Figure 5-32, five or more absences cause a student to fail automatically, regardless of his or her test average. To reflect this modified condition, you would replace the functions in the range F4..F9 with functions such as

F9: @IF(@AVG(B9..D9)>=75#AND#E9<5,"Pass","Fail")

The conditional test *@AVG(B9..D9)>=75#AND#E9<5* will be true only if both of the component tests are true, that is, if the student's test average is greater than or equal to 75 AND that student had less than five absences. If the student had a test average less than 75 or five or more absences or both, the combined conditional test would be false. Therefore, the result of this revised function would produce a failing grade for Bob.

#OR#

1-2-3's #OR# operator allows you to join two conditional tests in a "logical OR" fashion. When you use this operator to join two conditions, the combined conditional test will be true if either or both of the component conditions are true. A logical OR test will be false only when both component conditions are false.

For example, suppose you want 1-2-3 to return the string *Good* if either cell A1 contains a value greater than 3 or cell B2 contains a value less than 100 and return the string *Bad* otherwise. To achieve this effect, you would use the function

@IF(A1>3#OR#B2<100,"Good","Bad")

This function will return the string *Bad* only when both conditions (A1>3 and B2<100) are false.

#NOT#

1-2-3's final complex logical operator, #NOT#, gives you an alternative way to negate a conditional test. Unlike #AND# and #OR#, #NOT# does not join two conditions. Instead, it prefaces the condition that you want to negate.

For example, suppose that you want 1-2-3 to return the string *True* if the value in cell A1 is not equal to the value 123, and return the string *False* otherwise. To do this, you could use the function

@IF(#NOT#A1=123,"True","False")

Of course, the function *@IF(A1<>123,"True","False")* and the function *@IF(A1=123,"False","True")* return the same result.

> **TIP: NESTING @IF FUNCTIONS**
>
> Although many logical problems can be solved with individual @IF functions that include either simple or complex conditional tests, some situations require more sophisticated conditional tests. You often can use nested @IF functions to model these complex conditional situations. Nesting one @IF function within another creates a hierarchy of conditional tests that allow 1-2-3 to take different actions depending on the combined result of many different tests.
>
> For example, suppose that you want to enter formulas into cells F4 through F9 of the worksheet in Figure 5-32 that assign a letter grade to each student based on his or her average test score. To do this, you would use a formula like
>
> F4: @IF(@AVG(B4..D4)<60,"F",@IF(@AVG(B4..D4)<70,"D",
> @IF(@AVG(B4..D4)<80,"C",@IF(@AVG(B4..D4)<90,"B","A"))))
>
> As you can see, this formula is a set of four nested @IF functions. The first function, *@IF(GRADE<60,"F",...)*, returns the string *F* if the average is less than 60. If the average is greater than 60, 1-2-3 evaluates the function *@IF(@AVG (B4..D4)<70,"D",...)*. If the average is less than 70 (but greater than or equal to 60), 1-2-3 returns the string *D*. If the average is greater than or equal to 70, 1-2-3 evaluates the next @IF function, *@IF(@AVG(B4..D4)<80,"C",...)*. If the average is less than 80 (but greater than or equal to 70), 1-2-3 returns the string *C*. Otherwise, 1-2-3 evaluates the final @IF function, *@IF(@AVG(B4..D4)<90,"B","A")*. If the average is less than 90, 1-2-3 returns the string *B*. If the average is greater than or equal to 90, 1-2-3 returns the string *A*.

Other Logical Functions

In the previous examples of the @IF function, we used basic conditional operators (=, >, <, >=, <=, and) and complex conditional operators (#AND#, #OR#, and #NOT#) to create conditional tests. You also can use any of six special functions as the conditional test of an @IF function. These functions—@ISERR, @ISNA, @ISSTRING, @ISNUMBER, @TRUE, and @FALSE—test conditions that would be impossible to test with traditional conditional formulas.

The @ISERR and @ISNA Functions

1-2-3's @ISERR and @ISNA functions allow you to test whether a formula or function returns the special values ERR and NA, respectively. 1-2-3 returns the value ERR when it is unable to evaluate a formula or function due to incorrect syntax, the improper mixing of values and labels, and so forth. The value NA, which stands for not available, usually results from a use of the @NA function, which we will cover at the end of this chapter.

The forms of these two functions are

@ISERR(*argument*)
@ISNA(*argument*)

where *argument* is the formula or function that you want to test, or a reference to a cell that contains that formula or function. The @ISERR function is true when its argument returns the value ERR and is false otherwise. The @ISNA function is true only when its argument returns the value NA. If cell A2 contains the value 2 and cell B2 contains the label *'two*, for example, the function *@ISERR(A2+B2)* will be true, and the function *@IF(@ISERR(A2+B2),"Error","No Error")* will return the string *Error*. Similarly, the function *@ISNA(Z100)* will be true if the formula or function in cell Z100 returns the value NA and will be false otherwise.

The @ISSTRING and @ISNUMBER Functions

@ISSTRING and @ISNUMBER are special conditional-testing functions. 1-2-3 uses these to determine whether a cell contains or returns a label or a value. The forms of these commands are

@ISSTRING(*argument*)
@ISNUMBER(*argument*)

where *argument* usually is a reference to a cell. The @ISSTRING function returns the value 1 (True) if the cell referred to by its argument contains a label or string, and the number 0 (False) if it contains a value. Similarly, the function @ISNUMBER will return 1 if the function referred to by its argument contains a value, and the value 0 otherwise. If cell A1 contains the label *'abc*, for example, the function *@ISSTRING(A1)* will return the value 1, and the function *@ISNUMBER(A1)* will return the value 0. If cell A1 contains the value 123 instead, the function *@ISSTRING(A1)* will return the value 0, and the function *@ISNUMBER(A1)* will return the value 1.

@TRUE and @FALSE

1-2-3's @TRUE and @FALSE functions give you alternative ways to represent the logical conditions True and False (the values 1 and 0). The @TRUE function is equivalent to the value 1, while the @FALSE function is equivalent to the value 0. These functions accept no arguments. If you enter the function @TRUE into a cell, it will return the value 1. If you enter the function @FALSE instead, it will return the value 0.

STRING FUNCTIONS

1-2-3 offers a variety of functions that can operate on strings. In all, there are 17 string functions: @CHAR, @CODE, @FIND, @EXACT, @REPLACE, @LEFT, @RIGHT, @MID, @LENGTH, @LOWER, @UPPER, @PROPER, @STRING, @VALUE, @REPEAT, @TRIM, @CLEAN. These functions, which are not available in Release 1A, allow you to manipulate string entries in a variety of ways.

The @CHAR and @CODE Functions

All computers use numeric codes to represent the numbers, letters, and symbols you see on the screen. Although different computers use different sets of codes, all personal computers use a code system called ASCII, or American Standard Code for Information Interchange. The ASCII system uses a three-digit code to represent each number, letter, and symbol. For example, your computer knows the character *a* as the code 97, the number 1 as the code 49, the symbol $ as the code 36, and so forth. The ASCII system includes representations for 256 different characters.

1-2-3 uses a special character code system, called the Lotus International Character Set (LICS), to represent the letters, numbers, punctuation marks and other special characters you see on your 1-2-3 screen. The LICS is related to the ASCII character set since codes 000 to 127 are used to represent the same characters in both systems. However, the LICS uses the codes from 128 to 255 to represent special characters, such as the symbols π and ¿, which are not a part of the normal ASCII system. For the most part, you can think of ASCII and LICS as being identical. Only if you fool around with the characters with codes above 127 will you need to understand the differences between the two systems.

The @CHAR Function

Although you can use any of the 256 characters contained in the Lotus International Character Set (LICS) whenever you work within 1-2-3, only about 100 are represented by keys on the keyboard of your computer. You can enter common characters such as these just by pressing a single key or a combination of the [Shift] key and another key. To access the remaining characters, you can either use the [Compose] key, which we'll discuss in Appendix 2, or the @CHAR function. The form of this function is

   @CHAR(*value*)

where the single argument is an integer from 0 to 255. This integer specifies the LICS code of the character you want 1-2-3 to return. Appendix 2 at the end of Lotus 1-2-3 reference manual contains a table that lists each LICS code and the character it represents.

The worksheet shown in Figure 5-34 contains several examples of the @CHAR function. Because cell A4 contains the value 90, the function

   C4: @CHAR(A4)

in cell C4 returns the string Z (LICS character 90). Because cell A5 contains the value 122, the function @CHAR(A5) in cell C5 returns the character *z* (LICS character 122). Similarly, the function @CHAR(A6) in cell C6 returns the character £, the function @CHAR(A7) in cell C7 returns the character ±, and the function @CHAR(A8) in cell C8 returns the character ¿.

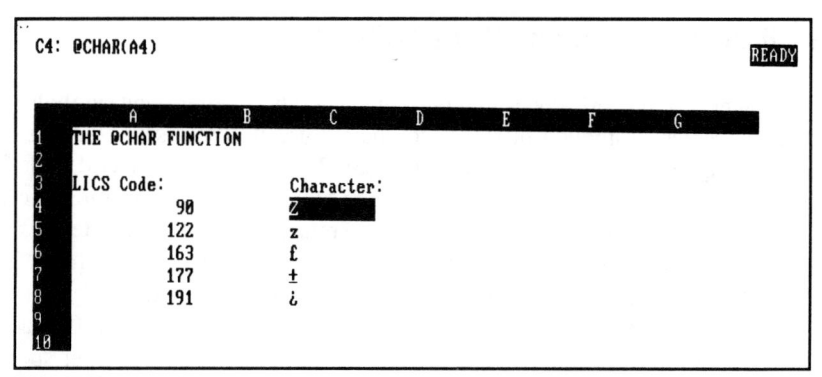

```
C4: @CHAR(A4)                                                    READY

         A         B         C         D         E         F         G
1   THE @CHAR FUNCTION
2
3   LICS Code:          Character:
4            90         Z
5           122         z
6           163         £
7           177         ±
8           191         ¿
9
10
```

FIGURE 5-34: The @CHAR function

The @CODE Function

The action of 1-2-3's @CODE function is opposite to that of the @CHAR function. While the @CHAR function returns a character, given a LICS code, the @CODE function returns a LICS code, given a character. The form of this function is

@CODE(*character*)

where the *character* argument specifies the character whose LICS code you want returned. This argument must be a string, enclosed in quotes, or a reference to a cell that contains a label.

The worksheet shown in Figure 5-35 contains several examples of the @CODE function. The function in cell C4

C4: @CODE(B4)

returns the value 33, indicating that the exclamation point (!) has the LICS code 33. The function *@CODE(B5)* in cell C5 returns the value 57, indicating that the character 9 has the LICS code 57. (Importantly, the entry in cell B5 is the label '9, not the value 9. If cell B5 had contained a value, 1-2-3 would have returned the value ERR.) The functions in cells C6, C7, and C8 indicate that the LICS codes for the characters *R, m,* and *}* are 82, 109, and 125, respectively.

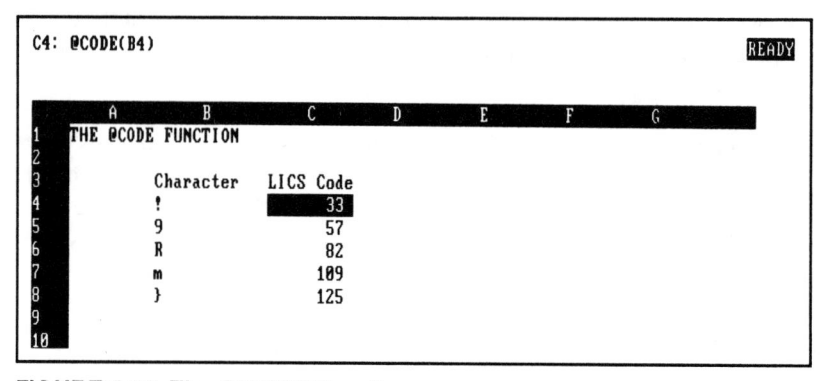

```
C4: @CODE(B4)                                                    READY

         A         B         C         D         E         F         G
1   THE @CODE FUNCTION
2
3            Character   LICS Code
4                !          33
5                9          57
6                R          82
7                m         109
8                }         125
9
10
```

FIGURE 5-35: The @CODE Function

If the argument of an @CODE function is made up of more than one letter, the function will return the ASCII code of the first letter in the argument.

The @FIND, @EXACT, and @REPLACE Functions

1-2-3's @FIND, @EXACT, and @REPLACE functions allow you to manipulate subsets of characters within a string. The @FIND function allows you to locate the position of a substring within a string. The @EXACT function determines whether two strings match. The @REPLACE function allows you to replace a group of characters in a string with another group of characters.

The @FIND Function

1-2-3's @FIND function allows you to locate one string within another. This function requires three arguments:

@FIND(*substring,string,offset*)

The first argument, *substring*, specifies the group of characters that you want 1-2-3 to locate within the second argument, *string*. The final argument, *offset*, allows you to specify where in *string* you want 1-2-3 to begin the search. In most cases, you'll want to specify an offset of 0 so that 1-2-3 will begin searching at the beginning of the string.

The result of the function is a number that specifies the offset of the first character of *substring* within *string*. If 1-2-3 cannot find the substring within the string, it returns the value ERR.

For example, cell B3 of the worksheet in Figure 5-36 contains the label *'Jones, John, President*. Suppose you want to determine the location of the first comma within this string. The function in cell B5

B5: @FIND(",",B3,0)

does the trick. Because the first comma is the fifth character to the right of the first character in the string (the *J* in Jones), this function returns the value 5. The offset of 0 instructs 1-2-3 to begin the search with the first character in cell B3.

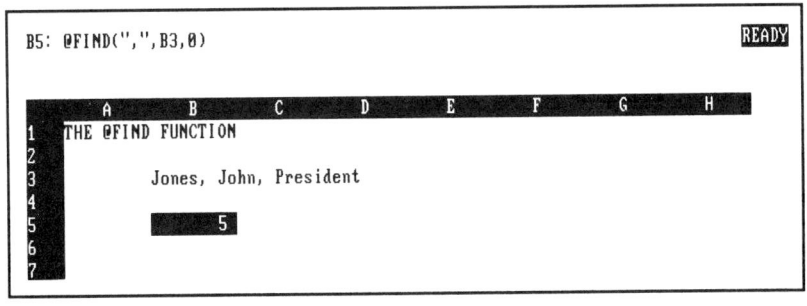

FIGURE 5-36: The @FIND function

The offset argument is included in the function so that you can search for multiple occurrences of the same substring within a given string. For instance, suppose you now want to locate the second comma in the string in cell B3. The function *@FIND(",",B3,6)* or the function *@FIND(",",B3,@FIND(",",B3,0)+1)* will return the correct result: 11. The offset argument in this function tells the function to skip to the sixth character in the string before beginning its search. As a result, it passes over the first occurrence of the comma and finds the second.

If you had specified an offset of 12 or greater in either function, 1-2-3 would have begun the search with the twelfth character in the string, would not have found a comma, and, therefore, would have returned the result ERR.

The @EXACT Function

1-2-3's @EXACT function allows you to compare one string to another. The form of this function is

@EXACT(*string1*,*string2*)

where *string1* and *string2* specify the two strings that you want to compare. If the two strings are identical in every way, including capitalization, the @EXACT function will be true and will return the value 1. If the two strings are not identical, the @EXACT function will be false and will return the value 0. In other words, @EXACT is a conditional-testing function that operates on strings.

As an example of the use of this function, suppose you want to know whether cell A1 contains the label *'abc*. To do this, you would use either the function

@EXACT(A1,"abc")

or the function *@EXACT("abc",A1)*. In either case, 1-2-3 would return the value 1 (True) if cell A1 contains the label *'abc*, *"abc*, or *^abc*, or any reference, formula, or function that returns the string *abc*. If cell A1 contains any other string, even only a variation of capitalization, such as *Abc*, this function would return the value 0 (False).

If you want to compare two strings, but don't care about differences in capitalization, use the = operator instead of the @EXACT function. For instance, while the function @EXACT(A1,"abc") will only be true if cell A1 contains the string *abc* (with any label prefix), the equation A1="abc" will be true if A1 contains any of the following strings: *abc*, *Abc*, *aBc*, *abC*, *ABc*, *AbC*, or *ABC*.

The @REPLACE Function

1-2-3's @REPLACE function allows you to replace a group of characters in one string with another group of characters. The form of this function is

@REPLACE(*original string*,*starting point*,*# of characters to replace*, *replacement string*)

The first argument, *original string*, must specify the string in which you want to replace some characters. The next two arguments, *starting point* and *# of characters to replace*, tell 1-2-3 which characters to replace within that string. The *starting point* argument specifies the offset of the first character you want to replace. A value of 0 specifies the first character, a value of 1 specifies the second character, and so forth. The *# of characters to replace* argument determines how many characters 1-2-3 will replace in the original string, starting with the character pinpointed by the *starting point* argument. The concluding argument of this function, *replacement string*, specifies the characters with which 1-2-3 will replace the characters that it just removed from the original string.

```
B5: @REPLACE(B3,7,4,"Sally")                                            READY

        A       B       C       D       E       F       G       H
  1   THE @REPLACE FUNCTION
  2
  3           Jones, John, President
  4
  5           Jones, Sally, President
  6
  7
```

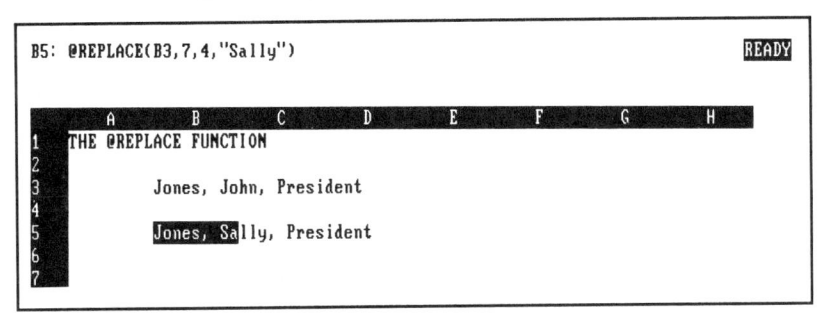

FIGURE 5-37: The @REPLACE function

For example, cell B3 in Figure 5-37 contains the label *'Jones, John, President*. Suppose that you want to replace the seventh through tenth characters from this label with the string *Sally*. To do this, you could use the function in cell B5,

B5: @REPLACE(B3,7,4,"Sally")

The first argument of this function, *B3*, specifies the entry in cell B3 as the string in which to replace some characters. The second and third arguments, *7* and *4*, tell 1-2-3 to remove four characters from the string, beginning with the one that is seven characters to the right of the first character in the string. The final argument, *"Sally"*, instructs 1-2-3 to replace the characters that it removes with the characters *Sally*. When 1-2-3 evaluates this function, it replaces the characters *John* with the characters *Sally*, to produce the string *Jones, Sally, President*.

The @LEFT, @RIGHT, and @MID Functions

1-2-3's next three string functions, @LEFT, @RIGHT, and @MID, extract groups of characters from within a string, based on a position within that string. The @LEFT function copies characters from the beginning, or left, of a string; the @RIGHT function copies characters from the end, or right, of a string; and the @MID function copies characters from anywhere in the middle of a string.

The @LEFT Function

1-2-3's @LEFT function allows you to extract any number of characters from a string, starting at the beginning, or left edge, of that string. The form of this function is

@LEFT(*string,# of characters*)

where *# of characters* tells 1-2-3 how many characters to extract from *string*. The function will always extract the requested characters beginning with the first, or leftmost, character in *string*. If the *# of characters* argument specifies more characters than there are in the string, 1-2-3 will return the entire string.

For example, cell B3 in Figure 5-38 contains the label entry *'Jones, John, President*. Suppose you want to extract the last name *Jones* from this label. To do this, you could use the function in cell B5

B5: @LEFT(B3,5)

which extracts the first five characters from the entry.

```
B5: @LEFT(B3,5)                                                    READY

        A         B          C           D         E        F        G        H
  1   THE @LEFT, @RIGHT, and @MID FUNCTIONS
  2
  3             Jones, John, President
  4
  5   Left:    Jones
  6   Right:   President
  7   Mid:     John
  8
  9
```

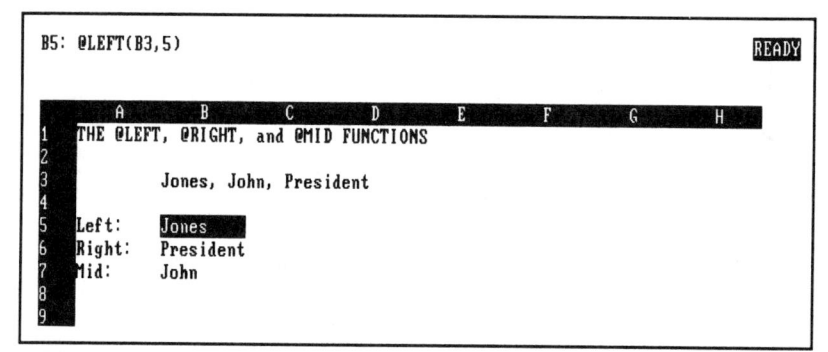

FIGURE 5-38: The @LEFT function

TIP: USING @FIND WITH @LEFT

If you don't know exactly how many characters you want to extract from a string, but you know that the last character you want to extract will be followed by a specified character, you can use @FIND to help pin down the *# of characters* argument. For example, the function

@LEFT(B3,@FIND(",",B3,0))

will extract the name *Jones* from the string in cell B3 of Figure 5-38. The @FIND function within this @LEFT function returns the offset of the first comma in the string. Since the comma follows the last character that you want to extract, the offset of the comma is equal to the absolute position of the last character you want to extract, which also is the number of characters you want to extract. Consequently, this function also returns the string *Jones*. The advantage of this form is that it is more flexible than the first and could be used to extract the last name from any string that had the same form as *Jones, John, President*.

The @RIGHT Function

1-2-3's @RIGHT function works in much the same way as the @LEFT function, except it extracts characters from the right edge (end) of a string. The form of this function is

@RIGHT(*string,# of characters*)

where *# of characters* tells 1-2-3 how many characters to extract from *string*. The function will always extract the requested characters beginning with the last, or rightmost, character in *string*. If the *# of characters* argument specifies more characters than there are in the string, 1-2-3 will return the entire string.

As an example of this function, suppose that you want to extract the word *President* from the label *'Jones, John, President*, which is stored in cell B3 in Figure 5-38. Since the letters in this word are the first nine characters at the right edge of the string, you could use the function in cell B6

B6: @RIGHT(B3,9)

to return that string.

The @MID Function

Unlike the @LEFT and @RIGHT functions, which allow you to copy characters only from the left or right edges of a string, the @MID function lets you copy characters from anywhere within that string. The form of this function is

@MID(*string,starting position,# of characters*)

The first argument, *string*, specifies the string from which you want to extract characters. The second argument, *starting position*, specifies the offset of the first character you want to extract. (Remember—the first character in a string has an offset of 0.) The final argument, *# of characters*, tells 1-2-3 how many characters you want to extract, starting with and including the character pointed out by the second argument.

As an example of this function, suppose that you want to extract the name *John* from the label *'Jones, John, President* in cell B3 of Figure 5-38. The function in cell B7

B7: @MID(B3,7,4)

does the trick. This function commands 1-2-3 to extract four characters from the string in cell B3, starting with the seventh character to the right of the first character in that string.

The @LENGTH Function

1-2-3's @LENGTH function measures the number of characters, including spaces, in a string. The form of this function is

@LENGTH(*string*)

The result of the function is the length of *string*. The *string* argument must specify a string. If the argument specifies a value, this function will return ERR.

The worksheet shown in Figure 5-39 contains several examples of the @LENGTH function. Since cell A2 contains the five-character label *'hello*, the function

B3: @LENGTH(A3)

returns the value 5. Similarly, the function in cell B4 *@LENGTH(A4)*, which refers to the label *'John Smith* in cell A4, returns the value 10. (Remember—the space counts.) Because cell A5 contains a value, the function in cell B5, *@LENGTH(A5)* in cell B6 returns the value result ERR.

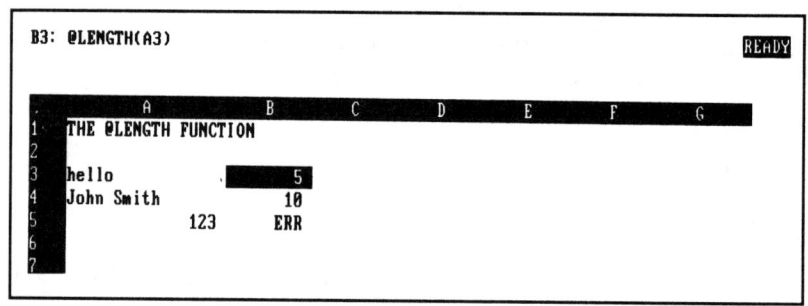

FIGURE 5-39: The @LENGTH function

The @LOWER, @UPPER, and @PROPER Functions

1-2-3's @LOWER, @UPPER, and @PROPER functions allow you to alter the capitalization of strings. The forms of these functions are

@LOWER(*string*)
@UPPER(*string*)
@PROPER(*string*)

The @LOWER function converts *string* to all lower-case characters. @UPPER converts *string* to all upper-case characters. @PROPER converts the first letter in *string* and the first letter after each space in *string* to upper-case form and the remaining letters to lower case.

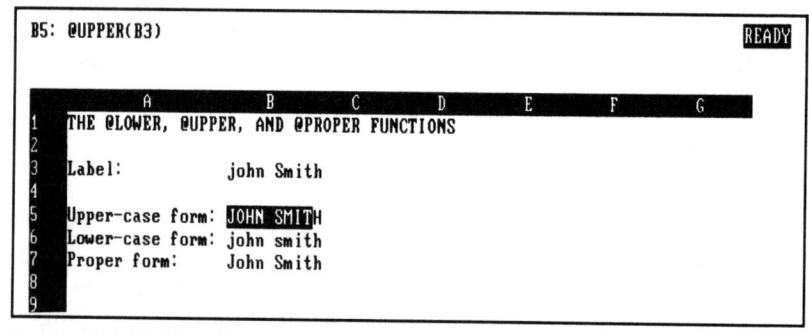

FIGURE 5-40: The @LOWER, @UPPER, and @PROPER Functions

The worksheet in Figure 5-40 contains examples of these three functions. The function

   B5: @UPPER(B3)

in cell B5 returns the string *JOHN SMITH*—an all upper-case version of the label in cell B3. The function

   B6: @LOWER(B3)

in cell B6 returns the string *john smith*—an all lower-case version of that string. Finally, the function

   B7: @PROPER(B3)

in cell B7 returns the string *John Smith*—the "proper" version of the string.

TIP: USING @UPPER, @LOWER, AND @PROPER

The @UPPER, @LOWER, and @PROPER functions are used most often to modify the form of strings that have been input from the keyboard during the execution of a macro. For example, suppose you have a macro that, among other things, requests the user to enter the address of a customer. The address includes the two-letter abbreviation of the name of a state. You want to make sure that the state abbreviation is stored in all upper-case form (as in KY or NY) instead of in some other form (such as ky or Ny). To do this, you could use the @UPPER function to transform whatever entry the user made into all upper-case form. You can use @LOWER and @PROPER in similar circumstances when you need strings in lower-case or proper form.

The @STRING and @VALUE Functions

1-2-3 offers two special string functions, @STRING and @VALUE, which convert values to strings and strings to values. The @STRING function acts upon a value and returns a numeric string. The @VALUE function acts upon a numeric string and returns a value.

To understand the importance of these functions, you must remember that 1-2-3 recognizes two types of entries: labels (or strings) and values. Although you can create formulas that concatenate one string to another or that use any of 1-2-3's math operators to manipulate values, you can't create a formula that refers to both a label and a value. Any formula that attempts to do so will return the value ERR.

The main purpose of the @STRING and @VALUE functions is to convert an entry that is of one type (string or value) into the other form so that it can be linked to other entries of the new type.

The @STRING Function

The form of the @STRING function is

@STRING(*value,decimals*)

where *value* specifies the value you want to convert into a string and *decimals* tells 1-2-3 how many decimal places to include in the resulting string.

Cells B5 through B10 in Figure 5-41 contain @STRING functions that convert the value 1234.56 in cell B3 into strings with various numbers of decimal places. For example, the function in cell B5

B5: @STRING(B3,0)

returns the string *1235*. As you can see, 1-2-3 rounded the value to zero decimal places as it converted it to a string. The function *@STRING(B3,1)* in cell B6 returns the result *1234.6*—the string version of the value 1234.56 rounded to one decimal place. The functions *@STRING(B3,2)* and *@STRING(B3,3)* in cells B7 and B8 return the strings *1234.56* and *1234.560*, respectively.

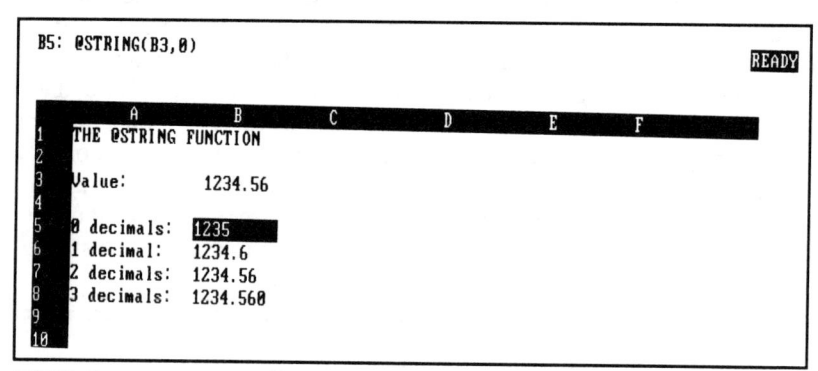

```
B5: @STRING(B3,0)                                          READY

        A           B          C        D        E        F
1   THE @STRING FUNCTION
2
3   Value:       1234.56
4
5   0 decimals:  1235
6   1 decimal:   1234.6
7   2 decimals:  1234.56
8   3 decimals:  1234.560
9
10
```

FIGURE 5-41: The @STRING function

The @VALUE Function

The form of the @VALUE function is

@VALUE(*numeric string*)

where *numeric string* specifies a numeric string or label: a label or string that contains only numerals (0, 1, 2, and so on) and special numeric symbols like $, %, commas, and parentheses. In other words, a numeric string is a string that looks like a value. *Numeric string* can be in the form of a value that has been assigned any of the 1-2-3 formats: Fixed, Currency, Comma, Scientific, or Percent. A numeric string can also be a label in the form of a fraction or a mixed number. The result of the function is a value.

TIP: USING @STRING

The most important use of the @STRING function is to convert value entries into strings so that they can be concatenated with other string entries. For example, suppose you've set up a table in the worksheet, like the one in Figure A, that includes the address of several of your friends. Also suppose that the zip code entries in column E are values and not numeric labels. Now suppose that you want to concatenate the city, state, and zip code for each person into a long string in the form

City, ST Zip

Since the entries in column E are values, they cannot be directly concatenated with the entries in the other columns. Thanks to the @STRING function, however, the task is still possible. The formula in cell F4

F4: +C4&", "&D4&" "&@STRING(E4,0)

does the trick. This formula converts the value entry in cell E4 into a string before concatenating to the entries in cells C4 and D4.

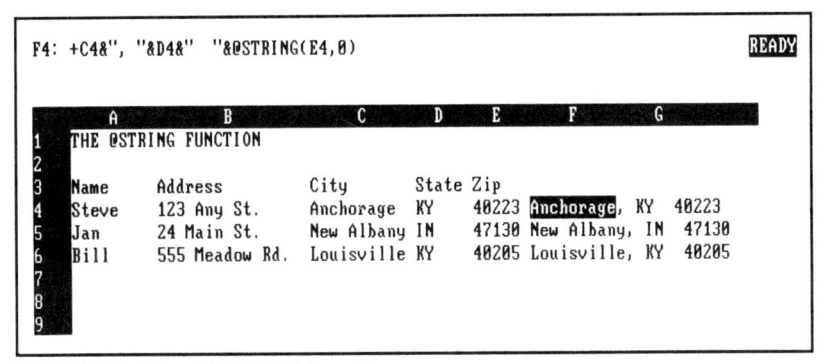

```
F4: +C4&", "&D4&" "&@STRING(E4,0)                                   READY

        A         B              C          D      E       F           G
  1  THE @STRING FUNCTION
  2
  3  Name      Address        City       State  Zip
  4  Steve     123 Any St.    Anchorage  KY     40223  Anchorage, KY  40223
  5  Jan       24 Main St.    New Albany IN     47130  New Albany, IN 47130
  6  Bill      555 Meadow Rd. Louisville KY     40205  Louisville, KY 40205
  7
  8
  9
```

FIGURE A: The @STRING function

The worksheet in Figure 5-42 contains several examples of the @VALUE function. As you can see, cell B4 of this worksheet contains the function

B4: @VALUE(A4)

Because cell A4 contains the numeric label '12345.67, this function returns the value 12345.67. The functions @VALUE(A5) in cell B5 and @VALUE(A6) in cell B6 return this same value. The function @VALUE(A7) in cell B7, which refers to the label '123.45% in cell A7, returns the value .12345. The function in cell B8, @VALUE(A8), refers to the label '1/2 in cell A8. This function converts that string into the value 0.5. Similarly, the function in cell B9, @VALUE(A9), converts the numeric label '4 1/8 into the value 4.125.

```
B4: [W11] @VALUE(A4)                                    READY

        A           B         C       D       E       F       G
   1 THE @VALUE FUNCTION
   2
   3  String        Value
   4  12345.67     12345.67
   5  $12,345.67   12345.67
   6  12,345.67    12345.67
   7  12.345%       0.12345
   8  1/2           0.5
   9  4 1/8         4.125
  10
```

FIGURE 5-42: The @VALUE function

The most important use of @VALUE is in converting data that has been imported from another program as numeric strings into values that can be manipulated mathematically by 1-2-3. If you import data from other programs—such as the *Dow Jones News Retrieval Service*—you will probably need to use this function.

The @REPEAT Function

1-2-3's @REPEAT function produces a string that repeats the characters you specify as many times as you wish. The form of this function is

   @REPEAT(*string,# of repeats*)

where *string* is the series of characters you want to repeat, and *# of repeats* specifies how many times you want to repeat those characters. If *string* is a literal string, it must be enclosed in quotes.

Unlike the strings produced by 1-2-3's repeating label prefix (\), the length of the string produced by this function is not limited to the length of the cell that contains the function. For example, the function

   A3: @REPEAT("=",20)

in cell A3 of Figure 5-43 creates the string ====================.

```
A3: @REPEAT("=",20)                                     READY

        A           B         C       D       E       F       G       H
   1 THE @REPEAT FUNCTION
   2
   3  ========================
   4
   5  +-+-+-+-+-+-+-+-+-+
   6
   7
```

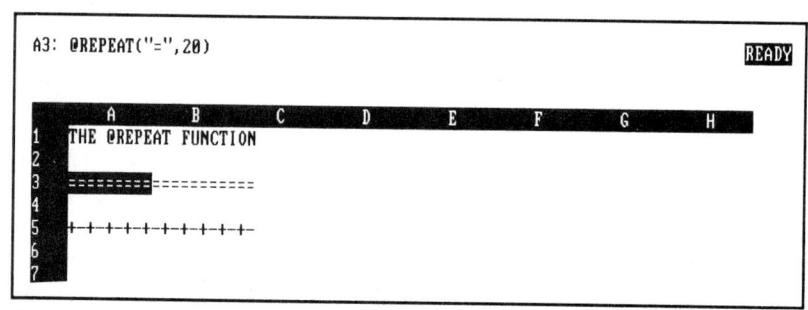

FIGURE 5-43: The @REPEAT function

While you will usually use a single character string as the *string* argument, @REPEAT will repeat a string that is made up of two or more characters. For example, suppose that you want to create a string that repeats the string +- ten times. To do this, you could type +, then -, then +, then -, and so forth. Alternatively, you could use the function in cell A5 of Figure 5-43

A5: @REPEAT("+-",10)

which returns the string +-+-+-+-+-+-+-+-+-+-. Notice that this string is 20 characters long. Whenever you use a string that contains two or more characters as the *string* argument of @REPEAT, the length of the resulting string will be equal to the number of characters in the *string* argument times the *# of repeats* argument. Remember—the *# of repeats* argument does not specify the length of the string returned by the function; it specifies the number of times the string argument is to be repeated.

The @TRIM and @CLEAN Functions

1-2-3's last two string functions—@TRIM and @CLEAN—strip unwanted characters from a string. The forms of these functions are

@TRIM(*string*)
@CLEAN(*string*)

If the *string* argument is a literal string, it must be enclosed in quotes.

The @TRIM Function

The @TRIM function removes leading and trailing spaces from a label. For example, if cell A1 contains the 20-character label '   this is a label (notice the five leading spaces), the function

@TRIM(A1)

would return the 15-character string *this is a label*.

The @CLEAN Function

1-2-3's @CLEAN function strips special control characters from strings. Control characters correspond to LICS codes 0 to 31. Text that you import from other programs may contain these characters. If the label in cell A1 contains control characters, for example, the function @CLEAN(A1) would return a copy of that label without those characters.

OTHER FUNCTIONS

In addition to the functions we've covered so far, 1-2-3 contains some other functions that are difficult to categorize. For that reason, we combine them under the classification "Other Functions." The nine functions in this class are @CELL, @CELL-POINTER, @COLS, @ROWS, @ERR, @NA, @N, @S, and @@.

The @CELL and @CELLPOINTER Functions

@CELL and @CELLPOINTER are functions that return information about the status of a cell. The @CELL function returns information about the cell you specify; the @CELLPOINTER function returns information about the cell on which the cell pointer is positioned when 1-2-3 calculates the function. In every other way, the two functions are identical.

The forms of the @CELL and @CELLPOINTER functions are

@CELL(*code,cell*)
@CELLPOINTER(*code*)

The *cell* argument of the @CELL function specifies the cell about which you want to return information. (Because the @CELLPOINTER function always acts upon the cell over which the cursor is positioned, it does not include a *cell* argument.) Although the @CELL function returns information about only a single cell, the *cell* argument must be stated as a range reference (for example, A1..A1). If you supply a reference to only a single cell (such as A1) when you create or edit the function, 1-2-3 will convert it to a range reference (in this case, A1..A1) when you press [Enter] to lock the function into the worksheet. If you specify a multiple-cell range (such as A1..D5), the function will act upon the upper-left cell of that range. The *cell* argument can also be a range name.

The *code* argument is a string that specifies the type of information that 1-2-3 will return. Table 5-2 shows the nine available code arguments and the information that each code returns. The first argument of both the @CELL and @CELLPOINTER function must specify one of these nine literal strings.

Code	Returns
"address"	the absolute address of the specified cell
"col"	the column number of the specified cell
"contents"	the contents of the specified cell
▶ "filename"	the file name of the file in which the current worksheet is saved ◀
"format"	the format code of the specified cell
"prefix"	the label prefix of the specified label-containing cell
"protect"	the protection status of the specified cell
"row"	the row number of the current cell
"type"	the type of entry in the specified cell
"width"	the width of the specified cell

TABLE 5-2: @CELL and @CELLPOINTER code arguments

Cells B5 through B14 of the worksheet shown in Figure 5-44 contain examples of the @CELL function. Each of these functions refers to cell B3, which contains the centered label ^test. The function in cell B5, *@CELL("address",B3..B3)*, returns the string *$B$3*—the absolute address of the specified cell. Since column B is the second column in the worksheet, the function *@CELL("col",B3..B3)* in cell B6 returns the value 2. Similarly, the function *@CELL("row",B3..B3)*, in cell B11, returns 3—the number of the row that contains cell B3. The function in cell B13, *@CELL("width",B3..B3)*, returns 9, the width of column B.

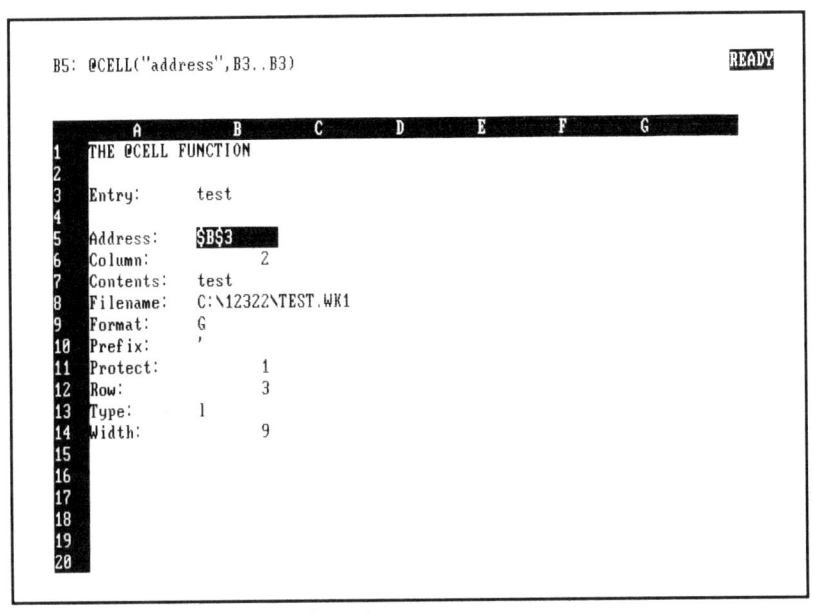

```
B5: @CELL("address",B3..B3)                                          READY

    A         B          C        D        E         F        G
 1 THE @CELL FUNCTION
 2
 3  Entry:    test
 4
 5  Address:  $B$3
 6  Column:        2
 7  Contents: test
 8  Filename: C:\12322\TEST.WK1
 9  Format:   G
10  Prefix:   '
11  Protect:       1
12  Row:           3
13  Type:     1
14  Width:         9
15
16
17
18
19
20
```

FIGURE 5-44: The @CELL function

The function in cell B7, *@CELL("contents",B3..B3)*, returns the contents of cell B3—the string *test*. If the entry in cell B3 had been a function, formula, or cell reference, the function would have returned the result of that entry, not the entry itself.

The function in cell B8, *@CELL("format",B3..B3)*, returns the string *G*, indicating that cell B3 has been assigned the General format. (Even though a cell contains a label, it still has a format.) If the cell had been assigned another format, the function would return the first letter in the name of that format, followed by a number indicating the number of decimals that have been assigned to the cell. For instance, if cell B3 had been assigned the Currency format with two decimal places, the function *@CELL("format",B3..B3)* would return the string *C2*.

The function in cell B9, *@CELL("prefix",B3..B3)*, returns the character ^, indicating that the entry in cell B3 is a centered label. If cell B3 contained a right-aligned entry, this function would return the character ". If the entry in B3 were left aligned, the function would return '. If B3 contained a value, this function would return an empty string.

The function in cell B10, *@CELL("protect",B3..B3)*, returns the value 1, indicating that cell B3 is protected. If cell B3 were unprotected, this function would return the value 0.

The function in cell B12, *@CELL("type",B3..B3)*, returns the string *l*, which stands for label. If cell B3 contained a value (including a formula or a function), this function would return the string *v*. If B3 were blank, the function would return the string *b*.

RELEASE ▶ 2.2 ◀
▶In 1-2-3 Release 2.2, you can use the @CELL and @CELPOINTER functions to return the name of the current worksheet. To do this, you simply use the string *filename* as the first argument of the @CELL function, or the only argument of the @CELLPOINTER function. If the worksheet has been saved previously, these functions will return a string that contains both the path and the name of that file. If you have not saved the worksheet, these functions will return a null label.

For example, cell B14 contains the function *@CELLPOINTER("filename")*. The result of this function—C:\12322\TEST.WK1—indicates that the worksheet shown in Figure 5-44 has been saved under the name TEST.WK1 in the C:\12322 directory.◀

The @COLS and @ROWS Functions

1-2-3's @COLS and @ROWS functions return the number of columns or rows in a range. The forms of these functions are

@COLS(*range*)
@ROWS(*range*)

Suppose that you have used the /Range Name Create command to assign the name TEST to cells A1..Z100. Given this range, the function

@COLS(TEST)

would return the value 26, indicating that the range spans 26 columns. The function

@ROWS(TEST)

would return the value 100, indicating that TEST encompasses 100 rows.

The @ERR Function

1-2-3's @ERR function allows you to enter the special value ERR into a worksheet. This function does not accept an argument.

When you enter the function @ERR into a cell, 1-2-3 will display the value result ERR—the same result it returns when you enter a function with the wrong syntax, attempt to add a label to a value, and so forth. Any cell that refers to the cell containing the @ERR function will also return the result ERR.

The @ERR function can be used to signal errors in your worksheets. For example, the function

@IF(C10<100,@ERR,C10)

will return the value ERR if cell C10 contains a value less than 100. You could use this function to flag an incorrect entry in cell C10.

The @NA Function

1-2-3's @NA function allows you to enter the special value NA into a worksheet. Like @ERR, @NA does not accept an argument. Unlike the value ERR, 1-2-3 will never return the value NA on its own; the @NA function provides the only way to enter this value into the worksheet.

The @NA function is useful as a "placeholder" in incomplete worksheets. If you do not yet have the correct entry for a cell in a worksheet, you can enter the function @NA into that cell. The NA result in that cell, and every cell that depends on that cell, will remind you that the worksheet is lacking a critical piece of information.

The @N and @S Functions

@N and @S are specialized functions that return the contents of the upper-left cell of a range. The forms of these functions are

@N(*range*)
@S(*range*)

where *range* specifies the block of cells that you want the function to act upon. If the upper-left cell of the specified range contains a value or a reference, function, or formula that contains a value, the @N function will return that value, and the @S function will return a blank string. If the upper-left cell of the specified range contains a label or a reference, formula, or function that returns a string, the @S function will return that string, and the @N function will return the value 0.

The @@ Function

1-2-3's @@ function allows you to make an indirect reference to a cell or range. Like the @CELLPOINTER function, this function is useful mainly within advanced command language programs.

The form of this function is

@@(*cell reference*)

The *cell reference* argument must be the address or name of a cell (the first cell) that contains the address or name of another cell (the second cell), in label form. The @@ function uses the address in the first cell to locate the second cell and returns the value from the second cell.

The worksheet shown in Figure 5-45 demonstrates the use of this function. Cell A3 of this worksheet contains the value 123. Cell A4 contains the label '*A3*. As you can see, the function

B5: @@(A4)

in cell B5 returns the value 123—the value stored in cell A3. When 1-2-3 evaluates this function, it looks in cell A4 (the argument of the function) for a label that specifies the address or name of another cell. In this case, cell A4 contains the label 'A3. Consequently, 1-2-3 looks to cell A3 and returns the entry from that cell, 123, as the result of this function.

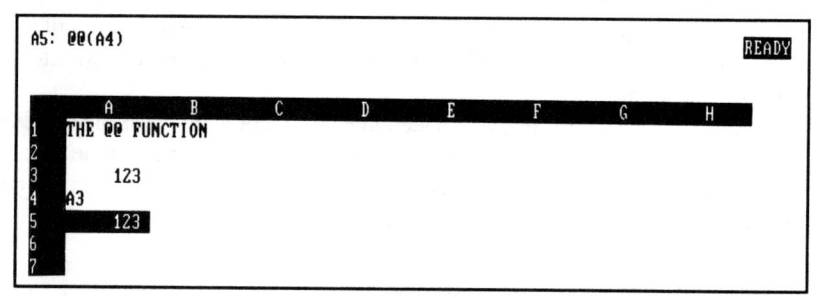

FIGURE 5-45: The @@ function

CONCLUSION

In this chapter, we've talked about functions—special built-in tools that allow you to manipulate values and strings in ways that would be difficult or impossible to do with traditional operators. We have presented seven groups of functions in this chapter: mathematical, statistical, financial, lookup, logical, string, and other. You will probably find functions to be among the most useful and most-used tools in 1-2-3.

We'll explore 1-2-3's date/time functions in Chapter 7 and will examine 1-2-3's data base functions in Chapter 12.

6

Worksheet Commands

Commands are the tools that you use to manipulate the entries in the 1-2-3 worksheet. We've already explained some of 1-2-3's commands, including / Range Name, / Range Format, and the cut-and-paste commands. In this chapter, we will consider 1-2-3's other worksheet commands. These commands are: / Worksheet Titles, / Worksheet Window, / Data Fill, / Data Distribution, / Data Table, / Data Regression, / Data Matrix, / System, / Range Unprot and / Range Prot, / Worksheet Global Protection, / Range Input, / Range Justify, and / Range Search.

CREATING TITLES

Most of the time, you'll enter labels in the first few rows and columns of a worksheet that identify the contents of the worksheet. For example, as you can see in Figure 6-1, the column headers are in rows 1 to 4, and the row headers are in columns A and B. The problem is that most worksheets are too large to fit on a single screen. When you scroll away from the upper-left corner of the worksheet, as shown in Figure 6-2, the column and row headers disappear off the top and left sides of the screen. This makes it difficult, if not impossible, to figure out the meaning of the entries in the worksheet.

The / Worksheet Titles command allows you to "freeze" a few rows and/or a few columns so that they always appear on the screen. Once you have frozen the rows and columns that contain the column and row headers, those headers will remain in view no matter where you scroll in the worksheet.

When you issue the / Worksheet Titles command, you'll see a menu with four options: Both, Horizontal, Vertical, and Clear. The option you choose determines which rows and/or columns 1-2-3 will lock onto the screen. If you want to lock the labels in the first few columns of the worksheet onto the screen, you should choose Vertical. Choosing Horizontal allows you to lock the first few rows onto the screen. Choosing Both will lock both the first few columns and the first few rows in place. The last option, Clear, eliminates any titles you have defined.

```
A1: [W18] \=                                                    READY

        A           B           C        D         E         F         G
1  =====================================================================
2  XYZ CORP. EXPENSE PROJECTION
3  OPERATING EXPENSES                    JUNE      JULY      AUG       SEPT
4  ====================================  ======    ======    ======    ======
5  SALARIES                              $19,917   $18,993   $17,601   $19,561
6  BONUS                                           $5,000
7  CONTRACT LABOR                        $423      $145      $1,294    $971
8  PAYROLL TAXES                         $1,400    $1,746    $1,256    $1,373
9  GROUP MEDICAL INS                     $933      $933      $964      $791
10 FUTA, SUTA, WORKMEN'S COMP            $698      $994
11 LIFE INSURANCE                        $124                $114
12 LIABILITY INSURANCE                   $346
13 OFFICE LEASE                          $3,125    $3,125    $3,125    $3,699
14 EQUIPMENT LEASE                       $168      $936      $85       $148
15 TELEPHONE                             $1,040    $1,600    $874      $1,153
16 SHIPPING & DELIVERIES                 $247      $355      $415      $410
17 OFFICE SUPPLIES                       $216      $322      $217      $196
18 COMPUTER SUPPLIES                     $219      $331      $416      $122
19 STATIONARY AND FORMS                  $44       $58       $300      $307
20 POSTAGE                                         $303      $150      $505
```

FIGURE 6-1: A sample worksheet

```
P31: @SUM(P4..P30)                                              READY

        I         J         K         L         M         N         O         P
13   $3,699    $3,699    $3,699    $3,699    $3,699    $3,699    $3,699    $42,666
14   $66                            $66       $66       $66       $66       $1,752
15   $1,372    $1,398    $1,769    $3,332    $3,332    $3,332    $3,332    $23,996
16   $391      $214      $353      $166      $166      $166      $166      $3,355
17   $339      $468      $462      $158      $158      $158      $158      $2,962
18   $625      $423      $36       $136      $136      $136      $136      $3,527
19   $606                $636      $435      $435      $435      $435      $3,963
20   $189      $1,254    $1,756    $1,500    $1,500    $1,500    $1,500    $11,207
21   $202      $795      $251      $123      $123      $123      $123      $2,496
22   $1,300              $814                                              $2,574
23   $245      $145      $217      $136      $136      $136      $136      $1,486
24   $500      $800      $880      $800      $800      $800      $800      $6,380
25   $150      $62       $89       $285      $285      $285      $285      $3,367
26   $18                 $334      $913      $913      $913      $913      $4,608
27   $434      $4,030              $1,503                        $0        $6,282
28   $647      $10                                                         $657
29                                 $15                                     $15
30   ------    ------    ------    ------    ------    ------    ------    ------
31   $38,033   $41,312   $40,952   $44,782   $42,011   $42,464   $41,978   $448,569
32   ======    ======    ======    ======    ======    ======    ======    ======
```

FIGURE 6-2: Scrolling away from the upper-left corner

1-2-3 uses the position of the cell pointer to determine which columns and rows you want to lock on the screen. Depending on which option you choose from the Titles menu, 1-2-3 will lock the rows above the cell pointer, or the columns to the left of the cell pointer, or both, onto the screen. Before you issue the / Worksheet Titles command, then, you must first move the cell pointer to a position that defines the rows and/or columns you want to lock onto the screen.

An Example

Suppose you want to freeze columns A and B and rows 1 to 4 in the sample worksheet in Figure 6-1. First, you must position the cell pointer. To do this, press [Home] to move the cell pointer to cell A1. Then move the cell pointer to cell C5. Why C5? Because when you issue / Worksheet Titles, 1-2-3 will lock the rows above the cell pointer—rows 1, 2, 3, and 4—and the columns to the left of the cell pointer—columns A and B—onto the screen.

When the cell pointer is in place, issue the / Worksheet Titles command. Since you want to lock both rows and columns in place, you should choose the Both option from the Titles menu. That's all there is to it. Although nothing seems to have changed in the worksheet, you have now locked rows 1, 2, 3, and 4 and columns A and B onto the screen. No matter where you move the cell pointer on the worksheet, the appropriate cells of columns A and B and rows 1, 2, 3, and 4 will remain in view.

For example, Figure 6-3 shows the screen as it will look when the cell pointer is in cell J29. Notice that the row numbers at the left edge of the screen now read 1, 2, 3, 4, 14, 15, 16, and so on, and that the column letters read A, B, F, G, H, and so on. As you can see, the labels in rows 1, 2, 3, and 4 and in columns A and B are now in view, making it easy to figure out the meaning of the worksheet.

```
J29:                                                              READY

            A            B           F         G         H         I         J
     ================================================================================
 1
 2   XYZ CORP. EXPENSE PROJECTIO
 3   OPERATING EXPENSES                AUG       SEPT      OCT       NOV       DEC
 4   ================================================================================
14   EQUIPMENT LEASE                   $85       $148      $85       $66
15   TELEPHONE                         $874      $1,153    $1,462    $1,372    $1,398
16   SHIPPING & DELIVERIES             $415      $410      $306      $391      $214
17   OFFICE SUPPLIES                   $217      $196      $110      $339      $468
18   COMPUTER SUPPLIES                 $416      $122      $811      $625      $423
19   STATIONARY AND FORMS              $300      $307      $272      $606
20   POSTAGE                           $150      $505      $1,050    $189      $1,254
21   SUBS, LIBRARY                     $365      $85       $306      $202      $795
22   CONSULTING FEES                   $460                          $1,300
23   COFFEE AND BEVERAGE SERVIC        $94       $147      $94       $245      $145
24   BANKCARD FEES                     $200      $200      $200      $500      $800
25   MAINTENANCE & REPAIR              $307      $949      $670      $150      $62
26   EQUIPMENT INSTALLATION                      $19       $585      $18
27   LEGAL & ACOUNTING                 $40                 $275      $434      $4,030
28   TAXES AND LICENSES                                              $647      $10
29   OTHER
```

FIGURE 6-3: The / Worksheet Titles command

Notes

You can include as many rows and as many columns in the Titles area as you wish. However, if you include more than a few rows and columns in the Titles area, you will severely limit the usefulness of the worksheet. As a rule, you should keep the Titles area as small as possible.

Once you have defined a Titles range, you will not be able to use the arrow keys, the [Home] key, or the [Pg Up] or [Ctrl] ← keys to move the cell pointer into that range. For example, after you lock rows 1 through 4 and columns A and B in the example worksheet, you cannot use the ↑ key to move the cell pointer from row 5 into row 4, or use the ← key to move the cell pointer from column C to column B. If you try to do either of these things, 1-2-3 will simply beep.

If you press [Home] after you use the / Worksheet Titles command, the cell pointer will move to the upper-left cell in the worksheet that is not in the Titles range. For example, if you press [Home] in the worksheet in Figure 6-3, the cell pointer will move to cell C5.

Although you can't use the arrow keys to move the cell pointer into the Titles range, it is not impossible to get it in there if you need to. First, you can use the [Goto] key ([F5]) to jump the cell pointer to any cell, including any cell in the Titles range. For example, to move the cell pointer to cell A1 in the example worksheet, you have to press [Goto], type A1, and press [Enter]. Doing this will move the cell pointer to cell A1. However, while the cell pointer is in the Titles range, 1-2-3 will display the rows and columns in the Titles range—rows 1 through 4 and columns A and B—twice! The result can be pretty confusing.

There is one other way to move the cell pointer into the Titles range. 1-2-3 will always let you move the cell pointer into any cell when it is in the POINT mode. Although your Titles range will usually include the first few rows and/or columns in the worksheet, you can define a Titles range that is remote from the upper-left corner of the worksheet. For example, suppose cells A41 to H60 are in view on your screen, and the cell pointer is in cell A43. If you issue / Worksheet Titles Horizontal, 1-2-3 will lock rows 41 and 42 onto the screen. As you move the cell pointer down through the worksheet, rows 41 and 42 will remain in view. Until you issue the / Worksheet Titles Clear command, you won't be able to move the cell pointer above row 44.

To remove titles from a worksheet, just issue the / Worksheet Titles Clear command. As soon as you issue this command, 1-2-3 will forget the Titles range you have defined and will cease to lock the Titles range onto the screen.

SPLITTING THE SCREEN

As we explained in Chapter 2, the 1-2-3 worksheet is far too large to be seen in its entirety on the screen. For this reason, when you first load 1-2-3, you view the worksheet through a window that is 20 rows deep and eight columns wide. To view remote portions of the worksheet, you use the cursor-movement keys to drag the window around on the worksheet.

For the most part, this arrangement works fine. There will be times, however, when you'll want to view two separate parts of the worksheet at once. In those cases, you can use / Worksheet Window to split the screen into separate windows.

When you issue the / Worksheet Window command, you'll see a menu with five options: Horizontal, Vertical, Sync, Unsync, and Clear. As you might expect, the Horizontal option allows you to split the screen horizontally and the Vertical option allows you to split the screen vertically. The Sync and Unsync options determine how the two windows will interact when you scroll through the worksheet. We'll talk about these options in depth in a moment. The last option, Clear, "unsplits" the screen.

1-2-3 uses the position of the cell pointer when you issue the / Worksheet Window command to determine where to split the window. If you choose the Vertical option from the Window menu, 1-2-3 will split the screen vertically to the left of the column that contains the cell pointer. If you choose the Horizontal option, 1-2-3 will split the screen horizontally above the row that contains the cell pointer. Before you issue the / Worksheet Window command, then, you must first move the cell pointer to the proper position.

An Example

For example, Figure 6-1 shows the upper-left corner of a worksheet that extends to column P and row 32. Suppose you want to be able to look at the totals in row 31 while you are making changes in the upper part of the worksheet. To begin, you must position the cell pointer. Since you want to be able to see only a couple of rows in the lower window, you can position the cell pointer near the bottom of the main window. We'll place it in cell A17. Now issue the / Worksheet Window Horizontal command. Figure 6-4 shows the result. As you can see, 1-2-3 has split the screen into two windows between rows 16 and 17.

The [Window] Key

Notice that the cell pointer is in the upper window in Figure 6-4. As in this case, whenever you split the screen horizontally, 1-2-3 will place the cell pointer in the upper window. When you split the screen vertically, the cell pointer will end up in the left-hand window.

Once you have split the screen, 1-2-3 allows you to move the cell pointer from one window to another. All you have to do is press the [Window] key ([F6] on the IBM PC). When you press [Window], the cell pointer will jump directly to the other window. For example, if you press [Window] when the screen looks like Figure 6-4, the cell pointer will jump to cell A17 in the lower window. Pressing [Window] again will move the cell pointer back to the other window.

```
A16: [W18] ' SHIPPING & DELIVERIES                                      READY

         A                   B         C         D         E         F         G
 1  ===============================================================================
 2  XYZ CORP. EXPENSE PROJECTION
 3  OPERATING EXPENSES                           JUNE      JULY       AUG      SEPT
 4  ===============================            ======    ======    ======    ======
 5  SALARIES                                  $19,917   $18,993   $17,601   $19,561
 6  BONUS                                                $5,000
 7  CONTRACT LABOR                               $423      $145    $1,294      $971
 8  PAYROLL TAXES                              $1,400    $1,746    $1,256    $1,373
 9  GROUP MEDICAL INS                            $933      $933      $964      $791
10  FUTA, SUTA, WORKMEN'S COMP                   $698      $994
11  LIFE INSURANCE                               $124                $114
12  LIABILITY INSURANCE                          $346
13  OFFICE LEASE                               $3,125    $3,125    $3,125    $3,699
14  EQUIPMENT LEASE                              $168      $936       $85      $148
15  TELEPHONE                                  $1,040    $1,600      $874    $1,153
16  SHIPPING & DELIVERIES                        $247      $355      $415      $410
         A                   B         C         D         E         F         G
17  OFFICE SUPPLIES                              $216      $322      $217      $196
18  COMPUTER SUPPLIES                            $219      $331      $416      $122
19  STATIONARY AND FORMS                          $44       $58      $300      $307
```

FIGURE 6-4: The / Worksheet Window Horizontal command

Moving the Cell Pointer

Once you have split the window, you can move the cell pointer around in either window in any way you wish. All of the keys you use to move the cell pointer in one window—→, ←, ↑, ↓, [Home], [End], [Pg Up], [Pg Dn], [Ctrl]→, and [Ctrl]←—can be used in either window on a split screen.

For example, the lower window in Figure 6-4 displays rows 17, 18, 19. We want this window to show us rows 30, 31, and 32, so we can view the totals. To move the cell pointer from row 17 to row 32, press [Window] to move the cell pointer in the lower window, then press ↓ repeatedly. Figure 6-5 shows the screen with the cell pointer in row 32.

Keep in mind that the [Pg Up], [Pg Dn], [Ctrl]→, and [Ctrl]← keys move the cell pointer up, down, left, or right by one windowful of cells. For this reason, when you use the \ Worksheet Window command to split the screen, you change the effect of these keys.

If you press [Pg Up] or [Pg Dn] after you've split the screen horizontally, 1-2-3 will not move the cell pointer up or down through the worksheet 20 rows at a time. Instead, the cell pointer will move up or down by one windowful of rows. For example, because the lower window in Figures 6-4 and 6-5 contains only three rows, pressing [Pg Dn] when the cell pointer is in that winedow will move it down by only three rows. Similarly, pressing [Pg Up] while the cell pointer is in the lower window will move the cell pointer up by just three rows.

```
A32: [W18]                                                                    READY

         A              B         C         D         E         F         G
   1   ================================================================================
   2   XYZ CORP. EXPENSE PROJECTION
   3   OPERATING EXPENSES                         JUNE      JULY       AUG      SEPT
   4   --------------------------------------   ------    ------    ------    ------
   5   SALARIES                                $19,917   $18,993   $17,601   $19,561
   6   BONUS                                              $5,000
   7   CONTRACT LABOR                             $423      $145    $1,294      $971
   8   PAYROLL TAXES                            $1,400    $1,746    $1,256    $1,373
   9   GROUP MEDICAL INS                          $933      $933      $964      $791
  10   FUTA, SUTA, WORKMEN'S COMP                 $698      $994
  11   LIFE INSURANCE                             $124                $114
  12   LIABILITY INSURANCE                        $346
  13   OFFICE LEASE                             $3,125    $3,125    $3,125    $3,699
  14   EQUIPMENT LEASE                            $168      $936       $85      $148
  15   TELEPHONE                                $1,040    $1,600      $874    $1,153
  16   SHIPPING & DELIVERIES                      $247      $355      $415      $410
         A              B         C         D         E         F         G
  30                                            ------    ------    ------    ------
  31   TOTAL OPERATING EPENSES                 $29,100   $35,041   $28,277   $30,636
  32                                            ======    ======    ======    ======
```

FIGURE 6-5: Moving the cell pointer

When you split the screen vertically, you change the effect of the [Ctrl]→ and [Ctrl]← combinations. If you press [Ctrl]→ or [Ctrl]← after you have split the screen vertically, 1-2-3 will move the cell pointer to the left or right by one windowful of columns.

Synchronizing and Unsynchronizing Windows

By default, the movement of the two windows on a split screen is usually synchronized; that is, they move together in the direction of the split. For example, Figure 6-6 shows the result of pressing → 15 times while your worksheet looks like the one shown in Figure 6-5. As you can see, 1-2-3 has shifted columns I through P into view in both windows—not just the bottom window (the one in which the cell pointer was positioned). If you subsequently press the ← key, the windows will scroll together to the left.

Importantly, 1-2-3 synchronizes the scrolling of windows only in the direction of the split. In other words, the horizontal scrolling of two horizontal windows will be synchronized, but the vertical scrolling of those windows will not be. For example, as we demonstrated in Figure 6-6, using the →, ←, [Ctrl]→, and [Ctrl]← keys to bring new columns into view in one horizontal window will bring the same columns into view in the other window. However, the ↑, ↓, [Pg Up], and [Pg Dn] keys will scroll new

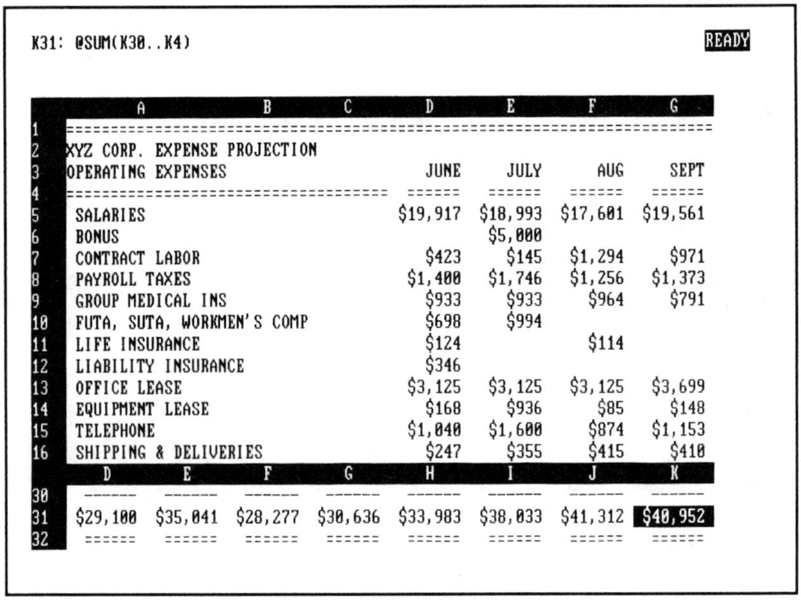

```
K31: @SUM(K30..K4)                                                    READY

           A              B         C         D        E        F        G
  1  ==========================================================================
  2  XYZ CORP. EXPENSE PROJECTION
  3  OPERATING EXPENSES                                JUNE     JULY     AUG     SEPT
  4  ==========================================    ======   ======   ======   ======
  5  SALARIES                                      $19,917  $18,993  $17,601  $19,561
  6  BONUS                                                   $5,000
  7  CONTRACT LABOR                                   $423     $145   $1,294     $971
  8  PAYROLL TAXES                                  $1,400   $1,746   $1,256   $1,373
  9  GROUP MEDICAL INS                                $933     $933     $964     $791
 10  FUTA, SUTA, WORKMEN'S COMP                       $698     $994
 11  LIFE INSURANCE                                   $124              $114
 12  LIABILITY INSURANCE                              $346
 13  OFFICE LEASE                                   $3,125   $3,125   $3,125   $3,699
 14  EQUIPMENT LEASE                                  $168     $936      $85     $148
 15  TELEPHONE                                      $1,040   $1,600     $874   $1,153
 16  SHIPPING & DELIVERIES                            $247     $355     $415     $410
           D         E         F        G         H        I        J        K
 30     ------    ------    ------   ------    ------   ------   ------   ------
 31    $29,100   $35,041   $28,277  $30,636   $33,983  $38,033  $41,312  $40,952
 32     ======    ======    ======   ======    ======   ======   ======   ======
```

FIGURE 6-6: Synchronized windows

rows into view in one horizontal window without affecting which rows are displayed in the other window. Similarly, the scrolling of two vertical windows will be synchronized in the vertical—but not horizontal—direction. For example, using the ↑, ↓, [Pg Up], and [Pg Dn] keys to bring new rows into view in one vertical window will bring the same rows into view in the other window. However, the →, ←, [Ctrl]→, and [Ctrl]← keys will scroll new columns into view in one vertical window without affecting which columns are displayed in the other window.

Although windows are usually synchronized when you first create them, you can unsynchronize them, if you wish. To do this, simply issue the / Worksheet Windows Unsync command. As soon as you issue the command, 1-2-3 will break the links between the two windows on the screen. Specifically, horizontal windows will scroll independently of one another in the horizontal direction as well as the vertical one; vertical windows will scroll independently of one another in the vertical direction as well as the horizontal one. For example, Figure 6-7 shows the result of pressing the ← key 15 times while the worksheet looks like the one shown in Figure 6-6, after issuing the / Worksheet Window Unsync command. As you can see, 1-2-3 has shifted columns A through G into view in the bottom window (the active window); however, columns I through P remain visible in the top window. If you issue the / Worksheet Windows Unsync command while only a single window is visible on the screen, the windows created by a subsequent \ Worksheet Windows (Horizontal or Vertical) command will be unsynchronized.

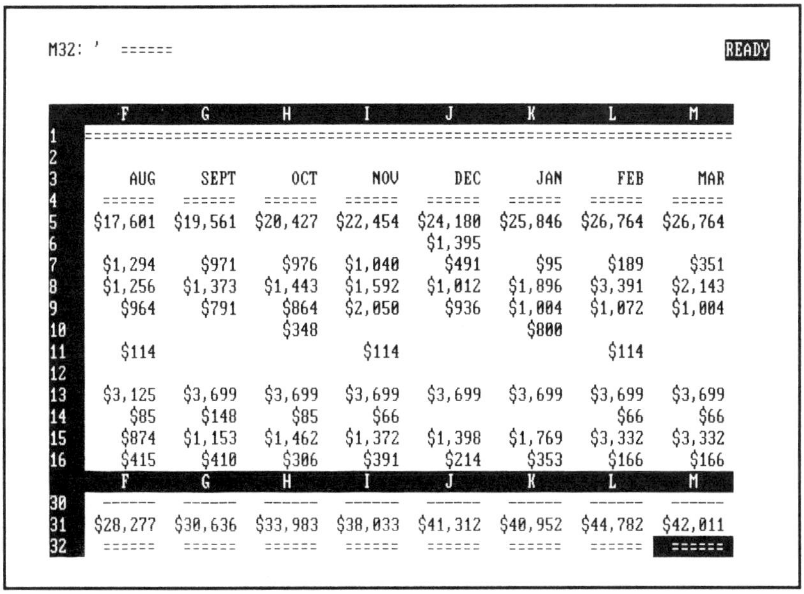

M32: ' ====== READY

	F	G	H	I	J	K	L	M
1	======	======	======	======	======	======	======	======
2								
3	AUG	SEPT	OCT	NOV	DEC	JAN	FEB	MAR
4	======	======	======	======	======	======	======	======
5	$17,601	$19,561	$20,427	$22,454	$24,180	$25,846	$26,764	$26,764
6					$1,395			
7	$1,294	$971	$976	$1,040	$491	$95	$189	$351
8	$1,256	$1,373	$1,443	$1,592	$1,012	$1,896	$3,391	$2,143
9	$964	$791	$864	$2,050	$936	$1,004	$1,072	$1,004
10			$348			$800		
11	$114			$114			$114	
12								
13	$3,125	$3,699	$3,699	$3,699	$3,699	$3,699	$3,699	$3,699
14	$85	$148	$85	$66			$66	$66
15	$874	$1,153	$1,462	$1,372	$1,398	$1,769	$3,332	$3,332
16	$415	$410	$306	$391	$214	$353	$166	$166

	F	G	H	I	J	K	L	M
30	------	------	------	------	------	------	------	------
31	$28,277	$30,636	$33,983	$38,033	$41,312	$40,952	$44,782	$42,011
32	======	======	======	======	======	======	======	======

FIGURE 6-7: Unsynchronizing windows

Once you have unsynchronized a pair of windows, you can re-synchronize them simply by issuing the Windows Sync command. If the worksheet is currently split into two horizontal window, this command shifts the inactive window (the one in which the cell pointer is not positioned) so that the same columns are visible in that window as are visible in the ative window (the one in which the cell pointer is positioned at the time), and synchronizes the horizontal scrolling of the windows. For example, if you issue the / Worksheet Windows Sync command while the worksheet looks like the one shown in Figure 6-7 (note that the bottom window is active), 1-2-3 will shift columns A through G into view in the top window. At that point, the worksheet will look like the one shown in Figure 6-6, except that the upper window would be active. If the worksheet is currently split into two vertical windows, the / Worksheet Window Sync command shifts the inactive window so that the same rows are visible in that window as are visible in the active window. If the worksheet contains only a single window, no shifting occurs. However, windows that you create subsequently will be synchronized.

The [Window] key, revisited

As we explained earlier, the [Window] key moves the cell pointer to the opposite window. However, the exact cell to which 1-2-3 moves the cell pointer depends on whether the windows are synchronized or not. If you press the [Window] key while the worksheet is divided into two unsynchronized windows, 1-2-3 will move the cell pointer to the opposite window and position it on the cell on which it was positioned the last time that window was active. For example, suppose you move the cell pointer to cell K3 in the upper window of the worksheet shown in Figure 6-7, then press the [Window] key to activate the lower window. If you press the [Window] key again at that point, 1-2-3 will reactivate the upper window and position the cell pointer on cell K3—no matter which cell it was on in the lower window.

The action of the [Window] key in synchronized windows depends on whether the windows are horizontal or vertical. If the worksheet is split horizontally, the [Window] key will activate the opposite window and position the cell pointer on the cell at the intersection of the current column (the one in which the cell pointer was positioned in the other window) and the row that the cell pointer was in the last time the newly-activated window was active. For example, suppose that, while the worksheet looks like the one shown in Figure 6-6, you press [Window] to move the cell pointer to the upper window, then move the cell pointer to column M. If you press [Window] again, 1-2-3 will activate the lower window and position the cell pointer on cell M32—not P32. Similarly, if the worksheet is split vertically, the [Window] key will activate the opposite window and position the cell pointer on the cell at the intersection of the current row (the one in which the cell pointer was positioned in the other window) and the column that the cell pointer was in the last time the newly-activated window was active.

The Clear Option

If you want to unsplit the screen, you issue /Worksheet Window Clear. As soon as you do this, 1-2-3 will unsplit the screen so it contains only one window.

When you issue the /Worksheet Window Clear command, the cell pointer will return to its last position in the upper window or the left window. After the screen is unsplit, the one window will show the same part of the worksheet that the upper window or the left window in the split screen had been displaying.

Notes

Although there are two windows on the screen in Figure 6-4, there is just one active 1-2-3 worksheet. When you split the screen into two windows, all you do is create a new "porthole" through which to view the worksheet. You do not create a second worksheet. Any entry you make through one window will be stored in the worksheet and will be displayed in the other window when it is properly positioned. Any command you issue in one window will affect the worksheet, and its effects will be visible in both windows.

If you want to, you can define separate titles in each window on a two-window screen. To do this, you just define the titles in the first window in the usual way, then press [Window] to move the cell pointer to the other window and define titles in that window as well. Similarly, if you issue the / Worksheet Titles Clear command when the screen is split, only the titles in the current window are cleared.

There can be only two windows at a time on the screen in 1-2-3. If the window is split and you try to split it again, 1-2-3 will simply beep. If you want to change the position of a split, or if you want to change the split from Vertical to Horizontal, you'll have to use the / Worksheet Window Clear command to unsplit the window before you resplit it in the new way.

As we have mentioned, you can split the screen vertically. For example, suppose you want to split the screen in Figure 6-1 so that you can view the totals in column P at the same time you are viewing the entries in the leftmost columns in the worksheet. To do this, move the cell pointer to column G in Figure 6-1, then issue the / Worksheet Window Vertical command. Figure 6-8 shows the result of this command. As you can see, the window is now split vertically between columns F and G. If you wanted to bring column P into view, you would press [Window], then press ➡ to move the cell pointer to column P. Of course, once you have split the screen vertically, you can use the [Window] key to move the cell pointer from window to window, you can unsynchronize the two windows, and you can create titles in either or both windows.

F1: \=   READY

	A B C	D	E	F		G
1	==	======	======	======	1	======
2	XYZ CORP. EXPENSE PROJECTION				2	
3	OPERATING EXPENSES	JUNE	JULY	AUG	3	SEPT
4	=================================	======	======	======	4	======
5	SALARIES	$19,917	$18,993	$17,601	5	$19,561
6	BONUS		$5,000		6	
7	CONTRACT LABOR	$423	$145	$1,294	7	$971
8	PAYROLL TAXES	$1,400	$1,746	$1,256	8	$1,373
9	GROUP MEDICAL INS	$933	$933	$964	9	$791
10	FUTA, SUTA, WORKMEN'S COMP	$698	$994		10	
11	LIFE INSURANCE	$124		$114	11	
12	LIABILITY INSURANCE	$346			12	
13	OFFICE LEASE	$3,125	$3,125	$3,125	13	$3,699
14	EQUIPMENT LEASE	$168	$936	$85	14	$148
15	TELEPHONE	$1,040	$1,600	$874	15	$1,153
16	SHIPPING & DELIVERIES	$247	$355	$415	16	$410
17	OFFICE SUPPLIES	$216	$322	$217	17	$196
18	COMPUTER SUPPLIES	$219	$331	$416	18	$122
19	STATIONARY AND FORMS	$44	$58	$300	19	$307
20	POSTAGE		$303	$150	20	$505

FIGURE 6-8: A vertical split

FILLING RANGES

The /Data Fill command allows you to fill a range of cells with an equally spaced series of numbers. This command comes in handy any time you need to create a series—for example, when you want to number the entries in a data base or enter a date series in the worksheet.

When you issue the / Data Fill command, 1-2-3 will display the prompt *Enter fill range:*. When you see this prompt, you select the range you want 1-2-3 to fill and press [Enter]. Next, 1-2-3 will prompt you to define the start value—the value you want 1-2-3 to place in the first cell of the range. The default start value is 0. You can press [Enter] to use this default, or you can type any value (including a formula or function) and press [Enter]. After you define the start value, 1-2-3 will prompt you to define the step value—the interval you want between each number in the range. The default step value is 1. You can press [Enter] to use this default, or you can type any value and press [Enter]. Finally, 1-2-3 will prompt you to define the stop value. The default stop value is 8191 (which just happens to be one less than the number of rows in the worksheet). The stop value should always be greater than or equal to the largest value you want 1-2-3 to place in the fill range.

When you press [Enter] to lock in the stop value, 1-2-3 will fill the range you selected with the series you defined.

An Example

Suppose you want to fill cells A1 to A10 in a blank worksheet with a series of numbers that begins with 0. You want the interval between the numbers in the list to be 1. To begin, move the cell pointer to cell A1, then issue the / Data Fill command. When 1-2-3 prompts you to define the fill range, select the range A1..A10 and press [Enter].

Now you must define the start, step, and stop values. Since the start value and the step value you want to use match the default start and step values, you can press [Enter] twice to accept these defaults. Since the default stop value, 8191, is larger than the largest value you want 1-2-3 to enter into the fill range, you can press [Enter] to accept this default as well.

As soon as you press [Enter] to lock in the stop value, 1-2-3 will execute the command. Figure 6-9 shows the result. Notice that cell A1 contains the value 0, cell A2 the value 1, cell A3 the value 2, and so on through cell A10, which contains the value 9.

Notes

When you issue the / Data Fill command for the first time, 1-2-3 will follow the prompt *Enter fill range:* with a reference to the current cell. This value is 1-2-3's guess at the fill range. Typically, you'll want to move the cell pointer to the first cell in the range you want to fill so that you can base the range on this guess.

```
A1: 0                                                    READY

     A      B      C      D      E      F      G      H
1    0
2    1
3    2
4    3
5    4
6    5
7    6
8    7
9    8
10   9
11
```

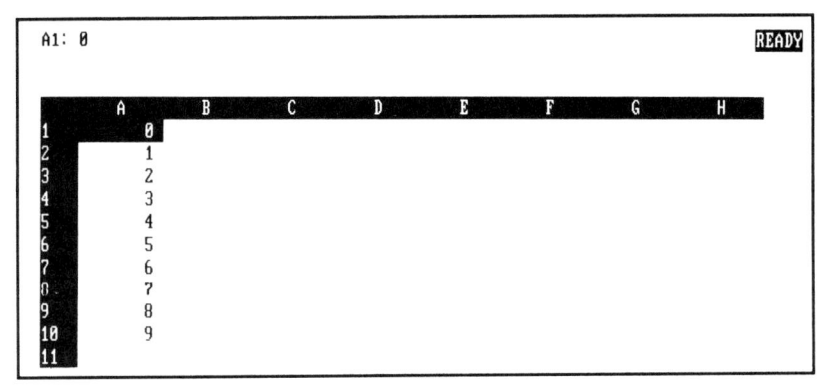

FIGURE 6-9: The / Data Fill command

After you use / Data Fill once in a worksheet, 1-2-3 will remember the fill range and the start, step, and stop values you have defined. The next time you issue the / Data Fill command, 1-2-3 will offer your previous settings as the new defaults. This makes it easy to fill the same range with a different series.

Filling a Rectangular Range

You can also use the / Data Fill command to fill a rectangular range. For example, suppose you want to fill the range A1..D5 of a blank worksheet with a series. You want 1-2-3 to enter 10 in the first cell of the range and use a step value of 1. To do this, issue the / Data Fill command, select the range A1..D5 and press [Enter] to define the fill range, type 10 and press [Enter] to define the start value; type 1 and press [Enter] to define the step value; and press [Enter] to accept the default stop value and execute the command.

Figure 6-10 shows the result. Notice that 1-2-3 has filled the range in column-by-column order. In other words, 1-2-3 has entered the values 10, 11, 12, 13, and 14 in column A, then the values 15 through 19 in column B, and so on. As in this case, / Data Fill always fills rectangular fill ranges column-by-column.

The Step Value

Although the step value can be a number of any size (including a negative number, as you'll see in a moment), it is always a constant. In other words, the interval between every number in the fill range will be the same. There is no way to use / Data Fill to create a series of numbers that have a variable interval.

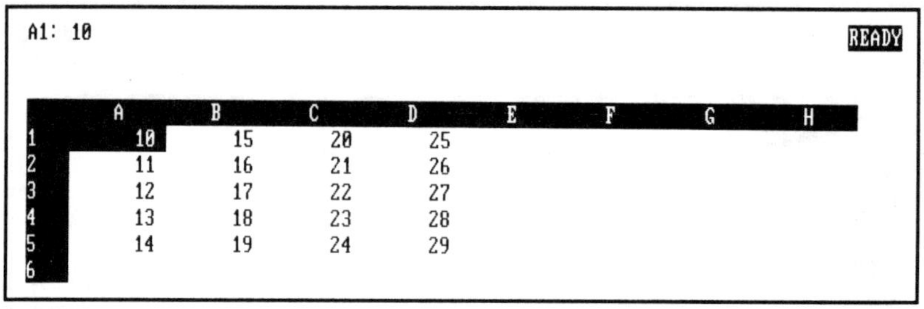

```
A1: 10                                                    READY

     A        B        C        D        E        F        G        H
1    10       15       20       25
2    11       16       21       26
3    12       17       22       27
4    13       18       23       28
5    14       19       24       29
6
```

FIGURE 6-10: Filling a rectangular range

The Stop Value

The stop value allows you to tell 1-2-3 to stop filling the fill range when the numbers it is entering in the range reach a certain value. You can think of the stop value and the fill range as being two separate braking systems for / Data Fill. 1-2-3 will stop filling when it reaches the end of the fill range or when the numbers that it enters in the range reach the stop value, whichever comes first.

For example, suppose you want to fill the range A1..A10 in a blank worksheet with a series of values. You want the series to begin with 0 and have an interval of 1. However, you also want 1-2-3 to stop filling the range when the numbers in the range reach 5. To do this, issue the / Data Fill command, select the range A1..A10, specify a start value of 0, a step value of 1, and a stop value of 5. Figure 6-11 shows the result. Notice that 1-2-3 has filled only part of the fill range you specified. 1-2-3 stopped filling the range because the number in cell A6, 5, equals the stop value.

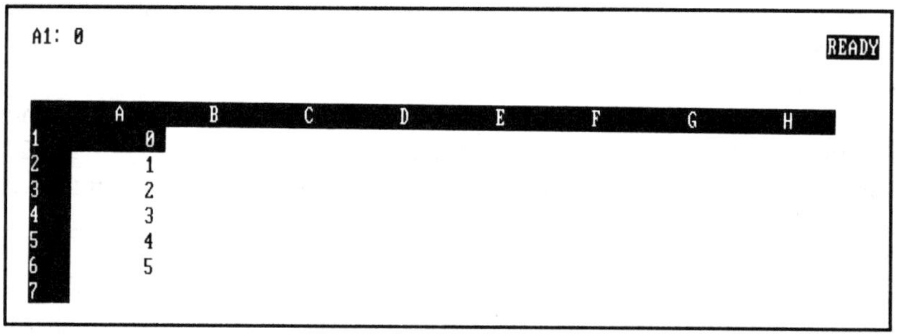

```
A1: 0                                                     READY

     A        B        C        D        E        F        G        H
1    0
2    1
3    2
4    3
5    4
6    5
7
```

FIGURE 6-11: The stop value

You may wonder why you would ever bother to use the stop value. Why not just define the fill range so that the last cell in the fill range contains the last value in the series? Here's why. When you are filling a large range, you won't always be able to figure out exactly what the last value in the fill range will be. In those cases, you can define a larger than necessary fill range, then use the stop value to make sure that 1-2-3 stops filling at the proper point.

Always be sure to set the stop value large enough for the series you are creating. If the start value is greater than the stop value, 1-2-3 will not fill any cells in the fill range. If the stop value is larger than the start value, but smaller than the largest number you want 1-2-3 to enter in the range, 1-2-3 will stop the fill prematurely.

Using Negative and Decimal Values

The start, step, and stop values can be positive or negative, and can be integer, decimal, or mixed numbers. There is one trick to watch out for, however. Whenever the step value is less than 0, you'll need to make sure that the stop value is *less* than the start value. If the step value is less than 0 and the start value is negative, the stop value must be negative as well.

Using Formulas and Functions

Although the start, step, and stop values will usually be simple numbers, they can also be formulas or functions. For example, you'll usually use an @DATE function as the start value in a date series. (We'll show you how to create a date series in Chapter 7.) To use a formula or function as the start, step, or stop value, you just type the formula or function when 1-2-3 prompts you to define the Start, Step, or stop value.

When you use a formula or function as the start, step, or stop value, 1-2-3 will convert that formula or function to a simple value as it creates the series. If you repeat the / Data Fill command, 1-2-3 will offer the value of the function or formula—and not the function or formula itself—as the default setting.

COMPUTING FREQUENCY DISTRIBUTIONS

The / Data Distribution command makes it possible to compute frequency distributions. A frequency distribution is a table that tells you how many values from a group fall within a certain range. For example, you might use a frequency distribution to determine the number of families responding to a survey that have incomes over $100,000; the number of families that have incomes between $75,000 and $100,000; the number of families that have incomes between $50,000 and $75,000; and so on.

Before 1-2-3 can compute a frequency distribution, you must enter two sets of numbers into the worksheet. The first set contains the values that you want 1-2-3 to group in the frequency distribution. 1-2-3 calls the range of cells containing the values you want to group the *values range*. Next, you must define the groups into which you want 1-2-3 to divide the values in the values range. 1-2-3 calls this range of cells the *bin range* since it defines the "bins" into which you want to group the entries in the values range.

Once you have entered these values into the worksheet, you issue the / Data Distribution command. When you issue this command, 1-2-3 will display the prompt *Enter values range:*, followed by a reference to the current cell. When you see this prompt, point to the range that contains the values you want to group and press [Enter] (you can also type the range reference). Next, 1-2-3 will display the prompt *Enter bin range:*, again followed by a reference to the current cell. This time, you should point to the range that contains the "bin" values (or type the range reference) and press

[Enter]. When you press [Enter], 1-2-3 will use the values in the values and bin ranges to compute a frequency distribution.

An Example

The range B1..B12 in Figure 6-12 contains a list of test scores. Suppose you want to compute a frequency distribution that tells you how many students scored 70 or less, how many scored 80 or less but more than 70, how many scored 90 or less but more than 80, and so on.

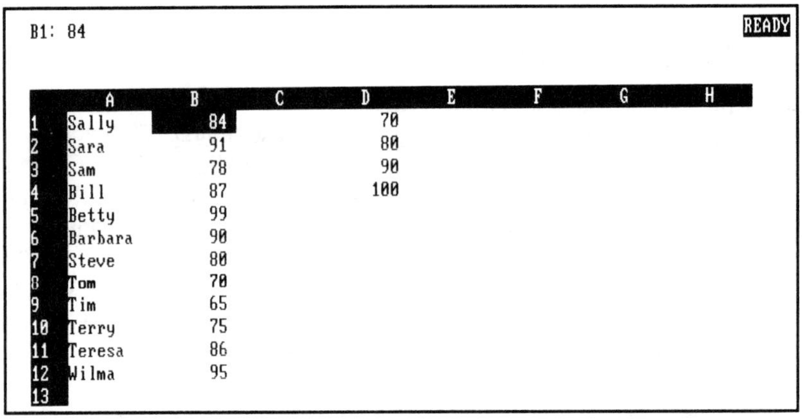

```
B1: 84                                                          READY

       A        B        C        D        E        F        G        H
 1   Sally     84                 70
 2   Sara      91                 80
 3   Sam       78                 90
 4   Bill      87                100
 5   Betty     99
 6   Barbara   90
 7   Steve     80
 8   Tom       70
 9   Tim       65
10   Terry     75
11   Teresa    86
12   Wilma     95
13
```

FIGURE 6-12: A set of values

The first step in computing a frequency distribution is to set up the values and bin ranges. In the example, the entries you want to group are in the range B1..B12 so that will be the values range. The bin range must include the values that define the groups you want 1-2-3 to use in computing the frequency distribution. Figure 6-12 shows the bin range values in the range D1..D4. These values—70, 80, 90, and 100—are the scores you want to use as dividing points when we compute the distribution.

Now, to compute the distribution, issue the / Data Distribution command. When you issue this command, 1-2-3 will prompt you to define the values range. You should point to the range B1..B12 and press [Enter]. Then 1-2-3 will prompt you to define the bin range. You should point to the range D1..D4 and press [Enter]. Once these ranges are defined, 1-2-3 will compute the distribution.

Figure 6-13 shows the result. The values in column E represent the number of items from the values range that fall into each of the bins defined by the numbers in column D. For example, the number 2 in cell E1 indicates that two students scored 70 or lower. The number 3 in cell E2 shows that three students scored 80 or less but more than 70.

```
B1: 84                                                    READY

      A         B      C      D      E      F      G      H
 1  Sally      84            70      2
 2  Sara       91            80      3
 3  Sam        78            90      4
 4  Bill       87           100      3
 5  Betty      99                    0
 6  Barbara    90
 7  Steve      80
 8  Tom        70
 9  Tim        65
10  Terry      75
11  Teresa     86
12  Wilma      95
13
```

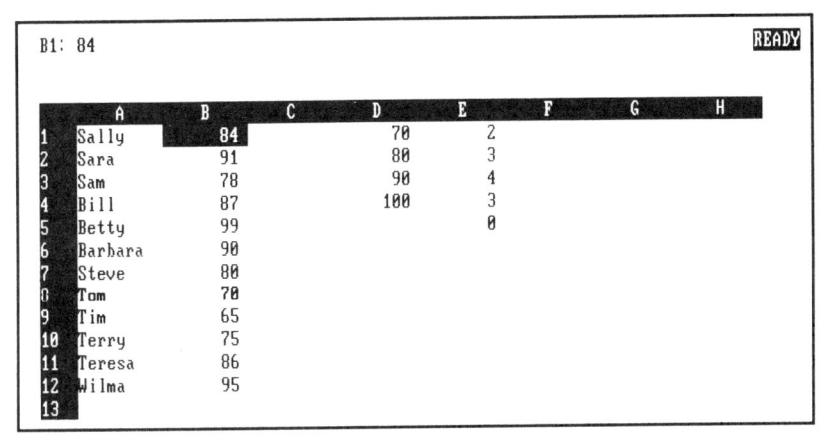

FIGURE 6-13: The / Data Distribution command

Notes

Notice that the first cell in the bin range, D1, includes the lowest bin range value, 70, and that the last cell, D4, contains the highest value, 100. You must always arrange the bin range values in ascending numeric order, beginning with the lowest value in the top cell of the bin range.

When 1-2-3 creates the distribution, it uses the values in the bin range as the upper limit for each bin. Each bin contains the values that are less than or equal to the bin value of that bin, but greater than the next lowest bin value. If a value is exactly equal to one of the bin range values, it will be placed in the bin next to that bin range value.

The number 0 in cell E5 tells you that no students scored above 100. As in this case, 1-2-3 will always include one more value in the result of the distribution than there are entries in the bin range. The "extra" entry tells you how many values are greater than the last value in the bin range.

Once you have defined the values and bin ranges, 1-2-3 will remember those ranges. If you want to recompute the distribution, you just reissue the / Data Distribution command and press [Enter] twice to accept the "remembered" values and bin range settings. Of course, if you want to use a different values or bin range, you must respecify that range. The values range and the bin range can be located anywhere in the worksheet and do not have to be located near one another. In most cases, however, you'll want the values range and the bin range to be adjacent. In addition, there are no limits on the number of values that can be included in the values range or the bin range, or on the sizes of those values. Both ranges, however, should contain only values—labels are not allowed.

DATA TABLES

One of the most important benefits of spreadsheet software is that it allows you to perform "what-if" analysis quickly and easily. You've probably performed what-if analysis manually many times. For example, suppose you are considering setting up an IRA (Individual Retirement Account). You plan to invest $2000 per year in the IRA for 30 years, at which time you will cash in the investment. You need to know how much the IRA will be worth in 30 years. Obviously, the value of the IRA in 30 years is affected directly by the rate of interest that the IRA will earn across that time.

To solve this problem manually, you might create a little table. The left-hand column of this table would list several different interest rates. The right-hand column would show the value of the IRA that results from each of those interest rates. (You would use a financial calculator to compute the future value of this investment.) By creating the table, you get a better feel for the effect of interest rates on the value of the IRA.

1-2-3's / Data Table command allows you to build this kind of "what-if" table in the 1-2-3 worksheet. In other words, this command lets you create a table that computes several outcomes for a formula or function using several different values for a variable. / Data Table is one of 1-2-3's most powerful—and, unfortunately, least used—commands.

Basics

Before you can use the / Data Table command, you must set up a data table in the worksheet. Every data table includes one or two sets of variables and at least one formula (called the table formula) that you want to compute. The precise form of the table depends on whether the table is a one-variable or two-variable table, and on how many formulas you will be testing. We'll explain the form of data tables in a few pages.

When you issue the / Data Table command, 1-2-3 will display a menu with three options: 1, 2, and Reset. / Data Table allows you to create two kinds of data tables: one-variable tables and two-variable tables. This menu lets you tell 1-2-3 how many variables are in the current table. The Reset option allows you to reset the ranges you have defined previously.

After you tell 1-2-3 how many variables it will be working with, you'll see the prompt *Enter table range:*, followed by a reference to the current cell. When you see this prompt, you should select the table range and press [Enter]. The table range is always the smallest rectangular range that includes the table formula and all of the variables.

Finally, 1-2-3 will prompt you to define the input cell (or cells if it is a two-variable table) for the table. The input cell of a data table is a cell that is referred to, at least indirectly, by the table formula. When 1-2-3 computes the data table, it will substitute the variables from the table into the input cell, one at a time, recalculating the table formula after each substitution. The results of each computation are stored in the table.

A One-Variable Table

Let's build a data table that computes the future value of an IRA at five different interest rates: 5%, 7.5%, 10%, 12.5%, and 15%. To build this table, you must first enter these interest rates (in the form .05, .075, etc.) in cells A4 to A8 of your worksheet.

We'll call the range A4..A8 the *input range*, or the *variable range*, because it contains the inputs, or variables, you want to run through the formula.

Next, enter the function @FV(2000,B1,30) in cell B3. Figure 6-14 shows the worksheet with this formula in place. We'll call the function in cell B3 the *table formula*. Notice that this function refers to cell B1. Because B1 is blank, the function returns the result ERR.

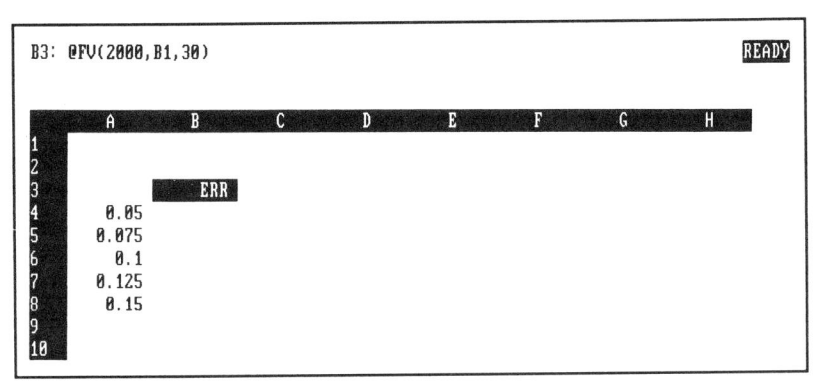

```
B3: @FV(2000,B1,30)                                                    READY

       A        B        C        D        E        F        G        H
 1
 2
 3              ERR
 4     0.05
 5     0.075
 6     0.1
 7     0.125
 8     0.15
 9
10
```

FIGURE 6-14: A data table

Issuing the Command

Once you've set up the table, issue the / Data Table command. Since this is a one-variable table, you should choose 1 from the Data Table menu. Next, 1-2-3 will display the prompt *Enter table range:*. When you see this prompt, you should select the range A3..B8 and press [Enter]. Notice that this is the smallest rectangular range that contains all of the variables and the table formula. Finally, 1-2-3 will display the prompt *Enter input cell:*. Remember that the input cell of a data table is a cell that is referred to, at least indirectly, by the table formula. Do you recall that our table formula (in cell B3) referred to the blank cell B1? In the example, B1 will be the input cell. You should select this cell and press [Enter].

As soon as you press [Enter] to lock in the input cell, 1-2-3 will compute the table. After a second or two, 1-2-3 will enter the five results of the table formula (one result for each input value) into the range B4..B8. Figure 6-15 shows the screen at this point.

How It Works

Here's how it works. When you pressed [Enter] to lock in the input cell, 1-2-3 automatically substituted the first value from the variable list, .05, into the input cell, B1. Then 1-2-3 computed the table formula in cell B3. Since the table formula refers to cell B1, it returns a different result whenever a new value is entered in cell B1. When B1 has the value .05, the formula in cell B3 has the value 132877.6. After it performed this calculation, 1-2-3 entered this result in cell B4—the cell to the right of the value .05 in the variable list.

Next, 1-2-3 substituted the second variable from column A, .075, into cell B1, and recomputed the table formula in cell A3. Since the value in cell B1 has changed, the formula in cell B3 will again take on a new value. 1-2-3 enters this new value, 206798.8, into the table in cell B5, next to the value .075 in the list.

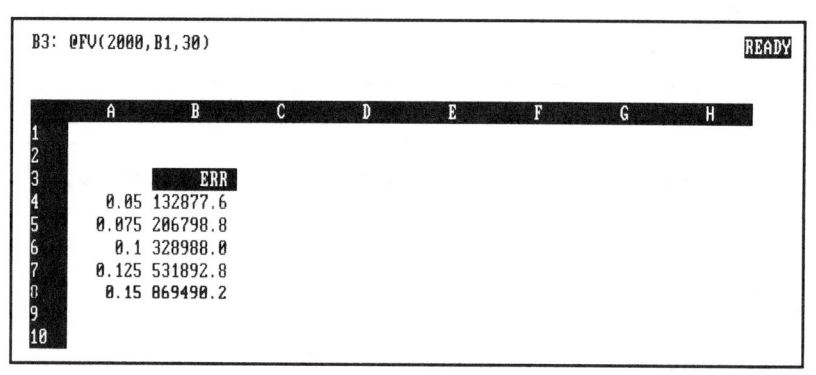

```
B3: @FV(2000,B1,30)                                              READY

         A        B        C        D        E        F        G        H
1
2
3                ERR
4      0.05   132877.6
5      0.075  206798.8
6      0.1    328988.0
7      0.125  531892.8
8      0.15   869490.2
9
10
```

FIGURE 6-15: A completed data table

This process of substitution and recalculation continues until all of the variables in the variable list have been used. When 1-2-3 runs out of variables, it stops recalculating the table.

The [Table] Key

Once you have built a table and defined the table range and the input cell, you might want to recompute the table using a different formula or a different set of variables. If you want to recompute the table, just change the variables or the table formula (or both), and then press the [Table] key ([F8] on the IBM PC). Pressing [Table] tells 1-2-3 to recompute the active data table.

For example, suppose you want to figure out how much better off you'd be if you invested $4000 per year in your IRA. To make this computation, change the formula in cell B3 to @FV(4000,B1,30) and then press the [Table] key. Immediately, 1-2-3 will recompute the table using this new formula.

A Table with Two Equations

You can include as many table formulas as you want in a one-variable data table. The second formula is entered in the cell immediately to the right of the first formula. Other formulas are entered in the same row to the right of the second formula. Of course, all of the formulas must refer, at least indirectly, to the table's input cell.

For example, suppose you want to compute the future value of the IRA assuming annual contributions of $2000 and $4000. You can modify the table in Figure 6-15 to make this calculation. To do this, just move the cell pointer to cell C3 and enter the function @FV(4000,B1,30). Like the first formula, the formula in cell C3 refers to cell B1, the input cell, and returns the result ERR.

After you have created this table, you must redefine the table range. As before, the table range will be the smallest rectangular range that includes the table formulas and all of the entries in the variable range. In this case, then, the table range would be A3..C8. To make this change, issue the /Data Table 1 command. When you issue this command, 1-2-3 will highlight the old table range. You should press → to change the range to A3..C8, then press [Enter] to lock in this new range. Since the input cell has not changed, you can press [Enter] to accept the existing setting.

As soon as you lock in the input cell, 1-2-3 will begin recomputing the table. After a moment, 1-2-3 will enter the results for the new equation in the range C4..C8, as shown in Figure 6-16. As before, 1-2-3 computes this table by substituting the values in the range A4..A8, one at a time, into the input cell, B1. After each substitution, 1-2-3 recomputes the table formulas in cells B3 and C3. Since both of these formulas refer to cell B1, they will both take on different values when the value in cell B1 changes. 1-2-3 stores these different results in columns B and C of the data table.

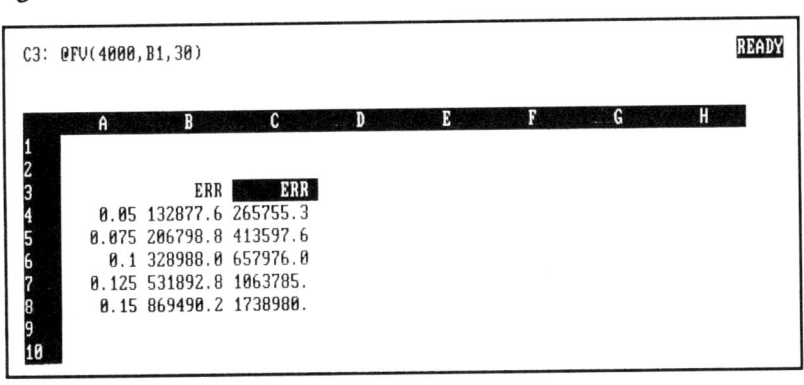

```
C3:  @FV(4000,B1,30)                                         READY

         A       B        C       D      E      F      G      H
1
2
3                       ERR      ERR
4              0.05  132877.6  265755.3
5              0.075 206798.8  413597.6
6              0.1   328988.0  657976.0
7              0.125 531892.8  1063785.
8              0.15  869490.2  1738980.
9
10
```

FIGURE 6-16: A two-formula table

A Two-Variable Table

In the examples we have considered so far, we computed the results of a formula as we changed a single variable (the interest rate). 1-2-3 also allows you to create data tables that compute the results of a formula as two variables change. For example, suppose that you want to build another data table that will compute the future value of your IRA. This time, you want to vary not only the interest rate, but also the term of the investment. You want to know what effect terms of 20, 25, 30, and 35 years will have on the future value of the IRA.

The first step in creating this table is to enter the five interest rates that you want to test in the range A4..A8 of a blank worksheet. Next, you must enter the different terms that you want to test—20, 25, 30, and 35 years—in the range B3..E3. Now you're ready to create the table formula. Because this is a two-variable table, the table formula must go in the cell at the intersection of the row and the column that contain the two sets of input values—in this example, cell A3. The table formula for this table is *@FV(2000,B1,B2)*. Notice that this formula refers to two blank cells, B1 and B2.

(Because both of these cells are blank, the table formula returns the value 0.) In a moment you will define cells B1 and B2 as the input cells for the table. Figure 6-17 shows the table.

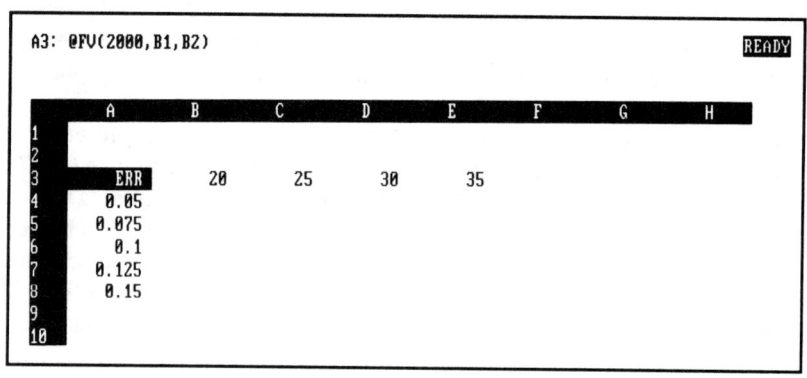

```
A3: @FV(2000,B1,B2)                                              READY

        A        B        C        D        E        F        G        H
1
2
3      ERR      20       25       30       35
4     0.05
5     0.075
6     0.1
7     0.125
8     0.15
9
10
```

FIGURE 6-17: A two-variable table

Next, issue the /Data Table command and, since this is a two-variable table, choose the 2 option. Next, 1-2-3 will prompt you to define the table range. Just as with the one-variable table, the table range for a two-variable table is the smallest rectangular range that includes all of the input values and the table formula. In the example, the table range is A3..E8. When 1-2-3 prompts you to define the table range, select the range A3..E8 and press [Enter].

Now 1-2-3 will prompt you to define the table's input cells. Because this is a two-variable data table, you must define two input cells—one for the variables in the first column of the table and one for the variables in the first row of the table. When it processes the table, 1-2-3 will substitute the variables from the first column of the table into input cell 1, and will substitute the values from the first row of the table into input cell 2. It is important that you do not reverse the input cells in a two-variable table. If you do, 1-2-3 will use the input values in the wrong places in the table formula, creating meaningless results.

As you may recall, the table formula for this table refers to cells B1 and B2. Since we want 1-2-3 to substitute the variables from column A into cell B1, that cell will be iinput cell 1 for this table. Input cell 2 will be cell B2.

When you press [Enter] to lock in input cell 2, 1-2-3 will compute the table. The result is shown in Figure 6-18. The numbers in the result range of this table are the future values of the IRA at each combination of interest rates and terms. For example, the number in cell C5, 135955.7, is the future value of the IRA at an interest rate of 7.5% and a term of 25 years.

As before, 1-2-3 computed this table using a process of substitution and recalculation. To begin, 1-2-3 substituted the first value from column A, 0.05, into cell B1, and the first value from row 3, 20, into cell B2, computed the table formula, and stored the result, 66131.90, in cell B4, next to the value 0.05 in the column A variable list and below the value 20 in the row 3 variable list. After this, 1-2-3 substituted the second variable in the column A variable list, 0.075, into cell B1, substituted the first variable from the row 3 list, 20, into cell B2 again, recomputed the table formula in cell A3, and stored that result in cell B5. The process continued until each pair of variables had been used.

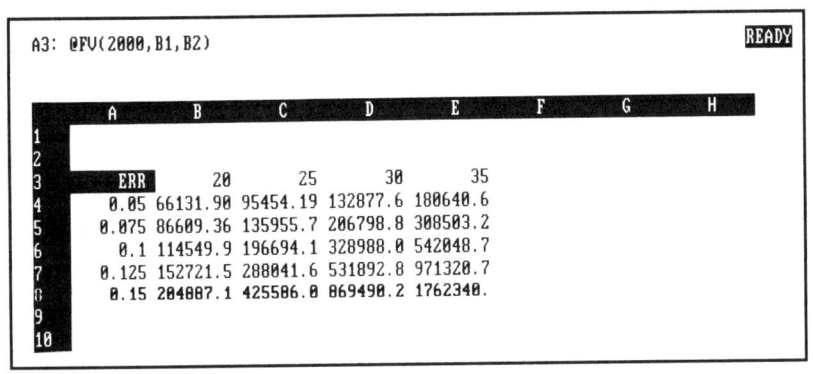

```
A3: @FV(2000,B1,B2)                                              READY

        A        B        C        D         E        F    G    H
1
2
3      ERR      20       25        30        35
4      0.05   66131.90  95454.19  132877.6  180640.6
5      0.075  86609.36 135955.7   206798.8  308503.2
6      0.1   114549.9  196694.1   328988.0  542048.7
7      0.125 152721.5  288041.6   531892.8  971320.7
8      0.15  204807.1  425586.0   869490.2 1762340.
9
10
```

FIGURE 6-18: A two-variable data table

Notes

For convenience, we positioned the example data tables in the upper-left corner of the worksheet. However, there are no restrictions on the position of a data table. You can create a data table in any part of the worksheet.

Similarly, we used cells B1 and B2 as the input cells in our examples, but there are no restrictions on the position of the input cell(s) either. The only rule about the input cell(s) are that they must be referred to, at least indirectly, by the table formula. In the examples, our table formulas referred directly to the input cell. However, you can also create data tables that have formulas that refer indirectly to the input cell (that is, formulas that refer to cells that contain formulas which refer to the input cell). As long as there is at least an indirect link between the table formula and the input cell, the table will work properly.

In addition, although the input cells in the previous examples were blank, the input cell you define may contain an entry. In fact, in most cases the input cell of your data tables will contain an entry. When the input cell contains an entry, 1-2-3 stores that entry temporarily while it substitutes and recalculates. When the entire process is finished, 1-2-3 returns the original entry to the input cell.

It is important that you understand that the entries in the results column of a data table are pure values, and not formulas or functions. For example, the entry stored in cell B5 of the table in Figure 6-15 is 206798.80504. Because these entries are pure values, they can be copied to any other location in the worksheet without any concern about absolute and relative references.

Once you have defined a data table, 1-2-3 will remember that definition. If you reissue the / Data Table command, 1-2-3 will use the previous definitions for the table range and the input cell(s) as the new defaults for those settings. If you want 1-2-3 to forget the previous settings, you should issue / Data Table Reset.

Although you can include as many formulas as you want in a one-variable table, you can include only one formula in a two-variable table. There is no way to test two formulas at once in a two-variable table. To test the second and subsequent formulas, you must recalculate the table repeatedly.

COMPUTING LINEAR REGRESSION

Linear regression is a technique that measures the extent to which one characteristic of a data set (the dependent variable) depends upon, or is influenced or determined by, another characteristic (the independent variable). For example, you can use linear regression to measure the extent to which the annual income of a group of people is determined by educational attainment, grade point average is determined by the amount of time spent studying, or weight is determined by height.

The / Data Regression command lets perform linear regression in your 1-2-3 worksheets. (This command is not available n 1-2-3 Release 1A.) ►If you are using 1-2-3 Release 2.2, you'll see the menu and the settings sheet shown in Figure 6-19 when you issue the / Data Regression command. (If you are using an earlier version of 123, you'll see only the menu; you won't see the settings sheet.)◄ To compute the regression statistics, you must define the X range, the Y range, and the Output range, and choose Go. The X range should be the range that contains the dependent values, and the Y range should be the range that contains the dependent values. The Output range should be a blank area of the worksheet where you want 1-2-3 to place the results of the command. You need specify only the address of the upper-left corner of the Output range you want 1-2-3 to use.

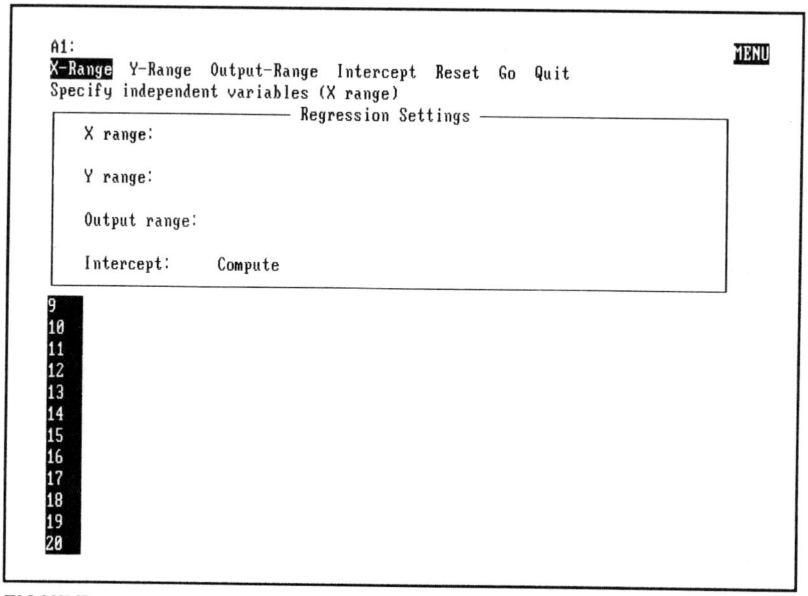

RELEASE ► 2.2 ◄

FIGURE 6-19: The / Data Regression menu

You can use the results of the / Data Regression command to plot a regression line, to predict the Y value that corresponds to a given X value, and to measure the certainty with which you can use the Y range values to predict the X range values. Let's look at an example of how this command can be used.

An Example

Figure 6-20 shows a worksheet that contains Age, Height, and Weight data for nine individuals. We'll assume that we selected these nine men at random from a large group, which we'll call the population. This group of nine men is a sample.

```
A1:                                                              READY

         A         B        C        D       E       F         G       H
 1                Age    Height   Weight
 2   John P.      35       72      220            Sample Age:
 3   Henry        17       60      135            Sample Height:
 4   Bill         22       66      150            Predicted Weight:
 5   Mike         25       76      220
 6   Dave         28       62      140
 7   John S.      19       65      140
 8   Mitch        18       70      150
 9   Milt         15       68      145
10   James        29       67      180
11
```

FIGURE 6-20: A sample worksheet

Suppose you want to use the / Data Regression command to perform linear regression on this data. To begin, you must determine which is the dependent (Y) variable and which is the independent (X) variable. In this case, we'll use height to predict weight. In other words, height will be the independent (or X) variable and weight will be the dependent (or Y) variable.

Once you have figured out the dependent and independent variables, you should issue the / Data Regression command. When you see the menu in Figure 6-19, choose the X-Range option, select the range C2..C10, and press [Enter]. Then choose the Y-Range option, select the range D2..D10, and press [Enter]. Next, choose Output-Range, point to cell A12, and press [Enter] again. Finally, choose Go to compute the regression. Figure 6-21 shows the result. Notice that 1-2-3 has created a small table in the range A12..D20 to hold the regression results.

Using the Results

The two most important results of the / Data Regression command are the Constant and the X Coefficient. The Constant is the y-axis intercept of the regression line. The X Coefficient is the slope of the regression line. In the example, cell D13 contains the Constant for the regression line: -219.656. This value is the y-axis intercept of the regression line that describes the relationship between height and weight. Cell C19 contains the X Coefficient for the regression: 5.704467. The X Coefficient predicts how much the dependent variable will change given a change of one unit in the independent variable—in other words, the slope of the regression line. The X Coefficient in the example, 5.704467, indicates that the value of Y (weight) will increase by 5.7 for each increase of 1 in the X variable (height).

```
A1:                                                                READY

            A       B        C         D       E       F       G       H
    1              Age    Height    Weight
    2    John P.    35      72        220           Sample Age:
    3    Henry      17      60        135           Sample Height:
    4    Bill       22      66        150           Predicted Weight:
    5    Mike       25      76        220
    6    Dave       28      62        140
    7    John S.    19      65        140
    8    Mitch      18      70        150
    9    Milt       15      68        145
   10    James      29      67        180
   11
   12              Regression Output:
   13    Constant                   -219.656
   14    Std Err of Y Est            20.56098
   15    R Squared                    0.680844
   16    No. of Observations                9
   17    Degrees of Freedom                 7
   18
   19    X Coefficient(s)  5.704467
   20    Std Err of Coef.  1.476192
```

FIGURE 6-21: The / Data Regression command

Making Predictions

You can use the Constant and the X Coefficient to predict the Y value for a given X value. The equation for predicting the value of Y for a given value of X is

Y=(X Coefficient*X)+Constant

(You may have seen this formula stated as y=mx+b. In this form, *m* represents the X Coefficient, or slope, and *b* represents the Constant, or y-intercept.)

For example, suppose you want to predict the value of Y for an X value of 76. To do this, move the cell pointer to cell H3 and enter the value 76. Then move to cell H4 and enter the formula ($C$19*H3)+$D$13, which will return the value 213.8831. This result is the predicted value of Y for the X value 76. In other words, the regression line predicts that a person who is 76 inches tall will weigh 213.88 pounds.

Creating the Regression Line

You can use the equation *Y=(X Coefficient*X)+Constant* to create a regression line that describes the relationship between the X and Y variables. For example, let's create the regression line that describes the relationship between height and weight in the example. To begin, move the cell pointer to cell E2 and enter the formula ($C$19*C2)+$D$13. (Notice that this formula is similar to the one in cell H4.) Next, use the / Copy command to copy the formula from cell E2 into the range E3..E10. Figure 6-22 shows the result.

```
E2: [W9] ($C$19*C2)+$D$13                                                READY

         A         B        C        D         E         F         G        H
 1                Age    Height   Weight
 2  John P.        35       72      220   191.0652 Sample Age:
 3  Henry          17       60      135   122.6116 Sample Height:        76
 4  Bill           22       66      150   156.8384 Predicted Weight: 213.88
 5  Mike           25       76      220   213.8831
 6  Dave           28       62      140   134.0206
 7  John S.        19       65      140   151.1340
 8  Mitch          18       70      150   179.6563
 9  Milt           15       68      145   168.2474
10  James          29       67      180   162.5429
11
12            Regression Output:
13  Constant                       -219.656
14  Std Err of Y Est                20.56098
15  R Squared                        0.680844
16  No. of Observations                    9
17  Degrees of Freedom                     7
18
19  X Coefficient(s)  5.704467
20  Std Err of Coef.  1.476192
```

FIGURE 6-22: Creating the regression line

The values in column E are the predicted Y values for the corresponding X values in column C. In other words, these values are the predicted weights for people who have the same height as the people in the sample. For example, this data predicts that a person who is 72 inches tall would weigh 191 pounds. As you can see, the predicted Y values in column E are close to, but are not exactly the same as, the actual Y values in column D. This is to be expected. The regression line is an estimate of the relationship between the X and Y variables. The Y values predicted by the regression are almost never exactly equal to the actual Y values. However, the predicted values depict the basic relationship between the X and Y values. In the example, the regression line predicts that weight will increase by 5.7 pounds for each one-inch increase in height.

Once you have created the regression line, you can plot it (along with the X and Y values) on an XY graph. (We'll show you how to create an XY graph and how to plot a regression line in Chapter 10.)

Interpreting the Results

So far, we have assumed that the regression results in Figure 6-21 do a good job of predicting the true relationship between height and weight. However, this is not always the case. Sometimes the results of a linear regression do not describe the relationship between the X and Y variables very precisely. Fortunately, there are statistics you can use to measure the reliability of a regression. The / Data Regression command computes several of these statistics: the Standard Error of Y Estimate, the R Squared Coefficient, the Degrees of Freedom, and the Standard Error of Coefficient.

Cell D14 contains the Standard Error of Y Estimate for the regression line: 20.56098. The Standard Error of Y Estimate helps to measure the certainty with which the independent values in the sample can be used to predict the dependent values. In general, the larger the Standard Error of Y Estimate is relative to the predicted Y (dependent) values, the less certain you can be about the prediction.

Cell D15 contains the R Squared value (also called the *coefficient of determination*) for the regression: 0.680844. The R Squared statistic tells you what percentage of the variation in the dependent variable (Y) is "explained" by the variation in the independent variable. The R Squared value can range from 1 (which would mean that the variation in the independent variable perfectly explains the variation in the dependent variable, or that the relationship between the two variables is very strong) to 0 (which would mean that there is no relationship between the variables). In general, the larger the R Squared value, the better the changes in the independent variable explain the variation in the dependent variable. The R Squared value in cell D15, 0.680844, means that about 68% of the variation in weight is explained by the variation in height.

Cell D16 contains the Number of Observations: 9. This number is simply the total number of values in the X or Y range. Cell D17 contains the Degrees of Freedom statistic for the X Coefficient: 7. For small populations like this one, degrees of freedom is computed by subtracting 2 from the number of observations.

Cell C20 contains the Standard Error of (the X) Coefficient: 1.476192. This value is an estimate of the standard deviation of the sampling distribution of the X Coeffiecient. As a rule, the larger the Standard Error of Coefficient is in relation to the X Coefficient, the less certain you can be about the prediction. In general, the larger the sample, the smaller the Standard Error of Coefficient will be. In this case, the sample was small, so the Standard Error of Coefficient is fairly large.

Multiple Regression

In the first example, we used the / Data Regression command to perform simple linear regression. In simple regression, you use one independent variable to attempt to explain the variation in a dependent variable. You can also use this command to perform multiple linear regression. In multiple regression, you use two or more independent variables to explain the dependent variable. When you use / Data Regression to perform multiple regression, 1-2-3 will return an X Coefficient and Standard Error of Coefficient for each of the independent variables.

For example, suppose you want to use both the age and height variables in Figure 16-21 to predict weight. To compute a regression based on this data, issue the / Data Regression command, choose X-Range, and select the range B2..C10. Notice that this range includes both columns that contain the independent variables. Next, choose

Y-Range and select the range D2..D10. Then choose Output-Range and select cell A12. Finally, choose Go to compute the regression. Figure 6-23 shows the result. Notice that 1-2-3 has computed X Coefficients for both independent variables, and has computed Standard Error of Coefficient statistics for both X Coefficients. Also notice that the confidence statistics have improved as a result of using a second independent variable.

```
A1:                                                              READY

        A         B         C         D         E       F        G       H
 1               Age     Height    Weight
 2  John P.       35        72       220              Sample Age:
 3  Henry         17        60       135              Sample Height:
 4  Bill          22        66       150              Predicted Weight:
 5  Mike          25        76       220
 6  Dave          28        62       140
 7  John S.       19        65       140
 8  Mitch         18        70       150
 9  Milt          15        68       145
10  James         29        67       180
11
12            Regression Output:
13  Constant                       -207.254
14  Std Err of Y Est                12.35088
15  R Squared                        0.901289
16  No. of Observations                     9
17  Degrees of Freedom                      6
18
19  X Coefficient(s)  2.537900  4.649189
20  Std Err of Coef.  0.693315  0.932426
```

FIGURE 6-23: Multiple regression

You can use the results of a multiple regression in much the same way you use the results of a simple regression. For example, suppose you want to predict the weight of an individual who is 76 inches tall and 30 years old. To do this, enter the value 30 in cell H2 and the value 76 in cell H3. Then enter the formula ($C$19*H2)+($D$19*H3)+$D$13 into cell H3. This function uses both X Coefficients and the Constant to compute the predicted value of the dependent variable, height. You could also use a similar formula to create the regression line using both X Coefficients.

The Intercept Option

The Intercept option on the / Data Regression menu allows you to compute a linear regression with a preset Constant, or y-axis intercept, of 0. In other words, when you use this option, 1-2-3 will set the y-axis intercept of the regression line at 0 and will adjust the other regression statistics (including, most importantly, the X Coefficient, or slope, of the regression line) to compensate.

When you choose the Intercept option, you'll see a menu with two options: Compute and Zero. Compute, the default, instructs 1-2-3 to compute the Constant. If you choose Zero, 1-2-3 will not compute the Constant, but instead will simply set the Constant to 0.

Setting the Constant to 0 is appropriate when a Constant of anything other than 0 would be absurd. For instance, recall that the Constants we've been working with so far are -219.656 and -207.254. These constants indicate that an individual with a height of zero inches would weigh -219 or -207 pounds— clearly absurd. It is a bit more realistic to assume that a person who is zero inches tall weighs zero pounds, so you might want to use the Intercept command to force 1-2-3 to place the y-intercept at 0 in this example. In most cases, however, you'll want 1-2-3 to compute the y-intercept for you.

MATRIX MATHEMATICS

The / Data Matrix command allows you to perform matrix mathematics in the 1-2-3 worksheet. While you may never use this command, it does have some exciting capabilites. (This command is not available in 1-2-3 Release 1A.)

When you issue the / Data Matrix command, you'll see a menu with two options: Invert and Multiply. The Invert command is used to invert a matrix. The Multiply option allows you to multiply one matrix by another. Together, these commands allow you to solve systems of simultaneous linear equations, and thus can be used to perform linear programming. In addition, the Multiply command can be used to compute expected values, given a set of probabilities and a set of possible outcomes.

The Multiply Option

The / Data Matrix Multiply command allows you to multiply one matrix by another. When you select this option, 1-2-3 will first display the prompt *Enter first range to multiply:*, which asks you to specify the range that contains the first matrix you want to multiply. Then it will display the prompt *Enter second range to multiply:*, which asks you to specify the range that contains the second matrix. Finally, 1-2-3 will display the prompt *Enter output range:*, which asks you to define the range where you want 1-2-3 to place the result of the multiplication.

Computing Expected Outcomes

One of the best uses for the / Data Matrix Multiply command is to compute the expected outcome of a forecast. Let's look at an example. Suppose you are about to launch a new product—say, a new book about 1-2-3. You think that the book could meet with an excellent reception, in which case it will sell 150,000 copies, a good reception (100,000 copies), a fair reception (75,000 copies), a marginal reception (50,000 copies), a poor reception (30,000 copies), or a disastrous reception (15,000 copies). You think that there is a 5% chance of an excellent reception, a 20% chance of a good reception, a 35% chance of a fair reception, a 25% chance of a marginal reception, a 10% chance of a poor reception, and a 5% chance of a disastrous reception. Figure 6-24 shows these values in a worksheet. You want to determine the expected level of sales of the book.

To compute the expected level of sales, you must multiply the percentage probabilities for each of the possible outcomes (Excellent, Good, and so on) by the sales level for that outcome. The sum of those products is the expected level of sales. You can use the / Data Matrix Multiply command to make this computation. To begin, issue the / Data Matrix command and choose the Multiply option. When you do this, 1-2-3 will display the prompt *Enter first range to multiply:*. When you see this prompt, select the range A11..F11 and press [Enter]. Next, 1-2-3 will display the prompt *Enter second range to multiply:*. When you see this prompt, select the range C2..C7 and press [Enter]. Finally, 1-2-3 will display the prompt *Enter output range:*. When you see this prompt, point to cell G2 and press [Enter] again. When you press [Enter] this last time, 1-2-3 will multiply the matrix A11..G11 by the matrix C2..C7. The result, the number 70000, will be stored in cell G2. As it turns out, this value is the expected level of sales for the book.

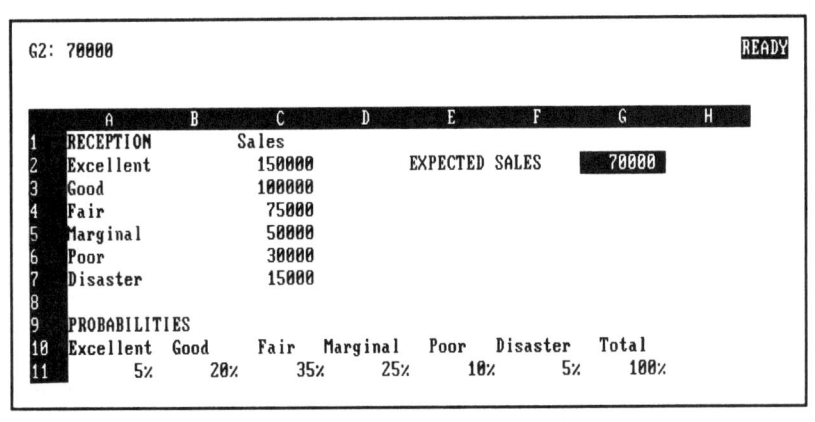

```
G2: 70000                                                              READY

         A         B         C         D         E         F         G         H
1    RECEPTION           Sales
2    Excellent           150000              EXPECTED SALES        70000
3    Good                100000
4    Fair                 75000
5    Marginal             50000
6    Poor                 30000
7    Disaster             15000
8
9    PROBABILITIES
10   Excellent  Good      Fair    Marginal    Poor    Disaster    Total
11        5%     20%       35%        25%      10%        5%       100%
```

FIGURE 6-24: The / Data Matrix Multiply command

Rules

The / Data Matrix Multiply command follows some very strict rules. First, you can use this command to multiply two matrices only if the number of rows in the first matrix is equal to the number of columns in the second matrix. This means that you could use this command to multiply two square matrices of the same size (for example, to multiply a 4 x 4 matrix by another 4 x 4 matrix) or to multiply a row vector by a column vector with the same number of elements (for example, a 3 x 1 matrix by a 1 x 3 matrix). Second, the number of columns in the first matrix multiplied by the number of rows in the second matrix must be less than 8192.

The result of a matrix multiplication is always a matrix with the same number of rows as the first matrix and the same number of columns as the second matrix. For instance, in the example we multiplied a 1 x 6 matrix by a 6 x 1 matrix. The result was a 1 x 1 matrix. If you multiply a 6 x 1 matrix by a 1 x 6 matrix, the result will be a 6 x 6 matrix. If you multiply a 5 x 5 matrix by a 5 x 5 matrix, the resulting matrix will be a 5 x 5 matrix.

If the Output range you specify contains entries, / Data Matrix Multiply will overwrite those entries. Always be sure that the Output range you select is big enough to hold the matrix that the command will produce.

Just like the numbers in a data table, the results of a / Data Matrix Multiply command are simple values—not formulas. Also as with the / Data Table command, once you've issued / Data Matrix Multiply, 1-2-3 will remember the First, Second, and Output ranges that you've defined. The next time you issue the command, 1-2-3 will use the previous ranges as the command's defaults.

The Invert Option

The / Data Matrix Invert command allows you to compute the inverse of a matrix. When you issue this command, 1-2-3 will display the prompt *Enter range to invert:*, which asks you to define the range that contains the matrix you want to invert. Next, 1-2-3 will display the prompt *Enter output range:*, which asks you to tell 1-2-3 where it should put the result of the command.

What is the inverse of a matrix? Here's the definition: The inverse of a matrix is another matrix of the same size as the original matrix. When you multiply the original matrix by its inverse matrix, the result will be an identity matrix: a matrix in which all the elements are 0, except for the first element in the first row, the second element in the second row, and so on, which are all 1.

As you might expect, the inverse matrix that results from the / Data Matrix Invert command has practical applications. Let's look at an example.

Linear Programming

Linear programming is a technique that can be used to determine how to achieve an optimal outcome given a set of constraints. For example, you could use linear programming to determine the optimal mix of two or more ingredients that are used in the production of two or more products. The optimal mix of ingredients is the mix that will achieve the highest possible sales (or profits). While a full discussion of linear programming is beyond the scope of this book, we will show one simple example of a linear programming problem and show how the / Data Matrix command can be used to solve linear programming problems.

Suppose you own a company that produces two products: Widgets and Wombats. Producing a Widget consumes one hour of time and seven pounds of raw material. Making a Wombat requires three hours of time and four pounds of raw material. Each Widget you make earns you $4 and each Wombat earns you $6. You have at your disposal 24 hours of time and 100 pounds of raw material. What is the most efficient way to employ these scarce resources?

To solve this problem, you must create this pair of equations:

1*Widgets+3*Wombats=24 hours
7*Widgets+4*Wombats=100 pounds of raw materials

These equations summarize the relationship between Widgets, Wombats, and the total available amounts of your scarce resources. The solutions to these equations are the number of Widgets and Wombats you should produce to achieve the optimal allocation of resources. As you might expect, you can use the / Data Matrix Invert and Multiply commands to solve this linear programming problem.

The first step would be to enter the coefficients of the variables and the constants into the worksheet as a matrix. Figure 6-25 shows a worksheet set up to make the computation. Now you're ready to compute the solution. First, issue the / Data Matrix Invert command. When you issue this command, 1-2-3 will display the prompt *Enter range to invert:*. When you see this prompt, select the range B2..C3—the range that contains the coefficients of the variables—and press [Enter]. Next, 1-2-3 will display the prompt *Enter output range:*. You should select a blank cell—we'll use B6—and press [Enter]. Figure 6-26 shows the result. As you can see, 1-2-3 has created a new matrix—the inverse of the original matrix in the range B2..C3—in cells B6..C7.

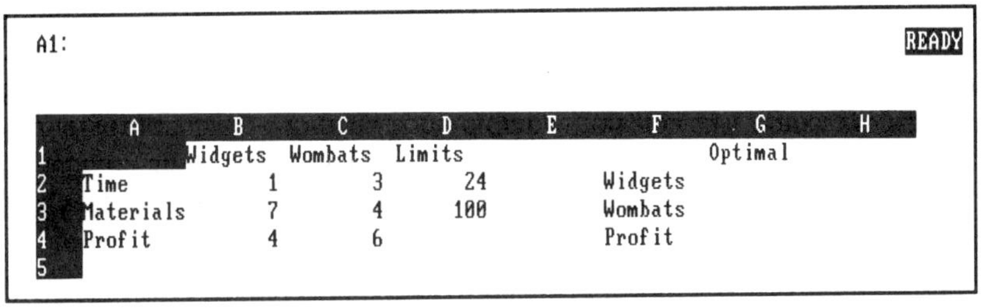

```
A1:                                                          READY

         A        B        C        D        E        F        G        H
 1              Widgets  Wombats  Limits                    Optimal
 2      Time       1        3       24                Widgets
 3      Materials  7        4      100                Wombats
 4      Profit     4        6                         Profit
 5
```

FIGURE 6-25: A linear system

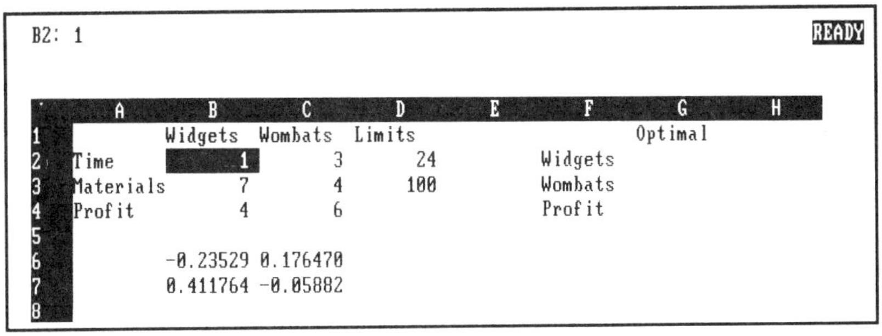

```
B2: 1                                                        READY

         A        B        C        D        E        F        G        H
 1              Widgets  Wombats  Limits                    Optimal
 2      Time       1        3       24                Widgets
 3      Materials  7        4      100                Wombats
 4      Profit     4        6                         Profit
 5
 6              -0.23529  0.176470
 7               0.411764 -0.05882
 8
```

FIGURE 6-26: The / Data Matrix Invert command

We can use this inverse matrix to solve the problem. When we multiply the inverse matrix by the matrix that contains the constants from the original equations (24 and 100), the result will be the optimal number of Widgets and Wombats that we should produce. To see how this works, issue the / Data Matrix Multiply command. When you see the prompt *Enter first range to multiply:*, select the range B6..C7 and press [Enter]. When you see the prompt *Enter second range to multiply:*, select the range D2..D3 and press [Enter]. Finally, when you see the prompt *Enter output range:*, select cell G2 and press [Enter]. Figure 6-27 shows the result. The numbers in cells G2 and G3 are the numbers of Widget and Wombats you should produce to achieve the most efficient use of your scarce resources.

```
B6: -0.2352941176                                                READY


          A         B        C        D        E        F        G        H
 1                Widgets  Wombats  Limits                     Optimal
 2       Time        1        3       24                Widgets    12
 3       Materials   7        4      100                Wombats     4
 4       Profit      4        6                         Profit
 5
 6                -0.23529  0.176470
 7                 0.411764 -0.05882
 8
```

FIGURE 6-27: Linear programming in 1-2-3

Now you need to figure out how much profit you will make at the most efficient level of production. The amount of profit you will make at any level of production can be expressed by the equation *4*Widgets + 6*Wombats=Profit*. To enter this equation into the worksheet, move the cell pointer to cell G4 and type +B4*G2+C4*G3. The result, 72, is the profit you will make at the optimal level of production.

This example only begins to scratch the surface of linear programming. If you already use linear programming, then it should be sufficient to show you how to use 1-2-3 to solve your linear programming problems. If you have not used linear programming before, you need to do some more reading before you begin to use this complex and powerful tool. You'll find many excellent books that explain linear programming at your library or bookstore.

Rules

Like the Multiply option, the Invert option follows a few strict rules. First, 1-2-3 can invert only square matrices—matrices in which the number of rows and the number of columns are equal. Second, you can invert matrices with up to 90 columns and 90 rows. Third, the determinant of the matrix you want to invert cannot be 0. (If you don't know what the determinant is, don't worry about it. This limitation does not come into play very often.)

If the Output range you specify contains entries, the / Data Matrix Invert command will overwrite those entries. Always be sure that the Output range you select is big enough to hold the matrix that the command will produce.

Just as with the / Data Matrix Multiply command, once you have issued the / Data Matrix Invert command, 1-2-3 will remember the Invert and Output ranges you have defined. The next time you issue the command, 1-2-3 will use the previous ranges as the command's defaults.

THE / SYSTEM COMMAND

The / System command allows you to exit from 1-2-3 to DOS without first saving your work. (This command is not available in 1-2-3 Release 1A.) The / System command can be a real lifesaver. Have you ever gotten to the point of saving a large worksheet, only to find that you have no formatted disks to save the worksheet on? Or have you ever wished you could exit to DOS, load your word processor, and dash off a quick memo without the need to save and then retrieve your 1-2-3 worksheet? If so, you can appreciate the value of / System.

To exit to DOS from 1-2-3, you simply issue the / System command. After a moment, you'll see a screen like the one in Figure 6-28. Notice the DOS prompt C:\12322> on this screen. While you are at the DOS level, you can issue DOS commands like FORMAT, ERASE, or COPY. You can even run some application programs—including 1-2-3's graph printing utility, PrintGraph. When you are finished with your work in DOS, you simply type *exit* and press [Enter] to return to 1-2-3. When the 1-2-3 worksheet comes back into view, your work will be just as you left it—you won't have lost anything.

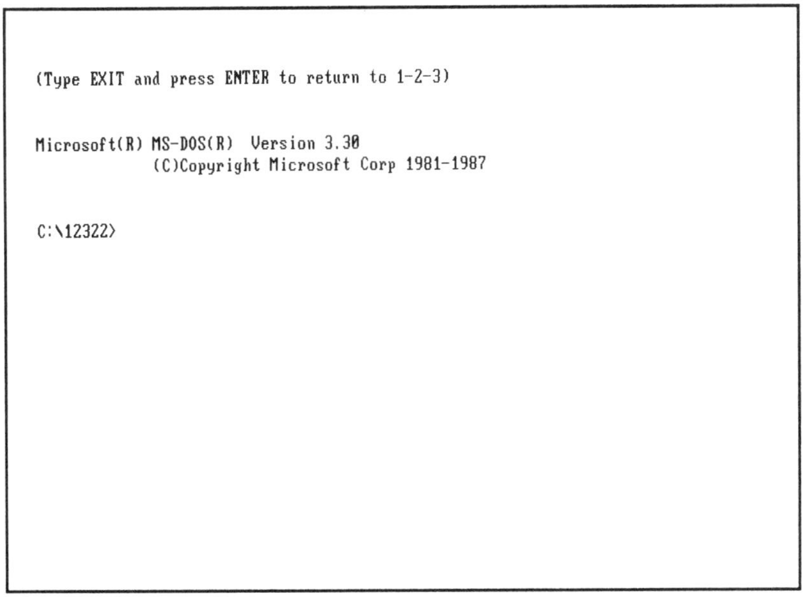

```
(Type EXIT and press ENTER to return to 1-2-3)

Microsoft(R) MS-DOS(R)  Version 3.30
          (C)Copyright Microsoft Corp 1981-1987


C:\12322>
```

FIGURE 6-28: The / System command

When you issue the / System command, 1-2-3 reboots DOS, loading a partial copy of DOS into memory in the area above the first copy of DOS, the 1-2-3 program code, and the contents of your 1-2-3 worksheet. This second copy of DOS consumes about

3000 bytes of memory. If there are less than about 3500 bytes of free memory when you issue the / System command, 1-2-3 will display the error message *Insufficient memory to invoke DOS*.

When you issue the / System command, 1-2-3 looks for DOS on the same drive and directory from which you booted your computer. For instance, if you booted DOS from a floppy disk in drive A, 1-2-3 will look to drive A for DOS. If you booted DOS from the root directory of drive C, 1-2-3 will look to drive C for DOS. If 1-2-3 can't find DOS on that drive and directory, it will beep, display the message *Cannot invoke DOS*, and will not take you to DOS. This type of error is most likely to occur if you use a floppy disk computer and have replaced the DOS disk in drive A with the 1-2-3 System disk.

We have successfully used WordStar and PrintGraph after issuing the / System command. However, while many progams will work successfully under these circumstances, some will not. For example, most memory-resident programs, like Sidekick and Spotlight, will cause problems if you try to run them "behind" 1-2-3. In fact, it is possible that you will not be able to return to 1-2-3 after you load a program. Unfortunately, you won't know about the problem until you type *exit* to return to 1-2-3. When you do, you'll see the error message *1-2-3 cannot be restarted because the memory that was formerly occupied by it is now in use by another program*. This message means that you can't return to 1-2-3, and that all of the unsaved work in your worksheet is lost. The moral? Be sure to test any program you want to run "behind" 1-2-3 before you put your work at risk.

PROTECTION

Like most other advanced electronic spreadsheets, 1-2-3 allows you to protect your worksheets against accidental or unauthorized changes. Protection comes in handy when you are creating worksheets that other people will use. By protecting certain key formulas and labels, you can prevent those people from accidentally destroying the contents of those cells. In much the same way, you can use protection to protect the key formulas in your own important worksheets. Using protection will keep you from destroying an important worksheet with simply one / Range Erase or / Worksheet Delete command. You can save a lot of work—and heartache—by protecting cells.

RELEASE ► 2.2 ◄

In 1-2-3, there are two elements to worksheet protection. First, each cell in the 1-2-3 worksheet has a protection attribute: Protected or Unprotected. ►The / Range Prot and / Range Unprot commands allow you to change the protection attributes of cells and ranges. (In earlier releases of 1-2-3, these commands had the names / Range Protect and / Range Unprotect.)◄ In addition, the entire worksheet has a protection setting: Protection Enabled or Protection Disabled. The / Worksheet Global Protection command controls the worksheets' protection setting. The worksheet setting and the protection attribute for individual cells combine to determine which cells are protected and which are not.

In a new 1-2-3 worksheet, every cell is protected. However, the worksheet protection setting in a new worksheet is Disabled. For this reason, you can make entries and issue commands without worrying about the effect of protection. If you issue the / Worksheet Global Protection Enable command, however, every cell in the worksheet will be protected. This will prevent you from making new entries, from making changes to existing entries, and from issuing commands that might erase, overwrite, or delete entries. If you want to make changes to selected cells, you must use the / Range Unprot command to unprotect those cells.

An Analogy

Here's an analogy that may help you understand how protection works. Imagine a lamp store. In this store, there are hundreds of lamps, each of which has its own on-off switch. In addition, in the back office there is a master switch that controls the power in the shop. In this analogy, the lamps in the store are equivalent to the cells in a worksheet. The on-off switches on the lamps are equivalent to the protection attributes of the cells. The master switch in the back room is equivalent to the worksheet protection setting.

Now let's assume that the individual switches on all the lamps are on, but that the master switch is off. In that situation, all of the lamps in the shop will be off. This situation is equivalent to the condition in a new worksheet—each of the cells in the worksheet is protected, but the worksheet protection setting is off.

Now suppose that the store manager comes in and turns on the master switch. Since each individual lamp in the store is turned on, every lamp will turn on when the master switch goes on. This is analogous to issuing the / Worksheet Global Protection Enable command in a new worksheet. As soon as you issue this command, every cell will be protected.

Finally, suppose that the manager walks into the showroom and flips off a few lamps. This is the equivalent of using the / Range Unprot command to unprotect a few cells in the worksheet.

Protecting the Worksheet

As we have said, every cell in a new 1-2-3 worksheet is protected. This means that all you have to do to protect every cell in the worksheet is issue the / Worksheet Global Protection Enable command. As soon as you enable worksheet protection, 1-2-3 will prevent you from making any changes to the worksheet.

As soon as you issue this command, the letters PR (for PRotected) will appear in the control panel next to the cell pointer indicator. 1-2-3 will display the letters PR in the control panel whenever you point to a protected cell when protection is enabled. This indicator is your hint that the current cell is protected.

You can use the / Worksheet Status command to check on the protection status of the worksheet. If you issue the / Worksheet Status command when protection is enabled, the last line of the status screen will read *Global Protection: On*. If protection is disabled, this line will read *Global Protection: Off*.

The / Range Unprot Command

Typically, you won't want to have every cell in a worksheet protected. If every cell is protected, you won't be able to do much of anything but look at the worksheet.

RELEASE ► 2.2 ◄ ►If you want to be able to make changes in a few cells, you'll need to use the / Range Unprot command to unprotect those cells. (In earlier releases of 1-2-3, this comand has the name / Range Unprotect.)◄

When you issue the / Range Unprot command, 1-2-3 will display the prompt *Enter range to unprotect:*, followed by a reference to the current cell as a range. When you see this prompt, you should select the cell or range you want to unprotect and press [Enter]. (You'll usually want to move the cell pointer to the cell or range you want to unprotect before you issue the command so that you can take advantage of the guess.) Immediately, 1-2-3 will unprotect that cell or range.

As soon as you issue this command, the letters PR in the control panel will be replaced with the letter U, for Unprotected. This indicator tells you that the current cell is unprotected. The letter U will always appear in the control panel when you point to an unprotected cell when worksheet protection is enabled.

In addition to displaying the letter U in the control panel, 1-2-3 displays unprotected cells in a different way. If you are using a monochrome monitor, the unprotected cells in your worksheet will be displayed in high-intensity. If you are using a color monitor, the unprotected cells will be displayed in a different color.

Protection Effects

1-2-3 will not let you do anything to destroy the contents of a protected cell. When a cell is protected and the worksheet protection setting is enabled, you will not be able to edit the contents of the cell or replace the contents of the cell with a different entry. If the protected cell is blank, you won't be able to make an entry into that cell. If you try to make an entry in any protected cell after you issue the / Worksheet Global Protection Enable command—including any of the blank cells—1-2-3 will beep and display the error message *Protected cell*.

As you might expect, you cannot use the / Range Erase command to erase a protected cell. Nor can you delete a row or column that contains a protected cell—if even only one cell in the row or column is protected. Similarly, you cannot move or copy the contents of one cell onto a protected cell. If you try to do any of these things, 1-2-3 will display the message *Protected cell*.

Of course, once you have unprotected a cell, you can make or edit an entry in that cell in the usual way. As long as the cell is unprotected, 1-2-3 will not block your change.

When you protect a cell that contains a formula, you do not "freeze" the value of the formula. If you make changes to the cells that are referred to by the formula, 1-2-3 will change the value of the formula—even though it is protected. Of course, protecting a cell that contains a formula makes it impossible to erase, delete, or overwrite that formula. If you want to freeze the value of a formula, you must use the / Range Values command.

You can use the /Worksheet Erase command to erase all of the entries in a protected worksheet. When you issue the /Worksheet Erase Yes command, 1-2-3 will erase the whole worksheet—including the protected cells.

▶When global protection is enabled, the contents of protected cells that have been assigned the Hidden format will not appear in the Control Panel of a 1-2-3 Release 2.2 worksheet. (Previous releases of 1-2-3 always display the contents of hidden cells in the Control Panel, regardless of whether those cells are protected or unprotected, or whether global protection is enabled or disabled.) Nevertheless, you can always display the contents of a hidden cell on the edit line by moving the cell pointer to that cell and pressing the [Edit] key, even if the cell is protected and global protection is enabled. This technique works in all releases.◀

RELEASE ▶ 2.2 ◀

Reprotecting Cells

▶If you want to assign the protected attribute to a cell that you have unprotected, just issue the / Range Prot command. (In earlier releases, this command has the name / Range Protect.)◀ When you issue this command, 1-2-3 will display the prompt *Enter range to protect:*, followed by a reference to the current cell as a range. When you see this prompt, you should highlight the cells you want to protect and press [Enter]. (Typically, you'll want to move the cell pointer to the cell or range you want to protect before you issue the command so that you can take advantage of 1-2-3's guess range.)

RELEASE ▶ 2.2 ◀

Unprotecting the Worksheet

You can unprotect the worksheet by issuing the /Worksheet Global Protection Disable command. This action will deactivate the worksheet's protection setting—sort of like turning off the master switch in the lamp store in our analogy. However, issuing this command does not change the protection attribute of any individual cells. When you want to reprotect the worksheet, you need only issue the / Worksheet Global Protection Enable command again.

CREATING INPUT FORMS

The /Range Input command allows you to create simple input forms in the cells of the 1-2-3 worksheet. You can use these forms to help inexperienced users make entries and to improve the appearance of your 1-2-3 applications.

Before you issue the / Range Input command, you should set up a portion of the worksheet to look like a simple form—for instance, like a check or a purchase order. When the form has been set up, you use the / Range Unprot command to unprotect the cells into which you want to make entries.

Once all of the input cells are unprotected, you're ready to issue the / Range Input command. When you issue this command, 1-2-3 will display the prompt *Enter data input range:*, followed by a range reference to the current cell. When you see the prompt, you should select the area of the worksheet that contains your entry form and press [Enter]. (As usual, you'll typically want to move the cell pointer to one corner of the input range before you issue the command so that you can take advantage of 1-2-3's guess.)

When you press [Enter] to lock in the input range, 1-2-3 will restrict the cell pointer to only the unprotected cells in the selected range. As you press →, ←, ↑, ↓, [Home], and [End], the cell pointer will move from one unprotected cell to another in the range. You can make entries in the unprotected cells, or edit the entries that are already there, as you move from cell to cell. This restriction will continue until you press [Esc] or [Enter]. When you press either of these keys, the cell pointer will return to where it was before you issued the / Range Input command.

An Example

Let's consider an example of the / Range Input command. Figure 6-29 displays a simple check template that we have created in a 1-2-3 worksheet. We want to use the / Range Input command to make entries into this form.

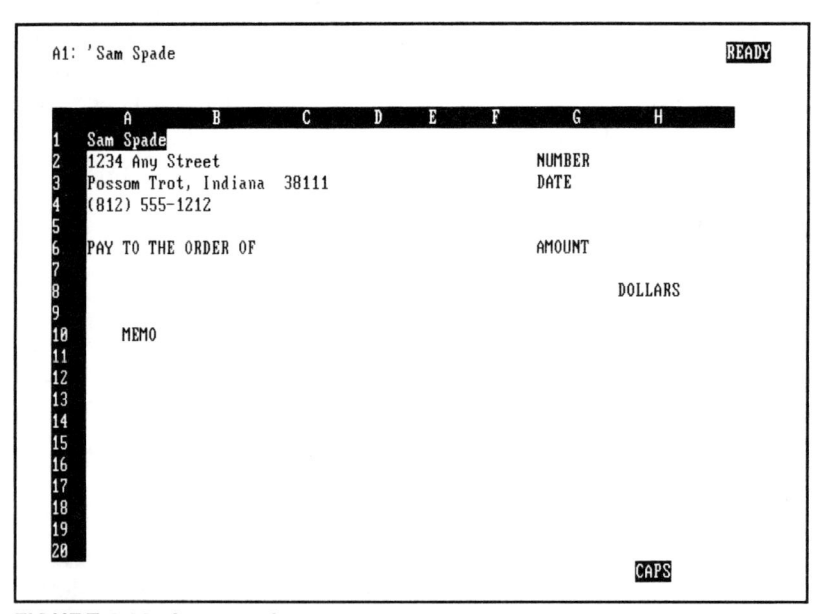

FIGURE 6-29: An entry form

The first step is to unprotect the cells into which we want to make entries. To do this, first issue the / Range Prot command, select the range A1..H10, and press [Enter]. This step ensures that all of the cells in the input form are protected. (While this step is not required, it is a good idea.) Next, move the cell pointer to cell H2, issue the / Range Unprot command, and press [Enter]. Then repeat this process for cells H3, C6, H6, A8, and B10.

Next, move the cell pointer to cell A1 and issue the / Range Input command. When 1-2-3 prompts you to define the input range, select the range A1..H10 and press

[Enter]. Immediately, the cell pointer will move to cell H2, the first unprotected cell in the input range. 1-2-3 is now in the INPUT mode (even though the mode indicator still reads READY).

You can now press →, ←, ↑, ↓, [End], and [Home] to move the cell pointer from unprotected cell to unprotected cell in the input range. (If you press any other cursor-movement key, 1-2-3 will simply beep.) For example, if you press →, the cell pointer will skip to the next unprotected cell in the range—in this case, cell H3. Pressing → again will move the cell pointer to cell C6. Pressing ← moves the cell pointer to the previous unprotected cell. For instance, if you press ← when the cell pointer is in cell C6 in the example, it will jump to cell H3. Pressing [Home] moves the cell pointer to the first unprotected cell in the input range. Pressing [End] moves it to the last unprotected cell.

If you press → or ↓ when the cell pointer is in the last cell of the input range, it will wrap around to the first cell. Similarly, pressing ↑ or ← with the cell pointer in the first unprotected cell will move it to the last cell.

As you move the cell pointer from cell to cell, you can make entries. For example, let's enter the following data into the sample entry form: Number, *1001*; Date, *December 31, 1989*; Payee, *Steven Cobb*; Amount, *1000* (also stated as *One Thousand and no/100*); Memo, *Loan payment for January*. To do this, press [Home] to move to cell H2, then type 1001. At this point, press → to lock this entry in and move the cell pointer to the next cell in the input range, cell H3. Then type *@DATE(89,12,31)*. Once again, press → to move to the next cell and enter the name *Steven Cobb*. You should continue in this way until the form is completely filled. When you're done, just press [Esc] to leave the INPUT mode. Figure 6-30 shows the completed form.

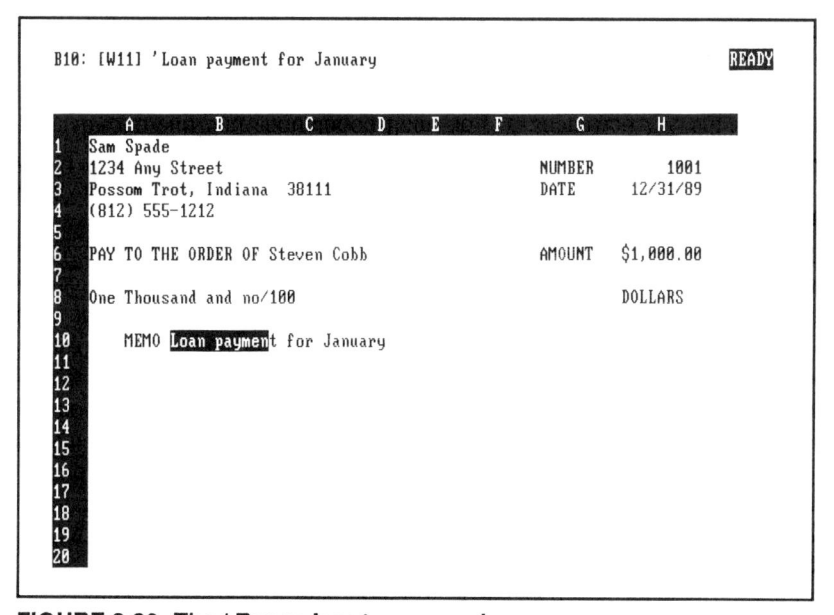

FIGURE 6-30: The / Range Input command

If you make an error in an entry, just move the cell pointer back to that cell and either retype the entry or edit it. To edit the entry, just do what you always do: press [Edit], use the arrow keys to reposition the cursor, and insert, delete, or replace characters. When you have made the change, press [Enter] to lock it in, then use the arrow keys to move on to the next cell.

Notes

You can use the [Enter] key as well as the arrow keys to lock in entries when 1-2-3 is in the INPUT mode. However, if you press the [Enter] key for any purpose other than to lock in an entry, 1-2-3 will leave the INPUT mode. Conversely, if you press [Esc] while you are making an entry, 1-2-3 will cancel that entry but will not leave the INPUT mode. You can also press [Help] while 1-2-3 is in the INPUT mode.

1-2-3 doesn't care about the order in which you unprotect the cells in the form. This means that there is no way to change the order in which the cell pointer moves through the form.

Typically, you'll use the /Range Input command in a macro. (Macros are covered in detail in Chapters 13 through 15. We'll just say enough here to show you how to use /Range Input in a macro.) For example, the simple macro statement */riA1..H20~* would allow a macro to use the simple form in Figure 6-29 to accept user input. When 1-2-3 processes this command, the macro will stop while you make entries in the form. Once you press [Enter] to exit from the INPUT mode, the macro would go on. The remaining commands in the macro would operate on the entries in the form. For example, in this case the macro might print this check or enter it into a 1-2-3 data base.

THE / RANGE JUSTIFY COMMAND

The /Range Justify command allows you to break one or more long labels into a series of shorter labels. This command makes it possible to perform crude word processing in the 1-2-3 worksheet. However, because 1-2-3 does not offer any other word-processing commands to support / Range Justify, this command has very limited application.

An Example

For example, suppose you have created the worksheet shown in Figure 6-31. As you can see, this worksheet is in the form of a memo from Sam to Dave. Cells A1, A2, and A3 contain simple, short labels. The range A11..E14 contains several simple labels and values that summarize the September and October results for a mythical company.

The labels in cells A5 and A6 are the body of the memo. Cell A5 contains a very long label that begins *As I feared, the results for October are not too great. As the figures....* Since the label in cell A5 is so long, only the first part of it is visible on the screen. If you print this worksheet, only a small part of the label will appear on the printed page. In order to bring the whole label into view, you must use the / Range Justify command to break it into several smaller labels.

```
A5: 'As I feared, the results for October are not too great. As the figure  READY

     A         B         C         D         E         F         G         H
 1  TO: Dave
 2  FROM: Sam
 3  RE: October Results
 4
 5  As I feared, the results for October are not too great. As the figures
 6  this disaster, you're history. Sorry.
 7
 8
 9
10
11                        Sept      Oct    Change
12  Unit Sales           40,000    30,000   10,000
13  Dollar Sales        $133,333  $100,000  $33,333
14  Net Income          $10,000  ($20,000)($30,000)
15
```

FIGURE 6-31: A memo in 1-2-3

To do this, move the cell pointer to cell A5 and issue the / Range Justify command. When you do so, 1-2-3 will display the prompt *Enter justify range:*, followed by a range reference to the current cell—in this case, the range A5..A5. When you see this prompt, press → and ↓ to select the range A5..G9. This range defines the maximum length of the short labels 1-2-3 will create when it breaks up the long label. In effect, this range sets the margins for the memo.

Once you've defined the range, press [Enter] to complete the command. Figure 6-32 shows the result. As you can see, 1-2-3 has justified the long label from cell A5 and the label from cell A6 into five shorter labels in cells A5, A6, A7, A8, and A9. Notice that all of these labels are short enough to fit within the "column A to column G" width we defined. In other words, 1-2-3 has justified the labels in cells A5 and A6 to fit within the margins we set.

```
A5: 'As I feared, the results for October are not too great. As       READY

     A         B         C         D         E         F         G         H
 1  TO: Dave
 2  FROM: Sam
 3  RE: October Results
 4
 5  As I feared, the results for October are not too great. As
 6  the figures below indicate, total units shipped fell by 10,000
 7  to 30,000. As a result, revenue fell to $100,000 and net
 8  income fell to ($20,000). Since you are responsible for this
 9  disaster, you're history. Sorry.
10
11                        Sept      Oct    Change
12  Unit Sales           40,000    30,000   10,000
13  Dollar Sales        $133,333  $100,000  $33,333
14  Net Income          $10,000  ($20,000)($30,000)
15
```

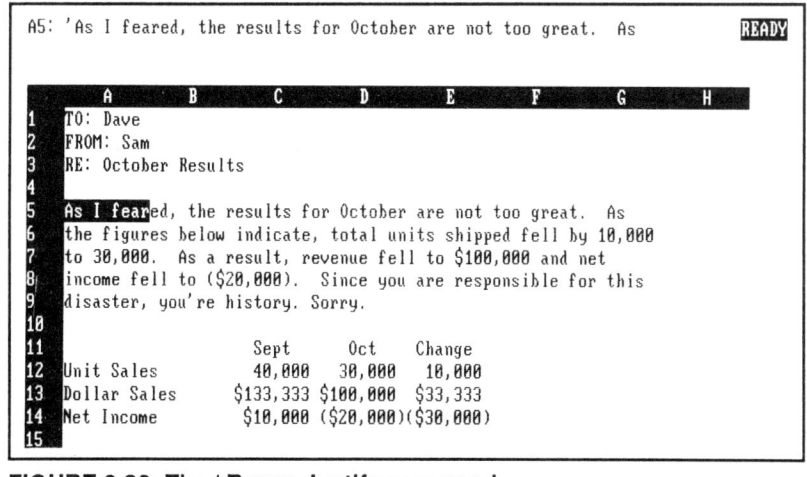

FIGURE 6-32: The / Range Justify command

Notes

In the example, we used a block of cells (a multiple-row range) as the justify range. You can also use a single-row range as the justify range. For example, suppose you want to use a single-row range to justify the labels in cells A5 and A6 in Figure 6-31. To do this, move the cell pointer to cell A5, issue the / Range Justify command, select the range A5..G5 (notice that this range includes only row 5) and press [Enter]. Figure 6-33 shows the result. As before, 1-2-3 has justified the long labels in cells A5 and A6. But at the same time, 1-2-3 has moved the entries in the range A12..A14 in Figure 6-31 to the range A15..A17 in Figure 6-33. This occurred because 1-2-3 inserted several blank cells in column A to hold the shorter labels that it created when it justified the long label. As in this case, when you use a single-row justify range, 1-2-3 will always insert blank cells to hold the justified labels.

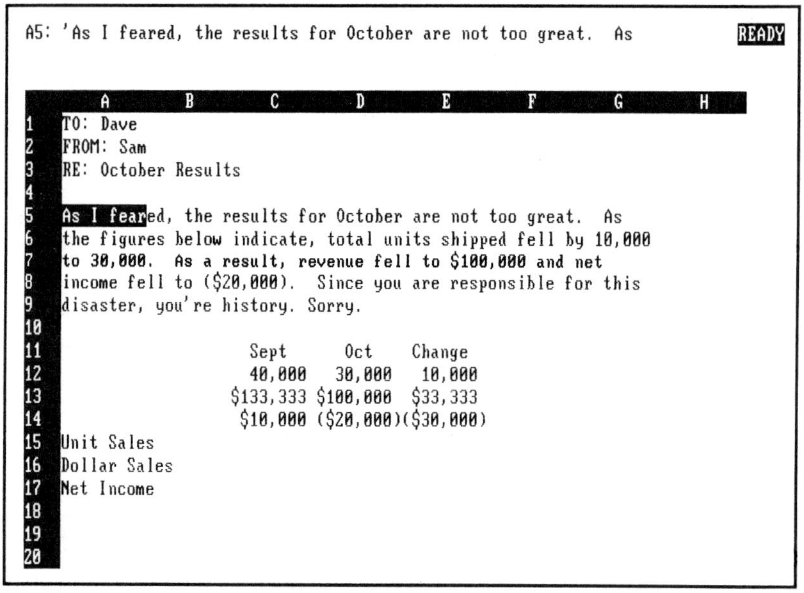

FIGURE 6-33: A single row justify range

The problem is that the entries in the range C11..E14 have not been moved. Although these entries are related to the labels that are now in the range A15..A18, 1-2-3 did not move them down when it justified the long label. Unfortunately, you'll usually encounter this problem if you use a one-row justify range. The only way to overcome this problem is to use the / Move command to restore the proper alignment to the worksheet.

If you decide to use a multiple-row justify range, be sure to include enough rows in the range to hold all of the justified labels. If the justify range is not large enough, you'll see the error message *Justify range is full or line too long*.

You can also use the / Range Justify command to unjustify a range of labels. For example, suppose you want to unjustify the labels in the range A5..A9 in Figure 6-32. To do this, move the cell pointer to cell A5 and issue the / Range Justify command. When 1-2-3 prompts you to define the justify range, select the range A5..Z9 and press [Enter]. When you press [Enter], 1-2-3 will unjustify the labels in the range A5..A9 into two labels in cells A5 and A6.

You can also use a single-row range when you unjustify labels. If you do so, however, 1-2-3 will delete one cell from the first column of the justify range for each label that is removed from the worksheet by the / Range Justify command. As a result, the entries in that column will lose their alignment relative to the other entries in the worksheet.

Finally, keep in mind that the absolute width of the justify range is determined by the widths of the columns in the range. If you want to adjust the width of the justify range precisely—say, to exactly 62 characters—you'll need to adjust the widths of the columns in the range.

SEARCHING AND REPLACING

▶/ Range Search is one of 1-2-3 Release 2.2's most useful new commands. This command lets you search for and, if you wish, replace occurrences of specified characters in labels, formulas, and functions in all or part of a worksheet.

RELEASE
▶ 2.2 ◀

When you issue this command, 1-2-3 Release 2.2 asks you to highlight the range you want to search. Once you do this, 1-2-3 prompts you to specify the characters you want to search for. This "search string" may be up to 239 characters long. As soon as you type the search string and press [Enter], 1-2-3 will present a menu that offers three choices: Formulas, Labels, and Both. The option you choose determines which type of entry 1-2-3 will search in for the search string you have specified. If you choose Formulas, 1-2-3 will search for the search string in all the formulas and functions in the selected range. This option makes it possible to search for cell references or range names in your formulas and functions. If you choose Labels, 1-2-3 will search for the search string in the labels in the selected range. If you choose Both, 1-2-3 will search for the search string in formulas, functions, and labels. (The Search command cannot search in values.)

As soon as you choose the type of entry 1-2-3 will search in, 1-2-3 will give you two more choices: Find and Replace. These options let you tell 1-2-3 whether you want to simply search for the string you have specified or replace the search string with another string as you search.

The Find Option

The Find option lets you find any or all occurrences of the search string you have specified in the search range you have defined. If you select the Find option, 1-2-3 will look for the search string in entries of the type you selected in the range you specified. 1-2-3 will begin searching at the upper-left corner of the range and will search through the range column-by-column. If it finds a formula or function that contains the search string, 1-2-3 will move the cell pointer to the cell that contains that entry, highlight the occurrence of the search string in that entry on the first line of the control panel, and give you two options: Next and Quit. If you choose Next, 1-2-3 will look for the next occurrence of the search string within the range. If you select Quit, 1-2-3 will cancel the Search command, leaving the cell pointer on the cell that contained the last match.

If 1-2-3 can't find a match for the search string you have specified, it will beep and display the message *String not found*. You'll need to press [Esc] to acknowledge this message before you go on.

An Example: Searching for Text

Let's look at an example of the / Range Search command. Suppose you are working in the worksheet shown in Figure 6-34. You need to look up some salary data for Dave Jones. Rather than search through the worksheet randomly for the cells that contain this information, you could use the / Range Search command to look for the label Dave Jones in the worksheet.

To do this, issue the / Range Search command and select the range A1..D17. When 1-2-3 prompts you for the search string, type Dave Jones and press [Enter]. Next, choose Labels to tell 1-2-3 that you want to search in labels. Finally, when 1-2-3 offers you the choice of find or replacing, choose Find. Almost instantly, the cell pointer will jump to cell A16, which contains the label 'Dave Jones. Figure 6-35 shows the worksheet at this point. You can now choose Next to continue the search or Quit to end it with the cell pointer on cell A16.

```
A1: [W17] 'SALARY WORKSHEET                                           READY

            A              B          C          D        E       F
     1  SALARY WORKSHEET
     2
     3                                FICA     BENEFITS
     4                    Salary      7.52%     20.00%
     5  Sally Smith       $94,206    $7,084    $18,841
     6  Betty Boop        $58,687    $4,413    $11,737
     7  Slim Pickens      $76,900    $5,783    $15,380
     8  Sue Michaels      $88,888    $6,684    $17,776
     9  Tom Beyers        $96,068    $7,224    $19,214
    10  Wilson Hareld     $51,607    $3,881    $10,321
    11  Connie Summe      $32,374    $2,435     $6,475
    12  Randy Michaels    $54,079    $4,067    $10,816
    13  Paul Roberts      $87,073    $6,548    $17,415
    14  Mike Mize         $54,387    $4,090    $10,877
    15  David Hilliard    $77,479    $5,826    $15,496
    16  Dave Jones        $21,763    $1,637     $4,353
    17  Jerry Abramson    $30,991    $2,331     $6,198
    18
    19
    20                                                              CAPS
```

FIGURE 6-34: A sample worksheet

Another Example: Searching in Formulas

You can also use / Range Search to search for a string in a formula. This makes it possible to search for cell references or range names in your formulas and functions. To see how this tool works, suppose you want to find all of the formulas in the worksheet in Figure 6-34 that contain a reference to cell B16. To do this, issue the / Range Search command and select the range A1..D17. (This range will already be selected if you worked along with the first example.) When 1-2-3 prompts you for the search string, type B16 and press [Enter]. Next, choose Formulas to tell 1-2-3 that you want to search in formulas. Finally, when 1-2-3 offers you the choice of find or replacing, choose Find. Almost instantly, the cell pointer will jump to cell C16, which contains the formula +B16*C$4. Figure 6-36 shows the worksheet at this point.

```
A16: [W17] 'Dave Jones                                              MENU
Next  Quit
Find next matching string
         A              B          C          D          E        F
 1  SALARY WORKSHEET
 2
 3                                FICA      BENEFITS
 4                    Salary      7.52%      20.00%
 5  Sally Smith      $94,206     $7,084     $18,841
 6  Betty Boop       $58,687     $4,413     $11,737
 7  Slim Pickens     $76,900     $5,783     $15,380
 8  Sue Michaels     $88,880     $6,684     $17,776
 9  Tom Beyers       $96,068     $7,224     $19,214
10  Wilson Hareld    $51,607     $3,881     $10,321
11  Connie Summe     $32,374     $2,435      $6,475
12  Randy Michaels   $54,079     $4,067     $10,816
13  Paul Roberts     $87,073     $6,548     $17,415
14  Mike Mize        $54,387     $4,090     $10,877
15  David Hilliard   $77,479     $5,826     $15,496
16  Dave Jones       $21,763     $1,637      $4,353
17  Jerry Abramson   $30,991     $2,331      $6,198
18
19
20
```

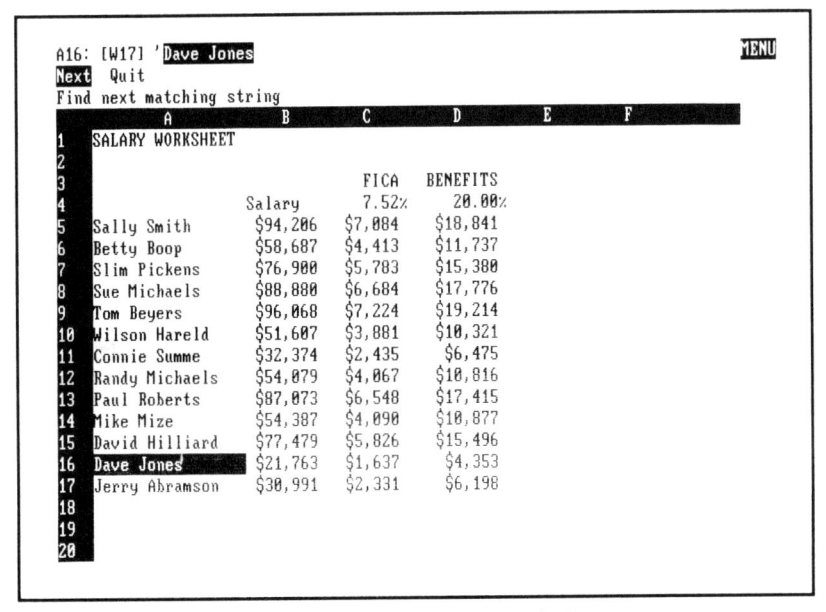

FIGURE 6-35: Using / Range Search to find a label

Now, choose Next to continue the search. Immediately, the cell pointer will jump to cell D16, which contains the formula +B16*D$4. Figure 6-37 shows the worksheet at this point.

If you choose Next again, 1-2-3 will search for the string B16 in the remainder of the search range. Since there are no more occurrences of the string in that range, 1-2-3 will return the message *No more matching strings*. The cursor will remain on cell D16. You'll need to press [Esc] to acknowledge this message before you go on.

```
C16: (C0) +B16*C$4                                              MENU
Next  Quit
Find next matching string
              A          B         C          D        E      F
   1  SALARY WORKSHEET
   2
   3                                FICA    BENEFITS
   4                    Salary      7.52%    20.00%
   5  Sally Smith       $94,206    $7,084    $18,841
   6  Betty Boop        $58,687    $4,413    $11,737
   7  Slim Pickens      $76,900    $5,783    $15,380
   8  Sue Michaels      $88,880    $6,684    $17,776
   9  Tom Beyers        $96,068    $7,224    $19,214
  10  Wilson Hareld     $51,607    $3,881    $10,321
  11  Connie Summe      $32,374    $2,435     $6,475
  12  Randy Michaels    $54,079    $4,067    $10,816
  13  Paul Roberts      $87,073    $6,548    $17,415
  14  Mike Mize         $54,387    $4,090    $10,877
  15  David Hilliard    $77,479    $5,826    $15,496
  16  Dave Jones        $21,763    $1,637     $4,353
  17  Jerry Abramson    $30,991    $2,331     $6,198
  18
  19
  20
```

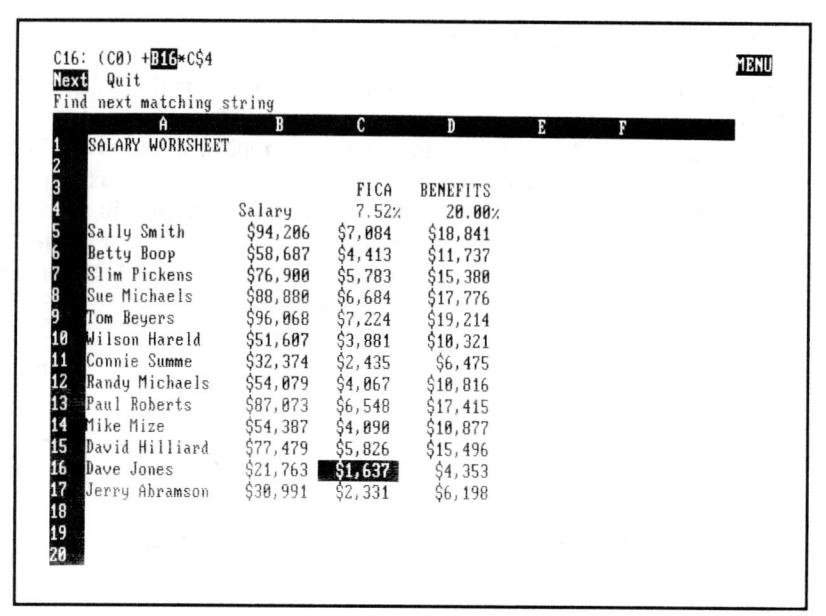

FIGURE 6-36: Using / Range Search to search in formulas

```
D16: (C0) [W11] +B16*D$4                                        MENU
Next  Quit
Find next matching string
              A          B         C          D        E      F
   1  SALARY WORKSHEET
   2
   3                                FICA    BENEFITS
   4                    Salary      7.52%    20.00%
   5  Sally Smith       $94,206    $7,084    $18,841
   6  Betty Boop        $58,687    $4,413    $11,737
   7  Slim Pickens      $76,900    $5,783    $15,380
   8  Sue Michaels      $88,880    $6,684    $17,776
   9  Tom Beyers        $96,068    $7,224    $19,214
  10  Wilson Hareld     $51,607    $3,881    $10,321
  11  Connie Summe      $32,374    $2,435     $6,475
  12  Randy Michaels    $54,079    $4,067    $10,816
  13  Paul Roberts      $87,073    $6,548    $17,415
  14  Mike Mize         $54,387    $4,090    $10,877
  15  David Hilliard    $77,479    $5,826    $15,496
  16  Dave Jones        $21,763    $1,637    $4,353
  17  Jerry Abramson    $30,991    $2,331     $6,198
  18
  19
  20
```

FIGURE 6-37: Using the Next option to continue the search

The Replace Option

The Replace option lets you search for the search string you have specified in the range you have defined, replace some or all of the occurrences of the search string with another string. If you choose Replace when 1-2-3 displays the Find/Replace menu, 1-2-3 will ask you to specify the replace string: the string you want to use to replace occurrences of the search string. When you type this string and press [Enter], 1-2-3 will search the range you specified for the first occurrence of the search string. As soon as it funds an occurrence of that string, 1-2-3 will move the cell pointer to that cell, highlight the occurrence within that entry on the first line of the control panel, and give you four options: Replace, All, Next, and Quit. If you choose Replace, 1-2-3 will replace the occurrence of the search string with the replacement string, then begin searching for the next occurrence of the search string within the range. If you choose All, 1-2-3 will replace the current occurrence of the search string, then locate and replace any remaining occurrences of the search string within the range automatically. If you choose Next, 1-2-3 will begin searching for the next occurrence of the search string without replacing the current occurrence of that string. If you choose Quit, 1-2-3 will cancel the Search command, leaving the cell pointer on the cell that contained the last match.

If 1-2-3 can't find a match for the search string you have specified, it will beep and display the message *String not found*. You'll need to press [Esc] to acknowledge this message before you go on.

For example, suppose one of the people in your table, Sue Michaels, has recently married. Her name is now Sue Bowers. To make this change, issue the / Range Search command and select the range A1..D17. (If you've been working along, this range should be selected already.) When 1-2-3 prompts you for the search string, type Michaels and press [Enter]. Next, choose Labels to tell 1-2-3 that you want to search in labels. When 1-2-3 offers you the choice of finding or replacing, choose Replace. When 1-2-3 prompts you for a replacement string, type Bowers and press [Enter]. Almost instantly, the cell pointer will jump to cell A16, which contains the label 'Sue Michaels, and will display the menu of replace options, as shown in Figure 6-38. You can now choose Replace to replace the string Michaels with the string Bowers. Immediately, 1-2-3 will make the replacement and will continue the search, moving the cursor to cell A12, which contains the label Randy Michaels. Figure 6-39 shows the worksheet at this point. Since you don't want to make any additional replacements, you can now choose Quit to stop the search.

Notes

The / Range Search command is not case-sensitive. For example, if you specify *Test* as the search string, 1-2-3 will locate occurrences of the letters *test*, *TEST*, *tEsT*, and so forth, in addition to *Test*. The Search command does treat the replacement string literally, however.

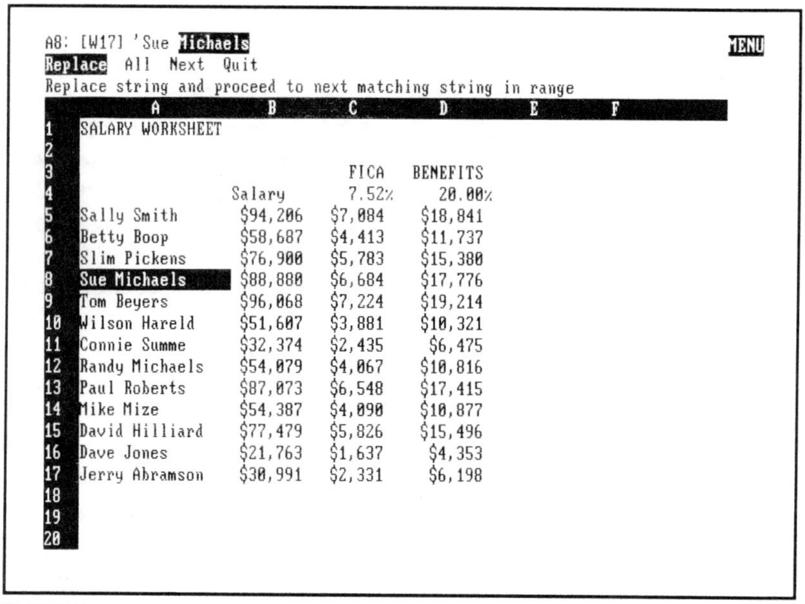

```
A8: [W17] 'Sue Michaels                                          MENU
Replace  All  Next  Quit
Replace string and proceed to next matching string in range
       A           B         C        D        E        F
 1  SALARY WORKSHEET
 2
 3                           FICA    BENEFITS
 4              Salary       7.52%   20.00%
 5  Sally Smith    $94,206   $7,084   $18,841
 6  Betty Boop     $58,687   $4,413   $11,737
 7  Slim Pickens   $76,900   $5,783   $15,380
 8  Sue Michaels   $88,880   $6,684   $17,776
 9  Tom Beyers     $96,068   $7,224   $19,214
10  Wilson Hareld  $51,607   $3,881   $10,321
11  Connie Summe   $32,374   $2,435    $6,475
12  Randy Michaels $54,079   $4,067   $10,816
13  Paul Roberts   $87,073   $6,548   $17,415
14  Mike Mize      $54,387   $4,090   $10,877
15  David Hilliard $77,479   $5,826   $15,496
16  Dave Jones     $21,763   $1,637    $4,353
17  Jerry Abramson $30,991   $2,331    $6,198
18
19
20
```

FIGURE 6-38: Using the Replace option

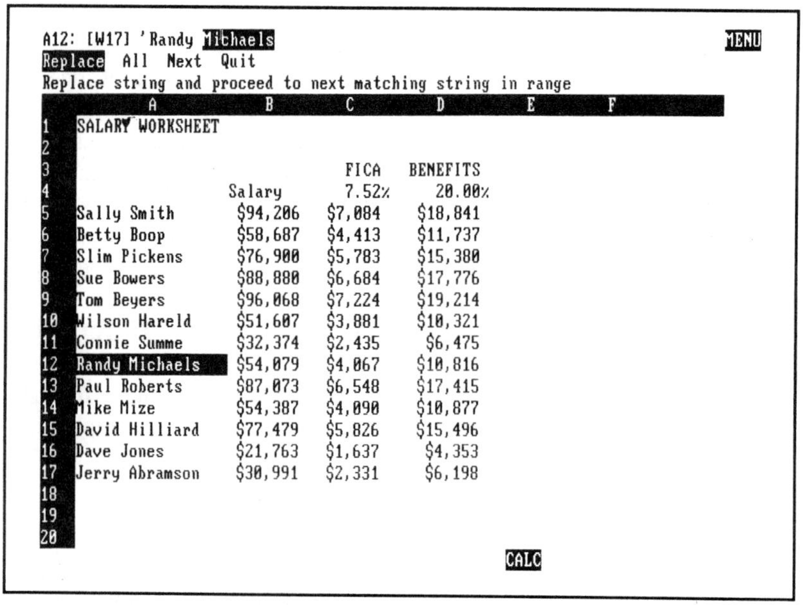

```
A12: [W17] 'Randy Michaels                                       MENU
Replace  All  Next  Quit
Replace string and proceed to next matching string in range
       A           B         C        D        E        F
 1  SALARY WORKSHEET
 2
 3                           FICA    BENEFITS
 4              Salary       7.52%   20.00%
 5  Sally Smith    $94,206   $7,084   $18,841
 6  Betty Boop     $58,687   $4,413   $11,737
 7  Slim Pickens   $76,900   $5,783   $15,380
 8  Sue Bowers     $88,880   $6,684   $17,776
 9  Tom Beyers     $96,068   $7,224   $19,214
10  Wilson Hareld  $51,607   $3,881   $10,321
11  Connie Summe   $32,374   $2,435    $6,475
12  Randy Michaels $54,079   $4,067   $10,816
13  Paul Roberts   $87,073   $6,548   $17,415
14  Mike Mize      $54,387   $4,090   $10,877
15  David Hilliard $77,479   $5,826   $15,496
16  Dave Jones     $21,763   $1,637    $4,353
17  Jerry Abramson $30,991   $2,331    $6,198
18
19
20                                                       CALC
```

FIGURE 6-39: Using the Quit option

While you will often use the Search command to search for complete strings, you can also use to it to find a string within a longer string. In fact, we used the command in this way in the example where we searched for the entry B16 in the formulas in a worksheet. 1-2-3 located this string even though it was just part of a longer string: +B16*C$6. Likewise, we used the command to find the string Michaels in the longer string Sue Michaels.

The /Range Search command retains the range and string settings you define until the end of your 1-2-3 session. If you use the command again, all of the settings you have defined will remain in effect. If the new search is similar to the previous one, you can use the existing settings. Alternatively, you can change the settings to define a new search.

You can use the /Range Search command as a substitute for the [Goto] key. For instance, suppose you know that the section of the worksheet you want to move to begins with the label "Income." Instead of trying to remember the address of the cell where that section begins, you could simply use the /Range Search command to search for the label "Income" in the worksheet.◄

CONCLUSION

In this chapter, we have explained 1-2-3's worksheet commands: / Worksheet Titles, / Worksheet Window, / Data Fill, / Data Distribution, / Data Table, / Data Regression, / Data Matrix, / System, / Range Prot and / Range Unprot, / Worksheet Global Protection, / Range Input, / Range Justify, and / Range Search. These commands allow you to perform many specialized tasks, such as computing frequency distributions and linear regressions, creating data tables and input forms, protecting the worksheet, and searching for and replacing entries.

7

Dates and Times

Like most other sophisticated spreadsheet programs, 1-2-3 can keep time. 1-2-3's ability to recognize dates and times makes it possible to time and date stamp your worksheets, to perform date and time arithmetic, and to sort worksheets and data bases into date or time order. In this chapter, we'll show you how to work with dates and times in 1-2-3.

DATES

1-2-3's basic unit for measuring time is a single day. In 1-2-3, dates are represented by integer values. The integer value that represents any given date is equal to the number of days that have elapsed between the fixed base date December 31, 1899, and that date. For example, 1-2-3 represents the date January 1, 1900, with the value 1 because it falls one day after the base date. Similarly, the date January 2, 1900, is represented by the value 2; the date January 31, 1900, is represented by the value 31, and so forth. Relatively current dates have much higher values, of course. For example, the date December 25, 1989, is represented by the value 32867. We'll refer to a value that 1-2-3 uses to represent a date as a *serial date value*.

Representing dates as values makes it possible for 1-2-3 to perform date arithmetic. For example, in 1-2-3 it is easy to calculate the interval between two dates or to determine the date that is a specific number of days after a given date. This representation also allows 1-2-3 to sort dates correctly—a topic we'll cover in Chapter 12.

There's only one problem: The serial values that 1-2-3 uses to represent dates don't look anything like dates. For instance, do you know what date is represented by the serial value 21099? If 1-2-3 forced us to work with serial date values, most of us would be in real trouble. Fortunately, 1-2-3 includes two tools that make it easy to work with dates: date functions and Date formats. In the next two sections, we'll show you how to use these special functions and formats to enter dates into your worksheets.

Entering Dates: The @DATE Function

The @DATE function makes it easy to enter dates into the 1-2-3 worksheet. The form of this function is

@DATE(*year,month,day*)

where *year* specifies the year of the date you want to enter, *month* specifies the month, and *day* specifies the day. The *year*, *month*, and *day* arguments may be literal values, references to cells that contain values, or formulas or functions that return values. The *year* argument must be a number between 0 (for the year 1900) and 199 (for the year 2099). For example, the *year* argument 89 would specify a date in the year 1989, and the *year* argument 105 would specify a date in the year 2005. The *month* argument must be a value between 1 (for January) and 12 (for December). For example, the *month* argument 2 would specify a date in the month of February.

The result of an @DATE function is the serial date value of the date specified by *year*, *month*, and *day*. For example, cell B3 in Figure 7-1 contains the function

B3: @DATE(89,7,4)

which represents the date July 4, 1989. As you can see, this function returns the value 32693. Similarly, the function *@DATE(56,7,4)*, which represents the date July 4, 1956, returns the serial value 20640. The function *@DATE(110,1,1)*, which represents the date January 1, 2010, returns the value 40179.

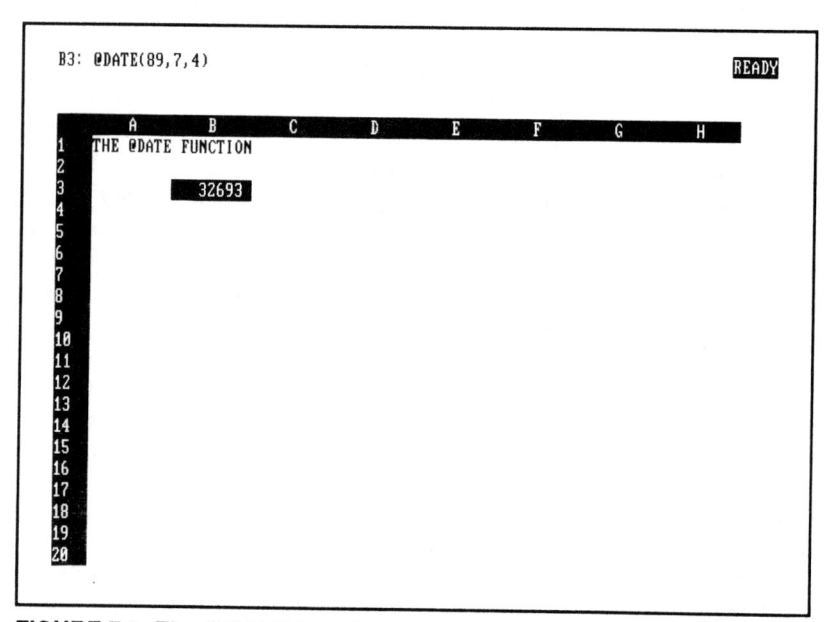

FIGURE 7-1: The @DATE function

1-2-3 can work with dates from January 1, 1900, (serial value 1) to December 31, 2099 (serial value 73050). To enter the serial value for December 31, 2099, you would use the function *@DATE(199,12,31)*. If you attempt to use the @DATE function to enter a date outside of this range, the function will return the value ERR. For example, the function *@DATE(200,1,1)* would return the result ERR.

1-2-3 will not allow you to use the @DATE function to enter dates that do not exist. For example, because the month of June has only 30 days, the function *@DATE(89,6,31)* will return the result ERR. The same thing will happen if you create an @DATE function with a month argument greater than 12 or less than 1. For example, the function *@DATE(89,13,1)* will return the result ERR. Similarly, because 1989 is not a leap year, the function *@DATE(89,2,29)* will also return ERR.

Formatting Dates

As you have seen, when you use an @DATE function to enter a date into a cell, that function will return a result like 32693. Although 1-2-3 knows which date this value represents, you probably do not. Fortunately, 1-2-3 lets you assign Date formats to the cells of a worksheet. Formatting a cell that contains a serial date value instructs 1-2-3 to display that value in a recognizable form, such as *4-Jul-89*.

The process of assigning a Date format to a cell is similar to that of assigning a numeric format to a cell—a process that we explained in Chapter 3. To assign a Date format to a cell, you issue the / Range Format Date command. When you issue this command, 1-2-3 will display the menu shown in Figure 7-2. The first five items on this menu represent the five Date formats that you can assign to a cell. (The final two date formnats are not available in 1-2-3 Release 1A). Table 7-1 lists these five formats. The sixth choice on this menu—Time— lets you select a Time format. We'll cover Time formats later in this chapter.

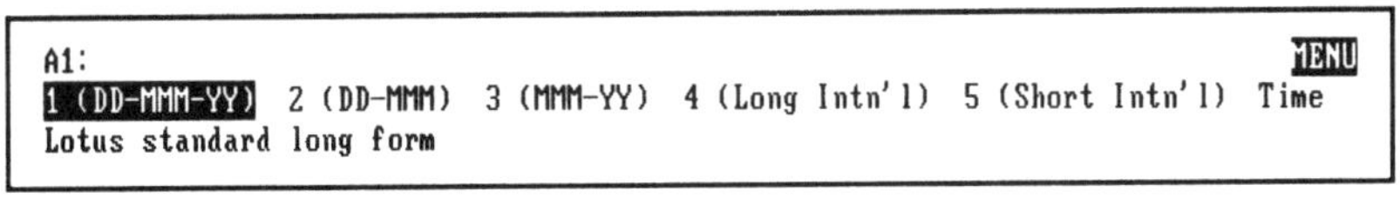

```
A1:                                                                    MENU
1 (DD-MMM-YY)  2 (DD-MMM)  3 (MMM-YY)  4 (Long Intn'l)  5 (Short Intn'l)  Time
Lotus standard long form
```

FIGURE 7-2: The / Range Format Date menu

Format	Code	Form	Example
1	D1	DD-MMM-YY	04-Jul-89
2	D2	DD-MMM	04-Jul
3	D3	MMM-YY	Jul-89
4 (Long Intn'l)	D4	MM/DD/YY	07/04/89
5 (Short Intn'l)	D5	MM/DD	07/04

TABLE 7-1: 1-2-3's default Date formats

To assign one of these formats to a cell, just select it from the menu, either by pointing and pressing [Enter] or by typing 1, 2, 3, 4, or 5. As soon as you select a format, 1-2-3 will prompt you to specify the range to be formatted and will offer the cell on which the cell pointer is positioned as the default option. If the cell pointer is on the cell you want to format, you can just press [Enter]. Otherwise, you can either type the address of the cell or range to which you want to assign the format, or point to that cell or range and press [Enter].

Importantly, assigning a Date format to a cell that contains a serial date value does not alter the value that is contained in that cell—it simply tells 1-2-3 to display that value in a different way.

An Example

For example, suppose you want to assign Date format 4 (Long Intn'l) to the date in cell B3 in Figure 7-1. To do this, you would move the cell pointer to cell B3, issue the / Range Format Date command, choose Date format 4, and press [Enter]. Figure 7-3 shows the worksheet with the formatted date. Notice the format memo, D4, which now appears in the control panel.

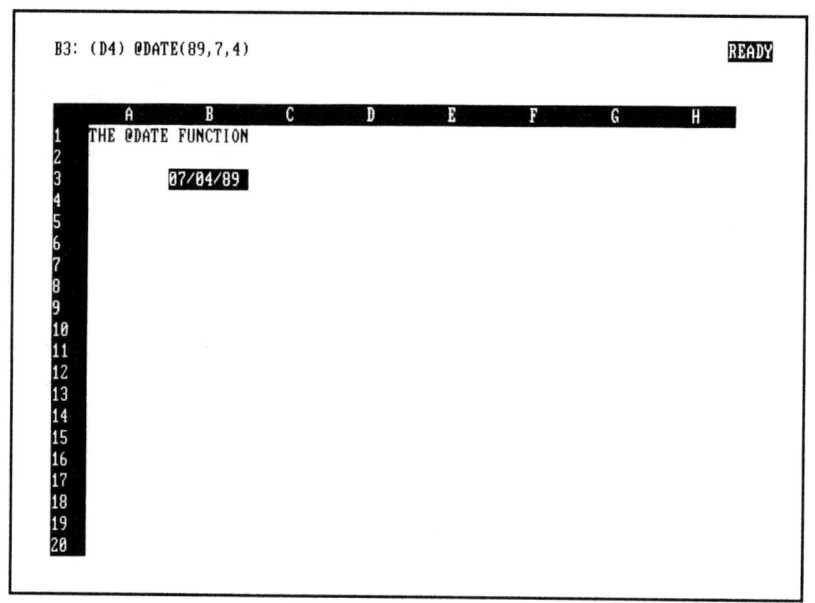

```
B3: (D4) @DATE(89,7,4)                                          READY

        A       B       C       D       E       F       G       H
 1  THE @DATE FUNCTION
 2
 3          07/04/89
 4
 5
 6
 7
 8
 9
10
11
12
13
14
15
16
17
18
19
20
```

FIGURE 7-3: A formatted date value

Column Width Considerations

As you may recall from Chapter 3, "Formatting the Worksheet," 1-2-3 will display a formatted value as a series of asterisks (*) if the column that contains that value is not at least one character wider than the number of characters in the formatted display. Because dates formatted with the D1 format are nine characters long, and because the default width of a column in 1-2-3 is nine characters, 1-2-3 displays dates in the D1 format in standard-width columns as a series of asterisks. For example, Figure 7-4 shows the sample worksheet after we assigned the D1 format to cell B3.

```
B3: (D1) @DATE(89,7,4)                                      READY
```

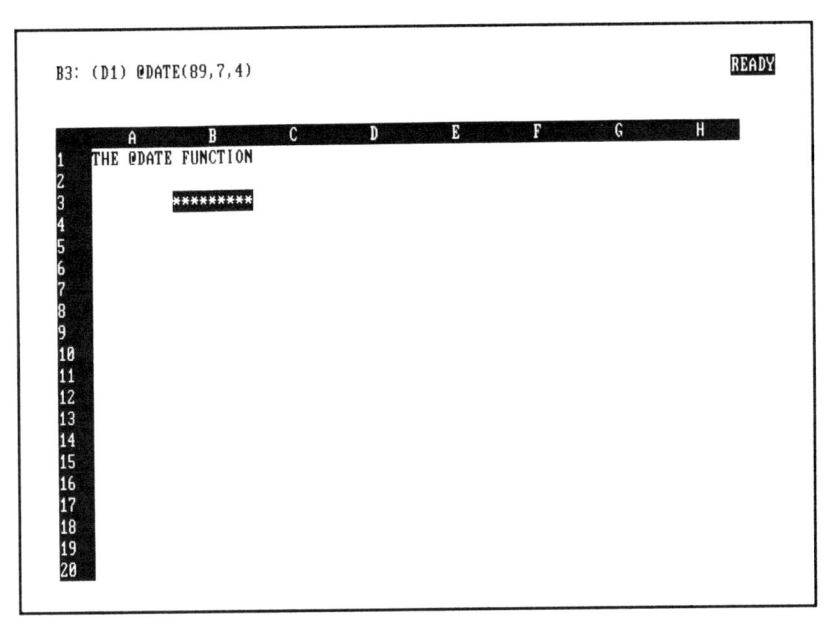

FIGURE 7-4: A formatting problem

To overcome this kind of problem, you can increase the width of the column that contains the formatted date to at least 10 characters. For example, Figure 7-5 shows the worksheet from Figure 7-4 after we used the / Worksheet Column Set-Width command to increase the width of column B to ten characters.

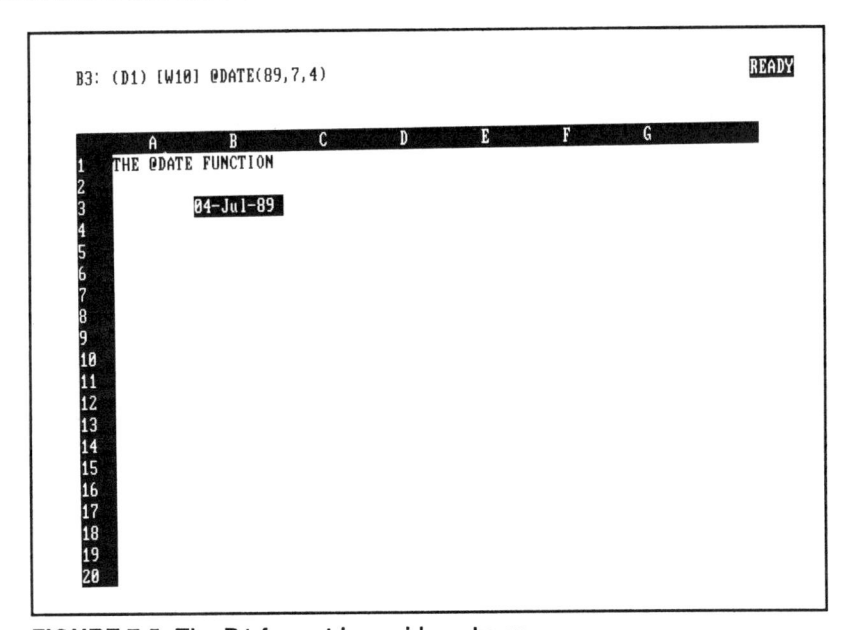

```
B3: (D1) [W10] @DATE(89,7,4)                                READY
```

FIGURE 7-5: The D1 format in a wide column

To avoid the inconvenience of widening columns, we suggest that you use the D4 (Long Intn'l) format instead of the D1 format. The D4 format supplies the same information as does the D1 format: day, month, and year. Because the D4 format requires only eight characters, however, 1-2-3 can display D4 dates in a default nine-character-wide column.

Changing the D4 and D5 Formats

If you issue the / Range Format Date command and point to either the D4 (Long International) or D5 (Short International) options, 1-2-3 will display a prompt like *Currently configured: MM/DD/YY* or *Currently configured: MM/DD* on the last line of the control panel, as shown in Figure 7-6. These prompts indicate that, unlike the forms of the other three Date formats, the forms of the D4 and D5 formats are variable.

```
A1:                                                                    MENU
1 (DD-MMM-YY)   2 (DD-MMM)   3 (MMM-YY)   4 (Long Intn'l)   5 (Short Intn'l)   Time
Currently configured: MM/DD/YY
```

FIGURE 7-6: The D4 prompt

RELEASE ▶ 2.2 ◀

To change the form of the D4 and D5 formats, you issue 1-2-3's / Worksheet Global Default Other International Date command. ▶If you are using 1-2-3 Release 2.2, you'll see the menu and settings sheet shown in Figure 7-7 when you issue this command. (If you are using an earlier version of 123, you'll see only the menu; you won't see the settings sheet.)◀ As you can see, this menu lists four format choices. These choices represent the alternative forms of the D4 and D5 formats. The message in the third line of the control panel

Format D4 will be MM/DD/YY   Format D5 will be MM/DD

explains how dates that have been assigned the D4 and D5 formats will appear if you select the highlighted option. As you point to each of the options, this message will change. Table 7-2 shows the Long and Short International forms associated with each of these four options.

Option	Long Intn'l	Short Intn'l
A	MM/DD/YY	MM/DD
B	DD/MM/YY	DD/MM
C	DD.MM.YY	DD.MM
D	YY-MM-DD	MM-DD

TABLE 7-2: Alternative forms for the D4 and D5 formats

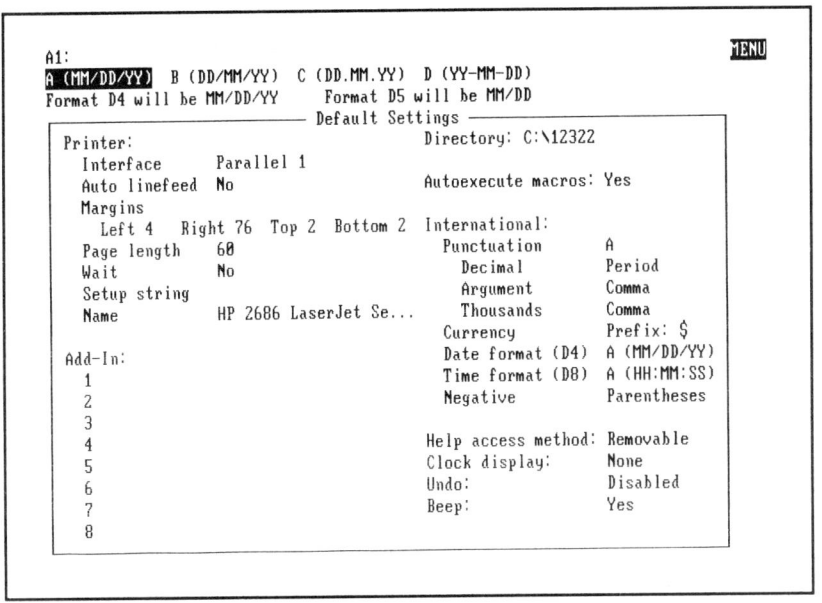

```
A1:
A (MM/DD/YY)  B (DD/MM/YY)   C (DD.MM.YY)   D (YY-MM-DD)
Format D4 will be MM/DD/YY    Format D5 will be MM/DD
                        ─── Default Settings ───
 Printer:                              Directory: C:\12322
   Interface      Parallel 1
   Auto linefeed  No                   Autoexecute macros: Yes
   Margins
     Left 4  Right 76  Top 2  Bottom 2  International:
   Page length    60                    Punctuation       A
   Wait           No                      Decimal         Period
   Setup string                           Argument        Comma
   Name           HP 2686 LaserJet Se...  Thousands       Comma
                                          Currency        Prefix: $
 Add-In:                                Date format (D4) A (MM/DD/YY)
   1                                    Time format (D8) A (HH:MM:SS)
   2                                    Negative         Parentheses
   3
   4                                    Help access method: Removable
   5                                    Clock display:      None
   6                                    Undo:               Disabled
   7                                    Beep:               Yes
   8
```

FIGURE 7-7: The / Worksheet Global Default Other International Date menu

As soon as you choose one of these options and press [Enter], 1-2-3 will change the active form of the D4 and D5 formats. The appearance of any cell in the worksheet to which you have assigned the D4 or D5 format will change to reflect the new forms of these formats. Any cells to which you subsequently assign the D4 or D5 formats also will appear in the new form of those formats.

Unless you issue the / Worksheet Global Default Update command after you change these defaults, 1-2-3 will use the D4 and D5 forms you specify only for the duration of the current 1-2-3 session. If you do choose Update, 1-2-3 will use the D4 and D5 forms you specified in all subsequent 1-2-3 sessions until you change these defaults again.

1-2-3 will always show the current form of the D4 format on the settings sheet it displays when you issue the / Worksheet Global Default Status command. In addition, if you issue the / Range Format Date command and point to either the D4 or D5 choice in the menu after changing the form of the D4 and D5 formats, you'll see that the prompt that appears in the third line of the control panel has changed. For example, if you change the forms of D4 and D5 to YY-MM-DD and MM-DD, the prompt you see when you point to the D4 option in the menu will read *Currently configured: YY-MM-DD*.

Working with Date Values

Once you have entered a date into a worksheet, you can work with that date in a number of different ways. First, you can operate upon it with 1-2-3's mathematical operators, like + and -. You also can act upon a serial date value with 1-2-3's mathematical functions or with any of three special functions that work only on dates.

Using Mathematical Operators and Functions

Because the results of @DATE functions are values, you can manipulate them with any of 1-2-3's mathematical operators or with mathematical functions like @MOD. These operators and functions allow you to calculate the number of days between two dates, the number of weeks between two dates, the date that is a specified number of days before or after a given date, and so forth.

By subtracting one date from another, you can compute the number of days that elapse between the two dates. For example, suppose that you want to calculate how many days elapse between March 26, 1989 (Easter) and December 25 of that year (Christmas). To do this, you would use the formula *@DATE(89,12,25)-@DATE(89,3,26)*. The result, 274, indicates that 274 days elapse between these two dates.

You also can use a simple formula to determine the date that is some specified number of days removed from any other date. For example, suppose you want to find out the date that was 90 days before November 23, 1989 (Thanksgiving). To do this, you could use the formula *@DATE(89,11,23)-90*. By formatting the result, 32745, you can see that the date 90 days before November 23, 1989, was August 25, 1989. Similarly, suppose you want to know the date that falls 45 days after September 4, 1989 (Labor Day). To do this, you would use the formula *@DATE(89,9,4)+45*. Formatting the result, 32800, reveals that the date in question is October 19, 1989.

You can divide the difference between two date values by 7 to determine how many weeks elapse between those dates. For example, the formula

(@DATE(89,12,25)-@DATE(89,3,26))/7

reveals that there are 39.14 weeks between Easter and Christmas of 1989.

You also can operate on serial date values with any of 1-2-3's mathematical functions. For example, the function *@MOD(@DATE(89,7,9),7)* returns the remainder of dividing the serial date value for July 4, 1989—32693—by 7. The result—3—can be used to determine the day of the week (Sunday, Monday, and so on) of the date. To learn how, see the tip at the bottom of the next page.

Special Date Functions

In addition to manipulating dates with traditional operators and mathematical functions, you can operate on date values with any of three special date functions: @DAY, @MONTH, and @YEAR. These functions, whose forms are

@DAY(*serial date value*)
@MONTH(*serial date value*)
@YEAR(*serial date value*)

return the day, month, and year components of a serial date value.

The @DAY Function

1-2-3's @DAY function returns the day of the month of the date referred to by its argument. The result of this function always will be a value from 1 to 31. For example, cell B3 in Figure 7-8 contains the function @DATE(89,7,4). Since this function returns the serial date value for July 4, 1989, the function in cell B5

   B5: @DAY(B3)

returns the value 4.

The @MONTH Function

1-2-3's @MONTH function returns a value from 1 to 12 that specifies the month of the year in which the date referred to by its argument falls. For example, the function in cell B6 in Figure 7-8, *@MONTH(B3)*, returns the value 7, which indicates that the date in cell B3 falls in July.

The @YEAR Function

1-2-3's @YEAR function returns a value from 0 to 199 that specifies the year in which the date referred to by its argument falls. For example, the function in cell B7 in Figure 7-8

   B7: @YEAR(B3)

returns the value 89.

TIP: COMPUTING THE DAY OF THE WEEK

Occasionally, you'll need to know on which day of the week a given date falls. For example, knowing that July 4, 1989, is a Saturday lets you know that July 3 will be a holiday. Although 1-2-3 does not have a function that will compute the day of the week of a date automatically, you can create a formula that will do the job nicely.

For example, suppose you want to figure out the day of the week on which July 4, 1989, falls. The formula

   @CHOOSE(@MOD(@DATE(89,7,4),7),"Saturday","Sunday",
       "Monday","Tuesday","Wednesday","Thursday","Friday")

will return the correct answer: *Tuesday*. The heart of this formula is the function @MOD(@DATE(89,7,4),7), which computes the remainder of dividing the serial date value of the date July 4, 1989, by 7: 3. The @CHOOSE function uses this result as its offset argument. Since an offset of 0 tells the @CHOOSE function to return the first item from its list of options, this function returns the string *Tuesday*.

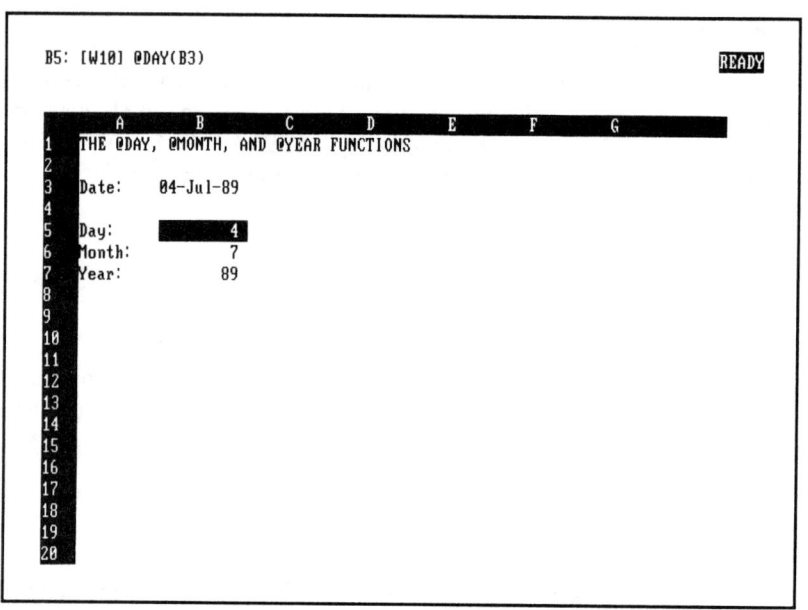

```
B5: [W10] @DAY(B3)                                              READY

       A         B         C         D         E         F         G
 1  THE @DAY, @MONTH, AND @YEAR FUNCTIONS
 2
 3  Date:     04-Jul-89
 4
 5  Day:             4
 6  Month:           7
 7  Year:           89
 8
 9
10
...
20
```

FIGURE 7-8: The @DAY, @MONTH, and @YEAR functions

TIP: RETURNING THE NAME OF A MONTH

The @MONTH function returns a number from 1 to 12 that specifies the month of the year in which a date falls. If you want 1-2-3 to return the name of the month, instead of just a number, you can enclose the @MONTH function in an @CHOOSE function. For example, if cell B3 contains the date function @DATE(89,7,4), the function

@CHOOSE(@MONTH(B3)-1,"January","February","March",
   "April","May","June","July","August","September",
      "October","November","December")

will return the string *July*. Because the @MONTH function returns a value from 1 to 12 but the @CHOOSE function starts counting with 0, it is necessary to subtract 1 from the result of the @MONTH function before that result can be used as the offset argument for the @CHOOSE function.

Creating Date Series

If you are like most 1-2-3 users, you will often use date series in your worksheets. A date series is a sequence of date entries with a constant interval—usually a day, a week, a month, or a year.

> **TIP: GETTING THE FULL YEAR**
>
> The @YEAR function returns a two-digit number representing the year portion of a date. If you want to get the full year number, you can use the formula
>
> @YEAR(A1)+1900
>
> If cell A1 contains the function *@DATE(89,7,4)*, this formula will return the full year number—1989.

Day and Week Series

In Chapter 6, you learned about 1-2-3's /Data Fill command. This command is an ideal tool for creating daily and weekly date series. For example, suppose you want to enter a series of dates in the range A1..A20 in a worksheet. You want the series to begin with the date January 1, 1989, and you want each of the dates in the series to be one day greater than the previous date. To create this series, issue the / Data Fill command, specify A1..A20 as the fill range, the function @DATE(89,1,1) as the start value, the value 1 as the step value, and the value 100000 as the stop value. When you press [Enter] to lock in the stop value, 1-2-3 will fill the range A1..A20 with the values 32509, 32510, and so on. Once the series is in place, you can use the / Range Format Date command to format these dates.

Did you notice that we used the value 100000 as the stop value? This large stop value is the result of the relatively large numbers that are used to represent dates in the 1980s. In fact, we could have used any value greater than about 40000 as the stop value; 100000 is just a convenient, easy-to-remember number. However, if we had simply accepted the default stop value, 8191, the series would have been stopped before it was started since 8192 is less than the first value in the series, 32509.

By specifying a different step value, you can create a series with an interval of two days, three days, or any other number of days. If you set the step value to 7, you can create a week series. For example, suppose you want to create a date series in the range A1..A20 that begins with the date July 15, 1989, (a Saturday) and includes the next 20 Saturdays. To create this series, issue the /Data Fill command, specify A1..A20 as the fill range (if you are following along, this range will already be set), the function @DATE(89,7,15) as the start value, the value 7 as the step value, and the value 100000 as the stop value. When you press [Enter] to lock in the stop value, 1-2-3 will fill the range A1..A20 with the values 32704, 32711, and so on. Once the series is in place, you can use the / Range Format Date command to format these dates.

Year and Month Series

The / Data Fill command requires the interval between any two items in the list to be the same as the interval between the other items. Since all months and years do not contain the same number of days, / Data Fill is not as good at creating monthly and yearly series as it is at building daily and weekly series. If you want the interval in your series to be a month or a year, you'll have to use a formula.

Month Series

Suppose you have taken out a loan that requires you to make a payment on the first day of each month, beginning on March 1, 1989. You want to create a schedule that shows the date, amount, and so on, of each payment. The interval between each of the dates in the schedule is exactly one month.

To begin, enter the date function @DATE(89,3,1) into the first cell in the series (we'll assume that this formula is in cell A1). Then enter the formula

A2: +A1+@CHOOSE(@MONTH
   (A1)-1,31,@IF(@MOD(@YEAR(A1),4)=0,
   29,28),31,30,31,30,31,31,30,31,30,31)

in cell A2. This complex formula uses the @MONTH function to determine the month of the date in cell A1, then adds the appropriate number of days to that date to arrive at the same date in the next month. The function *@IF(@MOD(@YEAR (A1),4)=0,29,28)* accounts for leap years, in which the second month, February, has an extra day.

Once you've entered this formula into cell A2, you can use the /Range Format Date command to give its result a Date format, then use the /Copy command to copy it down in column A.

This formula will create the proper interval for any month series, as long as the start date falls on or before the twenty-eighth of the month. Computing a month series that starts after the twenty-eighth of the month is far more complex.

As long as you don't care that the series falls on exactly the same day in each month, you can use the / Data Fill command to create the date series. For instance, suppose you want to create an imprecise monthly date series that starts with the date January 1, 1989, in the range A1..A20 in a worksheet. To do this, issue the /Data Fill command, specify A1..A20 as the fill range, the function @DATE(89,1,1) as the start value, the value 31 as the step value, and the value 100000 as the stop value. When you press [Enter] to lock in the stop value, 1-2-3 will fill the range A1..A20 with the values 32509, 32540, and so on. Once the series is in place, issue the / Range Format Date command, choose Date format 3, and select the range A1..A20. Figure 7-9 shows the result. As you can see, the entries in the range A1..A20 appear to be an even month series. Of course, the underlying date values are not exactly one month apart. However, thanks to the MMM-YY format, the result is close enough.

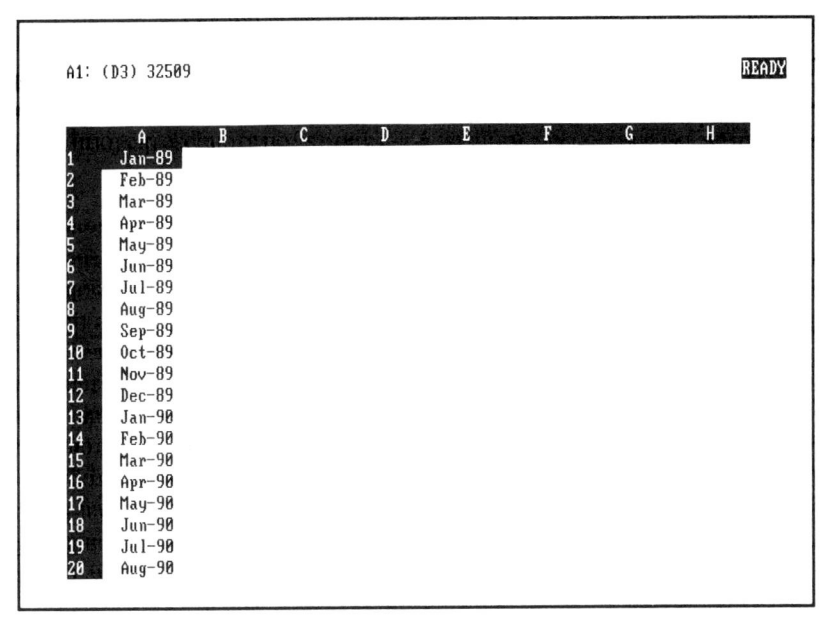

```
A1: (D3) 32509                                              READY

     A          B        C        D        E        F        G        H
 1   Jan-89
 2   Feb-89
 3   Mar-89
 4   Apr-89
 5   May-89
 6   Jun-89
 7   Jul-89
 8   Aug-89
 9   Sep-89
10   Oct-89
11   Nov-89
12   Dec-89
13   Jan-90
14   Feb-90
15   Mar-90
16   Apr-90
17   May-90
18   Jun-90
19   Jul-90
20   Aug-90
```

FIGURE 7-9: An imprecise month date series

Year Series

You can also create a formula that will result in a yearly date series. For example, suppose you want to create a yearly date series, beginning with the date January 1, 1989, in cell A1. To begin, enter the starting date of the series (@DATE(89,1,1)) into the first cell in the series (A1). Then enter the formula

A2: +A1+@IF(@MOD(@YEAR(A1),4)=3,
@IF(@MONTH(A1)>2,366,365),
@IF(@MOD(@YEAR(A1),4)=0,
@IF(@MONTH(A3)>2,365,366),365))

in cell A2. This complex formula determines whether the current year is or the previous year was a leap year, and whether the previous date in the series was in a month after February, and then adds the appropriate number of days to that date to arrive at the same date in the next year.

Once you have entered this formula into cell A2, you can use the / Range Format Date command to give its result a Date format, then use the / Copy command to copy it down in column A. The result will be a series of dates exactly one year apart.

TIMES

In addition to working with dates, 1-2-3 Releases 2, 2.01, and 2.2 also can work with times. (1-2-3 Release 1A cannot work with times.) As with dates, there are four things you need to know about working with times in 1-2-3: how 1-2-3 represents times, how to enter a time into a worksheet, how to format a cell that contains a time, and how to manipulate a time value once it is in a worksheet.

Since the base unit of time in 1-2-3 is a day, it makes sense that 1-2-3 represents hours, minutes, and seconds as fractions of a day. In 1-2-3, all times are represented by a fraction that equals the percentage of a day that has elapsed between the beginning of the day (midnight) and that time. For example, the time 12:00 noon is represented by the value .5 since 12:00 noon is exactly 1/2 of the way through a day. Similarly, the time 6:00 AM is represented by the value .25, and the time 6:00 PM is represented by the value .75. Time values usually are much more complex than this, however. For example, 1-2-3 uses the value .3958333333 to represent the time 9:30 AM and the value .6438078704 to represent the time 3:27:05 PM. We'll refer to a value that 1-2-3 uses to represent a time as a *time value*.

As with dates, the serial values that 1-2-3 uses to represent times are hard to understand. Fortunately, you don't have to master this way of keeping time. 1-2-3 provides a function, @TIME, that makes it easy to enter time values into your worksheets and a set of formats that displays time values in understandable forms.

Entering Times: The @TIME Function

The @TIME function allows you to enter a time value into a worksheet. The form of this function is

@TIME(*hours,minutes,seconds*)

where *hours*, *minutes*, and *seconds* describe the time you want to enter into the worksheet. The *hours* argument must specify a value from 0 to 23, where 0 is midnight, 6 is 6:00 AM, 12 is 12:00 noon, 18 is 6:00 PM, and so on. The minutes and seconds arguments must specify values from 0 to 59.

For example, cell B3 in the worksheet in Figure 7-10 contains the function

@TIME(13,27,0)

which represents the time 1:27 PM. The result of this function, .560416, is the time value of the time 1:27 PM. Similarly, the function *@TIME(2,30,0)*, which represents the time 2:30 AM, returns the value .104166. The function *@TIME(18,0,0)*, which represents the time 6:00 PM, returns the value .75.

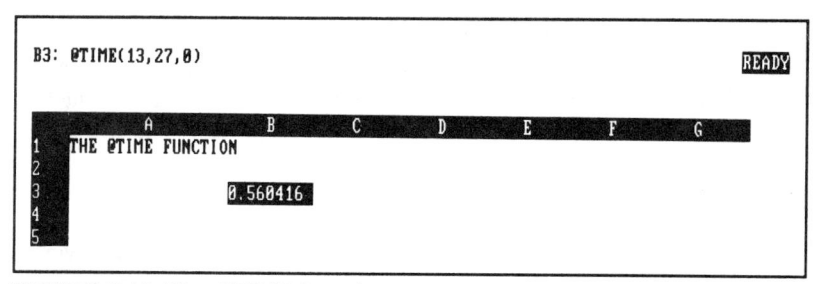

FIGURE 7-10: The @TIME function

Just as the @DATE function will not accept invalid dates, the @TIME function will not accept invalid times. If you specify an *hour* argument that is less than 0 or greater than 23, or if you specify a *minute* or *second* argument that is less than 0 or greater than 59, 1-2-3 will return the value ERR as the result of the @TIME function. For example, the function *@TIME(25,30,5)* returns the value ERR since its *hour* argument is outside the allowed range. The functions *@TIME(1,60,10)* and *@TIME(12,0,90)* will also return the result ERR.

Formatting Times

Although it is possible to estimate the time that is represented by a time value, it is virtually impossible to determine exactly what time corresponds to a time value in its "raw" form. For this reason, 1-2-3 allows you to format cells that contain time values so that those values are displayed in a recognizable form.

To assign a format to a cell that contains a time value, issue the / Range Format Date command. When 1-2-3 displays the Date format menu shown in Figure 7-2, choose the Time option. When you do this, 1-2-3 will display the menu shown in Figure 7-11. As you can see, this menu presents four Time format options. Table 7-3 explains the effect of each of these options. To choose a format, just type a number from 1 to 4, or point to the format you want to select and press [Enter]. Either way, after you make your selection, 1-2-3 will prompt you to specify the range to be formatted and will offer the cell on which the cell pointer is positioned as the default option. If the cell pointer is on the cell you want to format, you can just press [Enter]. Otherwise, you can either type the address of the cell or range to which you want to assign the format or point to that cell or range and press [Enter].

```
A1:                                                              MENU
1 (HH:MM:SS AM/PM)   2 (HH:MM AM/PM)   3 (Long Intn'l)   4 (Short Intn'l)
Lotus standard long form
```

FIGURE 7-11: The Time Format menu

As always, formatting a cell that contains a time value does not alter the value in that cell; it just tells 1-2-3 to display that value in a different way.

Format	Code	Form	Example
1	D6	HH:MM:SS AM/PM	2:53:27 PM
2	D7	HH:MM AM/PM	2:53 PM
3 (Long Intn'l)	D8	HH:MM:SS (24-Hour)	14:53:27
4 (Short Intn'l)	D9	HH:MM (24-Hour)	14:53

TABLE 7-3: 1-2-3's default Time formats

An Example

For example, suppose you want to assign Time format 2 (HH:MM AM/PM) to the time in cell B3 in Figure 7-10. To do this, you would move the cell pointer to cell B3, issue the / Range Format Date Time command, choose Time format 2, and press [Enter]. Figure 7-12 shows the worksheet with the formatted date.

Notice the format memo (D7), which now appears in the control panel next to the contents of cell B3. Apparently, 1-2-3 considers the four Time formats to be extensions of its set of Date formats. 1-2-3 gives the format code D6 to Time format 1, the code D7 to Time format 2, and so on.

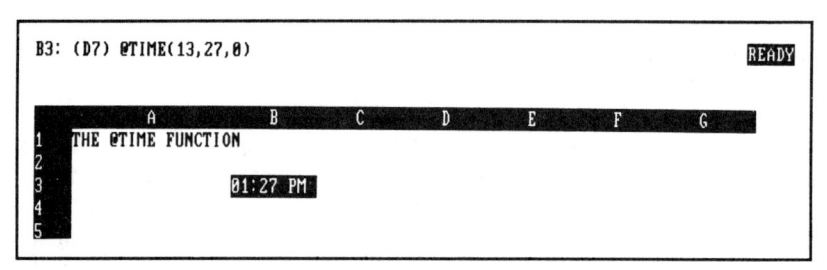

```
B3: (D7) @TIME(13,27,0)                                      READY

         A          B          C          D          E          F          G
1  THE @TIME FUNCTION
2
3                01:27 PM
4
5
```

FIGURE 7-12: A formatted time value

Column Width Considerations

Like the display produced by the D1 (DD-MMM-YY) format, the display produced by Time format 1 (HH:MM:SS AM/PM) is too long to be displayed in a standard nine-character-wide column. This means that 1-2-3 displays times in Time format 1 (format D6) in standard-width columns as a series of asterisks. To overcome this problem, you can increase the width of the column that contains the time to at least 12 characters.

Alternatively, you could choose one of the other available Time formats. Because time values that are formatted with any of 1-2-3's other Time formats occupy eight characters or less, 1-2-3 is able to display them in a default nine-character-wide column. Since in most cases you don't need the seconds portion of the time to be displayed anyway, you don't lose much by choosing an abbreviated format, like Time format 2 over Time format 1.

Changing the D8 and D9 Formats

Just as with the D4 and D5 Date formats, 1-2-3 allows you to choose the form in which it will display times formatted with the Long International (D8) and Short International (D9) Time formats. To specify the form in which 1-2-3 will display time values in cells to which you have assigned the D8 or D9 formats, you must issue 1-2-3's / Worksheet Global Default Other International Time command.

RELEASE ► 2.2 ◄ ►If you are using 1-2-3 Release 2.2, you'll see the the menu and settings sheet shown in Figure 7-13 when you issue this command. (If you are using an earlier release of 123, you'll see only the menu; you won't see the settings sheet.)◄ The four choices on this menu represent the ways that 1-2-3 will display times in cells assigned the D8 and D9 formats. The message in the third line of the control panel

Format D8 will be HH:MM:SS Format D9 will be HH:MM

explains the effects of the highlighted option. Table 7-4 shows the Long and Short International forms specified by each of these four options.

```
A1:                                                              MENU
A (HH:MM:SS)  B (HH.MM.SS)  C (HH,MM,SS)  D (HHhMMmSSs)
Format D8 will be HH:MM:SS    Format D9 will be HH:MM
─────────────────────── Default Settings ───────────────────────
 Printer:                           Directory: C:\12322
    Interface      Parallel 1
    Auto linefeed  No               Autoexecute macros: Yes
    Margins
      Left 4  Right 76  Top 2  Bottom 2  International:
    Page length    60                  Punctuation      A
    Wait           No                  Decimal          Period
    Setup string                       Argument         Comma
    Name           HP 2686 LaserJet Se... Thousands     Comma
                                       Currency         Prefix: $
 Add-In:                               Date format (D4) A (MM/DD/YY)
    1                                  Time format (D8) A (HH:MM:SS)
    2                                  Negative         Parentheses
    3
    4                               Help access method: Removable
    5                               Clock display:      None
    6                               Undo:               Disabled
    7                               Beep:               Yes
    8
```

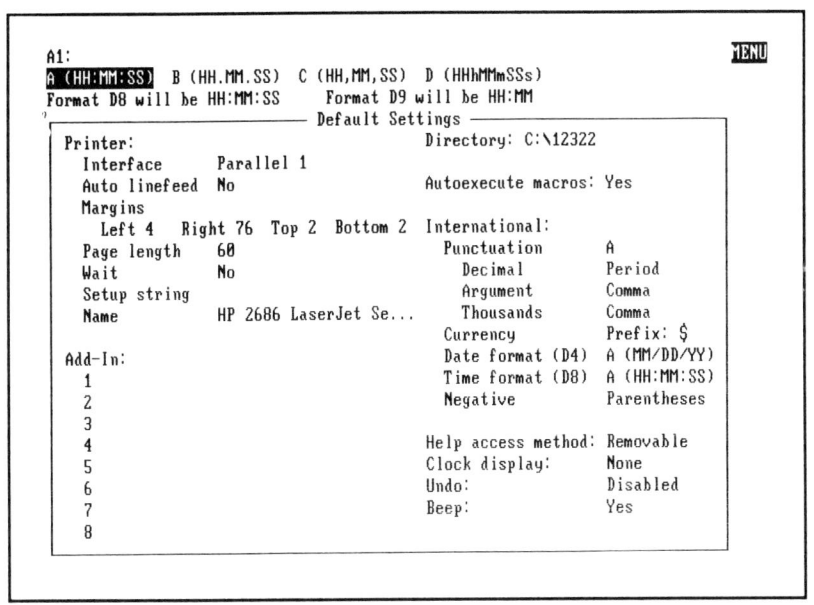

FIGURE 7-13: The / Worksheet Global Default Other International Time menu

Option	Long Intn'l Form	Short Intn'l Form
A	HH:MM:SS	HH:MM
B	HH.MM.SS	HH.MM
C	HH,MM,SS	HH,MM
D	HHhMMmSSs	HHhMMm

TABLE 7-4: Alternative forms for the D8 and D9 formats

As soon as you select one of these options, 1-2-3 will use the forms specified by that option to display time values in any cell to which you have assigned or subsequently assign the D8 or D9 formats. If you choose option D, for example, 1-2-3 will display time values in the form HHhMMmSSs in cells to which you have assigned the D8 format, and display time values in HHhMMm form in cells that have been assigned the D9 format.

To make the new forms of the D8 and D9 formats "permanent" (that is, to make them last longer than just the current 1-2-3 session), you must issue the / Worksheet Global Default Update command before you quit from 1-2-3. If you do not choose Update, these formats will revert to their previous default forms when you next load 1-2-3.

To determine which forms of the D8 and D9 formats 1-2-3 will use, you can issue the / Worksheet Global Default Status command and look at the resulting settings sheet. Alternatively, you can check the message in the third line of the control panel when you issue the / Range Format Date Time command and point to one of these commands.

Working with Time Values

Representing times as serial values makes it possible for 1-2-3 to manipulate them mathematically. You can do this with traditional mathematical operators or any of three special time functions.

Using Mathematical Operators

Calculating an elapsed time is probably the most common mathematical manipulation of time values. To calculate an elapsed time, you simply subtract one time value from another. For example, suppose that you have assigned the range name IN to cell A1, which contains the function *@TIME(8,30,0)* and that you have assigned the range name OUT to cell B1, which contains the function *@TIME(17,0,0)*. To calculate the amount of time that elapses between these two times, you would use either the formula *+OUT-IN* or the formula *+B1-A1*. Either way, the result is the time value .354166. Formatting the cell that contains this result reveals that 8 hours and 30 minutes elapse between these two times.

You can also add one time value to another. For example, suppose that you want to determine what time is 3 hours, 17 minutes, and 54 seconds after 3:37:52 PM. You would use the formula *@TIME(15,37,52)+@TIME(3,17,54)* to do this. Formatting the result, .78873, reveals that 6:55:46 PM is 3 hours, 17 minutes, and 54 seconds after 3:37:52 PM.

Problems with Time Arithmetic

Unlike date values, time values are cyclical in nature. That is, 3:00 PM on one day is represented by the same value as 3:00 PM on any other day. This can cause problems when you subtract time values. For example, suppose you want to determine the time that is 4 hours before 3:30 AM. Using the simple formula *@TIME(3,30,0)-@TIME(4,0,0)* would produce the result -.02083—a meaningless value. To correctly calculate this past time that falls in a previous day, you must use the function

@IF(@TIME(3,30,0)-@TIME(4,0,0)<0,1+@TIME(3,30,0)-@TIME(4,0,0),
@TIME(3,30,0)-@TIME(4,0,0))

This formula accounts for the cyclical nature of time values. If a subtraction produces a negative time value, indicating a time in the previous day, 1-2-3 will add 1 to that value to produce the correct time. If the result is a positive value, indicating that the result falls in the same day, 1-2-3 will return that value. (You can use this formula with any time values. Just substitute the values you want to use for the ones we used in the example.)

On the other hand, time addition that produces a result in a different day is not a problem. The result of such a formula is a value greater than 1. 1-2-3 ignores any digits to the right of the decimal place of a formatted time value. Thus, 1-2-3 has no problem interpreting the result of such an addition. For example, suppose you want to know the time that is 3 hours and 29 minutes after 11:47 PM. You would use the formula @TIME(23,47,0)+@TIME(3,29,0), which would return the value 1.136111. If you assigned the D7 format (HH:MM AM/PM) to the cell that contained this result, it would be displayed as 3:16 AM—the time 3 hours and 29 minutes after 11:47 PM.

Special Time Functions

In addition to using ordinary mathematical operators to manipulate time values, you can use three special time functions: @HOUR, @MINUTE, and @SECOND. These functions, whose forms are

@HOUR(*time value*)
@MINUTE(*time value*)
@SECOND(*time value*)

return the hour, minute, and second portion of a time value. The *time value* argument of these functions must be a literal time value or a function, formula, or cell reference that returns a time value.

The @HOUR Function

1-2-3's @HOUR function returns the hour represented by a time value. The result of this function always is a value between 0 and 23 inclusive. For example, cell B3 in Figure 7-14 contains the function @TIMEVALUE(13,2,15), which returns the time value .543229. The function in cell B5

B5: @HOUR(B3)

returns the value 13.

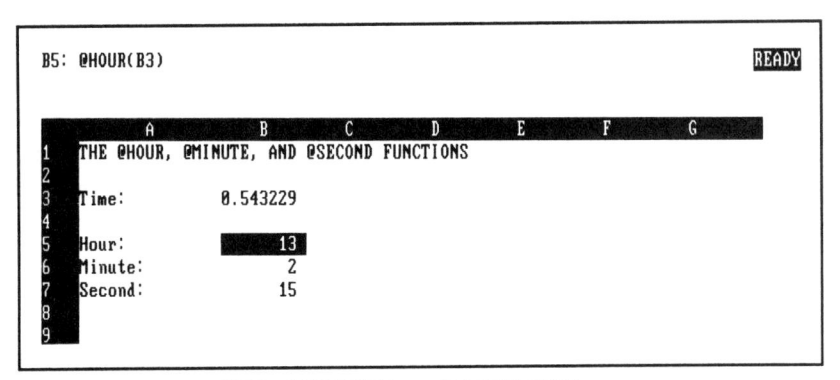

```
B5: @HOUR(B3)                                              READY

          A         B        C        D        E        F        G
1    THE @HOUR, @MINUTE, AND @SECOND FUNCTIONS
2
3    Time:     0.543229
4
5    Hour:           13
6    Minute:          2
7    Second:         15
8
9
```

FIGURE 7-14: @HOUR, @MINUTE, and @SECOND

The @MINUTE Function

1-2-3's @MINUTE function returns the minute represented by a time value. The result of this function always is a value between 0 and 59 inclusive. For example, the function in cell B6 of Figure 7-14

    B6: @MINUTE(B3)

returns the value 2.

The @SECOND Function

1-2-3's @SECOND function returns the second represented by a time value. Like the result of the @MINUTE function, the result of any @SECOND function will be a value between 0 and 59 inclusive. For example, the function in cell B7 in Figure 7-14

    B7: @SECOND(B3)

returns the value 15.

TIP: GETTING THE HOUR IN 12-HOUR FORM

The @HOUR function returns the hour represented by a time value. If you want the result in 12-hour form, you must use the formula

@IF(@HOUR(B3)>12,@HOUR(B3)-12,@HOUR(B3))

COMBINED DATE/TIME ENTRIES

So far, we've worked with date values and time values separately. 1-2-3 also allows you to create and work with combined date/time entries. As you recall, a date entry is an integer from 0 to 73050 that represents a number of days that have elapsed since a fixed base date, and a time entry is a value between 0 and 1 that represents a fractional day. Consequently, a date/time entry is represented by a single value that has both an integer portion and a decimal portion. The integer portion of the value specifies the day, while the digits to the right of the decimal point identify the time within that day. For example, the value 32787.25 represents the date/time October 6, 1989, 6 AM.

The @NOW Function

The @NOW function allows you to enter the current date and time into the worksheet. The form of this function is just @NOW; the function does not take any arguments.

    When you enter this function into a worksheet, 1-2-3 draws the current date and time from your computer's system clock and enters it into the worksheet as a combined date/time value. For example, if you entered the function @NOW into a worksheet at precisely 9:37:15 AM on August 1, 1989, it would return the value 32721.400868. The integer portion of this value, 32721, specifies August 1, 1989—the day 32,721 days after 1-2-3's base date: December 31, 1899. The decimal portion of this entry, .400868, specifies 9:37:15 AM—the additional portion of a day that has elapsed since that base date.

1-2-3 will update any @NOW functions in a worksheet each time you recalculate that worksheet. If 1-2-3 is in the Manual Recalculation mode, the value of @NOW will not be updated until you press the [Calc] key ([F9]). In that event, you may notice a difference between the result of @NOW and the clock display at the bottom of the 1-2-3 screen (which is constantly being updated). You can eliminate this discrepancy simply by calculating the worksheet.

Because the result of an @NOW function is based on the time and date in your computer's system clock, if the system clock is wrong, the result of @NOW also will be wrong. To set the system clock, you must exit from 1-2-3 to DOS (either by issuing the / Quit command or by issuing the / System command) and then run the resident DOS utilities DATE and TIME. Better yet, you might consider buying a battery-powered clock for your computer that will always keep the system clock up-to-date.

Because 1-2-3 Release 1A cannot work with times, the @NOW function is not available in that release of the program. In place of @NOW, 1-2-3 Release 1A offers the @TODAY function. When you enter this function into a 1-2-3 Release 1A worksheet, it draws only the current date from your computer's system clock and returns an integer that represents that date. If you enter the @TODAY function into a 1-2-3 Release 2.01 or 2.2 worksheet, they will automatically convert it into the combined function @INT(@NOW); 1-2-3 Release 2 converts the @TODAY function to @NOW.

TIP: LOCKING IN THE CURRENT DATE AND TIME

As you know, the result of any @NOW function in a worksheet is updated each time you recalculate that worksheet. This means that every cell that contains an @NOW function will display the date and time that the worksheet was last recalculated—not the date and time at which the @NOW function was entered into the worksheet. If you want to "freeze" the current value of an @NOW function, just position the cell pointer on the cell that contains the @NOW function, issue the / Range Values command, and press [Enter] twice. When you do this, 1-2-3 will replace the @NOW function with the current value of the function. Because the entry is no longer a function, it will not change when you subsequently recalculate the worksheet.

Formatting Combined Date/Time Entries

Although 1-2-3 permits you to create combined date/time entries, it does not provide a format that will display the date and time components of those entries together. In other words, you can format a combined date/time entry to display as a date or as a time, but not both at the same time.

For example, suppose that you entered the function @NOW into a worksheet at precisely 6:00 PM on January 1, 1989, so that 1-2-3 returned the combined date/time value 32509.75. If you issued the / Range Format Date command and chose D4, 1-2-3 would display the entry as 01/01/89. If you issued the / Range Format Date Time command and chose option B, 1-2-3 would display the value as 6:00 PM. There is no format that will display both the date and the time portion of the entry at once.

The only way to display the date and time components of a combined date/time value at the same time is to enter that value in two adjacent cells of the worksheet and then assign a Time format to one cell and a Date format to the other. For instance, cells G1 and H1 in Figure 7-15 both contain the function @NOW. We've assigned the D4 format (MM/DD/YY) to cell G1, and the D7 format (HH:MM AM/PM) to cell H1. Because the two cells are next to one another, the result looks like a single date/time entry.

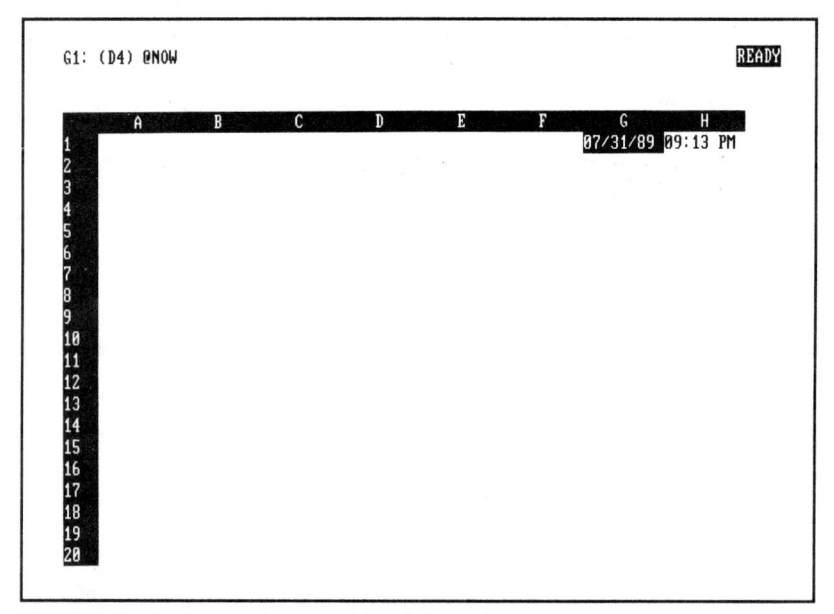

FIGURE 7-15: Formatting combined date/time entries

Creating Your Own Date/Time Entries

Although most combined date/time entries are the result of @NOW functions, you can create a combined date/time entry just by adding the result of an @DATE function to the result of an @TIME function. For example, suppose you want to create a single entry that identifies the time 7:00 AM on December 25, 1989. To create this entry, you would use the formula

@DATE(89,12,25)+@TIME(7,0,0)

The @DATE function, which specifies December 25, 1989, returns the value 32867. The @TIME function, which specifies 7:00 AM, returns the value .29167. The sum of these two values, 32867.29167, identifies 7:00 AM on December 25, 1989.

Working with Combined Date/Time Entries

Just as you can use 1-2-3's mathematical operators to add and subtract date values and time values, you can also use these tools to perform math with combined date/time values. For example, suppose you want to know what date and time is exactly 3 days and 11 hours after 6:00 PM on December 10, 1989. You can use the formula

(@DATE(89,12,10)+@TIME(18,0,0))+(3+@TIME(11,0,0))

to make this computation. The result of this formula is the value 32856.20. This value represents the date December 14, 1989, and the time 5:00 AM—the date and time exactly 3 days and 11 hours after 6:00 PM on December 10, 1989.

If you instead wanted to know the date and time that was 3 days and 11 hours before 6:00 PM on December 10, 1989, you would use the formula

(@DATE(89,12,10)+@TIME(18,0,0))-(3+@TIME(11,0,0))

The result of this function is the date/time value 32849.29, which represents the date December 7, 1989, and the time 7:00 AM.

Notice that we used the value 3, and not an @DATE function, to represent the days portion of the second date/time value. Since the base unit of time in 1-2-3 is a day, you can use simple integers to represent days when you are performing date/time arithmetic.

You can also subtract one date/time value from another to determine an interval. For example, the formula

(@DATE(89,12,10)+@TIME(18,0,0))-(@DATE(89,12,7)+@TIME(7,0,0))

determines the interval between 6:00 PM on December 10, 1989, and 7:00 AM on December 7, 1989. The result of this function is the date/time value 3.458333, which indicates that the interval between these two points in time is 3 days and 11 hours.

CONVERTING LABELS INTO DATES AND TIMES

In almost all cases, you'll use the @DATE, @TIME, and @NOW functions to enter dates and times into a worksheet. As you know, the results of these functions are serial values that can be manipulated mathematically by 1-2-3.

In some situations, however, your worksheet might contain labels in the forms of dates and times. This might occur if you import information into 1-2-3 from other programs or because someone less knowledgeable about 1-2-3 than you entered a set of dates and times into the worksheet as labels. As you have learned, 1-2-3 cannot work with dates and times unless they are in serial value form, so these labels that are in the form of dates and times are not of much value.

Fortunately, 1-2-3 includes functions, @DATEVALUE and @TIMEVALUE, that convert labels in the form of dates and times into serial value form. We'll cover those tools in this section.

The @DATEVALUE Function

1-2-3's @DATEVALUE function converts label dates into serial date values. The form of this function is

@DATEVALUE(*date label*)

where the *date label* argument is a label in the form of any of 1-2-3's standard Date formats, including whatever forms of the Long and Short International formats are current at the time. The result of the function is the serial date value of the date represented by the label.

Cells B3 through B9 in Figure 7-16 contain examples of the @DATEVALUE function. These functions convert the labels in cells A3 to A9 into date values. For example, the function in cell B3

B3: @DATEVALUE(A3)

converts the label in cell A3, *'6-Oct-89*, into the serial date value 32787.

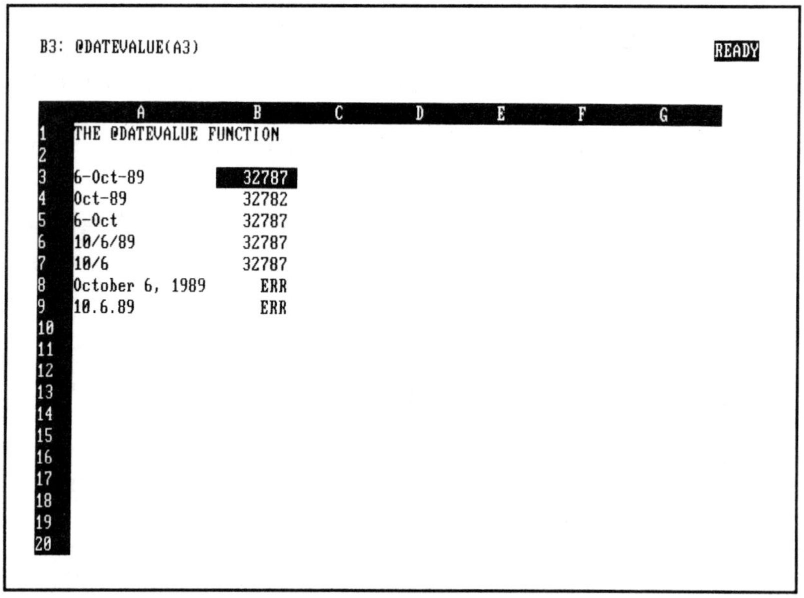

```
B3: @DATEVALUE(A3)                                               READY

         A              B        C        D        E        F        G
 1  THE @DATEVALUE FUNCTION
 2
 3  6-Oct-89        32787
 4  Oct-89          32782
 5  6-Oct           32787
 6  10/6/89         32787
 7  10/6            32787
 8  October 6, 1989 ERR
 9  10.6.89         ERR
10
11
12
13
14
15
16
17
18
19
20
```

FIGURE 7-16: The @DATEVALUE function

If the argument of an @DATEVALUE function is a label in the form of any of 1-2-3's Short International Date formats, like *'6-Oct* or *'Oct-89*, 1-2-3 will "guess" at the missing element. If the day component is missing, @DATEVALUE will return the serial date value of the first day in the indicated month. For example, notice that the label in cell A4 is *'Oct-89*. The function in cell B4, *@DATEVALUE(A4)*, returns the value 32782, which is the serial date value of October 1, 1989.

If the year component is missing, @DATEVALUE will assume that the date falls in the current year (in this case, 1989). For example, cell A5 contains the label *'6-Oct*. The function in cell B5, *@DATEVALUE(A5)*, returns the value 32787—the serial date value of October 6, 1989.

If the argument is in a form that 1-2-3 cannot recognize (including a Long or Short International form that is not active at the time), it will return the value ERR. For example, the function in cell B8 of Figure 7-16, @DATEVALUE(A8), returns the value ERR because the label in cell A8 is not in a form that 1-2-3 recognizes as a date. The function in cell B9, @DATEVALUE(A9), returns ERR even though the label in cell A9 is in the form of one of 1-2-3's International Date formats. This occurs because the format MM.DD.YY is not the currently selected Long International Date format.

The @TIMEVALUE Function

1-2-3's @TIMEVALUE functions convert labels in the form of times into time values. The form of this function is

@TIMEVALUE(*time label*)

where the *time label* argument is a label in the form of any of 1-2-3's Time formats, including whatever Long and Short International forms are current at the time. The result is the time value of the time represented by *time label*.

Cells B3 to B8 in Figure 7-17 contain examples of the @TIMEVALUE function. The functions in these cells convert the labels in the range A3..A8 into time values. For example, the function is cell B3

@TIMEVALUE(A3)

converts the label in cell A3, *'2:15:30 PM*, into the time value .594097. Similarly, the function in cell B5, *@TIMEVALUE(A5)*, converts the label *'14:15:30* into a time value. Notice that the label in cell A5 is in the Long International form.

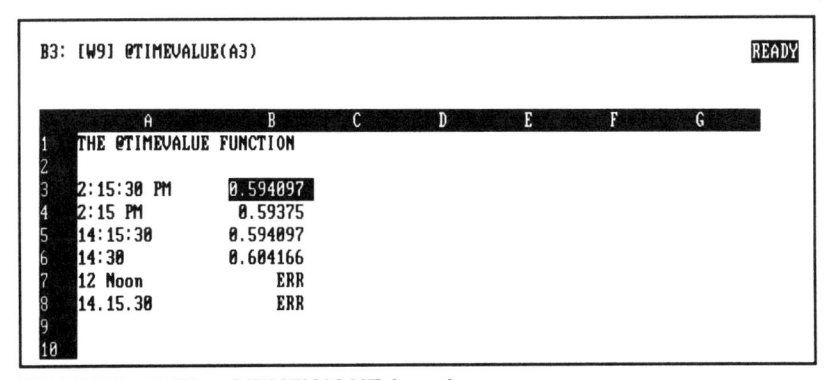

FIGURE 7-17: The @TIMEVALUE function

If the argument of an @TIMEVALUE function is in a form that 1-2-3 cannot recognize, including any Long or Short International form other than the current one, the function will return the value ERR. For example, the function in cell B7 in Figure 7-17, *@TIMEVALUE(A7)*, returns the value ERR because the label in cell A7 is not in a form that 1-2-3 recognizes as a time. The function in cell B8, *@TIMEVALUE(A8)*, returns ERR even though the label in cell A8 is in the form of one of 1-2-3's international Time formats. This occurs because the format HH.MM.SS is not the active Long International Time format.

CONCLUSION

In this chapter, we have shown you how to work with dates and times in a 1-2-3 worksheet. Because 1-2-3 represents times and dates as serial values, it's easy to perform date and time calculations, like projecting a future date or computing an elapsed time. Three functions—@DATE, @TIME, and @NOW—are the principal tools that you'll use for working with dates and times in 1-2-3.

8

Printing

Virtually all 1-2-3 users need to make printed copies of their worksheets at one time or another. The / Print command is the key to producing printed reports within 1-2-3. This command allows you to define, format, and print reports that are based on the data in your worksheets.

Printing your 1-2-3 worksheets can be very simple—the only information you must supply is the range of cells that you want to print. However, 1-2-3 offers quite a few options for formatting printed reports. You will probably want to take advantage of most of these options. Before we discuss 1-2-3's printing options, we'll show you how to create a simple report. Then, we'll explain how to use each of the different printing options to customize a report.

There are a couple of printing topics we will not cover in this chapter. First, we will not show you how to print graphs. Because graphs contain characters other than the standard letters, numbers, punctuation marks, and so forth, you must use a special program called PrintGraph—and not the / Print command—to print them. Chapter 11 explains in detail how you can use the PrintGraph program to print 1-2-3 graphs.

In addition, we won't cover the / Print File command in this chapter. When you issue the / Print command, you will see a menu of two choices: Printer and File. Choosing Printer tells 1-2-3 that you want to print to a printer. This is the option you will choose to create a report from a worksheet. The File choice allows you to "save" a worksheet into an ASCII text file, which can be imported into other programs that read the ASCII format. In this chapter, we will address only the Printer option. If you are interested in printing to files, see Appendix 1, "Exchanging Data with Other Programs."

HARDWARE SETUP

Before you print a 1-2-3 worksheet, you must take care of a few housekeeping details relating to your printer. The first step is to use the Install program to install a driver for the text printer (or printers) you plan to use. The 1-2-3 manuals explain how to use the 1-2-3 Install program to install a printer driver.

1-2-3 Releases 2, 2.01, and 2.2 allow you to install two or more text printers in a given driver set. However, because only one printer can be used for a particular print session, before you can print you must choose the text printer you plan to use. (If you have installed only one printer, then it will be chosen as the default automatically.) You also must choose a printer interface and make sure that the Auto-LF (Automatic Linefeed) setting is correct for your printer.

RELEASE ► 2.2 ◄ To configure 1-2-3 to work with your printer, you must issue the / Worksheet Global Default Printer command. ►If you are using 1-2-3 Release 2.2, you'll see the menu and the settings sheet shown in Figure 8-1 when you issue this command. (If you are using an earlier version of 123, you'll see only the menu; you won't see the settings sheet.)◄

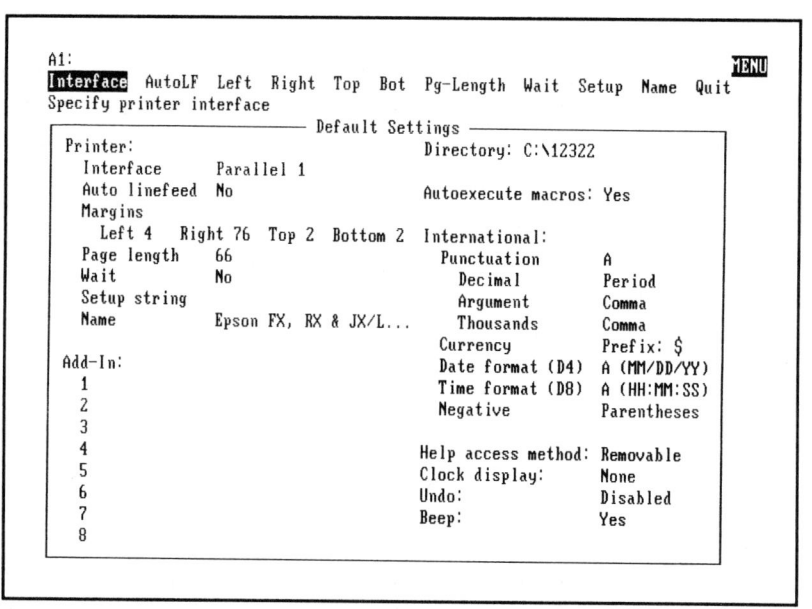

```
A1:                                                                    MENU
Interface AutoLF Left Right Top Bot Pg-Length Wait Setup Name Quit
Specify printer interface
┌─────────────────────── Default Settings ───────────────────────┐
│ Printer:                          Directory: C:\12322          │
│   Interface     Parallel 1                                     │
│   Auto linefeed No                Autoexecute macros: Yes      │
│   Margins                                                      │
│     Left 4   Right 76  Top 2  Bottom 2  International:         │
│   Page length   66                  Punctuation    A           │
│   Wait          No                    Decimal      Period      │
│   Setup string                        Argument     Comma       │
│   Name          Epson FX, RX & JX/L...  Thousands  Comma       │
│                                       Currency    Prefix: $    │
│ Add-In:                             Date format (D4) A (MM/DD/YY) │
│   1                                 Time format (D8) A (HH:MM:SS) │
│   2                                   Negative    Parentheses  │
│   3                                                            │
│   4                                 Help access method: Removable │
│   5                                 Clock display:  None       │
│   6                                 Undo:           Disabled   │
│   7                                 Beep:           Yes        │
│   8                                                            │
└────────────────────────────────────────────────────────────────┘
```

FIGURE 8-1: The default Printer menu and settings sheet

This menu offers a number of options that relate to printing. Right now, however, we're interested in the Name, Interface, and Auto-LF options. These related but separate commands allow you to select a printer, specify a printer interface, and change the automatic linefeed setting. We'll discuss the other printer defaults later in this chapter.

Choosing a Printer

Although you can install two or more printers, you can use only one printer for a particular printing session. If you have installed more than one printer, you must tell 1-2-3 which of those printers you want to use before you can begin printing. (If you have installed only one printer, then there will be only one choice on the Name menu. Since 1-2-3 automatically assumes that the one installed printer is the printer you want to use, you will not have to choose the Name option.)

To select the printer you want to use, issue the / Worksheet Global Default Printer Name command. Issuing this command will cause 1-2-3 to display a list of numbers (1, 2, 3, and so on). Each number in this list corresponds to one of the printers you have installed. As you point to a number on the menu, the name of the printer with which it is associated will appear in the prompt line. To choose the printer you plan to use, just point to the appropriate number and press [Enter], or type the number.

Choosing an Interface

Before you begin printing, you must tell 1-2-3 to which printer interface it should print. The printer interface is the physical connection between your computer and your printer—the place on your computer where you connect the printer cable. There are two basic types of printer interfaces: serial and parallel. Most computers have one parallel interface (or "parallel port") and one serial interface (or "serial port"), though some computers will have two or more parallel ports and/or two or more serial ports.

Many popular printers, such as the Epson printers, use a parallel interface to receive data from a computer. If your printer uses a parallel interface, you will probably not need to adjust the Interface setting. However, if your printer uses a serial interface—or if you have different printers connected to different interfaces—then you'll need to change the Interface setting before you begin printing. (If you are not sure what type of interface your printer uses, check the printer manual or ask your dealer or the PC guru at your company.)

To choose the printer interface, issue the / Worksheet Global Default Printer command and choose Interface. Issuing this command will bring up a menu that includes the numbers 1 through 8. Each of these numbers corresponds to a particular Interface setting. The default choice is 1, for Parallel 1, the first parallel port on your computer. The other choices for the Interface setting are Serial 1, Parallel 2, Serial 2, DOS Device LPT1, DOS Device LPT2, DOS Device LPT3, and DOS Device LPT4. The last four choices represent DOS logical devices. These options are included for users whose computers are connected to remote output devices through a network. Unless your computer is part of this kind of system, you do not need to be concerned with the four LPT options.

As we have said, if you are using a single parallel printer, you should leave the Interface setting at its default, Parallel 1. Otherwise, you should select the number corresponding to the interface to which the printer is connected. To choose the interface you plan to use, just point to the appropriate number and press [Enter], or type the number.

If you choose a serial interface (options 2 or 4 on the Interface menu), you must also specify a baud rate. The baud rate you choose determines how fast your computer will send information to the printer. The most important consideration in selecting a baud rate is to make sure that the rate you select is the rate at which your printer expects to receive data.

After you select either option 2 or option 4 from the Interface menu, you will see another menu containing the numbers 1 through 9. Each number on this menu corresponds to a baud rate, ranging from 110 baud to 19200 baud. To choose the correct baud rate for your printer, just type the appropriate number (1 through 9) or point to the number and press [Enter]. (If you are not sure what baud rate the printer can accept, check the printer manual or ask your dealer or PC expert.)

Changing the Auto-Linefeed Setting

The Auto-LF setting tells 1-2-3 whether it should send a carriage return and linefeed, or just a carriage return, to the printer after each line of a report. 1-2-3's default setting for Auto-LF is No. When Auto-LF is set to No, 1-2-3 will send a carriage return and a linefeed to the printer at the end of each printed line. The carriage return tells the printer to move the print head to the left edge of the paper, and the linefeed tells the printer to scroll the paper up by one line so that the next line of the report is printed on a new line.

The option you should choose for the Auto-LF setting depends on how your printer responds to a carriage return. Some printers interpret a carriage return as a carriage return plus a linefeed. In other words, when the printer receives a carriage return code, it will execute both a carriage return and a linefeed. If you are using this kind of printer, you must turn off 1-2-3's automatic linefeed. If you do not do this, your printer will execute a carriage return and *two* linefeeds after each line in the report, causing the report to be double spaced.

If the printer is adding a linefeed to each carriage return that it receives—in other words, if you see double-spacing when you print a few rows from a worksheet—you should set Auto-LF to Yes. To change the Auto-LF setting, issue the / Worksheet Global Default Printer Auto-LF command and choose Yes. This setting tells 1-2-3 that the printer performs a linefeed each time it executes a carriage return, and, therefore, 1-2-3 should not send a linefeed as well. In other words, when Auto-LF is set to Yes, 1-2-3 will send only a carriage return—and not a carriage return plus a linefeed—to the printer after it prints each line.

PRINTING BASICS

RELEASE ► 2.2 ◄

Once you have taken care of your hardware settings, you are ready to print. To begin printing, you issue the / Print Printer command. ►If you are using 1-2-3 Release 2.2, you'll see the menu and the settings sheet shown in Figure 8-2 when you issue this command. (If you are using an earlier version of 1-2-3, you'll see only the menu; you won't see the settings sheet.)◄ The options on this menu allow you to define the print range, advance the paper in the printer, define various formatting options for your report, and print. All you have to do to print is choose the Range option and select the range of cells you want to include in the report, align the paper in the printer, and then choose the Align and Go options from the Print menu.

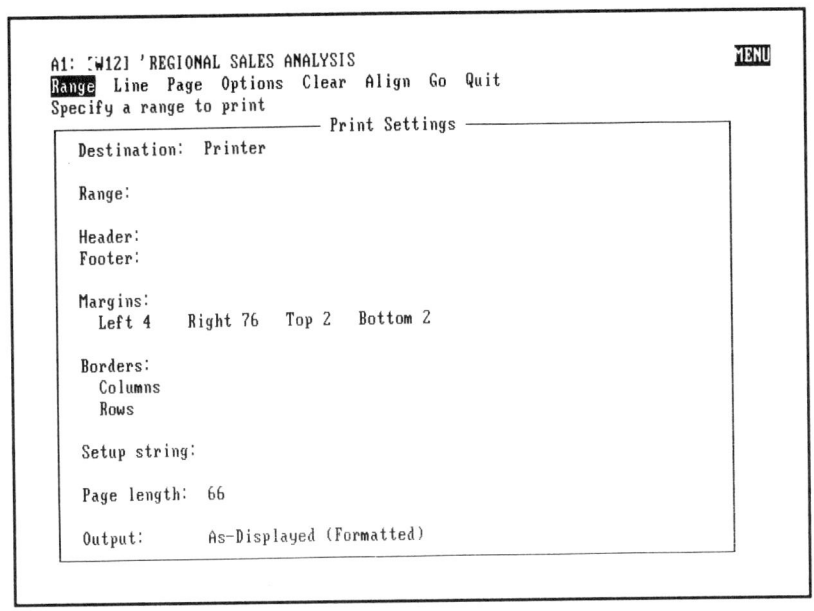

```
A1: [W12] 'REGIONAL SALES ANALYSIS                          MENU
Range  Line  Page  Options  Clear  Align  Go  Quit
Specify a range to print
                         ─── Print Settings ───
  Destination:  Printer

  Range:

  Header:
  Footer:

  Margins:
    Left 4      Right 76    Top 2    Bottom 2

  Borders:
    Columns
    Rows

  Setup string:

  Page length:  66

  Output:       As-Displayed (Formatted)
```

FIGURE 8-2: The Print menu and settings sheet

An Example

Figure 8-3 shows part of a worksheet that contains a regional sales analysis model. The worksheet includes six months' worth of month-by-month data extending from cell A1 to cell K86. In this worksheet, we have set the global column width to 12 and widened columns I and J (which contain the yearly totals) to 16 characters.

Suppose you want to print this worksheet. To begin, issue the / Print Printer command. When you see the Print menu, choose the Range command. 1-2-3 will then display the prompt *Enter print range:*, followed by the address of the current cell. When you see this prompt, you should specify the range A1..K86. Selecting a range of cells to print is no different than selecting any other range in 1-2-3. You can either type the range definition or you can point to one of the corner cells, press [period], and then point to the opposite corner and press [Enter].

Once you have selected the range, make sure the printer is on line, properly loaded with paper, and that the print head is aligned at the top of a new sheet of paper, then choose Align. This command tells 1-2-3 that the printer is positioned at the top of a new page. To print the report, choose Go. That's all there is to it! Figure 8-4 shows this worksheet printed by an Epson LQ-1500 printer on four 8 1/2-by-11-inch sheets of paper.

```
A1: 'REGIONAL SALES ANALYSIS                                              READY

         A          B            C           D           E           F
    1  REGIONAL SALES ANALYSIS
    2  ==========================================================================
    3
    4                          Jan-90      Feb-90      Mar-90      Apr-90
    5  SOUTHEASTERN REGION
    6    Alabama
    7      Actual Sales      $174,800    $180,700    $185,900    $193,660
    8      Target Sales      $175,000    $175,000    $180,000    $180,000
    9      Actual/Target       99.89%     103.26%     103.28%     107.59%
   10    Arkansas
   11      Actual Sales      $136,790    $140,200    $143,700    $147,290
   12      Target Sales      $135,000    $140,000    $145,000    $145,000
   13      Actual/Target      101.33%     100.14%      99.10%     101.58%
   14    Florida
   15      Actual Sales      $357,900    $366,840    $376,010    $385,410
   16      Target Sales      $354,000    $362,900    $372,000    $381,300
   17      Actual/Target      101.10%     101.09%     101.08%     101.08%
   18    Georgia
   19      Actual Sales      $225,000    $230,620    $236,680    $242,280
   20      Target Sales      $225,000    $230,600    $236,400    $242,300
```

FIGURE 8-3: A sample worksheet

Default Print Settings

When 1-2-3 printed the report in Figure 8-4, it automatically added a left, right, top, and bottom margin to each page and inserted a page break at the bottom of each page. Because you did not make any changes to 1-2-3's Print settings before you printed this report, 1-2-3 used its built-in defaults to fix the size of each of the margins and to determine the page length. Figure 8-5 uses the first page of the report in Figure 8-4 to illustrate 1-2-3's default Margin and Page-Length settings.

The default setting for the left margin is 4 characters. As you might expect, this setting means that 1-2-3 will add four blank spaces to the beginning of each line of the report. The default right margin setting is 76 characters. This setting determines the number of characters that can be printed on each line of the report. A setting of 76 characters indicates that each line in the report will be 76 characters long. However, since this total length includes the four-space left margin, only 72 characters from your worksheet can fit on each line.

The default setting for both the top and bottom margins is 2 lines. These settings mean that 1-2-3 will place two blank rows at the top and bottom of each page. If you look at Figure 8-5, however, you'll see that there are actually five blank lines at the top and bottom of each page. In addition to adding a two-line top margin and a two-line bottom margin to the report, 1-2-3 reserved three blank lines at the top and bottom of each page for a header and footer. These lines are inserted between the top and bottom margin and the printed data on the pages. As a result, the effective top and bottom margin on each page of the report is five lines. Unless you use /Print Printer Options Other Unformatted to turn off all page formatting, 1-2-3 will always include

FIGURE 8-4: A sample printed report

these three-line spaces on every page of every report—even if, as in this case, you do not define a header or footer.

The default Page-Length setting is 66 lines per page. These 66 lines include the two-line top and bottom margins and the three-line header and footer spaces. This means that each page of a standard report can include up to 56 rows of data (66–2–2–3 –3 = 56).

As you might expect, 1-2-3 allows you to change all of these default settings. We'll show you how to do that later in this chapter.

```
REGIONAL SALES ANALYSIS
=====================================================================
                          Jan-90        Feb-90        Mar-90        Apr-90
SOUTHEASTERN REGION
  Alabama
    Actual Sales        $174,800      $180,700      $185,900      $193,660
    Target Sales        $175,000      $175,000      $180,000      $180,000
    Actual/Target         99.89%       103.26%       103.28%       107.59%
  Arkansas
    Actual Sales        $136,790      $140,200      $143,700      $147,290
    Target Sales        $135,000      $140,000      $145,000      $145,000
    Actual/Target        101.33%       100.14%        99.10%       101.58%
  Florida
    Actual Sales        $357,900      $366,840      $376,010      $385,410
    Target Sales        $354,000      $362,900      $372,000      $381,300
    Actual/Target        101.10%       101.09%       101.08%       101.08%
  Georgia
    Actual Sales        $225,000      $230,620      $236,680      $242,280
    Target Sales        $225,000      $230,600      $236,400      $242,300
    Actual/Target        100.00%       100.01%       100.12%        99.99%
  Kentucky
    Actual Sales        $198,765      $203,725      $208,815      $214,035
    Target Sales        $200,000      $203,700      $208,800      $214,000
    Actual/Target         99.38%       100.01%       100.01%       100.02%
  Louisiana
    Actual Sales        $145,890      $149,530      $153,260      $157,090
    Target Sales        $145,000      $149,500      $153,300      $157,100
    Actual/Target        100.61%       100.02%        99.97%        99.99%
  Mississippi
    Actual Sales        $142,300      $145,850      $149,490      $153,220
    Target Sales        $140,000      $145,800      $149,500      $153,200
    Actual/Target        101.64%       100.03%        99.99%       100.01%
  South Carolina
    Actual Sales        $265,230      $271,860      $278,650      $285,610
    Target Sales        $250,000      $271,900      $278,600      $285,600
    Actual/Target        106.09%        99.99%       100.02%       100.00%
  Tennessee
    Actual Sales        $344,500      $353,110      $361,930      $370,970
    Target Sales        $340,000      $353,100      $361,900      $371,000
    Actual/Target        101.32%       100.00%       100.01%        99.99%
SOUTHEASTERN REGION SUMMARY
    Actual Sales      $1,991,175    $2,042,435    $2,094,435    $2,149,565
    Target Sales      $1,964,000    $2,032,500    $2,085,500    $2,129,500
    Actual/Target        101.38%       100.49%       100.43%       100.94%

NORTHEASTERN REGION
  Connecticut
    Actual Sales        $130,890      $134,160      $137,500      $140,940
    Target Sales        $126,000      $134,200      $137,500      $140,900
    Actual/Target        103.88%        99.97%       100.00%       100.03%
  Maine
    Actual Sales         $44,620       $45,730       $46,870       $48,040
    Target Sales         $45,000       $45,700       $46,900       $48,000
```

FIGURE 8-5: The first page of the report shown in Figure 8-4

> **TIP: USING [END][HOME]**
>
> You can define print ranges in 1-2-3 in the same way you define other ranges: either by typing the range reference or by pointing. However, there is one trick you can use to speed up the process of defining print ranges. Since you will usually want to include the entire active area of a worksheet in the print range, you can define the range quickly by issuing the /Print Printer Range command, pointing to cell A1, pressing [.], pressing [End][Home], and then pressing [Enter]. Since pressing [End][Home] moves the cell pointer to the lower-right corner of the active area of the worksheet, this technique will immediately define the print range to include the entire active area.

How 1-2-3 Divides a Report into Pages

When you print the entire worksheet in Figure 8-3, the result is a four-page report. Whenever you print a report that is too large to fit on a single page, 1-2-3 will divide that report into several pages. 1-2-3 uses the current Margin and Page-Length settings to determine how much of the worksheet can fit on each page.

Although a given worksheet may have more or fewer pages than the report in this example, 1-2-3 will always use the same general technique for dividing the worksheet into pages. The first page will always contain as many complete rows and columns from the upper-left portion of the worksheet as 1-2-3 can fit on one page. In our example, the first page includes columns A through F and rows 1 through 56. Assuming that the worksheet has more rows than can fit on one page, the second page of the report will contain the same columns as the first page, but different rows. In our example, the second page includes rows 57 through 86 of columns A through F.

When 1-2-3 has finished printing *all* of the data in the leftmost columns of the worksheet, it will then print another group of columns, starting at the top of the worksheet. In our example, the third page of the report includes columns G through K and rows 1 through 56. Once all of the data in this next group of columns is printed, 1-2-3 will go back to the top of the worksheet again and print another group of columns (if the worksheet is more than two pages wide). This process will continue until 1-2-3 has printed the entire range that you specified.

To figure out how many full columns will fit on each page of a report, first subtract the left margin setting from the right margin setting to compute the report's page width. If all the columns in the worksheet are of the same width, you can then just divide the page width by the column width to determine how many columns will fit on each page. For example, if the right margin is set to 76 characters and the left margin to 4 characters, the page width is 72 characters. If all the columns in the worksheet you are printing are 9 characters wide, then 1-2-3 will print 72/9, or 8, columns on each page.

When 1-2-3 divides a report into pages, it always divides the report between columns. 1-2-3 will never divide the entries within a column as it divides a report. For example, suppose the left margin setting is 4 and the right margin setting is 76, but that the width of all of the columns in the worksheet is 10 characters. Subtracting the left margin (4) from the right margin (76) again yields a page width of 72 characters. Dividing this result by the standard column width, 10, yields 7.2 columns. However, since 1-2-3 will not divide a column as it divides a report into pages, only 7 full columns will be printed on each page of the report.

Of course, calculating the number of columns that will fit on each page of a report is a bit trickier if the columns in the worksheet have different widths. In that case, you must add the widths of the individual columns, and then compare that number to the page width to determine how many columns will be printed on each page.

As we have said, the amount of information that will fit on a single page is determined by the current Margin and Page-Length settings. By changing these settings, you can change the amount of information that can fit on a page and thus control the way the report is divided into pages. In addition, you can insert manual page breaks in your documents. We'll show you how to do both of these things later in the chapter.

There are several utility programs—such as Sideways from Funk Software—that allow you to print your reports sideways. Printing sideways helps to eliminate 1-2-3's vertical page breaks. We'll discuss Sideways in Chapter 16.

Aligning the Paper in the Printer

As we have mentioned, before you begin printing, you should align the paper in the printer so that the print head is at the top of a new page, and then issue the Align command. The Align command tells 1-2-3 that the printer is positioned at the top of a new page. Issuing this command lets 1-2-3 know just where to insert page breaks in your document as it prints.

Once you issue the Align command, you should not adjust the paper in the printer manually. If you do, 1-2-3 will lose track of the printer's position on the page, and it may insert page breaks in weird places in your document. For example, suppose that you have just finished printing a worksheet that ended in the middle of a page. To remove the report from the printer, you turn the platen and tear off the paper, leaving the print head aligned at the top of a new page. If you were to print another report at this point, 1-2-3 would think that the print head was still positioned in the middle of a page instead of at the top of a new page. After printing a few lines, 1-2-3 would insert a page break in the report—right in the middle of the page.

There are two ways to avoid this problem. First, you can use 1-2-3's commands to scroll the paper in the printer and avoid the printer's controls altogether. To scroll a single line (or several lines), issue the / Print Printer Line command. Each time you choose Line, 1-2-3 will send a linefeed to the printer. When you issue the / Print Printer Page command, 1-2-3 will scroll to the top of a new page of paper. The amount of paper that 1-2-3 will scroll with this command depends on your Page-Length setting and where the print head is positioned when you issue the command.

Alternatively, you can manually align the paper in the printer and then issue the Align command each time you print. If you can make this a habit, then you should have no problems with misaligned page breaks.

Printing Part of a Worksheet

In the first example, we printed the entire contents of the worksheet. However, you can instruct 1-2-3 to print only a portion of the entries in a worksheet. In fact, you can print just a single cell at a time. All you have to do is set the print range to include just those cells you want to print.

```
REGIONAL SALES ANALYSIS
=================================================================
                              Jan-90        Feb-90        Mar-90
SOUTHEASTERN REGION
  Alabama
    Actual Sales            $174,800      $180,700      $185,900
    Target Sales            $175,000      $175,000      $180,000
    Actual/Target             99.89%       103.26%       103.28%
  Arkansas
    Actual Sales            $136,790      $140,200      $143,700
    Target Sales            $135,000      $140,000      $145,000
    Actual/Target            101.33%       100.14%        99.10%
  Florida
    Actual Sales            $357,900      $366,840      $376,010
    Target Sales            $354,000      $362,900      $372,000
    Actual/Target            101.10%       101.09%       101.08%
  Georgia
    Actual Sales            $225,000      $230,620      $236,680
    Target Sales            $225,000      $230,600      $236,400
    Actual/Target            100.00%       100.01%       100.12%
  Kentucky
    Actual Sales            $198,765      $203,725      $208,815
    Target Sales            $200,000      $203,700      $208,800
    Actual/Target             99.38%       100.01%       100.01%
  Louisiana
    Actual Sales            $145,890      $149,530      $153,260
    Target Sales            $145,000      $149,500      $153,300
    Actual/Target            100.61%       100.02%        99.97%
  Mississippi
    Actual Sales            $142,300      $145,850      $149,490
    Target Sales            $140,000      $145,800      $149,500
    Actual/Target            101.64%       100.03%        99.99%
  South Carolina
    Actual Sales            $265,230      $271,860      $278,650
    Target Sales            $250,000      $271,900      $278,600
    Actual/Target            106.09%        99.99%       100.02%
  Tennessee
    Actual Sales            $344,500      $353,110      $361,930
    Target Sales            $340,000      $353,100      $361,900
    Actual/Target            101.32%       100.00%       100.01%

SOUTHEASTERN REGION SUMMARY
    Actual Sales          $1,991,175    $2,042,435    $2,094,435
    Target Sales          $1,964,000    $2,032,500    $2,085,500
    Actual/Target            101.38%       100.49%       100.43%
```

FIGURE 8-6: A small report

For example, suppose you would like to print only the data for the first three months of 1990 for the Southeastern region (in other words, the range A1..E46). Begin by issuing the /Print Printer command. Then choose Range, select the range A1..E46, and press [Enter]. Once the range is defined, just align the paper in the printer, then choose Align and then Go. Figure 8-6 shows the printed report. As you can see, the range you have selected is small enough to fit on a single page, so 1-2-3 does not divide it into pages.

Aborting a Print

There may be times when you issue the Go command to begin printing a large worksheet, only to discover that you haven't set up the report correctly. Rather than waiting for the entire worksheet to be printed, you can halt the printer in mid-report by pressing [Ctrl][Break]. After you press these keys, 1-2-3 will take a few seconds to return to the READY mode. The printer probably will not stop printing immediately since it must empty its buffer first. Still, this is the best technique we know to interrupt the printing of a lengthy report, short of turning off the printer.

FORMATTING PRINTED REPORTS

As you have seen, it's very easy to print a simple report in 1-2-3 using the default Print settings. You may find that the default Print settings are perfectly adequate for most of your printing needs. However, by taking advantage of 1-2-3's formatting options, you can improve the appearance of your reports and present your data in a clearer, more understandable form. 1-2-3 offers commands that allow you to change a report's margins, define a header and footer, change the Page-Length setting, define a setup string, and designate certain rows and columns in your reports as borders. In this section, we will explain how to use each of these commands to format your reports.

Margins

If you make no changes to your original Print settings in 1-2-3, your reports will be formatted with a left margin of 4, a right margin of 76, a top margin of 2, and a bottom margin of 2. However, you can use the /Print Printer Options Margins command to change these default settings.

Left Margin

The left margin setting indicates how many spaces 1-2-3 will add before the first character in each line of the report. For example, if you use the default left margin setting of 4, then your worksheet will be printed with a four-character space at the left edge of the page. The first character of each line will be printed at the fifth space on the page. If you set your left margin to 0, 1-2-3 will print the first character of each line just within the left edge of your paper.

To change the left margin setting, issue the / Print Printer Options Margins Left command. When you issue this command, 1-2-3 will display the prompt *Enter left margin (0..240):*, followed by the current left margin setting. When you see the prompt, type the left margin you wish to use and press [Enter]. There is no need to erase the current left margin setting before you type a new one. 1-2-3 will automatically replace the initial Margin setting with the number you type.

You can specify a left margin setting of between 0 and 240 characters. Typically, however, your left margin setting will not be greater than around 10 characters. We often use a left margin setting of 0 in our reports so that we can squeeze as much information as possible onto each page. Of course, you should not set the left margin to be greater than the right margin.

TIP: LEFT MARGINS AND INDENTED ENTRIES

If the first character in an entry in the first column of the print range is not left-aligned, then it will be offset somewhat in your printed report, no matter what your Margin setting. For example, suppose cell A5 in your worksheet contains the value 20400, displayed in General format. Assuming that column A is the standard nine-characters wide, there will be three blank spaces between the left edge of cell A5 and the first character in the entry in that cell. These three blank spaces will appear in your printed report, in addition to any blank spaces in the left margin. For instance, if you have specified a left margin setting of 4, then there will be seven blank spaces between the left edge of the paper and the first printed character in row 5 (four spaces for the left margin plus the three spaces that appear in the cell).

Right Margin

The right margin setting specifies the total number of characters that can appear on each line of the report. This total includes the spaces in the left margin. For example, if you print a report using the default right margin setting of 76 and the default left margin setting of 4, then no more than 72 characters from the worksheet will be printed on each line of the report (since 4 + 72 = 76). If you've set your left margin setting to 0 and your right margin setting to 80, then 1-2-3 can squeeze 80 characters on each line.

To change the right margin setting, issue the / Print Printer Options Margins Right command. When you do this, 1-2-3 will display the prompt *Enter right margin (0..240):*, followed by the current right margin setting. When you see the prompt, type the right margin setting you wish to use and press [Enter]. 1-2-3 will automatically replace the initial Margin setting with the number you type.

Although the right margin setting can be any number between 0 and 240, it must be larger than the left margin setting. If the right margin setting is less than the left margin setting, 1-2-3 will be unable to print any data. You also must be careful that the difference between the right and left margin settings is at least equal to or greater than the width of the widest column in the worksheet you plan to print.

The right margin setting you specify must also be consistent with the width of the paper you are using and the setup string you have specified (if any). If the right margin setting you specify is longer than the maximum number of characters the printer can print on one line, each line of the report will wrap around to the next line on the page. Not only does this make for a very confusing appearance in your printed report, it also fouls up 1-2-3's page breaks. If you are using a narrow carriage printer, such as an Epson FX-80, the maximum line length will be about 80 characters. If you use a setup string to print in compressed type, this number increases to about 120 characters. If you have a wide carriage printer, such as an Epson FX-100, then the maximum line length is about 130 characters. However, if you use compressed print, this number increases to about 200 characters.

Top and Bottom Margins

The top and bottom margin settings indicate how many blank lines 1-2-3 should insert at the top of each page above the first printed line and at the bottom of each page below the last printed line. As we have said, the default top margin and bottom margin settings are both 2.

To change the top margin setting, issue the / Print Printer Options Margins Top command. When you issue this command, 1-2-3 will display the prompt *Enter top margin (0..32):*, followed by the current top margin setting. When you see the prompt, type the top margin you wish to use and press [Enter]. You change the bottom margin in much the same way: Issue the / Print Printer Options Margins Bottom command, then type the bottom margin you wish to use and press [Enter].

Although the top and bottom Margin settings can be any number between 0 and 32, they will rarely be greater than five lines or so. We often set the top margin and bottom margin to 0 in our reports.

As we mentioned earlier, 1-2-3 always reserves three blank lines at the top and bottom of each page for a header and footer. These blank lines are *in addition to* the top and bottom margins. As a result, the *de facto* default top and bottom margins are both five lines. If you change the top margin setting to 3, 1-2-3 will include six blank lines at the top of each page. If you set both the top and bottom margins to 0, 1-2-3 will still include three blank lines at the top and bottom of each page.

The only way to get rid of *all* blank lines at the top and bottom of each page is to use the / Print Printer Options Other Unformatted command, which is described on pages 335-336. Unfortunately, there is no way to print a report with just one or two blank lines at the top and/or bottom of each page. 1-2-3 forces you to have at least three blank lines (the header and footer lines) or no blank lines at all.

"Zeroing" Margins

▶1-2-3 Release 2.2's / Print Printer Options Margins None command is a timesaver: It lets you set the top, bottom, and left margins to 0 and the right margin to 240 in one step. This makes it easier to "zero-out" print margins in 1-2-3 Release 2.2 than it is in earlier releases of 1-2-3.◄

Changing the Default Margin Settings

You may find that 1-2-3's default margin settings are not applicable to many of the reports that you print. For example, if you always print your worksheets on a wide-carriage printer using 11-by-14-inch paper, then you will probably want to use a right margin setting of 120 or more on a regular basis. To save yourself some time and trouble, you can change the default right margin from 76 to 120. This way, you won't need to worry about changing the right margin setting each time you print a different worksheet.

To make a change to one of the default margin settings, issue the / Worksheet Global Default Printer command. This will bring up the menu that is shown in Figure 8-1. Notice the four margin choices on this menu: Left, Right, Top, Bottom. You should choose the option for the margin that you want to change, enter the new default, and press [Enter]. For example, to change the default right margin setting, choose Right, then type the new default, 120, and press [Enter].

If you want to save this new default, issue the / Worksheet Global Default Update command after you have entered the new Margin setting. If you do not save this change, then the new default will apply for only the current 1-2-3 session. The next time you use 1-2-3, the old default will be in effect. For more on changing your default Print settings, see page 331.

Changing the Page Length

As we mentioned earlier, the Page-Length setting in 1-2-3 determines the total number of lines that 1-2-3 will print on each page of a report. The default Page-Length setting is 66 lines. Since the total page length includes the top and bottom margins and the header and footer spaces, the number of rows of data from your worksheet that can be printed on a page is determined by subtracting these settings from the Page-Length setting. The default page-length setting is 66 lines per page, which means that a standard report can have up to 56 rows of data on each page (66–2–2–3–3 = 56).

The page-length setting is important because it tells 1-2-3 where to place page breaks in a report. The default page-length setting, 66 lines, assumes that you are printing on standard 11-inch-long paper and that the printer will print six lines per inch. Given those assumptions, the standard page-length setting will work just fine. On the other hand, if you use a setup string to print a report in expanded type or to change the number of lines per inch, then you will need to adjust the page-length setting accordingly. Also, if you are printing on special forms or labels that are not 11 inches long, you should change the page-length setting.

Let's suppose that you have defined a setup string that instructs 1-2-3 to print eight lines per inch instead of the standard six lines. In order for your page breaks to be correct, you must change the page-length setting to 88. To make this change, you would issue the / Print Printer Options Pg-Length command. When you issue this command, 1-2-3 will display the prompt *Enter lines per page (1..100):*, followed by the current page-length setting. To change the Page-Length setting, type 88 and press [Enter].

Notes

1-2-3 will accept any page-length setting from 1 to 100. However, you must be sure that the page-length setting you define is at least equal to the top and bottom margin settings, plus header and footer allowances, plus one line for data. For example, if the top and bottom margin settings are both 2, then the minimum page-length setting will be 11. This is computed by adding the two margins (2 + 2), the header and footer allowances (3 + 3), plus one line of data. If you enter a page-length setting that is too short, 1-2-3 will not alert you until you choose Go to print your report. Then 1-2-3 will display the error message *Margins, header and footer equal or exceed page length*.

If you are printing an unformatted report, then the page-length setting makes no difference. 1-2-3 ignores page breaks completely in unformatted reports. Unformatted reports are explained in detail on page 335.

If you decide to use a page-length setting other than 66 and you find that you are getting "double" page breaks at odd intervals, check your printer manual. Some printers have switches that control the default page length. Unless you adjust the printer's page-length setting to be in synch with the page-length setting in 1-2-3, your page breaks will not be where you want them.

Changing the Default Page Length

If you find that the default page length of 66 is not appropriate for the majority of your reports, you can save time by creating a new default. For example, suppose that you print the majority of your worksheets with eight-lines-per-inch spacing, which requires a page-length setting of 88. To change the default from 66 to 88, issue the / Worksheet Global Default Printer Pg-Length command. When you see the prompt, *Default lines per page (1..100):*, type 88 and press [Enter].

To save this new default, issue the / Worksheet Global Default Update command. If you do not save this change, then the new default will apply only for the current 1-2-3 session. The next time you load 1-2-3, the old default will be in effect. For more on changing default Print settings, see page 331.

Setup Strings

Most printers are set up to print six lines per inch vertically and either 10 or 12 characters per inch horizontally in some standard typestyle. However, many printers have the ability to print more lines per inch, to print compressed or expanded characters, or even to print in alternative fonts and typestyles (such as boldface or italics). In most cases, you can control these special print attributes by sending special character sequences, called setup strings, to the printer before you begin printing.

The / Print Printer Options Setup command allows you to define setup strings for your 1-2-3 reports. To define a setup string, you issue the / Print Printer Options Setup command, type the setup string you wish to use, and press [Enter]. A setup string consists of one or more three-digit numbers, each of which must be preceded by a backslash (\). The three-digit numbers are the ASCII codes (in decimal notation) of the character sequences that activate (or deactivate) the special printer features you want to use. For example, the character sequence that activates eight-lines-per-inch printing on Epson printers is [Esc]0. The 1-2-3 setup string representation for this character sequence is \027\048. The first part of this string, 027, is the ASCII representation for [Esc], and the second part, 048, is the ASCII representation for zero. The two backslashes are used as delimiters for the codes. Similarly, the code that activates compressed print on Epson printers is [Ctrl]O. Since 015 is the ASCII code for the character [Ctrl]O, the 1-2-3 representation for this code is \015.

Once you define a setup string, 1-2-3 will send that string to the printer each time you issue the / Print Printer Go command. The characters in the string are not printed—they simply tell the printer which of its special features to use in printing the report.

If you wish, you can create a single setup string that turns on several different Print settings. For example, the setup string \015\027\048 turns on compressed print and eight-line-per-inch printing on an Epson LQ-1500. The maximum length for a setup string is 39 characters (including the backslashes between codes). It is unlikely that you'll ever encounter this limit in your work with 1-2-3.

The particular print options that are available to you depend on what kind of printer you are using. For example, you cannot use a setup string to create italic type if your printer is not capable of generating italic characters. To find out what options are available on your printer, check the printer manual.

In addition, the setup string used to activate a given print attribute (such as compressed print) differs from printer to printer. Table 8-1 shows a few common setup strings for several popular families of printers. Depending on the make and model of the printer you are using, some or all of these codes may also work for you. To determine which codes activate your printer's special features, see your printer's manual. Be sure to look up the decimal ASCII representations for the controlling characters, and not the hexadecimal or octal representations.

Printing on HP LaserJet Printers

Hewlett-Packard LaserJet printers are some of the most popular printers on the market today. To learn how to print worksheets on these printers, see Appendix 5.

Deleting a Setup String

To delete a setup string, just issue the / Print Printer Options Setup command, press [Esc] to delete the string, then press [Enter] to lock in the change. The / Print Printer Clear All command will also reset the setup string—along with the other Print settings. For this reason, we don't recommend using it for that purpose.

DOUGLAS COBB'S 1-2-3 HANDBOOK RELEASE 2.2 EDITION

Feature	Epson	Okidata Microline	IBM Proprinter
Elite Print	\027\077	\028	\027\058
Normal Print (Pica)	\018	\030	\018
Enlarged Print	\027\087\049	\031	\027\087\049
Condensed Print	\015	\029	\015
Boldface	\027\069	\027\084	\027\069
Double-Strike	\027\071	na	\027\071
Underline	\027\045\049	\027\067	\027\045\049
Italic	\027\052	\027\033\047	na
8 Lines Per Inch	\027\048	\027\056	\027\048
Initialize Printer	\027\064	\027\024	\024

TABLE 8-1: Common setup strings

You may find that deleting a setup string seems to have no effect. Even though the string is gone, the special print features may still be in effect the next time you print. Here's why. Once you turn on a special attribute, it may remain in effect until you either turn the printer off or send the printer a new control sequence that turns off the activated attribute. For this reason, just deleting a setup string is usually not enough to reverse the effects of that string. To restore normal printing, you must both delete the setup string and turn the printer off and back on to reset it.

Alternatively, you can replace the existing setup string with a new setup string that resets the printer's special print features. For Epson printers, this setup string is \027\064. (To determine the "initialize printer" string for your printer, check your printer manual.) When 1-2-3 sends this string to the printer, it will reset all special formatting options—before the report begins printing. As a result, the report will be printed with the standard Print settings for your printer.

Creating a Default Setup String

If you find that you are always using the same setup string to print your worksheets, you will probably want to make that string the default for all your worksheets. As we explained earlier, 1-2-3 initially has no default setup string. To create a default, issue the / Worksheet Global Default Printer Setup command. When you see the prompt, *Enter setup string:*, type the string you wish to use and press [Enter].

To make this change permanent, issue the / Worksheet Global Default Update command. If you do not save this change, then the new default will apply only for the current session. The next time you use 1-2-3, the old default will be in effect. (For more on changing your Print defaults, see page 331.)

Embedding Setup Strings in Your Worksheet

When you use the /Print Printer Options Setup command to enter a setup string, that string will affect your entire worksheet, including headers and footers. However, you can also define printer setup strings that affect only a part of your worksheet. To do this, you simply enter the setup string directly into one of the cells of your worksheet. This kind of setup string is called an embedded setup string since it is embedded in your worksheet. When you print a report that contains an embedded setup string, 1-2-3 will print only that part of the report that follows the setup string with the special print attributes you specify. If the report contains a second embedded setup string that resets the printer's special features, then only that part of the report between the two embedded setup strings will have the special format.

To embed a setup string in a report, you must insert a row into the worksheet just above the first row that you want to print with the special format. Then you must move the cell pointer to the leftmost column in the print range in that row. (Typically, the first column in the print range will be column A.) When the cell pointer is in place, you should type two vertical bars (||), followed by the setup string that signals the beginning of the print attribute. The setup string should be in the normal form.

Typically, you will want to include a second embedded setup string somewhere in the report to turn off the special attribute that is activated by the first string. To insert this string, just move the cell pointer to the row below the last row that you want to print with the special format, insert another blank row, move the cell pointer to the leftmost cell in the print range in that row, and type two vertical bars (||) followed by the setup string that ends the print attribute.

For example, suppose you want to print the one-page report from Figure 8-6 and you want the text in row 1 of the worksheet (REGIONAL SALES ANALYSIS) to appear in expanded type. To begin, move the cell pointer to cell A1 and use the /Worksheet Insert Row command to insert one blank row above row 1. When the new row is in place, move the cell pointer to column A and type |\027\087\049 and press [Enter]. (The setup string \027\087\049 turns on expanded print on an Epson printer. If you are using a different printer, you may need to use a different setup string.) Now move the cell pointer to row 3, use the /Worksheet Insert Row command to add another blank row to the worksheet, move the cell pointer to column A in this row, and type |\027\087\048. (This setup string turns off expanded printing.)

Figure 8-7 shows the worksheet with the embedded setup strings. Notice that the first vertical-bar character in cells A1 and A3 do not appear on your screen. This first vertical bar is a special label prefix, which tells 1-2-3 that the numbers in this cell are printer setup codes and not normal values.

```
A1: !!\027\087\049                                                    READY

         A           B          C          D          E          F
1   !\027\087\049
2   REGIONAL SALES ANALYSIS
3   !\027\087\048
4   ===============================================================
5
6                            Jan-90     Feb-90     Mar-90     Apr-90
7   SOUTHEASTERN REGION
8     Alabama
9       Actual Sales       $174,800   $180,700   $185,900   $193,660
10      Target Sales       $175,000   $175,000   $180,000   $180,000
11      Actual/Target         99.89%    103.26%    103.28%    107.59%
12    Arkansas
13      Actual Sales       $136,790   $140,200   $143,700   $147,290
14      Target Sales       $135,000   $140,000   $145,000   $145,000
15      Actual/Target        101.33%    100.14%     99.10%    101.58%
16    Florida
17      Actual Sales       $357,900   $366,840   $376,010   $385,410
18      Target Sales       $354,000   $362,900   $372,000   $381,300
19      Actual/Target        101.10%    101.09%    101.08%    101.08%
20    Georgia
```

FIGURE 8-7: Embedded setup strings

After entering these setup strings, you are ready to print. To begin, you must issue the / Print Printer Range command and redefine the print range to include the range A1..E48. (This step is required because you inserted a new row 1 into the worksheet to hold the first embedded setup string. If you had placed the embedded setup string anywhere else in the report, you would not need to redefine the range.) Once the range is set, align the paper in the printer and choose Align and then Go from the Print menu.

Figure 8-8 shows the resulting report. As you can see, the text *REGIONAL SALES ANALYSIS* from row 2 of the worksheet has been printed in expanded print. Notice, however, that the remainder of the report is printed in normal print.

Also notice that rows 1 and 3 from the worksheet in Figure 8-7, which contain the embedded setup strings, were not included in the printed report in Figure 8-8. Rows 2 and 4 from the worksheet appear to be adjacent rows in the report, even though they are separated by one row in the worksheet. Keep in mind that whenever you embed a setup string in a worksheet, 1-2-3 will not print the row that contains the embedded setup string. Therefore, it's important that you not enter your setup strings on the same row as the data that you want to appear in the printed report. You should enter the string on a blank row or on a row of data that you do not want to include in your report.

Also remember that all embedded setup strings must be in the leftmost column of the range of cells you are printing—typically, column A. If a setup string is not in the first column of the print range, 1-2-3 will ignore it.

```
                    REGIONAL   SALES   ANALYSIS
       ================================================================

                                   Jan-90        Feb-90        Mar-90
       SOUTHEASTERN REGION
          Alabama
             Actual Sales         $174,800      $180,700      $185,900
             Target Sales         $175,000      $175,000      $180,000
             Actual/Target          99.89%       103.26%       103.28%
          Arkansas
             Actual Sales         $136,790      $140,200      $143,700
             Target Sales         $135,000      $140,000      $145,000
             Actual/Target         101.33%       100.14%        99.10%
          Florida
             Actual Sales         $357,900      $366,840      $376,010
             Target Sales         $354,000      $362,900      $372,000
             Actual/Target         101.10%       101.09%       101.08%
          Georgia
             Actual Sales         $225,000      $230,620      $236,680
             Target Sales         $225,000      $230,600      $236,400
             Actual/Target         100.00%       100.01%       100.12%
          Kentucky
             Actual Sales         $198,765      $203,725      $208,815
             Target Sales         $200,000      $203,700      $208,800
             Actual/Target          99.38%       100.01%       100.01%
          Louisiana
             Actual Sales         $145,890      $149,530      $153,260
             Target Sales         $145,000      $149,500      $153,300
             Actual/Target         100.61%       100.02%        99.97%
          Mississippi
             Actual Sales         $142,300      $145,850      $149,490
             Target Sales         $140,000      $145,800      $149,500
             Actual/Target         101.64%       100.03%        99.99%
          South Carolina
             Actual Sales         $265,230      $271,860      $278,650
             Target Sales         $250,000      $271,900      $278,600
             Actual/Target         106.09%        99.99%       100.02%
          Tennessee
             Actual Sales         $344,500      $353,110      $361,930
             Target Sales         $340,000      $353,100      $361,900
             Actual/Target         101.32%       100.00%       100.01%
       SOUTHEASTERN REGION SUMMARY
          Actual Sales          $1,991,175    $2,042,435    $2,094,435
          Target Sales          $1,964,000    $2,032,500    $2,085,500
          Actual/Target            101.38%       100.49%       100.43%
```

FIGURE 8-8: Report printed with embedded setup strings

The sample report in Figure 8-8 is just one page wide. When you use embedded setup strings in wider reports, you'll see that the special format defined by a string applies to all of the characters in the rows following the string—including entries that do not appear on the first page of the report. You'll want to keep this in mind if you use embedded setup strings in wide reports.

> **TIP: HIDING ROWS AND COLUMNS**
>
> As you learned in Chapter 4, the / Worksheet Column Hide lets you hide a column of your worksheet. As you might expect, if you print a worksheet that has one or more hidden columns, the hidden columns will not appear in the printed report. You can use this technique to remove columns that contain proprietary or confidential information from your printed reports. (For more on this command, see Chapter 4.)
>
> 1-2-3 does not offer a command for hiding a row. However, thanks to the vertical bar label prefix (|), you can tell 1-2-3 not to include certain rows in your printed reports. The technique for hiding a row is almost identical to that for embedding a setup string. To hide a row, just move the cell pointer to the first column in the print range of that row and type ||.
>
> For example, suppose that you want to print the range A1..H30 from a worksheet, and that you would like to hide row 6. To do this, you would move the cell pointer to cell A6 and type ||. When you print the worksheet, 1-2-3 will not print row 6. The contents of row 7 will appear on the line of the report immediately following the contents of row 5, just as if these two rows were adjacent in the worksheet.
>
> The || code must be entered in a blank cell. If there is already an entry in the first cell of the row you want to hide, you'll need to move that entry to another cell or insert a new blank column to hold the format code (or you can simply replace the current entry with the || code). Above all, there must not be any other characters in the cell that contains the || code. If there are other characters in that cell, 1-2-3 will not hide the row and may produce some strange results (such as triple spacing) when you print.

Headers and Footers

A header is a line of text that appears at the top of every page of a report. A footer is a line of text that is printed at the bottom of every page. 1-2-3 allows you to define a header, a footer, or both, for your reports. You can use headers and footers to include titles, page numbers, and the current date in your reports.

To create a header, issue the / Print Printer Options Header command. When you issue this command, 1-2-3 will display the prompt *Enter header:*. When you see this prompt, type the text that you want to appear at the top of each page and press [Enter]. That's all there is to it. The procedure for creating a footer is the same, except that you issue / Print Printer Options Footer to begin the process.

As we have mentioned before, 1-2-3 always reserves three lines at the top of each page of your reports for a header and three lines at the bottom of each page for a footer, even if you have not created a header or footer. If you have defined a header, it will be printed on the first of these three lines, with two blank lines below. Similarly, if you have defined a footer, it will be printed on the third line with two blank lines above.

These blank lines separate the header or footer from the body of the report. The position of the first character in the header or footer is determined by the left margin setting. Like the body of a report, the headers and footers are offset from the left edge of the page by the number of characters in the left margin.

Headers and footers can be up to 240 characters long. However, the number of characters that will actually be printed is determined by the current left and right margin settings. If your header or footer is too long to fit within your left and right margins, 1-2-3 will simply truncate part of the header or footer. In the default condition, where the left margin setting is 4 and the right margin setting is 76, your headers and footers can be up to 72 characters long.

For example, suppose you want to include the header *Sales Analysis for 1990* at the top of each page of the report in Figure 8-4. You want this header to be left-aligned. To create this header, issue the / Print Printer Options Header command and type the header line *Sales Analysis for 1990*. When you print your report, this line will appear at the top-left of each page, as shown in Figure 8-9. The first character in the header line will be aligned at the left margin of the report. (We used the default left and right margin settings of 4 and 76 in this report.)

Using Cell References in Headers and Footers

▶1-2-3 Release 2.2 allows you to use references to the entries in the cells of a worksheet in headers and footers. To do this, you first issue either the / Print Printer Options Header command or the / Print Printer Options Footer command, then type a backslash (\) and then the address (or name) of the cell that contains or returns the label or value you want to use in the header or footer. (Unfortunately, you must type these references; you cannot create them by pointing.) The cell that you refer to must contain the entire header or footer; you cannot use a cell reference as a part of a header or footer that also contains literal text.

RELEASE
▶ 2.2 ◀

For example, suppose that you want the words *REGIONAL SALES ANALYSIS* to appear at the top of each page of our example report. Since cell A1 contains the label 'REGIONAL SALES ANALYSIS, to create this header you could issue the / Print Printer Options Header command, type \A1, and then press [Enter].

One of the advantages to basing your headers and footers on cell entries is that doing so allows you to change your header or footer simply by changing the entry on which it is based. For example, if you changed the label in cell A1 to 'FY 1990 REGIONAL SALES ANALYSIS, 1-2-3 would print the words *FY 1989 REGIONAL SALES ANALYSIS* at the top of each page.◀

Controlling the Alignment of Headers and Footers

You can use the vertical bar character (|) to control the alignment of your headers and footers and to divide your headers and footers into sections. If you do not use this symbol, 1-2-3 will assume that your entire header or footer is to be printed left-aligned. Including one vertical bar in a header or footer tells 1-2-3 to divide that header or footer into two sections: one left-aligned and the other centered. Including a second vertical

```
Sales Analysis for 1990

REGIONAL SALES ANALYSIS
===============================================================================
                              Jan-90       Feb-90       Mar-90       Apr-90
SOUTHEASTERN REGION
  Alabama
    Actual Sales            $174,800     $180,700     $185,900     $193,660
    Target Sales            $175,000     $175,000     $180,000     $180,000
    Actual/Target              99.89%      103.26%      103.28%      107.59%
  Arkansas
    Actual Sales            $136,790     $140,200     $143,700     $147,290
    Target Sales            $135,000     $140,000     $145,000     $145,000
    Actual/Target             101.33%      100.14%       99.10%      101.58%
  Florida
    Actual Sales            $357,900     $366,840     $376,010     $385,410
    Target Sales            $354,000     $362,900     $372,000     $381,300
    Actual/Target             101.10%      101.09%      101.08%      101.08%
  Georgia
    Actual Sales            $225,000     $230,620     $236,680     $242,280
    Target Sales            $225,000     $230,600     $236,400     $242,300
    Actual/Target             100.00%      100.01%      100.12%       99.99%
  Kentucky
    Actual Sales            $198,765     $203,725     $208,815     $214,035
    Target Sales            $200,000     $203,700     $208,800     $214,000
    Actual/Target              99.38%      100.01%      100.01%      100.02%
  Louisiana
    Actual Sales            $145,890     $149,530     $153,260     $157,090
    Target Sales            $145,000     $149,500     $153,300     $157,100
    Actual/Target             100.61%      100.02%       99.97%       99.99%
  Mississippi
    Actual Sales            $142,300     $145,850     $149,490     $153,220
    Target Sales            $140,000     $145,800     $149,500     $153,200
    Actual/Target             101.64%      100.03%       99.99%      100.01%
  South Carolina
    Actual Sales            $265,230     $271,860     $278,650     $285,610
    Target Sales            $250,000     $271,900     $278,600     $285,600
    Actual/Target             106.09%       99.99%      100.02%      100.00%
  Tennessee
    Actual Sales            $344,500     $353,110     $361,930     $370,970
    Target Sales            $340,000     $353,100     $361,900     $371,000
    Actual/Target             101.32%      100.00%      100.01%       99.99%
SOUTHEASTERN REGION SUMMARY
    Actual Sales          $1,991,175   $2,042,435   $2,094,435   $2,149,565
    Target Sales          $1,964,000   $2,032,500   $2,085,500   $2,129,500
    Actual/Target             101.38%      100.49%      100.43%      100.94%

NORTHEASTERN REGION
  Connecticut
    Actual Sales            $130,890     $134,160     $137,500     $140,940
    Target Sales            $126,000     $134,200     $137,500     $140,900
    Actual/Target             103.88%       99.97%      100.00%      100.03%
  Maine
    Actual Sales             $44,620      $45,730      $46,870      $48,040
    Target Sales             $45,000      $45,700      $46,900      $48,000
```

FIGURE 8-9: A sample header

bar tells 1-2-3 to divide the header or footer into three sections: left-aligned, centered, and right-aligned.

To demonstrate how the | character works, suppose you want to create the header shown in Figure 8-10. To do this, issue the / Print Printer Options Header command and change the existing header to

Sales Analysis for 1990|CONFIDENTIAL|MainLine, Inc.

To make this change, you can either press [Esc] to erase the existing header, then type the new header from scratch, or you can edit the existing header in the same way you would edit the contents of a cell. As in this case, it is usually more efficient to edit the existing header than to start over.

```
Sales Analysis for 1990        CONFIDENTIAL              MainLine, Inc.

REGIONAL SALES ANALYSIS
=================================================================
                        Jan-90      Feb-90      Mar-90      Apr-90
SOUTHEASTERN REGION
   Alabama
      Actual Sales     $174,800    $180,700    $185,900    $193,660
      Target Sales     $175,000    $175,000    $180,000    $180,000
      Actual/Target      99.89%     103.26%     103.28%     107.59%
   Arkansas
      Actual Sales     $136,790    $140,200    $143,700    $147,290
      Target Sales     $135,000    $140,000    $145,000    $145,000
      Actual/Target     101.33%     100.14%      99.10%     101.58%
   Florida
      Actual Sales     $357,900    $366,840    $376,010    $385,410
      Target Sales     $354,000    $362,900    $372,000    $381,300
      Actual/Target     101.10%     101.09%     101.08%     101.08%
   Georgia
      Actual Sales     $225,000    $230,620    $236,680    $242,280
      Target Sales     $225,000    $230,600    $236,400    $242,300
      Actual/Target     100.00%     100.01%     100.12%      99.99%
   Kentucky
      Actual Sales     $198,765    $203,725    $208,815    $214,035
      Target Sales     $200,000    $203,700    $208,800    $214,000
      Actual/Target      99.38%     100.01%     100.01%     100.02%
   Louisiana
      Actual Sales     $145,890    $149,530    $153,260    $157,090
      Target Sales     $145,000    $149,500    $153,300    $157,100
      Actual/Target     100.61%     100.02%      99.97%      99.99%
   Mississippi
      Actual Sales     $142,300    $145,850    $149,490    $153,220
      Target Sales     $140,000    $145,800    $149,500    $153,200
      Actual/Target     101.64%     100.03%      99.99%     100.01%
   South Carolina
      Actual Sales     $265,230    $271,860    $278,650    $285,610
      Target Sales     $250,000    $271,900    $278,600    $285,600
      Actual/Target     106.09%      99.99%     100.02%     100.00%
   Tennessee
      Actual Sales     $344,500    $353,110    $361,930    $370,970
      Target Sales     $340,000    $353,100    $361,900    $371,000
      Actual/Target     101.32%     100.00%     100.01%      99.99%

SOUTHEASTERN REGION SUMMARY
      Actual Sales   $1,991,175  $2,042,435  $2,094,435  $2,149,565
      Target Sales   $1,964,000  $2,032,500  $2,085,500  $2,129,500
      Actual/Target     101.38%     100.49%     100.43%     100.94%


NORTHEASTERN REGION
   Connecticut
      Actual Sales     $130,890    $134,160    $137,500    $140,940
      Target Sales     $126,000    $134,200    $137,500    $140,900
      Actual/Target     103.88%      99.97%     100.00%     100.03%
   Maine
      Actual Sales      $44,620     $45,730     $46,870     $48,040
      Target Sales      $45,000     $45,700     $46,900     $48,000
```

FIGURE 8-10: A header with left-aligned, centered, and right-aligned portions

The two vertical bars in this header tell 1-2-3 to divide it into left-aligned, centered, and right-aligned sections. The portion of the header to the left of the first | character will be printed left-aligned. The portion between the two | characters will be centered between the left and right margins. The portion to the right of the second | character will be right-aligned. When you print this header, it will look like Figure 8-10.

You don't have to use two | characters in a header or footer; you can include just one or, as you have seen, none at all. In addition, you do not have to include characters in every portion of a header or footer. For example, suppose you want to center the header *Sales Analysis for 1990* at the top of each page of your report. To do this, issue the / Print Printer Options Header command and alter this header line to look like this:

|Sales Analysis for 1990

Because there is no text to the left of the | character in this header, 1-2-3 will simply skip the left-aligned portion and print the header text in the center of the page. Now suppose you issue the / Print Printer Options Header command and change the header line to

||Sales Analysis for 1990

Because there is no text to the left of the first or second | characters, 1-2-3 will skip *both* the left-aligned and centered portions of the header and print the header right-aligned.

Numbering Pages

You can also use headers and footers to number the pages in your reports. If you include the symbol # in a header or footer, 1-2-3 will substitute the page number for that symbol on each page of the printed report.

For example, suppose you would like to place the word *page* followed by the correct page number at the lower-right corner of each page in a report. To do this, you issue the / Print Printer Options Footer command and type ||page #. When you print the report, each page will include the word *page* followed by the correct page number.

After you've printed a report with numbered pages, 1-2-3 will not automatically reset the first page number to 1. For example, suppose you print a three-page report with the page number in the lower-right corner of each page. Then, without leaving the Print menu, you define a new print range and print another report that also has page numbers. 1-2-3 will "remember" the last page number in the first report and begin numbering the second report with page 4. In other words, the first page of the second report will have the page number 4 in the lower-right corner, the second page will be numbered 5, the third page 6, and so forth.

In order to reset the first page number to 1 before you print a report, you must issue the Align command or quit all the way out of the Print menu. Of course, there may be times when you *want* continuous page numbering from one report to the next. In these cases, be sure that you do *not* choose Align or Quit.

Dating Reports

1-2-3 also offers a special symbol, @, that allows you to include the current DOS date in a header or footer. If you include the symbol @ in a header or footer, 1-2-3 will substitute the current date for that symbol when it prints a report. The date will always appear in dd-Mmm-yy format, regardless of the current global date format. For example, suppose today is March 2, 1987. The header

|Summary of Operations|@

will cause 1-2-3 to print *Summary of Operations* at the top center of each page and the current date in the form *1-Jan-90* in the upper-right corner of each page.

Deleting a Header or Footer

If you want to get rid of a header or footer, issue the / Print Printer Options Header (or Footer) command. Then press [Esc] to erase the current header or footer and press [Enter] to lock in the change. Of course, deleting a header or footer simply removes the text from the header or footer lines. 1-2-3 will still insert three blank lines at the top and bottom of each page of the printed report.

You can also use the / Print Printer Clear All command to delete the current header and footer. However, this command will also reset all of the other print options to their default settings, so you should use it with care.

Borders

If you are like most 1-2-3 users, you probably enter labels across the top and down the left side of your worksheets to describe the entries in those worksheets. For example, in the worksheet shown in Figure 8-3, row 3 contains month names and column A contains region names and other labels. Labels like these are essential to interpreting a worksheet—especially if the person reading the worksheet is not the same person who built it.

As you learned in Chapter 6, when you scroll around in a large worksheet, these labels may disappear from view. A similar problem can crop up when you print a large worksheet. When 1-2-3 divides a large report into pages, some of those pages will lack some or all of the explanatory labels. For example, in Figure 8-4, only page 1 contains *both* the month labels in row 3 and the region labels in column A. Page 2 is missing the month labels in row 3, and page 3 does not have the region labels in column A. Page 4 is the most difficult to interpret since it has neither month labels nor region labels.

Fortunately, 1-2-3 includes a command—/ Print Printer Options Borders—that will force 1-2-3 to include the contents of selected rows and columns on every page of a report. This command is similar to the / Worksheet Titles command, which you learned about in Chapter 6. The difference is that / Print Printer Options Borders affects only printed reports, while / Worksheet Titles affects only the screen.

When you issue the / Print Printer Options Borders command, 1-2-3 will display a menu with two options: Columns and Rows. To define the columns that you want

1-2-3 to print on each page of your report, you should choose the Columns option. When 1-2-3 displays the prompt *Enter range for border columns:*, you should select a range that includes at least one cell in each of the columns you want 1-2-3 to print on each page. For example, to define columns A, B, C, and D as the border columns, you should select a range that includes at least one cell in each of these columns, such as A1..D1, A1..D3, and so on.

To define the rows you want 1-2-3 to include on each page of a report, you should issue the / Print Printer Options Borders Rows command and select a range that includes at least one cell in each of those rows. For example, to define rows 1 and 2 as the border rows, you should select a range that includes at least one cell in each of these rows, such as A1..A2, A1..B2, and so on.

Once you have defined the columns and/or rows that you want 1-2-3 to print on each page, you must adjust the print range to exclude these columns and rows. Otherwise, 1-2-3 will print the border columns and rows twice on some pages. To redefine the print range, you simply issue the /Print Printer Range command and select the new range.

An Example

For example, suppose you'd like every page in the printed report in Figure 8-4 to contain the appropriate month headings and region labels. To do this, you must define columns A and B and rows 1 through 4 as borders. To begin, you would issue the /Print Printer Options Borders command and choose the Columns option. When 1-2-3 prompts you to define the border columns range, select a range that includes at least one cell in both columns A and B, such as A1..B1. You do not need to mark entire columns, just a single cell in each column.

Similarly, to print the month names at the top of each page, you should designate rows 1 through 4 as row borders. To do this, issue the / Print Printer Options Borders Rows command (if you just defined the column borders, you can simply choose Borders from the Options menu and then select the Rows option), highlight the range A1..A4 (or any other range that includes at least one cell in rows 1, 2, 3, and 4), and press [Enter]. As with column borders, you only need to mark one cell in each row.

Changing the Print Range

Before you print a report with borders, you must redefine the print range (or define it for the first time) so that it does *not* include the rows and columns that you designated as borders. If you do not do this, 1-2-3 will print the entries in your border rows and columns twice on some pages of the report. For example, Figure 8-11 shows how the first page of our example report would look if we specified borders but did not change the original print range (A1..K86).

To change the print range, issue the / Print Printer Range command. Immediately, 1-2-3 will highlight the old print range (cells A1..K86 in our example). You must redefine this range so that it does not include columns A and B or rows 1 through 4. There are two ways to approach this task. First, you could press [Esc], which will cancel the current print range and move the cell pointer to cell A1. You would then move the cell pointer to cell C5, press the [period] key to anchor the cell pointer, and press [End][Home] to highlight the new range, C5..K86.

```
REGIONAL SALES ANALYSIS REGIONAL SALES ANALYSIS
=================================================================
                                                    Jan-90      Feb-90
REGIONAL SALES ANALYSIS REGIONAL SALES ANALYSIS
=================================================================
                                                    Jan-90      Feb-90
SOUTHEASTERN REGION     SOUTHEASTERN REGION
  Alabama                 Alabama
    Actual Sales            Actual Sales            $174,800    $180,700
    Target Sales            Target Sales            $175,000    $175,000
    Actual/Target           Actual/Target             99.89%     103.26%
  Arkansas                Arkansas
    Actual Sales            Actual Sales            $136,790    $140,200
    Target Sales            Target Sales            $135,000    $140,000
    Actual/Target           Actual/Target            101.33%     100.14%
  Florida                 Florida
    Actual Sales            Actual Sales            $357,900    $366,840
    Target Sales            Target Sales            $354,000    $362,900
    Actual/Target           Actual/Target            101.10%     101.09%
  Georgia                 Georgia
    Actual Sales            Actual Sales            $225,000    $230,620
    Target Sales            Target Sales            $225,000    $230,600
    Actual/Target           Actual/Target            100.00%     100.01%
  Kentucky                Kentucky
    Actual Sales            Actual Sales            $198,765    $203,725
    Target Sales            Target Sales            $200,000    $203,700
    Actual/Target           Actual/Target             99.38%     100.01%
  Louisiana               Louisiana
    Actual Sales            Actual Sales            $145,890    $149,530
    Target Sales            Target Sales            $145,000    $149,500
    Actual/Target           Actual/Target            100.61%     100.02%
  Mississippi             Mississippi
    Actual Sales            Actual Sales            $142,300    $145,850
    Target Sales            Target Sales            $140,000    $145,800
    Actual/Target           Actual/Target            101.64%     100.03%
  South Carolina          South Carolina
    Actual Sales            Actual Sales            $265,230    $271,860
    Target Sales            Target Sales            $250,000    $271,900
    Actual/Target           Actual/Target            106.09%      99.99%
  Tennessee               Tennessee
    Actual Sales            Actual Sales            $344,500    $353,110
    Target Sales            Target Sales            $340,000    $353,100
    Actual/Target           Actual/Target            101.32%     100.00%
SOUTHEASTERN REGION SUMMSOUTHEASTERN REGION SUMMARY
    Actual Sales            Actual Sales          $1,991,175  $2,042,435
    Target Sales            Target Sales          $1,964,000  $2,032,500
    Actual/Target           Actual/Target            101.38%     100.49%


NORTHEASTERN REGION     NORTHEASTERN REGION
  Connecticut             Connecticut
    Actual Sales            Actual Sales            $130,890    $134,160
    Target Sales            Target Sales            $126,000    $134,200
```

FIGURE 8-11: A problem report

There is another way to redefine the print range, however, without cancelling the current range. After you issue the / Print Printer Range command, press the [period] key twice. This will shift the anchored corner of the print range from the lower-right corner of the range to the upper-left corner. Instead of seeing columns G through K and rows 67 through 86 on your screen, you will see columns A through F and rows 1 through 20. At this point, you should press ↓ four times to remove rows 1 through 4 from the print range, then press → twice to remove columns A and B from the range. When you are finished, the print range should be C5..K86. You can press [Enter] to lock in this range.

TIP: CHANGING THE ANCHORED CORNER OF A RANGE

In explaining how to alter a print range, we demonstrated a very useful technique that applies to all ranges in 1-2-3. Whenever you are viewing a range highlighted on your screen—such as when you issue the / Range Name Create command and choose a range name—you can always change the anchored corner of the range by pressing the [period] key. As you press [period], 1-2-3 moves the anchored corner of the range clockwise from one corner of the range to another. If the range is too large to be viewed on your screen in its entirety, pressing [period] will change not only the anchored corner of the range, but also the portion of the range that is in view. For example, when you issue the / Print Printer Range command, 1-2-3 will show you the lower-right corner of the range you have chosen to print. When you press the [period] key, 1-2-3 will bring the lower-left corner of the range into view. Pressing [period] again will bring the upper-left corner into view.

Printing the Report with Borders

Once you have designated your border rows and columns and redefined your print range, you can print the report as usual. As 1-2-3 prints the reports, it will include the appropriate sections of the border columns and rows you have selected on each page of the report. In the example, 1-2-3 will include the labels from columns A and B and from rows 1, 2, 3, and 4 on each page of the report. For instance, Figure 8-12 shows the fourth page from the report in Figure 8-4. Figure 8-13 shows the fourth page from the report after we added border rows and columns.

Keep in mind that 1-2-3 will divide your pages somewhat differently after you add borders. For example, because 1-2-3 has printed part of columns A and B on page 4 in Figure 8-13, fewer columns of actual data can appear on that page. Instead of presenting the contents of columns G through K, page 4 in Figure 8-13 displays only columns G through I (plus the border columns A and B). Columns J and K (containing the 1985 sales totals and the percent change from 1985 to 1986) will appear on another page of the report, and the total length of the report will become six pages instead of four.

Also notice that the label *NORTHEASTERN REGION SUMMARY* appears partly truncated in Figure 8-13. In the worksheet, this label overlaps into column C. Because

```
           100.08%       99.94%        99.88%        99.50%

          $138,000     $141,500      $809,360      $698,973       15.79%
          $141,000     $144,600      $818,500      $695,700
            97.87%       97.86%        98.88%       100.47%

          $120,790     $123,800      $699,050      $609,500       14.69%
          $124,100     $127,200      $715,800      $608,400
            97.33%       97.33%        97.66%       100.18%

          $746,540     $765,200    $4,295,680    $3,870,200       10.99%
          $746,500     $765,200    $4,305,800    $3,845,600
           100.01%      100.00%        99.76%       100.64%

           $45,170      $46,290      $263,100      $257,690        2.10%
           $47,000      $48,100      $269,200      $262,400
            96.11%       96.24%        97.73%        98.21%

           $46,010      $47,160      $266,300      $289,450       -8.00%
           $46,000      $47,200      $264,600      $275,100
           100.02%       99.92%       100.64%       105.22%

        $1,290,210   $1,322,490    $7,454,480    $6,816,743        9.36%
        $1,298,300   $1,330,900    $7,490,400    $6,779,500
             0.00%        0.00%        99.52%         0.00%

        $3,496,355   $3,581,935   $20,197,680   $18,744,633        7.75%
        $3,487,700   $3,581,700   $20,142,100   $18,382,600
           100.25%      100.01%       100.28%       101.97%
```

FIGURE 8-12: A page from a large worksheet with no borders

we did not include column C in the Column Borders range, the portion of the label that overlaps into that column is not printed on page 4.

Clearing Borders

If you decide that you do not want to use borders when you print, you can delete them by issuing the /Print Printer Clear Borders command. Issuing this command will clear *both* the row borders and column borders. There is no way to clear only your row borders or only your column borders. (Unlike some of the other Print settings, such as the setup string or header, you cannot clear Borders by issuing the / Print Printer Options Borders Rows (or Columns) command and pressing [Esc].)

```
REGIONAL SALES ANALYSIS
================================================================
                           May-90        Jun-90          Totals
         Actual/Target    100.08%        99.94%          99.88%
  Massachusetts
         Actual Sales    $138,000      $141,500        $809,360
         Target Sales    $141,000      $144,600        $818,500
         Actual/Target     97.87%        97.86%          98.88%
  New Hampshire
         Actual Sales    $120,790      $123,800        $699,050
         Target Sales    $124,100      $127,200        $715,800
         Actual/Target     97.33%        97.33%          97.66%
  New York
         Actual Sales    $746,540      $765,200      $4,295,680
         Target Sales    $746,500      $765,200      $4,305,800
         Actual/Target    100.01%       100.00%          99.76%
  Rhode Island
         Actual Sales     $45,170       $46,290        $263,100
         Target Sales     $47,000       $48,100        $269,200
         Actual/Target     96.11%        96.24%          97.73%
  Vermont
         Actual Sales     $46,010       $47,160        $266,300
         Target Sales     $46,000       $47,200        $264,600
         Actual/Target    100.02%        99.92%         100.64%

  NORTHEASTERN REGION SUMM
         Actual Sales  $1,290,210    $1,322,490      $7,454,480
         Target Sales  $1,298,300    $1,330,900      $7,490,400
         Actual/Target      0.00%         0.00%          99.52%

  TOTAL ACTUAL SALES   $3,496,355    $3,581,935     $20,197,680
  TOTAL TARGET SALES   $3,487,700    $3,581,700     $20,142,100
  PERCENT OF GOAL MET     100.25%       100.01%         100.28%
```

FIGURE 8-13: A page from a large worksheet with borders

After you use the /Print Printer Clear Borders command to remove the borders you have defined, you'll want to redefine the print range once again to include the border rows and columns. Otherwise, 1-2-3 will not include these rows and columns in the report.

Saving Print Settings

The changes you make to the Print settings in a worksheet are unique to that worksheet. Any changes that you make to Print settings will be saved along with the worksheet when you issue the /File Save command. When you use the /File Retrieve command to retrieve a saved worksheet, any Print settings you defined for that worksheet will be retrieved with the worksheet.

Returning Print Settings to Their Defaults

After you format and print a worksheet, you may decide to return some or all of the Print settings to their default values. The /Print Printer Clear command offers a quick way to return your Print settings to their defaults.

To reset *all* of the Print settings to their defaults, issue the /Print Printer Clear All command. This command will delete your header and footer, erase your setup string, eliminate any borders you have defined, and reset the Margin and Page-Length settings to their defaults. It also will eliminate your print range selection so that no range is selected for printing. The only settings that are not affected by this command are manual page breaks you may have defined, any embedded setup strings, and the / Worksheet Global Default Printer Wait setting.

If you want to retain the header, footer, and borders that you have defined, but reset the margins, page length, and setup string, issue the / Print Printer Clear Format command. If you just want to reset the Borders setting, issue the / Print Printer Clear Borders command. If you just want to reset the print range, issue the / Print Printer Clear Range command.

Formatting—Final Comments

Although it's easy to change 1-2-3's Print settings, there are several things to keep in mind as you work with print options. For one thing, remember that the various Print settings often interact with one another. For example, if you use a setup string to change the typestyle of a report, you will likely need to change the report's margins and maybe the Page-Length setting as well. Second, it's easy to lose track of your changes as you experiment with different options. You may find that it's helpful to keep a written record of your Print settings as you go along, and then store a copy of these settings with the printed worksheet.

Fortunately, you do not have to worry about Print settings at all if you don't want to. As we demonstrated at the beginning of this chapter, all you need to do to print a report in 1-2-3 is specify the range of cells that you want to print.

CHANGING THE DEFAULT PRINT SETTINGS

So far, we have shown you how to change 1-2-3's Print settings to suit a particular worksheet. As we've mentioned in several places, 1-2-3 also offers a command— / Worksheet Global Default Printer—that lets you change the *default* values of some of its Print settings. For example, you can use this command to define new default margins or to specify a default setup string.

When you issue the / Worksheet Global Default Printer command, you will see the menu shown in Figure 8-1. ▶(If you use 1-2-3 Release 2.2, you'll also see the / Worksheet Global Default settings sheet.)◀ As we explained at the beginning of this chapter, three of the choices on this menu—Interface, Auto-LF, and Name—are used to configure 1-2-3 for your printing hardware. The Wait choice is used to specify whether or not 1-2-3 should pause between printing pages so you can load individual sheets into the printer (we'll cover this option in a few pages). The other options control the default Margin, Page-Length, and Setup String settings.

RELEASE
▶ 2.2 ◀

An Example

For example, suppose you'd like to change the default left margin setting from 4 to 2. To do this, issue the / Worksheet Global Default Printer command, choose Left, type

2, and press [Enter]. Once you do this, this new default left margin setting will remain active until you change it or exit from 1-2-3. Each time you begin a new worksheet in the current 1-2-3 session, that worksheet will automatically have a left margin setting of 2. When you issue the / Print Printer Clear All or / Print Printer Clear Format command, the left margin setting will change to 2.

The Update Option

The changes you make with the / Worksheet Global Default Printer command are only temporary. They remain in effect only until you exit from 1-2-3. Once you begin a new 1-2-3 session, the old defaults will once again be in effect.

If you would like to make the changes you make to one or more of the default Print settings permanent, you must use the / Worksheet Global Default Update command to save those changes. Issuing this command instructs 1-2-3 to rewrite the 1-2-3 configuration file (123.CNF), replacing the existing default settings in that file with your new default settings.

For example, suppose you want to make the new default left margin of 2 a permanent default. After you have used the / Worksheet Global Default Printer Left command to change the left margin default, issue the / Worksheet Global Default Update command. When you issue this command, 1-2-3 will save the current default settings (including the printer defaults) into the file 123.CNF. From that point on, each time you load 1-2-3, it will use the settings in the file 123.CNF—including your new default left margin setting—as its default settings.

Changing 1-2-3's default Print settings will *not* affect the Print settings of any worksheets that already have been saved to disk. When you retrieve a saved worksheet, you will find that it contains exactly the Print settings it contained when you saved it. This is true even if you have used the Update option to make the new default settings permanent.

The Status Option

If you want to review the current default Print settings, issue the / Worksheet Global Default Status command. Issuing this command will bring into view a the same settings sheet that 1-2-3 displays whenever you issue the / Worksheet Global Default command. In earlier releases of 1-2-3, the / Worksheet Global Default Status command provides the only way to see the default print settings.

Forcing the Printer to Pause between Pages

Normally, when you print a multiple-page report, 1-2-3 assumes that you are using continuous-feed paper. For this reason, after each page in the report is printed, 1-2-3 sends a signal to the printer that tells it to scroll to a new page without pausing and begin printing the next section of the report. If you want to print on single-sheet paper, such as your company's letterhead, you'll need to tell 1-2-3 to pause after it prints each page in the report while you insert a new sheet of paper. To do this, you must issue the

/ Worksheet Global Default Printer Wait command and choose the Yes option. (The initial default setting is No.)

When you print a report with the Wait setting on Yes, 1-2-3 will beep and pause after it prints the first and every subsequent page in the report. While 1-2-3 is waiting, you can position a new piece of paper in the printer. When you are ready to print again, you can press any key to resume printing.

If you later want to go back to using continuous-feed paper, you'll probably want to turn off 1-2-3's Wait setting. To do this, issue the / Worksheet Global Default Printer Wait command again and choose No.

We think it's a little odd that the Wait command is on the / Worksheet Global Default Printer menu. It would seem to fit better on the / Print Printer Options menu, along with the Margin and Borders commands. Apparently, 1-2-3 considers the Wait setting to be a default rather than a temporary setting. Nevertheless, if you know how to change the Wait setting, you can take advantage of 1-2-3's option of printing your reports on noncontinuous paper.

INSERTING MANUAL PAGE BREAKS

When you print a multiple-page report, you will often find that 1-2-3's automatic page breaks occur at rather awkward locations in your worksheet. In fact, just as Murphy's Law would predict, 1-2-3 always seems to place a horizontal page break between the last number in a column of figures that you are totaling and the total itself, or between the heading at the top of a column of entries and the entries in that column.

The / Worksheet Page command allows you to insert manual page breaks in worksheets. (This command is not available in 1-2-3 Release 1A.) To insert a manual page break into a worksheet, you just move the cell pointer to the row above which you want to insert the page break and to the first column in the print range (usually column A). Once the cell pointer is in place, you issue the / Worksheet Page command. When you issue this command, 1-2-3 will insert a new row into the worksheet at the position of the cell pointer, and then enter a special page-break symbol (::) in the new row. This symbol tells 1-2-3 to insert a page break in the report.

An Example

Suppose you would like to force a page break between rows 48 and 49 of the example worksheet in Figure 8-3. This page break will separate the sales data for the Southeastern region from the data for the Northeastern region. To insert this page break, move the cell pointer to cell A49 and issue the / Worksheet Page command. Immediately, 1-2-3 will insert a new blank row above the row that contains the cell pointer and place a page-break symbol at the beginning of that row. In this example, 1-2-3 would insert a new row at row 49 (the entries in row 49 will now be in row 50) and place a page-break symbol at the beginning of row 49. Figure 8-14 shows this symbol in place in the worksheet.

When you print the worksheet, 1-2-3 will issue a page break after it prints row 49 and before it prints row 50. However, the new row and the page-break symbol will not appear in your printout.

```
A49: |::                                                          READY

      A           B           C           D           E           F
 41   Actual/Target          101.32%     100.00%     100.01%      99.99%
 42
 43  SOUTHEASTERN REGION SUMMARY
 44   Actual Sales           $1,991,175  $2,042,435  $2,094,435  $2,149,565
 45   Target Sales           $1,964,000  $2,032,500  $2,085,500  $2,129,500
 46   Actual/Target          101.38%     100.49%     100.43%     100.94%
 47
 48
 49  ::
 50  NORTHEASTERN REGION
 51   Connecticut
 52    Actual Sales          $130,890    $134,160    $137,500    $140,940
 53    Target Sales          $126,000    $134,200    $137,500    $140,900
 54    Actual/Target         103.88%      99.97%     100.00%     100.03%
 55   Maine
 56    Actual Sales          $44,620     $45,730     $46,870     $48,040
 57    Target Sales          $45,000     $45,700     $46,900     $48,000
 58    Actual/Target          99.16%     100.07%      99.94%     100.08%
 59   Massachusetts
 60    Actual Sales          $127,000    $130,990    $134,260    $137,610
```

FIGURE 8-14: A manual page break

Notes

Before you issue the /Worksheet Page command, you must be sure that the cell pointer is positioned in the leftmost column of the print range so that the page-break symbol will appear at the left edge of your print range. If you insert the page break anywhere other than the leftmost column of the print range, 1-2-3 will ignore it. Usually, the leftmost column of your print range will be column A—the leftmost column in the worksheet.

When you print a report that contains a manual page break, 1-2-3 will adjust the position of any automatic page breaks that follow the manual page break. In other words, 1-2-3 will change the location of its automatic page breaks so that only full pages of data are printed.

If the report you are printing is more than one page wide, the manual page breaks in that report will apply across the entire report. For instance, when you print the example worksheet, the resulting report is two pages wide. When you insert the page break in row 49, 1-2-3 will include that page break in the report after it prints row 48 on every page of the report that includes that row.

Instead of issuing the /Worksheet Page command, you can enter a manual page break by typing the page-break symbol into a cell. To do this, first move the cell pointer to the row above which you want to insert the page break, and then issue the /Worksheet Insert Row command to create a new row. Next, move the cell pointer to the leftmost column in the print range and type |:: (a vertical bar followed by two colons). 1-2-3 interprets manually entered page breaks in the same way it interprets page breaks you enter with the / Worksheet Page command.

If you want to remove a manual page break, you need only use the / Worksheet Delete Row command to delete the row that contains the page-break symbol. Since there should not be any other entries in the row that contains the page break, deleting that row should have no effect on your worksheet—other than removing the page break.

UNFORMATTED REPORTS

So far, we have shown you how you can use the commands on the Print menu to change the format of your printed reports. In addition to the options we've looked at so far, 1-2-3 offers the choice of creating an "unformatted" report. When 1-2-3 prints an unformatted report, it ignores the top and bottom margin settings, the Page-Length setting, and any header or footer you have defined. Instead of inserting blank lines for the top margin and header at the top of each page, 1-2-3 will print the first line of the report on the first line of the page. Similarly, instead of inserting blank lines at the bottom of each page for the bottom margin and the footer, 1-2-3 will continue printing right to the bottom of the page.

There are no page breaks in an unformatted report. When 1-2-3 reaches the end of a page in an unformatted report, it will ignore the page break and continue printing, leaving no extra space between the bottom of one page and the top of the next page.

To create an unformatted report, issue the / Print Printer Options Other Unformatted command. To turn formatting back on, issue the / Print Printer Options Other Formatted command.

Although the Unformatted option will cause 1-2-3 to ignore page breaks and headers and footers, it will not affect your left and right margins or your setup string. 1-2-3 still uses the left and right margin settings to determine where the vertical page breaks in the report should occur. Similarly, if you have defined a setup string for a report, that string will affect the typestyle of the characters in the report even if you print the report unformatted.

The Unformatted option suppresses all horizontal page breaks, but it does not affect vertical page breaks. If your report is wider than a single page, 1-2-3 will still have to break the report into vertical sections. If you have defined column borders, those borders will appear on each vertical section of the report. However, because an unformatted report has no horizontal page breaks, the row borders you have defined will appear only once at the top of the report.

LISTING THE WORKSHEET

Instead of printing a worksheet as it appears on your screen, you can print a listing of the contents of the cells in that worksheet. This listing can be a useful way to document a model, and it provides a helpful tool for debugging a worksheet.

TIP: PRINTING REPORT DRAFTS

When printing a draft of a large worksheet, we recommend that you try to get as much information as possible on each page. This way, you will have fewer pages to tape together and keep track of, and you will be able to get a better overall view of the worksheet.

To achieve this goal, we recommend that you print your draft reports using the Unformatted option, with your left and right margins set as wide as possible. You should also use a setup string that will cause the printer to print in compressed print with a smaller line spacing.

For example, suppose you are using an Epson wide-carriage printer, such as the FX-100. To print a draft of a large worksheet, load the printer with 14-by-11-inch paper. Issue the / Print Printer Options Other Unformatted command. Then choose Setup from the Options menu and enter the setup string \027\048\015. (This setup string causes Epson printers to print in condensed print and eight lines per inch instead of the usual six lines per inch. If you use a different type of printer, check your printer manual for the equivalent ASCII codes.) Next, set the left margin to 0 and the right margin to 200. Then set the page length to 88.

When you print this report, your data may appear to be "crammed" onto the page. However, you will be able to print your worksheet in fewer pages. For example, Figure A shows the first page of the example worksheet from Figure 8-3 printed with all of the recommended settings. Notice that all of the worksheet fits on one page.

FIGURE A: A draft report

To print cell contents instead of the worksheet display, issue /Print Printer Options Other and choose Cell-Formulas. When you choose Go to begin printing, 1-2-3 will print a cell-by-cell list of all the entries in your selected print range. For example, Figure 8-15 shows one page of the listing of cell contents of the worksheet in Figure 8-3.

```
H32: (C0) 161000
I32: (C0) [W16] @SUM(C32..H32)
J32: (C0) [W16] 833900
A33: '    Actual/Target
C33: (P2) +C31/C32
D33: (P2) +D31/D32
E33: (P2) +E31/E32
F33: (P2) +F31/F32
G33: (P2) +G31/G32
H33: (P2) +H31/H32
I33: (P2) [W16] +I31/I32
J33: (P2) [W16] +J31/J32
A34: '  South Carolina
A35: '    Actual Sales
C35: (C0) 265230
D35: (C0) 271860
E35: (C0) 278650
F35: (C0) 285610
G35: (C0) 292750
H35: (C0) 300060
I35: (C0) [W16] @SUM(C35..H35)
J35: (C0) [W16] 1766590.1981
K35: (P2) (I35-J35)/J35
A36: '    Target Sales
C36: (C0) 250000
D36: (C0) 271900
E36: (C0) 278600
F36: (C0) 285600
G36: (C0) 292700
H36: (C0) 300100
I36: (C0) [W16] @SUM(C36..H36)
J36: (C0) [W16] 1650700
A37: '    Actual/Target
C37: (P2) +C35/C36
D37: (P2) +D35/D36
E37: (P2) +E35/E36
F37: (P2) +F35/F36
G37: (P2) +G35/G36
H37: (P2) +H35/H36
I37: (P2) [W16] +I35/I36
J37: (P2) [W16] +J35/J36
A38: '  Tennessee
A39: '    Actual Sales
C39: (C0) 344500
D39: (C0) 353110
E39: (C0) 361930
F39: (C0) 370970
G39: (C0) 380240
H39: (C0) 389740
I39: (C0) [W16] @SUM(C39..H39)
J39: (C0) [W16] 1925188.1015
K39: (P2) (I39-J39)/J39
A40: '    Target Sales
C40: (C0) 340000
D40: (C0) 353100
E40: (C0) 361900
```

FIGURE 8-15: A Cell-Formulas listing

Notice that this listing includes all the information you would see in the control panel when you point to a cell—its contents, its format (if any), the column width (when the width is different from the global default), and the label prefix for label entries—for each cell in the worksheet. The listing includes only cells that contain entries; blank cells are not included unless they have been assigned a format.

Overall, the listing created by the Cell-Formulas option is not very useful. Because 1-2-3 prints the contents of the cells as a list with only one cell on each line, instead of as a grid, it is very difficult to determine the relationships between the cells in the listing. Second, because 1-2-3 prints only one cell per line, the listing for even a relatively small worksheet can be quite long. Finally, while the listing 1-2-3 prints is accurate as far as it goes, it does not include some important information you might want to have. For example, it does not include a listing of the range names in your worksheet, or of the graph or data base settings.

Other programs, such as the Spreadsheet Auditor and the Cambridge Spreadsheet Analyst, correct these weaknesses. If you plan to print worksheet listings frequently, we suggest that you consider one of these programs.

CONCLUSION

In this chapter, you've learned how to create printed reports from your 1-2-3 worksheets. Like most other tasks in 1-2-3, printing is remarkably easy. As you have learned, 1-2-3's many formatting options give you quite a bit of control over the appearance of your printed reports. You can use these options to produce reports that are formatted in just about any way that you can imagine. Don't let the variety of print options overwhelm you. Experiment—no doubt you'll soon be creating your own custom reports with 1-2-3.

9

File Management

The commands on 1-2-3's File menu allow you to save your worksheets to disk and retrieve saved worksheets back into 1-2-3. In addition, the commands on this menu let you perform more complex tasks, such as extracting ranges from worksheets into files and combining one worksheet (or a part of a worksheet) into another. There also are commands, such as / File List and / File Erase, that help you manage your files. Understanding how to create and manage files is essential to using 1-2-3 effectively.

In this chapter, we will explain the following commands on 1-2-3's File menu: / File Save, / File Retrieve, / File Erase, / File Directory, / File Xtract, / File Combine, / File List, and / File Admin Table. We'll cover the / File Import command—which allows you to bring ASCII text files into a 1-2-3 worksheet in Appendix 1, "Exchanging Data with Other Programs." We'll cover the / File Admin Reservation and / File Admin Link-Refresh commands—which facilitate the use of 1-2-3 on a network—in Appendix 4, "Using 1-2-3 on a Network". (We talked briefly about the / File Admin Link-Refresh command in Chapter 2.)

SAVING WORKSHEETS

When you create a worksheet in 1-2-3, that worksheet resides in your computer's RAM (random access memory). Because RAM is not a permanent storage medium—it gets erased when your computer is turned off—you must save your worksheets in disk files to make them permanent. A disk file provides a parking place where the worksheet can reside until you need to use it again. The command that lets you save a worksheet into a file is / File Save.

Saving a Worksheet for the First Time

To save a worksheet to disk for the first time, you issue the / File Save command. When you issue this command, 1-2-3 will display the prompt *Enter name of file to save:*, followed by the default directory and the file-name descriptor *.wk1, as shown in

Figure 9-1. In addition, the descriptor *.wk1 causes 1-2-3 to display a list of all worksheet files (that is, files with the file-name extension .WK1) in the default directory. This list will be in alphabetical order in all releases of 1-2-3 except for Release 1A. When you see this prompt, you specify the name under which you want to save the worksheet and press [Enter] to save the worksheet.

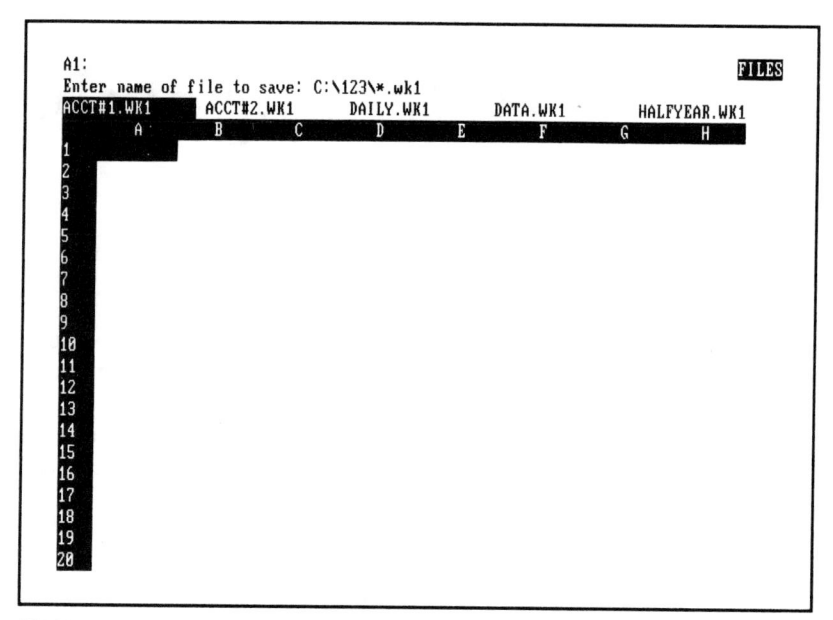

```
A1:                                                                    FILES
Enter name of file to save: C:\123\*.wk1
ACCT#1.WK1      ACCT#2.WK1      DAILY.WK1     DATA.WK1     HALFYEAR.WK1
       A            B            C            D            E            F            G            H
1
2
3
4
5
6
7
8
9
10
11
12
13
14
15
16
17
18
19
20
```

FIGURE 9-1: The / File Save prompt

Choosing a New Name

Chances are, when you save a worksheet for the first time, you will want to save it into a new worksheet file. To do this, you just issue the / File Save command, type the name under which you want to save the worksheet, and press [Enter]. For example, suppose that you would like to save a new worksheet in a file named BALANCES. To do this, issue the / File Save command and type BALANCES. When you press [Enter], 1-2-3 will save the contents of the worksheet to disk in a file named BALANCES.WK1. (As we'll explain in a few paragraphs, you don't have to supply a file-name extension. 1-2-3 automatically will give your worksheet files the extension .WK1.)

Choosing an Existing Name

As you can see in Figure 9-1, when you issue the / File Save command, 1-2-3 will display a list of all the worksheet files on the default directory. If you want to, you can choose one of these names when you save a worksheet for the first time. All you have to do to save a worksheet under an existing name is issue the / File Save command, point to the file name under which you want to save the worksheet, and press [Enter].

▶When you save a worksheet under the name of an existing file, 1-2-3 Release 2.2 will display a menu with three options: Cancel, Replace, and Backup. (Earlier versions of 1-2-3 offer only two options: Cancel and Replace.)◀ If you choose Replace, 1-2-3 will replace the existing file with the current worksheet. If you choose Cancel, the / File Save command will be aborted and 1-2-3 will return to the READY mode. ▶If you choose Backup, 1-2-3 will change the extension of the existing file to .BAK before saving the new file. That way, both the old file and the new one will still exist.◀

RELEASE
▶ 2.2 ◀

RELEASE
▶ 2.2 ◀

File Names

There are several important file-name rules you'll need to keep in mind when you save worksheets. First, the name you choose for a worksheet file can be no more than eight characters long. If you enter a file name that is longer than eight characters, 1-2-3 will simply truncate any characters beyond the eighth character. In addition to the eight-character name, you can specify a three-character file-name extension. (If you do not supply an extension, 1-2-3 will automatically supply the extension .WK1.)

A file name can include any letter of the alphabet (upper and lower case), the digits 0 through 9, and the underline character (_). You may include any of the following symbols in your file names:

! @ # $ % ^ & * ( ) - { } ~ ` '

For example, the following are all acceptable file names:

BOB'S	YOU&ME	ADS(75%)
JUN_23	6_23_87	FOUR@$30<

You do not have to supply a file-name extension when you specify the name for your 1-2-3 worksheets. If you do not supply an extension, 1-2-3 Release 2, 2.01, and 2.2 all automatically will supply the file-name extension .WK1. (Earlier releases of 1-2-3 saved worksheet files with the file-name extension .WKS.) For example, if you issue the / File Save command, type the name STATEMNT, and press [Enter], 1-2-3 will save the worksheet into the file *STATEMNT.WK1*.

In 1-2-3 Releases 2, 2.01, and 2.2, you can save a file with an extension other than .WK1. All you have to do is type the extension you want to use as part of the file name. For example, suppose you would like to save a worksheet into a file named EXPENSES.ASA. To do this, issue the / File Save command, type *expenses.asa* and press [Enter]. We will refer to file-name extensions other than .WK1 as "nonstandard extensions."

Although you are allowed to specify an extension other than .WK1, 1-2-3 makes it pretty inconvenient to do so. For one thing, when you issue the / File Retrieve or / File Save commands, 1-2-3 will show you a list of only those files that have an extension that begins with the letters WK. Similarly, when you issue the / File List command, 1-2-3 will show you a list of only those files that have an extension beginning with the letters WK. In addition, when you save a file with a nonstandard extension for the second time, 1-2-3 will attempt to save the file with the .WK1 extension. You'll have to type the nonstandard extension every time you save the worksheet.

Saving a Worksheet That Already Has Been Saved

When you save a worksheet that has been saved before, 1-2-3 will automatically assume that you want to save it under the same name. For example, suppose you are making some changes to a worksheet named CASH.WK1 and you decide to save those changes to disk. When you issue the / File Save command, 1-2-3 will not display the descriptor *.*wk1* and will not show you a list of all existing worksheet files, as it does when you save a file for the first time. Instead, 1-2-3 will automatically enter the original file name, CASH.WK1, on the prompt line, as shown in Figure 9-2.

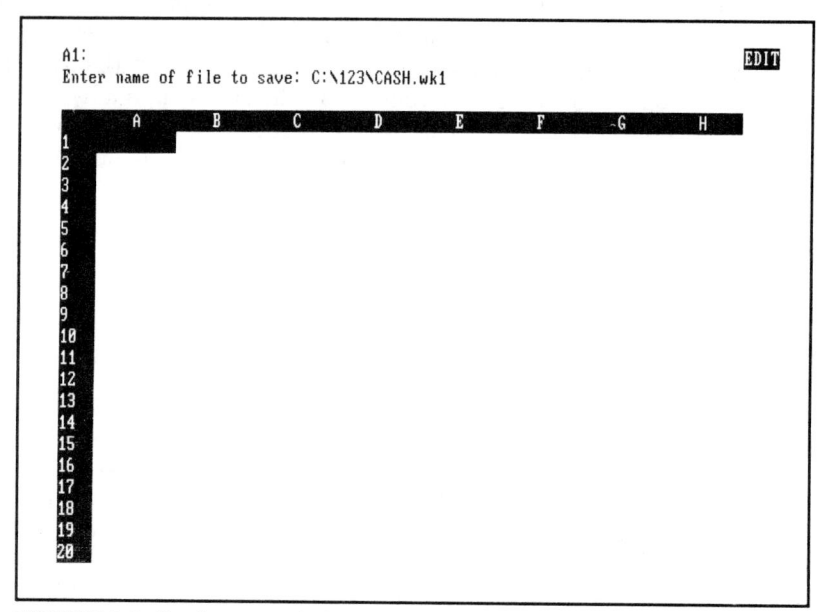

FIGURE 9-2: Saving a worksheet for the second time

RELEASE ▶ 2.2 ◀

If you want to save the altered worksheet under this name, you need only press [Enter]. ▶1-2-3 Release 2.2 will then present a menu with three options: Cancel, Replace, and Backup. (Earlier versions of 1-2-3 will present a menu with just two options: Cancel and Replace.)◀ You should select Replace if you want to replace the existing version of CASH.WK1 with the revised worksheet. If you don't want to save the file under the name you selected, you should choose Cancel, which will abort the command.

RELEASE ▶ 2.2 ◀

▶If you want to save both the existing version of the file and the new version, you should choose Backup. When you do this, 1-2-3 will change the extension of the existing file to .BAK before saving the new file. For example, if you choose the Backup when resaving a worksheet into a file named TEST.WK1, 1-2-3 will change the name of the existing file to TEST.BAK before saving the new version of the worksheet in a file named TEST.WK1. When the save is finished, both the old file and the new one will still exist.◄

Although you will usually save a worksheet under the same name each time you save it, you do not have to. You can always choose to save a worksheet under a new name, thereby creating a new worksheet file. For example, suppose that after you've made some changes to the CASH.WK1 worksheet, you decide to save the altered worksheet in a file named CASH2.WK1. Begin by issuing the / File Save command. 1-2-3 will then display a prompt like *Enter name of file to save: B:\CASH.WK1*. You should type the new name, CASH2, and press [Enter]. As soon as you start to type the new name, 1-2-3 will erase the original name in the prompt line. When you press [Enter], 1-2-3 will save the worksheet under the name CASH2.WK1. (1-2-3 will automatically supply the .WK1 extension.)

Choosing a new name for the new version of the worksheet allows you to save it without overwriting the old version. Because you decided to save the modified worksheet under the name CASH2, the original, unmodified version still exists in the file CASH.WK1. (►Of course, in 1-2-3 Release 2.2, you can use the Backup option to accomplish the same result.◄)

RELEASE
► 2.2 ◄

TIP: EDITING A FILE NAME

When you issue the / File Save command to save a worksheet that already has been saved, 1-2-3 will display the name of that worksheet file in the File Save prompt. If you want to save the worksheet under a different name, you can just type that name, and 1-2-3 will replace the original name with the name you enter. But if the new name for the worksheet is only slightly different from the original name, it seems a waste of effort to type the new name from scratch. Fortunately, you don't have to do this. If you want to make a slight change to the original file name, you can just edit the name. After you issue the / File Save command, press the [Spacebar] to enter the EDIT mode. Then you can use the cursor-movement keys, the [Backspace] key, and the [Delete] key to edit the original name. When you have completed your changes, press [Enter] to save the worksheet under the new name. (This capability is not available in Release 1A.)

By the way, we have noted that you must press the [Spacebar] to enter the EDIT mode when you want to change a file name. You might notice that the Mode indicator immediately says EDIT when you issue the / File Save command. However, if you try to edit the file name without pressing the [Spacebar], 1-2-3 will beep and will not accept your keystrokes. You must press [Spacebar] before 1-2-3 will accept your keystrokes.

Disk-Full Errors

If you are using a floppy-disk computer system, you will likely encounter disk-full problems from time to time as you save 1-2-3 worksheets. If the disk to which you are saving a worksheet becomes full, 1-2-3 will beep and display the message *Disk full* in the lower-left corner of the screen. You must press [Esc] to acknowledge the error and return to the READY mode, then take some action to free up enough memory to save the worksheet and repeat the / File Save command.

Avoiding Disk-Full Errors

If you aren't sure whether a worksheet will fit on a disk, you can issue / Worksheet Status to check the size of the worksheet, then check the amount of space available on the current disk. To check the amount of space available on the disk, you can issue the / System command and exit to DOS temporarily. Once you are at the DOS prompt, you can use the CHKDSK or DIR command to find out how much space is available.

By comparing the size of the worksheet to the available memory on disk, you can get a pretty good idea of whether the worksheet can be saved or not. However, you should be aware that there is not a one-to-one relationship between the number of bytes a worksheet consumes in RAM and the number of bytes it consumes on disk. Since 1-2-3 squeezes worksheets slightly as it saves them, most worksheets consume less memory on disk than they do in RAM.

Overcoming Disk-Full Errors

There are several things you can do to get around disk-full problems. The most obvious solution is simply to remove the current disk from the disk drive, insert a new formatted disk, and issue the / File Save command again. If you don't happen to have a formatted disk handy, you can use the / System command to return to DOS temporarily and format a new disk. (See Chapter 6 for a complete explanation of the / System command.)

Another solution is to use the / File Erase command to erase unneeded files from the current disk, thereby freeing up some space. (We'll talk about the / File Erase command in more detail later in this chapter.) If there aren't any expendable files on your current disk, you might try to shrink your worksheet. You can do this by deleting any unnecessary blank rows and/or columns at the edges of your worksheet and by using the / Range Format Reset command to reset the format of any blank cells that are outside of the working area of the worksheet.

If the worksheet you are saving is too large to fit on a single diskette, then you can use the / File Xtract command to save different sections of the worksheet on different disks. When you get ready to use the worksheet again, the / File Combine command allows you to put the sections back together in RAM. We'll talk about the Xtract and Combine commands in more detail later in this chapter.

A Word of Warning

The first thing 1-2-3 does when you ask it to save a worksheet is erase the old version of that worksheet file from disk. If 1-2-3 then runs out of disk space before it saves the worksheet, neither the old version of the file nor the new version will be saved. Be careful! If you don't find a way to save the new version of the worksheet, or if you forget to save it, all of your work will be lost.

RETRIEVING WORKSHEETS

The / File Retrieve command allows you to retrieve from disk worksheets that you have previously saved. When you issue the / File Retrieve command, 1-2-3 will display the prompt shown in Figure 9-3. Notice that this prompt includes the descriptor *.wk?, which causes 1-2-3 to display a list of all the worksheet files in the current directory (that is, all of the files in the directory with a file-name extension that begins with the letters WK, including .WK1 and .WKS files).

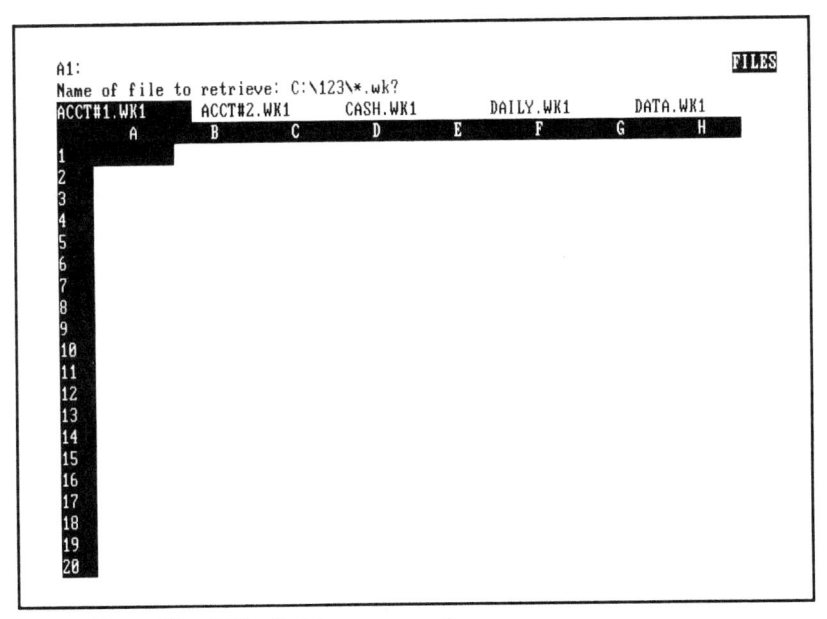

```
A1:                                                              FILES
Name of file to retrieve: C:\123\*.wk?
ACCT#1.WK1    ACCT#2.WK1    CASH.WK1    DAILY.WK1    DATA.WK1
      A       B       C       D       E       F       G       H
 1
 2
 3
 4
 5
 6
 7
 8
 9
10
11
12
13
14
15
16
17
18
19
20
```

FIGURE 9-3: The / File Retrieve prompt

To retrieve a file, you simply select its name from the list, either by pointing to its name and pressing [Enter] or by typing its name and pressing [Enter]. (Usually you'll find it easier to point than to type.) For example, suppose you want to retrieve the file named CASH.WK1, which is the third file in the list in Figure 9-3. To do this, issue the / File Retrieve command, press → to point to its name in the list, and press [Enter].

Alternatively, you could issue the / File Retrieve command, type CASH, and press [Enter]. Notice that you don't have to type the extension .WK1 to retrieve the file. As long as the file's file-name extension is .WK1 or .WKS, you only have to type the file name—you don't have to type the extension.

A Caution

The first thing 1-2-3 does when it begins to retrieve a file is erase the current contents of the worksheet. Once you select a name and press [Enter], whatever was in the worksheet will be gone. Be careful! If you don't want to lose the current contents of the worksheet, always be sure to use the / File Save command to save before you issue the / File Retrieve command.

Retrieving a File with a Nonstandard Extension

Retrieving a file with a nonstandard extension is a little more difficult than retrieving a file with the extension .WK1. If a file's file-name extension does not begin with the letters *WK*, 1-2-3 will not include the name of that file in the list it displays when you issue the / File Retrieve command. For this reason, you can't select a file with a nonstandard extension by pointing.

There are two ways to retrieve a file that has a nonstandard file-name extension. First, you can issue the / File Retrieve command, type the name of the file—including the file-name extension—and press [Enter]. Alternatively, you can issue the / File Retrieve command, press [Esc] to erase the descriptor **.wk?*, and type a new descriptor that tells 1-2-3 to list all the file names that contain certain characters. Then you can select the file that you wish to retrieve from this list.

For example, suppose you have saved a worksheet under the name SUMMARY.FIL. To retrieve this file, you could issue the / File Retrieve command, type *SUMMARY.FIL*, and press [Enter]. Instead of typing the file name, you could press [Esc] to erase the descriptor **.wk?*, then type the new descriptor **..fil* and press [Enter]. This descriptor tells 1-2-3 to display a list of all files that have the file-name extension .FIL. When you see this list on your screen, you can point to the name SUMMARY.FIL and press [Enter].

Loading a Worksheet from the DOS Prompt

RELEASE ► 2.2 ◄

▶1-2-3 Release 2.2 allows you to retrieve a file when you load 1-2-3. To do this, simply follow the characters *123* at the DOS prompt with a space, a hyphen, the letter w, and then the name of the worksheet file. If the file is not in the default directory (the directory whose name appears when you issue the / Worksheet Global Default Directory command), you must preface the name of the file with the path to that file. If the file has the extension .WK1, there is no need to include the extension with the file name. If the file name has a different extension, you'll need to include the extension.

> **TIP: USING WILDCARDS**
>
> You can use either of the DOS file-name wildcards—? and *—in file-name descriptors you design in 1-2-3. These wildcards have the same effect in 1-2-3 that they have in DOS. The ? character can be used in place of any one single character. The * character can be used in place of any number of characters. For example, the ? in the descriptor *.*wk?* tells 1-2-3 to display all the files with an extension that begins with the characters WK, including the extensions .WK1 and .WKS. The * in the descriptor *.*wk?* tells 1-2-3 to display a file with any name, as long as its extension begins with the characters WK.
>
> You can use these and other characters to your advantage when you retrieve files. For example, suppose you have a group of related worksheet files, the names of which begin with the letter D. To narrow the list 1-2-3 displays to include only those files, you could press [Esc] when the / File Retrieve prompt appears, then type D*.wk? and press [Enter].

For example, suppose you want to load 1-2-3 and at the same time retrieve a worksheet named TEST.WK1, which is stored in the *c:\12322\worksheets* directory. If *c:\12322\worksheets* is the default directory, you can type *123 -wtest* at the DOS prompt and then press [Enter]. If *c:\12322\worksheets* is not the default directory, you would have to type *123 -wc:\12322\worksheets\test*.

If you want to both load a worksheet and specify an alternative .SET file, you must type the names of both files. It doesn't matter which file name comes first. For example, to load 1-2-3 using a driver set file SPECIAL.SET (located in the directory that contains your 1-2-3 program files), and retrieve a worksheet named TEST.WK1 (located in the default directory), you could type either *123 special -wtest* or *123 -wtest special* at the DOS prompt.◄

Auto-Loading Worksheets

If there is a worksheet that you use nearly every time you load 1-2-3, you may want to bypass the normal / File Retrieve command by making that worksheet an Auto-Loading file. As the name implies, 1-2-3 will retrieve an auto-loading worksheet automatically each time you load 1-2-3.

To designate a worksheet as an auto-loading worksheet, just save it to the default directory under the name AUTO123. (We explain the concept of the default directory later in this chapter.) From that point on, each time you start 1-2-3, the file named AUTO123.WK1 will be loaded automatically. Instead of seeing a blank worksheet when you enter 1-2-3, you'll see the auto-load worksheet.

For example, suppose that you use the same worksheet each day for recording sales data. To save yourself a little time, you can save this worksheet under the name AUTO123.WK1 so that it will automatically be retrieved each time you start 1-2-3.

To do this, just retrieve that worksheet, issue the / File Save command, type AUTO123, and press [Enter].

You can designate only one worksheet file on a given diskette or directory as an auto-load worksheet. If you are using a floppy-disk-based computer, you can have an AUTO123 worksheet on each of several disks. 1-2-3 will retrieve the AUTO123 worksheet from the disk in the default directory (usually B:\) as it loads. If you are using a hard-disk-based computer, you can have AUTO123 worksheets on each of several subdirectories. However, 1-2-3 will always retrieve the AUTO123 worksheet from the default directory as it loads.

RELEASE ► 2.2 ◄   ►Suppose you use the techniques we explained in the previous section to retrieve a file when you load 1-2-3 Release 2.2, and you have previously designated an auto-loading worksheet. In that event, 1-2-3 will retrieve the worksheet you specified at the DOS prompt—rather than AUTO123.WK1—when it loads.◄

ERASING A FILE

The / File Erase command allows you to erase files while you're working in 1-2-3. In 1-2-3 Releases 2, 2.01, and 2.2, this command allows you to erase any type of file. (In 1-2-3 Release 1A, you can erase only worksheet, graph, and print files.)

To erase a file, you just issue the / File Erase command. Issuing this command causes 1-2-3 to display the menu shown in Figure 9-4. The options on this menu allow you to tell 1-2-3 what type of file you want to erase. You should choose the option that matches the type of file you want to erase: Worksheet for .WK1 and .WKS files, Print for .PRN files, or Graph for .PIC files. If you want to see a list of every file on the directory, choose Other. After you make a choice, 1-2-3 will display a list of all the files of the selected type on the default directory. You should select the file you want to erase (either by pointing to or typing its name) and press [Enter].

Before it erases the selected file, 1-2-3 will display a No/Yes menu and give you a chance to change your mind. To erase the selected file, choose Yes. If you're not sure, choose No, and 1-2-3 will abort the / File Erase command.

For example, suppose you want to erase the worksheet file DATA.WK1. To do this, issue the /File Erase command and choose the Worksheet option. When you make this choice, 1-2-3 will display the prompt shown in Figure 9-5 and a list of all the worksheet files in the current directory (all the files with the extension .WK1 or .WKS). To erase the file DATA.WK1, point to or type its name and press [Enter]. When you do this, 1-2-3 will display the No/Yes menu. To erase the file, choose Yes.

1-2-3 does not let you erase more than one file at a time. If you want to erase several files, you will have to issue / File Erase once for each of those files. If you want to erase a large number of files, you will probably find it better to issue the / System command and then use the DOS Erase command to erase those files.

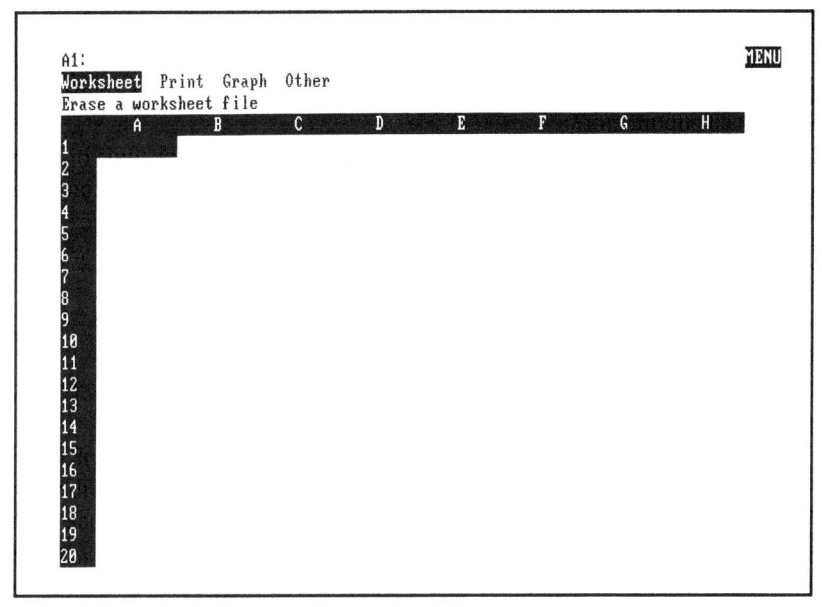

```
A1:                                                        MENU
Worksheet  Print  Graph  Other
Erase a worksheet file
          A          B          C          D          E          F          G          H
 1
 2
 3
 4
 5
 6
 7
 8
 9
10
11
12
13
14
15
16
17
18
19
20
```

FIGURE 9-4: The / File Erase menu

```
K31: @SUM(K30..K4)                                                             FILES
Enter name of file to erase: C:\123\*.wk?
ACCT#1.WK1      ACCT#2.WK1      CASH.WK1        DAILY.WK1       DATA.WK1
          A          B          C          D          E          F          G
 1  ================================================================================
 2  XYZ CORP. EXPENSE PROJECTION
 3  OPERATING EXPENSES                         JUNE       JULY        AUG       SEPT
 4  ----------------------------------        ------     ------     ------     ------
 5  SALARIES                                 $19,917    $18,993    $17,601    $19,561
 6  BONUS                                                $5,000
 7  CONTRACT LABOR                              $423       $145     $1,294       $971
 8  PAYROLL TAXES                             $1,400     $1,746     $1,256     $1,373
 9  GROUP MEDICAL INS                           $933       $933       $964       $791
10  FUTA, SUTA, WORKMEN'S COMP                  $698       $994
11  LIFE INSURANCE                              $124                  $114
12  LIABILITY INSURANCE                         $346
13  OFFICE LEASE                              $3,125     $3,125     $3,125     $3,699
14  EQUIPMENT LEASE                             $168       $936        $85       $148
15  TELEPHONE                                 $1,040     $1,600       $874     $1,153
16  SHIPPING & DELIVERIES                       $247       $355       $415       $410
          D          E          F          G          H          I          J          K
30  ------     ------     ------     ------     ------     ------     ------     ------
31 $29,100    $35,041    $28,277    $30,636    $33,983    $38,033    $41,312    $40,952
32  ======     ======     ======     ======     ======     ======     ======     ======
```

FIGURE 9-5: The / File Erase prompt

TIP: VIEWING FILE NAMES

When you execute most of the File commands (including Save, Retrieve, Combine, Erase, and Import), 1-2-3 will present a list of the worksheet files that are stored in the default directory. This list appears in the second line of the control panel at the top of your screen. For example, when you issue the / File Retrieve command, 1-2-3 will display a list like the one in Figure 9-3.

You can see only five names at a time in any of these file lists. To view the names of other files, you must use the →, ←, [End], [Home], [Pg Up], [Pg Dn], [Ctrl]→ and [Ctrl]← keys to move through the list. Pressing → will move the highlight one name to the right, and pressing ← will move it one name to the left. Pressing [End] will move the highlight to the last name in the list, and pressing [Home] will move it to the first name. Pressing either [Pg Dn] or [Ctrl]→ will move the highlight to the right by five names, while pressing [Pg Up] or [Ctrl]← will move it to the left five names.

If the current directory contains a large number of files, it may take a long time for you to scroll through the list and find a particular file. Fortunately, there is an easier way. If you press the [Name] key ([F3] on the IBM PC) while the list of files is displayed in your control panel, 1-2-3 will display a full-screen view of the list, like the one shown in Figure A. You can use the arrow keys to point to different files in this list, and press [Enter] to select a file. To return to the worksheet after viewing the full-screen list, just press the [Name] key again. (Release 1A does not have this capability.)

```
A1:                                                              FILES
Name of file to retrieve: C:\123\*.wk?
          ACCT#1.WK1      07/31/89        22:57         9153
ACCT#1.WK1        ACCT#2.WK1      CASH.WK1        DAILY.WK1     DATA.WK1
HALFYEAR.WK1
```

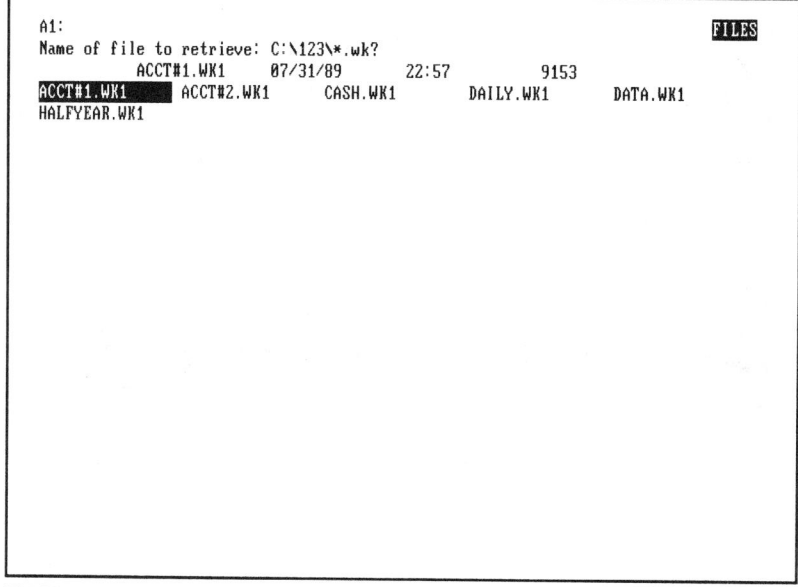

FIGURE A: A full-screen view of a list of files

CHANGING THE DIRECTORY

When you issue a File command, 1-2-3 assumes that you want that command to apply to one or more files on the default directory. If you want to work with files on a directory other than the default, you'll need to change the directory.

You can change the default directory in one of three ways. First, you can change the directory after you have issued a File command. This kind of change remains in effect only until the command is completed. Second, you can use the / File Directory command to change the directory for the duration of a 1-2-3 session. Third, you can use the / Worksheet Global Default Directory and Update commands to make a permanent change to the current directory. Let's look at each of these options in more detail.

Changing the Directory During Command Execution

When you issue a File command, 1-2-3 will present a prompt like *Enter name of file to save:* or *Name of file to retrieve:*, followed by the name of the default directory and a file-name descriptor like *.wk? or *.wk1. In addition, 1-2-3 will display a list of the files on the default directory of the type specified by the descriptor. If you want to work with the files on the default directory, you're in great shape. But if you want to work with the files on another directory, you'll have to change the directory before you continue with the command. There are two ways to do this.

Pressing [Esc]

To change the directory during the execution of a File command, you can press the [Esc] key twice after you issue the command to erase the descriptor and the name of the default directory. Then you can type the new directory name (including the drive name, the path, and the directory name, if applicable) and press [Enter]. When you press [Enter], 1-2-3 will display the descriptor and, after a moment, a list of the files of the specified type in the new directory. You can complete the command in the usual way.

For example, suppose the current drive/directory is B:\ and you would like to retrieve a file from the diskette in the A: drive. To begin, issue the / File Retrieve command, and then press [Esc] twice. The first time you press [Esc], 1-2-3 will erase the descriptor *.wk?. Pressing [Esc] again will erase the directory name *B:*. Now, type the name of the drive and directory that contains the file you want to retrieve, A:\, and press [Enter]. When you press [Enter], 1-2-3 will automatically display the descriptor *.wk?* along with a list of all the worksheet files on the diskette in the A:\ directory. You can select the file you want to retrieve by pointing to its name and pressing [Enter].

Similarly, suppose that the current directory is C:\123\Data and you would like to erase a worksheet file stored on the directory C:\123\Budgets. To erase this worksheet, first issue the / File Erase Worksheet command, then press [Esc] twice to erase the descriptor *.wk?* and the directory designation. Next, type the full name of the directory that contains the file you want to erase—in this example, C:\123\Budgets\—

and press [Enter]. When you do this, 1-2-3 will automatically display the descriptor *.wk? and a list of all of the .WK1 and .WKS files on the directory C:\123\Budgets. You can select the file you want to erase by pointing to its name and pressing [Enter].

If you want to use this technique to save a file that you have saved previously to a different directory, you'll need to press [Esc] three times instead of twice. Remember—when you issue the / File Save command to save a file that you have previously saved, 1-2-3 will display the name of the file in the / File Save prompt. The first time you press [Esc], 1-2-3 will replace the file name with the descriptor *.wkl. Pressing [Esc] again erases this descriptor, and pressing it a third time erases the directory name.

An Alternative Approach

If you have organized your 1-2-3 files in subdirectories, there is a more efficient way to access a different directory during the execution of a File command. As we have said, when you issue a file command, 1-2-3 will display a list of all of the files with the extension .WK1 or .WKS. If there are one or more subdirectories beneath the default directory, this list will also include the names of those subdirectories. To change the current directory to one of those subdirectories, you need only point to its name and press [Enter]. 1-2-3 will then display a list of all the files in that subdirectory.

Similarly, you can press the [Backspace] key when the file list is in view to jump to the next highest directory. When you do this, you will see a list of the files that are stored in that directory. Each time you press [Backspace], you will jump up another level in the directory path and see a different list of files until you are viewing the files on the root directory.

As you move up and down the hierarchical directory paths, you can select a file from any directory and then complete the / File command.

An Example

To demonstrate how this procedure works, consider this example: Suppose that you have organized your 1-2-3 worksheet files into two subdirectories named *C:\123\FINANCLS\STATMNTS* and *C:\123\FINANCLS\RECORDS*. As you can see, Figure 9-6 depicts the structure of these directories and the names of some of the files stored in each subdirectory.

Now, suppose that the default directory is *C:\123\FINANCLS\RECORDS*, and that you want to retrieve a file that is named APR_BAL from the directory *C:\123\FINANCLS\STATMNTS*. To begin, issue the / File Retrieve command. In response to this command, 1-2-3 will display the prompt shown in Figure 9-7. Notice that the prompt includes the name of the default directory, *C:\123\FINANCLS\RECORDS*, and that 1-2-3 is displaying a list of the worksheet files on that directory.

Next, press the [Backspace] key to jump into the FINANCLS directory. At this point, the control panel will look like Figure 9-8. Notice that the prompt now includes the name of the directory *C:\123\FINANCLS* and that the list has changed to include the .WK1 files in that directory.

Chapter 9: File Management 353

The last two items in the file list in Figure 9-8 are the subdirectories STATMNTS and RECORDS. Notice that the names of these subdirectories end with backslashes (\); 1-2-3 always marks directory names in this way so that you can distinguish the directory names from the file names.

Since you want to retrieve a file from the STATMNTS subdirectory, you should point to that name and press [Enter]. When you do this, the prompt will include the directory name *C:\123\FINANCLS\STATMNTS*, and 1-2-3 will display a list of the .WK1 files on that directory, as shown in Figure 9-9.

Now, to select the APR_BAL file, just point to its name in the list and press [Enter]. Immediately, 1-2-3 will retrieve that file.

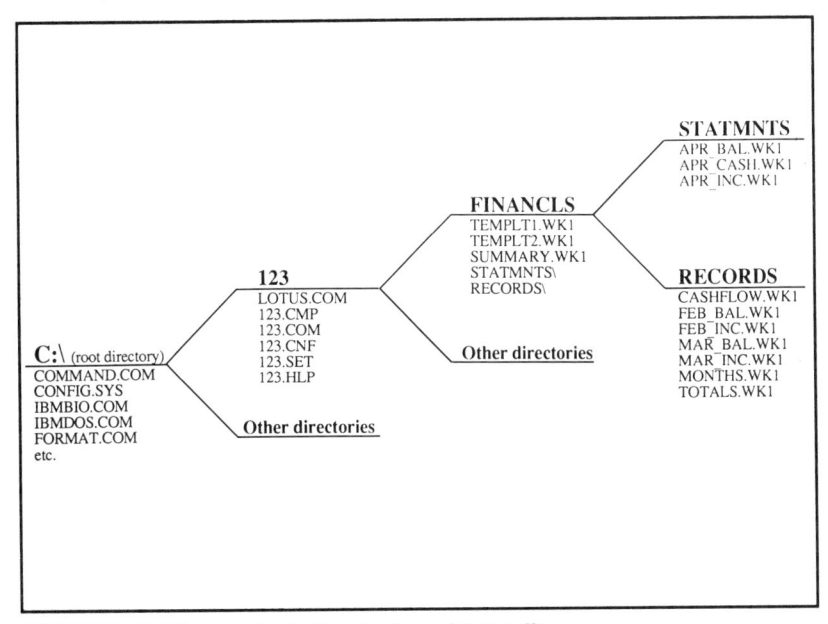

```
                                              STATMNTS\
                                              APR_BAL.WK1
                                              APR_CASH.WK1
                            FINANCLS          APR_INC.WK1
                            TEMPLT1.WK1
                            TEMPLT2.WK1
                            SUMMARY.WK1
              123           STATMNTS\         RECORDS\
              LOTUS.COM     RECORDS\          CASHFLOW.WK1
              123.CMP                         FEB_BAL.WK1
              123.COM                         FEB_INC.WK1
              123.CNF       Other directories MAR_BAL.WK1
C:\ (root directory)
              123.SET                         MAR_INC.WK1
COMMAND.COM   123.HLP                         MONTHS.WK1
CONFIG.SYS                                    TOTALS.WK1
IBMBIO.COM
IBMDOS.COM    Other directories
FORMAT.COM
etc.
```

FIGURE 9-6: Hierarchical directories of 1-2-3 files

```
A1:                                                        FILES
Name of file to retrieve: C:\123\FINANCLS\RECORDS\*.wk?
CASHFLOW.WK1   FEB BAL.WK1   FEB INC.WK1   MAR BAL.WK1   MAR INC.WK1
```

FIGURE 9-7: File Retrieve prompt in RECORDS subdirectory

```
A1:                                                        FILES
Name of file to retrieve: C:\123\FINANCLS\*.wk?
SUMMARY.WK1    TEMPLT1.WK1   TEMPLT2.WK1   RECORDS\      STATMNTS\
```

FIGURE 9-8: File Retrieve prompt after backing into FINANCLS directory

```
A1:
Name of file to retrieve: C:\123\FINANCLS\STATMNTS\*.wk?                    FILES
APR_BAL.WK1      APR_CASH.WK1     APR_INC.WK1
```

FIGURE 9-9: File Retrieve prompt after selecting the STATMNTS subdirectory

When This Technique Won't Work

By following a similar procedure, you can use any other File command to operate on files in a directory other than the default directory. However, there are a few instances when the technique we have described will not work. First, there must be at least one worksheet file in the default directory *or* at least one subdirectory beneath the default directory in order to use this technique. If the default directory is empty, pressing [Backspace] after you issue a File command will simply delete letters in the prompt line at the top of your screen. If the File command you are using requires you to specify a type of file—as do the /File Erase and /File List commands—then there must be one file of the type you select in the default directory, or a subdirectory beneath that directory, to use this technique.

Using this technique is also a bit tricky when you are saving a file you have saved before. If you want to use this technique to change the directory while you are saving a file you have saved before, you must press [Esc] once after you issue the /File Save command to delete the name of the file from the prompt line. Then, you can press [Backspace] to back up the directory hierarchy or choose a subdirectory from the list.

The Change Is Temporary

When you use either of these techniques to change the directory while you're in the midst of a File command, the directory will revert to the default as soon as the command is completed. In the previous example after the file APR_BAL is loaded, the directory will become C:\123\FINANCLS\RECORDS once again.

However, when you save a worksheet that you have retrieved from a directory other than the default, 1-2-3 will assume that you want to save that worksheet onto the directory from which it was retrieved. When you save the file APR_BAL, for example, 1-2-3 will try to save it in the C:\123\FINANCLS\STATMNTS directory, rather than saving it in the default directory. If you want to save it in the current subdirectory, just press [Esc] once, then type the name you wish to save it under, and press [Enter].

Changing the Default Directory Temporarily

If you plan to work with the files on one particular directory during an entire 1-2-3 session, you will probably want to make that directory the default directory. You can use the /File Directory command to change the default directory for the duration of the current 1-2-3 session.

For example, suppose that the default directory is C:\123\FINANCLS and you want to change it to C:\123\EMPLYEES for the duration of the current session. To make this change, issue the /File Directory command, then type C:\123\EMPLYEES, and press [Enter]. You don't have to press [Esc] or [Backspace] to erase the name of the current default; 1-2-3 will erase the name of the current directory as soon as you begin typing. Interestingly, though, you cannot edit the name of the current default directory as you are specifying the name of the new directory. You must type the full name of the directory.

Once you have used the /File Directory command to change the default directory, 1-2-3 will assume that you want to work with the files on the new default directory whenever you issue a File command. For example, if you issue the /File Retrieve command after changing the default directory from C:\123\FINANCLS to C:\123\EMPLYEES, 1-2-3 will display the prompt

Name of file to retrieve: C:\123\EMPLYEES*.wk?

along with a list of the files on the directory C:\123\EMPLYEES.

The new default will remain in effect for the duration of the current session (or until you use the /File Directory command to change it again). When you exit from 1-2-3, your change will be lost. The next time you load 1-2-3, the default directory will revert to its original setting.

Changing the Default Directory Permanently

To make a permanent change to the default directory, just specify a new default and then save that default to the disk. You can use the / Worksheet Global Default Directory command to change the default directory and the / Worksheet Global Default Update command to save the change.

For example, suppose that you would like to change the default directory from A:\ (1-2-3's initial default) to C:\123. To do this, issue the / Worksheet Global Default Directory command. This will bring up the prompt *Enter default directory: A:*. You must press [Esc] or use the [Backspace] key to delete the initial default, then type the new default directory C:\123 and press [Enter].

If you do nothing else at this point, the effect is the same as if you had issued the / File Directory command: The new default will remain in effect for the current 1-2-3 session only. To make the change permanent, you must choose Update from the Global Default menu. (If you have quit from the menu structure, you must issue the / Worksheet Global Default Update command.) 1-2-3 will then write the new directory specification to the 1-2-3.CNF file. (If you're using a floppy-disk system, be sure your 1-2-3 system disk is in the A drive before choosing Update.)

Once you have used Update to save the new default directory, it will remain in effect until you use the / Worksheet Global Default Directory and the Update commands to change it. Each time you load 1-2-3, it will read the new default directory specification from the 123.CNF file.

PASSWORD PROTECTING A WORKSHEET

In 1-2-3 Releases 2, 2.01, and 2.2 you can assign a password to a worksheet. Once you have assigned a password to a worksheet, 1-2-3 will not allow you to retrieve that worksheet (or combine it into another worksheet) until you supply that password. (You cannot password protect files in Release 1A.)

If you want to password-protect a worksheet, you must give that worksheet a password as you save it. After you issue the /File Save command and specify the name for the worksheet file, you press [Spacebar], type a *p*, and press [Enter]. When you do this, 1-2-3 will display the prompt *Enter password:*. You should type your password, which can be up to 15 characters long, and press [Enter].

After you press [Enter] to enter the password, 1-2-3 will display the prompt *Verify password:*. You should type your password again, exactly as you entered it the first time, and press [Enter] again. If the two passwords match, 1-2-3 will save your worksheet to disk in password-protected form. If the two passwords are not identical, then 1-2-3 will beep and display the error message, *Passwords do not match*. If you see this message, you'll have to press [Esc] and start the /File Save command again.

To retrieve a password-protected worksheet, you issue the /File Retrieve command as usual and point to or type the name of the file you want to retrieve. Immediately, your screen will go blank except for a prompt that says *Enter password:*. You should type the name of the password that protects that file and press [Enter]. If you type the password correctly, 1-2-3 will retrieve the file. Otherwise, 1-2-3 will abort the /File Retrieve command.

An Example

For example, suppose you want to assign the password *MyName* to the current worksheet as you save it into the file RATINGS. To do this, issue the /File Save command, type RATINGS p, and press [Enter]. When 1-2-3 prompts you to supply the password, type MyName and press [Enter] again. Then, in response to 1-2-3's second prompt, type MyName again and press [Enter] one more time. Provided that you type the password correctly both times, 1-2-3 will save the worksheet with the password MyName.

Now suppose that you want to retrieve the file RATINGS. To do this, issue the /File Retrieve command, either type RATINGS or point to the name RATINGS.WK1 in 1-2-3's list of files, and press [Enter]. When 1-2-3 prompts you to supply the password, type MyName and press [Enter]. Provided that you type the password correctly, 1-2-3 will retrieve the worksheet RATINGS.

Notes

Whenever you type a password in response to one of 1-2-3's prompts, 1-2-3 will not display the characters you type on the screen. Instead, it will display a rectangular block in place of each character. For example, Figure 9-10 shows the screen as it would look after you entered the password MyName. 1-2-3 does this to prevent someone who might be peeking over your shoulder from reading a worksheet's password off the screen.

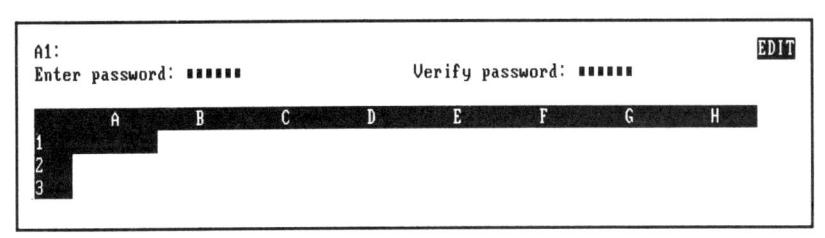

```
A1:                                                              EDIT
Enter password: ■■■■■■        Verify password: ■■■■■■
        A       B       C       D       E       F       G       H
1
2
3
```

FIGURE 9-10: The password prompt

If you mistype a character while you are entering a password, you can press the [Backspace] key to erase the mistake and then retype the character correctly. If you want to erase everything you've typed and start over, you can press [Esc].

When you are retrieving a password-protected file, you must type the password exactly as it has been defined. Every detail, including case, counts. For example, to retrieve the password-protected file RATINGS, you must type MyName exactly—not myname, Myname, or MYNAME.

To see why 1-2-3 asks you to verify the password you have assigned to a worksheet before it saves that worksheet, consider the following situation. You want to save a worksheet with the password PIPERCUB. Instead of typing PIPERCUB, however, you type PIPRECUB. If 1-2-3 saved the worksheet at this point, you might never be able to retrieve it. At best, you'd have to make a number of guesses at the password before you would be able to retrieve it. Because 1-2-3 asks you to verify the password, however, the chances are good that your error will be caught before the file is saved.

You can assign a password to a worksheet any time you save that worksheet—not just the first time you save it. For example, suppose that you have previously saved a worksheet named BUDGET without a password and that now you want to save the worksheet with the password Snowbird. When you issue the / File Save command, 1-2-3 will display the name under which you previously saved the worksheet, BUDGET.WK1, in the control panel. When you see the name, just press [Spacebar], type a p, and press [Enter]. 1-2-3 will ask you to enter and verify a password as we described above, and then it will save the file in password-protected form. The password-protected file will replace your original file of the same name.

We recommend that you use password protection very carefully. Once you password-protect a worksheet file, there is no way to retrieve that file without the password. Furthermore, 1-2-3 encrypts the data in the file so that you cannot use a special utility program to recover the data or search for the password. If you decide to use password protection, you should keep a written copy of the password so that you won't lose access to the file should you forget your password.

THE / FILE XTRACT COMMAND

1-2-3 offers a command—/ File Xtract—that allows you to save a range from the current worksheet into a separate worksheet file. The portion of the worksheet that you extract can be as small as a single cell or as large as the entire worksheet. Once you have extracted a range from a worksheet into a separate file, you can retrieve that file just as you would any other worksheet file or combine it into another worksheet. The / File Xtract command comes in handy when you need to break a large worksheet into smaller pieces or when you need to extract a range that contains some important information from one worksheet so that you can combine it into another worksheet.

Extract Basics

When you issue the / File Xtract command, 1-2-3 will present a menu with two options: Formulas and Values. The choice you make from this menu determines how 1-2-3 will treat the formulas in the range you select to extract. If you choose Formulas, 1-2-3 will save all the formulas in the range you extract as formulas. If you choose Values, on the other hand, 1-2-3 will save only the current results of the formulas in the extract range, and not the formulas themselves.

The option you choose depends on the nature of the range you plan to extract. If the range contains no formulas, you can choose either option with the same result. If the range includes formulas and all of the cells that are referred to by those formulas, you will probably want to choose Formulas. On the other hand, if the range includes formulas but does not include all of the cells those formulas refer to, you will probably want to choose the Values option. As you'll see, if the range includes formulas but does not include all of the cells those formulas refer to, choosing Formulas can create some problems for 1-2-3.

After you choose Formulas or Values, 1-2-3 will prompt you to supply a name for the file that will hold the extract range (the extract file) and will display a list of all the worksheet files in the current directory. You can either choose one of these existing names for the extract file or you can enter a new name. After you supply a file name, 1-2-3 will prompt you to enter the range of cells that you want to extract. (We will call this the extract range.) You can either point to the range in your worksheet or type the range coordinates.

Provided that you have selected a unique file name for the extracted file (and you usually will), 1-2-3 will then create the extract file and will store your extracted information in that file. ▶As you might expect, if you choose to save your extracted worksheet under the name of an existing file, 1-2-3 Release 2.2 will display a menu with three options: Cancel, Replace, and Backup. (Earlier versions of 1-2-3 offer only two options: Cancel and Replace.)◀ If you choose Replace, 1-2-3 will replace the existing file with the extracted worksheet. If you choose Cancel, the / File Xtract command will be aborted and 1-2-3 will return to the READY mode. ▶If you choose Backup, 1-2-3 will change the extension of the existing file to .BAK before extracting the new file. That way, both the old file and the new one will still exist.◀

The Formulas Option

The / File Xtract Formulas command causes 1-2-3 to save the formulas in the extract range as formulas. You can use this option when you want the extract file to have the same "dynamic" nature as the original worksheet. However, if the range includes formulas but does not include all of the cells those formulas refer to, choosing Formulas can lead to problems.

An Example

Consider the worksheet in Figure 9-11, which computes the sales commissions earned by two people, Jane Row and John Doe. Each one of the cells in column F in this worksheet contains a formula that computes a portion of the commission for one of the salespeople.

Suppose you want to extract the range A3..F10, which contains the commission computation for Jane Row, into a separate worksheet. You want the formulas in this range to be saved as formulas. To begin, issue the / File Xtract command. When you do this, 1-2-3 will present the Formulas/Values menu. Since you want 1-2-3 to extract the formulas in column F—and not just the current values of those formulas—into the new worksheet, you should choose Formulas. Since the range A3..F10 contains all of the cells that are referred to by the formulas in cells F6, F7, F8, F9, and F10, choosing Formulas will not cause 1-2-3 any problems.

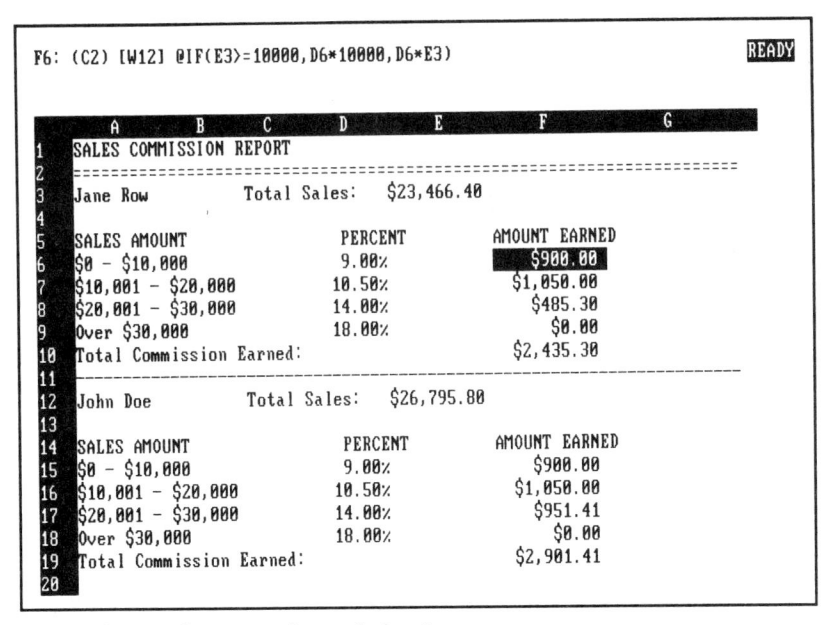

FIGURE 9-11: An example worksheet

Next, 1-2-3 will prompt you to supply a name for the extract file. You should type a new file name, such as JANEROW, and press [Enter]. When 1-2-3 prompts you to define the extract range, select the range A3..F10. When you press [Enter], 1-2-3 will extract the contents of the range A3..F10 in the file JANEROW.WK1.

Now suppose that you want to retrieve the file JANEROW. To do this, issue the / File Retrieve command, choose the file JANEROW from 1-2-3's list, and press [Enter]. Figure 9-12 shows the resulting worksheet.

Notice in Figure 9-12 that the range we extracted—which was the range A3..F10 in the original worksheet—appears in the upper-left corner of the new worksheet file. For example, the entry *Jane Row*, which was in cell A3 of our original worksheet, appears in cell A1 of the extract worksheet. Whenever you extract a range, the upper-left cell in the extract range will always be placed in cell A1 of the extract worksheet.

Because we selected the Formulas option, 1-2-3 has saved the formulas from the range F6..F10 in Figure 9-11 into the extract file. However, 1-2-3 has adjusted these formulas to account for their new position in the extract file. For example, in our original worksheet, cell F6 contains the formula

F6: @IF(E3>=10000,D6*10000,D6*E3)

In the extract file, this formula appears in cell F4 and has been changed to

F4: @IF(E1>=10000,D4*10000,D4*E1)

Both formulas return exactly the same result. Whenever you extract a range that includes formulas, 1-2-3 will adjust those formulas to reflect their new position in the extract file.

```
F4: (C2) [W12] @IF(E1)=10000,D4*10000,D4*E1)                         READY

          A         B         C         D         E         F         G
    1  Jane Row          Total Sales:     $23,466.40
    2
    3  SALES AMOUNT                PERCENT           AMOUNT EARNED
    4  $0 - $10,000                 9.00%              $900.00
    5  $10,001 - $20,000           10.50%            $1,050.00
    6  $20,001 - $30,000           14.00%              $485.30
    7  Over $30,000                18.00%                $0.00
    8  Total Commission Earned:                      $2,435.30
```

FIGURE 9-12: The extract worksheet

Also notice that the entries in the worksheet in Figure 9-12 have the same format and alignment as the entries in the extract range in Figure 9-11. When you extract a range from a worksheet, the cells in the extracted worksheet will have the same format and other attributes they had in the original worksheet.

When Formulas Won't Work

In the first example, we chose the Formulas option from the Formulas/Values menu. Because the extract range included all of the cells referred to by the formulas in the extract range, choosing Formulas created no problems for 1-2-3.

If, on the other hand, the extract range includes formulas that refer to cells outside of that range, you may run into problems if you choose Formulas. For one thing, since some of the values on which the formulas depend are not included in the extract range, the value of the formulas will be altered. In addition, because 1-2-3 adjusts the references in the formulas in the extract range, some of the formulas may be rather dramatically altered by the extraction. You might even end up with bizarre references to cells like IV8190 or IU1.

The Values Options

If you want to avoid these problems, you should use the Values option. Choosing the Values option causes 1-2-3 to save only the current values of the formulas in the extract range into the extract file.

For example, let's see what happens if we use this option to extract the range F15..F19 from Figure 9-11. To do this, issue the / File Xtract Values command, supply a name for the extract file (we'll use COMMIS2), select the range F15..F19, and press [Enter]. When the range has been extracted, use / File Retrieve to load the file COMMIS2 into the worksheet. Figure 9-13 shows the result.

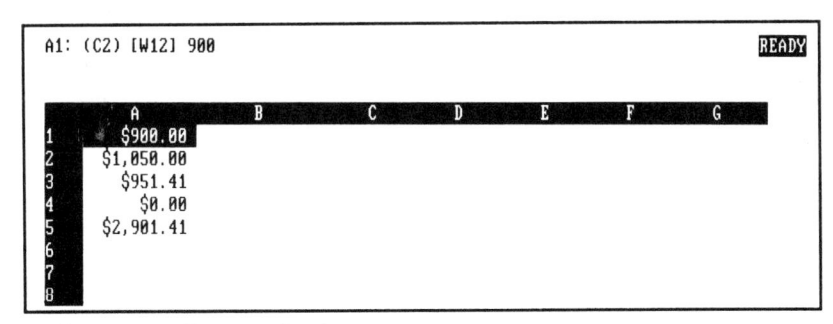

```
A1: (C2) [W12] 900                                              READY

          A          B         C         D         E         F         G
   1    $900.00
   2  $1,050.00
   3    $951.41
   4      $0.00
   5  $2,901.41
   6
   7
   8
```

FIGURE 9-13: Extracted values

Notice that the values in the range A1..A5 of Figure 9-13 are identical to those in the range F15..F19 in Figure 9-11. When 1-2-3 extracted the range F15..F19 from the worksheet in Figure 9-11, it saved only the current values of the formulas in that range, and not the formulas themselves, into the extract file. For example, cell A1 in Figure 9-13 contains the simple value 900. Because the entries in the COMMIS2 file are simple values and not formulas, it makes no difference that the cells to which the original formulas referred are not included in that file.

There are a couple of important points to keep in mind when you use the / File Xtract Values command. First, 1-2-3 does not recalculate the worksheet before it saves the contents of the extract range into the extract file. It simply saves the current results of the formulas in the extract range into the file. If the worksheet has not been recalculated, it is possible that the values in the extract file will not be up to date. Second, realize that there is no link between the entries in the extract file and the entries in the original worksheet. If you make changes to the values in the original worksheet, those changes will not be passed along to the extract file. If you want to update the extract file, you'll have to reissue the / File Xtract Values command.

COMBINING WORKSHEETS

The / File Combine command lets you combine all or part of the contents of a worksheet file into the current worksheet. Like / File Retrieve, / File Combine causes 1-2-3 to retrieve the contents of a worksheet file. Unlike / File Retrieve, however, which erases the contents of the current worksheet before loading the file you have selected, the / File Combine command combines the contents of the file you select into the current worksheet. This means that you can use the / File Combine command to consolidate information from two or more worksheet files into a single summary worksheet or to transfer data from one worksheet to another. There are several different ways to combine worksheets, each of which yields significantly different results. We'll discuss each of these methods separately. First, however, let's consider a few basic concepts.

Basics

When you issue the / File Combine command, 1-2-3 will display the menu shown in Figure 9-14. The options on this menu—Copy, Add, and Subtract—determine how 1-2-3 will combine the entries from a worksheet file into the current worksheet. If you choose Copy, 1-2-3 will simply load the entries from the file you select into the worksheet. If an entry in the file happens to fall on top of an entry in the worksheet, it will replace the entry in the worksheet.

The Add and Subtract options allow you to add the values in a worksheet file to, or subtract those values from, the values in the current worksheet. If a value from the file you are combining falls on top of a value in the worksheet, 1-2-3 will add or subtract those two values. The Add and Subtract options let you consolidate information in two or more worksheets into a single worksheet.

After you make a choice from the Copy/Add/Subtract menu, 1-2-3 will present a menu with two options: Entire-File and Named/Specified-Range. These options allow you to tell 1-2-3 how much of the worksheet file should be brought into the current worksheet. Choosing Entire-File tells 1-2-3 to combine all of the entries from the worksheet file into the worksheet. Choosing Named/Specified-Range tells 1-2-3 to combine only the entries in a range of the worksheet file. The range can be as small as a single cell or as large as an entire worksheet (although it is far more likely to be small). If you choose the Named/Specified-Range option, 1-2-3 will prompt you for the coordinates or name of the range.

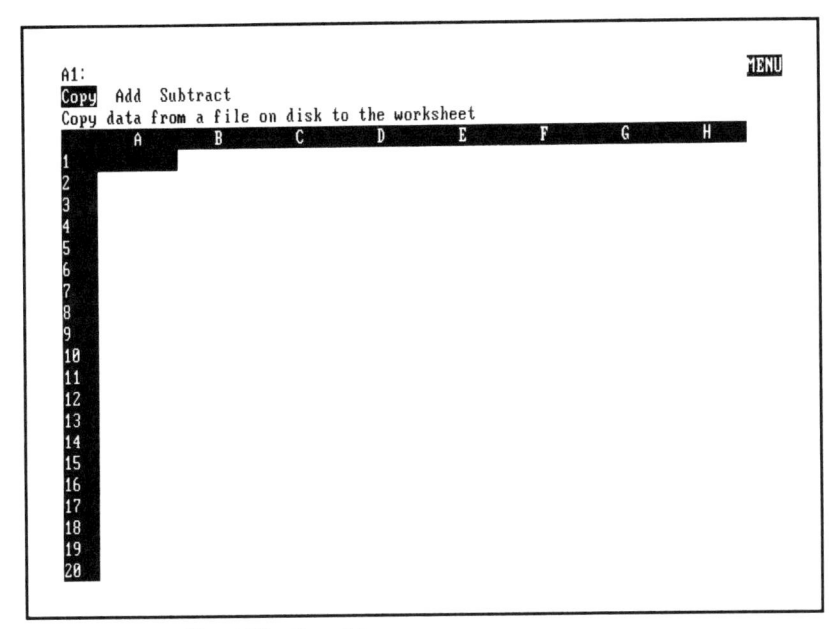

```
A1:                                                    MENU
Copy  Add  Subtract
Copy data from a file on disk to the worksheet
         A      B      C      D      E      F      G      H
1
2
3
4
5
6
7
8
9
10
11
12
13
14
15
16
17
18
19
20
```

FIGURE 9-14: The / File Combine menu

After you make your choice from the Entire-File/Named/Specified-Range menu, 1-2-3 will display the prompt *Enter name of file to combine: *.wk?*, along with a list of all the worksheet files in the current directory. You should point to or type the name of the file you want to combine. Once you select a name, 1-2-3 will combine the contents of that file into the current worksheet.

No matter which of the / File Combine options you select, 1-2-3 will always combine the contents of the worksheet file (or the selected portion of that file) into the current worksheet at the position of the cell pointer. That is, the contents of the upper-left cell in the worksheet file (or the selected range of that file) will be combined into the cell that contains the cell pointer. The contents of the other cells in the worksheet file will be combined into the cells below and to the right of the cell that contains the cell pointer. As a rule, then, you must be very careful to position the cell pointer properly before you issue the / File Combine command.

The Copy Option

The / File Combine Copy command allows you to copy the contents of a worksheet file into the current worksheet. This option is often used to transfer information from one worksheet to another.

An Example

For example, Figures 9-15 and 9-16 show two simple worksheets that summarize the sales by product for two different accounts. The first worksheet is saved in a file named

ACCT#1, and the second is saved in a file named ACCT#2. Suppose you want to combine the information from both the ACCT#1 and ACCT#2 worksheets into a single worksheet.

To begin, you must retrieve one of the worksheet files (we will use the file ACCT#1). To do this, issue the / File Retrieve command, select the file name ACCT#1, and press [Enter]. Next, move the cell pointer to the upper-left cell of the range where you want the combined worksheet to appear (we will use cell A11).

```
A11: [W13]                                                    READY

         A           B          C          D          E
 1  APRIL SALES FOR ACCOUNT #1
 2  ==========================================================
 3     Product   Unit Price Units Sold  Dollars
 4  Bats          $24.50        50      $1,225
 5  Balls          $4.28       120        $514
 6  Mitts         $34.50        20        $690
 7                                      ------    ------
 8  Totals                       190     $2,429
 9
10
11
```

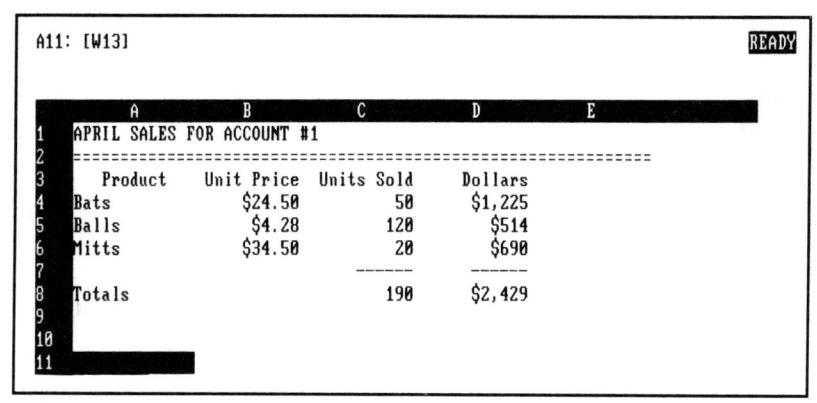

FIGURE 9-15: An example worksheet

```
D8: (C0) @SUM(D4..D6)                                         READY

         A           B          C          D          E       F
 1  APRIL SALES FOR ACCOUNT #2
 2  ==========================================================
 3     Product   Unit Price Units Sold  Dollars
 4  Bats          $24.50        44      $1,078
 5  Balls          $4.28       124        $531
 6  Mitts         $34.50        24        $828
 7                                      ------    ------
 8  Totals                       192     $2,437
 9
10
11
```

FIGURE 9-16: An example worksheet

Once you have positioned the cell pointer, issue the / File Combine Copy command. Since you want to combine the entire contents of ACCT#2 into ACCT#1, when 1-2-3 displays the Entire-File/Named/Specified-Range menu, you should choose Entire-File. Continuing with our example, you should choose the file ACCT#2 and press [Enter]. Immediately, 1-2-3 will read the file from disk and copy its contents in the current worksheet. The result will look like Figure 9-17.

```
D18: (C0) @SUM(D14..D16)                                    READY

        A           B          C           D         E
 1  APRIL SALES FOR ACCOUNT #1
 2  ========================================================
 3      Product   Unit Price  Units Sold   Dollars
 4  Bats          $24.50          50       $1,225
 5  Balls          $4.28         120         $514
 6  Mitts         $34.50          20         $690
 7                                        -------
 8  Totals                        190      $2,429
 9
10
11  APRIL SALES FOR ACCOUNT #2
12  ========================================================
13      Product   Unit Price  Units Sold   Dollars
14  Bats          $24.50          44       $1,078
15  Balls          $4.28         124         $531
16  Mitts         $34.50          24         $828
17                             -------    -------
18  Totals                        192      $2,437
19
20
```

FIGURE 9-17: Two files combined in one worksheet

Notes on / File Combine Copy

Notice in Figure 9-17 that the entries we combined into the worksheet retain their formats and, in the case of labels, their alignment. Whenever you use the / File Combine Copy command, 1-2-3 will combine the formats and label prefixes of the cells in the worksheet file as well as the entries in those cells.

If you move the cell pointer to cell C18 or cell D18, you'll see that they contain @SUM formulas like the ones in cells C8 and D8 in Figure 9-16. For example, the function in cell D8 in Figure 9-16 is *@SUM(D4..D6)*. The function in cell D18 in Figure 9-17 is *@SUM(D14..D16)*. The difference between the two formulas is accounted for by their positions. When you use the / File Combine Copy command, 1-2-3 always copies the formulas from the file you specify into the current worksheet and adjusts the cell references in those formulas to reflect their new position in the worksheet.

In the example, the area into which we combined the file was blank. If the area of the worksheet into which the file will be combined contains entries, then the entries in the file will overwrite the entries in the worksheet. For this reason, before you use the / File Combine Copy command, you must be sure that there is plenty of blank space to the right of and below the cell pointer. There is one exception to this rule. If the file contains blank cells, these will *not* overwrite existing cell entries.

If you would like to keep a permanent copy of your combined worksheet, then you should save it to disk. You may want to save it under a new name, such as COMBSLS, so that you don't overwrite the original files ACCT#1 and ACCT#2.

The Add and Subtract Options

When you issue the /File Combine Add command, 1-2-3 will add the values from the file you specify to the corresponding values in the current worksheet. Similarly, if you choose the Subtract option, 1-2-3 will subtract the values in the worksheet file from the corresponding values in the current worksheet. These options make it possible to consolidate and deconsolidate the information in different worksheets.

The Add Option

The /File Combine Add command allows you to add the values in a worksheet file to the values in the corresponding cells of the worksheet. You can use this option to consolidate the values in two or more different worksheets.

An Example

For example, Figures 9-18 and 9-19 show the sales reports for two salesmen. In each of these worksheets, cells B6, B7, and B8 contain the number of units sold for a particular product, and cell B10 contains the function *@SUM(B6..B8)*, which computes the total number of units sold. We have saved these worksheets in files named STEVE and TOM.

Suppose you want to total the sales for these two salesmen in a single worksheet. First, create a "form" worksheet like the one shown in Figure 9-20. As you can see, this form worksheet has the same layout as the individual worksheets in Figures 9-18 and 9-19. You'll use this worksheet as a base for consolidating the worksheets STEVE and TOM. As in the worksheets STEVE and TOM, cell B10 in the form worksheet contains the formula @SUM(B6..B8). Because cells B6, B7, and B8 are blank, this formula initially returns the value 0.

Once you have created the worksheet form, move the cell pointer to cell A1 and issue the /File Combine Add command. Next, choose Entire-File, select the file named STEVE from 1-2-3's list, and press [Enter]. Figure 9-21 shows the result. Notice that the values from the range B6..B8 in STEVE have been combined into the range B6..B8 in the form worksheet. Next, issue the /File Combine Add Entire-File command again, select the file named TOM, and press [Enter]. Figure 9-22 shows the result.

As you can see, 1-2-3 has added the numbers in the range B6..B8 of the worksheet TOM to the values in the range B6..B8 in the form worksheet. The values in cells B6, B7, and B8 in Figure 9-22 represent the sums of the values in those same cells in the worksheets STEVE and TOM. If you point to one of the cells in the range B6..B8 in the form worksheet, you will see that it contains a pure number—the result of adding the values from the two worksheets. For example, cell B6 in Figure 9-22 contains the value 35.

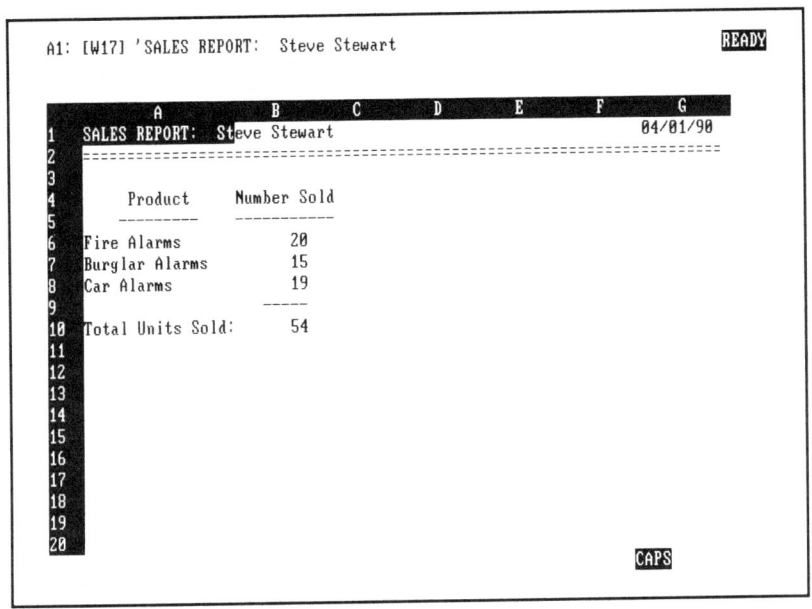

```
A1: [W17] 'SALES REPORT:   Steve Stewart                                    READY

           A           B           C         D         E         F         G
 1  SALES REPORT:   Steve Stewart                                        04/01/90
 2  ===============================================================================
 3
 4      Product     Number Sold
 5      ---------   -----------
 6  Fire Alarms         20
 7  Burglar Alarms      15
 8  Car Alarms          19
 9                     -----
10  Total Units Sold:   54
11
...
20                                                                          CAPS
```

FIGURE 9-18: The worksheet STEVE

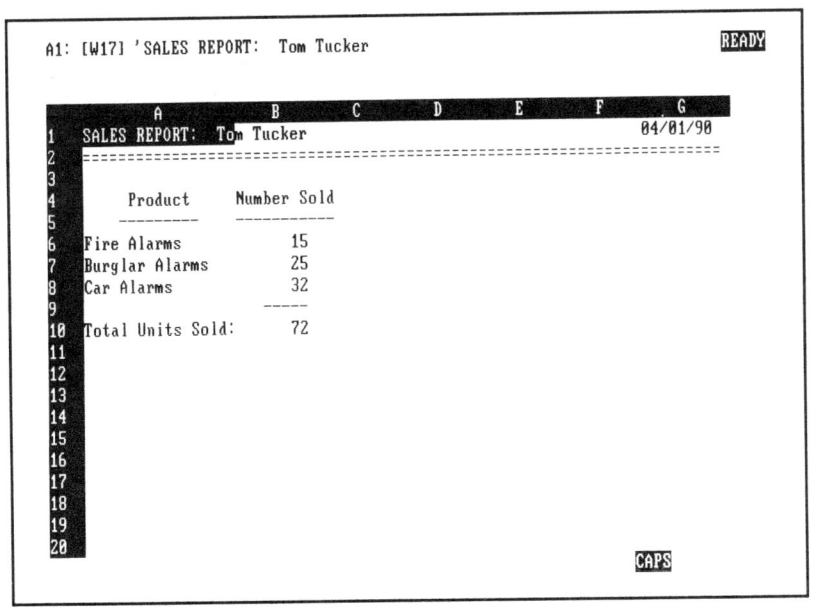

```
A1: [W17] 'SALES REPORT:   Tom Tucker                                       READY

           A           B           C         D         E         F         G
 1  SALES REPORT:   Tom Tucker                                           04/01/90
 2  ===============================================================================
 3
 4      Product     Number Sold
 5      ---------   -----------
 6  Fire Alarms         15
 7  Burglar Alarms      25
 8  Car Alarms          32
 9                     -----
10  Total Units Sold:   72
11
...
20                                                                          CAPS
```

FIGURE 9-19: The worksheet TOM

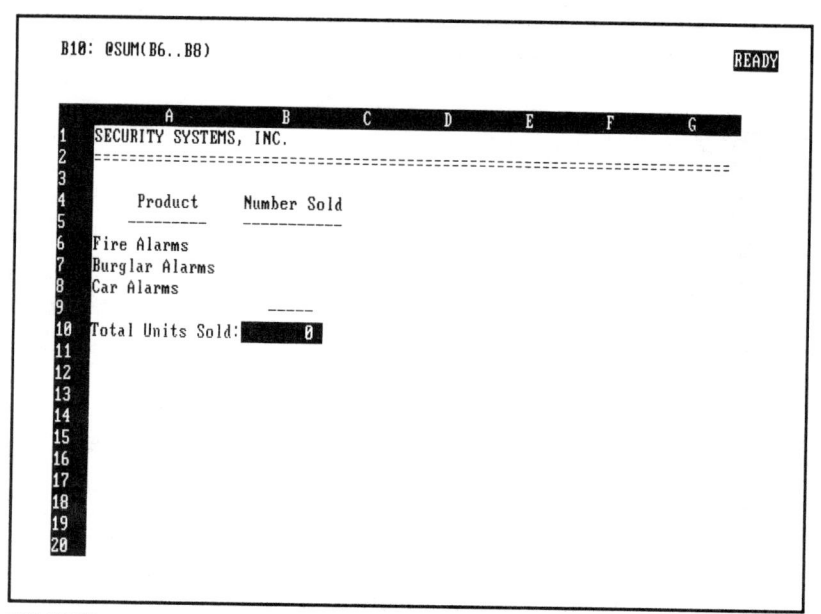

```
B10: @SUM(B6..B8)                                              READY

         A              B         C         D         E         F         G
 1  SECURITY SYSTEMS, INC.
 2  ==============================================================================
 3
 4       Product     Number Sold
 5       -------     -----------
 6  Fire Alarms
 7  Burglar Alarms
 8  Car Alarms
 9                      -----
10  Total Units Sold:     0
11
...
20
```

FIGURE 9-20: A "form" worksheet

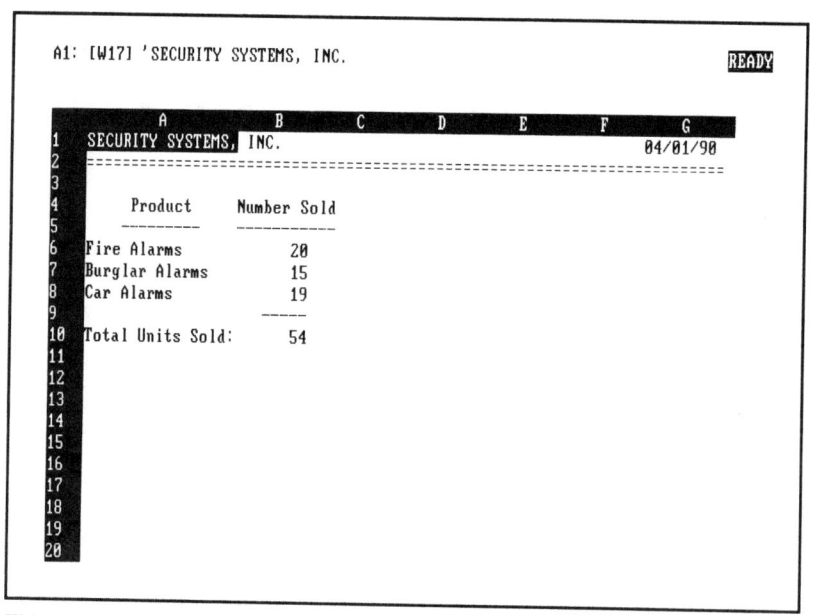

```
A1: [W17] 'SECURITY SYSTEMS, INC.                              READY

         A              B         C         D         E         F         G
 1  SECURITY SYSTEMS, INC.                                              04/01/90
 2  ==============================================================================
 3
 4       Product     Number Sold
 5       -------     -----------
 6  Fire Alarms         20
 7  Burglar Alarms      15
 8  Car Alarms          19
 9                      -----
10  Total Units Sold:   54
11
...
20
```

FIGURE 9-21: The / File Combine Add command

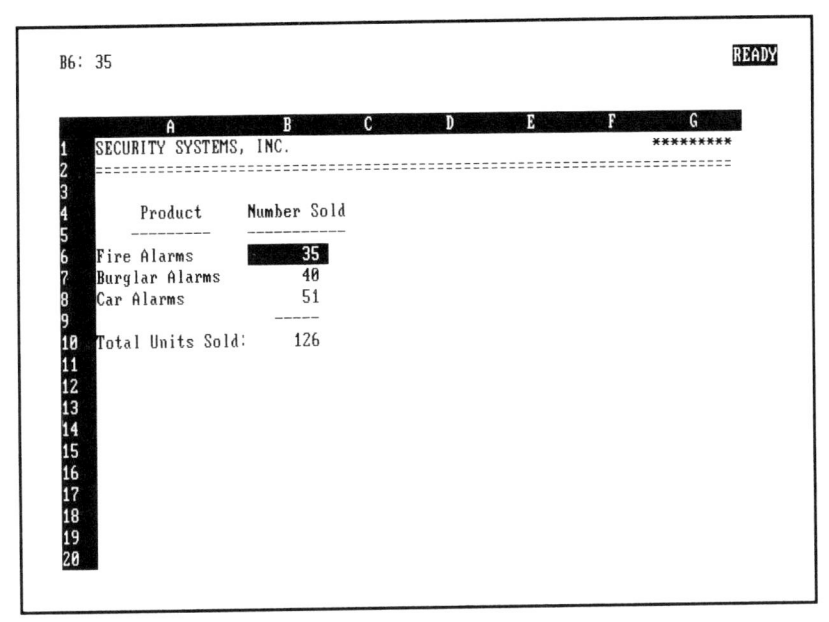

```
B6: 35                                                          READY

       A           B          C         D         E         F         G
  1 SECURITY SYSTEMS, INC.                                        *********
  2 ========================================================================
  3
  4      Product    Number Sold
  5      ---------  -----------
  6  Fire Alarms         35
  7  Burglar Alarms      40
  8  Car Alarms          51
  9                   -----
 10  Total Units Sold:  126
 11
 12
 ...
 20
```

FIGURE 9-22: Adding the second worksheet

How the Add Option Treats Labels

Unlike the Copy option, the Add option does *not* combine the labels from the worksheet file into the worksheet. For example, notice that the label in cell A1 of the form worksheet in Figure 9-22, 'SECURITY SYSTEMS, INC. is the same as the label in cell A1 in Figures 9-20 and 9-21. In other words, the labels in cell A1 of the TOM and STEVE worksheets did not overwrite the label in cell A1 of the form worksheet as you combined TOM and STEVE into the form.

How the Add Option Treats Formulas

What happens to the formulas in a worksheet file when you combine that file into the current worksheet using the Add or Subtract option depends on the entries in the cells of the current worksheet. If a cell in the worksheet file contains a formula, and the corresponding cell of the current worksheet is blank or contains a simple value, only the *results* of the formula (a pure value or a pure label) will be combined—not the underlying formula itself.

If the cell into which you combine a formula is not blank, the results will be somewhat different. If a cell in the worksheet file contains a formula, and the corresponding cell of the current worksheet contains a label, then the formula will not replace that label. The label will remain intact in the combined worksheet.

If a cell in the worksheet file contains a formula, and the corresponding cell of the current worksheet contains a value, 1-2-3 will add (or subtract) the result of the formula to the value in the worksheet.

Finally, if a cell in the worksheet file contains a formula, and the corresponding cell of the current worksheet also contains a formula, then the formula from the file will not replace the formula in the worksheet.

Unwanted Combinations

When you use the Add option, it's possible to add numbers inappropriately. This is most likely to happen when you are working with worksheets that contain serial date values or numbers that should remain constant.

For example, cells G1 in both the TOM and STEVE worksheets contain the function @DATE(90,4,1), as you can see in Figures 9-19 and 9-20. When you combined the STEVE worksheet into the form worksheet, 1-2-3 added the serial value of the @DATE function in cell G1 of STEVE—32964—to the blank cell G1 in the form worksheet, as you can see in Figure 9-21. When you combined the TOM worksheet into the form, 1-2-3 added the value of the @DATE function in cell G1 of TOM—again, 32964—to the value in cell G1 in the form worksheet. The result, 65928, is the serial date value for the date July 1, 2080—clearly not the result you had in mind. (This value is displayed as a series of asterisks because it is too long to be displayed in full in column G.)

To avoid this kind of problem, you could combine only selected ranges instead of combining the entire worksheets. This method lets you exclude the problem cells from the combination. Alternatively, you can enter any numbers or dates that you do not want to be affected by the combination—such as the dates in cell G1—as labels instead of values.

The "Form" Worksheet

Although we used a "form" worksheet to combine the STEVE and TOM worksheets, it is not essential that you do so. You can always just add the contents of one worksheet directly to another worksheet. However, it is a very good idea to use a forM worksheet since using a form worksheet helps to prevent you from damaging the data in the primary worksheets.

If you do decide to use a form worksheet, it's important that the layout of the form worksheet is identical to that of the individual worksheets you are combining. Otherwise, the consolidation will not work properly.

A Final Note

While the Add option of the / File Combine command is one of 1-2-3's most useful tools, it has one significant limitation. The worksheets you plan to combine (or, if you use the Named/Specified-Range, the ranges you plan to combine) with the Add option must have exactly the same layout. Unless you are very careful, this limitation can be crippling.

The Subtract Option

The Subtract option works just like the Add option, except that it subtracts the values in the worksheet file from the corresponding values in the current worksheet. In every other way, the two options are identical. Every rule we stated for the Add option in the previous pages also applies to the Subtract option.

To see how the Subtract option works, suppose that, after combining the worksheets TOM and STEVE into the worksheet in Figure 9-22, you discover that the worksheet TOM contains an error. In order to correct the error, you need to subtract the TOM worksheet from the consolidated worksheet, then correct the error in TOM and add it back to the consolidation.

To subtract TOM from the consolidated worksheet in Figure 9-22, move the cell pointer to cell A1 and issue the / File Combine Subtract Entire-File command. When 1-2-3 prompts you for the name of the file you want to combine, choose TOM and press [Enter]. Immediately, 1-2-3 will subtract the values in TOM from the values in the consolidated worksheet. The resulting worksheet will look just like Figure 9-21.

Once you have subtracted TOM from the consolidated worksheet, you can save the consolidated worksheet, retrieve TOM, make the needed changes, and then use the / File Combine Add command to add it back to the consolidated worksheet.

Combining a Range

The procedure for combining a range from a worksheet is almost identical to that for combining an entire worksheet. To combine a range from a worksheet file into the current worksheet, you must choose the Named/Specified-Range option from the Entire-File/Named/Specified-Range menu. When you do this, 1-2-3 will prompt you to supply the name or coordinates of the range you want to combine from the worksheet file. You should type the name or cell coordinates of the range you want to combine and press [Enter]. (In 1-2-3 Release 1A, you have to give a name to the range you want to combine and use that name to identify the range when you use the / File Combine command.) After that, 1-2-3 will prompt you for the name of the worksheet that contains the specified range.

You can select the Named/Specified-Range option after choosing the Copy, Add, or Subtract options from the File Combine menu. Exactly how 1-2-3 will combine the indicated range depends on which of these options you select. Just as when you choose the Entire-File option, if you select Copy, 1-2-3 will copy the entries from the worksheet file into the current worksheet at the position of the cell pointer. If you select Add or Subtract, 1-2-3 will add the values in the indicated range of the worksheet file to the values in the current worksheet.

An Example

To demonstrate how to combine a range, suppose you want to add the unit sales information from the ACCT#2 worksheet in Figure 9-16 to the unit sales information in the ACCT#1 worksheet in Figure 9-15. In other words, you want to use the / File

Combine Add command to add just the entries in the range C4..C6 in ACCT#2 to the entries in that same range of ACCT#1.

To begin, you might want to assign a range name to the range C4..C6 in ACCT#2. (This step is required in Release 1A and is optional in all other releases.) To do this, issue the / Range Name Create command, type the name SALES, and press [Enter]. Then, highlight the range C4..C6 and press [Enter]. Finally, be sure to save the ACCT#2 worksheet after you have created the range name. Otherwise, the name will not be a part of the file.

Next, load the file ACCT#1 and place the cell pointer on cell C4. Then issue the / File Combine Add Named/Specified-Range command. When you see the prompt *Enter range name or address:*, type either the range name, SALES, or enter the coordinates for that range, C4..C6. After you specify the range, 1-2-3 will prompt you to supply the name of the file that contains that range. You should type ACCT#2 (or point to its name in the file list) and press [Enter]. 1-2-3 will immediately retrieve the entries from the range C4..C6 in that file and add them to the entries in the same range of the ACCT#1 worksheet. The results will look like Figure 9-23.

As you can see, 1-2-3 has added the values from the range C4..C6 in ACCT#2 to the values in the same range of ACCT#1. The formulas in the range D4..D6 in ACCT#2 have been updated to reflect the new values in column C so that the worksheet now shows the unit and dollar sales for both accounts for April. (As a final step, you might want to change the title in cell A1 of ACCT#1 to reflect the new contents of that worksheet.)

```
C4: 94                                                              READY


            A              B           C           D             E
    1  APRIL SALES FOR ACCOUNT #1
    2  =========================================================
    3     Product    Unit Price  Units Sold   Dollars
    4  Bats           $24.50          94      $2,303
    5  Balls           $4.28         244      $1,044
    6  Mitts          $34.50          44      $1,518
    7                             --------    --------
    8  Totals                        382      $4,865
    9
```

FIGURE 9-23: Combining a range

Another Example: Combining a Range of Formulas

In the preceding example, the range we combined contained only values. If the range you want to combine contains formulas, and you use the Copy option instead of the Add option, things can be a good deal trickier.

For example, suppose you want to combine the entries from cells C8 and D8 in the worksheets ACCT#1 (Figure 9-15) and ACCT#2 (Figure 9-16) into cells C5, D5, C6, and D6 of the worksheet in Figure 9-24. As you may recall, cells C8 and D8 in ACCT#1 and ACCT#2 contain formulas that sum the values in columns C and D in those worksheets. You want to combine only the current results of those formulas into the worksheet in Figure 9-24.

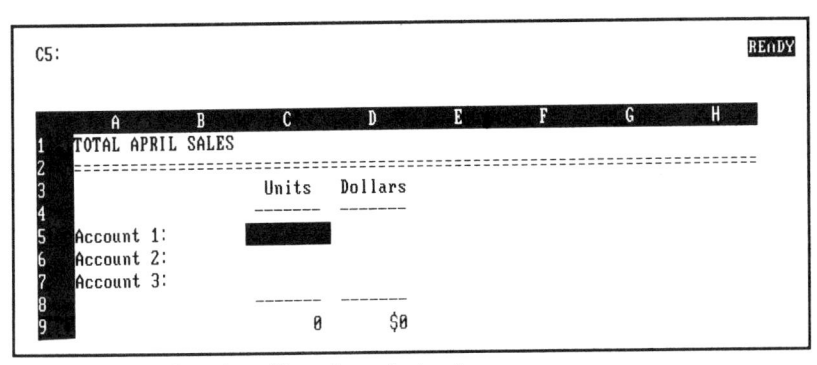

```
C5:                                                                          READY

         A         B         C         D         E         F         G         H
  1  TOTAL APRIL SALES
  2  ===========================================================================
  3                        Units    Dollars
  4                        ------   -------
  5  Account 1:           ███████
  6  Account 2:
  7  Account 3:
  8                        ------   -------
  9                           0        $0
```

FIGURE 9-24: Another "form" worksheet

In order to bring the current values of the formulas in ACCT#1 and ACCT#2 into the new worksheet, you must first use the / File Xtract command to extract the current values of those formulas into separate files, then combine the values from those files into the worksheet. To begin, retrieve the ACCT#1 worksheet, move the cell pointer to cell C8, issue the / File Xtract Values command, specify a name for the extract file (we'll use VALS1) and press [Enter]. Next, point to cells C8..D8 to specify the extract range, then press [Enter]. When 1-2-3 has extracted the values of the formulas from ACCT#1, retrieve the ACCT#2 worksheet, move the cell pointer to cell C8, issue the / File Xtract Values command, specify a name for the extract file (we'll use VALS2) and press [Enter]. Again point to cells C8..D8 as the extract range and press [Enter].

Now you're ready to combine the values into the worksheet in Figure 9-24. To begin, retrieve that worksheet, move the cell pointer to cell C5, issue the / File Combine Copy Entire-File command, specify VALS1 as the file to combine, and press [Enter]. Figure 9-25 shows the result. As you can see, this time the proper values have been combined into cells C5 and D5. To complete the process, move the cell pointer to cell C6, issue the / File Combine Copy Entire-File command, specify VALS2 as the file to combine, and press [Enter].

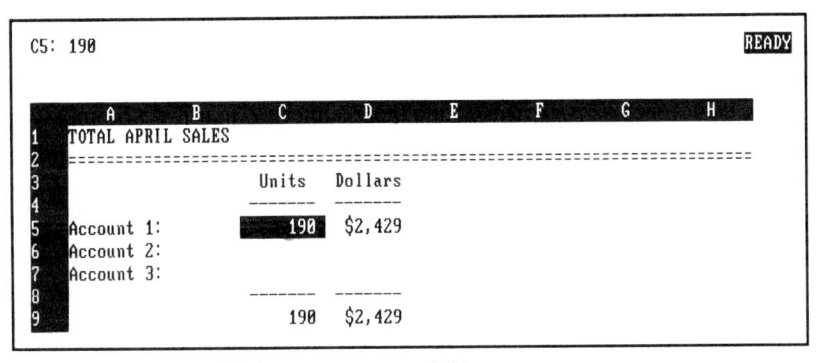

```
C5: 190                                                                      READY

         A         B         C         D         E         F         G         H
  1  TOTAL APRIL SALES
  2  ===========================================================================
  3                        Units    Dollars
  4                        ------   -------
  5  Account 1:            190     $2,429
  6  Account 2:
  7  Account 3:
  8                        ------   -------
  9                         190     $2,429
```

FIGURE 9-25: Combining an extracted file

It is important that you understand that the entries in the range C5..D5 in Figure 9-25 are not linked to the entries in cells C8 and D8 of ACCT#1. If the values in ACCT#1 and ACCT#2 change, the values in Figure 9-25 will not be updated automatically. Instead, you'll need to repeat the /File Xtract and /File Combine commands to update those values.

Notes

To take advantage of the Named/Specified-Range option, you must be able to remember the correct range name or cell coordinates for the range you plan to combine. 1-2-3 will not help you by showing you a list of range names in the file you are combining. If the file you specify does not contain the range name you supplied, 1-2-3 will just beep and display the error message *Named range not found in worksheet file*. If you see this error, you'll have to start over from scratch.

For this reason, it's a good idea to write down the name or coordinates of the range you plan to combine. If you will be performing the same combination many times, you might want to write a macro that will perform the entire operation automatically.

File Combine—Final Notes

When we explained password protection earlier in this chapter, we mentioned that you must enter the correct password in order to retrieve or combine a password-protected file. Whether you are combining the entire file or just a range, 1-2-3 will prompt you to supply the password for the worksheet file. 1-2-3 will not allow the data to come into your current worksheet unless you enter the correct password. We have mentioned several times in this section that the position of the cell pointer is critical to the success of the /File Combine command. If the cell pointer is in the wrong place, the contents of the incoming worksheet file may overwrite the contents of the worksheet. For this reason, we strongly recommend that you *always* save the current worksheet to disk before you issue the /File Combine command. This way, if the procedure does not work properly, you will have preserved a clean copy of your original worksheet.

LISTING FILES

RELEASE ▶ 2.2 ◀

1-2-3's /File List command allows you to see a full-screen list of files. ▶When you issue this command, 1-2-3 Release 2.2 will display a menu with five options: Worksheet, Print, Graph, Other, and Linked.◀ (In earlier versions of 1-2-3, this menu offers only four options: Worksheet, Print, Graph, and Other.) This menu allows you to include only Worksheet (.WK1 and .WKS) files, only graph (.PIC) files, or only text (.PRN) files in the file list. You also can choose Other to view a list of every file in the current directory. ▶The last option, Linked, creates a list of all of the files that are linked to the current worksheet; that is, all the files that are referred to by linking formulas in the current worksheet.◀

RELEASE ▶ 2.2 ◀

For example, suppose you would like to see a list of all the worksheet files in the current directory. To obtain this list, issue the /File List command and choose the

Worksheet option. Immediately, 1-2-3 will replace the worksheet on your screen with a list of file names like that shown in Figure 9-26.

```
B6: 35                                                          FILES
Enter extension of files to list: C:\123\*.wk?
          ACCT#1.WK1      07/31/89      22:57         9153
ACCT#1.WK1      ACCT#2.WK1      CASH.WK1      DAILY.WK1      DATA.WK1
FORM.WK1        HALFYEAR.WK1    STEVE.WK1     TOM.WK1
```

FIGURE 9-26: The / File List command

You can use the arrow keys to move the highlight from file name to file name in the list. As you point to each file name, 1-2-3 will display at the top of the screen that name, the date and time when that file was last saved, and its size.

If the current directory contains subdirectories, you can view the files in that sudirectory by pointing to the name of the directory in the file name list and pressing [Enter]. 1-2-3 will then display a list of all the files in that subdirectory. Similarly, you can press the [Backspace] key when the file list is in view to jump to the next highest directory. When you do this, you will see a list of the files that are stored in that directory. Each time you press [Backspace], you will jump up another level in the directory path and see a different list of files until you are viewing the files on the root directory.

THE / FILE ADMIN TABLE COMMAND

▶Like previous releases of 1-2-3, Release 2.2 offers a / File List command, which displays a listing of the files of the type you specify on the screen. In addition, however, 1-2-3 Release 2.2 offers a command—/ File Admin Table—that enters a table of file names into the worksheet, in much the same way that the / Range Name Table command creates a table of range names. When you issue this command, 1-2-3 presents a menu with five options: Worksheet, Print, Graph, Other, and Linked. This menu allows you to include only Worksheet (.WK1 and .WKS) files, only graph (.PIC)

RELEASE
▶ 2.2 ◀

files, or only text (.PRN) files in the file table. You also can choose Other to view a list of every file in the current directory. The last option, Linked, lets you create a list of all of the files that are linked to the current worksheet; that is, all the files that are referred to by linking formulas in the current worksheet.

Once you specify the type of file you want to list, 1-2-3 asks you to specify the directory in which the files you want to list are located. (1-2-3 skips this step if you choose the Linked option.) Next, 1-2-3 asks you to specify the upper-left corner of the table. As soon as you do this and press [Enter], 1-2-3 will enter a three-column table into the worksheet. The first column contains the names of the files of the type you specified in the directory you specified. (If you selected Linked, 1-2-3 will list all the files referenced by linking formulas in the current worksheet, regardless of which directories those files are in.) The second column contains the dates those files were created or last modified; the third column contains the times of day at which those files were created or last modified; and the fourth column contains the sizes of those files. ◄

CONCLUSION

In this chapter, we have explained how you can use 1-2-3's File commands to save worksheets into worksheet files, retrieve worksheets from files, erase files, extract a portion of a worksheet into a file, combine a worksheet file into another worksheet, and list the files on a directory. Since File commands are so important to using 1-2-3 effectively, you'll want to be sure you understand them thoroughly.

10

Creating Graphs

1-2-3's graphic capabilities make it easy to create graphs from the data in your worksheets. With just a few keystrokes, you can create a simple line, bar, pie, or XY graph. Once you have created a graph, you can add enhancements like titles, data labels, legends, and grids. In addition, because 1-2-3 graphics are so tightly integrated with the rest of the program, they allow you to perform visual "what-if" analysis—using a graph to illustrate changes you make to the worksheet.

In this chapter, we will walk through the steps required to create and enhance all of 1-2-3's graph types. We'll begin by explaining some fundamental concepts. Then we'll show you how to create each of 1-2-3's graph types and how to enhance each type of graph. Finally, we'll show you how to save a graph for printing.

GRAPH BASICS

Building a graph in 1-2-3 is a two-step process. First, you select the type of graph and the range or ranges in the worksheet that contain the data you want to graph. We call this process creating the graph. After the graph has been created, you can enhance the graph by adding titles, legends, and other refinements to it.

The / Graph Command

The / Graph command is the key to 1-2-3's graphics capabilities. ▶If you are using 1-2-3 Release 2.2, you'll see the menu and the settings sheet shown in Figure 10-1 when you issue the / Graph command. (If you are using an earlier version of 1-2-3, you'll see only the menu; you won't see the settings sheet.)◀ The options on this menu allow you to create, enhance, name, and save graphs.

RELEASE ▶ 2.2 ◀

The Type option lets you select the type of graph you want to create. 1-2-3 offers five different graph types: line, bar, stacked-bar, pie, and XY. The letters X, A, B, C, D, and so forth on the menu allow you to define the data ranges 1-2-3 should use as the basis for the graph. A graph can include just one data range (usually the A range) or as many as six ranges.

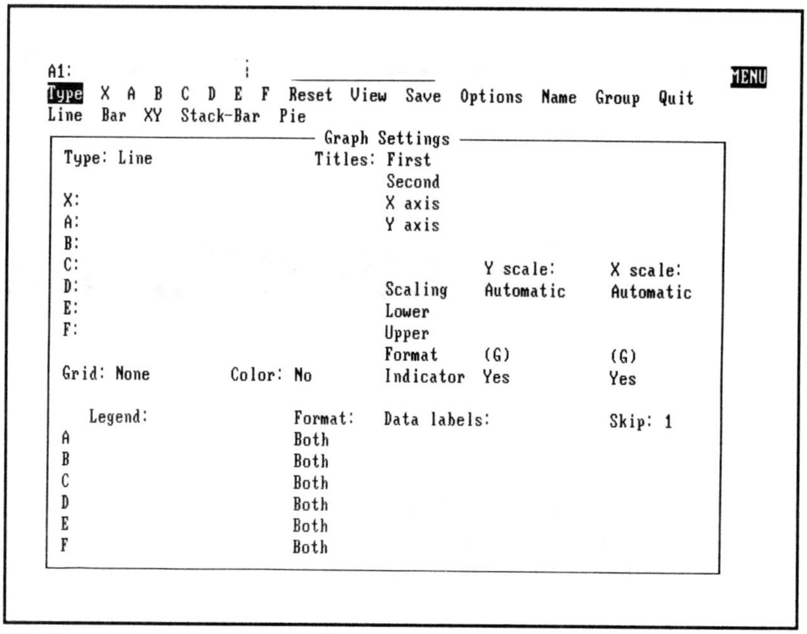

```
A1:                                                                    MENU
Type  X  A  B  C  D  E  F  Reset  View  Save  Options  Name  Group  Quit
Line  Bar  XY  Stack-Bar  Pie
                           ─ Graph Settings ─
   Type: Line             Titles: First
                                  Second
   X:                             X axis
   A:                             Y axis
   B:
   C:                                     Y scale:       X scale:
   D:                             Scaling  Automatic     Automatic
   E:                             Lower
   F:                             Upper
                                  Format    (G)           (G)
   Grid: None    Color: No        Indicator Yes           Yes

      Legend:                Format:   Data labels:     Skip: 1
   A                         Both
   B                         Both
   C                         Both
   D                         Both
   E                         Both
   F                         Both
```

FIGURE 10-1: The Graph menu

The other options allow you to reset the current Graph settings, view a graph, save and name graphs, and add enhancements to graphs. We'll cover each of these options later in this chapter.

Data Ranges

Every graph in 1-2-3 is based on values stored in the cells of a worksheet. In order to create a graph, then, you must begin with some worksheet data. This data can be a few simple numbers that you have typed into several cells, or it can be a selected range of cells from a large and complex worksheet.

There are two important restrictions on the data you can graph in 1-2-3. First, 1-2-3 can graph only values. If you include a cell that contains a label or a blank cell in a graph range, 1-2-3 will simply ignore that cell in the graph. If there are no values in one of the graph ranges you specify, 1-2-3 will not graph that range.

Second, the values you want to graph must be located in adjacent cells of a single row or a single column of the worksheet. These groups of values in a single row or column are called data series or data ranges. In 1-2-3, a graph can include up to six data ranges as well as one X range. (We'll explain the X range more in a few pages.)

TIP: GRAPHING DISCONTINUOUS DATA

Suppose you want to create a graph from the entries in cells P25, P50, P75, and P100 of a worksheet. Since these cells are not adjacent to one another, you won't be able to graph them as they are. However, you could enter the formulas +P25, +P50, +P75, and +P100 in four adjacent cells, such as Q1, Q2, Q3, and Q4. These formulas will return the values from cells P25, P50, P75, and P100. And since cells Q1, Q2, Q3, and Q4 are adjacent, they can serve as the basis for a graph.

Creating a Graph

There are two basic ways to create a graph in 1-2-3. First, you can issue the / Graph command and define the series that make up the graph individually. ▶Alternatively, in 1-2-3 Release 2.2, you can use the / Graph Group command to create a graph from a block of data in a worksheet.◀

RELEASE
► 2.2 ◄

Defining the Series Individually

To create a graph in 1-2-3, you issue the / Graph Type command and select the type for the graph, then use the A, B, C, D, E, and F options on the Graph menu to specify the ranges you want to graph. For example, suppose you would like to create a line graph that depicts the sales of Wombats in row 6 of the worksheet in Figure 10-2. To create this one-range graph, first issue the / Graph command, select the Type option, and choose Line. (Actually, this step is not required when you create a line graph, since Line is the default graph type.)

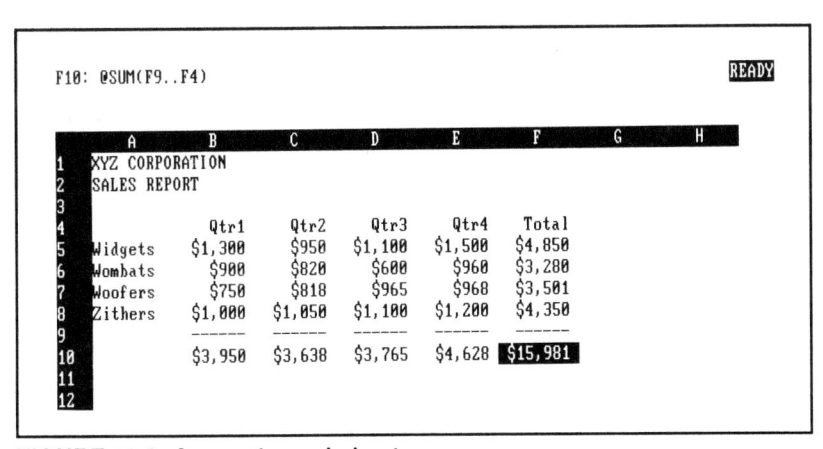

FIGURE 10-2: A sample worksheet

Next, select A from the Graph menu (by either pointing to that choice or by typing A). When you see the prompt *Enter first data range:*, specify B6..E6 as the range you want to graph. You can do this in the same way you define any other range in 1-2-3: either by typing the range reference B6..E6 or by pointing to those cells. When you have selected the range, press [Enter]. That's all there is to it! You have just created a graph, even though you don't see it yet on the screen.

The / Graph Group Command

RELEASE ► 2.2 ◄

►In 1-2-3 Release 2.2, you can also create a graph using the / Graph Group command. This new command allows you to create a graph simply by highlighting the range of cells that contain the data you want to graph. This command comes in handy when you need to create a graph with a number of ranges, since it allows you to create such a graph with just one command instead of several. It also allows you to define the X range for a graph at the same time you define the graph. (We'll cover the X range in detail in a few pages.)

Basics

When you issue the / Graph Group command, 1-2-3 Release 2.2 first asks you to highlight the range that contains the data ranges. Then, it will give you two choices: Columnwise or Rowwise. If each data series occupies a column of the range, you should choose Columnwise. When you do, 1-2-3 will define the first column of the highlighted range as the X range, the second column of the highlighted range as the A range, the third column of the highlighted range as the B range, and so forth. If each data series occupies a row of the range, you should choose Rowwise. If you choose this option, 1-2-3 will define the first row of the highlighted range as the X range, the second row of the highlighted range as the A range, the third row of the highlighted range as the B range, and so forth.

An Example

Let's use this command to create a simple graph from the data in the worksheet shown in Figure 10-2. We'll create a line graph that depicts the sales of Widgets. To begin, issue the / Graph Group command. When 1-2-3 asks you to highlight the range that contains the data ranges, highlight the range B4..E5. Next, when 1-2-3 displays the Columnwise/Rowwise menu, you should choose Rowwise. It's as simple as that.

Notes

The / Graph Group command has one major limitation. To define a graph using this command, all of the data you want to graph must be located in one contiguous block, without empty rows or columns and without extraneous labels and values. If you want to use this command, you'll need to be very careful about how you set up your worksheets.

When you use / Graph Group to create a graph, it will overwrite any existing graph settings you have defined. For example, the settings for the graph we created in the previous section were overwritten when we used /Graph Group to create the graph for Widgets sales. If you want to avoid this problem, you'll need to save your existing graph settings before you use / Graph Group to create a new graph. We'll show you how to do that in a few pages.◄

Viewing Graphs

Once you've created a graph, you'll usually want to view it. To view a graph you've just created, all you have to do is choose the View option from the Graph menu. For example, to view the graph you've just created with the / Graph Group command, choose the View option from the Graph menu. Figure 10-3 shows the graph on the screen.

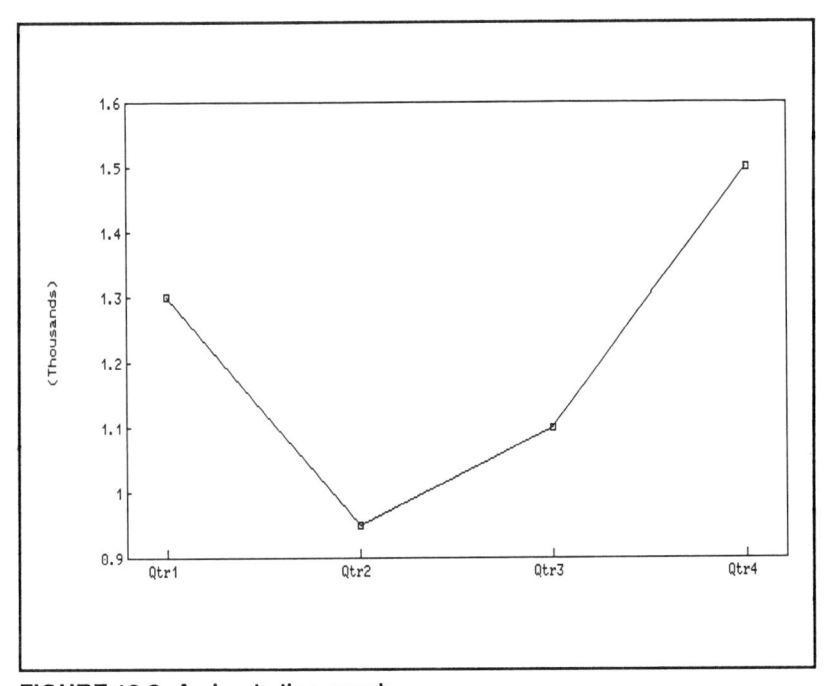

FIGURE 10-3: A simple line graph

Issuing the / Graph View command will always bring the active graph into view. You can issue this command at any time to view the active graph. If you issue this command before you have defined a graph, or after you have reset the Graph settings, 1-2-3 will simply beep.

How 1-2-3 Displays Graphs

Exactly what happens when you issue the / Graph View command depends on your hardware configuration and on how you installed 1-2-3. Most users have only a single monitor. If this is true for you, when you choose the View option, the active graph will replace the worksheet on the screen. When you are finished looking at the graph, you can return to the worksheet (and the Graph menu) by pressing any key.

If, on the other hand, you have installed 1-2-3 to use two monitors, 1-2-3 will draw the graph on the second (graphics) monitor. The worksheet will stay in view on your first monitor. If you do not have a graphics monitor or a graphics display adaptor, or if you have not installed 1-2-3 to display graphs, 1-2-3 will simply beep when you choose View. You will not be able to view your graphs.

The [Graph] Key

You can also view graphs by pressing the [Graph] key ([F10] on the IBM PC keyboard). Pressing this key causes 1-2-3 to bring the active graph into view. When you have finished with the graph, just press any key. Immediately, 1-2-3 will bring the worksheet back into view.

The [Graph] key is very handy for getting a quick view of the active graph after you make changes to your worksheet. You can press [Graph] at any time except when you are in a 1-2-3 menu (including the Graph menu). If you want to view a graph from within the Graph menu, you'll have to choose the View option. If you press [Graph] before you define any Graph settings, or after you have reset the settings you have defined, 1-2-3 will simply beep.

Notes

**RELEASE
▶ 2.2 ◀**

▶There is one major difference between graphs in 1-2-3 Release 2.2 and graphs in earlier releases of 1-2-3. Notice the position of the x-axis tick marks in the graph in Figure 10-3. In earlier versions of 1-2-3, the first and last x-axis tickmarks were at the far left and right edges of the graph. In fact, the first and last x-axis tick marks blended into the y-axis and the right border of the graph. In 1-2-3 Relase 2.2, however, the first and last tick marks are indented from the borders of the graph. As a result, the first and last data points in each series are also indented. This change improves the appearance of the graph significantly, especially in graphs that have data labels and x-axis labels.◀

Multiple-Range Graphs

Although many of your graphs will contain only one data range, you can include up to six data ranges in any 1-2-3 graph (except for pie graphs). Typically, the first range in a graph will be the A range. If you want to include a second data range in a graph, you need only select the B option from the Graph menu and identify the appropriate range of data. To add a third range, choose the C option and identify the range. The D, E, and F options on the Graph menu allow you to identify a fourth, fifth, and sixth data range.

An Example

For example, suppose you want to add a line representing the sales of Wombats to the graph in Figure 10-3. To do this, issue the / Graph B command, point to the range B6..E6, and press [Enter]. Finally, choose View to bring the graph shown in Figure 10-4 into view.

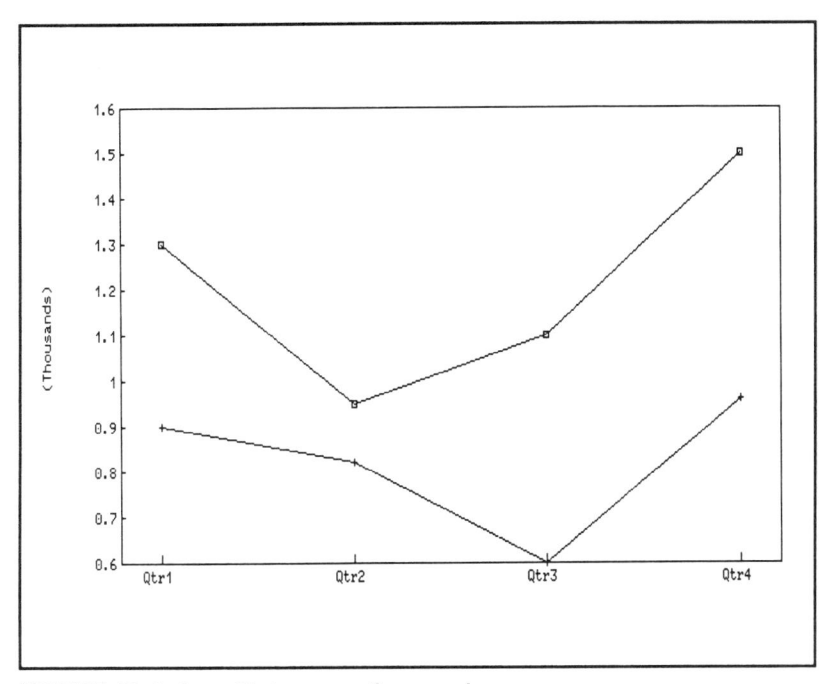

FIGURE 10-4: A multiple-range line graph

Notice that 1-2-3 uses a different symbol to mark the data points on each of the two lines in the graph. In multiple-range bar graphs, 1-2-3 uses different shading patterns to distinguish one bar from another. If you have a color monitor, you can also instruct 1-2-3 to display each range in a different color. In addition, you can add a legend to a graph that explains what each of these symbols (or shading patterns, in the case of bar graphs) represents. We'll show you how to do both of these things later in this chapter.

Deleting a Range

The / Graph Reset command allows you to delete a range from a graph. When you issue this command, 1-2-3 will display the menu shown in Figure 10-5. The options on this menu allow you to reset the ranges and options you have defined for a graph. ▶(Two of the options on this menu, Ranges and Options, are new in 1-2-3 Release 2.2.)◀

RELEASE
▶ 2.2 ◀

```
A1:                                                                    MENU
Graph  X  A  B  C  D  E  F  Ranges  Options  Quit
Clear all current graph settings
                        ─── Graph Settings ───
  Type: Line                     Titles: First
                                         Second
  X:                                     X axis
  A:                                     Y axis
  B:
  C:                                             Y scale:      X scale:
  D:                                     Scaling Automatic     Automatic
  E:                                     Lower
  F:                                     Upper
                                         Format  (G)           (G)
  Grid: None          Color: No          Indicator Yes         Yes

     Legend:                   Format:   Data labels:          Skip: 1
  A                            Both
  B                            Both
  C                            Both
  D                            Both
  E                            Both
  F                            Both
```

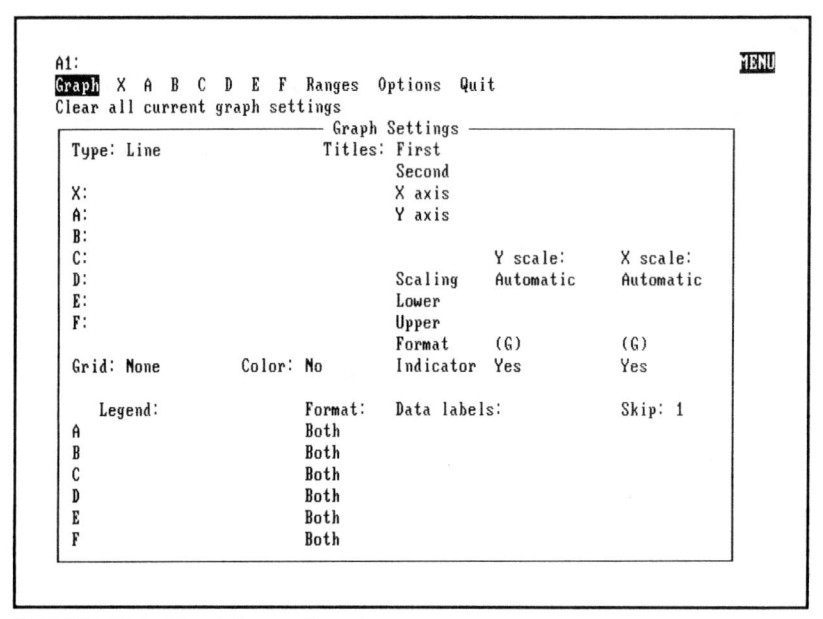

FIGURE 10-5: The / Graph Reset menu

Options A through F on this menu each allow you to reset, or delete, a single range in a graph. To delete a range from a graph, just choose the letter for that range. (This also deletes the data labels you've defined for the selected ranges, if any. We'll explain data labels in a few pages.) When you have deleted the unwanted range (or ranges), choose Quit to return to the Graph menu.

RELEASE
▶ 2.2 ◀
▶The Ranges option, which is new to Release 2.2, allows you to reset all of the data ranges in a graph with a single command. The result will be a graph that no longer contains any data, but which retains all of the options you have defined for it. For this reason, the Range option comes in handy when you want to replace all of the data in a graph with new data but you don't want to redefine all of the graph's options. (We'll explain graph options in detail in a few pages.)

The other options on this menu, Graph and Options, let you reset either all of the setting that make up a graph, or just the options settings. (We'll cover these options in a few pages.)◀

Graph Enhancements

Once you have created a graph, you can use the / Graph Options command to enhance it in many ways. When you issue this command, 1-2-3 will display the menu shown in Figure 10-6. Each of these options controls a particular enhancement option. For example, the Titles option allows you to add two titles at the top of a graph and to add titles along both the x-axis and y-axis, and the Scale option allows you to control the format and scaling of the y-axis.

```
A1:                                                    MENU
Legend  Format Titles Grid Scale Color B&W Data-Labels Quit
Create legends for data ranges
                         ─── Graph Settings ───
 Type: Line              Titles: First
                                 Second
 X:                              X axis
 A:                              Y axis
 B:
 C:                                      Y scale:    X scale:
 D:                              Scaling Automatic   Automatic
 E:                              Lower
 F:                              Upper
                                 Format  (G)         (G)
 Grid: None     Color: No        Indicator Yes       Yes

     Legend:             Format:  Data labels:       Skip: 1
  A                       Both
  B                       Both
  C                       Both
  D                       Both
  E                       Both
  F                       Both
```

FIGURE 10-6: The / Graph Options menu

Not all enhancements apply to all types of graphs. For example, you can add x- and y-axis titles to any type of graph except for pie graphs. On the other hand, the / Graph Options Scale X Scale command, which allows you to control the scaling of the x-axis, applies only to XY graphs. In addition, some enhancements affect different types of graphs in different ways.

We'll cover graph enhancements in detail in the section of this chapter entitled "Enhancing Graphs." Before we go on, however, we'll look at a brief example of enhancing graphs and explain how you can delete options from a graph.

A Brief Example

Let's add a few enhancements to the sample graph in Figure 10-4. To begin, choose Options from the Graph menu and issue the Titles First command, type *XYZ Corporation*, and press [Enter]. Then choose Titles Second, type *Sales of Widgets and Wombats*, and press [Enter]. Next, choose Titles X-Axis, type *Quarter*, and press [Enter]. Then choose Titles Y-Axis, type *Sales*, and press [Enter] again. These commands add two top titles, an x-axis title, and a y-axis title to the graph.

Now, issue the Scale Y Scale Manual command from the Graph Options menu, then choose Lower and press [Enter], and choose Upper and type *1600*. These commands redefine the scale of the y-axis. Then choose Format from the Y Scale menu, select the Currency option and press [Enter]. This command changes the format of the numbers along the y-axis to currency with two decimal places.

Next, choose Quit from the Y Scale menu, then Legend from the Options menu. Select the A option, type *Widgets*, and press [Enter]. Then choose Legend again, choose the B option, type *Wombats*, and press [Enter] once more. These commands add a legend to the graph.

Figure 10-7 shows the enhanced graph. As you can see, the graph now includes titles, x-axis labels, and a legend. In addition, the scale of the y-axis has been changed and the values along that axis have been formatted.

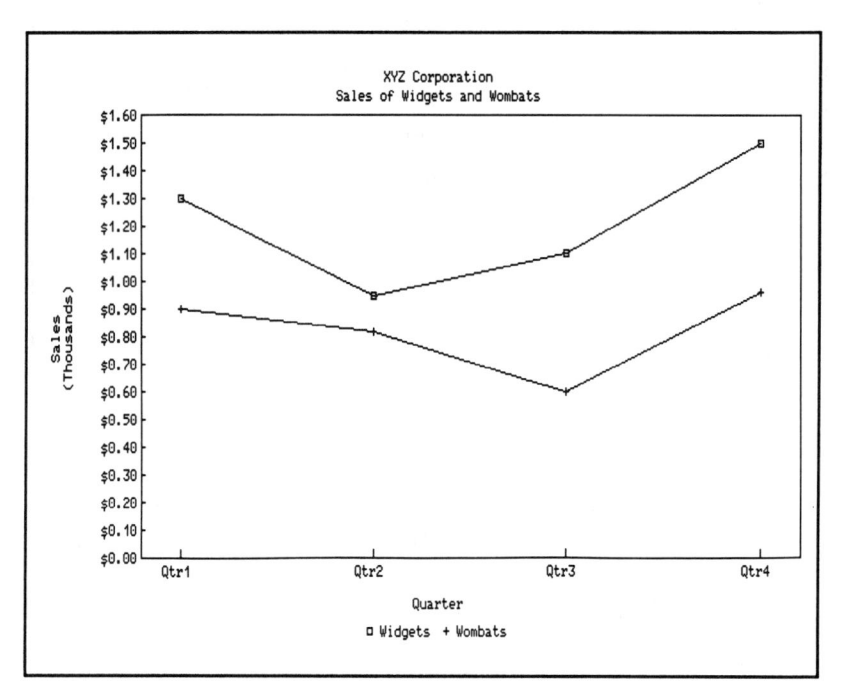

FIGURE 10-7: An enhanced graph

Resetting Options

**RELEASE
► 2.2 ◄**

►1-2-3 Release 2.2. offers a command, /Graph Reset Options, that allows you to reset all the graph options settings you have defined (including the data labels), but does not clear the definitions of the data ranges. This command makes it possible to delete the enhancements from a graph without deleting any of the data ranges you have defined.◄

Naming Graphs

1-2-3 allows you to have many different graphs associated with one worksheet. However, only one graph can be "active" at any time. It is the active graph that you see when you press the [Graph] key. Also, whenever you issue commands from the Graph menu, those commands affect only the active graph.

If you want to create more than one graph in a worksheet, you will have to give each of your graphs a name. Naming a graph saves its settings. Once you have named a graph, you can reset the Graph settings and create a new graph, or modify those settings to create a revised version of the named graph.

To name the active graph, you issue the / Graph Name Create command. When 1-2-3 displays the prompt *Enter graph name:*, you should type a name for the graph. When you press [Enter], 1-2-3 will save the active graph and all its settings (titles, legends, and so forth) under the name you specify. For example, suppose that you want to name the line graph in Figure 10-7. To do this, issue the / Graph Name Create command, type the name *LineGraph*, and press [Enter].

The names you specify for your graphs must conform to the same rules that apply to range names. The maximum length for a graph name is 15 characters. Graph names can include any alphabetic, numeric, or punctuation characters.

When you name a graph, you are *not* saving that graph to disk. All you are doing is storing that graph under a name in the current worksheet. Named graphs are saved to disk *only* when you save the worksheet file in which they were created. If you name a graph, then issue the / Worksheet Erase command to erase the worksheet, the named graph will be lost.

In addition to any named graphs, 1-2-3 will also save the active graph when you save a worksheet to disk. Consequently, if you have created only one graph in a worksheet, you do not need to name it before you save that worksheet to disk. The graph will be saved automatically along with the worksheet.

Recalling a Named Graph

Once you have named a graph, you can make that graph the active graph at any time by issuing the / Graph Name Use command. When you issue this command, 1-2-3 will display a list of all the named graphs in the current worksheet. To recall a graph, you simply point to its name in the list and press [Enter]. When you do this, 1-2-3 will immediately make the selected graph the active graph and will display it on the screen.

Once you have recalled a named graph, any / Graph commands you issue will affect that graph. This means that you can modify the graph in any way you wish. However, the changes you make to the graph will not be saved unless you reissue the / Graph Name Create command and rename the graph.

When you use the / Graph Name Use command to recall a named graph, the graph you select will become the active graph and will replace the currently active graph. If you have not named the active graph, it will be lost.

Deleting a Named Graph

The / Graph Name Delete command allows you to delete named graphs. When you issue this command, 1-2-3 will display a list of all the named graphs in the current worksheet. All you have to do to delete a named graph is point to its name in the list (or type the graph name) and press [Enter]. As soon as you press [Enter], 1-2-3 will delete the graph—there is no warning or second chance.

If you want to get rid of all the named graphs in a worksheet, issue the / Graph Name Reset command. Be careful! As soon as you choose Reset from the Graph Name menu, all named graphs in your worksheet will be eliminated—1-2-3 will not display a Yes/ No menu or offer any warning before it deletes all the graphs. As a safeguard, you may want to save your worksheet to disk before you issue the / Graph Name Reset command. Then, if you decide that you need to recall one of the named graphs, you can retrieve the worksheet file from disk.

Creating a Table of Graph Names

RELEASE 2.2 ►1-2-3 Release 2.2 offers a command—/ Graph Table—that lets you enter a table of named graphs into the cells of a worksheet. This command is similar to the / Range Name Table and / File Table commands. To create a table of named graphs, issue the / Graph Name Table command, point to the cell that you want 1-2-3 to use as the upper-left corner of the table, and press [Enter]. As soon as you do this, 1-2-3 will create a three-column table, starting at the cell you highlighted. The first column will contain the names of all the named graphs in the current worksheet, listed in alphabetical order; the second column will contain the type of each graph; and the third column will contain the first title line (if any).◄

Starting a New Graph

As we mentioned earlier, there can be more than one graph associated with a worksheet. Before you create the second and subsequent graphs in a worksheet, you should use the / Graph Name Create command to save the currently active graph under a name. Otherwise, the settings for that graph will be lost when you begin creating the new graph.

Once you have named the current graph, you are ready to begin creating a new graph. There are two different approaches you can take to creating a new graph: you can start from scratch or you can build on your current Graph settings. Let's look at both of these approaches.

Resetting the Current Graph Settings

If the new graph you want to create is entirely different from the previous graph, then you will probably want to reset the current settings and start from scratch. The / Graph Reset command allows you to reset the current Graph settings. When you issue the / Graph Reset command, you'll see the menu shown in Figure 10-5.

The options on this menu allow you to reset a single range in a graph or all of the graph's settings. If you want to cancel the entire graph, just choose the Graph option. Choosing this option resets all of the data ranges in the active graph, plus any enhancements, such as titles and formats. The Graph option also cancels the current Type setting. Once you have used the / Graph Reset Graph command, you can start with a clean slate to build the next graph.

Building on the Current Graph Settings

If the new graph you want to build is similar to the current graph, you might want to build on the current settings rather than starting from scratch. In that case, all you need to do is issue the / Graph Name Create command to save the current settings under a name, then issue / Graph commands to change the graph.

For example, suppose you would like to plot the data in the line graph in Figure 10-7 as a bar graph. You could, of course, build the bar graph from scratch. However, you could instead simply modify the settings you have already defined for the line graph named LineGraph. To do this, issue the / Graph Name Use command to make LineGraph the active graph, then issue the / Graph Type command and choose Bar as the graph type. Once you have changed the graph's type, choose View to bring it into view. Figure 10-8 shows the new bar graph.

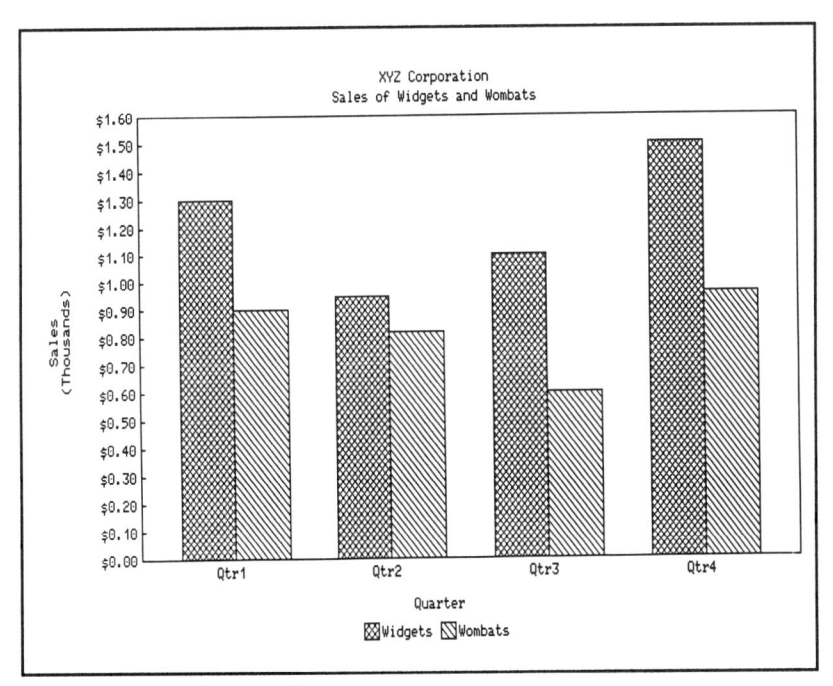

FIGURE 10-8: A bar graph

Notice that this bar graph has all the same enhancements that were added to the original line graph, including titles, legends, and x-axis labels. If you wanted to, at this point you could add further enhancements and additional data ranges, or you could delete some of the existing enhancements. However you decide to proceed, you've managed to save a lot of steps in creating this graph by using the pre-existing Graph settings.

If you want to save this new graph and create yet another, issue the / Graph Name Create command to save the graph under a name. Then use the / Graph Reset Graph command to reset the Graph settings and start over from scratch, or use the / Graph commands to make further modifications to the graph.

GRAPH TYPES

In this section, we'll show you how to create each of 1-2-3's different graph types. We'll use the simple worksheet in Figure 10-9 to demonstrate how to create several different kinds of 1-2-3 graphs.

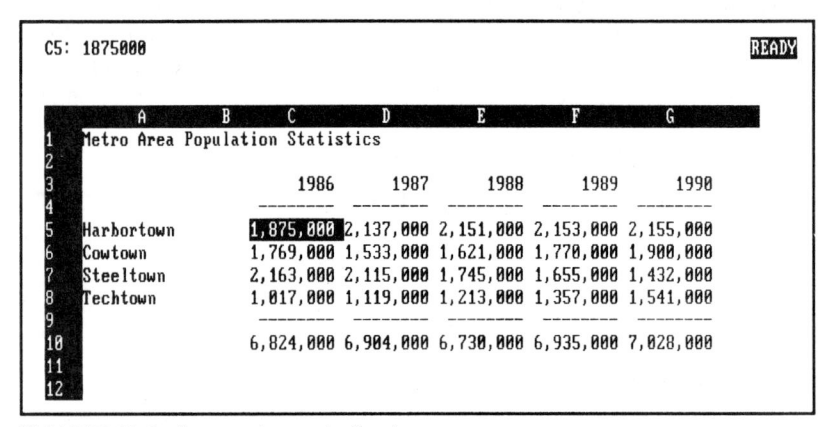

```
C5: 1875000                                                          READY


           A      B       C          D          E          F         G
     1  Metro Area Population Statistics
     2
     3                    1986       1987       1988       1989      1990
     4                   --------   --------   --------   --------  --------
     5  Harbortown       1,875,000  2,137,000  2,151,000  2,153,000 2,155,000
     6  Cowtown          1,769,000  1,533,000  1,621,000  1,770,000 1,900,000
     7  Steeltown        2,163,000  2,115,000  1,745,000  1,655,000 1,432,000
     8  Techtown         1,017,000  1,119,000  1,213,000  1,357,000 1,541,000
     9                   --------   --------   --------   --------  --------
     10                  6,824,000  6,904,000  6,730,000  6,935,000 7,028,000
     11
     12
```

FIGURE 10-9: A sample worksheet

RELEASE
▶ 2.2 ◀

▶Because of the way the data in this worksheet is arranged, we won't be able to use the /Graph Group command to defiine the graphs. Instead, we'll define each range individually. This is not an unusual problem—we expect that most of your worksheets will be set up in such a way that / Graph Group will not be usable.◀

Line Graphs

Line is 1-2-3's default graph type. Line graphs, which are probably the most commonly used type of business graph, are useful for illustrating the trend of data across time.

To create a line graph, you need only define the range or ranges of data that you want to graph. Since 1-2-3's default graph type is line, if you create a graph without specifying a type, that graph will be a line graph.

For example, suppose you want to create a line graph that depicts the population growth for Techtown from the worksheet in Figure 10-9. To create this graph, issue the / Graph command, choose A from the Graph menu, select the range C8..G8, and press [Enter]. (You could also choose the Type option and select Line, but you don't need to.) When you have defined the A range, choose View to bring the graph into view. Figure 10-10 shows the graph.

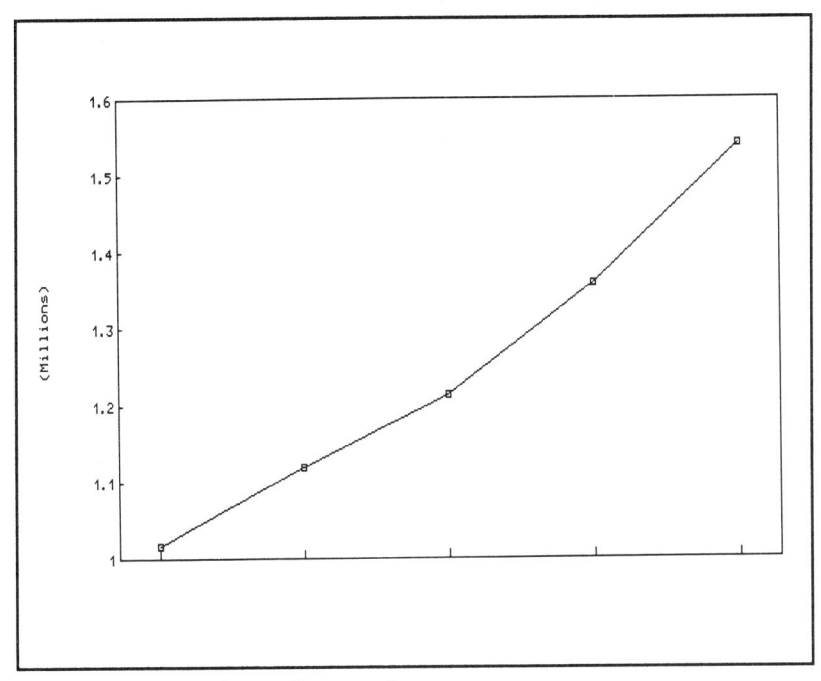

FIGURE 10-10: A simple line graph

Once you create a line graph, you can enhance it by adding titles, x-axis labels, and data labels; by formatting the values on the y-axis; by adding a grid; and by changing the symbols 1-2-3 uses to mark the points on the graph. We'll show you how to do these things later in this chapter.

There is one problem with line graphs that you should be aware of. One of the classic devices for creating a misleading line graph is to place the y-axis origin at some value greater than zero. (This can be particularly confusing when someone tries to compare two different graphs that have different origins for the y-axis.) If you look carefully at Figure 10-10, you'll see that the origin of the y-axis is not at 0 but at 1 (for 1,000,000). This is typical; when you create a line graph in 1-2-3, the y-axis will usually start at some number greater than zero. Fortunately, you can use the / Graph Options Scale Y Scale Manual command to correct this problem. We'll show you how to do that later in this chapter.

Multiple-Range Line Graphs

You can include up to six ranges in a line graph. To define the second through sixth ranges in a graph, you choose the B, C, D, E, and F ranges from the Graph menu and select the ranges of cells that contain the data you want to graph.

Multiple-line graphs are useful for illustrating the trends in several series of related data. For example, suppose you want to create a line graph that depicts the trend of population growth for all four towns in the worksheet in Figure 10-9. To do this, issue the /Graph Reset Graph command to reset the current Graph settings (you might want to save the existing settings under a name first), then choose the A option, select the range C5..G5, press [Enter]; choose B, select the range C6..G6, press [Enter]; choose C, select the range C7..G7, press [Enter]; choose D, select the range C8..G8, and press [Enter] one more time. (Since this is a line graph, you don't have to define its type.) When you are finished, choose View. Figure 10-11 shows the completed graph.

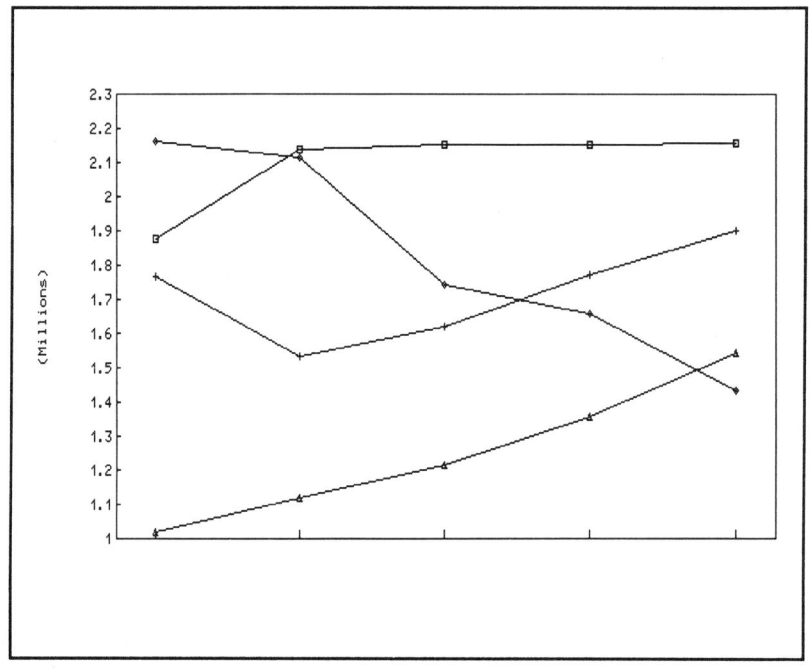

FIGURE 10-11: A multiple-range line graph

Notice that 1-2-3 has used different symbols to mark the different ranges in this graph. Since a graph can include up to six different data ranges, 1-2-3 offers six different symbols for marking the data points. Table 10-1 shows these symbols.

Range	Symbol
A	□
B	+
C	◊
D	Δ
E	X
F	∇

TABLE 10-1: Line-graph data symbols

Once you create a multiple-line graph, you can enhance it by adding titles, x-axis labels, and data labels; by formatting the values on the y-axis; by adding a grid; and by changing the symbols 1-2-3 uses to mark the points on the graph. We'll show you how to do these things later in this chapter.

Multiple-line graphs have the same problem with the y-axis origin as other line graphs. You'll usually want to use the / Graph Options Scale Y Scale Manual, Lower, and Upper commands to adjust the scaling of the y-axis in multiple-line graphs to overcome this problem.

Bar Graphs

Bar graphs are closely related to line graphs—in fact, in many cases either type of graph can be used to depict the same information. However, line graphs are best used to illustrate trends across time, while bar graphs are best used to compare two or more values at a point in time. For example, you could use a bar graph to compare the maximum income tax rates of different states in a given year or to compare the sales of several different products for a period of time.

For example, you could use a bar graph to compare the total populations for Harbortown, Cowtown, and so on, for 1987. To do this, issue the / Graph Reset Graph command to reset any existing Graph settings (you might want to save the previous graph under a name first), then choose the Type option and select Bar, choose the A option, select the range D5..D8, and press [Enter]. When you have defined the graph, choose the View option to display it. Figure 10-12 shows the completed graph on the screen.

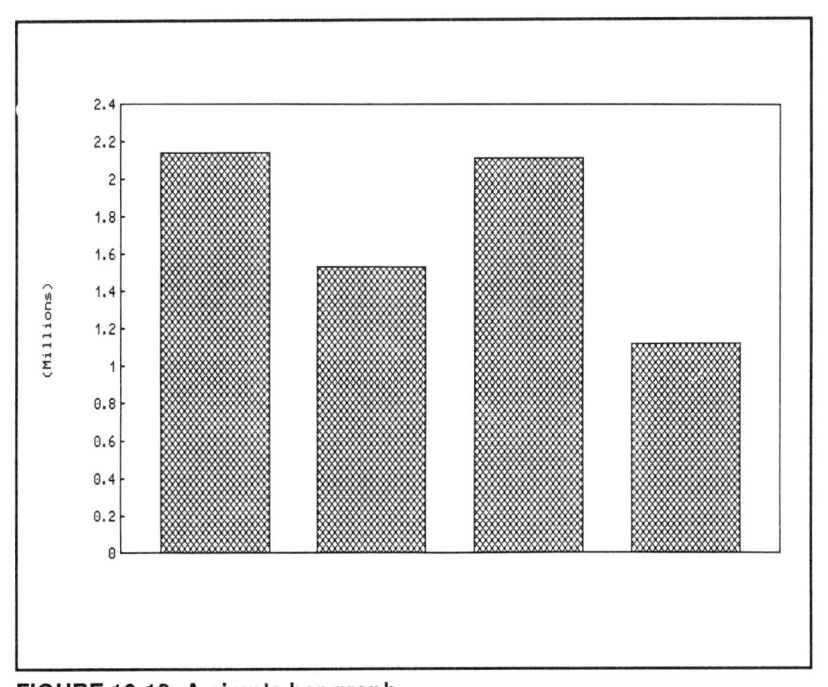

FIGURE 10-12: A simple bar graph

Once you create a bar graph, you can enhance it by adding titles, x-axis labels, and data labels; by formatting the values on the y-axis; by adding a grid; and by changing the shading patterns and colors in the bars. We'll show you how to do these things later in this chapter.

RELEASE ► 2.2 ◄ ▶Recall that in 1-2-3 Release 2.2 the first and last tick marks on the x-axis are indented from the left and right edges of the graph. Now, the first and last bars in bars graphs do not touch the left and right borders of the graph frame, as they do in earlier releases of 1-2-3. This simple change really helps to improve the appearance of bar charts in Release 2.2.◄

Multiple-Range Bar Graphs

If you include more than one range in a bar graph, 1-2-3 will place the bars for the two ranges side-by-side. Such side-by-side, or clustered, bar graphs allow you to build comparisons of several different data ranges into one graph.

For example, suppose you want to graph the population data from the worksheet in Figure 10-9, using a different bar for each town. To create this graph, first issue the / Graph Reset Graph command to clear any existing Graph settings (you might want to save the previous graph under a name first). Then choose Type Bar from the Graph menu. Next, choose A from the main graph menu, select the range C5..G5, press [Enter]; choose B, select the range C6..G6, press [Enter]; choose C, select the range C7..G7, press [Enter]; choose D, select the range C8..G8, and press [Enter] one last time. When you are finished, choose View to bring the graph shown in Figure 10-13 into view.

As you can see, the bars in the new graph are clustered around each of the x-axis tick marks. The first cluster illustrates the 1986 populations of all four towns; the second cluster, the 1987 populations of the towns; and so on.

Although we defined the ranges in the graph in Figure 10-13 in order (row 5, then row 6, and so on), 1-2-3 doesn't care about the order in which you define the ranges. We could have defined the A range to include cells C6 through G6, the B range to include cells C8 through G8, and so on. However, 1-2-3 will place the bar for the A range (if there is one) at the left of each cluster, with the bar for the B range (if it exists) immediately to the right, and so on. If you define the ranges out of sequence, you'll need to be careful when you define legends and data labels.

Notice that 1-2-3 has used different shading patterns for the different sets of bars in the graph. 1-2-3 has six different patterns that it uses for bar graphs (a different one **RELEASE ► 2.2 ◄** for each of six data ranges). These patterns or colors are shown in Table 10-2. ▶(By the way, in 1-2-3 Release 2.2 Lotus has changed the order of the patterns in bar charts. This change should have little or no practical significance, however.)◄

If your bar graph has less than six data ranges, you can control the selection of patterns to some extent. Instead of using the A option for the first data range, B for the second data range, and so on, you can skip a range or two to omit a particular pattern. For example, we used the ranges A, B, C, and D to define the graph in Figure 10-13. If we had used the B, D, E, and F ranges instead, the bars in the graph would be shaded differently.

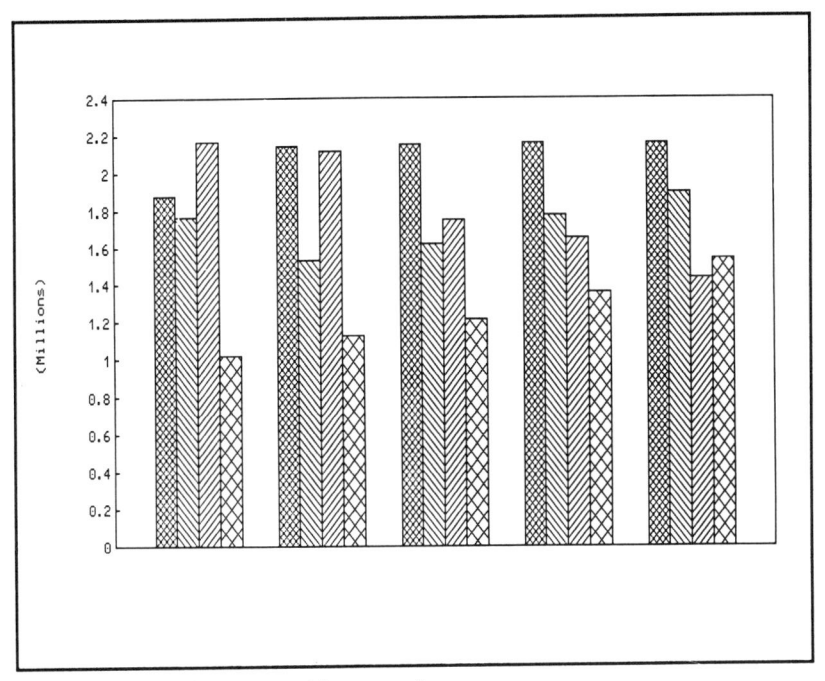

FIGURE 10-13: A clustered-bar graph

Range	Pattern	Range	Pattern
A		D	
B		E	
C		F	

TABLE 10-2: Bar Graph Patterns

Of course, the graph in Figure 10-13 needs some enhancements to make it easier to interpret. You could enhance this graph by adding titles, x-axis labels, and a legend; by formatting the values along the y-axis; and by changing the shading patterns 1-2-3 uses to display the bars. We'll show you how to make these enhancements later in this chapter.

Stacked-Bar Graphs

Stacked-bar graphs are similar to side-by-side bar graphs. However, in a stacked-bar graph the different data ranges you select are placed one on top of the other to create a stacked bar. Stacked-bar graphs are useful for depicting the relationships among the components of a series of data.

An Example

Suppose you want to create a stacked-bar graph from the data in Figure 10-9. You want each bar in the graph to represent the total population of all four towns in a given year. You further want each bar to be divided into four sections—one for each of the towns. To create this graph, issue the / Graph Reset Graph command (you might want to save the previous graph under a name first), then choose the Type option and select Stack-Bar as the graph's type. Next, choose the A option, point to the range C8..G8, press [Enter]; choose B, point to the range C7..G7, press [Enter]; choose C, point to the range C6..G6, press [Enter]; choose D, point to the range C5..G5, and press [Enter] one more time. When you are finished, choose View. The result will look like Figure 10-14.

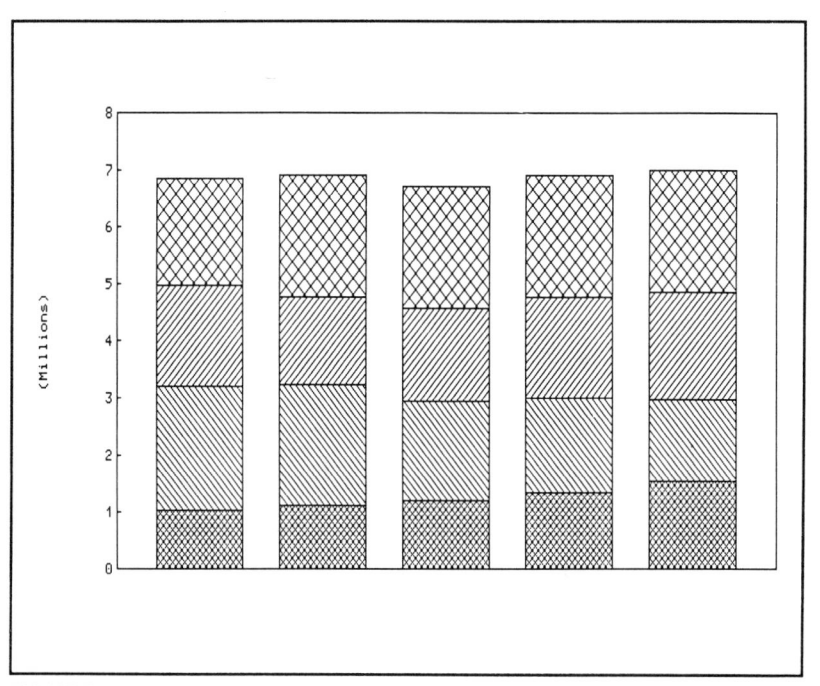

FIGURE 10-14: A stacked-bar graph

Notes

After you have defined the four data ranges, you can enhance the graph by adding titles, x-axis labels, and data labels, and by formatting the values along the y-axis. You are especially likely to want to add legends to your stacked-bar graphs. We'll show you how to do that later in this chapter.

As with clustered-bar graphs, 1-2-3 does not care about the order in which you define the ranges in a stacked-bar graph. However, 1-2-3 will always place the bar segment for the A range at the bottom of the stacks, with the segment for the B range just above that segment, and so on.

As with multiple-range bar graphs, you can vary the patterns in a stacked-bar graph by skipping ranges as you make your selections. For example, instead of choosing A, B, C, and D as the data ranges in a four-range stacked-bar graph, you could choose A, B, D, and F.

▶1-2-3 Release 2.2 handles negative values in stacked bar charts differently than earlier releases of 1-2-3 do. In 1-2-3 Releases 1A, 2, and 2.01, you cannot plot a combination of positive and negative values in a stacked-bar graph. If the graph includes both negative and positive values, the segments in the graph will overlap, and the result will be a real mess. 1-2-3 Release 2.2, on the other hand, draws the segments that correspond to any negative values in your data ranges below the x-axis. This makes for a cleaner and easier to read graph.◀

**RELEASE
▶ 2.2 ◀**

Of course, if all the values in the data ranges are negative, then 1-2-3 will simply plot the graph upside down, with the A range at the top of the stack (next to the x-axis), the B range below that, and so on.

Pie Graphs

Pie graphs are similar to stacked-bar graphs because both illustrate the individual components of a total. However, pie graphs can show only as much information as a single bar in a stacked-bar graph. In a pie graph, each value in the data range is represented by a "slice" of the pie. The total of all the values is represented by the "pie" itself.

Pie graphs are different from other 1-2-3 graphs. First, pie graphs include only one data range: the A range. (You can also use the B range in a pie graph to explode and shade segments.) In addition, many of the enhancements you use with other graphs—including x- and y-axis titles, data labels, legends, grids, and formats—do not apply to pie graphs. X-axis labels also serve a different purpose in pie graphs than in other types of graphs.

An Example

Suppose you want to create a pie graph of the 1987 population figures for all four towns from the range D5..D8 in Figure 10-9. Before you start, issue the / Graph Reset Graph command to reset any active Graph settings (you might want to save the previous graph under a name first). Then choose Type Pie from the main Graph menu, select A, point to the range D5..D8 (or type the range reference), and press [Enter]. When you are finished, choose View to bring the pie graph shown in Figure 10-15 into view.

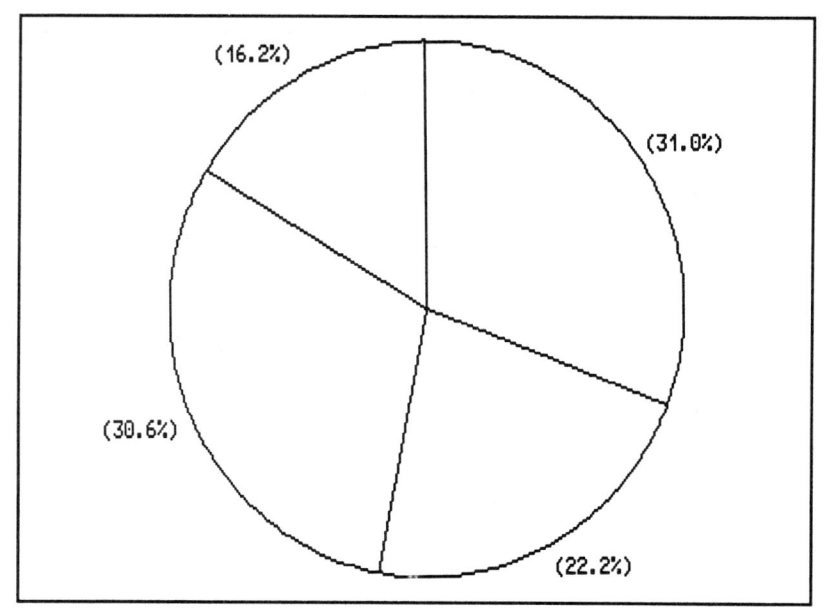

FIGURE 10-15: A pie graph

Notes

When 1-2-3 graphs the data in a pie graph, it begins with the first (top or leftmost) cell in the range. The first segment in the pie (that is, the segment to the right of the 12 o'clock position) represents this value. The second segment represents the second value, and so on.

Notice that 1-2-3 has automatically placed percentages that represent the portion of the total accounted for by the segment next to each wedge of the pie. 1-2-3 will always place these percentages in your pie graphs, and there is no way to remove them. All 1-2-3 pie graphs have percentages like these.

While pie graphs are among 1-2-3's most useful and attractive graph types, they have one significant limitation. You cannot plot a negative value in a pie graph. There is simply no way to picture a negative value in a pie graph.

Obviously, the pie graph in Figure 10-15 is pretty meaningless as it now stands since there is no easy way to figure out what each segment represents. As you will see, you can solve this problem by defining an X range for the graph. As you might expect, you can also define two titles for the graph. We'll show you how to do those things later in this chapter.

Shading and Exploding Pie Segments

You can shade and explode (pull out) selected segments in a pie graph. Shading the segments in a pie graph makes the graph more attractive and easier to read. By exploding, or pulling out, selected segments, you can draw attention to the data represented by those segments. (This capability is not available in Release 1A.)

To explode and shade segments in a pie graph, you enter special codes in the worksheet—one code for each value in the A range—and specify the range that contains those codes as the graph's B range. 1-2-3 uses the codes to determine how it should shade and/or explode the graph's segments.

1-2-3 offers eight different shading codes: 0, 1, 2, 3, 4, 5, 6, and 7. Each of the codes in the range 1 to 7 represents a different shading pattern. You can use the code 0 (or a blank cell) to indicate no shading for a segment. In addition, 1-2-3 offers another set of codes, 100 through 107, that causes segments to be exploded and/or shaded. The shading effects of each of the codes in the range 100 to 107 is equivalent to the corresponding code in the range 0 to 7. However, the codes in the range 100 to 107 also cause 1-2-3 to explode segments from the pie. For example, suppose you have assigned the code 2 to one segment of your pie graph and the code 102 to another segment. These two segments will be shaded with exactly the same pattern, but the segment with code 102 will also be exploded. Code 100 indicates that you want to explode, but not shade, a segment.

An Example

Suppose you want to add shading and exploded segments to the example pie graph in Figure 10-15. To begin, you must enter the shading and exploding codes you want to use into the cells of the worksheet. There should be one code (or a blank cell) for each value in the graph's A range. For example, to create the worksheet shown in Figure 10-16, enter the codes 1, 0, 5, and 107 in cells D12..D15.

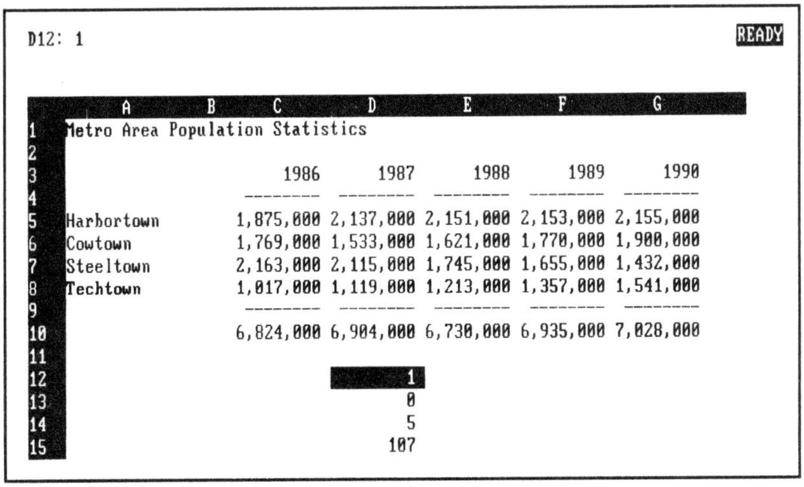

```
D12: 1                                                              READY

      A         B         C         D         E         F         G
1  Metro Area Population Statistics
2
3                       1986      1987      1988      1989      1990
4                   --------  --------  --------  --------  --------
5  Harbortown      1,875,000 2,137,000 2,151,000 2,153,000 2,155,000
6  Cowtown         1,769,000 1,533,000 1,621,000 1,770,000 1,900,000
7  Steeltown       2,163,000 2,115,000 1,745,000 1,655,000 1,432,000
8  Techtown        1,017,000 1,119,000 1,213,000 1,357,000 1,541,000
9                   --------  --------  --------  --------  --------
10                 6,824,000 6,904,000 6,730,000 6,935,000 7,028,000
11
12                                   1
13                                   0
14                                   5
15                                 107
```

FIGURE 10-16: A worksheet with shading codes

After entering these codes, you have to define the range that contains the codes as the graph's B range. To do this, issue the / Graph B command, select the range

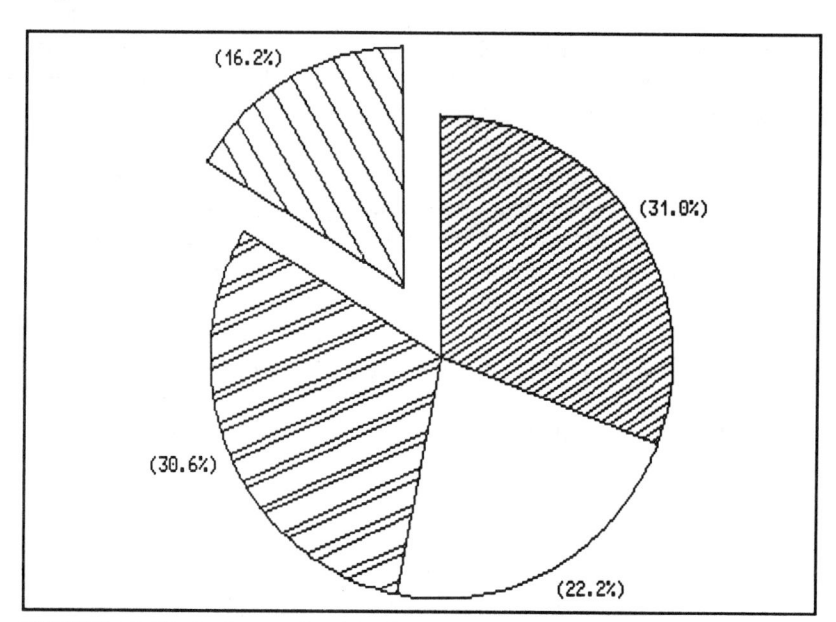

D12..D15, and press [Enter]. When you issue the View command, the graph will look like Figure 10-17.

FIGURE 10-17: A pie graph with shaded and exploded segments

As you can see, 1-2-3 has shaded the first, third, and fourth segments in the pie. These segments correspond to the first, third, and fourth cells in the B range (cells D12, D14, and D15). In addition, the fourth segment, which corresponds to the code 107 in cell D15, is exploded.

Because the second cell in the B range (cell D13) contains the value 0, the second segment in the graph is not shaded. We could have achieved the same effect by leaving cell D13 blank.

Notes

As a rule, it is a good idea not to explode more than one or two segments in a pie graph. Exploding all or most of the segments in a pie graph misses the point of explosion, which is to draw attention to a particular segment.

If you have a color monitor, you can instruct 1-2-3 to display the segments of a pie graph in different colors. To do this, you just issue the / Graph Options Color command. We'll cover that command later in this chapter.

XY Graphs

XY graphs allow you to plot the relationship between two quantifiable characteristics of a set of data. XY graphs come in handy when you are trying to use one characteristic (the independent characteristic or variable) to predict another characteristic (the dependent characteristic or variable). For example, you can use this type of graph to plot the relationship between years of education (the independent variable) and income (the dependent variable), or between height (the independent variable) and weight (the dependent variable). XY graphs are sometimes also called scatter diagrams.

To create an XY graph, you must designate two data ranges: the X range and at least one other range (usually the A range). The values in these ranges work together to determine the position of the points in the graph. The X range should contain the values for the independent variable. These values determine the horizontal position of each point in the graph. The other range should contain the values for the dependent variable. The values in this range determine the vertical position of each point in the graph.

An Example

Suppose you have created the worksheet shown in Figure 10-18, which lists some data on mortgage rates and the number of houses sold in a city. You would like to plot the relationship between mortgage rates and house sales. In this case, you would assume that the number of houses sold in a given month is *dependent upon* the average mortgage rate, and not vice versa. Thus, the average mortgage rate is the independent variable—and will be plotted as the X range—while the number of houses sold is the dependent variable.

```
A1: [W16] 'Harbortown Realty                                          READY

          A              B          C          D     E     F     G
1   Harbortown Realty
2   Mortgage Rate Analysis
3
4                      Average             Houses
5                       Rate                Sold
6                      -------             -------
7   January            11.750%               257
8   February           11.250%               285
9   March              10.875%               348
10  April              10.500%               420
11  May                10.500%               795
12  June               11.000%               679
13  July               10.875%               625
14  August             11.250%               647
15  September          10.750%               542
16  October            10.250%               600
17  November           10.250%               665
18  December           10.000%               702
19
20
```

FIGURE 10-18: A sample worksheet

To create the graph, issue the / Graph Type command and choose XY as the graph type. Then choose A from the main Graph menu and designate cells C7..C18 as the A range. Next, choose X from the main Graph menu, point to cells B7..B18 (or type the cell references), and press [Enter]. Finally, choose View to view the graph, which should look like Figure 10-19.

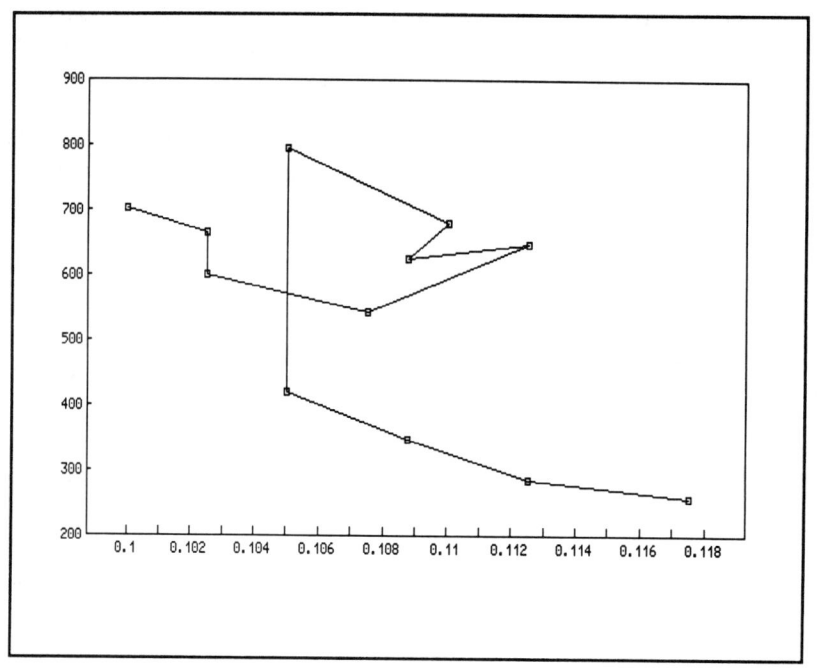

FIGURE 10-19: An XY graph

Removing the Lines

As you can see, the graph in Figure 10-19 is a confused mess. The mess occurs because 1-2-3 automatically connects the points in a new scatter diagram with lines, just as it connects the points in a line graph. Most of the time, however, you will not want 1-2-3 to draw connecting lines in your XY graphs.

To remove these lines, you must issue the / Graph Options Format command, choose Graph (or A), and select Symbols. Once you have completed this command, issue the View command again to view the graph, which now should look like Figure 10-20.

Adjusting the Scale

Just as when it draws a line graph, when 1-2-3 draws an XY graph it almost never places the origin for either the x-axis or the y-axis at 0. Instead, it draws the graph so that the upper and lower limits of the two axes are just large enough to hold the points in the graph. As with line graphs, this technique is almost certain to create a misleading graph. For example, in this XY graph, the relationship between mortgage rates and house sales almost appears to be random because of the tight borders of the graph.

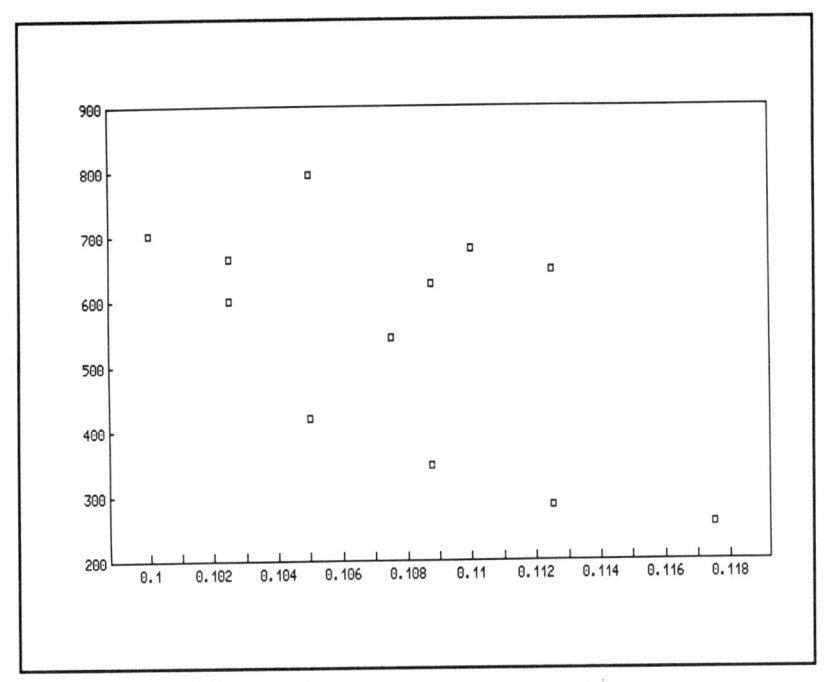

FIGURE 10-20: XY Graph formatted for symbols only

To correct this problem, issue the / Graph Options Scale Y Scale command, choose the Manual option, choose Lower, type 0, press [Enter], choose Upper, type a suitable upper limit, say 1000, and press [Enter]. Then choose Quit to return to the Options menu, choose Scale X Scale, choose Manual, choose Lower, type 0.01, and press [Enter]. Then choose Upper, type an appropriate upper limit, such as .12, and press [Enter]. When you are finished, press [Esc] or choose Quit to return to the main menu and choose the View option. Figure 10-21 shows the results.

You can also enhance an XY graph by adding titles, data labels, and a grid. We'll show you how to make all of these changes in the section titled "Enhancing Graphs." (We'll also cover the / Graph Scale command in detail in that section.)

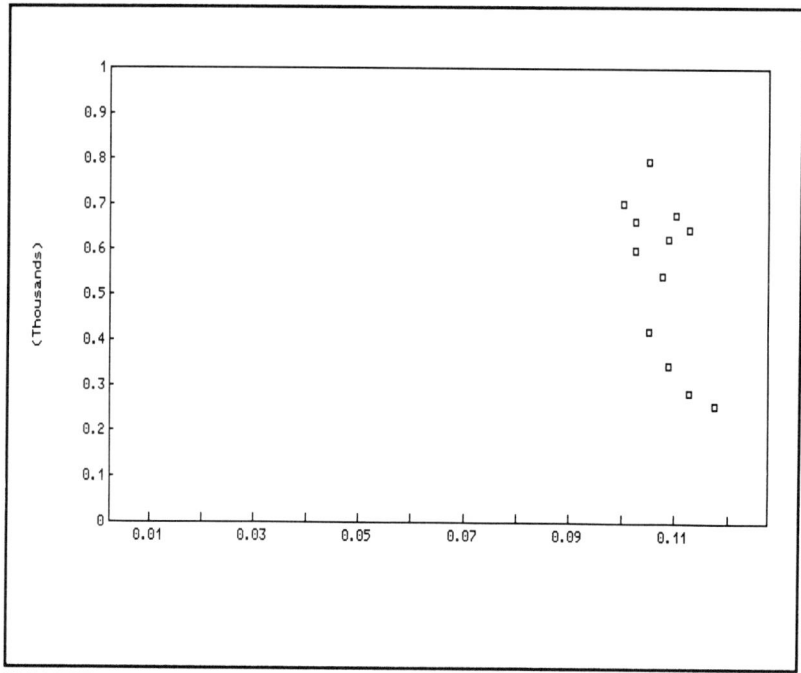

FIGURE 10-21: An XY graph with adjusted scales

Plotting a Regression Line

When you are analyzing the relationship between two characteristics of a population, you'll often want to go beyond a basic scatter diagram and perform some simple regression analysis. The / Data Regression command allows you to do just this. We introduced you to this command in Chapter 6, so we won't discuss it in detail here. Rather, we will show you how you can use the output from this command to plot a regression line in XY graphs.

To plot a regression line, you first need to compute the slope and the y-axis intercept of the line. You can use the / Data Regression command to compute these values. Once you have computed the slope and y-intercept, you can use the equation $y=mx+b$, where m is the slope of the line and b is its y-axis intercept, to compute the coordinates of the points along the regression line.

To create a regression line for the XY graph shown in Figure 10-21, first issue the / Data Regression command. To define the range that contains the X values, choose X-Range and select the range B7..B18. (Notice that this range is also the X range in our XY graph.) Next, to define the range that contains the Y values, choose Y-Range and select the range C7..C18. (Notice that this range is also the A range in our graph.) Then choose Output-Range, point to a cell in a blank area of the worksheet—we'll use cell A21—and choose Go. The results will look like Figure 10-22.

You can use the Constant and the X Coefficient and the numbers in the X range (cells B7..B18) to compute the Y value of points on the regression line. To do this, enter the formula +$C$28*B7+$D$22 in cell F7 and then use the / Copy command to copy this formula into the range F8..F18. The values in the range F7..F18 are the y-axis coordinates of the points on the regression line. To plot these points into our graph, you need only issue the / Graph B command, select the range F7..F18, and press [Enter]. Then choose Options Format B and select Lines as the format for this part of the graph. When you have completed these steps and view your graph, it should look like Figure 10-23.

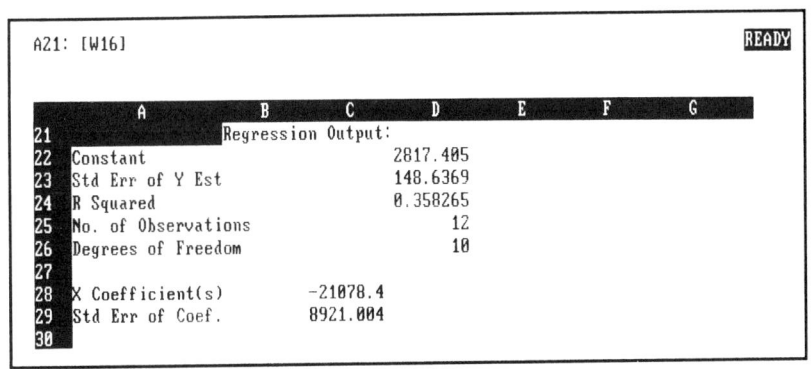

FIGURE 10-22: Output from the / Data Regression command

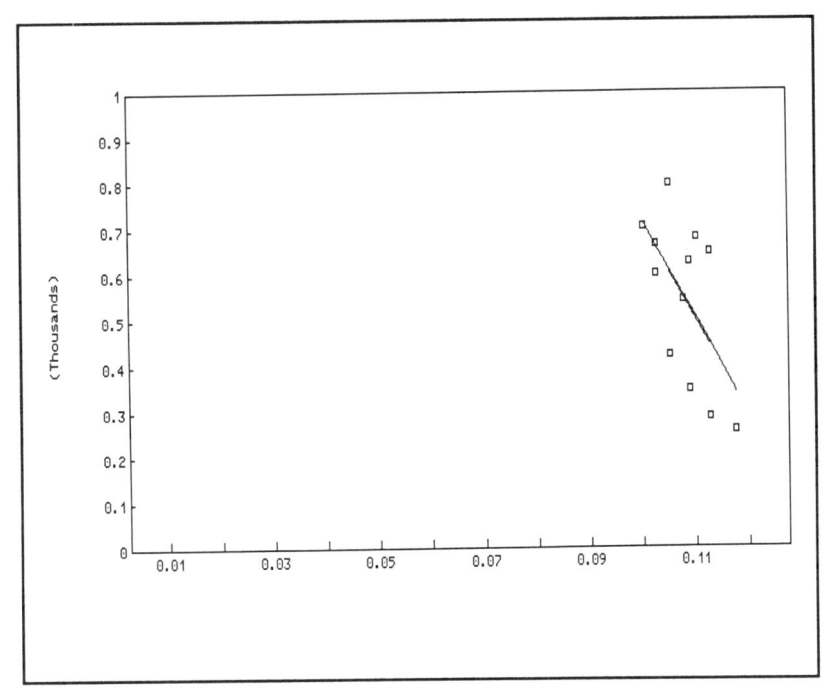

FIGURE 10-23: The regression line

TIP: SETTING THE LOWER LIMIT IN XY GRAPHS

Notice that we set the lower limt for the X sales in Figure 10-21 to .01 instead of 0. Here's why. In 1-2-3 2.2, the first x-axis tick mark in a graph is indented slightly from the y-axis. This is true in all graphs, including XY graphs, and is a great improvement in all types of graphs but XY graphs. In XY graphs, though, the x-axis origin should be 0 and should be at the y-axis origin. Unfortunately, there is no way to force 1-2-3 to place the x-axis origin at the y-axis origin. If you use the / Graph Options Scale X-Scale Lower command to specify a lower limit for the x-axis of 0, your graph will look like Figure A. Notice that there are now two lines at the left edge of the graph: the y-axis and a line representing the origin of the x-axis.

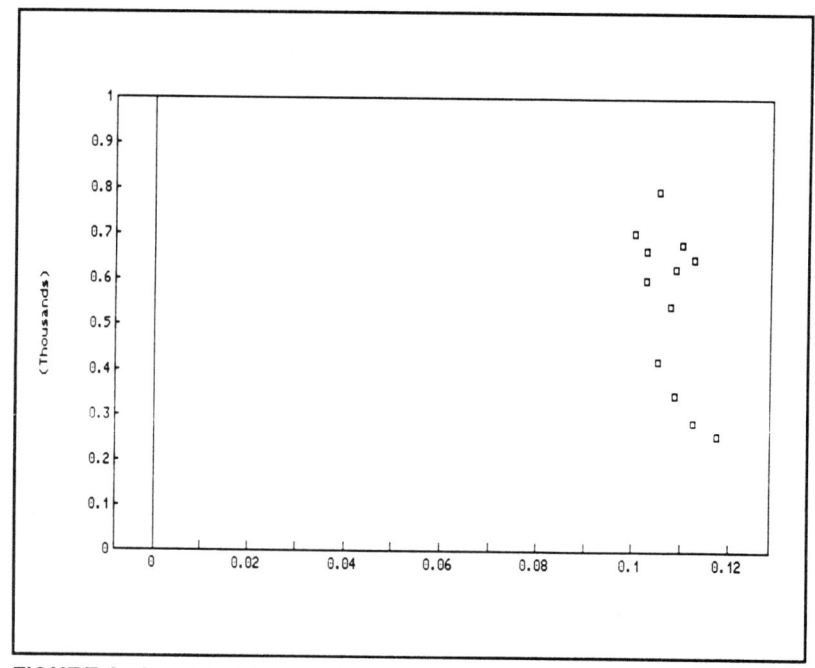

FIGURE A: A quirk of XY graphs

As a result of this quirk, you usually will not want to set the lower limit of the x-axis in an XY graph to 0. Instead, you'll want to choose a lower limit that will give the impression that the lower limit of the x-axis is at 0. In the example, we achieved this effect by setting the lower limit of the x-axis to .01.

ENHANCING GRAPHS

As you've seen, 1-2-3 lets you add many enhancements, such as titles and legends, to your graphs. These enhancements help to make graphs easier to interpret and far more useful. Now that we've explained how to create each of 1-2-3's graph types, let's take a closer look at all of 1-2-3's graph enhancements.

As we mentioned earlier in this chapter, not every type of enhancement applies to every type of graph. For this reason, we'll use several different graphs in this section to illustrate 1-2-3's graph enhancements. Since most enhancements apply to line graphs, however, we'll use the simple two-range line graph in Figure 10-24 as our basic example. This graph is based on the population worksheet shown in Figure 10-9. To create this graph, we issued the / Graph command, selected the A option, selected the range C7..G7, pressed [Enter], selected the B option, specified the range C8..G8, and pressed [Enter] again.

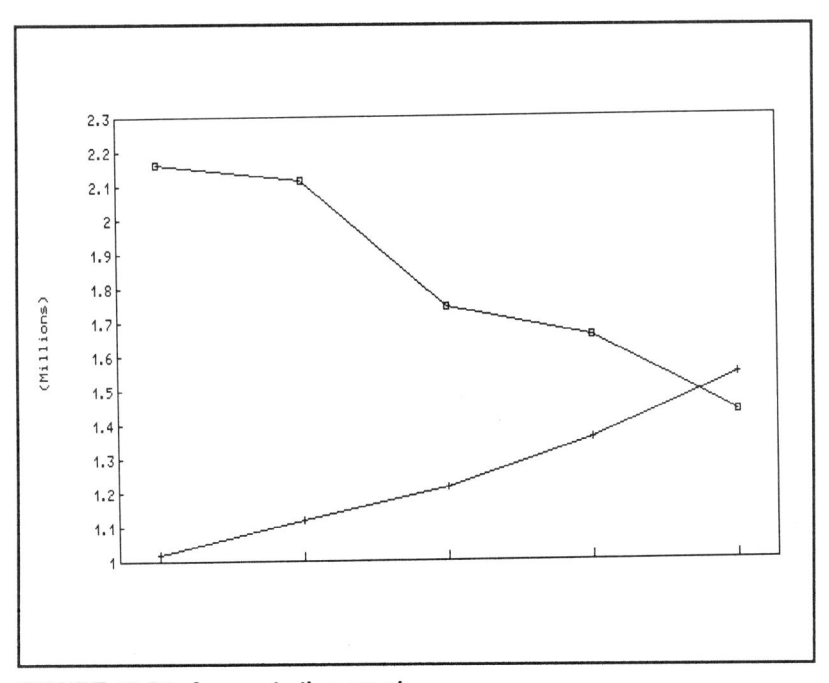

FIGURE 10-24: A sample line graph

Adding Titles

Perhaps the most helpful additions you can make to a basic graph are titles that explain what the graph depicts. 1-2-3 allows you to add four titles to a graph: two titles at the top of the graph, one under the x-axis, and one beside the y-axis.

To add a title to a graph, you issue the / Graph Options Titles command. Issuing this command brings up a menu with four options: First, Second, X-Axis, and Y-Axis. The first and second titles are the main graph titles that appear at the top of the graph on separate lines. The x-axis title appears beneath the graph's horizontal axis, and the y-axis title appears along the vertical axis. To add one of these titles to the graph, just select that option, type the title, and press [Enter]. You can add first and second titles to every type of 1-2-3 graph. You can add x- and y-axis titles to every type of graph except for pie graphs.

An Example

For example, suppose you want to add titles to the line graph in Figure 10-24. To do this, issue the /Graph Options Titles command and choose First from the Titles menu. When you see the prompt, *Enter first line of graph title:*, type *Population Projections* and press [Enter]. Similarly, to create the second title, choose Titles Second, and at the prompt, type *For Steeltown and Techtown.*

Adding axis titles is just as easy. To add an x-axis title, choose the Titles X-Axis command, type *Year*, and press [Enter]. Similarly, to create the y-axis title, choose Titles Y-Axis, type *Population*, and press [Enter]. If you choose Quit from the Options menu and then choose View, the graph will look like Figure 10-25.

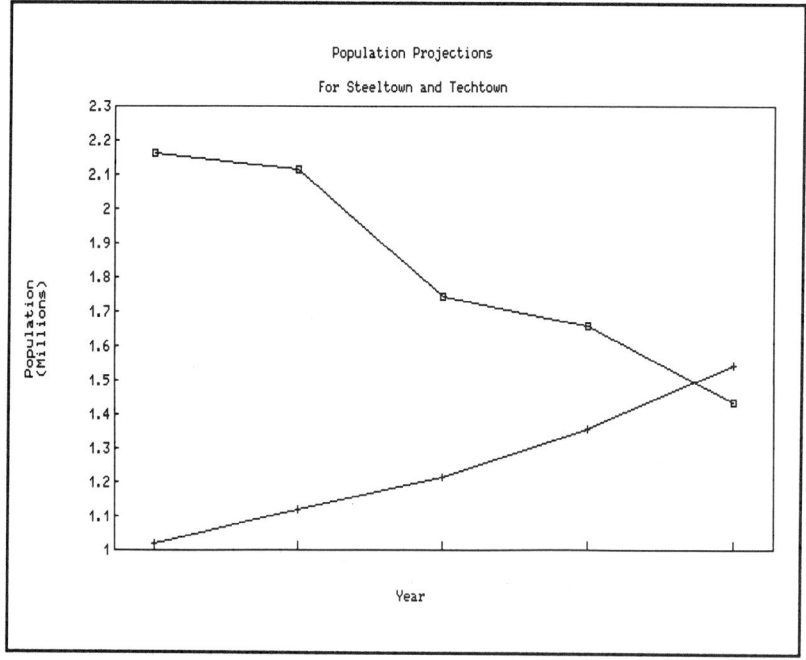

FIGURE 10-25: A graph with titles

Notes

1-2-3 allows you to type up to 39 characters when you are defining a title. However, the y-axis title, which is displayed vertically, has a practical limit of only about 32 characters, since no more than 32 characters of a y-axis title can be displayed on the screen. If you create a y-axis title that is more than 32 characters long, the first few and last few characters in the title will be truncated.

There isn't any difference between the size and intensity of the first and second titles in the screen display of a graph. However, when you print a graph, 1-2-3 will print the first title in larger type than the second title. In addition, you can select a different type style for the first title when you print the graph if you wish.

Removing Titles

To remove titles from a graph, just issue the / Graph Options Titles command, select the option for the title you want to remove (First, Second, X-Axis, or Y-Axis), press [Esc], and press [Enter]. 1-2-3 will remove the selected title from the graph; 1-2-3 does not offer a warning or second chance. If you want to remove all the titles from the graph, you'll have to repeat this process for every title.

Of course, you can also use the / Graph Reset Options command to delete titles—along with all other options—from a graph.

Labeling the X-Axis

When you create a bar, stacked-bar, or line graph, 1-2-3 will automatically label the tickmarks on the y-axis of that graph. However, 1-2-3 does not label the tickmarks along the x-axis. If you want to label the x-axis tickmarks, you can do so by defining an X range from the graph. Unlike the other graph ranges (A through F), the X range does not represent a data series (except in the case of XY graphs). Instead, it represents the range of cell entries that you want to use to label the x-axis of your graph.

To add x-axis labels to a graph, you issue the / Graph X command, point to the cells that contain the entries you want to use as the x-axis labels (you could also type the coordinates of that range), and press [Enter]. For instance, suppose you want to use the year numbers in row 3 of the worksheet in Figure 10-9 as the x-axis labels in the sample graph. To do this, issue the / Graph X command, highlight cells C3..G3 (or type C3..G3) and press [Enter]. If you issue the View command at this point, the graph will look like Figure 10-26. Notice the labels 1986, 1987, and so on, along the x-axis.

▶Remember that in 1-2-3 Release 2.2, the first and last x-axis tick marks are indented from the borders of the graph. As you can see in Figure 10-26, this change improves the appearance of the x-axis labels in a graph significantly.

Also remember that 1-2-3 Release 2.2's / Graph Group command lets you create a graph and define x-axis labels in one step. If your worksheet is arranged properly, you can use this command to perform two steps in one.◀

RELEASE
▶ 2.2 ◀

TIP: USING CELL ENTRIES AS TITLES

If you want to, you can use the entries in your worksheet as titles in your graphs. To use an entry as a title, issue the / Graph Options Titles command, choose the title option you wish to define (First, Second, X-Axis, or Y-Axis), and then type a backslash (\) followed by the address of the cell that contains the entry you want to use as the title.

For example, you could use the entry in cell A1 in Figure 10-9 as the first title in the line graph shown in Figure 10-25. To do this, you would issue the / Graph Options Titles First command, press [Esc] to erase the existing title (if necessary), and type \A1. When you are done, choose Quit and then View to bring the graph in Figure A into view.

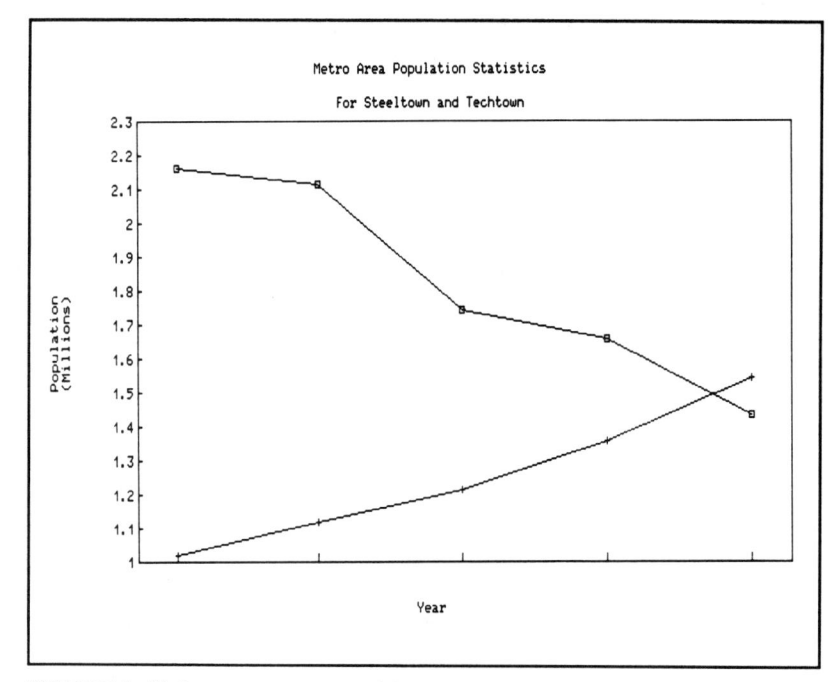

FIGURE A: Using an entry as a title

There are a few points to keep in mind if you use this technique. If the cell has been given a range name, you can type a backslash followed by that name. For example, if you had given the name TITLE to cell A1 in Figure 10-9, you could type \TITLE to define the title. In addition, the cell you refer to can contain either a value or a label. If the cell contains a value, 1-2-3 will treat that value as a label in the graph title. Third, the backslash is a critical part of the title

(Tip continued on next page.)

reference. If you forget the backslash, 1-2-3 will use the cell address (like A1 or Z100) as the literal title of the graph.

Using cell references instead of literal text offers a couple of advantages. First, you can change the title of a graph just by entering a new label into the title cell. Second, by using cell references, you can create titles that are, theoretically, up to 240 characters long. Of course, the practical limit for a graph title will be determined by the number of characters you can view across your screen.

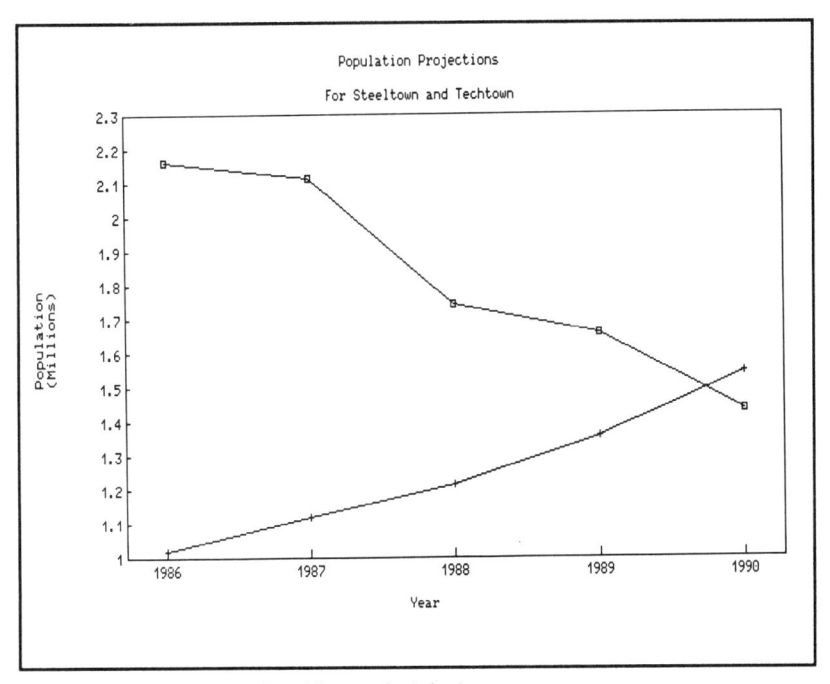

FIGURE 10-26: A graph with x-axis labels

Notes

The entries in the range you specify as the X range of a graph can be values or labels. 1-2-3 makes no distinction between labels and values in the X range (except in XY graphs, where the entries in the X range must be values).

The x-axis labels in your graphs will always be centered under the x-axis tick marks. The alignment of the X range entries in the worksheet has no effect on the alignment of the labels in the graph. However, if the entries in the X range are formatted values, the x-axis labels will have the same format as the values.

In most cases, your worksheets will contain a range of entries that would make appropriate x-axis labels. If a given worksheet does not contain an appropriate range of entries, you can simply create those entries in the worksheet and then use the / Graph X command to specify those entries as x-axis labels.

**RELEASE
► 2.2 ◄**

►If the entries in the X range are so long that they might overlap one another, 1-2-3 Release 2.2 will "stagger" the x-axis labels to prevent overlap. (Previous releases of 1-2-3 simply allow the labels to overlap.) This helps to make the graph easier to read, and prevents you from having to worry about the lengths of the labels you want to use in your X range.

To demonstrate how this works, let's create a line graph from the worksheet in Figure 10-27. Cells B3 through B28 contain the estimated national debt for the years 1985 through 2010. To create this graph, issue the / Graph command, choose the A option, select the range B3..B28, and press [Enter]. Now suppose that you want to use the entries in the range A3..A28 as x-axis labels. To define the X range, choose the X option from the Graph menu, select the range A3..A28, and press [Enter] again.

Figure 10-28 shows the resulting graph. As you can see, the x-axis labels are staggered and do not overlap. In earlier release of 1-2-3, these labels would overlap, making the graph quite hard to understand.◄

Skipping Labels along the X-Axis

If your graph includes a lot of data points, you might be able to improve the appearance of your graph by specifying a skip factor for your x-axis labels. To specify a skip factor, you issue the / Graph Options Scale Skip command and type a number representing the skip factor you want 1-2-3 to use. 1-2-3's default skip factor is 1, which means that every tickmark on the x-axis will have a label. If you change the skip factor to 2, then only every second x-axis tick mark will be labeled. Similarly, a skip factor of 3 means that only every third x-axis label will be displayed, and so forth.

An Example

To see how this works, we could use a skip factor for the x-axis lables in the graph in Figure 10-28. To do this, issue the / Graph Options Scale Skip command. When you see the prompt *Enter skip factor (1..8192):*, type 5 and press [Enter]. When you are finished, choose Quit and View to display the graph, which will look like Figure 10-29. As you can see, 1-2-3 is now displaying only every fifth x-axis label.

Notes

After you have defined a skip factor, you can change the skip factor back to 1 by reissuing the / Graph Options Scale Skip command and entering 1. The next time you display the graph, 1-2-3 will display every x-axis label.

Although you can set the X range skip factor to any value between 1 and 8192, in most cases a skip factor of only 2, 3, 4, or 5 will be sufficient to overcome problems with overlapping labels.

Chapter 10: Creating Graphs 413

```
A1: 'NATIONAL DEBT PROJECTIONS                              READY

         A           B           C       D       E       F
 1  NATIONAL DEBT PROJECTIONS
 2
 3      1985   $3,000,000,000,000
 4      1986   $3,600,000,000,000
 5      1987   $4,320,000,000,000
 6      1988   $5,184,000,000,000
 7      1989   $6,220,800,000,000
 8      1990   $7,464,960,000,000
 9      1991   $8,957,952,000,000
10      1992  $10,749,542,400,000
11      1993  $12,899,450,880,000
12      1994  $15,479,341,056,000
13      1995  $18,575,209,267,200
14      1996  $22,290,251,120,640
15      1997  $26,748,301,344,768
16      1998  $32,097,961,613,722
17      1999  $38,517,553,936,466
18      2000  $46,221,064,723,759
19      2001  $55,465,277,668,511
20      2002  $66,558,333,202,213
```

FIGURE 10-27: A sample worksheet

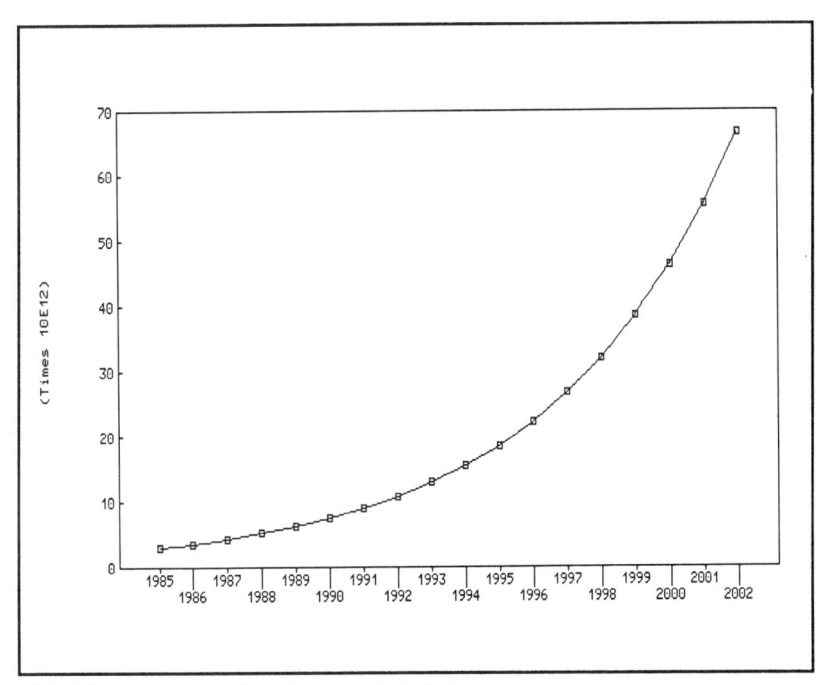

FIGURE 10-28: Overlapping x-axis labels

Removing X-Axis Labels

To remove x-axis labels from a graph, just issue the / Graph Reset X command. As soon as you choose X, 1-2-3 will remove the X labels from the graph. Remember that 1-2-3 does not offer a warning or second chance.

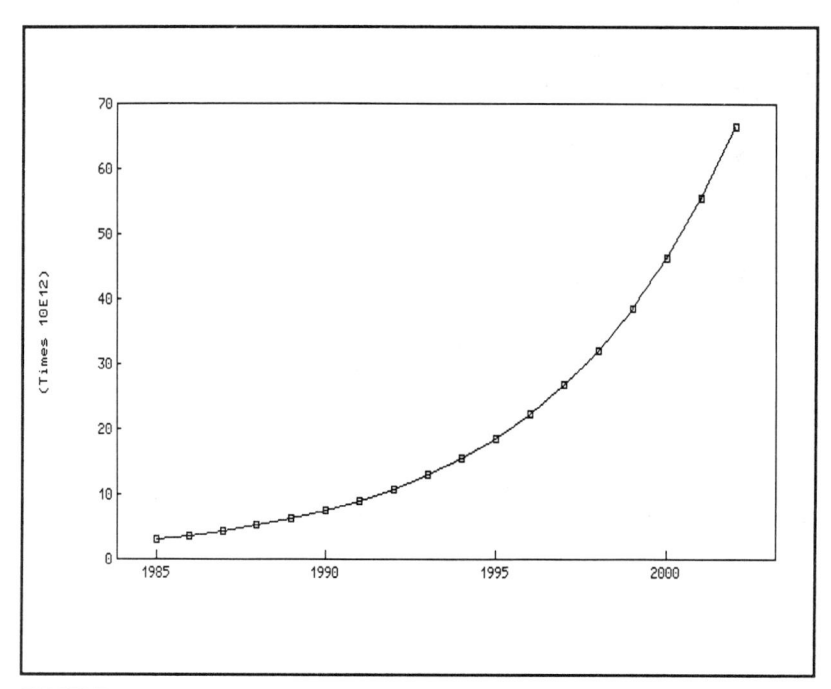

FIGURE 10-29: The / Graph Options Scale Skip command

XY Graphs

As we have said, when you create an XY graph, you must define an X range. The entries in the X range of an XY graph are not merely labels; instead, those entries are values that set the scale of the x-axis and help determine the position of the points in the graph. The entries in the X range of an XY graph must be values.

Interestingly, you cannot set a skip factor for the X range of an XY graph. Apparently, 1-2-3 sets its own skip factor automatically in XY graphs.

Pie Graphs

Because pie graphs do not have axes, they cannot have x-axis labels. However, you can use the X range in a pie graph to create labels for the segments in the graph. All you have to do is issue the / Graph X command and select the range of cells that you want 1-2-3 to display as segment labels. When 1-2-3 draws the graph, it will display the entry in the first cell of the X range next to the first segment in the pie, the second entry in the X range next to the second segment, and so on.

Using Labels

For example, suppose you want to add segment labels to the pie graph in Figure 10-17. (Recall that this graph is based on the entries in the range D5..D8 in the worksheet in Figure 10-9.) You might use the entries in the range A5..A8 of the worksheet as the segment labels. To do this, first issue the /Graph X command, select the range A5..A8 (or type the cell references), and press [Enter]. When you are finished, choose View to display the graph shown in Figure 10-30.

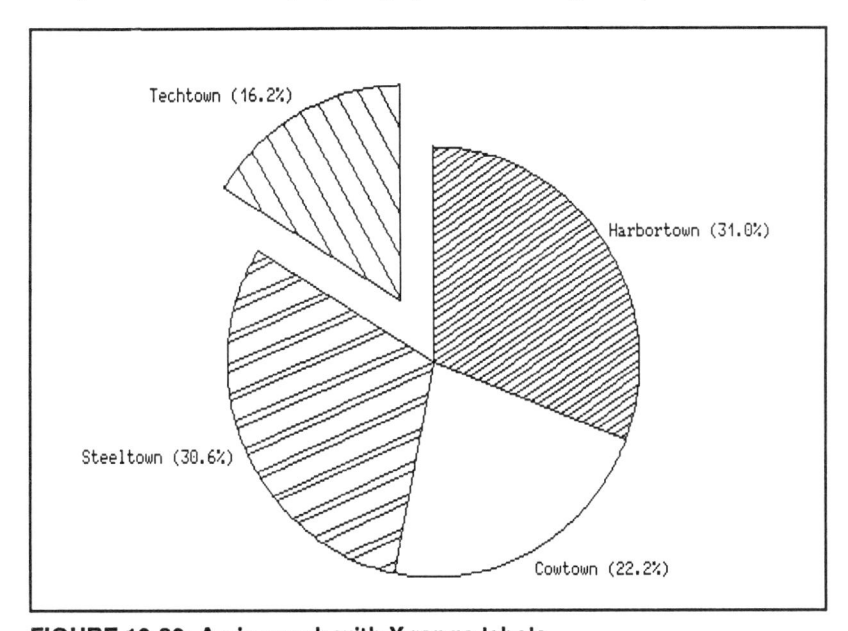

FIGURE 10-30: A pie graph with X range labels

Notice that 1-2-3 still displays the percentages next to each pie segment, in addition to the X range labels. There is no way to delete these percentages; they will always appear after whatever segment labels you define.

Using Values

You can also use values as the segment labels in a pie graph. In fact, many 1-2-3 users like to use the same values on which a pie graph is based as the segment labels. To do this, you must define the X range of the graph to include the same cells as the A range.

For example, instead of using the labels in column A of Figure 10-9 as segment labels, you might want to use the values on which the pie graph is based as the segment labels. To do this, issue the / Graph X command, press [Esc] to erase the existing X range (if necessary), select the range D5..D8, and press [Enter]. If you choose View to display the graph, it will look like Figure 10-31. As you can see, 1-2-3 is now using the values in the range D5..D8 as segment labels. As always, the segment labels have the same format as the values in the range.

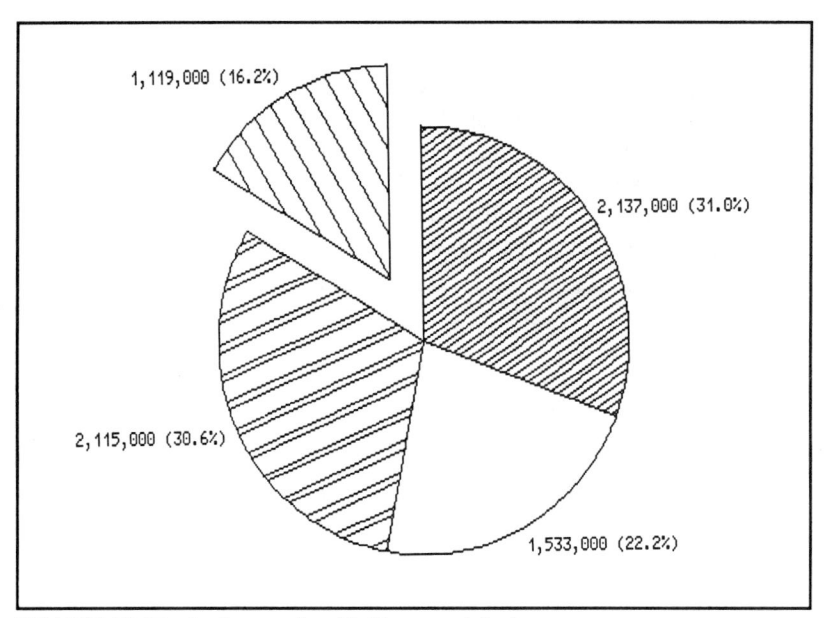

FIGURE 10-31: A pie graph with X range labels

One advantage of using the values on which the graph is based as segment labels is that doing so makes the segment labels dynamic. In other words, if you change the values on which the graph is based, the segment labels will change.

The / Graph Options Scale Command

The / Graph Options Scale command allows you to adjust and format the y-axis of line, bar, stacked-bar, and XY graphs, and the x-axis of XY graphs. When you issue this command, 1-2-3 will display a menu with three options: Y Scale, X Scale, and Skip. We've already explained the Skip command (see the section "Skipping Labels along the X-Axis"). The Y Scale option allows you to adjust or format the y-axis of a graph. The X Scale option, which applies only to XY graphs, allows you to adjust or format the x-axis of a graph.

When you choose either of these options, 1-2-3 will display the menu shown in Figure 10-32. The options on this menu allow you to choose manual or automatic scaling for the selected axis, to set the upper limit and lower limit of the axis, to format the values displayed along the axis, and to change the indicator that 1-2-3 displays along the axis.

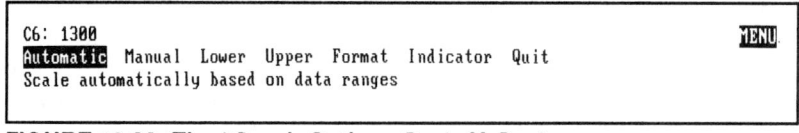

```
C6: 1300                                                              MENU
Automatic  Manual  Lower  Upper  Format  Indicator  Quit
Scale automatically based on data ranges
```

FIGURE 10-32: The / Graph Options Scale Y Scale menu

TIP: LABELING PIE SEGMENTS

As we have said, the X range of a pie graph can include labels or values. However, there may be times when you want to use *both* a label and a value to describe each pie segment. Through the clever application of string arithmetic, you can create just such a combination.

Using the worksheet in Figure 10-9 as an example, suppose you would like to combine each label in column A with the corresponding value in column D and then use these label/number combinations in the pie graph. To do this, enter the string formula *+A5&" "&@STRING(D5,0)* into cell A12 (or any other blank cell), then copy it into the three cells immediately below (the range A13..A15). Figure A shows our example worksheet with this string formula in cells A12..A15. These formulas join the labels in column A with the values in column D, creating a combined label/value string.

```
A12: [W13] +A5&" "&@STRING(D5,0)                                    READY


         A         B       C         D         E         F         G
  12  Harbortown  2137000             1
  13  Cowtown     1533000             0
  14  Steeltown   2115000             5
  15  Techtown    1119000           107
```

FIGURE A: Worksheet with string formulas

Next, you must redefine the X range of the pie graph to include the cells that contain these string formulas. To do this, issue the / Graph X command, press [Esc] to erase the existing X range (if necessary), select the range A12..A15, and press [Enter]. When you are finished, choose View to bring the graph shown in Figure B into view.   (*Tip continued on next page.*)

Since the / Graph Options Scale X Scale command applies only to XY graphs, we'll use the / Graph Options Scale Y Scale command to demonstrate the effects of the options listed in Figure 10-32. After we've covered each of these options in detail, we'll show you how to use the / Graph Options Scale X Scale command to adjust the x-axis of an XY graph.

Manual Scaling

You will often find that 1-2-3 automatically sets the y-axis origin in your line graphs at some number other than zero, and sets the upper limit of the axis just barely high enough to accommodate the data in the graph. Both of these characteristics are evident in the example graph in Figure 10-26. The problem is that setting the origin of a graph at a value other than 0 can make the graph confusing or even misleading.

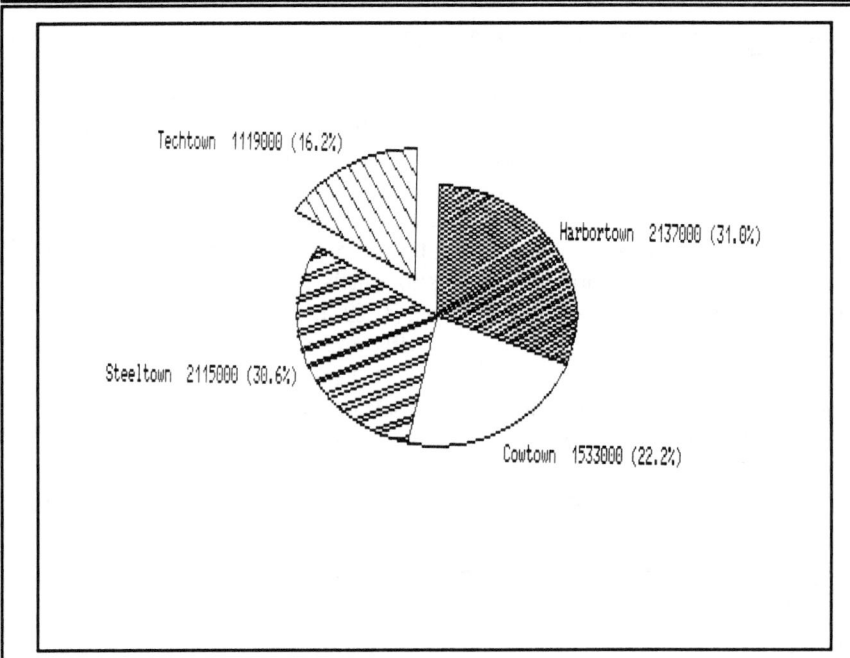

FIGURE B: Pie graph with string segment labels

When you are using this technique, it is very easy to create labels that are too long for 1-2-3 to display in full. If the labels are too long to be fully displayed, 1-2-3 will simply truncate them.

The Manual, Lower, and Upper options of the / Graph Options Scale Y Scale command are the keys to correcting these kinds of problems. To override 1-2-3's automatic scaling, you can select the Manual option from the Y Scale menu. This command tells 1-2-3 that you want to set specific upper and lower limits for your graph's y-axis. Once you have selected Manual, you need to choose Lower to set the desired lower limit for the y-axis and Upper to set the upper limit for the axis.

An Example

For example, suppose you want to change the y-axis of the graph shown in Figure 10-26 so that its origin is 0 and its upper limit is 2500000. To make this change, issue the /Graph Options Scale Y Scale Manual command. Next, choose Lower, type 0, and press [Enter]. Then choose Upper, type 2500000, and press [Enter] once again. When you are finished, choose Quit twice to return to the Graph menu and choose View to display the graph. Figure 10-33 shows the result.

As you can see, changing the upper and lower limits of the y-axis has significantly changed the appearance of the graph. Notice that the curves representing the populations of Steeltown and Techtown are now less steep. In fact, the graph in Figure 10-33 gives a much more accurate picture of the changes in the populations of the two towns. In addition, the graph looks cleaner and is easier to read.

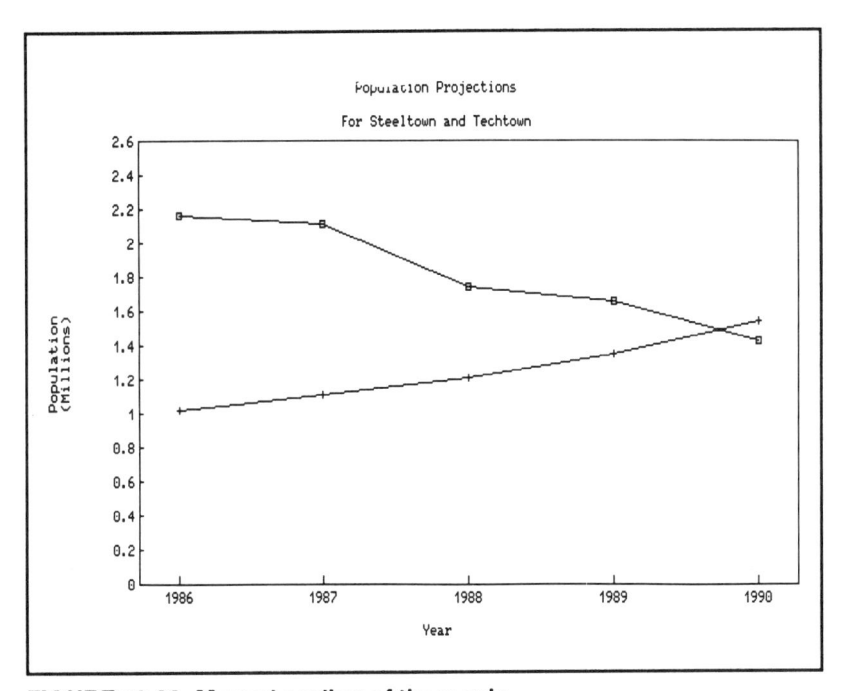

FIGURE 10-33: Manual scaling of the y-axis

Notes

Once you select manual scaling, you *must* specify both an upper and lower limit for the y-axis or you may get very strange results—such as a lower limit of zero with an upper limit of 1. In addition, the upper limit you set must be greater than the lower limit. If not, 1-2-3 will be unable to draw the graph.

Both the upper limit and the lower limit can be negative numbers. You will usually use a negative lower limit only in graphs that have some values that fall below 0. You will use a negative upper limit only when every value in the graph is less than 0.

Notice that the upper limit of the axis in Figure 10-33 is 2600000 (2.6 million) and not, as we specified, 2500000. 1-2-3 uses the upper limit you specify as a guideline instead of a strict limit. If you use a number like 2300000 as the upper limit, 1-2-3 will usually round it up to a number that will allow it to create nice, even divisions along the y-axis.

Although 1-2-3 will often adjust the upper limit in this way, it will never set the top value on the y-axis to be less than the limit you specify. In other words, the value you specify sets the minimum value for the top end of the y-axis.

Unfortunately, there is no way to change the position of the tick marks along the y-axis and thus change the upper limit of that axis. 1-2-3 always determines the position of the tick marks automatically as it draws the graph, and then sets the upper limit of the axis accordingly.

You should be careful to choose upper and lower limits for your graphs that will allow 1-2-3 to display all of the data in the graph. If you choose a lower limit that is greater than some of the values in the graph, or an upper limit that is less than some of those values, 1-2-3 will truncate a part of your graph. At the same time, you do not want to set the lower limit too low or the upper limit too high. If the limits you set define too wide a range, the graph will lose its detail and, therefore, much of its meaning.

Bar Graphs

While you can use the / Graph Options Scale command to adjust the upper and lower limits of a bar or stacked-bar graph, you will rarely need to do so. 1-2-3 always sets the y-axis origin in bar and stacked-bar graphs to 0, eliminating the need to manually reset the lower limit of the y-axis.

The Indicator Option

When 1-2-3 draws a line, bar, stacked-bar, or XY graph, it will never show more than three digits to the left of the decimal point in the values along the y-axis of the graph. Instead, it will divide each number along the axis by 1000, 1000000, or some other number in order to limit the number of digits to no more than three. When it does so, it displays a magnitude indicator like *(Thousands)*, *(Millions)*, or *(times 10E9)* (which means "multiply each number by 10^9"), along the y-axis to let you know what the numbers along the y-axis actually represent.

For example, 1-2-3 has divided the numbers along the y-axis in Figure 10-33 by 1,000,000. In other words, the value .5 on the y-axis stands for the value 500,000, the value 1 stands for the value 1,000,000, and so on. Notice the message *(Millions)* along the y-axis in this graph. This message tips you off to what 1-2-3 has done.

There is one case in which 1-2-3's technique can result in a misleading graph. If the values you are graphing have already been divided by 1000 or 1,000,000, then 1-2-3's message *(Thousands)* or *(Millions)* may not accurately reflect the data in the graph. For example, suppose you decide to modify the worksheet in Figure 10-9 to eliminate the extraneous zeros at the end of each population number. For example, you want to change the number in cell C5 to 1875, the number in cell C6 to 1769, and so on. In other words, you want to state the numbers in the worksheet as thousands.

If you create a graph from the modified worksheet, 1-2-3 will divide the numbers along the y-axis by 1000 and will display the magnitude indicator *(Thousands)* beside the y-axis. Unfortunately, this magnitude indicator does not fit the data in the graph. As we have noted, the numbers in the worksheet are *already* stated in thousands. For this reason, the numbers along the y-axis will actually represent millions, not thousands.

You can partially alleviate this problem by removing the *(Thousands)* indicator. The Indicator option of the / Graph Options Scale Y Scale command allows you to eliminate this indicator from the graph. When you choose this option, 1-2-3 will present a Yes/No menu. Choosing No tells 1-2-3 not to display the magnitude indicator. Choosing Yes from the Indicator menu tells 1-2-3 to display the magnitude indicator again. To remove an erroneous indicator from a graph, then, you issue the / Graph Options Scale Y Scale Indicator command and choose No.

Once you have eliminated the indicator, you might also want to add or change the y-axis title to explain the magnitude of the y-axis values. For example, you might want to add the y-axis title *Population in Millions* to the example graph to clarify the meaning of the graph. To do this, issue the / Graph Options Titles Y-Axis command, type Population in Millions, and press [Enter].

Although you can use the Indicator option to remove an erroneous magnitude indicator, there is no way to override 1-2-3's decision to divide the numbers along the y-axis. In other words, you cannot force 1-2-3 to display the numbers along the scale "as is." As we have said, 1-2-3 will never display more than three digits to the left of the decimal point in these values. Unless the values in your graph are all less than 1000, 1-2-3 will always divide the values along the y-axis.

Formatting the Numbers along the Y-Axis

The / Graph Options Scale Y Scale Format command lets you choose a format for the numbers along the y-axis in line, bar, stacked-bar, and XY graphs. When you issue this command, 1-2-3 will present the menu in Figure 10-34. Notice that this menu is almost identical to the menu that 1-2-3 displays when you issue / Range Format. To change the format of the numbers along the y-axis, you need only choose a format, specify the number of decimals you want 1-2-3 to display, and then press [Enter].

An Example

For example, suppose that you want to display the numbers along the y-axis in the Fixed format with three decimal places. To do this, you would issue the / Graph Options Scale Y Scale Format Fixed command. When 1-2-3 displays the prompt *Enter number of decimal places (0..15):*, you would type 3 and press [Enter]. Figure 10-35 shows the result.

Notes

1-2-3's y-axis formats have a few quirks that you should keep in mind. First, even though some of the formats (such as Fixed, Currency, and Percent) allow you to specify that 1-2-3 display as many as 15 decimal places, the number of decimal places that you actually can see in the graph is limited by the amount of room next to the y-axis. You may find that you can't display numbers with lots of decimals in full, especially when you have added a y-axis title to the graph.

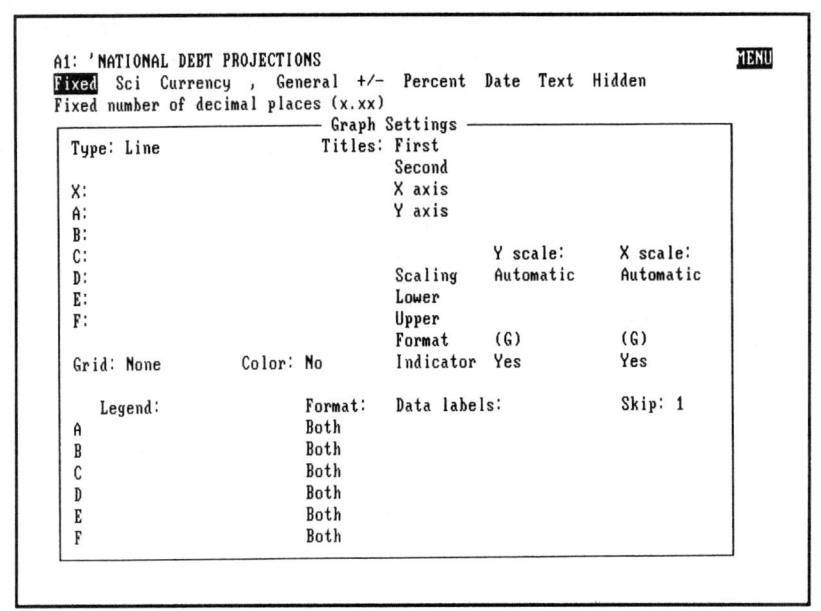

```
A1: 'NATIONAL DEBT PROJECTIONS                                    MENU
 Fixed  Sci Currency , General +/- Percent Date Text Hidden
Fixed number of decimal places (x.xx)
                      ┌─── Graph Settings ───────────────────────┐
  Type: Line             Titles: First
                                 Second
  X:                             X axis
  A:                             Y axis
  B:
  C:                                     Y scale:      X scale:
  D:                             Scaling Automatic     Automatic
  E:                             Lower
  F:                             Upper
                                 Format    (G)           (G)
  Grid: None    Color: No        Indicator Yes           Yes

    Legend:              Format:  Data labels:         Skip: 1
  A                      Both
  B                      Both
  C                      Both
  D                      Both
  E                      Both
  F                      Both
```

FIGURE 10-34: The / Graph Options Scale Y Scale Format menu

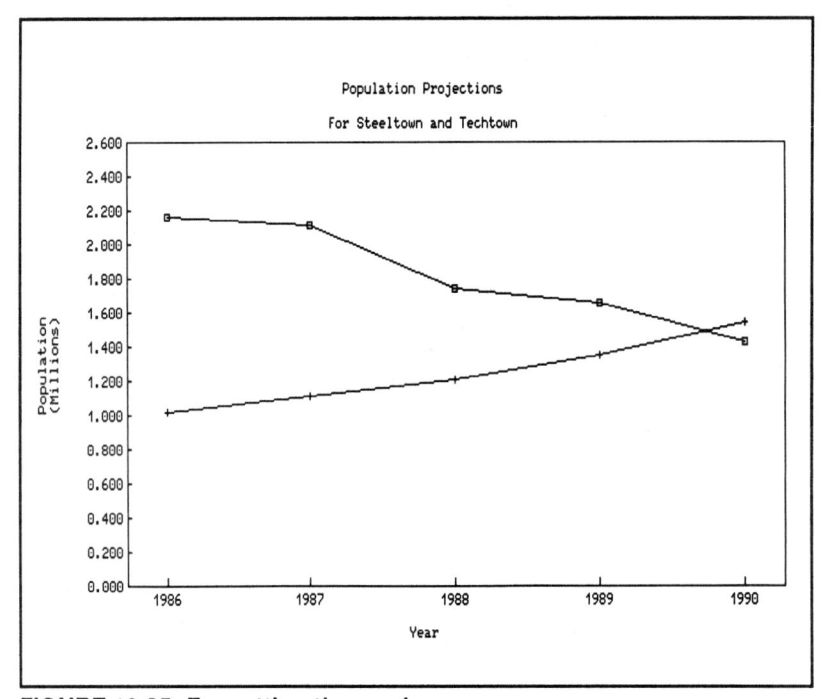

FIGURE 10-35: Formatting the y-axis

As you may recall, both the Comma (,) and Currency formats insert commas between the hundreds and thousands, thousands and millions, and so on, in formatted values. Since 1-2-3 never displays more than three digits to the left of the decimal place in the values along the y-axis, this feature of these formats never comes into play in graphs.

Although the /Graph Options Scale Y Scale Format command offers a Text option, this option has absolutely no effect in graphs.

XY Graphs

In an XY graph, you can use the / Graph Options Scale command to change both the y-axis and the x-axis. In fact, the / Graph Options Scale X Scale option applies only to XY graphs since only XY graphs have a numeric x-axis.

The X Scale option of the /Graph Options Scale command offers the same choices as the Y Scale option. You can use this command to change the upper and lower limits of the x-axis in XY graphs, to format the values along the x-axis in XY graphs and to remove the magnitude indicator along the x-axis in those graphs. This command works in exactly the same way as the Y Scale command, except that it affects only the x-axis in XY graphs.

For an example of using the / Graph Options Scale X Scale command, see the section "XY Graphs" under the heading "Creating Graphs" earlier in this chapter.

Adding Data Labels

Data labels are labels you can place on or near the data points in a graph. Unlike x-axis labels and titles, which appear outside a graph's axes, data labels appear within the axes, next to the points or bars that make up the graph. You can add data labels to line, XY, bar, and stacked-bar graphs. You can't add them to pie graphs.

Data labels are drawn directly from entries in the worksheet. To define data labels, you issue the / Graph Options Data-Labels command. ►When you issue this command, 1-2-3 Release 2.2 will present a menu with eight choices: A, B, C, D, E, F, Group, and Quit. (Earlier versions of 1-2-3 do not include the Group option on this menu.)◄ Each of the first six options, A through F, corresponds to one of the data ranges in the graph. To assign data labels to a range, you choose the appropriate option from this menu and select a range that contains the entries you want to use as data labels and press [Enter]. 1-2-3 will then display a menu with five options—Center, Left, Above, Right, or Below—and prompt you to specify where you want to place the data labels in relation to the actual data points on the graph.

►The Group option, which is new to 1-2-3 Release 2.2, lets you define the data labels for more than one range at a time. To do this, issue the / Graph Options Data-Labels command and choose the Group option. As soon as you issue this command, 1-2-3 Release 2.2 will ask you to highlight the range that contains the data labels. Then, 1-2-3 will present you with the same two choices that the / Graph Group command does: Columnwise and Rowwise. If you choose Columnwise (as you should if the data labels for each data range occupy a single column), 1-2-3 will define the leftmost

RELEASE
► 2.2 ◄

RELEASE
► 2.2 ◄

column of the highlighted range as the data label range for the A range, the second column of the highlighted range as the data label range for the B data range, and so forth. If you choose Rowwise (as you should if the data labels for each data range occupy a single row), 1-2-3 will define the topmost row of the highlighted range as the data label range for the A range, the second row of the highlighted range as the data label range for the B data range, and so forth. Of course, the data labels for the various ranges must be situated in adjacent cells in order for this command to produce the desired effect.

Once you choose one of these two options, 1-2-3 will present you with the same position options that the / Graph Options Data-Labels (A, B, C, D, E, and F) commands do: Center, Left, Above, Right, and Below. The option you select determines the position of the data labels for every data range. ◄

An Example

Many 1-2-3 users choose to use the values on which a graph is based as data labels. For example, you could use the values in cells C7..G7 and C8..G8 of the worksheet in Figure 10-9 as data labels in the graph in Figure 10-35. To create these labels, you would issue the / Graph Options Data-Labels command. When you see the Data Labels menu, select A, select the range C7..G7, and press [Enter]. Then, when 1-2-3 prompts you to position the data labels, choose Below. Next, select B, select the range C8..G8, press [Enter], and choose Above. When you are finished, choose Quit twice to return to the main graph menu and choose View to bring the graph shown in Figure 10-36 into view.

You could also use the Group option to create these labels. To do this, you would issue the / Graph Options Data-Labels Group command, select the range C7..G8, and press [Enter]. Then, when 1-2-3 displays the Columnwise/Rowwise menu, you would choose Rowwise to tell 1-2-3 that the labels are arranged in rows.

Notes

The entries in the range you select can be values or labels. If the entries are labels, they can be as long as you wish (up to the 240-character limit 1-2-3 places on all labels). As with titles and legends, however, the practical limit on the length of data labels is much less than 240 characters. If the entries in the data-labels range are values, then the data labels in the graph will have the same format as the values on which they are based.

As you've seen, after you select the range of cells that you want to use as data labels, 1-2-3 lets you specify the alignment of those labels relative to the points in the graph. You can choose Center, meaning that the data labels will be centered right on top of the data points, or you can choose Above, Right, Left, or Below. Whatever position you choose, it will apply to *all* of the data labels in that range. There is no way to choose different alignments for the data labels in a single range. Of course, different ranges of data labels can have different alignments.

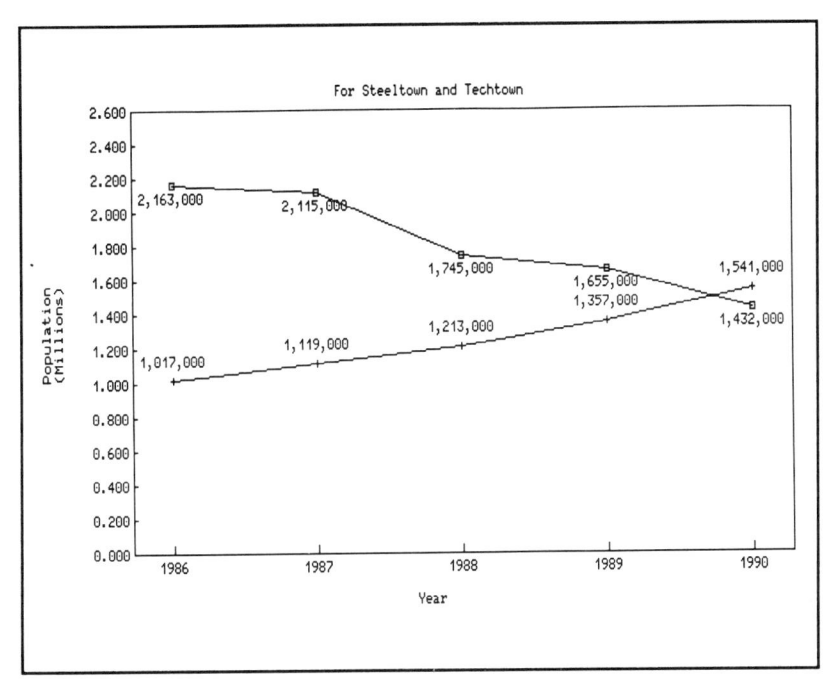

FIGURE 10-36: A graph with data labels

Data-Label Problems

There are several problems you are likely to encounter when you use data labels in your 1-2-3 graphs. For one thing, the leftmost labels for any range in the graph may overlap the values along the y-axis, making both the data labels and the y-axis values unreadable. In addition, the data labels for corresponding data points in different ranges may overlap. Finally, the rightmost labels in any range in the graph may overlap the right border of the graph.

▶While these problems were very common in older releases of 1-2-3, in Release 2.2 they are less of a problem. Because Release 2.2 indents the first and last data point in each data series from the borders of the graph, data labels are not nearly as likely to overlap the y-axis and the right border of the graph. Nevertheless, it is still possible for data labels to overlap the borders of a graph and for data labels from different ranges to overlap one another.◀

RELEASE ▶ 2.2 ◀

Fortunately, there are a couple of ways to deal with these problems. The simplest is just to eliminate the data labels from the graph altogether (we'll show you how to do that in a few pages). Short of that, you can eliminate the first and last data label in each range. You can do this by assigning the Hidden format to the first and last cells in each of the data-labels ranges. Hiding the first and last labels for each range will prevent the labels from overlapping the graph's borders.

Bar Graphs

You can also use data labels in bar and stacked-bar graphs. However, there are a few limitations to using data labels in bar graphs. For one thing, you will usually use the Above option to position data labels in bar graphs above the data points with which they are associated. Otherwise, the data labels may overlap the bar, making them difficult to read.

When you use data labels in a stacked-bar graph, you'll usually not want to assign labels to any range except the topmost range in the graph. Since the ranges in a stacked-bar graph are stacked one above another, if you assign data labels to every range in a stacked-bar graph, then the labels for all but the top range will overlap the bars.

In addition, you may want to use data labels in a slightly different way in a stacked-bar graph. Instead of using the values on which the top bar segment is based as the data labels for that segment, you might want to use the totals of all the values that make up the graph as the labels for the bars. For example, suppose that you want to create data labels for each of the stacked bars in the graph in Figure 10-14. You may recall that this graph is based on the ranges C5..G5, C6..G6, C7..G7, and C8..G8 in Figure 10-9. To create these labels, just issue the / Graph Options Data-Labels command and choose D from the Data-Labels menu. (The D range is represented by the top segment in each stacked bar.) Then select the range C10..G10—the range that contains the totals of the values that make up the graph—as the data-labels range, and choose Above to position the labels above the bars. Figure 10-37 shows the result. As you can see, 1-2-3 has displayed the totals from the range C10..G10 above the stacked bars in this graph.

Deleting Data Labels

It's a lot harder to get rid of data labels than it is to create them. 1-2-3 does not offer a command that directly deletes only data labels. Nor can you issue the / Graph Options Data-Labels command, choose a range, and press [Esc].

There are three possible ways to delete the data labels from a graph. First, you can use the / Graph Reset command to reset each data range to which you have assigned data labels. Resetting the ranges will also reset the data labels. Once you have done this, you will need to redefine each of the graph's data ranges. ▶Alternatively, in 1-2-3 Release 2.2 you can issue the / Graph Reset Options command. This command will delete the data labels you have defined—along with any titles, legends, or other options you have defined for the graph.◀ Finally, you can substitute a blank range of cells for the existing data-labels range. To do this, you issue the / Graph Options Data-Labels command, choose the appropriate range, select a range of blank cells, and press [Enter].

RELEASE
▶ 2.2 ◀

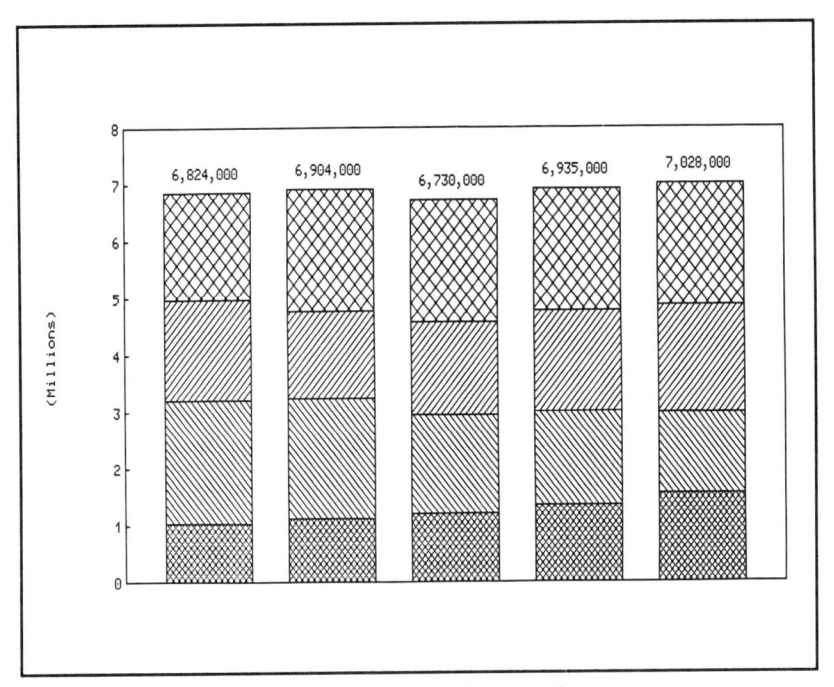

FIGURE 10-37: Data labels in a stacked-bar graph

The / Graph Options Format Command

When you create a line or XY graph, 1-2-3 will place a symbol (such as + or ∆) to identify each data point in the graph and will connect those symbols with lines. The / Graph Options Format command allows you to change this basic format. You can use this command to instruct 1-2-3 to display only the line without symbols at each data point, or only the symbols without the connecting line. Finally, you can format the graph to show neither lines nor symbols.

To change the format of a line or XY graph, issue the / Graph Options Format command. When you issue this command, 1-2-3 will bring the menu shown in Figure 10-38 into view. The options on this menu allow you to choose the data range whose format you want to change. If you select Graph, then 1-2-3 will format every line in the graph—assuming, of course, that your graph contains more than one data range. Any new ranges that you add to the graph will also appear in the format you specify for the entire graph. If you choose one of the ranges, A through F, then 1-2-3 will change the format of that range only.

```
C6: 1300                                                MENU
Graph  A  B  C  D  E  F  Quit
Set format for all ranges
```

FIGURE 10-38: The / Graph Options Format menu

After you choose either Graph or one of the data ranges, you'll see a menu with four choices: Lines, Symbols, Both, and Neither. The default choice, Both, causes 1-2-3 to display symbols for each data point and to connect those points with a line. Choosing Lines causes 1-2-3 to remove the symbols and display only the connecting lines, while choosing Symbols will remove the line and display only symbols. Choosing Neither does what you would expect: It causes 1-2-3 to display neither symbols nor lines.

Figures 10-39 and 10-40 show the example graph from Figure 10-35 with lines only and with symbols only.

Notes

The best choice of format for a given graph is really a matter of taste. As a rule, we prefer to use Lines in single-range line graphs and Both in multiple-range line graphs. Lines is usually not a good choice for multiple-range graphs since taking the symbols out of the graph makes it difficult to tell one range from another. This is especially true if you have a monochrome graphics monitor.

We prefer to use the Symbols option for XY graphs. The lines that 1-2-3 automatically includes in XY graphs usually have little meaning and are often confusing. However, when we use a regression line in an XY graph, we use the both.

You'll rarely, if ever, use the Neither option. When you choose Neither, 1-2-3 will not display either lines or symbols, making it difficult or impossible to figure out exactly where the points in the graph are located. Interestingly, 1-2-3 will continue to display data labels in graphs to which you assign the Neither format. You can use this quirk to create floating labels in graphs.

The / Graph Options Format command applies only to line and XY graphs. It does not affect bar, stacked-bar, or pie graphs.

TIP: ADDING INFORMATION LABELS TO A GRAPH

Though you will rarely use the Neither option to format line or XY graphs, there are a couple of specialized applications for this format. For one thing, you can use the Neither option in conjunction with data labels to create floating labels in your graphs.

For example, suppose you want to place the label *Based on Census Bureau Data* in the upper-right corner of the graph in Figure 10-35, as shown in Figure A. To begin, you must add a new, artificial data range to the worksheet shown in Figure 10-9. The value in this range should be just right to position the floating data label where you want it in the graph. To define this value, move to cell F12 and enter the value 2300000. Next, you must create the label you want 1-2-3 to display. To do this, move to cell F13 and enter the label *'Based on Census Bureau Data*.

Now, you must identify the new data range and data label for 1-2-3. To do this, issue the / Graph command, choose the C option, point to the range

(Tip continued on next page.)

C12..G12, and press [Enter]. Then choose Options Format, choose C, and choose Neither to hide the point in this range from View. Now choose Quit to return to the Options menu, choose Data-Labels, choose the C range, point to the range C13..G13, press [Enter], and choose Center. Finally, choose Quit twice to return to the Graph menu and choose View to display the graph in Figure A.

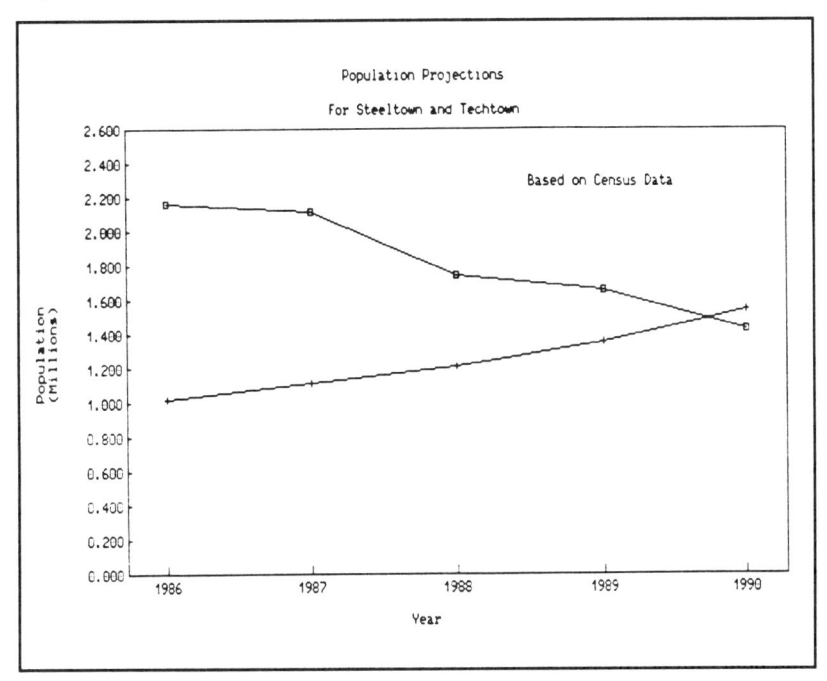

FIGURE A: A graph with a floating label

Here's how it works: The new C range includes just one value, 2300000, which corresponds to the year 1989 in the graph. This new range causes 1-2-3 to plot a single point above the X value 1989 at the Y value 2300000. The data label for this point, *Based on Census Bureau Data*, is centered on this point. However, because you have selected the Neither option for the C range, only the data label is displayed; the point is hidden from view. The result is a floating label in the graph.

There are a couple of things to keep in mind about this technique. First, you must include as many cells in the artificial data range as there are in the "real" ranges upon which the graph is based. For instance, in the example there are five cells in the C range and five cells in the A range. Otherwise, the label may not be positioned properly. Of course, every cell in the artificial range does not have to contain an entry. As in this case, you need only include one positioning entry in the artificial range. Also, be sure that the value you use to position the data label is not greater than the upper limit of the y-axis. Otherwise, the label may not be displayed.

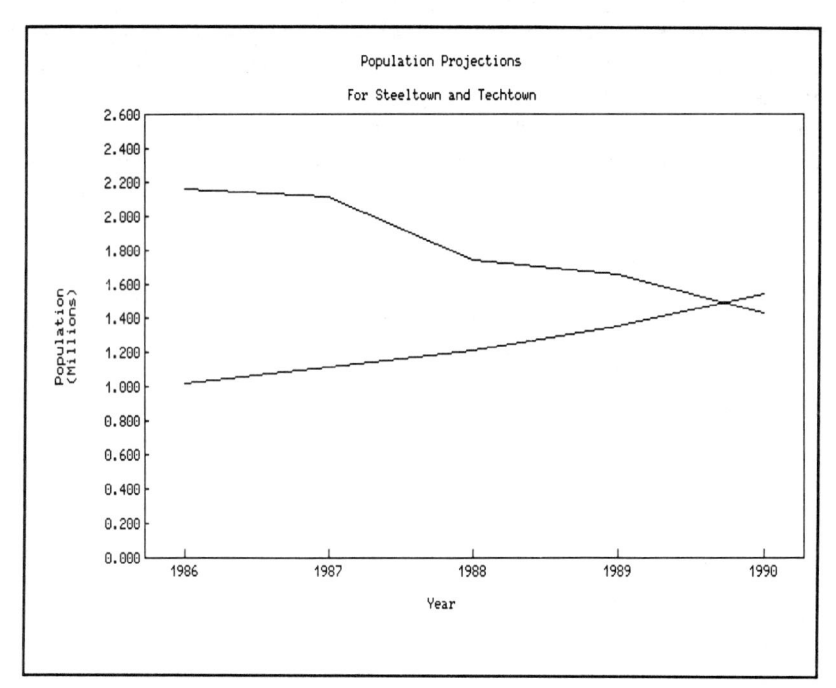

FIGURE 10-39: Line graph formatted for lines only

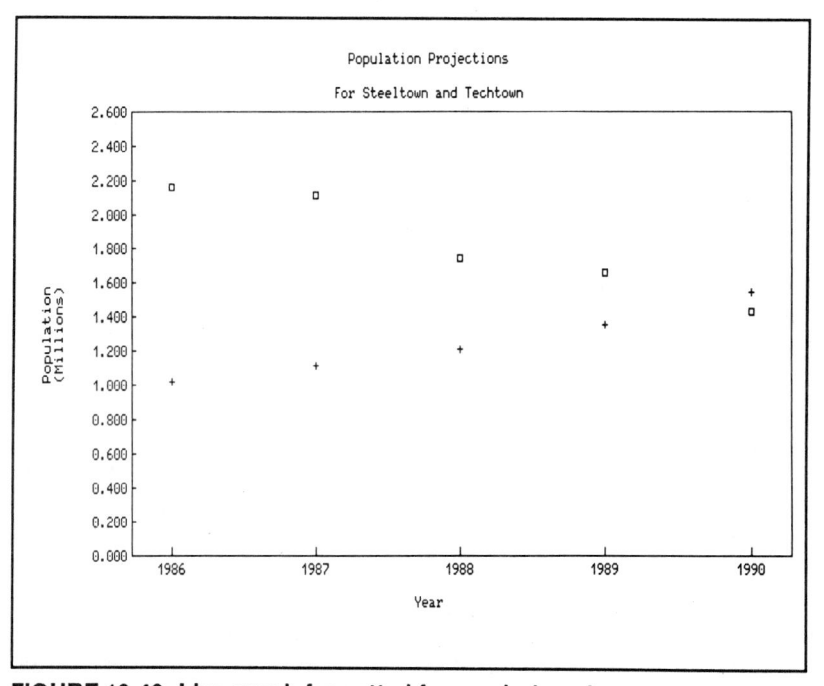

FIGURE 10-40: Line graph formatted for symbols only

Using Color and Shading

As we have explained, 1-2-3 will use a different symbol to mark every point in a line graph and a different shading pattern to mark each bar in a bar graph. If you have a color monitor, you can choose to display each data range in a different color as well. To do this, issue the / Graph Options Color command. When you issue this command, 1-2-3 will begin using different colors for each of the ranges in the graph. If the graph has a legend, the legend for each range will be displayed in the same color as the range itself.

If your computer has an Enhanced Graphics Adaptor (EGA) or a Video Graphics Array (VGA) and a high resolution monitor, 1-2-3 will be able to display up to seven different colors in a graph—one color for each of the six data ranges and a color for the graph border and the x-axis labels. Table 10-3 shows the color 1-2-3 will use for each data range in a graph if you have an EGA- or VGA-equipped computer.

Range	Color
A	yellow
B	magenta
C	blue
D	red
E	light blue
F	green
Border	white

TABLE 10-3: Colors in 1-2-3 graphs with an EGA or VGA monitor

If you are using a Color Graphics Adaptor (CGA), 1-2-3 will display only three colors in a graph: magenta (deep pink), cyan (bright blue), and white. If your graph has more than three data ranges, then one or more of these colors will be repeated in the graph. Table 10-4 shows how 1-2-3 assigns colors to the ranges in a graph.

Range	Color
A	magenta
B	cyan
C	white
D	magenta
E	cyan
F	white

TABLE 10-4: Colors in 1-2-3 graphs with a CGA monitor

You can use the / Graph Options Color command to display any type of graph in color. If the active graph is a bar graph, choosing color will cause 1-2-3 to display the bars for each of the ranges in the graph in a different color. ▶(1-2-3 Release 2.2 also draws a thin white line around each bar in a bar graph and each section of the bars in

RELEASE ▶ 2.2 ◀

a stacked-bar graph when you view those graphs in color. Earlier releases of 1-2-3 do not display this line, which serves as a boundary between the colors of various bars.)◄ If you use this command to display a bar graph on a monochrome monitor, 1-2-3 will display every bar in the graph in a solid color. For example, with a green-on-black monitor, all the bars will appear solid green. The result is rarely very attractive.

If the active graph is a pie graph, issuing the / Graph Options Color command will cause 1-2-3 to display each segment in a different color. (If the pie has more than three segments, 1-2-3 will have to repeat one or more colors.) In addition to displaying the segments in color, 1-2-3 will display a pattern in each segment.

Adding Legends

Legends are almost always an appropriate addition to graphs that have more than one data range. Legends allow you to add text to a graph that explains what each range in the graph represents. You can add legends to line, bar, stacked-bar, and XY graphs. Since pie graphs have only one data range, you cannot add a legend to a pie graph. You must use the labels next to each segment of the pie (the X range) to identify what the segments represent.

To add a legend to a graph, you issue the / Graph Options Legend command. ►When you issue this command, 1-2-3 Release 2.2 will display a menu with seven options: A, B, C, D, E, F, and Range. (Earlier versions of 1-2-3 do not include the Range option on this menu.)◄ Each of the first six options corresponds to one of the ranges in the graph. When you see this menu, select the range for which you wish to create a legend, type the text of the legend, and press [Enter]. After you create a legend for one data range, you can choose another graph range, type its legend, and press [Enter]. You can continue this process until you have created a legend for each range.

An Example

Suppose you want to add a legend to the sample graph in Figure 10-35. To begin, issue the / Graph Options Legend command. Since this graph includes two ranges, you'll want to define legends for the A and B ranges. To do this, choose A, type *Steeltown*, and press [Enter]. Then choose Legends again, select B, type *Techtown*, and press [Enter] again. When you are finished, choose Quit and then View to display the graph in Figure 10-41.

As you can see, 1-2-3 has positioned the legend at the bottom of the screen. Next to the legend text for each range, 1-2-3 displays a symbol that identifies the range to which the legend text applies. For example, the symbol + next to the legend text *Techtown* indicates that that legend applies to the second data range. Notice that the points along the line for Techtown in the graph are also marked with the symbol +. If you are using color in the graph, each legend will also appear in the same color as its corresponding data range.

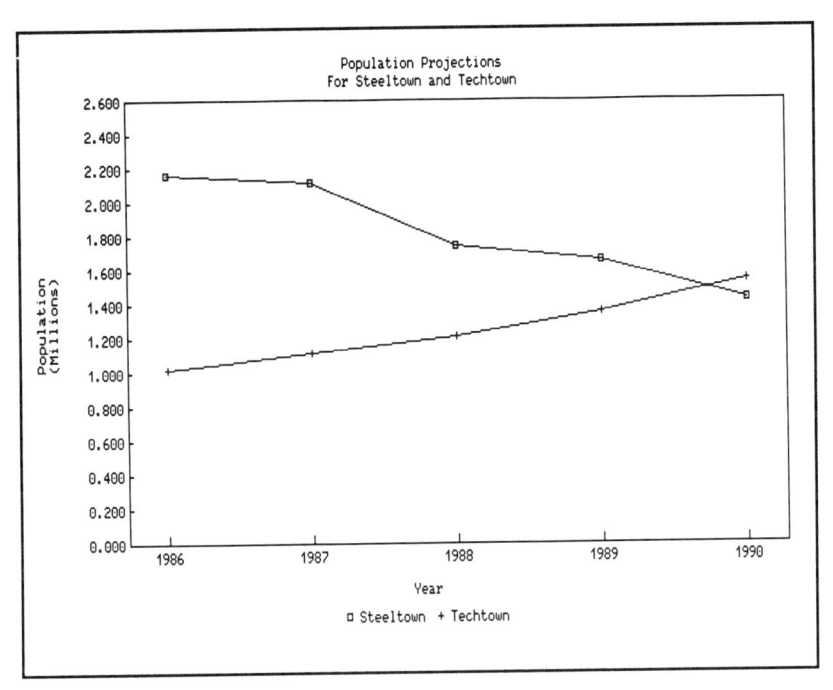

FIGURE 10-41: A legend

Using Worksheet Entries as Legends

As with titles, you can use entries from the worksheet as the legends in your graphs instead of typing the literal legend text. To do this, you type a backslash (\) followed by the address of the cell that contains the entry you want to use as the legend when 1-2-3 prompts you for the legend text. 1-2-3 will use the contents of the cell you specify as the legend text.

For example, you could use the entries in cells A7 and A8 of the worksheet shown in Figure 10-9 as the legend text in Figure 10-41. To do this, you would issue the / Graph Options Legend command, choose the A option, press [Esc] (if necessary) to erase the existing legend text, type \A7, and press [Enter]. Next, you would select Legend again, choose B, press [Esc] (if necessary) to erase the existing legend text, type \A8, and press [Enter]. The resulting graph would look just like Figure 10-41.

If you use this method, the legend text for any range can be up to 240 characters long, instead of just 19 characters. However, the practical limit for the legend text for each range in a graph is determined by the number of legends in the graph and by the number of characters your monitor can display on a single line. On our Compaq computers, the total length of the legend text cannot exceed 77 characters. If a graph has just two ranges, the legend text for each range can be up to about 36 characters long. If the graph includes six ranges, on the other hand, the legend text for each range can be only about 12 characters long.

The / Graph Options Legend Range Command

RELEASE ▶ 2.2 ◀

▶1-2-3 Release 2.2 offers a command—/Graph Options Legends Range—that allows you to define the legends for all of the data ranges in a graph at once. This command is similar to the / Graph Group and / Graph Options Data-Labels Group commands. When you issue this command, 1-2-3 asks you to highlight the range that contains the legends for the various data ranges. When you highlight a range and press [Enter], 1-2-3 Release 2.2 will define the legends for the various ranges in the chart, using references in the form \ref, where *ref* is the address of one of the cells in the range you highlighted. (You can use references of this sort in any release of 1-2-3 to "link" cells of the worksheet to the legends in a chart.)

In most cases, you'll highlight only a single-column or single-row range. When you do, 1-2-3 will use a reference to the first cell of the range as the legend for the A range, a reference to the second cell of the series as the legend for the B range, and so forth. If you highlight multiple-row, multiple-column range, things get more complex. 1-2-3 will work down the first column of the range, using references to those cells as the legends for as many data ranges as there are rows in the range. If the range contains fewer than six rows, 1-2-3 will begin using references to the cells of the second column; when all of the cells in the second column have been used, it will go on to the third column, and so on.

You could use the Range option to create the legend in Figure 10-41. To do this, you would issue the / Graph Options Legend Range command, select the range A7..A8, and press [Enter]. 1-2-3 will use the legend in cell A7 for the first range in the graph and the label in cell A8 as the legend for the second range.◀

Bar Graphs

You will usually want to define a legend for your multiple-range and stacked-bar graphs. The process of defining a legend for a bar graph is identical to that of defining a legend in a line graph. When 1-2-3 displays a legend in a bar graph, it places a shaded or colored block next to the legend text for each data range. The pattern or color in the box will match the color or pattern of the range to which the legend text applies.

Notes

RELEASE ▶ 2.2 ◀

▶In 1-2-3 Release 2.2, a legend can be as long as you wish. However, only about 100 or so characters in the legend will be displayed. The remaining characters will be truncated when the graph is displayed. (In earlier releases of 1-2-3, you can type up to 19 characters when you are entering the legend for a data range. If you try to type more than 19 characters, 1-2-3 will simply beep.)

If there is not enough room to display the legends for all of the ranges in a graph on one line, 1-2-3 Release 2.2 will wrap part of the legend onto a second line. If the complete legend won't fit on two lines, portions of both lines may be truncated. (In earlier releases of 1-2-3, if there is not enough room to display the legends for all of the ranges in a graph on one line, the first and last legends will be truncated.)◀

Because different types of monitors can display different numbers of characters on a line, the maximum length of legend text for your computer may be greater or less than it is on ours. You may want to experiment to determine exactly how many characters will fit in your legends.

Unfortunately, 1-2-3's graph printing utility PrintGraph cannot fit as many characters in the legends of printed graphs as 1-2-3 can display on the screen. If your legends contain too many characters, the rightmost legend in the printed graph will be truncated. For more on legends in printed graphs, see Chapter 11.

Removing a Legend

If you decide that you do not want to display legends on a graph, it's easy to remove them. Just issue the / Graph Options Legend command, choose one of the ranges to which you have assigned a legend (such as A), press [Esc] to delete the legend text or cell reference, and press [Enter] to lock in the change. Then choose the next range to which you assigned a legend, press [Esc] again, and press [Enter] again. You should continue in this way until you have reset the legend text for every range in the graph.

▶Of course, if you use 1-2-3 Release 2.2, you can also use the / Graph Reset Options command to delete legends—along with all other options—from a graph.◀

RELEASE
▶ 2.2 ◀

Adding a Grid

The / Graph Options Grid command allows you to superimpose a grid of vertical and/ or horizontal lines across a graph. When you issue this command, 1-2-3 will display a menu with four options: Horizontal, Vertical, Both, and Clear. If you choose Horizontal, 1-2-3 will place horizontal lines across the graph. Similarly, if you choose Vertical, 1-2-3 will place vertical lines across the graph. As you might expect, the Both option will create a grid of horizontal and vertical lines.

Suppose you want to add a grid to the graph in Figure 10-41. To do this, issue the / Graph Options Grid Both command. Figure 10-42 shows the result. Notice how the grid lines up with the tick marks along the graph's axes.

Grid lines are designed to help you read a graph. Unfortunately, they often just clutter the graph image so that it is more difficult to interpret. For example, the grid lines in Figure 10-42 don't do much except clutter the graph and obscure the data labels. In general, you probably will want to avoid grids.

▶Lotus has made one improvement to grid lines in 1-2-3 Release 2.2. In Release 2.2, grid lines do not overlap the bars in bar charts, as they do in previous releases of 1-2-3. The grid lines in a Release 2.01 bar graph are superimposed on the bars; the bars in the Release 2.2 bar graph are superimposed on the gridlines.◀

RELEASE
▶ 2.2 ◀

If you add a grid to a graph and then decide you don't want to use it, you can delete it by issuing / Graph Options Grid and choosing the Clear option.

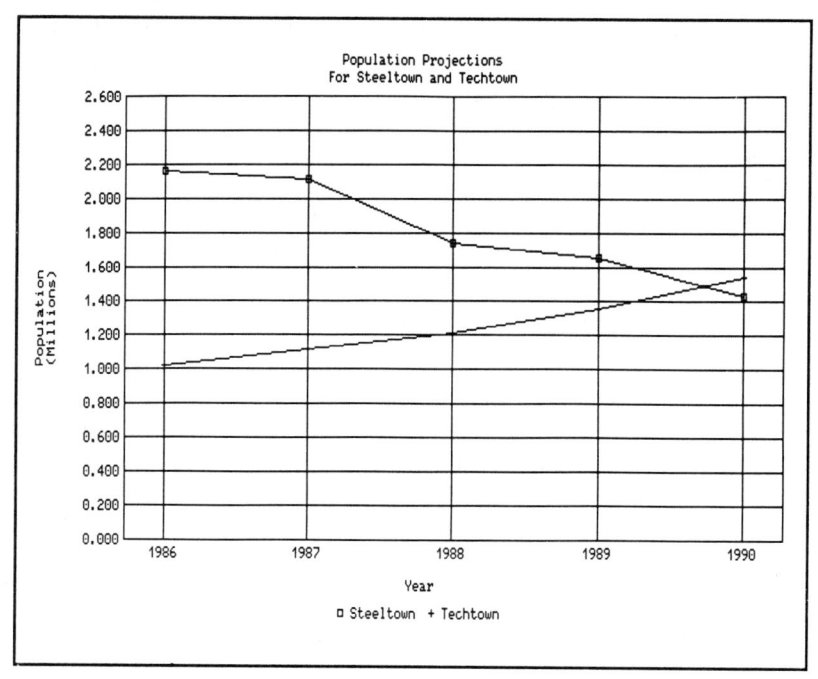

FIGURE 10-42: A graph with a grid

SAVING A GRAPH FOR PRINTING

The biggest problem with 1-2-3 graphics is that you cannot print a graph directly from 1-2-3. In order to print a graph, you must save it to a special file, called a .PIC file. Once you have created the .PIC file, you must exit from 1-2-3, load the PrintGraph program, load the .PIC file into PrintGraph, and then print the graph. (We will explain how to use the PrintGraph program to print a .PIC file in the next chapter.)

You may have noticed that the main Graph menu in 1-2-3 includes a Save command. You use this command to save a graph image into a .PIC file. Saving to a .PIC file is very easy. First, make sure that the graph you want to save is the active graph. (You can tell which graph is active by pressing the [Graph] key, or by issuing the / Graph View command.) If the graph that you want to save is not active, use the / Graph Name Use command to make it active. Next, be sure that you have made all the enhancements and changes that you want to appear in the printed graph. You cannot make these kinds of changes to the graph image in a .PIC file.

Once the graph is as you want it, just issue the / Graph Save command. Next, 1-2-3 will display the prompt *Enter graph file name:* and a list of any .PIC files that are already on the current directory. To save the graph, just type a name for the .PIC file and press [Enter]. 1-2-3 will automatically supply the .PIC extension to the file name.

For example, suppose you would like to save the line graph in Figure 10-42 so that you can print it. After making all the final enhancements to the graph, issue the / Graph Save command, enter a file name, such as Line, and press [Enter]. 1-2-3 will automatically save the graph image to a file named LINE.PIC.

If there is already a .PIC file on the current directory with the name you specify for the graph you are saving, 1-2-3 will display a Cancel/Replace menu. If you want to replace the existing .PIC file with a file containing the current graph image, choose Replace. If you want to preserve the existing file, choose Cancel, reissue the / Graph Save command, and specify a new name for the current image.

If you want to save the current graph into a .PIC file on a directory other than the current directory, you should press [Esc] twice when you see the prompt *Enter graph file name:*, then type the new directory and the name of the .PIC file. For example, suppose the current directory is C:/123/Data. You want to save the active graph into the file TEST.PIC on the directory C:/123/Pictures. To do this, you would press [Esc] twice when you see the prompt *Enter graph file name:*, then type C:/123/Pictures/TEST and press [Enter].

Every graph image that you want to print must be saved in a separate .PIC file. For example, suppose you would like to print the same graph, both with and without legends. You must create both versions of this graph in 1-2-3 and use the Save command twice to save each version into its own .PIC file.

Saving a graph is *not* the same as naming a graph. Giving a graph a name stores it permanently in the current worksheet's graph library. If you want to view a graph you have named, you issue the / Graph Name Use command and type the graph's name. Saving a graph, on the other hand, simply saves the image of the graph into a .PIC file.

You can't retrieve a graph from a .PIC file into 1-2-3. If you issue the / Graph Reset Graph command after you have saved a graph but before you give it a name, the graph is gone. If you want to view or modify the graph, you'll have to recreate it from scratch.

CONCLUSION

In this chapter, we have shown you how to create and format 1-2-3 graphs. One of the best ways to learn 1-2-3's graphics is to experiment. We would encourage you to work along with the examples in this chapter (or create your own examples) and then try out different combinations of the various enhancement options until you feel comfortable with creating graphs.

In the next chapter, we'll show you how to print graphs using 1-2-3's graphics printing utility, PrintGraph.

11

Printing Graphs

In Chapter 10, we showed you how easy it is to create and enhance graphs in 1-2-3. As we pointed out in that chapter, however, it's not quite as easy to print a graph. In order to print a graph you have created with 1-2-3, you must save that graph into a .PIC file, exit from 1-2-3, and then load the special graph-printing utility program, PrintGraph. Once you have loaded PrintGraph, you must retrieve the .PIC file that contains the image you want to print and adjust a few settings. After you have done all of this, you can print.

As you are reading this chapter and working with PrintGraph, you'll notice that there are quite a few commands you must issue to configure the program for your needs. You should not be intimidated by PrintGraph, however. Once you understand what each selection does, you should have no trouble setting up the program and printing graphs.

The structure of the PrintGraph program for 1-2-3 Releases 2, 2.01, and 2.2 is significantly different from that of Release 1A's PrintGraph program. The capabilities of both programs are almost identical, but the menus for accessing the various options are different. As we explain PrintGraph's commands in this chapter, we will assume that you're using Release 2, 2.01, or 2.2. Table 11-2 (located at the end of this chapter) lists each 1A PrintGraph command and its Release 2/2.01/2.2 equivalent.

PREPARING TO PRINT GRAPHS

Before you can print a graph with PrintGraph, you must first create that same graph in 1-2-3, then use the / Graph Save command to save it into a .PIC file. If you do not save the graph into a .PIC file before you leave 1-2-3 and load PrintGraph, you will not be able to retrieve and print the graph with PrintGraph.

Although PrintGraph offers a few options for altering the appearance of your printed graphs, it does not allow you to enhance your graphs as you can in 1-2-3. Therefore, before you save a graph for printing, you should be certain that you have added all the "bells and whistles" that you want to appear in the final printed graph.

If you find that a graph you are about to print (or have already printed) is not in the desired form, you'll have to leave PrintGraph and return to 1-2-3 to make the necessary changes.

In addition, you will not be able to use PrintGraph to print a graph unless you have used the Install program to install the graphics output device (or devices) to which you will print. If you have not installed one or more graphics printers and/or plotters, you must do so before you can use PrintGraph. (For a detailed explanation of the Install program, see your 1-2-3 manuals.)

LOADING PRINTGRAPH

You can load PrintGraph either from the Lotus Access menu or directly from DOS. To enter PrintGraph from the Lotus Access menu, choose the PrintGraph option when that menu is in view. If you're using a floppy disk system, the Access System will prompt you to insert the PrintGraph disk into drive A. You should follow this instruction and press [Enter] when the disk is in place. If you're using a hard disk system, the PrintGraph program file should be on the same directory as the Access System, so you won't need to insert any disks or change directories.

You don't have to go through the Access System to load PrintGraph. If you are using a floppy disk system, all you have to do is insert the PrintGraph disk in the system drive (usually A) and type PGRAPH at the DOS prompt. (In 1-2-3 Release 1A, you simply type GRAPH.) If you have copied the PrintGraph files to a hard disk, just change the active directory to the directory that contains the PrintGraph files and type PGRAPH.

Usually you will want to load PrintGraph immediately after you have completed a 1-2-3 session. For example, suppose you have been working in 1-2-3 and have created several graphs that you have saved to .PIC files. You now want to print those graphs. To do this, first save the current worksheet, then issue the /Quit Yes command. Depending on how you entered 1-2-3, you'll see either the Lotus Access menu or the DOS prompt when you leave 1-2-3. Either way, you can load PrintGraph using the steps explained in the previous paragraphs.

You can load PrintGraph without permanently exiting from 1-2-3. All you have to do is issue the /System command from within 1-2-3. As you learned in Chapter 6, this command suspends 1-2-3 temporarily and returns you to DOS. Once you see the DOS prompt, you can load PrintGraph in the usual way. When you are finished printing graphs and have exited from PrintGraph, you can return to 1-2-3 just by typing *exit* next to the DOS prompt.

This method is a great deal faster than exiting from 1-2-3 and loading PrintGraph each time you want to print graphs. However, it has one disadvantage. PrintGraph requires at least 256K of free memory. If the worksheet you are working on is very large, there may not be enough memory to load PrintGraph after you issue the /System command. If there is not enough memory, you'll see the message *Insufficient memory. 256K FREE memory required to run PGRAPH.* If you see this message, you'll have to return to 1-2-3 and then enter PrintGraph in the conventional way.

Chapter 11: Printing Graphs

As soon as PrintGraph is loaded, you will see the screen shown in Figure 11-1. This screen displays all the PrintGraph settings and the main PrintGraph menu. Unlike 1-2-3, you don't have to press the / key to reveal PrintGraph's main menu—it appears automatically. You can choose commands from this menu either by typing their first letter or by pointing to the command and pressing [Enter]—just as you do in 1-2-3.

```
Copyright 1986, 1989 Lotus Development Corp.  All Rights Reserved. V2.2   MENU

Select graphs to print or preview
Image-Select  Settings  Go  Align  Page  Exit

    GRAPHS     IMAGE SETTINGS                    HARDWARE SETTINGS
    TO PRINT   Size               Range colors   Graphs directory
               Top       .395   X                  A:\
               Left      .750   A                Fonts directory
               Width    6.500   B                  A:\
               Height   4.691   C                Interface
               Rotation  .000   D                  Parallel 1
                                E                Printer
               Font             F
                 1 BLOCK1                        Paper size
                 2 BLOCK1                          Width     8.500
                                                   Length   11.000

                                                ACTION SETTINGS
                                                  Pause  No   Eject  No
```

FIGURE 11-1: The main PrintGraph screen

CONFIGURING PRINTGRAPH

Before you print a graph with PrintGraph, you must adjust several settings that tell the program about your hardware. These settings are controlled by the Settings Hardware command. When you issue this command, PrintGraph will bring the menu shown in Figure 11-2 into view.

Choosing a Graphs Directory and a Fonts Directory

The Settings Hardware Graphs-Directory and Settings Hardware Fonts-Directory commands allow you to tell PrintGraph where your .PIC files and the PrintGraph font files are stored. If you are using a computer with two floppy disk drives, you'll want to keep the PrintGraph disk (which contains the font files) in drive A and your disk containing .PIC files in drive B. If your computer has a hard disk, then both your .PIC files and the PrintGraph font files are probably on the hard disk, though perhaps in different subdirectories. If you have just one floppy disk drive, then both the .PIC files and font files will be accessed through the drive A.

```
Copyright 1986, 1989 Lotus Development Corp. All Rights Reserved. V2.2  MENU
Specify directory containing graphs
Graphs-Directory  Fonts-Directory  Interface  Printer  Size-Paper  Quit

  GRAPHS    IMAGE SETTINGS                    HARDWARE SETTINGS
  TO PRINT  Size            Range colors      Graphs directory
            Top      .395   X                   A:\
            Left     .750   A                 Fonts directory
            Width   6.500   B                   A:\
            Height  4.691   C                 Interface
            Rotation .000   D                   Parallel 1
                            E                 Printer
            Font            F
            1 BLOCK1                          Paper size
            2 BLOCK1                            Width     8.500
                                                Length   11.000

                                              ACTION SETTINGS
                                              Pause No    Eject No
```

FIGURE 11-2: The Settings Hardware menu

Specifying the Location of .PIC Files

To tell PrintGraph where your .PIC files are stored, issue the Settings Hardware Graphs-Directory command. When you see the prompt *Enter directory containing graph(.PIC)files,* type the name of the directory that contains your .PIC files and press [Enter]. If you are using a two-floppy system and your .PIC files are stored on a disk in the B drive, you should type B:\ and press [Enter].

If you're using a hard disk and you've stored your .PIC files in a subdirectory, then you should type the appropriate path for that subdirectory. For example, suppose you have stored your .PIC files on your hard disk in a subdirectory named PICTURES, which is part of another directory called LOTFILES. You should specify your Graphs directory as C:\LOTFILES\PICTURES\.

You don't need to erase the name of the default Graphs directory before you can specify a new directory. As soon as you begin to type the name of the new directory, the current setting will disappear.

Specifying the Location of Font Files

When you are setting up a graph to print, you can specify one or two fonts for all of the graph text. (We will cover fonts in more detail in a few pages.) These fonts are stored in special files, which are found on your PrintGraph disk. If you have copied the PrintGraph files over to your hard disk, the font files also will be on your hard disk.

The command for specifying the Fonts-Directory setting is Settings Hardware Fonts-Directory. The default for the Fonts-Directory setting is A:\. If you are using a two-floppy system, with your PrintGraph disk in drive A and your .PIC files in drive B (or if your computer has only one disk drive), you will not need to change the default Fonts-Directory setting.

If you are using a computer with a hard disk, you must specify the path for the subdirectory that contains your font files. For example, suppose your font files are stored in the PGRAPH subdirectory, which is part of the LOTFILES directory. To change the Fonts directory, issue the Settings Hardware Fonts-Directory command, enter C:\LOTFILES\PGRAPH\, and press [Enter].

Choosing a Printer or Plotter

The next step in configuring PrintGraph is to select a graphics output device. PrintGraph supports many graphics output devices, including a wide variety of plotters and color printers, as well as most popular dot-matrix and laser printers.

Your choice of output devices in PrintGraph is limited to those devices you installed when you ran the 1-2-3 Install program. PrintGraph allows you to choose an output device only from the printers or plotters that are already installed. If you have not installed any graphics output devices, you'll have to exit from PrintGraph, run the Install program, and install one or more graphics printers and/or plotters before you can select an output device in PrintGraph.

Although you can install several graphics printers and/or plotters when you run the Install program, only one device can be selected within PrintGraph for a particular print session. This means that you must choose the device you want to print before you begin printing graphs. Even if you installed only one graphics printer or plotter, you still must select the device in PrintGraph before you can begin printing.

To select the printer or plotter that you want to use, issue the Settings Hardware Printer command. When you issue this command, 1-2-3 will display a list of all of the currently installed graphics output devices like the one shown in Figure 11-3.

You may find the choices on this list to be broader than you expected. That's because PrintGraph automatically offers more than one density option for some printers. For example, if you specify the HP LaserJet Series II printer as one of your graphics printers, PrintGraph will offer two choices: HP LaserJet+ or LaserJet II Medium Density and HP LaserJet+ or LaserJet II High Density.

When you see the list of the installed devices, use the ↓ and ↑ keys to highlight the name of the printer or plotter you plan to use, then press [Spacebar] to mark that choice. PrintGraph will place a # next to the device you select. When you've made your selection, press [Enter] to lock in that choice and return to the Settings Hardware menu. If you change your mind, you can just repeat this procedure and select a different device from the list.

```
Copyright 1986, 1989 Lotus Development Corp.  All Rights Reserved. V2.2    POINT
Select graphics printer or plotter
─────────────────────────────────────────────────────────────────────
  Printer or Plotter name and Resolution
  ─────────────────────────────────────────  Space bar marks or unmarks selection
  HP-LaserJet+ or LaserJet II-Med den.       ENTER selects marked device
  HP-LaserJet+ or LaserJet II-High den.      ESC exits, ignoring changes
  HP-7470A Plotter - 8 1/2 x 11 transp.      HOME moves to beginning of list
  HP-7470A Plotter - 8 1/2 x 11 paper        END moves to end of list
  Epson-LQ-800, 1000 and 1500-Low density    ↑ and ↓ move highlight
  Epson-LQ-800, 1000 and 1500-Hi density        List will scroll if highlight
                                                moved beyond top or bottom
```

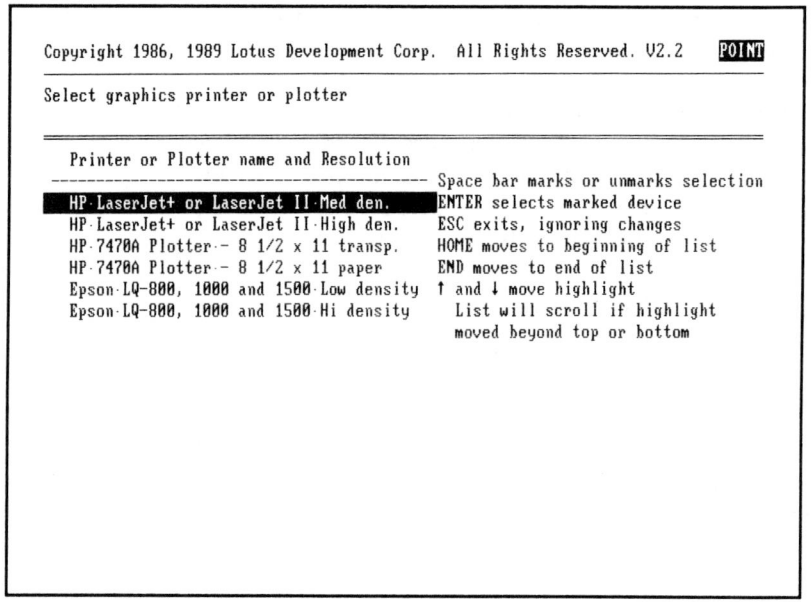

FIGURE 11-3: Installed graphics output devices

TIP: PRINT DENSITY

As we have mentioned, PrintGraph will offer you two or more density options for some graphics printers. These options may be Low Density, Medium Density, and High Density, or they may be Single Strike, Double Strike, and Triple Strike. In most cases, the higher density options will produce better looking graphs. However, higher density graphs take *much* more time to print. The first time you print a graph, you should use a low density (or single strike) option so you can see the printed result as soon as possible. You might consider this first printed graph a draft, which you can check for any adjustments that need to be made. After you are certain that all your settings are correct, use a higher density option for the final printed graph.

Choosing the Interface

The interface is the physical connection between your computer and the graphics output device (printer or plotter) you have chosen. PrintGraph offers eight choices for the Interface setting: Parallel 1, Serial 1, Parallel 2, Serial 2, DOS Device LPT1, DOS Device LPT2, DOS Device LPT3, and DOS Device LPT4.

Most computers are equipped with one parallel interface (or "parallel port") and one serial interface (or "serial port"). Most popular computer printers, such as the Epson printers, use the parallel port to receive data from a computer. Some printers (and many plotters) accept data through a serial port. If you are not sure which type of interface is appropriate for your graphics output device, check the printer manual or ask your dealer.

The default Interface setting is *Parallel 1*, which means the first parallel port. The chances are good that this is appropriate for your hardware configuration, especially if you are printing to a graphics printer. However, if you are using a serial device (including many plotters) or if you are using two printers—one for text and one for graphics—you may need to change the Interface setting. For example, suppose you have two parallel interfaces on your computer. A text printer is attached to the first parallel interface, and your graphics printer is attached to the second parallel port. To print graphs to the second printer, you would need to change the Interface setting to Parallel 2. To make this change, issue the Settings Hardware Interface command, select 3, and press [Enter].

If you choose a serial interface, PrintGraph will ask you to supply a baud rate. The baud rate you choose determines how fast the graph image information will be sent from your computer to the printer or plotter. The most important consideration in selecting a baud rate is to make sure that the rate you specify is the rate at which your output device expects to receive information. Otherwise, the graph will not be transmitted correctly. Most serial graphics output devices support 1200 baud or 9600 baud communication.

The last four Interface choices represent the DOS logical devices LPT1 through LPT4 (these choices are not available in 1-2-3 Release 1A). These Interface settings have been included for users whose computers are connected to remote output devices (for example, computers that are hooked into a network). If your computer is connected to a network and you plan to use a remote output device to print graphs, you should ask your system operator which logical device you should choose. Unless your computer is part of this kind of system, you should not be concerned with these choices.

Specifying Paper Size

The Settings Hardware Size-Paper command allows you to specify the size of the paper on which you will be printing. PrintGraph's default paper size is 8.5 inches wide by 11 inches long. While this setting will probably be appropriate for most applications, if you plan to print graphs larger than usual, you will need to change the Size-Paper setting.

To specify a different paper size, you just issue the Settings Hardware Size-Paper command. Issuing this command will reveal a menu with two options: Length and Width. To change the Page Width setting, choose the Width option and specify the new page width in inches. For example, to change the paper size to 14 by 11 inches (the dimensions of standard computer paper), issue the Settings Hardware Size-Paper command, then choose Width, type 14, and press [Enter].

To change the Page-Length setting, you must choose the Length option and specify the new length in inches. In addition, you must manually adjust your printer's Page-Length (or Form Length) setting. For example, if you want to change the page length to 6 inches, issue the Settings Hardware Size-Paper Length command, type 6, and press [Enter]. Next, adjust your printer's Form Length setting to 6 inches. (The procedure for changing the Form Length setting varies from printer to printer. You should read your printer's manual for instructions.)

The page size you specify does not affect the size of the printed graph image nor its position on the page. (You can alter both of these with other PrintGraph commands, which we'll discuss in a few pages.) In fact, the only use for the Size-Paper setting is to increase the default page size to accommodate larger graphs. If you plan to print standard-size graphs, you do not need to adjust this setting.

If you specify a paper size that is too small to hold the graph image you are printing, PrintGraph will print as much of the graph as possible within the page dimensions you have set, then will truncate the remainder of the graph.

The Pause and Eject Settings

The Pause and Eject settings affect the action of your printer or plotter when you are printing several graphs in one session. The Pause setting tells PrintGraph whether or not it should pause after it prints each graph in a series. If Pause is set to No (the default), PrintGraph will print all of the graphs in sequence without pausing. If you set Pause to Yes, then PrintGraph will pause after it prints each graph and will begin beeping. You will have time to load a new piece of paper into your printer or plotter, change a setting on your printer or plotter, or change your plotter pens before PrintGraph prints the next graph. When you are ready to print, just press [Spacebar], and PrintGraph will resume printing with the next graph in the sequence. If you are using a printer or plotter that does not have continuous paper or automatic sheet feed, you should be sure that Pause is set to Yes before you print several graphs in one session.

To change the Pause setting, issue the Settings Action Pause command. Choose the Yes option to tell PrintGraph to pause after printing each graph. To tell PrintGraph to print all of the graphs in a session without pausing, choose No.

Although you can alter your printer settings or change paper while PrintGraph pauses, you will not be able to adjust any PrintGraph settings such as Color, Size, or Fonts. PrintGraph will always print all of the graphs in a sequence with the same settings. Once you have begun printing, there is no way to change a setting.

The Eject option specifies whether or not PrintGraph should send a page-feed command to the printer after printing each graph in a series. The Eject setting is controlled by the Settings Action Eject command. This setting is useful only for printers with continuous-feed paper.

When you issue the Eject command, you'll see two choices: Yes and No. If you want each of your graphs on a separate page, then you should set Eject to Yes. This will force your printer to advance to the top of the next page before printing a new graph. If you set Eject to No, PrintGraph will not advance your printer to the next page between graphs, enabling you to print more than one graph on a page. However, if there is not enough room to print an additional graph on the current page, PrintGraph will automatically advance the paper to the top of the next page.

CHOOSING GRAPHS TO PRINT

The Image-Select command on the main PrintGraph menu allows you to retrieve .PIC files into PrintGraph. When you issue the Image-Select command, you will see a screen, like the one in Figure 11-4, that lists all of the .PIC files stored in the current Graphs directory. Notice that the files appear in alphabetical order and that PrintGraph displays the creation date and time, as well as the size, of each file. To select a graph, use the ↓ and ↑ keys to position the cursor over the name of a file that you want to print. Then press [Spacebar] to select that graph. A # will appear next to the file name to indicate that it has been selected. If you want to deselect a selected graph, highlight it and press [Spacebar] again.

```
Copyright 1986, 1989 Lotus Development Corp. All Rights Reserved. V2.2    POINT

Select graphs to print


    GRAPH FILE  DATE      TIME    SIZE
    ─────────────────────────────────────
                                          Space bar marks or unmarks selection
    ALPHA3      07-09-86  14:40    6660   ENTER selects marked graphs
    BAR         07-09-86  12:39    6648   ESC exits, ignoring changes
    FORUM       07-08-86  14:49     788   HOME moves to beginning of list
    FOUR        07-09-86  14:38    6632   END moves to end of list
    LINES       07-02-86   9:02     909   ↑ and ↓ move highlight
    LOTUS       07-08-86  14:50     788     List will scroll if highlight
    PIE         07-02-86   9:07    2164     moved beyond top or bottom
    REGLINE     07-02-86   9:08    1141   GRAPH (F10) previews marked graph
    STACKED     07-02-86   9:05    3878
    TEST        06-23-86  11:23    1629
    THREE       07-09-86  14:41    6539
    TRENDS      07-09-86  14:53    1324
    XY          07-02-86   9:07    1030
```

FIGURE 11-4: A list of .PIC files

You can select more than one graph for printing. All you have to do is highlight the name of the first .PIC file that you want to print, press [Spacebar], then highlight the second one, press [Spacebar] again, and so on. Keep in mind that PrintGraph will print all of the graphs that you select. The order in which you select the graphs will determine the order in which they will be printed.

After you have marked the graph(s) you want to print, press [Enter]. At that point, PrintGraph will lock in your selection(s) and return you to the main PrintGraph menu.

If there are no .PIC files in the directory you specified in your hardware setup, you'll see an error message when you choose Image-Select. If this happens to you, press [Esc] to acknowledge the error and change the Graphs directory to a directory that contains .PIC files. If you have not created any .PIC files, you must quit PrintGraph, load 1-2-3, and save one or more graphs before you can go on.

> ### TIP: PREVIEWING GRAPHS
>
> While you are selecting the graphs you want to print, you can get an on-screen preview of any graph in your list of .PIC files. To preview a graph, just highlight the name of the graph you want to see and press the [Graph] key ([F10]). When you do this, PrintGraph will replace the list of .PIC files with a display of the graph whose name is highlighted. (The graph you preview does not have to be selected.)
>
> The graph image you see on your screen is a fair approximation of the printed graph. However, the screen image will *not* reflect your choices of fonts, graph size, or rotation. In fact, this preview capability is most useful for helping you select the graph or graphs you want to print. For example, suppose you have two .PIC files with very similar names, such as BAR1 and BAR2. To make sure you select the correct graph for printing, use the [Graph] key to preview one or both of these graphs on screen. After you've seen them, you can select the correct one and then go ahead with printing.

FORMATTING YOUR GRAPHS

PrintGraph offers several options for altering the format of your printed graphs. These options let you choose the size of the printed graph, its position on the paper, and the fonts used for graph text. If you are using a color output device, such as a plotter, you can also specify how you want to use color in the graph.

Choosing a Text Font

PrintGraph lets you choose the font in which the text in your graph (titles, legends, and so on) will be printed. You can choose one or two fonts. If you choose only one font, then all the text in the graph will be printed with that font. If you choose two fonts, then the first title will appear in Font 1, while the rest of the graph text (the second title, labels, legends, and so forth) will appear in Font 2. PrintGraph offers eleven fonts to choose from: BLOCK1, BLOCK2, BOLD, FORUM, ITALIC1, ITALIC2, LOTUS, ROMAN1, ROMAN2, SCRIPT1, and SCRIPT2. (1-2-3 1A's PrintGraph program does not offer the LOTUS, BOLD, or FORUM fonts.) Figure 11-5 shows a sample of each font printed on an Epson LQ-1500 printer in the High Density mode.

The default font setting is BLOCK1. You do not have to change this setting if you do not want to; in fact, Block1 is one of the best font options, especially if you are printing to a dot-matrix printer.

If you want to specify different fonts for your graph, issue the Settings Image Font command. You will then see a menu with two choices: 1 and 2. To specify the first font, select Font 1. This choice will bring up a list, like the one in Figure 11-6, of the fonts stored in the current Fonts directory. If there are no fonts on the directory that you have specified as the Fonts directory, PrintGraph will display an error message and instruct you either to place the disk containing the font files in the specified directory or to change the Fonts directory to the directory that contains the font files.

1. This is a Sample of the BLOCK1 Font
2. This is a Sample of the BLOCK2 Font
3. **This is a Sample of the BOLD Font**
4. **This is a Sample of the FORUM Font**
5. *This is a Sample of the ITALIC1 Font*
6. *This is a Sample of the ITALIC2 Font*
7. *This is a Sample of the LOTUS Font*
8. This is a Sample of the ROMAN1 Font
9. This is a sample of the ROMAN2 Font
10. *This is a Sample of the SCRIPT1 Font*
11. *This is a Sample of the SCRIPT2 Font*

FIGURE 11-5: PrintGraph fonts

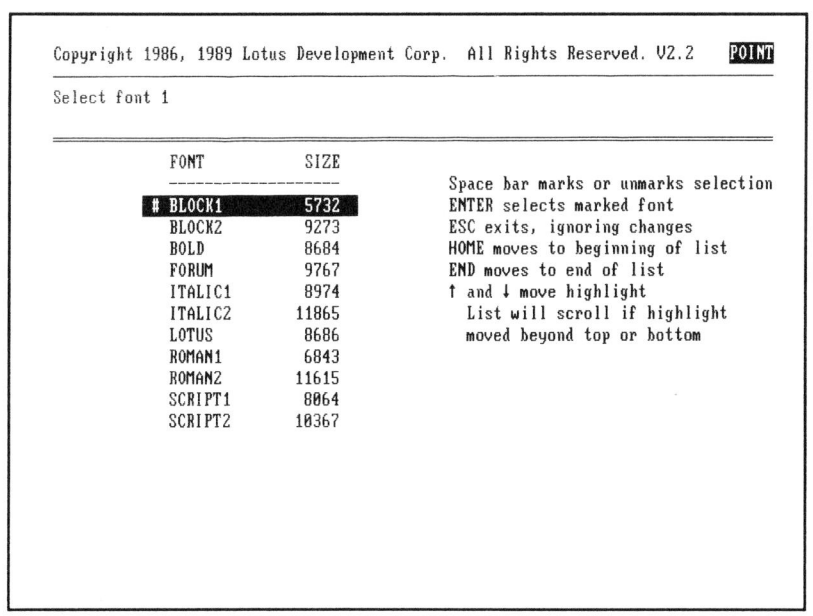

```
Copyright 1986, 1989 Lotus Development Corp.  All Rights Reserved. V2.2   POINT

Select font 1
================================================================================
           FONT        SIZE
           ----        ----         Space bar marks or unmarks selection
         # BLOCK1      5732         ENTER selects marked font
           BLOCK2      9273         ESC exits, ignoring changes
           BOLD        8684         HOME moves to beginning of list
           FORUM       9767         END moves to end of list
           ITALIC1     8974         ↑ and ↓ move highlight
           ITALIC2     11865            List will scroll if highlight
           LOTUS       8686             moved beyond top or bottom
           ROMAN1      6843
           ROMAN2      11615
           SCRIPT1     8064
           SCRIPT2     10367
```

FIGURE 11-6: The list of fonts

You should choose the font you wish to use by highlighting its name and pressing [Spacebar] to select it. A # will appear next to the name of the font you have chosen. You can select only one font from the list. If you try to select another font, PrintGraph will deselect the first choice and select the new one. When you've made your selection, press [Enter] to return to the Settings Image menu.

If you want to use two fonts in your printed graph, issue the Settings Image Font 2 command and follow the same procedure that you used to select Font 1. If no font is selected for Font 2, then PrintGraph will use your selection for Font 1 as the default for Font 2.

Specifying the Size and Rotation of a Printed Graph

The Size command on the main PrintGraph menu allows you to control the size of a printed graph, as well as its orientation on the page. When you select this command, PrintGraph will display three options: Full, Half, and Manual.

Full and Half Size

In most cases, you will want to use either the Full or Half options. When you choose either of these settings, PrintGraph automatically will adjust the width and height of your graph, the margins, and the graph's orientation on the page. If you choose to print a graph half size (the default), it will be printed 4.691 inches high and 6.5 inches wide. If you print the graph full size, it will be 6.852 inches wide, 9.445 inches tall, and rotated 90 degrees on the page.

Since half size is the default size setting, you don't need to do anything if you want to print graphs in half size. To specify full size for a printed graph, you would issue the Settings Image Size Full command. When you issue this command, the Top, Left, Width, Height, and Rotate settings on the PrintGraph screen will change to reflect the new setting. To change the setting back to half size, you would issue the Settings Image Size Half command.

Figures 11-7 and 11-8 show the same graph printed full size and half size. Notice that the half-size graph in Figure 11-7 fills half of an 8 1/2-by-11 inch page and is oriented with the top of the graph at the top of the page. The full-size graph in Figure 11-8 is rotated 90 degrees so that the top of the graph is at the left edge of the page. The full-size graph fills the 8 1/2-by-11-inch page.

Manual Sizing

If you want to specify a size other than full or half, you must select the Manual option. This option allows you to define the height, width, top and left margins, and rotation of a graph manually. Figure 11-9 shows the menu that results when you issue the Settings Image Size Manual command.

When you use manual sizing, you do not have to change *all* of these settings. If you want, you can use PrintGraph's defaults for all the settings except one or two (such as margins). In this way, manual sizing can be very helpful for making minor adjustments to the size and position of a printed graph.

Chapter 11: Printing Graphs 451

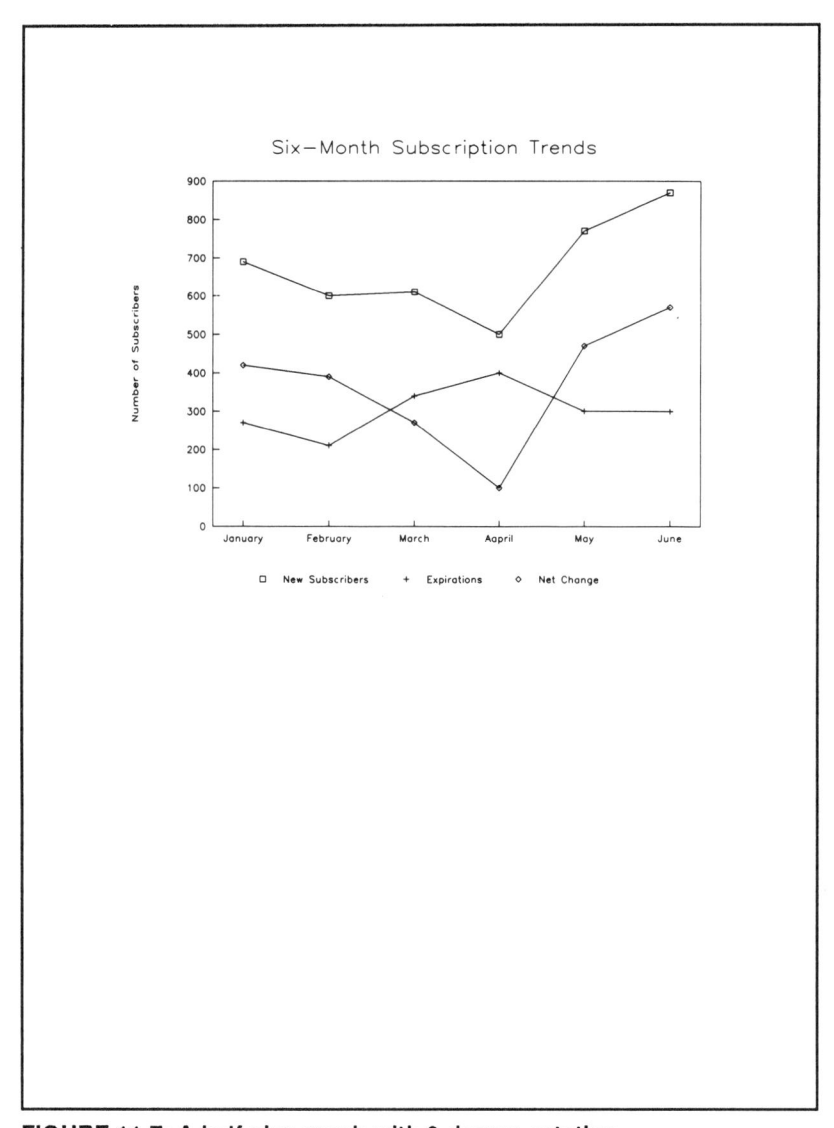

FIGURE 11-7: A half-size graph with 0-degree rotation

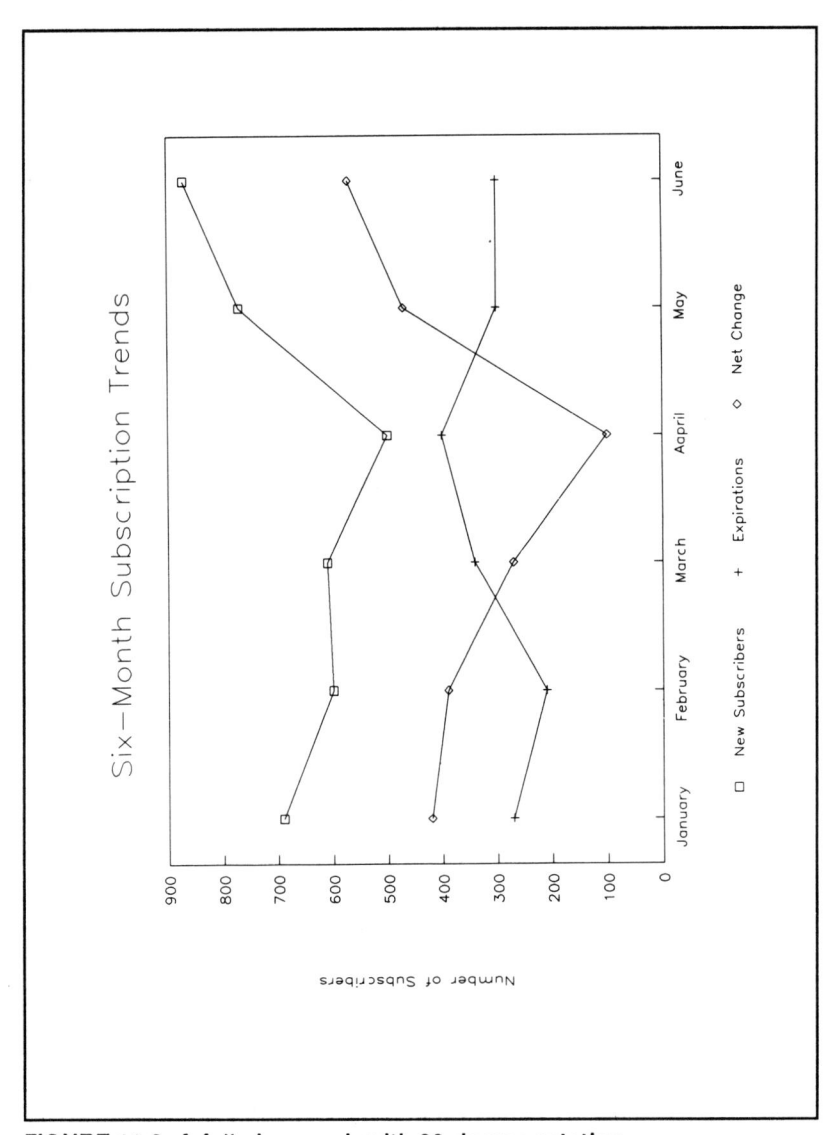

FIGURE 11-8: A full-size graph with 90-degree rotation

Margins

The Top and Left Margin settings control how a graph is positioned on the page. The Top Margin setting determines the space between the top of the page and the top of the graph; the Left Margin setting determines the space between the left edge of the page and the left edge of the graph. These settings are very easy to change. All you have to do is select either the Top or Left option from the Size Manual menu and specify the new Margin setting in inches.

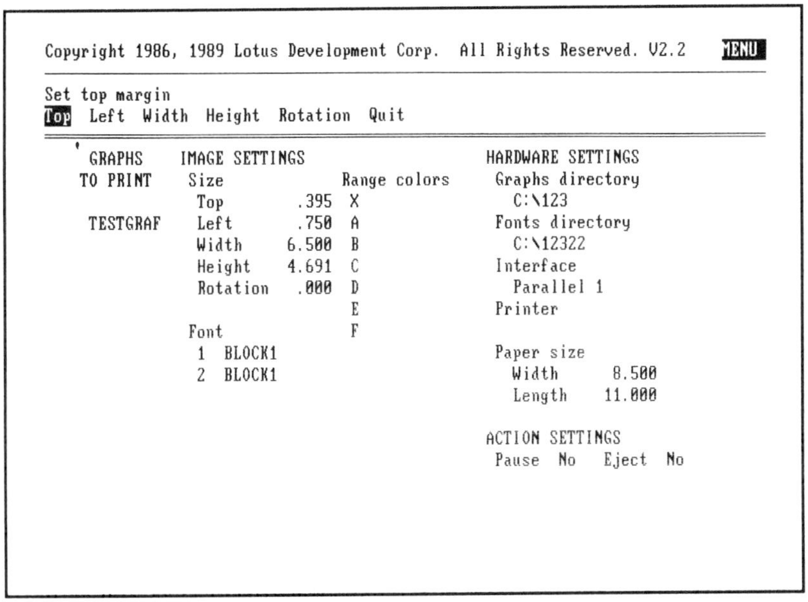

```
Copyright 1986, 1989 Lotus Development Corp.  All Rights Reserved. V2.2    MENU

Set top margin
Top  Left  Width  Height  Rotation  Quit

        GRAPHS      IMAGE SETTINGS                        HARDWARE SETTINGS
        TO PRINT    Size              Range colors        Graphs directory
                    Top       .395    X                     C:\123
        TESTGRAF    Left      .750    A                   Fonts directory
                    Width    6.500    B                     C:\12322
                    Height   4.691    C                   Interface
                    Rotation  .000    D                     Parallel 1
                                      E                   Printer
                    Font              F
                    1 BLOCK1                              Paper size
                    2 BLOCK1                                Width     8.500
                                                           Length    11.000

                                                         ACTION SETTINGS
                                                          Pause  No   Eject  No
```

FIGURE 11-9: The Size Manual menu

For example, suppose you want to print a half-size graph in the center of a 14- by-11-inch page. You can use the Settings Image Size Half command to set the basic proportions of the graph and then use the Manual option to adjust the margins only. When you choose Half, PrintGraph will automatically set the size of the graph to 6.5 inches wide and 4.691 inches tall. In addition, PrintGraph will automatically set the top margin to .395 inch and the left margin to .75 inch, which means that the graph will be .395 inch from the top and .75 inch from the left edge of the page. To print this graph in the center of the page, just choose Manual from the Size menu, select Top, then type 3.15 and press [Enter]. (You don't have to press [Esc] to erase the current setting; it will disappear when you begin typing the new setting.) Then choose the Left option, type 3.75, and press [Enter]. When both settings have been changed, choose Quit four times to return to the main menu. When you print the graph, it should appear in the center of the 14-by-11-inch page.

Rotation

The Rotation setting allows you to control the rotation of a printed graph on the page. A graph's Rotation setting determines whether it will be printed vertically, horizontally, or diagonally on a page. As you have already seen (in Figures 11-7 and 11-8), PrintGraph normally prints half-size graphs with 0 degrees of rotation and full-size graphs with 90 degrees of rotation. PrintGraph always rotates graphs in a counterclockwise direction, so a Rotation setting of 90 will cause PrintGraph to place the top of the graph along the left edge of the page.

To change the Rotation setting, issue the Settings Image Size Manual Rotation command, type a Rotation setting (from 0 to 360 degrees), and press [Enter]. In most cases, you will want either 0-degree or 90-degree rotation. (We don't recommend diagonal rotation since it makes most graph text unreadable.)

Setting the Height and Width Manually

The Height and Width options on the Size Manual menu allow you to change the height and width of a graph. These settings allow you to print graphs in sizes other than the standard half and full size. Before you use these commands to change the size of a graph, however, you need to understand the relationship between rotation and height and width.

The Relationship between Rotation and Size

In addition to determining the orientation of a printed graph, the Rotation setting determines which axis of the graph is associated with the Width setting and which axis is associated with the Height setting. PrintGraph does *not* automatically associate the Width setting with the x-axis and the Height setting with the y-axis. Instead, the Width setting always determines the horizontal size of the graph, and the Height setting always determines the vertical size of the graph. (The menus in PrintGraph are misleading in this respect since the prompt for the Width setting is *Set width of the graph (horizontal distance)*, and the prompt for the Height setting is *Set height of the graph (vertical distance)*.)

Depending on the rotation of the graph, the Height setting may correspond to the x-axis or the y-axis. Similarly, the Width setting may correspond to either axis. If a graph has 0-degree rotation, then the x-axis will be printed horizontally, and the Width setting will correspond to the x-axis direction. On the other hand, if a graph has 90-degree rotation, the y-axis is printed horizontally, and the width measure will correspond to the y-axis. Remember—the Width setting always determines the horizontal size of the graph, and the Height setting always determines the vertical size of the graph.

The Golden Ratio

When PrintGraph sets the height and width of a graph, it always maintains a certain ratio between the width and height of the graph. In a graph with 0-degree rotation, the width-to-height ratio is 1.385 to 1. In a graph with 90-degree rotation, the width-to-height ratio is 1 to 1.385. Although it's not essential that you maintain this ratio when you specify the width and height manually, you may want to do so in order to assure that your printed graphs have the same proportions they do when 1-2-3 displays them.

Setting the Height and Width

Once you know the standard width-to-height ratio, it is easy to determine the proper height for a graph of any width or the proper width for a graph of any height. Table

11-1 shows the formulas you would use to determine either the height or width of a graph, given the other dimension, for graphs with 0-degree rotation and for graphs with 90-degree rotation.

Rotation 0 Width: x-axis Height: y-axis	Width = Height * 1.385	Height = Width / 1.385
Rotation 90 Width: y-axis Height: x-axis	Width = Height / 1.385	Height = Width * 1.385

TABLE 11-1: Determining the Height and Width settings

For example, suppose you want to print a graph with 0-degree rotation that is five inches tall. What should your Width setting be? Using PrintGraph's standard ratio, you could calculate the Width setting with the formula *5 * 1.385*. This formula returns the result 6.925, which is the Width setting you should use if you want to preserve the ideal relationship between height and width. To specify the size of this graph, you should issue the Settings Image Size Manual Height command, type 5 as the graph height, and press [Enter]. To change the width, issue the Settings Image Size Manual Width command, type 6.925, and press [Enter].

Similarly, suppose you want to print a graph with 90-degree rotation that is to be 10 inches high. The ideal Width setting for this graph would be 7.22 inches, or 10/1.385. To specify the size of this graph, you should issue the Settings Image Size Manual Height command, type 10 as the graph height, and press [Enter]. To change the width, you would issue the Settings Image Size Manual Width command, type 7.22, and press [Enter]. Because this graph will be printed with a 90-degree rotation, the x-axis of the graph will correspond to the longer dimension, and the proportion of the graph will be preserved.

When you are thinking about the relationship between rotation, width, and height, it might be helpful to remember that, in most cases, the x-axis of a graph should be longer than the y-axis. Thus, a graph with 0-degree rotation should have a Width setting that is greater than its Height setting. Similarly, a graph with 90-degree rotation should have a Height setting that is greater than its Width setting.

Specifying Paper Size

If you increase the width or height of a graph so that the graph won't fit on a standard 11-by-8-1/2-inch sheet of paper, you'll need to use the Settings Hardware Size-Paper command to increase the Size-Paper setting before you print. Otherwise, PrintGraph will print as much of the graph as possible within the existing page dimensions and then will truncate the remainder of the graph.

Choosing Colors in a Graph

If you are using a color output device such as a plotter or color printer, PrintGraph lets you assign specific colors to different parts of a graph. In line, bar, stacked-bar, and XY graphs, you can assign a different color to each data range and yet another color to the other parts of the graph—the axes, titles, grid, and so forth. For example, you might choose to print your graph box and text in black, with your data ranges in red, blue, and green. (You also can use colors in pie graphs. To learn how, see the tip on page 458.)

The command for assigning colors in a graph is Settings Image Range-Colors. When you issue this command, you will see the menu shown in Figure 11-10. Each of the items on this menu corresponds to one of the ranges in the graph: A to the A range, B to the B range, and so on. The X choice represents not only the X labels in the graph, but also the graph "box" and everything outside the box (titles, y-axis labels, and so forth) except legends. Each legend will be printed in the same color as the data range it describes. Likewise, data labels are printed in the same color as the range to which they're associated.

```
Copyright 1986, 1989 Lotus Development Corp.  All Rights Reserved. V2.2    MENU
Select color for X data range
X  A  B  C  D  E  F  Quit

     GRAPHS     IMAGE SETTINGS                     HARDWARE SETTINGS
     TO PRINT   Size              Range colors     Graphs directory
                Top       .395    X Black            C:\123
     TESTGRAF   Left      .750    A Black          Fonts directory
                Width    6.500    B Black            C:\12322
                Height   4.691    C Black          Interface
                Rotation  .000    D Black            Parallel 1
                                  E Black          Printer
                Font              F Black            HP 7470A-trans.
                1 BLOCK1                           Paper size
                2 BLOCK1                             Width     8.500
                                                    Length   11.000

                                                  ACTION SETTINGS
                                                    Pause  No  Eject  No
```

FIGURE 11-10: The Image Range-Colors menu

To assign a color to a particular range, select that range from the Range-Colors menu. You will then see a menu of color options. The number of colors on the menu is determined by the output device you have selected. For example, if your output device is an IBM PC Color Printer, you will see a menu of eight colors. When you see this menu, you should choose the color that you want to assign to the range you have selected. (To choose a color, you should point to its name and press [Enter]. You should be careful about choosing a color by typing its first letter since sometimes a menu will contain two colors that begin with the same letter, such as Black and Brown.) Once you have chosen a color for one range, PrintGraph will return you to the menu of graph ranges. You should then choose another range and select its color. You can repeat this process until you have assigned a color to each graph range.

For example, suppose you are printing a line graph with two data ranges, A and B, and you would like to plot this graph on an HP 7470A plotter. You want the graph box and text to be printed in blue, the A range in red, and the B range in green. To assign these colors, issue the Settings Image Range-Colors command and choose X. Point to the color you want to use for the graph axes and titles—Blue—and press [Enter]. Then choose A, point to the Red choice, and press [Enter]. Finally, select the B range, point to the Green choice, and press [Enter]. Before you plot this graph, PrintGraph will instruct you to load your plotter pens in the correct order so that your colors are assigned properly in the finished graph.

You can print a graph in color even if your computer has only a monochrome monitor. All that is required to print graphs in color is a color printer or plotter.

If you have a monochrome monitor, you probably used the / Graph Options B&W command to tell 1-2-3 to use cross-hatch patterns instead of color to distinguish the different ranges in your bar graphs and stacked-bar graphs. Those patterns will be saved when you save a graph image into a .PIC file and will appear in the printed graph, even if you use the Range-Colors command to assign colors to the graph. If you are going to use a color output device, and you don't want *both* patterns and color, you must use the / Graph Options Color command in 1-2-3 to display the graph in "color" before you save it into a .PIC file.

You cannot choose colors for your graph until you have selected an output device. If the device you select does not offer color, PrintGraph will not allow you to assign colors to the ranges in the graph. While you can issue the Settings Image Range-Colors command, PrintGraph will offer only one color—Black—for any range in the graph.

Printing More Than One Graph

Keep in mind that the formatting options you choose will apply to *all* graphs that you print in a single batch. If you want to print several graphs and use different options for each one, you should select only one graph with the Image-Select command and then choose your settings for that graph. When the graph is printed, select another graph, alter your settings, and then print that graph. You must repeat this process for each graph if you want them all to have different formatting.

TIP: ASSIGNING COLORS TO PIE GRAPHS

Assigning colors to a pie graph is a little trickier than assigning colors to line and bar graphs. You might recall that a pie graph has only one data range, the A range. The numbers in this range determine the size of each wedge in the pie. In order to color or shade the wedges in a pie graphs, you must enter color/explosion codes into a range of cells in the worksheet, and then designate that range as the B range for the graph. (Chapter 10 explains this use of the B range in detail.)

Like 1-2-3, PrintGraph also uses the codes in the B range to assign colors to the ranges in a pie graphs. Here's how it works: Each number in the B range corresponds to one of the ranges on the PrintGraph Range-Colors menu. Table A summarizes the relationship between the B range and the corresponding ranges on the PrintGraph Range-Colors menu.

For example, suppose you have entered the number 5 in the first cell of the B range in your worksheet. This number will correspond to the first segment of the pie (the segment that is drawn first on your screen when you view the graph in 1-2-3). When you print the pie graph, PrintGraph will use the color you have assigned to the D range on the Range-Colors menu to print the first segment of the pie graph. Similarly, if the second cell in the B range contains the code 3, PrintGraph will use the color you have assigned to the B range on the Range-Colors menu to print the second segment in the pie. If the third cell of the B range contains the number 104, the third segment of the pie will be printed in the color you have assigned to range C on the Range-Colors menu, and will be exploded.

Value in B Range	Corresponding Range
1 or 101	X
2 or 102	A
3 or 103	B
4 or 104	C
5 or 105	D
6 or 106	E
7 or 107	F

TABLE A: How PrintGraph uses B range values to assign color

Remember: Once you're in PrintGraph, you will not be able to view the numbers in the graph's B range, nor will you be able to change those numbers. Before you exit 1-2-3 and load PrintGraph, you should make a copy of the B-range values for reference in PrintGraph.

PRINTING

Once you've configured PrintGraph, selected one or more .PIC files to print, and selected the settings you want to use to print those graphs, you're ready to produce the finished product. Before you begin, make sure your printer or plotter is properly attached to your computer and is on-line. If you're printing to a printer, be sure that the print head is aligned at the top edge of a new page. Then issue the Align command to tell PrintGraph that you are at the top-of-form. Finally, choose Go from the main menu to begin printing.

Before the printing actually begins, PrintGraph will take a few seconds to load the font files you have selected—you'll see a message on your screen to this effect. Then, it may take a few seconds for PrintGraph to form the image before output begins. Once these tasks are out of the way, PrintGraph will begin printing.

If you have set Eject to Yes, PrintGraph will advance the printer to the top of a new page after it prints each graph in a series. If you set Pause to Yes, PrintGraph will stop after it prints each graph and beep. You can make any needed adjustments to your printer or to the paper during this pause. When you are ready to begin printing again, press [Spacebar].

If you are printing to a plotter, PrintGraph may stop during printing and give you instructions to change the active pen. You should follow these instructions, then press [Spacebar] when you are ready to resume printing.

Generally, graph printing is very slow, especially if you are using a high-density printing option. This is especially true if you have selected several different graphs for printing. If you want to stop printing before the graph is complete, press [Ctrl][Break] then [Esc].

Once your graphs are printed, you can issue the Page command, which will advance the printer to the top of the next page. This can be helpful for removing your printed output at the end of a print session.

TIP: LEAVE YOUR PRINTER ALONE!

The Align command on the PrintGraph menu allows you to tell PrintGraph that the paper in your printer is properly aligned, with the print head at the top of a new page. Once you have issued this command, PrintGraph keeps track of its position on the page, using the Size-Paper settings.

If you change the position of the paper in your printer manually, however, PrintGraph will lose its place. This may lead to all kinds of problems, including page breaks in the middle of graphs. Therefore, once you issue the Align command, leave your printer alone! Use the Page command—and not your printer's controls—to advance the paper to the top of a new page. If you must scroll the paper in your printer manually or use the printer's controls to move the paper, be sure to use the Align command to tell PrintGraph where the top-of-form is *before* you print another graph.

AN EXAMPLE

Figure 11-12 shows a printed version of the 1-2-3 graph in Figure 11-11. This graph was printed on an HP LaserJet Series II printer using high-density print. We also chose to print this graph full size, so it was rotated 90 degrees. We used the Forum option for Font 1 and the Roman1 option for Font 2.

To print this graph, we first saved it into a .PIC file in 1-2-3, then exited from 1-2-3, loaded PrintGraph, and used the Image-Select command to load the .PIC file into PrintGraph. Next, we issued the Settings Image Size Full command to specify full size and chose Quit to return to the Settings Image menu. Then, we chose Font from this menu, selected option 1, and chose Forum from the list of fonts. To specify Font 2, we selected 2 from the Font menu and chose the Roman1 option. Once these settings had been selected, we aligned the paper in our printer, issued the Align command, and issued the Go command. Figure 11-12 shows the result.

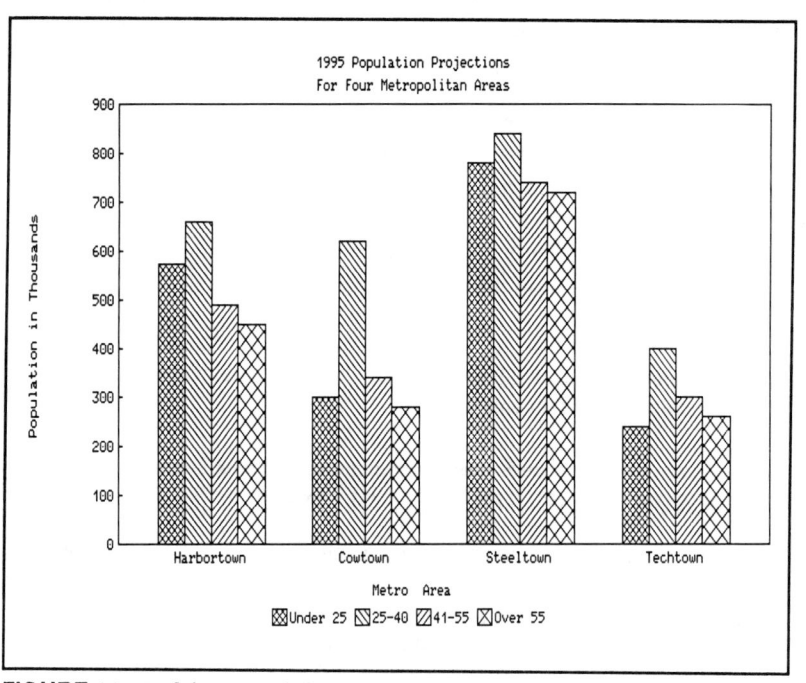

FIGURE 11-11: A bar graph in 1-2-3

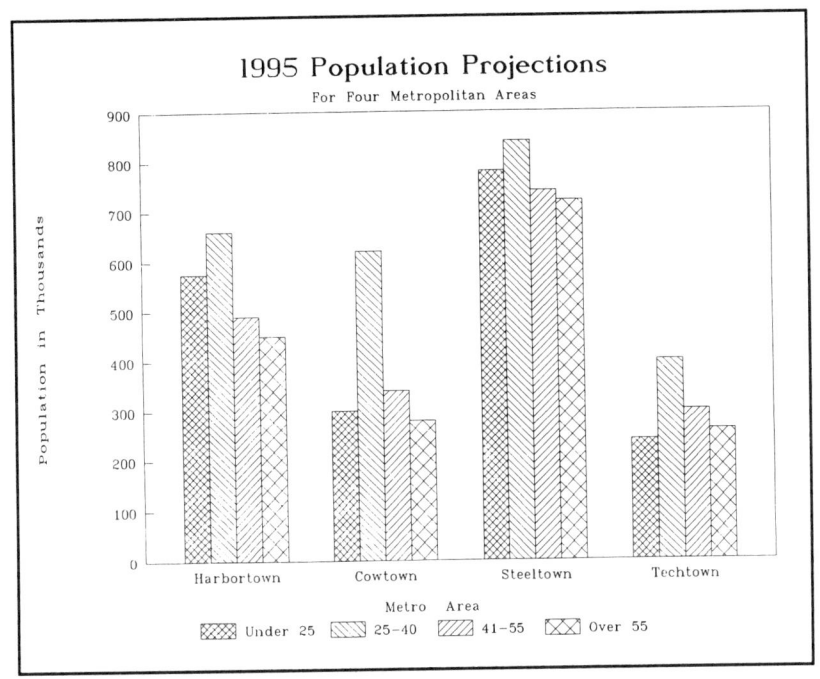

FIGURE 11-12: A printed bar graph

You may notice that there are some differences between the appearance of the printed graph in Figure 11-12 and the on-screen graph in Figure 11-11. First, notice that the first title in the printed graph is larger than the rest of the text in that graph. In the on-screen version of the graph, all of the text is the same size. In addition, the legends in the printed graph are spaced farther apart than the legends in the on-screen version (see the tip on the next page for more on this problem). Also notice that the shading patterns in the printed graph are not exactly the same as those you see in the screen display. Finally, the overall proportions of the printed version are different from those of the on-screen graph. These differences are typical; you'll see them in all of the graphs you print.

SAVING PRINTGRAPH SETTINGS

It's possible to save your PrintGraph settings so that you do not have to configure the program more than once. To save your PrintGraph settings, just issue the Settings Save command. This command saves all of the current PrintGraph settings into a configuration file on the default directory.

Once you have used this command to save your PrintGraph settings, those settings become the new defaults. Each time you load PrintGraph, it will read the saved settings from the configuration file and use them as its default settings.

> **TIP: PRINTING GRAPHS WITH LEGENDS**
>
> When you view a graph with a legend on your screen, you'll notice that 1-2-3 places the legends fairly close together. In printed graphs, you will encounter just the opposite problem. Instead of being crowded together, the legends will be spread out across the bottom of the printed page. Unfortunately, this means that 1-2-3 cannot fit as many characters in the legends of printed graphs as it can on your screen. If your legends contain too many characters, the rightmost legend in the printed graph will be truncated.
>
> To avoid this problem, you should limit the number of characters in your legends. Table A shows the maximum number of characters you can include in a legend in each type of 1-2-3 graph if you plan to print that graph. The numbers in the Total Characters columns represent the maximum combined lengths of legend text for all the ranges in the graph.
>
> | Line and XY Graphs | | Bar and Stacked-bar Graphs | |
> |---|---|---|---|
> | *Legend Entries* | *Total Characters* | *Legend Entries* | *Total Characters* |
> | 2 | 42 | 2 | 39 |
> | 3 | 36 | 3 | 33 |
> | 4 | 30 | 4 | 27 |
> | 5 | 24 | 5 | 21 |
> | 6 | 18 | 6 | 15 |
>
> **TABLE A:** Limits on legend lengths in printed graphs

Chances are you'll want to save your basic hardware settings (such as Fonts directory and Printer Interface) and use them every time you print a graph. Your formatting options, on the other hand, probably won't be as permanent. Each time you select a new graph or batch of graphs to print, you will most likely want to specify formatting options that are appropriate for those graphs. However, *all* your current PrintGraph settings will be saved when you issue the Save command, including those that you may want to change from time to time. Only your .PIC file selections are not saved.

Keep in mind that you can save only one group of settings. When you issue the Save command, your current PrintGraph settings will overwrite whatever you had saved before. Therefore, you should use this command with caution.

The Settings Reset command lets you call up your saved PrintGraph settings at any time. When you issue this command, 1-2-3 reads the settings from the configuration file into PrintGraph. If you have never saved PrintGraph settings, issuing this command resets the PrintGraph settings to their original defaults.

The Settings Reset command assures that you can make temporary changes to your PrintGraph settings without losing your saved settings. For example, suppose you normally use an Epson printer to print your .PIC files, so you have configured PrintGraph to work with this device. However, a friend has lent you a plotter, which you plan to use for a couple of days instead of your printer. After installing the plotter driver, you can change all your PrintGraph settings to work with this new output device. You should *not* save the new PrintGraph settings. After you have finished plotting the graphs, you can return to your original settings by issuing the Settings Reset command. Of course, this command will wipe out all your temporary PrintGraph settings, so you should be sure that you no longer need these settings before you choose Reset.

Interestingly, when you issue the Reset command, PrintGraph will not reset your selected .PIC files. These will remain selected until you deselect them or exit from PrintGraph.

LEAVING PRINTGRAPH

Once you have finished using PrintGraph, you can exit the program by choosing Exit Yes. After a moment, you will be returned to the level from which you entered PrintGraph—either the Lotus Access menu or the DOS prompt. If you entered PrintGraph after issuing the / System command, you'll be returned to DOS. You can return to 1-2-3 just by typing Exit.

PRINTING GRAPHS IN 1-2-3 RELEASE 1A

As we mentioned at the begining of this chapter, printing graphs in 1-2-3 Release 1A is similar to printing graphs in Releases 2, 2.01, and 2.2. However, some commands have different names, and many are located in different places. Table 11-2 lists these command differences.

1-2-3 Release 1A	1-2-3 Releases 2, 2.01, and 2.2
Accessing PrintGraph:	
A>GRAPH	A>PGRAPH
Specifying Hardware Parameters:	
Configure Device	Settings Hardware Printer
Configure Files Pictures	Settings Hardware Graphs-Directory
Configure Files Fonts	Settings Hardware Fonts-Directory
Configure Interface	Settings Hardware Interface
Configure Page	Settings Hardware Size-Paper
Options Pause	Settings Action Pause
Options Eject	Settings Action Eject
Selecting Graphs to Print:	
Select	Image-Select
Choosing Format Options:	
Options Color	Settings Image Range-Colors
Options Color Grid	Settings Image Range-Colors X
Options Font	Settings Image Font
Options Size	Settings Image Size
Saving and Recalling PrintGraph Settings:	
Configure Save	Settings Save
Configure Reset	Settings Reset
Leaving PrintGraph:	
Quit Yes	Exit Yes

TABLE 11-2: PrintGraph command equivalents

CONCLUSION

This chapter concludes our look at 1-2-3 graphs. In it, we showed you how to print the graphs that you create and save in 1-2-3. In the next chapter, we'll explore 1-2-3's data base powers.

12

Data Base Management

So far, we've explored spreadsheets and graphics—the "1" and "2" of 1-2-3. In this chapter, we'll examine 1-2-3's third environment—its data base manager.

A data base is simply a structured collection of information. You probably use data bases every day—maybe without realizing it. For example, the telephone book in your desk drawer is a data base. So is your dictionary. The 1-2-3 data base manager makes it possible to store many kinds of data bases—such as mailing lists, employee records, price lists, stock price histories, and cash receipts records—in the cells of a 1-2-3 worksheet.

The value of a data base manager like 1-2-3 is that it lets you access and manipulate the information in a data base quickly and easily. Once you have created a data base in 1-2-3, you can use the program's commands to sort the information in the data base. For instance, you could sort a mailing list data base into alphabetical order by last name. You can also find, delete, or extract from the data base the information that matches the conditions you define. For instance, you could ask 1-2-3 to find the information for employee number 10001 in an employee data base, or to delete the information in a prospect data base for all the people who have not bought anything from you in the last three years. You can even compute statistics about the information—or a part of the information—in a data base. For example, you might ask 1-2-3 to compute the average salary for the employees in an employee data base, or the average salary for those employees who work in one particular division. Best of all, because 1-2-3 stores your entire data base in RAM while you work with it, 1-2-3 can sort and query the data base much faster than most other data base managers.

BASICS

A 1-2-3 data base is nothing more than a specially structured collection of entries in a 1-2-3 worksheet. However, there are a few rules you need to know before you begin working with data bases in 1-2-3. We'll explain those rules in this section, and then we'll show you how to sort and query a 1-2-3 data base.

The Structure of 1-2-3 Data Bases

When we say that a data base is structured, we mean that the information it contains is presented in some consistent form. For example, think about how your telephone book is structured. Each entry in the phone book occupies a single line. This line is divided into four columns: the last name, first name, address, and phone number. In data base terminology, each line of information—the name, address, and phone number for one individual—is called a *record*. Each of the columns—Last Name, First Name, Address, and Number—is called a *field*.

The structure of a 1-2-3 data base is similar to the structure of a telephone directory. Each record in a 1-2-3 data base occupies a single row in a worksheet. Each field occupies a single column. For example, Figure 12-1 shows a 1-2-3 data base. As you can see, this data base contains ten records, the first of which is stored in row 2. The data base includes six fields—Last Name, First Name, Street, City, State, and Zip—which occupy columns A through F in a worksheet. Notice that these fields are in adjacent columns. Although you can skip columns between fields, doing so just wastes space and memory.

```
A1: [W11] 'Last Name                                                    READY

         A          B           C                  D             E      F
   1  Last Name  First Name  Street             City          State  Zip
   2  Cook       James       301 Blair Ct.      Chicago       IL     60631
   3  Logsdon    Morton      4406 W. 71st St.   New York      NY     10023
   4  Callahan   Viola       1402 Central Ave.  Atlanta       GA     30331
   5  Powers     Donald      3510 Fairway Dr.   Phoenix       AZ     85019
   6  Schultz    Louis       310 Oxford Ln.     Philadelphia  PA     19125
   7  Miller     Nancy       1076 Chadwick Dr.  St. Louis     MO     63129
   8  Hudson     William     211 Merriman Rd.   Los Angeles   CA     90013
   9  Jackson    Frances     2317 Hillside Dr.  Denver        CO     80234
  10  Clark      Andrew      1820 Garden Way    Dallas        TX     75212
  11  McCoy      David       11203 Shoreline Rd. Miami        FL     33180
  12
  13
```

FIGURE 12-1: An example data base

The labels in cells A1 to F1 are the field names for the six fields in the data base. The first row of a 1-2-3 data base must contain field names—label entries that describe what sort of information each field contains. Field names must be labels. Like any label entry, field names can be up to 240 characters in length. For practical reasons, however, you usually will want to keep your field names as short as possible.

Field names serve two purposes. First, they help you to identify the information in each column of the worksheet. More importantly, they are the means by which 1-2-3 links selection conditions (criteria) to the correct fields of the data base. You'll learn about selecting records later in this chapter.

The example data base in Figure 12-1 begins in cell A1—the field names are in row 1 and the first field is in column A. Although you will usually position your 1-2-3 data bases in the upper-left corner of the worksheet, you don't have to. You can create a data base in any part of a worksheet. In fact, you can create more than one data base in a single worksheet.

The Size of 1-2-3 Data Bases

The size of your 1-2-3 data bases is limited by the size of the 1-2-3 worksheet and the amount of RAM in your computer. As you know, 1-2-3 Releases 2, 2.10, and 2.2 worksheets contain 8192 rows and 256 columns. Because each record in a 1-2-3 data base occupies one row, and one row must be reserved for field names, no 1-2-3 Release 2, 2.01, or 2.2 data base can contain more than 8191 records. Since a 1-2-3 Release 1A worksheet has only 2048 rows, a 1-2-3 Release 1A data base can contain only 2047 records. Similarly, because each field in a 1-2-3 data base occupies a single column, no 1-2-3 data base can have more than 256 fields.

Because 1-2-3 stores your data base in the cells of the worksheet, the maximum size of a 1-2-3 data base also depends on how much RAM is installed in your computer. Although it is theoretically possible to create an 8191-record, 256-field data base in 1-2-3 Releases 2, 2.01, and 2.2, in most cases memory constraints will limit your 1-2-3 data bases to a fraction of that size. For example, if your computer has 640K of RAM, you will be able to build a data base with approximately 5000 records and six fields. (Of course, the exact number of records and fields depends on the length and type of the entry in each field.) If your computer is fitted with an Above Board or other expanded memory card, then you will be able to build much larger data bases.

Data Base Entries

The entries in a 1-2-3 data base are just labels, values, functions, and (less commonly) formulas. For this reason, entering records into a data base is no different from making any other entries into a worksheet.

Remember that if you want to enter a label that begins with a number, you must type a label prefix before you type the first character in the entry. You'll need to keep this in mind when you enter telephone numbers, Social Security numbers, zip codes, and so on, into your data bases.

In most cases, you'll want to fill in the data base one record at a time, starting with the leftmost field in each record. In some cases, however, you may wish to make entries column-by-column. In general, all of the entries in a given field should be of the same type. You usually won't want to mix labels and values, or labels and formulas, in one field.

Although the entries in your data bases usually will be literal labels and literal values, they also can be functions or formulas. In those cases when you use formula or function entries, you must follow some special rules. First, if a formula or function refers to another entry in the same record (as it usually will), it should do so with a relative reference. For example, suppose columns A and B contain the Price and SqFt fields of a data base, and column C contains the Price/SqFt field. To compute the entries in the Price/SqFt field, you would enter the formula *+A2/B2* into cell C2, the formula *+A3/B3* into cell C3, and so on. If a formula or function in a data base refers to a cell outside of the data base, it should do so with an absolute reference or a mixed reference with a fixed row component. Unless you follow these rules, your formulas or functions will refer to the wrong cells after you sort the data base—a topic we'll cover later.

Cleaning Up a Data Base

Once you have entered records into a 1-2-3 data base, you might want to take a couple of steps to improve the appearance of the data base. First, you might want to use 1-2-3's / Range Format command to format the entries in one or more fields. For instance, if a field contains numbers that represent dollar amounts, you might want to assign the entries in that field the Currency format. If one or more fields contain date entries, you might want to use one of the Date formats to make the serial date values understandable.

There's no trick to formatting data base entries—you just issue the / Range Format command, select the format you want to use, and select the range you want to format. Typically, you'll format all of the entries in a field in the same way. You can format the cells of a field before you make entries into them. However, because even blank formatted cells use up memory, this can be wasteful. We recommend that you format the cells of your data base after you make entries into them—not before.

In addition to formatting the entries in a data base, you might want to increase or decrease the widths of some of the columns in the data base. If a field contains long entries, widening the column that contains that field will allow you to view those entries in full. If a field contains short entries (like State name abbreviations), you can narrow the column that contains that field, perhaps allowing you to see more fields on the screen at once. As you might expect, you change the width of a column in a data base in the same way you change the width of any other column—you move the cell pointer to the column you want to widen or narrow, issue the / Worksheet Column Set-Width command, and either type or point to define the width.

Editing a Data Base

You can edit the entries in a 1-2-3 data base in exactly the same way you edit any other entries in a worksheet. You can use the / Copy command to copy entries, the / Move command to move entries, or the / Range Erase command to erase entries. To edit an entry, just move the cell pointer to that entry, press the [Edit] key, and then add and delete the characters you choose. To replace an entry, just position the cell pointer on the cell that contains that entry, type a new one, and then press [Enter].

You also can add records and fields to a data base and delete records and fields from a data base. To add a field, just move the cell pointer to the first blank column to the right of the data base, type a field name in the correct row of the new column, and begin making entries. If you want to insert a new field between existing fields, use the / Worksheet Insert Column command to add a blank column where you want the new field to be, then type a field name and begin making entries. To add a record, just move to the bottom of the data base and begin typing. If you would like to add a new record between existing records, use the / Worksheet Insert Row command to add a new blank row to the data base, then type the new record.

Later in this chapter, you'll learn that you must formally define the dimensions of the data base before you can sort it or use criteria to select records from it. In some cases, you'll have to redefine the boundaries of the data base after you insert or delete rows or columns. We'll address those situations when we introduce the use of criteria.

Saving and Printing a Data Base

Because 1-2-3 data bases are stored in the cells of the 1-2-3 worksheet, and because the entries in a data base are just labels, values, and formulas, you can save and print data bases in the same ways you save and print other 1-2-3 worksheets. To save a data base, simply issue the / File Save command, choose a name for the worksheet that contains the data base, and press [Enter]. To retrieve a saved data base, issue the / File Retrieve command, choose the right file name, and press [Enter].

To print a data base, you issue the / Print Printer command, choose the Range option, select the range that contains the field names and all of the records, set any print options, then choose Align and Go. The result will be a simple tabular listing of the data base. Instead of printing a simple listing of the entire data base, you might want to sort the data base, select a subset of the records to print, or compute a few statistics to include in the report. We'll show you how to do these things later in the chapter.

Creating a 1-2-3 Data Base: An Example

Suppose you want to create the 1-2-3 data base shown in Figure 12-2. The first step in building a data base in 1-2-3 is to enter the field names for the data base into adjacent cells of a single row of a worksheet. To begin creating this data base, then, enter the labels 'Name, 'ID#, 'Date of Hire, 'Region, 'Sales, and 'Quota into cells A1 to F1 of a blank worksheet.

```
C2: (D1) [W13] @DATE(85,5,17)                                    READY

         A            B            C          D         E          F
 1   Name           ID#      Date of Hire  Region    Sales      Quota
 2   Gibson         705G1      17-May-85   North   $163,293   $150,000
 3   Williams       356W3      01-Feb-82   South   $351,951   $375,000
 4   Johnson        585J2      04-Aug-80   East    $410,227   $400,000
 5   Franklin       128F4      06-Oct-81   West    $427,498   $450,000
 6   Logan          512L3      24-May-84   South   $253,944   $250,000
 7   Christensen    274C1      12-Sep-85   North   $155,960   $175,000
 8   Stewart        215S4      23-Jun-86   West    $128,922   $125,000
 9   Murphy         173M3      05-Apr-79   South   $458,132   $475,000
10   Adams          600A2      18-Jul-83   East    $235,526   $225,000
11   Parks          778P4      12-Jan-81   West    $304,887   $325,000
12   Wheeler        533W1      11-Nov-84   North   $209,575   $200,000
13   Foster         653F2      27-Mar-82   East    $337,400   $350,000
```

FIGURE 12-2: A simple data base

Entering Records

Once you have entered the field names, you can begin to enter records. To do this, move the cell pointer to the cell immediately below the first field name (in this case, to cell A2) and type the label 'Gibson. Next, press ➡ to lock in the entry and move to the second field of the first record (cell B2) and type the identification number '705G1. Because this entry begins with a number but contains alphabetic characters, you must begin it with a label prefix. Otherwise, 1-2-3 will beep when you try to lock in the entry. Then, press ➡ to move to the Date of Hire field. Since this field will hold date information, you should make the entries in the form of @DATE functions. To enter the date May 17, 1985, for example, you should first type the function @DATE(85,5,17). Next, you should press ➡ again and type the label 'North into the Region field. Then, press ➡ and type the value 163293 into the Sales field. Finally, press ➡ one last time to move the cell pointer to the Quota field, type 150000, and press [Enter].

After you have entered the first record, you're ready to enter another. To do this, first move the cell pointer to the second cell below the first field name, then enter the second record in the same way that you entered the first one. When you're finished with the second record, move to cell A4 and enter the third. You can continue in this way until you've entered all 12 records. After you enter all 12 records, the data base should look like Figure 12-3.

```
F13: 350000                                                          READY

      A         B        C         D        E       F       G       H
 1  Name       ID#    Date of H Region    Sales    Quota
 2  Gibson     705G1     31184  North     163293   150000
 3  Williams   356W3     29983  South     351951   375000
 4  Johnson    585J2     29437  East      410227   400000
 5  Franklin   128F4     29865  West      427498   450000
 6  Logan      512L3     30826  South     253944   250000
 7  Christens  274C1     31302  North     155960   175000
 8  Stewart    215S4     31506  West      128922   125000
 9  Murphy     173M3     28950  South     458132   475000
10  Adams      600A2     30515  East      235526   225000
11  Parks      778P4     29598  West      304887   325000
12  Wheeler    533W1     30997  North     209575   200000
13  Foster     653F2     30037  East      337480   350000
14
```

FIGURE 12-3: A new 1-2-3 data base

Cleaning Up the Data Base

Once you've entered the records in the data base, you may want to format the entries in some of its fields. For example, if you look again at the data base shown in Figure 12-3, you'll notice that 1-2-3 is displaying the results of the @DATE functions in column C as serial date values—not in an understandable Date format. Second, 1-2-3 is displaying the values in columns E and F in the default General format, rather than as currency. You can use 1-2-3's / Range Format command to format these entries.

To make the dates in column C understandable, move the cell pointer to cell C2, issue the / Range Format Date command, choose the D1 format, select the range C2..C13, and press [Enter]. To display the values in columns E and F in the Currency format, move the cell pointer to cell E2, issue the / Range Format command again, choose the Currency option, type 0 and press [Enter] to specify zero decimal places, select the range E2..F13, and press [Enter].

At this point, the widths of the columns in the worksheet cause 1-2-3 to truncate the labels in column A and the field name at the top of column C and to display the formatted date entries in that column as a series of asterisks. To improve the appearance of this data base, therefore, you probably will want to widen columns A and C. To do this, move the cell pointer to column A, issue the / Worksheet Column Set-Width command, type 15, and press [Enter]. Then move the cell pointer to column C, issue the / Worksheet Column Set-Width command, type 13, and press [Enter]. Figure 12-2 shows the completed data base.

SORTING

Once you build a 1-2-3 data base, you can use the / Data Sort command to sort it. You can use this command to sort any data base into either ascending or descending order based on the entries in one or two fields. Why would you want to sort a data base? First, sorting a data base makes it easier to find a particular record. Second, sorting makes it easier to compare the entries in the same field of different records.

Sort Basics

To sort a data base, you issue the / Data Sort command. ▶If you are using 1-2-3 Release 2.2, you'll see the menu and the settings sheet shown in Figure 12-4 when you issue the / Data Sort command. (If you are using an earlier version of 1-2-3, you'll see only the menu; you won't see the settings sheet.)◄ To specify the group of entries you want to sort, you should choose the first item on this menu: Data-Range. When you select this option, 1-2-3 will display the prompt *Enter data range:* at the top of the screen and wait for you to highlight or type the coordinates of the range you want to sort. In response to this prompt, you should select every field of every record in the data base. However, you should not include the row of field names in the range.

Once you've defined the range of entries you want to sort, you must tell 1-2-3 which field(s) to use as the basis for the sort and whether to sort the data base into ascending or descending order based on the entries in those fields. To specify the first sort field, you choose the Primary-Key option from the Data Sort menu. When you select this option, 1-2-3 will present the prompt *Primary sort key:* at the top of the screen and will allow you to select a field. When you see this prompt, you should move the cell pointer to any cell in the column that contains the field whose entries you want to use as the basis of the sort. The cell you select doesn't have to be within the data base—it can be anywhere in the correct column.

RELEASE
▶ 2.2 ◄

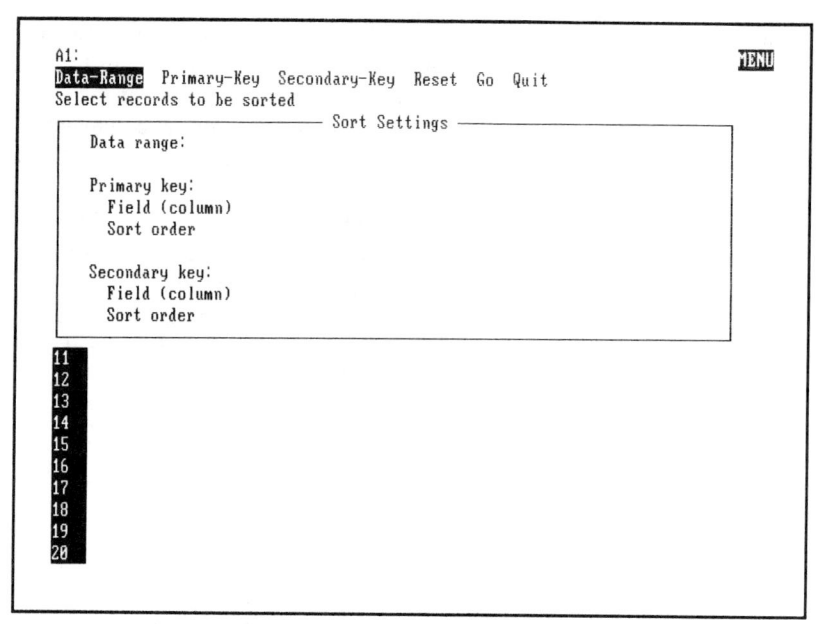

```
A1:
Data-Range Primary-Key Secondary-Key Reset Go Quit                    MENU
Select records to be sorted
┌─────────────────────────── Sort Settings ───────────────────────────┐
│  Data range:                                                         │
│                                                                      │
│  Primary key:                                                        │
│    Field (column)                                                    │
│    Sort order                                                        │
│                                                                      │
│  Secondary key:                                                      │
│    Field (column)                                                    │
│    Sort order                                                        │
└──────────────────────────────────────────────────────────────────────┘
11
12
13
14
15
16
17
18
19
20
```

FIGURE 12-4: The / Data Sort menu and settings sheet

When you press [Enter] to lock in the coordinates of the cell you chose, 1-2-3 will display the prompt *Sort order (A or D):*, followed by a letter representing the default sort order: either D (for Descending) or A (for Ascending). If you have sorted the data base previously, the default order will be the one you chose when you performed the most recent sort. If you have not yet sorted the worksheet, Descending will be the default order. If you want to sort the data base into the default order, just press [Enter] to accept the default. If you want to sort the data base into the other order, type A or D and then press [Enter].

As soon as you select a sort order, 1-2-3 again will return you to the Data Sort menu. At this point, you can either define a Secondary sort key or you can go ahead and sort the data base. To define a Secondary sort key, you choose the Secondary-Key option, point to the field you want 1-2-3 to use as the Secondary key, press [Enter], and choose a sort order. To sort the data base, you just choose Go. When you choose this option, 1-2-3 will rearrange the records in the data base into the order you have specified.

Once you've defined a data range, 1-2-3 will remember the coordinates of that range until you change them, cancel them, or load another worksheet. 1-2-3 also will remember the fields you specified as the Primary and Secondary keys, as well as the sort order. (If you save the worksheet after defining these settings, 1-2-3 will remember them when you next load the worksheet.) For this reason, you don't have to redefine the sort range, the sort keys, or the sort order when you want to resort the data base.

Of course, you can change any of these settings before you re-sort if you want to. In some cases, you may want to sort a group of entries that is completely different from the ones you last sorted. This often happens when you have more than one data base in your worksheet. To prevent 1-2-3 from highlighting the previous data range and sort key(s) when you reissue the / Data Sort Data-Range and / Data Sort Primary-Key commands, you simply issue the / Data Sort Reset command beforehand. As soon as you issue this command, 1-2-3 will clear the current definitions of the data range and sort key(s) from its memory.

Sorting on a Single Field: An Example

To understand how sorting works, suppose you want to sort the data base shown in Figure 12-2 into descending order based on the values in the Sales field. To do this, issue the / Data Sort command. Then choose the Data-Range option from the Data Sort menu, select the range A2..F13 and press [Enter]. Notice that this range includes all of the fields and records in the data base, but that it does not include the field names in row 1.

Now you have to tell 1-2-3 which field you want to sort on. In this case, you want to sort the data base on the basis of the entries in the Sales field. To do this, choose the Primary-Key option, point to any cell in column E, and press [Enter]. Next, 1-2-3 will prompt you to define the sort order. Because you want to sort the data base into descending order (the default order) you need only press [Enter].

As soon as you select a sort order, 1-2-3 will return you to the Data Sort menu. At this point, you are ready to perform the sort. To sort the data base, just choose Go. When you choose this option, 1-2-3 will rearrange the records so that your data base looks like Figure 12-5. As you can see, 1-2-3 has rearranged the data base so that the record with the highest Sales entry is at the top of the data base, and the record with the lowest Sales entry is at the bottom.

```
E2: (C0) 458132                                                    READY

        A           B            C         D         E         F.
 1   Name          ID#       Date of Hire  Region   Sales     Quota
 2   Murphy        173M3      05-Apr-79    South    $458,132  $475,000
 3   Franklin      128F4      06-Oct-81    West     $427,498  $450,000
 4   Johnson       505J2      04-Aug-80    East     $410,227  $400,000
 5   Williams      356W3      01-Feb-82    South    $351,951  $375,000
 6   Foster        653F2      27-Mar-82    East     $337,480  $350,000
 7   Parks         778P4      12-Jan-81    West     $304,887  $325,000
 8   Logan         512L3      24-May-84    South    $253,944  $250,000
 9   Adams         600A2      18-Jul-83    East     $235,526  $225,000
10   Wheeler       533W1      11-Nov-84    North    $209,575  $200,000
11   Gibson        705G1      17-May-85    North    $163,293  $150,000
12   Christensen   274C1      12-Sep-85    North    $155,960  $175,000
13   Stewart       215S4      23-Jun-86    West     $128,922  $125,000
14
```

FIGURE 12-5: A Descending sort on the Sales field

> **TIP: UNDOING A SORT**
>
> Although it's easy to sort a data base, it can be difficult to return that data base to its pre-sort order. If you have saved your worksheet prior to sorting the data base, you can return the data base to its original order just by retrieving the saved copy of the worksheet. Unless you saved the worksheet immediately prior to sorting the data base, however, you'll lose some of your work.
>
> Fortunately, there is a more foolproof way to return a data base to its original order. If the data base includes a field that numbers the records—such as a Customer Number, Check Number, or Employee Number field—you can return the data base to its original order by performing an Ascending sort on that field. If the data base does not include this kind of field, you can add one before you sort the data base and fill that column with an ascending (or descending) series of values. (The easiest way to do this is with the / Data Fill command.) When you sort the data base, include that column in the data range. Then, to return the data base to its original order, just perform an Ascending sort on the basis of the entries in the "counter" column.

Sorting on a Text Field

In the previous example, we sorted a 1-2-3 data base on the basis of the entries in a value field. You also can sort the records in a data base according to the entries in a text field. When you sort on the basis of the entries in a text field, 1-2-3 will rearrange the data base so that the entries in that field are in ascending or descending alphabetical order.

An Example

For example, suppose that you want to sort the records in the data base shown in Figure 12-5 into ascending order based on the entries in the Region field. To do this, issue the / Data Sort command. Next, if you have not already done so, choose the Data-Range option, select the range A2..F13, and press [Enter]. (If you have already defined the data range, 1-2-3 will remember that range, and you can skip this step.) Next, choose the Primary-Key option, move the cell pointer to any cell in column D, and press [Enter]. Then type A to specify an Ascending sort and press [Enter] again. When you choose Go, 1-2-3 will perform the sort and present the result shown in Figure 12-6.

Because the sort field (Region) contains text entries and we specified an Ascending sort, 1-2-3 has arranged the records so that the entries in that field are arranged in ascending alphabetical order by region. For example, the records with the Region entry *'East* come before the records with the other Region entries.

In addition, because there are duplicate entries in the Region field, the sorting process has grouped the records in the data base by Region. As you can see, all the records that have the entry *'East* in their Region field are grouped together, as are the records that have the Region entries *'North*, *'South*, and *'West*.

```
D2: 'East                                                         READY

           A         B          C         D        E        F
  1   Name       ID#        Date of Hire Region  Sales    Quota
  2   Foster     653F2      27-Mar-82    East    $337,400 $350,000
  3   Johnson    585J2      04-Aug-80    East    $410,227 $400,000
  4   Adams      600A2      18-Jul-83    East    $235,526 $225,000
  5   Wheeler    533W1      11-Nov-84    North   $209,575 $200,000
  6   Gibson     705G1      17-May-85    North   $163,293 $150,000
  7   Christensen 274C1     12-Sep-85    North   $155,960 $175,000
  8   Logan      512L3      24-May-84    South   $253,944 $250,000
  9   Murphy     173M3      05-Apr-79    South   $458,132 $475,000
 10   Williams   356W3      01-Feb-82    South   $351,951 $375,000
 11   Parks      778P4      12-Jan-81    West    $304,887 $325,000
 12   Franklin   128F4      06-Oct-81    West    $427,498 $450,000
 13   Stewart    215S4      23-Jun-86    West    $128,922 $125,000
 14
```

FIGURE 12-6: An Ascending sort on the Region field

Sort Orders

The way that 1-2-3 arranges the records in a sorted data base depends primarily on the sort order you choose. When you sort on the basis of a field that contains text entries, however, another factor influences the result of a sort: the collating sequence specified by the driver set you used when you loaded 1-2-3.

Because the choice of collating sequence is an advanced installation option, you probably didn't select one when you installed 1-2-3. In that case, 1-2-3 will sort your data bases in accordance with the *Numbers first* collating sequence. According to this collating sequence, upper- and lower-case versions of the same letter have the same value, and text numbers have lower values than alphabetic characters.

For example, the first column in Table 12-1 shows the original order of a set of label entries. If you were to sort this list into ascending order using the *Numbers first* collating sequence, the result would look like the second column of the table. As you can see, the lower-case letter 'b comes between the upper-case letters 'A and 'C, and the labels '1, '2, and '3 come before any of the letters.

Original Order	Ascending, Numbers first	Ascending, Numbers last	Ascending, ASCII Order
'A	'1	'A	'1
'1	'2	'b	'2
'b	'3	'C	'3
'2	'A	'1	'A
'C	'b	'2	'C
'3	'C	'3	'b

TABLE 12-1: Alternative collating Sequences

Sorting this same list into ascending order using either of 1-2-3's other collating sequences will produce different results. According to the *Numbers last* collating sequence, upper- and lower-case versions of the same letter have the same value, but text numbers have higher values than alphabetic characters. Sorting the sample list of labels into ascending order using the *Numbers last* collating sequence will produce the result shown in the third column of Table 12-1.

1-2-3's third collating sequence, *ASCII*, produces yet a different sort order. According to this collating sequence, text numbers have lower values than letters, just as they do with the *Numbers first* sequence. Instead of treating upper- and lower-case versions of the same letter equally, however, the *ASCII* collating sequence assigns lower-case letters a higher value than every upper-case letter. Consequently, an Ascending sort of the sample list of labels under the *ASCII* collating sequence will produce the results in the fourth column of Table 12-1.

The default collating sequence, *Numbers first*, probably will be suitable for most of your sorts. If you want 1-2-3 to use a different collating sequence, you'll have to change your driver set. To do this, you must exit from 1-2-3 and enter the Install program. Once you are in the Install program, you should choose Advanced Options, then Modify Current Driver Set. Next, choose the Collating option, then choose one of the three options that the Install program presents: ASCII, Numbers first, or Numbers last. Once you have selected a new collating driver, save the new driver set, exit from the Install program, and reload 1-2-3. The next time you sort, 1-2-3 will use the new collating sequence.

TIP: SORTING OTHER WORKSHEET ENTRIES

You usually will use the / Data Sort command to sort 1-2-3 data bases. However, you can use this command to sort almost any group of entries in adjacent rows of a worksheet. For example, you can use this command to rearrange a vertical lookup table so that the entries in the key column are in ascending numeric order. All you have to do is issue the / Data Sort command, use the Data-Range option to define the range you want to sort, choose one or two sort keys, and choose Go.

Sorting on Two Fields

Although 1-2-3 has grouped the records in the data base in Figure 12-6 by region, the records in the Region groups are not arranged in any particular order. The data base would be more meaningful if the records within each Region group were also sorted—for instance, into descending order based on the entries in the Sales field.

To achieve this effect, you must perform a two-key sort. To perform a two-key sort, you must define both a Primary key and a Secondary key. To define the Secondary key, you issue the / Data Sort Secondary-Key command, point to any cell in the column that contains the field you want to use as the secondary key, press [Enter], then choose

Ascending or Descending. When you choose Go after defining both a Primary key and a Secondary key, 1-2-3 will sort the data base based on the entries in the Primary key field. If there are any duplicate records in the Primary key field—as there are in the Region field in the example data base— 1-2-3 will arrange those records according to the entries in the Secondary key field.

For example, suppose you want to sort the example data base using the Region field as the Primary key and the Sales field as the Secondary key. You want 1-2-3 to sort the entries in the Region field into ascending order and the entries in the Sales field into descending order. To do this, first issue the / Data Sort command. Next, if you have not already done so, choose the Data-Range option, select the range A2..F13, and press [Enter], then choose the Primary-Key option, point to any cell in column D, press [Enter], type A to specify an Ascending sort, and press [Enter] again. (If you have already defined the data range and Primary key, you can skip this step.) Now, to specify a secondary Descending sort on the Sales field, choose Secondary-Key, highlight any cell in column E (the column that contains the Sales field), press [Enter], specify Descending order, and press [Enter] again.

When you choose Go, 1-2-3 will rearrange the data base into the order shown in Figure 12-7. As you can see, the data base is still grouped by Region, just as it is in Figure 12-6. Within each Region group, however, the records now are arranged in descending order according to the entries in the Sales field.

```
D2: 'East                                                           READY

          A          B          C            D        E          F
     1  Name       ID#      Date of Hire  Region   Sales      Quota
     2  Johnson    585J2    04-Aug-80     East     $410,227   $400,000
     3  Foster     653F2    27-Mar-82     East     $337,400   $350,000
     4  Adams      600A2    18-Jul-83     East     $235,526   $225,000
     5  Wheeler    533W1    11-Nov-84     North    $209,575   $200,000
     6  Gibson     705G1    17-May-85     North    $163,293   $150,000
     7  Christensen 274C1   12-Sep-85     North    $155,960   $175,000
     8  Murphy     173M3    05-Apr-79     South    $458,132   $475,000
     9  Williams   356W3    01-Feb-82     South    $351,951   $375,000
    10  Logan      512L3    24-May-84     South    $253,944   $250,000
    11  Franklin   128F4    06-Oct-81     West     $427,498   $450,000
    12  Parks      778P4    12-Jan-81     West     $304,887   $325,000
    13  Stewart    215S4    23-Jun-86     West     $128,922   $125,000
    14
```

FIGURE 12-7: A two-key sort

Unfortunately, 1-2-3 is unable to sort on the basis of more than two keys at a time. Although some other spreadsheet software packages allow you to do this by performing successive single-field sorts, starting with the least important field, that technique produces unpredictable results in 1-2-3.

CRITERIA

In the previous section, we showed you how to use the / Data Sort command to sort the records in a 1-2-3 data base. 1-2-3 can do a lot more than just sort a data base, however. 1-2-3's / Data Query commands allow you to find, extract, and delete records that meet selection conditions (called criteria) that you specify. In addition, 1-2-3 offers data base statistical functions that compute common statistics, such as sums and averages, for the records in a data base that match criteria you define.

Before you can use the / Data Query commands or compute data base statistics, you need to know how to define criteria. Criteria are the conditional tests that tell 1-2-3 which records to select from a data base when you issue a / Data Query command or create a statistical function. To define criteria, you first create a special range in the worksheet called the Criteria range. Then you make entries in this range that tell 1-2-3 which records to select.

The Criteria Range

The structure of a Criteria range is quite similar to that of the data base with which it is associated. The top row of a Criteria range must contain one or more of the field names from that data base. For example, cells A15 to F15 of the worksheet in Figure 12-8 contain the field names of a Criteria range for the example data base. The second and subsequent rows of the Criteria range hold the criteria themselves.

```
A15: [W15] 'Name                                                         READY


         A            B            C          D         E         F
 1  Name          ID#         Date of Hire Region    Sales     Quota
 2  Gibson        705G1        17-May-85   North    $163,293  $150,000
 3  Williams      356W3        01-Feb-82   South    $351,951  $375,000
 4  Johnson       585J2        04-Aug-80   East     $410,227  $400,000
 5  Franklin      128F4        06-Oct-81   West     $427,498  $450,000
 6  Logan         512L3        24-May-84   South    $253,944  $250,000
 7  Christensen   274C1        12-Sep-85   North    $155,960  $175,000
 8  Stewart       215S4        23-Jun-86   West     $128,922  $125,000
 9  Murphy        173M3        05-Apr-79   South    $458,132  $475,000
10  Adams         600A2        18-Jul-83   East     $235,526  $225,000
11  Parks         778P4        12-Jan-81   West     $304,887  $325,000
12  Wheeler       533W1        11-Nov-84   North    $209,575  $200,000
13  Foster        653F2        27-Mar-82   East     $337,480  $350,000
14
15  Name          ID#         Date of Hire Region    Sales     Quota
16
17
```

FIGURE 12-8: The first row of a Criteria range

Notice that the field names in row 15 are the same as those in the first row of the data base. A Criteria range must contain at least the names of those fields for which you will specify selection conditions. In most cases, however, you'll want to include the name of every field from the data base in the Criteria range, as we did in Figure

12-8. That way, you won't have to redefine the Criteria range each time you specify a criterion for a new field.

Each field name in the first row of a Criteria range must be identical to the corresponding field name in the data base, with two exceptions: differences in capitalization and label prefixes do not matter. The easiest way to create the field names for the Criteria range—and the best way to avoid spelling errors—is to use the / Copy command to copy the field names from the data base to the first row of the Criteria range.

The order of the names at the top of the Criteria range does not have to match the order of the names at the top of the data base. However, you'll find the Criteria range much easier to work with if they do.

Unlike a data base, which can include as many as 256 fields, a Criteria range can include a maximum of only 32 fields. If your data base contains more than 32 fields, you'll only be able to create criteria for 32 of those fields at a time. If you issue a / Data Query command after specifying a Criteria range that covers more than 32 columns, 1-2-3 will beep, flash ERROR in the Mode indicator, and display the message *Too many fields (32 max)* at the bottom of the screen.

You can create a Criteria range in any part of the worksheet. We usually put the Criteria range below the data base, as we have in Figure 12-8. Positioning the Criteria range in this way makes it easy to visualize the relationship between the data base and the Criteria range. On the other hand, positioning the Criteria range below the data base means that you'll have to use the / Worksheet Insert Row command to add records to the data base. One way around this problem would be to place the Criteria range above the data base in the worksheet.

Defining Criteria

The second and subsequent rows of the Criteria range contain the criteria that tell 1-2-3 which records to operate on. The simplest sort of criteria consists of a label or value entry beneath one of the field names. More complex criteria involve the use of wildcards (like ? and *), comparison operators (like <, >, and =), special operators (like #AND# and #NOT#), formulas and functions, and entries in more than one cell and/or row.

Exact-Match Criteria

The simplest selection conditions select records that have a particular entry in a particular field. To define these "exact-match" conditions, you simply type the criteria you want 1-2-3 to match into the Criteria range below the name of the field that contains the entries you want to match. The Criteria range entry can be a value, a label, or a function or formula.

Label Criteria

If you want to select records based on the entries in a field that contains label entries, you must enter a label into the Criteria range. For example, suppose that you want

1-2-3 to select the records from the data base in Figure 12-8 that have the label 'East in the Region field. To do this, enter the label 'East into cell D16—the cell of the Criteria range immediately below the field name Region—as shown in Figure 12-9. The entry tells 1-2-3 what to look for. The position of the entry tells 1-2-3 in which field of the data base to look for matching entries. If you use this criterion with a / Data Query command or a data base statistical function, then 1-2-3 will select the records in rows 4, 10, and 13—the records that have the label *'East* in their Region field.

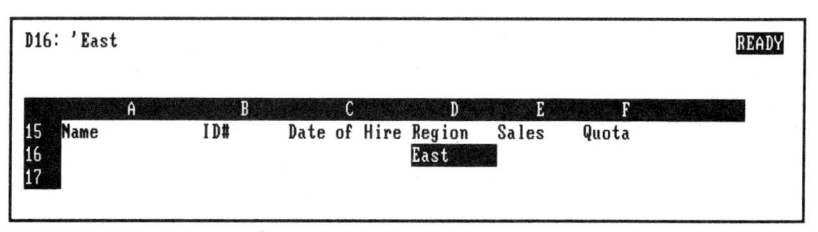

```
D16: 'East                                                              READY

             A           B           C          D         E        F
    15  Name          ID#      Date of Hire  Region    Sales    Quota
    16                                       East
    17
```

FIGURE 12-9: An exact-match label criterion

When 1-2-3 evaluates exact-match label criteria, it ignores any capitalization differences between the criteria and the entries in the data base. For example, the criterion *'East* would match the labels *'East*, *'east*, *EAST*, and so forth; the criteria *'east*, *'EAST*, *'East*, and so on, would match exactly the same entries. We'll show you how to make 1-2-3 recognize capitalization differences later.

1-2-3 also ignores differences between the label prefixes of the entries in the data base and the entry in the Criteria range. If the two entries are identical except for the label prefix, 1-2-3 will consider them to be a match. Although we'll use the left-aligned prefix (') in our examples, you can use any prefix.

Value Criteria

You also can use values as exact-match criteria. To do this, just enter the value you want to match into the appropriate cell of the Criteria range. For example, suppose you want to select the record in the example data base that has the value 250000 in its Quota field. To do this, you would enter the value 250000 into cell F16—the cell of the Criteria range below the field name Quota—as shown in Figure 12-10. (If the Criteria range contained other entries, you'd want to erase them before you use the Criteria range. When you use a Criteria range, 1-2-3 tries to use all of the criteria in that range. If you don't want 1-2-3 to consider the old criteria, you must erase them.) If you use this criterion with a / Data Query command or a data base statistical function, 1-2-3 will select the record in row 16—the only record that has the value 250000 in the Quota field.

You can use a similar technique to select records based on the entries in a date or time field. Instead of entering a value into the appropriate cell of the Criteria range, however, you'll probably enter a date or time function. For example, to select those records that have the serial date value for September 12, 1985, in the Date of Hire field, you would enter the function *@DATE(85,9,12)* immediately below the field name *'Date of Hire* in the Criteria range.

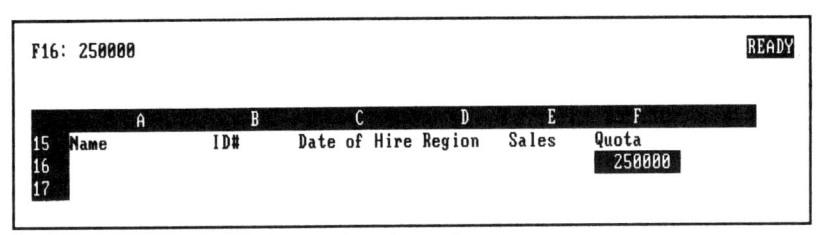

```
F16: 250000                                                   READY

        A          B          C         D      E       F
   15 Name        ID#    Date of Hire Region  Sales  Quota
   16                                                250000
   17
```

FIGURE 12-10: An exact-match value criterion

Wildcards

1-2-3 allows you to use three special "wildcard" characters—?, *, and ~ —as a part of any text criterion. The ? wildcard takes the place of any single character in a label. The * wildcard takes the place of any series of adjacent characters. The ~ wildcard negates the stated text condition.

The ? Wildcard

1-2-3's ? wildcard takes the place of any single text character in an exact-match label criterion. The ? wildcard can be used anywhere in a label criterion.

To demonstrate the use of the ? wildcard, suppose that you want to find a certain salesman's record in the example data base, but you can't remember if his name is spelled *Christensen* or *Christenson*. To select either entry, you could enter the label *'Christens?n* into cell A16 of the Criteria range—the cell below the field name *Name*—as shown in Figure 12-11. (If the Criteria range contained other entries, you'd want to erase them.) This criterion will match the entries *Christensen, Christenson*, and any other similar entry.

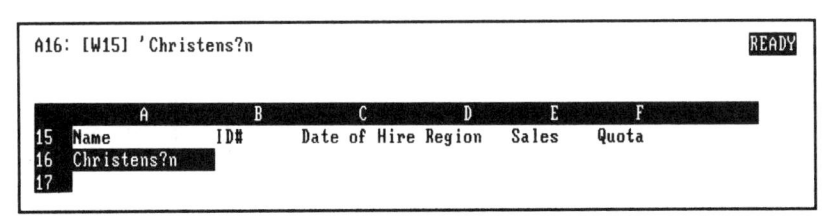

```
A16: [W15] 'Christens?n                                       READY

        A          B          C         D      E       F
   15 Name        ID#    Date of Hire Region  Sales  Quota
   16 Christens?n
   17
```

FIGURE 12-11: The ? wildcard

The ? wildcard will not match a nonexistent character. For example, the criterion *'Park?* would match the entry *'Parks* but not the entry *'Park*.

The * Wildcard

1-2-3's * wildcard takes the place of any number of adjacent text characters at the end of an entry. The * wildcard can be used only at the end of a label criterion.

To demonstrate the use of the * wildcard, suppose that you want to find a certain salesman's record in the example data base, but you can't remember how his name is spelled. All you know is that the name begins with the letters *Christ*. To select this record, you could enter the label criterion *'Christ** into cell A16—the cell below the field name Name. This criterion will match the entries *'Christiansen,* '*Christensen*, or any other entry that begins with the letters *Christ*.

The * wildcard will match a nonexistent character. For example, the criterion *'Park** would match the entry *'Parks* as well as the entry *'Park*.

You should be aware that a series of ? wildcards is not identical to a single * wildcard. For instance, the criterion *'Christ??????* is not identical to the criteria *'Christ**. Although the criterion *'Christ??????* would match the label *'Christiansen*, which has six characters following *Christ*, it would not match *'Christensen*, which has only five. Remember, the ? wildcard stands for a single character and will not match a noncharacter.

Unfortunately, you cannnot use the * wildcard to match groups of characters at the beginning or in the middle of a text entry. Whenever 1-2-3 encounters a * wildcard in a criterion, it ignores all characters that follow. For this reason, the criteria *Christ** and *Christ*nsen* are functionally identical—they both match any entry that begins with the letters *Christ*. For the same reason, the criterion **sen* causes 1-2-3 to match any entry in the specified field—not just the ones that end with the characters *sen*.

The ~ Wildcard

1-2-3's last text wildcard character, ~, negates the stated text condition. To see how this wildcard works, suppose you want 1-2-3 to select all the records from the example data base that have an entry other than *'Christensen* in their Name field. To do this, you would enter the criterion *'~Christensen* into cell A16.

You can use the ~ wildcard with the ? and * wildcards. For example, suppose you want 1-2-3 to select all the records from the example data base that have an entry other than *'Christensen* in their Name field, but you aren't sure of the spelling of the name. You could use the criterion *'~Christ** to make the selection.

A Restriction

Important: these three wildcards work only within text criteria; you cannot use them to replace digits in value entries. For example, you cannot use the criterion ~250000 to select the records that have entries other than the value 250000 in the Quota field. To make this selection, you'd have to use the comparison operator . We'll show you how to do that later.

You can use these wildcards within text fields that contain digits, however. For example, you could use the criterion *'2** to select all the records with ID# field entries that begin with the character 2.

Comparison Criteria

Although you can select records on the basis of an exact match in any type of field, you will use this technique most often to select records on the basis of text entries. When you select records on the basis of the value entries, you usually will be looking for a range of values. For example, you might want to select the records for salesmen whose sales exceeded 250000, the records for salesmen whose quota was 150000 or less, or the records for salesmen who have been with the company less than two years.

Basics

The form of comparison criteria is more complex than that of exact-match criteria. For example, suppose you want to select those records in the example data base that have an entry greater than 250000 in their Sales fields. To make this selection, you would enter the criterion *+E2>250000* into cell E16 of the Criteria range. (If the Criteria range contained other entries, you would want to erase them.) Figure 12-12 shows this criterion in place.

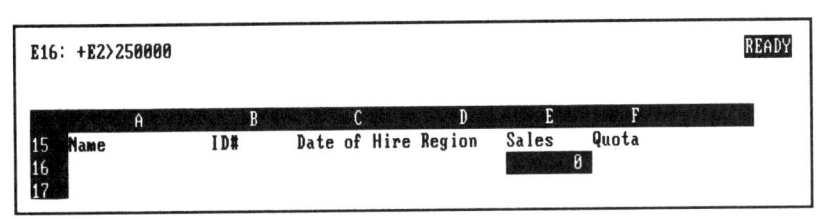

```
E16: +E2>250000                                              READY

              A         B         C        D       E      F
         15  Name      ID#   Date of Hire Region  Sales  Quota
         16                                         0
         17
```

FIGURE 12-12: A comparison criterion

Like most comparison criterion, this one has three parts: a cell reference, a comparison operator, and a value. The first part must be a relative reference to the cell in the first record of one of the fields of the data base. This reference determines which field the criterion will apply to. For example, the criterion *+E2>250000* refers to cell E2. Since cell E2 is the first cell in the Sales field, this reference tells 1-2-3 that this criterion applies to the Sales field.

Although comparison criteria refer directly to the first cell in the field to which they apply, when you use a comparison criterion with a / Data Query command or a data base statistical function, 1-2-3 will use the criterion to test every entry in the field. For example, the criterion *+E2>250000* refers to cell E2, the first cell in the Sales field of the example data base. When you use this criterion with a / Data Query command or a data base statistical function, 1-2-3 will use it to test every entry in the Sales field. For this process to work properly, however, the reference to the cell in the first record of the field must be relative.

Because the field reference for a comparison criterion is built into the criterion, the position of the criterion has no effect on the field to which it applies. You can place a comparison criterion underneath any of the field names in the Criteria range without changing its meaning. For instance, you could enter the comparison criterion *+E2>250000* in any cell in the range A16..F16. For the sake of orderliness, however, we prefer to place a comparison criterion underneath the name of the field to which it applies.

The second part of most comparison criterion will be a comparison operator: > (greater than), < (less than), >= (greater than or equal to), <= (less than or equal to), = (equal to), or <> (not equal to). Our example criterion uses the > operator. The third part of a typical comparison criterion specifies the value to which 1-2-3 should compare the entries in the specified field. In this case, the value 250000 tells 1-2-3 to select records that have values greater than 250000 in the Sales field.

As you can see, comparison criteria are simply conditional tests, not unlike the ones you use as the first argument of an @IF function. Like any conditional test, comparison criteria are either True or False. If the test is true for a particular record, 1-2-3 will select that record. If the test is false for a particular record, 1-2-3 will not select it.

Notice that the criterion in cell E16 in Figure 12-12 returns the value 0. This result simply means that the first record in the data base doesn't meet this criterion. As we explained in Chapter 5, 1-2-3 assigns the value 0 to a conditional test that is false, and the value 1 to a conditional test that is true. In this case, 1-2-3 returns the value 0 because cell E2 contains the value 163293, which is not greater than 250000. This result has absolutely no impact on the function of the criterion, however, other than to tell you that the criterion will not select the first record. When you use this criterion with a / Data Query command or a data base statistical function, 1-2-3 will apply it to every entry in the Sales field.

Referring to Cells Outside the Data Base

In some cases, you may wish to compare the entries in a field to an entry in a cell outside of the data base. When you do this, the reference to the outside cell must be absolute, or mixed with an absolute row reference. Otherwise, 1-2-3 will alter the reference as it moves down through the data base.

For example, suppose that you want to select the records from the example data base that have a Sales field value that is less than the value stored in cell Z100. To select these records, you would enter either the criterion +E2<Z$100 or the criterion +E2<$Z$100 into cell E16 (or any other cell in the second row of the Criteria range). Fixing the row component of the reference assures that 1-2-3 will compare each record's Amount field entry to the value in cell Z100. If the reference to cell Z100 was relative, 1-2-3 would compare the first record's Sales field entry to the entry in cell Z100, the second record's Sales field entry to the entry in cell Z101, and so forth.

Using the = Operator

In most cases, you will use the <, >, <=, >=, and <> operators in comparison criteria. However, you also can use the = operator. For example, if you want to select all the records from the example data base with the value 250000 in the Quota field, you could enter the criterion +F2=250000 in any cell in the second row of the Criteria range. Of course, you could specify this same exact-match condition by entering the value 250000 into cell F16, as we did in Figure 12-10.

Using the <> Operator

The <> (not equal) operator allows you to select records that have an entry in a specified field that does not equal some other value. For example, suppose you want to select those records from the example data base that do not have the entry 250000 in the Quota field. To make this selection, you could enter the criterion +*F2<>250000* into one of the cells in the second row of the Criteria range.

Using Comparison Criteria on Date Fields

You can use comparison criterion to make selections from date fields. When you do this, the third part of the criterion—the comparison operator—will usually be a date function. For example, suppose you want 1-2-3 to select the records for salesmen who were hired on or after January 1, 1986. You would use the criterion +*C2>=@DATE(86,1,1)* to make this selection. Similarly, suppose you want to select the records for salesmen who were hired before December 31, 1982. You would use the criterion +*C2<@DATE(82,12,31)* to make this selection.

Using Comparison Criteria on Text Fields

Although you usually will use comparison criteria to operate on value fields, you also can use this form of criteria to operate on text fields. For example, you could use the criterion +*D2="East"* to select all the records from the example data base that have the label *'East* in their Region field. (Of course, it would be simpler to enter the label *'East* into cell D16, as we did in Figure 12-9.) Notice that the string *East* is enclosed in quotes in this criteria. If you use a literal string in a comparison criterion, you must enclose the comparison string in quotes.

You can even use the operators >, <, >=, and <= to make selections based on the entries in a text field. When you use these operators, 1-2-3 will use the current collating sequence to determine whether an entry in a field is "greater than" or "less than" the comparison string. For example, suppose you want to select all records from the example data base that have a Name field entry that begins with a letter that is "greater than" the letter G. To make this selection, you could enter the criterion +*A2>"G"* in one of the cells of the Criteria range.

The operators <, >, <=, and >= come in handy when you need to make selections based on text fields that include numeric entries, such as Telephone Number, Social Security Number, Zip Code, and ID# fields. For example, suppose you want to select all records from the example data base that have an ID# field entry that begins with a number less than 3. To make this selection, you could enter the criterion +*B2<"3"* in one of the cells of the Criteria range.

You cannot use wildcard characters in text comparison criteria. If you include a wildcard in a text comparison criterion, 1-2-3 will treat that character literally.

Complex Comparison Criteria

As you have seen, a comparison criterion is simply a conditional test that references a cell in the first record of a data base. Although most comparison criteria will be in the form we've shown so far, they also can include formulas and functions. For example, you could use the criterion *@LENGTH(D2)>4* to select all records whose Region field entry is more than four characters long. You could use the criterion

@YEAR(C2)=86 to select those records with a Date of Hire field entry that represents a date in 1986—in other words, the records for salesmen who were hired in 1986. The criterion *+E2<F2* would select any record with a Sales field entry that is less than the same record's Quota field entry—in other words, the records for salesmen who did not meet their quotas. You could use the criterion *@MOD(@CELL("row",A2..A2),2)=0* to select every second record.

There usually are a number of ways to state any comparison criteria. For example, you could use either the criterion *+E2>250000* or the criterion *250000<E2* to select records with Sales field entries that exceed 250000. Similarly, you could use the criteria *+F2<E2* or *+E2-F2>0* instead of *+E2>F2* to select the records for salesmen who exceeded their quota.

TIP: EXACT-MATCH TEXT CRITERIA

Earlier in this chapter, we showed you that 1-2-3 ignores capitalization differences when it evaluates an exact-match text criterion. If you want 1-2-3 to consider capitalization, you must use the logical function @EXACT. For example, suppose you want to select those records that have the entry *'East*—and not *'east* or *'EAST*—in the Region field. You would use the criterion *@EXACT(C2,"East")* to make this selection. Because @EXACT is a logical function (one that returns either the value 1 or the value 0), this criterion does not require a conditional operator.

Multiple Criteria

In many cases, you'll want 1-2-3 to select records that meet some or all of several different selection conditions. For example, you may want 1-2-3 to select records that have the label *'East* in their Region field and a value greater than 250000 in their Sales field. Or you might want to select the records that have either the label *'East* or the label *'West* in their Region field. To achieve these effects, you must combine two or more criteria within the same Criteria range.

Logical AND Conditions

When you enter two or more selection conditions into the same row of a Criteria range, 1-2-3 will select only those records that meet all the conditions specified on that row. This situation is called a logical AND combination because 1-2-3 combines each of the criteria with the word AND when it uses the criterion: *Select the records that meet this condition AND this condition AND this condition, and so on*. For a record to be selected, all of the stated conditions must be true.

TIP: NAME THE CELLS OF THE FIRST RECORD

Because all comparison criteria must refer to a cell in the first record of a data base, your comparison criteria usually will contain cell references like +B2, +C2, and so forth. Although 1-2-3 understands these references, you might have a hard time determining which field a criterion refers to.

You can make criteria more understandable by assigning range names to the cells of the first record in a data base. You'll usually want to assign those cells the names of the fields in which they are situated. The easiest way to do this is to issue the / Range Name Labels Down command, highlight the row of field names at the top of the data base, and press [Enter]. After you do this for the example Sales data base, cell A2 will be named NAME, cell B2 will be named ID#, cell C2 will be named DATE OF HIRE, and so on. Once these cells are named, you can use those range names in your criteria.

As an example of this technique, suppose that you want to select all the records from the example data base that have the entry *'East* in the Region field and a value greater than 250000 in the Amount field. To specify this criterion, you would enter the label *'East* into cell D16 and enter the condition *+E2>250000* into cell E16 (or another cell of that row), as shown in Figure 12-13. (If the Criteria range contained other entries, you would want to erase them.) Since these criteria are both on the same row of the Criteria range, 1-2-3 will select only records that meet both of them: those records with the label *'East* in the Region field AND a value greater than 250000 in the Sales field. In this case, 1-2-3 will select only the records in rows 4 and 13.

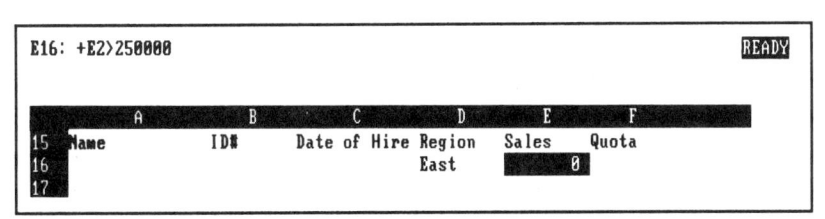

```
E16: +E2>250000                                              READY

          A         B         C         D        E       F
     15  Name      ID#    Date of Hire Region  Sales   Quota
     16                                 East            0
     17
```

FIGURE 12-13: A logical AND condition

Logical OR Conditions

In some cases, you'll want 1-2-3 to select records that meet at least one of several criteria. To make this kind of selection, you enter criteria into two or more rows of a Criteria range. When you use this kind of criterion, 1-2-3 will select those records that meet the conditions specified on any one of the rows of the Criteria range. This situation is called a logical OR combination because 1-2-3 combines each of the criteria with the word OR when it uses the criterion: *Select the records that meet this condition OR this condition OR this condition, and so on.* For a record to be selected, only one of the stated conditions must be true.

For example, suppose you want 1-2-3 to select all the records from the example data base that have either the entry 'East or the entry 'West in the Region field. To specify this condition, enter the label 'East into cell D16 and the label 'West into cell D17 (or vice versa), as shown in Figure 12-14. (If the Criteria range contained other entries, you'll want to erase them.) When you use this criterion with a / Data Query command or a data base statistical function, 1-2-3 will select records that have either the label 'East or the label 'West in the Region field—in this case, the records in rows 4, 5, 8, 10, 11, and 13.

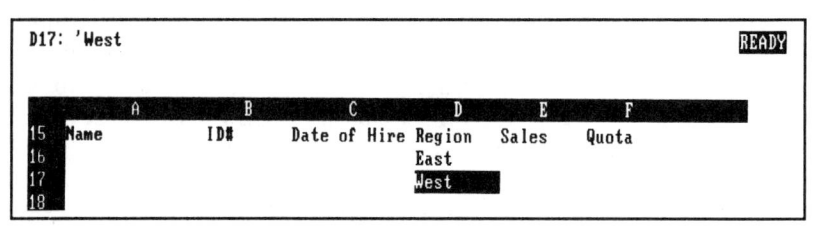

```
D17: 'West                                                          READY

           A           B            C         D        E        F
    15  Name          ID#      Date of Hire  Region  Sales    Quota
    16                                       East
    17                                       West
    18
```

FIGURE 12-14: A logical OR condition

Although many of your logical OR criteria will refer to a single field, you can combine references to different fields in a logical OR criterion. For example, suppose that you want 1-2-3 to select all the records that have either a Sales field entry less than $160,000 or a Quota field entry less than $160,000. To select these records, you'd enter the formula +E2<160000 into any cell of row 16, and enter the formula +F2<160000 into any cell of row 17, as shown in Figure 12-15. (In fact, you could enter either condition in either row 16 or 17, as long as one is in one row and one is in the other.)

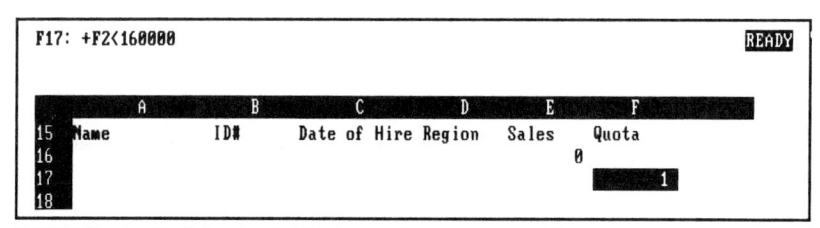

```
F17: +F2<160000                                                     READY

           A           B            C         D        E        F
    15  Name          ID#      Date of Hire  Region  Sales    Quota
    16                                                         0
    17                                                                 1
    18
```

FIGURE 12-15: A logical OR that references two fields

When you use this criterion with a / Data Query command or a data base statistical function, 1-2-3 will select all the records that have a value less than 160000 in the Sales field or a value less than 160000 in the Quota field, or both. In this case, 1-2-3 will select the records in rows 2, 7, and 8. The record in row 7 meets only the first criterion (+E2<160000); the record in row 2 meets only the second criterion (+F2<160000); and the record in row 8 meets both criteria.

Combining ANDs and ORs

By making entries into several cells in each of several rows of a Criteria range, you can create combined AND/OR situations. For example, suppose you want to select those records that have a Date of Hire field entry less than (before) January 1, 1982, or those records that have a Quota field entry greater than or equal to 250000 AND a Sales field entry greater than or equal to the Quota field entry. To make this selection, enter the criteria +C2<@DATE(82,1,1) in cell C16, the criteria +F2>=250000 in cell F17, and the criteria +E2>=F2 in cell E17. Figure 12-16 shows these criteria.

```
E17: +E2>=F2                                              READY

         A          B         C        D       E       F
    15  Name        ID#    Date of Hire Region Sales  Quota
    16                           0
    17                                          1      0
    18
```

FIGURE 12-16: A combined AND/OR criterion

The entry in row 16 of the Criteria range tells 1-2-3 to select all the records with a Date of Hire field entry less than (before) January 1, 1982. The entries in row 17 tell 1-2-3 to select all the records that have a Quota field entry greater than or equal to 250000 and a Sales field entry greater than or equal to its Quota field entry. When you use this criteria, 1-2-3 will join the criteria on rows 16 and 17 with a logical OR, and will select any records that meet either set of criteria—in this case, the records in rows 4, 5, 6, 9, and 11.

Let's consider another example. Suppose you want 1-2-3 to select all the records that have either the label 'East or the label 'West in the Region field, and a value greater than 250000 in the Sales field. To do this, you would enter the label 'East in cell D16 of the Criteria range, the label 'West in cell D17, and the comparison criterion +E2>250000 into cell E16 and cell E17. Figure 12-17 shows the completed Criteria range.

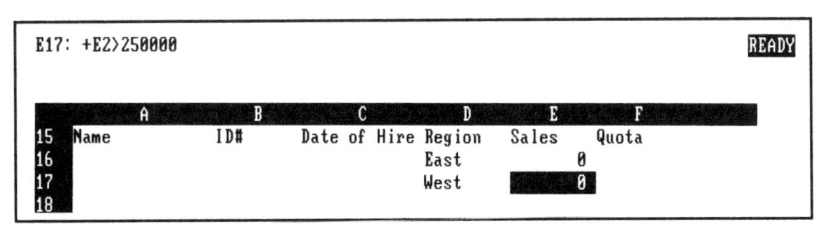

```
E17: +E2>250000                                           READY

         A          B         C        D       E       F
    15  Name        ID#    Date of Hire Region Sales  Quota
    16                                  East          0
    17                                  West    0
    18
```

FIGURE 12-17: A combined AND/OR criterion

The entries in row 16 of the Criteria range tell 1-2-3 to select all the records with the label 'East in the Region field and a value greater than 250000 in the Sales field. The entries in row 17 tell 1-2-3 to select all the records with the label 'West in the Region field and a value greater than 250000 in the Sales field.

When you use this criterion, 1-2-3 will select only those records that meet all the criteria on either row. In this case, 1-2-3 will select the records in rows 4 and 13, which meet the criteria on the first row, as well as the records in rows 5 and 11, which meet the criteria on the second row. 1-2-3 would select the same records even if you switched the order of the two records in the Criteria range.

Notice that we entered the criterion +E2>250000 into both rows of the Criteria range in Figure 12-17. This is absolutely necessary. If we had not entered this criteria into both rows of the Criteria range, the meaning of the criterion would have been completely different. For example, consider the criterion shown in Figure 12-18. Notice that cell E17 in this Criteria range is blank. This criterion asks 1-2-3 to select those records that have the entry 'East in the Region field and a value greater than 250000 in the Sales field, OR those records with the entry 'West in the Region field and any entry in the Sales field. When you use this criterion, 1-2-3 will select the records in rows 4 and 13 and those in rows 5, 8, and 11.

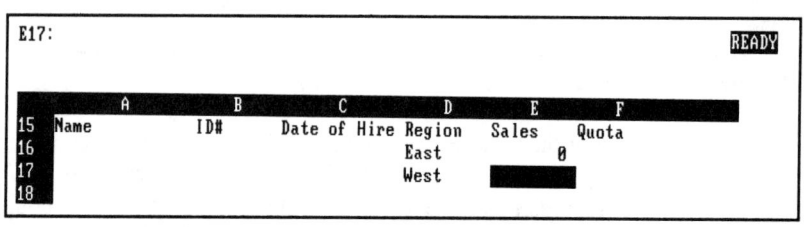

```
E17:                                                               READY
            A           B           C           D       E       F
     15 Name            ID#        Date of Hire Region  Sales   Quota
     16                                         East            0
     17                                         West
     18
```

FIGURE 12-18: A combined AND/OR criterion

Special Operators: #AND#, #OR#, and #NOT#

1-2-3 has two special logical operators—#AND# and #OR#—that offer an alternative way to specify logical AND and OR conditions. Another special operator, #NOT#, allows you to negate comparison criteria.

The #AND# Operator

1-2-3's #AND# operator links two criteria in a logical AND relationship (both criteria must be true for the record to be selected). This operator is most useful for making logical #AND# combinations of criteria that relate to the same field. For example, suppose you want to select those records from the Sales data base that have a value between 200000 and 300000 in the Sales field. To do this, you could enter the criteria +E2>=200000 and +E2<=300000 into different cells of the same row of the Criteria range. Alternatively, you could enter the combined criteria +E2>=200000#AND#E2<=300000 into a single cell, as shown in Figure 12-19. Both alternatives select the records in rows 6, 10, and 12. However, the #AND# operator makes it possible to use only a single cell.

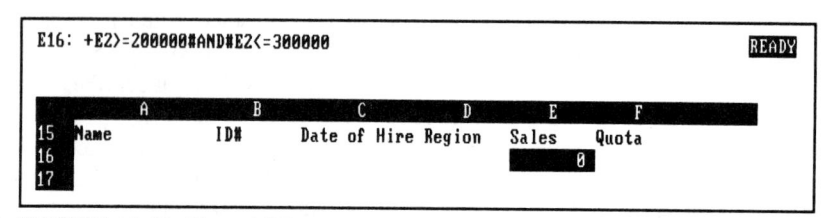

```
E16: +E2>=200000#AND#E2<=300000                                    READY
            A           B           C           D       E       F
     15 Name            ID#        Date of Hire Region  Sales   Quota
     16                                                         0
     17
```

FIGURE 12-19: The #AND# operator

The #OR# Operator

1-2-3's #OR# operator makes it possible to specify logical OR criteria on a single row of the Criteria range. Traditionally, you would specify a logical OR situation by making entries into more than one row of that range. For example, suppose that you want 1-2-3 to select all the records from the example data base that have either the label *'East* or the label *'West* in the Region field. To do this, you could use the two-row criterion shown in Figure 12-14. Alternatively, you could use the criterion +D2="East"#OR#D2="West" as shown in Figure 12-20.

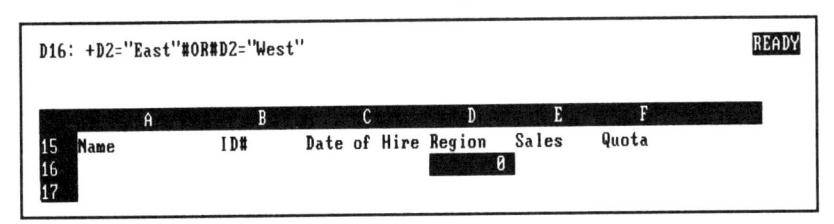

```
D16: +D2="East"#OR#D2="West"                                    READY

         A           B           C            D        E       F
   15  Name         ID#     Date of Hire   Region    Sales   Quota
   16                                         0
   17
```

FIGURE 12-20: The #OR# operator

Although this criterion probably takes more time to enter than the alternative of typing the label *'East* into one cell and *'West* into another, it occupies one line instead of two. The space savings is even greater when you combine three or more criteria with this operator.

Combining the #AND# and #OR# Operators

If you wish, you can create complex criteria that use both the #AND# and #OR# operators within a single cell. For example, the criterion

   +E2>250000#AND#(D2="East"#OR#D2="West")

selects those records with a Sales field entry greater than 250000 and either the label *'East* or the label *'West* in the Region field—just like the Criteria range shown in Figure 12-17. The advantage of this approach is that it requires only a single entry.

The #NOT# Operator

1-2-3's third special operator—#NOT#—allows you to negate comparison criteria. To use this operator to negate a criterion, you simply use it as a prefix for the criterion. For example, the criterion *#NOT#E2>250000* would select all records that have a value less than or equal to 250000 in the Sales field.

In most cases, there is a different (usually simpler) way to state a criterion that uses the #NOT# operator. For instance, it probably would be simpler just to use the criterion *+E2<=250000* instead of the criteria *#NOT#E2>250000*.

You also can use this operator to negate compound criteria. For example, the criterion *#NOT#(D2="East"#AND#E2>250000)* would select those records that do not have the label *'East* in the Region field and that do not have an entry greater than 250000 in the Sales field. This criterion is identical to the criterion *+D2"East"#OR#E2<=250000*.

Defining the Criteria Range

So far, we have shown you how to create criteria. Before you can use criteria with / Data Query commands or data base statistics, however, you have to tell 1-2-3 which range in the worksheet contains the criteria it should use to select records. To define the Criteria range for / Data Query commands, you must issue / Data Query Criteria command and select the range that contains the criteria. To define criteria for a data base statistical function, you must use the third argument of the function to specify the range that contains the criteria. We'll show you how to do this when we explain 1-2-3's / Data Query commands and data base functions.

QUERYING

RELEASE
► 2.2 ◄

1-2-3's / Data Query commands offer four commands that allow you to find, extract, and delete records that match criteria. ►If you are using 1-2-3 Release 2.2, you'll see the menu and the settings sheet shown in Figure 12-21 when you issue the / Data Query command. (If you are using an earlier version of 1-2-3, you'll see only the menu; you won't see the settings sheet.)◄ The / Data Query Find command highlights the records in a data base that match the criteria you specify. The / Data Query Extract command copies selected fields of those records that match the criteria you specify to other cells of the worksheet. The / Data Query Unique command does the same thing as the / Data Query Extract command, but it only copies one occurrence of any duplicate records. The / Data Query Delete command deletes all the records that match the criteria you specify.

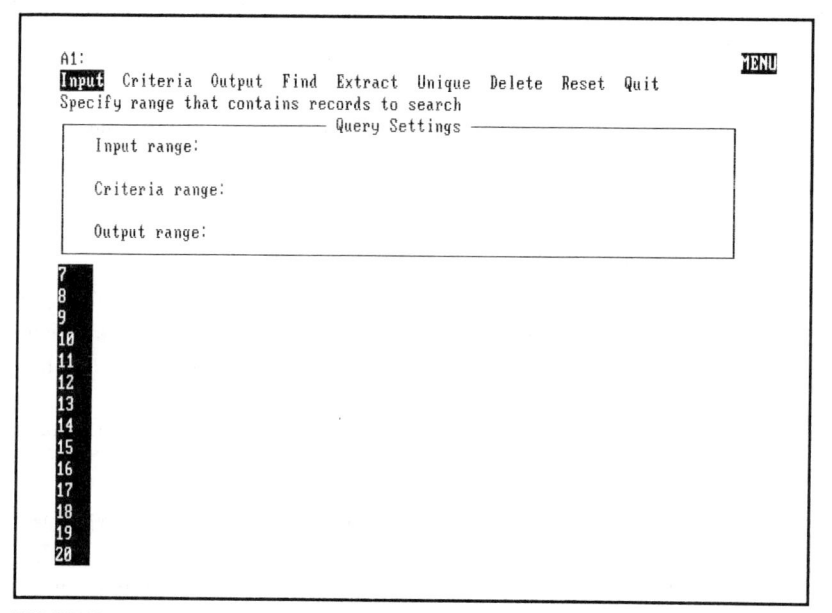

FIGURE 12-21: The / Data Query menu and settings sheet

Using any of these commands is a three-step process. First, you must create the criteria that tell 1-2-3 which records to operate on. (We've already shown you how to do this.) Second, you must formally define the ranges that contain the data base and the criteria. (The / Data Query Extract and / Data Query Unique commands also require you to define an additional range called the Output range.) After you complete these steps, you can use the appropriate / Data Query command to query the data base.

Defining the Ranges

Although you may recognize the entries in cells A1 to F13 of the worksheet shown in Figure 12-22 as a data base, and the entries in cells A15 to F16 as a Criteria range, 1-2-3 doesn't—to 1-2-3, these are simply entries in the worksheet. Before 1-2-3 can execute any / Data Query command, you must tell it which cells contain the data base it should act upon, and which cells contain the criteria. To define these two ranges, you must use 1-2-3's / Data Query Input and / Data Query Criteria commands.

```
A1: [W15] 'Name                                                    READY

        A           B          C            D         E         F
 1   Name          ID#      Date of Hire  Region    Sales     Quota
 2   Gibson        705G1    17-May-85     North    $163,293  $150,000
 3   Williams      356W3    01-Feb-82     South    $351,951  $375,000
 4   Johnson       585J2    04-Aug-80     East     $410,227  $400,000
 5   Franklin      128F4    06-Oct-81     West     $427,498  $450,000
 6   Logan         512L3    24-May-84     South    $253,944  $250,000
 7   Christensen   274C1    12-Sep-85     North    $155,960  $175,000
 8   Stewart       215S4    23-Jun-86     West     $128,922  $125,000
 9   Murphy        173M3    05-Apr-79     South    $458,132  $475,000
10   Adams         600A2    18-Jul-83     East     $235,526  $225,000
11   Parks         778P4    12-Jan-81     West     $304,887  $325,000
12   Wheeler       533W1    11-Nov-84     North    $209,575  $200,000
13   Foster        653F2    27-Mar-82     East     $337,480  $350,000
14
15   Name          ID#      Date of Hire  Region    Sales     Quota
16
```

FIGURE 12-22: A data base and Criteria range

Defining the Input Range

The / Data Query Input command defines the Input range—the group of cells that contain the data base you want to query. When you issue this command, 1-2-3 will present you with the prompt *Enter input range:* and wait for you to highlight the block of cells that contain the data base. When you define the Input range, you *must* include the row of field names at the top of the data base. For example, to define the Input range in Figure 12-22, you'd issue the / Data Query Input command, select the range A1..F13, and press [Enter].

As you add records to and delete records from your data base, you'll need to keep track of the Input range setting. If you add new records to the bottom of the data base, you'll need to use the / Data Query Input command to expand the Input range. If, on the other hand, you use the / Worksheet Insert Row command to insert a new row for a new record within the current Input range, you won't have to redefine the Input range. Like other ranges in 1-2-3, the Input range will grow if you use the / Worksheet Insert Row command to insert a row between the top and bottom rows of the range.

Similarly, if you use the / Worksheet Delete Row command to delete records from the data base, 1-2-3 will shrink the Input range to conform to the new size of the data base. As with other ranges, when you delete a row between the top and bottom rows in the Input range, 1-2-3 will automatically contract the range. However, if you delete the last record from a data base—the record in the last row of the Input range—1-2-3 will lose track of the range. If you delete the last row in the Input range, then, you'll need to use the / Data Query Input command to redefine that range before you next issue a / Data Query command.

Defining the Criteria Range

RELEASE
▶ **2.2** ◀

▶To define a Criteria range, you must use 1-2-3's / Data Query Criteria command (the / Data Query Criterion command in releases of 1-2-3 prior to 2.2).◀ When you issue this command, 1-2-3 will present the prompt *Enter criteria range:* and wait for you to mark the block of cells that contain the Criteria range. The range should begin with the row of field names at the top of the range and should include every row below that row that contains a criterion. At a minimum, the range you select needs to include two rows and one field—the field for which you have specified a criterion. Usually, however, you'll want to include all of the fields in the range you select—even those for which you have not specified criteria. That way, you won't have to redefine the Criteria range each time you specify a criterion for another field.

For example, to define the Criteria range in Figure 12-22, you would issue the / Data Query Criteria command, select the range A15..F16, and press [Enter]. (Typically, you'll wait until after you've entered criteria into the Criteria range before you define the range.)

Most of your Criteria ranges will include just two rows. If you are creating an OR criterion, however, the range might span three, four, or more rows. For example, if you were defining the Criteria range in Figure 12-14, you would select the range A15..F17.

If, after you have defined the Criteria range, you add rows or delete rows from the criterion, you'll need to redefine the Criteria range. If you remove one row of criteria from the Criteria range, you'll need to use the / Data Query Criteria command to shrink the range. If you add a new row of criteria, you'll need to expand the range to include that row.

> ### TIP: BLANK ROWS IN A CRITERIA RANGE
> If you include a blank row in a Criteria range you select, and then issue one of the / Data Query commands, 1-2-3 will select every record in your data base—even if the Criteria range contains other nonblank rows. A blank cell in any field of a Criteria range tells 1-2-3 to match any entry in that field. Consequently, an entire blank row tells 1-2-3 to match those records that contain any entry in any field—in other words, every record in the data base. Whenever you issue a / Data Query command, 1-2-3 selects any records that meet all of the conditions specified by any single row of the Criteria range. For this reason, a blank row "overrides" any criteria in any other row and causes 1-2-3 to select every record from the data base. You should avoid including blank rows in your Criteria ranges.

The Output Range

Two of 1-2-3's / Data Query commands—Extract and Unique—require a third range: the Output range. This is the range to which 1-2-3 will copy data base records that match the criteria you have defined when you issue either of these commands. We will discuss this range later in this chapter in our discussion of the / Data Query Extract command.

Redefining and Cancelling Range Definitions

Once you define the Input, Criteria, and Output ranges, 1-2-3 will remember the coordinates of those ranges for the duration of the current 1-2-3 session. If you save the worksheet after defining those ranges, 1-2-3 will remember them the next time you load the worksheet. Because 1-2-3 remembers these ranges, you don't need to redefine them each time you issue a / Data Query command.

In some cases, of course, you may want to (or need to) change the coordinates of one or more of the ranges. When you issue the / Data Query Input, Criteria, or Output command to redefine one of the ranges, 1-2-3 will highlight the current coordinates of that range. You can then use any of the pointing techniques discussed in Chapter 2 to resize the range.

If the coordinates of the new ranges will be significantly different from their current coordinates (for example, if you have two data bases in the same worksheet), you may wish to clear the definitions of those ranges entirely before defining the new ones. You can use the / Data Query Reset command to do this. When you issue this command, 1-2-3 "forgets" the coordinates of the Input, Criteria, and Output ranges. Before you can use one of the / Data Query commands to query the data base, you'll need to redefine those ranges.

The / Data Query Find Command

The / Data Query Find command instructs 1-2-3 to highlight the records in a data base that match the criteria you have defined. When you issue this command, then 1-2-3 looks for records that match the criteria in the Criteria range, starting at the top of the data base. If the data base doesn't contain any matching records, 1-2-3 will simply beep and redisplay the / Data Query menu. If 1-2-3 finds a matching record, it will highlight the entire record, and display the message FIND in the Mode indicator. Once 1-2-3 has highlighted a matching record, you can edit that record. You can also press ↓ or ↑ to highlight other matching records.

An Example

Suppose you want 1-2-3 to highlight the records in the example data base in Figure 12-22 that have the label 'East in the Region field. To do this, first enter the label 'East in cell D16 in the Criteria range. Then issue the / Data Query command, choose the Input option, select the range A1..F13, press [Enter], choose the Criteria option, select the range A15..F16, and press [Enter] again. (If you have already defined these ranges, you can skip this step.) Now, choose the Find option from the / Data Query menu. Figure 12-23 shows the screen after you issue this command. As you can see, 1-2-3 has highlighted the record in row 4—the first record that has the label 'East in its Region field.

```
A4: [W15] 'Johnson                                              FIND

         A          B           C         D        E         F
    1  Name        ID#    Date of Hire  Region   Sales     Quota
    2  Gibson      705G1     17-May-85  North    $163,293  $150,000
    3  Williams    356W3     01-Feb-82  South    $351,951  $375,000
    4  Johnson     585J2     04-Aug-80  East     $410,227  $400,000
    5  Franklin    128F4     06-Oct-81  West     $427,498  $450,000
    6  Logan       512L3     24-May-84  South    $253,944  $250,000
    7  Christensen 274C1     12-Sep-85  North    $155,960  $175,000
    8  Stewart     215S4     23-Jun-86  West     $128,922  $125,000
    9  Murphy      173M3     05-Apr-79  South    $458,132  $475,000
   10  Adams       600A2     18-Jul-83  East     $235,526  $225,000
   11  Parks       778P4     12-Jan-81  West     $304,887  $325,000
   12  Wheeler     533W1     11-Nov-84  North    $209,575  $200,000
   13  Foster      653F2     27-Mar-82  East     $337,480  $350,000
   14
   15  Name        ID#    Date of Hire  Region   Sales     Quota
   16                                   East
   17
```

FIGURE 12-23: The / Data Query Find command

Moving Around in the FIND Mode

While 1-2-3 is in the FIND mode, you can move the highlight from one matching record to another. Pressing the ↓ key moves the highlight to the next matching record in the data base. If you press ↓ while your screen looks like Figure 12-23, 1-2-3 will highlight the record in row 10. If you press ↓ again, 1-2-3 will highlight the record in row 13.

Pressing ↑ while 1-2-3 is in the FIND mode will move the highlight to the previous matching record. If you press ↑ while 1-2-3 is highlighting the record in row 13, for example, 1-2-3 will move the highlight back to row 10.

If you press ↓ while the last matching record in the data base is highlighted, or if you press ↑ while the first matching record is highlighted, 1-2-3 will simply beep. The same thing will happen if you press ↓ while the only matching record in the data base is highlighted.

If you press [Home] while 1-2-3 is in the FIND mode, it will highlight the first record in the data base—even if that record does not match the criteria you have defined. If you press [End], 1-2-3 will highlight the last record in the data base—even if that record does not match the criteria. For example, if you press [Home] in the example, 1-2-3 will highlight the record in row 2. If you press [End], 1-2-3 will highlight the record in row 13.

Editing in the FIND Mode

1-2-3 Releases 2, 2.01, and 2.2 allow you to edit highlighted records while 1-2-3 is in the FIND mode. (1-2-3 Release 1A does not). Here's how it works. If you look closely at the highlighted record in Figure 12-23, you'll see a small underline character underneath the highlighted record's Name field entry. This character, which we'll call the cursor, marks the "active" cell in the highlighted range—the cell that will be affected if you type something. You can use the → and ← keys to move the cursor to different fields in the highlighted record. If you press → while the screen looks like Figure 12-23, for example, 1-2-3 will move the cursor to cell B4.

Once you have positioned the cursor on the entry you want to change, you can either replace or edit that entry. If you want to replace the contents of a field in the highlighted record, just move the cursor to that entry and type the replacement. For example, to replace the entry in the Sales field of the selected record in Figure 12-23 with the entry 475000, you would press → to move the cursor to the Sales field and type 475000. When you press [Enter] to lock in the change, 1-2-3 will display the revised entry and remain in the FIND mode.

If you want to edit the entry in a field in the highlighted record, just move the cursor to that entry, press [Edit] to bring that entry to the control panel, and then make the correction just as you normally would. For example, to change the entry in the ID# field of the selected record in Figure 12-23 from '585J2 to '585J3, press → to move the cursor to the ID# field and press [Edit] to bring the entry '585J2 into the control panel. Then press [Backspace] to delete the character 2 and type 3. When you press [Enter] to lock in the change, 1-2-3 will display the revised entry and remain in the FIND mode.

Leaving the FIND Mode

When you are ready to leave the FIND mode, you can press either [Esc], [Enter], [Ctrl][Break], or [Query] ([F7]). If you press [Esc] or [Enter] while 1-2-3 is in the FIND mode, 1-2-3 will return you to the /Data Query menu. If you press [Ctrl][Break], 1-2-3 will take you all the way to the READY mode. In either case, 1-2-3 will position the cell pointer where it was when you issued the /Data Query Find command. If you press the [Query] key instead of [Esc], [Enter], or [Ctrl][Break], 1-2-3 will return to the READY mode but leave the cell pointer where it is—in a criteria-matching record.

Extracting Records

The /Data Query Extract and /Data Query Unique commands make it possible to extract—or copy—to another part of the worksheet the entries in any or all of the fields in the data base records that match the criteria you define. These commands allow you to extract subsets of records from your data base for analysis or printing.

Before you issue either of these commands, you must first enter the appropriate selection criteria into the Criteria range, then use the /Data Query Input and Criteria commands to specify the Input and Criteria ranges. The Input and Criteria ranges tell 1-2-3 where the records are stored and which records to select, respectively—just as they do for the /Data Query Find command. You must also use the /Data Query Output command to define an Output range.

The Output Range

The Output range plays a major role in the process of extracting records from a data base. 1-2-3 copies the records it selects when you issue the /Data Query Extract and /Data Query Unique commands to the Output range you have defined. In addition, the entries in this range tell 1-2-3 from which fields to copy entries. Depending on how you define it, the Output range may also limit the number of records that 1-2-3 can copy.

Creating the Output Range

To create the Output range, you first must enter one or more field names from the data base into a single row of the worksheet. These names serve as the first row of the Output range. Like the field names at the top of the Criteria range, these names must be identical to the corresponding names at the top of the data base, except that capitalization and label prefix differences do not matter.

You can place the field names for the Output range anywhere in the worksheet. We typically put the Output range below the data base in the worksheet.

The field names you include at the top of the Output range determine which fields 1-2-3 will extract information from. If you include the name of every field at the top of the Output range, 1-2-3 will copy the entries from every field of every matching record in the data base to the Output range. If you include the names of only some fields at the top of the Output range, 1-2-3 will extract the entries from only those fields.

The order of the field names at the top of the Output range does not have to match the order of the names at the top of the data base. However, when 1-2-3 extracts the matching records, the order of the field names in the Output range determines the order of the fields in the extracted records.

You can create the field names for the Output range either by typing them or by using the /Copy command to create a copy of the field names for the data base. If you plan to include all of the field names from the data base in the Output range, you'll probably find it easier to use the /Copy command. If you only want to use selected field names in the Output range, you'll probably want to type the names.

Defining the Output Range

After you enter the names of the fields from which you want 1-2-3 to extract information, you can formally define the Output range. To do this, you issue the /Data Query Output command. When you issue this command, 1-2-3 will display the prompt *Enter output range:* and wait for you to highlight a range.

There are two different ways to define the Output range. First, you can define the range to include just the row of field names. Alternatively, you can define the range to include the field names and as many rows as you wish below the names.

In general, we prefer to use the one-row method to define Output ranges. Here's why. The size of the range you select determines how many records 1-2-3 can extract. If you select only the row of field names, 1-2-3 can extract as many records as there are rows between those names and the bottom of the worksheet. For example, suppose the field names for your Output range are in the range A100..F100. Since there are 8092 rows between row 100 and the bottom of the worksheet (row 8192), if you define cells A100..F100 as the Output range, 1-2-3 will be able to extract up to 8092 records. Of course, the actual number of records that it can extract will be limited by the number of records in the data base and by the amount of memory in your computer.

If you select more than one row when you define the Output range, 1-2-3 will be able to extract only as many records as there are rows in the selected range, minus one. For example, if you specify a two-row Output range—the row of field names and one blank row—1-2-3 will be able to extract only a single record. If you specify a five-row Output range, 1-2-3 will be able to extract up to four records. If there are more matching records in your data base than there are rows in your Output range, when you issue the /Data Query Extract command, 1-2-3 will extract as many records as it can. Then it will beep, present the message *Too many records for output range* at the bottom of the screen, and flash ERROR in the Mode indicator. You can avoid this problem by including a large number of rows in the Output range, or by defining the Output range as a single row.

> **TIP: ONE-ROW OUTPUT RANGES**
>
> Although one-row Output ranges are more flexible than multiple-row ranges, they are subject to one major hazard. The first thing 1-2-3 does when you issue the / Data Query Extract command is erase every cell in the Output range (it does not erase the field names at the top of the range). If you defined the Output range as a multiple-row range, 1-2-3 will erase the cells within the range you specified. If you defined the Output range as a single-row range, however, 1-2-3 will assume that the Output range includes every cell below the row of labels you specified to the bottom of the worksheet. When you issue the / Data Query Extract command, therefore, 1-2-3 will erase every cell between the Output range field names and the bottom of the worksheet. For example, if you define your Output range to be A18..B18, 1-2-3 will erase the range A19..B8192 when you issue the / Data Query Extract command. Any entries in the cells of columns A and B below row 18 will be erased.
>
> Be careful! If you choose to define single-row Output ranges, be sure to place the field names in cells that have no entries below them.

The / Data Query Extract Command

The / Data Query Extract command allows you to extract from a data base the contents of selected fields for those records that match the criteria you define. To use this command, you must first create the Criteria and Output ranges, specify the criteria you want to use to select records, and define the Input, Criteria, and Output ranges. When all three ranges have been defined, you issue the / Data Query Extract command. When you issue this command, 1-2-3 will copy the records that match the criteria you have defined to the Output range.

An Example

Suppose you want to use the / Data Query Extract command to extract every field of those records from the data base in Figure 12-22 that have the Region field entry *'East*. To begin, you must enter the criterion 'East in cell D16.

Next, you have to set up the Output range. We want this range to include every field name from the data base. We'll enter these field names for the Output range in row 18. To create the range, move the cell pointer to cell A18, and then either type the field names from the data base, one per cell, across row 18, or use the / Copy command to copy those names from row 1 to row 18. Figure 12-24 shows the Output range field names in place.

When the worksheet is set up, issue the / Data Query command, choose the Input option, select the range A1..F13, press [Enter], choose the Criteria option, select the range A15..F16, and press [Enter] again. (If you have already defined these ranges, you can skip this step.) Now you need to define the Output range. To do this, choose the Output option, select the range A18..F18, and press [Enter] again.

```
A18: [W15] 'Name                                                      READY


       A            B           C              D         E          F
 1  Name         ID#        Date of Hire   Region    Sales      Quota
 2  Gibson       705G1      17-May-85      North     $163,293   $150,000
 3  Williams     356W3      01-Feb-82      South     $351,951   $375,000
 4  Johnson      585J2      04-Aug-80      East      $410,227   $400,000
 5  Franklin     128F4      06-Oct-81      West      $427,498   $450,000
 6  Logan        512L3      24-May-84      South     $253,944   $250,000
 7  Christensen  274C1      12-Sep-85      North     $155,960   $175,000
 8  Stewart      215S4      23-Jun-86      West      $128,922   $125,000
 9  Murphy       173M3      05-Apr-79      South     $458,132   $475,000
10  Adams        600A2      18-Jul-83      East      $235,526   $225,000
11  Parks        778P4      12-Jan-81      West      $304,887   $325,000
12  Wheeler      533W1      11-Nov-84      North     $209,575   $200,000
13  Foster       653F2      27-Mar-82      East      $337,480   $350,000
14
15  Name         ID#        Date of Hire   Region    Sales      Quota
16                                         East
17
18  Name         ID#        Date of Hire   Region    Sales      Quota
19
20
```

FIGURE 12-24: Creating an Output range

Now, choose the Extract option from the Data Query menu. When you issue this command, 1-2-3 first will erase the cells of the Output range—in this case, cells A19..F8192. After these cells have been erased, 1-2-3 will copy the records that match the criteria from the data base into the Output range. Figure 12-25 shows the screen after you issue this command. (We've scrolled the screen up so that the entire Output range is visible.)

Extracting Partial Records

You can also use the /Data Query Extract command to extract just selected fields from the records that match the criterion you define. For example, suppose you want 1-2-3 to extract just the Name and Sales field entries for the records in the data base in Figure 12-22 that have the Region field entry 'East. To begin, you must enter the criterion 'East in cell D16.

Next, you have to set up the Output range. Since you want 1-2-3 to extract only the data in the Name and Sales fields, you must create an Output range that includes just those fields. To do this, move the cell pointer to cell A18, enter the field name 'Name, move the cell pointer to cell B18, and enter the field name 'Sales. (If your worksheet already includes an Output range, you'll want to use the / Range Erase command to erase that range before you create this new one.)

```
D16: 'East                                                            MENU
Input Criteria Output Find Extract Unique Delete Reset Quit
Copy all records that match criteria to output range
┌─────────────────────────── Query Settings ───────────────────────────┐
│  Input range:        A1..F13                                         │
│                                                                       │
│  Criteria range:     A15..F16                                        │
│                                                                       │
│  Output range:       A18..F18                                        │
└───────────────────────────────────────────────────────────────────────┘
15  Name              ID#        Date of Hire  Region    Sales      Quota
16                                              East
17
18  Name              ID#        Date of Hire  Region    Sales      Quota
19  Johnson           585J2      04-Aug-80     East      $410,227   $400,000
20  Adams             600A2      18-Jul-83     East      $235,526   $225,000
21  Foster            653F2      27-Mar-82     East      $337,480   $350,000
22
23
24
25
26
27
28
```

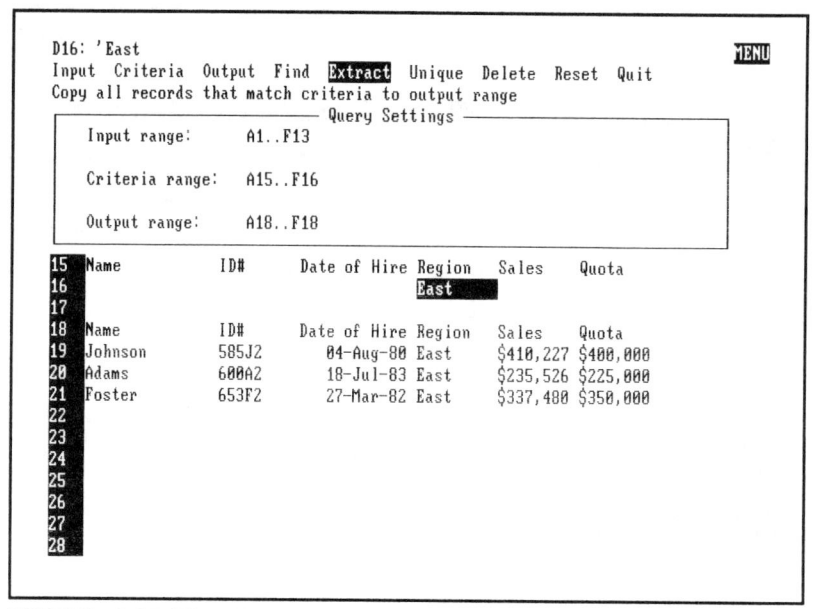

FIGURE 12-25: The / Data Query Extract command

When the worksheet is set up, issue the / Data Query command, choose the Input option, select the range A1..F13, press [Enter], choose the Criteria option, select the range A15..F16, and press [Enter] again. (If you have already defined these ranges, skip this step.) Next, define the Output range by choosing the Output option from the Data Query menu, selecting cells A18..B18, and pressing [Enter].

Now, to extract the selected records, choose Extract from the Data Query menu. After you issue this command, your worksheet will look like Figure 12-26. As you can see, 1-2-3 has copied the Name and Sales field entries for the three East region records (the records in rows 4, 10, and 13) into the range A19..B21.

TIP: EXTRACTING FORMULAS AND FUNCTIONS

Most of the entries in your data bases will be literal labels and values. In some cases, however, your data bases will contain formulas and functions. When you extract a field that contains formulas and functions, 1-2-3 copies the current value of those formulas and functions to the cells of the Output range.

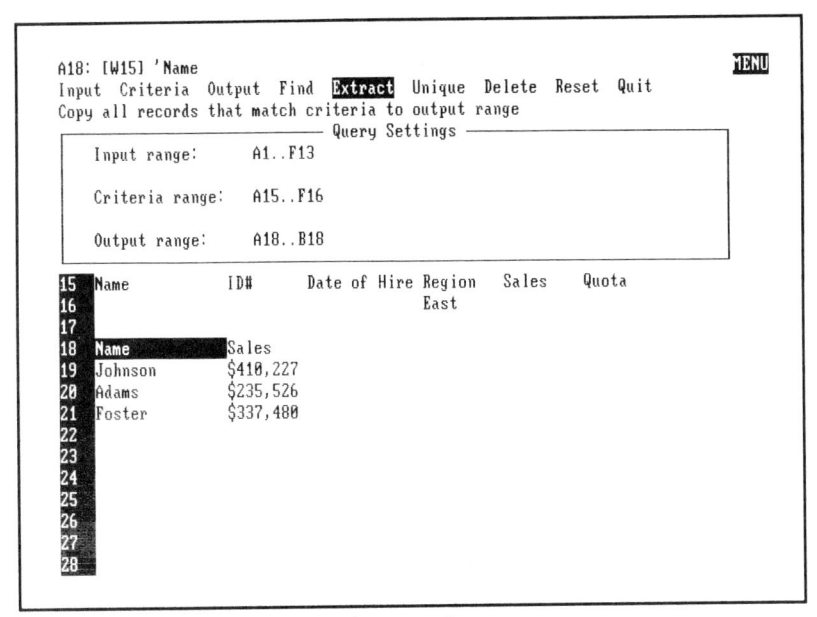

```
A18: [W15] 'Name                                                          MENU
Input  Criteria  Output  Find  Extract  Unique  Delete  Reset  Quit
Copy all records that match criteria to output range
┌─────────────────────── Query Settings ───────────────────────┐
│  Input range:     A1..F13                                     │
│                                                               │
│  Criteria range:  A15..F16                                    │
│                                                               │
│  Output range:    A18..B18                                    │
└───────────────────────────────────────────────────────────────┘
15  Name         ID#       Date of Hire  Region   Sales    Quota
16                                       East
17
18  Name         Sales
19  Johnson      $410,227
20  Adams        $235,526
21  Foster       $337,480
22
23
24
25
26
27
28
```

FIGURE 12-26: Extracting partial records

The / Data Query Unique Command

As we have explained, the / Data Query Extract command copies the specified fields of every data base record that matches the criterion you define into the cells of the Output range. If two or more records have the same entries in their extracted fields, the Output range will contain two or more identical records.

1-2-3's / Data Query Unique command also copies matching records into the Output range. However, if two or more records in the data base are identical, 1-2-3 will copy only one of those records into the Output range. When the command is completed, the Output range will contain only unique records.

Two records do not need to have identical entries in every field in the data base to be considered as duplicates by the / Data Query Extract command. / Data Query Unique will consider two records to be identical—and thus will copy only one of the two into the Output range—if they have the same entries in all of the fields that you have included in the Output range.

For example, suppose you want to extract one copy of each unique entry in the Region field from the data base in Figure 12-22. In this case, you want 1-2-3 to work with all the records in the data base—not a particular subset. To make this possible, you need to erase all criteria from the Criteria range.

Next, you need to set up an Output range. Since you want to extract only the entries in the Region field, your Output range needs to include just one field name: Region. To do this, move the cell pointer to cell A18 and enter the field name 'Region. (If your worksheet already includes an Output range, you'll want to erase that range before you create this new one.)

When the worksheet is set up, issue the / Data Query command, choose the Input option, select the range A1..F13, press [Enter], choose the Criteria option, select the range A15..F16, and press [Enter] again. (If you have already defined these ranges, you can skip this step.) Next, choose the Output option from the Data Query menu, select the range A18..A18, and press [Enter].

Once you have redefined the Output range, you can perform the extraction by issuing the / Data Query Unique command. When you issue this command, 1-2-3 will select the unique Region entries from the data base and copy those records into the Output range. Figure 12-27 shows the result. Notice that the Output range contains only one copy of each unique Region field entry.

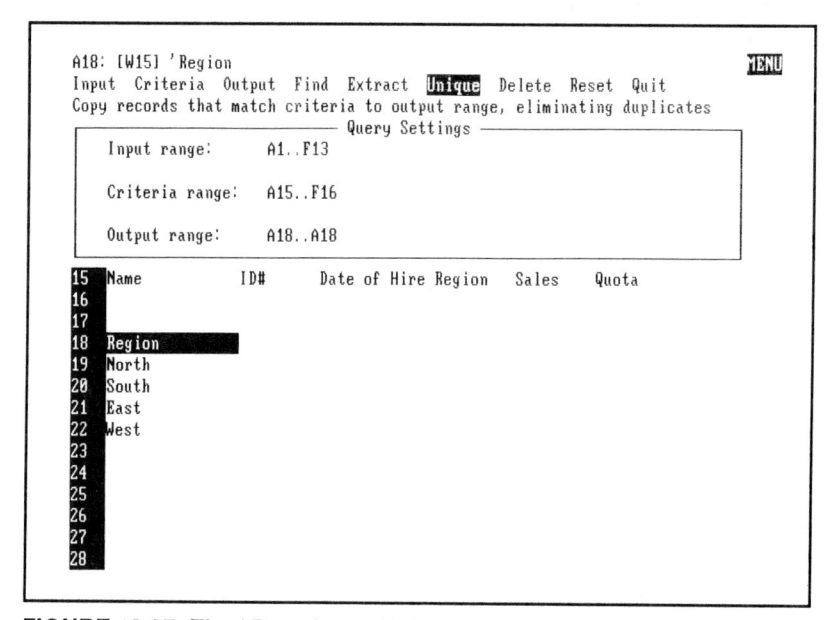

```
A18: [W15] 'Region                                                    MENU
Input  Criteria  Output  Find  Extract  Unique  Delete  Reset  Quit
Copy records that match criteria to output range, eliminating duplicates
─────────────────── Query Settings ───────────────────
  Input range:      A1..F13

  Criteria range:   A15..F16

  Output range:     A18..A18

15  Name          ID#      Date of Hire Region   Sales    Quota
16
17
18  Region
19  North
20  South
21  East
22  West
23
24
25
26
27
28
```

FIGURE 12-27: The / Data Query Unique command

The / Data Query Delete Command

1-2-3's / Data Query Delete command deletes every record that matches the criteria you have defined from a data base. Like 1-2-3's other / Data Query commands, this powerful command acts upon the records in the Input range that meet the criteria specified in the Criteria range.

An Example

For example, suppose you want to delete from the data base in Figure 12-22 the records for all the salesmen who did not meet their quota. To do this, you must enter the criterion +E2<F2 into any cell in row 16 of the Criteria range (the range must otherwise be blank). Next, issue the / Data Query command, choose the Input option, select the range A1..F13, press [Enter], choose the Criteria option, select the range A15..F16,

and press [Enter] again. (If you have already defined these ranges, you can skip this step.)

Once you have created the criterion and defined the ranges, then you can issue the / Data Query Delete command. When you issue this command, 1-2-3 will present a menu with two choices: Cancel and Delete. If you choose Cancel, 1-2-3 will leave the data base intact and return you to the / Data Query menu. If you choose Delete, 1-2-3 will remove the matching records from the data base.

Figure 12-28 shows the result of choosing Delete. As you can see, 1-2-3 has removed six records from the data base: the ones originally in rows 3, 5, 7, 9, 11, and 13 of the worksheet. 1-2-3 also has shifted the location of the remaining six records to fill in the space left by the deleted records. Although you can't tell it just by looking, 1-2-3 has also contracted the Input range so that it encompasses only the range A1..F7.

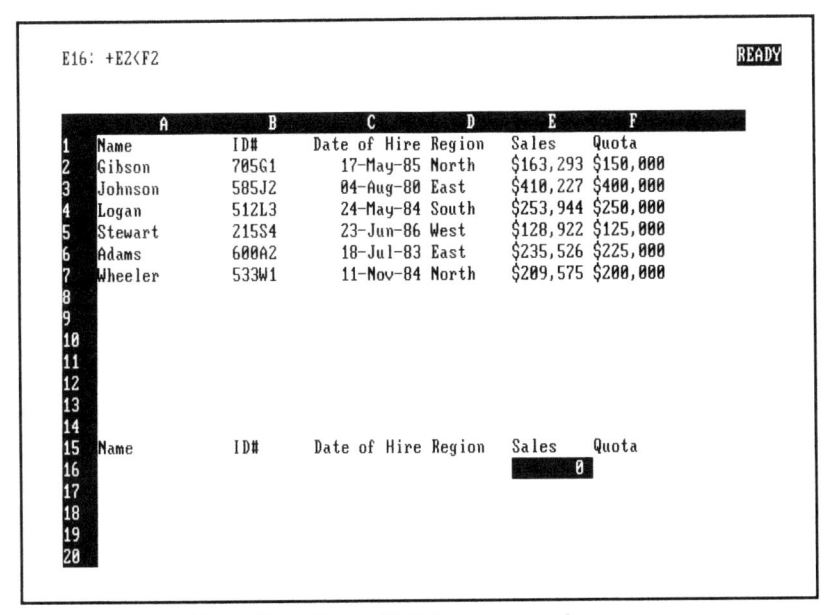

```
E16: +E2<F2                                                      READY

         A          B            C         D         E        F
1   Name          ID#      Date of Hire  Region    Sales     Quota
2   Gibson        705G1      17-May-85   North    $163,293  $150,000
3   Johnson       585J2      04-Aug-80   East     $410,227  $400,000
4   Logan         512L3      24-May-84   South    $253,944  $250,000
5   Stewart       215S4      23-Jun-86   West     $128,922  $125,000
6   Adams         600A2      18-Jul-83   East     $235,526  $225,000
7   Wheeler       533W1      11-Nov-84   North    $209,575  $200,000
8
9
10
11
12
13
14
15  Name          ID#      Date of Hire  Region    Sales     Quota
16                                                             0
17
18
19
20
```

FIGURE 12-28: The / Data Query Delete command

Notes

Once you use the / Data Query Delete command to delete records, those records are gone. Obviously, the / Data Query Delete command can have disastrous results. If you don't specify quite the right criteria before issuing this command, 1-2-3 will delete records that you didn't want it to delete. If you leave a blank row in your Criteria range—which tells 1-2-3 to select every record—the / Data Query Delete command will wipe out your entire data base.

Although 1-2-3 does not offer a command that can "undo" a deletion, you can reverse the effects of the / Data Query Delete command if you do one of two things ahead of time. First, you can save your worksheet immediately prior to issuing the / Data Query Delete command. That way, if the command doesn't do what you intended, you can use the / File Retrieve command to bring the worksheet back to its original form.

Alternatively, you can use the / Data Query Extract command to make a copy of every field of the records you are going to delete just before you issue the / Data Query Delete command. This technique has two benefits. First, by looking at the extracted records, you can tell which records 1-2-3 will delete. If 1-2-3 hasn't selected the records you intended for it to select, you can change the criteria and try again. Second, if you do happen to delete the wrong records, then you can use the / Move or / Copy commands to add the deleted records back to the data base.

Unless you save the worksheet or extract the deleted records to another part of the worksheet before you issue the / Data Query Delete command, there is no way to recover what has been deleted. It almost goes without saying—be careful! Always save or extract before you delete records.

TIP: USING THE [QUERY] KEY

1-2-3's [Query] key ([F7]) commands 1-2-3 to reissue the / Data Query command (Find, Extract, Unique, or Delete) that you issued most recently. If you press [Query] after issuing the / Data Query Find command, for example, 1-2-3 will repeat the Find operation. If you press the [Query] key after issuing the / Data Query Extract command, 1-2-3 will repeat the extraction.

The [Query] key is most useful when you want to perform the same operation repeatedly using different criteria. To do this, just change the criteria, redefine the Criteria range (if necessary), and press the [Query] key.

DATA BASE STATISTICAL FUNCTIONS

1-2-3 offers seven special data base functions: @DSUM, @DCOUNT, @DAVG, @DMAX, @DMIN, @DSTD, and @DVAR. Like the "regular" functions @SUM, @AVG, and so forth, these functions calculate common statistics like sums and averages. Unlike those functions, however, these special functions compute statistics about the entries in a data base. Specifically, they calculate statistics about the entries in a specified field of the records in a data base that match a criterion that you define.

There is almost no limit to the usefulness of these functions. For example, you could use an @DAVG function to calculate the average price of the three-bedroom Cape Cod houses in a real estate data base. You could use an @DCOUNT function to count the number of people with the area code 40205 in your mailing list data base, or you could use an @DMAX function to find the sales of the top salesman for the East region in your sales data base.

The Form of @D Functions

Although each of 1-2-3's data base statistical functions calculate a different statistic, they all have the same form. For example, the form of the @DSUM function is

@DSUM(*Input range,field offset,Criteria range*)

The first two characters, @D, identify the function as a data base statistical function. The next three letters tell 1-2-3 what statistic to calculate—in this case, a sum. Similarly, @DAVG calculates an average, @DSTD calculates a standard deviation, and so forth.

The three arguments of any data base statistical function determine which entries that function will act upon. The *Input range* argument identifies the data base from which the function will draw information. This argument should be a range reference (or a range name) that includes the field names and all of the records in the data base—the same range you would highlight if you used the / Data Query Input command to define the Input range for a / Data Query command.

The second argument, *field offset,* is a number that tells the function on which field to base its calculation. This argument identifies the field by its position relative to the leftmost field in the data base. For example, the *field offset* argument 0 tells the function to base its calculation on the entries in the first field in the data base. The *field offset* argument 1 tells the function to base its calculation on the entries in the second field, and so on.

All data base statistical functions except @DCOUNT must refer to fields that contain value entries. If the second argument of a data base statistical function refers to a field that contains labels, the function will return the value ERR.

The *Criteria range* argument identifies the function's Criteria range. The entries in this range determine which records the function will act upon—just like the entries in the Criteria range determine which entries are selected by a / Data Query command. The argument range should include at least one field name and one cell below that field name—in other words, the same range you would highlight if you used the / Data Query Criteria command to define the Criteria range for a / Data Query command. If the Criteria range includes several rows of criteria—as in an OR criterion—you'll need to include all those rows in the range.

Although the ranges specified by the *Input range* and *Criteria range* arguments will usually be the same ranges you would select if you issued the / Data Query Input or / Data Query Criteria commands, you don't have to issue these commands before you use a data base statistical function. Similarly, even if you already have created one or more data base statistical functions in a worksheet, you must use the / Data Query Input and / Data Query Criteria commands to define the Input and Criteria ranges before you use a / Data Query Find, Extract, Unique, or Delete command to query the data base.

The @DSUM Function

The @DSUM function sums the values in the specified field of the records in a data base that match the criterion you have defined. For example, suppose you want to calculate the total sales for the Eastern region in our example data base. To do this, erase the existing entries in the Criteria range, then enter the label 'East into cell D16. Once you have specified this criterion, you can calculate the total sales for the East region just by entering the function

@DSUM(A1..F13,4,A15..F16)

into any cell of the worksheet. Figure 12-29 shows this function in cell A18.

```
A18: [W15] @DSUM(A1..F13,4,A15..F16)                               READY

          A             B          C          D         E         F
   1  Name           ID#       Date of Hire  Region    Sales    Quota
   2  Gibson         705G1     17-May-85     North    $163,293  $150,000
   3  Williams       356W3     01-Feb-82     South    $351,951  $375,000
   4  Johnson        585J2     04-Aug-80     East     $410,227  $400,000
   5  Franklin       128F4     06-Oct-81     West     $427,498  $450,000
   6  Logan          512L3     24-May-84     South    $253,944  $250,000
   7  Christensen    274C1     12-Sep-85     North    $155,960  $175,000
   8  Stewart        215S4     23-Jun-86     West     $128,922  $125,000
   9  Murphy         173M3     05-Apr-79     South    $450,132  $475,000
  10  Adams          600A2     18-Jul-83     East     $235,526  $225,000
  11  Parks          778P4     12-Jan-81     West     $304,887  $325,000
  12  Wheeler        533W1     11-Nov-84     North    $209,575  $200,000
  13  Foster         653F2     27-Mar-82     East     $337,480  $350,000
  14
  15  Name           ID#       Date of Hire  Region    Sales    Quota
  16                                         East
  17
  18        983233
  19
  20
```

FIGURE 12-29: The @DSUM function

The first argument, *A1..F13*, tells 1-2-3 to work with the data base in the range A1..F13. The second argument, *4*, tells 1-2-3 that you want it to use the values in the fourth field to the right of the leftmost column in the data base—the Sales field. The third argument, *A15..F16*, identifies the Criteria range that determines which records the function will operate on. The entry in cell D16 of this range, *'East*, tells the function to compute the sum of just those entries with the Region field entry *East*.

As soon as you press [Enter] to lock in this function, 1-2-3 will evaluate it and will return the value 983233. To calculate this result, 1-2-3 totaled the Sales entries from the three records that have the entry *'East* in their Region field: the records in rows 4, 10, and 13.

> **TIP: REUSING DATA BASE STATISTICAL FUNCTIONS**
>
> Once you have entered a data base statistical function into a worksheet, you can use it to calculate statistics for different subsets of records. All you have to do is change the entries in the Criteria range. For example, suppose that having used the function @DSUM(A1..F13,4,A15..F16) to calculate the total sales for the East region, you now want 1-2-3 to calculate the total sales for the West region. To do this, you can simply replace the label 'East in cell D16 with the label 'West, and (if 1-2-3 is in the Manual recalculation mode) press the [Calc] key. Because you have changed the criterion, the function will operate on a different group of records and return a different result. In this case, 1-2-3 will add the Sales field entries for the records that have the Region field entry 'West (the records in rows 5, 8, and 11) and will return 861307.

The @DCOUNT Function

1-2-3's @DCOUNT function counts the nonblank entries in the specified field of the records in a data base that match the criterion you have defined. Unlike 1-2-3's other data base statistical functions, @DCOUNT can operate on fields that contain any type of entry—not just fields that contain values.

For example, suppose you want to determine how many of the sales in the data base shown in Figure 12-22 came from the East region. To calculate this statistic, enter the label 'East into cell D16 in the Criteria range. Then enter the function

@DCOUNT(A1..F13,3,A15..F16)

into any cell of the worksheet. The first argument of this function directs 1-2-3 to use the entries from the data base in the range A1..F13. The second argument, 3, instructs 1-2-3 to count the entries in the Region field. The third argument instructs 1-2-3 to use the entries only from records that meet the criteria specified in the range A15..F16. Because cell D16 contains the entry 'East, the function will operate only on those records with the State field entry *East*. For this reason, the function will return the value 3—the number of nonblank entries in the Region field of those records that have the Region field entry *East*.

You'll usually use @DCOUNT to count the number of records in a data base that match the criterion you specify—not just the nonblank entries in a specific field of those records. If you are using @DCOUNT in this way, it usually doesn't matter which field you ask the @DCOUNT function to operate on. As long as there are entries in every field of every record, the @DCOUNT function will return the same result no matter which field you ask it to count. For example, you could use any of the values 0, 1, 2, 3, 4, or 5 as the *field offset* argument in the example function since there are no blank fields in the data base.

If there are blank entries in some of the fields of a data base, you might want to ask @DCOUNT to count the entries in the same field you use to select records. For instance, the example function commands 1-2-3 to count the entries in the Region field and uses the entries in that same field to select the records to count. Counting the entries in the field you use to select records ensures that there will be a one-to-one relationship between the selected records and the count.

Of course, you can also use @DCOUNT to count the number of nonblank entries in a specific field. If you are using @DCOUNT in that way, the function must refer specifically to that field.

The @DAVG Function

1-2-3's @DAVG function calculates the average of the values in the specified field of the data base records that match the criterion you define. For example, suppose you want to calculate the average amount of the East region sales in the example data base. To calculate this statistic, first enter the label 'East into cell D16 in the Criteria range. Then enter the function

@DAVG(A1..F13,4,A15..F16)

into any cell of the worksheet. When you press [Enter], 1-2-3 will calculate this function and return the value 327744.33333—the average, or arithmetic mean, of the Sales field entries for those records that have the entry *'East* in the Region field—the records in rows 4, 10, and 13.

The @DMAX and @DMIN Functions

1-2-3's @DMAX and @DMIN functions return the highest and lowest values, respectively, from the specified field of the data base records that match the criterion you define. For example, suppose you want 1-2-3 to compute the largest and smallest values from the Sales field for those records with the Region field entry East. To calculate these statistics, first enter the label 'East into cell D16 of the Criteria range. Then, to determine the amount of the largest sale, enter the function @DMAX(A1..F13,4,A15..F16) into any cell of the worksheet. This function returns the value 410227—the largest Sales field entry for those records with the Region field entry East. To determine the amount of the smallest sale, enter the function @DMIN(A1..F13,4,A15..F16) into another cell. This function returns 235526—the smallest Sales field entry for those records with the Region field entry *East*.

The @DSTD and @DVAR Functions

1-2-3's @DSTD and @DVAR functions calculate the standard deviation and variance of the values in a specified field of the records in a data base that match the criterion you specify. As we explained in Chapter 5, the standard deviation and variance are measures of the dispersion of a set of values.

> **TIP: LOCATING THE MAX AND MIN VALUES**
>
> Although @DMAX and @DMIN do not tell you which records in the data base contain the maximum and minimum values in the specified field, you can use the results of these functions to locate those records yourself. To do this, first use the /Range Value command to copy the result of the @DMAX or @DMIN function to the appropriate cell of the Criteria range. Then use the /Data Query Find command to find the record that matches the criterion.
>
> For example, suppose you want to find out which record in the example data base contains the maximum East region sales field entry—410227. To begin, use the /Range Value command to copy the result of the @DMAX function into cell E16 of the Criteria range—the cell immediately below the field name Sales. This criterion will cause 1-2-3 to select those records with the Sales field entry 410227 when you issue a /Data Query command.
>
> After copying this entry, use the /Data Query Input command to define cells A1..F13 as the Input range, and the /Data Query Criteria command to define cells A15..F16 as the Criteria range. Then issue the /Data Query Find command. When you do this, 1-2-3 will highlight the record in row 4—the record that contains the maximum value in the Sales field.

For example, suppose you want 1-2-3 to calculate the standard deviation and variance of the entries in the Sales field for those records with the Region field entry East. To calculate these statistics, first enter the label 'East into cell D16 of the Criteria range. Then, to compute the standard deviation, enter the function @DSTD(A1..F13,4,A15..F16) into any cell. This function returns the value 71,652.854115—the standard deviation of the entries in the Sales field for those records with the Region field entry East. Then, to compute the variance, enter the function @DVAR(A1..F13,4,A15..F16) into any cell. This function returns the value 5,134,131,052.9—the variance of the entries in the Sales field for those records with the Region field entry East.

TIP: USING A DATA TABLE

1-2-3's / Data Table command makes it easy to calculate data base statistics for different sets of records in a data base. For example, suppose you want 1-2-3 to calculate the total sales for each of the regions in the example data base in Figure 12-22. To begin, you must set up a Criteria range. We'll use the range A15..F16 as the Criteria range in the example. If this range contains entries, you might want to erase them.

Now you need to set up a data table. To do this, enter the labels 'North, 'South, 'East, and 'West into cells B21 to B24 (actually, any four adjacent cells in a single column would do). Notice that this list contains all of the unique entries from the Region field of the data base. If you wanted to, you could use a / Data Query Unique command to create this list.

Next, enter the function @DSUM(A1..F13,4,A15..F16) into cell C20 (or the cell above and to the right of the first variable). This function is the Table formula for the data table. As you can see, this function refers to the Database range A1..F13 and to the Criteria range A15..F16.

Now you are ready to process the table. To do this, issue the / Data Table 1 command. In response to the prompt Enter Table range:, highlight the range B20..C24 and press [Enter]. Next, 1-2-3 will prompt you to define the Input cell for the data table. Since the entries in the Variable range are Region field entries, we'll use the cell under the field name Region in the Criteria range—cell D16—as the Input cell. When you process the data table, 1-2-3 will substitute the entries in the Variable range, one at time, into this cell.

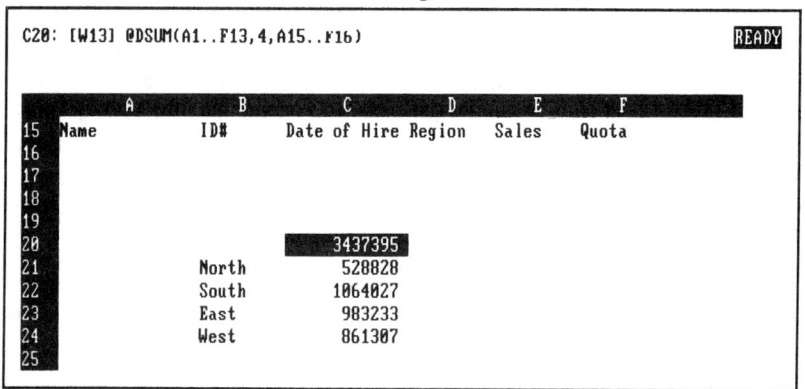

```
C20: [W13] @DSUM(A1..F13,4,A15..F16)                              READY

              A           B           C           D           E           F
    15   Name           ID#       Date of Hire  Region     Sales       Quota
    16
    17
    18
    19
    20                            3437395
    21                 North       520828
    22                 South      1064027
    23                 East        903233
    24                 West        861307
    25
```

FIGURE A: A data table

(Tip continued on next page.)

As soon as you press [Enter], 1-2-3 will process the table and present the results shown in Figure A. As you can see, 1-2-3 has processed the @DSUM function four times—once for each of the four criteria. For example, to produce the result shown in cell C21, 1-2-3 substituted the label 'North from cell B21 into cell D16 of the Criteria range. Consequently, 1-2-3 acted only upon the records with the label 'North in their Region field when it evaluated the @DSUM function. Because the Criteria range contained different entries during each calculation, the function returned a different result each time.

TIP: NAME THE RANGES

So far, we have used cell coordinates to refer to the Input and Criteria ranges in data base statistical functions. If you want to, however, you can assign names to your Input and Criteria ranges. To assign names to these ranges, just issue the / Range Name Create command, type the name, and point to the range you want to name. Be sure to include the entire data base (including the field names) in the one named range and the entire Criteria range in the other. Although you can use any names you want for these ranges, you might want to use the name INPUT for the data base (Input range) and the name CRIT for the Criteria range.

Once you have named these ranges, you can use the names in your data base statistical functions. For example, you could use the function *@DSUM(INPUT,4,CRIT)* to calculate the sum of the entries in the fourth field of the records in INPUT that meet the criteria contained in CRIT.

CONCLUSION

In this chapter, we have explored 1-2-3's third environment—the 1-2-3 data base manager. At the beginning of the chapter, we showed you how to create and edit a data base. Then we showed you how to sort a data base. Next, we showed you how to create criteria and how to use 1-2-3's four / Data Query commands—Find, Extract, Unique, and Delete—to query a data base. Finally, we demonstrated the use of 1-2-3's powerful data base statistical functions.

13

Macros

Macros are a special kind of computer program that work entirely within a 1-2-3 worksheet. In their simplest form, macros are just representations of keystrokes stored as labels in the cells of a worksheet. This kind of macro automates tasks that you normally would perform by pressing keys on the keyboard of your computer—making entries into cells, moving the cell pointer, and issuing commands from 1-2-3's menus.

In many ways, a macro is like the scroll of music that drives a player piano. Just as the scroll of music in a player piano is a recorded series of keystrokes for the piano, a macro is a recorded sequence of keystrokes and commands for 1-2-3. When you turn on a player piano, it reads and plays the notes stored on the scroll of music. When you run a macro, 1-2-3 reads and executes the keystrokes and commands stored in that macro. Although the keys on your computer's keyboard do not move during the execution of a macro, 1-2-3 performs the same actions that it would if you had pressed those keys yourself.

As you will see, macros add much power to 1-2-3. For one thing, 1-2-3 executes macros with amazing speed. Even if you are an exceptionally fast typist, you won't be able to type as fast as 1-2-3 can "type" the keystrokes in a macro. This means that you can use macros to speed up processes that must be repeated over and over, saving time. In addition, once you have removed all of the errors, or bugs, from a macro, 1-2-3 will always read and execute the instructions in that macro perfectly. This means that macros can be used to automate complex processes that must be performed correctly every time.

In addition to stored keystrokes, 1-2-3 macros also can contain a variety of special programming commands. These commands let you do things from within a macro that you can't do simply by pressing keys. For example, the {MenuBranch} and {MenuCall} commands let you set up custom menus; the {GetNumber} and {GetLabel} commands let you solicit input from the user of the macro; and the {For} command lets you set up counter-controlled loops. Collectively, these commands make up the Lotus Command Language (LCL). Although the LCL has many of the powers of stand-alone languages like Basic, C, and Pascal, it works entirely within a 1-2-3 worksheet.

In this chapter, we'll show you how to create and use simple macros. We'll cover macros that move the cell pointer, make entries in cells, and issue menu commands. We'll also show you how to debug a macro, and how to create auto-executing macros. We'll cover the LCL in Chapter 14.

Before you begin to work with macros, you should have a good working knowledge of 1-2-3. You should be familiar enough with the layout of 1-2-3's menus to feel comfortable with selecting commands by typing the first letter in their names, rather than by pointing and pressing [Enter]. Of course, you don't need to know everything about 1-2-3 before you begin to explore the world of macros. As long as you feel fairly comfortable with 1-2-3, you should have no trouble getting started with macros.

A SIMPLE EXAMPLE

So that you can begin to understand how macros work, let's create and run a simple macro. Suppose you are about to build a new spreadsheet in 1-2-3. In the course of building this spreadsheet, you'll have to enter the labels *Qtr1*, *Qtr2*, *Qtr3*, *Qtr4*, and *Total* into five adjacent cells in a row many times. So that you won't have to type these entries manually each time you want to enter them, you decide to create a macro that commands 1-2-3 to type them for you.

Creating the Macro

RELEASE ▶ 2.2 ◀

To create a macro, you enter the keystrokes you want 1-2-3 to "press" when the macro is run as a series of labels in consecutive cells in a column. ▶(In 1-2-3 Release 2.2, you can also create a macro by recording keystrokes. We'll show you how to do that in a few pages.)◀ To create the example macro, then, first enter the following labels into cells B5 through B14 of an otherwise empty worksheet:

B5: 'Qtr1	B10: '{Right}
B6: '{Right}	B11: 'Qtr4
B7: 'Qtr2	B12: '{Right}
B8: '{Right}	B13: 'Total
B9: 'Qtr3	B14: '~

After these labels have been entered, your worksheet will look like Figure 13-1.

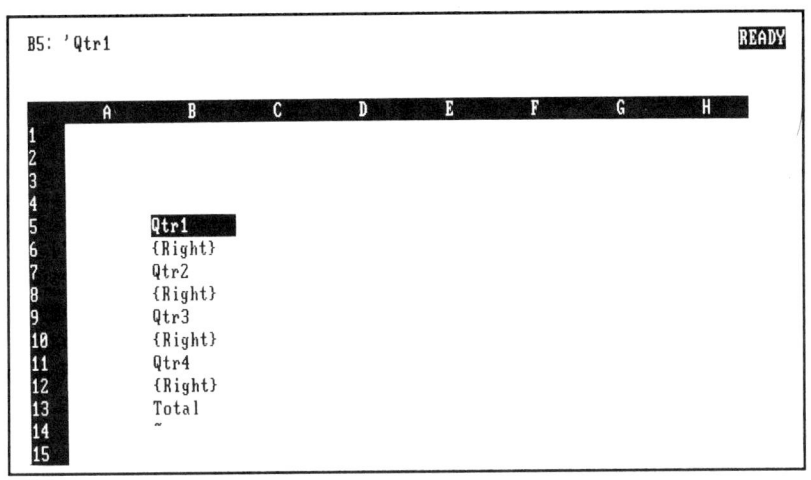

```
B5: 'Qtr1                                          READY

        A       B       C       D       E       F       G       H
1
2
3
4
5       Qtr1
6       {Right}
7       Qtr2
8       {Right}
9       Qtr3
10      {Right}
11      Qtr4
12      {Right}
13      Total
14      ~
15
```

FIGURE 13-1: A simple macro

Naming the Macro

Before you use a macro, you should give it a name, since naming a macro makes it easier to run the macro. To name a macro, you just assign a range name to the first cell of the macro. ▶In 1-2-3 Release 2.2, you can use any valid range name as a macro name. However, you will be able to run your macros more easily if you give them special names consisting of a backslash (\) and a single letter (such as \a, \k, or \c). In earlier releases of 1-2-3, you are limited to using backslash-letter names for macros.◀

RELEASE
▶ 2.2 ◀

To continue with our example, suppose you want to give your simple macro the name \a. To do this, move the cell pointer to cell B5, issue the / Range Name Create command, type \a, and press [Enter] twice. We'll discuss macro names in more detail in a few pages.

Running the Macro

Once you've named a macro, you're ready to run it. If you've given your macro a name that consist of a backslash followed by a letter, you can run it by pressing the [Alt] key and the letter that follows the backslash in the macro's name at the same time. When you press an [Alt]-letter combination, 1-2-3 will check to see if the current worksheet contains a macro with that name. If so, 1-2-3 will begin to execute the macro. Otherwise, 1-2-3 will just beep.

▶(In 1-2-3 Release 2.2, you can also run a macro by pressing the [Run] key ([Alt][F3]) and supplying the macro's name or address. We'll cover the [Run] key in a few pages.)◀

RELEASE
▶ 2.2 ◀

For example, suppose you want to use the example macro to enter these labels in the range B3..F3. To do this, move the cell pointer to cell B3 and press [Alt]a. As soon as you do this, 1-2-3 will begin "pressing" the keystrokes stored in the macro. You'll see the screen flicker quickly as 1-2-3 types, moves the cell pointer, and issues commands. (1-2-3 runs macros much too rapidly for you to see each individual keystroke.) While 1-2-3 is executing a macro, the message CMD will appear in inverse video at the bottom of the screen.

How It Works

Figure 13-2 shows the result of running the macro. As you can see, 1-2-3 has entered the labels 'Qtr1, 'Qtr2, 'Qtr3, 'Qtr4, and 'Total into cells B3, C3, D3, E3, and F3.

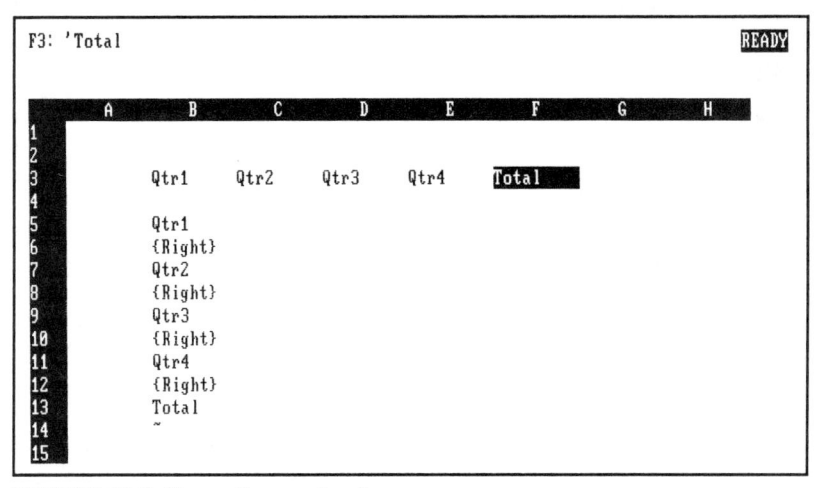

```
F3: 'Total                                                          READY


          A         B        C        D        E        F        G        H
   1
   2
   3             Qtr1      Qtr2     Qtr3     Qtr4    Total
   4
   5             Qtr1
   6             {Right}
   7             Qtr2
   8             {Right}
   9             Qtr3
  10             {Right}
  11             Qtr4
  12             {Right}
  13             Total
  14             ~
  15
```

FIGURE 13-2: Executing a simple macro

When you command 1-2-3 to execute a macro, it looks for the macro with the name you have specified in the current worksheet. If the macro you have specified exists, 1-2-3 will begin "pressing" the keys you have stored in that macro, beginning with those in the first cell in the macro. (The first cell of the macro is the cell to which you assigned the macro's name.) In the example, the macro starts in cell B5, to which you assigned the name \a. Because this cell contains the characters 'Qtr1, 1-2-3 types the characters Q, t, r, and 1. 1-2-3 displays these characters in the control panel as it types them, just as it would if you had typed the same characters from the keyboard. Because the cell pointer was in cell B3 when you ran the macro, these characters are entered into cell B3—just as they would be if you typed them from the keyboard.

Once 1-2-3 has read all the characters that are stored in the first cell in the macro, it looks to the cell immediately below that cell. If that cell contains a label, then the macro will continue by processing the characters in that label. If that cell is blank, or if it contains a value, then the macro will stop.

In this case, after 1-2-3 processes the keystrokes stored in cell B5, it looks to cell B6. Cell B6 contains the label '{Right}, which is the Lotus Command Language's representation of the ➡ key. This command instructs 1-2-3 to do the same things it would do if you were to press the ➡ key in the same situation. First, it moves the cell pointer one cell to the right to cell C3. At the same time, it locks in the characters that 1-2-3 just typed into cell B3.

Since {Right} is the only command in cell B6, 1-2-3 next looks to cell B7. The label 'Qtr2 in that cell commands 1-2-3 to type the characters *Q*, *t*, *r*, and *2*. 1-2-3 then looks to cell B8, where it finds another occurrence of the command *{Right}*. This command locks in the entry into cell C3 and moves the cell pointer to cell D3. As the macro continues, it will enter the label 'Qtr3 into cell D3, move the cell pointer to cell E3, enter the label 'Qtr4, move the cell pointer to cell F3, and type *Total*.

The entry ~ in cell B14 is the LCL's representation of the [Enter] key. This command locks the entry into cell F3. Then, since the cell immediately below cell B14 is blank, 1-2-3 ends the macro and returns to the READY mode.

MACRO BASICS

Now that you have learned how to create and run macros, we need to go back and cover a few fundamental concepts in a bit more depth. In this part of the chapter, we'll cover macro syntax (including macro representations of special keys), look at macro names in more detail, and explain the worksheet specificity of macros. We'll also show you how to document macros and offer some hints about where you should place your macros.

Macro Syntax

All macros have the same basic form as the simple example in Figure 13-1. As in this case, the instructions that make up a macro almost always will be labels that represent the keys you want 1-2-3 to "press" as it runs the macro. Also as in this example, the labels that make up a macro must be entered in consecutive cells in a column of the worksheet. We chose to enter this macro in column B; however, you can enter the labels that make up a macro in any column.

Labels and Label Prefixes

In almost all cases, the entries that make up your macros will be labels. (As we will explain in Chapter 14, the statements in a macro can also be formulas and functions that return string results.) The labels that make up a macro are just like any other labels, except that they represent keystrokes and commands. We'll sometimes call the labels that make up a macro instructions or statements. No matter what we call them, though, at heart they are simply labels.

Because every statement in a macro is a label, 1-2-3 always ignores the first label prefix it finds in any cell in a macro. For example, when 1-2-3 processed the label in cell B5, 'Qtr1, it didn't "type" the label prefix '. Similarly, when 1-2-3 processed the label in cell B6, '{Right}, it ignored the label prefix that precedes the instruction {Right}.

The way 1-2-3 treats label prefixes in macro instructions can be confusing. For example, we said that when 1-2-3 processed the label 'Qtr1, it ignored the label prefix '. However, the result of this instruction is the label *'Qtr1* in cell B3 of the worksheet. If 1-2-3 ignores the label prefix in cell B5, where does the prefix in cell B3 come from? Because the first character in the label in cell B5, *Q*, is a letter, 1-2-3 supplies a label prefix automatically as it "types" this character—just as it would if you typed *Qtr1* from the keyboard. In other words, because 1-2-3 is "typing" a label that begins with a letter, it will supply the label prefix automatically.

Now suppose you want 1-2-3 to enter a label that begins with a numerical character from within a macro. In that case, you'll need to put two label prefixes in front of the macro instruction that types the label. For example, suppose you want to change the macro so that it enters the labels *1st Qtr*, *2nd Qtr*, and so on, into the worksheet. To do this, you would change the entry in cell B5 to *"1st Qtr*. Notice that this label has two label prefixes. The first label prefix tells 1-2-3 that the entry in cell B5 is a label. 1-2-3 will ignore this prefix as it plays the macro. 1-2-3 will not ignore the second prefix, however. When it reads the instruction in cell B5, it "types" ', then *1*, *s*, *t*, and so on. The second label prefix is required because the first character in the label, *1*, is a numeral—just as it would be if you entered this kind of label from the keyboard.

What if you want 1-2-3 to enter a value into a cell from within a macro? In that case, you should place just a single label prefix in front of the macro instruction that types the value. For example, suppose you want to modify the macro so that it enters the values *1986*, *1987*, *1988*, and *1989* into adjacent cells of the worksheet. To do this, you would change the entry in cell B5 to *'1986*. The label prefix in this entry identifies the entry as a label. 1-2-3 will ignore this prefix as it plays the macro, then will "type" the characters *1*, *9*, *8*, and *6*. Since the first character 1-2-3 "types" is a number, this entry will be a value.

If you simply entered the value *1986* in cell B5, the macro would not work correctly. In fact, the macro would simply stop running as soon as it started. Remember: The entries that make up a macro must be labels or formulas that return strings—not values, formulas that return values, or blank cells. When 1-2-3 encounters a value or a blank cell as it is processing a macro, the macro ends.

Combining and Dividing Instructions

When we designed the simple macro in Figure 13-1, we chose to enter one instruction into each of ten cells. While it is often a good idea to "spread out" your macros in this way, you can combine two or more instructions in a single cell if you want to. For example, the macro in Figure 13-3 is functionally identical to the one in 13-1. As you can see, however, each line of this macro contains two instructions.

You can even stuff all of the instructions in a macro into a single cell. For example, the macro in Figure 13-4 is made up of only one label that contains all of the same instructions as the macros in Figures 13-1 and 13-3.

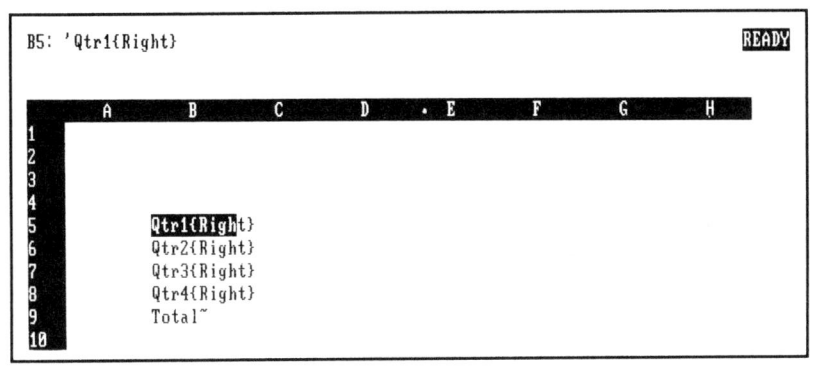

```
B5: 'Qtr1{Right}                                          READY

      A        B         C        D    . E        F        G        H
    1
    2
    3
    4
    5          Qtr1{Right}
    6          Qtr2{Right}
    7          Qtr3{Right}
    8          Qtr4{Right}
    9          Total~
   10
```
FIGURE 13-3: Two commands per line

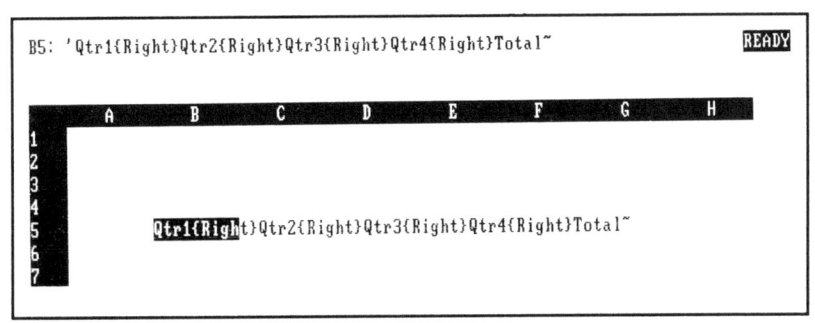

```
B5: 'Qtr1{Right}Qtr2{Right}Qtr3{Right}Qtr4{Right}Total~    READY

      A        B         C        D        E        F        G        H
    1
    2
    3
    4
    5          Qtr1{Right}Qtr2{Right}Qtr3{Right}Qtr4{Right}Total~
    6
    7
```
FIGURE 13-4: Ten commands per line

The number of commands that you can place in a single cell is limited only by the maximum length of a label in 1-2-3—240 characters. However, if you include too many commands on a single line, as we have in Figure 13-4, then your macros will be hard to decipher. On the other hand, if you include too few instructions per cell, as we have in Figure 13-1, your macros will occupy more space (and memory) than is necessary. In general, you'll want to strive for a balance between length and understandability when you design your own macros. For example, Figure 13-3 shows what is probably the best form for the example macro. It's easy to understand but doesn't take up too much room.

Special Key Representations

As you have already seen, 1-2-3 offers a special set of symbols you can use to represent "special" keys like [Esc], [Enter], [Goto], and ➡ in macros. You've already seen two of these key representations: {Right} and ~. The command {Right} represents the ➡ key, and the command ~ represents the [Enter] key.

Table 13-1 shows a complete listing of 1-2-3's special key representations. Notice that, in almost every case, the representation for a key is simply the name of that key enclosed in braces ({ }). For example, the macro representation for the [Esc] key is {Esc} and the macro representation for the [Home] key is {Home}. The macro representations for the ↑, ↓, ←, and → keys—{Up}, {Down}, {Left}, and {Right}—describe the action of those keys. Notice that the representations for the [Ctrl]→ and [Ctrl]← combinations are {BigRight} and {BigLeft}.

When 1-2-3 encounters one of these key representations in a macro, it "presses" the key represented by that symbol. For example, when 1-2-3 runs across the symbol ~ in a macro, it presses the [Enter] key. In the same way, when 1-2-3 encounters the representation {Calc} in a macro, it "presses" the [Calc] key and recalculates the worksheet.

Key	Representation	Key	Representation
↓	{Down} or {D}	[Enter]	~
↑	{Up} or {U}	[Help] ([F1])	{Help}
→	{Right} or {R}	[Edit] ([F2])	{Edit}
←	{Left} or {L}	[Name] ([F3])	{Name}
[Home]	{Home}	[Abs] ([F4])	{Abs}
[End]	{End}	[Goto] ([F5])	{Goto}
[Pg Up]	{PgUp}	[Window] ([F6])	{Window}
[Pg Dn]	{PgDn}	[Query] ([F7])	{Query}
[Ctrl]←	{BigLeft}	[Table] ([F8])	{Table}
[Ctrl]→	{BigRight}	[Calc] ([F9])	{Calc}
[Esc]	{Escape} or {Esc}	[Graph] ([F10])	{Graph}
[Backspace]	{BackSpace} or {BS}	[App1] ([Alt][F7])	{APP1}
[Break]	{Break}	[App2] ([Alt][F8])	{APP1}
[Del]	{Delete} or {Del}	[App3] ([Alt][F9])	{APP1}
/	/ or {Menu}	[App4] ([Alt][F10])	{APP1}

TABLE 13-1: Special key representations

Alternative Forms

Several of 1-2-3's special key representations have two alternative forms. For example, the →, ←, ↑, and ↓ keys can be represented in macros either by {Right}, {Left}, {Up}, and {Down}, or by {R}, {L}, {U}, and {D}. Similarly, the [Esc] key can be represented in macros by {Escape} or just {Esc}. Likewise, the [Backspace] key can be represented in macros by {Backspace} or just {BS}, and the [Del] key can be represented in macros by {Delete} or just {Del}. In most cases, you'll find it more convenient to use the abbreviated representation.

Arguments

You can include a numeric argument with any of 1-2-3's macro key representations (except ~ and /) to multiply its effect. For example, instead of using the statement

'{Down}{Down}{Down}{Down}

to move the cell pointer down four cells, you can use the statement {Down 4}. Similarly, the statement {Up 3} causes 1-2-3 to "press" the ↑ key three times, and the statement {Esc 3} causes 1-2-3 to "press" the [Esc] key three times.

Although you usually will use literal values as the arguments of special key representations, you also can use formulas, functions, or references that return values as arguments. If cell A1 contains the value 5, for example, the command {Right A1} will move the cell pointer five cells to the right. Similarly, if the cell named COUNT contains the value 2, the command {PgDn COUNT*2} will move the cell pointer down four screens.

Unrepresented Keys

Although 1-2-3 includes representations for most of the keys on your computer's keyboard, there are a few keys that cannot be represented in macros—they are [Alt], [Num Lock], [Caps Lock], [Prt Sc], and [Scroll Lock]. There is no way to ask 1-2-3 to "press" these keys from within a macro.

Capitalization

Table 13-1 presents 1-2-3's macro key representations in "proper" form; that is, the first letter of each word is capitalized, and the remaining letters are lower case. This is the form we prefer to use. 1-2-3 is not picky about capitalization, however. As long as the representation of a key is spelled correctly, begins with an opening brace ({), and ends with a closing brace (}), 1-2-3 will understand it, no matter what capitalization convention you choose to use.

Naming Macros

As we have said, before you use a macro, you should give it a name. To name a macro, you just assign a range name to the first cell of the macro. ►In 1-2-3 Release 2.2, you can use any valid range name as a macro name. However, if you want to be able to run a macro by pressing [Alt] and a single key, you'll have to give it a special name consisting of a backslash (\) and a single letter (such as \a, \k, or \c). (In earlier releases of 1-2-3, you were limited to using backslash-letter names for macros.) If you use another kind of name for a macro, you'll have to use the [Run] key ([Alt][F3]) to run the macro. For this reason, we almost always use backslash-letter names for our macros.◄

While we prefer to use backslash-letter names for macros, there are a couple of disadvantages to using this kind of name. Because there are only 26 letters in the alphabet, there can be only 26 macros with backslash-letter names in a given worksheet at any time. Of course, you can create more than 26 macros in the worksheet; however, only 26 of those can have backslash-letter names. ►If you need to create and use more than 26 macros in a single worksheet, and you are using 1-2-3 Release 2.2, you can give some of your macros other kinds of names. Of course, you'll have to use the [Run] key to run those macros.◄

There is one other way around this limitation. In Chapter 14 you'll learn how to make one macro run another macro. Because 1-2-3 does not require macros that are invoked by other macros to have \-letter names, there can be an unlimited number of this type of macro in any worksheet.

RELEASE
► 2.2 ◄

RELEASE
► 2.2 ◄

RELEASE
▶ 2.2 ◀

A second disadvantage to backslash-letter names is that they are not very descriptive. For instance, the name /f is not nearly as descriptive as the name FORMAT. ▶If it is important to you that your macro names be descriptive, you'll want to take advantage of 1-2-3 Release 2.2's ability to run a macro with any name. (In earlier releases of 1-2-3, you should try to give your macros descriptive names—to the extent that it is possible to do so when your universe of options includes just 26 alternatives.)◀

The \0 Macro

Every 1-2-3 worksheet can have one macro named \0. Giving this special name to a macro will cause 1-2-3 to run that macro whenever you retrieve the worksheet that contains the macro. However, you cannot invoke a \0 macro by pressing [Alt]0. We'll cover this special type of macro later in this chapter.

Using / Range Name Labels Right to Name Macros

To name the macro in Figure 13-1, we moved the cell pointer to cell B5, issued the / Range Name Create command, typed the name \a, and pressed [Enter] twice. However, we usually prefer to name our macros in a slightly different way. Typically, we enter the name that we want to assign to the macro as a label in the cell to the left of the first cell of that macro. Then we issue the / Range Name Labels Right command to assign that name to the first cell of the macro.

For example, suppose you want to use this technique to name the macro in Figure 13-3. To assign the name \a to this macro, first enter the label \a in cell A5, as shown in Figure 13-5. After entering this label, issue the / Range Name Labels Right command, point to cell A5 (the cell that contains the label), and press [Enter] to assign the range name \a to cell B5.

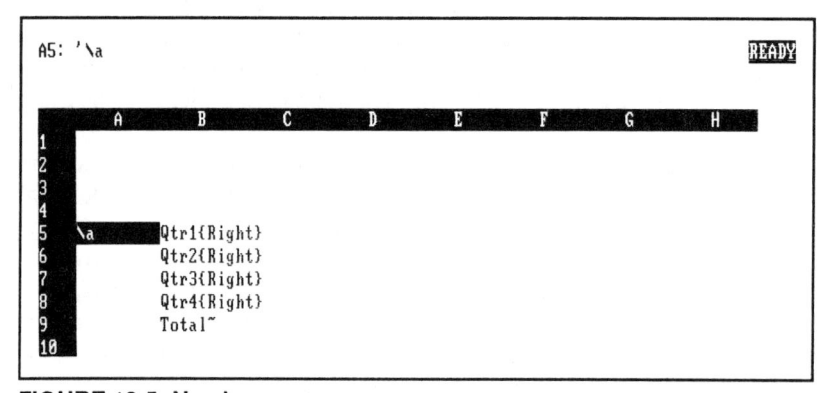

```
A5: '\a                                                       READY


          A         B         C         D         E         F         G         H
     1
     2
     3
     4
     5   \a        Qtr1{Right}
     6             Qtr2{Right}
     7             Qtr3{Right}
     8             Qtr4{Right}
     9             Total~
    10
```

FIGURE 13-5: Naming a macro

Important: the label in cell A5 does not have any effect on the execution of the macro. It does, however, serve to remind you of the macro's name. Without this reminder, it's easy to forget what name you have assigned to a macro.

When you enter the name of a macro into the worksheet, be sure to begin with a label prefix like ', ", or ^. Otherwise, 1-2-3 will interpret the \ in the macro name as a repeating label prefix, and will repeat the next character you type across the cell.

Naming the Whole Macro

Although it is only necessary to name the first cell of a macro, you can assign that name to the entire macro or to any range that has the first cell of the macro in its upper-left corner. No matter how many cells you name, 1-2-3 will execute the macro in exactly the same way. In almost all cases, however, you'll find it simpler just to name a macro's first cell.

Names Are Optional

▶In 1-2-3 Release 2.2 you do not have to name your macros. You can use the [Run] key ([Alt][F3]) to run a macro in 1-2-3 Release 2.2 whether it is named or not. While this new capability can come in handy in some situations, we recommend that you give a name—preferably a backslash-letter name—to each of your macros.◀

RELEASE
▶ 2.2 ◀

Running Macros

▶In 1-2-3 Release 2.2, there are two different ways to run macros. If you give your macros backslash-letter names, you can run them by pressing [Alt] and a single key. As we have said, we recommend that you use backslash-letter names so that you can use the [Alt] key to run your macros. (In earlier releases of 1-2-3, you didn't have a choice—you were required to use backslash-letter names.)

RELEASE
▶ 2.2 ◀

To invoke a macro that has an unconventional (nonbackslash) name (or no name at all), you must use the [Run] key ([Alt][F3]). (Of course, macros named with a backslash and a letter can be invoked in this way as well). When you press the [Run] key, 1-2-3 Release 2.2 displays the prompt *Select the macro to run:*, followed by a single-line list of range names. (If you press the [Name] key ([F3]), 1-2-3 will expand the list of range names to full-screen size.) To invoke a named macro, simply choose its name from the list or type the name and press [Enter]. To invoke an unnamed macro, simply type the address of the cell that contains its first command to the right of the *Select macro to run:* prompt, then press [Enter].◀

Stopping Macros

As we have said, when you invoke a macro, 1-2-3 first reads and executes the instructions stored in the first cell of the macro. After it has finished with those instructions, it begins processing the instructions in the cell immediately below the first cell in the macro. 1-2-3 will continue executing the macro in this way until it encounters a blank cell, a cell that contains a value, a {Quit} command, an error, or until you press [Ctrl][Break].

First, 1-2-3 will stop executing a macro as soon as it encounters a blank cell or a cell that contains a value. In the case of the macro in Figure 13-1, for example, 1-2-3 stops processing the macro and returns to the READY mode when it comes to cell B15, which is blank.

Second, 1-2-3 will stop executing a macro when it encounters a {Quit} command or an /xq command in the macro. {Quit} and /xq are two forms of an LCL command that instructs 1-2-3 to stop executing a macro. Although a blank cell and a {Quit} command have the same effect on a macro, {Quit} has one advantage: you can use it in the same cell as other macro commands. We'll use the {Quit} and /xq commands in several example macros in Chapter 14.

Third, 1-2-3 will stop executing a macro if you press [Ctrl][Break] while the macro is running. This "emergency stop" combination is most often used to cancel the execution of a macro that is not doing what you want it to do or a macro that you invoked accidentally. When you press this combination, 1-2-3 will beep, flash ERROR in the Mode indicator, display the word *Break* in the lower-left corner of the screen, and erase the CMD indicator. Pressing [Esc] at this point returns 1-2-3 to the READY mode.

Of course, any changes that the macro has made to the worksheet prior to your pressing [Ctrl][Break] will remain. [Crtl][Break] does not undo the effects of a macro; it just keeps the macro from doing anything else.

Finally, 1-2-3 will stop executing a macro if it encounters a command that it does not recognize or that it cannot perform. When this happens, 1-2-3 will beep, flash ERROR in the Mode indicator, and present a brief explanation of the cause and location of the error at the bottom of the screen. At that point, you can press [Esc] to clear the error and return to the READY mode, and edit the macro to correct the error. We'll show you how to edit a macro at the end of this chapter.

TIP: PAUSING MACROS

Pressing [Ctrl][Break] while a macro is running stops the macro cold. Once you stop a macro with [Ctrl][Break], there is no way to restart it. All you can do is press [Alt] and the appropriate letter key to start the macro over from the beginning.

If you want to stop a macro temporarily, but want to be able to restart it, you can press the [Pause] key ([Ctrl][Num Lock] on older computers). If you press [Pause] or [Ctrl][Num Lock] while a macro is running, 1-2-3 suspends the execution of that macro temporarily. As soon as you press any other key, 1-2-3 will resume executing the macro at the point where it left off. You can use this technique as many times as you wish during the execution of any macro.

Macros Are Worksheet Specific

As you have learned, the instructions that make up a macro are simply labels in the cells of a worksheet. Similarly, the name you assign to a macro is simply a range name in the current worksheet. While these may seem like trivial concepts, they have some important implications for the way you work with macros.

▶1-2-3 Release 2.2 offers an add-in, the Macro Library Manager (MLM), that lets you use macros that do not exist in the current worksheet. With the MLM, you create a macro in a worksheet, then export it from the worksheet into a macro library that is accessible to all worksheets. Once a macro has been handed over to the MLM, it can be run from any worksheet.

RELEASE
▶ 2.2 ◀

The MLM allows you to work around many of the issues we are about to explain, since it allows you to remove your macros from your worksheets. However, if you are like many users, you won't use the MLM all that often, and most of your macros will continue to exist in worksheets. For this reason, what follows is still important. As you read it, though, remember that the MLM offers solutions to most of these problems. We'll cover the MLM in Chapter 16.◀

Saving Macros

Like all other labels, the labels that make up a macro are saved when you save the worksheet that contains them. For this reason, all you have to do to save a macro is save the worksheet that contains the macro. When you use the / File Save command to save the worksheet that contains a macro, you save that macro. When you retrieve a worksheet that contains a macro, you also retrieve the macro.

There may be times when you'll want to save a macro independently from the worksheet in which it was created. If you need to do this, just issue the / File Xtract Formulas command, specify a name for the file into which you want to save the macro, and then select the range of cells that contains the macro as the Extract range. When you press [Enter], 1-2-3 will extract the labels that make up the macro into a separate worksheet file.

▶(Remember that 1-2-3 Release 2.2's Macro Library Manager lets you export macros from worksheets into macro libraries. As we'll explain in Chapter 16, storing a macro in a library eliminates the need to "save" it as a part of the current worksheet.)◀

RELEASE
▶ 2.2 ◀

Cut-and-Paste Commands and Macros

Because macros exist within the cells of a worksheet, they are affected by cut-and-paste commands such as / Move, / Copy, / Worksheet Delete, / Worksheet Insert, and / Range Erase. On the plus side, this means that you can use the / Move command to move a macro from one place to another in a worksheet and can use the / Copy command to make a copy of a macro or a portion of a macro.

On the minus side, this means that you can do all kinds of damage to your macros with the / Worksheet Delete, / Worksheet Insert, and / Range Erase commands. For example, if you delete a row that contains one of the labels that make up a macro, then you will delete that label and foul up the macro. If you use the / Worksheet Delete Column command to delete the column that contains a macro, you'll delete the entire macro. Similarly, if you use the / Worksheet Insert Row command to insert a row in the middle of a macro, you'll damage the macro. Since 1-2-3 will stop processing a macro when it comes to a blank cell, inserting a row in the middle of a macro will cause 1-2-3 to stop running the macro prematurely. Of course, using the / Range Erase command to erase a portion of a macro will also destroy the macro.

You also must be careful about issuing commands like / Worksheet Erase and / File Retrieve, which erase the entire worksheet. If you use either of these commands to erase a worksheet that contains macros, and you have not saved those macros, they will be destroyed when the worksheet is erased.

Running Macros

When you press an [Alt]-letter combination to invoke a macro, 1-2-3 looks for the macro with the name you have specified in the current worksheet. If 1-2-3 finds the macro in the current worksheet, it will begin to execute the macro. If 1-2-3 does not find the macro, it will just beep. 1-2-3 will not look in other worksheets for the macro you have named.

In other words, if you plan to use a macro in a given worksheet, you must create the macro in that worksheet—even if it already exists in another worksheet. If you have created a macro that you plan to use in several worksheets, you'll need to recreate it in each of those worksheets.

RELEASE 2.2 ▶(In 1-2-3 Release 2.2, you can get around this limitation by using the Macro Library Manager, which lets you use macros that are stored in macro libraries, independent of any one worksheet. We'll cover the MLM in Appendix 4.)◀

You can use the / File Combine command to transfer macros from one worksheet to another. To transfer a macro, first use the / File Save command to save the worksheet containing the macro you want to transfer, then use the / File Retrieve command to load the worksheet into which you want to move the macro. When that worksheet is loaded, use the / File Combine Copy Named/Specified-Range command to combine the range of cells that contains the macro you want to transfer into the new worksheet.

Because 1-2-3 cannot invoke macros that exist in any worksheet but the current worksheet, you won't run into any problems if you use the same name for macros in different worksheets. In fact, since the number of backslash-letter macro names is limited, it is likely that you will use the same name for different macros in different worksheets. For example, the macro named /a in one worksheet may type a series of month labels, while the macro named /a in another worksheet may draw a graph. No matter how many worksheets contain a macro with the same name, 1-2-3 always will execute the one that is stored in the current worksheet.

TIP: WHERE IS THE CELL POINTER?

When 1-2-3 executes a macro, it reads and performs the commands in the first cell of that macro, then the second cell, and so forth. It is important that you understand that the cell pointer does not "step down" through the cells of the macro as 1-2-3 reads the commands in those cells. The position of the cell pointer is completely independent of the location of the macro.

For example, before you invoked the macro in Figure 13-1, you moved the cell pointer to cell B3. When you pressed [Alt]a to invoke the macro, 1-2-3 read the instruction in the first cell of the macro—cell B5. However, the cell pointer did not move from its location in cell B3. As a result, 1-2-3 typed the characters Q, t, r, and I into cell B3. As you can see, the location of the instruction and the location of the cell pointer are totally unrelated.

Of course, you can include instructions in your macros that move the cell pointer. For example, after 1-2-3 had exhausted the instructions in cell B5, it looked at cell B6 and executed the instruction stored there. This command, {Right}, caused the cell pointer to move to cell C3. Even though the instruction in cell B6 affects the position of the cell pointer, however, the location of that instruction is completely independent of the location of the cell pointer.

Documenting Macros

As your macros become longer and more complex, it will become harder for you to remember exactly what they do and how they work—especially when you haven't looked at them in weeks or months. So that you don't waste a lot of time, you should get into the habit of including explanatory comments in the cells adjacent to your macros.

Typically, you'll enter your comments into a column of cells to the right of the column that contains the macro. For example, Figure 13-6 shows an annotated version of the macro originally in Figure 13-5. As you can see, we have entered labels into the cells in the range D5..D9 that explain the commands in the range B5..B9. For example, the entry in cell D5, *Types Qtr1, moves CP right*, describes the instructions in cell B5. These explanatory entries are not an executable part of the macro; they merely help to remind you what the macro does or how it works.

Although you probably will not bother to document simple macros like this one, you should use this technique to document macros that are long and/or complex. You'll begin to understand how important these comments are when you begin to work with the LCL.

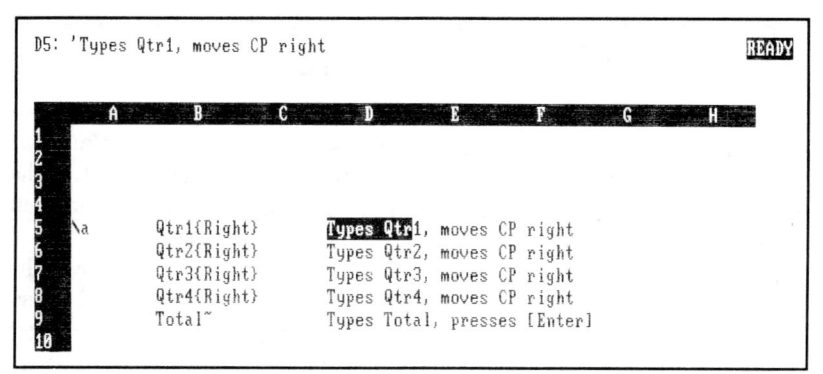

```
D5: 'Types Qtr1, moves CP right                                    READY

         A         B         C         D         E         F         G         H
   1
   2
   3
   4
   5    \a        Qtr1{Right}         Types Qtr1, moves CP right
   6              Qtr2{Right}         Types Qtr2, moves CP right
   7              Qtr3{Right}         Types Qtr3, moves CP right
   8              Qtr4{Right}         Types Qtr4, moves CP right
   9              Total~              Types Total, presses [Enter]
  10
```

FIGURE 13-6: An annotated macro

Where to Place Macros

Because macros are really nothing more than a series of label entries, you can place them anywhere in the worksheet that you wish. Although we positioned the macro in Figure 13-1 into the range B5..B14, for example, we could have placed it into the range A1..A10, B1..B10, A1000..A1010, AA1..AA10, or any other ten-cell columnar range.

Typically, you'll want to put your macros in a part of the worksheet that is unlikely to be affected when you insert and delete rows and columns. Otherwise, you might accidentally delete a command or two from the macro when you delete a row, or add an unwanted blank cell in the middle of a macro when you insert a row. Even worse, you might delete an entire macro when you delete a column.

We prefer to position our macros in columns A, B, and C below the "working area" of the worksheet. Placing the macros there makes them easy to find, and since we rarely delete columns A, B, or C, this eliminates problems with the / Worksheet Delete command. Other experts recommend placing your macros far out to the right of the active portion of the worksheet. We don't like this approach because it makes the macros harder to find and exposes them to the problems caused by the / Worksheet Insert Rows command. Still others believe that macros should be placed both below and to the right of the working area, or above and to the left of the working area.

RECORDING MACROS

RELEASE ► 2.2 ◄ ►1-2-3 Release 2.2 offers a new command, / Worksheet Learn, that gives it the ability to record macros. (To record macros in Releases 2 and 2.01 of 1-2-3, you had to use the LEARN.APP add-in application.) This new ability means that you no longer have to create macros by typing. Instead, you can ask 1-2-3 to create a macro by recording your keystrokes.

Before you begin recording a macro, you must tell 1-2-3 Release 2.2 where to place the macro. To do this, issue the / Worksheet Learn Range command, highlight a range that includes two or more cells in a single column, and press [Enter]. The range you select should be large enough to accommodate all of the keystrokes you want 1-2-3 to record All of the cells in the range should be blank; if they are not, 1-2-3 will begin recording in the cell below the last one that contains an entry, rather than at the beginning of that range.

Once you have selected a learn range, you can record your keystrokes. Before you begin recording, however, you should make sure that the cell pointer is properly positioned and that the worksheet is set up correctly to perform the task you are about to record. If you wait until after you begin recording to set up your worksheet, then your macro will include extra commands that really aren't needed.

To begin recording, press the [Learn] key ([Alt][F5]). When you press this key, 1-2-3 will display the indicator LEARN at the bottom of the screen. While this indicator is visible, 1-2-3 will record the macro representations of what ever keys you press. Of course, 1-2-3 will also perform whatever actions those keystrokes normally command it to do. For example, if you press the ↓ key, 1-2-3 Release 2.2 will enter {D} into the Learn range, as well as moving the cell pointer down one cell.

Once 1-2-3 starts recording your keystrokes, it will continue until one of two things happens: it reaches the end of the Learn range, or you press the [Learn] key. In the first case, you'll have to redefine or expand the Learn range before you can continue recording. in the second case, you can resume recording simply by pressing the [Learn] key again.

An Example

Let's use the recorder to recreate the simple macro shown in Figure 13-1 in a blank worksheet. To begin, issue the / Worksheet Learn Range command, highlight the range B5..B14, and press [Enter]. Now, move the cursor to cell B3 and press the [Learn] key ([Alt][F5]) to begin recording. When you press this key, 1-2-3 will display the indicator LEARN at the bottom of the screen. Now, type Qtr1, press →, type Qtr2, press →, type Qtr3, press →, type Qtr4, press →, type Total, and press [Enter]. When you finished, press [Learn] again to stop recording. Figure 13-7 shows the worksheet after you have recorded the macro.

The Cancel and Erase Options

The / Worksheet Learn command offers two options that let you erase and reset the record range. The / Worksheet Learn Erase command erases the Learn range. Be careful! This command will erase all of the recorded keystrokes in the Learn range, destroying your recorded macro in the process. For this reason, you'll usually want to copy your recorded macro to another part of the worksheet before you use this command to erase the Learn range.

The / Worksheet Learn Cancel command simply cancels the existing Learn range setting. This command does not erase the Learn range—it just causes 1-2-3 to "forget" the Learn range you have defined. You'll have to use the / Worksheet Learn Range command to redefine the Learn range before you can record again.

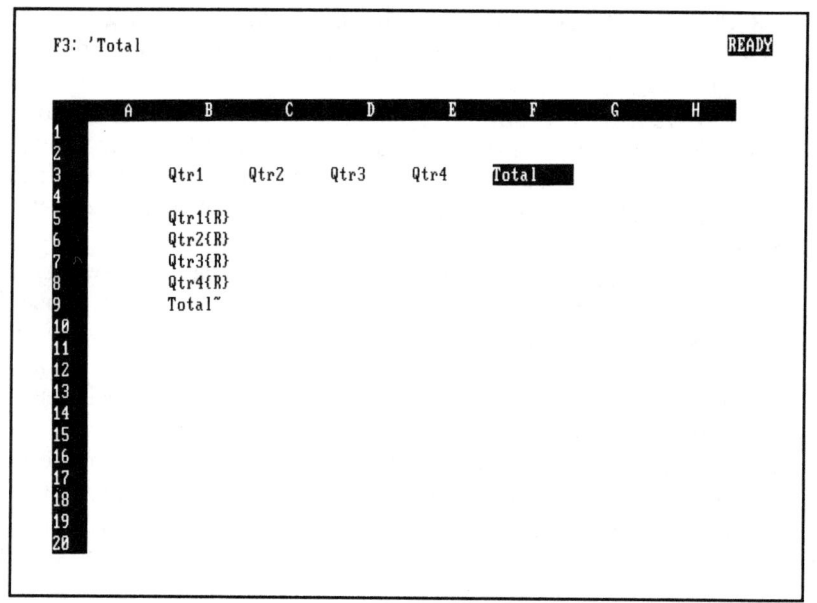

```
F3: 'Total                                                           READY

      A        B        C        D        E        F        G        H
 1
 2
 3           Qtr1     Qtr2     Qtr3     Qtr4     Total
 4
 5           Qtr1{R}
 6           Qtr2{R}
 7           Qtr3{R}
 8           Qtr4{R}
 9           Total~
10
11
12
13
14
15
16
17
18
19
20
```

FIGURE 13-7: Recording macros

Notes

When you finish recording a macro, you can name the first cell of your macro and execute it. In most cases, however, you will want to modify the macro you have recorded in some way. You may want to add some Lotus Command Language commands to the macro, or you may want to use the / Copy command to incorporate what you recorded into another macro.

You may also need to edit the recorded macro to remove the record of any typos you made while you were recording. The recorder is very literal—it records the mistakes you make as well as the keystrokes you mean to type.

The [Learn] key is a toggle switch. If you wish, you can use press [Learn] to suspend recording for a moment in the middle of recording a macro—to go "off the record"—then press it again to turn recording back on. When 1-2-3 resumes recording, it will begin storing keystrokes in the first cell under the last cell in the record range that contains an entry.◄

USING MENU COMMANDS IN MACROS

So far, you've learned how to create macros that move the cell pointer from cell to cell, make entries, and "press" 1-2-3's special function keys. In addition to doing these things, macros can also issue 1-2-3 commands as they run. In this section, we'll show you how to create macros that issue 1-2-3 commands.

An Example

Suppose that you are creating a brand new model in 1-2-3. As you create the model, you will be assigning range names to many cells and ranges. So that you won't have to issue the /Range Name Create command each time you want to define a range name, you decide to create a simple macro that issues this command for you.

Figure 13-8 shows a simple macro that will do the trick. As you can see, this macro includes only one statement, the simple label

'/rnc

To create this macro, we entered this label in cell B100 of a worksheet. Then we entered the label \n in cell A100 (the cell immediately to the left of the first cell in the macro), and then used the / Range Name Labels Right command to assign the name \n to cell B100.

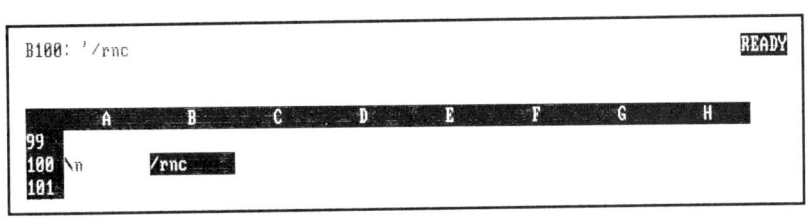

```
B100: '/rnc                                              READY


        A       B       C       D       E       F       G       H
  99
 100   \n      /rnc
 101
```

FIGURE 13-8: A simple command macro

Notice that the keystrokes stored in the macro in cell B100 are exactly the same keystrokes you would type to issue the / Range Name Create command: /, r, n, and c. When 1-2-3 executes this macro, it simply reads and presses the keystrokes stored in the macro—just as it would when it executes any other macro. The first character in the label, /, causes 1-2-3 to "press" the slash key (/), bringing the main 1-2-3 menu into view. The next character, r, causes 1-2-3 to choose the Range command from the main menu. The next keystroke, n, causes 1-2-3 to select the Name option from the Range menu, and the last keystroke, c, causes it to choose the Create option from the Range Name menu, bringing the prompt *Enter name:* into view in the control panel.

After 1-2-3 reads and presses all of the keystrokes stored in cell B100, it checks to see if there is another instruction in cell B101. Since that cell is blank, the macro stops. Once the macro is completed, all you have to do to define a new range name is type a new name and specify the range to which you want the name to apply.

In effect, the macro condenses the four-keystroke command / Range Name Create into a two-keystroke sequence: [Alt]n. Instead of having to issue the / Range Name Create command each time you want to name a range, all you have to do is press [Alt]n, type the name you want to create, and specify the range to which the name applies. If you have to define 50 range names, this macro will save you 100 keystrokes—not too bad for a macro that might take all of 15 seconds to create.

This macro is an example of what we call an "open ended" macro—a macro that begins a task that it does not finish. Instead of actually assigning a name to a range, this macro simply automates the "dumb" part of that job—pressing the /, r, n, and c keys. Then it stops, allowing you to do the "smart" part of the job—defining the name and range.

Another Example

Let's consider another example of using 1-2-3 commands in macros. Suppose you are creating a new worksheet, like the one in Figure 13-9. In the course of building this worksheet, you will frequently assign the Currency format with zero decimal places to a cell that contains a formula, and then copy that formula into the 11 cells to the right of the cell that contains the formula. Rather than repeat these steps, you decide to write a macro that performs them automatically.

```
C9: +C8*$B9                                                    READY

         A          B         C         D         E         F         G
1      ================================================================
2      XYZ CORP. FINANCIAL PLAN
3      ================================================================
4                  Unit
5                  Price    Jan       Feb       Mar       Apr       May
6                          ------    ------    ------    ------    ------
7      Widgets
8        Units              1000      1100      1300      1350      1450
9        Dollars  $24.95   24950
10     Wombats
11       Units               500       500       500       500       500
12       Dollars  $60.00
13     Woofers
14       Units               750       800       850       900       950
15       Dollars  $70.00
16     Zithers
17       Units              1200      1100      1000       900       900
18       Dollars  $22.95
19
20
```

FIGURE 13-9: A sample worksheet

Figure 13-10 shows our version of this macro. This macro includes two statements. The first of these,

'/rfc0~~

causes 1-2-3 to issue the / Range Format command, choose the Currency option, specify 0 decimal places, and assign that format to the current cell only. The second statement

'/c~{Right}.{Right 10}~

causes 1-2-3 to issue the / Copy command, select the current cell as the FROM range, define the TO range by pointing one cell to the right, pressing period (.), and pointing ten cells to the right, and pressing [Enter].

```
B102: '/rfc0~~                                          READY

         A         B         C         D       E       F       G
 99
100  \n            /rnc
101
102  \c            /rfc0~~
103            /c~{Right}.{Right 10}~
104
```

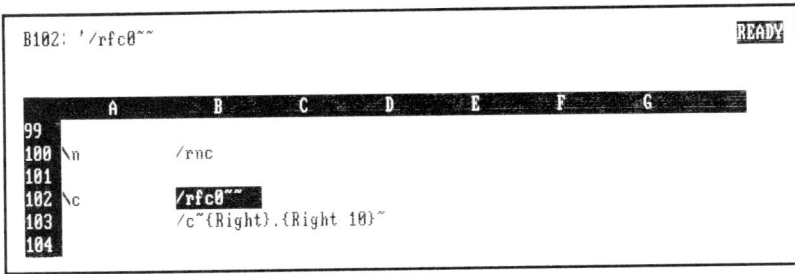

FIGURE 13-10: A command macro

To create this macro, we entered these labels in cells B102 and B103 of the worksheet in Figure 13-9 (we assumed that this macro and the previous one exist in the same worksheet). Then we entered the label \c in cell A102 (the cell immediately to the left of the first cell in the macro), and then used the /Range Name Labels Right command to assign the name \c to cell B102.

To see how this macro works, suppose we have just entered a formula into cell C9 in Figure 13-9. Now we want to format this cell and then copy the formula and the format from cell C9 to the range D9..N9. To do this, we simply press [Alt]c. Immediately, the macro will format cell C9, then copy the format and the formula into the range D9..N9. Figure 13-11 shows the resulting worksheet.

```
C9: (C0) +C8*$B9                                        READY

         A         B         C         D       E       F       G
 1   ================================================================
 2   XYZ CORP. FINANCIAL PLAN
 3   ================================================================
 4              Unit
 5              Price    Jan      Feb      Mar     Apr     May
 6              ------   ------   ------   ------  ------  ------
 7   Widgets
 8     Units             1000     1100     1300    1350    1450
 9     Dollars  $24.95   $24,950  $27,445  $32,435 $33,683 $36,178
10   Wombats
11     Units             500      500      500     500     500
12     Dollars  $60.00
13   Woofers
14     Units             750      800      850     900     950
15     Dollars  $70.00
16   Zithers
17     Units             1200     1100     1000    900     900
18     Dollars  $22.95
19
20
```

FIGURE 13-11: The results of a macro

Yet Another Example

As you learned in Chapter 8, in 1-2-3 only one set of Print settings is "active" at any time. If you use different Print settings to print different parts of a worksheet, you must redefine those settings each time you print. To save yourself the trouble and time of redefining these settings manually, you can create a macro that defines them for you. That way, you can define the settings for a report and then print it just by running a simple macro.

For example, suppose you want to create a macro that prints the report in Figure 13-13 from the worksheet in Figure 13-12 (this figure shows only a portion of the entire 88-row by 12-column worksheet). The Print range for this report is A5..L88. Rows 1-4 are Border rows. The report includes a header which prints the current date in the top-left corner of each page and a footer which prints the word *Page* followed by the current page number centered at the bottom of each page. It uses the default Page-Length setting of 66 lines per page, and the default left, top and bottom margins of 4, 2, and 2, respectively. Because the report will be printed on standard computer paper, however, the right margin is set to 132.

```
A1: [W21]                                                              READY


              A             B        C        D        E        F
   1                   =====A SAMPLE COMPANY: 10-YEAR BUSINESS PLAN=====
   2
   3                         1986     1987     1988     1989     1990
   4                        ------   ------   ------   ------   ------
   5      SALES
   6        Product 1      $30,800  $72,630  $53,309  $21,440  $28,452
   7        Product 2       $1,178   $6,195     $950
   8        Product 3      $13,680   $5,688   $2,274   $2,000   $2,000
   9        Product 4      $88,684 $107,996  $92,819 $112,125  $74,750
  10        Product 5      $18,598  $11,030   $3,572   $7,475   $3,738
  11        Product 6       $6,057   $2,451     $948   $2,451   $2,451
  12        Product 7                        $112,301 $15,629  $22,425  $59,800
  13        Product 8                                          $59,800  $29,900
  14        Product 9                                                   $29,950
  15        Product 10
  16        Product 11
  17        Product 12
  18        Product 13
  19        Product 14
  20        Product 15
```

FIGURE 13-12: A sample worksheet

Figure 13-14 shows a macro that will control this printing process. To create this macro, we first entered the labels shown in Figure 13-14 into the range B100..B106 of the worksheet in Figure 13-12. (Of course, we could have entered these labels into any seven blank cells in one column in the worksheet.) Next, we entered the label \p into cell A100 and used the /Range Name Labels Right command to assign the name \p to cell B100—the first cell of the macro.

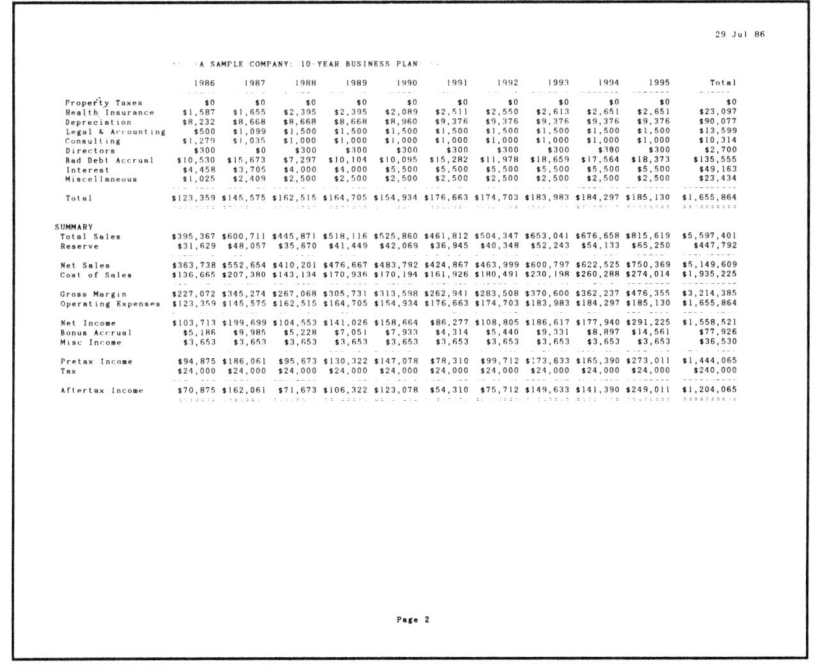

FIGURE 13-13: A sample report

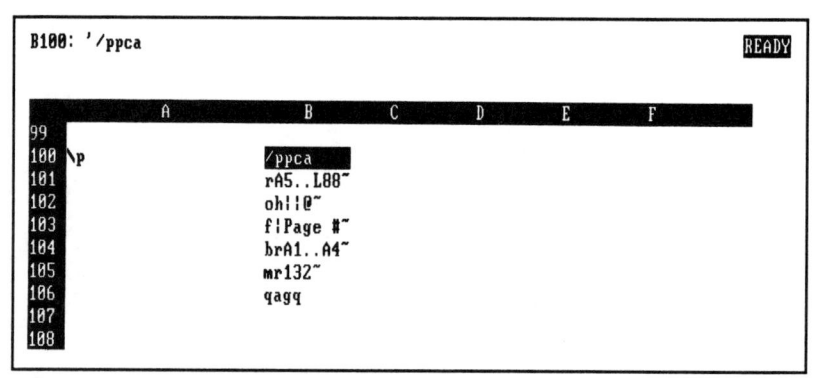

```
B100: '/ppca                                                    READY

            A           B           C           D           E           F
  99
 100  \p              /ppca
 101                  rA5..L88~
 102                  oh||@~
 103                  f|Page #~
 104                  brA1..A4~
 105                  mr132~
 106                  qagq
 107
 108
```

FIGURE 13-14: The printing macro

When 1-2-3 executes this macro, it first "presses" the / key, which reveals the main 1-2-3 menu. Next, 1-2-3 "types" a *p*, which selects the Print option from the main menu and reveals the Print submenu. Then it "types" another *p*, which selects the Printer option from the Print submenu, then a *c*, which selects the Clear option from the Print Printer menu, and then an *a*, which chooses the All option from the Print Printer Clear menu. This command resets all of the Print settings to their defaults, clearing any Print settings that you specified for an earlier printing of the worksheet.

Because this command leaves 1-2-3 in the Print Printer menu, the next statement, '*rA5..L88~*, instructs 1-2-3 to choose the Range option, type A5..L88, and press [Enter]. This command specifies the range A5..L88 as the Print range.

The next four statements in the macro set the header, footer, borders, and right margin. Because the instruction in cell B101 leaves 1-2-3 in the main Print menu, the statement '*oh||@~* causes 1-2-3 to issue the Options Header command, type ||@—the symbols necessary to produce a right-aligned date header—and press [Enter] to lock in that selection. This command leaves 1-2-3 in the Print Options menu.

The next statement in the macro, '*f|Page #~*, chooses the Footer option from the Options menu and types |Page #—the character sequence required to produce a centered footer—and press [Enter], to lock it in that footer. The statement in cell B104, '*brA1..A4~*, then commands 1-2-3 to choose Borders from the Print Options menu, select the Rows option, type A1..A4, and then press [Enter], specifying rows 1-4 as the Border rows for the report. Finally, the statement, '*mr132~*, instructs 1-2-3 to choose Margins Right from the Print Options menu, type 132, and then press [Enter] to lock in that Right Margin setting.

The final statement in the macro, '*qagq*, commands 1-2-3 to print the worksheet. The *q* selects Quit from the Print Options menu, returning 1-2-3 to the main Print menu. The *a* selects the Align option, and the *g* commands 1-2-3 to print the report. Once 1-2-3 has printed the report, the final *q* chooses Quit from the Print menu, which returns 1-2-3 to the READY mode.

Notes

As you can see, issuing 1-2-3 commands from within macros is very simple. All you have to do is include in the macro the keystrokes 1-2-3 should press to issue the command. For example, to ask 1-2-3 to issue the / Print Printer Clear All command from within a macro, we simply created the macro statement *'/ppca*. As 1-2-3 "types" the keystrokes represented by this statement, it issues the / Print Printer Clear All command—just as it would if you typed these keystrokes from the keyboard.

You can issue any 1-2-3 command from within a macro. (As you'll see in several pages, however, there are a few commands you probably will not want to include in macros.) You can use macros that include commands to automate processes that must be performed perfectly every time, or to issue commands that must be repeated frequently. For example, you might want to write a macro that automates the process of combining one or more worksheets into another worksheet, or that automates the process of extracting a range from a worksheet. Similarly, you can use this sort of macro to save keystrokes in your data base and graphics applications.

Conventions

Notice that we've used lower-case letters to represent the names of 1-2-3 commands in our macros. Like our preference for capitalizing the first letter of special key representations, this use of lower case is simply a convention we like to use. 1-2-3 does not care whether you use upper- or lower-case letters and will allow you to use any combination of upper- and lower-case letters in a macro statement. For example, the statement

    '/RNCTEMP~~

does the same thing as the statement

    '/rncTEMP~~.

We find the second form to be significantly easier to read and understand, however, so we recommend it.

Pointing to Menu Commands

In the macros in Figures 13-8, 13-10, and 13-14, we instructed 1-2-3 to choose menu items by typing the first letters of their names. To choose Range from the Main menu, for example, we used the letter r. To choose Name from the Range menu, we used the letter n, and so forth.

TIP: USE RANGE NAMES, NOT CELL REFERENCES

In the macro in Figure 13-14, we used the range reference A5..L88 to define the Print range. As a rule, however, we would have been much better off assigning a name, like PRINT, to this range, and then using that name in the macro instead of the range reference. Here's why: As you have learned, the statements that make up a macro are labels. Like any other labels, these labels will not change to reflect the insertion or deletion of rows or columns or the moving of ranges. This can lead to problems.

For example, suppose that after you had written the macro in Figure 13-14 you decided to add three new rows to the worksheet somewhere between row 1 and row 88. The addition of these new rows changes the range you want 1-2-3 to print when you run the macro from A5..L88 to A5..L91. However, because the statement in the macro that refers to the Print range

'rA5..L88~

is a label, it will not change to reflect the addition of the new rows. At best, you'll remember to edit this label to define the new range before you print; at worst, you'll run the macro "as is," creating a printed report that is lacking the last three rows of the worksheet, then go back and make the change.

If you use a range name to describe the Print range, however, you can avoid this problem. For example, suppose you give the name PRINT to the range A5..L88 in the original worksheet, and change the second statement in the macro to

'rPRINT~

When you issue the /Worksheet Insert Rows command to add three new rows to the worksheet, 1-2-3 will change the range described by PRINT from A5..L88 to A5..L91. Since the macro uses the name PRINT to refer to the Print range, the change in the range referred to by the name PRINT automatically changes the range referred to by the macro.

Because this technique is so important, it is worth repeating the rule—always use range names, and not cell coordinates, to refer to cells and ranges from within macros. Putting this rule into practice will save you a lot of time and aggravation.

Although this is by far the preferred way to select menu items from within a macro, it is not the only way. Instead of choosing menu items by their first letter, 1-2-3 can choose them by pointing and pressing [Enter]. However, programming 1-2-3 to select menu items by pointing is considerably more cumbersome than programming it to select items by their first letter. In addition, 1-2-3 cannot execute macros that choose commands in this way nearly as rapidly as it can execute macros that choose commands by their first letter. Furthermore, macros written in this style are almost impossible to decipher. For these reasons, we strongly recommend that you program 1-2-3 to choose commands by their first letter, not by pointing.

Commands You Should Avoid

You should be careful about using the / Worksheet Erase Yes and / File Retrieve commands in a macro. Here's why: Both of these commands cause 1-2-3 to erase the current worksheet. Since any macro that is running must be a part of the current worksheet, erasing the current worksheet will also erase that macro. Obviously, when you erase a macro, 1-2-3 cannot read any more instructions from that macro. In other words, if you use either of these commands in a macro, that macro will stop running as soon as 1-2-3 issues the command.

Of course, you can use these commands in your macros. In fact, there may be times when you'll want to end a macro with one of these commands. If you use them in the middle of a macro, however, the macro will not work correctly.

Another command you'll probably want to avoid is / Range Name Reset. This command causes 1-2-3 to delete all range names from the current worksheet—including the name of the macro that is running. If you use this command in a macro, you'll need to rename the macro after each time you run it.

TIP: DON'T FORGET THE LABEL PREFIX

When you enter a macro statement that begins with a /, you must remember to type a label prefix first. If you forget the prefix, 1-2-3 will assume that you are issuing a command, instead of creating a macro statement, when you press the / key. For example, suppose you want to create the macro statement

/rfc0~{End}{Right}

which assigns the Currency format with zero decimal places to a range of cells. As you are entering this label, however, you forget to type the label prefix. As a result, 1-2-3 will assume that you are issuing the / Range Format command instead of typing a macro statement.

One way to avoid this problem is to use the alternative form for the / character, {Menu}, in your macros, as in the macro line

{Menu}rfc0~{End}{Right}

Because the first character in this representation, {, is a simple label character, 1-2-3 will assume you are entering a label as soon as you type this character. Although typing this alternative representation requires more keystrokes than typing the / character, you might still want to consider using it for this reason.

DEBUGGING MACROS

Even if you are an experienced 1-2-3 programmer, you'll often make mistakes as you create your macros. If a macro contains a mistake—such as a misspelled word or an incorrect cell reference—it won't execute properly when you run it. To make a flawed macro work properly, you must edit it to correct the mistakes it contains. Because programming errors are often called bugs, the process of finding and correcting mistakes in a program is called debugging. Fortunately, 1-2-3 offers several tools that make it relatively easy to track down and correct mistakes in macros. In this section, we'll show you how to use those debugging tools.

Types of Errors

There are almost as many different kinds of macro errors as there are macros. However, most errors are caused by one of three simple mistakes on your part. You'll either omit characters (particularly tildes) that are required for the macro to work properly, supply an invalid response to a menu command prompt, or misspell or use the incorrect form of a special key representation or LCL command. Although all of these errors stop the execution of a macro, 1-2-3 responds differently to each one.

Omitting Keystrokes

Omitted keystrokes are probably the most common macro error for beginning programmers. The simple macro

'/mA1A2~

contains an example of this sort of error. When you invoke this macro, 1-2-3 will issue the / Move command. Next, the macro is supposed to supply A1 as the FROM range and A2 as the TO range. Because there is no tilde after A1, however, 1-2-3 does not "press" [Enter] to lock in the FROM range. It just keeps on "typing" the characters stored in the macro, and ends up supplying the nonsensical reference A1A2 as the FROM range. Because this reference makes no sense, 1-2-3 will beep, stop the macro, flash ERROR in the Mode indicator, and display the message *Invalid cell or range address* at the lower-left corner of the screen. The control panel will display the prompt *Enter range to move FROM: A1A2*. To clear this error and return to the READY mode, you must press [Esc].

In some cases, omitting a keystroke from a command sequence will result in a valid but unintended command. For example, suppose that you want to delete the range name REVENUE from the worksheet from within a macro. To do this, you write the macro

'/rnREVENUE~

Notice that there is no *d* (for Delete) following the *n* in this macro. The omission of the *d* gives this macro a completely different meaning. When 1-2-3 executes the macro, it issues the / Range Name command. Then, instead of choosing the Delete option, typing the name of the range to be deleted, REVENUE, and pressing [Enter], 1-2-3 chooses the Reset option, which immediately deletes every range name in the worksheet. Why does 1-2-3 choose the Reset option? Because the next keystroke following the *n* in the macro is *R*. After resetting all of the range names, the macro will simply type the letters *EVENUE* into the current cell, then press [Enter] to lock in the entry.

Invalid Responses to Command Prompts

Supplying an invalid response to a command prompt is another common cause of macro errors. Trying to delete a range name that does not exist is a classic example of this sort of error. For instance, suppose 1-2-3 encounters the statement

'/rndTEMP~

within a macro. When 1-2-3 processes this statement, it will issue the / Range Name Delete command, then supply TEMP as the name to be deleted. If the worksheet contains the range name TEMP, 1-2-3 will delete that name. If the worksheet does not contain that name, however, 1-2-3 will beep, stop the macro, flash ERROR in the Mode indicator, and display the message *Range name does not exist* in the lower-left corner of the screen. Pressing [Esc] will clear the error and return you to the READY mode.

Errors in the Syntax of a Key Representation or LCL Command

Macro errors also often result from misspelling a key name or LCL command or from using an incorrect form of a key name or LCL command. The macro in Figure 13-15 contains an example of this sort of error. This simple macro types the label *'January* into the current cell, moves the cell pointer down and types *'February*, moves the cell pointer down again and types *'March*, and so forth. 1-2-3 continues in this fashion until it reaches the command *'{Dwn}* in cell B8. Because 1-2-3 cannot recognize misspelled commands, when it comes to this command, it will beep, stop the macro, and flash ERROR in the Mode indicator, just at it does for any other type of error.

In addition, however, 1-2-3 will display the message *Unrecognized key/range name {...} (B8)* at the bottom of the screen. Notice that, in addition to describing the error, this message points out the location of the statement that contains the error. Whenever 1-2-3 encounters a word that it does not recognize enclosed in braces, it will stop running the macro and display a message like this one.

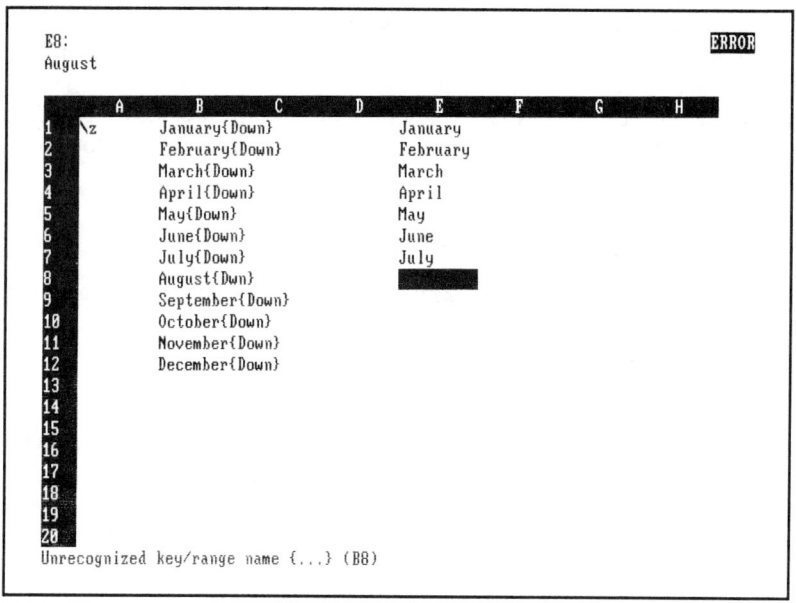

```
E8:                                                    ERROR
August
              A         B          C         D         E         F         G         H
         1   \z      January{Down}                  January
         2           February{Down}                 February
         3           March{Down}                    March
         4           April{Down}                    April
         5           May{Down}                      May
         6           June{Down}                     June
         7           July{Down}                     July
         8           August{Dwn}                    ▓▓▓▓▓
         9           September{Down}
        10           October{Down}
        11           November{Down}
        12           December{Down}
        13
        14
        15
        16
        17
        18
        19
        20
Unrecognized key/range name {...} (B8)
```

FIGURE 13-15: A misspelled key representation

TIP: SAVE THE WORKSHEET BEFORE RUNNING A MACRO FOR THE FIRST TIME

Because you're only human, some of your macros will not work right the first time you run them. For example, suppose you intended to write the macro

/re{Right}~

which erases the current cell and the cell to its right, but instead you wrote

/we{Right}~

which erases the entire worksheet. If you don't discover the mistake until after you've run the macro, you're out of luck.

You can protect yourself from the potentially disastrous consequences of programming mistakes, however, simply by saving the worksheet that contains a macro prior to executing that macro. That way, if the macro does something to the worksheet that you didn't anticipate, you can retrieve the version of the worksheet that you just saved, edit the macro, and try it again.

The STEP Mode

Although errors in simple macros are usually easy to find, errors in complex macros are often more difficult to pinpoint. In those cases, 1-2-3's STEP mode comes in handy. Normally, 1-2-3 executes the commands in a macro so quickly that it is virtually impossible to determine exactly where an error occurs. In the STEP mode, however, 1-2-3 executes macros one keystroke at a time, making it easy for you to see the effect of each keystroke and command in the macro. As a result, you easily can determine the location of any errors in the macro.

To enter the STEP mode, press the [Step] key ([Alt][F2]) before you begin running a macro or while a macro that is already running has paused as a result of a {?}, {MenuBranch}, or {MenuCall} command. When you press this key, the word STEP will appear at the bottom of the screen. Once you are in the STEP mode, you can invoke the macro you want to debug. As soon as you invoke the macro, the STEP indicator will be replaced by the flashing letters SST. 1-2-3 will wait for you to press a key before it executes the first command in the macro. When you press a key (any key will do), 1-2-3 will execute the first keystroke or command in the macro, then pause and wait for you to press another key. Each time you press a key, 1-2-3 will execute another keystroke or command. You can continue to step through the macro one step at a time until you find the error.

You can turn off the STEP mode at any time. To do this, you simply press the [Step] key a second time. When you turn off the STEP mode during the execution of a macro, 1-2-3 will replace the SST indicator with the indicator CMD. After you turn off the STEP mode, 1-2-3 will wait for you to press a key before it resumes running the macro. Once you press a key, 1-2-3 will begin executing the macro at its normal speed.

▶When you use the STEP mode in Release 2.2, 1-2-3 displays on the Status line a copy of the macro statement that contains the commands it is currently executing. At any moment, the command that 1-2-3 will execute the next time you press a key will be highlighted. This makes it easier to figure out exactly where you are in the macro and, if the macro contains an error, exactly where that error resides.◀

RELEASE ▶ 2.2 ◀

Let's look at an example. The macro in Figure 13-16 contains an error. Suppose you want to use the STEP mode to pinpoint the error. To do this, begin by pressing the [Step] key to enter the STEP mode, then press [Alt]p to run the macro. The first time you press any key (we prefer to use the [Spacebar]), 1-2-3 will execute the command /, which reveals the main 1-2-3 menu. When you press the [Spacebar] a second time, 1-2-3 will read the character *p*, which chooses the Print command from the main menu. Figure 13-17 shows the screen at this point. When you press the [Spacebar] for the third time, 1-2-3 will read the character *c*, which produces a beep. Why? Because the Print menu does not have an option that begins with the letter C. Once 1-2-3 alerts you that this is the location of the error, it is relatively easy to determine that the error is the result of a missing p (for Printer), prior to the c (for Clear). To correct the error, press [Ctrl][Break] to cancel the macro, and press [Esc] to return to the READY mode. Then you can edit the macro.

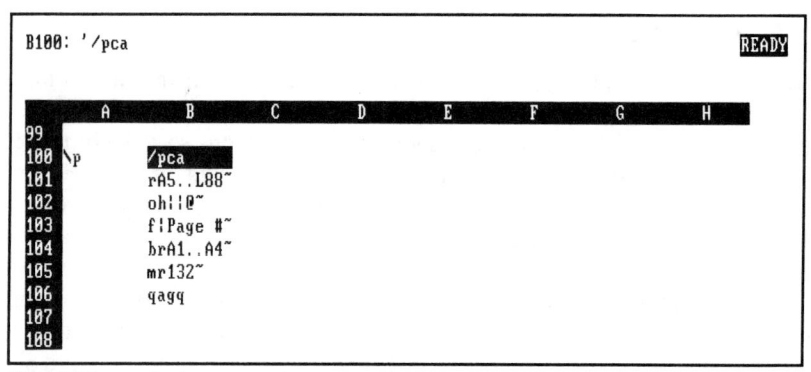

FIGURE 13-16: A macro that contains an error

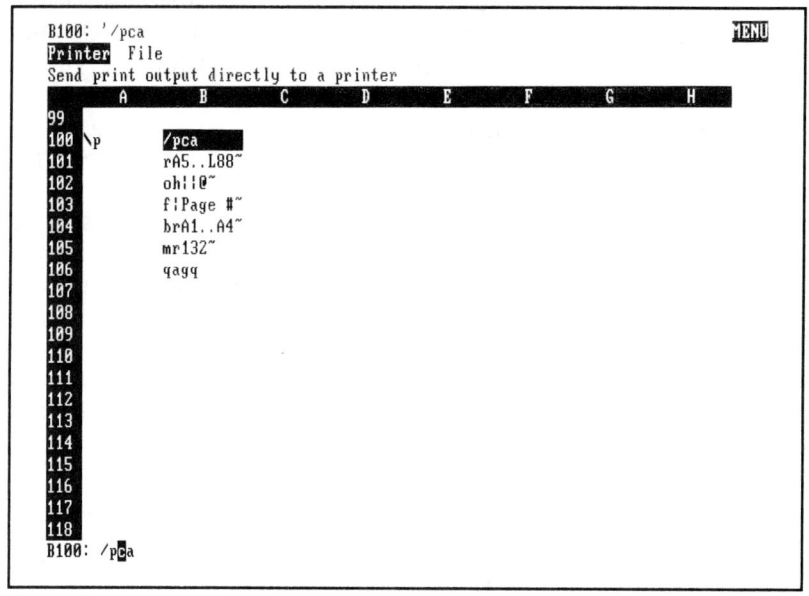

FIGURE 13-17: Using the STEP mode to debug a macro

Editing Macros

Once you have pinpointed the source of a macro error, editing the macro to correct that error is simple. Since the statements in a macro are simply labels (or formulas that return strings), you can edit them in the same way you would edit any other label or formula. To correct an error, you first move the cell pointer to the cell that contains the erroneous statement and press the [Edit] key to enter the EDIT mode. Once 1-2-3 is in the EDIT mode, you can add or delete characters to correct the error. Once the error has been eliminated, you press [Enter] to lock in the change. If, instead of editing the erroneous statement you want to replace it with a new statement, you can simply position the cell pointer on the cell, type a new entry, and press [Enter].

Once you have corrected the macro, you must save the worksheet that contains the macro so that the version of the macro stored on disk will be up-to-date. If you forget this step, the macro in the worksheet will work correctly; however, when you use the / Worksheet Erase command, the / File Retrieve command, or the / Quit Yes commands to erase the current worksheet, the corrected version of the macro will be lost.

For example, suppose you want to edit the error out of the first statement in the macro in Figure 13-16. To do this, move the cell pointer to cell B100, press [Edit], press ← two times, type a p, and then press [Enter]. When you next run the macro, it will work properly. To save the corrected macro, you must issue the / File Save command.

AUTO-EXECUTING MACROS

Occasionally, you'll create a macro that you want 1-2-3 to run automatically as soon as the worksheet that contains the macro is retrieved. In other words, you might want to make the macro an *auto-executing macro*. To make a macro an auto-executing macro, you need only give the macro the special name \0. Assigning this name to a macro commands 1-2-3 to execute that macro automatically as soon as it retrieves the worksheet that contains that macro.

An Example

For example, suppose you have created a system of three worksheets named SUMMARY, REVENUE, and EXPENSES. The SUMMARY worksheet summarizes the results from REVENUE and EXPENSES. To make the job of managing these three worksheets simpler, you might create a macro that combines the information from REVENUE and EXPENSES into SUMMARY (using / File Combine) and then recalculates SUMMARY. Figure 13-18 shows such a macro.

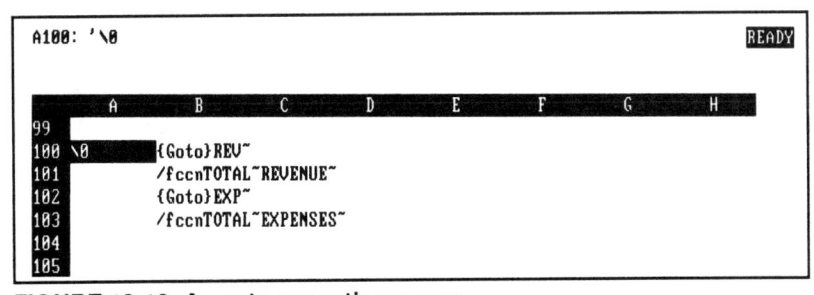

```
A100: '\0                                                    READY

      A        B          C         D      E      F      G     H
 99
100  \0      {Goto}REV~
101          /fccnTOTAL~REVENUE~
102          {Goto}EXP~
103          /fccnTOTAL~EXPENSES~
104
105
```

FIGURE 13-18: An auto-executing macro

Since the results in SUMMARY will not be up-to-date until this macro is run, you might want to tell 1-2-3 to run the macro automatically whenever SUMMARY is retrieved. To do this, you need only assign the name \0 to cell B100, the first cell in the macro. Once the macro is named, you'll want to save the worksheet containing the macro. From that point on, whenever you load the worksheet SUMMARY, 1-2-3 will run the \0 macro automatically.

Notes

In some cases, you might want to execute an auto-executing macro again after you have retrieved the worksheet that contains it. Unfortunately, 1-2-3 won't allow you to invoke an auto-executing macro by typing [Alt]0. If you try this, 1-2-3 will just beep at you. If you want to manually invoke an auto-executing macro, you must assign that macro a second name—one that consists of a backslash followed by a letter. That way, you can invoke the macro by pressing [Alt] followed by that letter.

Since assigning a range name to a cell does not delete any names that have been previously assigned to the cell, assigning a "regular" name to a macro does not cancel its auto-executing properties. If you have assigned both the names \a and \0 to the first cell of a macro, for example, 1-2-3 will execute that macro whenever you retrieve the worksheet that contains the macro. In addition, 1-2-3 will execute the macro whenever you press [Alt]a.

If you no longer want a macro to be auto-executing, just use the / Range Name Delete command to remove the name \0, then resave the worksheet. Once you remove the name \0 from the macro, it will no longer be an auto-executing macro.

Since only one range in a worksheet can have the name \0 (or any other name, for that matter), there can be only one auto-executing macro in each worksheet. Of course, that one macro can be as long and complex as you wish and may contain commands that run other related macros.

In some cases, you won't want 1-2-3 to execute an auto-executing macro when you retrieve the worksheet that contains it. ▶If you are using 1-2-3 Release 2.2, you're in luck. Release 2.2 includes a new command—/ Worksheet Global Default Autoexec—that allows you to disable the automatic execution of auto-executing macros. To do this, you must issue the / Worksheet Global Default Autoexec command and choose No. If you then retrieve a worksheet that contains an auto-executing macro, the macro will not run automatically. To reenable the recognition of auto-executing macros, simply reissue the / Worksheet Global Default Autoexec command and choose Yes. If you wish to turn off the auto-executing feature permanently, first use the / Worksheet Global Default Autoexec command to turn it off, then use the / Worksheet Global Default Update command to save the new setting. (For more on the Update command, see Appendix 3.)◀

In earlier releases of 1-2-3, you can prevent the execution of an auto-executing macro by entering the STEP mode prior to retrieving the worksheet that contains the macro. That way, when 1-2-3 retrieve the worksheet, it will pause after executing the first command in the macro. At that point, you can press [Ctrl][Break] to cancel the execution of the macro.

While most auto-executing macros are designed to perform simple housekeeping chores, you can use auto-executing macros to create complete turnkey applications in 1-2-3. If you are developing complex 1-2-3 applications for other 1-2-3 users, you might find this capability to be worth considering.

CONCLUSION

In this chapter, we have introduced you to macros—the special computer programs that run inside your 1-2-3 worksheet. We began by creating and running a simple macro and explaining the basics of working with macros. Next, we showed you how a macro can select items from 1-2-3's menus. Finally, we discussed macro errors and showed you how to debug a macro.

In Chapter 14, we'll build upon the basics covered here. In that chapter, we'll show you how 1-2-3's special programming commands can expand the scope and power of a macro.

14

Lotus Command Language Basics

In Chapter 13, we showed you how to create simple macros that move the cell pointer, make entries, and issue 1-2-3 commands. The macros we presented in that chapter are collections of keystrokes that automate processes that would be difficult or tedious to perform manually.

Macros can do a lot more than just automate keystrokes, however. 1-2-3 has its own built-in programming language—The Lotus Command Language (LCL)— which allows you to create sophisticated macro programs in your 1-2-3 worksheets. In this chapter, we'll introduce you to the Lotus Command Language. First, we'll explain the basic form and function of the LCL's commands. Then we'll demonstrate the use of 14 of the most commonly used LCL commands. In Chapter 15, we'll continue our discussion of the LCL with a presentation of the remaining LCL commands and a look at some advanced programming techniques.

The LCL is available only in 1-2-3 Release 2. However, all releases of 1-2-3 support a set of special macro commands (called the /x commands) that duplicate the actions of eight of the most useful LCL commands. If you use 1-2-3 Release 2, 2.01, or 2.2, you can use both LCL commands and these special /x commands. However, if you use 1-2-3 Release 1A, only the /x commands will be available to you. In this chapter, we'll present each /x command immediately following the discussion of its LCL equivalent.

COMMAND LANGUAGE BASICS

The LCL is a high-level progamming language that works entirely within 1-2-3. The LCL includes commands that allow you to set up loops, perform conditional testing, solicit input from the keyboard, create custom menus, branch, call subroutines, read and write to text files, and so on—all from within macros. Table 14-1 lists all of the LCL commands and provides a brief description of what each one of them does.

Command:	What It Does:
{?}	Allows user input; pauses the macro until user presses [Enter].
{Beep pitch}	Sounds a tone.
{Blank location}	Erases the entries from location.
▶{BordersOff}	Turns off worksheet borders.◀
▶{BordersOn}	Turns on worksheet borders.◀
{Branch location}	Branches execution of a macro to location.
{BreakOff}	Disables [Ctrl][Break].
{BreakOn}	Enables [Ctrl][Break].
{Close}	Closes an open text file.
{Contents destination,source}	Copies the contents of source into destination as a label.
{Define location1:type 1, location 2:type 2...}	Specifies cells that will store the arguments passed to a subroutine.
{Dispatch location}	Branches to a cell whose address or name is stored in location.
{FileSize location}	Stores number of bytes in open text file in location.
{For counter,start,stop,step,routine}	Executes commands at routine as long as start<=stop. Increases counter by step after each pass.
{ForBreak}	Breaks 1-2-3 out of current {For} loop.
▶{FrameOff}	Turns off worksheet borders.◀
▶{FrameOn}	Turns on worksheet borders.◀
{Get location}	Captures the first subsequent keystroke and stores in location.
{GetLabel prompt,location}	Displays **prompt**, waits for input followed by [Enter], stores response in location as a string.

TABLE 14-1: The Lotus Command Language (*Part 1*)

Chapter 14: Lotus Command Language Basics

{GetNumber **prompt**,*location*}	Displays **prompt**, waits for numeric input followed by [Enter], stores response in *location* as a value.	
{GetPos *location*}	Determines position of pointer in open text file, stores result in *location*.	
▶{GraphOff}	Ends display of current graph.◀	RELEASE ▶ 2.2 ◀
▶{GraphOn}	Displays current graph until macro encounters a {GraphOff} command.◀	RELEASE ▶ 2.2 ◀
{If CONDITION}	Determines if CONDITION is true or false. If true, continues on same line of macro. If false, skips to next line.	
{Indicate **message**}	Displays **message** in Mode indicator.	
{Let *location*,<u>number</u> or **string**}	Enters <u>number</u> or **string** (usually the result of a formula or function) at *location*.	
{Look *destination*}	Extracts the first character from the keyboard buffer and places it in *destination*.	
{MenuBranch *location*}	Branches to custom menu at *location*.	
{MenuCall *location*}	Calls a custom menu at *location* as a subroutine.	
{OnError *location*}	Resumes execution of macro at *location* when certain macro errors occur.	
{Open **filename**,**mode**}	Opens the text file **filename** for access in the specified **mode**.	

TABLE 14-1: The Lotus Command Language (*Part 2*)

{PanelOff clear}	Prevents 1-2-3 from redrawing the control panel during the execution of a macro. Optional keyword clear erases control panel from screen befor freezing.
{PanelOn}	Resumes redrawing of the control panel.
{Put *range*,column offset,row offset,**calc**}	Places the result of **calc** in the cell of range specified by the column offset and row offset arguments.
{Quit}	Cancels the execution of a macro.
{Read count,*location*}	Reads the number of characters specified by count from an open text file and stores in *location* as a label.
{ReadLn *location*}	Reads from current position in text file to next carriage return and places characters in *location* as a label.
{Recalc *location*}	Recalculates the entries in the range *location* in row-by-row order.
{RecalcCol}	Recalculates the entries in the range *location* in column-by-column order.
{Restart}	"Resets the stack" so that 1-2-3 executes the next statement as if it were beginning a new macro.
{Return}	Returns 1-2-3 from a subroutine.

TABLE 14-1: The Lotus Command Language (*Part 3*)

{SetPos position}	Moves pointer to position in open text file.
{subroutine,argument 1,argument 2,...}	Calls a subroutine and, optionally, passes one or more arguments to it.
▶{System name}	Exits from 1-2-3 to DOS and runs program with filename name.◀ RELEASE ▶ 2.2 ◀
{Wait time}	Pauses execution of a macro until time.
{WindowsOff}	Prevents 1-2-3 from redrawing the window area during the execution of a macro.
{WindowsOn}	Resumes redrawing of the window area. Also, enables display of settings sheets during macro execution.
{Write string}	Writes string to open text file.
{WriteLn string}	Writes string to open text file, followed by a carriage return/linefeed.

Key to argument types:
Literal arguments appear in plain print.
Location arguments appear in *italic print*.
String arguments appear in **bold print**.
Numeric arguments appear in underlined print.
Conditional arguments appear in CAPS.

TABLE 14-1: The Lotus Command Language (*Part 4*)

The Form of LCL Commands

As you can see in Table 14-1, all LCL commands have a similar form. First, all LCL commands consist of a command name (such as *MenuBranch* or *If* or *For*) surrounded by braces. In addition, many (but not all) LCL commands accept or require one or more arguments. These arguments tell 1-2-3 what the command is to act upon, when the command should perform its action, where to place the command's result, and so forth.

For example, the form of the {Branch} command is

{Branch *location*}

The location argument of the {Branch} command is a reference to a cell. When 1-2-3 encounters this command in a macro, it will "branch" the macro to the cell specified by *location*. Notice that the command name, Branch, and the argument, *location*, are enclosed together in braces.

The first argument in an LCL command must be separated from the command name by a single space. For example, notice the space between the argument *location* and the command name Branch in the previous example. If a command includes two or more arguments, those arguments must be separated from one another by the default argument separator (usually a comma) or by a semicolon. (To learn how to change the default argument separator, see Appendix 3.)

Argument Types

Different LCL commands require different types of arguments. For example, the argument of the {Branch} command must be a cell reference, while the arguments of the {Let} command must be a string and a cell reference.

Some LCL commands accept numeric arguments. A numeric argument can be a literal value, a reference to a cell that contains or returns a value, or a formula or function that returns a value.

RELEASE ► 2.2 ◄
Other LCL commands require string arguments. ►In 1-2-3 Release 2.2, a string argument can be a literal string or a formula or function that returns a string. (In earlier releases of 1-2-3, string arguments must be literal strings.)◄ Unlike the string argument of a function, the string argument of an LCL command does not need to be enclosed in quotation marks unless it contains the default argument separator (usually a comma), a semicolon, a colon, or the closing brace character (}), or unless the spelling of the string is identical to the spelling of an existing range name. In any of these cases, 1-2-3 will not evaluate the command correctly unless the argument is enclosed in quotation marks. To avoid problems, we usually enclose string arguments in quotation marks, even when they are not required.

RELEASE ► 2.2 ◄
Many LCL commands require one or more arguments that specify the location of a cell or range in a worksheet. ►In 1-2-3 Release 2.2, a location argument can be a range name, a cell reference, range reference, or a formula or function that returns a cell address or range name. (In earlier releases of 1-2-3, you cannot use a formula or function as a location argument in a macro command.)◄

The first argument of the LCL command {If} must be a conditional test. We'll explain conditional test arguments when we explain the {If} command.

One command, {PanelOff} takes a literal argument (the word clear). We'll explain this command in Chapter 15.

In Table 14-1 and throughout this chapter, literal arguments appear in plain type, numeric arguments appear <u>underlined</u>, string arguments appear in **boldface**, location arguments appear in *italics*, and conditional-testing arguments appear in CAPITAL LETTERS.

> **TIP: USE RANGE NAMES AS LOCATION ARGUMENTS**
>
> In Chapter 13, we suggested that you always use range names instead of cell references to refer to cells and ranges from within macros. Using range names in your macros instead of cell references allows those macros to adapt to changes you make in the worksheet with the / Move, / Worksheet Insert, and / Worksheet Delete commands.
>
> The same advice holds true for the location arguments in LCL commands. If you use range names instead of cell references as the location arguments in LCL commands, those commands will be able to adapt to changes you make in the worksheet with / Move, / Worksheet Insert, and / Worksheet Delete.

Using LCL Commands

As explained in Chapter 13, the statements that make up macros are simply labels in the cells of your worksheets. LCL commands are no exception to this rule. When you use an LCL command in a macro, just enter that command as a label into the appropriate cell in a worksheet. For example, the simple macro in Figure 14-1 uses two LCL commands: {GetNumber} and {Quit}. This macro prompts you to enter a number. When you type a number and press [Enter], the macro stores the number in the cell named INPUT (cell B5), then assigns the Currency format with zero decimal places to that cell. The entries that make up this macro are

B1: '{GetNumber "Enter a number: ",INPUT}
B2: '/rfc0~INPUT~
B2: '{Quit}

As you can see, all of the entries in the macro—including the LCL commands {GetNumber} and {Quit}—are labels.

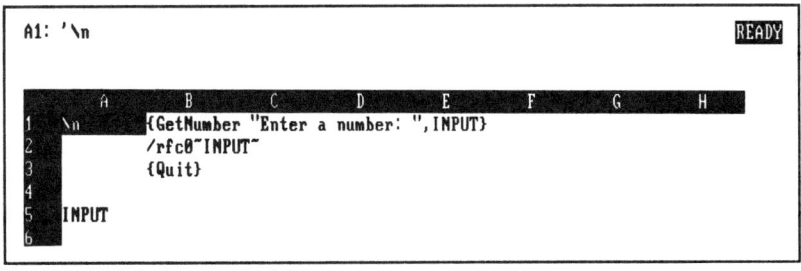

FIGURE 14-1: A sample LCL macro

You don't need to type a label prefix when you enter an LCL command. 1-2-3 considers the opening brace character ({)—which is the first character in every LCL command—to be a label character. As soon as you type {, 1-2-3 will assume that the entry is a label.

Conventions

In Table 14-1 and throughout the rest of this chapter, you'll see that we capitalize the first letter of each LCL command. In most cases, we use the lower-case form of the remaining letters in the command. For "multiple-word" commands like {WindowsOff} and {GetLabel}, however, we capitalize the first letter of each "word" in the command name. These capitalization patterns are our conventions, not 1-2-3's rules. 1-2-3 will understand any LCL command that is spelled correctly, no matter what combination of upper- and lower-case letters it contains.

FUNDAMENTAL LCL TECHNIQUES

In all, there are 49 unique commands in the LCL. The chances are good, however, that you'll use 14 of these commands far more than any of the others and that you will never use many of them at all. In this section, we'll explain the most commonly used LCL commands. We'll present these commands in the context of eight fundamental techniques: stopping macros, soliciting user input, making entries in cells, conditional testing, looping, branching, calling subroutines, and creating custom menus.

Stopping Macros: The {Quit} Command

In Chapter 13, we explained that a macro will continue to run until it encounters a blank cell or a cell that contains a value, until an error occurs, or until the macro encounters the LCL command {Quit}. {Quit}, which takes no arguments, is perhaps the simplest LCL command.

When 1-2-3 encounters a {Quit} command in a macro, it will immediately stop executing that macro. For example, we used a {Quit} command to mark the end of the macro in Figure 14-1. When 1-2-3 encountered this command in the macro, the macro stopped running.

You can use the {Quit} command to mark the end of any macro. However, since 1-2-3 always ends a macro when it encounters a blank cell, in most cases you won't need to use the {Quit} command to end your macros. For example, instead of entering the command {Quit} in cell B3 in Figure 14-1, we could have simply left that cell blank. Either way, the macro would stop after it processed the command in cell B2.

{Quit} is far more useful when you need to stop a macro in midstream. For example, {Quit} is often used with the LCL command {If} to stop a macro if some conditional test is true. We'll look at an example of using {Quit} and {If} together later in this chapter.

Like other LCL commands, {Quit} is available only in 1-2-3 Releases 2, 2.01, and 2.2. However, 1-2-3 offers another command, /xq, which has the same function as {Quit} and which is available in all releases of 1-2-3, including Release 1A. When 1-2-3 encounters an /xq command in a macro, the macro stops.

Soliciting User Input

The LCL includes five commands that allow macros to accept input from the keyboard: {?}, {GetNumber}, {GetLabel}, {Get}, and {Look}. Of these commands, you'll probably use the first three most often. We'll cover those commands in this chapter and the {Get} and {Look} commands in Chapter 15.

The {?} Command

The {?} command instructs 1-2-3 to pause the execution of a macro until you press the [Enter] key. Depending on what mode 1-2-3 is in when the macro pauses, you can type, issue commands, move the cell pointer, select ranges, and so on, during the pause. Unlike other LCL commands, {?} is available in Release 1A as well as Releases 2, 2.01, and 2.2.

The macro shown in Figure 14-2 demonstrates the {?} command. This simple one-line macro assigns the range name TEST to the range of cells you specify. When 1-2-3 executes this macro, it begins by issuing the /Range Name Create command, typing TEST, and pressing [Enter] to lock in that name. At that point, while 1-2-3 is presenting the prompt Enter range:, it reads the {?} command, which causes it to pause. During the pause, you can do just what you could do if you had issued the /Range Name Create command yourself: Specify a range, either by pointing or typing.

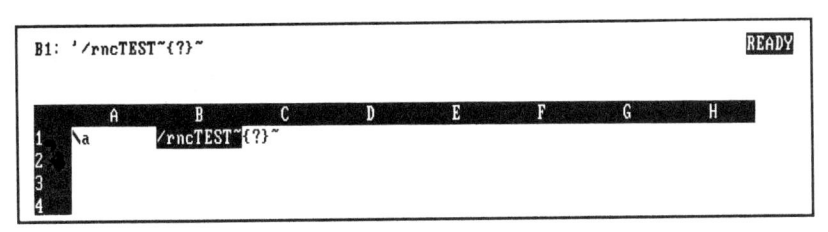

```
B1: '/rncTEST~{?}~                                                READY

        A       B       C       D       E       F       G       H
    1  \a     /rncTEST~{?}~
    2
    3
    4
```

FIGURE 14-2: The {?} command

After you have chosen the cell or cells you want to name, you must press [Enter]. Importantly, pressing [Enter] at this point does not complete the /Range Name Create command—it simply ends the pause caused by the {?} command. The final command in the macro, ~, locks in your range selection to complete the process of naming the range.

You can use this command to solicit input at almost any point during the execution of a macro. For example, the {?} command in the statement

'{Goto}C5~{Edit}{?}~

lets you edit the contents of cell C5. This macro moves the cell pointer to cell C5 and "presses" {Edit}, then pauses. While the macro is paused, you can add and delete characters in that cell, just as you normally would. When you press [Enter] to end the pause, 1-2-3 will read the ~ keystroke, which locks in the changes you have made. Similarly, the {?} command in the statement '/fs{?}~ lets you specify the name of the file to which you want to save the worksheet. When you type a file name and press [Enter], 1-2-3 will save the worksheet under that name.

The {GetNumber} and {GetLabel} Commands

{GetNumber} and {GetLabel} are two of the most commonly used LCL commands. Like {?}, these commands allow you to solicit input during the execution of a macro. Like {?}, these commands cause 1-2-3 to pause until you press [Enter]. Unlike {?}, these two commands allow you to display a prompt that tells the user what sort of information to supply.

The only difference between the {GetNumber} and {GetLabel} commands is the type of information they accept. The {GetNumber} command accepts numeric input, while the {GetLabel} command accepts strings.

GetNumber and GetLabel have similar forms:

{GetNumber **prompt**,*destination*}
{GetLabel **prompt**,*destination*}

RELEASE ► 2.2 ◄ The first argument—which must be a literal string ►or, in 1-2-3 Release 2.2, a formula or function that returns a string◄—is the prompt that 1-2-3 will display during the execution of the command. If the string you use for the prompt argument contains a semicolon, colon, comma, or closing brace, ►or, if you are using 1-2-3 Release 2.2, the string has the same spelling as an existing range name◄, you must enclose it in quotes.

RELEASE ► 2.2 ◄

The length of the prompt argument is limited only by the fact that, like any label, a {GetNumber} or {GetLabel} statement cannot be more than 240 characters long. Because 1-2-3 can display only about 72 characters across a line of the screen, however, you'll want to keep your prompts to less than 72 characters. If your prompt is longer than 72 characters, 1-2-3 will display only the first 72 characters; however, the commands will still work properly.

The destination argument instructs 1-2-3 where to store the response to the prompt. This argument may be a cell address, range address, or range name. Because 1-2-3 always stores the response in a single cell, only a reference to one cell is necessary. If you specify a range, 1-2-3 will place the response in the upper-left cell of that range.

The {GetNumber} Command

The {GetNumber} command allows you to solicit numeric input from the keyboard during the execution of a macro. The macro shown in Figure 14-3 demonstrates this command. This macro begins with the command *{GetNumber "Please enter a value: ",RESPONSE}*. When 1-2-3 reads this command, it will display the prompt *Please enter a value:* on the second line of the control panel, as shown in Figure 14-4, and then wait for your response. As you type characters in response to this prompt, 1-2-3 will display those characters immediately to the right of the last character in the prompt. For example, Figure 14-5 shows the result of typing 100 in response to this prompt.

Assuming that you type a value in response to a {GetNumber} prompt, 1-2-3 will store that value in the destination cell as soon as you press [Enter]. For example, if you type 100 and then press [Enter] in response to the prompt shown in Figure 14-4, 1-2-3 will place the value 100 into the cell named RESPONSE (B3).

Chapter 14: Lotus Command Language Basics

```
B1: '{GetNumber "Please enter a value: ",RESPONSE}            READY

       A         B         C       D  /     E         F         G         H
1     \b      {GetNumber "Please enter a value: ",RESPONSE}
2
3     RESPONSE
4
```

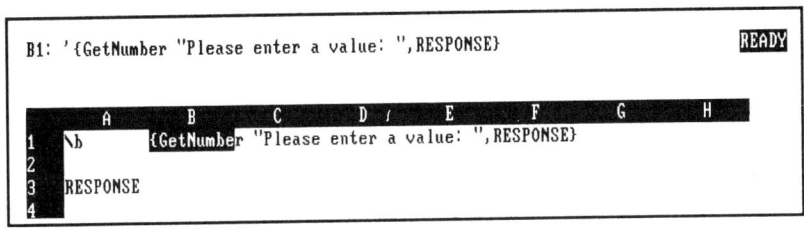

FIGURE 14-3: The {GetNumber} command

```
A1: '\b                                                        READY
Please enter a value:

       A         B         C         D         E         F         G         H
1     \b      {GetNumber "Please enter a value: ",RESPONSE}
2
3     RESPONSE
4
```

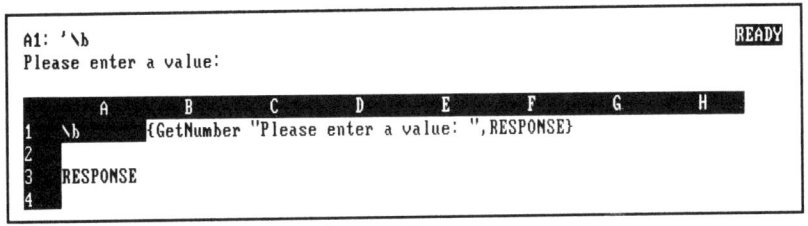

FIGURE 14-4: A {GetNumber} prompt

```
A1: '\b                                                        READY
Please enter a value: 100

       A         B         C         D         E         F         G         H
1     \b      {GetNumber "Please enter a value: ",RESPONSE}
2
3     RESPONSE
4
```

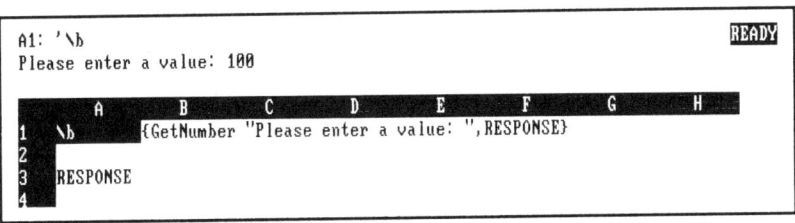

FIGURE 14-5: A response to a {GetNumber} prompt

Although you usually will type a literal value in response to a {GetNumber} prompt, you also can type a formula or function that produces a value result. When you press [Enter] to lock in this type of response, 1-2-3 will evaluate the formula or function and enter its result in the destination cell. For example, if you type .12/12 in response to the {GetNumber} prompt in Figure 14-4, 1-2-3 will store the value .01 in cell B3.

1-2-3 will even allow you to enter a literal string or a string-producing formula or function in reponse to a {GetNumber} command. If you do, however, 1-2-3 will store the value ERR in the destination cell when you press [Enter]. The same thing happens when you press [Enter] in response to a {GetNumber} prompt without typing anything, or when you type an invalid formula or function.

The {GetLabel} Command

The {GetLabel} command is like the {GetNumber} command, except that it allows you to solicit string input. The simple macro shown in Figure 14-6 demonstrates this command. The first command in this macro *{GetLabel "Please enter a label: ",ANSWER}* commands 1-2-3 to display the prompt *Please enter a label:* in the second line of the control panel and wait for your input. As you begin to type characters, 1-2-3 will display them to the right of the prompt. As soon as you press [Enter], 1-2-3 will store your response as a label in the destination cell—in this case, cell B3, which we have named ANSWER. For example, if you type hello in response to the prompt displayed by the {GetLabel} command in Figure 14-6, 1-2-3 will enter the label 'hello in cell B3 when you press [Enter].

```
B1: '{GetLabel "Please enter a label: ",ANSWER}                                    READY

         A         B         C         D         E         F         G         H
1       \c        {GetLabel "Please enter a label: ",ANSWER}
2
3       ANSWER
4
```

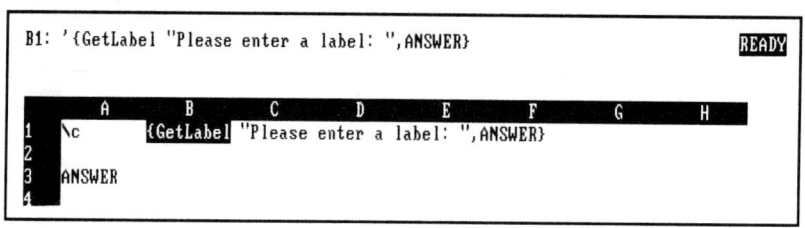

FIGURE 14-6: The {GetLabel} command

1-2-3 always assumes that the response to a {GetLabel} command is a literal string. Therefore, 1-2-3 will convert value, formula, and function responses to labels before it enters them into the destination cell. If you type the value 999 in response to a {GetLabel} prompt, 1-2-3 will enter the label '999 into the destination cell. If you type the formula +A1&A2, 1-2-3 will enter the label '+A1&A2. If you press [Enter] without typing a response, 1-2-3 will enter a label prefix into the destination cell.

The response to a {GetLabel} command cannot be more than 79 characters long. If you try to type more than 79 characters, 1-2-3 will simply beep.

Notes

Although 1-2-3 will enter your response to a {GetNumber} or {GetLabel} statement into the destination cell as soon as you press [Enter], that entry will not be visible in the worksheet until 1-2-3 next redraws the screen. Although this does not prevent 1-2-3 from using the value (for calculations and so forth), you still may want 1-2-3 to display it immediately. The easiest way to make 1-2-3 display the response to a {GetNumber} or {GetLabel} command is to follow that command with the symbol ~. This keystroke representation commands 1-2-3 to press the [Enter] key, which redraws the screen and, therefore, displays your response.

Notice that 1-2-3 has left a space between the prompt and the response in Figure 14-5. This space is included only because we included a blank space at the end of our prompt, as you can see if you look carefully at Figure 14-3. If we had not included this space in the macro, 1-2-3 wouldn't have included a space between the prompt and the response in the control panel. So that your macros will be easier to read and understand, we suggest you always include a single space at the end of your prompt arguments in {GetNumber} and {GetLabel} commands.

The /xn and /xl Commands

The {GetNumber} and {GetLabel} commands are not available in 1-2-3 Release 1A. However, there are two other commands—/xn and /xl—that do essentially the same thing as the {GetNumber} and {GetLabel} command and which are available in all releases of 1-2-3.

The forms of the / xn and /xl commands are

/xn**prompt**~*destination*~
/xl**prompt**~*destination*~

The first argument, **prompt**, must be a literal string that specifies the message 1-2-3 will display in the control panel when it executes this command. Unlike the prompt argument of the {GetNumber} and {Get Label} commands, the prompt argument of /xn and /xl cannot be longer than 39 characters. The second argument, *destination*, must be the name or address of the cell in which you want 1-2-3 to place your response to the command. The tildes that follow these two arguments are required.

The /xn Command

1-2-3's /xn command allows you to solicit numeric input from a user during the execution of a macro, in much the same way as the {GetNumber} command does. For example, you could use the command */xnPlease enter a value: ~RESPONSE~* instead of the command *{GetNumber "Please enter a value: ", RESPONSE}* in cell B1 in Figure 14-3 without changing the function of the macro in any way.

Like the {GetNumber} command, the /xn command will accept literal values and formulas and functions that return values as responses. If the response is a literal value, 1-2-3 will place that value into the destination cell. If the response is a formula or function, 1-2-3 will place the result of that formula or function in the destination cell.

However, the /xn command responds differently to string and null responses than does the {GetNumber} command. Instead of entering the value ERR into the destination cell when you press [Enter], 1-2-3 beeps and displays the message *Invalid number input* at the bottom-left corner of the screen. When you see this message, you can press [Esc] to clear your original entry and try again. This process continues until you supply a value response.

1-2-3 will automatically redraw the screen after it executes an /xn command. Consequently, your response will be visible in the destination cell as soon as you press [Enter].

Finally, although the {GetNumber} command requires a destination argument, the /xn command does not. If you neglect to include a final argument in an /xn statement, as in the statement */xnPlease enter a value: ~~*, 1-2-3 will place your response in the cell in which the cell pointer is positioned when it executes the command. Although a destination argument is not required, the final tilde is. Without this character, 1-2-3 will not evaluate the /xn command properly.

The /xl Command

1-2-3's /xl command is to the {GetLabel} command what /xn is to the {GetNumber} command. Both {GetLabel} and /xl allow 1-2-3 to accept string inputs during the execution of a macro. For example, you could substitute the command */xlPlease enter a label: ~ANSWER~* for the command *{GetLabel "Please enter a label: ",ANSWER}* in cell B1 in Figure 14-6.

Like the {GetLabel} command, the /xl command assumes that the response you type is a literal string. Also like the {GetLabel} command, the length of the response to an /xl command is limited to 79 characters.

As with /xn, the destination argument of the /xl command is optional. If you do not include a destination argument in an /xl command, 1-2-3 will store the response in the current cell. Even if you don't use a destination argument, you must include the second tilde in the command. Without this character, 1-2-3 will not execute the command properly.

Making Entries in Cells: The {Let} Command

The {Let} command instructs 1-2-3 to place an entry (usually the result of a calculation) into a specified cell of a worksheet. The form of this command is

{Let *destination*,value or **string**}

RELEASE
► 2.2 ◄

The first argument, *destination*, specifies the cell in which 1-2-3 will place the number or string specified by the second argument. This argument can be a cell reference, a range reference, a range name, ►or, if you use 1-2-3 Release 2.2, a formula or function that returns the name or address of a cell or range.◄ If this argument refers to a range, 1-2-3 will place the number or string in the upper-left cell of that range.

The second argument tells 1-2-3 what to place in the destination cell. Although this argument usually will be a formula or function, it can be a literal value or string. If the second argument is a formula or function, 1-2-3 will evaluate it and place its result in the destination cell. If the second argument is a literal value or string, 1-2-3 will simply place that value or string into the destination cell. {Let} is only available in 1-2-3 Releases 2, 2.01, ans 2.2. There is no equivalent command in 1-2-3 Release 1A.

An Example

The macro in Figure 14-7 demonstrates the {Let} command. This macro prompts the user to supply a principal amount, a rate of interest, and a term and uses his responses to calculate a periodic payment. The first three commands prompt the user to supply the principal borrowed, the periodic interest rate, and the term of the loan and store those responses in the cells named PRINCIPAL (B7), RATE (B8), and TERM (B9). The fourth command

{Let PAYMENTS,@PMT(PRINCIPAL,RATE,TERM)}

uses the values in PRINCIPAL, RATE, and TERM to calculate the periodic payment. The first argument, PAYMENTS, instructs 1-2-3 to place the result of the calculation in the cell named PAYMENTS (B10). The second argument, *@PMT (PRINCIPAL,RATE,TERM)*, defines the calculation 1-2-3 should perform.

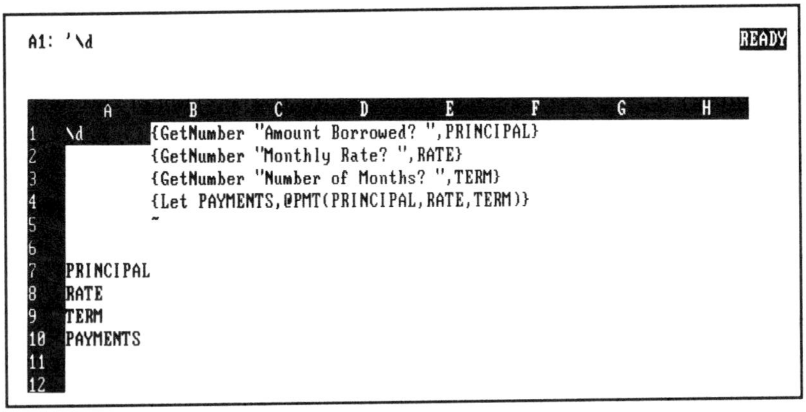

```
A1: '\d                                                    READY

      A        B           C           D        E       F      G      H
 1   \d      {GetNumber "Amount Borrowed? ",PRINCIPAL}
 2           {GetNumber "Monthly Rate? ",RATE}
 3           {GetNumber "Number of Months? ",TERM}
 4           {Let PAYMENTS,@PMT(PRINCIPAL,RATE,TERM)}
 5           ~
 6
 7   PRINCIPAL
 8   RATE
 9   TERM
10   PAYMENTS
11
12
```

FIGURE 14-7: The {Let} command

For example, if you run this macro and enter 5600 in response to the *Amount Borrowed?* prompt, .115/12 in response to the *Monthly Rate?* prompt, and 36 in response to the *Number of Months?* prompt, the cells named PRINCIPAL, RATE, and TERM will contain the values 5600, .009583, and 36. When 1-2-3 evaluates the {Let} command in cell B4, it will store the result of the function *@PMT(5600,.009583,36)*, 184.67, in PAYMENTS (B10).

The final character in the macro, ~, instructs 1-2-3 to press the [Enter] key to redraw the screen so that the result of the {Let} command is visible. As with {GetLabel} and {GetNumber}, 1-2-3 won't redraw the screen automatically after executing a {Let} command. Until 1-2-3 redraws the screen, the result of the {Let} command won't be visible, although 1-2-3 has entered it into the destination cell.

Invalid Arguments

If you use an invalid formula or function as the second argument of a {Let} command, 1-2-3 will treat that argument as though it is a literal string. For example, when 1-2-3 evaluates the command *{Let A3,@SUM(A1..A5}*, it will place the label '@SUM(A1..A5 in the destination cell, since *@SUM(A1..A5* is an incomplete function. Whenever 1-2-3 is unable to evaluate the second argument of a {Let} command, it treats that argument as a literal string.

Optional Arguments

When you use the {Let} command in its basic form, the type of entry (value or label) that 1-2-3 makes in the destination cell is determined by the form of the second argument. If the argument is a value or a formula that returns a value, then 1-2-3 will place that value in the destination cell. If the argument is a string or a formula that returns a string, 1-2-3 will place that string in the destination cell. However, two special suffixes—*:string* and *:value*—let you alter the way 1-2-3 treats the second argument of a {Let} command.

The *:string* Suffix

The *:string* suffix instructs 1-2-3 to treat the second argument of a {Let} command as a literal string. If you append the suffix *:string* to the end of a literal value argument, 1-2-3 will enter that value in the destination cell as a label. For example, when 1-2-3 evaluates the command *{Let A1,12345}*, it will place the value 12345 in cell A1. On the other hand, when 1-2-3 evaluates the command *{Let A1,12345:string}*, it will place the label *'12345* in that cell.

If you append the *:string* suffix to the end of a formula or function argument, then 1-2-3 will store that formula or function as a label—not the result of that formula or function—in the destination cell. For example, suppose that cell A1 of a worksheet contains the value 100, and that cell A2 contains the value 50. When 1-2-3 evaluates the command *{Let A3,+A1+A2}*, it will place the value 150 in cell A3. When 1-2-3 evaluates the command *{Let A3,+A1+A2:string}*, however, it will place the string *'+A1+A2* in that cell. In the same manner, if cell A1 contains the string *John* and cell A2 contains the string *Smith*, then the command *{Let A3,A1&" "&A2}* will put the label *'John Smith* in cell A3, while the command *{Let A3,+A1&" "&A2:string}* will put *'+A1&" "&A2* in that cell.

The *:string* suffix has no effect on a literal string argument. Whether you use the suffix or not, 1-2-3 will enter the argument into the destination cell as a label.

The *:value* Suffix

The optional *:value* suffix allows you to override this default treatment of invalid formulas and functions. Whenever you append this suffix to the end of a formula or function argument, 1-2-3 will always attempt to evaluate that argument. If the formula or function is valid, 1-2-3 will store the result in the destination cell, just as it would if you had not used the *:value* suffix. If the formula or function is not valid, however, 1-2-3 will not treat it as a label. Instead, 1-2-3 will beep, stop the macro, and display a message like *Macro: Invalid string in LET (B1)* at the bottom of the screen.

Because the *:value* suffix commands 1-2-3 to treat the second argument of a {Let} command as a value, it has no effect if the second argument is a literal value. If the second argument is a literal string, however, the *:value* suffix will always produce an error. Why? Because the *:value* suffix tells 1-2-3 to enter a string as a value—something it cannot do.

Conditional Testing

1-2-3 offers two commands—{If} and /xi—that allow you to build conditional tests into your macros. If the conditional test presented by the {If} or /xi command is true, then 1-2-3 will execute one set of commands. If the test is false, the macro will execute a different set of commands. The {If} does not work in 1-2-3 Release 1A. The /xi command works in all releases of 1-2-3.

The {If} Command

The form of the {If} command is

{If CONDITION}

where the single argument, CONDITION, is a conditional test—a formula or function that compares two values or strings using a conditional operator and returns the result *True* (the value 1) or *False* (the value 0). If the conditional test is true, 1-2-3 will execute the next instruction in the cell that contains the {If} command. If the conditional test is false, 1-2-3 will skip the remaining instructions in the cell that contains the {If} command and execute the instructions in the cell below that cell.

The conditional tests you'll use with the {If} command have exactly the same form and follow the same rules as the conditional tests you use as the first argument of an @IF function. (For a complete discussion of conditional tests, see the discussion of the @IF function in Chapter 5.)

An Example

The macro in Figure 14-8 uses an {If} command to evaluate the user's response to a {GetLabel} command. The first command in this macro causes 1-2-3 to display the message *Save worksheet as BACKUP.WK1 (y/n)?* in the control panel and wait for a response from the user. When the user types a response, 1-2-3 will store that response in the cell named RESPONSE (B5). Next, 1-2-3 will execute the commands *{If RESPONSE="n"}{Quit}*. The {If} command that begins this statement compares the entry in RESPONSE to the literal string *"n"*. If the user types *n* or *N* in response to the prompt, *RESPONSE* will contain the label *'n* or *'N*. Because capitalization does not affect the result of a conditional test, either of these responses makes the conditional test *RESPONSE="n"* true. Thus, 1-2-3 will evaluate the next instruction in the same cell. That command, *{Quit}*, tells 1-2-3 to cancel the execution of the macro and return to the READY mode.

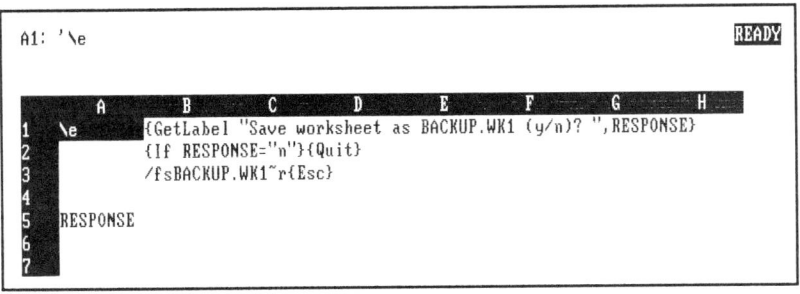

```
A1: '\e                                                          READY


       A      B         C        D        E        F        G        H
  1   \e    {GetLabel "Save worksheet as BACKUP.WK1 (y/n)? ",RESPONSE}
  2         {If RESPONSE="n"}{Quit}
  3         /fsBACKUP.WK1~r{Esc}
  4
  5   RESPONSE
  6
  7
```

FIGURE 14-8: The {If} command

If the user types anything but *n* or *N* in response to the {GetLabel} prompt, the conditional test *RESPONSE="n"* will be false. When the conditional test of an {If} command is false, 1-2-3 will skip any instructions that follow in the same cell and execute the instructions in the next cell. In this case, 1-2-3 will skip the *{Quit}* command that follows the {If} command in cell B2, and execute the statement in cell B3. When 1-2-3 evaluates this statement, it begins by issuing the /File Save command, typing the name BACKUP.WK1, and pressing [Enter]. If there is already a file with that name, 1-2-3 will present you with two choices: Cancel and Replace. In response to this menu, 1-2-3 will type *r*, which chooses the Replace option and saves the file.

(The final {Esc} accounts for the case in which there is no file with the name BACKUP.WK1. In that case, {Esc} simply cancels the unnecessary keystroke *r*.)

A Note

In many cases, you'll follow the {If} command with the LCL command {Branch}. The {Branch} command tells 1-2-3 to "branch" the macro to a different part of the worksheet. Following an {If} command with a {Branch} command tells 1-2-3 to branch to the location specified by the {Branch} command if the conditional test specified by the {If} command is true. We'll explain {Branch} in a few pages.

The /xi Command

1-2-3 offers another conditional-testing command: /xi. The /xi command is nearly identical to the {If} command. Unlike the {If} command, however, the /xi command works in all releases of 1-2-3.

The form of the /xi command is

/xiCONDITION~

where the single argument, CONDITION, is a conditional test. The ending tilde is an essential part of this command.

The operation of the /xi command is the same as that of the {If} command. If the conditional test is true, 1-2-3 will execute the instructions in the cell that contains the /xi command. If the conditional test is false, 1-2-3 will skip the remaining instructions in the cell that contains the /xi command and execute the instruction in the next cell. For example, you could use the command */xiRESPONSE="n"~* in place of the command *{IF REPONSE="n"}* in cell B2 in Figure 14-8 without affecting the function of the macro.

Looping: The {For} Command

The LCL also gives you the ability to create loops in your macros. Loops allow 1-2-3 to repeat selected commands a specific number of times.

The best way to program a loop within a 1-2-3 macro is to use the {For} command. The form of this command is

{For *counter*,start,stop,step,*routine*}

RELEASE
► 2.2 ◄

where *routine* is an address, range name, ►or, if you use 1-2-3 Release 2.2, a formula or function that returns the name or address of a cell.◄ In any case, the argument should specify the starting location of the set of commands you want 1-2-3 to execute repeatedly. The remaining arguments— *counter*, start, stop, and step—control how many times 1-2-3 should execute those commands (that is, how many "passes" it should make through the loop).

The looping process works in the following way. Before 1-2-3 makes the first pass through the loop, it stores the value specified by the <u>start</u> argument (the Start value) in the cell specified by the *counter* argument (the counter cell). If the value stored in *counter* doesn't exceed the value specified by the <u>stop</u> argument (the Stop value), 1-2-3 executes the instructions that begin at the cell specified by *routine*.

As soon as 1-2-3 reaches a blank cell or a {Return} command, it ends the first pass through the loop. Before making another pass, 1-2-3 adds the value specified by the <u>step</u> argument (the Step value) to the value in the counter cell, then compares the new counter value to the Stop value. If the value of counter still does not exceed the Stop value, 1-2-3 makes another pass through the loop.

1-2-3 continues this process of increasing the counter, testing it against the Stop value, and making another pass through the loop until the value stored in the counter cell exceeds the Stop value. At this point, instead of making another pass through the loop, 1-2-3 breaks out of the {For} command and executes the next instruction in the macro.

An Example

Suppose you want 1-2-3 to print a worksheet a specified number of times using the current Print settings. The looping macro shown in Figure 14-9 makes this possible. The first command in this macro displays the prompt *Print how many copies?* and stores your response as a value in the cell named COPIES (cell B8). If you type 5, for example, 1-2-3 will store the value *5* in that cell. After you have specified the number of copies you want to print, 1-2-3 will execute the statement in cell B2, which instructs 1-2-3 to issue the / Print Printer Align command. This command prepares 1-2-3 for printing and leaves it within the Print Printer menu.

```
B3: '{For COUNT,1,COPIES,1,PRINT}                          READY

        A         B            C          D         E       F       G       H
   1   \f        {GetNumber "Print how many copies? ",COPIES}
   2             /ppa
   3             {For COUNT,1,COPIES,1,PRINT}
   4             q
   5
   6   PRINT     gp
   7
   8   COPIES
   9   COUNT
  10
  11
```

FIGURE 14-9: The {For} command

After 1-2-3 has completed these two steps, it will execute the command in cell B3, *{For COUNT,1,COPIES,1,PRINT}*. In this command, the counter argument is a reference to the named range COUNT (B9). The Start value is 1, the Stop value is a reference to the cell named COPIES (B8), and the Step value is 1. The location argument is a reference to the cell named PRINT (B6). This {For} command instructs 1-2-3 to execute the commands that begin in PRINT (cell B6) repeatedly until the value in COUNT exceeds the value in COPIES—the value you typed in response to the {GetNumber} prompt.

To show how the {For} loop works, suppose you press [Alt]f to invoke this macro, then enter the value 3 in response to the prompt *Print how many copies?* When 1-2-3 first executes the {For} command in cell B3, it will place the value 1 (the Start value) in COUNT and then will compare that value to the value stored in COPIES (3). Since 1 is not greater than 3, 1-2-3 will execute the instructions in PRINT. These keystrokes tell 1-2-3 to print the worksheet and then advance to the top of the next page.

After 1-2-3 has executed all the keystrokes in PRINT (cell B6), it will look to the next cell (B7) for more instructions. Since cell B7 is blank, 1-2-3 will end the first pass through the loop and reevaluate the {For} command in cell B3. Executing the {For} command for a second time causes 1-2-3 to increase the value in COUNT by the Step value, 1. Since the new value in COUNT, 2, does not exceed 3 (the Stop value in COPIES), 1-2-3 will again execute the keystrokes in PRINT, printing another copy of the report. After it executes these keystrokes for a second time, 1-2-3 will reevaluate the {For} command in cell B3 again and increase the value in COUNT to 3. Because the value of COUNT still does not exceed the Stop value (3), 1-2-3 will print the report again.

After 1-2-3 prints the worksheet for the third time, it will repeat the {For} command for a fourth time. As before, when 1-2-3 executes the {For} command, it will increase the value in COUNT by one. Because the new value in COUNT (4) now exceeds the Stop value in COPIES (3), 1-2-3 will not make another pass through the loop. Instead, it will look for the next instruction in the macro. Because {For} is the only command in cell B3, 1-2-3 will look to cell B4 for the next command. The single keystroke in this cell instructs 1-2-3 to choose Quit from the Print Printer menu and return 1-2-3 to the READY mode. Because cell B7 is blank, 1-2-3 will then stop the macro.

Controlling the Execution of Loops

In most cases, you'll want 1-2-3 to execute the instructions in a loop as many times as prescribed by the Start, Stop, and Step values. In some cases, however, you may not want 1-2-3 to execute all of the instructions in a loop during each pass through that loop. In other cases, you may wish to break out of the loop before the value of the counter exceeds the Stop value. The LCL includes two commands—{Return} and {ForBreak}—that make it possible to do these things.

The {Return} Command

The {Return} command instructs 1-2-3 to return to the {For} command that controls a loop without executing the remaining instructions in the loop. For example, suppose that you want to create a macro that will enter zeros in all of the blank cells in a column but leave the contents of any occupied cells in place. To do this, you could use an {If} command and a {Return} command in a {For} loop, as shown in Figure 14-10.

```
A1: '\g                                                              READY

         A         B         C         D         E         F         G         H
  1     \g        {For COUNT,1,8192-@CELLPOINTER("row")+1,1,FILL}
  2
  3     FILL      {If @CELLPOINTER("type")<>"b"}{Down}{Return}
  4               0{Down}
  5
  6     COUNT
  7
```

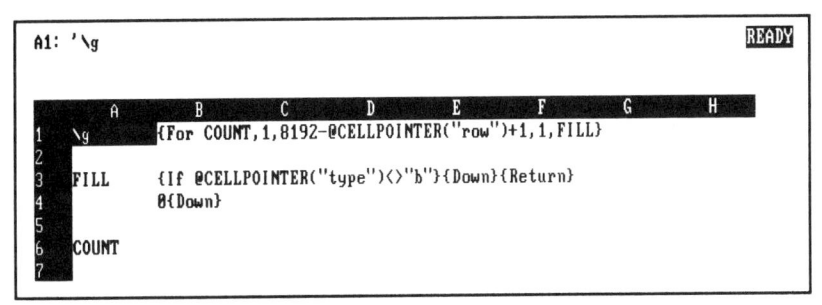

FIGURE 14-10: Using {Return} in a {For} Loop

Let's look at how this macro works. The first command

{For COUNT,1,8192-@CELLPOINTER("row")+1,1,FILL}

sets up the {For} loop that commands 1-2-3 to execute the instructions that begin in FILL (cell B3) until the cell pointer reaches the bottom of the worksheet. The counter argument is a reference to the cell named COUNT. The Start value and Step value are both 1. The Stop value is *8192-@CELLPOINTER("row")+1*, which sets the Stop value equal to the number of rows between the current row and the bottom of the worksheet.

The {If} command in cell B3 determines whether the current cell is blank or occupied. If the cell is blank, the @CELLPOINTER function will return the result "b", and the {If} statement will be true. In that case, 1-2-3 will skip the commands that follow the {If} statement in cell B3 and execute the statement in cell B4 instead. This statement tells 1-2-3 to enter 0 into the current cell, then move the cell pointer down to the next cell. Because cell B5 is blank, 1-2-3 then returns to the {For} command in cell B1.

However, if the current cell is not blank (that is, if the @CELLPOINTER function returns a string other than "b"), 1-2-3 follows a different course of action. Because a result other than "b" makes the {If} statement in cell B3 true, 1-2-3 will execute the commands that follow that statement. The command *{Down}* instructs 1-2-3 to move the cell pointer down one cell. The *{Return}* command tells 1-2-3 to return to the beginning of the loop (the {For} command in cell B1) without executing the remaining commands in that loop (in this case, the commands in cell B4). Consequently, 1-2-3 does not replace the existing contents of the current cell with the value 0.

When 1-2-3 reevaluates the {For} command, it increases the value of the counter (COUNT) by the Step value (1). As long as the new value in COUNT does not exceed the Stop value, 1-2-3 will make another pass through the loop.

In most cases, including this one, you can eliminate the need for a {Return} statement by reversing the conditional test. For example, the macro shown in Figure 14-11 does the same thing as the one shown in Figure 14-10. By reversing the conditional test, however, we are able to remove both a {Return} command and a

{Down} command from the macro. In general, it is better to define your conditional tests to avoid using the {Return} command.

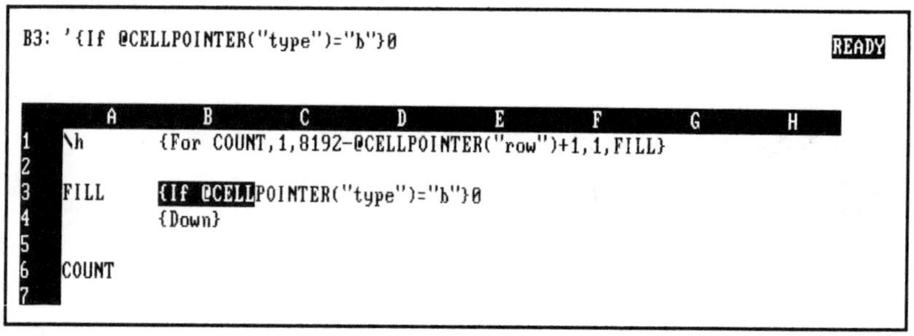

```
B3: '{If @CELLPOINTER("type")="b"}0                                    READY

        A           B           C         D       E       F       G       H
1   \h          {For COUNT,1,8192-@CELLPOINTER("row")+1,1,FILL}
2
3   FILL        {If @CELLPOINTER("type")="b"}0
4               {Down}
5
6   COUNT
7
```

FIGURE 14-11: An alternative approach

The {ForBreak} Command

The {ForBreak} command instructs 1-2-3 to cancel the execution of a {For} loop entirely and execute the instruction that follows the {For} command that controls the loop. To see how {ForBreak} works, suppose you want to modify the multiple-printing macro shown in Figure 14-9 so that it prints a maximum of ten copies. To do this, you can use an {If} and {ForBreak} command within the {For} loop, as shown in Figure 14-12.

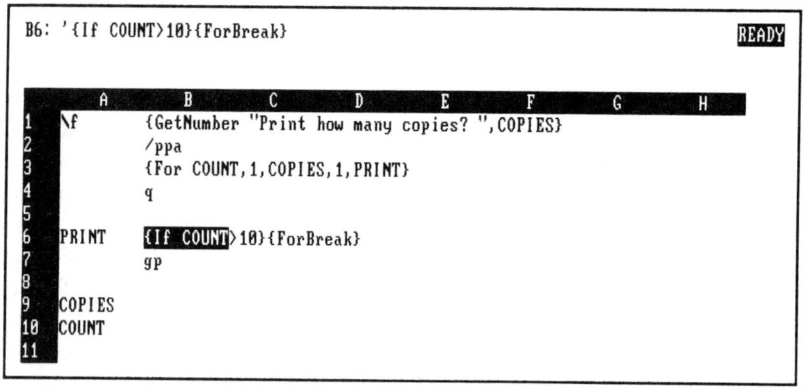

```
B6: '{If COUNT>10}{ForBreak}                                           READY

        A           B           C         D       E       F       G       H
1   \f          {GetNumber "Print how many copies? ",COPIES}
2               /ppa
3               {For COUNT,1,COPIES,1,PRINT}
4               q
5
6   PRINT       {If COUNT>10}{ForBreak}
7               gp
8
9   COPIES
10  COUNT
11
```

FIGURE 14-12: The {ForBreak} command

As you can see, the macro shown in Figure 14-12 begins in exactly the same way as the one in Figure 14-9: by asking how many copies you want to print and storing your response in the cell named COPIES (B9). After you tell 1-2-3 how many copies to print, 1-2-3 issues the / Print Printer Align command. Then it executes the {For} command in cell B3, which tells it to execute the instructions that begin in the cell named PRINT (B6) until the value in COUNT exceeds the value in COPIES.

The difference between these two macros is in the first line of the PRINT routine. The routine in Figure 14-12 begins with the command *{If COUNT>10}*, which commands 1-2-3 to test the value of COUNT at the beginning of each pass through the loop. During the first ten passes through the loop, this statement will be false, so 1-2-3 will skip the remaining instructions in cell B6 and execute the instructions in cell B7, which print the report. As 1-2-3 begins the eleventh pass through the loop, however, COUNT will contain the value 11. Since 11 is greater than 10, the {If} statement in cell B6 will be true, and 1-2-3 will execute the {ForBreak} command in that cell. That command instructs 1-2-3 to exit from the loop and continue executing the macro with the instruction that follows the {For} statement. In this case, 1-2-3 executes the keystroke in cell B4, which instructs it to quit from the Print menu and return to the READY mode.

Branching

In most cases, 1-2-3 will execute the statements in a macro in order. First, 1-2-3 will execute all the instructions in the first cell of the macro, then all the instructions in the cell below the first cell, and then the instructions in the cell below the second cell, and so forth. When 1-2-3 encounters a blank cell or a {Quit} command, the macro ends.

The LCL command {Branch} lets you redirect the flow of a macro. When 1-2-3 encounters a {Branch} command in a macro, it stops executing the current series of instructions and continues with the instructions in the cell specified by the command. In other words, the macro "branches" to the cell specified by the {Branch} command.

Because {Branch} is an LCL command, it is not available in 1-2-3 Release 1A. However, 1-2-3 offers another branching command—/xg—that works in all releases of 1-2-3.

The {Branch} Command

The form of the {Branch} command is

{Branch *location*}

where the single argument, *location*, specifies the cell that contains the statement you want the macro to process next—the cell you want the macro to branch to. This argument can be a cell reference, a range reference, a range name, ▶or, if you use 1-2-3 Release 2.2, a formula or function that returns the name or address of a cell or range.◀ If *location* refers to a multiple-cell range, the macro will branch to the upper-left cell of that range.

RELEASE ▶ 2.2 ◀

When 1-2-3 branches to another location, it starts executing the instructions at that location, just as it would any other set of instructions. First, 1-2-3 will execute all the instructions in the cell specified by the {Branch} command. After that, 1-2-3 will execute all the instructions in the cell below that cell, then the instructions in the cell below the second cell, and so forth. 1-2-3 will continue in this fashion until it encounters a blank cell, a {Quit} command, or another {Branch} command. If 1-2-3 encounters a blank cell or a {Quit} command, it will stop the macro at that point—it will not "return" to the original macro. If 1-2-3 encounters another {Branch} command, it will branch to the indicated location and execute the instruction it finds there.

You'll almost always use the {Branch} command in conjunction with the {If} command, as in the simple statement *{IF TEST=1}{Branch TRUE}*. You'll use the {If} command to define a conditional test. If that test is true, the {Branch} command will redirect the macro. In this situation, for example, if the value in the cell named TEST is 1, the {Branch} command will branch the macro to the cell named TRUE.

An Example

As you recall from our discussion of the {GetNumber} command earlier in this chapter, 1-2-3 will place the value ERR in the destination cell if the response to a {GetNumber} prompt is not a value. This result causes problems for most macros. In the case of the macro shown in Figure 14-12, for example, this result causes 1-2-3 to keep printing copies of the worksheet indefinitely.

The macro shown in Figure 14-13 uses the LCL's {Branch} command to avoid this problem. As you can see, this macro begins in the same way that the macro shown in Figure 14-9 does—by asking you for the number of copies you want to print and storing your response in the cell named COPIES (B9). The next statement tests your response to the {GetNumber} command. We have given the name TEST to the cell that contains this statement—cell B2.

```
B2: '{If @ISERR(COPIES)}{Branch REDO}                              READY

         A          B          C          D          E          F          G          H
1       \f         {GetNumber "Print how many copies? ",COPIES}
2       TEST       {If @ISERR(COPIES)}{Branch REDO}
3                  /ppa
4                  {For COUNT,1,COPIES,1,PRINT}
5                  q
6
7       PRINT      gp
8
9       COPIES
10      COUNT
11      REDO       {GetNumber "Try again. How many copies? ",COPIES}
12                 {Branch TEST}
13
```

FIGURE 14-13: The {Branch} command

If you entered a value, the conditional test *@ISERR(COPIES)* will be false, and 1-2-3 will print the number of copies that you have requested. If you typed a label or an invalid formula or function, however, COPIES will contain the value ERR, and the conditional test *@ISERR(COPIES)* will be true. In that case, 1-2-3 will execute the command *{Branch REDO}*, which instructs it to stop executing the macro at the current point and continue at the cell named REDO (B11). The command in that cell causes 1-2-3 to display the prompt *Try again. How many copies?* and await your response, which it will store in the cell named COPIES (the same destination as the original {GetNumber} command in cell B1).

After you enter a response, 1-2-3 will execute the command *{Branch TEST}*, which instructs 1-2-3 to branch back to the cell named TEST (B2). If you have typed a valid response, the conditional test *@ISERR(COPIES)* will be false, and 1-2-3 will print the number of copies that you specified. If your response was invalid, the conditional test will be true, and 1-2-3 will branch to cell B11 again. 1-2-3 will continue this process until you enter a valid response, or until you press [Ctrl][Break] to exit from the macro.

More Examples

Figure 14-14 shows another example of the {Branch} command. This simple macro is designed to overcome the limitation of the IBM PC keyboard that makes it impossible to use the numeric keypad to enter numbers and to move the cell pointer at the same time. The macro steps down through a column of cells, pausing on each cell for you to enter a number. Since the macro handles the movement of the cell pointer, you can use the keypad to enter the numbers.

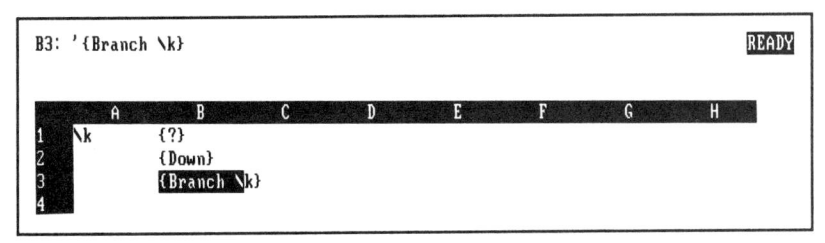

```
B3: '{Branch \k}                                    READY

        A        B        C        D        E        F        G        H
1      \k       {?}
2               {Down}
3               {Branch \k}
4
```

FIGURE 14-14: The keypad macro

When you run the macro, 1-2-3 will read the {?} command, which will make the macro stop and wait for you to do something. When you press [Enter], the macro will execute the {Down} command, which will move the cell pointer down one cell, and then will execute the command {Branch\k}, which causes the macro to start over from the top. The macro will keep running until you press [Ctrl][Break] to stop it.

By the way—you can use the basic structure of the macro in Figure 14-14 to create all sorts of simple repeating macros. For example, you'll notice that the macro in Figure 14-15 is very similar in structure to the one in Figure 14-14. This macro causes 1-2-3 to step down through a column of label entries, adding a single space at the beginning of each of those labels. When 1-2-3 executes the macro, it presses the [Edit] key to enter the EDIT mode. Then it presses the [Home] key to move to the beginning of the current entry, then the → key to move one space to the right. Next, the macro simply types a space and then presses ↓ to end the edit and move the cell pointer down one cell. Finally, 1-2-3 will execute the command {Branch\i}, which causes the macro to start over from the top. The macro will keep running until you press [Ctrl][Break].

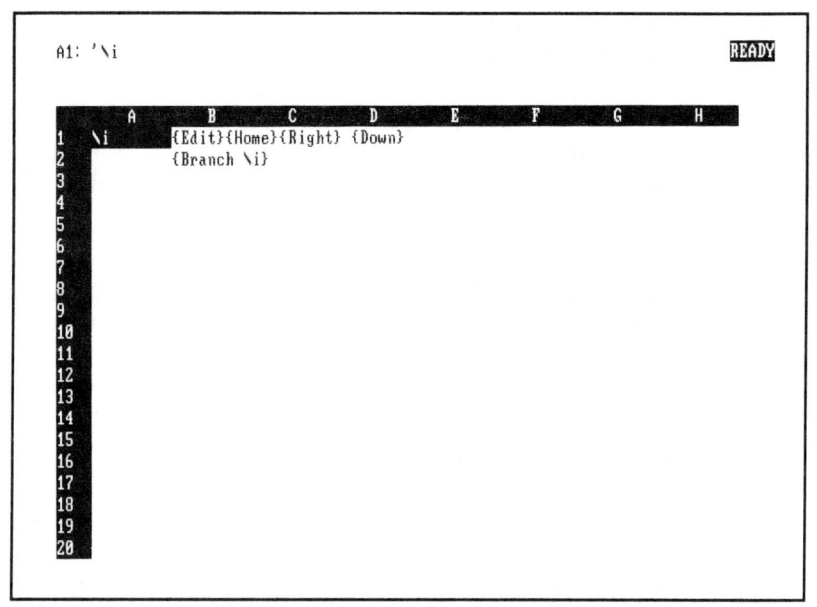

```
A1: '\i                                              READY

         A       B        C        D        E        F        G       H
    1   \i    {Edit}{Home}{Right} {Down}
    2         {Branch \i}
    3
    4
    ...
   20
```

FIGURE 14-15: The indent macro

The /xg Command

The form of the /xg command is

  /xglocation~

where *location* specifies the cell to which you want the macro to branch. This argument must be a cell address, a range address, or a range name. The ending tilde is a required part of the command.

The /xg command works just like the {Branch} command. When 1-2-3 encounters an /xg command in a macro, it immediately branches the macro to the location specified by the argument of that command. For example, you could substitute the commands */xgREDO~* and */xgTEST~* for the commands *{Branch REDO}* and *{Branch TEST}* in cells B2 and B12 of the macro in Figure 14-13 without changing the function of the macro in any way.

Subroutine Calls

The {Branch} and /xg commands allow you to redirect the flow of a macro. When 1-2-3 encounters a {Branch} or /xg command in a macro, it stops executing the current series of instructions and continues with the instructions in the cell specified by the command. Importantly, once 1-2-3 has branched to the specified destination, it will not execute any more instructions in the original macro (unless you use another {Branch} or /xg command to loop the macro back onto itself).

> **TIP: WHERE IS THE CELL POINTER?**
>
> In Chapter 13, we pointed out that when 1-2-3 is running a macro, the cell pointer does not "step down" through the cells of the worksheet that contain the labels that define that macro. The position of the cell pointer is completely independent of the location of the macro. You will want to keep this concept in mind as you work with the {Branch} and /xg commands. When you use {Branch} or /xg to redirect the flow of a macro, you are not telling 1-2-3 to move the cell pointer but to branch the execution of the macro to the instructions in another cell. To repeat: The position of the cell pointer is independent of the location of the macro commands 1-2-3 is executing.

In some cases, you may want a macro to process a group of instructions in a remote location and then return to the original macro. In these cases, you probably don't want to use the {Branch} command. Instead, you'll want to call the remote instructions as a subroutine.

The form of a subroutine call is simply

{*subroutine*}

where *subroutine* specifies the name or address of the cell or range where the instructions that you want 1-2-3 to process begin. ▶In 1-2-3 Release 2.2, this argument can be a formula or function that returns the name or address of a cell or range. In earlier releases of 1-2-3, it must be a literal name or address.◀ For example, the subroutine call {Z100} tells 1-2-3 to execute the instructions in cell Z100 and the command {TEST} tells 1-2-3 to execute the instructions in the cell named TEST.

RELEASE ▶ 2.2 ◀

1-2-3 processes subroutines in exactly the same way it processes other macros. First, 1-2-3 will execute all the instructions in the first cell of the subroutine, then all the commands in the cell below that cell, and then the instructions in the cell below the second cell, and so forth. However, when 1-2-3 reaches the end of a subroutine (which is usually marked by a blank cell), it does not end the macro. Instead, it returns control of the macro to the instruction that follows the subroutine call.

As you begin to create more complex LCL programs, there will be times when you'll need a macro to perform the same task over and over. This kind of repeating task is a perfect application for subroutines. Instead of repeating the instructions that control a task over and over in your macro, you can store those instructions in a single subroutine. Then, when you need to perform the task, you can simply call the subroutine. Storing the instructions that perform a repeating task in subroutines saves a lot of time and effort.

An Example

For example, consider the simple worksheet in Figure 14-16. The formulas in the range C8..F15 in this worksheet all depend on the rate assumption stored in cell B20, which we have named RATE. Suppose you want to print this worksheet three times: once with an inflation rate assumption of 5%, once with an inflation rate assumption of 7.5%, and once with an inflation rate assumption of 10%.

```
A1: [W14]                                                              READY

              A         B         C         D         E         F         G
 1                        Amalgamated Widgets, Incorporated
 2                             5-Year Expense Projection
 3                         (Amounts in Thousands of Dollars)
 4
 5                      1987      1988      1989      1990      1991     Total
 6                     --------  --------  --------  --------  --------  ----------
 7    Expense
 8    COGS            $136,665  $150,332  $165,365  $181,901  $200,091  $834,353
 9    Salaries         $41,118   $45,230   $49,753   $54,728   $60,201  $251,030
10    Insurancce          $595      $655      $720      $792      $871    $3,633
11    Telephone         $4,867    $5,354    $5,889    $6,478    $7,126   $29,714
12    T&E               $1,349    $1,484    $1,632    $1,796    $1,975    $8,236
13    Supplies          $7,638    $8,402    $9,242   $10,166   $11,183   $46,631
14    Advertising      $17,092   $18,801   $20,601   $22,749   $25,024  $104,348
15    Depreciation      $1,368    $1,505    $1,655    $1,821    $2,003    $8,352
16                     --------  --------  --------  --------  --------  ----------
17    Total           $210,692  $231,761  $254,937  $280,431  $308,474  $1,286,296
18                     ========  ========  ========  ========  ========  ==========
19
20   Inflation Rate       10%
```

FIGURE 14-16: A sample worksheet

Figure 14-17 shows the macro that will print the worksheet. As you can see, the macro begins by instructing 1-2-3 to issue the /Print Printer Range command, specify cells A1..G20 as the Print range, and then quit from the Print menu. The second statement commands 1-2-3 to store the value .05 (the first inflation assumption) in cell B20. The third statement, {PRINT}, is a subroutine call. When 1-2-3 reads this statement, it calls the subroutine that begins in cell B30 (which we named PRINT). The keystrokes in this cell instruct 1-2-3 to issue the /Print Printer Align Go command, which causes it to recalculate the worksheet (see the accompanying Tip) and print the report. The final two instructions, *pq*, instruct 1-2-3 to advance the paper to the top of the next page, then quit out of the Print menu.

Once 1-2-3 has executed the instructions in the first cell of the subroutine, it looks to the next cell in column B (cell B31) for more instructions. Because cell B31 is blank, however, 1-2-3 returns to the instruction that follows the subroutine call in the main macro. Because the call to the PRINT subroutine is the last command in cell B24, 1-2-3 next executes the {Let} command in cell B25. This command instructs 1-2-3 to replace the value in RATE (cell B20) with the value .075. The next command, {PRINT}, is another call to the PRINT subroutine, which recalculates the worksheet, prints it, and quits out of the Print menu.

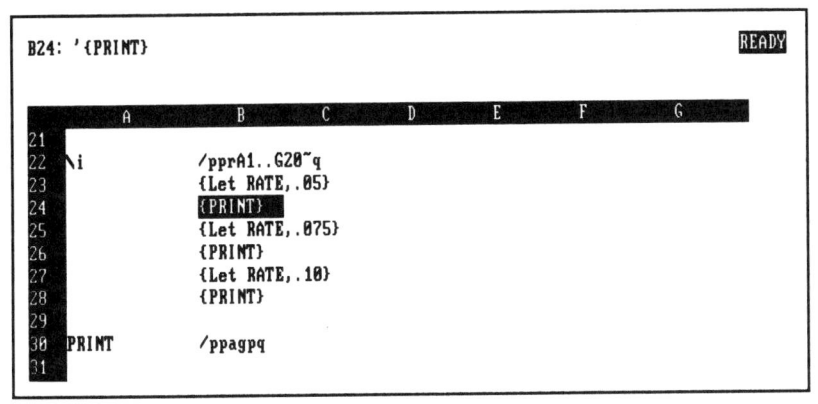

```
B24: '{PRINT}                                                    READY

          A              B         C         D         E         F         G
     21
     22    \i           /pprA1..G20~q
     23                 {Let RATE,.05}
     24                 {PRINT}
     25                 {Let RATE,.075}
     26                 {PRINT}
     27                 {Let RATE,.10}
     28                 {PRINT}
     29
     30    PRINT        /ppagpq
     31
```

FIGURE 14-17: A macro that uses a subroutine

As soon as 1-2-3 has finished this second execution of the PRINT subroutine, it returns the macro to cell B26, then skips to the command in cell B27, which stores the value .10 in cell B20. Next, 1-2-3 reads the statement, *{PRINT}*, in cell B28, which again calls the PRINT subroutine.

When 1-2-3 has finished printing the worksheet for the third time, it again returns control to the main macro. Because the subroutine call is the only command in cell B28, 1-2-3 looks to cell B29 for more instructions. Because cell B29 is blank, the macro ends.

TIP: AUTOMATIC RECALCULATION WITH THE /P COMMAND

When 1-2-3 encounters the keystrokes /p (which is the macro representation for the / Print command), in a macro immediately following a {GetLabel}, {GetNumber}, {Let}, or {Define} command, it will automatically recalculate the worksheet. 1-2-3 apparently assumes that since these commands make entries in cells of the worksheet, it is a good idea to recalculate before it prints. 1-2-3 will also recalculate automatically if the /p command is the first command in a subroutine, and the subroutine call is the command immediately following the {GetLabel}, {GetNumber}, {Let}, or {Define} command—as in the macro in Figure 14-17.

The /xc Command

In the previous examples, we called a subroutine by enclosing its name in braces. This type of subroutine call does not work in 1-2-3 Release 1A. However, 1-2-3 offers another command, /xc, which you can use to call a subroutine in all releases of 1-2-3. The form of this command is

/xc*location*~

where *location* is the literal address or name of the first cell in the subroutine. The final tilde is required.

The action of the /xc command is identical to that of the subroutine calls we've considered so far. When 1-2-3 encounters the /xc command, it temporarily suspends execution of the macro that contains the command and transfers control to the specified subroutine. 1-2-3 processes the instructions in the subroutine in the same way it processes the instructions in any other macro. As soon as 1-2-3 encounters a cell that does not contain a value or a string-producing formula, or a {Return} command, it will transfer control back to the calling macro and resume execution with the instruction that follows the subroutine call. For example, we could substitute the command */xcPRINT~* for the command *{PRINT}* in cells B24, B26, and B28 in Figure 14-17 without affecting the performance of the macro.

The {Return} Command in Subroutines

When 1-2-3 encounters the LCL command {Return} while it is processing a subroutine, it immediately stops processing the subroutine and returns the macro to the cell that contains the subroutine call. If you wish, you can use the {Return} command to mark the end of the subroutine. For example, in the macro in Figure 14-17, the subroutine PRINT ended with a blank cell. When 1-2-3 encountered this cell, it ended the subroutine and returned to the main macro. Instead of ending this subroutine with a blank cell, we could have ended it by placing the command {Return} in cell B31.

In most cases, you'll use a {Return} command to break out of a subroutine prematurely. For example, suppose that you want to let the user of the macro in Figure 14-17 tell 1-2-3 whether to print the worksheet or not. If the user chooses not to print the worksheet, 1-2-3 will return from the subroutine without printing the worksheet and will continue executing the macro.

To make this change, we'll insert a {GetLabel} command and an {If} command at the beginning of the PRINT subroutine. Figure 14-18 shows the revised macro. As you can see, the statements in the range B22..B28 are exactly the same as the ones in the same cells of the original macro. The instructions in the PRINT subroutine in Figure 14-18 are different, however. When 1-2-3 calls the PRINT routine in this revised macro, it executes the command in cell B30, which presents the prompt *Print the revised worksheet (y/n)?* at the top of the screen, and then places your response in the cell named ANSWER (B34). The next command evaluates the response. For example, if you typed *n* or *N*, the {If} command will be true and 1-2-3 will evaluate the command {Return}. This command tells 1-2-3 to break from the subroutine and return to the main macro without printing the worksheet. If you typed anything but *n* or *N*, the {If} statement will be false. In that case, 1-2-3 will evaluate the keystrokes in cell B32, which instruct it to print the worksheet.

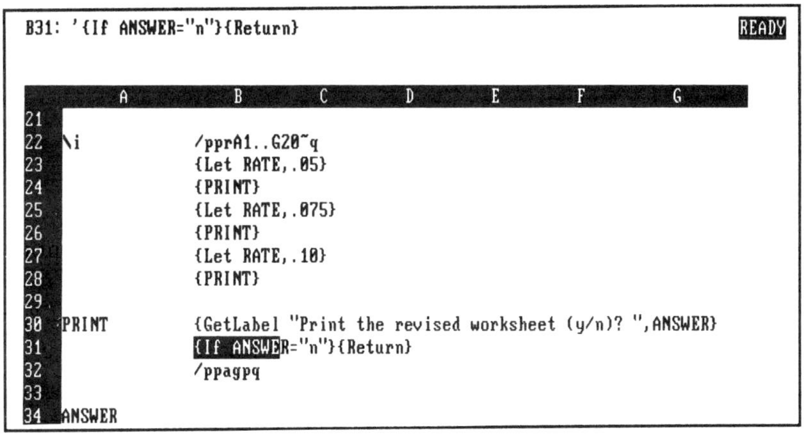

```
B31: '{If ANSWER="n"}{Return}                              READY

           A           B          C         D         E         F         G
21
22   \i              /pprA1..G20~q
23                   {Let RATE,.05}
24                   {PRINT}
25                   {Let RATE,.075}
26                   {PRINT}
27                   {Let RATE,.10}
28                   {PRINT}
29
30   \PRINT          {GetLabel "Print the revised worksheet (y/n)? ",ANSWER}
31                   {If ANSWER="n"}{Return}
32                   /ppagpq
33
34   ANSWER
```

FIGURE 14-18: Another {Return} command

Don't confuse the {Quit} command with the {Return} command. {Return} breaks out of the current subroutine and returns you to the calling macro. {Quit} completely cancels the execution of the entire macro. If 1-2-3 encounters a {Quit} command while it is processing a subroutine, it will stop processing both the subroutine and the calling macro.

The /xr Command

The {Return} command does not work in 1-2-3 Release 1A. However, 1-2-3 provides an alternative to the {Return} command—the /xr command—that works in any release. Like the {Return} command, /xr instructs 1-2-3 to suspend the execution of a subroutine and resume execution with the statement that follows the subroutine call in the main macro. Because the actions of these two commands are identical, you can use /xr wherever you would use the {Return} command, with exactly the same results. For example, you could substitute the /xr command for the {Return} command in cell B31 in Figure 14-18 without changing the function of the macro in any way.

Passing Arguments to Subroutines

As we have explained, you can use subroutines to streamline macros that command 1-2-3 to perform the same task over and over. In the previous example, the subroutine performed exactly the same action each time; it printed the current worksheet. In many cases, however, you'll want a subroutine to perform a slightly different task each time. In that event, you'll need to pass information to the subroutine when you call it so that it will know exactly what it is supposed to do.

For example, you may want to create a subroutine named ADDER that adds three values. Each time you call that subroutine, you'll want it to add three different values; therefore, each time you call the subroutine, you'll need to pass to it the three values you want it to add.

> **TIP: DON'T USE KEY WORDS AS SUBROUTINE NAMES**
>
> As you have seen, a subroutine call is simply the name of a range enclosed in braces ({}). As you also have seen, most LCL commands have essentially the same structure as subroutine calls. Unfortunately, this similarity of form can cause problems when the name of a subroutine is spelled the same way as an LCL command or key representation. When this happens, 1-2-3 will press the indicated key or perform the LCL command instead of passing control to the subroutine.
>
> For example, suppose you have assigned the name DELETE to the first cell of a subroutine. To call the subroutine, you would use the command {DELETE}. Because {Delete} is 1-2-3's macro representation for the [Del] key, 1-2-3 will "press" that key instead of calling the subroutine when it reads that command.
>
> There are two ways to avoid this kind of problem. The best way is not to use any of 1-2-3's keywords as the name of a subroutine. The second way is to use the /xc command to call your subroutines. Because this command does not use braces, there is no chance of confusing 1-2-3. If you must use a reserved keyword as the name of a subroutine, call it with the /xc command.

Although passing information to a subroutine increases the flexibility of the subroutine, it also increases the complexity of the subroutine call and of the subroutine itself. To pass information to a subroutine, you must include that information as arguments in the subroutine call, as shown below:

{*subroutine argument1,argument2,argument3,...*}

The arguments are the values, labels, formulas, or functions that you want to use in the subroutine. For example, the subroutine call

{ADDER 10,25,50)

calls the subroutine ADDER and passes the values 10, 25, and 50 to it.

The {Define} Command

When you pass arguments to a subroutine, the subroutine itself must begin with the LCL command {Define}. The form of this command is

{Define *location1*:**type1**,*location2*:**type2**,*location3*:**type3**,...}

The *location*:**type** argument pairs tell 1-2-3 where and in what form to store the arguments passed to it by the subroutine call. The first location:type pair instructs 1-2-3 how to deal with the first argument passed by the subroutine call, the second location:type pair tells 1-2-3 how to deal with the second argument passed to the subroutine, and so forth.

Each of the location arguments of a {Define} command should be the name address or name of a cell or range. ►(In 1-2-3 Release 2.2, it can be a formula or function that returns a name or address.)◄ These arguments tell 1-2-3 where to store the arguments passed to the subroutine. The {Define} command must include a location argument for every argument passed by the subroutine call.

RELEASE ► 2.2 ◄

The type suffixes, which are optional, tell 1-2-3 how to interpret the arguments that are passed to the subroutine by the subroutine call. There are two possible type arguments: *string* and *value*. If you don't specify a type suffix, or if you use the suffix *:string*, 1-2-3 will store the argument as a label. If you use the suffix *:value*, 1-2-3 will treat that argument as a value.

For example, if you want to pass values to the ADDER subroutine, you need to begin it with a command like

{Define A1:value,A2:value,A3:value}

The location arguments *A1*, *A2*, and *A3* tell 1-2-3 to store the arguments that will be passed to the subroutine in cells A1, A2, and A3. Since each of these location arguments is followed by the suffix *:value*, the arguments of the subroutine will be stored as values.

An Example

Let's consider how argument passing can streamline the printing macro shown in Figure 14-17. As you recall, that macro prints the range A1..G20 three times, changing the inflation factor in cell B20 (which is named RATE) before it prints each time. Figure 14-19 shows a revised version of this macro. As you can see, this macro begins just as the macro in Figure 14-17 does. The first statement in the macro commands 1-2-3 to issue the /Print Printer Range command, specify A1..G20 as the Print range, and then quit from the Print menu.

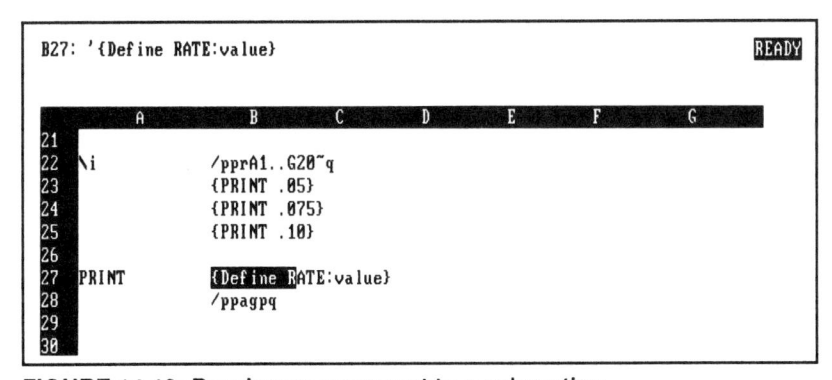

```
B27: '{Define RATE:value}                                    READY

       A          B           C       D       E       F       G
21
22    \i         /pprA1..G20~q
23               {PRINT .05}
24               {PRINT .075}
25               {PRINT .10}
26
27    PRINT     {Define RATE:value}
28               /ppagpq
29
30
```

FIGURE 14-19: Passing an argument to a subroutine

The use of argument passing streamlines the remainder of the macro. The second statement, *{PRINT .05}*, calls the subroutine named PRINT, which begins in cell B27, and passes the argument .05 to it. As you can see, the subroutine begins with the command *{Define RATE:value}*, which tells 1-2-3 to treat the argument passed by the subroutine call (in this case, the characters .05) as a value and store them in the cell named RATE (B20). After 1-2-3 has stored this value in RATE, it executes the keystrokes in cell B28, which cause 1-2-3 to recalculate the worksheet, print, advance the paper, and then quit from the Print menu.

Since cell B29 is blank, 1-2-3 returns control of the main macro after it prints. Because the subroutine call was the last statement in cell B23, 1-2-3 next executes the command {PRINT .075}, which again calls the PRINT subroutine. This time, 1-2-3 passes the value .075 to the subroutine, and the {Define} command stores this value in cell B20. The subroutine then recalculates the worksheet and prints.

After the macro has printed the report for the second time, it returns to cell B25, which contains the statement {PRINT .10}. This statement calls the subroutine PRINT and passes the value .10 to it. The {Define} command in cell B27 stores the value .10 in cell B20 as a value. The rest of the subroutine recalculates the worksheet and prints. Because the subroutine call is the last command in cell B25, and because cell B26 is blank, the macro ends at that point.

As you can see, passing the rates to the subroutine as arguments allows you to substitute a single {Define} command for three {Let} commands. The more times you repeat a process within a macro, the more efficient the use of argument passing will make your macro.

TIP: USE SINGLE WORD NAMES FOR YOUR SUBROUTINES

As you learned in Chapter 3, 1-2-3 allows you to include spaces within range names. For example, FIRST CELL, JAN RENT, and PAYROLL TAX are all valid range names. Unfortunately, you'll run into problems if you include spaces within the name of a subroutine. When you call a subroutine that has a multiple-word name, 1-2-3 will think you're trying to pass an argument rather than just making a simple subroutine call. In most cases, a macro error will result.

Fortunately, there are two ways to avoid this. First, you can enclose the name of the subroutine in quotation marks. To call the subroutine named PRINT IT, for example, you would use {"PRINT IT"}. The quotation marks tell 1-2-3 that both words are part of the routine name. Second, you can use the /xc command to call the subroutine. Because this command doesn't support argument passing, there's no chance of confusing 1-2-3.

Creating Custom Menus: The {MenuBranch} and {MenuCall} Commands

One of the LCL's most useful features is its ability to create custom menus. These custom menus look and work just like the ones that 1-2-3 presents when you press the / and issue commands. You can use this capability to create menus that ask the user simple yes/no questions to summarize frequently performed tasks, or to create complex menu-driven applications within 1-2-3.

Macro Menu Basics

The LCL commands that allow you to create custom menus are {MenuBranch} and {MenuCall}. The forms of these commands are

{MenuBranch *location*}
{MenuCall *location*}

where *location* is the name or address of the cell in the upper-left corner of the range that contains the statements that define the custom menu. ▶In 1-2-3 Release 2.2, it can be a formula or function that returns a name or address.◀

RELEASE
► 2.2 ◄

The difference between {MenuBranch} and {MenuCall} is the same as the difference between {Branch} and a subroutine call. The {MenuBranch} command "branches" the macro to the entries that define the menu. After 1-2-3 displays the menu and executes the instructions that correspond to your choice, it will not automatically return to the macro that contains the {MenuBranch} command. The {MenuCall} command calls the custom menu as a subroutine. After 1-2-3 displays the menu and executes the instructions that correspond to your choice, it will return to the statement that follows the {MenuCall} command in the main macro. Otherwise, the two commands are identical.

The location argument of the {MenuBranch} and {MenuCall} commands directs 1-2-3 to the area of the worksheet where you have defined a custom menu. For example, the command in cell B10 in Figure 14-20, *{MenuBranch PRINTIT}*, directs 1-2-3 to a menu that begins at the cell named PRINTIT (cell B12).

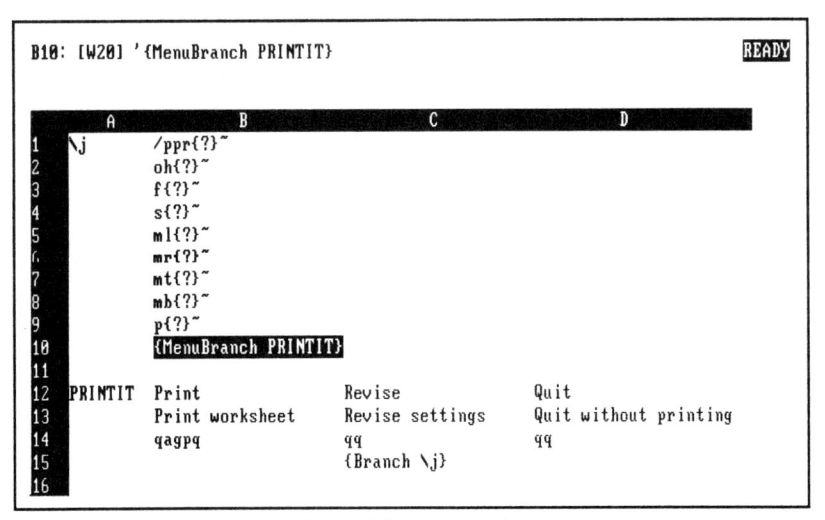

```
B10: [W20] '{MenuBranch PRINTIT}                              READY

         A         B              C              D
 1    \j        /ppr{?}~
 2              oh{?}~
 3              f{?}~
 4              s{?}~
 5              ml{?}~
 6              mr{?}~
 7              mt{?}~
 8              mb{?}~
 9              p{?}~
10              {MenuBranch PRINTIT}
11
12    PRINTIT   Print          Revise         Quit
13              Print worksheet Revise settings Quit without printing
14              qagpq          qq             qq
15                             {Branch \j}
16
```

FIGURE 14-20: The {MenuBranch} command

Before 1-2-3 can display a custom menu, you must define that menu in a range of the worksheet. All custom menus are structured in the same basic way. For example, the entries in the range B12..D15 in Figure 14-20 define a custom menu. The labels in cells B12, C12, and D12—the first row of the range—define the options in the menu. Notice that the first option is in cell B12, the cell referred to by the {MenuBranch} command in cell B10. The labels in cells B13, C13, and D13—the cells immediately below the ones that contain the menu choices—define the prompts for those choices. These prompts are just like the prompts 1-2-3 displays when you point to an option in one of its standard menus.

The entries in cells B14, C14, C15, and D14—the third and fourth rows of the menu range—define the action 1-2-3 will take after you make a choice from the menu. The choice you make determines which instructions 1-2-3 will execute. When you make a choice, 1-2-3 will execute the instructions in the cells below the label that defines that choice. For example, suppose you choose Print from the menu. 1-2-3 will execute the keystrokes in cell B14—the cell below the Print option in the menu definition. If you choose Quit, 1-2-3 will execute the keystrokes in cell D14.

All custom menus have this same basic form. The first option in the menu must be in the cell specified by the argument of the {MenuBranch} or {MenuCall} command—in this case, cell B12. The other options in the menu must be in the columns immediately to the right of the column that contains the first option, and in the same row as that option. 1-2-3 always assumes that the cell immediately beneath each option contains the prompt it should display when that option is highlighted. The cells in the third row of the menu definition contain the instructions 1-2-3 should execute after you make a choice.

A Simple Example

We'll use the simple macro in Figure 14-20 to demonstrate the {MenuBranch} command and the fundamentals of working with custom menus. This macro leads you through the process of establishing the Print settings for a worksheet, then, depending on the item you choose from a custom menu, either prints the worksheet, lets you revise the settings, or quits from the macro without printing.

The first nine statements in this macro allow you to select various Print settings. Each of these statements issues a 1-2-3 command and then uses the {?} command to pause the macro while you define a Print setting. For example, the statement in cell B1, */ppr{?}~*, issues the /Print Printer Range command and allows you to define the Print range. If you want to change the current setting, you type a new setting and press [Enter]. If you do not want to make a change, you just press [Enter].

Once you have specified the Print settings for the report, 1-2-3 executes the command in cell B10, *{MenuBranch PRINTIT}*. This command tells 1-2-3 to branch control of the macro to the cell named PRINTIT (cell B12) and execute the statements in that cell and the ones around it as a custom menu. As soon as 1-2-3 executes the {MenuBranch} command, it will display the custom menu shown in Figure 14-21.

```
A10:                                    MENU
Print  Revise  Quit
Print worksheet
```

FIGURE 14-21: A custom menu

The Custom Menu

As you can see, this menu looks very much like one of 1-2-3's standard menus. The first line of the menu displays the options from which you can choose. The choices in the menu—Print, Revise, and Quit—correspond to the labels in cells B12, C12, and D12. Notice that the first option in the menu, Print, is highlighted. When 1-2-3 first presents a custom menu, it always highlights the first choice on that menu.

The second line of the menu presents a prompt that explains the highlighted choice. 1-2-3 uses the labels in cells B13, C13, and D13—the cells immediately below the ones that contain the menu choices—as the prompts for those choices. For example, in Figure 14-21, 1-2-3 displays the prompt *Print worksheet* (which is defined by the label in cell B13) as the prompt for the highlighted option *Print* (which is defined by the label in cell B12). If you press → or ← to move the highlight from choice to choice, the prompt in the second line of the menu will change. For example, if you press → to move the highlight to the *Revise* choice, which is defined by the label in cell C12, 1-2-3 will use the label *'Revise settings* from cell C13 as the prompt.

Using the Menu

After 1-2-3 displays a custom menu, it pauses the macro and waits for you to make a choice. You make selections from custom menus in the same way you make selections from standard 1-2-3 menus. You can either press → or ← to point to the option you want to choose and then press [Enter] to select that option, or you can type the first letter in the name of the choice you want to select. For example, you could choose Quit from the menu shown in Figure 14-21 by pressing → twice and then pressing [Enter], or just by typing *q* or *Q*.

When you choose an item from a custom menu, 1-2-3 will execute the instructions in the cells below the label that defines the selected choice. For example, if you select the Print option—which is defined by the label in cell B12—from the menu in Figure 14-21, 1-2-3 will execute the keystrokes in cell B14. These keystrokes instruct 1-2-3 to choose Quit from the Print Options menu, issue the Align command, and print. After it prints, the macro will advance the paper and quit from the Print menu. Similarly, if you select Quit, which is the final item on the menu, 1-2-3 will transfer control of the macro to cell D14. The keystrokes in this cell instruct 1-2-3 to quit from the Print menu and the main menu and return to the READY mode.

After 1-2-3 executes the instructions in the first cell under an option, it looks to the next cell in the same column for more instructions. For example, if you choose the Print option, 1-2-3 will first execute the keystrokes in cell B14. After the macro executes the keystrokes in that cell, it looks to the next cell in column B—cell B15— for more instructions. Because that cell is blank, the macro ends.

If there are more instructions in the next cell, the macro will execute those instructions, then look at the next cell for more instructions, and so on. The macro will continue until it comes to a {Quit} command or a blank cell. For example, if you select Revise from the menu in Figure 14-21, 1-2-3 will execute the keystrokes in cell C14. These keystrokes instruct 1-2-3 to quit from the Print Options menu to the Print menu, then quit from the Print menu back to the READY mode. After 1-2-3 executes these keystrokes, it looks to cell C15, where it finds the command {Branch \j}, which instructs 1-2-3 to branch back to cell B1 (which is named \j) and execute the macro again.

Because we used the {MenuBranch} command to branch to this menu, the macro will stop running when it encounters a blank cell or a {Quit} command under one of the menu options. As we'll explain in a few pages, the macro would behave differently if we used the {MenuCall} command to call the menu.

Menu Rules

As you have seen, custom menus are relatively simple to design and use. However, there are a number of important rules that you should keep in mind whenever you program a custom menu.

Menu Choices Must Be Labels

The entries that define the options in custom menus must be labels (or formulas or functions that return strings) arranged in adjacent cells of a single row. The first option must be in the cell referred to by the location argument of the {MenuBranch} or {MenuCall} command that calls the menu.

You cannot use values or formulas that return values to define menu options. Similarly, there cannot be any blank cells in the row of cells that defines the menu options. If the cell referred to by the {MenuBranch} command contains a value or is blank, 1-2-3 will beep, display the message *Invalid use of Menu macro command*, and stop the macro. If any of the other cells in the row that defines the menu contain a value or are blank, 1-2-3 will truncate the menu at that point. For example, if cell C12 in Figure 14-20 were blank or contained a value, 1-2-3 would display a menu with only one item—Print—when it calls the menu.

1-2-3 always capitalizes the first letter in each option in a custom menu, even if the label that defines the option begins with a lower-case letter. 1-2-3 does not change the capitalization of the remaining letters in a menu choice, however.

Prompts Must Be Labels or Blanks

The entries that define the prompts for a custom menu should be labels (or formulas or functions that return strings). If a cell in the row of prompts contains a value, 1-2-3 will truncate the menu at that point, even if the entry that defines the corresponding menu option contains a label. 1-2-3 does allow you to include blank cells in the Prompt range, however. If you leave a cell in the Prompt range blank, 1-2-3 will simply leave the prompt line of the menu blank when you highlight the corresponding menu option.

TIP: BEGIN EACH OPTION WITH A DIFFERENT LETTER

As we have said, you can select an option from a custom menu by typing the first letter in the name of that option. If you intend to choose items from a custom menu in this way, each of those options should begin with a different letter. If two or more items on a menu begin with the same letter and you type that letter, 1-2-3 will select the one closest to the left edge of the menu. For example, Figure A shows a menu that includes two options that begin with the letter *S*. If you type the letter *s* while 1-2-3 is displaying this menu, it will execute the instructions that correspond to the Start option.

```
A1: '\k                                                              MENU
Start  Stop
Begin execution
          A              B              C              D       E
1       \k        {MenuBranch TEST}
2
3       TEST      Start          Stop
4                 Begin execution  Cancel Execution
5                 {Branch START}  {Branch STOP}
6
7
```

FIGURE A: A poorly designed menu

Controlling the Order of the Choices on a Custom Menu

The order of the options on a custom menu is determined by the order of the labels that define the menu in the cells of the worksheet. The entry in the cell referred to by the {MenuBranch} or {MenuCall} command will be the first option in the menu, the entry in the cell immediately to the right of that cell will be the second option, and so on. Consequently, the way you construct the menu determines the order in which 1-2-3 will display the items on a custom menu.

TIP: PLACE THE DEFAULT OPTION FIRST

Since 1-2-3 always highlights the first item on a menu when it first presents that menu to you, you can choose that item simply by pressing [Enter]; you don't have to point to another entry or press another letter. For this reason, it's a good idea to make the option you will choose most often the first option in the menu. To do this, just place that option in the cell that is referred to by the {MenuBranch} or {MenuCall} command.

Menus are Limited to Eight Options and 72 Characters

No custom menu can contain more than eight options. If you try to define more than eight options for a menu, 1-2-3 will display only the first eight options in the menu. The additional options are simply ignored.

1-2-3 also restricts the combined lengths of the options in a custom menu. When 1-2-3 displays a custom menu, it leaves one space in between each option. If the combined lengths of the characters in all the menu choices plus these spaces exceed 72 characters, 1-2-3 will not be able to display the menu at all. Instead, it will beep and display the message *Invalid use of Menu macro command*.

Column Widths Do Not Affect Custom Menus

There is a good chance that the length of the labels that define the options, prompts, and instructions in your menus will be greater than 1-2-3's default column width of nine characters. For this reason, you'll probably have a hard time reading the labels that define a menu unless you increase the widths of the columns that contain those labels. In the worksheet shown in Figure 14-20, for example, we have increased the widths of columns B, C, and D to 20 characters each. Figure 14-22 shows the same worksheet with the widths of columns B, C, and D set to 9 (the default width). Although expanding the widths of the columns that contain a menu can make it easier for you to read, it does not have any effect on 1-2-3's execution of the macro or on the appearance of the menu.

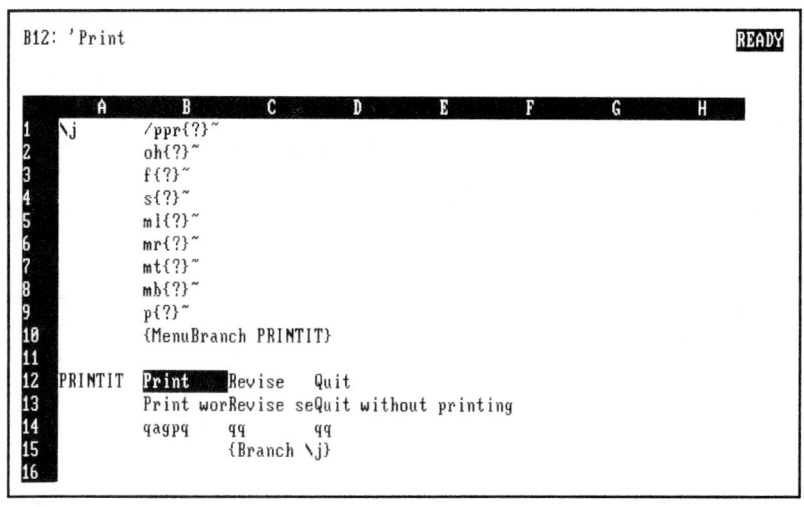

```
B12: 'Print                                                        READY

         A      B          C         D        E        F       G       H
1       \j     /ppr{?}~
2              oh{?}~
3              f{?}~
4              s{?}~
5              ml{?}~
6              mr{?}~
7              mt{?}~
8              mb{?}~
9              p{?}~
10             {MenuBranch PRINTIT}
11
12     PRINTIT Print      Revise     Quit
13             Print worRevise seQuit without printing
14             qagpq      qq        qq
15                        {Branch \j}
16
```

FIGURE 14-22: The effect of column widths

Using [Esc] to Escape from Custom Menus

If you press [Esc] in response to a custom menu, 1-2-3 will suspend the execution of the menu and return control of the macro to the cell that contains the command that called or branched to that menu. If there are instructions that follow in the same cell as the {MenuBranch} or {MenuCall} command, 1-2-3 will execute those instructions. If the {MenuBranch} or {MenuCall} command is the last instruction in its cell, 1-2-3 will look to the cell below that cell for more instructions. If that cell is blank, the macro will end. If that cell contains instructions, 1-2-3 will continue running the macro until it reaches a blank cell or a {Quit} command.

For example, if you press [Esc] while viewing the menu that is shown in Figure 14-21, 1-2-3 will pass control back to cell B10. Since the {MenuBranch} command is the only instruction in that cell, 1-2-3 will look to cell B11 for another instruction. Since that cell is blank, the macro ends.

The /xm Command

Like other LCL commands, {MenuBranch} is not available in 1-2-3 Release 1A. However, 1-2-3 offers an alternative menu-branching command, /xm, that can be used in any release of the program. The form of this command is

/xm*location*~

where *location* is the literal range name or address of the upper-left cell in a range that contains a menu definition. The tilde (~) is an essential part of this command.

The action of the /xm command is identical to that of the {MenuBranch} command. This command causes the macro to branch to the specified location and to treat the entries it finds there as a custom menu. For example, you could substitute the command */xmPRINTIT~* for the command *{MenuBranch PRINTIT}* in cell B10 of Figure 14-20 without changing the function of the macro.

The {MenuCall} Command

The LCL's {MenuCall} command lets you call a menu as a subroutine. As you may recall, after 1-2-3 executes the commands in the subroutine, it returns to the instruction that follows the subroutine call. When you call a custom menu with {MenuCall}, 1-2-3 will display the menu in exactly the same way that it does when you branch to the menu with {MenuBranch}. However, when 1-2-3 has completed the instructions under the menu option you select, it will return control of the macro to the instruction that follows the {MenuCall} command.

To see how this works, suppose you want to add a second menu to the macro in Figure 14-20 that allows you to choose one of three print styles: Normal, Expanded, or Compressed. Figure 14-23 shows the revised macro. As you can see, we have substituted the command *{MenuCall STYLE}* for the command *'s{?}~* in the fourth line of the macro. When 1-2-3 reads this command, it transfers the macro to the cell named STYLE (B17) and presents the menu that is shown in Figure 14-24. As you can see, the three choices on this menu—Normal, Compressed, and Expanded—correspond to the entries in cells B17, C17, and D17. The entries in the range B18..D18 serve as prompts for these choices.

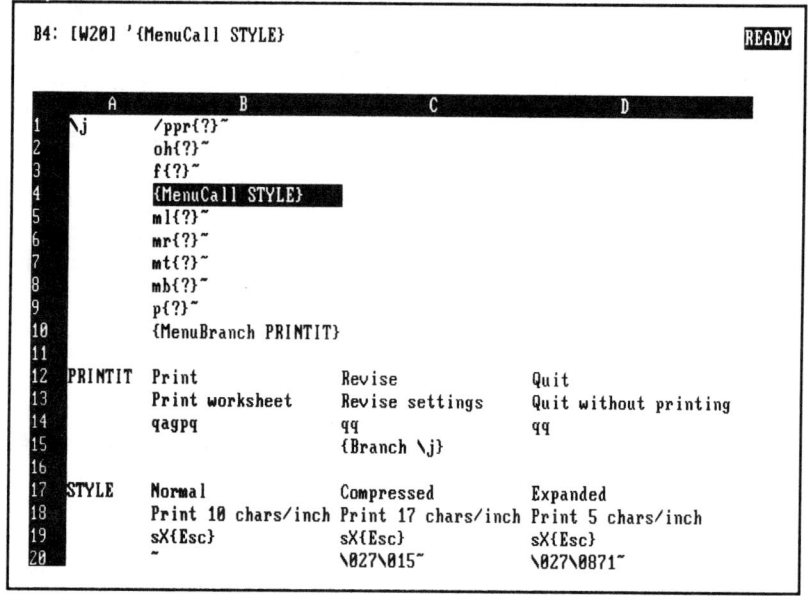

```
B4: [W20] '{MenuCall STYLE}                                              READY

        A           B                  C                    D
    1  \j          /ppr{?}~
    2              oh{?}~
    3              f{?}~
    4              {MenuCall STYLE}
    5              ml{?}~
    6              mr{?}~
    7              mt{?}~
    8              mb{?}~
    9              p{?}~
   10              {MenuBranch PRINTIT}
   11
   12  PRINTIT     Print              Revise              Quit
   13              Print worksheet    Revise settings     Quit without printing
   14              qagpq              qq                  qq
   15                                 {Branch \j}
   16
   17  STYLE       Normal             Compressed          Expanded
   18              Print 10 chars/inch Print 17 chars/inch Print 5 chars/inch
   19              sX{Esc}            sX{Esc}             sX{Esc}
   20              ~                  \027\015~           \027\0871~
```

FIGURE 14-23: The {MenuCall} command

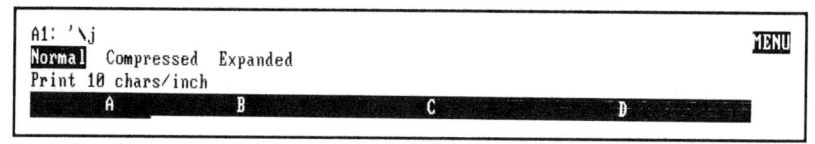

```
A1: '\j                                                                   MENU
Normal  Compressed  Expanded
Print 10 chars/inch
        A           B                  C                    D
```

FIGURE 14-24: Another custom menu

As soon as you choose one of the options from this menu, 1-2-3 will execute the instructions in the column under that choice. If you choose the Compressed option, for example, 1-2-3 will execute the instructions in cell C19. The first keystroke in this cell, *s*, instructs 1-2-3 to choose the Setup option from the Print Options menu. Next, 1-2-3 types a capital *X* and then presses the [Esc] key. (These keystrokes clear any existing setup strings from the prompt line. The *X* is necessary in case no setup string is active at the time 1-2-3 issues this command. If the macro pressed [Esc] when no setup string was present, 1-2-3 would return to the Options menu. Typing a character first assures that pressing [Esc] will have its intended effect. We used *X*, but any character would do.)

After 1-2-3 has cleared any existing setup strings, it reads the keystrokes in cell C20, types the setup string \027\015, and presses [Enter] to lock in that string. This string instructs an Epson printer to print compressed characters.

After 1-2-3 has executed all of the keystrokes in cell C20, it looks to cell C21. Because cell C21 is blank and 1-2-3 called this menu as a subroutine, 1-2-3 returns the macro to cell B4. Because the {MenuCall} command is the only instruction in cell B4, 1-2-3 resumes execution of the macro with the statement in cell B5, which allows you to choose a left margin. The remainder of the macro is identical to the one in Figure 14-20.

Multiple-level Custom Menus

Most of your custom menus will be simple one-level menus like the ones we've presented so far. However, it is possible to create custom menus that have multiple levels, as many of 1-2-3's standard menus do. To do this, you must "nest" one {MenuBranch} or {MenuCall} command within another.

Figure 14-25 shows an example of this technique. As you can see, this macro is a revision of the printing macro shown in Figure 14-20. The difference between these two macros is the substitution of a {MenuBranch} command for the keystrokes *qq* in cell D14. When 1-2-3 executes the *{MenuBranch PRINTIT}* command in cell B10, it presents the menu shown in Figure 14-21. If you choose Quit from this menu, 1-2-3 will not immediately quit from the Options and Print menus. Instead, 1-2-3 will execute the command *{MenuBranch VERIFY}*, which instructs it to transfer control to the cell named VERIFY (B17), and will display the custom menu shown in Figure 14-26.

```
D14: '{MenuBranch VERIFY}                                          READY

          A         B               C               D           E
1       \j       /ppr{?}~
2                oh{?}~
3                f{?}~
4                s{?}~
5                ml{?}~
6                mr{?}~
7                mt{?}~
8                mb{?}~
9                p{?}~
10               {MenuBranch PRINTIT}
11
12      PRINTIT  Print           Revise          Quit
13               Print worksheet Revise settings Quit without printing
14               qagpq           qq              {MenuBranch VERIFY}
15                               {Branch \j}
16
17      VERIFY   Yes             No
18               Quit without printing? Quit without printing?
19               qq              {MenuBranch PRINTIT}
20
```

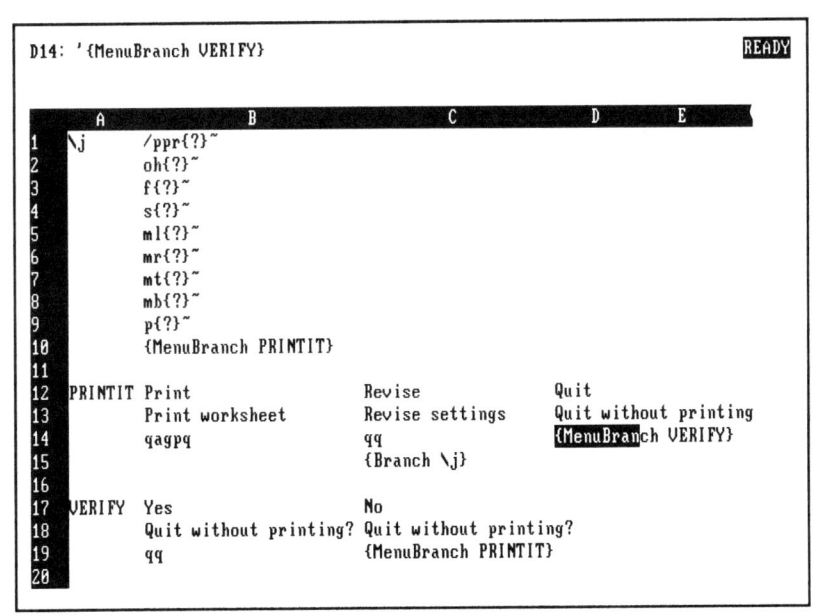

FIGURE 14-25: A multiple-level menu macro

```
A1: '\j                                                            MENU
Yes  No
Quit without printing?
```

FIGURE 14-26: A second-level custom menu

CONCLUSION

In this chapter, we've introduced the Lotus Command Language (LCL). In the first part of this chapter, we explained the form, function, and purpose of 1-2-3's LCL commands. In the second part of this chapter, we presented 14 of the most commonly used LCL commands and their /x equivalents, and showed examples of their use.

In the next chapter, we'll continue and conclude our coverage of the LCL. In that chapter, we will present the remaining 35 LCL commands and then demonstrate some advanced techniques.

15

More LCL Techniques

In Chapter 14, we explained the basics of the Lotus Command Language (LCL) and demonstrated 14 fundamental LCL commands. In this chapter, we'll explore the remaining 35 LCL commands. Then we'll present two important advanced programming techniques: self-modifying macros and computed macro statements.

OTHER LCL COMMANDS

In addition to the commands we presented in Chapter 14, 1-2-3 features a variety of other LCL commands. Although you probably won't use these commands as often as the ones explained in Chapter 14, you almost certainly will find uses for most of them as you become an experienced 1-2-3 programmer. We'll structure the discussion of the commands by functional groups.

Controlling the Interface

The LCL offers twelve commands that allow you to control the user interface—specifically, your computer's screen and bell—during the execution of a macro. The {WindowsOff}, {PanelOff}, {WindowsOn}, and {PanelOn} commands let you "freeze" and "unfreeze" the screen during the execution of a macro; the {FrameOn}, {FrameOff}, {BordersOn}, and {BordersOff} commands hide and reveal the worksheet frame; the {GraphOn} and {GraphOff} commands allow you to display and hide graphs; the {Indicate} command lets you place a custom message in the Mode indicator; and the {Beep} command instructs 1-2-3 to sound a tone.

The {WindowsOff} and {PanelOff} Commands

The LCL's {WindowsOff} and {PanelOff} commands allow you to "freeze" the screen during the execution of a macro. The {WindowsOff} command freezes the window area of the screen—the portion below the row of column letters and to the right of the column of row numbers. The {PanelOff} command freezes (and, optionally, clears) the control panel (the top three lines on the 1-2-3 screen) and the status line (the last line on the 1-2-3 screen).

The form of the {WindowsOff} is simply {WindowsOff}—it accepts no arguments.

RELEASE ► 2.2 ◄ ►The form of the {PanelOff} command is

{PanelOff clear}

where clear is an optional keyword that can be used only in 1-2-3 Release 2.2. If you omit this keyword, the 1-2-3 will simply freeze the control panel and status line. If you include this keyword, 1-2-3 will erase the control panel and status line before it freezes them.◄

There are two principal reasons for freezing the screen during the execution of a macro. First, freezing the screen increases the speed at which 1-2-3 executes macros. Normally, 1-2-3 redraws the screen after each command in a macro. Although each redrawing takes only a fraction of a second, the total redrawing time for a long macro can be a minute or more. Freezing the screen eliminates this redrawing time and, consequently, accelerates the macro.

The second reason for freezing the screen is aesthetic. Unless the screen is frozen, images will flicker across it quickly, sort of like an old silent movie, while 1-2-3 is executing the macro. If you like this effect, fine. If not, you can eliminate it through the use of the {WindowsOff} and {PanelOff} commands.

In general, the {WindowsOff} and/or {PanelOff} commands are useful in almost any macro that issues a lot of commands. We use these commands in almost all of our macros.

The {WindowsOn} and {PanelOn} Commands

As soon as 1-2-3 encounters a {WindowsOff} command in a macro, it will immediately freeze the window area of the screen until one of two things happens: it reaches the end of the macro, or it encounters a {WindowsOn} command. When either of these things happens, 1-2-3 will immediately redraw the screen, showing the effects of the macro on the worksheet up to that point. If you want to redraw the screen before a macro is finished executing, you should embed a {WindowsOn} command within the macro. In most cases, however, you will want the screen to remain frozen until the end of the macro. To do this, you could end the macro with a {WindowsOff} command. Since 1-2-3 automatically redraws the screen at the end of a macro, however, it is not necessary to do so.

RELEASE ► 2.2 ◄ ►In 1-2-3 Release 2.2, the {WindowsOn} command also controls the display of settings sheets during the execution of a macro. As we explained earlier, 1-2-3 Release 2.2 displays settings sheets when you issue various commands (for example, / Print and / Graph). However, it does not normally display them during the execution of a macro.

To make 1-2-3 Release 2.2 display settings sheets during the execution of a macro, you must use the {WindowsOn} command. Once 1-2-3 encounters this command in a macro (other than an occurrence that turns off a previous {WindowsOff} command), it will display settings sheets from that point until it encounters a {WindowsOff} command or reaches the end of the macro. If a {WindowsOff} command is "active," two {WindowsOn} commands are required to turn on the display of settings sheets—one to unfreeze the screen, and the second to display the settings sheet. While a settings sheet is visible, you can use the {Window} command (the representation of the [F6] key) to toggle between that settings sheet and the worksheet.◄

Just as the {WindowsOn} command unfreezes the windows area, the {PanelOn} command unfreezes and redraws the control panel and status line. If you want to reactivate the control panel and status line in the middle of a macro, you'll need to embed a {PanelOn} command in the macro. Since 1-2-3 automatically unfreezes and redraws the control panel and status line at the end of the execution of any macro, you don't have to end your macros with {PanelOn}.

A Caution

Although many of your macros can benefit from the use of {WindowsOff} and {PanelOff}, you should use these commands with care in macros that use the {?} command. If the {WindowsOff} and {PanelOff} commands are active when 1-2-3 reads a {?} command, 1-2-3 will pause as usual and wait for you to type a response, select a range, or select a command from a menu. However, you won't be able to see any prompts or menus 1-2-3 might be displaying, or determine where the cell pointer is. Consequently, you won't be able to figure out what to do. In fact, you'll be inclined to think your computer has "frozen" since nothing you do (except pressing [Enter]) will seem to have any effect.

Fortunately, this problem is easy to overcome. Just remember to include a {WindowsOn} and/or {PanelOn} command in the macro before the {?} command. If you want to turn the control panel and screen back off after the {?} has done its job, include another {WindowsOff} and/or {PanelOff} command in the macro right after the {?} command.

The {PanelOff} command does not affect the prompts displayed by the {GetLabel} and {GetNumber} commands, the custom mode indicators displayed by the {Indicate} command, or the menus created by the {MenuBranch} and {MenuCall} commands—even when you use the optional keyword: clear.

The {FrameOn}, {FrameOff}, {BordersOn}, and {BordersOff} Commands

►Unlike previous releases of 1-2-3, Release 2.2 allows you to turn the borders of a worksheet on and off during the execution of a macro. To turn off the borders of a 1-2-3 worksheet, you can use either the {Frameoff} or {BordersOff} commands. When 1-2-3 encounters either of these commands in a macro, it hides inverse-video row of column letters and column of row numbers that appear at the top and left edge, respectively, of the 1-2-3 worksheet. Figure 15-1 shows this effect.

RELEASE
► 2.2 ◄

```
A1: '\a                                                    WAIT


        \a      {FrameOff}
                {Wait @NOW+@TIME(0,0,5)}
















                                        CMD
```

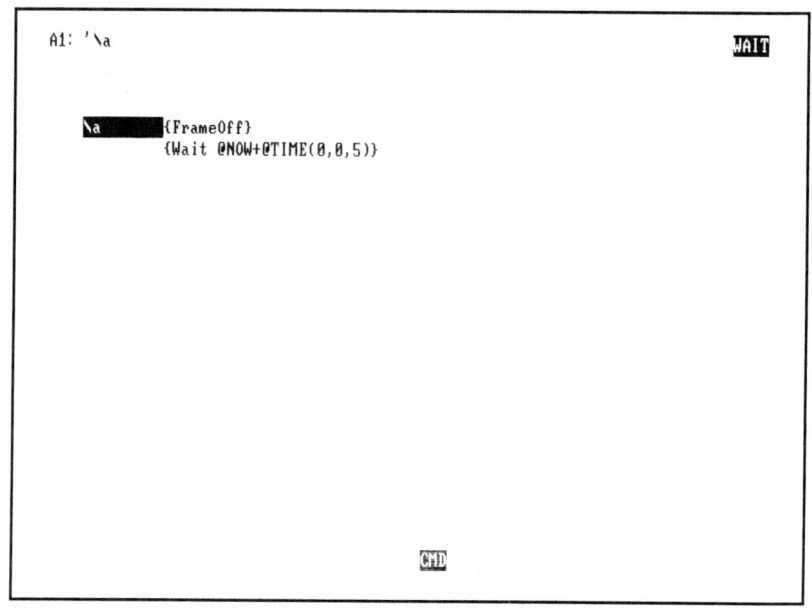

FIGURE 15-1: The {FrameOff} and {BordersOff} commands

Once you have turned off the borders of a 1-2-3 Release 2.2 worksheet, you can use the {FrameOn} or {BordersOn} commands to turn them back on. However, 1-2-3 will unhide the worksheet border automatically when it ends the execution of a macro. ◄

The {Indicate} Command

The LCL's {Indicate} command lets you place a custom message in the Mode indicator area of the screen. The form of this command is

{Indicate **message**}

RELEASE ► 2.2 ◄ where **message** is the message you want to display in the Mode indicator. ►In 1-2-3 Release 2.2, this message can be up to 240 characters in length (however, practical limitation is the number of characters that can be displayed on a single line of the screen—usually 80); in previous releases of 1-2-3, the limitation is 5 characters. ◄

When 1-2-3 executes an {Indicate} command in a macro, it replaces the current contents of the Mode indicator with the message string. If you are using 1-2-3 Releases 2 or 2.01, and the argument of an {Indicate} command is longer than 5 characters, 1-2-3 will display only the first five characters of the argument. If you are using 1-2-3 Release 2.2, 1-2-3 will truncate the message if it contains more characters than will fit across the screen.

Once 1-2-3 has placed a custom message in the Mode indicator, that message will remain until you tell 1-2-3 to clear it; it is not erased automatically at the end of the macro. To clear a custom message from the Mode indicator area, you must use an

{Indicate} command that doesn't include an argument. When 1-2-3 reads a plain {Indicate} command, it immediately erases the custom message and regains control of the Mode indicator.

The worksheet shown in Figure 15-2 contains a macro that uses the {Indicate} command. When 1-2-3 Release 2.2 runs this macro, it will display the message *Please Wait...* in the Mode indicator, as shown in Figure 15-2. (1-2-3 Releases 2 and 2.01 would display only the letters *Pleas*—the first five characters of the message.) The second command in this macro instructs 1-2-3 to pause for five seconds. (We'll discuss that command—{Wait}—later in this chapter.) The final command clears the custom mode indicator from the screen. Without this command, the custom mode indicator would remain on the screen after the execution of this macro.

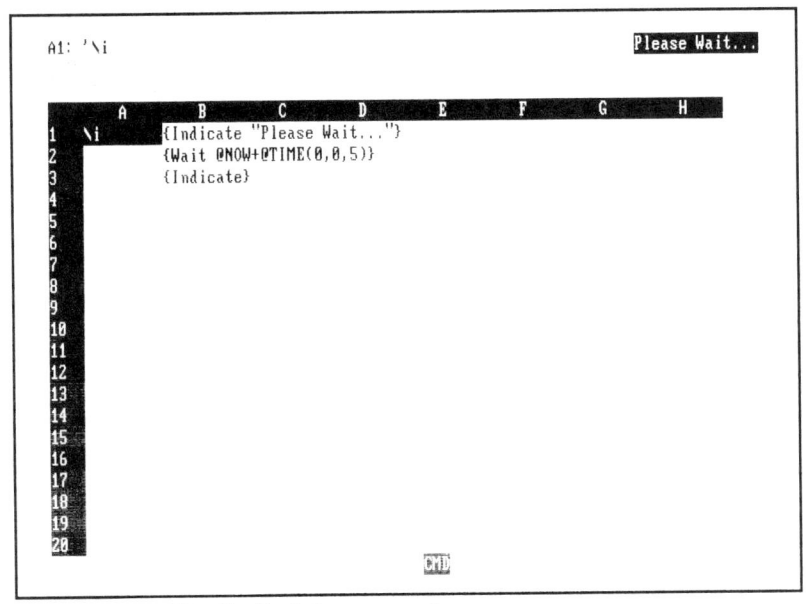

```
A1: '\i                                                   Please Wait...

        A       B          C           D          E       F       G      H
   1   \i    {Indicate "Please Wait..."}
   2         {Wait @NOW+@TIME(0,0,5)}
   3         {Indicate}
   4
   5
   6
   7
   8
   9
  10
  11
  12
  13
  14
  15
  16
  17
  18
  19
  20
                                       CMD
```

FIGURE 15-2: The {Indicate} command

▶In most cases, you'll use literal string as the arguments of your {Indicate} commands. If you use 1-2-3 Release 2.2, however, you can use a a string formula or function. If you do, 1-2-3 Release 2.2 will use the result of that formula or function as the custom mode indicator. For example, if cell A1 contains the label *'Please* and cell A2 contains the label *'Wait*, you could use the macro command

    '{Indicate A1&" "&A2&"..."}

to display the message *Please Wait...* in the mode indicator. In previous releases of 1-2-3, you have to use the calculated statement

    +"{Indicate "&A1&" "&A2&"...}"

to create this message. We'll explain more about calculated macro statements at the end of this chapter.

RELEASE
▶ 2.2 ◀

Since 1-2-3 Release 2.2's {Indicate} command accepts string formulas, you need to be careful when specifying a literal string as the argument of that command. If the string you specify is the name or address of a range, and you do not enclose that string in quotes, 1-2-3 Release 2.2 will attempt to use the contents of the upper-left cell of that range as the custom mode indicator. If the upper-left cell of the range contains a label or a string-producing formula or function, 1-2-3 Release 2.2 will display that label (or the result of the formula or function) in the mode indicator. For example, if cell A1 is named TEST and contains the label 'abc, the command

{Indicate TEST}

would cause 1-2-3 to display the message *abc*—not *TEST*. The command {Indicate A1} would do the same thing.

Fortunately there is an easy way to avoid this problem: enclose string arguments in quotes. For example, the command

{Indicate "TEST"}

causes 1-2-3 to display the message *TEST*—even though TEST is the name of a range. Since 1-2-3 Releases 2 and 2.01's {Indicate} commands won't accept string formulas, there is no need to enclose their arguments in quotes. ◄

The {GraphOn} and {GraphOff} Commands

RELEASE ► 2.2 ◄

►In releases of 1-2-3 prior to Release 2.2, there is no way to continue the execution of a macro automatically after displaying a graph on the screen for some period of time. To make a 1-2-3 Release 1A, 2, or 2.01 macro display a graph, you have to use the /gv command. Once a macro executes this command, it pauses until you press a key. At that point, it removes the graph from the screen and continues executing the macro.

The {GraphOn} and {GraphOff} commands solve this problem. (The commands are not available in 1-2-3 Releases 1A, 2, and 2.01.) When 1-2-3 encounters a {GraphOn} command in a macro, it displays the current graph on the screen—just as it does when it encounters the /gv command. However, it does not pause. Instead, it continues executing the macro. The graph will remain on the screen until 1-2-3 encounters a {GraphOff} command or it reaches the end of the macro, whichever comes first.

To display a graph on the screen for a specified period of time, you must use the {GraphOn} and {GraphOff} commands in conjunction with a {Wait} command. (We'll talk about the {Wait} command in detail later in this chapter.) For example, to make the current graph appear on the screen for five seconds, you would use the macro shown in Figure 15-3. The first statement in this macro, {GraphOn}, commands 1-2-3 Release 2.2 to display the current graph on the screen; the second command

B2: {Wait @NOW+@TIME(0,0,5)}

pauses the execution of the macro for five seconds; and the third statement removes the graph from the screen. ◄

```
A1: '\g                                                    READY

      A      B         C        D       E      F      G      H
  1   \g    {GraphOn}
  2         {Wait @NOW+@TIME(0,0,5)}
  3         {GraphOff}
  4
  5
  6
  7
  8
  9
 10
 11
 12
 13
 14
 15
 16
 17
 18
 19
 20
```

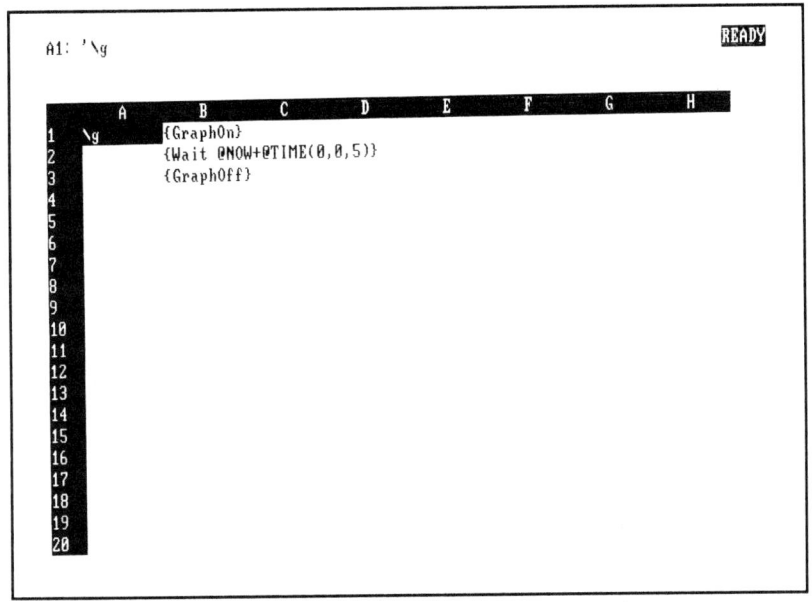

FIGURE 15-3: The {GraphOn} and {GraphOff} commands

The {Beep} Command

The {Beep} command allows you to instruct 1-2-3 to sound a tone at any point during the execution of a macro. The form of this command is

{Beep pitch}

where the optional argument pitch is a value from 0 to 3 (or a formula or function that returns one of those values) that controls the pitch of the tone. The value 0 produces the lowest tone, while the value 3 produces the highest tone. If you do not provide an argument, 1-2-3 will sound the same tone that results from the argument 1.

The {Beep} command is mainly useful for alerting the user to something that is happening during the course of a macro. For example, the simple macro in Figure 15-4 uses the {Beep} command to warn you of an error. As you can see, the macro begins with a {GetLabel} statement that requests one of two responses: *y* or *n*. If you type any response other than *y*, *Y*, *n*, or *N*, 1-2-3 will execute the commands in the range B4..B6. The commands in cell B4, *'{Beep}{Beep}{Beep}*, tell 1-2-3 to sound three regular tones. The {GetLabel} command in cell B5 gives you another chance to respond to the question. *{Branch TEST}*, the final command, tells 1-2-3 to transfer control to the statement in cell B2, which tests the validity of the new response. 1-2-3 will continue in this fashion until you type a correct answer.

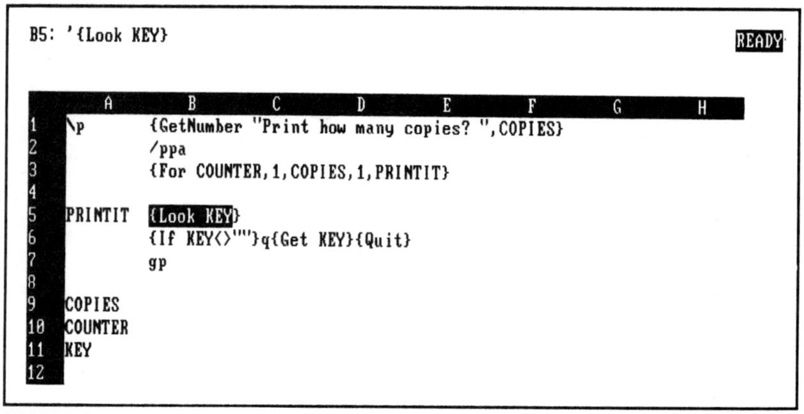

```
B5: '{Look KEY}                                                    READY

        A         B         C         D         E         F         G         H
   1   \p        {GetNumber "Print how many copies? ",COPIES}
   2             /ppa
   3             {For COUNTER,1,COPIES,1,PRINTIT}
   4
   5   PRINTIT   {Look KEY}
   6             {If KEY<>""}q{Get KEY}{Quit}
   7             gp
   8
   9   COPIES
  10   COUNTER
  11   KEY
  12
```

FIGURE 15-4: The {Beep} command

Interacting with the User

In Chapter 14, we demonstrated five commands—{?}, {GetNumber}, {GetLabel}, {MenuBranch}, and {MenuCall}—that let a macro interact with a user. In addition to these five commands, the LCL features two other commands—{Get} and {Look}—that, like {GetNumber}, {GetLabel}, and {?}, allow 1-2-3 to accept input from the keyboard during the execution of a macro. Unlike the {GetNumber} and {GetLabel} commands, however, {Get} and {Look} accept only a single character. Also unlike these commands, {Get} and {Look} don't contain built-in prompts.

The {Get} Command

The {Get} command allows 1-2-3 to pause to accept a single character from the keyboard during the execution of a macro. The form of this command is

{Get *destination*}

where *destination* specifies the cell in which you want 1-2-3 to store the character that it accepts. This argument can be a literal name or address, ►or, in 1-2-3 Release 2.2, a formula or function that returns a name or address.◄ When 1-2-3 encounters a {Get} command in a macro, it pauses (without displaying any prompt) until you press any single key. As soon as you press a key, 1-2-3 will store the representation of that key as a label in the cell named by the destination argument. In contrast to the {GetNumber} and {GetLabel} commands, there is no need to press [Enter] to end the pause; 1-2-3 will continue with the macro as soon as you press a key.

Typically, you will type an alphabetic, numeric, or punctuation character in response to a {Get} command. However, you can also press any of the special keys or key combinations that 1-2-3 understands, such as [Enter], [Calc], ►or, if you use 1-2-3 Release 2.2, [Help].◄ If you press one of these special keys, 1-2-3 will store the label representation of that key in the destination cell. These representations are the

RELEASE
► 2.2 ◄

RELEASE
► 2.2 ◄

same ones that you use within your macros. For example, if you press [Enter] in response to a {Get} statement, 1-2-3 will store the label '~ in the destination cell. (See Table 13-1 in Chapter 13 for a complete list of the key representations used in macros.)

An Example

The {Get} command comes in handy when you need to get a single-letter response (like y or n) from a user. For example, the macro in Figure 15-5 uses a {Get} command instead of a {GetLabel} command to ask whether you want to save the current worksheet under the name BACKUP.WK1. The first statement, *'Save the worksheet as BACKUP.WK1 (y/n)?*, provides a prompt for the {Get} command. When 1-2-3 encounters this statement, it will type *Save the worksheet as BACKUP.WK1 (y/n)?*. As 1-2-3 types this label, it will appear on the second line of the control panel.

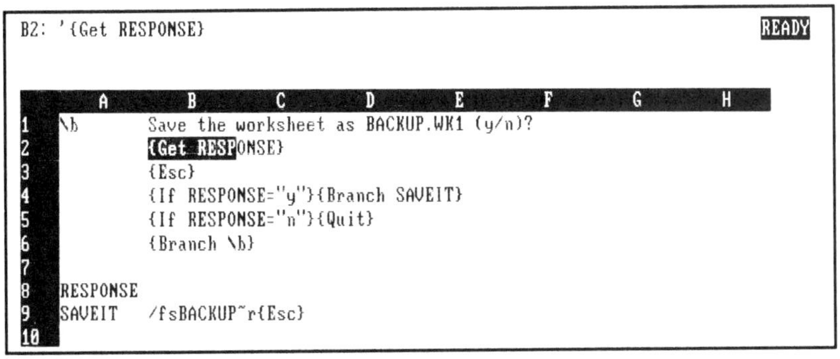

```
B2: '{Get RESPONSE}                                          READY

        A         B        C        D        E        F        G        H
1      \b        Save the worksheet as BACKUP.WK1 (y/n)?
2                {Get RESPONSE}
3                {Esc}
4                {If RESPONSE="y"}{Branch SAVEIT}
5                {If RESPONSE="n"}{Quit}
6                {Branch \b}
7
8      RESPONSE
9      SAVEIT    /fsBACKUP~r{Esc}
10
```

FIGURE 15-5: The {Get} command

Once 1-2-3 has typed this prompt, it reads the command located in cell B2, '{GetRESPONSE}, which instructs 1-2-3 to wait until you type a single letter. As soon as you type a response, 1-2-3 will store it in the cell named RESPONSE (B8). Then it will read the keystroke {Esc} in cell B3, which removes the label *Save the worksheet as BACKUP.WK1 (y/n)?* from the control panel.

After 1-2-3 has cleared this prompt, it reads the {If} command in cell B4. If you pressed the *y* key in response to the {Get} command, RESPONSE will contain the label *'y*, and this {If} statement will be true. Consequently, 1-2-3 will execute the *{Branch SAVEIT}* command, which instructs it to branch to the cell named SAVEIT (B9). The instructions in SAVEIT tell 1-2-3 to save the work-sheet under the name BACKUP.WK1.

If you pressed any key other than *y* or *Y*, 1-2-3 will next execute the {If} command in cell B5. If you pressed *n* or *N* in response to the {Get} command, the conditional test of this command will be true. In this case, 1-2-3 will evaluate the command {Quit}, which instructs it to exit from the macro. If you typed anything other than *n* or *N*, 1-2-3 will evaluate the {Branch} command in cell B6. This command instructs 1-2-3 to transfer control back to cell B1 and begin again.

The Keyboard Buffer

In most cases, 1-2-3 will pause and wait for you to press a key when it encounters a {Get} command in a macro. There's one situation in which it won't, however— when there are unprocessed characters waiting in the keyboard buffer. Like many software programs, 1-2-3 stores keystrokes that it is unable to process immediately in a small section of RAM called the keyboard buffer. If you type unsolicited characters during the execution of a macro, 1-2-3 will store those characters in the keyboard buffer.

If there are one or more keystrokes stored in the buffer when 1-2-3 encounters a {Get} command, 1-2-3 will use the first keystroke in the buffer as your response, store a representation of that key in the destination cell, and continue with the macro without ever pausing. If you know what 1-2-3 is going to ask, then you can type your {Get} responses in advance. If you are wrong, however, 1-2-3 won't give you a chance to correct your mistake before it continues processing the macro.

Displaying the Result

Although 1-2-3 will enter a representation of a key into the destination cell as soon as you press that key, it will not display that response until it next redraws the screen. To force 1-2-3 to redraw the screen, simply add a tilde (~) at the end of the {Get} command.

The {Look} Command

The LCL's {Look} command instructs 1-2-3 to retrieve a single character from the keyboard buffer. The form of this command is

{Look *destination*}

RELEASE ► 2.2 ◄

where *destination* specifies the address or name of the cell in which you want 1-2-3 to store the representation of the character it retrieves. ►In 1-2-3 Release 2.2, this argument can be a formula or function that returns the name or address of a cell; in earlier releases of 1-2-3, it must be a literal name or address.◄

When 1-2-3 executes a {Look} command, it looks to see if there are any unprocessed characters waiting in the keyboard buffer. If so, 1-2-3 will place a representation of the first character in the buffer into the destination cell. If the keyboard buffer is empty, 1-2-3 will place a null label (a label prefix without an accompanying label) into the destination cell and continue executing the macro; it will not pause and wait for you to type a character.

The {Look} command is useful in situations where you want to be able to interrupt the execution of a macro without making 1-2-3 wait for your input. For example, the {Look} command in the macro in Figure 15-6 lets you stop the macro by typing any character at any point during the execution of the macro.

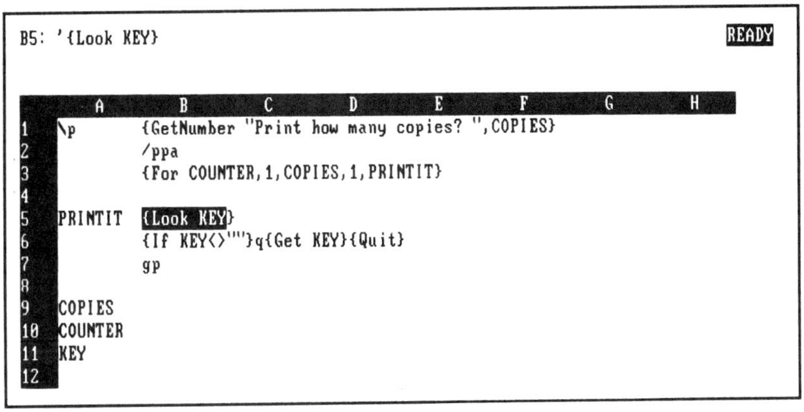

```
B5: '{Look KEY}                                              READY

      A         B         C         D         E         F         G         H
1    \p        {GetNumber "Print how many copies? ",COPIES}
2              /ppa
3              {For COUNTER,1,COPIES,1,PRINTIT}
4
5    PRINTIT   {Look KEY}
6              {If KEY<>""}q{Get KEY}{Quit}
7              gp
8
9    COPIES
10   COUNTER
11   KEY
12
```

FIGURE 15-6: The {Look} command

The first statement in this macro asks you how many copies you want to print and stores your response in the cell named COPIES (B9). The second statement issues the / Print Printer Align command. The {For} command in cell B3 sets up a loop that causes 1-2-3 to execute the instructions that begin in PRINTIT (cell B5) as many times as you specified in your response to {GetNumber}.

The first command in the loop, *{Look KEY}*, tells 1-2-3 to check the keyboard buffer. If the buffer contains a character (as it will if you have pressed any key since this macro began), 1-2-3 will retrieve it and store it in the cell named KEY (B11). If not, 1-2-3 will enter a null label in cell B11.

Either way, 1-2-3 will then execute the command *{If KEY<>""}* in cell B6. If you haven't typed a character between the time 1-2-3 began executing the macro and the time 1-2-3 executes the {Look} command, KEY will contain a null label, and this {If} statement will be false. Consequently, 1-2-3 will skip the remaining commands in cell B6 and execute the instructions in cell B7 instead. These instructions, *gp*, tell 1-2-3 to print the worksheet and advance the paper to the top of a new page. 1-2-3 then will increase the value of COUNTER by 1, and, if COUNTER does not exceed COPIES, make another pass through the loop.

If you have pressed one or more keys since the macro began, however, KEY will contain a representation of the key that you pressed. In that case, the {If} statement in cell B6 will be true, and 1-2-3 will evaluate the instructions that follow the {If} command in cell B6. The first of these, *q*, instructs 1-2-3 to choose Quit from the Print menu, returning it to the READY mode.

Notice the command {Get KEY} in cell B6. Why does the macro contain this command? Because, as we said, the {Look} command does not remove the character it finds from the keyboard buffer. Consequently, there will be a character in the buffer when 1-2-3 quits from the macro. If the keyboard buffer contains any characters when the execution of the macro ends, your computer will pass any characters in the buffer on to 1-2-3, just as if you had typed them yourself after the macro was over. By following the {Look} command with a {Get} command, however, you can force

1-2-3 to clear the characters that the {Look} command found in the keyboard buffer. Consequently, those characters will not be in the buffer when the macro ends.

Controlling Program Flow

In Chapter 14, we demonstrated three commands that control the flow of 1-2-3 macros: {For}, {Branch}, and *subroutine*. In addition to these three commands, the LCL features seven other commands that affect the flow of a 1-2-3 macro: {OnError}, {Wait}, {BreakOff}, {BreakOn}, {Dispatch}, {Restart}, and {System}.

The {OnError} Command

At the end of Chapter 13, we explained the process of debugging macros. In that discussion, we presented three common causes of macro errors: omitted keystrokes, invalid responses to command prompts, and errors in the syntax of a key representation of an LCL command. As you recall, we stated that all three types of errors will stop the execution of a macro.

The {OnError} command allows you to "trap" errors of the second type—invalid responses to a 1-2-3 command prompt. You can use the {OnError} command to instruct 1-2-3 to branch to a specified location when this type of error occurs. The form of this command is

{OnError *location*}

RELEASE ► 2.2 ◄

where *location* is a range name, a cell reference, ►or, in 1-2-3 Release 2.2, a formula or function that returns a name or address.◄ If 1-2-3 has processed an {OnError} command before it encounters an invalid response to a 1-2-3 command prompt, it will ignore the erroneous response and continue executing the macro at the cell specified by the argument of the {OnError} command.

For example, the macro in Figure 15-7 is designed to assign the name HERE to the current cell. The macro assumes that the name HERE already exists in the worksheet. For this reason, it first issues the / Range Name Delete command to delete the name HERE. Next, it issues the / Range Name Create command and assigns the name HERE to the current cell.

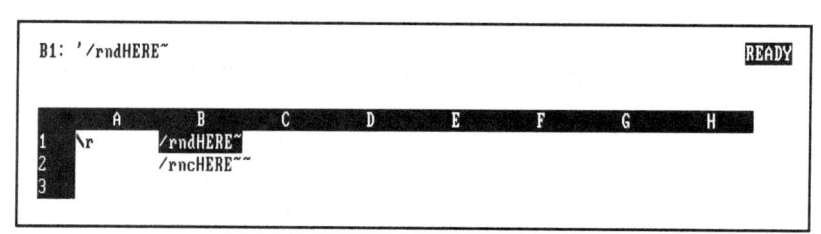

```
B1: '/rndHERE~                                          READY

         A          B          C     D     E     F     G     H
1       \r        /rndHERE~
2                 /rncHERE~~
3
```

FIGURE 15-7: A potential macro error

Unfortunately, an error will occur if a range named HERE does not already exist when you execute this macro. If there is no range named HERE when the macro issues the / Range Name Delete command, types HERE, and presses [Enter], 1-2-3 will beep, display the message *Range name does not exist* at the bottom of the screen, and stop the macro.

Figure 15-8 shows how you would use the {OnError} command to overcome this error. As you can see, the modified version begins with the command *{OnError NAMEIT}*. Once 1-2-3 executes this command, it knows to continue executing at the cell named NAMEIT (B3) if it encounters an invalid response to a command prompt at any point within the macro. If a range named HERE exists when 1-2-3 executes the commands *'/rndHERE~* in cell B2, it will delete the range name and then proceed to cell B3. If there is no range named HERE in the worksheet, an error will result. Instead of stopping the macro, however, this error will "trip" the {OnError} command, which instructs 1-2-3 to proceed directly to cell B3 and assign the range name HERE to the current cell.

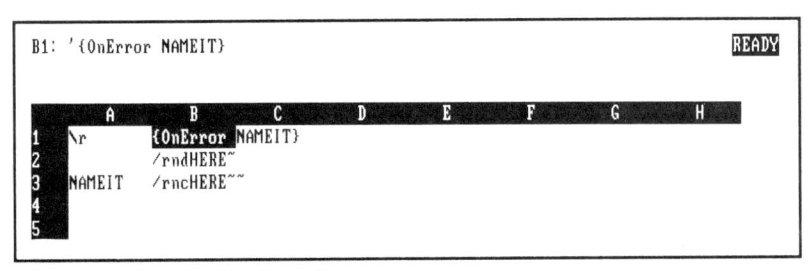

```
B1: '{OnError NAMEIT}                                          READY

        A       B           C       D       E       F       G       H
1      \r      {OnError NAMEIT}
2              /rndHERE~
3      NAMEIT  /rncHERE~~
4
5
```

FIGURE 15-8: The {OnError} command

The Lifespan of an {OnError} Command

An {OnError} command remains active until it is tripped, until 1-2-3 reads another {OnError} command, or until 1-2-3 reaches the end of the macro that contains the command. Once an error trips an {OnError} command, that command is no longer in effect. The macro will no longer be protected from macro errors unless 1-2-3 subsequently reads another {OnError} command. If 1-2-3 reads a second {OnError} command while another one is still active (that is, has not been tripped), the new {OnError} command will cancel the old one. The {OnError} command that 1-2-3 has read most recently always will control 1-2-3's reaction to an error.

Storing the Error Message

In addition to rerouting the macro in the event of an error, the {OnError} command also can record the error message that 1-2-3 would have displayed at the bottom of the screen had the error not been trapped. To do this, you must include a second location argument in the command. For example, the command

    {OnError CONTINUE,ERRMSG}

routes the macro to the cell named CONTINUE in the event of an invalid response to a 1-2-3 command prompt and stores the error message that would have appeared at the bottom of the screen in the cell named ERRMSG. If you wanted to, you could include an {If} command in the macro that tries to evaluate the error message and takes different actions depending upon exactly which error has occurred.

The {Wait} Command

1-2-3 usually executes macro at breakneck speed. As soon as 1-2-3 executes one command, it will execute the next one, the one after that, and so on, until it reaches the end of the macro. However, the LCL offers a command, {Wait}, which instructs 1-2-3 to pause during the execution of a macro. This command is useful for delaying the macro while the user reads messages, views graphs, and so forth.

The form of the {Wait} command is

{Wait time}

where time is a time value or a formula or function that returns a time value. Unlike the {GetNumber}, {GetLabel}, and {?} commands, the {Wait} command does not expect input from the keyboard. Instead, it pauses the macro until the time specified by the time argument. The time argument specifies the time at which you want 1-2-3 to resume executing the macro—not the length of the delay. For the {Wait} command to have its intended effect, of course, your computer's system clock must be set for the correct time.

For example, the command

{Wait @TIME(17,0,0)}

instructs 1-2-3 to wait until 5:00 PM before it executes the next statement in the macro. The absolute length of the pause depends on when the macro is run. If the macro is run at 4:59 PM, the pause will last only one minute. If the macro is run at 5:01 PM, the pause will last 23 hours and 59 minutes.

TIP: PAUSING FOR A SPECIFIED INTERVAL

If you're like most people, you'll probably want to use {Wait} to introduce a pause of a specified duration in a macro. For that reason, the arguments of your {Wait} commands probably will be equations that add an @TIME function to an @NOW function. The @TIME function controls the length of the pause. For example, the command

{Wait @NOW+@TIME(0,0,30)}

instructs 1-2-3 to wait 30 seconds before it executes the next command.

The {BreakOff} and {BreakOn} Commands

In Chapter 13, you learned that you can press [Ctrl][Break] to stop a macro. In some cases, however, you may not want the user of a macro to be able to use these keys to stop the macro. Fortunately, the LCL offers a simple command— {BreakOff}—that disables the [Ctrl][Break] key during the execution of a macro. Once 1-2-3 has processed a {BreakOff} command, pressing [Ctrl][Break] will not stop the macro.

The [Ctrl][Break] combination will remain disabled until 1-2-3 encounters the end of the macro or a {BreakOn} command.

You'll commonly use a {BreakOff} command at the beginning of an auto-executing macro. That way, inexperienced users won't inadvertently press [Ctrl][Break] and find themselves in the middle of an unfamiliar 1-2-3 worksheet, and advanced users won't be able to "crack" your macro. If you want to reactivate the [Ctrl][Break] keys in the middle of a macro, just include a {BreakOn} command in the macro. You might want to end a macro that begins with the {BreakOff} command with a {BreakOn} command; however, it is not necessary to do so.

We strongly suggest that you debug your macros before you include the {BreakOff} command in them. If you preface a macro with a {BreakOff} command before you debug it, you won't be able to stop the macro if it doesn't work the way you intended.

The {Dispatch} Command

The {Dispatch} command provides you with an alternative, indirect way to branch a macro. The form of this command is

{Dispatch *location*}

where *location* specifies the name or address of the cell whose contents identify the cell to which you want 1-2-3 to branch. ►In 1-2-3 Release 2.2, this argument can be a formula or function that returns the name or address of a cell or range; in earlier releases of 1-2-3, it must be a literal name or address.◄

RELEASE
► 2.2 ◄

To understand how this command works, suppose that the cell named WHERE contains the label 'PRINTIT. When 1-2-3 encounters the command {Dispatch WHERE} in a macro, it won't branch the macro to the cell named WHERE. Instead, it will look at the contents of WHERE and branch the macro to the cell named PRINTIT—the cell identified by the label in WHERE.

The partial macro shown in Figure 15-9 uses the {Dispatch} command. This macro begins with a {GetLabel} command that pauses the macro, displays the prompt *Continue (y/n)?*, and waits for your response. When you type a response and press [Enter], 1-2-3 will store that response in the cell named ANSWER (B9). The {If} command in cell B2 evaluates your response. If you typed *y*, *Y*, *n*, or *N*, the {If} statement will be true, and 1-2-3 will evaluate the command *{Dispatch ANSWER}*. If you have typed a *y* or a *Y*, ANSWER will contain the label '*y* or '*Y*. Consequently, 1-2-3 will branch to the cell named Y (B5) and execute the commands it finds in that cell. In this case, 1-2-3 will just move the cell pointer to cell H20 and enter the value 123. If you typed *n* or *N* in response to the {GetLabel} command, ANSWER will contain the label '*n* or '*N*. In that case, the {Dispatch} command will instruct 1-2-3 to branch to the cell named N (B7) and execute the instructions it finds there. In this case, 1-2-3 will read the command {Quit} and end the macro.

```
B2: '{If ANSWER="y"#OR#ANSWER="n"}{Dispatch ANSWER}                    READY

         A           B          C         D         E         F         G         H
1       \d        {GetLabel "Continue (y/n)? ",ANSWER}
2                 {If ANSWER="y"#OR#ANSWER="n"}{Dispatch ANSWER}
3                 {Branch \d}
4
5        Y        {Goto}H20~123~
6
7        N        {Quit}
8
9     ANSWER
10
```

FIGURE 15-9: The {Dispatch} command

If you typed a response other than *y*, *Y*, *n*, or *N*, the {If} statement in cell B2 will be false. Consequently, 1-2-3 will skip the {Dispatch} command and evaluate the command *{Branch \d}* in cell B3 instead. This command causes 1-2-3 to branch back to the beginning of the macro and start it again.

The {Restart} Command

The LCL's {Restart} command instructs 1-2-3 to clear the subroutine stack during the execution of a macro. In effect, the {Restart} command turns a subroutine call into a branch. When 1-2-3 encounters a {Restart} command within a subroutine, it "forgets" the location of the command that called the subroutine. When the subroutine is finished, 1-2-3 will not return to the subroutine call.

The simple macro in Figure 15-10 demonstrates the {Restart} command. The first statement in this macro asks you for a positive value and stores your response in the cell named VALUE (B9). The next statement, *{CHECKIT}*, is a call to the subroutine CHECKIT, which begins in cell B5. The first command in this subroutine checks to see if you have entered a positive value. If so, 1-2-3 executes the {Return} statement, which causes it to exit from the subroutine and execute the remainder of the macro.

```
B6: '{Restart}                                                         READY

         A           B          C         D         E         F         G         H
1       \r        {GetNumber "Enter a positive value, please: ",VALUE}
2                 {CHECKIT}
3                 {Let ANSWER,@SQRT(VALUE)}
4                 ~
5     CHECKIT     {If VALUE>=0}{Return}
6                 {Restart}
7                 {Branch \r}
8
9     VALUE
10    ANSWER
11
```

FIGURE 15-10: The {Restart} command

If you have entered a negative value in response to the {GetNumber} prompt, however, 1-2-3 takes a different action. Because the value is less than 0, the {If} statement in cell B5 (CHECKIT) will be false. Consequently, 1-2-3 will skip the {Return} command and execute the {Restart} command in cell B6. This command instructs 1-2-3 to forget that it is in a subroutine. The next statement, *{Branch \r}*, passes control back to the command in cell B1, which again asks you to supply a positive value. 1-2-3 then calls the CHECKIT subroutine again. If the value is negative, 1-2-3 again will clear the stack and branch back to cell B1. 1-2-3 will continue in this fashion until you type a positive value, at which point it will break from the subroutine, calculate the square root, and end the macro.

The {System} Command

As we explained in Chapter 6, you can use 1-2-3's / System command to access DOS without unloading 1-2-3. Once you access DOS, you can run a program by typing its name at the DOS prompt. Then, you can return to 1-2-3 by typing *exit* and pressing [Enter].

You can represent the / System command in a macro as /s. However, once 1-2-3 accesses DOS, the execution of the macro suspends temporarily. Consequently, you have to type the name of the program you want to run; then you have to type exit to return to 1-2-3. Once you return to 1-2-3, it resumes executing the macro with the command that follows the /s command.

▶The {System} command automates the process of accessing DOS, issuing a command, and returning to 1-2-3. (This command is available only in 1-2-3 Release 2.2—not in Releases 1A, 2, or 2.01). The form of this command is

RELEASE
► 2.2 ◄

{System *name*}

where *name* is the name of the progam you want to execute, or a formula or function that returns that name. If the progam is stored in the default directory (the one whose name appears when you issue the /Worksheet Default Directory command), you don't need to include a path; if it is not, you do.

When 1-2-3 Release 2.2 encounters a {System} command in a macro, it accesses DOS and runs the specified program. As soon as it finishes, returns from DOS and continues executing the macro. For example, the macro shown in Figure 15-11 causes 1-2-3 to access DOS, create a file that contains the names of the files in the current directory, and then import that file into the current worksheet.

The rules for which programs you can and cannot use the {System} command to run are the same as for the / System command. For details, see the discussion of the / System command in Chapter 6.◄

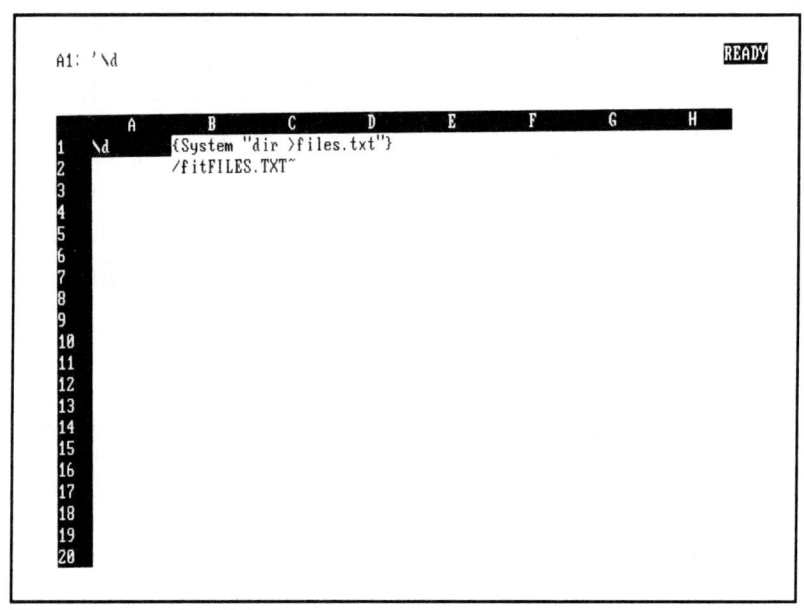

```
A1: '\d                                                    READY

     A       B          C        D       E      F      G      H
1   \d    {System "dir >files.txt"}
2          /fitFILES.TXT~
3
...
20
```

FIGURE 15-11: The {System} command

Manipulating Information

In addition to the {Let} command, which we covered in Chapter 14, the LCL offers five other commands that allow you to manipulate the information in a worksheet during the execution of a macro: {Recalc}, {RecalcCol}, {Put}, {Blank}, and {Contents}. The {Recalc} and {RecalcCol} commands let you recalculate selected portions of a worksheet. The {Put} command lets you store the results of calculations in specific cells of a range. The {Blank} command gives you an alternative way to erase the entries in a range. And the {Contents} command allows you to make special copies of the contents of worksheet cells.

The {Recalc} and {RecalcCol} Commands

When 1-2-3 reads a {Calc} command in a macro, it recalculates the entire worksheet. If the worksheet is small, this recalculation will take a few seconds at most. If the worksheet is large, however, and especially if it contains a lot of formulas and functions, the recalculation process can take minutes. That's a lot of time to waste if you just need to recalculate a few formulas.

Fortunately, the LCL features two commands—{Recalc} and {RecalcCol}—that make it possible to recalculate only selected portions of a 1-2-3 worksheet. The basic forms of these commands are

{Recalc *location*}
{RecalcCol *location*}

where *location* specifies the cell or group of cells that you want to recalculate. This argument may be a cell reference (like A1), a range reference (like A1..B5), a range name (like TEST), ►or, in 1-2-3 Release 2.2, a formula or function that returns the name or address of a cell or range.◄

RELEASE
► 2.2 ◄

The only difference between these two commands is the order in which they recalculate the specified range. When 1-2-3 executes a {Recalc} command, it recalculates the argument range in a row-by-row fashion. For example, when 1-2-3 executes the command *{Recalc A1..B2}*, it recalculates cell A1, then cell B1, then cell A2, and finally cell B2. When 1-2-3 executes a {RecalcCol} command, on the other hand, it recalculates the indicated range in column-by-column order. For example, the command *{RecalcCol A1..B2}* instructs 1-2-3 to recalculate cell A1, then cell A2, then cell B1, and finally cell B2.

Extra Arguments

In most cases, you'll use {Recalc} and {RecalcCol} in their basic forms. However, these commands accept two optional arguments, as shown below:

{RecalcCol *location*,CONDITION,iterations}

These arguments command 1-2-3 to recalculate the specified range more than one time. The second argument, CONDITION, must be a conditional test. If you include this second argument in a {Recalc} or {RecalcCol} command, 1-2-3 will continue to recalculate the range as long as the conditional test is false. After each recalculation, 1-2-3 will again evaluate the conditional test. Then, if the test is false, 1-2-3 will perform the calculation again. If the test is true, 1-2-3 will stop recalculating. The third argument, iterations, allows you to specify the maximum number of times that 1-2-3 will perform the recalculation.

When you use both a CONDITION argument and an iterations argument, 1-2-3 will continue to recalculate the range until the conditional test is true or until it has calculated the range the number of times specified by the iterations argument, whichever comes first. For example, the command

{Recalc B1..B10,@ABS((B10*.08)-B3)<.0002,100}

instructs 1-2-3 to recalculate the range B1..B10 until the conditional test @ABS((B10*.08)-B3)<.0002 is true or until it has calculated the range 100 times.

You can use a CONDITION argument without an iterations argument. When you use only a CONDITION argument, 1-2-3 will continue recalculating the specified range until the conditional test is true, regardless of how long it takes.

Unfortunately, you cannot use an iterations argument without a CONDITION argument. However, there is an easy way to make the iterations argument alone control the number of times 1-2-3 recalculates the range. To do this, simply use the value 0 or a conditional test that always evaluates the CONDITION argument as false. For example, both the commands *{Recalc B1..B10,0,100}* and *{Recalc B1..B10,@FALSE,100}* make 1-2-3 recalculate the range B1..B10 100 times.

The {Put} Command

The LCL's {Put} command is a variant of the {Let} command. Like {Let}, {Put} performs a calculation and places the result in a cell. The difference between these two commands is in the way they identify the destination cell. As we explained in Chapter 14, the destination argument of a {Let} command is a simple cell or range reference. For example, the command *{Let A1,@SQRT(VALUE)}* places the result of the function *@SQRT(VALUE)* into cell A1.

Identifying the destination cell for a {Put} command is a bit more complex. To do this, you must specify a destination range and use row and column offsets to pinpoint a cell within that range. Accordingly, the {Put} command requires four arguments, as shown below:

{Put *range*,column offset,row offset,**calculation**}

The first argument, *range*, defines the block of cells in which the {Put} command should place the result of its fourth argument, **calculation**. The second argument, column offset, specifies a column within that range. The third argument, row offset, specifies a row within that range. Together, these two arguments pinpoint the single cell in which 1-2-3 will place the result of the calculation. As usual, 1-2-3 assumes that the first row and first column of the range have the offset of 0. The first argument can be a literal address or name, ▶or, in 1-2-3 Release 2.2, a formula or function that returns an address or name.◀ The second and third arguments can be literal values or formulas or functions that return values; the final argument can be a literal value, a literal string, or a formula or function that returns a value or a string.

RELEASE ▶ 2.2 ◀

For example, suppose you've assigned the name TABLE to the range C3..E5, and that you've entered the value 10 into cell A1 and the value 5 into cell A2. If you then run a macro that contains the command

{Put TABLE,0,0,A1*A2}~

1-2-3 will store the value 50 (the result of the formula *A1*A2*) in cell C3—the first cell in the range TABLE. 1-2-3 places this result in cell C3 because column C has the column offset of 0 in the range TABLE and row 3 has the row offset of 0 in the same range. (The tilde causes 1-2-3 to press the [Enter] key to redraw the screen.) Similarly, the macro command

{Put TABLE,1,2,A1/A2}~

will place the result of the formula *A1/A2*, 2, in cell D5—the cell with the column offset of 1 and the row offset of 2 in the range TABLE.

The {Blank} Command

The {Blank} command erases the contents of the range specified by its argument. The form of this command is

{Blank *location*}

where *location* identifies the cell or cells you want to erase. This argument can be a cell reference, range reference, range name, ▶or, in 1-2-3 Release 2.2, a formula or function that returns a reference or name.◀

RELEASE
▶ 2.2 ◀

The effect of the {Blank} command is identical to that of the / Range Erase command. For example, the commands *{Blank A1..A5}* and */reA1..A5~* both erase the entries from cells A1, A2, A3, A4, and A5; the commands *{Blank TEST}* and */reTEST~* both erase the cells in the range named TEST.

So what are the differences between these commands? First, 1-2-3 usually can execute a {Blank} command a bit faster than it can execute a / Range Erase command. Second, you can use a {Blank} command within the middle of a menu command sequence. For example, the command

/cA1..A3~{Blank A2}B1~

issues the / Copy command, specifies cells A1..A3 as the FROM range, and erases cells A2 (the second cell of the FROM range) before specifying cell B1 as the upper-left corner of the TO range. Consequently, after the copy, cell B1 will contain a copy of the entry in cell A1; cell B2 will be blank; and cell B3 will contain a copy of the entry in cell A3. Of course, we could have erased cell A2 prior to issuing the / Copy command. Overall, there probably won't be many cases in which you'll need (or want) to embed a {Blank} command within another command.

The {Contents} Command

The {Contents} command is a special copying command. {Contents} converts the display of one cell into a label and places that label into another cell. Contrary to its name, the {Contents} command does not copy the contents of a cell, like the / Copy command does. Instead, it copies what you see on the screen, complete with formats, and so forth. The basic form of this command is

{Contents *destination,source*}

where *destination* specifies the cell into which you want to place the label form of what is displayed in the cell specified by *source*. Both arguments can be literal cell addresses, literal range names, ▶or, in 1-2-3 Release 2.2, formulas or functions that return cell addresses or range names.◀

RELEASE
▶ 2.2 ◀

An Example

For example, suppose cell A2, to which you have assigned the C2 format, contains the formula +A1. Suppose further that cell A1 contains the value 77 and that column A is nine characters wide. Figure 15-12 shows this worksheet.

Cells B5 and B6 in this worksheet contain a simple macro. The first command in this macro, *{Contents A3,A2}*, tells 1-2-3 to copy what is displayed in cell A2 into cell A3. The second instruction, ~, causes 1-2-3 to press the [Enter] key. This key forces 1-2-3 to redraw the screen and to display the result of {Contents}.

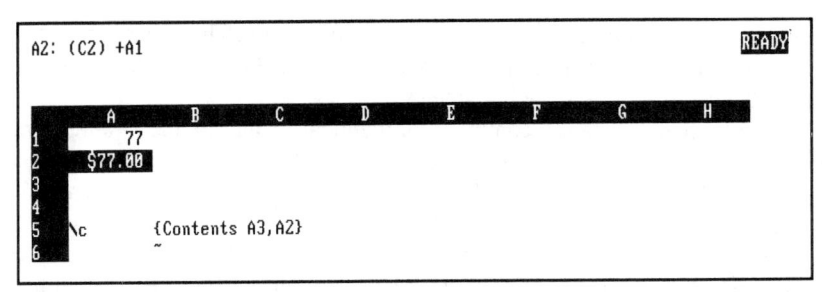

```
A2: (C2) +A1                                        READY

       A         B         C         D         E         F         G         H
1            77
2       $77.00
3
4
5    \c        {Contents A3,A2}
6              ~
```

FIGURE 15-12: The {Contents} command

After you run this macro, your worksheet will look like Figure 15-13. If you look at cells A2 and A3 without glancing at the control panel, you will probably think that both cells contain the same entry. They don't, however. Cell A3 contains the label ' *$77.00*, while cell A2 contains the formula *+A1*. When you ran the macro, 1-2-3 made an exact copy of what it was displaying in cell A2 at that time and placed the copy in cell A3. Because cell A2 was assigned the C2 format, then the resulting label includes a $, a decimal point, and two digits to the right of that decimal. Because the source cell was nine spaces wide, then the label contains nine characters—the six you see, plus two leading spaces and one trailing space. The location of these spaces is determined by the amount of empty space visible between the characters displayed in the source cell and the left and right borders of that cell.

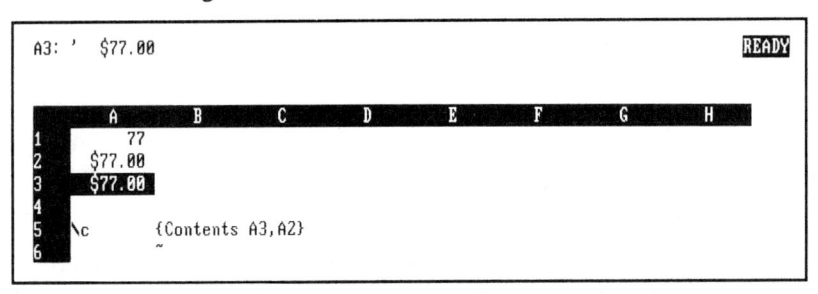

```
A3: '   $77.00                                      READY

       A         B         C         D         E         F         G         H
1            77
2       $77.00
3       $77.00
4
5    \c        {Contents A3,A2}
6              ~
```

FIGURE 15-13: The result of the {Contents} command

Optional Arguments

As you have seen, a {Contents} command in its basic form produces a label that exactly mimics what is displayed in the source cell. However, this command also accepts two optional arguments that instruct it to alter the number of leading spaces and/or change the format of the value that it converts. In its full form, then, the {Contents} command has four arguments:

{Contents *destination*,*source*,width,format}

Normally, the number of characters in the label result of a {Contents} command will be equal to the width of the source cell. The optional width argument allows you to specify a different number of characters. An argument of 15 would produce a label with 15 characters, an argument of 3 would produce a three-character label, and so forth. 1-2-3 adds leading spaces to change the width of the resulting label. If we changed the {Contents} command in cell B5 of Figure 15-12 to *{Contents A3,A2,20}*, for example, 1-2-3 would place the 20-character label ' $77.00 in cell B3. This label has 13 leading spaces and one trailing space.

If you specify a width that is narrower than the number of characters displayed in the source cell, the {Contents} command will produce a series of asterisks. For example, 1-2-3 would place the label '****** in cell A3 when it executed the command {Contents A3,A2,6}.

The second optional argument of the {Contents} command allows you to alter the format of the display as 1-2-3 converts it into a label. This argument must be one of the special codes shown in Table 15-1. To specify the Scientific format with two digits to the right of the decimal place, for example, you would use the value 18. To specify the D3 format, you would use the value 116. Because the <u>format</u> argument follows the <u>width</u> argument, it cannot be used independently of that argument.

Code	Format
0-15	Fixed, 0 to 15 digits to the right of the decimal place
16-31	Scientific, 0 to 15 digits to the right of the decimal place
32-47	Currency, 0 to 15 digits to the right of the decimal place
48-63	Percentage, 0 to 15 digits to the right of the decimal place
64-79	Comma, 0 to 15 digits to the right of the decimal place
112	Bar graph
113	General
114-116	D1 (DD-MMM-YY), D2 (DD-MMM), D3 (MMM-YY)
121-122	D4 (Full International Date), D5 (Partial International Date)
119-120	D6 (HH:MM:SS AM/PM), D7 (HH:MM AM/PM)
123-124	D8 (Full International Time), D9 (Partial International Time)
117	Literal (display formulas)
118	Hidden
127	Default format for worksheet

TABLE 15-1: Format codes for the {Contents} command

Working with Files

1-2-3's / Print File command lets you write information from a 1-2-3 worksheet into an ASCII text file; its / File Import command allows you to read information from an ASCII text file into a 1-2-3 worksheet. These commands—which we'll explore in detail in Appendix 1—are well suited for working with large blocks of information.

The LCL's file input/output (or file i/o) commands—{Open}, {Close}, {SetPos}, {FileSize} {Read}, {ReadLn}, {Write}, {WriteLn}, and {GetPos}— provide an alternative way to import and export text. You can use these commands to read and write small chunks of text at specific places in a text file. Using these commands to work with a text file is a three-step process. First, you must use the {Open} command to open the file with which you want to work. Once the file is open, you can use the

{Write} or {WriteLn} commands to write information to it, or use the {Read} or {ReadLn} commands to read information from it. Once you have finished manipulating the open file, you can use {Close} to close it up again.

DOS uses a "pointer" to keep track of its position within an open file. While a file is open, you can use the {GetPos} command to determine the current location of the pointer in that file. You also can use the {SetPos} command to move the pointer around within the file, and the {FileSize} command to determine the number of bytes occupied by the file.

Opening a Text File: The {Open} Command

The {Open} command lets you open a file so that it can be accessed by 1-2-3's other file i/o commands. The form of this command is

{Open **filename,mode**}

The first argument, **filename**, specifies the name of the file you want 1-2-3 to open. This argument may be a literal string that names a file (like "TESTFILE.PRN"), the address or range name of a cell that contains the name of a file (like A1 or FILE), or a string formula or function that returns a file name.

Access Modes

The mode argument specifies the manner in which you want to access the file named by the filename argument. There are four possible options for this argument: the strings Read, Write, Modify, and Append (you can abbreviate these strings to R, W, M, or A).

The access mode you choose determines what you can do with the file once it is open. If you use Write or W, 1-2-3 will create a new file with the name you specify. If a file with that name exists, 1-2-3 will automatically overwrite it. Once you have opened a file in the Write mode, you can both write information to the file and read information from it.

If you open a file with Modify or M, 1-2-3 will allow you to write to and read from the file, just as it does when you are in the Write mode. Unlike the Write option, Modify and M do not create a new file. Instead, they open an existing file and position the pointer at the beginning of the file.

Like the Modify option, the Append and A arguments allow you to open an existing file. However, the Append mode only allows you to write information into the file. Also, the Append mode automatically places the pointer at the end of the file you open. As you will see, this makes it easy to write new information into a file without overwriting existing information.

Like Modify and Append, the Read and R options open an existing file. Unlike these two options, however, the Read mode allows you only to read information from a file, not write information to it. When you open a file with the Read option, 1-2-3 places the pointer at the beginning of that file.

Restrictions

As we have just explained, the Modify, Append, and Read options are designed to access existing files. However, no macro error results when you use those options in an attempt to access files that do not exist. Instead, 1-2-3 will execute any commands that follow on the same line of the macro, then skip to the next line and continue executing the macro. If 1-2-3 is able to execute the {Open} command, it will skip any remaining commands in the same cell as that command and continue executing the macro in the cell below that cell.

Closing a Text File: The {Close} Command

Once you open a file, it will remain open until 1-2-3 encounters a {Close} command, encounters another {Open} command (only one file can be open at a time), or reaches the end of the macro. Any of these three actions close the file.

It is very important that you close every text file that you open. When DOS creates a file, it writes the name of the file into the directory of the disk on which it will save the file. Then it writes the information that you want to save in the file onto the available sectors of the disk. While the file is open, DOS uses RAM to keep track of the locations of that information on the disk. DOS does not write the locations of that information into the directory until you close the file. If you do not close the file, DOS will not link the name of the file to the information in that file. As a result, the file will be unusable.

If you reboot your computer or lose power (by turning off your computer, tripping over the cord, etc.) while a file is still open, the addresses of the information in the file will not be written to the directory. Consequently, you will be unable to retrieve the file. To prevent this from happening, you should close any file as soon as you have finished working with it.

Controlling the Pointer

The position of the pointer in a file determines where 1-2-3 writes information into that file and what information 1-2-3 reads from the file. When you open a file in any mode except for the Append mode, 1-2-3 places the pointer at the beginning of the file. When you open a file in the Append mode, 1-2-3 places the pointer at the end of the file. Every time you write information to a file or read information from it, 1-2-3 will move the pointer to the character that follows the last one you wrote or read.

1-2-3's {SetPos} command allows you to move the pointer around within an open file. Together with two other commands, {GetPos} and {FileSize}, this command gives you complete control over the position of the pointer within an open text file.

The {SetPos} Command

1-2-3's {SetPos} command allows you to move the pointer within an open file. The form of this command is

{SetPos position}

where position specifies where you want 1-2-3 to place the pointer within the file. This argument may be a literal value, a reference to a cell that contains a value, or a formula or function that returns a value.

1-2-3 begins numbering the characters in a file with the number 0, not 1. To move the pointer to the first character in a file (the beginning of that file), you must use the command {SetPos 0}. The command {SetPos 1} moves the pointer to the second character in a file, not the first, the command {SetPos 2} moves the pointer to the third character in the file, and so on. If you specify a position that is greater than the number of characters in a file, 1-2-3 will move the pointer one space beyond the last character in the file.

The {GetPos} Command

1-2-3's {GetPos} command allows you to determine the current position of the pointer within an open file. The form of this command is

{GetPos location}

RELEASE
▶ 2.2 ◀

where *location* is the address or range name of the cell in which you want to store the current position of the pointer. ▶(In 1-2-3 Release 2.2, it can be a formula or function that returns the name or address of a cell.)◀ When 1-2-3 reads the command {GetPos A1}, for example, it will enter the current location of the pointer as a value in cell A1. For purposes of the {GetPos} command, the first character in a file has the position 0.

The {FileSize} Command

The {FileSize} command allows you to determine the total number of characters in the file that currently is open. The form of this command is

{FileSize location}

where *location* is an address or range name of the cell in which you want 1-2-3 to store the size of the file.

Restrictions

Like 1-2-3's other file i/o commands, the {SetPos}, {GetPos}, and {FileSize} commands work on the file that currently is open. If a file is open when 1-2-3 encounters one of these commands, 1-2-3 will execute the command, skip any remaining commands in the same cell, and continue executing the macro in the cell below that cell. If no file is open when 1-2-3 encounters one of these commands, however, it will execute any remaining commands in the same cell as the {SetPos}, {GetPos}, or {FileSize} command before it moves to the next cell.

Writing Information to a Text File

Once you have used the {Open} command with any mode option other than Read (or R), you can write information to it. 1-2-3 provides two commands for writing information to an open file: {Write} and {WriteLn}. When 1-2-3 executes either of these commands, it writes the information you specify into the file that is currently open, starting at the current position of the pointer within that file. (We'll show you how to move the pointer within a file later.)

The {Write} Command

The {Write} command allows you to write characters into a text file. The form of this command is

{Write **string**}

where **string** is a string that you wish to write to the file. **String** can be in the form of a literal sting, a reference to a cell that contains that string, or a formula or function that produces that string. If the argument is a literal string, it does not have to be enclosed in quotation marks unless it contains a colon or a comma, or unless the string names a range in the worksheet. If you wish to write a value to a text file, you first must use the @STRING function to convert it to a string. You can write a maximum of 239 characters to a file with a single {Write} command.

The {WriteLn} Command

The {WriteLn} command provides a second way to write information into an open file. The form of this command is

{WriteLn **string**}

where **string** is the string you want to write into the file. **String** can be in the form of a literal string, a reference to a cell that contains a string, or a formula or function that returns a string. If **string** is a literal string, it does not have to be enclosed in quotation marks unless it contains a colon or a comma, or unless the string names a range in the worksheet.

Like the {Write} command, the {WriteLn} command writes the string specified by its argument into the text file that currently is open, starting at the position of the pointer. However, the {WriteLn} command writes the string into the file as an entire line. In other words, {WriteLn} instructs 1-2-3 to add a carriage return (ASCII 13) and a linefeed (ASCII 10) at the end of the string as it writes the string into the file. When you use a {WriteLn} command to write information to a file, therefore, 1-2-3 always will write two more characters than the string contains.

Restrictions

The {Write} and {WriteLn} commands can write information only to files that are open in the Write, Modify, or Append modes. If 1-2-3 encounters one of these commands while no file is open, or while a file is open in the Read mode, no macro error will result. Instead, 1-2-3 will execute any commands that follow on the same line as the {Write} or {WriteLn} command. If a file is open in the appropriate mode, 1-2-3 will write the requested information into the file, then skip to the commands in the next cell below the {Write} or {WriteLn} command.

Reading Information from a Text File

In addition to writing information to an open text file, you also can read information from it. Two commands make this possible: {Read} and {ReadLn}. Each of these commands retrieves information from the open file and stores it as a left-aligned label in the cell that you specify. 1-2-3 will not display the result on the screen until you make an entry into another cell of the worksheet or press [Calc] to calculate the worksheet, however. 1-2-3 can read information only from files that are open in the Read, Write, or Modify modes.

Whenever 1-2-3 executes a {Read} or {ReadLn} command, it starts reading at the current position of the pointer within the open file. Exactly how much information 1-2-3 reads from the file, however, depends on which of these commands you've used.

The {Read} Command

1-2-3's {Read} command allows you to read up to 240 characters at a time from an open text file and store them in a cell of the 1-2-3 worksheet. The form of this command is

{Read *count,location*}

RELEASE
► 2.2 ◄

where *count* is the number of characters you want 1-2-3 to read from the file, and *location* is the cell into which you want 1-2-3 to place what it reads. The first argument can be a literal value, a reference to a cell that contains a value, or a formula or function that contains a value. The second argument can be a cell address, a range name, ►or, in 1-2-3 Release 2.2, a formula or function that returns the name or address of a cell or range.◄ When 1-2-3 executes a {Read} command, it will read as many characters as you specify, up to a maximum of 239 characters. After 1-2-3 executes a {Read} command, it moves the pointer to the character that follows the last one it read from the file.

The {ReadLn} Command

Just like the {Read} command, 1-2-3's {ReadLn} command reads information from the currently open text file, starting at the current position of the pointer within that file. Instead of reading the number of characters that you specify, 1-2-3 reads until it reaches a carriage return/linefeed combination.

The form of the {ReadLn} command is

{ReadLn *location*}

where *location* is the address or name of the cell in which you want 1-2-3 to write the information that it reads from the file. ►(In 1-2-3 Release 2.2, this argument can be a formula or function that returns the name or address of a cell.)◄ This command tells 1-2-3 to store the characters it reads in the cell specified by *location*. 1-2-3 will continue reading characters until it encounters a carriage return/linefeed or the end of the file, or until it has read 239 characters. 1-2-3 does not enter the carriage return or linefeed characters into the specified cell of the worksheet. After 1-2-3 executes a {ReadLn} command, it moves the pointer to the character that follows the linefeed.

RELEASE
► 2.2 ◄

Restrictions

The {Read} and {ReadLn} commands can read information from a file only if that file is open in the Read, Write, or Modify modes. If 1-2-3 encounters one of these commands when no file is open or when a file is open in the Append mode, however, no macro error will result. Instead, 1-2-3 will execute any commands to the right of the unexecutable {Read} or {ReadLn} command in the same cell. Then 1-2-3 will continue executing the macro in the cell below the one that contains the {Read} or {ReadLn} command.

An Example

You probably will not use the file i/o commands very often. However, you can use them to do a number of things—including creating a disk-based data base management system in 1-2-3. We'll use a stripped-down, simplified version of such a system to demonstrate the use of the file i/o commands.

Creating a Text File

To begin, you need to create a file to work with. We'll do this by printing the contents of the range A1..C4 in Figure 15-14 into a file named PHONE.PRN. To do this, issue the / Print File command, type PHONE, and press [Enter]. Next, choose Range and select the range A1..C4. Once the range is selected, issue the Options Other Unformatted command, then choose Margins Left, type 0, and press [Enter]. Finally, choose Quit to return to the Print menu and choose Go to print the range A1..C4 into the file PHONE.PRN. 1-2-3 will automatically add the extension .PRN to the file name. (For more on the / Print File command, see Appendix 1.)

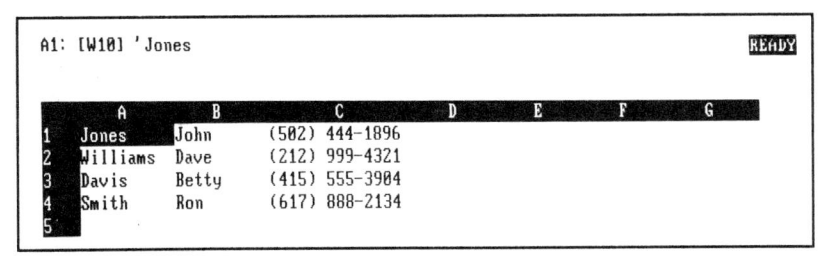

```
A1: [W10] 'Jones                                              READY

        A          B          C           D        E        F        G
1    Jones      John      (502) 444-1896
2    Williams   Dave      (212) 999-4321
3    Davis      Betty     (415) 555-3904
4    Smith      Ron       (617) 888-2134
5
```

FIGURE 15-14: A sample worksheet

There are a couple of things to point out about this file before we go on. First, because column A in Figure 15-14 is ten characters wide, column B is ten characters wide, and column C is 14 characters wide, each line in the text file includes 34 characters of information (including blank spaces). In addition, 1-2-3 has inserted a carriage return and a linefeed at the end of each line, bringing the total length of each line in the file to 36 characters. Since 1-2-3's file i/o commands consider the first character in a text file to occupy position 0, this means that the second line begins at position 36, the third line at 72, and the fourth line at 108. It also means that the file contains a total of 144 characters.

Reading Data from the File

Suppose you want to read the entire third line from the file PHONE.PRN. Figure 15-15 shows a macro that will do the trick. The first line of this macro uses the {Open} command to open the file PHONE.PRN in the Modify mode. (We could have also used the Read mode to open the file since all we plan to do is read information from it.) The {SetPos} command in cell B2 moves the pointer to position 72 in the file. Since every line in the file is 36 characters long, the third line begins at position 72. The {ReadLn} command on the third line tells 1-2-3 to read the entire third line from the file and store the retrieved characters in the cell named RETRIEVE (cell B7). The {Close} command in cell B4 closes the file PHONE.PRN, and the ~ instruction in cell B5 causes 1-2-3 to redraw the screen. Figure 15-15 shows the screen after the macro has been run. As you can see, 1-2-3 has entered the label *'Davis Betty (415) 555-3904* into cell B7.

```
B7: [W10] 'Davis      Betty     (415) 555-3904                          READY

        A         B              C            D        E        F        G
1      \r        {Open PHONE.PRN,"Modify"}
2                {SetPos 72}
3                {ReadLn RETRIEVE}
4                {Close}
5                ~
6
7      RETRIEVE  Davis     Betty     (415) 555-3904
8
```

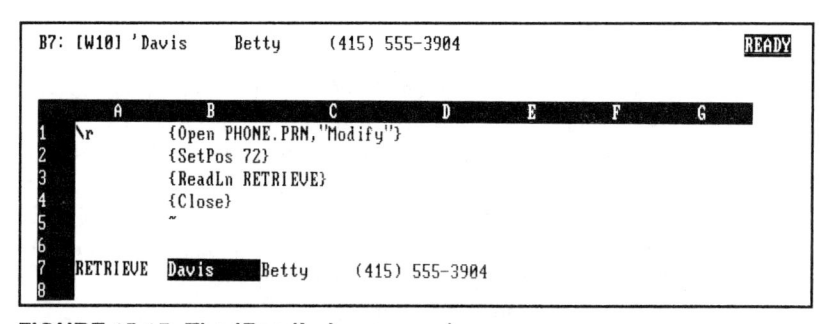

FIGURE 15-15: The {ReadLn} command

Now suppose you want to retrieve only the last name from the second line of the text file. Figure 15-16 shows a macro that will do this. In fact, this macro is very similar to the one in Figure 15-15. The first line opens the file PHONE. The second line of the macro moves the pointer to position 36 in the file—the first character in the second line. The command in cell B3, *{Read 10,RETRIEVE}* tells 1-2-3 to read the next ten characters from the file PHONE.PRN, beginning at the position of the pointer, and to store the retrieved characters in the cell RETRIEVE (cell B7). Figure 15-16 shows the screen after this macro has been run. As you can see, 1-2-3 has entered the label 'Williams into cell B7.

```
B7: [W10] 'Williams                                                    READY

       A        B              C           D      E      F      G
  1   \r      {Open PHONE.PRN,"Modify"}
  2           {SetPos 36}
  3           {Read 10,RETRIEVE}
  4           {Close}
  5           ~
  6
  7   RETRIEVE  Williams
  8
```

FIGURE 15-16: The {Read} command

Now let's use the file i/o commands to write some information into PHONE.PRN. To begin, suppose you want to replace the first name in the first line of the file ("John") with the text *Jane*. Figure 15-17 shows a macro that will make this change. Again, the macro begins by opening the file in the Modify mode. (Since you want to write characters to the file, you could open the file in the Write mode instead.) Next, the {SetPos} command in the second line moves the pointer to position 10—the first character in the name *John*. How do we know that the name *John* begins at position 10 in the file? Because column A of the worksheet in Figure 15-14, from which we created the file, was ten characters wide. The command in cell B3, *{Write Jane}*, will replace the characters *John* in the first line of the file with the characters *Jane*.

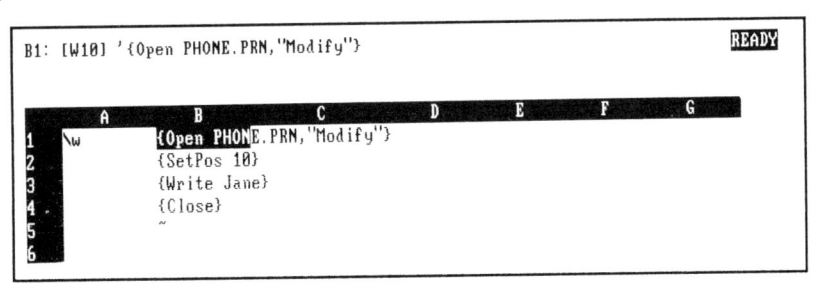

```
B1: [W10] '{Open PHONE.PRN,"Modify"}                                  READY

       A        B              C           D      E      F      G
  1   \w      {Open PHONE.PRN,"Modify"}
  2           {SetPos 10}
  3           {Write Jane}
  4   .       {Close}
  5           ~
  6
```

FIGURE 15-17: The {Write} command

Finally, suppose you want to add a line to the file PHONE. The characters you want to add to the file, *Rogers John (502) 555-1414* are shown in cell B6 of Figure 15-18. We've given this cell the name ADDITION. Note that the spacing of the characters in this cell matches that of the entries in the text file. If you want to maintain the consistency of the spacing in the file, it is critical that any lines you write to the file have the same spacing as the original entries in the file.

```
B6: [W10] 'Rogers     John        (502) 555-1414                          READY

          A         B           C           D         E        F        G
    1   \w        {Open PHONE.PRN,"Append"}
    2             {WriteLn ADDITION}
    3             {Close}
    4             ~
    5
    6   ADDITION  Rogers      John        (502) 555-1414
    7
```

FIGURE 15-18: The {WriteLn} command

The macro that writes these characters into the file begins in cell B1. The command in that cell opens the file PHONE.PRN in the Append mode. Recall that when you open a file in the Append mode, 1-2-3 places the pointer at the end of the file. Since we want to add the new line at the end of the file, this means that we don't need to reposition the pointer before we write the information to the file. The command in cell B2, *{WriteLn ADDITION}*, writes the entire line from cell B6 (ADDITION) into the file at the position of the pointer. The commands in cells B3 and B4 close the file PHONE and redraw the screen.

Figure 15-19 shows the text file PHONE.PRN after it has been modified by the macros in Figures 15-17 and 15-18. As you can see, the first line now contains the text *Jane* instead of *John*, and the file now includes a fifth line.

```
C:\123>type PHONE.PRN
Jones      Jane       (502) 444-1896
Williams   Dave       (212) 999-4321
Davis      Betty      (415) 555-3904
Smith      Ron        (617) 888-2134
Rogers     John       (502) 555-1414
```

FIGURE 15-19: The result of the {Write} and {WriteLn} commands

TIP: RANGE NAMES WITH {WRITE} AND {WRITELN}

In the macro in Figure 15-18, we used the name ADDITION as the argument for {WriteLn}. 1-2-3 lets you use a range name as the argument of the {WriteLn} and {Write} commands. When you use a range name as the argument in one of these commands, 1-2-3 will write the contents of the cell identified by the name into the text file. If the range name you specify does not exist, however, 1-2-3 will write the name into the file as literal text.

ADVANCED TECHNIQUES

In Chapter 14 and the previous part of this chapter, we've presented each of 1-2-3's LCL commands. As you've seen, the use of these commands can add a tremendous amount of power to your 1-2-3 macros. We'll finish our discussion of the LCL by presenting two advanced LCL programming techniques: self-modifying macros and computed macro statements.

Self-Modifying Macros

As you learned in Chapter 13, a macro is a collection of labels, arranged in a column of a 1-2-3 worksheet, that represent keystrokes and commands. In most cases, all of the cells of a macro will contain instructions before the macro begins running. In some cases, however, you'll want to leave one or more cells in a macro blank so that 1-2-3 can fill them with commands as it executes the macro. By the time 1-2-3 reaches the originally blank cells, they will contain one or more commands, and 1-2-3 will continue executing the macro.

The simple macro in Figure 15-20, which automates the process of adjusting the width of a column, demonstrates this technique. The {GetLabel} command in cell B1 asks you to supply the new width for the current column, and stores your response as a label in the cell named WIDTH (cell B3). If you type 25 in response to this prompt, for example, 1-2-3 will place the label '25 in cell B3. The second statement in the macro, '/wcs, commands 1-2-3 to issue the /Worksheet Column Set-Width command. Because the s (for Set-Width) is the final instruction in this cell, 1-2-3 then looks to cell B3, where it finds your response to the {GetLabel} command. In this case, cell B3 will hold the label '25, so 1-2-3 will type 25 as the new width for the current column. Finally, 1-2-3 will execute the ~ in cell B4, which commands it to press the [Enter] key, locking in the new width.

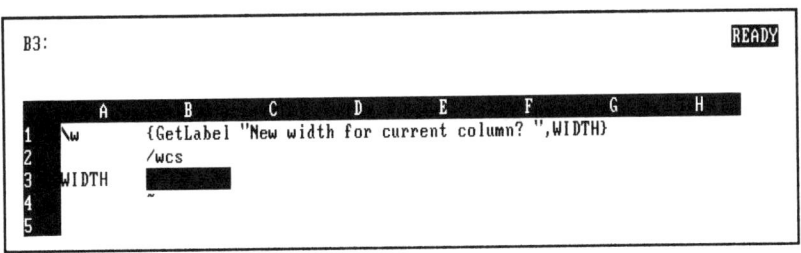

FIGURE 15-20: A self-modifying macro

Why did we use a {GetLabel} statement rather than a {GetNumber} statement to solicit the column width? Because the {GetNumber} statement places a value—rather than a label—in its destination cell. As you recall, 1-2-3 stops the execution of a macro when it reaches a cell that contains a value. For 1-2-3 to be able to read the new width, that width must be in the form of a label. If we had used a {GetNumber} command, we would have had to follow it with the command

{Let WIDTH,@STRING(WIDTH,0)}

which converts the value into a label.

Computed Macro Statements

Every statement in each of the example macros presented in Chapters 13, 14, and (so far) 15 have been labels. However, macro statements do not have to be labels—they can be formulas that return strings. If the string result of a formula is a valid macro statement, 1-2-3 will execute that statement just as if it were a label entry. We'll refer to this kind of string formula as a "computed" macro statement.

An Example

Computed macro statements are an alternative to self-modifying macros. For example, the macro shown in Figure 15-21 does the same thing as the one shown in Figure 15-20—it sets the current column to the width you specify. However, it uses a computed macro statement to do so. The first statement in this macro is identical to the one that begins the macro shown in Figure 15-20. Like that statement, it solicits a width, and enters your response into the cell named WIDTH (in this case, cell B5). The second statement in this macro, {Recalc NEXT}, commands 1-2-3 to recalculate the cell named NEXT (B3). As you can see, this cell contains the formula

+"/wcs"&WIDTH&"~"

(Before you enter this formula into the worksheet, you should assign the name WIDTH to cell B5). When recalculated, this formula returns a macro statement that commands 1-2-3 to set the current column to the width you specified. For example, if WIDTH contained the label '20 (as it would if you typed 20 in response to the {GetLabel} prompt), this formula would return the string */wcs20~*. Since the cell that contains this formula is the next cell in the macro, 1-2-3 executes the result of the formula—a valid macro statement that commands 1-2-3 to set the width of the current column to 20—as soon as it recalculates that formula.

Other Uses for Computed Macro Statements

As we explained in Chapter 14, all releases of 1-2-3 allow you to use formulas and functions in place of numeric arguments. However, only 1-2-3 Release 2.2 allows you to use formulas and functions in place of reference and string arguments. For example, in 1-2-3 Release 2.2, the statement

{GetNumber B4,@CELLPOINTER("address")}

will use the label from cell B4 as a prompt, and enter the user's response into the current cell—the cell on which the cell pointer is positioned at the time. In 1-2-3 Releases 2 and 2.1, this statement would cause a macro error.

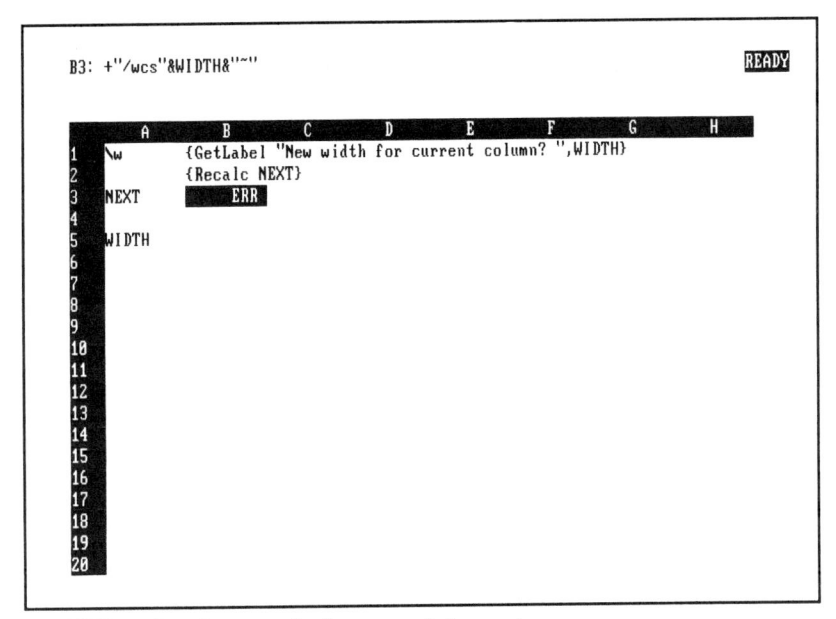

```
B3: +"/wcs"&WIDTH&"~"                                              READY

       A         B          C         D         E         F         G         H
  1   \w     {GetLabel "New width for current column? ",WIDTH}
  2          {Recalc NEXT}
  3   NEXT       ERR
  4
  5   WIDTH
  6
  ...
 20
```

FIGURE 15-21: A computed macro statement

Fortunately, you can use computed macro statements to make up for the inability of 1-2-3 Releases 2 and 2.01 to use formulas and functions as reference and string arguments. For example, you could use the macro routine shown in Figure 15-22 to duplicate the effect of the statement *{GetNumber B4,@CELLPOINTER("address")}* in 1-2-3 Release 2.2. The first statement in this macro, '{Recalc NEXT}, commands 1-2-3 to recalculate the cell named NEXT (B2), which contains the formula

+"{GetNumber "&B4&" ,"&@CELLPOINTER("address")&"}"

Since cell B4 contains the label *Value?* and the cell pointer is on cell B6, this formula returns the string *{GetNumber Value? ,$B$6}*, which commands 1-2-3 to display the prompt *Value?* at the top of the screen and enter the user's response into cell B6.

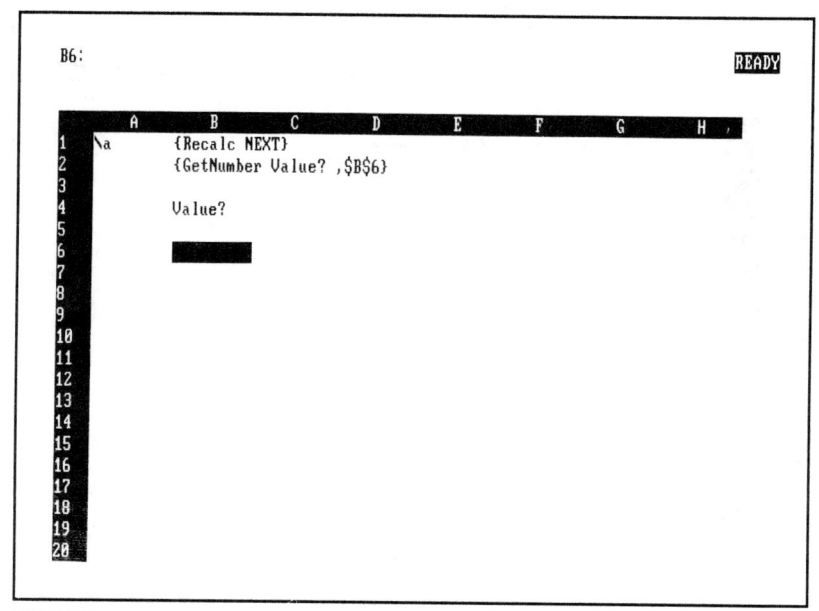

```
B6:                                                    READY

        A         B         C         D       E       F       G       H
    1  \a    {Recalc NEXT}
    2        {GetNumber Value? ,$B$6}
    3
    4        Value?
    5
    6        ████████
    7
    ...
   20
```

FIGURE 15-22: Another computed macro statement

CONCLUSION

This chapter concludes our discussion of 1-2-3 macros and the Lotus Command Language. We began this chapter by demonstrating the use of the remaining 35 LCL commands. Although you probably will use these commands less frequently than the ones presented in Chapter 14, you'll find them indispensable in certain programming situations. At the end of this chapter, we showed you how to develop self-modifying macros and how to use computed macro statements.

16

Add-in Applications

In the previous chapters of this book, we've explored the myriad of features built into 1-2-3. If 1-2-3 went only that far, it would be a fine program. However, you can expand the functionality of 1-2-3 Releases 2, 2.01, and 2.2 through the use of add-in add-in applications, or *add-ins*. (You cannot use add-ins with 1-2-3 Release 1A). Add-ins are programs that are designed to add additional powers to 1-2-3. Unlike RAM-resident utilities, add-in applications actually become a part of the 1-2-3 program code. Therefore, they allow you to do things that RAM-resident utilities cannot. For example, some add-ins add new @ functions to 1-2-3; others add word-processing powers; one expands the functionality of the Edit line; and one allows you to see more of a worksheet on the screen at one time.

In this chapter, we'll show you how to use add-in applications with 1-2-3. ▶Then, we'll examine in detail the two add-ins that come with 1-2-3 Release 2.2: Allways and the Macro Library Manager.◀ Then, we'll take a brief look at several other add-in applications that work with 1-2-3.

RELEASE
▶ 2.2 ◀

USING ADD-IN APPLICATIONS

Since add-in applications are not a part of the 1-2-3 program itself, you must do a couple of things before you can use them. First, you must attach them to 1-2-3. Attaching an add-in loads the program code for that add-in into RAM, essentially "merging" it into 1-2-3. Second, in order to use most applications, you must invoke them. Invoking an add-in activates the program code for that add-in, allowing it to do whatever it was intended to do.

▶The commands that allow you to attach and invoke add-ins are built into 1-2-3 Release 2.2. However, they must be added to 1-2-3 Releases 2 and 2.01. In this section of this chapter, we'll show you how to attach and invoke add-ins in 1-2-3 Release 2.2. We'll show you how to use add-ins in 1-2-3 Releases 2 and 2.01 at the end of this section.

RELEASE
▶ 2.2 ◀

Attaching Add-in Applications

Before you can use any add-in application, you must attach it to 1-2-3. Attaching an add-in application loads it into RAM. To attach an add-in application to 1-2-3, begin by issuing the / Add-In command (or, if you have not already linked an add-in application to the [Alt][F10] combination, press that combination of keys). When you do this, 1-2-3 will display the menu shown in Figure 16-1. The commands on this menu allow to to attach, detach, invoke, and clear add-in applications.

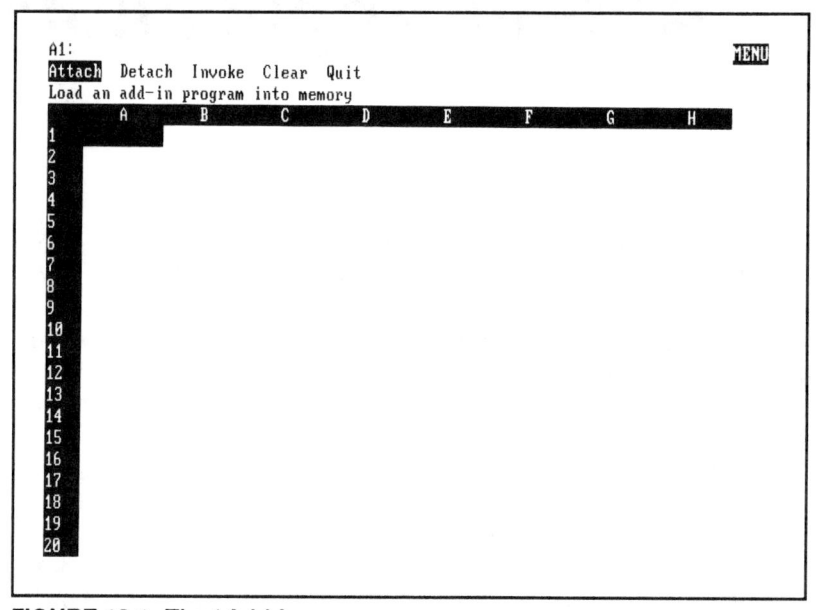

```
A1:                                                                  MENU
Attach Detach Invoke Clear Quit
Load an add-in program into memory
         A       B       C       D       E       F       G       H
1
2
3
4
5
6
7
8
9
10
11
12
13
14
15
16
17
18
19
20
```

FIGURE 16-1: The / Add-In menu

Next, choose the Attach option from the menu shown in Figure 16-1. As soon as you select this option, 1-2-3 will present a list of the add-in applications in the directory that contains your 1-2-3 program files. Unless you have purchased additional add-ins for use with 1-2-3, only two will be listed: ALLWAYS.ADN (an add-in that allows you to embellish printed worksheets) and MACROMGR.ADN (an add-in that allows you to store and use macros in a nonworksheet portion of RAM). To choose an add-in from this list, simply highlight its name and press [Enter]. (If the add-in application you want to attach is in a directory other than the one in which your 1-2-3 progam files are stored, you can use the any of the techniques mentioned in Chapter 9 to select that file from another directory.)

As soon as you select the add-in you want to attach, 1-2-3 will present the menu shown in Figure 16-2. The choices on this menu allow you to specify the key combination (if any) to which you want to link the application. If you select the 7 option, 1-2-3 will link the add-in to the [Alt][F7] combination; if you select 8, 1-2-3 will link the add-in to the [Alt][F8] combination; if you select 9, 1-2-3 will link the add-in to the [Alt][F9] combination; and if you select 10, 1-2-3 will link the add-in to the

[Alt][F10] combination. Linking an add-in application to one of these four combinations of keys gives you an alternative way to invoke it: by pressing that combination of keys. For example, if you link an add-in to the [Alt][F7] combination, you can invoke it simply by pressing [Alt][F7]. (If you link an add-in to the [Alt][F10] combination, 1-2-3 will invoke that application—rather than revealing the menu shown in Figure 16-1—when you press that combination of keys.)

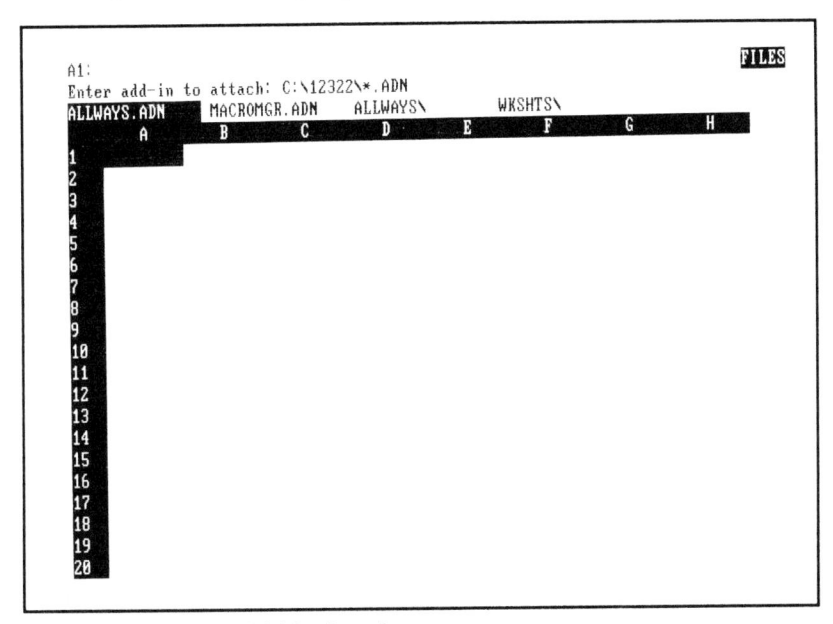

FIGURE 16-2: The / Add-In Attach menu

If you don't want to link the add-in to one of these four combinations of keys, you should select the No-Key option. If you do, you'll have to use the / Add-In Invoke command to invoke the add-in. (Of course, you can also use this command to invoke macros that you have linked to one of the four [Alt]-key combinations).

More than one add-in application can be attached to 1-2-3 at a time. If you atttach an add-in while one or more add-ins are already attached, the key combinations (if any) to which those add-ins are attached will not appear on the menu shown in Figure 16-2.

As soon as you choose one of the items from the menu shown in Figure 16-2, 1-2-3 will load the add-in into RAM. Some add-ins display an identification screen while they are loading; some do not. In any case, 1-2-3 will return you to the menu shown in Figure 16-1 after it finshes loading the add-in. At that point, you can invoke the add-in you just attached, attach another add-in, remove one or more add-ins from RAM, or choose Quit to return to the READY mode.

The amount of RAM that an add-in occupies depends on the add-in. For example, the Macro Library Manager occupies 13,366 bytes of RAM; Allways occupies at least 62,504 bytes.

Invoking Add-in Applications

When you attach most add-in applications to 1-2-3, 1-2-3 simply loads them into RAM; it does not execute ("invoke") them until you tell it to do so.

The way you invoke an application depends on whether or not you have linked it to a combination of the [Alt] and [F7], [F8], [F9], and [F10] keys. If you have, you can invoke the add-in simply by pressing the combination of keys to which it is linked. For example, if you selected 7 from the menu shown in Figure 16-2 when you attached an add-in, you can invoke that add-in by pressing [Alt][F7]. If you haven't linked the add-in to one of these four key combinations, you must use the / Add-In Invoke command to invoke it. When you issue this command, 1-2-3 will display a list of the names of all the add-ins that are attached to 1-2-3 at the time. To invoke the application, you simply highlight its name and press [Enter]. (Of course, you also can use this command to invoke add-in that are linked to one of the four key combinations.)

What happens when you invoke an application depends on the application itself. When you invoke the Macro Library Manager, 1-2-3 will reveal a special menu; when you invoke Allways, it will replace the 1-2-3 sceen with a graphical image of that screen. (We'll explore these two add-ins in detail later in this chapter.) Other add-ins will change the appearance of the screen in other ways, change the action of the function keys, and so forth.

Some add-in applications invoke themselves automatically as soon as you attach them. For example, Personics' SeeMore (which allows you to see a larger portion of a 1-2-3 worksheet on the screen at one time) changes the screen display as soon as you attach it. However, pressing the key combination to which it is attached (or issuing the / Add-In Invoke command and choosing its name) reveals a menu that allows you customize the display. Some add-ins cannot be invoked. For example, a number of add-ins add new @ functions to 1-2-3. Attaching these add-ins activates those functions; to use them, you simply type them into the worksheet.

Detaching Add-in Applications

Because add-in applications occupy RAM, they decrease the potential size of your worksheets. If you are bumping up against memory constraints, and you no longer need to use an attached application, you can remove it from RAM. This process is called "detaching." To detach an application, simply issue the / Add-In command and choose Detach from the menu shown in Figure 16-1. When you do this, you'll see a listing of all the applications currently attached to 1-2-3—the same listing that appears when you issue the / Add-In Invoke command. To detach an application, simply highlight or type its name and press [Enter]. When you do this, 1-2-3 will empty the RAM occupied by the application, making it available for worksheet information.

In some cases, you'll want to detach all of the add-in applications currently attached to 1-2-3 at once. The / Add-In Clear option makes this possible. When you issue this command, 1-2-3 will detach all add-in applications currently attached to 1-2-3, clearing the RAM occupied by those applications.

Auto-attaching and Auto-invoking Add-ins

In some cases, you'll want to attach and invoke one or more add-in applications every time you work with 1-2-3. To do this, you can make them auto-attaching (and, optionally, auto-invoking) applications.

To make an add-in application auto-attaching and/or auto-invoking, you must use the / Worksheet Global Default Other Add-In command. When you issue this command, 1-2-3 will display a menu with three choices: Set (which allows you to specify which add-ins will be auto-attached and, optionally, auto-invoked); Cancel (which allows you to specify that an add-in no longer be automatically attached or invoked); and Quit (which returns you to the / Worksheet Global Default menu). The changes you make with the Set and Cancel commands will be reflected in the Default Settings settings sheet, which will be visible on the screen at the time.

The Set option allows you to select up to eight add-in applications that you want 1-2-3 to attach (and, if you wish, invoke) automatically whenever you load it. When you select this option, 1-2-3 will reveal a menu with eight choices: 1, 2, 3, 4, 5, 6, 7, and 8. The number you choose from this menu determines the order in which 1-2-3 will attach the application you select relative to other auto-attaching applications. As soon as you choose a number, 1-2-3 will display a list of the add-ins in the directory from which you loaded 1-2-3 (1-2-3 can only auto-attach applications that are in that directory). As soon as you choose an add-in, 1-2-3 will let you select the [Alt] key combination (if any) to which you want to link that add-in. Finally, 1-2-3 will let you choose whether or not you want it to invoke that add-in automatically.

As soon as you complete this selection process, 1-2-3 will record your choices on the appropriate line of the settings sheet. The name of the add-in will appear first. If you specified that the add-in be linked to an [Alt] key combination, the name of that combination will follow the name of the add-in. If you specified that the add-in be invoked automatically, the words *(Auto invoke)* will follow the name of the key combination. Important: it will also attach that add-in you specified—just as if you had issued the / Add-In Attach command.

Once 1-2-3 has done these things, it will return you to the / Worksheet Global Default Other Add-In menu. At this point, you can choose other auto-attaching/auto-invoking applications (up to eight total). Alternatively, you can erase choices that you selected previously. To do this, simply choose Clear from the / Worksheet Global Default Other Add-In menu. When you issue this command, 1-2-3 will display the same eight-item menu it displays when you issue the / Worksheet Global Default Other Add-In Set command. To cancel an add-in application, simply choose its number from that menu. When you do this, 1-2-3 will remove the description of that add-in from the Default settings sheet, and, important, remove that add-in from RAM—just as if you had issued the / Add-In Detach command.

Once the Default settings sheet specifies the application(s) that you want, you should choose Update. When you do this, 1-2-3 will save the specifications from this settings sheet in a file named 123.CNF. As we explain in Appendix 3, 1-2-3 reads this file whenever it loads. Consequently, 1-2-3 will attach (and, if you instructed it to, invoke) the add-ins that you specified. If you neglect to choose Update, the effects of the / Worksheet Global Default Other Add-In Set and / Worksheet Global Default Other Add-In Clear commands will be the same those of the / Add-In Attach and / Add-In Detach commands—they will simply attach and detach the specfied add-ins for the current 1-2-3 session. ◄

Using Add-in Applications in Releases 2 and 2.01

The ability to use add-in applications is not built into 1-2-3 Releases 2 and 2.01. However, it can be added to them by merging the Add-In Manager (the contents of a driver file named ADN_MGR.DRV) into the driver set you use to load 1-2-3. This file, along with two related files—ADN_MGR.DRV and ADD_MGR.EXE—are included with every 1-2-3 add-in application.

To merge the Add-In Manager into a driver set file, make current the directory that contains the ADN_MGR.DRV and ADD_MGR.EXE. files. Then, type add_mgr, a space, and the name of the .SET file into which you want to add the Add-In Manager. (You must include the .SET extension). As soon as you press [Enter], your computer will display the message *Updating driver set to include ADN_MGR. . ..* After your computer reads and writes for a few seconds, it will display the message *Driver set update complete.* and return you to the DOS prompt. Merging the Add-In Manager into a .SET file increases the size of that file by 20,128 bytes.

In order to use an add-in application with 1-2-3, you must load 1-2-3 with a driver set that contains the Add-In Manager. When you do this, the Add-In Manager becomes a part of 1-2-3. In the process of loading the Add-In Manager, 1-2-3 looks for a file named 123.DYN in the directory that contains your 1-2-3 program files. (This file is stored on the 1-2-3 PrintGraph disk.) If this file is not present, 1-2-3 will load successfully, the Add-In Manager will not.

To access the Add-In Manager in 1-2-3 Releases 2 and 2.01, you must press the [Alt][F10] combination (there is no / Add-In command in these releases of 1-2-3). When you do this, 1-2-3 Releases 2 ands 2.01 will display a menu like the one shown in Figure 16-1, but with one additional option: Setup. The Attach, Detach, and Clear options work the same way they do in 1-2-3 Release 2.2, except that 1-2-3 Releases 2 and 2.01 do not allow you to link add-ins to the [Alt][F10] combination. The Setup option allows you to set and erase auto-attaching, auto-invoking add-ins, like the / Worksheet Global Default Other Add-In command in 1-2-3 Release 2.2. The third option on the [Alt][F10] Setup menu, Update, saves a record of the auto-attaching, auto-invoking add-ins in a file named ADN.CFG. 1-2-3 Releases 2 and 2.01 look for this file whenever you load them with a .SET file that contains the Add-In Manager.

ALLWAYS

One of 1-2-3's most significant shortcomings is the extremely limited number of tools that it provides for customizing the appearance of a printed worksheet. Unlike Microsoft Excel, 1-2-3 does not allow you to shade portions of the worksheet, draw lines of varying thicknesses, and so forth. Although you can print different portions of a 1-2-3 worksheet in different fonts and styles, you must embed complex setup strings in that worksheet in order to do so. To draw boxes around cells and ranges, you must use complex formulas that produce upper-level ASCII characters.

Fortunately, 1-2-3 Release 2.2 includes an add-in that eliminates these shortcomings. This add-in—Allways—adds Excel-like formatting features to 1-2-3. Allways is a complete printing and formatting system that enables you to get presentation-quality output from your 1-2-3 worksheets on almost any printer. Allways makes it easy to

—assign different fonts to individual cells or ranges in a worksheet
—boldface and underline the contents of individual cells or ranges
—assign different colors and shadings to individual cells or ranges
—adjust the heights of the rows in a worksheet
—assign any of three levels of shading to any cell or range
—draw vertical and horizontal lines of any thickness you desire
—draw complete or partial outlines around cells or ranges

In addition to these powers, Allways allows you to embed a graph within a worksheet, so that it prints on the same page as that worksheet. Allways also makes it possible to print your spreadsheets in color from color printers. (Allways also will work with 1-2-3 Releases 2 and 2.01, but must be purchased separately.)

Figure 16-3 shows a printout of a 1-2-3 worksheet that has been enhanced with Allways. As you can see, this printout combines the worksheet shown in Figure 16-4 and the graphs shown in Figures 16-5 and 16-6 on one page. (Figure 16-4 shows how the worksheet looks when printed from 1-2-3; Figures 16-5 and 16-6 show graphs of the information in that worksheet printed from within PrintGraph.) As you can see, using fonts, shadings, lines, and other print attributes, as well as combining graphs and numbers on the same page, creates a significantly more professional-looking printout than 1-2-3 alone can produce.

Installing Allways

Allways comes on five disks. Before you can use Allways with 1-2-3, you must install it. To do this, insert the Allways Setup Disk into your computer's A drive, type *awsetup* at the A> prompt, and press [Enter]. A few seconds after you do this, the Allways setup program will display an introductory screen. After pressing [Enter] to bypass this screen, choose First-Time Setup from the menu that the setup program display at that point. Then, press [Enter] to bypass the next screen, type the name of the directory that contains your 1-2-3 program files, and press [Enter] again. Next, choose the type of video card that is in your computer, and then select the printer(s) that you will be using with Allways. After you make those selections, the setup program will ask you to insert the remaining four Allways disks, one at a time, as it copies the necessary files. One file—ALLWAYS.ADN—will be copied to the directory that contains your 1-2-3 program files. The remaining files (15 or so) will be copied to a subdirectory named ALLWAYS, which the setup program creates.

Amalgamated Hardware, Inc.
Five-Year Sales Analysis

Product	FY 1986	FY 1987	FY 1988	FY 1989	FY 1990	Total
Hammers	$53,326	$47,993	$57,591	$46,072	$64,500	$269,482
Screwdrivers	$88,846	$79,961	$95,953	$76,762	$107,466	$448,988
Pliers	$10,569	$9,512	$11,414	$9,131	$12,783	$53,409
Wrenches	$32,547	$29,292	$35,150	$28,120	$39,368	$164,477
Saws	$28,921	$26,028	$31,233	$24,986	$34,980	$146,148
Drills	$70,850	$63,765	$76,518	$61,214	$85,699	$358,046
Levels	$98,937	$89,043	$106,851	$85,480	$119,672	$499,983
Chisels	$50,499	$45,449	$54,538	$43,630	$61,082	$255,198
Files	$58,332	$52,498	$62,997	$50,397	$70,555	$294,779
Planes	$26,509	$23,858	$28,629	$22,903	$32,064	$133,963
Toolboxes	$83,368	$75,031	$90,037	$72,029	$100,840	$421,305
Putty Knives	$11,955	$10,759	$12,910	$10,328	$14,459	$60,411
Total	$285,059	$256,551	$307,859	$246,285	$344,796	$1,440,550

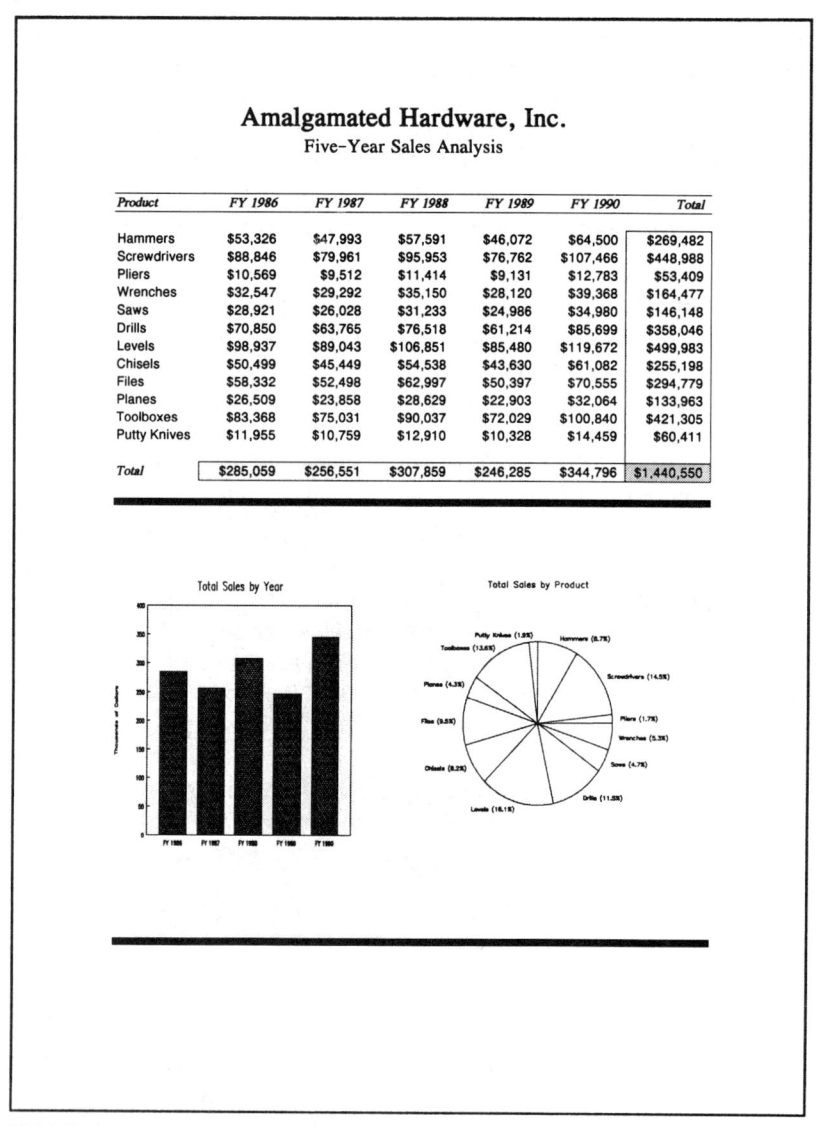

FIGURE 16-3: A report produced with Allways

Attaching and Invoking Allways

Since Allways is an add-in application, it allows you to enhance your worksheets without exiting from 1-2-3. However, you first must attach it to 1-2-3. To do this, simply issue the / Add-In Attach command (or press [Alt][F10]) and select ALLWAYS.ADN from the list that 1-2-3 presents, and, optionally, choose a key to link it to. While 1-2-3 is attaching Allways, it displays an identification screen. After Allways has been loaded, 1-2-3 will return you to the / Add-In menu.

```
              Amalgamated Hardware, Inc.
                Five-Year Sales Analysis

Product         FY 1986   FY 1987   FY 1988   FY 1989   FY 1990       Total

Hammers         $53,326   $47,993   $57,591   $46,072   $64,500    $269,482
Screwdrivers    $88,846   $79,961   $95,953   $76,762  $107,466    $448,988
Pliers          $10,569    $9,512   $11,414    $9,131   $12,783     $53,409
Wrenches        $32,547   $29,292   $35,150   $28,120   $39,368    $164,477
Saws            $28,921   $26,028   $31,233   $24,986   $34,980    $146,148
Drills          $70,850   $63,765   $76,518   $61,214   $85,699    $358,046
Levels          $98,937   $89,043  $106,851   $85,480  $119,672    $499,983
Chisels         $50,499   $45,449   $54,538   $43,630   $61,082    $255,198
Files           $58,332   $52,498   $62,997   $50,397   $70,555    $294,779
Planes          $26,509   $23,858   $28,629   $22,903   $32,064    $133,963
Toolboxes       $83,368   $75,031   $90,037   $72,029  $100,840    $421,305
Putty Knives    $11,955   $10,759   $12,910   $10,328   $14,459     $60,411

Total          $285,059  $256,551  $307,859  $246,285  $344,796  $1,440,550
```

FIGURE 16-4: The worksheet printed with 1-2-3

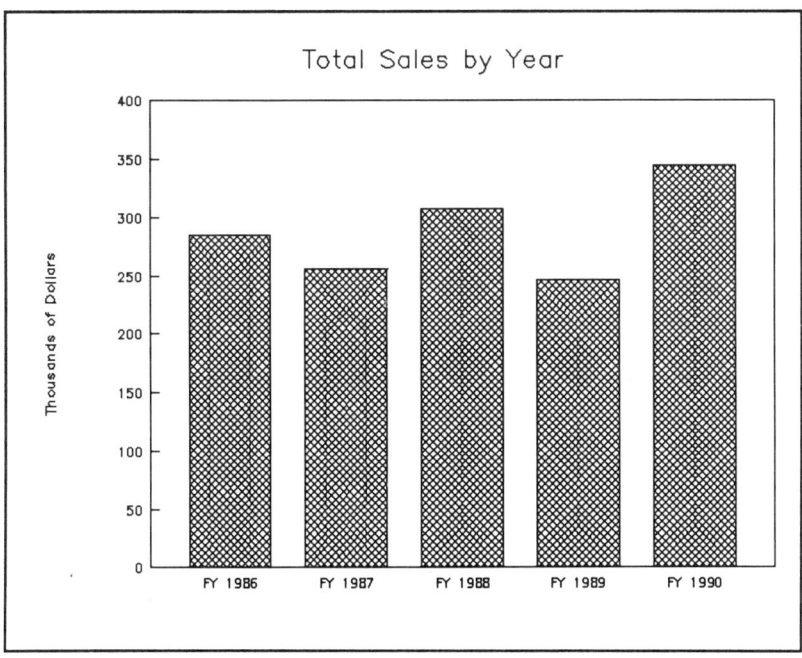

FIGURE 16-5: The first graph printed in PrintGraph

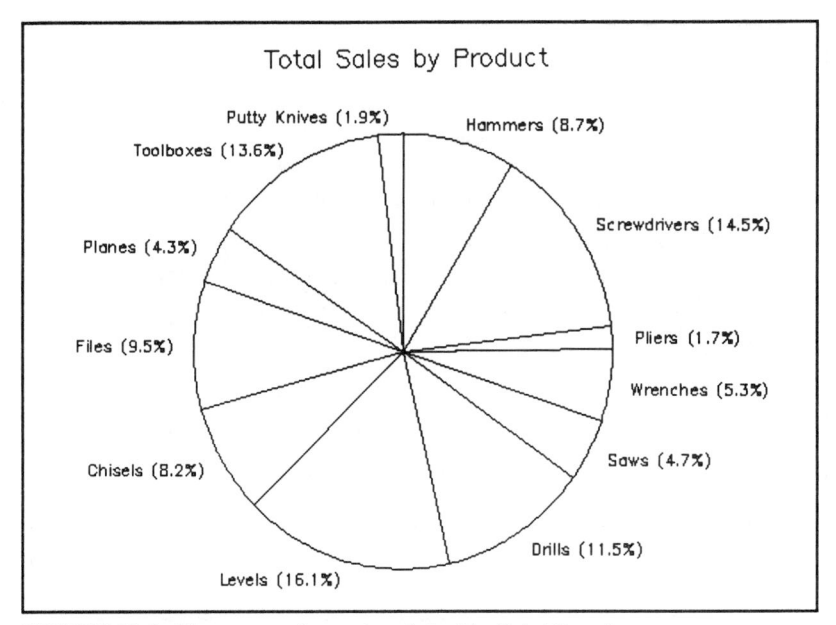

FIGURE 16-6: The second graph printed in PrintGraph

Once you have attached Allways, you can invoke it any time 1-2-3 is in the READY mode, either with the / Add-In Invoke command or by pressing the combination of keys to which Allways is linked. When you invoke Allways, it will replace the standard 1-2-3 worksheet with a modified version of that worksheet. If Allways is operating in the graphics mode, it will present a bit-mapped image of the worksheet. In that mode, any enhancements that you make to the worksheet will be visible on the screen. If Allways is operating in the text mode, the worksheet will look much the same as it does in 1-2-3. In either case, the first line of the control panel will list the attributes (font, color, and so forth) of the current cell. Although Allways operates more slowly in the graphics mode than it does in the text mode, the ability to see formats, colors, and so forth on the screen makes the graphics mode the mode of choice.

Once you have invoked Allways, you can enhance the current 1-2-3 worksheet in a variety of ways. To do this, you use commands on Allways menus. If you press the / key while Allways is active, you'll see Allways' main menu, which is shown in Figure 16-7. Selecting commands from this menu reveals other menus, just as it does in 1-2-3. Some of the commands on these menus can be invoked by pressing [Alt] key combinations. Like many of 1-2-3's commands, many of Allways' commands require you to highlight the range that you want to modify. Just like in 1-2-3, you can highlight the range after you issue the command. However, you can highlight the range ahead of time, if you wish.

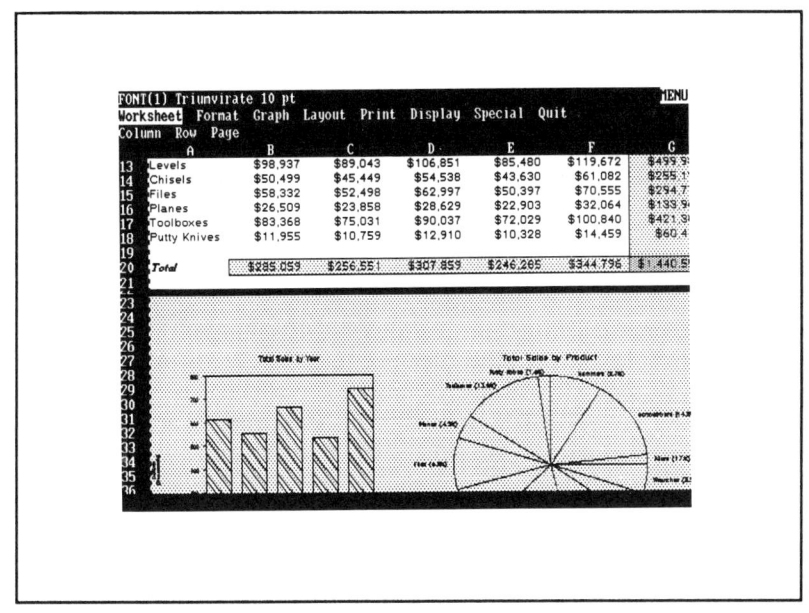

FIGURE 16-7: The main Allways menu

Formatting the Worksheet

The commands on Allways' Format menu allow you to format cells and ranges in the current worksheet in a variety of ways. The first command, Font, allows you to assign one of the eight fonts in the current font set to any cell or range in the worksheet, replace one or more fonts in the current font set, save the current font set, and make another font set current. (Any font set can contain any of the fonts that your printer is capable of reproducing.) The second and third commands on the Format menu, Bold and Underline, let you assign or remove the Bold and Underline attributes from any cell or range in a worksheet. The fourth command, Color, allows you to assign one of seven colors (black, red, green, blue, cyan, magenta, or white) to the contents of any cell or cells in the worksheet. It also allows you to specify that Allways display negative values in red.

The fifth item on the Format menu, Lines, allows you to draw a line at the left, right, top, bottom, or all edges of the cell or range you specify. The Left, Right, Top, and Bottom options command Allways to draw a line at the left, right, top, or bottom edges, respectively, of each of the cells in the range that you highlight. The Outline option draws a line around all four edges of the range you specify; the All option draws a line around all four edges of each of the cells in that range. If you highlight only one cell, these two options produce the same result. The / Layout Options LineWeight command allows you to specify whether the thickness of these lines will be normal, light, or heavy.

The sixth item on the Format menu, Shade, allows you to assign one of three shadings—light, dark, or black—to any cell or range in the worksheet. Light and dark shading options are useful as the background for occupied cells, or as a "shadow" around a box that you created with the Line command. The Black option is most useful for creating vertical or horizontal lines. To do this, you simply assign the black shading to adjacent cells in a row or column, then alter the height of that row or the width of that column.

Altering the Column Widths and Row Heights

The Worksheet command on the main Allways menu enables you to adjust the width of columns, alter the height of rows, and to embed page breaks within a worksheet. The first command on the Worksheet menu, Column, allows you to adjust the width of a column in increments as small as 1/10 of a character with the arrow keys, and in increments as small as 1/100th of a character if you type the width. The second command, Row, allows you to adjust the height of rows in increments as small as a single point—1/72 of an inch. (The default row height setting—Auto—commands Allways to set the height of the row one point greater than the point size of the largest character in that row.) The third command, Page, allows you to set or clear a page break between any two rows or columns in the worksheet.

Embedding a Graph Within a Worksheet

The third option on the main Allways menu, Graph, allows you to embed a graph within a worksheet and customize that graph. The first command on the Graph menu, Add, lets you embed a graph within a worksheet. When you issue this command, Allways will present a list of all the .PIC files in the current directory. As soon as you select a file from that directory (or any other directory that you specify), Allways will ask you to highlight the range that you want to overlay with that graph. As soon as you press [Enter], Allways will complete the command, bringing the graph that you specify into the current worksheet, and placing it in the range you choose.

If Allways is operating in the Graphics mode, and you have set it to display embedded graphs, Allways will draw an actual copy of the graph in the range you specify, sized so that it fits within that range. Since drawing the graph takes a few seconds each time Allways refreshes the screen, Allways gives you the option of marking the position of the graph with a crosshatching pattern instead of drawing the actual graph. (If Allways is operating in the text mode, it will fill the area that the graph will occupy with the letter G.)

The second command on the Graph menu, Remove, allows you to remove a graph from the worksheet. The third command, Goto, moves the cell pointer to the upper-left cell of the range that contains the graph you specify. This option is useful for identifying a particular graph when Allways is set not to display the actual graph on the screen. The fourth command, Settings, allows you to alter the fonts, colors, or margins for the graph; specify a new range in which to embed the graph; or specify a new graph to be placed in that range. The fifth option, Font-Directory, allows you to specify the directory that contains the PrintGraph program's font files. Without these files, Allways can't display or print graphs.

Controlling the Layout of a Printed Worksheet

The fourth command on Allways' main menu—Layout—allows you to control the positioning of the current worksheet when it is printed. The first item on the Layout menu, PageSize, enables you to specify the dimensions of the paper on which you will be printing the worksheet. The second option, Margins, allows you to specify the minimum amount of white space that will appear at the top, bottom, left edge, and right edge of each page. The third option, Titles, lets you specify a header and/or footer. The fourth option, Borders, allows you to specify that one or more columns appear at the left edge of every page, or that one or more adjacent rows appear at the top edge of every page. The fifth option, Options, allows you to control the intensity of the cell borders (if any), and specify whether Allways will display (and print) a gridwork of dotted lines (one between each row and column in the worksheet). The sixth and seventh options, Default and Library, allow you to save layout settings, recall them for future use, and make a particular set of layout settings the default.

Printing a Worksheet

The fifth command on Allways' main menu, Print, allows you to print the enhanced worksheet. The first item on this menu, Go, commands Allways to print the current worksheet, according to the way you have enhanced it in Allways. If you want to send the output to a print file (so that you can print it later with the DOS Copy command), you should choose the second command—File—instead.

The third, fourth, and fifth options on this menu (Range, Configuration, and Settings) allow you to control the printing process. The Range option lets you specify the range that you want to print. Just as in 1-2-3, you can specify this range either by pointing to it or by typing its coordinates. The Configuration option enables you to specify the printer to which you will be printing the worksheet, the port to which it is connected, the orientation (portrait or landscape), the graphic resolution, and so forth. The Settings option allows you to specify which pages you want to print, the page number (if any) that should be printed on the first page, how many copies you want to print, and whether the printer should pause between pages.

Controlling the Display

The sixth command on Allways' main menu, Display, lets you control several features determining the way a worksheet is displayed on the screen of your computer. The first item on this menu, Mode, allows you to specify whether Allways will operate in the graphics or text modes. The second item on this menu, Zoom, lets you magnify or reduce the worksheet. The Tiny or Small options allow more of the worksheet to be displayed on the screen at one time; the Large and Huge options allow you to see small fonts more clearly. These options do not affect the appearance of the printed worksheet.

The third option on the Display menu, Graphs, allows you to specify whether Allways will draw embedded graphs on the screen. If you choose Yes, Allways will draw each graph within the range that you specify for it. If you choose No, Allways will fill that range with a pattern. Choosing No reduces the amount of time it takes to refresh the screen; choosing Yes allows you to see the worksheet as it will be printed.

The fourth option on the Display menu, Colors, enables you to control the colors of the foreground, background, and cell pointer. Like the other options on the Display menu, these options only affect the way that the worksheet is displayed on the screen—not the way that it will be printed.

Other Commands

The next-to-last command on Allways' main menu—Special—provides some other worksheet-enhancing tools. The first item on the Special menu, Copy, allows you to copy the formats (fonts, shadings, underlines, and so forth) from one cell or range into another cell or range in the same worksheet. This command is useful, since Allways does not copy these formats when you use 1-2-3's / Copy command. The second command, Move, moves the Allways formats from one cell or range into another. When you issue this command, Allways removes the formats from the cell or cells in the source range and assigns them to the cell or cells in the destination range. Of course, the contents of the cells are not altered. Allways also moves the formats that were assigned to the source range when you issue 1-2-3's / Move command.

The next-to-last command on the Special menu, Justify, does the same thing as 1-2-3's / Range Justify command—it justifies the text within the range you specify. Duplicating the / Range Justify command in an Allways menu saves you the time and trouble of returning to 1-2-3 whenever you need to justify text—something that you'll do fairly often as you use Allways to enhance your worksheets. The final command on the Special menu—Import—allows you to import the Allways formats and settings from a worksheet that you have enhanced with Allways previously.

Returning to 1-2-3

The final command on Allways' main menu—Quit—allows you to return to 1-2-3. While you are within Allways, you can't edit your worksheet. For example, you can't make, erase, copy, or move entries; insert or delete rows; and so forth. Consequently, you'll find yourself going back and forth between Allways and 1-2-3 frequently as you enhance a worksheet. You also can return to 1-2-3 by pressing [Esc] from the ALLWAYS mode, or by pressing the [Alt] key combination (if any) to which you linked Allways.

Saving Enhancements

Whenever you use 1-2-3's / File Save command while Allways is attached to 1-2-3, Allways will save the formats (if any) that you have assigned to that worksheet in a file with the same name as the worksheet, but with the extension .ALL instead of

.WK1. When you retrieve a file while Allways is attached to 1-2-3, Allways will automatically retrieve the file that contains the formats for that worksheet. To ensure that Allways adjusts the enhancements as you edit a worksheet, make sure that Allways is attached whenever you make changes to an enhanced worksheet from within 1-2-3.

THE MACRO LIBRARY MANAGER

▶Unlike previous releases of 1-2-3, Release 2.2 can store macros in an area of RAM outside the current worksheet. There are a number of obvious advantages to storing and executing macros outside of a worksheet. First, you can use a macro in any number of worksheets without storing a copy of that macro in each worksheet. Second, you can create macros that retrieve worksheets. Since the macro is not situated in the worksheet that is overwritten by the retrieved worksheet, it will continue to run after the worksheet has been retrieved. Third, you can insert rows and columns in and delete rows and columns from a worksheet without disturbing the macro.

RELEASE
▶ 2.2 ◀

The second of the two add-ins bundled with 1-2-3 Release 2.2—the Macro Library Manager—makes this possible. (Throughout the remainder of this section, we'll use the abbreviation MLM to refer to the Macro Library Manager.) To attach the MLM to 1-2-3 Release 2.2, issue the / Add-In command, choose Attach, select MACROMGR.ADN, and press [Enter]. When attached, the MLM occupies approximately 13K of RAM.

Using the Macro Library Manager

Once you have attached the MLM to 1-2-3, you can use it to create macro libraries, edit the macros in those libraries, and execute the macros that are stored in those libraries. Whenever you want to use the MLM, you must invoke it, either by pressing the [Alt] key combinatin to which it is linked, or by choosing it from the list that 1-2-3 presents when you issue the / Add-In Invoke command. In either case, 1-2-3 will reveal the Macro menu that is shown in Figure 16-8.

As you can see, the MLM's menu has six commands: Load, Save, Edit, Remove, Name-List, and Quit. The Load command lets you bring a macro library from disk into RAM so that you can execute the macros that it contains. The Save command lets you save a macro into a macro library, which 1-2-3 stores both in RAM and on disk. The Edit command lets you bring a library to the cells of a worksheet where you can edit existing macros or add new ones to that library. The Remove command tells 1-2-3 to remove a macro library from RAM. The Name-List command instructs 1-2-3 to enter a list of the range names in a macro library into the cells of the worksheet. The Quit command returns you to the command state. These six commands control the storage, editing, and use of macros in the nonworksheet portions of RAM.

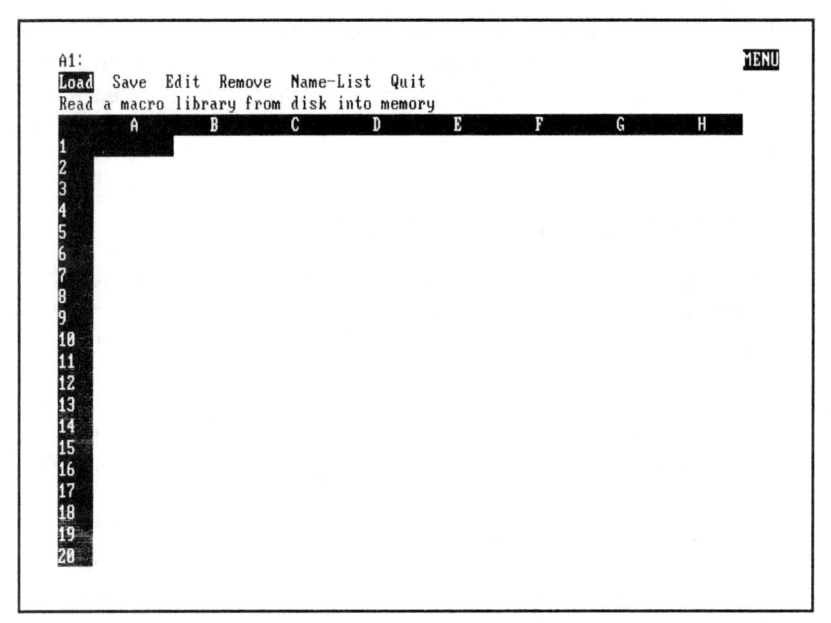

FIGURE 16-8: The Macro Library Manager's main menu

Creating a Macro Library

A macro library is a collection of one or more macros, stored in a single macro library (.MLB) file. Macro library (.MLB) files are similar to but not the same as worksheet (.WK1) files. Like .WRK files, macro library files contain labels, values, formulas, functions, and range names. However, they do not have the same structure as .WK1 files and, therefore, cannot be retrieved with the / File Retrieve command. .MLB files can be used only in conjuction with the Macro Library Manager.

Creating a macro library is a two-step process. First, you must create and name one or more macros in the cells of a 1-2-3 worksheet in the same way that you would create them without the MLM. Once you have created the macros, you must use the Save command on the MLM's main menu to save those macros into a .MLB file.

For example, suppose you wanted to create a macro library that contains a single macro—one that allows you to print multiple copies of a document. To create this macro library, enter the labels

A1: '\p
B1: '{Getnumber "Print how many copies? ",COPIES}
B2: '{For COUNTER,1,COPIES,1,PRINT}
A4: 'PRINT
B4: '/ppagpq
A6: 'COPIES
A7: 'COUNTER

into cells A1..B7 of a 1-2-3 worksheet (actually, any block of cells with a similar structure will do). Next, assign the range names \p, PRINT, COPIES, and COUNTER to cells B1, B4, B6, and B7, respectively. The result is the fully usable macro shown in Figure 16-9.

```
A1: '\p                                                              READY

       A          B         C         D         E         F       G       H
 1    \p     {GetNumber "Print how many copies? ",COPIES}
 2           {For COUNTER,1,COPIES,1,PRINT}
 3
 4    PRINT  /ppagpq
 5
 6    COPIES
 7    COUNTER
 8
 9
10
11
12
13
14
15
16
17
18
19
20
```

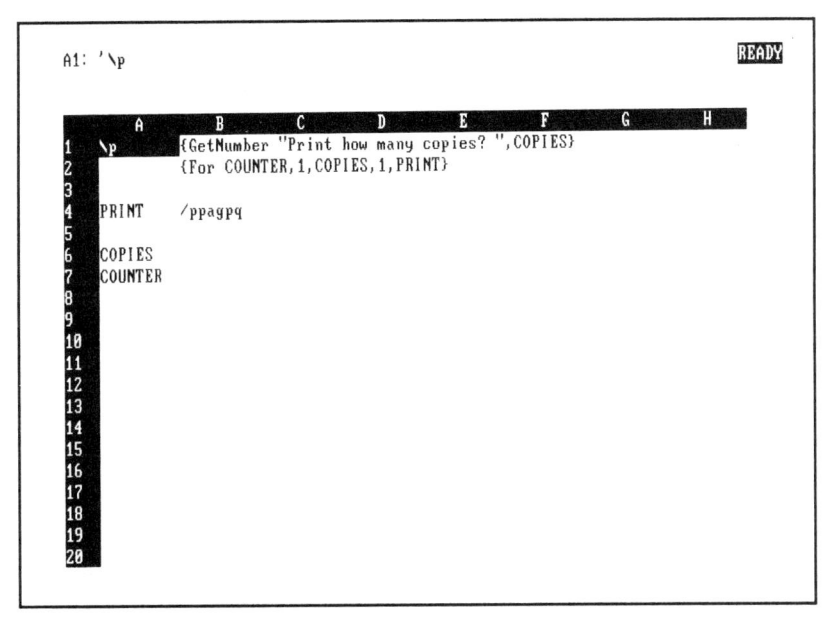

FIGURE 16-9: An example macro

Once you have created this working macro, you can use the Macro Library Manager to save it in a macro library. To do this, invoke the MLM and choose Save from its main menu. When you issue this command, 1-2-3 will present the prompt *Enter name of macro library to save:* followed by the path to the default directory, and display the names of all the .MLB files in that directory. At this point, you should type in a name for the library in which you want to save this macro. We'll use the name PRNTMACS.MLB by typing PRNTMACS. (There's no need to include the extension, unless you want to use one other than .MLB.) When you press [Enter], 1-2-3 will display the prompt *Enter macro library range:*, followed by the range coordinates of the cell over which the cell pointer is positioned at the time. At this point, you should use the arrow keys to highlight the range that contains the macro you want to save (in this case, cells A1..B7) and then press [Enter].

After you have specified the range of cells you want to store in the macro library, 1-2-3 will display the prompt *Use password to lock library?* and offer you two choices: No and Yes. If you choose Yes, 1-2-3 will ask you to supply a password, which may be up to 80 characters in length. (As we will show you later, the use of a password prevents anyone who does not know that password from editing the macros in the library.) In most cases, you probably will not want to password-protect a macro library. Consequently, you should choose No instead of Yes.

After you complete these steps, 1-2-3 will do three things. First, it will save the macro into a macro library file named PRNTMACS.MLB. This file will contain the contents of the cells you highlighted (A1..B7), as well as the range names associated with those cells (\p, PRINT, COPIES, and COUNTER). Unless you specify otherwise, 1-2-3 will save the .MLB file in the default directory (the one whose name 1-2-3 displays when you issue the / File Directory command).

In addition to saving the library into a .MLB file, 1-2-3 will store the library (cell contents and range names) in a nonworksheet portion of RAM under the name PRNTMACS. Finally, 1-2-3 will erase the worksheet cells (A1..B7) that contain the saved macro and delete the range names associated with those cells (\p, PRINT, COPIES, and COUNTER) from the worksheet.

Executing a Macro from a Library

Once you have saved a macro into a macro library, you can execute that macro without ever bringing it into a worksheet. However, the library that contains that macro must be in the RAM of your computer at the time—you cannot execute a macro directly from a .MLB file that is on disk. Since the MLM's Save command stores a macro library both on disk and in a nonworksheet portion of RAM, the macros in any library are ready to be invoked as soon as you save them.

Invoking a macro that is stored in a macro library is no different than invoking a macro that is stored in the cells of a worksheet. If you have named the macro with a backslash and a single letter (like \p), you can invoke the macro by holding down the [Alt] key and typing that letter. To execute a macro with any other name, press the [Run] key, type the name of the macro, and then press [Enter].

Loading and Removing Macro Libraries

When you attach the MLM, 1-2-3 loads the code that allows it to access macros that are stored outside of the worksheet. If you save any library after you have attached the MLM, 1-2-3 will store that library in a nonworksheet portion of RAM. If you want to use macros that you have saved in previous 1-2-3 sessions, however, you must command 1-2-3 to bring that library from disk into RAM. 1-2-3 does not bring any macro libraries into RAM automatically when you load the MLM.

To load a library into RAM from a .MLB file, you must use the Load command on the MLM's menu. When you issue this command, 1-2-3 will read from the default drive and display a list of all the .MLB files in that drive. To load one of the listed libraries into RAM, just highlight the name of that library and press [Enter]. Once the library is in RAM, you can invoke any macro that it contains in the same way that you would invoke any other macro.

While a macro library is in RAM, it occupies space that otherwise could be used for the contents of a 1-2-3 worksheet. To conserve your computer's RAM, it is a good idea to keep your macro libraries on disk until you need to use them. When you need to use a macro that is stored in a .MLB file, you can load that library into RAM and execute the macro.

The Remove command on the MLM's menu deletes macro libraries from RAM. When you issue this command, 1-2-3 will display a list of the names of the libraries that are currently in RAM (in our example, 1-2-3 will display only the single name PRNTMACS). To remove a library from RAM, just highlight its name and press [Enter]. Instantly, 1-2-3 will clear the memory that contained the library. Of course, 1-2-3 still retains the removed library on disk in its .MLB file.

Editing Macro Libraries

Sometime after you first create a macro library, you'll probably want to modify the macros that are contained in that library, delete macros from that library, or add macros to that library. 1-2-3 lets you edit a macro library in each of these three ways.

Editing a macro library is a three-step process. First, you must bring the library into the cells of a 1-2-3 worksheet. Once the macro is within the cells of the worksheet, you can edit it in the same way you would any "traditional" macro. Once you are finished editing the macros in the library, you must resave the macro library. You must go through these three steps whenever you want to make any change to a macro library.

Editing Existing Macros

Suppose you've saved the multiple-print macro shown in Figure 16-9 into the library named PRNTMACS.MLB. Now suppose you want to revise that macro so that it looks like the one in Figure 16-10. To revise this macro, first make sure that the library that contains this macro (PRNTMACS) is currently in RAM. If it is not, use the MLM's Load command to load it from disk.

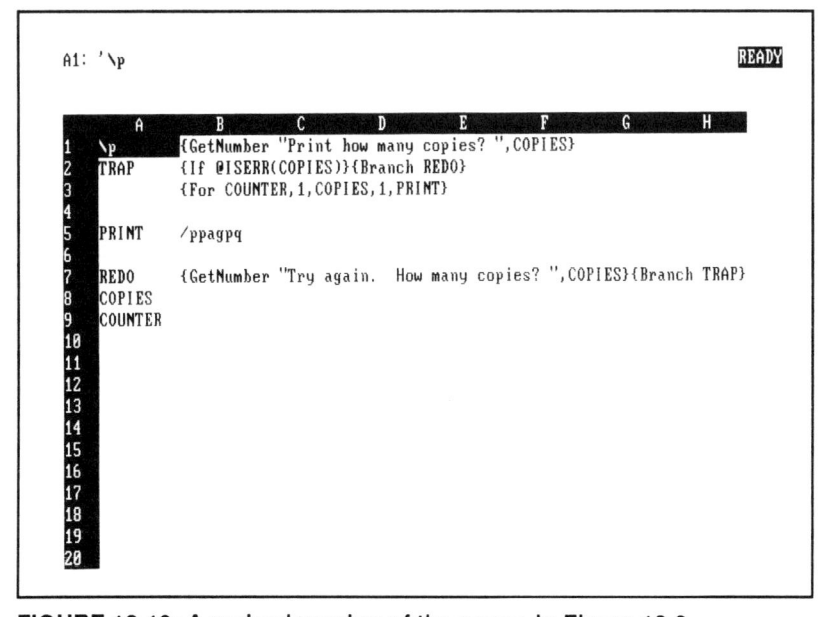

```
A1: '\p                                                          READY

       A         B           C          D         E        F         G        H
 1   \p         {GetNumber "Print how many copies? ",COPIES}
 2   TRAP       {If @ISERR(COPIES)}{Branch REDO}
 3              {For COUNTER,1,COPIES,1,PRINT}
 4
 5   PRINT      /ppagpq
 6
 7   REDO       {GetNumber "Try again.  How many copies? ",COPIES}{Branch TRAP}
 8   COPIES
 9   COUNTER
10
11
12
13
14
15
16
17
18
19
20
```

FIGURE 16-10: A revised version of the macro in Figure 16-9

Once the library is in RAM, you must bring it into the cells of the worksheet before you can edit any macro that it contains. To bring a macro from non-worksheet RAM into the worksheet, invoke the MLM and choose Edit from its menu. When you issue this command, 1-2-3 will list the names of the macro libraries currently in RAM. Choose the name of the library you want to edit by highlighting its name and pressing [Enter].

If you have password-protected the macro library that you want to edit, 1-2-3 will prompt you to enter the password for that library. If you type the incorrect password, 1-2-3 will cancel the Edit command and "bump" you back to the READY mode. If you type the correct password, 1-2-3 will move to the next step of the edit process.

After you choose the library you wish to edit and then type the correct password (if you have password-protected the library), 1-2-3 will display two choices: Ignore and Overwrite. These commands tell 1-2-3 how to deal with range names in the library that conflict with range names in the worksheet into which you are bringing the library. If you choose Ignore, 1-2-3 will ignore any range names in the library that conflict with range names that already are in the worksheet. However, 1-2-3 will bring in any nonconflicting range names. If you choose Overwrite, 1-2-3 will overwrite any range names in the worksheet that conflict with names in the library.

For example, suppose cell Z100 of the current worksheet is named PRINT and you want to edit the library named PRNTMACS (which also contains a range named PRINT) in that worksheet. If you choose the Ignore option, 1-2-3 will not bring the range name PRINT into the worksheet when it brings PRNTMACS into that worksheet. In that case, the range name PRINT will still refer to cell Z100 even after PRNTMACS is in the worksheet. If you choose Overwrite, however, 1-2-3 will bring the name PRINT into the worksheet with the library. In the resulting worksheet, the range name PRINT will refer to a cell of the macro, not to cell Z100.

Your choice of these two options depends on your reasons for bringing the library into the worksheet. If you just want to look at the library to determine what macros it contains, you won't need to bring in the range names from the library. In that case, you'll want to choose Ignore so that any conflicting range names in the worksheet will remain intact.

If you are bringing the library into the worksheet so you can edit it, however, you'll want to choose the Overwrite option. Otherwise, the library will not contain the conflicting range names when you again save it to disk, and the resulting macro will not work correctly. When you choose Overwrite, of course, any conflicting range names will no longer refer to the proper cells in the original worksheet. To avoid these range-name problems, you should always try to edit macro libraries in a worksheet that contains no range names (such as a new, blank worksheet).

Once you choose either Ignore or Overwrite, 1-2-3 will prompt you to specify the area of the worksheet where you want the library to be placed. To specify this area, you only need to highlight the single cell at the upper-left corner of the chosen range, then press [Enter]. Make sure there are enough blank cells below and to the right of the cell you select to accommodate the entire contents of the library because 1-2-3 will overwrite the contents of any occupied cells in that area. In this example, we'll bring the macro into cells A1..B7 by highlighting cell A1 and pressing [Enter] so that the worksheet looks like Figure 16-9 again.

Once you return the library to the worksheet, you can edit the cells that contain its macros the same way you would edit any other macro. In this case, we'll edit the macro so that it looks like the one in Figure 16-10. To do this, first position the cell pointer in row 2 and issue the / Worksheet Insert Row command to add a new row below the {Getnumber} statement. Then make the entries

A2: 'TRAP
B2: '{If @ISERR(COPIES)}{Branch REDO}

into cells A2 and B2. Next, position the cell pointer in row 7, again issue the / Worksheet Insert Row command, and make the entries

A7: 'REDO
B7: '{Getnumber "Try again. How many copies? ",COPIES}{Branch TRAP}

into cells A7 and B7. Finally, use the / Range Name Labels Right command to assign the labels in cells A2 and A7 as the range names of cells B2 and B7.

Once you have brought a macro library into the worksheet and edited one or more of its macros, you'll want to resave the library to its original .MLB file. To do this, invoke the MLM, issue the Save command, and choose the name of the .MLB file from which you "retrieved" the library you just edited (in this case, PRNTMACS.MLB). When you press [Enter] to choose this file name (or the name of any other existing file), 1-2-3 will display the prompt

Macro library already exists in memory and on disk. Write over it?

If you choose Yes, 1-2-3 will save the edited library on top of the old version. If you choose No, 1-2-3 will return the READY mode without saving the library. If you want to save the edited library without overwriting the old version, you must issue the Save command again and type in a previously unused file name.

Once you choose Yes to overwrite the existing library, 1-2-3 will ask you to specify the block of cells that you want to save in the library. Like before, you'll want to highlight the smallest block of cells that contains every cell of the macro(s) you want to save in the library. In this case, you'll need to highlight or type in the coordinates of cells A1..B9. When you press [Enter], 1-2-3 will replace the original contents of the designated .MLB file with the contents and range names of the cells that you highlighted. 1-2-3 will then erase the contents and range names of the highlighted cells from the worksheet.

Adding a New Macro to a Library

Instead of (or in addition to) editing an existing macro in a library, you can add one or more macros to that library. Like editing an existing macro, adding a macro to a library is a three-step process. First, you must bring the contents of the library to the worksheet. Second, you must enter the new macro into the cells of that worksheet adjacent to the original contents of that library. Finally, you must resave the entire revised library—the original macros plus the macros that you wish to add to the library. You cannot just use the Save command to append a new macro to an existing file; you first must bring the library to the worksheet, then add the macro, then resave the entire file.

For example, suppose that you want to add a simple macro like the one shown in cells A11..B11 of the worksheet in Figure 16-11 to the PRNTMACS library. This macro adjusts 1-2-3's Print settings so that it prints 88 lines on each page. To add this macro to the library, first invoke the MLM and use the Edit command to bring the current contents of PRNTMACS into cells A1..B9 of the worksheet. Next, create the new macro by entering

A11: \l
B11: /ppos\027\048~p88~qq

into cells A11..B11. Next, name the macro \l by positioning the cell pointer on cell A11, issuing the / Range Name Labels Right command, and pressing [Enter].

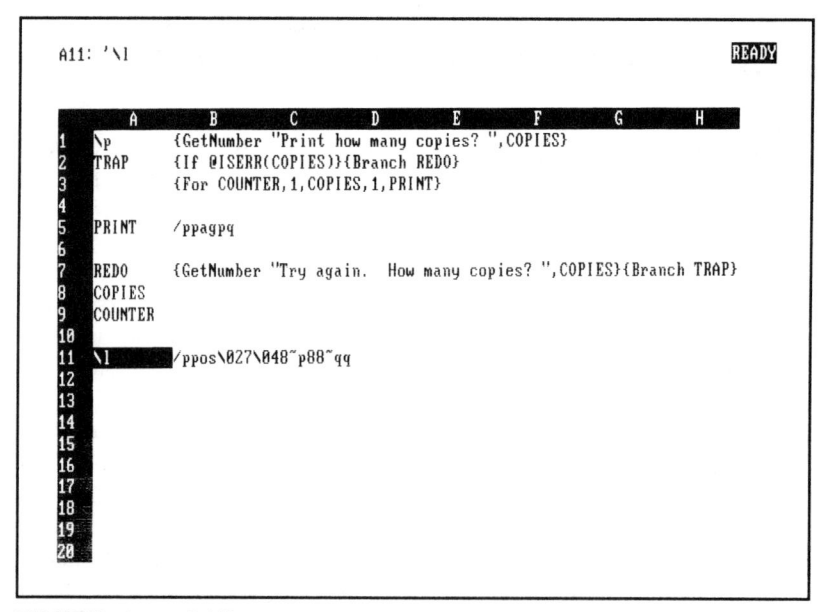

```
A11: '\l                                                          READY


       A           B           C           D           E           F           G           H
 1    \p          {GetNumber "Print how many copies? ",COPIES}
 2    TRAP        {If @ISERR(COPIES)}{Branch REDO}
 3                {For COUNTER,1,COPIES,1,PRINT}
 4
 5    PRINT       /ppagpq
 6
 7    REDO        {GetNumber "Try again.  How many copies? ",COPIES}{Branch TRAP}
 8    COPIES
 9    COUNTER
10
11    \l          /ppos\027\048~p88~qq
12
13
14
15
16
17
18
19
20
```

FIGURE 16-11: Adding a new macro to an existing library

Once you have created this new macro in the worksheet, you will want to resave PRNTMACS so that it includes the new macro. To do this, invoke the MLM, issue the Save command, highlight PRNTMACS, press [Enter], and choose Yes to tell 1-2-3 to overwrite the existing library. Next, highlight cells A1..B11—the cells that contain both the old and new macros. When you press [Enter], 1-2-3 will overwrite the old contents of PRNTMACS.MLB with these two macros and will erase the contents and range names of cells A1..B11 from the worksheet.

Creating a Second Macro Library

Most users of the MLM will create more than just a single macro library. In most cases, the macros within each library will share a common purpose. For example, they could perform related tasks, like printing, filing, or window management. Because the number of macro libraries that you can create is limited only by disk space, and you can save .MLB files on any disk, you can create a virtually unlimited number.

Let's look at an example of a second macro library. Suppose that you want to save the label-underlining macro shown in Figure 16-12 into a library named UTILITY.MLB. This macro underlines the label on which the cell pointer is positioned at the time. To create this macro, make the following entries in a 1-2-3 worksheet:

A1: \u
B1: \c~{Down}~{Down}
B2: '{If @CELLPOINTER("type")<>"l"}{Beep}/re~{Quit}
B3: '{Edit}{BS @LENGTH(@CELLPOINTER("contents"))}
B4: '{For COUNT,1,@LENGTH(@CELLPOINTER("contents")),1,CHAR}
B5: '~
A7: 'COUNT
A8: 'CHAR
B8: '-

Then, issue the / Range Name Labels Right command, highlight cells A1..A8, and press [Enter].

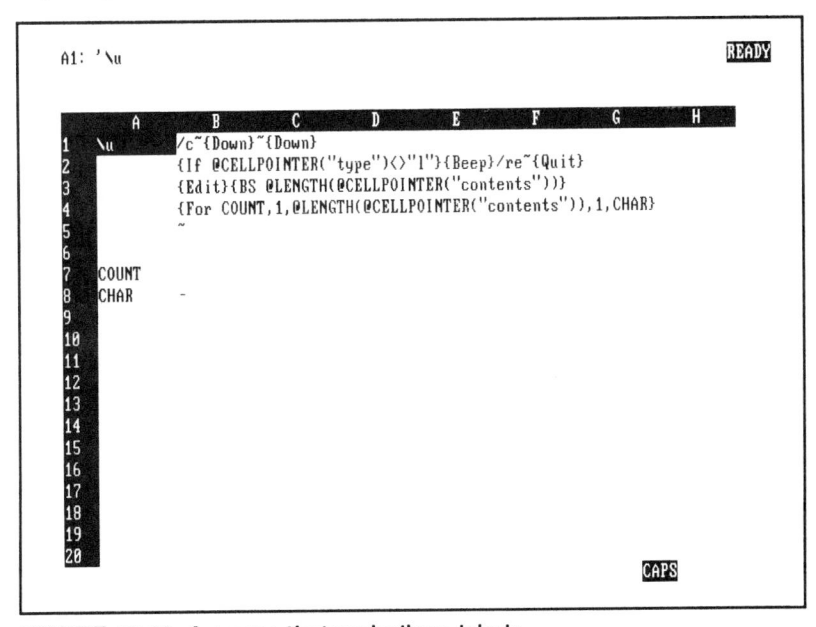

FIGURE 16-12: A macro that underlines labels

To save this macro into a new library named UTILITY.MLB, invoke the MLM, issue the Save command, type UTILITY, press [Enter], highlight cells A1..B6, and press [Enter] again. After you select either No or Yes in response to the password-protection prompt, 1-2-3 will save the macro into a nonworksheet portion of RAM, write it to disk as UTILITY.MLB, and erase the macros and macro range names from the worksheet.

Once you have created a new library, you can use the MLM's Remove and Load commands to take the library in and out of RAM, independent of any other macro libraries. You also can use the MLM's Edit command to bring the library into a worksheet so you can edit it. Of course, you can invoke the macro named \u by pressing [Alt]u any time UTILITY.MLB is in RAM.

Limitations

Although 1-2-3 does not place any limitation on the number of macro library files you can create, it does limit the number of macro libraries you can have in RAM at one time to ten. If you issue the {Services} Macro Load command when 10 libraries are already in RAM, 1-2-3 will beep, display the message

Maximum number of macro libraries reached

and refuse to load the new library. Before you can load the library into RAM, you must use the MLM's Remove command to remove one or more libraries from RAM.

As you recall, 1-2-3 automatically loads a macro library into RAM when you save it into a .MLB file by issuing the MLM's Save command. If you already have ten libraries in RAM when you issue this command, 1-2-3 cannot save the library into RAM. Consequently, 1-2-3 will abort the Save command and will not save the library into a .MLB file. To save the library, you first must remove an existing library from RAM and then reissue the Save command.

Because each active macro library occupies a portion of your computer's RAM, you usually will want to keep as few libraries as possible in RAM at one time. Although macro libraries do not exist in the worksheet, they compete with the contents of your worksheets for RAM. As a rule, the fewer libraries that you have in RAM at one time and the smaller each of those libraries is, the more RAM will be left for worksheet applications. Because you must load an entire library into RAM when you need to use any single macro from that library, you can save RAM by creating many small libraries, each with only a few macros rather than a few large libraries. (Remember, however, that you can have only a maximum of 10 macro libraries in RAM at one time.)

A Macro that can be Executed only from a Library

So far, we have used some rather ordinary macros to explain the mechanics of creating, editing, and using macro libraries. However, the ability to store and execute macros outside of a 1-2-3 worksheet allows you to do things in macros that you never could do before—such as retrieve files and clear the worksheet. If you include commands like / File Retrieve and / Worksheet Erase Yes within a worksheet-resident macro, 1-2-3 will overwrite or erase the macro as soon as it executes one of those statements. However, if you store the macros containing these commands outside of the worksheet they affect, 1-2-3 will execute these commands without destroying the macros.

For example, suppose you want to create a macro that will retrieve and print four worksheets (1STQTR, 2NDQTR, 3RDQTR, and 4THQTR) one after the other. (The print settings for each of these four worksheets are preset within each worksheet.) To build this macro (shown in Figure 16-13), enter the following into the cells of a worksheet:

A1: '\p
B1: '/fr1STQTR~{PRINT}
B2: '/fr2NDQTR~{PRINT}
B3: '/fr3RDQTR~{PRINT}
B4: '/fr4THQTR~{PRINT}
A6: 'PRINT
B6: '/ppagp

To name this macro (and the cell named PRINT within it), issue the / Range Name Labels Right command, highlight cells A1..A6, and press [Enter].

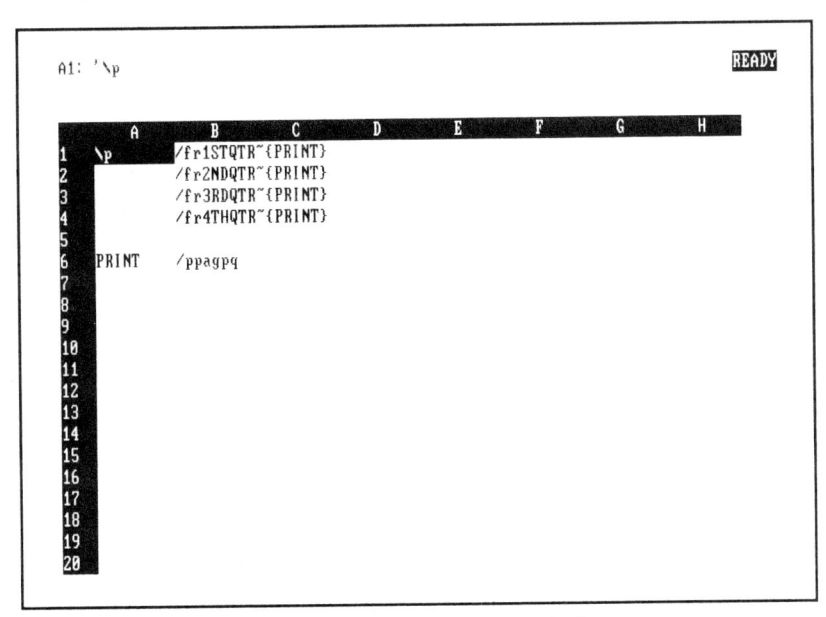

FIGURE 16-13: A macro that prints multiple worksheets

Once you have named this macro, you can execute it directly from the worksheet by pressing [Alt]p. However, as soon as 1-2-3 retrieved the file 1STQTR, the macro would be gone, because the worksheet that contains it would be overwritten by 1STQTR. Consequently, 1-2-3 would stop executing the macro.

If you store this macro within a macro library, however, it will not be affected when the worksheets are retrieved into 1-2-3. To save this macro into a new library, invoke the MLM, issue the Save command, type in a name like MULTPRNT, and press [Enter]. Next, highlight cells A1..B6 as the range to save and press [Enter] again. Finally, choose No to tell 1-2-3 not to lock the library with a password. When you press [Enter], 1-2-3 will save the one-macro library in a nonworksheet portion of RAM and on disk in the file MULTPRNT.MLB, and will remove the macro and its range names from the worksheet.

Once you have saved the macro to the library, you can invoke it by pressing [Alt]p. (If the library is not in RAM, you first must invoke the MLM and use the Load command to bring it back.) When you invoke the macro, 1-2-3 will retrieve the first worksheet and print it, then retrieve the second worksheet and print it, and so forth, until all four worksheets have been retrieved and printed. Since the macro is not in a worksheet, it will not be overwritten when 1-2-3 retrieves the four files.

Range Name Confusion

1-2-3 identifies any macro by the range name that you assign to the first cell in the macro. Whenever you invoke a macro, either with the [Run] or [Alt] keys, 1-2-3 looks for the range name of the starting cell of that macro. If you are not using the Macro Library Manager, range names (and therefore macros) can exist only in the cells of the current worksheet. When you use the Macro Library Manager, however, the macro that you want to invoke could be stored in any of 10 RAM-resident macro libraries as well.

Whenever you invoke a macro while the MLM is attached, 1-2-3 has no way of knowing exactly where that macro is stored. Instead of searching for the macro randomly, however, 1-2-3 searches for the macro in a predefined pattern. First, it looks for the starting cell of the macro in the cells of the current worksheet. If it does not find the named range in the worksheet, it looks for that range in the RAM-resident macro libraries in the order that 1-2-3 lists them when you issue the Edit, Remove, or Name-List commands. (In most cases, this will be the order in which you loaded the libraries into RAM.) If 1-2-3 cannot find the macro in the worksheet or in any of the RAM-resident libraries, it will beep instead of executing the macro.

In addition to beginning with a named range, most macros call upon other named ranges as they execute. When a macro refers to another named range, 1-2-3 will look first for that range in the cells of the worksheet, then in the RAM macro libraries in the order those libraries are stored. 1-2-3 does not search first the location in which it found the macro (either a library or the worksheet).

Because 1-2-3 can store range names in a variety of locations, and searches for those named ranges in a particular order, it is extremely important to avoid duplicating range names when you use the Macro Library Manager. For example, suppose you have a macro library in RAM that contains a macro named TOTAL. However, suppose cell E15 of the current worksheet is also named TOTAL, and it contains the function @SUM(E1..E5). When you press [Run], type TOTAL, and press [Enter], 1-2-3 will not invoke the macro named TOTAL from the macro library as you intended. Instead, 1-2-3 will move to cell E15 and "execute" that formula. The range in the worksheet "blocks" 1-2-3 from finding the macro in the library.

A similar problem can occur if two macro libraries contain the same range name. For example, suppose that two macro libraries, MACONE and MACTWO, are currently in RAM with MACONE "before" MACTWO. MACTWO contains a macro named PRINT, and MACONE contains a subroutine named PRINT. The worksheet does not contain a range named PRINT. Given this situation, if you press [Run], type PRINT, and press [Enter], 1-2-3 will not execute the macro in MACTWO as you intended it to do. Instead, because 1-2-3 looks for range names in macro libraries in the order in which they are stored in RAM, it will execute the subroutine in MACONE.

There are two ways to avoid these problems. First, you can try not to use a range name in any worksheet or library that you have used in any other worksheet or library. The best way to do this is to use a unique set of range names for each library. For example, you could begin the macros in each library with a different "prefix" coded to the name of that library. For instance, you might begin all range names in the library named PRNTMACS with the letters PR (like PRCOUNT) and begin all macros in the library named FILEMACS with the letters FI (like FICOUNT).

Unfortunately, even the most disciplined macro user will occasionally forget to use this system and will, therefore, create duplicate range names. There are two ways to prevent these duplicate range names from inhibiting the proper execution of a macro. First, use the MLM's Remove command to remove from RAM all macro libraries except the one that contains the macro that you wish to use. Alternatively, if you don't want to remove any macros from RAM, use the MLM's Load command to "reload" all macro libraries except for the macro you wish to use. This technique moves the library you choose to the "top of the stack" so that 1-2-3 sees it first when you invoke a macro.

1-2-3 also lets you check for range-name duplications between a macro library and a worksheet. To check for range name duplications, first use the / Range Name Table command to bring the listing of range names in the current worksheet into a block of cells in that worksheet. Next, use the MLM's Name-List command to bring into the worksheet the list of range names in the macro library. By comparing these two lists, you can determine whether duplicate range names exist. If they do, you can eliminate the duplication by renaming one range name in each pair of duplicates.

Macros that Use Other Libraries and the Worksheet

In some cases, you'll want macros stored in a library to call on, branch to, store data in, or retrieve data from the worksheet or from another library. Similarly, you might want a macro stored in a worksheet to call on, branch to, store data in, or pull data from a macro library. For example, you could use a macro within a library to format a block of cells in the current worksheet. Alternatively, you might want to use a macro stored in a worksheet to use an @VLOOKUP function to pull a result from a lookup table that is stored in a macro library. Or you might want a macro in one library to continue executing at a certain point in another library. The Macro Library Manager allows you to do all these things as long as you follow three rules.

RULE 1: All information references in a macro library must be by range name, not cell reference. 1-2-3 always will look to the worksheet whenever it finds a cell reference in a macro.

We'll use the two simple macros contained in cells B7 and B9 of the worksheet shown in Figure 16-14 to explain this first rule. Cell B7, which we have named \a, contains the macro

B7: '{Let B11,@SUM(A1..A5)}

which sums the entries in cells A1..A5 and places the result in cell B11. Cell B9, which we have named \b, contains the macro

B9: '{Let B11,@SUM(VALUES)}

Since cells A1..A5 in this worksheet are named VALUES, this macro is identical in effect to the one in cell B7. If you execute either of these macros while they are still within the worksheet, 1-2-3 will add the entries in cells A1..A5 and place the value 15 in cell B11.

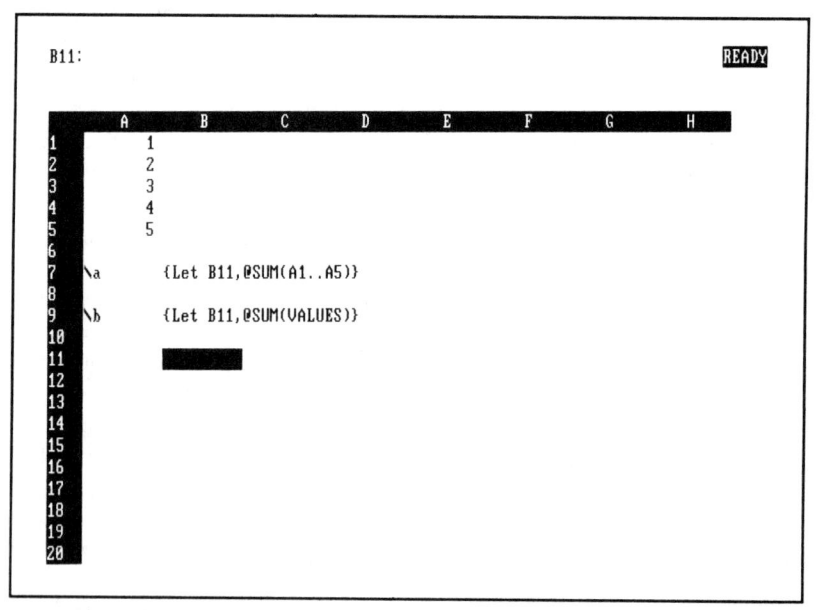

```
B11:                                                              READY

        A       B       C       D       E       F       G       H
 1              1
 2              2
 3              3
 4              4
 5              5
 6
 7     \a       {Let B11,@SUM(A1..A5)}
 8
 9     \b       {Let B11,@SUM(VALUES)}
10
11              ███████
12
13
14
15
16
17
18
19
20
```

FIGURE 16-14: Library macros must use range names

Once you save cells A1..B9 into a macro library, however, these two macros have different effects. To save this block of cells into a library named SUM, invoke the MLM, issue the Save command, type SUM, and highlight cells A1..B9 (the macro statement and the cells to which it refers). When you press [Enter], 1-2-3 will save cells

A1..B9 and the range names \a and \b to the library. 1-2-3 also will erase cells A1..B9 in the worksheet and delete the range names \a, \b, and VALUES from that worksheet.

Once these macros and their data are saved in the library, you can execute the macro named \a by pressing [Alt]a. This time, 1-2-3 places the value 0 instead of the value 15 in cell B11. Although "cells" A1..A5 in the SUM library contain the values 1-5, cells A1..A5 in the worksheet are blank. Since cell references in a macro can refer only to the cells of a worksheet, 1-2-3 adds the "values" of five blank cells in the worksheet and returns the value 0.

Now let's execute the macro named \b and see what happens. Unlike \a, which contains cell references as the second argument of the {Let} statement, \b refers to the range that is named VALUES. When 1-2-3 executes this macro, it looks for the range of cells named VALUES. Since we assigned the range name VALUES to cells A1..A5 of the original worksheet before we saved cells A1..B9 into the library named SUM, the range name VALUES now refers to "cells" A1..A5 in that macro library. Because A1..A5 in SUM contain the values 1, 2, 3, 4, and 5, respectively, 1-2-3 places the value 15 in cell B11 of the worksheet.

RULE 2: All references to the information in any macro library must be contained within Lotus Command Language (LCL) commands (like {Let}, {Put}, or {Branch}). You cannot refer to ranges in a library from the formulas and functions you enter into the cells of a worksheet or from within menu commands.

We'll explain this rule by working through an example. To begin, suppose that you have created the simple lookup table shown in Figure 16-15 (cells A1..D5) and have assigned it the range name TABLE. Instead of storing this table in the worksheet, you want to save it in a macro library so that you can access it from a number of different macros. To store this table, invoke the MLM, issue the Save command, choose the name LOOKUP, highlight cells A1..D5, and press [Enter] twice. Instantly, 1-2-3 will save the contents of cells A1..A5 and its range name TABLE to the library named LOOKUP. It will then load the contents into RAM and erase those cells and their range names from the worksheet.

Now suppose that you want to pull a value from the lookup table into cell C10 of the worksheet. To do this, you might try to enter the function

@VLOOKUP(3,TABLE,2)

into cell C10. 1-2-3 will not accept this entry, however. Whenever a formula or function that is not within an LCL command refers to a named range, 1-2-3 can look for that range only in the cells of the current worksheet. Since the range TABLE is in a macro library—not in the worksheet—1-2-3 is unable to find it. 1-2-3 assumes you are including a nonexistent range name in the function. For this reason, 1-2-3 will beep and reject the function when you press [Enter].

To access the range named TABLE from the macro library named LOOKUP, you must embed the reference within an LCL statement like {Let}, then execute that statement as part of a macro. For example, to pull the result of the function @VLOOKUP(3,TABLE,2) into cell C10 of a worksheet, you must first enter the statement

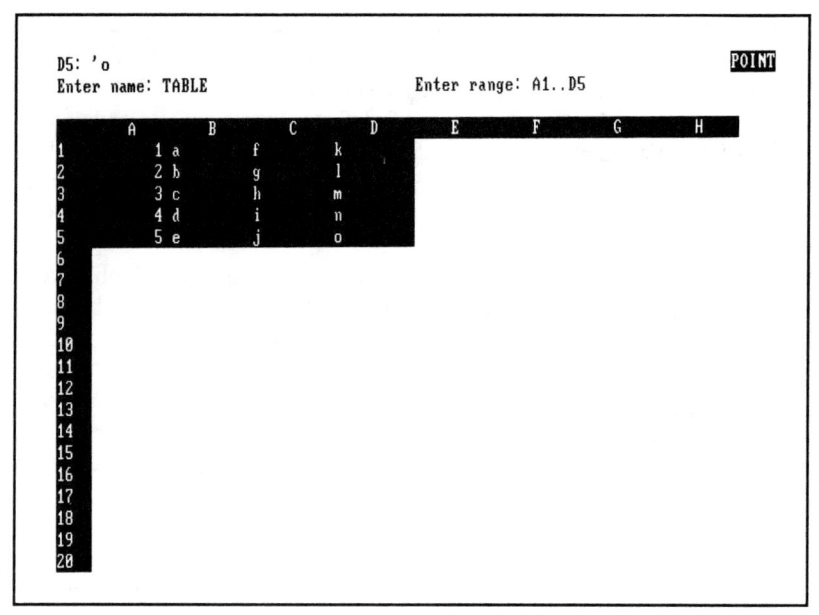

FIGURE 16-15: Formulas and functions cannot reference cells in macro libraries

{Let C10,@VLOOKUP(3,TABLE,2)}

into any cell of the worksheet except C10. Next, assign a range name to that cell so that you can execute it as a macro. When you invoke this single-line macro, 1-2-3 will evaluate the {Let} statement and place the result (the label 'm) into cell C10. Because the @VLOOKUP function is within an LCL command, 1-2-3 is able to look in every RAM-resident macro library for the range name TABLE, as well as in the worksheet. As long as the library that contains TABLE is in RAM, 1-2-3 will be able to use that range just as it would any range in the worksheet.

RULE 3: 1-2-3 always looks for referenced ranges first in the cells of the worksheet, then in any RAM-resident macro libraries in the order they exist in RAM. 1-2-3 will not look first in the library that contains the reference.

Again, we'll explain this rule by working through an example. To begin, suppose that you have only two macro libraries, MACLIB1 and MACLIB2, within the nonworksheet portion of your computer's RAM. MACLIB1 is the "first" library in RAM and MACLIB2 is the "second." MACLIB1 contains a macro named \a, and MACLIB2 contains a second part of that macro in a range named CONTINUE.

Suppose you press [Alt] a to invoke the macro in MACLIB1. When 1-2-3 encounters the statement

{Branch CONTINUE}

in the MACLIB1 macro, it will search for the range named CONTINUE and resume executing the macro at that cell. Although CONTINUE is contained within MACLIB2,

1-2-3 will look for that range in the worksheet first. If 1-2-3 cannot find the range in the worksheet, it will then look in the "first" library (in this case, MACLIB1). If 1-2-3 cannot find a range named CONTINUE in MACLIB1, it will search the "second" library (in this case, MACLIB2). Since MACLIB2 contains the range named CONTINUE, 1-2-3 will resume the execution of the macro at that cell.

In this example, the macro will execute just as you expected it to because neither the worksheet nor MACLIB1 contained a range named CONTINUE. If a cell of the worksheet had been named CONTINUE, 1-2-3 would have branched to that cell rather than the intended range in MACLIB2. Similarly, if MACLIB1 had contained a range named CONTINUE, 1-2-3 would have branched to that range rather than the one in MACLIB2. Always remember that when duplicate range names exist, 1-2-3 may use a range other than the one you intended for it to use.◄

OTHER ADD-IN APPLICATIONS

So far, we've only explored the two add-in applications that come with 1-2-3 Release 2.2: Allways and the Macro Library Manager. However, these add-ins represent only a small portion of the total number of add-ins available for use with 1-2-3.

Two other add-ins—SpeedUp and Learn—were packaged with 1-2-3 Releases 2 and 2.01. These add-ins add minimal recalculation and a macro learn mode to those releases of 1-2-3. However, most of the add-ins available for 1-2-3 were developed by third parties, rather than Lotus. Three of the biggest players in the add-in market are Personics, Symantec, and Funk Software.

One of the most popular add-in applications for 1-2-3 is SeeMORE. Developed by Personics, this add-in alters the 1-2-3 display so that more columns and rows are visible on the screen at one time. Personics also developed Look and Link—an add-in that adds file-linking capabilities to 1-2-3 Releases 2 and 2.01, and expands 1-2-3 Release 2.2's built-in file linking powers—and @BASE, which extends 1-2-3's database capabilities.

SQZ! Plus is another popular 1-2-3 add-in. Developed by Symantec, this add-in saves disk space by compressing worksheet files when you save them with the / File Save command, and expands them when you retrive them with the / File Retrieve command. Symantec also developed several other popular 1-2-3 add-ins, including Note-It Plus (an add-in that allows you to attach explanatory nortes to cells and files), The Cambridge Spreadsheet Analyst (a worksheet-auditing add-in), Spellin! (a spelling checker), 4WORD (an add-in that adds word processing powers to 1-2-3), 4VIEWS (an add-in that enhances 1-2-3's database powers), and The Budget Express (an add-in that streamlines the process of building budgets in 1-2-3).

Perhaps the most popular 1-2-3 add-in of all time is SideWays. This add-in, developed by Funk Software (the same people who developed Allways), allows you to print 1-2-3 worksheets "sideways"; that is, in landscape rather then portrait orientation. Since most worksheets are wider than they are tall, this saves a lot of cutting and pasting. Funk Software also developed a number of other popular 1-2-3 add-ins, including The Worksheet Utilities (which does things like allowing you to see an entire fromula—rather than just its first 80 characters—on the Edit line), InWord (a word processing add-in), and NoteWorthy (a cell-annotation add-in).

A number of smaller companies offer useful add-ins as well. For example, Intex Solutions offers a number of add-ins that add @ functions to 1-2-3, as well as one (3D Graphics) that expands 1-2-3's graphing capabilities; General Optimization offers What's Best!, a linear-programming add-in; FrontLine Systems offers 3-2-1 GOSUB, an add-in that allows you to create your own custom @ functions, and Goldata offers SOS, which saves your worksheet automatically at the intervals you specify.

CONCLUSION

1-2-3's powers can be expanded through the use of add-in applications: programs that merge with 1-2-3 and, therefore, allow you to do things that RAM-resident utilities cannot. In this chapter, we showed you how to use add-ins, explored the two add-ins that are bundled with 1-2-3 Release 2.2 (Allways and the Macro Library Manager), and briefly discussed a number of the third-party add-ins available for 1-2-3.

Appendix 1

Exchanging Data with Other Programs

If you are like most 1-2-3 users, you probably use several programs in addition to 1-2-3. If you work in an office with several computers, it's also likely that different people in your office use different programs. If this is true for you, then from time to time you'll probably want to transfer information from one program to another—for example, from 1-2-3 Release 1A to 1-2-3 Release 2, from Symphony to 1-2-3, from dBASE II or III to 1-2-3, or from ASCII text files to 1-2-3. Unfortunately, files that are created in one program usually cannot be loaded directly into another program. However, 1-2-3 offers a set of tools that allow you to overcome most of the obstacles you usually encounter when exchanging data between programs.

Data exchange between 1-2-3 and other programs can be divided into two broad categories: data exchange with programs that read the ASCII file format and data exchange with other kinds of programs. These "other kinds of programs" are a handful of spreadsheet and data base programs including dBASE II and III and Symphony. In order to exchange data between 1-2-3 and these other programs, you must use the Translate program, which is delivered on the 1-2-3 Utility disk. To exchange data with programs that read ASCII text files, you don't need to use a special utility program. Instead, you use a couple of 1-2-3 commands: / Print File and / File Import. We'll talk about these commands in more detail later in this chapter. Let's begin, however, with an overview of 1-2-3's Translate program.

THE TRANSLATE UTILITY

The Translate program is a tool that allows you to convert a file stored on disk in one format into another format. You will find that the Translate program is very easy to use. It contains an abundance of on-screen prompts and instructions that guide you through each step of the file translation.

▶Our discussion of the Translate program is based on the Release 2.2 version. The Translate programs for 1-2-3 Releases 2 and 2.01 are essentially the same as Release 2.2's. 1-2-3 Release 1A's Translate program offers less file translation options and has a slightly different menu structure.◄

RELEASE
▶ 2.2 ◄

Loading the Translate Program

There are two ways to load the Translate program. First, you can choose the Translate option from the Lotus Access menu. If you are using a floppy-disk computer, you will then see a message instructing you to insert the Translate disk (the Utility disk in earlier releases of 1-2-3) in drive A and press [Enter]. If you are using a hard disk and you have stored the Translate program in the same directory as the 1-2-3 program files, you won't see this message; the Translate program will load automatically.

You also can access the Translate program directly from DOS. To do this, just place the Translate disk in drive A, type TRANS at the DOS prompt, and press [Enter]. (If you are using a hard disk, just make the directory that contains the Translate program the current directory and then type TRANS at the prompt.)

Specifying the Translation

Once you load the Translate program, you'll see the screen shown in Figure A1-1, which asks you to specify the kind of file format you wish to translate from. You simply point to the file type and press [Enter]. 1-2-3 will then show you another list of file types and ask you to specify the kind of file format you want to translate to. The list of choices that you see on this second screen is determined by the type of file you specified to translate from. Files from any Lotus spreadsheet product (1-2-3 Release 1A; 1-2-3 Releases 2, 2.01, and 2.2; Symphony 1.0; and Symphony 1.1, 1.2, and 2.0) can be translated into files for any other Lotus spreadsheet product, plus dBase II, dBase III, and DIF. Files from non-Lotus products can only be translated into files for any Lotus spreadsheet product.

```
                Lotus  1-2-3  Release 2.2 Translate Utility
         Copr. 1985, 1989  Lotus Development Corporation  All Rights Reserved

    What do you want to translate FROM?

              1-2-3  1A
              1-2-3  2, 2.01 or 2.2
              dBase II
              dBase III
              DIF
              Multiplan (SYLK)
              Symphony  1.0
              Symphony  1.1, 1.2 or 2.0
              VisiCalc




                    Highlight your selection and press ENTER
                    Press ESC to end the Translate utility
                    Press HELP (F1) for more information
```

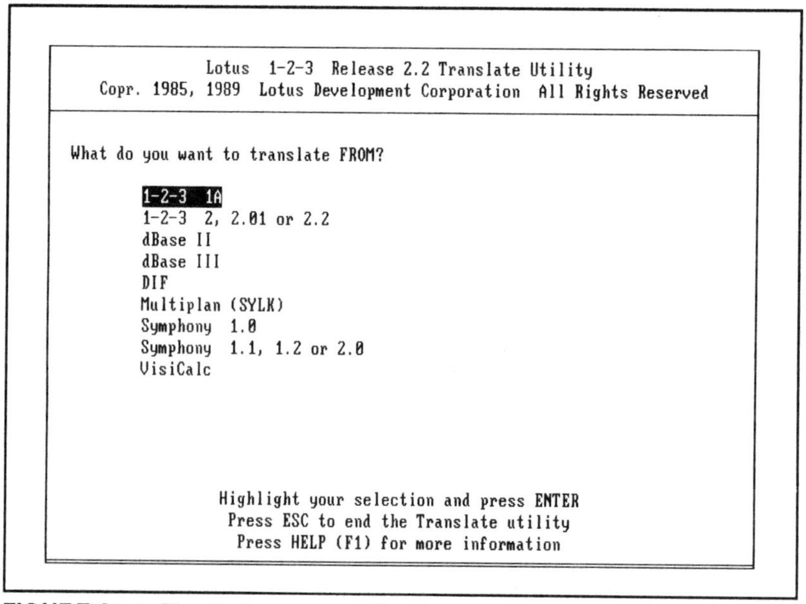

FIGURE A1-1: The first screen of the Translate program

Interestingly, the Translate program lets you perform file translations that have nothing to do with 1-2-3. For example, you can translate a Symphony file into DIF format. In this appendix, we will explain only the file translation options that relate to 1-2-3 Release 2.2.

We also should point out that some of the file translation choices are just placebos. For example, you do not have to translate a 1-2-3 Release 1A file in order to use it in 1-2-3 Releases 2, 2.01, and 2.2. If you choose this option in the Translate program, you will just see a message telling you that you do not need to translate.

Built-in Help

After you have selected the kind of files you want to translate from and to, the Translate program will display one or more screens of instructions and explanations relating to the type of file translation you wish to perform. If there is more than one screen, pressing [Enter] moves you to the next screen; pressing [Backspace] moves you back to the previous screen. To proceed with the translation, just press [Esc].

Choosing the File to Translate

At this point, the Translate program will search the current drive and directory for any files of the type you wish to translate from. For example, if you have chosen to translate from a 1-2-3 Release 2, 2.01, or 2.2 file into a dBASE III file, the program will search for all .WK1 files in the current drive and directory. Figure A1-2 shows how your screen would look at this point.

```
               Lotus  1-2-3  Release 2.2 Translate Utility
      Copr. 1985, 1989  Lotus Development Corporation  All Rights Reserved


    Translate FROM: 1-2-3 2.2          Translate TO: 1-2-3 1A

    Source file: A:\*.WK1

       ┌─────────────────────────────────────────────────────┐
       │No files were found that match the source file specification│
       │       If appropriate, insert a new disk and          │
       │       press ENTER to search again, or press          │
       │       ESC to edit source file specification.         │
       └─────────────────────────────────────────────────────┘




              Highlight the file you want to translate and press ENTER
                  Press ESC to edit the source file specification
                       Press HELP (F1) for more information
```

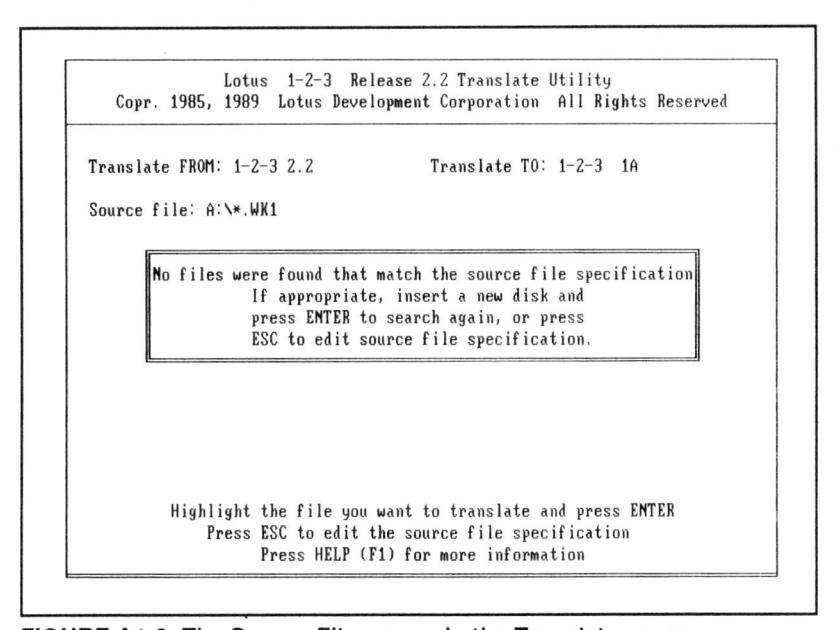

FIGURE A1-2: The Source File screen in the Translate program

There are a couple of things you should notice about the screen in Figure A1-2. First, at the top of the screen, you will see the kind of file format you have chosen to translate from (*1-2-3 2, 2.01 or 2.2* in this example), as well as the kind of file format you have chosen to translate to (*dBase III* in this example). Just below this, you see the words *Source file: A:*.WK1*. This message tells you that the Translate program is searching the root directory on the A drive for all files that have the .WK1 file-name extension. If you were using a hard disk, you might see a message like *Source file: C:\123*.WK1*. This indicates that the Translate program is looking in the C:\123 directory for files that have a .WK1 extension.

The term *Source file* refers to the file that you will be translating. We will refer to the **.WK1* portion of the message as the *source file descriptor*. When you are translating a 1-2-3 Release 2, 2.01, or 2.2 file, the Translate program will assume that the source file will be a .WK1 file. If you are translating another kind of file, then the Translate program will assume a different file-name extension. For example, when you translate a dBASE II or dBASE III file, the Translate program will look for files with the extension .DBF.

Changing the Directory

If the directory that contains the Translate program contains no files of the type that the program is looking for, you will see an error message like the one in the middle of the screen in Figure A1-2. To get around this problem, you can remove the Utility disk from the A drive (either before or after you see the error message), then insert the disk that contains the file you want to translate, and press [Enter]. Alternatively, you can tell the Translate program to search a different drive. To do this, first press [Esc] to delete the error message and enter the EDIT mode. Then use the standard editing keys—[Backspace], [Del], and the arrow keys—to edit the drive/directory name, as well as the source file descriptor. Instead of editing the drive/directory name and the source file descriptor, you can press [Esc] a second time to erase both the entire drive/directory name and the source file descriptor. Then you can type the names of the drive/directory and the source file descriptor that you wish to use. Once you have entered this information, press [Enter] to lock it in.

If you enter only a drive/directory name (such as B:\), the Translate program will automatically supply the appropriate source file descriptor for the type of file you select to translate from. (For example, if you choose to translate from a 1-2-3 Release 2, 2.01, or 2.2 file, 1-2-3 will automatically display the source file descriptor **.WK1*.) However, you can supply your own source file descriptor if you want. For example, if you would like to choose a source file from among files with *any* name and extension, you can enter *.* after you type the drive/directory name.

After you enter the name of the drive/directory that contains your source file (and the descriptor, if you so choose), the Translate program will display a list of all appropriate files in the directory you specified. For example, Figure A1-3 shows a list of all the .WK1 files in the C:\12322 directory.

Appendix 1: Exchanging Data with Other Programs

```
              Lotus  1-2-3  Release 2.2 Translate Utility
   Copr. 1985, 1989  Lotus Development Corporation  All Rights Reserved

Translate FROM: 1-2-3 2.2           Translate TO: 1-2-3  1A

Source file: C:\12322\*.WK1

   3-20     WK1    7/31/89   5:23p      3669

            3-20     WK1
            3-21     WK1
            3-3      WK1
            4-1      WK1
            4-19     WK1
            5-44     WK1
            6-29     WK1
            —More—


          Highlight the file you want to translate and press ENTER
               Press ESC to edit the source file specification
                   Press HELP (F1) for more information
```

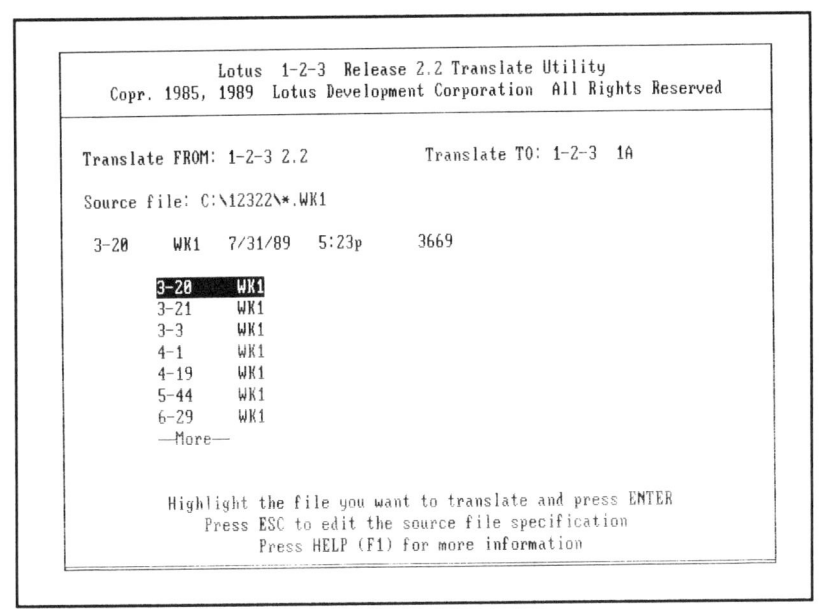

FIGURE A1-3: List of possible files to translate

Only seven or eight file names can fit on the screen at one time. If the directory you specify contains more than eight files of the appropriate type, then you will see seven names with the message —More— at the bottom of the list. In this case, you can use the ↓, ↑, [Pg Dn], [Pg Up], [End], and [Home] keys to scroll through the list. As you point to each file in the list, the Translate program will display its name, the date and time it last was saved, and its size in bytes.

To select a file to translate, just point to its name and press [Enter]. If you accidentally choose the wrong file name, you can back out of your mistake by pressing [Esc] twice. This will take you back to the list of file names, where you can choose the correct file.

Specifying the Name for the Target File

Once you have selected a source file, the Translate program will suggest a name for the file that will contain the translated data. This file is called the *target file*. The target file name suggested by the Translate program will be identical to the source file name, except that it will have a different file-name extension. For example, if you are translating the 1-2-3 Release 2, 2.01, or 2.2 file named ACCRUALS.WK1 to dBASE III, the Translate program will suggest the name ACCRUALS.DBF for the target file. The program also will assume that you want to save the target file in the same directory as the source file. As you can see, Figure A1-4 shows how your screen will look during a file translation after you select the file named ACCRUALS.WK1 as your source file.

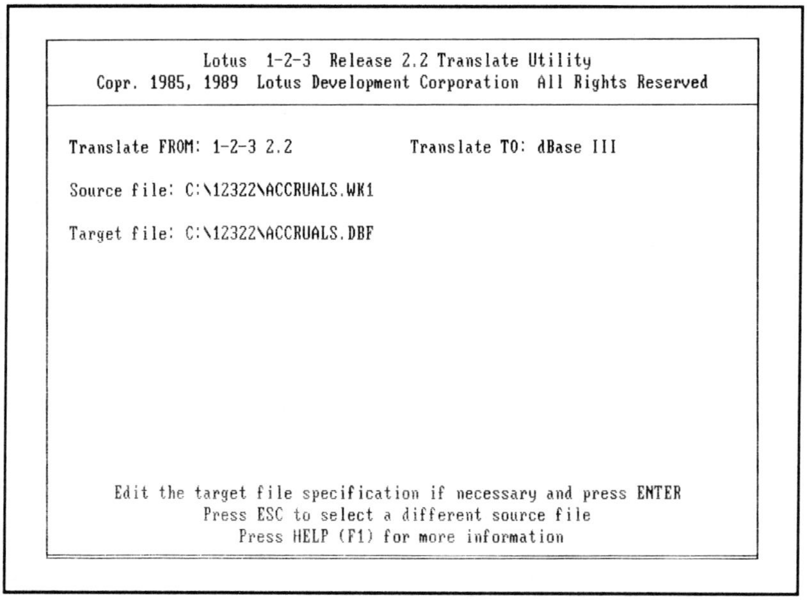

```
          Lotus  1-2-3  Release 2.2 Translate Utility
    Copr. 1985, 1989  Lotus Development Corporation  All Rights Reserved

Translate FROM: 1-2-3 2.2          Translate TO: dBase III

Source file: C:\12322\ACCRUALS.WK1

Target file: C:\12322\ACCRUALS.DBF




          Edit the target file specification if necessary and press ENTER
                Press ESC to select a different source file
                   Press HELP (F1) for more information
```

FIGURE A1-4: Source file selected in the Translate program

As you might expect, you can edit the suggested target file name at this point. To change the suggested name, you can either press the [Backspace] key to delete individual characters in the file name or press [Esc] to delete the entire file name and the directory name. You can then type the new target file name and, if you want, the new directory name. (If you delete the directory name and then don't reenter it, the program will assume that you would like to use the same directory that the source file is stored in.) You also can use the other keys you normally would use in editing worksheet entries in 1-2-3, such as the arrow keys and the [Del] key, to edit the file and directory name.

Of course, if you choose to specify a different name, that name must conform to all the normal file name rules. In addition, the name you select for the target file must be different from the name of the source file.

If the name you choose for the target file is identical to a file name that is already in the current directory, you will see the message, *The target file already exists. Should it be written over?* followed by *Yes* and *No*. If you select Yes, the translation will proceed and the translated file will overwrite the existing file. If you select No, you will go back to the point of editing the target file name. In the Release 1A version of the 1-2-3 Translate program, you do not get any warning before a translated file overwrites an existing file.

Performing the Translation

After you have specified the file name you want to use for the target file and pressed [Enter], the Translate program will present three options: Yes, No, and Quit. If you choose Yes, the program will proceed with the translation. If you choose No, the program will go back to the screen shown in Figure A1-3. If you choose Quit, the program will back up all the way to the first screen (shown in Figure A1-1) and will ask what kind of file you want to translate.

As the Translate program performs the translation, it will draw a bar across the screen, indicating the progress of the translation (from 0 to 100%). Once the translation is complete, you will see one of several different messages on your screen. If the file was translated without a hitch, then you'll see the message *Translation successful*. If the file or part of the file could not be translated, you will see an error message. This error message does not necessarily mean that the file was not translated. It may just tell you that one entry in the file could not be translated. The particular message that you see will depend on what kind of file you are attempting to translate and the specific problem that occurs. As we explain the different file translation options, we will discuss the various kinds of traps that can interfere with smooth file translation.

After translating a file, you have two options. First, you can choose to translate another file using the same file types for both the destination and the source file. For example, if you have translated a 1-2-3 Release 2, 2.01, or 2.2 file to dBASE III format, you can translate another 1-2-3 Release 2, 2.01, or 2.2 file to dBASE III. To do this, just press [Enter]. The Translate program will then bring up the list of possible source files, like the one shown in Figure A1-3.

If you don't want to perform another file translation using the same file types, you should press [Esc] after you have completed a file translation. This will return you to the first screen of the Translate program. Then you can choose other types of files to translate from and to. You also can exit from the Translate program by pressing [Esc] once more. You will then see the message, *Do you want to leave Translate?* followed by a No/Yes menu. To exit from the Translate program, choose Yes.

Final Comments

The steps that we have described for using the Translate program are almost identical for every kind of file translation. Of course, the screens of instructions and explanations that you see after you choose a source file type and a target file type will be different, depending on which types of files you choose. In addition, some kinds of translations require an extra step or two. For example, when you are translating a 1-2-3 worksheet into dBASE format, you must specify whether you want to translate the entire worksheet or only a named range. However, these differences are minor. Once you've translated one or two files of any type, you should be quite familiar with the workings of the Translate program.

Now that we have explained the basics of using the Translate program, let's examine the specifics of exchanging data between 1-2-3 and other programs. We will begin by looking at how you can exchange files between 1-2-3 Releases 1A, 2, 2.01, and 2.2 and 3.

EXCHANGING DATA BETWEEN DIFFERENT RELEASES OF 1-2-3

1-2-3 Releases 2, 2.01, and 2.2 all save files in the same format: the .WK1 format. Consequently, you can retrive a file that you have created in any one of those releases of 1-2-3 into either of the other two releases. That is, you can retrieve files you created in 1-2-3 Release 2 into 1-2-3 Releases 2.01 and 2.2; you can retrieve files you created in 1-2-3 Release 2.01 into 1-2-3 Releases 2 and 2.2; and you can retrieve files you created in 1-2-3 Release 2.2 into 1-2-3 Releases 2 and 2.01.

When you retrieve a file created in 1-2-3 Release 2 into 1-2-3 Release 2.01 or 2.2 (or from 1-2-3 Release 2.01 into 1-2-3 Releases 2 or 2.2), all entries and attributes (including cell formats, cell alignments, range names, print settings, global and individual column widths, the global format, the default label prefix, recalculation settings, protection settings, graph settings, and so forth) will be the same as they would be if you had retrieved the worksheet into the release of 1-2-3 in which the file was created.

RELEASE ► 2.2 ◄ ►When you retrieve a 1-2-3 Release 2.2 file into 1-2-3 Releases 2 or 2.01, everything will be the same as it is in 1-2-3 Release 2.2 except for linking formulas (formulas the reference cells in other worksheets) and *@CELL("filename",cell)* and *@CELLPOINTER("filename")* functions. In Releases 2 and 2.01, these entries return the value ERR. (Interestingly, linking formulas are retrieved into 1-2-3 Releases 2 and 2.01 as @@ functions. For example, the formula +<<*test.wk1*>>*A1* becomes *@@("<<test.wk1>>A1")*.)◄

Translating 1-2-3 Release 1A Files into Releases 2, 2.01, and 2.2

1-2-3 Releases 2, 2.01, and 2.2 can read files created in Release 1A with no translation. All you need to do is place the disk that contains the Release 1A .WKS file in your disk drive (or, if you have a hard disk, set the directory to the one that contains the Release 1A file you want to transfer) and issue the /File Retrieve command. When you do this, 1-2-3 will display a list of all the files in the current directory that have .WK as the first two letters of the file-name extension, including 1-2-3 Release 1A's .WKS files. When you see this list, just point to the name of the file you wish to retrieve and press [Enter]. 1-2-3 will immediately retrieve the Release 1A worksheet file into Release 2.

Once you have loaded a 1-2-3 Release 1A file into 1-2-3 Releases 2, 2.01, or 2.2, you probably will want to use the /File Save command to resave it to disk as a .WK1 file. When you issue the /File Save command, 1-2-3 automatically will attempt to save the worksheet into a file with the extension .WK1 instead of the original extension .WKS. For example, suppose you have loaded the Release 1A file named CASH.WKS file into Releases 2, 2.01, or 2.2. When you issue the / File Save command, these releases of 1-2-3 will "suggest" the name CASH.WK1 as the file name for the translated worksheet. This is an important safeguard. If 1-2-3 did not specify the extension .WK1, you might accidentally overwrite the original 1-2-3 Release 1A file with the translated file.

Translating 1-2-3 Release 2, 2.01, and 2.2 Files into Release 1A

You cannot simply retrieve a 1-2-3 Release 2, 2.01, or 2.2 worksheet into 1-2-3 Release 1A. Before you can load a worksheet file created in 1-2-3 Release 2, 2.01, or 2.2 into Release 1A, you'll have to use the Translate utility program to convert that file into a form Release 1A can read.

To translate a Release 2, 2.01, or 2.2 file into Release 1A form, first load the Translate program, select *1-2-3 2, 2.01 or 2.2* as the type of the source file, and choose *1-2-3 1A* as the type of the target file. Then follow the standard steps described above for using the Translate program. In choosing a name for the Release 1A target file, you should be sure to use the .WKS file-name extension; otherwise, you will not be able to retrieve the translated worksheet into 1-2-3 Release 1A.

Once you have translated a 1-2-3 Release 2, 2.01, or 2.2 worksheet, you can retrieve the translated file into Release 1A just as you would any other Release 1A worksheet. When the worksheet is loaded, you may need to make some changes, such as replacing formulas that could not be transferred. Overall, however, the worksheet should look virtually identical to the worksheet that you created originally in 1-2-3 Releases 2, 2.01, or 2.2.

If the Release 2, 2.01, or 2.2 file that you have chosen to translate is password protected, the Translate program will not be able to complete the translation. Before you can translate the file, you'll need to retrieve it into 1-2-3 and then save it again, this time without a password.

What Does and Does Not Get Translated

Because of the differences between 1-2-3 Release 1A and later releases of 1-2-3, it is likely that the Translate program will not be able to translate some parts of your Release 2, 2.01, and 2.2 worksheets. If the Release 2, 2.01, or 2.2 worksheet contains formulas, functions, or special characters that cannot be translated into Release 1A, or if the worksheet contains entries below row 2048, the Translate program will display a message telling you that part of the worksheet could not be translated. This does not mean that the translation did not take place; it only means that part of the worksheet file was not translated.

In most cases, the differences between Releases 2, 2.01, and 2.2 and Release 1A should not cause any major problems. However, you almost certainly will need to make some adjustments to the translated Release 1A worksheet to compensate for the items that do not get translated. Let's look at a few of these potential problems.

Functions and Formulas

1-2-3 Releases 2, 2.01, and 2.2 include a number of functions that are not available in Release 1A. When the Translate program translates a worksheet that contains these functions (or any formulas that use these functions), it converts them into labels. For example, if your Release 2, 2.01, or 2.2 worksheet includes the function

@CELL("Width",A1..A1)

the Translate program will convert it to the label *'@CELL("Width",A1..A1)*. Instead of seeing the result of the function in the resulting Release 1A worksheet, you will see this label.

Table A1-1 lists all of the Release 2, 2.01, and 2.2 functions that will be converted into labels in a Release 1A worksheet.

String Functions	Date & Time Functions	Logical Functions
@CHAR	@DATEVALUE	@ISNUMBER
@CODE	@TIMEVALUE	@ISSTRING
@RIGHT	@TIME	
@LEFT	@HOUR	Other Functions
@MID	@MINUTE	@INDEX
@EXACT	@SECOND	@CELL
@FIND		@CELLPOINTER
@REPLACE	Financial Functions	@COLS
@LENGTH	@RATE	@ROWS
@LOWER	@TERM	@N
@UPPER	@CTERM	@S
@PROPER	@DDB	@@
@STRING	@SLN	
@VALUE		
@REPEAT		
@TRIM		
@CLEAN		

TABLE A1-1: Release 2, 2.01, and 2.2 functions that cannot be translated into Release 1A format

Because 1-2-3 Release 1A does not recognize the & operator, any string formulas in your Release 2, 2.01, and 2.2 worksheet files also will not be translated into the Release 1A file. Instead, the Translate program will convert each string formula into a label. There is one exception to this rule. If a string formula is a simple reference to a cell that contains a label—such as +A1—that formula will come into the Release 1A worksheet intact where it will return the value 0.

> **TIP: SPURIOUS ERROR MESSAGES**
>
> Sometimes the Translate program will display the error message *FORMULA TRANSLATION ERROR* for no apparent reason whatsoever during the translation of a 1-2-3 Release 2, 2.01, or 2.2 worksheet to Release 1A format. We've even seen this error when the Translate program was translating a worksheet that contained no formulas. If the Translate program encounters a real problem in translating a formula, you'll be able to tell where the problem occurred when you load the translated worksheet in Release 1A. You should see the label *'FORMULA TRANSLATION ERROR* in the cell that contained the formula.

Upper-Level LICS Characters

If your Release 2, 2.01, or 2.2 worksheet contains a character from the Lotus International Character Set (LICS) whose LICS code is 128 or greater, that character will not be translated into a Release 1A worksheet. (Appendix 2 gives more information about the LICS.) Instead, the Translate program will substitute a lower-level character. For example, if the Release 2, 2.01, or 2.2 worksheet you are translating contains the character ¥ (a yen sign), that character will be converted into the letter Y in the Release 1A worksheet. The explanation screens that you see as you are using the Translate program list all of the LICS character substitutions that will be made during the translation.

Worksheet Attributes

When you translate a worksheet from Release 2, 2.01, or 2.2 into Release 1A, that worksheet will maintain nearly every attribute that you have assigned it, including range names, print settings, global and individual column widths, the global format, the default label prefix, recalculation settings, protection settings, graph settings (including named graphs), and the various / Data command ranges. The only worksheet attribute that will *not* appear in the translated 1A file is zero suppression.

Entries Beyond Row 2048

The 1-2-3 Release 1A worksheets contains only 2048 rows; Release 2, 2.01, and 2.2 worksheets contains 8192 rows. If the worksheet file you are translating contains entries in the rows below row 2048, the Translate program will truncate the worksheet to include only 2048 rows as it is translated. After the translation is complete, you will see the following message:

WARNING: The SOURCE file extended below row 2048. Cells below row 2048 will not appear in the output file. The resulting 1-2-3 worksheet may not be usable due to missing data.

There are two other things to keep in mind when you translate 1-2-3 Release 2, 2.01, and 2.2 worksheets with entries below row 2048 into Release 1A. First, if rows

1 to 2048 of the source worksheet contain formulas that refer to cells below row 2048, those formulas will not return meaningful results after the translation is completed. In many cases, this will make the translation impossible or at least highly impractical. Second, if the Release 2, 2.01, or 2.2 worksheet contains entries below row 2048, it is extremely likely that the translated worksheet will consume too much memory to be loaded into Release 1A. This occurs because of the different memory allocation schemes of Releases 2, 2.01, and 2.2 and Release 1A.

Memory Considerations

1-2-3 Release 1A uses a different memory allocation scheme than later releases of 1-2-3. In Release 1A, blank cells sometimes will consume memory, while in later releases, only cells that contain entries (or are formatted or unprotected) consume memory. Therefore, it's quite possible that a worksheet that you created in Releases 2, 2.01, or 2.2 will not fit in Release 1A. When you try to load the translated file, you will get a *Memory Full* message.

The only way to get around this problem is to rearrange your worksheet in Release 2, 2.01, or 2.2, save the file, and then translate it again. When you rearrange the worksheet, you should try to condense your entries into as small an area as possible, eliminating blank rows and columns. You also should place your cell entries as close to the top and left edge of the worksheet as possible.

Of course, you may not be able to compress your Release 2, 2.01, or 2.2 worksheet enough so that it will fit into 1-2-3 Release 1A. If this is the case, you can use the / File Xtract command to break the source worksheet into several smaller pieces, and then translate and retrieve each of these smaller worksheets to Release 1A individually.

Exchanging information with 1-2-3 Release 3

Unlike 1-2-3 Release 1A (which saves files in the .WKS format) and 1-2-3 Releases 2, 2.01, and 2.2 (which save files in the .WK1 format), 1-2-3 Release 3 saves files in the .WK3 format. However, you can load files created in 1-2-3 Releases 1A, 2, 2.01, and 2.2 directly into 1-2-3 Release 3. To do this, simply issue the / File Retrieve or / File Open commands, select the name of the file you want to retrieve, and press [Enter]. (Like 1-2-3 Releases 2, 2.01, and 2.2, 1-2-3 Release 3 lists all files whose extension begins with the letters WK. Consequently, the names of files created in 1-2-3 Releases 1A, 2, 2.01, and 2.2 will be listed.) Since 1-2-3 Release 3 has all the features of other releases of 1-2-3, all of the information and settings from the 1-2-3 Release 1A, 2, 2.01, or 2.2 worksheet will be brought into 1-2-3 Release 3.

Getting information from 1-2-3 Release 3 into 1-2-3 Releases 2, 2.01, and 2.2 is also easy. To save a 1-2-3 Release 3 worksheet in a form that 1-2-3 Releases 2, 2.01, and 2.2 can use, simply issue the / File Save command, type the name of the file— making sure to include the extension .WK1—and press [Enter]. When you do this, 1-2-3 Release 3 will save the worksheet into a .WK1 file instead of a .WK3 file.

Getting information from 1-2-3 Release 3 into 1-2-3 Release 1A is more difficult. To do this, save the file either in the .WK3 or .WK1 formats. Then, use 1-2-3 Release 3's Translate program to convert the file into .WKS format. (If you saved the file in

.WK1 format, you can use 1-2-3 Release 2, 2.01, or 2.2's Translate utility to convert the file to .WKS form).

EXCHANGING DATA BETWEEN 1-2-3 AND SYMPHONY

You do not have to perform any kind of translation to exchange worksheets between Symphony Releases 1.1, 1.2, and 2.0 and 1-2-3 Releases 2, 2.01, or 2.2. Worksheets created in these releases of Symphony can be loaded into these releases of 1-2-3 directly, and worksheets created in these releases of 1-2-3 can be loaded directly into these releases of Symphony.

Data exchange between 1-2-3 Releases 2, 2.01, and 2.2 and Symphony Releases 1 and 1.01 is only slightly more inconvenient. You can load Symphony Release 1 and 1.01 worksheet into 1-2-3 Release 2, 2.01, and 2.2 directly—no translation is required. You also can load a 1-2-3 Release 1A worksheet directly into any release of Symphony with no translation. If you want to load a 1-2-3 Release 2, 2.01, or 2.2 worksheet into Symphony Releases 1 and 1.01, however, you must first translate the file.

In this section, we will first examine what happens when you load a Symphony worksheet into 1-2-3. Then we will explain how you can use a 1-2-3 worksheet in Symphony. As you'll see, it's pretty easy to exchange Symphony and 1-2-3 worksheets. However, you will lose a few worksheet attributes when you move worksheet files from one program to the other.

Using Symphony Worksheets in 1-2-3

To use a Symphony worksheet in 1-2-3 Releases 2, 2.01, or 2.2, you just retrieve that file. However, when you issue the /File Retrieve command, 1-2-3 will not include the Symphony files with the file-name extensions .WRK or .WR1 in the list of file names. To retrieve a Symphony file, you must type the entire file name, including the .WRK or .WR1 extension, and press [Enter]. Alternatively, you can change the file descriptor from *.*WK?* to *.*WR?* and press [Enter] to display a list that includes the Symphony files on the current directory. You can then point to the name of the file you wish to retrieve and press [Enter].

When a Symphony file comes into 1-2-3, some of its worksheet attributes will be missing. Table A1-2 on the next page summarizes which worksheet attributes do and do not get transferred from Symphony to 1-2-3. This table applies to both Symphony Releases 1 and 1.01 and Symphony 1.1.

You might notice that many more attributes are lost in the Symphony-to-1-2-3 exchange than in the exchange between 1-2-3 Releases 2, 2.01, or 2.2 and 1-2-3 Release 1A. After you load a Symphony worksheet into 1-2-3, you most likely will want to redefine some of the worksheet attributes, such as Print settings and Titles.

When you retrieve a Symphony worksheet into 1-2-3, any range names in the Symphony worksheet will be brought into the 1-2-3 worksheet. In addition, if the Symphony worksheet contains a word-processing document, the labels that make up that document will be brought into the 1-2-3 worksheet. Of course, since 1-2-3 has no word-processing capabilities, you will not be able to manipulate the document in 1-2-3 as you could in Symphony.

Using 1-2-3 Worksheets in Symphony

As we mentioned earlier, you do not have to translate a 1-2-3 Release 2, 2.01, or 2.2 worksheet in order to use it in Symphony Releases 1.1, 1.2, or 2.0. After you have loaded Symphony, you can simply issue the {Services} File Retrieve command, type the name and extension of the 1-2-3 Release 2, 2.01, or 2.2 worksheet you want to retrieve, and press [Enter] to retrieve that file. You can also modify the file-name descriptor to obtain a list of 1-2-3 files, then choose a file from that list.

Attributes That Will be Transferred from Symphony to 1-2-3	Attributes That Will *Not* Be Transferred from Symphony to 1-2-3
Individual Cell Formats	Global Formats
Individual Column Widths	Global Column Width
Global Label Prefix	Print Settings
Individual Label Alignments	Graph Settings
Global Protection	Windows
Individual Cell Protection Status	Titles
Recalculation Method	Database-Related Ranges (Input,
Recalculation Order	Criterion, and Output Ranges)
Recalculation Iterations	
Data Distribution Ranges	
Data Fill Range	
Data Table Range	

TABLE A1-2: Transfer of worksheet attributes from Symphony to 1-2-3 Releases 2, 2.01, and 2.2

What Does Not Get Translated

When you load a 1-2-3 Release 2, 2.01, or 2.2 worksheet into Symphony Release 1.1, 1.2, or 2.0, or translate a 1-2-3 Release 2, 2.01, or 2.2 file into Symphony Release 1 and 1.01 format (we'll explain that in a few paragraphs), a few of the attributes of the 1-2-3 worksheet will be lost. Table A1-3 summarizes what happens to various worksheet attributes when you use a 1-2-3 Release 2, 2.01, or 2.2 file in Symphony. After you load a 1-2-3 Release 2, 2.01, or 2.2 worksheet into Symphony, you most likely will want to redefine some of the worksheet attributes, such as Print settings and Graph settings. You will not need to redefine range names, however, since they will become a part of the Symphony worksheet.

Attributes That Will be Transferred from 1-2-3 to Symphony	Attributes That Will *Not* Be Transferred from 1-2-3 to Symphony
Global Format	Print Settings
Individual Cell Formats	Graph Settings
Global Column Width	Database-Related Ranges (Input, Criterion, and Output Ranges)
Individual Column Widths	Windows
Global Label Prefix	
Individual Label Alignments	
Global Protection	
Individual Cell Protection Status	
Recalculation Method	
Recalculation Order	
Recalculation Iterations	
Data Distribution Ranges (both Values and Bin Ranges)	
Data Fill Range	
Data Table Range	
Titles	

TABLE A1-3: Transfer of worksheet attributes from 1-2-3 Releases 2, 2.01, and 2.2 to Symphony

Translating from 1-2-3 Releases 2, 2.01, and 2.2 to Symphony Releases 1 and 1.01

Loading a 1-2-3 Release 2, 2.10, or 2.2 file into Symphony Releases 1 and 1.01 is not as simple as loading a 1-2-3 Release 2, 2.01, or 2.2 file into Symphony Release 1.1, 1.2, or 2.0. In order to load a 1-2-3 Release 2 file into Symphony Releases 1 and 1.01, you must first translate the file. To do this, load the Translate utility, choose *1-2-3 2, 2.01, or 2.2* as the type of file to translate from, and choose *Symphony 1.0* as the type of file to translate to. After this, the Translate program will direct you step by step through the translation process.

What Is Not Translated

In addition to the worksheet attributes listed in Table A1-3, there are six functions in 1-2-3 Release 2 that will not be translated into Symphony Releases 1 and 1.01: @TERM, @CTERM, @RATE, @SLN, @SYD, and @DDB. The Translate program will simply convert each of these functions into a label as it translates the worksheet.

Memory Considerations

When you translate a 1-2-3 Release 2, 2.01, or 2.2 file into Symphony Release 1 or 1.01 format, you may run into the same memory problem that can occur when you translate from 1-2-3 Releases 2, 2.01, and 2.2 to 1-2-3 Release 1A. Like 1-2-3 Release 1A, Symphony Releases 1 and 1.01 use a memory allocation scheme in which blank cells sometimes consume memory. Therefore, when you try to load a translated 1-2-3 Release 2, 2.01, or 2.2 worksheet into Symphony Releases 1 and 1.01, you may get a *Memory Full* message, indicating that the file requires too much memory to fit in Symphony Releases 1 and 1.01. Again, the only ways around this problem are to try to compress the worksheet in 1-2-3, eliminating as many blank rows and columns as you can, or to use the /File Xtract command to save the 1-2-3 worksheet in sections, then translate each section individually.

There's another kind of memory problem that you may encounter when you try to load a 1-2-3 Release 2, 2.01, or 2.2 worksheet into Symphony. These releases of 1-2-3 occupy considerably less RAM than any releases of Symphony. This means that you can build bigger worksheets in 1-2-3 than in Symphony. Not surprisingly, it's possible to build a worksheet model in 1-2-3 that is too large to fit into Symphony. If this happens, you must eliminate some entries from the 1-2-3 worksheet then retranslate it.

EXCHANGING DATA BETWEEN 1-2-3 AND dBASE

If you are one of the thousands of 1-2-3 users who also use dBASE II or dBASE III, there probably will be times when you will want to transfer data between 1-2-3 and dBASE. For example, when a 1-2-3 data base outgrows the worksheet (or, more likely, outgrows your computer's RAM), you can preserve that data base by transferring it to a dBASE file. On the other hand, although dBASE can handle larger amounts of information than 1-2-3, it's not as fast for sorting and analyzing data, and it does not allow you to perform computations as quickly and as easily as 1-2-3. You may want to transfer part or all of a dBASE file into a 1-2-3 worksheet so that you can analyze data quickly and easily.

You must use the Translate program to exchange data between 1-2-3 and dBASE. The rules and procedures for exchanging data are almost identical for dBASE II and dBASE III. When we talk about "dBASE" (without specifying II or III), you can assume that the discussion applies to either version of the program. We will, however, point out those cases where data exchange with 1-2-3 is different, depending on the particular version of dBASE that you're using.

Translating a dBASE File into a 1-2-3 Worksheet

Translating a file from dBASE to 1-2-3 is really quite easy. All you have to do is load the Translate utility, choose *dBase II* or *dBase III* as the type of file to translate from, and then choose *1-2-3 2, 2.01 and 2.2* as the type of file you want to translate to. After you do this, the Translate program will direct you step by step through the translation process.

Translation Rules

The Translate program can convert just about any dBASE data base into a 1-2-3 worksheet. The Translate program uses the structure of the dBASE data base to determine the structure of the 1-2-3 data base that results from the translation. The Translate program will place the field names from the dBASE data base in the first row of a new 1-2-3 worksheet. These names will then serve as the field names in the 1-2-3 data base. The data base records will be placed in the rows immediately below the row that contains the field names. Each field of information will be in a different column of the worksheet.

1-2-3 uses the widths of the fields in the dBASE data base to set the widths of the columns in the 1-2-3 worksheet. Columns that receive data from Character fields will have the same width as the corresponding Character fields in the data base. Columns that receive data from Numeric fields will be one character wider than the corresponding fields in the dBASE data base. The contents of Character fields are translated as labels in the 1-2-3 worksheet. This is true even for entries that are made up entirely of numerals. The contents of Numeric fields are translated as values.

Columns that receive data from Logical fields in the dBASE data base will be two characters wide. The Translate program automatically converts each entry in a dBASE logical field to either @TRUE, which will display a 1 in the worksheet, or @FALSE, which will display a 0 in the worksheet. The entries Y and T will be converted to @TRUE, while the entries N and F will be converted to @FALSE. This is an improvement over the Release 1A Translate program, which recognizes only the entries T and F in dBASE logical fields.

If the dBASE file being translated contains a Date field (only dBASE III offers Date fields), then 1-2-3 will convert the data from that field into serial date values. In addition, 1-2-3 will assign the DD-MMM-YY format to the cells in a column that receives data from a Date field and will set the width of that column to ten characters. (The Translate program does this so that the formatted values can be displayed.) Since dBASE II does not offer a Date field type, all the "dates" in dBASE II files are Character fields. If you translate a dBASE II data base that contains dates, they will come into your 1-2-3 worksheet as labels. If you want to convert those labels into dates, you can use the @DATEVALUE function— provided that the date labels appear in one of the Date formats that 1-2-3 can recognize.

Translation Problems

There are some cases where part of a dBASE file will not be translated. First, if your dBASE data base contains more than 8191 records, then no records after record 8191 will be translated. The reason for this truncation is obvious—1-2-3 Release 2, 2.01, and 2.2's worksheets have only 8192 rows. Since the first row will be occupied by field names, and each record occupies another row, the 1-2-3 Release 2 worksheet can hold only 8191 records. If the dBASE file contains more than 8191 records, you will need to use the dBASE COPY command to break that data base into two or more files and then translate each file separately.

If the dBASE file contains an extremely wide Character field, the Translate program may truncate the entries in that field. The Translate program will truncate any Character field entries in the dBASE file that are more than 240 characters long. This makes sense, given the 240-character limit for label entries in 1-2-3. However, it's not likely that you will encounter this limit very often, if at all.

If you have used the dBASE DELETE command to select some records in the dBASE file for deletion, then those records will not be translated. Also, if you are translating a dBASE III file that has an associated memo (.DBT file), then that .DBT file will not be translated along with the rest of the dBASE data.

An Example

To demonstrate how to translate a dBASE file into a 1-2-3 worksheet, let's consider an example. (We will use a dBASE III file in this example, but the procedure is identical for translating a dBASE II file.) Figure A1-5 shows a simple 11-record dBASE III data base named SLS_JAN. Figure A1-6 shows the structure of this data base. Notice that the second field in this data base (PREFERRED) is a Logical field and the third field is a Date field.

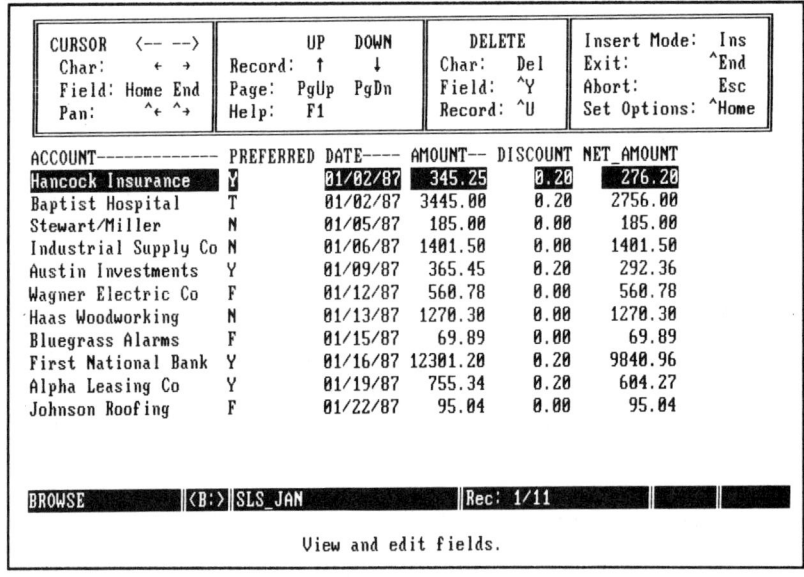

```
┌─────────────────────┬─────────────────┬───────────────┬─────────────────────┐
│ CURSOR   <-- -->    │        UP  DOWN │ DELETE        │ Insert Mode:   Ins  │
│ Char:     ← →       │ Record:  ↑   ↓  │ Char:    Del  │ Exit:          ^End │
│ Field: Home End     │ Page:  PgUp PgDn│ Field:   ^Y   │ Abort:         Esc  │
│ Pan:    ^← ^→       │ Help:  F1       │ Record:  ^U   │ Set Options:  ^Home │
├─────────────────────┴─────────────────┴───────────────┴─────────────────────┤
│ ACCOUNT------------- PREFERRED DATE---- AMOUNT-- DISCOUNT NET_AMOUNT         │
│ Hancock Insurance    Y         01/02/87   345.25    0.20      276.20         │
│ Baptist Hospital     T         01/02/87  3445.00    0.20     2756.00         │
│ Stewart/Miller       N         01/05/87   185.00    0.00      185.00         │
│ Industrial Supply Co N         01/06/87  1401.50    0.00     1401.50         │
│ Austin Investments   Y         01/09/87   365.45    0.20      292.36         │
│ Wagner Electric Co   F         01/12/87   560.78    0.00      560.78         │
│ Haas Woodworking     N         01/13/87  1270.30    0.00     1270.30         │
│ Bluegrass Alarms     F         01/15/87    69.89    0.00       69.89         │
│ First National Bank  Y         01/16/87 12301.20    0.20     9840.96         │
│ Alpha Leasing Co     Y         01/19/87   755.34    0.20      604.27         │
│ Johnson Roofing      F         01/22/87    95.04    0.00       95.04         │
│                                                                              │
│ BROWSE      <B:> SLS_JAN              Rec: 1/11                              │
│                          View and edit fields.                               │
└──────────────────────────────────────────────────────────────────────────────┘
```

FIGURE A1-5: A sample dBASE III data base

```
Structure for database: B:sls_jan.dbf
Number of data records:      11
Date of last update   : 08/29/86
Field  Field Name  Type      Width    Dec
  1    ACCOUNT     Character    20
  2    PREFERRED   Logical       1
  3    DATE        Date          8
  4    AMOUNT      Numeric       8     2
  5    DISCOUNT    Numeric       4     2
  6    NET_AMOUNT  Numeric       8     2
** Total **                     50
```

FIGURE A1-6: The dBASE III data base structure

To translate this data base into a 1-2-3 worksheet, first load the Translate program. Choose *dBase III* as the type of file to translate from and *1-2-3 2, 2.01, and 2.2* as the kind of file to translate to. Then follow the standard translation procedures that we described at the beginning of this appendix. When the translation has been completed, exit from the Translate program, load 1-2-3, and use the / File Retrieve command to retrieve the newly translated file. Figure A1-7 shows how the data base from Figure A1-5 will look when you load it into 1-2-3.

```
A1: [W20] 'ACCOUNT                                                    READY

              A              B    C          D       E       F         G
 1   ACCOUNT                     PRDATE      AMOUNT  DISCONET_AMOUN
 2   Hancock Insurance       1 02-Jan-87     345.25  0.20    276.20
 3   Baptist Hospital        1 02-Jan-87    3445.00  0.20   2756.00
 4   Stewart/Miller          0 05-Jan-87     185.00  0.00    185.00
 5   Industrial Supply Co    0 06-Jan-87    1401.50  0.00   1401.50
 6   Austin Investments      1 09-Jan-87     365.45  0.20    292.36
 7   Wagner Electric Co      0 12-Jan-87     560.78  0.00    560.78
 8   Haas Woodworking        0 13-Jan-87    1270.30  0.00   1270.30
 9   Bluegrass Alarms        0 15-Jan-87      69.89  0.00     69.89
10   First National Bank     1 16-Jan-87   12301.20  0.20   9840.96
11   Alpha Leasing Co        1 19-Jan-87     755.34  0.20    604.27
12   Johnson Roofing         0 22-Jan-87      95.04  0.00     95.04
13
```

FIGURE A1-7: The translated dBASE file after it has been loaded into 1-2-3

There are a few things you should notice about the worksheet in Figure A1-7. First, notice that the width of column A, which contains the translated field ACCOUNT, has been set to 20 characters—the same width as the Character field ACCOUNT in the dBASE data base. Similarly, columns D, E, and F, which contain data from the Numeric fields in the dBASE data base are each one character wider than the corresponding dBASE field. Column B in the worksheet, which matches up with the Logical field PREFERRED, is two characters wide. Notice that the cells in this field all display either the value 1 (for True) or the value 0 (for False). Finally, notice that the entries in column C, which correspond to the entries in the field DATE, are displayed in DD-MMM-YY format and that column C is ten characters wide.

Before you begin working with this or any other translated data base, you probably will want to make a few changes to your worksheet. If you want to query the data base, you will need to define an Input range and set up a Criterion range and Output range. Second, although 1-2-3 has used the widths of the fields in the dBASE data base to set the widths of the columns in the worksheet, some of the field names are still not completely visible. To make the data more readable, you can change the column widths and format the numeric fields.

Translating from 1-2-3 into dBASE

The Translate utility program also allows you to translate a 1-2-3 data base to dBASE II or III. You can use this tool to transfer data bases that are becoming too large for 1-2-3 or to return to dBASE data that you have imported into 1-2-3 and manipulated. All you have to do to translate a 1-2-3 file into dBASE format is load the Translate utility program, choose *1-2-3 2, 2.01, and 2.2* as the type of file to translate from, and choose *dBase II* or *dBase III* as the type of file to translate to. After this, the Translate program will direct you step by step through the translation process.

Translation Rules

While the procedure for translating from 1-2-3 to dBASE is similar to that for translating any other type of file, there is one important difference. When you translate data from a 1-2-3 worksheet to dBASE, you can either translate the entire 1-2-3 worksheet or just a named range from that worksheet. If you want to translate only a range of a worksheet and not the entire worksheet, you *must* name the range you wish to translate. You cannot use cell coordinates to specify the range you wish to translate.

Whichever option you choose, the data you want to translate must be in the form of a 1-2-3 data base. In other words, the first row of the worksheet or range must contain field names. The remaining rows of the worksheet or range should contain the data to be translated. The worksheet or range cannot include stray entries or formatted cells outside of the Database range.

If you are translating to dBASE III format, the 1-2-3 data base can contain a maximum of 128 fields (128 columns in the worksheet or range). For dBASE II translations, the maximum number of fields is 32.

The field names in the first row must be valid dBASE field names. Each name must be a label entry that is no longer than ten characters. Although the field names can include both letters and numbers, they must begin with a letter. If you are translating to dBASE III format, you also can include an embedded underscore in your field names.

In order for the translation to work properly, there cannot be any blank cells in the row below the field names (the first record of the 1-2-3 data base). The type of entry in each cell of this row will determine the field type in dBASE. If the entry is a label, then the corresponding field in dBASE will be a Character field. If the first entry is a value, then the corresponding field in the dBASE data base will be a Numeric field.

If your data base contains formulas or functions, only the result of those formulas and functions will be transferred to the dBASE data base. If the first entry in a column is a formula, the corresponding field in the dBASE data base will be a Numeric field.

A Caution

Most 1-2-3 worksheets will not meet the conditions we have described here. Typically, a worksheet will contain a data base and at least a few other entries. Therefore, in order to translate the 1-2-3 data base to dBASE format, you must assign a range name to the range that contains the field names and records and then translate just that named range. Or you can use the / File Xtract command to save only the data base portion of the worksheet into a separate file and then translate that entire file.

Even in cases where a worksheet contains only a data base, it's a good idea to assign a range name to that data base. Then, if there are any stray entries or formatted cells in the worksheet, you can still translate the data by translating only the named range. (You may not discover that the worksheet is not in acceptable form until you have loaded the Translate program. If you have created a range name for the data you want to translate, you won't have to leave the Translate program, go back into 1-2-3, and delete extraneous worksheet entries. You can just use the Range option offered by the Translate program.)

Dates

What happens to the date entries in a 1-2-3 worksheet depends on several factors. When you are translating to dBASE III, if the first entry in a column is a formatted serial date value, that column will become a Date field. If the first entry is an unformatted serial date value, however, that column will become a Numeric field. When you are translating to dBASE II, which does not offer a Date type field, and the first cell in a column contains a serial date value, that column will become a Numeric field in dBASE. If you want to transfer dates from 1-2-3 to dBASE II, you must enter the dates as labels in your 1-2-3 worksheet. Those label entries will then become entries in a dBASE II Character field.

Since neither dBASE II nor dBASE III has a Time field type, any column that contains time values in the 1-2-3 worksheet will become a Numeric field in dBASE. The values in that field will be the decimal values of the times in the worksheet. For example, the time 1:00 PM would appear in the dBASE file as the value .54166.

Formats

In translating worksheet values other than serial date values, the Translate program generally ignores formats. Special symbols, such as % and $, will not be transferred from a 1-2-3 worksheet to dBASE. However, if you format the entry in the first row of a field in the 1-2-3 data base to display a certain number of decimal places, then that number of decimal places will also appear in the dBASE field. If the first entry in a column is an unformatted value, then the corresponding dBASE field will always display two decimal places.

1-2-3 offers three formats—Text, +/, and Hidden—which do not actually display numbers in your worksheet. Values that have been assigned one of these formats will all be transferred to dBASE as unformatted numbers.

Column Widths

When you translate a data base from 1-2-3 to dBASE, the column widths within the 1-2-3 worksheet determine the field widths in dBASE. For this reason, you must be sure that your worksheet columns are wide enough to display all the entries in a particular field. Only the characters that actually are displayed in the worksheet will be transferred to the dBASE file. If a label entry is too long to be displayed in a column in the worksheet, then that entry will be truncated when you translate from 1-2-3 to dBASE. If a value entry is too long to be displayed in a column, then 1-2-3 will display the entry in scientific notation. When the entry is transferred to dBASE, however, it will be truncated. Only the number of digits that can fit in the field width will be translated. For example, if your 1-2-3 worksheet contains the number 1,231,231,231 in a standard nine-character column, then 1-2-3 will display the number as *1.2E+09*. In dBASE, this number will be translated as 123123123. In other words, only the first nine digits will be translated since the field width in dBASE is nine characters.

Interestingly, if a field name is too long to be displayed in the 1-2-3 worksheet, it will not be truncated. As long as the field name is within dBASE's ten-character limit, it will be transferred correctly, even if part of the name cannot be displayed in the 1-2-3 worksheet.

An Example

To demonstrate how 1-2-3-to-dBASE file translation works, let's consider an example. In this example, we will translate a 1-2-3 Release 2, 2.01, or 2.2 worksheet into a dBASE III file. However, the procedure we will describe works the same for translating a 1-2-3 worksheet to dBASE II format.

Figure A1-8 shows a sample worksheet named PAYROLL that we have created in 1-2-3. This worksheet contains a small data base with five fields. The first field, WeekEnding, contains serial date values formatted in the Date1 format. We have widened column A to 10 characters in order to display this format. The second field, Name, contains label entries. The next field, Rate, contains numbers that we have formatted to display in Currency format with three decimal places. The fourth field, Hours, contains numbers in the General format. Notice that some entries in this field have digits to the right of the decimal point and some entries are whole numbers. The last field in the data base, Gross, contains formulas that compute each employee's gross pay based on the hourly rate and the number of hours worked. For example, the formula in cell E2 is *+D2*C2*.

```
E2: (C2) +D2*C2                                              READY

       A          B        C        D       E        F     G
 1  WeekEnding  Name     Rate     Hours   Gross
 2  08-Feb-87   Clark    $5.450      40   $218.00
 3  08-Feb-87   Fraser   $6.850    42.5   $291.13
 4  08-Feb-87   Logan    $4.275      40   $171.00
 5  08-Feb-87   Powell   $7.300      39   $284.70
 6  08-Feb-87   Sayers   $4.150   40.75   $169.11
 7  15-Feb-87   Clark    $5.450      41   $223.45
 8  15-Feb-87   Fraser   $6.850      40   $274.00
 9  15-Feb-87   Logan    $4.275      41   $175.28
10  15-Feb-87   Powell   $7.300      42   $306.60
11  15-Feb-87   Sayers   $4.150      40   $166.00
12
13
```

FIGURE A1-8: A sample worksheet containing a data base

We have purposely designed this worksheet to be in a form that can be translated to dBASE—there are no entries other than those in the data base itself, and the worksheet does not contain any blank formatted cells. However, we have assigned the name DATA to the range A1..E11 so that we can demonstrate how to translate a named range. Notice that the range named DATA includes both the field names in row 1 and the data records in rows 2 through 11.

To translate this worksheet into dBASE III format, begin by loading the Translate program. At the first screen, choose *1-2-3 2, 2.01 and 2.2* as the type of file to translate from. Then choose *dBase III* as the type of file to translate to. Next, follow the standard file translation steps that we described at the beginning of this appendix. After you specify a target file name, you will see a menu on the screen with two choices, *Worksheet* and *Range*. If you want to translate the entire worksheet, choose the Worksheet option. However, since the data base in this worksheet has been assigned the range name DATA, you also could choose the Range option. If you select Range, the Translate program will then ask you to enter the range name. Just type DATA and press [Enter].

Once the translation is complete, you can exit from the Translate program, load dBASE III, and view the newly translated PAYROLL.DBF file. Figure A1-9 shows the records in this file, while Figure A1-10 displays the file structure. The results shown in these figures are the same, whether you translate the entire worksheet or just the range named DATA.

There are several things that are worth pointing out about this data base. First, the Translate program has used the field names from the 1-2-3 data base as the field names in the dBASE data base. In addition, the widths of the fields in the dBASE data base match the widths of the columns in the 1-2-3 worksheet.

Also notice that the Translate program has correctly translated the first field from the 1-2-3 data base, WEEKENDING, into a dBASE III Date field. This translation occurred because the entry in cell A2 in the 1-2-3 worksheet was a formatted date value.

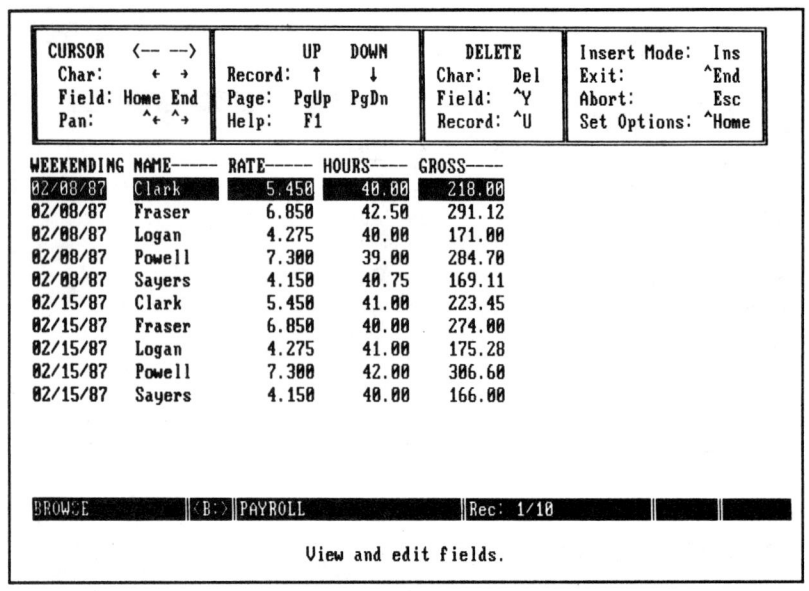

```
        CURSOR    <-- -->       UP    DOWN      DELETE       Insert Mode:  Ins
        Char:      ←  →    Record:  ↑    ↓      Char:  Del   Exit:         ^End
        Field: Home End    Page:  PgUp PgDn     Field: ^Y    Abort:        Esc
        Pan:     ^← ^→     Help:   F1           Record: ^U   Set Options:  ^Home

        WEEKENDING  NAME-----  RATE-----  HOURS----  GROSS----
        02/08/87    Clark       5.450      40.00     218.00
        02/08/87    Fraser      6.850      42.50     291.12
        02/08/87    Logan       4.275      40.00     171.00
        02/08/87    Powell      7.300      39.00     284.70
        02/08/87    Sayers      4.150      40.75     169.11
        02/15/87    Clark       5.450      41.00     223.45
        02/15/87    Fraser      6.850      40.00     274.00
        02/15/87    Logan       4.275      41.00     175.28
        02/15/87    Powell      7.300      42.00     306.60
        02/15/87    Sayers      4.150      40.00     166.00




        BROWSE         <B:> PAYROLL             Rec: 1/10
                           View and edit fields.
```

FIGURE A1-9: Sample data base after conversion to dBASE III

```
    Structure for database: B:PAYROLL.dbf
    Number of data records:      10
    Date of last update    : 09/18/86
    Field  Field Name  Type         Width    Dec
        1  WEEKENDING  Date           10
        2  NAME        Character       9
        3  RATE        Numeric         9      3
        4  HOURS       Numeric         9      2
        5  GROSS       Numeric         9      2
    ** Total **                       47
```

FIGURE A1-10: Structure of the sample data base

As you can see, none of the Numeric fields in the dBASE data base have a format. For example, the entries in the Rate and Gross fields are not formatted as currency in dBASE although they were in the Currency format in 1-2-3. Notice, however, that the entries in the Rate field display three decimal places, just like the formatted values in the Rate field in 1-2-3. In addition, notice that the entries in the Hours field all have two decimal places. These values were not formatted in the 1-2-3 worksheet.

Finally, realize that the entries in the Gross field in the dBASE data base are pure values and not formulas. For example, the entry in the first record of the Gross field is 218.00, not a formula like *Rate*Hours*.

WORKING WITH ASCII TEXT FILES

Most of the business software that runs on the IBM PC (and compatibles) can read and write ASCII text files. An ASCII text file is a special kind of file that contains only the characters you can type from the keyboard of your computer: letters, numbers, punctuation marks, and so on. In general, ACSII text files include only those characters with ASCII codes 9 (Tab), 10 (Linefeed), 13, (Carriage Return), and codes 32 to 127. Because most programs can read and write ASCII text files, these files serve as a kind of "least common denominator" for transferring data from one program to another.

Some programs regularly save data into ASCII text files. For example, the files created by many popular word processors, including Microsoft Word and WordStar, are ASCII text files. In addition, if you use a communications program, such as CrossTalk, to capture information from an on-line data service, that information will usually be stored as an ASCII file. Even programs that do not normally save data into ASCII text files offer commands that allow them to read and write ASCII text files. For example, dBASE II and III both have the ability to write data into ASCII text files and to read data from these files.

The worksheet files that 1-2-3 creates when you issue the / File Save command are not ASCII text files. Since 1-2-3 does not use the ASCII format, you cannot load a standard 1-2-3 worksheet file into a word-processing program or another program that uses the ASCII file format. Also, you can't retrieve an ASCII file into 1-2-3 as you would a normal worksheet file. However, 1-2-3 offers a couple of commands that let you exchange data with programs that read and write ASCII files. The / Print File command saves a worksheet in ASCII format, and the / File Import command allows you to import an ASCII file into 1-2-3. In this section, we will explain what happens when you use each of these commands.

Creating ASCII Files in 1-2-3

The / Print File command allows you to write a worksheet or a portion of a worksheet into an ASCII text file. You can use this command to create ASCII text files that can be used by word processors and other programs that read text files. When you do this, each row in the worksheet or range will be saved as a line of text in the ASCII file. In this format, the value entries of the worksheet will no longer be true numbers that can be operated on mathematically. Instead, they will be stored simply as strings of numeric characters. Similarly, formulas and functions will not be stored in the ASCII file—only the numbers that result from these calculations.

An Example

Let's consider a simple example of the / Print File command. Suppose you want to convert the worksheet shown in Figure A1-11 into ASCII format so that you can incorporate it into a word-processing document. To begin, issue the / Print File command. 1-2-3 will then ask you to supply the name of the file in which you want to save the ASCII version of your worksheet. You respond by typing a file name and pressing [Enter]. Unless you type an extension to the file name, 1-2-3 will automatically save the file with the extension .PRN. If you want to save the file with a different extension, you can do so by entering that extension as you type the file name. For our example, enter the name PETS and press [Enter].

```
A4:                                                              READY

           A           B        C        D        E        F        G
 1   POLLY'S PET STORE
 2   SALES BY CATEGORY
 3   ==========================================================
 4                   Qtr. 1   Qtr. 2   Qtr. 3   Qtr. 4    Total  Percent
 5                   ------   ------   ------   ------   ------  -------
 6   Puppies         $1,800   $2,400   $2,100   $1,950   $8,250   41.04%
 7   Kittens         $1,200   $1,950   $1,800   $1,350   $6,300   31.34%
 8   Birds             $450     $450   $1,050     $900   $2,850   14.18%
 9   Fish              $300     $600     $750   $1,050   $2,700   13.43%
10                   ------   ------   ------   ------   ------
11                   $3,750   $5,400   $5,700   $5,250  $20,100
12
13
14
15
16
17
18
19
20
```

FIGURE A1-11: A sample worksheet in 1-2-3

As soon as you do this, your disk drive will whir for a second as 1-2-3 opens the file on your disk. At this point, 1-2-3 is writing the file name, PETS.PRN, to disk and reserving a place to store the ASCII version of your worksheet.

After you have specified the name of the file in which you want to print your worksheet, 1-2-3 will display the same menu you see when you issue the /Print Printer command. All the options on this menu work exactly as they do when you are printing to a printer. We won't discuss each of these options in detail since they are covered thoroughly in Chapter 8.

After you supply a file name, the next step is to choose the Range option from the Print File menu and then specify the Print range—the cell entries that you want to include in the ASCII file. You mark this range just as you would mark any other range in 1-2-3: either by highlighting cells or by typing the coordinates of the range and pressing [Enter]. For our example, you should highlight cells A1..G11 and press [Enter].

> **TIP: MARKING THE PRINT RANGE**
>
> As we explained in Chapter 2, when you enter a long label into the 1-2-3 worksheet, 1-2-3 will allow that label to overlap into the adjacent cells of the worksheet. The label is contained in only one cell, but appears to span two, three, or more cells in the worksheet.
>
> When you are printing to disk, the Print range you select should include any cells that long labels overlap into. For example, if cell G1 of the sample worksheet contained a long label that spilled over into column H, then you would need to include column H in the Print range. If you did not, then 1-2-3 would truncate that label at the right edge of column G.

Specifying the Print Settings

If you choose Options from the Print File menu, 1-2-3 will display the same Options menu that you see when you issue the / Print Printer Options command. With one exception, all of the options on the Print File Options menu work exactly as they do when you are printing to a printer. (The exception is the Setup option, which has no effect when you print to a file.) Of course, when you choose File instead of Printer as the destination for your printing, the information you print, including any special formatting options, ends up "printed" on disk instead of on paper.

When you are printing to an ASCII text file, you probably will not want to use most of the Print options. For example, you can create a header and footer for your worksheet, but then these will be printed on each "page" of the ASCII file. When you load that file into another program, you'll see the header and footer text on your screen. (Normally, headers and footers appear only on printed reports and not on your screen.)

In most cases, you'll probably want your ASCII files to contain just the entries from your worksheet and no extraneous text or formatting features. Therefore, we will describe the settings that we think work best for printing a worksheet to disk as an ASCII file.

Use the Unformatted Option

First of all, we recommend that you use the Unformatted option when you print to a file. This option suppresses any headers or footers, as well as top and bottom margins and the breaks between "pages." If you do not use the Unformatted option, 1-2-3 will insert extra blank lines at the beginning of the ASCII file and between each "page" in the file. To specify the Unformatted option, choose Options Other Unformatted from the Print File menu.

Margins

We also recommend that you set the left margin to 0 when you print to a file. If you do not set the left margin to 0, 1-2-3 will insert a few blank spaces at the beginning of each line in the file. To do this, choose Options Margins Left, type a 0, and press [Enter].

The proper setting for the right margin depends on how you plan to use the file. In most cases, however, you'll want to set the right margin to 240—the maximum allowed by 1-2-3. You can do this in any release of 1-2-3 by issuing the /Print File Margins Right command, typing 240, and pressing [Enter]. ▶In 1-2-3 Release 2.2, you can use the /Print File Options Margins None command to set the left margin to 0 and the right margin to 240 all in one step. In addition to adjusting the left and right margins, this command sets the top and bottom margins to 0. However, the top and bottom margin settings don't matter if you've selected the Unformatted option.◀

In our current example, the Right Margin setting is not critical since we have only seven columns of data. Therefore, we will use 1-2-3's default right margin of 76. If you want to use a different right margin, choose Options Margins Right, enter the setting you wish to use, and press [Enter].

RELEASE ▶ 2.2 ◀

Printing to Disk

After you have selected a range and specified all the settings you wish to use, you are ready to print to disk. To do this, choose Quit from the Options menu, then choose Go from the main Print File menu. (You do not need to choose Align since 1-2-3 will automatically start printing your worksheet at the top of a new file.) After you choose Go, your disk drive will whir for a few seconds as 1-2-3 begins to write the worksheet to disk in ASCII form. However, DOS will store all or part of the file in a disk buffer, so the file on disk will not be complete. (In fact, if the range you have selected is fairly small, it may be stored entirely in the buffer at this point, and you won't hear your disk drive whir at all.) In order to complete the print-to-file procedure, you must choose Quit from the Print File menu. This empties the information in the buffer to disk and closes the ASCII file by writing an end-of-file character in the file.

Using a .PRN File in Another Program

Once you have used the /Print File command to create an ASCII text file, you can load that file into any program that reads the ASCII file format. When you do, you'll see that the worksheet looks virtually the same as it does in 1-2-3. For example, Figure A1-12 shows our example file PETS.PRN after it has been loaded into Microsoft Word.

As you can see, the formats we assigned to the numbers in 1-2-3 appear on the word-processing screen, and the spacing between the columns is consistent with our original worksheet. Of course, since Word is not a spreadsheet program, you cannot mathematically manipulate the numbers in it the way you can in 1-2-3. However, you can edit any character in the worksheet just as you would edit text in a file that you created in Word. For example, you can delete characters and spaces, insert new characters and spaces, and delete and insert words and lines.

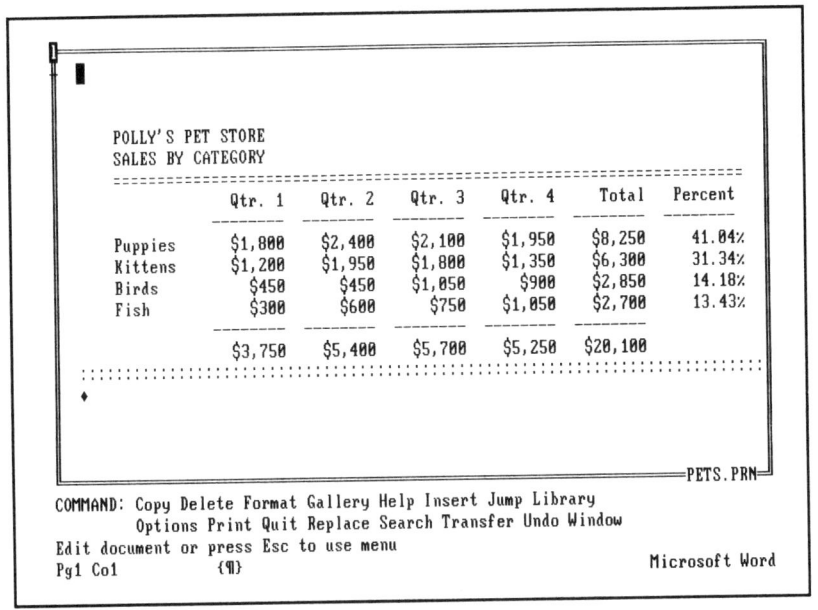

```
POLLY'S PET STORE
SALES BY CATEGORY
=================================================================
            Qtr. 1    Qtr. 2    Qtr. 3    Qtr. 4     Total   Percent
           --------  --------  --------  --------  --------
Puppies    $1,800    $2,400    $2,100    $1,950    $8,250    41.04%
Kittens    $1,200    $1,950    $1,800    $1,350    $6,300    31.34%
Birds        $450      $450    $1,050      $900    $2,850    14.18%
Fish         $300      $600      $750    $1,050    $2,700    13.43%
           --------  --------  --------  --------  --------
           $3,750    $5,400    $5,700    $5,250   $20,100
```

FIGURE A1-12: A .PRN file loaded into Microsoft Word

TIP: PRINTING MORE THAN ONE COPY

The procedure that we have described so far will write only one copy of the range you select into an ASCII file. However, you can create an ASCII file that contains multiple copies of your worksheet. To do this, just choose Go from the Print File menu before you choose Quit. Each time you select Go, another copy of your selected range will be written to the file. Each new copy will be appended to whatever information is already in the file.

If you would like to insert a few blank lines between copies, you can choose the Line command before you select Go the second time. Each time you choose Line, 1-2-3 will insert another blank line into the file. You can also use the Page command, which will cause 1-2-3 to skip to the top of a new "page" in the file before it prints the next copy of your worksheet.

When you use this technique, you do not have to print the same range each time. If you want, you can select a new range before you choose Go the second time. You also can change the Print options before you choose Go. As long as you make all these changes before you choose Quit, each of your selected ranges will be printed in the same ASCII file. When you choose Quit from the Print File menu, 1-2-3 closes the ASCII file it has created and will no longer append new information to that file.

Importing ASCII Text Files into 1-2-3

There may be times when you want to import data that is stored on disk in ASCII format into 1-2-3. For example, when you a communications programs to capture information from an on-line data service or mainframe computer into a disk file, that file will be in ASCII format. Also, if you create a table of data using your word-processing program, that table will probably be stored in an ASCII text file. If you want to use that data in 1-2-3, you'll need to import it into your worksheet.

The / File Import command allows you to bring ASCII text files into 1-2-3. When you issue the / File Import command, you'll see a menu with two options: Text and Numbers. If you choose Text, 1-2-3 will import the file you select as a series of long labels. Each line in the file will be one label that is stored *entirely* within the column where the cell pointer is located when you issue the / File Import command. The Numbers option, on the other hand, will divide the characters in the text file into values and labels. Any numbers in the file will be imported as values. Any text that is enclosed in quotation marks will be imported as labels. Any text that is not enclosed in quotation marks will not be imported. When you choose the Numbers option, 1-2-3 will automatically divide the data into different columns and will enter each number from the file into a separate cell as a value.

After you choose Text or Numbers, 1-2-3 will display the prompt *Enter name of file to import:*, followed by the name of the current directory and the file descriptor **.prn*. This descriptor causes 1-2-3 to display a list of the files on the current directory with the file-name extension .PRN. If the file you want to import has the extension .PRN, you can choose its name from the list. If not, you can either type the full file name and press [Enter] , or modify the descriptor to bring up a list of files that includes the file you want to import. You can also import a file that is stored on another directory. (Chapter 9 contains more information about file names, descriptors, and changing directories.)

No matter which option you choose—Text or Numbers—the / File Import command brings the ASCII file into your current worksheet at the current location of the cell pointer. To keep the data in the ASCII file from overwriting entries in your current worksheet, you should be sure that there is plenty of blank space below and to the right of the cell pointer before you issue the / File Import command.

Since the Text and Numbers options yield radically different results when you import a file, we will discuss them separately. As you'll see, there are advantages and disadvantages to each option, and the option you choose will depend upon the contents of the file you are importing.

The Numbers Option

The / File Import Numbers command allows you to import so-called *delimited* ASCII text files into 1-2-3. When you use this option to import a file, all of the numbers in the file will be entered as values in the 1-2-3 worksheet. Any text in the file that is enclosed in quotation marks will be imported as labels. Any text that is not enclosed in quotation marks will not be imported. The Numbers option is useful in cases where the ASCII file you want to import contains mostly unformatted numbers, or in cases where the text in the file is delimited by quotation marks and separated by commas or tabs.

An Example

For example, suppose you would like to import the file NAMES.PRN, which is shown in Figure A1-13. This file is an example of a delimited file. Notice that all of the text in the file (except for the last word on each line) is enclosed in quotation marks. Notice also that commas to separate the information on each line.

```
A:\>type names.prn
"Don Schroeder","123 Any St","Louisville","KY","40205",97000,Partner
"Kristy Callahan","999 Main St","Anchorage","NY","10987",76300,President
"Mike Mize","444 Elm Ln","San Francisco","CA","43125",56000,VP Finance

A:\>
```

FIGURE A1-13: A delimited file

Let's assume that you will be importing this file into a completely blank worksheet. To begin, move the cell pointer to cell A1 and issue the / File Import Numbers command. 1-2-3 will then display a list of all files in the current directory that have .PRN as the file-name extension. You can select a file by pointing to or typing its name and pressing [Enter]. If the file you want to import has a different extension, you can either type its full name and press [Enter], or you can modify the descriptor to bring up a new list and select the file from that list. For this example, you would select the file NAMES.PRN and press [Enter].

1-2-3 will immediately load the file into your worksheet. Figure A1-14 shows the result (we've widened the columns in this worksheet as necessary so that all of the imported data are visible). As you can see, all of the text from the file NAMES.PRN that was enclosed in quotation marks has been imported into the worksheet as labels. For example, cell A1 contains the label 'Don Schroeder and cell B2 contains the label '999 Main St.

```
A1: [W17] 'Don Schroeder                                    READY

         A              B           C            D    E      F         G
1   Don Schroeder   123 Any St   Louisville    KY  40205   97000
2   Kristy Callahan 999 Main St  Anchorage     NY  10987   76300
3   Mike Mize       444 Elm Ln   San Francisco CA  43125   56000
4
5
```

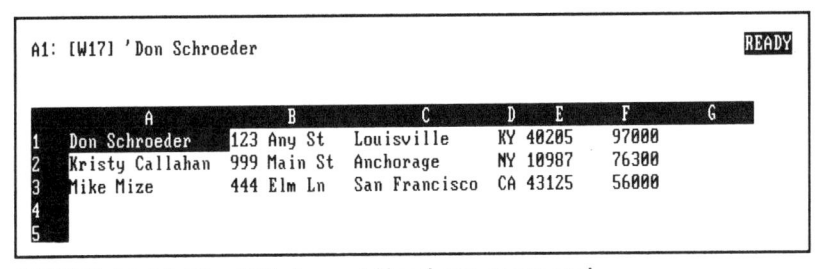

FIGURE A1-14: The / File Import Numbers command

Next, notice that column F in Figure A1-14 contains the numbers 97000, 76300, and 56000. The Numbers option always imports the numbers it finds in the text file as values. However, you'll notice in column E that the "zip codes" from the file, which were enclosed in quotation marks, have been imported as labels. The / File Import

Numbers command always treats any characters it finds enclosed in quotation marks as text.

Finally, notice that 1-2-3 has not imported the last word from each line of the text file. This occurred because these text characters were not enclosed in quotation marks. When you choose the Numbers option, 1-2-3 will not import any text that is not enclosed in quotation marks. For this same reason, 1-2-3 did not import the commas that we used to separate the "fields" in the text file.

A Note

The numbers in the file you want to import should not be formatted in any way—no dollar signs, commas, or any other formatting symbols. If the numbers are formatted, 1-2-3 may divide them into several values as it imports the file. For example, suppose that the number on the first line of the file NAMES.PRN was formatted like this: $97,000. When 1-2-3 imported the file, it would have ignored the dollar sign and imported the number 97,000 as two values: 97 and 0.

There are a couple of exceptions to this rule. First, if the numbers in the file contain decimal points, 1-2-3 will recognize and import those decimal points. For example, if the number in the first line of the file NAMES.PRN had been 97000.99, then 1-2-3 would have imported it as the value 97000.99.

Second, 1-2-3 apparently recognizes the percent sign when it imports numbers. For example, if the number in the first line of the file NAMES.PRN had been 97.99%, 1-2-3 would have imported that number as the value 0.9799.

The Text Option

The / File Import Text command imports the data from a text file as a series of long labels. The Text option imports all of the characters from the text file. However, it does not import the numbers from the text file as values. The Text option allows you to import ASCII files that are not in delimited form. For example, you might use this option to import a text file that results from a communication session, or to import text from a word-processing document.

For example, Figure A1-15 shows a simple sales log. Let's suppose that we've just downloaded this data from your company's mainframe computer and that it is saved in a file named LOG.DTA. Let's see what happens when you import this file into 1-2-3.

We'll assume that you will be importing this file into a completely blank worksheet. With the cell pointer on cell A1, issue the / File Import Text command. When you see the prompt *Enter name of file to import:*, type the name LOG.DTA and press [Enter]. Figure A1-16 shows the result of this command.

At first glance, this worksheet looks pretty much like any other 1-2-3 worksheet. However, if you move the cell pointer around, you'll see that only column A in this worksheet contains entries, and each of these entries is a long label. For example, cell A2 contains the label

'R. Baird $45.50 $2.5025 $48.00 4/13/87 10:15 AM

```
A>type b:log.dta
Name           Amount      Sales Tax    Total     Date      Time
R. Baird       $45.50      $2.5025      $48.00    4/13/87   10:15 AM
C. Reeves      $9.67       $0.5318      $10.20    4/13/87   10:34 AM
D. Ford        $125.00     $6.8750      $131.88   4/13/87   11:02 AM
R. Sommers     $25.09      $1.3799      $26.47    4/13/87   2:35 PM
P. Finch       $18.95      $1.0423      $19.99    4/13/87   3:20 PM
S. Roberts     $67.75      $3.7263      $71.48    4/13/87   4:20 PM
A. Bennetto    $55.20      $3.0360      $58.24    4/13/87   4:30 PM
               -------     -------      -------
               $347.16     $19.0938     $366.26
A>
```

FIGURE A1-15: An example ASCII text file

```
A2: 'R. Baird      $45.50    $2.5025     $48.00    4/13/87   10:15 AM         READY

          A            B          C           D         E         F        G        H
   1  Name          Amount     Sales Tax   Total     Date      Time
   2  R. Baird      $45.50     $2.5025     $48.00    4/13/87   10:15 AM
   3  C. Reeves     $9.67      $0.5318     $10.20    4/13/87   10:34 AM
   4  D. Ford       $125.00    $6.8750     $131.88   4/13/87   11:02 AM
   5  R. Sommers    $25.09     $1.3799     $26.47    4/13/87   2:35 PM
   6  P. Finch      $18.95     $1.0423     $19.99    4/13/87   3:20 PM
   7  S. Roberts    $67.75     $3.7263     $71.48    4/13/87   4:20 PM
   8  A. Bennetto   $55.20     $3.0360     $58.24    4/13/87   4:30 PM
   9                -------    -------     -------
  10                $347.16    $19.0938    $366.26
  11
```

FIGURE A1-16: Sales log imported into 1-2-3

Since all of the entries in this worksheet are long labels, there is no way to use the numeric data in the worksheet or to perform queries on the data. If you want to change this worksheet from a set of labels into a "true" worksheet containing label and value entries in individual cells, you must parse the long label entries. In other words, you must break each long label into its components.

Parsing Data

The / Data Parse command allows you to parse long labels into separate value and label entries. When you issue this command, you will see the menu ▶(and, if you are using 1-2-3 Release 2.2, the settings sheet) shown in Figure A1-17.◀

RELEASE
▶ 2.2 ◀

There are basically four steps to parsing long labels in 1-2-3. First, you must use the / Data Parse Format-Lines Create command to create one or more format lines. These lines contain special symbols that tell 1-2-3 where to break apart the long labels you are parsing and what type of entries are contained in each section of the divided label. The second step is to edit the format line to make sure that it works correctly. (In some cases, you'll be able to skip this step.) Third, you must use the / Data Parse Input-Column and Output-Range commands to tell 1-2-3 what you want to parse and where you want it to put the parsed data. Once the format lines are in place and the ranges have been defined, the last step is to choose Go to parse the labels.

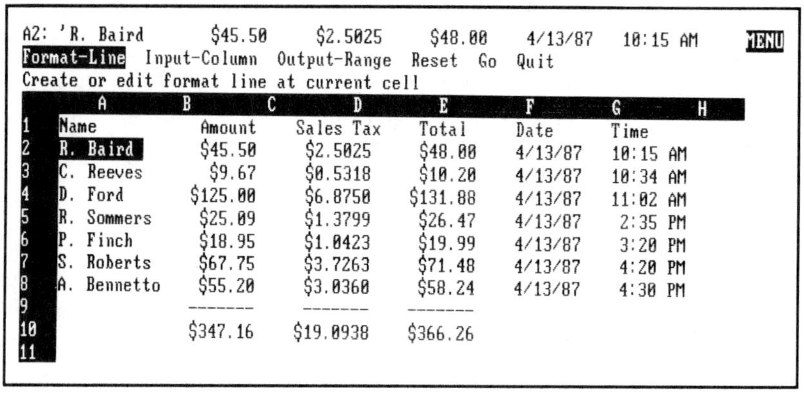

```
A2: 'R. Baird        $45.50      $2.5025      $48.00    4/13/87   10:15 AM    MENU
Format-Line Input-Column Output-Range Reset  Go  Quit
Create or edit format line at current cell
         A              B            C           D         E         F         G         H
   1  Name            Amount      Sales Tax    Total     Date      Time
   2  R. Baird        $45.50      $2.5025      $48.00    4/13/87   10:15 AM
   3  C. Reeves        $9.67      $0.5318      $10.20    4/13/87   10:34 AM
   4  D. Ford        $125.00      $6.8750     $131.88    4/13/87   11:02 AM
   5  R. Sommers      $25.09      $1.3799      $26.47    4/13/87    2:35 PM
   6  P. Finch        $18.95      $1.0423      $19.99    4/13/87    3:20 PM
   7  S. Roberts      $67.75      $3.7263      $71.48    4/13/87    4:20 PM
   8  A. Bennetto     $55.20      $3.0360      $58.24    4/13/87    4:30 PM
   9                 --------    --------     --------
  10                 $347.16     $19.0938     $366.26
  11
```

FIGURE A1-17: The / Data Parse menu

An Example

Let's use the /Data Parse command to parse the labels in Figure A1-16. In the example, row 1 contains the labels *Name, Amount,* and so forth. Rows 2 through 8 contain values, row 9 contains dashed underlines, and row 10 contains more values. Because of the different types of entries in the range we are parsing, we will need to create two format lines. The first format line will appear just above the labels in row 1, and the second format line will be placed just above the values in row 2.

Creating the Format Line

To begin, move the cell pointer to cell A1 (it's important that the cell pointer be positioned on the cell that contains the label you will be parsing.) Then issue the /Data Parse Format-Line Create command. 1-2-3 will immediately insert a new row above row 1 (the label in row 1 will now be in row 2) and place a format line in that row. Next, choose Quit to exit from the Data Parse menu. Then move the cell pointer to row 3, issue the /Data Parse Format-Line Create command again, and choose Quit. Figure A1-18 shows the worksheet at this point.

Notice that each of these format lines is divided into sections or blocks. When you created each of these format lines, 1-2-3 guessed about where it should break the long labels and about what type of entry appears in each section of the labels. The symbols in the format lines indicate how 1-2-3 thinks it should divide the long labels. For example, 1-2-3 will group the characters that fall below the symbol L>>>>>> into seven-character-long labels. (The L stands for the first character, and each > stands for a single character.) Similarly, 1-2-3 will group the characters that fall below the symbol V>>>>> into values with six digits.

Each *L* in the format line indicates the beginning of a label block. Each *V* indicates the start of a value block, each *D* indicates a date block, and each *T* indicates a time block. The >>>> that follow each letter indicate the length of the different sections or blocks of the format line. The **** symbols in the format lines stand for blank spaces. Table A1-4 summarizes the different kinds of symbols that can be used in format lines.

```
A3: !L)*L)>>>>*******U)>>>>>*****U)>>>>>*****U)>>>>>****D)>>>>>>***T)>>>*L>                READY

        A         B          C          D         E         F          G         H
1  L)>>>************L)>>>>****L)>>>>*L)>****L)>>>*****L)>>>******L)>>>
2  Name          Amount    Sales Tax    Total     Date      Time
3  L>*L)>>>*******U)>>>>>*****U)>>>>>*****U)>>>>*****D)>>>>>***T)>>>*L>
4  R. Baird      $45.50    $2.5025     $48.00    4/13/87   10:15 AM
5  C. Reeves     $9.67     $0.5318     $10.20    4/13/87   10:34 AM
6  D. Ford       $125.00   $6.8750     $131.88   4/13/87   11:02 AM
7  R. Sommers    $25.09    $1.3799     $26.47    4/13/87   2:35 PM
8  P. Finch      $18.95    $1.0423     $19.99    4/13/87   3:20 PM
9  S. Roberts    $67.75    $3.7263     $71.48    4/13/87   4:20 PM
10 A. Bennetto   $55.20    $3.0360     $58.24    4/13/87   4:30 PM
11               -------   --------    --------
12               $347.16   $19.0938    $366.26
13
```

FIGURE A1-18: Sales log in 1-2-3 with format lines added

Symbol	Meaning
L	Beginning of label block
V	Beginning of value block
D	Beginning of date block
T	Beginning of time block
S	Beginning of skip block
>	1 character in block
*	Blank space between blocks

TABLE A1-4: Format line symbols

Besides *L, V, D, T, >* and *, there is one more symbol that 1-2-3 allows in format lines: *S*. An *S* in a format line stands for *skip*. It tells 1-2-3 to eliminate some characters in the long label when performing the parse. This symbol will not be included in the format lines that initially appear on your screen.

1-2-3 stores each format line as a long label in the same column that contains the labels you plan to parse. For example, the format line in row 1 is stored in cell A1, and the line in row 3 is stored in cell A3.

Format-line Problems

If you examine the format lines in Figure A1-18, you will see that 1-2-3 has done a pretty good job of guessing how it should break up each long label. For example, 1-2-3 has guessed correctly that the characters in row 2 should be parsed into a series of labels. In addition, 1-2-3 has guessed correctly that the second, third, and fourth columns of data in rows 4 through 12 should be parsed as values, that the fifth column of data should be parsed as dates, and that the sixth column should be parsed as times. In general, 1-2-3 will do a good job of figuring out how the data in an imported text file should be parsed.

However, there typically will be one or two problems with the format lines that 1-2-3 creates. For example, notice that in the second format line, 1-2-3 has divided the Name column into two separate label blocks. Second, although 1-2-3 has correctly guessed that the last column of information contains time data, notice how the AM/PM portion of the times are assumed to be labels, rather than part of the time data. Third, notice that 1-2-3 has divided the Sales Tax column in the first format line into two label blocks. These problems occurred because of the spaces between the first and second parts of the entries in these columns. This kind of problem can also arise if there are "mixed" character strings like *Qtr 1* or *123 Any Street* in the long labels. You'll need to correct these problems before you parse the data. To correct this kind of error, you must edit the format line.

Editing the Format Lines

To edit a format line, first place the cell pointer on the cell in which the format line is stored, then issue the / Data Parse Format-Line Edit command. The format line will appear highlighted on your screen with a small blinking cursor just below the first character of the line. You can use the → and ← keys to move this cursor to any position on the format line. [Home] will move the cursor to the beginning of the line, and [End] will move it to the end of the format line. Pressing [Ctrl]] → will move the cursor five characters to the right, while [Ctrl]|← will move it five characters to the left. If you need to view more rows of the labels you plan to parse, you can press the ↓ or [Pg Dn] key, which will scroll additional rows onto your screen. The ↑ and [Pg Up] keys will scroll the rows back down.

To change the format line, you can insert new characters or edit the existing characters. When you first begin editing a format line, you'll be in the Overwrite mode—in other words, any character you type will write over existing characters in the format line. However, by pressing the [Ins] key, you can toggle between the Insert and Overwrite modes. Any new characters that you type must be legitimate format-line characters. 1-2-3 will not accept any characters other than those listed in Table A1-5. To erase characters in the format line, use the [Backspace] and [Del] keys. If you want to delete the entire format line, just press [Esc].

In the example, you need to edit the second format line to create only one eight-character label block for the Name column. To do this, place the cell pointer on cell A3 and issue the / Data Parse Format-Line Edit command. Then press → to move the cursor to the first * in the format line and type >> to replace the characters *L with two character markers (>>).

Next, you need to let 1-2-3 know that the AM/PM portion of the times in the Time column are part of the time data. To do this, move the cursor to the last * in the second format line and type >>> to replace the characters *L> with the characters >>>. After you have made these changes, press [Enter] to lock them in and choose Quit to exit from the Data Parse menu.

Before parsing the data, you need to make one minor change to the top format line as well. Move the cell pointer to cell A1 and issue the / Data Parse Format-Line Edit command. Then edit the block over the words *Sales Tax* to be a single nine-character-long label block (*L>>>>>>>>*). Again, press [Enter] to lock in the change, and choose Quit to exit from the Data Parse menu. At this point, your worksheet should look like Figure A1-19.

```
A1:  |L>>>***********L>>>>>****L>>>>>>>>****L>>>>*****L>>>******L>>>                    READY


              A          B          C          D          E          F        G         H
 1     L>>>*****|******L>>>>>****L>>>>>>>>****L>>>>*****L>>>******L>>>
 2     Name        Amount     Sales Tax  Total      Date       Time
 3     L>>>>>>>*******U>>>>>*****U>>>>>>*****U>>>>>****D>>>>>>***T>>>>>>>
 4     R. Baird    $45.50     $2.5025    $48.00     4/13/87    10:15 AM
 5     C. Reeves   $9.67      $0.5318    $10.20     4/13/87    10:34 AM
 6     D. Ford     $125.00    $6.8750    $131.88    4/13/87    11:02 AM
 7     R. Sommers  $25.09     $1.3799    $26.47     4/13/87     2:35 PM
 8     P. Finch    $18.95     $1.0423    $19.99     4/13/87     3:20 PM
 9     S. Roberts  $67.75     $3.7263    $71.48     4/13/87     4:20 PM
10     A. Bennetto $55.20     $3.0360    $58.24     4/13/87     4:30 PM
11                 ------     -------    -------
12                 $347.16    $19.0938   $366.26
13
```

FIGURE A1-19: Worksheet with edited format lines

Adding a Skip Block

Skip blocks let you instruct 1-2-3 to ignore the data in certain columns when you parse long labels. Skip blocks are marked with the symbol *S*. Although 1-2-3 will never include a skip block in the format lines it creates, you can edit those lines to add skip blocks.

For example, suppose you want to leave off the last two digits in each number in the Sales Tax block when you parse these labels. You can do this by using a skip block. First, move the cell pointer back to cell A3 and issue the / Data Parse Format-Line Edit command. Then move the cursor to the right and change the block marker for the Sales Tax column from *V>>>>>>* to *V>>>>S>*. When you are finished making the change, press [Enter] to lock in the change, then choose Quit to exit from the Data Parse menu. At this point, your worksheet should look like Figure A1-20. The segment *V>>>>S>* tells 1-2-3 that the third column of data should be parsed into a five-character value block, and that any characters beyond the first five should be skipped.

You may wonder why we did not simply change the last two characters in this block to ** so that the block looked like this: *V>>>>***. In fact, changing the format line in this way would have no effect on the result of the parse. It does not matter if the block size in the format line is shorter than some of the entries in the labels below. 1-2-3 will still parse the longer entries correctly, as long as there are enough blank spaces (as indicated by the * characters) before the next block begins.

```
A3: |L>>>>>>********U>>>>*****U>>>S>*****U>>>>****D>>>>>>***T>>>>>>                    READY

         A          B         C           D         E           F           G         H
 1   L>>>***********L>>>>****L>>>>>>>****L>>>>*****L>>>******L>>>
 2   Name       Amount    Sales Tax   Total     Date        Time
 3   L>>>>>>>*****U>>>>*****U>>>S>*****U>>>>****D>>>>>>***T>>>>>>
 4   R. Baird   $45.50    $2.5025     $48.00    4/13/87     10:15 AM
 5   C. Reeves  $9.67     $0.5318     $10.20    4/13/87     10:34 AM
 6   D. Ford    $125.00   $6.8750     $131.88   4/13/87     11:02 AM
 7   R. Sommers $25.09    $1.3799     $26.47    4/13/87      2:35 PM
 8   P. Finch   $18.95    $1.0423     $19.99    4/13/87      3:20 PM
 9   S. Roberts $67.75    $3.7263     $71.48    4/13/87      4:20 PM
10   A. Bennetto $55.20   $3.0360     $58.24    4/13/87      4:30 PM
11              -------   -------     -------
12              $347.16   $19.0938    $366.26
13
```

FIGURE A1-20: A skip block

Parsing the Data

After you have edited your format line(s) to correctly represent the breaks in your long labels, you are ready to parse the data. To do this, you must use the / Data Parse Input-Column command to tell 1-2-3 which column contains the labels you want to parse. Then you use the Output-Range option on the Data Parse menu to tell 1-2-3 where to put the parsed entries. Once you have done these two things, you choose Go to parse the labels.

To parse the labels in the range A1..A12, choose Input-Column from the Data Parse menu and highlight the cells that contain the format line(s) and the long labels you will be parsing. In the example, you should select the range A1..A12 and press [Enter]. Next, select Output-Range from the Data Parse menu and select the range of cells where you want 1-2-3 to place the parsed data. You can either select the entire range or simply indicate the upper-left cell of the range. Just be sure that there are no entries below and to the right of the cell you indicate. If there are entries in those cells, they may be overwritten by the parsed data. In the example, specify cell A14 as the upper-left cell in the Output range and press [Enter].

Assuming that everything is okay, you are now ready to parse the labels. To do this, choose Go from the Data Parse menu. Figure A1-21 shows the result.

Notes

There are a few things you should notice about the parsed data that appears in Rows 14 through 23 in Figure A1-21. First, the entries in the range A14..F23 are now individual value and label entries, not just parts of long labels. For example, the entry in cell A15 is the label *R. Baird*, and the entry in cell D16 is the value *10.2*. As you can see, none of the numbers in the parsed range are formatted. When 1-2-3 parses long labels, it strips all non-numeric characters—including format symbols—out of value blocks.

In addition, the parsed data does not contain any formulas, only pure values. The entries in column D and in cells B23, C23, and D23 are all simple values. The Parse command does not have the power to deduce formulas from the values in the labels being parsed.

```
A14: 'Name                                                          READY

       A         B         C         D        E         F        G    H
14  Name      Amount   Sales Tax  Total    Date      Time
15  R. Baird    45.5      2.5        48    31880  0.427083
16  C. Reeves   9.67     0.53      10.2    31880  0.440277
17  D. Ford      125     6.87    131.88    31880  0.459722
18  R. Sommer  25.09     1.37     26.47    31880  0.607638
19  P. Finch   18.95     1.04     19.99    31880  0.638888
20  S. Robert  67.75     3.72     71.48    31880  0.680555
21  A. Bennet   55.2     3.03     58.24    31880   0.6875
22          -------   -----   -------
23            347.16    19.09    366.26
24
```

FIGURE A1-21: Parsed sales log data

Third, notice that we used only two format lines to parse this worksheet. We did not create a third format line to parse the series of dashed-line labels in row 13; we just included these labels under the V>>>>> block in the second format line. Here's why this works. 1-2-3 will attempt to convert the characters under a value block into values. If it encounters some characters that cannot be interpreted as a value, then 1-2-3 will simply convert those characters into a label—as it did with these dashed lines. For that reason, if there are entries under a value block that you want 1-2-3 to parse as labels, you don't need to do anything special.

Also note that the entries in column C contain only two decimal places, while the characters on which they are based in the long labels contain four decimal places. Because of the skip block you defined in the second format line, 1-2-3 did not parse the last two decimals in each of these entries.

Columns E and F in Figure A1-21 contain the parsed date and time information from the original sales log. When 1-2-3 parsed the date and time portions of the long labels, it converted these dates and times into their corresponding serial date or time values. As with other values, however, 1-2-3 did not format the parsed information. You will probably want to give these entries a format in order to make these entries more understandable.

Now that you have parsed the long labels, you probably will want to make a few changes to the parsed data. First, you'll probably want to format all the numeric entries and replace pure values with formulas where appropriate. Also, you may need to use the /Range Label command to change the alignment of some of the label entries in the range of parsed data. 1-2-3 always uses left alignment for labels in the Output range—even if your global default label alignment is right or center. Once you have completed these changes, you may want to copy the parsed data from rows 14 through 23 into the top of the worksheet (replacing the imported long labels) and then erase the Output range.

Parse Problems

There are a couple of things to watch out for when you use / Data Parse. First, there cannot be any spaces or alphabetic characters in the numbers in the value blocks of the labels you plan to parse. If there are spaces or letters mixed in with a number, 1-2-3 will parse the numbers as a label. For example, suppose the number in the second row of the Sales Tax column was *$ .5318* instead of *$0.5318*. Notice that there is a space between the dollar sign and the decimal point in this number. When you parse the label that contains this number, 1-2-3 will parse it as the label *'$ .53*.

The dates and times in the long labels that you plan to parse must be in one of 1-2-3's standard Date or Time formats. Otherwise, 1-2-3 will not be able to parse those dates and times into date and time values, but will instead parse them into labels. For example, suppose the entry in the sixth row of the Date column in the LOG.DTA file is 4-13-87 instead of 4/13/87. When you parse the label that contains this date, 1-2-3 will parse it as the label *'4-13-87*. For a complete list of 1-2-3's Date and Time formats, see Chapter 7.

OTHER KINDS OF DATA EXCHANGE

In addition to the kinds of data exchange that we have discussed in this appendix, you can use the Translate utility program to transfer VisiCalc, DIF, and SYLK files into 1-2-3. The procedure that you follow to execute these kinds of transfers is virtually identical to the standard procedure that we described at the beginning of this appendix.

CONCLUSION

If you are like most 1-2-3 users, you will never need to worry about exchanging data with other programs. However, for those occasions when you must tackle this job, the guidelines in this appendix—and 1-2-3's built-in capabilities—should help you perform the exchange quickly and easily.

Exchanging data between 1-2-3 and other programs is, at best, a less-than-perfect process. We have spent much of this appendix explaining the kinds of problems you might encounter when you perform data exchanges, and how you can get around those problems. Nevertheless, 1-2-3's tools for translating data—the Translate program, the / Print File command, the / File Import command, and the / Data Parse command—are relatively easy to use and do a pretty good job of what might otherwise be a difficult task.

Appendix 2

The [Compose] Key

In Chapter 5, you learned about the @CHAR function, which allows you to enter special characters like £, ¿, and ¢ into the 1-2-3 Release 2, 2.01, or 2.2 worksheet. In addition to this function, 1-2-3 Releases 2, 2.01, and 2.2 offer another tool that allows you to enter these special characters into the worksheet: the [Compose] key ([Alt][F1] on the IBM PC). (This key is not available in 1-2-3 Release 1A).

HOW COMPUTERS REPRESENT CHARACTERS

All computers use numeric codes to represent the numbers, letters, and symbols you see on the screen. Although different computers use different sets of codes, all personal computers use a system called ASCII, or American Standard Code for Information Interchange. The ASCII system uses a three-digit code to represent each number, letter, and symbol. For example, your computer knows the character *a* as the code 97, the number 1 as the code 49, the symbol $ as the code 36, and so forth. The ASCII system includes representations for 256 different characters.

1-2-3 uses a special character code system, called the Lotus International Character Set (LICS), to represent the letters, numbers, punctuation marks and other special characters you see on your 1-2-3 screen. The LICS is related to the ASCII character set since codes 0 to 127 are used to represent the same characters in both systems. However, the LICS uses the codes from 128 to 255 to represent special characters, such as the symbols π and ¿, which are not a part of the normal ASCII system. For the most part, you can think of ASCII and LICS as being identical. However, if you work with characters with codes above 127, you'll need to understand the differences between the two programs.

Although you can use any of the 256 characters contained in the Lotus International Character Set (LICS) whenever you work within 1-2-3, only 94 are represented by keys on the keyboard of your computer. You can enter common characters such as these just by pressing a single key or a combination of the [Shift] key and another key. To access the remaining characters, you must use the @CHAR function, which we covered in Chapter 5, or the [Compose] key.

THE [COMPOSE] KEY

To enter a character using the [Compose] key, you move the cell pointer to the cell into which you want to enter the character, press [Compose] ([Alt][F1]), and type a two-character sequence (called a compose sequence) that represents the character you want to enter. For example, to enter the character π into cell B3, you would move the cell pointer to cell B3, press [Compose], and type PI, pi, or Pi (any of these two-character compose sequences will work). As soon as you type the second character in the compose sequence, the character π will appear on the Edit line.

You can use the [Compose] key to enter all kinds of characters that cannot be accessed directly from the keyboard. For instance, you can use [Compose] to enter foreign-language characters like ¿ and ç. You can also use [Compose] to enter legal characters, mathematical symbols, foreign currency symbols, and Greek alphabet characters. Table A2-1 shows the compose sequences for some of the most common compose characters. Appendix A in your *1-2-3 Reference Manual* contains a complete list of these characters and their compose sequences.

To enter...	Press [Compose] and type...	To enter...	Press [Compose] and type...
©	co or Co or CO	1/2	12
™	tm or Tm or TM	1/4	14
¶	!p or !P	£	l= or l- or L= or L-
§	so or So or SO	¥	y= or y- or Y= or Y-
•	^.	ƒ	ff
≥	>=	¢	c| or c\ or C| or C\
≤	<=	π	pi or Pi or PI
+	:-	Δ	dd or DD
±	+-		

TABLE A2-1: Commonly-used compose sequences

You can enter regular characters in the same cell with compose characters. For example, to enter the label *'Douglas Cobb's 1-2-3 Handbook, © 1987* into a cell, you would type *Douglas Cobb's 1-2-3 Handbook,*, press [Compose], type *co, Co,* or *CO,* and then type *1987*.

Many computers cannot display every character in the LICS. For example, many cannot represent the characters © or ™. If you attempt to compose a character that your computer cannot display, 1-2-3 will use a "fallback representation" for that character. For example, the fallback representation for the © character is simply c. The fallback representation for the character ™ is T.

Similarly, many printers cannot print some of the characters in the LICS. This is particularly true of daisy-wheel and thimble printers. When you try to print a character that your printer cannot represent, it will use a fallback representation for that character. For example, the fallback representation for the character π is pi.

The keyboards of some computers lack a few keys that are found on the standard IBM PC keyboard. If you have such a computer, you may need to use [Compose] to enter characters that can be typed directly on an IBM PC. For example, suppose your computer's keyboard does not have a key for the character #. To enter this character, you would press [Compose] and type ++.

A special [Compose] sequence—[Compose]mg—instructs 1-2-3 to "merge" characters when they are printed; that is, to print them one on top of the other. For example, suppose you want the label 'Test to be underlined when it is printed. To make this happen, you would enter the label by typing T, pressing [Compose], typing mg, and typing _; typing [Enter], pressing [Compose], typing mg, and typing _; typing s, pressing [Compose], typing mg, and typing _; typing t, pressing [Compose], typing mg, and typing _; and then pressing [Enter]. On the screen, the entry will look like T← _e←_s←_t←_; however, it will print as Test.

USING UPPER-LEVEL ASCII CHARACTERS

If you use 1-2-3 Releases 2.01 and 2.2, you can display either LICS or ASCII character on the screen. (1-2-3 Releases 1A and 2 do not give you this option). If you want to display ASCII characters rather than LICS characters, you must load 1-2-3 with a driver set that specifies the Universal Text Display—ASCII—No LICS screen driver.

Unfortunately, 1-2-3 does not allow you to specify the Universal Text Display—ASCII—No LICS screen driver when you select the First-Time Installation and Change Selected Equipment options from the Install program's main menu. To specify this driver, you must select the Advanced Options option from the main Install menu, select the Modify Current Driver Set option from the Advanced Options menu, select the Text Display option from the Modify Current Driver Set menu, select Text Display from the Text Display menu, and select Universal Text Display—ASCII—No LICS (the final option in the list of screen drivers). At that point, choose Return to Main Menu to return to the main Install menu, choose Save Changes, and then press [Enter] to exit the Install program. Once you make this change, 1-2-3 will display upper-level ASCII characters—rather than upper-level LICS characters—whenever you load it with the modified driver set.

Unfortunately, 1-2-3 will print upper-level LICS characters even if it displays upper-level LICS characters. To make 1-2-3 print upper-level ASCII characters, you must alter bytes in your .SET file manually—a topic that is beyond the scope of this book.

Appendix 3
Changing 1-2-3's Global and Default Settings

As we've explained in various places throughout this book, 1-2-3 allows you to change many of its global and default settings. 1-2-3's global settings are controlled by the commands on the / Worksheet Global menu; its default settings and are controlled by the commands on the / Worksheet Global Default menu. In this appendix, we'll explain the difference between these two groups of settings, and explore the settings that we have not already covered in previous chapters of this book.

GLOBAL SETTINGS

1-2-3's Global settings are controlled by the commands (other than Default) on the / Worksheet Global menu. ►This menu and the settings sheet that appears with it in 1-2-3 Release 2.2 are shown in Figure A3-1.◄ (Only the menu appears in 1-2-3 Releases 1A, 2, and 2.01. To see the Global settings sheet in those releases of 1-2-3, you must issue the / Worksheet Global Status command.) The settings controlled by these commands affect only the current worksheet—not any other worksheets that you create or retrieve during the current or any future 1-2-3 sessions.

RELEASE
► 2.2 ◄

We've already talked about 1-2-3's /Worksheet Global settings in previous chapters of this book. Specifically, we covered the Format option (which changes the worksheet's global format), the Label-Prefix option (which changes the global label prefix), and the Zero option (which controls the display of zeros) in Chapter 3; we covered the Column-Width option (which changes the global column width) in Chapter 4; we covered the Recalculation option (which controls both the order and method of recalculation) in Chapter 2; and we covered the Protection option (which enables and disables global protection) in Chapter 6.

When you save a worksheet, 1-2-3 saves all of these settings (except, for some reason, zero-supression) along with it. Consequently, the same settings will be in effect the next time you retrieve the worksheet. Once again: the settings controlled by the commands on the / Worksheet Global menu (other than Default) affect only the current worksheet.

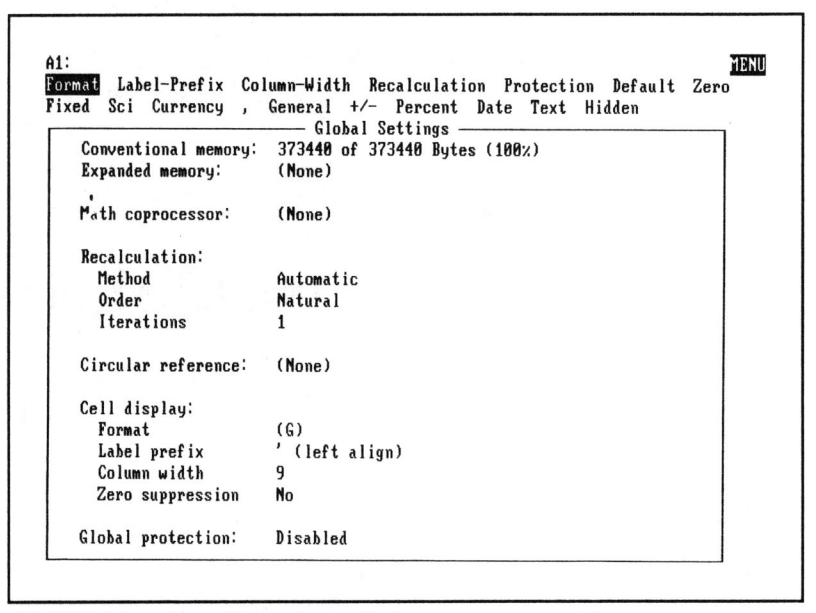

```
A1:                                                              MENU
Format Label-Prefix Column-Width Recalculation Protection Default Zero
Fixed  Sci  Currency ,  General +/-  Percent  Date  Text  Hidden
┌──────────────────── Global Settings ────────────────────┐
│ Conventional memory:  373440 of 373440 Bytes (100%)      │
│ Expanded memory:      (None)                             │
│                                                          │
│ Math coprocessor:     (None)                             │
│                                                          │
│ Recalculation:                                           │
│   Method              Automatic                          │
│   Order               Natural                            │
│   Iterations          1                                  │
│                                                          │
│ Circular reference:   (None)                             │
│                                                          │
│ Cell display:                                            │
│   Format              (G)                                │
│   Label prefix        ' (left align)                     │
│   Column width        9                                  │
│   Zero suppression    No                                 │
│                                                          │
│ Global protection:    Disabled                           │
│                                                          │
└──────────────────────────────────────────────────────────┘
```

FIGURE A3-1: The / Worksheet Global menu and settings sheet

DEFAULT SETTINGS

RELEASE
▶ 2.2 ◀

▶1-2-3's Default settings are controlled by the commands on the / Worksheet Global Default menu and are listed in the settings sheet that appears when you issue the / Worksheet Global Default command in 1-2-3 Release 2.2 or the / Worksheet Global Default Status command in any release of 1-2-3.◀ This menu and settings sheet are shown in Figure A3-2.

Unlike the settings controlled by the other commands on the / Worksheet Global menu, the settings controlled by the Default command affect every worksheet that you create or retrieve during the current 1-2-3 session (that is, from the point you make the changes until you issue the / Quit command)—not just the current worksheet. In fact, the default settings can remain in effect for future 1-2-3 sessions. We'll show you how to make that happen at the end of this appendix.

```
A1:                                                          MENU
Printer  Directory Status Update Other Autoexec Quit
Specify printer interface and default settings
                        ── Default Settings ──
 Printer:                          Directory: C:\123
  Interface       Parallel 1
  Auto linefeed   No               Autoexecute macros: Yes
  Margins
   Left 4  Right 76  Top 2  Bottom 2  International:
  Page length     60                 Punctuation      A
  Wait            No                 Decimal          Period
  Setup string                       Argument         Comma
  Name            HP 2686 LaserJet Se... Thousands    Comma
                                     Currency         Prefix: $
 Add-In:                             Date format (D4) A (MM/DD/YY)
  1                                  Time format (D8) A (HH:MM:SS)
  2                                  Negative         Parentheses
  3
  4                                 Help access method: Removable
  5                                 Clock display:      None
  6                                 Undo:               Disabled
  7                                 Beep:               Yes
  8
```

FIGURE A3-2: The / Worksheet Global Default menu

Settings We've Explored Previously

We've covered seven of 1-2-3's default settings in earlier chapters of this book. Specifically, we discussed the / Worksheet Global Default Printer command (which controls the default print settings) in Chapter 8; we discussed the / Worksheet Global Default Directory command (which changes the default directory) in Chapter 9; we discussed the / Worksheet Global Default Other International Date and Time commands (which control the form of the D4, D5, D8, and D9 formats) in Chapter 7; we discussed the / Worksheet Global Default Other Undo command (which turns 1-2-3's undo feature on and off) in Chapter 2; we discussed the / Worksheet Global Default Other Add-In command (which allows you to specify auto-attaching, auto-invoking add-ins) in Chapter 16; and we discussed the / Worksheet Global Default Autoexec command (which enables and disables the execution of auto-executing macros) in Chapter 13. Consequently, we won't talk about them in detail in this appendix. However, we will talk about the remaining / Worksheet Global Default settings—ones that we only alluded to in previous chapters.

The Punctuation Setting

1-2-3 uses punctuation marks in four different ways: as decimal points in numbers; to separate the thousands from the millions, the millions from the billions, and so on, in formatted values; to separate the arguments in functions; and to separate the arguments in advanced macro commands. Normally, 1-2-3 uses periods for decimal points (as in the number 123.45); commas to separate the hundreds from the thousands, the thousands from the millions, and so on, in formatted numbers (as in the number 123,456,789); and commas to separate the arguments in functions (for example, @SUM(A1,A5,A10) and macro commands (for example, '{Let A2,A1^2}). However, you can use the /Worksheet Global Default Other International Punctuation command to change the punctuation mark 1-2-3 will use for any of these tasks.

To change the punctuation default, you just issue the / Worksheet Global Default Other International Punctuation command and choose the option you want. 1-2-3 will display the menu shown in Figure A3-3. This menu offers eight punctuation alternatives, each of which includes three punctuation marks: one for the decimal; one for the argument separator (for both functions and macro commands); and one for the 000 separator, which separates the thousands from millions and so on, in formatted values. The second line of the control panel shows which punctuation mark will be used for each of these purposes if you select the highlighted option from the menu. As you point to the other alternatives, the second line will change to reflect the settings defined by those options. Table A3-1 shows the effect of each of these options.

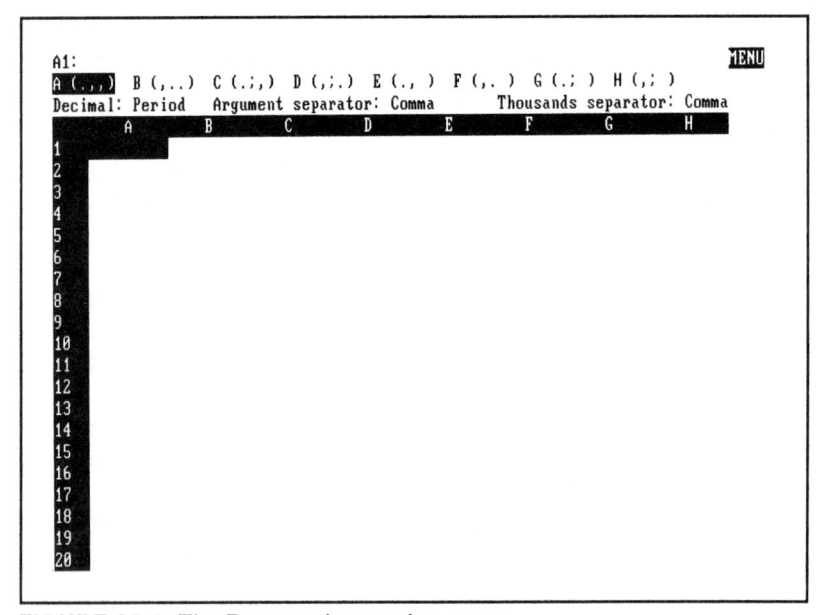

FIGURE A3-3: The Punctuation setting menu

Interestingly, you always can use a semicolon as the argument seperator for functions and macro commands, no matter what character is the default. For example, even if you select option B (which specifies a period as the default argument separator, you can use the function @SUM(A1;A2) to sum the values in cells A1 and A2 of a worksheet. Of course, you also can use the function @SUM(A1...A2). Similarly, you can use either the command {Let A2;A1^2} or {Let A2.A1^2} to enter the square of the value in cell A1 into cell A2.

Option	Formatted Value	Argument Separator
A (.,,)	1,234.56	@SUM(A1,A5,A10)
B (,..)	1.234,56	@SUM(A1.A5.A10)
C (.;,)	1,234.56	@SUM(A1;A5;A10)
D (,;.)	1.234,56	@SUM(A1;A5;A10)
E (.,)	1 234.56	@SUM(A1,A5,A10)
F (,.)	1 234,56	@SUM(A1.A5.A10)
G (.;)	1 234.56	@SUM(A1;A5;A10)
H (,;)	1 234,56	@SUM(A1;A5;A10)

TABLE A3-1: The Punctuation setting options

The Currency Setting

The / Worksheet Global Default Other International Currency command allows you to change the character 1-2-3 uses as the currency sign in numbers that have been assigned the Currency format. You can use any string of up to 15 characters, including the special LICS characters f, ¥, £, and Pts as the currency sign. In addition, you can tell 1-2-3 that the currency symbol should appear before or after the formatted number.

When you issue the / Worksheet Global Default Other International Currency command, 1-2-3 will display the prompt *Enter currency sign:*, followed by the character that is currently defined as the currency sign. Unless you have previously used this command to change the currency sign, it will be $. To change the sign, first press [Backspace] to erase the default, then type the new sign (if it can be typed from the keyboard) or press the [Compose] key and type the compose sequence that defines the character. (For more on the [Compose] key, see Appendix 2.)

When you press [Enter] to lock in the sign, 1-2-3 will ask you whether the sign should be a Prefix or a Suffix. If you choose Prefix, the sign will appear before the formatted value (as in $1,234). If you choose Suffix, the sign will appear after the formatted value (as in 1,234$).

For example, Figure A3-4 shows a worksheet that contains entries that have been assigned the Currency format with zero decimal places. Suppose you want to change the currency sign to £ and that you want this sign to appear after the formatted values. To make this change, issue the / Worksheet Global Default Other International Currency command, press [Backspace], press [Compose], type L-, and press [Enter]. When 1-2-3 displays the Prefix/Suffix menu, choose Suffix Figure A3-5 shows the results. As you can see, the form of all the formatted values in this worksheet have changed to reflect the new Currency format.

While you will generally use a single character as the currency sign, you can designate any string of up to 15 characters as the currency sign. For example, suppose you want to define the string *US$* as the currency sign. You want this sign to be a prefix. To do this, you would issue the / Worksheet Global Default Other International Currency command, press [Backspace], type US$, press [Enter], and choose Prefix. Figure A3-6 shows the sample worksheet after we made this change. You could also use strings like *US Dollars*, *Duetsche Marks*, or *Francs* as the currency sign.

```
B3: (C0) 65428                                                    READY

       A           B           C           D           E        F
1                1987        1988        1989       Total
2              ----------  ----------  ----------  ----------
3   Widgets    $65,428     $70,799     $76,286     $212,512
4   Wombats    $54,305     $55,067     $60,148     $169,521
5   Woofers    $68,699     $69,960     $74,244     $212,904
6              ----------  ----------  ----------  ----------
7   Total      $188,433    $195,826    $210,678    $594,937
8              ==========  ==========  ==========  ==========
```

FIGURE A3-4: A sample worksheet

```
B3: (C0) 65428                                                    READY

       A           B           C           D           E        F
1                1987        1988        1989       Total
2              ----------  ----------  ----------  ----------
3   Widgets    65,428£     70,799£     76,286£     212,512£
4   Wombats    54,305£     55,067£     60,148£     169,521£
5   Woofers    68,699£     69,960£     74,244£     212,904£
6              ----------  ----------  ----------  ----------
7   Total      188,433£    195,826£    210,678£    594,937£
8              ==========  ==========  ==========  ==========
```

FIGURE A3-5: Changing the currency default

```
B3: (C0) 65428                                                    READY

       A           B           C           D           E        F
1                1987        1988        1989       Total
2              ----------  ----------  ----------  ----------
3   Widgets    US$65,428   US$70,799   US$76,286   US$212,512
4   Wombats    US$54,305   US$55,067   US$60,148   US$169,521
5   Woofers    US$68,699   US$69,960   US$74,244   US$212,904
6              ----------  ----------  ----------  ----------
7   Total      US$188,433  US$195,826  US$210,678  US$594,937
8              ==========  ==========  ==========  ==========
```

FIGURE A3-6: Another change to the currency default

There are some limits to 1-2-3's ability to use different currency signs. First, only one format can be active in any worksheet. This means that you cannot have some numbers formatted as dollars and others as British pounds sterling within one worksheet. In addition, the currency sign you define must be either a prefix or a suffix. You cannot define a sign that has both a prefix portion and a suffix portion. For example, you cannot define a currency sign that would display the value 1234 as $1,234 (US).

The Negative Setting

▶As we explained in Chapter 3, 1-2-3 usually displays negative Currency and Comma-formatted values with leading minus signs. However, 1-2-3 Release 2.2 can display these values with leading minus signs (-) instead (previous releases of 1-2-3 cannot). To make 1-2-3 display Currency and Comma-formatted values with leading minus signs, issue the / Worksheet Global Default Other International Negative command and choose Sign. To switch back to parentheses, issue the same command, but choose Parentheses. For example, Figure A3-7 shows a 1-2-3 worksheet while the Negative setting is Sign; Figure A3-8 shows the same worksheet with the Negative setting as Parentheses.◀

RELEASE
▶ 2.2 ◀

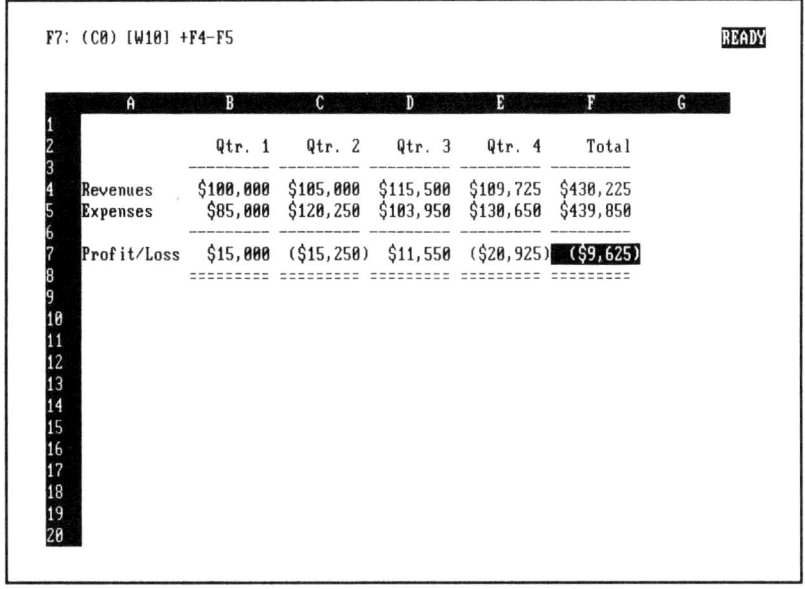

```
F7: (C0) [W10] +F4-F5                                          READY

          A         B          C          D          E          F          G
 1
 2                 Qtr. 1     Qtr. 2     Qtr. 3     Qtr. 4     Total
 3                ---------  ---------  ---------  ---------  ---------
 4   Revenues    $100,000   $105,000   $115,500   $109,725   $430,225
 5   Expenses     $85,000   $120,250   $103,950   $130,650   $439,850
 6                ---------  ---------  ---------  ---------  ---------
 7   Profit/Loss  $15,000   ($15,250)   $11,550   ($20,925)   ($9,625)
 8                =========  =========  =========  =========  =========
 9
10
11
12
13
14
15
16
17
18
19
20
```

FIGURE A3-7: Negative Currency-formatted values displayed in parentheses

The Help Setting

If you are using 1-2-3 on a floppy-disk-based computer, occasionally you'll need to have a disk other than the disk that contains the 123.HLP file in drive A. For example, if you are using 1-2-3 on a computer with only one floppy disk drive (like an IBM PCjr) you'll need to use the single floppy disk drive for saving and retrieving worksheet files. If you will be removing the disk that contains the 123.HLP file from drive A, you need to let 1-2-3 know that the disk that contains the 123.HLP file may not be in drive A at the time you press [Help].

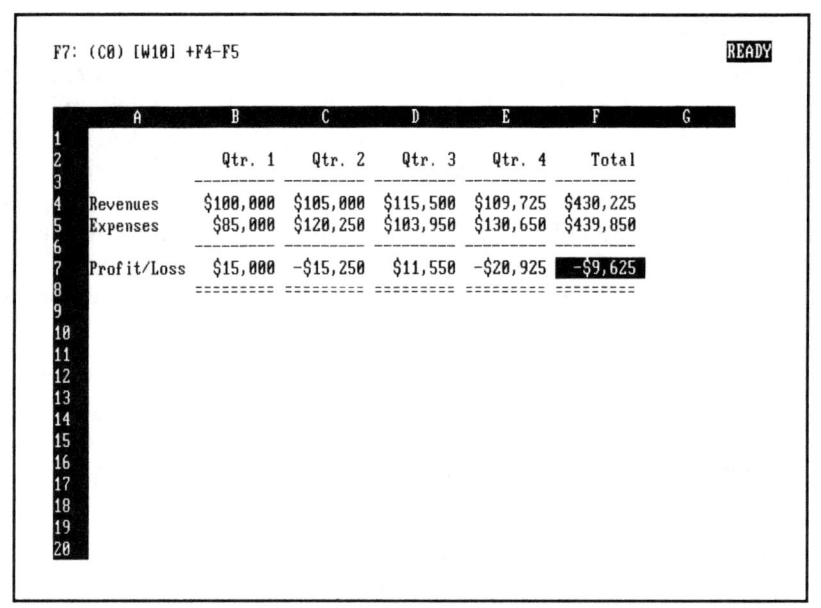

```
F7: (C0) [W10] +F4-F5                                              READY

         A         B         C         D         E         F         G
1
2                  Qtr. 1    Qtr. 2    Qtr. 3    Qtr. 4    Total
3                  --------  --------  --------  --------  --------
4   Revenues       $100,000  $105,000  $115,500  $109,725  $430,225
5   Expenses        $85,000  $120,250  $103,950  $130,650  $439,850
6                  --------  --------  --------  --------  --------
7   Profit/Loss     $15,000  -$15,250   $11,550  -$20,925   -$9,625
8                  ========  ========  ========  ========  ========
9
10
...
20
```

FIGURE A3-8: Negative Currency-formatted values displayed with leading minus signs

The / Worksheet Global Default Other Help command allows you to control the way 1-2-3 accesses Help when you press the [Help] key. When you issue this command, you'll see the menu shown in Figure A3-9. The default setting, Instant, tells 1-2-3 that the disk containing the file 123.HLP (usually the 1-2-3 System Disk) will always be in drive A. You should choose this option if you plan to keep the disk containing the 123.HLP file in drive A.

When the Help setting is Instant, 1-2-3 will not close the 123.HLP file after you access Help. The next time you press [Help], 1-2-3 will be able to access Help instantly. If the disk containing the .HLP file is not in drive A, however, when you press [Help], 1-2-3 will display the error message *divide overflow* and then will exit from 1-2-3 directly to DOS (or to the Lotus Access System). Any work that you have not saved will be lost.

You might remove the disk containing the 123.HLP file from drive A from time to time; therefore, you should choose the Removable option. Choosing this option tells 1-2-3 that the disk in drive A may not contain the file 123.HLP. For that reason, 1-2-3 will close the 123.HLP file after each time that you access Help. As a result, it will take a bit longer for 1-2-3 to bring the help screens into view. However, if the disk in drive A does not contain the 123.HLP file, 1-2-3 will simply display the error message *Cannot find 1-2-3.HLP file* when you press [Help]. All you have to do is press [Esc] to acknowledge the error message, then place the disk containing the 123.HLP file in drive A and press [Help] again. You won't lose any work.

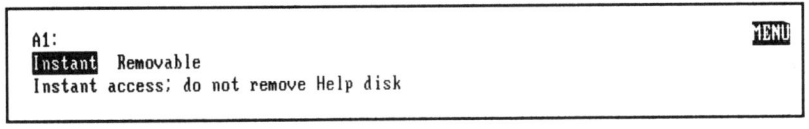

```
A1:                                                          MENU
Instant  Removable
Instant access; do not remove Help disk
```

FIGURE A3-9: The Help setting menu

The default Help setting, Instant, is the correct setting for hard-disk systems. If you are using 1-2-3 on a computer with a hard disk, you should not use the / Worksheet Global Default Other Help command.

The Clock Setting

The / Worksheet Global Default Other Clock command lets you control what appears at the left edge of the Status line (the bottom-most line on the 1-2-3 screen). By default, 1-2-3 displays the current date and time, in DD-MMM-YY and HH:MM AM/PM form, respectively, in this area. However, you can change the format of this display, remove it,▶ or, in 1-2-3 Releases 2.2, replace it with the name of the current worksheet.◀ The / Worksheet Global Default Other Clock command makes this possible.

RELEASE ▶ 2.2 ◀

When you issue the / Worksheet Global Default Other Clock command, command, 1-2-3 will display the menu shown in Figure A3-10. The first item on this menu, Standard, instructs 1-2-3 to display the current date in DD-MMM-YY form and the current time in HH:MM AM/PM form on the Status line. For example, at 5:30 PM on November 24, 1989, 1-2-3 would display *24-Nov-89 05:30 PM* on the Status line.

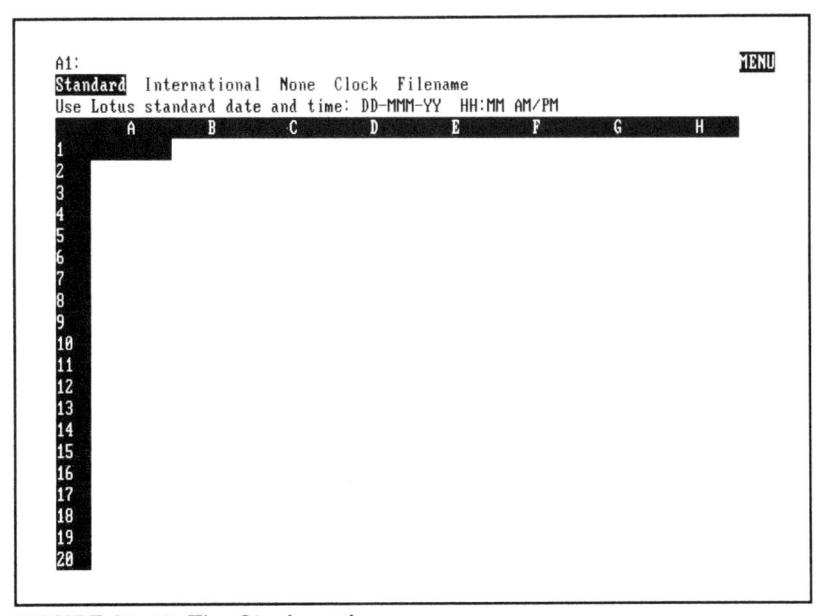

```
A1:                                                          MENU
Standard  International  None  Clock  Filename
Use Lotus standard date and time: DD-MMM-YY  HH:MM AM/PM
```

FIGURE A3-10: The Clock setting menu

The International option instructs 1-2-3 to display the current time and date on the Status line in the form specified by the current Long International Date format (D4) and Short International Time format (D9). The actual form of the clock display is determined by the selection you have made for the form of the Long International Date and Short International Time formats. If you have not changed these formats, the clock will be displayed in the form *MM/DD/YY HH:MM*. Consequently, 1-2-3 would display the *11/24/89 18:30* on the Status line at 5:30 PM on November 24, 1989. If you have changed the D4 and/or D9 formats, 1-2-3 will display the date and time in whatever form you specified. For example, if you have changed the D4 format to DD/MM/YY (Option B) and changed the D9 format to HHhMMm (Option D), 1-2-3 would display *November 24, 1989, 5:30 PM* on the Status line at 5:30 on the afternoon on 11/24/58.

▶The Filename option instructs 1-2-3 to display the name of the file (if any) in which the current worksheet is stored—in place of the the date and time—on the Status line. (This option is available only in 1-2-3 Release 2.2.) If the worksheet has not been saved, 1-2-3 will display the date and time at the bottom of the screen until you save the current worksheet or retrieve another one. In most cases, this date will be displayed in Standard format; however, 1-2-3 will use the International format if it was displaying the date and time in that format when you selected the Filename option.

The Clock option (also new to 1-2-3 Release 2.2) commands 1-2-3 Release 2.2 to replace the file name with the current time and date—even if the None option was in effect before you selected the Filename option. 1-2-3 will display the date and time in Standard format unless it was using the International format before you selected the Filename option.◀

The remaining option on the Clock menu, None, removes the clock display from the screen altogether. Once you have hidden the display, you can bring it back into view by choosing one of the other options from the / Worksheet Global Default Other Clock menu.

The Beep Setting

The / Worksheet Global Default Other Beep command controls whether or not 1-2-3 "beeps" when you do something wrong (for example, enter an invalid formula or function) or are about to do something wrong (like exiting from 1-2-3 without saving your work). To prevent 1-2-3 from beeping in these situations, issue the / Worksheet Global Default Other Beep command and choose No. To re-enable the beep, issue the same command, but choose Yes.

Saving the Default Settings

Also unlike the global settings (the ones controlled by the commands other than Default on the / Worksheet Global menu), the default settings (the ones controlled by the commands on the / Worksheet Global Default menu) are not saved as a part of any worksheet. However, you can save these settings so that they affect future 1-2-3 sessions. To do this, simply choose the Update option from the / Worksheet Global

Default menu. When you issue this command, 1-2-3 saves the current default settings into a special file named 123.CNF. Each time you load 1-2-3, it reads the 123.CNF file. Consequently, the settings specified by that file will be in effect during the new 1-2-3 session.

If you don't use the Update command to save your changes to the defaults, any changes you make to the settings controlled by the commands on the / Worksheet Global Default menu will remain in effect only until the end of the current 1-2-3 session. The next time you load 1-2-3, all of the defaults you changed will revert to the settings stored in the 123.CNF file.

Appendix 4

Using 1-2-3 on a Network

▶1-2-3 Release 2.2 has several features that facilitate its use on networks. (Earlier releases of 1-2-3 do not have these features). In this appendix, we'll explain 1-2-3 Release 2.2's network features and related commands.

RELEASE
▶ 2.2 ◀

FILE RESERVATIONS

When used on a network, 1-2-3 assigns reservations to worksheet files. Although more than one person can use the same worksheet at the same time when 1-2-3 is used on a network, only one of the multiple users—the person with the file's "reservation"— can resave the file under its current name. If you retrieve a file while no one else is using it, you automatically get the file's reservation. If you retrieve a file whose reservation is held by someone else, the indicator *RO* will appear at the bottom of your screen. This indicator denotes that you have accessed the file in the "read only" mode. Consequently, 1-2-3 will not allow you to resave the worksheet under its original name. However, you can save the worksheet under a different name, if you wish.

The user who has a file's reservation gives it up when any of the following things happen: he retrieves another file, he issues the / Worksheet Erase command, he quits from 1-2-3, or he issues the / File Admin Reservation Release command (which does nothing other than releasing a file's reservation). If you are using the file in the read-only mode when its reservation becomes available, you can obtain the reservation, either by issuing the / File Admin Reservation Get command or by saving the file under its original name. Unfortunately, you cannot get the file's reservation in either of these ways if the file was resaved under its original name while you were working with it in the read-only mode. In that case, the only way to get the file's reservation is to re-retrieve the file.

UPDATING LINKING FORMULAS

In Chapter 2, we explained that 1-2-3 Release 2.2 allows you to enter references to other worksheets. On single-user systems, only one worksheet can be open at a time. Consequently, there's no way to make changes to a worksheet that is referenced by a linking formula while the worksheet that contains the linking formula is open. This fact, combined with the fact that 1-2-3 recalculates the linking formulas in a worksheet whenever you retrieve a worksheet, means the result of a linking formula on a single-user system always will be up-to-date.

When 1-2-3 Release 2.2 is used on a network, however, other people may have access to the files referenced by linking formulas in the worksheet you are working with at the time. If another user saves changes to a file that is referenced by a linking formula in the worksheet you are using, the linking formulas may need to be updated. Fortunately, you don't have to save your worksheet and then retrieve it again in order to update those formulas. Instead, you can simply issue the /File Admin Link-Refresh command. When you issue this command, 1-2-3 will recalculate all the linking formulas in your worksheet, using the values from the most recently saved version of the referenced files.◄

Appendix 5

Printing with an HP LaserJet

The HP LaserJet is probably the most popular printer on the market today. It is also one of the most versatile printers around. Many 1-2-3 users have picked the HP LaserJet as their printer of choice for 1-2-3 worksheets and graphs. In this appendix, we'll show you how to use 1-2-3 to generate both professional reports and attractive graphs on your HP LaserJet printer.

HARDWARE SETUP

Before you can print either a 1-2-3 worksheet or a 1-2-3 graph on an HP LaserJet printer, you need to use 1-2-3's Install Program to tell 1-2-3 a few things about the printer. You'll probably need to run through this installation procedure only once—from that point on, you'll be able to print your worksheets without any hardware setup.

Running the Install Program

Lotus 1-2-3's Install Program lets you tell 1-2-3 about your computer equipment. When you run the Install Program, 1-2-3 will present a main menu with four options: First-Time Installation, Change Selected Equipment, Advanced Options, and Exit Install Program. Since the Install Program can be used either to tell 1-2-3 about your equipment for the first time or to modify some specific information you've already told 1-2-3, you'll use one of two different approaches to set up your HP LaserJet printer with the Install Program.

Running Install for the First Time

If you're using the Install Program for the first time to tell 1-2-3 about your computer equipment, you'll want to choose the First-Time Installation option from the main install menu. When you do this, 1-2-3 will ask you some questions about your computer, including whether your computer can display graphs and how many monitors you have. After you've answered these questions, 1-2-3 will present the question *Do you have a text printer?* When this question appears, you should choose the Yes option to bring up the list of supported printer manufacturers. When you see this list, choose the HP option to bring up the list of supported HP printers, and choose the 2686 LaserJet Series option from the list.

After you answer another question or two, 1-2-3 will present the prompt *Do you want to print graphs?* You should answer Yes to this prompt to bring up another list of printer manufacturers. When you see this list, choose the HP option from the list of printer manufacturers to bring up the list of supported HP printers. If you have an original HP LaserJet printer, choose the *LaserJet* option. If you have a LaserJet Plus, a LaserJet 500 Plus, a LaserJet Series II, or a LaserJet IID printer, choose the *LaserJet+* or *LaserJet II* option.

After you answer another question or two, 1-2-3 will save your driver set under the name 123.SET, which contains all of the information you provided during the installation procedure. Once 1-2-3 has saved your driver set, you can exit the Install Program and load the 1-2-3 spreadsheet program. (For more information on the Install Program, see your 1-2-3 manuals.)

Modifying the Existing Driver Set

If you've previously saved a driver set with the Install Program and you want to add the HP LaserJet printer's driver to your existing driver set, you should run the Install Program and choose the Change Selected Equipment option from the main printgraph menu. When you choose this option, the Install Program presents a menu with several options, two of which are Text Printer(s) and Graphics Printer(s). You should choose the Text Printer(s) option from this menu, choose the *HP* option from the list of printer manufacturers, and choose the *2686 LaserJet Series* option from the list of HP printers. At this point, the Change Selected Equipment menu will reappear.

If you intend to print graphs on your HP LaserJet printer, choose Graphics Printer(s) from the Change Selected Equipment menu, choose the *HP* option from the list of printer manufacturers, and choose the *LaserJet* or *LaserJet+* or *LaserJet II* option from the list of HP printers. (Lotus 1-2-3 Release 2.01 does not have a driver for the LaserJet 500 Plus, LaserJet Series II, or LaserJet IID printer; if you have any of these printers, just choose the *LaserJet+* or *LaserJet II* option.)

After you've completed the procedures for installing the HP LaserJet as both a text printer and a graphics printer, you must save your changes in 1-2-3's driver set. To do this, just choose the Save Changes option from the Change Selected Equipment menu, and press [Enter] to save the changes to the current file containing the driver set. After you've saved your changes, you can exit the Install Program and load 1-2-3's spreadsheet program. (For more information on the Install Program, see your 1-2-3 manuals.)

You'll probably need to use the Install Program to tell 1-2-3 about your LaserJet printer only once—just before you use 1-2-3 with your LaserJet for the first time. From that point on, you'll be able to print using the settings you've defined.

Configuring the Printer

After you've used the Install Program to tell 1-2-3 that you're using an HP LaserJet printer, you need to load 1-2-3 and configure your printer with 1-2-3's / Worksheet Global Default Printer command. ►When you issue this command, 1-2-3 Release 2.2 will present the menu and settings sheet shown in Figure A5-1. (If you are using an earlier release, you'll see just the menu.)◄ Before you try to print a 1-2-3 worksheet on the LaserJet, you need to adjust the following settings on this menu: Interface, Name, Pg-Length, Left, Right, Top, and Bottom.

RELEASE
► 2.2 ◄

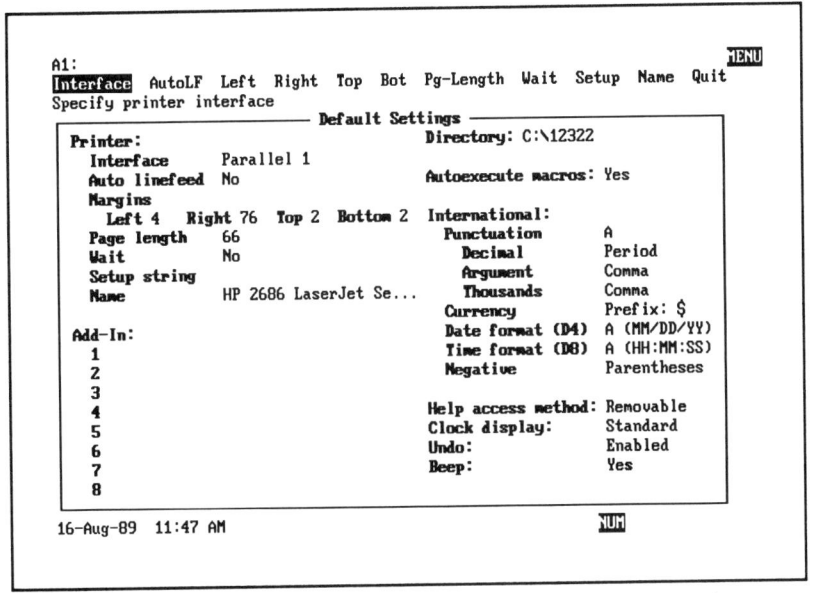

```
A1:                                                             MENU
Interface AutoLF Left Right Top Bot Pg-Length Wait Setup Name Quit
Specify printer interface
                        ─ Default Settings ─
  Printer:                          Directory: C:\12322
    Interface      Parallel 1
    Auto linefeed  No               Autoexecute macros: Yes
    Margins
      Left 4    Right 76  Top 2  Bottom 2  International:
    Page length    66                Punctuation      A
    Wait           No                  Decimal        Period
    Setup string                       Argument       Comma
    Name           HP 2686 LaserJet Se...  Thousands  Comma
                                     Currency         Prefix: $
  Add-In:                            Date format (D4) A (MM/DD/YY)
    1                                Time format (D8) A (HH:MM:SS)
    2                                Negative         Parentheses
    3
    4                                Help access method: Removable
    5                                Clock display:   Standard
    6                                Undo:            Enabled
    7                                Beep:            Yes
    8

16-Aug-89   11:47 AM                                        NUM
```

FIGURE A5-1: The / Worksheet Global Default Printer command

The Interface Setting

As we said in Chapter 1, you can run the LaserJet Series II and the LaserJet Plus printer as either a parallel or serial printer. Since most PC printers are parallel printers, 1-2-3's default Interface setting is Parallel 1. If your LaserJet is connected to your computer's primary parallel interface, you probably won't need to adjust the Interface setting. However, if your LaserJet is connected to a second or third parallel interface, or if you are running your LaserJet as a serial printer, you must specify the appropriate Interface setting before you can print.

To select a printer interface, choose the Interface option from the menu in Figure A5-1. When you do this, 1-2-3 will present the menu shown in Figure A5-2.

As we said earlier, if your LaserJet is using your computer's primary parallel interface, you should leave the Interface setting at Parallel 1 (the default). If you are using anything other than the primary parallel interface, you should choose the option that corresponds to the interface used by your LaserJet. To choose the appropriate interface, just point to that option (or type the number of that option) and press [Enter].

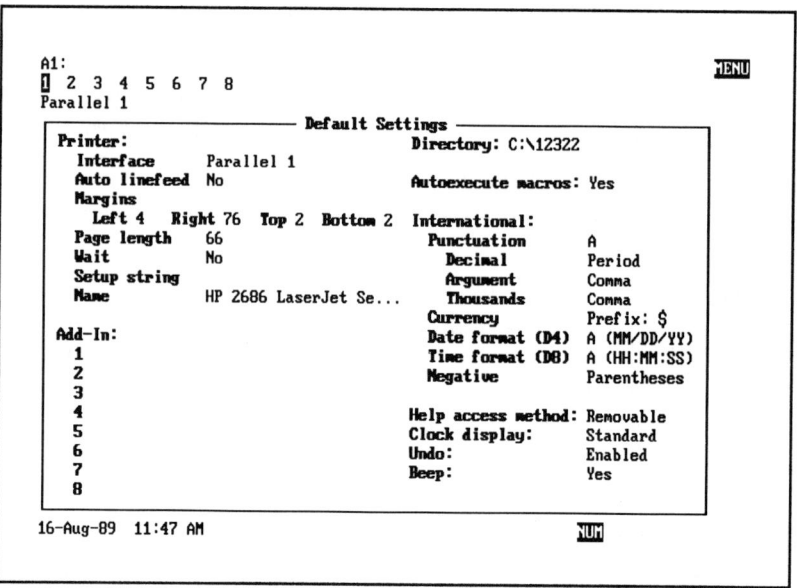

```
A1:                                                                    MENU
 1 2 3 4 5 6 7 8
Parallel 1
                         ┌─── Default Settings ───┐
 Printer:                    Directory: C:\12322
   Interface      Parallel 1
   Auto linefeed  No         Autoexecute macros: Yes
   Margins
     Left 4   Right 76  Top 2  Bottom 2  International:
   Page length    66                       Punctuation        A
   Wait           No                         Decimal          Period
   Setup string                              Argument         Comma
   Name           HP 2686 LaserJet Se...     Thousands        Comma
                                             Currency         Prefix: $
 Add-In:                                   Date format (D4)   A (MM/DD/YY)
   1                                       Time format (D8)   A (HH:MM:SS)
   2                                       Negative           Parentheses
   3
   4                                       Help access method: Removable
   5                                       Clock display:      Standard
   6                                       Undo:               Enabled
   7                                       Beep:               Yes
   8

16-Aug-89  11:47 AM                                              NUM
```

FIGURE A5-2: The Interface option

Although the HP LaserJet Series II and the HP LaserJet Plus are equipped with both a parallel and a serial interface, the original HP LaserJet is equipped with only a serial interface. If you have an original LaserJet printer, or if you want to run your LaserJet Plus or LaserJet Series II as a serial printer, you need to choose the appropriate serial interface setting from the Interface menu (options 2 or 4). You must also ensure that you've used DOS's MODE command to define the baud rate, number of stop bits, and parity for your printer. (Parallel printers don't require you to specify a Baud, Stop Bits, and Parity setting.) For instance, suppose you have connected your LaserJet to your computer's primary serial interface (COM1:). To define the baud, parity, data bits, and stop bits for COM1:, you must issue the DOS command

MODE COM1:9600,n,8,1,p

before you load 1-2-3. Once you have issued this MODE command and have started your 1-2-3 session, just choose the appropriate Interface setting for the serial port you defined in your MODE command (Serial 1 in this case).

The Name Setting

The Printer menu's Name setting specifies which printer driver you want 1-2-3 to use when it prints your 1-2-3 worksheet. If you've installed more than one printer driver, you should choose the option that corresponds to the *HP 2686 LaserJet Series* printer driver. (If you don't see the *HP 2686 LaserJet Series* option on the Name menu, you need to run 1-2-3's Install Program.)

The Pg-Length Setting

The Pg-Length setting specifies the default page length for your 1-2-3 reports. Since most PC printers automatically print 66 lines on a standard size page, 1-2-3's default page length is 66. Because LaserJet printers automatically print only 60 lines per page, however, you'll need to change 1-2-3's default Pg-Length setting from 66 to 60. If you print a worksheet on the LaserJet printer with a Pg-Length setting of 66, 1-2-3 will not break the pages of the report in the proper locations.

To specify a page length setting of 60, simply choose the Pg-Length option from the Printer menu, type 60, and press [Enter].

Margin Settings

The left, right, top, and bottom margin settings specify the default margins for your 1-2-3 reports. You should set the left, top, and bottom margin settings to 0 and the right margin setting to 80.

To set the left margin setting to 0, choose the Left option from the Printer menu in Figure A5-8, type 0, and press [Enter]. Similarly, to set the top and bottom margin settings to 0, choose Top (or Bottom), type 0, and press [Enter]. Finally, to set the right margin setting to 80, choose Right, type 80, and press [Enter].

Other Settings

You should not change 1-2-3's default Auto-LF, Wait, and Setup settings. The Auto-LF and Wait settings should remain No, and the Setup setting should remain blank. If you inadvertently change these default settings, use the / Worksheet Global Default Printer command to restore them.

Saving Your Changes

After you've defined all of the appropriate settings on the / Worksheet Global Default Printer menu, press [Esc] to return to the Default menu and choose the Update option. Once you've updated the default settings, 1-2-3 will use those defaults every time it prints a worksheet.

PRINTING WORKSHEETS

1-2-3 offers several tools that allow you to create attractive worksheet reports with your HP LaserJet printer. In this section, we'll show you how to use these tools to create worksheet reports that suit your specific needs.

Printing Basics

RELEASE ▶ 2.2 ◀

The / Print Printer command is the tool you will use to print reports in 1-2-3. ▶When you issue this command, 1-2-3 Release 2.2 presents the menu and settings sheet shown in Figure A5-3. (If you are using an earlier release, you'll see only the menu.)◀ The options on this menu allow you to define the area of the worksheet you want to print, set up various formatting options, advance the paper in the printer, and print.

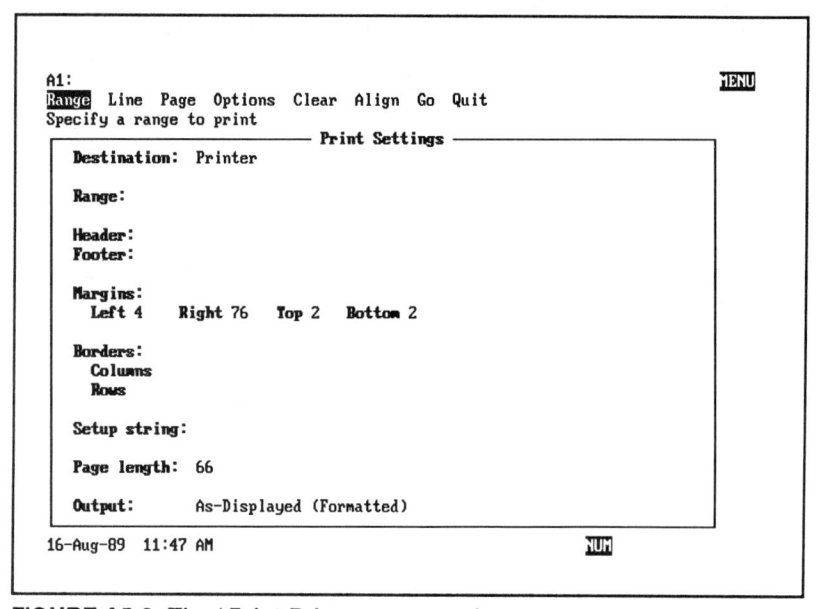

```
A1:                                                              MENU
Range Line Page Options  Clear  Align  Go  Quit
Specify a range to print
                          ─── Print Settings ───
   Destination:  Printer

   Range:

   Header:
   Footer:

   Margins:
      Left 4      Right 76    Top 2    Bottom 2

   Borders:
      Columns
      Rows

   Setup string:

   Page length:  66

   Output:         As-Displayed (Formatted)

16-Aug-89  11:47 AM                                       NUM
```

FIGURE A5-3: The / Print Printer command

To print a worksheet, you need to choose the Range option from the Print menu, select the range of cells you want to include in the report, align the paper in the printer, choose the Align command from the Printer menu, and then choose Go. The Options command on the Printer menu lets you customize your reports in a number of ways. We'll show you how to use these options to produce different kinds of reports on the LaserJet in a few pages.

Aligning Paper

As with other types of printers, you must align the paper in the HP LaserJet printer before you send the data to be printed. To align paper in the LaserJet, press the ON LINE key on the LaserJet's control panel to take the printer off line, and then press the FORM FEED key to eject the current page. After you press the ON LINE key again to put the printer back on-line, issue 1-2-3's / Print Printer Align command. This command tells 1-2-3 that the LaserJet is ready to begin printing on a new sheet of paper. If you do not follow this aligning procedure, 1-2-3 may insert page breaks in the wrong places in your report.

Figure A5-4 shows part of a worksheet that contains a sales forecast for a fictitious company. The worksheet shows the expected level of sales for many different cities beginning in January 1990. The worksheet extends from cell A1 to cell L69.

```
A1: [W22] 'Sales Forecast by Region                                    READY

                A           B         C         D         E         F
 1  Sales Forecast by Region
 2  ==========================================================================
 3                        Jan-90    Feb-90    Mar-90    Apr-90    May-90
 4                        ------    ------    ------    ------    ------
 5  East
 6    Raleigh, NC         $1,145    $1,264    $1,383    $1,502    $1,621
 7    Providence, RI        $873      $882      $891      $900      $909
 8    Baltimore, MD       $1,179    $1,298    $1,417    $1,536    $1,655
 9    Washington, DC      $1,196    $1,315    $1,434    $1,553    $1,672
10    Virginia Beach, VA    $736      $848      $960    $1,072    $1,184
11    Carson City, NJ       $792      $904    $1,016    $1,128    $1,240
12    Syracuse, NY        $1,213    $1,332    $1,451    $1,570    $1,689
13    Boston, MA          $1,230    $1,349    $1,468    $1,587    $1,706
14    Atlantic City, NJ   $1,247    $1,366    $1,485    $1,604    $1,723
15    Hartford, CT          $945      $956      $967      $978      $989
16                        ------    ------    ------    ------    ------
17    East Total          $9,611   $10,558   $11,505   $12,452   $13,399
18                        ======    ======    ======    ======    ======
19
20  South
```

FIGURE A5-4: A sample worksheet

To print this worksheet, first issue the / Print Printer command and choose the Range option. When 1-2-3 prompts you to specify the range of the worksheet you want to print, select the range A1..L69 (either by typing or by pointing), and press [Enter]. Next, check the LaserJet's printer tray to make sure that it contains paper and that the ON LINE light is on. When the printer is ready, choose Align from the Printer menu to tell 1-2-3 that you're ready to begin printing at the top of a new sheet of paper. Finally, print the report by choosing Go. As soon as you choose the Go option, 1-2-3's Mode indicator will change from MENU to WAIT, and 1-2-3 will begin sending the worksheet data to the printer. When 1-2-3 returns to the MENU mode, you'll need to choose the Page option from the Printer menu to eject the last page. Figure A5-5 shows the resulting report as it will appear when printed on any HP LaserJet printer.

Printing Partial Pages

Because the HP LaserJet does not eject a printed page until it receives a full page of information, you'll need to issue 1-2-3's / Print Printer Page command to eject the last page of your worksheet almost every time you print a report. Issuing this command has exactly the same effect as pressing the FORM FEED key on the LaserJet's control panel—it tells the printer that the current page is finished and should be ejected from

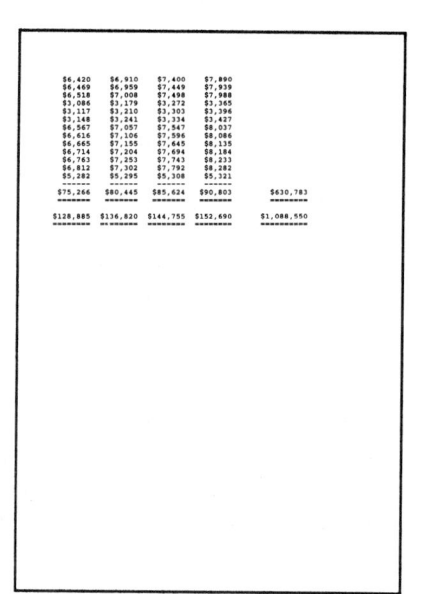

FIGURE A5-5: A sample printout

the printer. Of course, you can always tell when a partial page has been sent to the LaserJet by observing the FORM FEED light on the LaserJet's control panel. When this light is on, you can use either the LaserJet's FORM FEED key or 1-2-3's / Print Printer Page command to eject the current page.

Formatting Reports

1-2-3 offers several formatting options that you can use to improve the appearance and clarity of the reports you can print on the HP LaserJet. In addition to modifying the report's margins, you can change the page length, define a header and footer, define a setup string, and designate certain rows and columns in your report as headings. In this section, we'll demonstrate how to make these kinds of changes to your reports.

Margin Settings

Figure A5-6 shows a larger view of page 1 from the report in Figure A5-12. We will use this page to illustrate how 1-2-3's margin settings affect the format of the printed report.

The Unprintable Area

As you probably know by now, the LaserJet printer does not print at the very top, bottom, left, and right edge of the page. This "unprintable" area occupies the first three and last three lines of the page, and the first $2^1/_2$ and last $2^1/_2$ character spaces of each row. In other words, the unprintable area on a standard $8^1/_2$- by 11-inch page is $^1/_2$ inch at the top and bottom and $^1/_4$ inch at the left and right edges of each page.

Top and Bottom Margins

We have recommended that you use a default top and bottom margin setting of 0 for your reports so that you can fit as much information as possible onto each page. As you probably know, 1-2-3 reserves three rows at the top of each page for a header. When you consider the three unprintable lines along with a three-line header, you'll see that a top margin setting of 0 creates an effective top margin of six lines for each page in the report. Similarly, since there are three unprintable lines at the bottom of the page, along with a three-line footer, a bottom margin setting of 0 produces an effective bottom margin of six lines as well.

If you want to change the top margin setting for any of your 1-2-3 worksheets, first retrieve the worksheet, then issue the / Print Printer Options Margins Top command. Issuing this command causes 1-2-3 to display the prompt *Enter top margin (0..32):*, followed by the current top margin setting. When you see this prompt, type the new top margin setting, and press [Enter]. You change the bottom margin setting in much the same way: Issue the / Print Printer Options Margins Bottom command, type the new bottom margin, and press [Enter].

Although you may specify top and bottom margin settings ranging from 0 lines to 32 lines, you will rarely use a setting greater than 2 or 3 lines when printing to a LaserJet printer. As we have said, you'll almost always want to use top and bottom margin settings of 0 so that you can fit as much information as possible onto each page. Remember that even when you specify a top margin of 0, the LaserJet will still have an effective six-line top and bottom margin—three lines which are unprintable, and three lines which are reserved for a header or a footer.

```
Sales Forecast by Region
================================================================
                         Jan-90     Feb-90     Mar-90     Apr-90     May-90
                         ------     ------     ------     ------     ------
East
  Raleigh, NC            $1,145     $1,264     $1,383     $1,502     $1,621
  Providence, RI           $873       $882       $891       $900       $909
  Baltimore, MD          $1,179     $1,298     $1,417     $1,536     $1,655
  Washington, DC         $1,196     $1,315     $1,434     $1,553     $1,672
  Virginia Beach, VA       $736       $848       $960     $1,072     $1,184
  Carson City, NJ          $792       $904     $1,016     $1,128     $1,240
  Syracuse, NY           $1,213     $1,332     $1,451     $1,570     $1,689
  Boston, MA             $1,230     $1,349     $1,468     $1,587     $1,706
  Atlantic City, NJ      $1,247     $1,366     $1,485     $1,604     $1,723
  Hartford, CT             $945       $956       $967       $978       $989
                         ------     ------     ------     ------     ------
    East Total           $9,611    $10,558    $11,505    $12,452    $13,399
                         ======    =======    =======    =======    =======

South
  Miami, FL                $879     $1,023     $1,167     $1,311     $1,455
  Atlanta, GA              $903     $1,047     $1,191     $1,335     $1,479
  Jackson, MS              $927     $1,071     $1,215     $1,359     $1,503
  Nashville, TN          $1,001     $1,047     $1,093     $1,139     $1,185
  Hilton Head, SC        $1,024     $1,070     $1,116     $1,162     $1,208
  Louisville, KY           $951     $1,095     $1,239     $1,383     $1,527
  Knoxville, TN            $975     $1,119     $1,263     $1,407     $1,551
  Tallahassee, FL        $1,325     $1,367     $1,409     $1,451     $1,493
  Boca Raton, FL         $1,346     $1,388     $1,430     $1,472     $1,514
  Myrtle Beach, SC       $1,162     $1,281     $1,400     $1,519     $1,638
  Birmingham, AL           $999     $1,143     $1,287     $1,431     $1,575
                         ------     ------     ------     ------     ------
    South Total         $11,492    $12,651    $13,810    $14,969    $16,128
                        =======    =======    =======    =======    =======

Midwest
  Indianapolis, IN       $2,179     $2,270     $2,361     $2,452     $2,543
  Chicago, IL            $2,192     $2,283     $2,374     $2,465     $2,556
  Dayton, OH             $2,205     $2,296     $2,387     $2,478     $2,569
  Springfield, IL        $2,218     $2,309     $2,400     $2,491     $2,582
  St. Louis, MO          $2,231     $2,322     $2,413     $2,504     $2,595
  Fort Wayne, IN         $2,244     $2,335     $2,426     $2,517     $2,608
  Milwaukee, WI          $3,210     $3,223     $3,236     $3,249     $3,262
  Kansas City, MO        $2,257     $2,348     $2,439     $2,530     $2,621
                         ------     ------     ------     ------     ------
    Midwest Total       $18,736    $19,386    $20,036    $20,686    $21,336
                        =======    =======    =======    =======    =======

West
  Denver, CO             $3,921     $4,411     $4,901     $5,391     $5,881
```

FIGURE A5-6: A sample page

If you want 1-2-3 to remove the lines that are reserved for the header and footer, you can issue the /Print Printer Options Other Unformatted command. Unfortunately, this command affects more than just the header and footer—it also causes 1-2-3 to ignore the top and bottom margin, manual page breaks, and the page length. We'll discuss this command in more detail in the section "Printing unformatted reports". As you might expect, 1-2-3 either reserves a full three lines for the header or footer, or no lines at all. Consequently, when you set your top margin to 0, your effective top margin will either be three lines (the LaserJet's three unprintable lines), or six lines (the three unprintable lines plus the three lines reserved for the header or footer). There is no way you can print a report with an effective top margin of zero lines.

Left and Right Margins

We've recommended that you set your default left margin to 0, which tells 1-2-3 to insert no blank characters at the beginning of each line in the report. However, since the LaserJet cannot print in the first $1/4$-inch area at the left edge of each page, a left margin setting of 0 produces an effective left margin of $2^1/_2$ characters.

If you want to insert additional spaces at the beginning of each line in the report, you can use the / Print Printer Options Margins Left command to change the left margin setting. When you issue this command, 1-2-3 will present the prompt *Enter left margin (0..240):*, followed by the current left margin setting. When you see this prompt, just type the left margin setting you want to use and press [Enter].

As the prompt indicates, you can enter a left margin setting ranging from 0 to 240 characters. However, the left margin setting must always be less than the right margin setting. You will seldom use a left margin setting of more than eight characters. We almost always use a left margin setting of 0 in our reports so that we can fit as much information as possible onto each page.

1-2-3's right margin setting is a little different from the other margin settings. While the top, bottom, and left margin settings tell 1-2-3 how many blank rows or characters to reserve at the edge of a page, the right margin setting tells 1-2-3 how many characters to print on each line of the page. A default right margin setting of 80 means that each line of the report may contain a maximum of 80 characters. If you've specified a non-zero left margin setting, however, then those characters count as part of the 80. For instance, a left margin setting of 4 along with a right margin setting of 80 allows 1-2-3 to print a maximum of 76 characters on each line of the report.

As you can see in Figure A5-6, a left and right margin setting of 0 and 80, respectively, keeps the report centered on the page. When you print a report with compressed characters, however, or in Landscape orientation, you'll need to change the right margin setting in order to print more characters per line and to keep the lines centered on the page.

To change the right margin setting, issue the / Print Printer Options Margins Right command. This command causes 1-2-3 to display the prompt *Enter right margin (0..240):*, followed by the current Right Margin setting. When you see this prompt, type the new Right margin setting, and press [Enter].

The right margin setting can range from 0 to 240 and must be larger than the left margin setting. In fact, the difference between the right margin setting and the left margin setting must be at least equal to or greater than the widest column in your Print range. If the right margin setting is less than the left margin setting, 1-2-3 will not be able to print any data.

Always remember to use a right margin setting that is consistent with the paper size you are using and with the setup string you have specified (if any). If you specify a right margin setting that is greater than the maximum number of characters your printer can print on one line, each line of the report will wrap around to the next page. Not only does this make a confusing mess of the printout, it also disrupts 1-2-3's page breaks.

The maximum line length you use for 10 cpi type on a standard $8\frac{1}{2}$- by 11-inch sheet of paper is 80 characters. If you use a setup string to print in compressed type, the maximum length increases to about 132 characters. If you print a report with normal type in Landscape orientation, then the maximum line length can be as much as 106 characters. However, if you use compressed print and Landscape orientation, the maximum length increases to about 176 characters. We've included a summary of some popular report formats and their associated right Margin and setup string settings in the table on pages 735 and 736.

Page Length

The number of lines that 1-2-3 prints on each page of a report is determined by the page length setting. Since the LaserJet cannot print on the first or last three lines of a page, 60 lines is the maximum the LaserJet can print on a standard size sheet of paper. Consequently, you must make certain that 1-2-3's default page length is 60 before printing on a standard size sheet of paper with the LaserJet.

Since the page length setting determines where 1-2-3 will place page breaks in a report, it is very important that you specify the appropriate page length. As we have said, a page length setting of 60 assumes that you are using the LaserJet to print text that occupies six vertical lines-per-inch on $8\frac{1}{2}$- by 11-inch size paper in Portrait orientation. If you use a setup string that changes the character size or the paper orientation, or if you use paper that is longer or shorter than 11 inches (including legal paper, mailing labels, and special forms), you will need to adjust the page length setting accordingly.

To change the page length setting, issue the / Print Printer Options Pg-Length command. This command causes 1-2-3 to display the prompt *Enter lines per page (1..100):*, followed by the current page length setting. When you see this prompt, just type the new page length setting and press [Enter].

You can specify any page length setting from one line to 100 lines. However, you must make sure that the page length you specify is at least as long as the sum of the the top and bottom margins, the header and footer spaces, the lines that fall in the page's unprintable area, and one line of data. For example, if the top and bottom margin settings are both 0, then the minimum page length setting will be 13. We obtained this result by adding the two margin settings (0+0), the header and footer spaces (3+3), the lines that fall in the unprintable area at the top and bottom of the page (3+3), plus one line of data. If you enter a page length setting that is too short, 1-2-3 will alert you when you select Go to print your report by displaying the error message *Margins, header and footer equal or exceed page length.*

If you issue the /Print Printer Options Other command and choose the Unformatted option, 1-2-3 will completely ignore the Page length setting. We'll discuss the Unformatted command in more detail later.

Headers and Footers

1-2-3 lets you define a header, a footer, or both for your printed reports. A header is a line of text that is printed once at the top of every page in a report, while a footer is a line of text that is printed at the bottom of every page. You will probably use headers and footers to title your reports or to date and number the pages in your report.

As we've explained, the LaserJet will not print on the first three or last three lines of a page. 1-2-3 reserves three additional lines just below the unprintable area at the top of the page for the header, and three lines just above the unprintable area at the bottom of each page for the footer, even if you haven't defined a header or a footer. If you have defined a header, it will be printed on the first of the three header lines, with two blank lines between it and the first line of the report. Similarly, if you've defined a footer, it will appear on the third footer line at the bottom of the page, with two blank lines between it and the last line of the report.

The position of the first character in the header or footer is determined by the left margin setting. (Of course, the "built-in" $1/_4$ inch margin at the left edge of the page affects the header line—just as it affects the printed lines in the worksheet.) Although headers and footers may contain up to 240 characters, the left and right margin settings determine the number of characters that can actually fit on the page. If your header or footer is too long to fit within your left and right margins, 1-2-3 will truncate the header or footer. The default left margin (4) and right margin (76) allow 1-2-3 to print a header or footer that is up to 72 characters long.

Font Options

Since 1-2-3 is a character-based product, it can display only fixed-spaced characters on your screen, and it expects your printer to use only fixed-space characters in printed reports. For this reason, you'll find that it is impractical to print worksheet reports with proportionally-spaced fonts on the HP LaserJet. If you want to use proportionally spaced fonts in your printed worksheets, you'll have to use a graphics-based spreadsheet application like Microsoft Excel.

Each LaserJet printer is equipped with a few internal fonts. Almost every LaserJet printer is equipped with both Courier and Line Printer fonts. If your LaserJet is not equipped with the font you want to use, you'll have to purchase an optional font cartridge for your LaserJet.

When you are purchasing a font cartridge, you should decide which fonts you'll most want to use in your printed worksheets, then identify the font cartridge(s) that best suits your needs. You need to consider more than just the size of the fonts when purchasing a font cartridge. You should also consider the style of the fonts on each cartridge (Medium, Bold, Italics), and the orientations in which the fonts are available (Portrait, Landscape). One of the most popular font cartridges for 1-2-3 users with older LaserJet models is the "L" cartridge (HP part # 92286L), which contains Courier 12 Bold and Italic fonts along with the Line Printer Compressed font (both fonts are offered in Portrait and in Landscape orientation). If you own a LaserJet Series II printer, you'll find that the "S1" cartridge (HP part # 92290S1) supplements the Series II's internal fonts quite nicely.

Although 1-2-3 is capable of using the LaserJet's soft fonts, we recommend that you not use soft fonts with 1-2-3 for two reasons. First of all, almost all soft fonts are proportionally-spaced, which usually fouls up the spacing of your rows and columns in the printed worksheet. Second, soft fonts occupy a portion of your printer's RAM, which reduces the amount of printer RAM available for printing graphs. (We'll talk about printing graphs on the LaserJet in the next section of this chapter.) You'll save yourself plenty of time and trouble by using font cartridges instead of soft fonts when printing your 1-2-3 reports.

Setup Strings

By default, the LaserJet uses the Courier 12 font to print 1-2-3 reports. This font occupies six lines per inch vertically and ten characters per inch horizontally. As you know, however, the LaserJet also has the ability to print more lines per inch, to print in boldface and in italics, to print in Portrait or in Landscape orientation, or even to print in completely different fonts. You can take advantage of the LaserJet's special print features by sending special strings of characters called setup strings.

The /Print Printer Options Setup command allows you to specify a setup string for your printed reports. When you issue this command, 1-2-3 will present the prompt *Enter setup string:*. When you see this prompt, simply type the setup string that activates the print feature you want to use and press [Enter]. If you use a setup string that changes the size of the type or the orientation of the page, you'll also need to change either the page length setting, the right margin setting, or both.

The particular print options that are available to you depend on the LaserJet model you own and on the font options you've installed. Setup strings don't import any special features—they merely ask the LaserJet to use the features that are already there. For example, since none of the LaserJet printers contain a built-in italic font, you cannot use a setup string to create italic type on your LaserJet printer unless you've installed a font cartridge or a soft font that provides italic type. Make sure your printer has access to the font you want to use before you attempt to activate that font with a setup string.

Table A5-1 shows the common setup strings that are used for all LaserJet printers. As you can see, all of these setup strings have a similar form: They begin with \Ø27, are followed by various strings of characters, and end with a capital letter. For example, the character sequence that activates 12 cpi printing is *\Ø27(sØp12H*, while the sequence that activates 16 cpi printing is *\Ø27(s16.66H*. When you use the /Print Printer Options Setup command to define a setup string, you should type the appropriate string exactly as it appears in Table 6-1. Make sure you distinguish the number Ø from the capital letter O, and the number 1 from the lowercase letter l. If you confuse these characters with one another, your setup strings will not produce the results you expect.

Appendix 5: Printing with an HP LaserJet

	Setup	Page Length	Right Margin
Portrait			
Letter size paper			
60 lines per page			
10 cpi	\Ø27E	60	80
12 cpi	\Ø27(sØp12H	60	96
16.66 cpi	\Ø27(s16.66H	60	132
66 lines per page			
10 cpi	\Ø27&"7.27C	66	80
12 cpi	\Ø27&"7.27C\Ø27(sØp12H	66	96
16.66 cpi	\Ø27&"7.27C\Ø27(s16.66H	66	132
89 lines per page			
10 cpi	\Ø27&"5.39C	89	80
12 cpi	\Ø27&"5.39C\Ø27(sØp12H	89	96
16.66 cpi	\Ø27&"5.39C\Ø27(s16.66H	89	132
Legal size paper (legal tray)			
78 lines per page			
10 cpi	\Ø27E	78	80
12 cpi	\Ø27(sØp12H	78	96
16.66 cpi	\Ø27(s16.66H	78	132
104 lines per page			
10 cpi	\Ø27&"8D	100	80
12 cpi	\Ø27&"8D\Ø27(sØp12H	100	96
16.66 cpi	\Ø27&"8D\Ø27(s16.66H	100	132
150 lines per page			
16.66 cpi	\Ø27&"4.16C\Ø27(s16.66H	100	132
Legal size paper (manual feed)			
78 lines per page			
10 cpi	\Ø27&"84p2H	78	80
12 cpi	\Ø27&"84p2H\Ø27(sØp12H	78	96
16.66 cpi	\Ø27&"84p2H\Ø27(s16.66H	78	132
104 lines per page			
10 cpi	\Ø27&"84p2hØo8D	100	80
12 cpi	\Ø27&"84p2hØo8D\Ø27(sØp12H	100	96
16.66 cpi	\Ø27&"84p2hØo8D\Ø27(s16.66H	100	132
150 lines per page			
16.66 cpi	\Ø27&"84p2hØo4.16C\Ø27(s16.66H	100	132

TABLE A5-1: Common setup strings (*continued on next page*)

Landscape
　Letter size paper
　　45 lines per page

10 cpi	\027&"1O	45	106
12 cpi	\027&"1O\027(sØp12H	45	127
16.66 cpi	\027&"1O\027(s16.66H	45	176

　　66 lines per page

10 cpi	\027&"1o5.45C	66	106
12 cpi	\027&"1o5.45C\027(sØp12H	66	127
16.66 cpi	\027&"1o5.45C\027(s16.66H	66	176

　Legal size paper (legal tray)
　　45 lines per page

10 cpi	\027&"1O	45	136
12 cpi	\027&"1O\027(sØp12H	45	163
16.66 cpi	\027&"1O\027(s16.66H	45	226

　　66 lines per page

10 cpi	\027&"1o5.45C	66	136
12 cpi	\027&"1o5.45C\027(sØp12H	66	163
16.66 cpi	\027&"1o5.45C\027(s16.66H	66	226

　Legal size paper (manual feed)
　　45 lines per page

10 cpi	\027&"84p2h1O	45	136
12 cpi	\027&"84p2h1O\027(sØp12H	45	163
16.66 cpi	\027&"84p2h1O\027(s16.66H	45	226

　　66 lines per page

10 cpi	\027&"84p2h1o5.45C	66	136
12 cpi	\027&"84p2h1o5.45C\027(sØp12H	66	163
16.66 cpi	\027&"84p2h1o5.45C\027(s16.66H	66	226

TABLE A5-1 (*continued*):Common setup strings

After you have defined a setup string, 1-2-3 will automatically send that string to the printer each time you print a worksheet. Once a setup string has told the printer to use a particular print feature, the printer will continue using that feature until you use another setup string to turn off the feature or power off the printer. Any setup string you define with the / Print Printer Options Setup command will affect your entire worksheet, including headers and footers.

Using Setup Strings with Soft Fonts

If you download a soft font to your LaserJet printer before you load 1-2-3, you can tell 1-2-3 to use that font when you print your worksheet by sending the appropriate setup string. There are two ways to activate a downloaded soft font with a 1-2-3 setup string.

First, you can specify the string that describes the soft font's orientation, pitch, and so forth, just as you would to activate a cartridge font. Alternatively, you can send a setup string that activates the font I.D. number of the font you've downloaded. (You must assign a font ID number between Ø and 32767 to each font you download.) For more information on how to activate soft fonts with setup strings, refer to the documentation included with your soft fonts.

Troubleshooting

If you can't make a setup string correctly alter the format of your printed report, use these tips to help debug the problem:

- First reset your LaserJet. If you have a Series II model, take the printer off line, and then press and hold the ENTER/RESET MENU button on the printer's control panel until the message *09 MENU RESET* appears. If you have a LaserJet Plus or 500 PLUS, press and hold the *HOLD TO RESET* key until *07* appears. If you have an original LaserJet printer, you must power the printer off and back on again.

- Check to see if your setup string has been typed correctly. The most common causes of setup string problems are the accidental use of the number one (1) in place of the lowercase letter ", and the use of the number zero (Ø) in place of the capital letter O. Also make sure you've used a backslash (\) instead of a forward slash (/). All of the letters within the setup string should be lowercase letters, except for the last letter, which must be uppercase.

- Make sure your printer is equipped with the print feature you are trying to activate. If you are attempting to use a particular font, make sure that that font is either one of your LaserJet's built-in fonts or that you've installed a font cartridge or a soft font that contains the font you're trying to use. If you're using a font cartridge, take the printer off line, remove the cartridge, reinsert it firmly in the printer, and then put the printer back on line before you test the setup string again.

Deleting a Setup String

After you've entered a setup string, you may want to remove that string so you can print a report in the LaserJet's standard typeface (Courier 12). To delete a setup string, issue the / Print Printer Options Setup command, press [Esc] to delete the existing string, then press [Enter] to lock in the change.

You will find that deleting a setup string has no immediate effect on your printer. Although you've deleted the string, you'll still see the current special print features the next time you print. As we have said, once you turn on a special print attribute, that attribute remains in effect until you either turn off the printer or send another control sequence that turns off the special attribute. Consequently, just deleting a setup string is usually not enough to reverse that string's effect. To restore normal printing, you must delete the setup string and reset the printer by turning it off and on again.

Instead of simply deleting a setup string, you can replace the existing setup string with a new string that resets the printer to its default condition. For all LaserJet printers, this setup string is \Ø27E. When 1-2-3 sends this string to the printer, it will reset all formatting options.

Embedded Setup Strings

If you want to assign some special attributes to just a portion of your worksheet, you can embed setup strings that control those attributes directly in the worksheet. To embed a setup string in your worksheet, you must first insert a blank row directly above the first row that you want to print with the special attribute. Then, you must move the cell pointer to the leftmost column in the Print range in that row (this is usually column A). When the cell pointer is in place, type two vertical bars (||), followed by the setup string that signals the beginning of the print attribute.

You'll usually want to include a second embedded setup string that turns off the special print attribute activated by the first string. You use the same procedure to insert a second embedded setup string that you use to insert the first string, except that you move the cell pointer to the row below the last row that you want to print with the special attribute. Table A5-2 shows a few popular setup strings you can embed in your 1-2-3 worksheets.

Feature	Setup String
Underline On	\Ø27&dD
Underline Off	\Ø27&d@
Boldface On	\Ø27(s3B
Boldface Off	\Ø27(sØB
Italic On	\Ø27(s1S
Italic Off	\Ø27(sØS
Printer Reset	\Ø27E

TABLE A5-2: Embeddable setup strings

As an example of how you might use these strings, consider the worksheet shown in Figure A5-7. As you can see, we've embedded the setup string that turns on underlining (\Ø27&dD) in row 1 of this worksheet, and we've embedded the string that turns off underlining (\Ø27&d@) in row 3 of the worksheet. (Notice that the first vertical bar characters of the embedded setup strings are not displayed in the cells of the worksheet.) When we print this worksheet on an HP LaserJet printer, we will generate the report shown in Figure A5-8. As you can see, the entry in cell A3, "Sales Forecast for 1989", is underlined, while the rest of the page is printed without an underline.

```
A2: ||\027&dD                                              READY

         A         B         C         D         E         F         G
    FORGED WIDGETS, INC.
    :\027&dD
    Sales Forecast for 1989
    !\027&d@


                   Qtr 1     Qtr 2     Qtr 3     Qtr 4     Total
                   -------   -------   -------   -------   -------
    Region 1       13,500    14,320    15,140    15,960    58,920
    Region 2       23,450    24,270    25,090    25,910    98,720
    Region 3       19,930    20,750    21,570    22,390    84,640
    Region 4       25,000    26,620    27,440    28,260   108,120
    Region 5       15,300    16,120    16,940    17,760    66,120
                   -------   -------   -------   -------   -------
    Total          97,980   102,080   106,180   110,280   416,520
```

FIGURE A5-7: A sample worksheet

If your embedded setup string does not generate the report you expect, first make sure you have typed the embedded setup string correctly. Make sure you have not confused any number Ø's with capital O's, or any number 1's with lower case letter l's. Also make sure you've preceded the setup string with two vertical bar characters (||).

If you're certain that you've entered the setup string correctly, make sure you've defined the correct Print range. If you've inserted a blank row above the first row in your worksheet to hold an embedded setup string, you'll probably need to redefine the Print range to include the new row 1. Also remember that your embedded setup string must appear in the leftmost column of the Print range (usually column A) in order to work properly.

Finally, make sure that your LaserJet is capable of printing with the special attribute you are attempting to invoke. If you're attempting to turn on bold printing, for example, make sure your printer has access to a bold font in the appropriate typeface. Remember that the setup string does not "pump in" any special print features, it merely activates the print features that already exist inside your LaserJet.

Sample Reports

The sample reports and accompanying page layout settings in this section should help you decide which style to use for your 1-2-3 reports. You'll notice that most of these reports require either a LaserJet Series II Printer or a font cartridge. In all of these examples, we've set the top, bottom, and left margins to 0.

```
              FORGED WIDGETS, INC.
              Sales Forecast for 1989

                         Qtr 1      Qtr 2      Qtr 3      Qtr 4      Total
                         -------    -------    -------    -------    -------
              Region 1   13,500     14,320     15,140     15,960      58,920
              Region 2   23,450     24,270     25,090     25,910      98,720
              Region 3   19,930     20,750     21,570     22,390      84,640
              Region 4   25,800     26,620     27,440     28,260     108,120
              Region 5   15,300     16,120     16,940     17,760      66,120
                         -------    -------    -------    -------    -------
              Total      97,980    102,080    106,180    110,280     416,520
```

FIGURE A5-8: A printed worksheet

If you need to fit more than 80 characters on a single line of the report, then you'll want to use the settings in Figure A5-9 to generate compressed characters in Portrait orientation:

Requires: Series II or font cartridge
Right: 105
Page Length: 45
Setup String: \Ø27E\Ø27&l1O

```
Sales Forecast by Region
==========================================================================================================
                    Jan-90    Feb-90    Mar-90    Apr-90    May-90    Jun-90    Jul-90    Aug-90    Sep-90     TOTALS
                    ------    ------    ------    ------    ------    ------    ------    ------    ------     ------

East
  Raleigh, NC       $1,145    $1,264    $1,383    $1,502    $1,621    $1,740    $1,859    $1,978    $2,097
  Providence, RI      $873      $882      $891      $900      $909      $918      $927      $936      $945
  Baltimore, MD     $1,179    $1,298    $1,417    $1,536    $1,655    $1,774    $1,893    $2,012    $2,131
  Washington, DC    $1,196    $1,315    $1,434    $1,553    $1,672    $1,791    $1,910    $2,029    $2,148
  Virginia Beach, VA  $736      $848      $960    $1,072    $1,184    $1,296    $1,408    $1,520    $1,632
  Carson City, NJ     $792      $904    $1,016    $1,128    $1,240    $1,352    $1,464    $1,576    $1,688
  Syracuse, NY      $1,213    $1,332    $1,451    $1,570    $1,689    $1,808    $1,927    $2,046    $2,165
  Boston, MA        $1,230    $1,349    $1,468    $1,587    $1,706    $1,825    $1,944    $2,063    $2,182
  Atlantic City, NJ $1,247    $1,366    $1,485    $1,604    $1,723    $1,842    $1,961    $2,080    $2,199
  Hartford, CT        $945      $956      $967      $978      $989    $1,000    $1,011    $1,022    $1,033
                    ------    ------    ------    ------    ------    ------    ------    ------    ------
      East Total    $9,611   $10,558   $11,505   $12,452   $13,399   $14,346   $15,293   $16,240   $17,187   $120,591
                    ======   =======   =======   =======   =======   =======   =======   =======   =======   ========

South
  Miami, FL           $879    $1,023    $1,167    $1,311    $1,455    $1,599    $1,743    $1,887    $2,031
  Atlanta, GA         $903    $1,047    $1,191    $1,335    $1,479    $1,623    $1,767    $1,911    $2,055
  Jackson, MS         $927    $1,071    $1,215    $1,359    $1,503    $1,647    $1,791    $1,935    $2,079
  Nashville, TN     $1,001    $1,047    $1,093    $1,139    $1,185    $1,231    $1,277    $1,323    $1,369
  Hilton Head, SC   $1,024    $1,070    $1,116    $1,162    $1,208    $1,254    $1,300    $1,346    $1,392
  Louisville, KY      $951    $1,095    $1,239    $1,383    $1,527    $1,671    $1,815    $1,959    $2,103
  Knoxville, TN       $975    $1,119    $1,263    $1,407    $1,551    $1,695    $1,839    $1,983    $2,127
  Tallahassee, FL   $1,325    $1,367    $1,409    $1,451    $1,493    $1,535    $1,577    $1,619    $1,661
  Boca Raton, FL    $1,346    $1,388    $1,430    $1,472    $1,514    $1,556    $1,598    $1,640    $1,682
  Myrtle Beach, SC  $1,162    $1,281    $1,400    $1,519    $1,638    $1,757    $1,876    $1,995    $2,114
  Birmingham, AL      $999    $1,143    $1,287    $1,431    $1,575    $1,719    $1,863    $2,007    $2,151
                    ------    ------    ------    ------    ------    ------    ------    ------    ------
      South Total  $11,492   $12,651   $13,810   $14,969   $16,128   $17,287   $18,446   $19,605   $20,764   $145,152
                   =======   =======   =======   =======   =======   =======   =======   =======   =======   ========

Midwest
  Indianapolis, IN  $2,179    $2,270    $2,361    $2,452    $2,543    $2,634    $2,725    $2,816    $2,907
  Chicago, IL       $2,192    $2,283    $2,374    $2,465    $2,556    $2,647    $2,738    $2,829    $2,920
  Dayton, OH        $2,205    $2,296    $2,387    $2,478    $2,569    $2,660    $2,751    $2,842    $2,933
  Springfield, IL   $2,218    $2,309    $2,400    $2,491    $2,582    $2,673    $2,764    $2,855    $2,946
  St. Louis, MO     $2,231    $2,322    $2,413    $2,504    $2,595    $2,686    $2,777    $2,868    $2,959
  Fort Wayne, IN    $2,244    $2,335    $2,426    $2,517    $2,608    $2,699    $2,790    $2,881    $2,972
  Milwaukee, WI     $3,210    $3,223    $3,236    $3,249    $3,262    $3,275    $3,288    $3,301    $3,314
  Kansas City, MO   $2,257    $2,348    $2,439    $2,530    $2,621    $2,712    $2,803    $2,894    $2,985
                    ------    ------    ------    ------    ------    ------    ------    ------    ------
      Midwest Total $18,736  $19,386   $20,036   $20,686   $21,336   $21,986   $22,636   $23,286   $23,936   $192,02
                   =======  =======   =======   =======   =======   =======   =======   =======   =======   ========

West
  Denver, CO        $3,921    $4,411    $4,901    $5,391    $5,881    $6,371    $6,861    $7,351    $7,841
  Reno, NV          $3,970    $4,460    $4,950    $5,440    $5,930    $6,420    $6,910    $7,400    $7,890
  Salem, OR         $4,019    $4,509    $4,999    $5,489    $5,979    $6,469    $6,959    $7,449    $7,939
  Albuquerque, NM   $4,068    $4,558    $5,048    $5,538    $6,028    $6,518    $7,008    $7,498    $7,988
  Columbia, WA      $2,621    $2,714    $2,807    $2,900    $2,993    $3,086    $3,179    $3,272    $3,365
```

FIGURE A5-9: Portrait orientation at 16.66 cpi and 60 lines per page

If your worksheet report is relatively small (fewer than 45 lines), and is wider than it is tall, you may prefer to print the report in uncompressed print in Landscape orientation. To do this, you should use the settings in Figure A5-10:

Requires: Series II, or font cartridge
Right: 132
Page Length: 60
Setup String: \Ø27E\Ø27(s16.66H

```
Sales Forecast by Region
===============================================================================
                       Jan-90    Feb-90    Mar-90    Apr-90    May-90    Jun-90    Jul-90
                       ------    ------    ------    ------    ------    ------    ------
East
  Raleigh, NC          $1,145    $1,264    $1,383    $1,502    $1,621    $1,740    $1,859
  Providence, RI         $873      $882      $891      $900      $909      $918      $927
  Baltimore, MD        $1,179    $1,298    $1,417    $1,536    $1,655    $1,774    $1,893
  Washington, DC       $1,196    $1,315    $1,434    $1,553    $1,672    $1,791    $1,910
  Virginia Beach, VA     $736      $848      $960    $1,072    $1,184    $1,296    $1,408
  Carson City, NJ        $792      $904    $1,016    $1,128    $1,240    $1,352    $1,464
  Syracuse, NY         $1,213    $1,332    $1,451    $1,570    $1,689    $1,808    $1,927
  Boston, MA           $1,230    $1,349    $1,468    $1,587    $1,706    $1,825    $1,944
  Atlantic City, NJ    $1,247    $1,366    $1,485    $1,604    $1,723    $1,842    $1,961
  Hartford, CT           $945      $956      $967      $978      $989    $1,000    $1,011
                       ------    ------    ------    ------    ------    ------    ------
       East Total      $9,611   $10,558   $11,505   $12,452   $13,399   $14,346   $15,293
                       ======   =======   =======   =======   =======   =======   =======
South
  Miami, FL              $879    $1,023    $1,167    $1,311    $1,455    $1,599    $1,743
  Atlanta, GA            $903    $1,047    $1,191    $1,335    $1,479    $1,623    $1,767
  Jackson, MS            $927    $1,071    $1,215    $1,359    $1,503    $1,647    $1,791
  Nashville, TN        $1,001    $1,047    $1,093    $1,139    $1,185    $1,231    $1,277
  Hilton Head, SC      $1,024    $1,070    $1,116    $1,162    $1,208    $1,254    $1,300
  Louisville, KY         $951    $1,095    $1,239    $1,383    $1,527    $1,671    $1,815
  Knoxville, TN          $975    $1,119    $1,263    $1,407    $1,551    $1,695    $1,839
  Tallahassee, FL      $1,325    $1,367    $1,409    $1,451    $1,493    $1,535    $1,577
  Boca Raton, FL       $1,346    $1,388    $1,430    $1,472    $1,514    $1,556    $1,598
  Myrtle Beach, SC     $1,162    $1,281    $1,400    $1,519    $1,638    $1,757    $1,876
  Birmingham, AL         $999    $1,143    $1,287    $1,431    $1,575    $1,719    $1,863
                       ------   -------   -------   -------   -------   -------   -------
       South Total    $11,492   $12,651   $13,810   $14,969   $16,128   $17,287   $18,446
                      =======   =======   =======   =======   =======   =======   =======
Midwest
  Indianapolis, IN     $2,179    $2,270    $2,361    $2,452    $2,543    $2,634    $2,725
  Chicago, IL          $2,192    $2,283    $2,374    $2,465    $2,556    $2,647    $2,738
  Dayton, OH           $2,205    $2,296    $2,387    $2,478    $2,569    $2,660    $2,751
```

FIGURE A5-10: Landscape orientation at 10 cpi and 45 lines per page

If you need to squeeze a few more characters on each line of a Landscape-oriented report, use the layout settings in Figure A5-11 to set up your LaserJet for compressed print in landscape orientation:

Requires: Series II or font cartridge
Right: 175
Page Length: 45
Setup String: \Ø27E\027&l1O\Ø27(s16.66H

If your worksheet is extremely wide in comparison to its length (as will be the case with a five-year sales forecast), you may prefer to use the layout settings in Figure A5-12, which produce a compressed report in landscape orientation on legal paper:

Requires: Series II or font cartridge
Right: 225
Page Length: 66
Setup String: \Ø27E\027&l84p2h1o5.45C\Ø27(s16.66H

Appendix 5: Printing with an HP LaserJet 743

FIGURE A5-11: Landscape orientation at 16.66 cpi and 45 lines per page

FIGURE A5-12: Landscape orientation on legal paper at 16.66 cpi and 45 lines per page

Printing Unformatted Reports

1-2-3 offers you the option of printing "unformatted" reports—that is, reports that ignore the top and bottom margin settings, the page length setting, and any header or footer you have defined. Instead of reserving lines for the header, footer, top margin, and bottom margin areas at the top and bottom of each page, 1-2-3 will begin printing on the first printable line of the page and will continue printing to the last printable line of the page. Of course, the first and last printable lines of the page are $1/2$ inch from the top and bottom edges of the page.

To create an unformatted report, issue the / Print Printer Options Other Unformatted command. To turn formatting back on, issue the / Print Printer Options Other Formatted command.

Although the Unformatted option causes 1-2-3 to ignore the headers, footers, and manual page breaks, it will not affect your left and right margins or your setup string. The left and right margin settings still determine where the vertical page breaks in the report should occur. In addition, the printer will use whatever setup string you have defined.

If you have defined column headings before printing an unformatted report, those headings will appear on each vertical section of the report. However, because an unformatted report has no horizontal page breaks, the row headings will appear only once at the top of the report.

Resetting Print Defaults

After you change the default print settings for a worksheet, you might decide to return some or all of the print settings to their default values. The quickest way to do this is to issue the / Print Printer Clear command.

If you want to reset all of the print settings to their defaults, issue the / Print Printer Clear All command. This command will delete your header and footer, remove any headings you have defined, and return the settings for the setup string, margins, and page length to their defaults. It also will remove the range you have defined as your Print range. The only settings that are not affected by this command are the manual page breaks you have defined, embedded setup strings, and the printer settings defined by the / Worksheet Global Default Printer command.

If you want to retain the current settings for the Print range, left heading, and top heading, but reset the header, footer, margins, page length, and setup string, issue the / Print Printer Clear Format command. If you just want to clear the headings settings, issue the / Print Printer Clear Borders command. Finally, if you want to reset the Print range, issue the / Print Printer Clear Range command.

PRINTING GRAPHS

The process of printing a 1-2-3 graph on an HP LaserJet printer is entirely different from the process of printing a 1-2-3 worksheet. In this section, we'll tell you how to take advantage of the LaserJet's graphics capabilities, and we'll walk you through the process of printing some sample 1-2-3 graphs.

As you probably know, in order to print a graph you have created with 1-2-3, you must save that graph into a .PIC file, exit from 1-2-3, and then load 1-2-3's graph-printing utility program, PrintGraph. Once you've loaded PrintGraph, you must retrieve the appropriate .PIC file and adjust a few of the print settings. After you've done all of this, you can print the graph on your LaserJet.

You will not be able to use PrintGraph to print a graph on your LaserJet unless you have used the Install Program to install the LaserJet's graphics output driver with 1-2-3's Install Program. For an explanation of how to use the Install Program to install graphics output drivers, see the section entitled "Hardware Setup" at the beginning of this chapter, or refer to your 1-2-3 manuals.

Configuring PrintGraph

Before you can use PrintGraph to print a 1-2-3 graph on your LaserJet printer, you need to tell 1-2-3 a few things about your printer. Specifically, you must indicate what kind of printer you have and how your printer is connected to your computer. The command you will use to define these settings is the Settings Hardware command. When you issue the Settings Hardware command, PrintGraph will present the menu shown in Figure A5-13.

Choosing an Interface

Just as you told 1-2-3 where to send your printed worksheets, you must tell PrintGraph which printer interface your LaserJet is using. To select a printer interface, choose the Interface option from the menu in Figure A5-13. When you do this, 1-2-3 will present a menu with eight options, as shown in Figure A5-14. You'll notice that these are the same eight options 1-2-3 presents when you are defining a printer interface with 1-2-3's / Worksheet Global Default Printer Interface command.

If your LaserJet is using your computer's primary parallel interface, you should leave the Interface setting at Parallel 1 (the default). If you are using anything other than the primary parallel interface, you should choose the option that corresponds to the interface used by your LaserJet. To choose the appropriate interface, just point to that option (or type the number of that option) and press [Enter].

```
Copyright 1986, 1989 Lotus Development Corp. All Rights Reserved. V2.2    MENU
Specify directory containing graphs
Graphs-Directory  Fonts-Directory  Interface  Printer  Size-Paper  Quit

  GRAPHS     IMAGE SETTINGS                      HARDWARE SETTINGS
  TO PRINT   Size              Range colors      Graphs directory
             Top      .395  X                      A:\
             Left     .750  A                    Fonts directory
             Width   6.500  B                      A:\
             Height  4.691  C                    Interface
             Rotation .000  D                      Parallel 1
                            E                    Printer
             Font           F
             1 BLOCK1                            Paper size
             2 BLOCK1                              Width    8.500
                                                  Length  11.000

                                                 ACTION SETTINGS
                                                  Pause  No   Eject  No
```

FIGURE A5-13: The Settings Hardware command

```
Copyright 1986, 1989 Lotus Development Corp. All Rights Reserved. V2.2    MENU
Parallel 1
1 2 3 4 5 6 7 8

  GRAPHS     IMAGE SETTINGS                      HARDWARE SETTINGS
  TO PRINT   Size              Range colors      Graphs directory
             Top      .395  X                      A:\
             Left     .750  A                    Fonts directory
             Width   6.500  B                      A:\
             Height  4.691  C                    Interface
             Rotation .000  D                      Parallel 1
                            E                    Printer
             Font           F
             1 BLOCK1                            Paper size
             2 BLOCK1                              Width    8.500
                                                  Length  11.000

                                                 ACTION SETTINGS
                                                  Pause  No   Eject  No
```

FIGURE A5-14: The Interface menu

Although the HP LaserJet Series II and the HP LaserJet Plus are equipped with both a parallel and a serial interface, the original HP LaserJet is equipped with only a serial interface. If you have an original LaserJet printer, or if you want to run your LaserJet

Plus or LaserJet Series II as a serial printer, you need to choose the appropriate serial Interface setting from the Interface menu (options 2 or 4). You must also make sure that you've used DOS's MODE command to define the baud rate, number of stop bits, and parity for your printer. (Parallel printers don't require you to specify a Baud, Stop Bits, and Parity setting.) For instance, suppose you have connected your LaserJet to your computer's primary serial interface (COM1:). To define the baud, parity, data bits, and stop bits for COM1:, you must issue the DOS command

MODE COM1:9600,n,8,1

before you load PrintGraph. Once you have issued this MODE command and have started your PrintGraph session, choose the appropriate Interface setting for the serial port you defined in your MODE command (Serial 1 in this case).

Choosing a Printer

The Printer setting specifies which printer driver you want PrintGraph to use when it prints your 1-2-3 graphs. When you choose the Printer option, PrintGraph brings up a list of the printers you've installed with the Install Program. If you've installed the drivers for both of HP's LaserJet printers—LaserJet and LaserJet Plus—PrintGraph will present a screen like the one shown in Figure A5-15 when you choose the Printer option.

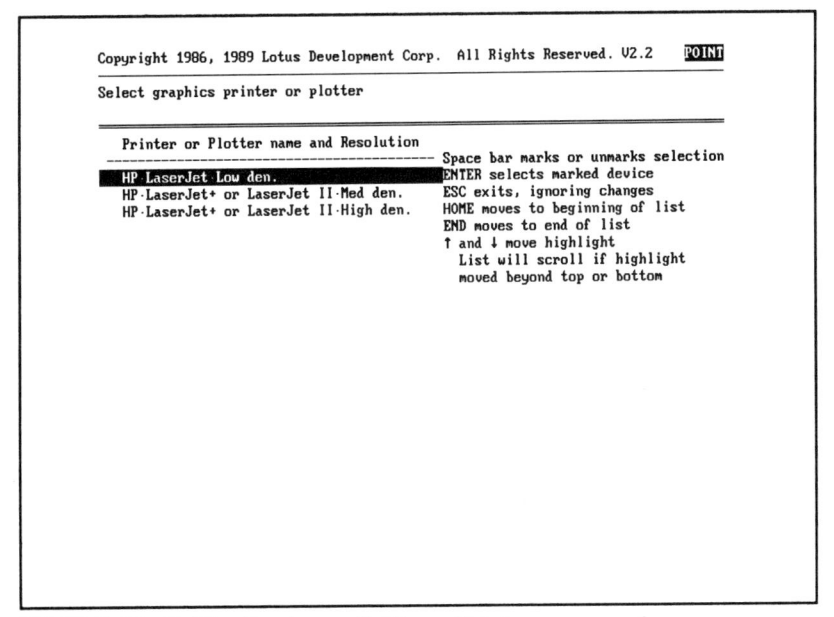

```
Copyright 1986, 1989 Lotus Development Corp.  All Rights Reserved. V2.2   POINT
Select graphics printer or plotter

  Printer or Plotter name and Resolution
  --------------------------------------  Space bar marks or unmarks selection
  HP-LaserJet-Low den.                    ENTER selects marked device
  HP-LaserJet+ or LaserJet II-Med den.    ESC exits, ignoring changes
  HP-LaserJet+ or LaserJet II-High den.   HOME moves to beginning of list
                                          END moves to end of list
                                          ↑ and ↓ move highlight
                                            List will scroll if highlight
                                            moved beyond top or bottom
```

FIGURE A5-15: The Hardware Settings Printer command

If you have an original LaserJet printer, you need to choose the HP LaserJet option, which prints graphs in a resolution of 75 x 75 dpi. If you have a LaserJet Plus, LaserJet

500+, or LaserJet Series II printer, you'll have to choose one of the LaserJet Plus printer drivers: low density (100 x 100 dpi) and high density (300 x 300 dpi). A full page of 300 dpi graphics requires about 1.5 MB of printer memory. If you want to print full-page 300 dpi graphs and your printer has less than 2 MB of memory, you'll need to upgrade the memory on your printer.

After you use the ↓ and ↑ keys to highlight the appropriate LaserJet printer option, press the [Spacebar] to mark that choice. PrintGraph will place a # next to the device you select. When you've made your selection, press [Enter] to lock in that choice and return to the Hardware Settings menu. If you change your mind, just repeat this procedure and select a new printer driver from the list.

Specifying Paper Size

The Settings Hardware Size-Paper command lets you specify the size of the paper you'll be using in your printer. PrintGraph's default paper size is $8^1/_2$ inches wide by 11 inches long. While this setting will probably be appropriate for most applications, you may need to change the Size-Paper setting in certain situations.

To specify a different paper size, just issue the Settings Hardware Size-Paper command to reveal the options Length and Width. To change the page length setting, choose the Length option and specify the new length in inches. Similarly, to change the page width setting, choose the Width option and specify the new page width.

One common situation where you will need to change the page length setting is when you are using legal size paper ($8^1/_2$ inches wide by 14 inches long) to hold your printed graphs. To set up PrintGraph for legal size paper, simply issue the Settings Hardware Size-Paper Length command, type 14, and press [Enter].

Defining the Graphs-Directory and Fonts-Directory

As you probably know, you must use the Graphs-Directory option to tell PrintGraph where you have stored the .PIC files you intend to print. Similarly, you must use the Fonts-Directory option to tell PrintGraph where you've installed PrintGraph's font files. If you do not define these two settings correctly, PrintGraph will be unable to print your graphs.

The Pause and Eject Settings

The Pause and Eject settings are used to control the action of your printer when you are printing multiple graphs with one command. The Pause setting tells PrintGraph whether or not it should pause after it prints each graph in a series. If Pause is set to No (the default), PrintGraph will print all of the graphs in sequence without pausing. If Pause is set to Yes, however, PrintGraph will pause after it prints each graph and will make a beeping noise.

You'll probably want PrintGraph to pause between graphs whenever you are manually feeding sheets of paper to the LaserJet. To change the Pause setting from No (the default) to Yes, issue the Settings Action Pause command and choose the Yes option.

When you issue the Settings Action Eject command, PrintGraph will offer you two choices: Yes and No. If you want to print each of your graphs on a separate page, then you should set Eject to Yes, which forces the LaserJet to eject the current page before printing a new graph. If you set Eject to No, PrintGraph will not advance your printer to the next page between graphs, enabling you to print more than one graph on a page. You must remember, however, that if there is not enough room to print an additional graph on the current page, PrintGraph will automatically eject the current page from the LaserJet.

Graph Printing Basics

After you've configured PrintGraph for your LaserJet printer, you're ready to print your graphs. The Image-Select command on the main PrintGraph menu is the tool you use to retrieve .PIC files into PrintGraph. When you issue the Image-Select command, a list of all the .PIC files stored in the current Graphs directory will appear on the screen, as shown in Figure A5-16.

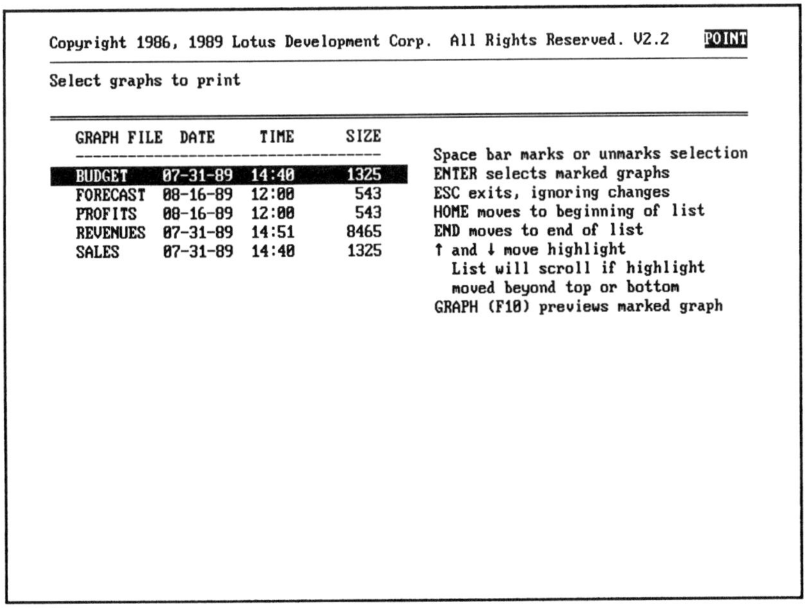

```
Copyright 1986, 1989 Lotus Development Corp. All Rights Reserved. V2.2    POINT
Select graphs to print

    GRAPH FILE  DATE      TIME    SIZE
    ----------------------------------      Space bar marks or unmarks selection
    BUDGET      07-31-89  14:40   1325      ENTER selects marked graphs
    FORECAST    08-16-89  12:00   543       ESC exits, ignoring changes
    PROFITS     08-16-89  12:00   543       HOME moves to beginning of list
    REVENUES    07-31-89  14:51   8465      END moves to end of list
    SALES       07-31-89  14:40   1325      ↑ and ↓ move highlight
                                               List will scroll if highlight
                                               moved beyond top or bottom
                                            GRAPH (F10) previews marked graph
```

FIGURE A5-16: The Image-Select command

To select a graph, use the ↓ and ↑ keys to position the cursor over the name of the graph you want to print, then press the [Spacebar] to select that graph. A # will appear next to the file name to indicate that it has been selected. If you want to deselect a selected graph, highlight it and press the [Spacebar] again.

If you want, you can select multiple graphs for printing. All you have to do is highlight the name of the first .PIC file that you want to print, press the [Spacebar], then highlight the name of the second graph, press the [Spacebar] again, and so forth. After you've marked all the graphs you want to print, press [Enter] to lock in your selections and return to the main PrintGraph menu.

Printing

Once you've selected a graph and returned to the main Print Graph menu, you issue the Align command to tell PrintGraph that the LaserJet is ready to print a new page, and then you issue the Go command to print the graph. As soon as you issue the Go command, PrintGraph will take a few seconds to load the appropriate font files and to form the print image. While this is taking place, 1-2-3 will display a message that informs you of the situation. When all of these preliminary tasks are out of the way, PrintGraph will begin sending data to the printer.

You'll find that the process of printing graphs on the LaserJet is relatively slow compared to printing worksheets. If your patience runs out and you want to stop printing before the graph is complete, press [Ctrl][Break] then [Esc].

As an example, suppose you have created the graph shown in Figure A5-17, and that you want to print this graph using PrintGraph's default print settings. To do this, simply select the graph with the Image-Select command, make sure that the LaserJet printer is on-line and has no information in the print buffer, issue the Align command, and then issue the Go command to print the graph. As soon as you choose the Go command, PrintGraph's mode indicator will change to WAIT while PrintGraph loads the graph's fonts and generates the picture. When PrintGraph has finished printing the graph, the Mode indicator will change from WAIT to MENU to let you know that the graph is finished. Since the Eject option is set to No by default, you'll need to issue the Page command to eject the graph from the LaserJet. Figure A5-18 shows the printed graph as it appears when printed with PrintGraph's original default settings.

Notes

As you will recall, the LaserJet will not eject the current page until the page becomes full or until it receives a form feed command. If you have set the Eject setting to Yes, PrintGraph will automatically eject the current page after it prints each graph in the series. If, instead, you have set the Eject setting to No, you will need to issue the Page command on PrintGraph's main menu to eject the last page.

If you are using manual feed and you have set the Pause setting to Yes, PrintGraph will stop and beep after it prints each graph. During this time, you can insert a new sheet of paper and make any necessary adjustments to the printer. When you are ready to resume printing, press the [Spacebar].

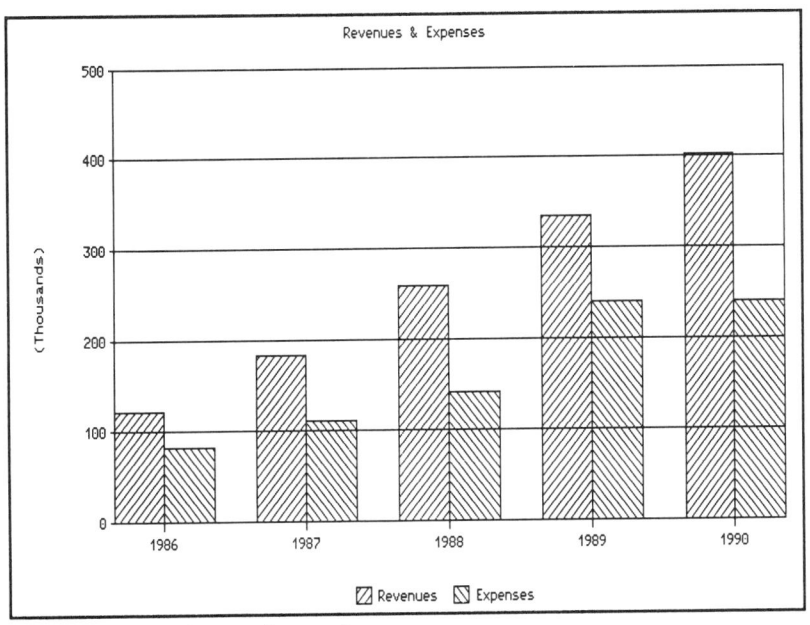

FIGURE A5-17: A sample graph

Formatting the Graph

As you can see in Figure A5-18, PrintGraph's default settings cause graphs to be printed on half of the page in Portrait orientation. Although this format may be appropriate in most situations, you'll sometimes find that PrintGraph's default graph print settings do not suit your needs. Fortunately, the Settings Image command gives you control over the dimensions of the printed graph, its position on the page, and the fonts used in your printed graphs.

Specifying the Size and Rotation of a Printed Graph

The Size options in PrintGraph let you change the size of a graph and its orientation on the page. The command for controlling graph size is Settings Image Size. There are three main choices for graph size: Full, Half, and Manual.

Full Size

You can use the Full size option to make PrintGraph automatically adjust the width, height, margins, and orientation of your graph for a full-page graph. To do this, just issue the Settings Image Size Full command. When you issue this command, the top, left, width, height, and rotate settings on the PrintGraph screen will change to reflect the new setting. Figure A5-19 shows the graph in Figure A5-18 printed full size. Notice that the full size graph is rotated 90 degrees and completely fills the 8 $\frac{1}{2}$- by 11-inch page.

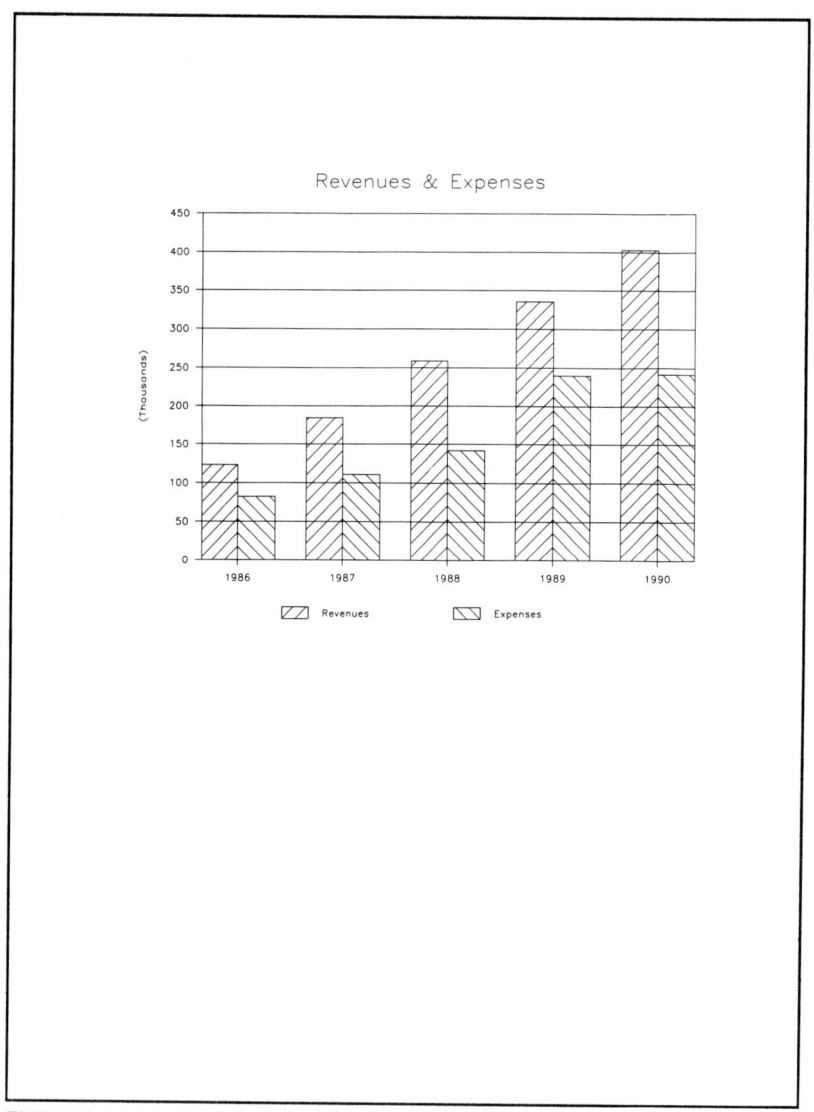

FIGURE A5-18: A printed graph

Half Size

With most printers, PrintGraph's Half option automatically adjusts the width, height, margins, and orientation settings for a half-page graph. When printing to a LaserJet printer, however, PrintGraph's Half settings do not allow you to print two half-size graphs on the same page, because PrintGraph does not take into account the LaserJet's "built-in" $1/2$-inch margins at the top and bottom of each page. If you attempt to print two graphs on the same page with PrintGraph's Half settings, the second graph will spill over to the next page.

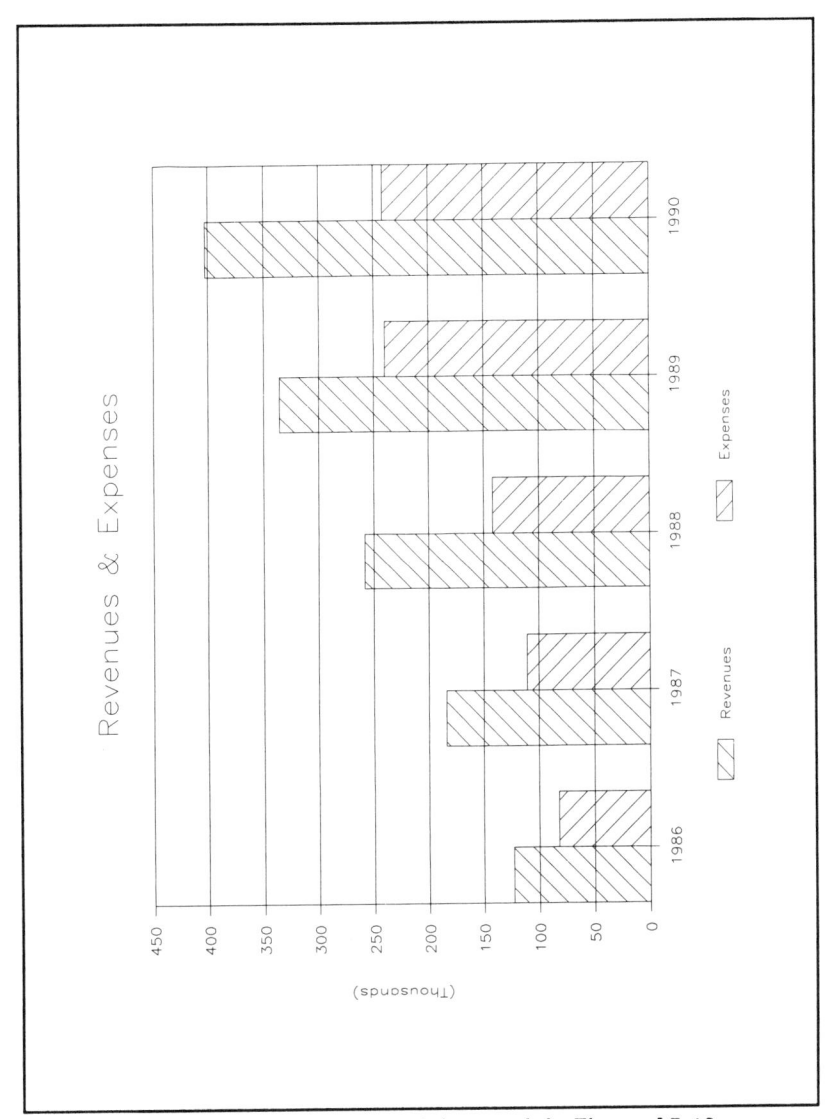

FIGURE A5-19: A full-size version of the graph in Figure A5-18

If you want to print a single graph that occupies only half of the page, you can issue the Settings Image Size Half command and print with PrintGraph's built-in Half page settings. If you need to print two graphs on a single page, however, or if you want to print a graph that occupies a true half page on the LaserJet printer, you'll have to manually change the sizing of the graph. Specifically, you need to define a left margin of 1.102, a width of 5.805, and a height of 4.191 (you can leave the top margin at the default setting of .395). We'll show you how to define these settings in the next section.

Manual Sizing

If you want to specify a size other than PrintGraph's full or half sizes, you'll need to select the Manual option. When you select the Manual option, PrintGraph presents the menu shown in Figure A5-20. As you can see, this option allows you to define the height, width, top, and left margins, and rotation of a graph manually.

When using manual sizing, you don't have to change all of the settings. If you want, you can use all of PrintGraph's default settings except for the one or two you want to change manually. Manual sizing can come in handy when you need to make minor adjustments to the size and position of a printed graph.

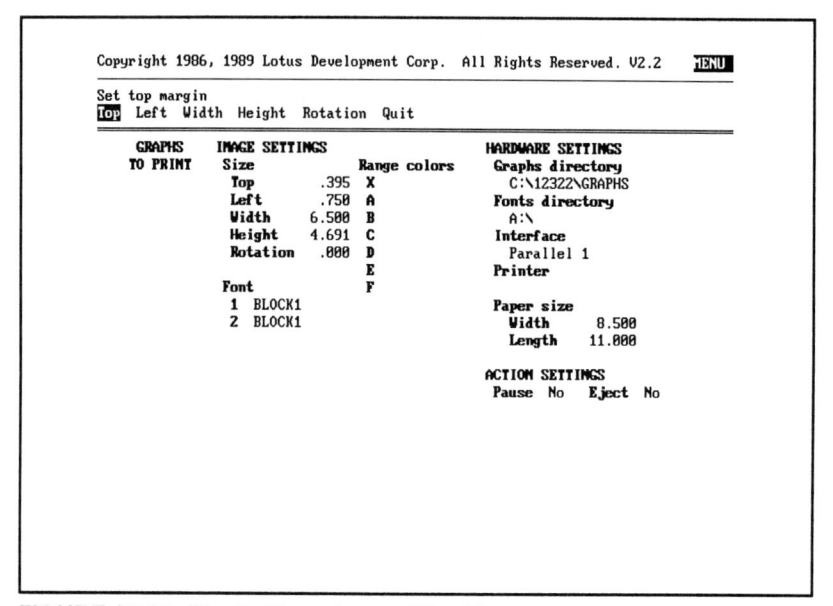

```
Copyright 1986, 1989 Lotus Development Corp. All Rights Reserved. V2.2   MENU
Set top margin
Top Left Width Height Rotation Quit

   GRAPHS      IMAGE SETTINGS                    HARDWARE SETTINGS
   TO PRINT    Size              Range colors    Graphs directory
               Top      .395     X                 C:\12322\GRAPHS
               Left     .750     A               Fonts directory
               Width   6.500     B                 A:\
               Height  4.691     C               Interface
               Rotation .000     D                 Parallel 1
                                 E               Printer
               Font              F
               1 BLOCK1
               2 BLOCK1                          Paper size
                                                   Width     8.500
                                                   Length   11.000

                                                 ACTION SETTINGS
                                                   Pause  No   Eject  No
```

FIGURE A5-20: The Settings Image Size Manual menu

Redefining the Half Settings

As we mentioned earlier, you'll need to manually change PrintGraph's Half settings if you want to print two graphs on the same page. To print two graphs on the same page, first issue the Settings Image Size Half command to display PrintGraph's default Half settings on the screen. Next, choose Manual to bring up the menu in Figure A5-28, select Left, type 1.102, and press [Enter]. Once you've changed the Left setting, choose Width, type 5.805, and press [Enter]. Finally, choose Height, type 4.191, and press [Enter]. After you've redefined these settings, use the Image-Select command to select the two graphs you want to print, and then issue the Align and Go commands. When you do this, both graphs will fit nicely on a single page, as shown in Figure A5-21.

If you will often want to use the LaserJet to print two graphs on the same page, you'll probably want to make the adjusted half-page settings your defaults. To do this, first follow the instructions above to define the new half-page settings, then issue the Settings Save command to save your changes.

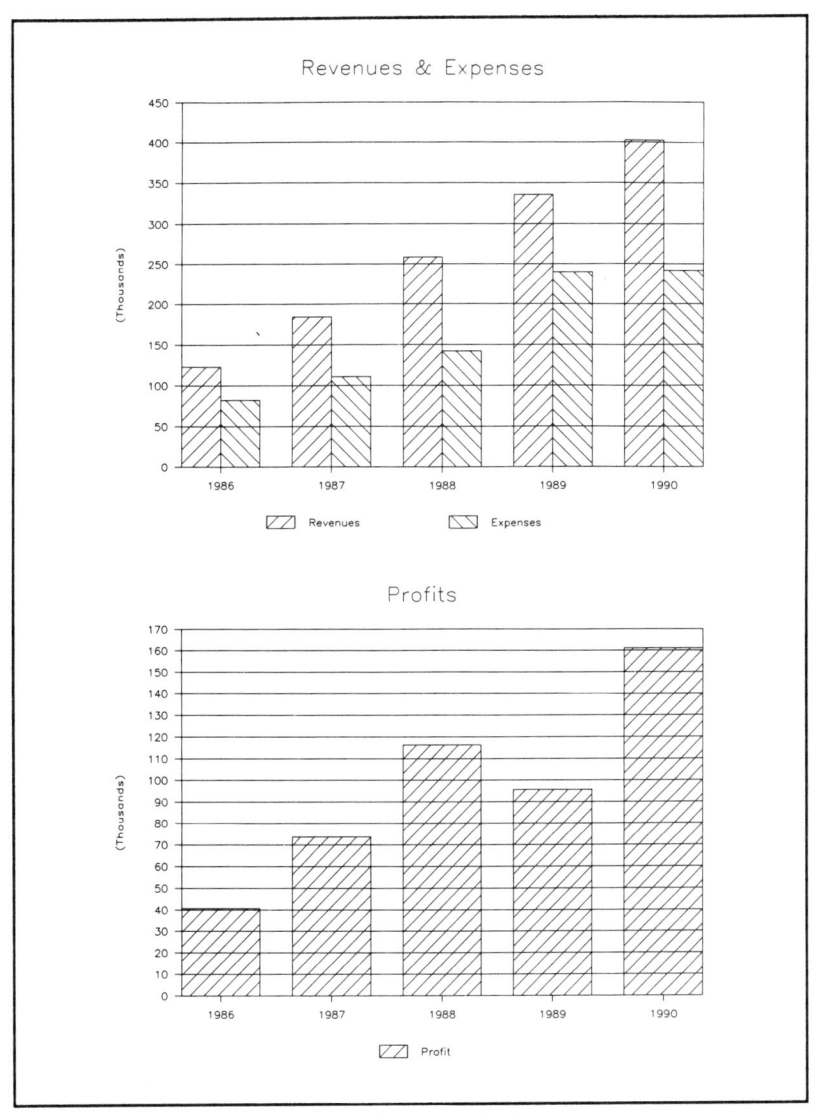

FIGURE A5-21: Printing two graphs on a single page

Accounting for Unprintable Areas

Keep in mind that the margin settings you define with the Manual command do not take into account the LaserJet's "unprintable" area at the edges of the page. As you will recall, the LaserJet has a built-in margin of $1/2$ inch at the top and bottom of the page (regardless of orientation), and $1/4$ inch at the left and right of the page. For this reason, if you define a top margin setting of 1 inch, the effective top margin will be 1.5 inches. Similarly, a left margin setting of 1 inch results in an effective $1 1/4$ inch left margin.

The Golden Ratio

In order to keep your graphs from looking disproportionate, you should maintain a width-to-height ratio of 1.385 to 1. Although you can use manual sizing to produce any ratio you want, you'll want to maintain this ratio for almost all of your printed graphs.

Choosing a Text Font

PrintGraph allows you to specify the font in which your graph's text (titles, legends, and so forth) will be printed. There is nothing different about choosing text fonts for your LaserJet printer than for any other type of printer. The fonts that PrintGraph uses in its graphs are simply graphical fonts that are sent along with the graph—PrintGraph cannot take advantage of the LaserJet's font cartridges or soft fonts.

Resetting and Saving Print Settings

After you've defined some new PrintGraph settings, you can save your changes to disk. To do this, just issue the Settings Save command. This command saves all of the current PrintGraph settings into a configuration file on the default directory. Once you've used this command to save your PrintGraph settings, those settings become the new defaults.

The Settings Reset command lets you call up your saved PrintGraph settings at any time. When you issue this command, 1-2-3 reads the settings from the configuration file into PrintGraph. The Settings Reset command lets you experimentally modify your permanent PrintGraph settings without losing your saved settings. Just remember to avoid the Settings Save command when you are experimenting with new PrintGraph settings that you don't want to save.

CONCLUSION

The HP LaserJet is the ideal printer for serious 1-2-3 users. The LaserJet's multiple font offerings let 1-2-3 print worksheet reports in many different styles and sizes, and the LaserJet's graphics capabilities allow 1-2-3's PrintGraph program to generate handsome graphs from the data in your worksheets. In this appendix, we've shown you how to get the most out of 1-2-3 and an HP LaserJet printer.

Index

\# character
  in headers and footers, 324
& operator, 33
* character
  as wildcard in criteria, 481-482
  as wildcard in file names, 347
? character
  as wildcard in criteria, 481
  as wildcard in file names, 347
{?} command, 559
@ character
  in headers and footers, 325
@@ function, 219-220
\ character
  in references for headers and footers, 321
/ key
  macro representation of, 521-522
| character
  in embedded setup strings, 317-319
  in headers and footers, 321-324
  to hide rows, 320
~ character
  as wildcard in criteria, 482
  in macros, 522
123.CNF file, 716-717
123.HLP file, 713-715
1-2-3 Release 1A
  exchanging data with, 670-674
1-2-3 Releases 2 and 2.01
  exchanging data with, 670
1-2-3 Release 3, 1
  exchanging data with, 674-675
3-2-1 GOSUB, 662
4VIEWS, 661
4WORD, 661

A

@ABS function, 157
Absolute references, 32, 138-142
Absolute value, 157
[Abs] key, 14, 33, 139
@ACOS function, 165
Add-in applications, 46, 631-662
  3-2-1 GOSUB, 662
  4VIEWS, 661
  4WORD, 661
  Allways, 636-645
  attaching, 632-633
  auto-attaching, 635-636
  auto-invoking, 635-636
  @BASE, 661
  Budget Express, 661
  Cambridge Spreadsheet Analyst, 661
  detaching, 634
  invoking, 634
  InWord, 662
  Learn, 661
  LEARN.APP, 530
  Look and Link, 661
  Macro Library Manager, 645-661
  NoteWorthy, 662
  Note-It Plus, 661
  SeeMORE, 661
  SideWays, 661
  SOS, 662
  SpeedUp, 661
  SQZ! Plus, 661
  using, 631-636
  What's Best!, 662
  with 1-2-3 Release 2 and 2.01, 636
  Worksheet Utilities, 661
/ Add-In commands, 632-636
Add-ins
  (see Add-in applications)
Alignment
  (see Label alignment)
Allways, 636-645
  attaching, 638-639
  changing column widths and row heights, 642
  controlling layout, 643
  embedding graphs with, 642-643
  formatting with, 641
  installing, 637
  invoking, 640
  options, 643-644
  printing with, 643
  saving enhancements, 644-645
[Alt][F1] key, 14, 703-705
[Alt][F2] key, 14, 545-546
[Alt][F3] key, 14, 517, 525
[Alt][F4] key, 14
[Alt][F5] key, 14, 531-532
[Alt][F6] key, 14
[Alt][F7] key, 14, 632, 634
[Alt][F8] key, 14, 632, 634
[Alt][F9] key, 14, 632, 634
[Alt][F10] key, 14, 632, 634

#AND# operator, 199-200, 490, 491
[App1] key, 14, 632, 634
[App2] key, 14, 632, 634
[App3] key, 14, 632, 634
[App4] key, 14, 632, 634
Argument separators, 709-711
Arguments
  of functions, 155-157
  of LCL commands, 556-557
  of macro key representations, 522-523
  passing to subroutines, 581-584
Arrow keys, 15-19
  in EDIT mode, 37-38, 39
  in INPUT mode, 260
  locking in entries with, 22
  macro representation of, 521-522
  pointing to commands, 41
  with [Ctrl] key, 19
  with [End] key, 18-19
ASCII, 203-205
ASCII characters, 703-705
ASCII text files
  (see Text files)
@ASIN function, 165
@ATAN function, 165
@ATAN2 function, 166
AUTO123.WK1, 347-348
Auto-executing macros, 547-548
Auto-LF setting, 302
Auto-loading worksheets, 347-348
Averages, 170-171
@AVG function, 170-171

B

[Backspace] key
  in EDIT mode, 38
  macro representation of, 521-522
  to change directory, 352
Bar graphs, 393-395
  adjusting Y scale, 420
  data labels in, 426
  legends for, 434
@BASE, 661
Baud rate
  for serial printers, 301-302
Beep
  deactivating, 716
{Beep} command, 601-602
{Blank} command, 614-615
Borders
  hiding, 597-598
  print, 325-331
{BordersOff} command, 597-598
{BordersOn} command, 597-598
Branching
  in macros, 573-576
{Branch} command, 573-576
{BreakOff} command, 608-609

{BreakOn} command, 608-609
[Break] key
  macro representation of, 521-522
Budget Express, 661
Buffer
  keyboard, 604

C

CALC indicator, 13, 51
[Calc] key, 14
Cambridge Spreadsheet Analyst, 661
CAPS indicator, 13
@CELL function, 216-218
Cell pointer, 11
  moving, 14-20
  moving in partial-screen windows, 226-227
  position during macro execution, 529, 577
Cell protection, 256-259
  disabling, 258
  effects of, 258-259
  enabling, 257
  with /Range Input command, 259-262
Cell references
  to define headers and footers, 321
  (see also References)
@CELLPOINTER function, 216-218, 571-572
Cells, 10-11
  erasing, 112-116
  formatting, 69-93
    (see also Formats)
  hiding, 85-87
  pointing to, 31-32
  protecting, 256-259
  unprotecting, 258
@CHAR function, 203-204
Charts
  (see Graphs)
@CHOOSE function, 186-188
CIRC indicator, 13, 53-56
Circular references, 53-57
  finding, 54-55
  fixing, 55
  solvable, 55-56
  unsolvable, 53
@CLEAN function, 215
Clock, 13
  at bottom of screen, 715-716
{Close} command, 619
CMD indicator, 13, 518, 526
@CODE function, 204-205
Color
  in displayed graphs, 431-432
  in printed graphs, 456-457
@COLS function, 218

Column widths, 76, 101-109
  changing
    multiple columns, 105-106
    single column, 102-105
  effect on custom menus, 590
  effect on date formats, 276-278
  effect on time formats, 288
  global, 106-109
  resetting
    multiple columns, 106
    single column, 105
Columns, 10-11
  changing widths of, 101-109
    (see also Column widths)
  counting, 216-218
  deleting, 122-123
  hiding, 109-111
  inserting, 119-121
  locking onto screen, 221-224
  title, 221-224
  unhiding, 111-112
Combining
  information from files, 362-374
Commands, 40-44
  cancelling, 44
  cut-and-paste, 101-153
  issuing, 40-41
  range names in, 59
  worksheet, 221-271
Commands by name
  / Add-In, 632-636
  / Copy, 130-144
  / Data Distribution, 235-237
  / Data Fill, 283-284
  / Data Matrix, 250-256
  / Data Parse, 43, 695-702
  / Data Query, 43
  / Data Query Criteria, 494-495
  / Data Query Delete, 504-506
  / Data Query Extract, 500-503
  / Data Query Find, 496-498
  / Data Query Input, 493-494
  / Data Query Output, 498-500
  / Data Query Unique, 503-504
  / Data Regression, 43, 244-250, 404-405
  / Data Sort, 43, 471-477
  / Data Table, 237-244
  / File Admin Link-Refresh, 720
  / File Admin Reservation Get, 719
  / File Admin Reservation Release, 719
  / File Admin Table, 375-376
  / File Combine, 362-374, 528
  / File Combine Add, 366-371
  / File Combine Copy, 362-365
  / File Combine Subtract, 366, 371
  / File Directory, 354-355
  / File Erase, 348-349

/ File Extract Values, 361-362
/ File Import Numbers, 692-694
/ File Import Text, 694-695
/ File List, 374-375
/ File Retrieve, 345-348, 357
/ File Save, 339-345, 356-357, 527
/ File Xtract, 527
/ File Xtract Formulas, 358-361
/ Graph A, 380
/ Graph B-F, 382-383
/ Graph Delete, 387-388
/ Graph Group, 380-381
/ Graph Name Create, 386-387, 388, 389
/ Graph Name Use, 387
/ Graph Options, 384-386
/ Graph Options B&W, 431-432
/ Graph Options Color, 431-432
/ Graph Options Data-Labels A-F, 423-426
/ Graph Options Data-Labels Group, 423-424
/ Graph Options Format, 427-430
/ Graph Options Format Graph Symbols, 402
/ Graph Options Grid, 435-436
/ Graph Options Legend A-F, 432-435
/ Graph Options Legend Range, 434
/ Graph Options Scale Skip, 412-414
/ Graph Options Scale X-Scale, 423
/ Graph Options Scale X-Scale Lower, 406
/ Graph Options Scale Y-Scale, 403
/ Graph Options Scale Y-Scale Format, 421-423
/ Graph Options Scale Y-Scale Indicator, 421
/ Graph Options Scale Y-Scale Lower, 417-420
/ Graph Options Scale Y-Scale Manual, 417-420
/ Graph Options Scale Y-Scale Upper, 417-420
/ Graph Options Titles, 407-409, 410
/ Graph Reset A-F, 384
/ Graph Reset Graph, 388
/ Graph Reset Options, 386, 426
/ Graph Reset Range, 384
/ Graph Save, 436-437
/ Graph Table, 388
/ Graph Type, 379
/ Graph Type Bar, 393
/ Graph Type Line, 390
/ Graph Type Pie, 397
/ Graph Type Stack-Bar, 396
/ Graph Type XY, 401
/ Graph View, 381-382
/ Graph X, 409-416

/ File Admin Link-Refresh command, 35-36
/ Move, 124-130
/ Print File, 687-690
/ Print Printer, 302-338, 536-538
/ Print Printer Align, 303, 308
/ Print Printer Clear, 331
/ Print Printer Go, 303
/ Print Printer Line, 308
/ Print Printer Options Borders, 325-331
/ Print Printer Options Footer, 320-325
/ Print Printer Options Header, 320-325
/ Print Printer Options Margins Bottom, 312
/ Print Printer Options Margins Left, 310-311
/ Print Printer Options Margins None, 312-313
/ Print Printer Options Margins Right, 311-312
/ Print Printer Options Margins Top, 312
/ Print Printer Options Other Cell Formulas, 336-338
/ Print Printer Options Other Formatted, 335
/ Print Printer Options Other Unformatted, 304-305, 335
/ Print Printer Options Pg-Length, 313-314
/ Print Printer Options Setup, 315-316
/ Print Printer Page, 308
/ Print Printer Range, 302-303, 309-310
/ Quit, 66-67
/ Range Erase, 112-116
/ Range Fill, 232-235
/ Range Format, 71-73, 275-278, 287-288, 534-535
/ Range Format Reset, 77
/ Range Input, 259-262
/ Range Justify, 262-265
/ Range Label, 96-98
/ Range Name Create, 57, 63, 533-534
/ Range Name Delete, 62
/ Range Name Labels, 63-65
/ Range Name Labels Right, 524-525
/ Range Name Table, 60-62
/ Range Prot, 256-259
/ Range Search, 265-271
/ Range Trans, 148-153
/ Range Unprot, 258
/ Range Value, 145-147
/ System, 344

/ Worksheet Column Column-Range, 105-106
/ Worksheet Column Column-Range Set-Width, 76
/ Worksheet Column Display, 111-112
/ Worksheet Column Hide, 109-111
/ Worksheet Column Reset-Width, 105, 109
/ Worksheet Column Set-Width, 76, 102-105, 277-278, 288
/ Worksheet Delete Column, 122-123
/ Worksheet Delete Row, 121-122
/ Worksheet Erase, 65
/ Worksheet Global, 42, 707-708
/ Worksheet Global Column-Width, 106-108
/ Worksheet Global Default, 42
/ Worksheet Global Default Autoexec, 548
/ Worksheet Global Default Directory, 355
/ Worksheet Global Default Other Add-in, 635
/ Worksheet Global Default Other Beep, 716
/ Worksheet Global Default Other Clock, 715-716
/ Worksheet Global Default Other Help, 713-715
/ Worksheet Global Default Other International Currency, 711-712
/ Worksheet Global Default Other International Date, 278-279
/ Worksheet Global Default Other International Negative, 713
/ Worksheet Global Default Other International Punctuation, 709-711
/ Worksheet Global Default Other International Time, 288-289
/ Worksheet Global Default Other Undo, 45
/ Worksheet Global Default Other Update, 716-717
/ Worksheet Global Default Printer Auto-LF, 302
/ Worksheet Global Default Printer Bottom, 313
/ Worksheet Global Default Printer Interface, 301-302
/ Worksheet Global Default Printer Left, 313
/ Worksheet Global Default Printer Name, 300-301
/ Worksheet Global Default Printer Pg-Length, 314
/ Worksheet Global Default Printer Right, 313

/ Worksheet Global Default Printer
  Top, 313
/ Worksheet Global Default Printer
  Update , 332
/ Worksheet Global Default Printer
  Wait, 332-333
/ Worksheet Global Format, 88-89
/ Worksheet Global Label-Prefix,
  98-99
/ Worksheet Global Protection,
  256-257, 258, 259
/ Worksheet Global Recalculation, 52
/ Worksheet Global Recalculation
  Iteration, 56-57
/ Worksheet Global Status, 332
/ Worksheet Global Zero, 91-94
/ Worksheet Insert Column, 119-121
/ Worksheet Insert Row, 116-119
/ Worksheet Learn, 530-532
/ Worksheet Page, 333-335
/ Worksheet Status, 46-47,
  54-55, 344
/ Worksheet Titles, 221-224, 231
/ Worksheet Window, 225-231
[Compose] key, 14, 703-705
Computed macros, 628-630
Concatenation, 33
Conditional operators
  complex, 199-200
  simple, 196-197
Conditional testing
  in macros, 566-568
Conditional tests
  in @IF function, 196-197
Consolidating worksheets, 362-374
{Contents} command, 615-617
Control Panel, 12
Conventions, 4
/ Copy command, 130-144
Copying, 130-153
  absolute references, 138-142
  formulas and functions, 135-144
  mixed references, 142-144
  relative references, 135-138
  special kinds of, 145-153
@COS function, 164-165
@COUNT function, 170
Criteria, 478-492
  comparison, 482-490
  exact-match, 479-481
  label, 479-480
  logical AND, 486-487, 488-490, 491
  logical operators, 482-486
  logical OR, 487-490, 491
  multiple, 486-490
  value, 480-481
  wildcards, 481-482
Criteria range, 492, 494-495
@CTERM function, 182-183

[Ctrl] key, 37-38
  with arrow keys, 19, 22
[Ctrl][Break] key
  disabling, 608-609
  to cancel commands, 44
  to stop macro execution, 525-526
  to stop printing, 310
[Ctrl][Left] key
  macro representation of, 521-522
[Ctrl][Right] key
  macro representation of, 521-522
Currency symbol, 711-712
Custom menus, 585-593
Cut-and-paste commands
  effect on macros, 527-528

D

@D functions
  (see Database statistical functions)
Data bases, 465-513
  creating, 469-471
  criteria, 478-492
    #AND# operator, 490, 491
    comparison, 482-48486
    exact-match, 479-481
    logical AND, 486-487,
      488-490, 491
    logical OR, 487-490, 491
    #NOT# operator, 491-492
    #OR# operator, 491
    using, 492-506
    * wildcard, 481-482
    ? wildcard, 481
    ~ wildcard, 482
  Criteria range, 478-479, 492, 494-495
  deleting matching records, 504-506
  editing, 468-469
  entering records into, 470
  entries in, 467-468
  extracting matching records, 498-503
  extracting unique records, 503-504
  fields, 466
  finding matching records, 496-498
  formatting, 468
  Input range, 493-494, 495
  Output range, 495, 498-500
  printing, 469
  querying, 492-506
  Query] key, 498, 506
  records, 466
  saving, 469
  size limits, 467
  sorting, 471-477
    labels, 474-475
    order, 475-476
    one-field, 473-476
    two-field, 476-477

statistical functions, 506-513
    @DCOUNT, 509-510
    @DMAX, 510
    @DMIN, 510
    @DSTD, 510-511
    @DSUM, 508-509
    @DVAR, 510-511
    form of, 507
    structure of, 466-467
/ Data Distribution command, 235-237
/ Data Fill command, 283-284
Data labels, 423-427
/ Data Matrix commands, 250-256
/ Data Parse command, 43, 695-702
/ Data Query command, 43
/ Data Query Criteria command,
    494-495
/ Data Query Delete command, 504-506
/ Data Query Extract command, 500-503
/ Data Query Find command, 496-498
/ Data Query Input command, 493-494
/ Data Query Output command, 498-500
/ Data Query Unique command, 503-504
Data ranges
    in graphs, 378-381, 383-384
/ Data Regression command, 43,
    244-250, 404-405
/ Data Sort command, 43, 471-477
/ Data Table commands, 237-244
Data tables, 237-244
    basics, 238
    calculating @D functions in, 512
    one-variable, 238-241
    two-variable, 241-244
Database statistical functions, 506-513
    @DAVG, 510
    @DCOUNT, 509-510
    @DMAX, 510
    @DMIN, 510
    @DSTD, 510-511
    @DSUM, 508
    @DVAR, 510-511
    form of, 507
@DATE function, 274-275, 292-293
Dates, 273-285, 292-298
    entering, 274-275
    formatting, 275-279
    in data bases, 485
    in formulas and functions, 279-282,
        284-285, 294-295
    in headers and footers, 325
    series of, 282-285
@DATEVALUE function, 296-297
@DAVG function, 510
@DAY function, 280-282
dBASE
    exchanging data with, 678-686
.DBF files, 678-686
@DCOUNT function, 509-510

@DDB function, 185-186
Debugging macros, 542-547
Default settings, 708-717
{Define} command, 582-584
Deleting
    columns, 122-123
    criteria-matching records, 504-506
    rows, 121-122
[Del] key
    in EDIT mode, 38
    macro representation of, 521-522
Depreciation, 184-186
.DIF files, 702
Directories, 351-355
    changing the default, 354-355
    default, 351
    overriding the default, 351-354
Disks
    printing to, 687-691
{Dispatch} command, 609-610
Distributions, frequency, 235-237
@DMAX function, 510
@DMIN function, 510
DOS
    accessing in macro, 611-612
[Down] arrow key
    (see Arrow keys)
Driver sets, 8-9
    (see also .SET files)
@DSTD function, 510-511
@DSUM function, 508
@DVAR function, 510-511

E

EDIT mode, 12, 37-39
Editing
    cell entries, 36-39
    in FIND mode, 497
[Edit] key, 14, 37-39
Encrypting
    files, 356-357
END indicator, 13
[End] key, 18-19
    in EDIT mode, 37-38
    in INPUT mode, 260
    locking in entries with, 22
    macro representation of, 521-522
    with [Home] key, 20
[End][Home] key
    for defining print ranges, 307
[Enter] key
    in INPUT mode, 260
    locking in entries with, 22
    macro representation of, 522
Entries, 21-39
    cancelling, 23
    combined date and time, 292-295
    copying, 130-153
        (see also Copying)

Index

date, 273-285, 292-298
  (see also Dates)
  editing, 36-39
  erasing, 112-116
  formulas, 28-36
  labels, 25-28
  listing, 335-338
  locking in, 21-22
  moving, 124-130
    (see also Moving entries)
  replacing, 36-37, 269
  searching for, 265-268
  time, 285-298
    (see also Times)
  using a graph titles, 410-411
  using as legends, 433-434
  values, 23-25
  with {Let} command, 564-566
Entry forms, 259-262
  creating, 259-260
  using, 260-262
Erasing cells, 112-116
Erasing worksheets, 65
@ERR function, 218-219
Error messages, 13
ERROR mode, 12
Error values, 34
  trapping, 201-202
Errors
  in macros, 542-544
  trapping in macros, 606-607
[Esc] key
  in custom menus, 590-591
  in INPUT mode, 260
  macro representation of, 521-522
  to change directory, 351-352
@EXACT function, 206
Exchanging data
  with 1-2-3 Release 1A, 670-674
  with 1-2-3 Releases 2 and 2.01, 670
  with 1-2-3 Release 3, 674-675
  with dBASE, 678-686
  with other programs, 687-702
  with Symphony, 675-678
Exiting
  from 1-2-3, 66-67
@EXP function, 163-164
Expanded memory, 47, 49-50
Extracting
  information from worksheets, 358-362
Extracting records, 498-503

F

[F1] key, 14, 713-715
[F2] key, 14
[F3] key, 14
  to list file names, 350
  to list macro names, 525

[F4] key, 14, 33, 139
[F5] key, 14
[F6] key, 14, 225-226
[F7] key, 14
  to exit FIND mode, 498
  to reissue / Data Query commands, 506
[F8] key, 14, 240
[F9] key, 14
[F10] key, 14, 382
  to preview graphs in PrintGraph, 448
@FALSE function, 202
Fields
  in data bases, 466
File
  name at bottom of screen, 715-716
/ File Admin Link-Refresh command, 35-36, 720
/ File Admin Reservation Get command, 719
/ File Admin Reservation Release command, 719
/ File Admin Table command, 375-376
/ File Combine Add command, 366-371
/ File Combine command, 362-374
  to transfer macros, 528
/ File Combine Copy commands, 362-365
/ File Combine Subtract command, 366, 371
/ File Directory command, 354-355
/ File Erase command, 348-349
/ File Extract Values command, 361-362
/ File Import Numbers command, 692-694
/ File Import Text command, 694-695
File i/o commands, 617-626
/ File List command, 374-375
File pointer, 619-620
File reservations, 719
/ File Retrieve command, 345-348, 357
/ File Save command, 339-345, 356-357
  to save macros, 527
/ File Xtract command
  to save macros, 527
/ File Xtract Formulas command, 358-361
Files, 339-376
  accessing with macros, 617-626
  auto-loading, 347-348
  backing up, 342-343
  changing directories, 351-355
  combining information from, 362-374
  default directory, 351
  disk-full errors, 344-345
  erasing, 348-349

extracting information into, 358-362
listing names of, 374-375
loading from DOS prompt, 346-347
names, 340-342
password-protecting, 356-357
printing to, 687-691
replacing, 342
resaving, 342
reservations, 719
retrieving, 345-348
saving, 339-345
tables of names, 375-376
text, 687-695
translating, 663-686
updating links to, 720
viewing names of, 350
FILES mode, 12
{FileSize} command, 620
@FIND function, 205-206
FIND mode, 12
Finding records, 496-498
Font files
   for PrintGraph program, 442-443
Fonts
   for printed graphs, 449-450
Footers
   (see Headers and footers)
{ForBreak} command, 572-573
Format lines, 696-702
Formats, 69-91
   assigning, 71-77
   column widths and, 76
   combined date and time, 293-294
   Comma, 79
   copying, 74
   Currency, 79-81, 711-712
   date, 275-279
   default, 88-91
   Fixed, 78
   General, 69-70
   global, 69
   Hidden, 85-87, 259
   of graph scales, 421-423
   Percent, 81-82
   resetting, 77
   Sci, 82-83
   Text, 87-88
   time, 287-289
   +/-, 84-85
Formulas, 28-36
   absolute references in, 138-142
   as macro statements, 628-630
   cell references in, 29-33
   copying, 135-144
   date values in, 279-282, 284-285, 290-292
   editing, 39
   effect of /Range Trans command on, 150-153

entering, 28-33
extracting from data bases, 502
for /Range Fill command, 235
in databases, 467-468
linking, 34-36, 720
mixed references in, 142-144
moving, 124-130
operators, 29
pointing, 31-32
range names in, 59
relative references in, 135-138
replacing with results, 145-147
string, 33
{For} command, 568-573
{FrameOff} command, 597-598
{FrameOn} command, 597-598
Frequency distributions, 235-237
FRMT mode, 12
Functions
   for /Range Fill command, 235
Function keys, 14
Functions, 155-220
   absolute references in, 138-142
   arguments, 156-157
   copying, 135-144
   depreciation, 184-186
   effect of /Range Trans command on, 150-153
   extracting from data bases, 502
   financial, 172-186
   form of, 155-157
   in databases, 467-468
   logarithmic, 162-164
   logical, 196-202
   lookup, 186-196
   mathematical, 157-162
   mixed references in, 142-144
   moving, 124-130
   names, 155-156
   not available in 1-2-3 Releases 2 and 2.01, 670
   not available in 1-2-3 Release 1A, 672
   other, 215-220
   relative references in, 135-138
   replacing with results, 145-147
   statistical, 166-172
   string, 202-215
   trigonometric, 164-166
Functions by name
   @@, 219-220
   @ABS, 157
   @ACOS, 165
   @ASIN, 165
   @ATAN, 165
   @ATAN2, 166
   @AVG, 170-171
   @CELL, 216-218
   @CELLPOINTER, 216-218, 571-572

Index

@CHAR, 203-204
@CHOOSE, 186-188
@CLEAN, 215
@CODE, 204-205
@COLS, 218
@COS, 164-165
@COUNT, 170
@CTERM, 182-183
@DATE, 274-275, 292-293
@DATEVALUE, 296-297
@DAVG, 510
@DAY, 280-282
@DCOUNT, 509-510
@DDB, 185-186
@DMAX, 510
@DMIN, 510
@DSTD, 510-511
@DSUM, 508
@DVAR, 510-511
@ERR, 218-219
@EXACT, 206
@EXP, 163-164
@FALSE, 202
@FIND, 205-206
@FV, 180-181
@HLOOKUP, 194-196
@HOUR, 291-292
@IF, 196-201
@INDEX, 188-189
@INT, 160-162
@IRR, 177-179
@ISERR, 201-202, 574-575
@ISNA, 201-202
@ISNUMBER, 202
@ISSTRING, 202
@LEFT, 207-208
@LENGTH, 209-210
@LN, 162-163
@LOG, 162
@LOWER, 210-211
@MAX, 171
@MID, 209
@MIN, 171
@MINUTE, 291-292
@MOD, 157-158
@MONTH, 280-282
@N, 219
@NA, 219
@NPV, 175-177
@PI, 164
@PMT, 179-180
@PROPER, 210-211
@PV, 172-175
@RAND, 158
@RATE, 183-184
@REPEAT, 214-215
@REPLACE, 206-207
@RIGHT, 209
@ROUND, 159-160

@ROWS, 218
@S, 219
@SECOND, 291-292
@SIN, 164-165
@SLN, 185
@SQRT, 158-159
@STD, 171-172
@STRING, 211-212
@SUM, 167-169
@SYD, 186
@TAN, 164-165
@TERM, 181-182
@TIME, 286-287
@TIMEVALUE, 297-298
@TODAY, 293
@TRIM, 215
@TRUE, 202
@UPPER, 210-211
@VALUE, 212-214
@VAR, 172
@VLOOKUP, 189-194
@YEAR, 280-282
Future value, 180-181
@FV function, 180-181

G

{GetLabel} command, 560, 561-562
{GetNumber} command, 560-561
{GetPos} command, 620
{Get} command, 602-604
Global settings, 707-708
[Goto] key, 14, 20
  using to move into Titles area, 224
/ Graph A command, 380
/ Graph B-F command, 382-383
/ Graph Delete command, 387-388
/ Graph Group command, 380-381
/ Graph Name Create command, 386-387, 388, 389
/ Graph Name Use command, 387
/ Graph Options B&W command, 431-432
/ Graph Options Color command, 431-432
/ Graph Options command, 384-386
/ Graph Options Data-Labels A-F command, 423-426
/ Graph Options Data-Labels Group command, 423-424
/ Graph Options Format command, 427-430
/ Graph Options Format Graph Symbols command, 402
/ Graph Options Grid command, 435-436
/ Graph Options Legend A-F command, 432-435
/ Graph Options Legend Range command, 434

/ Graph Options Scale Skip command, 412-414
/ Graph Options Scale X-Scale command, 423
/ Graph Options Scale X-Scale Lower command, 406
/ Graph Options Scale Y-Scale, 403
/ Graph Options Scale Y-Scale Format command, 421-423
/ Graph Options Scale Y-Scale Indicator command, 421
/ Graph Options Scale Y-Scale Lower command, 417-420
/ Graph Options Scale Y-Scale Manual command, 417-420
/ Graph Options Scale Y-Scale Upper command, 417-420
/ Graph Options Titles command, 407-409, 410
/ Graph Reset A-F command, 384
/ Graph Reset Graph command, 388
/ Graph Reset Options command, 386, 426
/ Graph Reset Range command, 384
/ Graph Save command, 436-437
/ Graph Table command, 388
/ Graph Type Bar command, 393
/ Graph Type command, 379
/ Graph Type Line command, 390
/ Graph Type Pie command, 397
/ Graph Type Stack-Bar command, 396
/ Graph Type XY command, 401
/ Graph View command, 381-382
/ Graph X command, 409-416
{GraphOff} command, 600-601
{GraphOn} command, 600-601
Graphs, 377-437, 439-464
   bar, 389, 393-395, 420, 426, 434
   B-range
      in Pie charts, 399
   color in, 431-432
   creating, 377-381, 388-390
   data labels, 423-427
   data ranges
      defining, 378-381
      deleting, 383-384
   deleting, 387-388
   enhancing, 384-386, 407-436
   formatting, 427-432
   gridlines, 435-436
   in macros, 600-601
   legends, 432-435
      in printed graphs, 462
   line, 390-393
   multiple-range, 382-383, 391-393, 394-395, 395-397
   names
      assigning, 386-387
      deleting, 387-388
   tables of, 388
   using, 387
   pie, 397-400, 414-416, 417-418
   printing, 439-464
      (see also Printing graphs, PrintGraph program)
   resetting, 388
   saving, 436-437
   stacked-bar, 395-397, 420, 426, 434
   titles, 407-409
   types of, 390-406
   viewing, 381-382
   XY, 400-406, 414, 423
   X-axis labels, 409-416
   Y-axis, 416-423
      formatting, 421-423
      indicator, 420-421
      manual scaling, 417-420
[Graph] key, 14, 382
   to preview graphs in PrintGraph, 448
Gridlines, 435-436

H

Hardware requirements, 7-9
Headers and footers, 320-325
   alignment of, 321-324
   dates in, 325
   defining with cell references, 321
   deleting, 325
   page numbers in, 324
Help, 65-66
HELP mode, 12, 713-715
[Help] key, 14, 65-66, 713-715
Hiding
   cells, 85-87
   columns, 109-112
Hiding cells
   protection effects, 259
@HLOOKUP function, 194-196
[Home] key, 19-20
   in EDIT mode, 37-38
   in INPUT mode, 260
   locking in entries with, 22
   macro representation of, 521-522
@HOUR function, 291-292
HP LaserJet printers, 721-756

I

@IF function, 196-201
{If} command, 567-568, 571-572
Importing
   text files, 692-695
@INDEX function, 188-189
{Indicate} command, 598-600
INIT program, 8-9
Initializing 1-2-3 Release 2.2, 8
Input forms
   (see Entry forms)

Input range, 493-494
Insert mode, 38
Inserting
 columns, 119-121
 rows, 116-119, 121
Install program, 8-9, 721-722
Installing 1-2-3, 8-9
[Ins] key, 38
@INT function, 160-162
Integers, 160-162
Internal rate of return, 177-179
InWord, 662
@IRR function, 177-179
@ISERR function, 201-202, 574-575
@ISNA function, 201-202
@ISNUMBER function, 202
@ISSTRING function, 202

J

Justifying labels, 262-265

K

Keyboard buffer, 604, 605-606

L

Label alignment, 25-26, 94-99
 default, 94, 98-99
 overriding, 95-98
LABEL mode, 12
Label prefixes, 25-26, 94-99
 in macro commands, 519-520, 525, 541
 (see also Label alignment)
Labels, 25-28
 alignment of, 25-26
 as macro statements, 519-520
 converting to values, 212-213
 entering, 25
 in databases, 467-468
 justifying, 262-265
 long, 27
 numeric, 28
 parsing, 695-702
 prefixes, 25-26
 repeating, 26
LCL commands, 551-630
 arguments, 556-557
 {Beep}, 601-602
 {Blank}, 614-615
 {BordersOff}, 597-598
 {BordersOn}, 597-598
 {Branch}, 573-576
 {BreakOff}, 608-609
 {BreakOn}, 608-609
 /xc, 579-580
 {Close}, 619
 {Contents}, 615-617

{Define}, 582-584
{Dispatch}, 609-610
file i/o, 617-626
{FileSize}, 620
{ForBreak}, 572-573
form of, 555-556
{For}, 568-573
{FrameOff}, 597-598
{FrameOn}, 597-598
/xg, 576
{GetLabel}, 560, 561-562
{GetNumber}, 560-561
{GetPos}, 620
{Get}, 602-604
{GraphOff}, 600-601
{GraphOn}, 600-601
/xi, 568
{If}, 567-568, 571-572
{Indicate}, 598-600
/xl, 563, 564
{Let}, 564-566
{Look}, 604-606
/xm, 591
{MenuBranch}, 584-591
{MenuCall}, 591-593
/xn, 563
{OnError}, 606-607
{Open}, 618-619
{PanelOff}, 595-596
{PanelOn}, 596-597
{Put}, 614
{Quit}, 558
/xr, 581
{ReadLn}, 622-623
{Read}, 622
{RecalcCol}, 612-613
{Recalc}, 612-613
{Restart}, 610-611
{Return}, 570-573, 580-581
{SetPos}, 619-620
{subroutine}, 576-579
{System}, 611-612
{table of, 552-555
{Wait}, 598, 599, 600-601, 608
{WindowsOff}, 595-596
{WindowsOn}, 596-597
{WriteLn}, 621
{Write}, 621
{?}, 559
Learn, 661
LEARN indicator, 13
LEARN.APP, 46, 530
[Learn] key, 14, 531-532
@LEFT function, 207-208
[Left] arrow key
 (see Arrow keys)
Legends, 432-435
 in printed graphs, 462
@LENGTH function, 209-210

{Let} command, 564-566
LICS, 203-205
LICS characters, 673, 703-705
Line graphs, 390-393
Linear programming
  (see Matrices, inverting)
Linear regression
  (see Regression)
Linking formulas, 34-36, 720
@LN function, 162-163
Loading 1-2-3, 9-10
@LOG function, 162
Logarithms
  base 10, 162
  natural, 162-164
Logical operators, 482-486
Look and Link, 661
{Look} command, 604-606
Looping, 568-573
  in macros
Lotus Access System, 9-10
  loading PrintGraph from, 440
Lotus Command Language, 551-630
  accessing files, 617-626
  basics, 558
  branching, 573-576
  computed macro statements, 599, 628-630
  conditional testing, 566-568
  controlling program flow, 606-612
  controlling the interface, 595-602
  custom menus, 584-593
  form of commands, 555-556
  fundamental techniques, 558-593
  interacting with user, 602-606
  looping, 568-573
  manipulating information, 612-617
  self-modifying macros, 627-628
  soliciting input, 559-564
  subroutines, 576-584
  table of commands, 552-555
  using, 557-558
  (see also LCL commands)
Lotus Development Corporation, 1
Lotus/Intel/Microsoft Expanded
  Memory Specification, 49-50
@LOWER function, 210-211

M

Macro libraries, 645-661
  adding macros to, 651-652
  creating, 646-648, 653-654
  editing macros in, 649-652
  executing macros from, 648
  loading into RAM, 648-649
  range names problems, 656-657
  referencing information in, 657-661
  unloading from RAM, 649

Macro Library Manager, 527, 645-661
  attaching, 645
  invoking, 645
  using, 646-661
  (see also Macro libraries)
Macros
  accessing DOS with, 611-612
  advanced commands, 551-630
  auto-executing, 547-548
  auto-invoking, 524
  branching, 573-576, 609-610
  computed statements, 599, 628-629
  conditional testing, 566-568
  controlling the interface, 595-602
  copying information with, 615-617
  creating, 516
  custom menus, 584-593
  debugging, 542-547
  displaying graphs with, 600-601
  documenting, 529
  editing, 546-547
  entering information with, 564-566
  erasing ranges with, 614-615
  errors in, 542-544
  executable only from libraries, 654-656
  file i/o, 617-626
  key representations, 521-523, 582
  LCL commands, 551-630
  libraries, 645-661
  looping, 568-573
  Lotus Command Language, 551-630
  menu commands in, 532-541
  naming, 517, 523-525
  pausing, 526, 608
  positioning, 530
  recalculating worksheet with, 612-614
  recording, 530-532
  running, 517-519, 525, 528
  saving, 527
  self-modifying, 627-628
  soliciting input, 559-564, 602-606
  stopping, 525-526, 558
  subroutines, 576-584
  syntax, 519-523
  trapping errors, 606-607
  worksheet-specific, 527
  (see also Lotus Command Language)
Margins
  for printed worksheets, 310-313
Mathematical operators
  (see Operators, mathematical)
Matrices, 250-256
  inverting, 252-256
  multiplying, 250-252
@MAX function, 171
MEM indicator, 13
Memory, 45-50
  conventional, 46
  expanded, 49-50

Index 769

free, 46
Memory-full errors, 47-48
recovering, 48-49
required by 1-2-3, 45-46
used by 1-2-3 Release 1A, 674
used by undo feature, 45, 48
Memory management, 45-50
(see also Memory)
Menu commands
using in macros, 532-541
MENU mode, 12, 40-41
{MenuBranch} command, 584-591
{MenuCall} command, 591-593
Menus, 40-42
custom, 585-593
@MID function, 209
@MIN function, 171
@MINUTE function, 291-292
Mixed references, 32, 142-144
@MOD function, 157-158
Mode indicators, 12
custom, 598-600
Modes, 12
Modulus, 157-158
@MONTH function, 280-282
/ Move command, 124-130
Moving
cell pointer, 14-20
Moving entries, 124-130
effect on named ranges, 129
on top of referenced entries, 128
referenced by formulas, 127-128

N

@N function, 219
@NA function, 219
Names
graph, 386-388
of macros, 517, 523-524
range, 57-65
(see also Range names)
NAMES mode, 12
[Name] key, 14, 59-60
to list file names, 350
to list macro names, 525
Negative values
in Stacked-Bar graphs, 397
Net present value, 175-177
Networks
using 1-2-3 on, 36, 719-720
NoteWorthy, 662
Note-It Plus, 661
#NOT# operator, 200, 491
@NPV function, 175-177
NUM indicator, 13
[Num Lock] key, 16
Numbers
(see Values)

O

{OnError} command, 606-607
{Open} command, 618-619
Operators
mathematical, 29
precedence of, 29
#OR# operator, 200, 491
Output range, 498-500
Overwrite mode, 38
OVR indicator, 13, 38

P

Page breaks
automatic, 304-308
manual, 333-335
Page length
for printed worksheets, 313-314
Page numbers
in headers and footers, 324
{PanelOff} command, 595-596
{PanelOn} command, 596-597
Paper
aligning in printer, 308
Parsing labels, 695-702
Password-protection
of files, 356-357
Patterns
in graphs, 395
Payments
calculating with @PMT function, 179-180
[period] key
to change anchor cell, 328
[Pg Dn] key, 19
locking in entries with, 22
macro representation of, 521-522
to enter POINT mode, 39
[Pg Up] key, 19
locking in entries with, 22
macro representation of, 521-522
to enter POINT mode, 39
@PI function, 164
.PIC files, 436-437, 439, 441, 442, 447, 745
Pie graphs, 397-400
printing in color, 458
shading and exploding, 398-400
x-axis labels in, 414-416, 417-418
Plotters, 443-444
@PMT function, 179-180
POINT mode, 12, 31-32, 39
moving into Titles area, 224
Pointing, 31-32, 39
to commands in macros, 539
to define ranges, 43-44
Prefixes
(see Label prefixes)
Present value, 172-175
/ Print File commands, 687-690

/ Print Printer Align command, 303, 308
/ Print Printer Clear command, 331
/ Print Printer command, 302-338
/ Print Printer commands
  in macros, 536-538
/ Print Printer Go command, 303
/ Print Printer Line command, 308
/ Print Printer Options Borders command, 325-331
/ Print Printer Options Footer command, 320-325
/ Print Printer Options Header command, 320-325
/ Print Printer Options Margins Bottom command, 312
/ Print Printer Options Margins Left command, 310-311
/ Print Printer Options Margins None command, 312-313
/ Print Printer Options Margins Right command, 311-312
/ Print Printer Options Margins Top command, 312
/ Print Printer Options Other Cell-Formulas command, 336-338
/ Print Printer Options Other Formatted command, 335
/ Print Printer Options Other Unformatted command, 304-305, 335
/ Print Printer Options Pg-Length command, 313-314
/ Print Printer Options Setup command, 315-316
/ Print Printer Page command, 308
/ Print Printer Range command, 302-303, 309-310
Printers
  choosing, 300-301
  configuring, 299-302, 723-725
  for graphs, 443-444
  HP LaserJet, 721-756
PrintGraph program, 439-464, 745-756
  Commands by name
    Align, 459
    Exit, 463
    Go, 459
    Image-Select, 447-448
    Settings Action Eject, 446
    Settings Action Pause, 446
    Settings Hardware Fonts-Directory, 442-443
    Settings Hardware Graphs-Directory, 441-442
    Settings Hardware Interface, 444-445
    Settings Hardware Paper-Size, 445-446
    Settings Hardware Printer, 443-444
  Settings Hardware Size-Paper, 455
  Settings Image Font, 448-449
  Settings Image Range-Colors, 456-457
  Settings Image Size Full, 450
  Settings Image Size Half, 450
  Settings Image Size Manual Height, 454-455
  Settings Image Size Manual Left, 452-453
  Settings Image Size Manual Right, 452-453
  Settings Image Size Manual Rotation, 453-454
  Settings Image Size Manual Width, 454-455
  Settings Save, 461-463
  configuring, 441-446
  exiting from, 463
  in 1-2-3 Release 1A, 463-464
  loading, 440-441
  (see also Printing graphs)
Printing data bases, 469
Printing graphs, 439-464
  colors, 456-457
  Eject setting, 446
  fonts, 448-450
  Fonts-Directory setting, 442-443
  Graphs-Directory setting, 442
  Height setting, 454-455
  Interface setting, 444-445
  Margin settings, 452-453
  Paper size setting, 455
  Pause setting, 446
  previewing graphs in, 448
  printers, 443-444
  printing graphs with, 459
  printing multiple graphs, 457-459
  Rotation setting, 453-454
  saving settings, 461-463
  selecting graphs in, 447-448
  Size settings, 450-455
  Size-Paper setting, 445-446
  Width setting, 454-455
  with Allways, 636-645
  with HP LaserJet printers, 745-756
Printing worksheets, 229-338
  aborting, 310
  aligning paper, 308
  auto-LF setting, 302
  basics, 302-310
  borders, 325-331
  choosing a printer, 300-301
  choosing an interface, 301-302
  default print settings, 304-307
    changing, 331-333
  dividing into pages, 304-308
  footers, 320-325
  hardware setup, 299-302

headers, 320-325
hiding rows, 320
listing cell entries, 335-338
margins, 310-313
on HP LaserJet printers, 315, 721-744
page breaks
  automatic, 304-308
  manual, 333-335
page length, 313-314
partial, 309-310
setup strings, 314-320
to files, 687-691
unformatted reports, 335
with Allways, 636-645
.PRN files, 688-695
@PROPER function, 210-211
Protection
  (see Cell protection)
Punctuation setting, 709-7111
{Put} command, 614
@PV function, 172-175

Q

Querying
  (see also Data bases), 492-506
[Query] key, 14
  to exit FIND mode, 498
  to reissue / Data Query commands, 506
/ Quit command, 66-67
Quitting from 1-2-3, 66-67
{Quit} command, 525-526, 558

R

@RAND function, 158
Random numbers, 158
/ Range Erase command, 112-116
/ Range Fill command, 232-235
/ Range Format command, 71-73, 275-278, 287-288
  in macros, 534-535
/ Range Format Reset command, 77
/ Range Input command, 259-262
/ Range Justify command, 262-265
/ Range Label command, 96-98
/ Range Name Create command, 57, 63
  in macros, 533-534
/ Range Name Delete command, 62
/ Range Name Labels command, 63-65
/ Range Name Labels Right command
  to name macros, 524-525
/ Range Name Table command, 60-62
Range names, 57-65
  changing, 63
  creating, 57-58, 63-65
  deleting, 62
  effect of / Move command on, 129

for data base ranges, 513
in macros, 540
listing, 59-60
rules for, 58
tables of, 60-62
using, 59-60
/ Range Prot command, 256-259
/ Range Search command, 265-271
/ Range Trans command, 148-153
/ Range Unprot command, 258
/ Range Value command, 145-147
Ranges
  defining for commands, 43-44
  erasing, 112-116
  filling, 232-235
  naming, 57-65
    (see also Range names)
  selecting in commands, 112-116
  transposing, 148-153
@RATE function, 183-184
Rate of interest, 183-184
{ReadLn} command, 622-623
READY mode, 12
{Read} command, 622
{RecalcCol} command, 612-613
Recalculation, 50-57
  automatic, 51
  columnwise, 52-53
  in 1-2-3 Release 2.2, 50
  iterative, 56-57
  manual, 51
  methods of, 50-51
  minimal, 50
  natural, 52
  of linking formulas, 720
  orders of, 51-53
  rowwise, 52-53
  with macro, 612-613
{Recalc} command, 612-613
Recording macros, 530-532
Records
  in data bases, 466
References
  absolute, 32, 138-142
  circular, 53-57
    (see also Circular references)
  effect of deleting columns and rows on, 123-124
  effect of inserting columns and rows on, 120-121
  effect of / Move command on, 127-128
  in formulas, 29-33
  mixed, 32, 142-144
  relative, 32, 135-138
  to other worksheets, 34-36
Regression, 244-250
  intercept option, 249-250
  multiple, 248-249

plotting line, 404-405
using results, 246-248
Relative references, 32, 135-138
@REPEAT function, 214-215
@REPLACE function, 206-207
Replacing
    (see Searching and replacing)
Reservations
    of files, 719
{Restart} command, 610-611
Retrieving
    files, 345-348
{Return} command, 570-573, 580-581
@RIGHT function, 209
[Right] arrow key
    (see Arrow keys)
RO indicator, 13, 719
Rotation
    of printed graphs, 453-454
@ROUND function, 159-160
Rounding values, 159-160
Rows, 10-11
    counting, 216-218
    deleting, 121-122
    hiding in printed report, 320
    inserting, 116-119, 121
    locking onto screen, 221-224
    title, 221-224
@ROWS function, 218
[Run] key, 14, 517, 525

S

@S function, 219
Saving
    worksheets, 339-376
        (see also Files)
Screen
    freezing, 595-597
    splitting
        (see Windows)
    tour of, 10-13
SCROLL indicator, 13
[Scroll Lock] key, 17
Searching and replacing, 265-271
    Find option, 265-268
    in formulas and functions, 267-268
    in text, 266
    Replace option, 269
@SECOND function, 291-292
SeeMORE, 661
Self-modifying macros, 627-628
Serial date values, 273
    converting from labels, 295-297
Serial time values, 286
    converting from labels, 297-298
Series
    of numbers, 232-235
        (see also / Range Fill command)

SET files, 8-9
{SetPos} command, 619-620
Settings sheets
    Data Query, 492
    Data Regression, 244-245
    Data Sort, 471-472
    Default settings, 708-709
    general, 42-43
    Global settings, 707-708
    Graph, 377-378, 383-384, 385
    Print, 300, 302
    Sort, 471-472
    Worksheet Global, 88-89, 707-708
    Worksheet Global Default, 278-279, 288-289, 331, 708-709
Setup strings, 314-320
    embedded, 317-319, 738-739
    for HP LaserJet printers, 734-739
[Shift][Tab] key, 19
    locking in entries with, 22
Sideways, 308, 661
@SIN function, 164-165
@SLN function, 185
sorting, 471-478
    one field, 473-476
    text, 474-475
    two fields, 476-477
SOS, 662
[Spacebar]
    in STEP mode, 545-546
    selecting graphs to print, 447
SpeedUp, 661
SPEEDUP.APP, 46
@SQRT function, 158-159
Square roots, 158-159
SQZ! Plus, 661
SST indicator, 13, 545-546
Stacked-bar graphs, 395-397
    adjusting Y scale, 420
    data labels in, 426
    legends for, 434
Standard deviation, 171-172
STAT mode, 12
Status indicators, 13
@STD function, 171-172
STEP indicator, 13, 545-546
STEP mode, 545-546
[Step] key, 14, 545-546
String formulas, 33
@STRING function, 211-212
Strings, 33, 202-215
Subroutines, 576-584
{Subroutine} command, 576-579
@SUM function, 167-169
@SYD function, 186
SYLK files, 702
Symbols
    in graphs, 392

Index

Symphony
  exchanging data with, 675-678
/ System command, 344
  running PrintGraph with, 440
{System} command, 611-612

T

[Table] key, 14, 240
[Tab] key, 19
  locking in entries with, 22
@TAN function, 164-165
@TERM function, 181-182
Term of loan, 181-183
Text files, 687-702
  creating, 687-690
  importing into 1-2-3, 692-695
  parsing information from, 695-702
  using in other programs, 690-692
@TIME function, 286-287
Times, 285-298
  entering, 286-287
  formatting, 287-289
  in formulas and functions, 290-292, 294-295
@TIMEVALUE function, 297-298
Titles
  graph, 407-409
  in windows, 231
  in worksheet, 221-224
@TODAY function, 293
Translate utility, 663-686
  changing directory, 666-667
  choosing source file, 665-666
  choosing target file, 667-668
  help, 665
  loading, 664
  specifying translation, 664-665
  with 1-2-3 Release 1A, 670-674
  with 1-2-3 Releases 2 and 2.01, 670
  with 1-2-3 Release 3, 674-675
  with dBASE, 678-686
  with other programs, 687-702
  with Symphony, 675-678
Translating files, 663-686
  (see also Exchanging data, Translate utility)
Transposing ranges, 148-153
@TRIM function, 215
@TRUE function, 202

U

UNDO indicator, 13, 44-45
[Undo] key, 14, 44-45
Unique records
  extracting from data base, 503-504
@UPPER function, 210-211
Upper-level characters, 703-705

[Up] arrow key
  (see Arrow keys)

V

@VALUE function, 212-214
VALUE mode, 12
Values, 23-25
  adding with @SUM function, 167-169
  converting to labels, 212-213
  display of, 24
  entering, 23
  error, 34
  in databases, 467-468
  long, 24
  negative
    display of, 713
  precision of, 24-25
@VAR function, 172
Variance, 172
Visicalc, 1, 702
@VLOOKUP function, 189-194

W

WAIT mode, 12
{Wait} command, 598, 599, 600-601, 608
What's Best!, 662
What-if analysis
  (see Data tables)
Windows, 11-12, 224-231
  clearing, 230
  creating, 225
  moving between, 225-226
  synchronizing, 227-229
  unsynchronizing, 227-229
{WindowsOff} command, 595-596
{WindowsOn} command, 596-597
[Window] key, 14, 225-226
  in synchronized windows, 230
.WK1 files, 670-675
.WK3 files, 674-675
.WKS files, 670
/ Worksheet Column Column-Range command, 105-106
/ Worksheet Column Column-Range Set-Width command, 76
/ Worksheet Column Display command, 111-112
/ Worksheet Column Hide command, 109-111
/ Worksheet Column Reset-Width command, 105, 109
/ Worksheet Column Set-Width command, 76, 102-105, 277-278, 288
/ Worksheet Delete Column command, 122-123

/ Worksheet Delete Row command, 121-122
/ Worksheet Erase command, 65
/ Worksheet Global Column-Width command, 106-108
/ Worksheet Global command, 42
/ Worksheet Global Default Autoexec command, 548
/ Worksheet Global Default command, 42
/ Worksheet Global Default Directory command, 355
/ Worksheet Global Default Other Add-in commands, 635
/ Worksheet Global Default Other International Date command, 278-279, 288-289
/ Worksheet Global Default Other Undo command, 45
/ Worksheet Global Default Printer Auto-LF command, 302
/ Worksheet Global Default Printer Bottom command, 313
/ Worksheet Global Default Printer Interface command, 301-302
/ Worksheet Global Default Printer Left command, 313
/ Worksheet Global Default Printer Name command, 300-301
/ Worksheet Global Default Printer Pg-Length command, 314
/ Worksheet Global Default Printer Right command, 313
/ Worksheet Global Default Printer Top command, 313
/ Worksheet Global Default Printer Update command, 332
/ Worksheet Global Default Printer Wait command, 332-333
/ Worksheet Global Format command, 88-89
/ Worksheet Global Label-Prefix command, 98-99
/ Worksheet Global Protection commands, 256-257, 258, 259
/ Worksheet Global Recalculation command, 52
/ Worksheet Global Recalculation Iteration command, 56-57
/ Worksheet Global Status command, 332

/ Worksheet Global Zero command, 91-94
/ Worksheet Insert Row command, 116-119
/ Worksheet Learn commands, 530-532
/ Worksheet Page command, 333-335
/ Worksheet Status command, 46-47, 54-55, 344
/ Worksheet Titles commands, 221-224, 231
Worksheet Utilities, 661
/ Worksheet Window commands, 225-231
Worksheets
  auto-loading, 347-348
  consolidating, 362-374
  description of, 10-12
  erasing, 65
  extracting information from, 358-362
  formatting, 69-99
    (see also Formats)
  printing
    (see Printing worksheets)
  saving, 339-376
    (see also Files)
.WR1 files, 675-678
{WriteLn} command, 621
{Write} command, 621
.WRK files, 675-678

X

/xc command, 579-580
/xg command, 576
/xi command, 568
/xl command, 563, 564
/xm command, 591
/xn command, 563
/xr command, 581
XY graphs, 400-406
  formatting X-axis of, 423
  x-axis labels in, 414

Y

@YEAR function, 280-282

Z

Zero supression, 91-94
  Label option, 93
  undoing, 93-94